Contemporary Asian America

Contemporary Asian America

A Multidisciplinary Reader

EDITED BY

Min Zhou and James V. Gatewood

New York University Press

NEW YORK AND LONDON

NEW YORK UNIVERSITY PRESS
New York and London

© 2000 by New York University
All rights reserved

Library of Congress Cataloging-in-Publication Data
Contemporary Asian America : a multidisciplinary reader / edited by Min Zhou and
James V. Gatewood.
    p. cm.
Includes bibliographical references and index.
ISBN 0-8147-9690-7 (cloth : alk. paper)—ISBN 0-8147-9691-5 (paper : alk. paper)
    1. Asian Americans. 2. Asian Americans—Study and teaching. I. Zhou, Min, 1956–   II.
Gatewood, James V., 1972–
E184.O6 C66 1999
973'.0495073—dc21   99-053532

New York University Press books are printed on acid-free paper, and
their binding materials are chosen for strength and durability.

Manufactured in the United States of America

10 9 8 7 6 5 4 3 2 1

For Nan Guo—M.Z.
For Bill Gatewood, June Gatewood Nagao, and Ken Nagao—J.G.

Contents

Preface   *xiii*

Introduction: Revisiting Contemporary Asian America   1
Min Zhou and James V. Gatewood

PART I: Claiming Visibility: The Asian American Movement

  1 "On Strike!" San Francisco State College Strike, 1968–1969:
The Role of Asian American Students   49
Karen Umemoto

  2 The "Four Prisons" and the Movements of Liberation: Asian
American Activism from the 1960s to the 1990s   80
Glenn Omatsu

    Study Questions   *113*
    Suggested Readings   *113*
    Films   *114*

PART II: Making History: The Asian American Experience

  3 From a Different Shore: Their History Bursts with Telling   117
Ronald Takaki

  4 When and Where I Enter   132
Gary Y. Okihiro

    Study Questions   *150*
    Suggested Readings   *150*
    Films   *151*

PART III: Traversing Borders: Contemporary Asian Immigration to the
United States

  5 U.S. Immigration Policies and Asian Migration   155
Paul Ong and John M. Liu

6   Vietnamese, Laotian, and Cambodian Americans   175
     Rubén G. Rumbaut

7   The Social Construction of Gendered Migration from the
     Philippines   207
     James A. Tyner

     Study Questions   229
     Suggested Readings   229
     Films   230

P A R T   I V : Struggling to Get Ahead: Life and Work in Asian America

8   Life and Work in the Inner City   233
     Paul Ong and Karen Umemoto

9   Work and Its Place in the Lives of Immigrant Women:
     Garment Workers in New York City's Chinatown   254
     Min Zhou and Regina Nordquist

10   Striving for the American Dream: Struggle, Success, and
     Intergroup Conflict among Korean Immigrant Entrepreneurs   278
     Jennifer Lee

     Study Questions   295
     Suggested Readings   295
     Films   296

P A R T   V : Ties That Bind: The Asian American Family and Community

11   Children of Inmates: The Effects of the Redress Movement
     among Third-Generation Japanese Americans   299
     Yasuko I. Takezawa

12   Social Capital in Chinatown: The Role of Community-Based
     Organizations and Families in the Adaptation of the
     Younger Generation   315
     Min Zhou

13   New Household Forms, Old Family Values: The Formation
     and Reproduction of the Filipino Transnational Family in
     Los Angeles   336
     Rhacel Salazar Parreñas

     Study Questions   352
     Suggested Readings   352
     Films   353

PART VI: Keeping the Faith: Spiritual Practices among Asian Americans

14   Sangha of the South: Laotian Buddhism and Social
     Adaptation in Rural Louisiana   357
     Carl L. Bankston III

15   The Structure and Social Functions of Korean Immigrant
     Churches in the United States   372
     Pyong Gap Min

16   Asian Indian and Pakistani Religions in the United States   392
     Raymond Brady Williams

     Study Questions   408
     Suggested Readings   409
     Films   409

PART VII: Women in Asian America

17   Doing Gender with a Feminist Gaze: Toward a Historical
     Reconstruction of Asian America   413
     Shirley Hune

18   Power, Patriarchy, and Gender Conflict in the Vietnamese
     Immigrant Community   431
     Nazli Kibria

     Study Questions   444
     Suggested Readings   444
     Films   445

PART VIII: The Construction and Deconstruction of the "Model
Minority"

19   Asian Americans as the Model Minority: An Analysis of the
     Popular Press Image in the 1960s and 1980s   449
     Keith Osajima

20   The "Model Minority" Deconstructed   459
     Lucie Cheng and Philip Q. Yang

21   A Quota on Excellence? The Asian American Admissions
     Debate   483
     Don T. Nakanishi

     Study Questions   497
     Suggested Readings   497
     Films   498

PART IX: Confronting Adversity: Racism, Exclusion, and the Burden of Double Standards

22 The Murder of Navroze Mody: Race, Violence, and the
    Search for Order   501
    Deborah N. Misir

23 Race, Class, Citizenship, and Extraterritoriality: Asian
    Americans and the 1996 Campaign Finance Scandal   518
    L. Ling-chi Wang

24 A Letter to My Sister   535
    Lisa Park

    Study Questions   542
    Suggested Readings   543
    Films   543

PART X: Queering Asian America

25 Maiden Voyage: Excursion into Sexuality and Identity
    Politics in Asian America   547
    Dana Y. Takagi

26 Stories from the Homefront: Perspectives of Asian American
    Parents with Lesbian Daughters and Gay Sons   561
    Alice Y. Hom

27 Searching for Community: Filipino Gay Men in New York
    City   572
    Martin F. Manalansan IV

    Study Questions   584
    Suggested Readings   584
    Films   585

PART XI: The Complexity of Ethnic Identity: Interracial Marriage and Multiethnic Asian Americans

28 In Search of the Right Spouse: Interracial Marriage among
    Chinese and Japanese Americans   589
    Colleen Fong and Judy Yung

29 What Must I Be? Asian Americans and the Question of
    Multiethnic Indentity   606
    Paul R. Spickard

Study Questions   622
Suggested Readings   622
Films   623

PART XII: Visual Culture

30   Is There an Asian American Aesthetics?   627
     Transcribed by Gargi Chatterjee and edited by Augie Tam

31   Art, Activism, Asia, and Asian Americans   636
     Dorinne Kondo

     Study Questions   663
     Suggested Readings   663
     Films   664

**PART XIII: Mapping the Terrain: New Paradigms in Asian American
Studies**

32   Rethinking Race: Paradigms and Policy Formation   667
     Shirley Hune

33   Heterogeneity, Hybridity, Multiplicity: Marking Asian
     American Differences   677
     Lisa Lowe

     Study Questions   698
     Suggested Readings   698
     Film   699

     Contributors   701
     Permissions   703
     Index   707

Preface

The purpose of this anthology is to provide undergraduate and graduate students and all those interested in the Asian American community with some of the most central readings informing Asian America and Asian American Studies today. Of critical importance in selecting the readings is our goal of making the entire project a reflexive undertaking. The readings, while important in and of themselves to the evolution of Asian American Studies and to the development of the community, have been selected on the basis of what the authors can tell our readers about themselves or their own lives and, essentially, about the ways in which our readers' experiences may resonate within the larger framework of what we call the "Asian American experience."

We feel that it is important at the outset to state the limitations of an anthology such as this one. No one reader can capture the diversity of voices, experiences, and people that constitute different Asian American communities today. In privileging one topic of discussion, we must necessarily exclude another. It would be disingenuous for us to state otherwise. One of the most noticeable absences, one that will be readily apparent to students and teachers, is that of literary works produced by Asian American authors—the novels, short stories, poetry, plays. These literary works have played a fundamental role both in defining the curriculum in Asian American Studies and in providing a valuable window through which to evaluate identity formation within the community itself. Our decision not to include literary works as such is not by happenstance. Initially, we agreed to include these works, but we found it extremely difficult to devise ways to excerpt pieces without losing sight of their original meaning and context. It is unfair to the writers of these literary works to break apart chapters in their books or even short stories and to print selections that cannot be fully understood out of context. We feel that most of the excellent literary works that exist in Asian American Studies should be read and experienced in their entirety. Another reason for our decision is that this anthology is meant to accompany a college-level introductory course in Asian American Studies. It has been our experience in teaching Asian American Studies courses that classes almost always include a number of monographs and novels by Asian American authors that frame the discussion of certain historical, cultural, and social themes in the community. We have therefore decided to provide a focus that frames these discussions in a social science context.

Although there are a number of anthologies that focus on Asian American immigration, community development, and socialization, none really attempt to integrate the intersection of these themes and their effects on the contemporary Asian American community. The basis for our choice of material to include in each section of this anthology is our own introspection on those issues that students find meaningful in Asian American Studies classes today. The issue of identity is a central concept in these classes, and we have made a conscious effort to include various abstractions of Asian American identity—abstractions that deal with the intersections of generation, class, gender, sexuality, religion, and the cultural reconstruction of identity. The sections are meant to read not merely chronologically but rather as illustrations of different themes framing the reflexive bent that we assume. To get around spatial limitations on this book, we have included in each section's suggested reading list a number of excellent works that have emerged in recent years, as well as some of the "classic" readings in Asian American Studies.

A project of this scope is never a solitary undertaking. We gratefully acknowledge the support and assistance of all those individuals who offered their precious time and invaluable help in shaping this anthology and in making it better. First, we thank Tim Bartlett, former editor at New York University Press, who initiated the project and pushed it through with his keen foresight and enthusiasm. Jennifer Hammer, our current editor at New York University Press, has graciously offered her unlimited support for this project as well as her own commitment to its underlying goals, which greatly facilitated our ability to make this project happen. We would also like to acknowledge the four anonymous reviewers who, at an early stage of our work, read carefully the pieces we originally selected and critiqued the manner in which we organized this reader. Their critical comments greatly strengthened the theoretical framework that we ultimately employed.

This project was partially supported by a research grant from the Asian American Studies Center at the University of California at Los Angeles. We are particularly indebted to the Center director, Don Nakanishi, who has always been committed to supporting faculty and students in teaching and research. We would like to thank our colleagues in the Department of Sociology and at the Asian American Studies Center at UCLA for their insightful ideas, helpful comments, constructive critiques, and moral support. We especially thank Shirley Hune, Yuji Ichioka, Jennifer Lee, Margi Lee, Russell Leong, David Lopez, Valerie Matsumoto, Bob Nakamura, Don Nakanishi, Glenn Omatsu, Henry Yu, and Roger Waldinger. At other academic institutions, we specially thank Carlos Chan, Carla Tengan, Lane Hirabayashi, and Horacio Chiong. We also thank our colleagues at the Japanese American National Museum for their support, specially Karin Higa, Darcie Iki, Sojin Kim, Eiichiro Azuma, Karen Ishizuka, Cameron Trowbridge, Debbie Henderson, Nikki Chang, and Grace Murakami. A special thanks goes to Krissy Kim for her friendship and encouragement. We send a special note of appreciation to all the students in Asian American Studies, among them Teresa Ejanda, Lynn Itakagi, Lakandiwa M. de Leon, Gina Masequesmay, Derek Mateo, Randall Park, Steven Wong, and the many others with whom we have worked and who gave us the incentive to compile this anthology. Diana Lee, Amy Chai, and April Shen provided tremendous research assistance for this project.

Finally, we would like to express our deepest gratitude to our families, who sacrificed a considerable amount of time with us to enable us to see this project through to completion.

Min Zhou
James V. Gatewood

Introduction
Revisiting Contemporary Asian America

Min Zhou and James V. Gatewood

At the dawn of the new millenium, one cannot help but examine the development and growth of the Asian American community. What is the state of Asian America in 1999? How has it evolved since the 1960s, a turbulent decade in America's history that witnessed the birth of the nation's ethnic-consciousness movements? To what extent has the Asian American community asserted itself socially and politically and constructed an "Asian American" identity? These are but a few of the questions posed by this anthology, an introductory reader for those interested in the issues facing the Asian American community today. We have selected a number of themes that critically inform the current state of the community. Our goal in compiling this anthology was to make it personally meaningful to our readers, incorporating ideas that expose individuals to the evolution of Asian American Studies and to the broader social transformations in American society that have historically affected (and continue to affect) people of Asian descent and their communities.

Activism, the Movement, and the Development of Asian American Studies

> For Asian Americans, the struggles transformed our communities. They spawned numerous grassroots organizations. They created an extensive network of student organizations and Asian American Studies classes. They recovered a buried cultural tradition as well as produced a new generation of writers, poets, and artists. But most importantly, the struggles profoundly altered Asian American consciousness. They redefined racial and ethnic identity, promoted new ways of thinking about communities, and challenged prevailing notions of power and authority.
>
> —Glenn Omatsu (this volume)

The Significance of the Asian American Movement

The birth of the Asian American Movement coincided with the largest student strike in the nation's history. At San Francisco State College, members of the Third

World Liberation Front (TWLF), a coalition of African Americans, Latino Americans/Chicanos, Native Americans, and Asian Americans, launched a student strike in November 1968. The strike made demands on the university for curricular reform, initially aimed at three specific goals. First, student strikers sought to redefine education and to make their curriculum at once more meaningful to their own lives, experiences, and histories and more reflective of the communities in which they lived. Second, they demanded that racial and ethnic minorities play a more active role in the decision-making process and that university administrators institute an admissions policy to give minorities equal access to advanced education. Third, they attempted to effect larger changes in the institutional practices by urging administrators to institutionalize ethnic studies at San Francisco State College. The strike, in which Asian Americans played an integral role, brought about significant institutional changes; in particular, it led to the establishment of the nation's first School of Ethnic Studies at San Francisco State College. More than just a token concession to the students, the School began to implement the students' objectives of curricular reform and equal access to education.

In his seminal article, "The 'Four Prisons' and the Movements of Liberation" (this volume), Glenn Omatsu, a veteran activist of the Movement and a longtime resident scholar at UCLA's Asian American Studies Center, contends that the San Francisco student strike not only marked the beginning of the Asian American Movement but also set the agenda for the articulation of an Asian American "consciousness." Omatsu argues that those involved in the Movement were not simply seeking to promote their own legitimacy or representation in mainstream society. Rather, the Movement raised questions about subverting ideals and practices that rewarded racial or ethnic minorities for conforming to white mainstream values. The active involvement of Asian Americans extended well beyond college campuses on which many of these issues were being raised; it reached the working-class communities from which many students originated. Omatsu highlights several emerging themes that exerted a profound impact on the Asian American struggles in the 1970s:(1) building a coalition between activists and the community, (2) reclaiming the heritage of resistance,(3) forming a new ideology that manifested in self-determination and the legitimization of oppositional practices as a means of bringing about change to the racist structures inherent to American society,(4) demanding equal rights and minority power, and (5) urging mass mobilization and militant action. For Omatsu, the Asian American Movement was a grassroots working-class community struggle for liberation and self-determination.

The political actions of the 1960s unleashed shock waves that have continued to reverberate in the larger Asian American community today. As both Karen Umemoto and Glenn Omatsu recount in their articles on the Movement (this volume), the spirit that initially infused the period carried over into the next two decades, despite a changing political climate that marked the onset of what Omatsu deems "the winter of civil rights and the rise of neo-conservatism." The Movement has evolved to incorporate a broader range of diverse viewpoints and voices, helping frame the ways in which many students approach Asian American Studies today. Not only does the Movement provide students with an understanding of the strategies employed by racial and ethnic minorities in their fight against racism and oppression in American society; it also suggests specific ways in which these strategies can be effectively used for minority empowerment.

Institutional Development

Shortly after the founding of the first ethnic studies program at San Francisco State College in 1968, other universities across the United States set to work on developing their own academic programs. According to a survey conducted by Don Nakanishi and Russell Leong in 1978, at least fourteen universities established Asian American studies programs, including the Berkeley, Los Angeles, Davis, and Santa Barbara campuses of the University of California; the San Francisco, Fresno, San Jose, Sacramento, and Long Beach campuses of the California State University; the University of Southern California; the University of Washington; the University of Colorado; the University of Hawaii; and City College of New York. The programs at UC Berkeley and San Francisco State University had the largest enrollment, with 1,500 each, and offered sixty and forty-nine courses respectively. The programs on other campuses offered four to sixty courses per academic year and enrolled 100 to 650 students. All Asian American Studies programs, with the exception of UCLA's, listed teaching as their primary goal, with community work and research ranked as second and third priorities. UCLA, in contrast, made research and publications its top priority, with teaching ranked second. By 1978, at least three universities—UCLA, San Francisco State University, and the University of Washington—offered graduate courses (Nakanishi and Leong 1978).

In the span of only twenty-five years, Asian American Studies has experienced unparalleled growth as Asian American student enrollment has increased at unprecedented rates at American universities. Today, Asian Americans account for 4 percent of the U.S. population, but Asian American students make up more than 6 percent of total college enrollment and a significantly larger proportion at prestigious public and private universities. In 1995, for example, Asian American students represented more than 10 percent of the student populations at all nine UC campuses and at twelve of the twenty CSU campuses, as well as at Harvard, Yale, the Massachusetts Institute of Technology, Columbia, and other first-ranked universities. The UC system, in particular, has seen its Asian American population grow rapidly, representing 22 percent to 39 percent of students at seven of the nine campuses (Editors of the *Chronicle of Higher Education* 1995). The *Los Angeles Times* reported, in 1998, that Asian Americans made up more than 58 percent of the undergraduates at UC Irvine and more than 40 percent at three other UC campuses (41 percent at Berkeley, 40 percent at UCLA, and 43 percent at Riverside). The nations leading universities also reported disproportionate increases in enrollment of Asian Americans, who made up 28 percent of the undergraduates at MIT, 27 percent at Caltech, 24 percent at Stanford, 23 percent at Wellesley, 22 percent at New York University, 19 percent at Harvard, 17 percent at Yale, and 17 percent at Columbia.[1]

In response to these demographic changes, major public universities and a growing number of private universities in which Asian American student enrollments are disproportionately large have established Asian American Studies departments or interdepartmental programs. Today, all the University of California and the California State University campuses have established Asian American Studies programs, some of which have evolved into Asian American Studies departments. Outside California, many universities and colleges have established similar programs, often in response to student protests and even hunger strikes, as was the case in 1994 at Columbia University, where an Asian American Studies program is still struggling to get off the ground (Monaghan 1999). The current directory of Asian American Studies programs, complied at Cornell University, shows an incomplete count of forty-one departments, centers, or programs nationwide. These departments or interdepartmental/interdisciplinary programs offer a wide range of courses on the diversity of Asian American experiences. UCLA has the largest teaching programs in Asian American Studies in the nation and for the past twenty-five years has been one of two major sites for the training of Asian American Studies scholars. It has an M.A. program (the nation's only graduate program in the field and one that has been training future researchers and community leaders for the past fifteen years), a B.A. major and an undergraduate specialization minor. Each year it offers fifty to sixty classes, which enroll more than 2,000 students.

Despite the current boom, however, institutional development has often met with obstacles, ranging from the loss of faculty and staff positions to the retirement of veteran or founding faculty to budget cuts arbitrarily imposed on relatively young but growing departments. Although continued expansion of programs and departments is not inevitable, and is likely to be a matter of ongoing conflict, demographic pressure and the political weight of the Asian American community, as well as the continuing intellectual development of Asian American Studies as a field, make the prospects for growth very promising.

Asian American Studies as an Interdisciplinary Field

What is Asian American Studies? Is it an academic field with a perspective of its own and with intellectually cohesive themes, or is it a field that brings together people of different disciplines who share common interests and who work on similar topics?

At the early stage of its development, Asian American Studies understood itself as the offspring of the social movement from which it emerged. Thus, in its self-conceptualization, Asian American Studies sought to reproduce central aspects of the broader movement for social change in which it started out, as an oppositional orientation preoccupied with refuting the prevailing theoretical paradigm of assimilation and fostering self-determination through a Third-World consciousness (Chan 1978; Nakanishi and Leong 1978; Omatsu, this volume; Umemoto, this volume). Both curricular development and research in the field focused on history, identity, and community (Tachiki et al. 1971). Meanwhile, Asian American Studies explicitly served as an institutionalized training center for future community leaders, trying to connect scholars and students with grassroots working-class communities. Since the students and Asian American faculty of the 1960s and 1970s were mostly Japanese Americans and Chinese Americans, with a smaller number of Filipino Americans, most of the teaching and research were focused on these ethnic populations.

Of course, the guiding theoretical principles and self-understanding of the founders, themselves, still very much present and influential in the field, cannot be accepted without question. The founders' views carry the characteristic traces of the baby boom generation of which the founders are a part: namely, the sense of constituting a unique group whose actions mark a rupture with the past. Indeed, in the late 1960s and the 1970s, both the Asian American Movement and the academic field were intent on distancing themselves from the traditional academic disciplines and the more established, or "assimilated," components of the Asian American community. For example, the ethnic consciousness movements of the 1960 also fundamentally changed how historians and other social scientists interpreted Asian American history. The pre-Movement historiography of the wartime incarceration of Japanese Americans tended to interpret this experience as a grave national mistake but one that had been corrected by the postwar acceptance of Japanese Americans into American society. The Movement challenged this established interpretation and influenced Japanese Americans and others to reexamine the internment experience within the context of the ongoing debate over past and present racism in American society. Although redress was successfully obtained, the issue of Japanese American internment continues to be linked with contemporary issues of racial justice.[2]

In retrospect, it is clear that contemporary Asian American Studies stands in continuity with earlier attempts by Asian American intellectuals, within and outside the academy, to rethink their own experience and to link it to the broader sweep of American history. The connection is most evident in sociology: Paul Siu, Rose Hum Lee, and Frank Miyamoto, who were members of an older cohort, and Tamotsu Shibutani, Harry Kitano, James Sakoda, Eugene Uyeki, Netsuko Nishi, John Kitsuse, and many others, who were members of a younger cohort, all made important contributions to the study of Asian America, as well as to broader areas in sociology. To the extent that Asian American Studies involves activities that derive from an attempt at self-understanding, one also needs to point out the crucial literary, autobiographical, and polemical works of an earlier period: we note the writings of Jade Snow Wong, Monica Sone, Carlos Bulosan, Louis Chu, and John Okada, among others, a corpus that has now become the subject of considerable academic work within Asian American Studies. Also noticeable is a small group of Euro-American researchers who work within the mainstream disciplines, but without the assimilatory, condescending assumptions that mar earlier work and who have made significant contributions to the study of Asian America *prior* to the advent of the Asian American Movement, providing notice to the disciplines that this was a topic worthy of their attention. The historians Alexander Saxton, Roger Daniels, and John Modell and the sociologist Stanford Lyman deserve particular mention.

In its recent development, Asian American Studies is facing a new reality that is at odds with the Asian American community of the 1960s and 1970s. Asian American scholars have keenly observed several significant trends that have transformed Asian America, with attendant effects on Asian American Studies within the academy: an unparalleled demographic transformation from relative homogeneity to increased diversity; an overall political shift from progressive goals of making societal changes toward more individualistic orientations of occupational achievements; unprecedented rates of socioeconomic mobility and residential desegregation of native-born generations; and a greater separation between academia and the community (Fong 1998; Hirabayashi 1995; Kang 1998, Wat 1998). These trends mirror the broader structural changes that have occurred in American society since the late 1970s, which we shall discuss in greater detail shortly, and create both opportunities and challenges for the field.

To a large extent, Asian American Studies has been energized by the interdisciplinary dynamism that exists not only in history, literature and literary works, and cultural studies, but also in anthropology, sociology, psychology, education, political science, social welfare, and public policy. The field has traditionally been guided by varying theoretical concerns—Marxism, internal colonialism, racial formation, postmodernism, and postcolonialism, among others—and has steadily widened its purview of topics and subject matters. Interdisciplinary course offerings and research have touched on the daily experiences of the internally diverse ethnic populations; course subjects range from the histories and experiences of specific national origin groups to Asian American literature, film and art, and religion, as well as to special topics such as gender studies, gay and lesbian studies, immigration, and health. The field has also expanded into comparative areas of racial and ethnic relations in America, diasporic experiences, transnational communities, and the interconnectedness of Asians and Asian Americans, while maintaining a community focus through extensive internship and leadership development programs. These interdisciplinary and comparative approaches allow Asian American scholars and students to get beyond the simple assumption that, because people share certain phenotypes, they must also share the same experiences, values, and beliefs. Asian American Studies has also injected historical and ethnic sensibility into various academic disciplines and prevented itself from being trapped as an isolated elective subdiscipline.

On the academic front, however, there has been a debate over the relationship between theory and practice. Michael Omi and Dana Takagi voice a central concern over the lack of a sustained and coherent radical theory of social transformation, arguing that this absence may lead to a retreat to "more mainstream, discipline-based paradigmatic orientations." These scholars see the "professionalization" of the field at universities, the demands of tenure and promotion for faculty, and new faculty's lack of exposure to and experience of the Movement of the earlier period as the main contributing factors to this trend of retreat. They suggest that the field should be "transdisciplinary" rather than "interdisciplinary" and that it should be revisited, rethought, and redefined according to three main themes—the scope and domain of theory, the definition of core theoretical problems and issues, and the significance of Asian American Studies as a political project (Omi and Takagi 1995).

Meanwhile, some scholars and students are concerned that Asian American Studies is being diverted from its original mission of activism, oppositional ideology, and community-oriented practices (Endo and Wei 1988; Hirabayashi 1995; Kiang 1995; Loo and Mar 1985–1986). As the field gains legitimacy at universities, it is increasingly uprooted from the community. Although students have continued to involve themselves in community affairs, their activities tend to be framed in terms of service provision, since the social infrastructure in many Asian American communities is always almost in need of volunteers, as one might expect. But volunteering is all too often a part-time event, in which students may pass through the community and then ultimately maintain a distance from it. Lane Ryo Hirabayashi (1995) points out that the divergence goes beyond the institutional "reward structure" that prioritizes theoretical contributions over applied research. He alludes to the problems of essentialized notions of race and ethnicity, the presumed unity of the community, and the impacts of poststructural and postmodern critiques aiming at deconstructing academic dominance. He believes that these concerns can be effectively addressed by redefining the community as a multidimensional entity with ongoing internal class, generational, political, gender, and sexual divisions, reconceptualizing Asian American communities as a dynamic social construct, and incorporating new theories and methodologies into community-based research.

Finding a common ground from which to approach issues in Asian American Studies is a challenging task. Many scholars have made concerted efforts to develop alternative paradigms and perspectives to deal with issues confronting a new Asian America that has become more dynamic and diverse. For example, Lisa Lowe reconceptualizes contemporary Asian American in terms of heterogeneity, hybridity, and multiplicity to capture the material contradictions among Asian Americans (this volume). L. Ling-chi Wang (1995) proposes a dual-domination model for understanding Asian American experiences that takes into account the diplomatic relations between the United States and Asian countries and the extraterritorial interaction between Asian American communities and their respective homelands. Sau-Ling C. Wong (1995) uses the term "denationalization" to address transnational concerns that have emerged from the intrinsic relations between Asia and Asian America. Sylvia Yanagisako (1995) advances the idea of contextualizing meanings, social relations, and social action and of liberalizing the confines of social borders that cut across nation, gender, ethnicity, kinship, and social class in Asian American history. Shirley Hune (this volume) calls for the rethinking of race. She suggests that theoretical paradigms be shifted to articulate the multiplicity of racial dynamics that has moved beyond the black-white dichtomy and that more attention be paid to the differential power and agency of minority communities in the United States and to the situation of Asian America in connection to disaporic communities around the globe.

While the ongoing discussion of goals and methodologies is at once refreshing and evident of the field's continuing vitality, it also testifies to the degree to which intellectual and organizational tensions are built into the field. On the one hand, the very language of the debate, often filled with jargon and trendy concepts, stands in conflict with the self-professed orientation toward the community and its needs. On the other hand, there is a certain nostalgia among veteran activists, now mainly tenured professors, for the spirit of the 1960s and, to some extent, that yearning for the past ironically threatens to produce a divide between U.S.-born (and/or U.S.-raised) scholars and some of their Asian-born counterparts, especially those whose education in the United States was more likely to begin at the college and graduate level, and who may not share the same connection to a history that they never experienced.[3] Moreover, the ideological presuppositions of the scholars oriented toward the Movement has the potential to create distance between them and the growing number of Asian American (often Asian-born) scholars who work on Asian American topics, but from the standpoint of the more traditional disciplines of history, sociology, demography, economics, political science, and so on. Of course, work in the traditional disciplines is by no means value free, but the ideological presuppositions do not preclude the potential for expanding our understanding of the Asian American experience. Finally, we note the irony in the unspoken consensus about which groups are eligible for consideration as "Asian American," namely, everyone with origins east of Afghanistan. As Henry Yu has pointed out, the very definition of Chinese and Japanese as an "Asian American community" was itself the product of earlier externally imposed definitions of America's "Oriental Problem." (Yu 1998). The field has indeed initially organized itself around the study of peoples of East Asian descent, leaving others who are no less eligible on intellectual grounds nor, for that matter, any less vulnerable to discrimination or stigmatization than the "official" Asian American categories to different schools of "Oriental" studies.[4]

In our view, Asian American Studies is best construed in the broadest possible terms, understood as that body of scholarship devoted to the study of Asian American populations, conducted from any number of standpoints, from within the frameworks most commonly found among scholars affiliated with Asian American Studies as well as from standpoints more closely connected to the traditional disciplines. Just as we reject the conventional disciplinary boundaries, we also opt for an expanded view of the field's geographical scope, in particular, emphasizing a transnational framework that enables us to "better understand the ways that flows of people, money, labor, obligations, and goods between nations and continents have shaped the Asian American experience" (Gupta and Ferguson 1992; see also Lowe, this volume). Next, we describe these transnational linkages through the process of immigration and examine the ways in which contemporary immigration affects Asian American communities and challenges the founding principles of Asian American Studies.

Trans-Pacific Movement: Contemporary Immigration from Asia

Anyone who rides the subway in New York, drives on the freeway in California, or walks into any urban classroom will immediately feel the impact of contemporary immigration, the large-scale, non-European immigration to the United States that has accelerated since the late 1960s after a long period of restricted immigration (Massey 1995). Between 1971 and 1995, approximately 17.1 million immigrants came to the United States, almost matching the total number of immigrants who arrived during the first quarter of the century (17.2 million admissions between 1901 and 1925), when immigration was at its peak.[5] Unlike turn-of-the-century immigrants, today's newcomers have come predominantly from non-European countries. Since the 1980s, 88 percent of the immigrants admitted to the United States come from the

Americas (excluding Canada) and Asia; only 10 percent come from Europe, compared to more than 90 percent at the earlier peak. The share of immigrants from Asia as a proportion of the total admissions grew from a tiny 5 percent in the 1950s to 11 percent in the 1960s and 33 percent the 1970s and has remained at 35 percent since 1980.[6] The Philippines, China/Taiwan, Korea, India, and Vietnam have been on the list of top-ten sending countries since 1980 (USINS 1997). What caused this massive human movement in recent years, particularly from Asia? Who are these newcomers? How does the host society receive them? How do the immigrants impact the host society and the native peoples of Asian descent who share their cultural heritage? These questions are of central importance, as they will certainly determine the future of Asian America.

The Driving Forces behind Contemporary Immigration from Asia

Immigration Legislation. U.S. immigration legislation has always claimed to be humanitarian in principle and democratic in ideology. However, beginning with the Chinese Exclusion Act of 1882, various laws were passed by Congress to prohibit immigration from the "barred zone" (known as the Asia-Pacific triangle) and to single out Asian immigrants for exclusion. Asian immigrants were not only barred from re-entering the country but were also considered "aliens ineligible to citizenship," which prevented them from owning land, attaining professional occupations, sending for their family members, out-marrying, and becoming equal participants in American society. World War II marked a watershed for Asian Americans since their homelands, Japan excepted, were allies of the United States. Congress repealed the Chinese Exclusion Act in 1943 and other Asian exclusion acts at the end of the war and passed the War Brides Act in 1945 to allow American GIs to reunite with their Asian wives in the U.S. In 1947 more Asian wives were allowed to join their Asian American husbands by an amendment to the War Brides Act. The public began to shift its perception of Asian Americans from "yellow peril" to the "model minority." Postwar Japanese Americans also experienced a public image transformation from potential saboteurs to loyal Americans, even though more than 110,000 Japanese Americans along the Pacific coast (two-thirds of whom were citizens) were confined to American-style concentration camps during World War II. In 1952, Congress passed the McCarran-Walter Act, making all national origin groups eligible for naturalization and eliminating race as a bar to immigration but still keeping the national origins quota systems.

During the 1960s, the United States was entangled in an unpopular war against Vietnam while also in the throes of the civil rights movement. Both international and domestic crises pushed Congress to clean up the remaining discriminatory immigration legislation. Meanwhile, labor market projections showed that an acute shortage of engineering and medical personnel would soon materialize unless the United States opened its door to foreign labor. As a result, Congress passed the Hart-Cellar Act in 1965. This landmark piece of legislation abolished the national origins quota system, aiming at two goals: a humanitarian goal of reuniting families and an economic goal of meeting the labor market demand for skilled labor. Since the law went into effect in 1968, immigration from Asia and the Americas has increased rapidly, with little sign of slowing down. Between 1971 and 1996, a total of 5.8 million Asians were admitted into the United States as legal immigrants (not counting the thousands of refugees). The majority of contemporary Asian immigrants were either family-sponsored migrants (more than two-thirds) or employer-sponsored skilled workers (about one-fifth). Without a doubt, the Hart-Cellar Act has had a profound impact on Asian immigration. But the main driving forces are beyond the scope of U.S. immigration policy. Recent changes worldwide—global economic restructuring, rapid economic development in Asia, and increasing U.S. political, economic, and military involvement in Asia—have all combined to perpetuate Asian immigration into the United States.

Globalization. The globalization of the U.S. economy since the 1960s has forged an extensive link of economic, cultural, and ideological ties between the United States and many developing countries in the Pacific Rim. Globalization perpetuates emigration from developing countries in two significant ways. First, direct U.S. capital investments into developing countries transform the economic and occupational structures in these countries by disproportionately targeting production for export and taking advantage of raw material and cheap labor. Such twisted development, characterized by the robust growth of low-skilled jobs in export manufacturing, draws a large number of rural, and particularly female, workers into the urban labor markets. Increased rural-urban migration, in turn, causes underemployment and displacement of the urban work force, creating an enormous pool of potential emigrants (Sassen 1989). Second, economic development following the American model in many developing countries stimulates consumerism and consumption and raises expectations regarding the standard of living. The widening gap between consumption expectations and the available standards of living within the structural constraints of the developing countries, combined with easy access to information and migration networks, in turn create tremendous pressure for emigration (Portes and Rumbaut 1996). Consequently, U.S. foreign capital investments in developing countries have resulted in the paradox of rapid economic growth and high emigration from these countries to the United States.

On the U.S. side, unprecedented growth in capital-intensive, high-tech industries and in services has created a severe shortage of skilled workers. American businesses and policy makers believe that importing skilled labor is the quickest solution. Since the 1980s, about one-third of the engineers and medical personnel in the U.S. labor market have come from abroad—mostly from India, China, Taiwan, and the Philippines. However, the shortage of skilled labor is not a sufficient explanation for the trends in highly skilled migration, since skilled immigration disproportionately originates from selected countries in Asia (almost 60 percent of the total skilled immigration in 1995). It is the global integration of higher education and advanced training in the United States in interaction with the opportunity structure in the homelands that have set in motion the highly skilled immigration. The infusion of the educational systems with globalization in many developing countries—notably India, Korea, the Philippines, and Taiwan—has given rise to a sizable professional class. Many members of this emerging middle class are frustrated by the uneven economic development and lack of mobility opportunities at home that devalue their education and skills, and they feel powerless to make changes because of repressive political systems in their homelands. They therefore aggressively seek emigration as the preferred alternative, and the change in U.S. immigration policy facilitates their move (Liu and Cheng 1994). Also, the emergence of the United States as the premier training ground for international students has been instrumental in supplying the U.S. economy with needed skilled labor (Ong et al. 1992). Many foreign students have found permanent employment in the United States after completing their studies or practical training. For example, in fiscal year 1995, close to 40 percent of the immigrants from mainland China were admitted under employment-based preferences. Almost all of them had received higher education or training in the United States.

U.S. Military Involvement in Southeast Asia and the Refugee Exodus. Southeast Asian refugees constitute a significant share of contemporary Asian immigration. Since 1975, more than 1 million refugees have arrived from Vietnam, Laos, and Cambodia as a direct result of the failed U.S. intervention in Southeast Asia. The United States originally had little economic interest in the region but was drawn in because of the threat of Communist takeovers in several countries in the region, according to the then popular "domino" theory. The development of the Communist bloc, dominated by the former Soviet Union, the Communist takeover in China in the late 1940s, and the direct confrontation with Communist troops in the Korean War prompted a U.S. foreign policy aimed at "containing" communism, which ultimately pushed Americans into Indochina. The Vietnam War, its expansion into Southeast Asia and political turmoil in the region left millions of people living in poverty, starvation, and constant fear, while forcing many others to flee from their homelands. One ironic consequence of the U.S. involvement in Indochina is that sizable parts of the populations of Vietnam, Laos, and Cambodia are now in America (Rumbaut 1995). As of 1996, more than 700,000 refugees from Vietnam, 210,000 from Laos, and 135,000 from Cambodia had been admitted to the United States.

Southeast Asian refugees fled their countries in different waves. Although Saigon, Vientiane, and Phnom Penh fell to the Communist forces roughly at the same time in 1975, only the Vietnamese and a small number of the Hmong resistance force had the privilege of being "paroled" (being allowed under special provision of the law) into the United States immediately after the war. Approximately 130,000 Vietnamese refugees and only 3,500 Hmong refugees landed on U.S. soil in 1975 (Chan 1994), while the majority of Hmong resistance forces, Laotian royalists, and Cambodians sought refuge in Thailand. A large refugee exodus occurred at the end of the 1970s, during what is known as the second wave, when thousands of refugees fled Vietnam by boat, creating the "boat people" crisis, while many others fled on land to China and Thailand. About a quarter of a million Vietnamese refugees went to China, and some half a million were floating in the open sea to be picked up by the national guards of whichever country they happened be near. It was reported that almost half of the "boat people" perished at sea, and the remaining half ended up in camps in

Thailand, Indonesia, Malaysia, Singapore, the Philippines, and Hong Kong. Thousands of refugees also fled Laos and Kampuchea (formerly Cambodia) on land to seek refuge in crowded camps along the Thai border. Despite harsh repatriation efforts by the Thai government, about 600,000 Cambodians (15 percent of the country's population) and some 100,000 Hmong and 200,000 lowland Laotians (10 percent of the country's population) fled on land to Thailand, awaiting resettlement in a third country (Chan 1991). The refugee exodus continued in large numbers in the early 1980s. Although the new governments in Southeast Asia did not plunge the three countries into a bloodbath as so many had once feared, continuing political and religious repression, economic hardship, incessant warfare, and contacts with the outside world led many Southeast Asians to escape in search of a better life (Zhou and Bankston 1998).

Migration Network. Once set in motion, international migration is perpetuated by extensive and institutionalized migration networks. Networks are formed by family, kinship, and friendship ties, facilitating and perpetuating international migration because they lower the costs and risks of movement and increase the expected net returns to such movement (Massey et al. 1987). U.S. immigration policy has been instrumental in sustaining and expanding family migration networks. The Hart-Cellar Act of 1965 and its subsequent amendments give preference to family reunification, providing immediate relatives of U.S. citizens with unlimited visa numbers and other relatives with the majority of visa allocations subject to the numerical cap. More than two-thirds of the legal immigrants admitted to the United States since the 1970s have been family-sponsored immigrants. Even among employer-sponsored migrants and refugees, the role of networking is crucial. Family, kin, and friendship networks also tend to expand exponentially, serving as a conduit to additional and thus potentially self-perpetuating migration. In the next decade or so, immigration from Asia is expected to continue at its high volume because many recent immigrants and refugees will have established citizenship status and will become eligible sponsors who can send for family members to reunite in the United States.

Overall, contemporary immigration has been influenced and perpetuated not simply as a result of the Hart-Cellar Act but also by the interplay of a complex set of macro- and microstructural forces. Understanding its dynamics requires a reconceptualized framework that takes into account the effects of globalization, uneven political and economic developments in developing and developed countries, and the role of the United States in world affairs, as well as the social processes of international migration. One significant implication arising from these processes is that high levels of immigration will continue to remain an inseparable part of Asian American life for years to come.

Population Dynamics

Immigration is transforming Asian America in ways unanticipated by long-time Asian immigrants and their U.S.-born children. Although Asian Americans as a group are relatively few in number, making up less than 4 percent of the United

States population, they have aggressively asserted their presence in the American milieu, fighting their way, with varied success, into mainstream economic, social, and political institutions. Before the immigration surge in the late 1960s, the Asian American population was a tiny fraction of the total U.S. population—about 0.3 percent in 1900 and 0.7 percent in 1970—and was composed mainly of three national-origin groups—Japanese, Chinese, and Filipino. Figure I.1 shows the percentage distribution of the Asian American population from 1900 to 1970 (Barringer et al. 1993). During the first three decades of the twentieth century Asians in America were mainly either Chinese or Japanese adult immigrants. The next four decades saw a significant increase in the proportion of Filipinos, who were mostly brought into the United States to fill the labor shortage caused by anti-Asian legislation and the restrictive National Origins Act of 1924. By 1970, Japanese Americans were the largest national-origin group, making up 41 percent of the Asian American population, followed by Chinese Americans (30 percent) and Filipino Americans (24 percent). Members of other national-origin groups (mostly Koreans) represented less than 5 percent of the total.

Pre–World War II immigrants from Asia represented less than 5 percent of the total new arrivals admitted to the United States, a direct result of anti-Asian prejudice and various restrictive immigration laws. Most of the earlier Asian immigrants came from China and Japan, with a smaller number from the Philippines, India, and Korea. These earlier immigrants, like "the tired, huddled masses" from Europe, were typically poor and uneducated peasants, and many of them intended to make a quick

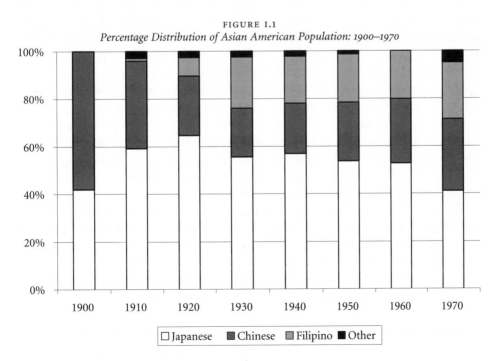

FIGURE I.1
Percentage Distribution of Asian American Population: 1900–1970

□ Japanese   ■ Chinese   ▨ Filipino   ■ Other

SOURCE: Barringer et al. 1993. *Asians and Pacific Islanders in the United States,* p. 42.

fortune to bring back to their homelands. Because of the drastic differences in migration histories among the earlier Asian-origin groups, only Japanese immigrants were able to develop family-based communities with a significant U.S.-born population in the pre–World War II period. Chinatowns, the rather dispersed Filipino enclaves, and other Asian immigrant communities were primarily bachelor societies, with single adult males overrepresented and with few women, children, and families (Chan 1991; Takaki 1989; Zhou 1992).

The distorted population growth in Asian American communities was living evidence of decades of legal exclusion and discrimination. From the time of their arrival, Asian immigrants were subject to laws that served to exclude them from the social and economic opportunities available to most white immigrants. Despite the repeal of the Chinese exclusion laws and the passage of the War Brides Act during World War II and the further relaxation of Asian exclusion laws in the 1950s, the Asian American population grew very slowly, making up barely 0.5 percent of the total U.S. population in 1950. The number of people in some Asian-origin groups was so minuscule, in fact, that the U.S. Census did not even categorize them until 1980 (Nash 1997).[7] Nonetheless, the relaxation of immigration legislation during the early 1940s and 1950s, combined with a postwar baby boom, did give rise to a notable native-born youth cohort, most of whom lived on the West Coast. This age cohort, comprising mostly Japanese and Chinese, came of age in the late 1960s to form the core force of the Asian American movement at college campuses on the West Coast and in the Northeast.

The diversity of the Asian American population started to take shape during the 1970s. The dramatic increase in Asian immigration marked the beginning of contemporary Asian American. In sheer numbers, the U.S. Asian and Pacific Islander population grew from a total of 1.4 million in 1970, to 7.3 million in 1990, and to almost 9 million in 1997 (in contrast to 205,000 in 1900), an impressive fivefold increase in just two decades. Much of this growth is attributed to immigration, which has accounted for more than two-thirds of the total population growth. The populations of most of the new national-origin groups—Indians, Koreans, Vietnamese, Cambodians, Laotians, and the Hmong—grew at spectacular rates, almost entirely because of immigration. It is estimated that, if the current levels of net immigration, intermarriage, and ethnic affiliation hold, the size of the Asian population will increase from 9 million in 1995 to 34 million in 2050, growing from 3 to 8 percent of the total U.S. population (Smith and Edmonston 1997).

The recency of Asian immigration highlights two distinct demographic characteristics of the Asian American population: a disproportionately large foreign-born component and a disproportionately young U.S.-born component. As indicated in the upper panel of figure I.2, the foreign-born component dominates all Asian American groups, except for Japanese Americans; 64 percent of Filipinos, and nearly 80 percent of Vietnamese and other Asians are foreign born. While many immigrant children move with their parents, the great majority of the immigrant generation is of working age. By contrast, the U.S.-born Asian American population is an extremely youthful group. As shown in the lower panel of figure I.2, more than half of U.S.-born Asian Americans are under fifteen years of age; again, Japanese Americans are the exception. Among the new groups, more than 75 percent were in this young age cohort. One implication about this emerging new second generation is that it will grow up in an era of continuously high immigration, joined by a sizable foreign-born cohort—the 1.5 generation—whose members are far more diverse in ethnic backgrounds, the timing of immigration, degrees of acculturation, orientation, and outlooks. This is a situation quite distinct from that which faced the second generation of immigrants in the 1950s and 1960s, because of restrictive immigration.

Diversity

Diversity in National Origins. The dramatic growth in absolute numbers of Asian Americans has been accompanied by increasing ethnic diversity within the Asian American population itself. As of 1990, the U.S. Census recorded seventeen national-

FIGURE I.2
Asian American Population: Nativity and Age

Nativity: Proportion Foreign Born, 1980 v. 1990

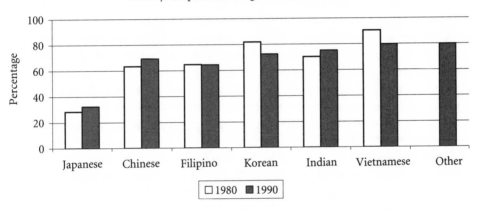

Age: US-Born Age Cohort 0–14, 1990

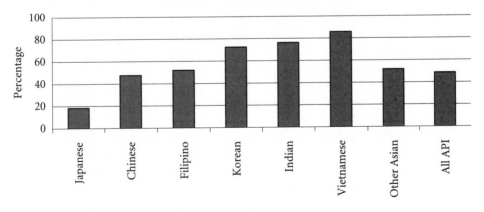

SOURCE: U.S. Census of the Population, 1980, 1990.

TABLE I.1
Asian American Population: 1980–1990

	1980	% Total	1990	% Total
Chinese	812,178	21.6%	1,645,472	22.8%
Filipino	781,894	20.8%	1,406,770	19.5%
Japanese	716,331	19.0%	847,652	11.7%
Indian	387,223	10.3%	815,447	11.3%
Korean	357,393	9.5%	798,849	11.1%
Vietnamese	245,025	6.5%	614,547	8.5%
Cambodian	16,044	0.4%	149,047	2.1%
Laotian	5,204	0.1%	147,375	2.0%
Hmong	47,683	1.3%	94,439	1.3%
Thai	45,279	1.2%	91,360	1.3%
Other Asian	97,585	2.6%	265,436	3.7%
Hawaiian	172,346	4.6%	211,014	2.9%
Guamanian	39,520	1.1%	49,345	0.7%
Samoan	30,695	0.8%	62,964	0.9%
Other Pacific Islander	8,040	0.2%	27,269	0.4%
Total	3,762,440	100.0%	7,226,986	100.0%

SOURCE: U.S. Census of the Population, 1980, 1990.

origin groups, and eight Pacific Islander groups, as revealed in table I.1. Since 1980, no single group has accounted for more than one-third of the Asian American population. While major national-origin groups—Japanese, Chinese, Filipino, Korean, Indian, and Vietnamese—were proportionally represented in 1990, other national-origin groups—Cambodian, Laotian, Hmong—marked their presence in Asian America for the very first time. Because of the unique migration patterns in each of the originating countries, national origins are strongly associated with the type of legal admission (family-sponsored, employer-sponsored, or refugees) and with the skill levels of immigrants. For example, many Filipino immigrants to the United States are college graduates with transferable job skills; many are physicians and nurses sponsored by U.S. employers in the health care industry. Indian immigrants are mostly employed as physicians and computer programmers, as well as small entrepreneurs. Koreans are predominantly middle-class professionals but tend to be disproportionately self-employed in small-scale retail trade. Chinese immigrants are more mixed, including fairly even proportions of rural peasants, urban workers, and the highly skilled. Southeast Asian refugees, in contrast, were pushed out of their homelands by force and suffer tremendous postwar trauma and social displacement, compounded by a lack of education and professional skills, which negatively affects their resettlement.

Socioeconomic Status. Another distinguishing characteristic of contemporary immigrants from Asia is their diverse socioeconomic status. The 1990 U.S. census attests to the vast differences in their levels of education, occupation, and income by national origins. For example, more than 60 percent of immigrants (age 25 years or older) from India and Taiwan reported having attained college degrees, three times the proportion of average Americans, but fewer than 5 percent of those from Cambodia and Laos so reported. Among the employed workers (age 16 years or older), about 45 percent of immigrants from India and Taiwan held managerial or professional occupations, more than twice the proportion of average American workers, but fewer than 5 percent of those from Laos and only about 10 percent of those from Cambodia so reported. Further, immigrants from India, the Philippines, and Taiwan reported a median household income of about or above $45,000, compared to $30,000 for average American households; those from Cambodia and highland Laos (Hmong) reported a median household income below $20,000. Poverty rates for Asian immigrants ranged from a low of 7 percent for Filipinos, Indians, and Japanese to a high of more than 60 percent for Hmongs and 42 percent for Cambodians, compared to about 10 percent for average American families (Zhou 1999).

Settlement Patterns. A third salient feature of contemporary immigration from Asia is the diverse geographic settlement patterns of immigrants. Historically, most Asian immigrants in the United States have been concentrated in Hawaii and in states along the Pacific coast, with a small number of Chinese moving east to settle in New York. Within each area of settlement, they have been highly segregated in ethnic enclaves, such as Chinatowns, Little Tokyos, and Little Manilas. Today, geographic concentration continues to be significant as newcomers follow the footsteps of their predecessors to settle on the West Coast in disproportionate numbers. California has become the preferred destination for immigrants from Asian countries and has 40 percent of the nation's Asian American population. Tables I.2 and I.3 show the geographic distribution of Asian Americans by metropolitan areas, further confirming historical and contemporary patterns of ethnic concentration.

Nonetheless, the Asian American population has begun to disperse throughout the Northeast, the Midwest, and the South. For example, sizable ethnic communities are found in New Orleans (Vietnamese), Houston (Vietnamese and Chinese), and Minneapolis (the Hmong), cities that traditionally received few Asian immigrants. Although there is still evidence of clustering along national or ethnic lines at the local level, there are very few examples of the large and distinctly monoethnic enclaves that were common in the past. In San Francisco, Los Angeles, and New York, there are no new Chinatowns where more than half of the residents are coethnics; Koreatowns in New York and Los Angeles and Little Saigon in Orange County are no

TABLE I.2

Asian and Pacific Islander Population by U.S. Metropolitan Area

	Population	Percent of total
Los Angeles-Long Beach, CA	925,561	12.72%
New York, NY	553,443	7.61%
Honolulu, HI	413,349	5.68%
San Francisco, CA	316,751	4.35%
Oakland, CA	259,002	3.56%
San Jose, CA	254,782	3.50%
Anaheim-Santa Ana, CA	240,703	3.31%
Chicago, IL	227,742	3.13%
Washington, DC-MD-VA	200,113	2.75%
San Diego, CA	184,596	2.54%
Seattle, WA	128,656	1.77%
Houston, TX	125,529	1.73%
Top-12 Subtotal	3,830,227	52.66%
Total API Population in the US	7,273,662	100.00%

SOURCE: U.S. Census of the Population, 1990.

TABLE 1.3
Top Three Metropolitan Areas of Concentration by National Origin (1990)

	Largest concentration	2d Largest concentration	3d Largest concentration	All U.S.	Top 3 as a percentage of total
Chinese	New York, NY 246,817	LA–Long Beach, CA 245,033	San Francisco, CA 162,636	1,645,472	39.77%
Filipino	LA–Long Beach, CA 219,653	Honolulu, HI 120,029	San Diego, CA 95,945	847,562	51.40%
Japanese	Honolulu, HI 195,149	LA–Long Beach, CA 129,736	Anaheim–Santa Ana, CA 29,704	1,460,770	24.27%
Indian	New York, NY 106,270	Chicago, IL 53,702	LA–Long Beach, CA 43,829	815,447	24.99%
Korean	LA–Long Beach, CA 145,431	New York, NY 74,632	Washington, DC–MD–VA 39,850	798,849	32.54%
Vietnamese	Anaheim–Santa Ana, CA 71,882	LA–Long Beach, CA 62,594	San Jose, CA 54,212	614,547	30.69%
Cambodian	LA–Long Beach, CA 27,819	Stockton, CA 10,350	Lowell, MA–NH 6,516	147,411	30.31%
Laotian	Fresno, CA 8,174	Sacramento, CA 7,861	San Diego, CA 7,025	149,014	15.48%
Hmong	Fresno, CA 18,321	Minneapolis–St. Paul, MN–WI 16,435	Merced, CA 6,458	90,082	45.75%

SOURCE: U.S. Census of the Population, 1990.

exception. Filipinos Americans and Indian Americans are comparatively more spread out across the urban landscape, with few identifiable ethnic enclaves. For example, in 1990, only 12 percent of Los Angeles County's Chinese Americans lived in China-town, 22 percent of Korean Americans lived in Koreatown, and a tiny number of Japanese Americans (about 700) lived in Little Tokyo. Overall, trends of spatial integration (moving into white, middle-class neighborhoods) and suburbanization among Asian Americans have been particularly strong in recent years, resulting in decreasing levels of residential segregation even in areas of high concentration (Massey and Denton 1987).

The Impacts of Immigration on Asian America

The impact of diversity in national origins is straightforward. National origins evoke drastic differences in homeland cultures, such as languages, religions, food-ways, and customs; histories of international relations; contexts of emigration; reception in the host society; and adaptation patterns. Such differences persist most significantly in the private domain, affecting not only the immigrant generation but also the native-born generations. For some national origin groups, such as the Chinese and Asian Indians, internal differences in languages or dialects and religions are quite substantial. It is therefore extremely difficult to group everybody under a pan-Asian umbrella at the individual level, creating an obstacle for panethnic coalitions. However, ethnic diversity among the second and third generations associated with homeland cultures is blurred because of these groups' rapid language switch to English and high rates of out-marriages.

Second, socioeconomic diversity gives rise to diverse mobility patterns. New immigrants may continue to follow the traditional bottom-up route to social mobility, starting their American life in isolated urban enclaves, but some segment of this urban population may be permanently trapped in poverty with dim prospects for the future. Those with sufficient social and economic resources may simply bypass the bottom starting line, moving directly into mainstream labor markets and settling directly into suburban middle-class communities (Portes and Zhou 1993). These trajectories to social mobility not only affect life chances of the first generation but also have a profound implication for the new second generation, since the current state and future prospects of immigrant offspring are related to the advantages or disadvantages that accrue through parental socioeconomic status.

Third, socioeconomic diversity leads to divergent destinies, creating a bifurcated distribution of the Asian American population along class lines. Some national-origin groups, such as the Chinese, Filipino, Japanese, Koreans, and Asian Indians, have converged with the general U.S. population, with the rich and the poor on the ends and an ever-growing affluent class in the middle. But, many others, especially the most recent refugee groups, are struggling in the most underprivileged segment of U.S. society. Consequently, class bifurcation toward two ends of society's class spectrum will likely lead to fragmentation of the larger Asian American community, creating new obstacles for political mobilization and ethnic solidarity. Bifurcation also affects the new second generation. Unlike the second generation of the 1960 and 1970s, most of whom grew up in segregated urban enclaves, a visible proportion of today's second generation is growing up in affluent Euro-American neighborhoods in suburbia. Members of the suburban middle class maintain little contact with their working-class coethnics in urban enclaves and show limited interest in working-class issues.

Fourth, settlement patterns have long-term implications for the state of Asia America. Those who are currently segregated in the inner city are confronted with a reality more daunting than the one faced by their earlier counterparts. Today, the United States has an emerging "hourglass" economy in which movement from bottom to top has gotten progressively more difficult. Those newcomers who are poorly educated and who lack marketable skills may find themselves stalled or, even worse, stumbling beneath the ranks of the lower working class, either because they are unable to obtain employment or because the jobs they do obtain do not pay a decent family wage. Consequently, they and their children may become trapped in poverty, poor schools, and a generally disruptive social environment plagued with social ills. In contrast, those who have achieved residential mobility are undoubtedly more privilege, enjoying comfortable homes, safe neighborhoods, quality schools, and more channels to mobility. They may, however, become politically powerless in the face of racism and racial discrimination or strained U.S. relations with the ancestral homeland precisely because they "melt" into a mainstream that has not yet welcomed them wholeheartedly.

Last but not least, immigration complicates intergenerational relations and ethnic solidarity. Native-born children and grandchildren of Asian ancestry have felt the intense cultural and social impact of contemporary immigration and settlement. Almost overnight, native-born Asian Americans, especially those assumed to be "assimilated," are faced with a renewed image of "foreigners." Stereotyped images of "American" create both psychological and practical problems for native-born Americans who phenotypically resemble the new arrivals. Harassment of a native-born Mexican American suspected of being an undocumented immigrant and comments about a third-generation Japanese American's "good English" are frequently heard. The children, U.S.-born and similar to other American children, suffer from persistent disadvantages merely because they look "foreign" (U.S. Commission on Civil Rights 1988, 1992). While they are infuriated by their unfair treatment as foreigners, native-born Asian Americans are also caught between including immigrants in their struggle for racial equality and excluding them. Similar to other Americans in speech, thought, and behavior, native-born Asian Americans often hold values about labor rights, individualism, civil liberty, and, ultimately, the ideology of assimilationism that are different from those of their foreign-born counterparts. These differences, intertwined with the acculturation gap between immigrant and native-born generations, have impeded ethnic coalition, ideological consensus, and collective action (Zhou 1998).

Contemporary Asian America: Identity, Emerging Ethnicity, and the Assimilation Problem

"Who Am I?"

We ABC [American-born Chinese] were ridiculed by the old immigrants as "Bamboo Stick" for not being able to speak Chinese and not being accepted as "white people." We are not here. We are not there. . . . We are different. Most of us are proud of the Chinese cultural heritage, but due to the pressure to assimilate and the lack of opportunity, we don't know much about the Chinese way.[8]

The issue of identity has always occupied a central place in the minds of Asian Americans. Changing demographics and residential mobility in contemporary Asian America make it more salient than ever before. However, this issue has concerned native-born generations more than the first generation, because native-born generations are caught in the insider/outsider divide: they suffer from the paradoxical experience of being in America but not fully a part of it. Both immigrants and their native-born children encounter this paradoxical experience, yet their feelings about it are different.

"While in America, do what the Americans do and become an American" has long been an ideal goal that all immigrants are pressured to attain. However diverse and initially disadvantaged, immigrants are expected to assimilate into mainstream society as quickly as possible. Behind this ideology of assimilationism, however, there is an invisible force for inclusion and exclusion. J. Hector St. John de Crèvecoeur described an American as "either an European or the descendant of an European" (1904 [1782]). More than a century later, Israel Zangwill characterized an American as an "immaculate, well-dressed, accent-free Anglo" (1914). These kinds of definitions of "American," widely if often unconsciously held, make it hard, if not impossible, for people to feel fully American if they happen to be nonwhite, including those whose ancestors settled on this land long before the first Europeans reached American shores. The 1790 National Origin Act prohibited immigrants of certain national origins from becoming U.S. citizens. Thus, not all outsider groups were afforded the privilege of becoming American. A second-generation Chinese American in her sixties explained her isolation from mainstream American society and her socially imposed otherness in these words:

The truth is, no matter how American you think you are or try to be, you do not look "American." If you have almond-shaped eyes, straight black hair, and a yellow complexion, you are a foreigner by default. People will ask where you come from but won't be satisfied until they hear you name a foreign country. And they will naturally compliment your perfect English.[9]

Immigrants are deemed "outsiders," and they tend to cope with their alienation from the immigrant perspective. Historically, people of Asian descent were considered members of "inferior races" and were negatively portrayed as the "indispensable enemy" and as the "yellow peril." No matter how hard they tried to accommodate to American ways, they were considered undesirable and uinassimilable aliens and were legally, socially, and economically excluded from the "melting pot" (Chan 1991).

The Chinese Exclusion Act of 1882, the first immigration act in U.S. history to exclude an entire category of immigrants purely on the basis of national origin, is a prime example. The forced removal and incarceration of Japanese Americans during World War II is another case in point. The federal government, under provision of President Franklin Delano Roosevelt's Executive Order 9066, justified these actions as a "military necessity" vital to the national defense of the United States. In contrast, no such categorical treatments were imposed on German Americans and Italian Americans.

As a reactive strategy to resist subjugation and discrimination, Asian immigrants retreated into their own ethnic communities, rebuilding ethnic institutions that resembled those found in the homeland and relying on one another for moral and practical supports. Extreme adversity allowed them to develop a clear sense of their position in the host society as "foreigners" and to maintain tangible ties to their ethnic community and their homeland, which became internalized as part of their shared experience. Since most Asian immigrants chose to come to the United States to seek better opportunities either for themselves or for their children, their shared experience of marginalization reinforced their determination to push their children into the mainstream by choosing a path of least resistance (Kitano 1969). For example, prewar *Issei* (first generation) drew on extensive ethnic resources in developing trade and business associations to negotiate favorable arrangements with the larger economy and to support their children's education (Matsumoto 1993; Nishi 1995). War-traumatized Japanese American parents or grandparents were reluctant to share wartime memories with their children and grandchildren for fear of hurting their children's chances of social integration (Takezawa, this volume). Post-1965 Korean immigrants pushed their children toward prestigious universities because they looked to their children to regain the social status the parents had lost in the host society (Kim 1999).

Unlike members of the first generation, who tend to avoid arousing antagonism by subscribing to the dominant society's mode of behavior—hard work, education, delayed gratification, nonconfrontational attitudes in the face of injustice—their offspring, American citizens by birth, are likely to fully embrace the principles of freedom, equality, and civil liberties on which citizenship is based. They are unlikely to think of their parents' home country as a place to which they might return, nor do they use it as a point of reference by which to assess their progress in the new land. Rather, their expectations are governed by the same standards to which other Americans aspire, and it is by those standards that native-born Asian Americans assess themselves and are assessed by others. However, American society is not color-blind, and the phenotypes of the second generation subject them to the same types of discrimination and injustice faced by the first generation, regardless of how long they have been in the United States. A third-generation Japanese American from Monterey Park, California, expressed frustration at being objectified as a "foreigner":

> Asian Americans fought for decades against discrimination and racial prejudice. We want to be treated just like everybody else, like Americans. You see, I get real angry when people come up to me and tell me how good my English is. They say: "Oh, you have no accent. Where did you learn English?" Where did I learn English? Right here in America. I was born here like they were. We really hated it when people assume that

just because Asian Americans look different we were foreigners. It took us a long time to get people to see this point, to be sensitized to it. Now the new immigrants are setting us back. People see me now and they automatically treat me as an immigrant. I really hate that. The worst thing is that these immigrants don't understand why I am angry (Cheng and Yang, this volume).

An examination of today's Asian American populations highlights the demarcation between the different generations. Because of legal exclusion in the past, Asian Americans remain primarily an immigrant group, in which the first generation makes up 62 percent of the total Asian American population.[10] It is only among Japanese Americans and Chinese Americans that we notice a sizable third or fourth generation. Among Asian American children under eighteen years of age, more than 90 percent are either foreign-born or children of foreign-born parents. Growing up in the context of an immigrant family is extremely difficult for Asian American children. Parents often place multiple pressures on their children to "do and say the right things" or to "act white" as a means of moving into the mainstream and accessing resources typically reserved for "insiders." In the process of growing up, the children often find themselves vacillating between the outsider's world from which they came and an insider's world into which they were born; they are increasingly ambivalent about their conflicting identities.

Many second-generation Asian Americans of the 1960s and 1970s went through a period of profound confusion, feeling trapped by the ironies of being in America but not a part of it. In the wake of the Asian American Movement, young Asian Americans who entered American institutions of higher education began to confront these identity issues. The Movement forged a space in which these young people not only shared their own personal experiences of racism and suffering in American society but also began to articulate an Asian American consciousness and to refashion their own identities in ways that were meaningful to their experiences—an Asian American identity. At a time when Asian Americans began to empower themselves across panethnic lines and raise ethnic consciousness to a new level for future generations, it is ironic that much of the shame and frustration that previously engulfed the second generation has resurfaced among the children of contemporary immigrants from Asia. Some of the children, especially those who live in suburban, white, middle-class neighborhoods, internalize the negative stereotypes that the society imposes upon their parents' generation and have undergone traumatic, even suicidal, identity crises, in which they feel ashamed of who they are, try to become who they are not, and end up being neither, as so vividly described in *A Letter to My Sister* (Park, this volume). A Chinese-American college student, born in the early 1980s, reveals her confusion as a teenager:

As a child, I had a very difficult time coping with my ethnic identity. I was hesitant to call myself American because as I perceived it, American meant all the beautiful Anglo children in my classes. Yet I was also hesitant to call myself Chinese for two reasons. First, I had no clear concept of what Chinese was besides the fact that my parents were from China. [Second,] I did not feel Chinese. I did not want to be Chinese. I wanted to be White. . . . I tried to hide my identity. I buried it deep within my subconscious, became oblivious to it. Yet every so often, it would be invoked. . . . Perhaps the most notorious manifestation of my shame was my inability to answer the simple question, "What are you?" ... When I was confronted with questions concerning my racial background, I found myself unable to answer. . . . Unable to utter the simple words, "I am Chinese." I just could not do it. It was too painful for some reason. The words seemed too dissonant and distasteful. So many times I simply shrugged and said: "I don't know."[11]

The pressure to assimilate and the conditional acceptance by mainstream society take a heavier toll on the second generation growing up in suburban, white, middle-class neighborhoods than on those who live in ethnic enclaves in the inner-city (Sung 1987). Within the enclave, the homeland is transplanted, ancestral culture and values are honored and practiced as a way of life, and ethnic pride is invigorated. Outside the enclave, ethnicity is subject to the rank order of the racial stratification system, operating under the assumption that ethnic traits should be abandoned in order to become "American." In the midst of an identity crisis, native-born children who are seemingly assimilated structurally may find that they lack a homeland on which they can fall back and an ethnic space in which they can express their fear and anxieties. This explains, in part, why so many Asian American college students demand ethnic studies classes. These ethnic studies classes do not merely serve to disseminate information or transport knowledge but provide a space in which Asian Americans address the issue of identity, allowing them to release negative feelings about themselves as well as inner tensions and anxieties. The classes let them rebuild a sense of self-worth and a group identity as a means of ethnic empowerment.

The Salience of Ethnicity

Identity crises are not uncommon among adolescents as they grow into adulthood, but they are not necessarily defining experiences for all members of native-born generations. Since the birth of the Asian American Movement, a vibrant and multi-faceted ethnic culture has emerged and been reconstructed among native-born Asian Americans in their attempt to reclaim their identity. This culture is neither mainstream American nor clearly associated with the immigrant generation. It is a hybrid form that has come to assume tremendous significance among Asian Americans as a viable means of resistance and compromise within the existing power structure. This phenomenon indicates the fluid nature of ethnicity.

Emergent Ethnicity. The sociologist William Yancey and his colleagues argue that the emergence of an ethnic culture has relatively little to do with the country of origin but more to do with the structure of opportunity in America. Instead of viewing the transplanted cultural heritage as the principal defining characteristic of an ethnic group, these scholars suggest that the development and persistence of ethnicity is a paradoxical process. On the one hand, it is defined in the context of frequent association and interaction with others of common origins and cultural heritage. On the other hand, it is dependent on structural conditions that characterize the positions of groups in American society and create common experiences and interests, thereby setting the potential for collective mobilization around shared goals. Ultimately, it is "a manifestation of the way populations are organized in terms of interaction patterns, institution, personal values, attitudes, lifestyle, and presumed consciousness of kind"—the result of a process that continues to unfold (Yancey et al. 1976, 400). Drawing on this reasoning, we see that Asian Americans develop different patterns of ethnic identification according to the length of time they are in the United States, internal group dynamics, and structural situations that the particular immigrant group and its descendants have encountered.

As we have discussed, identity formation varies across generations and national origin groups. The immigrant generation generally reaffirms its ethnic identity on the basis of homeland cultures and life experiences not only through ethnic practices but also through memories of its lived experiences in the homeland or during the process of movement. For example, Southeast Asian refugees share the common experience of having lived through internal power struggles in their home countries, the horrors of war, and the ordeal of exile and death. These life-threatening experiences become the basis for ethnic solidarity. Drastic cultural changes and adverse societal treatments or disadvantages associated with immigrant status in the host society can reinforce ethnic identity, as in the case of ethnic enclaves where transnational ties and kinship networks remain strong and homeland cultures are often frozen in time as the result of a collective, concerted effort to preserve them.

U.S.-born Asian Americans and those who arrived in the United States as infants or school-age children, in contrast, usually do not seize on traditional cultural symbols as a mode of defining their ethnicity. Rather, they tend to build their identities largely on the basis of mediating *interpretive memories* of homeland cultures in which they have never personally lived and their own diverse life experiences in the United States. Living in immigrant families and in (or close to) ethnic communities has made life in the homeland a continuing reality because parents often communicate to children with a strong sense of determination and instill in them a sense of origin. Close proximity to kinship networks and ethnic enclaves certainly exerts an important effect on the native born, providing an infrastructure that keeps alive the memories of homeland cultures. The collective memory of Chinese exclusion, the U.S. colonization of the Philippines, and the incarceration of Japanese Americans serve as pivotal organizational principles for ethnic identity among native-born Chinese Americans, Filipino Americans and Japanese Americans, respectively. The Museum of the Chinese in the Americas in New York and the Japanese American National Museum in Los Angeles are living proof that even the most "assimilated" of Asian Americans clearly retain vital links to their ethnic culture and to the community that sustains it.

Often, however, actual experiences in American society outweigh memories. Transplanted cultural heritage is no longer the requirement or the defining characteristic of ethnicity for the native born. Rather, the emergence and persistence of ethnicity depend on the structural conditions of the host society and the position that the immigrants group occupies in that social structure. The treatment of Asian Americans as foreigners, the glass-ceiling barrier, and racially motivated hate crimes all serve to reaffirm ethnic identity. However, this ethnic identity, even when it is affiliated with a national origin, differs for the first generation and for its native-born offspring in that the ethnicity of the first generation has a taken-for-granted nature, whereas that of native-born generations is derived both from the collective memory of the historical experience and from the native-born generations' actual experience, in a more self-conscious, reflexive way.

This vibrant emergent ethnic culture transcends the spatial boundaries of ethnic enclaves as well as the symbolic meaning of ethnicity. It is a culture characterized by structures that promote cooperation among coethnics while adopting activities and organizations (e.g., ethnic churches, sports clubs, trade guilds, political organizations) as a means of resistance (Espiritu 1992; Tuan 1999). Yet, what ethnicity means, stands for, or symbolizes differs from region to region, city to city, town to town in the vast expanse of the United States. Being Japanese American in Hawaii or Chinese American in Monterey Park or Vietnamese American in Little Saigon, is not the same as having those identities in New York, Houston, or New Orleans.

Symbolic or Instrumental Ethnicity. Is this emergent ethnicity symbolic? The sociologist Herbert Gans asserts that "as the functions of ethnic cultures and groups diminish and identity becomes the primary way of being ethnic, ethnicity takes on an expressive rather than instrumental function in people's lives, becoming more of a leisure-time activity" (Gans 1979, 9). Among the features of symbolic ethnicity is that it does not carry with it material consequences and does not serve to enhance group solidarity. Indeed, ethnic identity associated with a homeland has become blurred among the second or third generations, who have lost their ancestral languages, intermarried at rates far exceeding the national average, and no longer involved themselves with their ethnic communities on a daily basis, making their ethnicity "symbolic." Our argument about interpretive memories of homeland culture points to the importance of symbolic ethnicity. Clearly, ethnicity is not an either/or matter but rather a variable outcome that varies in its intensity. As we have noted earlier, Asian Americans, both foreign- and native-born, experience high levels of educational attainment, occupational mobility, and residential integration, have high rates of intermarriage, and rapidly lose facility in the native language; hence, much of Asian ethnicity may be optional. As they climb up the socioeconomic ladder in American society, many established Asian Americans may have more choices as to whether they want to be Asian and how Asian they should be when they want to.

At the societal level, however, we argue that the notion of symbolic ethnicity does not always apply well to Asian Americans or to other racial minority groups, since being nonethnic American is still not an option for them, as it is for most European immigrants and their offspring (Waters 1990; see also Takezawa, this volume). The outcry that "America does not include me, only a part of me" is heard here from many native-born, "well-assimilated" Asian Americans. This suggests that unless the whole racial perception of Americans changes and includes other groups as Americans, emergent ethnicity, often in the form of panethnicity, will continue to remain instrumental for the excluded social groups.

Panethnicity. Ethnicity is situational and structurally conditioned. Under certain circumstances, it can evolve into panethnicity, a form of ethnic aggregation typically oriented toward achieving certain material ends and empowerment. In thinking about panethnicity, we draw on the work of the sociologists David Lopez and Yen Espiritu, who link it to a set of cultural and structural preconditions: shared cultural values and life experiences in American society, imposed societal perception and treatment as one phenotypical group, and the internal need for political mobilization to fight for minority rights and to protect group interests (Lopez and Espiritu 1990). We add to these rapid language switch to English and increasing interethnic and interracial marriages, which also contribute to the formation of panethnicity. Today, Asian Americans intermarry extensively with members of other racial or ethnic groups. In Los Angeles County, for example, about one-third of Asian Americans and about half of all second-generation Asian Americans marry outside their ethnic groups. Ambiguous phenotype and social constraints imposed by the existing racial stratification system may foster a strong sense of panethnicity among multiracial Americans.

However, lumping together all peoples of Asian ancestry complicates the notion of ethnicity and its subsequent application to a particular ethnic group, because panethnicity accounts neither for regional or national differences nor for the historical legacies of intergroup conflicts. At this juncture, the term "Asian American," in and of itself, assumes a political agenda for those who subscribe to it, and panethnicity remains a political identity for instrumental purposes. The Asian American community today is, and continues to be, marked by tremendous diversity in the era of high immigration. Diverse languages and religions and differing historical legacies of domination and colonization in Asia make it unlikely that a panethnic coalition will develop in the near future. Differences in class background among the immigrant generation and divergent modes of incorporation of that generation can also deter the formation of panethnicity. The success of Asian Americans' integration into American society as individuals can both enhance and weaken their ability to act collectively. Also, while it is true that discrimination and violence against one Asian group serve to unite Asian Americans, it can also create intragroup conflicts. During World War II, the United States government singled out Japanese Americans as enemies and targets for incarceration. Fearing similar treatment, some Chinese Americans found themselves constantly invoking their Chinese ethnicity and even wore buttons with derogative anti-Japanese words to distinguish themselves. The negative stereotypes about welfare dependency and gang violence among southeast Asians also cause some Asian American groups to distance themselves from them and even to blame them for their plight.

The Assimilation Problem

The issue of assimilation has been at the core of a classic scholarly debate on immigration and racial and ethnic relations. Classical assimilation theory predicts a linear trajectory toward structural integration into the mainstream of society. In this view, the children and the grandchildren of immigrants move beyond the status of the first generation and progressively become less distinct from other Americans. This particular perspective shares a series of assumptions: outsider groups, however diverse and initially disadvantaged, all absorb a common culture and gain equal access to the opportunity structure; they do so in a more or less natural way, gradually deserting old cultural and behavioral patterns in favor of new ones; and the whole process, once set in motion, moves inevitably and irreversibly toward the dissolution of the original group. Consequently, observable ethnic differences are largely a function of time and generational status in the United States. In some cases, the time span for assimilation may be prolonged, but, in the end, distinctive ethnic characteristics eventually fade, retaining only some symbolic importance (Alba 1985; Gans 1979; Gordon 1964; Warner and Srole 1945).

Assimilation theories arose as an abstraction from the experience of earlier European immigration. The theoretical reflections developed largely while the process of immigrant adaptation was under way. Now that it is over, one can safely conclude that the descendants of the 1880–1920 wave have overcome earlier disadvantages, achieving parity with, if not outdistancing, "white" Americans of English ancestry, or what Milton Gordon calls the "core cultural group" (Gordon 1964). Unfortunately, assimilation theories provide no account of why this outcome should have transpired—unless one subscribes to that variant of the modernization theory that most earlier writers embraced but many contemporary social scientists have now challenged. Most important, past success may be due to the specific circumstances encountered by earlier immigrants and their offspring—the fact that between the 1920s and the 1950s, America experienced a long period of restricted immigration, which almost certainly weakened immigrants' attachment to their culture and patterns of group affiliation. Should this be the case, the past is unlikely to prove a useful guide to the future, since we appear to be headed for more, not less, immigration in the years to come.

Assimilationism—the ideology that imposes the dominant core culture on all immigrants to American society—is highly exclusive. The "melting pot" does not wholeheartedly embrace non-European immigrants. The experiences of African Americans are a case in point. Nathan Glazer (1993) shows how racism serves to exclude African Americans from assimilating or sharing in the opportunities of economic and social mobility. Racism and prejudice have also affected the situation of Asian Americans, although to a different degree. Examples are ample, but we point out three of the most obvious.

First, the perception of Asian Americans as "foreigners" has imposed and perpetuated the "otherness" on the group. As we have discussed in detail in the previous section, it is the socially imposed category based on phenotype, rather than acculturation and social mobility, that governs how group members are received and treated in American society. Speaking perfect English, effortlessly practicing mainstream cultural values, and even intermarrying members of the dominant group may help reduce this "otherness" at the individual level but have little effect on the group as a whole, given the relatively small size of the third or later generations of the Asian American population (only 12 percent of the total) and the high levels of recent immigration.

Second, the image of "the yellow peril," although largely repudiated in the post–World War II period, has repeatedly resurfaced throughout American history, especially when the United States is at odds with immigrants' ancestral homelands in Asia. The bombing of Pearl Harbor during World War II turned Japanese immigrants and Americans of Japanese ancestry into potential enemies who were forceably exiled from their homes and put into internment camps. The Communist takeover of China in the late 1940s and the subsequent Cold War made Chinese Americans of the 1950s prime suspects of treason and espionage. The perceived economic threat from Japan in the 1980s led to the murder of Vincent Chin, a Chinese American, mistaken for a Japanese, who was beaten to death by disgruntled unemployed auto workers in Detroit. The renewed spy stereotype is currently manifested in the case of a Taiwan-born scientist, Wen Ho Lee, who was convicted of stealing nuclear secrets for China in the court of public opinion before ever appearing in a court of law. This litany of examples is endless.

Third, the "model minority" stereotype has reinforced the "otherness" of Asian Americans. It is important to note that this stereotype derives from a larger political agenda, serving the ideological function of delegitimizing African American (in particular) claims for equalization of outcomes as opposed to equalization of opportunities. Although Asian Americans as a group are above average on just about any socioeconomic indicator that counts, the "model minority" stereotype obscures the very real problems that many highly "successful" Asians encounter. In particular, highly skilled professionals, who are most definitely part of the middle if not the upper-middle class, are not doing quite as well as their non-Hispanic white counterparts; they experience disproportionate underemployment because of overqualification and overwork (Zhou 1993, 1997; Zhou and Kamo 1994). Furthermore, the stereotype paints a one-sided picture of the Asian American population, obscuring the plight of those who are not doing well and thus further absolving the broader society of any responsibility for redress. There are immigrant workers who are doing poorly; some subjected to severe exploitation. Some groups—Laotians, Hmong, and Cambodians—are still struggling at the very bottom of the social ladder, facing the risk of being trapped in the urban underclass, and others—perhaps the Filipinos— may be stuck in the lower middle class, showing trends of downward mobility (Oropesa and Landale 1997).

In sum, the notion of assimilation, whether it is manifested in a straight line or a bumpy line, seems to clearly imply a *single* line—an idea that is very difficult to reconcile with the historical record of large and significant differences in the rate at which various groups move ahead in American society. Because of the complexity of the reality, with its multifaceted and dynamic nature, it is difficult to comprehend the experiences of today's racial minorities, Asian Americans included, within the assimilationist framework that makes explicit or implicit Anglo-conformist assumptions. Assimilationism may still be a social or moral imperative imposed on immigrants by the dominant culture, but it may not necessarily be the imperative toward which all immigrant groups and their succeeding generations are striving.

The Contents of This Volume

It is evident that Asian American communities are in a state of transition as we approach the beginning of the twenty-first century. The broad themes covered in this volume speak to the nature of these transitions and some of the core debates about the future of Asian American Studies as both a political process and an academic discipline. The range of issues—the Asian American Movement, historical interpretations of the Asian American experience, immigration, family and community, religion, gender, sexuality, the construction of identity among Asian Americans, representation, and the future direction of Asian American Studies—are clearly some of the emerging themes in the field today. More important, these issues are some of the subject matters with which students must contend if they are to have an informed knowledge of the field's development and continued importance.

The chapters in the selection vary in content and information. Some are meant to raise larger issues pertinent to Asian American Studies and to provoke critical thinking, while others provide substantial data to enlighten students about the makeup of the community and its evolution over time. We hope that these two kinds of sources provide students with the background to raise their own questions, to respond to the readings, and to generally make up their own minds about the contemporary issues facing Asian America today. At the end of each section, we provide a list of reading response questions for use in conjunction with course material to enable students to seek out the most important information from each chapter and to raise other questions for discussion.

Claiming Visibility: The Asian American Movement

The first section introduces two landmark pieces written about the genesis of Asian American Studies and the underlying ideologies that were instrumental in its early development. Umemoto's piece surveys the history of the 1968 San Francisco State strike and its importance to the development of the Asian American Movement. She reveals the complexity of the 1960s struggles to which Asian Americans were a part. She argues that the student strike did not occur in a political vacuum, but rather was centrally informed by other ethnic consciousness movements and international Third World Movements for liberation and self-determination. She asserts that the Asian American movement, specifically the outcome of the San Francisco State strike for Asian American students, has left a legacy for the Asian American community and continues to influence Asian American student life on college campuses.

Framing his discussion in a much larger historical context, Omatsu positions the Asian American Movement as a phenomenon centrally informed by the militant struggles against war and racism and by the multiple oppressions that many Americans were only beginning to understand during the 1960s. He contends that the Asian American Movement, while born of these struggles in the early 1960s, comprises diverse segments of the community and works toward one clear goal: liberation. He acknowledges the decline of the Movement's vitality during the 1970s and 1980s but nonetheless argues that the future of Asian American Studies hinges on the community's ability to "forge a new moral vision, reclaiming the militancy and moral urgency of past generations and reaffirming the commitment to participatory democracy, community building, and collective style of leadership."

Making History: The Asian American Experience

The second section focuses on the works of two scholars who are on the cutting edge of Asian American historical production. Takaki's piece is excerpted from his widely acclaimed *Strangers from a Different Shore*. Two themes emerge in this chapter. The first deals specifically with historical agency. Takaki "revisions" the Asian American experiences in its diversity, arguing that the lessons from history can come only from our understanding of Asian Americans not as objects for study but as agents of their own destinies. The second theme deals specifically with the comparative immigration experience. Takaki writes that Asian immigrants who came to the United States did so for many of the same reasons that motivated their European counterparts on the East Coast: they came for better economic lives, to "find a new beginning." The major distinction between these two streams of immigrant groups was their reception in the United States. While it was possible for European immigrants to begin their new lives by fashioning their immigrant identities (by changing their names, for example) into American ones, Asian immigrants were prevented from doing so by law on the basis of their race and places of origin. In fact, racism was endemic to their early lives. Economic exploitation, overt vigilantism, and even legislated bigotry ultimately aimed at excluding Asian immigrants from the privileges of naturalization.

Okihiro asks the important question: When and where do Asian Americans enter the mindset of mainstream American society? Breaking away from some of the more formulaic studies that date Asian American history to the founding of gold at Sutter's Mill in 1848, Okihiro looks to the point at which Asians first entered the mindset of Europeans and how these Orientalist constructions not only framed the reception of European settlers and immigrants to the United States but supported European expansion and colonialism in Asia. His work raises a number of important questions about the oppression encountered by Asian immigrants to the United States and continued attempts to legislate their exclusion from mainstream American life, as well as their social and economic disenfranchisement.

Traversing Borders: Contemporary Asian Immigration to the United States

The third section takes us into the present, examining the effects of contemporary immigration policies on Asian immigrants and their families. Ong and Liu provide a comprehensive overview of immigration policies and their evolution over time. Of interest to students are questions focusing on World War II as a watershed for Asian Americans with respect to changes in immigration and naturalization laws. After World War II, the forces supporting Asian exclusion began to wane, and the United States embarked on a goal to make immigration more equitable for Asian immigrants, which culminated in the passage of the 1965 Hart-Cellar Act. The authors map these changes over time by looking at the primary forces—global forces—that perpetuate high immigration from Asia.

Rumbaut goes to great detail to tease out the various differences, both subtle and overt, that distinguish Southeast Asian refugees and discusses the unique and enormous challenges that face Southeast Asians in the United States. He illustrates significant intragroup and intergroup differences among refugees from Vietnam, Laos, and Cambodia in the contexts of exit and reception. The refugees who were airlifted from the homeland immediately after the Vietnam War were spared lengthy hardships while in flight, but the later arrivals had it much worse. The second and third wave of Southeast Asian refugees, especially those from Laos and Cambodia in the late 1970s and early 1980s, had to endure prolonged periods of extreme difficulties in overseas refugee camps before resettlement. Most of the refugees were poor, uneducated, and unprepared for the displacement. Rumbaut argues that the differential starting points, especially the internal socioeconomic diversification of particular waves and "vintages" within the same nationalities over time, presage differential modes of incorporation and assimilation outcomes that cannot be extrapolated simply from the experience of earlier immigrant groups of the same nationality, let alone from the experiences of immigrants as an undifferentiated whole.

Tyner focuses on the social construction of gendered migration in the Philippines. He shows that the labor recruitment processes, which channel women migrants into domestic services and entertainment industries in foreign countries, are not the result of the formally instituted labor-export policy in the Philippines but simply reflect an acquiescence in global demands predicated on racist and sexist assumptions. In particular, he argues, the socialization into gendered and racial stereotypes predispose the women to take the roles of domestic helpers or entertainers. The social construction of gender, he concludes, accounts for a range of exploitation—mental, physical, and sexual—that women endure, and labor export highlights the manifestation of gendered and racialized stereotypes of migration flows.

Struggling to Get Ahead: Life and Work in Asian America

The fourth section delves into the question of how immigrants cope with the exigencies of life in their new land. Ong and Umemoto highlight an important context of immigrant reception—inner-city neighborhoods that conjure images of social decay, abject poverty, and an overwhelming sense of hopelessness—and argue that the urban plight is primarily the result of the suburbanization of the middle class, regional realignment, and the growing globalization of the economy. They show that, despite the "model minority" image, there are still a substantial number of impoverished Asian Americans, chiefly post-1965 immigrants and refugees, who are struggling to make ends meet and to get out of poverty. Asian Americans play multiple roles in the inner city, they contend, as residents, merchants, workers, and employers. Some Asian American residents receive substantial transitional benefits from their own ethnic economies but meanwhile face the risk of being trapped in poverty in the cities. Asian American entrepreneurs, on the other hand, tend to develop tenuous relationships with non-coethnic residents, customers, and employees, and their economic roles ultimately complicate inner-city living.

Zhou and Nordquist address the importance of gender in the process of immigrant adaptation and the social meaning of women's work in the context of employment and family responsibilities. They approach this theme from the perspective of female workers in Chinatown and consider women's labor force participation as an inseparable part of a family strategy for upward social mobility under extremely difficult circumstances. For Chinatown's immigrant women, they argue, the double burden is compounded by a lack of three things—knowledge of English, transferable education and skills, and knowledge of the larger economy. Employment in low-wage jobs is undesirable but is perceived by immigrant Chinese women as the only viable option to help lift their families out of poverty.

Lee's chapter focuses on Korean immigrant entrepreneurship and race and ethnic relations. Lee sets out to answer four comprehensive questions about the nature of Korean immigrant entrepreneurship in the United States: Why are Korean immigrants employed at a rate higher than any other ethnic group? What resources do Korean immigrants utilize to start their businesses and sustain them over time? What retail niches do Korean immigrants dominate, and why do they concentrate their businesses in economically depressed areas of the inner city? Finally, what are the structural forces that affect the nature of the tensions that have developed between African Americans and Korean immigrants? Lee states that self-employment is a symbol of downward mobility for many Korean immigrants who are educated and trained as white-collar professionals. However, their inability to transfer their pre-immigrant skills to the United States makes entrepreneurship the most effective means for them to achieve the American dream of upward mobility. This dream was shattered after the Los Angeles riots in 1992, which brought black-Korean conflicts to the fore. Although the media have focused on the conflict between the two communities, Lee illustrates that most encounters between Korean merchants and black customers are not fraught with racial animosity but instead are attended by the customary civility. Further, she suggests that, against the backdrop of inner-city poverty, simple economic arguments sometimes become racially coded and in only a few cases lead to interethnic conflict such as boycotts or urban riots.

Ties That Bind: The Asian American Family and Community

The fifth section focuses on the family and the ethnic community. Takezawa provides a detailed analysis of the redress movement and its impact on the reconfiguration of ethnic identity among Japanese Americans in Seattle. Her work explores the process through which Japanese Americans learned to overcome the shame that pervaded their memories of their wartime incarceration and used their understanding of these experiences to mediate their own ethnic identities. This process, as she painstakingly illustrates, is neither uniform nor complete but rather is complicated along generational lines.

Zhou's chapter provides new insight into the role of community-based organizations and families in facilitating the adaptation of second-generation Chinese Americans. She raises a number of questions that are important for the study of the new second generation: Why are the children of immigrant Chinese in Chinatown adapted so well in American schools? What forces (community, family, and peers) affect the adaptation process of the younger generation? Of what import is the ethnic enclave as a form of social capital for immigrants? And what are the implications of ethnicity for the second generation? She shows that new immigration forces the existing ethnic social structures in the enclave to change in order meet the needs of the emerging family-based community. These transformed ethnic organizations, in turn, reinforce immigrant families' expectations of the second generation and support their goal of educational achievement and integration into mainstream American society. She argues that it is the interplay of ethnic patterns of responding to structural disadvantages and family and community forces that affects the adaptation of immigrant Chinese children in inner-city enclaves.

Parreñas deals with the transnational Filipino household, broadly defined as "a family whose core members are located in at least two or more nation-states." Drawing on interviews with Filipina domestic workers in Los Angeles and Rome, she documents the formation and reproduction of transnational households among Filipino labor immigrants as one of many mechanisms available to immigrants as they cope with the exigencies of their new lives. She argues that transnational households have long existed among Filipino migrant workers, who have historically faced legal and economic barriers to full incorporation into the host society. The revival of this immigrant tradition by contemporary Filipino immigrants is the result of intersecting structural and cultural forces.

Keeping the Faith: Spiritual Practices among Asian Americans

The sixth section looks into the spiritual lives of Asian Americans. Bankston's study of a small Laotian refugee community in Iberia, Louisiana, examines the degree to which Laotian refugees to the United States utilize their religion (Therevada Buddhism) to mediate between their own life experiences in Laos and the new environments they encounter in the United States. What role does religion play in enabling these refugees to make sense of the world around them? How does it enable them to adapt to their new social environment? How must Buddhism itself adapt to meet the changing needs of these refugees as well as to accommodate the tensions between the preindustrial economy associated with life in Laos and the postindustrial economy of the United States? These are some of the questions considered by Bankston as he attempts to map out (painstakingly, at times) the differences in religious practices and religious symbols in the homeland and in the host society. He argues that the religious experiences of Laotians have been subtly reshaped by the American context and that this reshaped religion provides the socially displaced refugees with a sense of identity and a comprehensive moral order.

Min examines the social functions of Korean immigrant churches, which he groups into four categories: providing fellowship, maintaining homeland traditions, providing social services, and sustaining social positions. He argues that, in their effort to preserve Korean culture and identity, Korean Americans "Koreanize" Christianity, making it more conducive than mainstream Christian churches to providing social and economic services to the Korean American community and meeting the pressing needs of immigrants.

Williams's critical study explores how the rapid influx of South Asians since 1965—those who claim affiliations as Hindus, Jains, Sikhs, and Muslims, as well as Christians—has complicated the religious landscape of American life, altering the Judeo-Christian patterns that have become a considerable part of our understanding of American religion. Such a change, he argues, calls for a new conceptualization of religious adaptations as pluralistic rather than as reflecting a single Judeo-Christian tradition. He also points out the transnational nature of religious diversity as a result of new modes of communication and social mobility; transnational networks, in turn, affect religious organizations and practices in the host society as well as those in the homelands. He concludes that the future development of religious pluralism hinges on immigration legislation, the strength of the transnational community, and the level of individual mobility and integration into mainstream society.

Women in Asian America

The seventh section examines issues pertaining to gender. Hune's chapter serves the overall purpose of raising important questions about the social status of Asian American women—why women's issues are important to Asian American Studies, what we can do to make women's experiences more central in our research and writing, and ultimately, what our responsibilities are as intellectuals in Asian American Studies to the study of gender. She organizes her study around four specific themes in Asian American history: immigration, work, community, and family. In each instance, she argues, the importance of Asian American women in producing Asian American history cannot be dismissed. As immigrants, Asian American women are agents in their own destiny, often making painful decisions to come to America but, more often than not, having some control over their choices. They play an active role in the workplace and act as equal partners in the family and in the community. Hune concludes her article by reaffirming the importance of women in Asian American history, noting that the women have "actively negotiated and contested traditional hierarchical gender relations and flexed their gender roles to fulfill personal goals and to pursue household and community interests."

Kibria's study centers on Vietnamese refugee women in Philadelphia, focusing on their positions relative to their lives in both Vietnam and the United States. She traces gender roles within the patriarchy in Vietnam and the conditions that reinforced these roles. She notes that the weakening of men's positions had already occurred in Vietnam before the refugee flight, which resulted from, first, the French colonization and, later, the U.S. military intervention. Further changes took place when refugees resettled in the United States, where women usually assume economic responsibilities at least equal to and often greater than those of men. Men's declining economic power weakens the patriarchal structure of the refugee community. Also, women play a crucial role in reestablishing ethnic networks and social structures, which gives them greater power in determining family and community affairs and in challenging male-dominant ideologies and practices. However, Kibria points out the possibility that men may restate their authority over women once they achieve social mobility.

The Construction and Deconstruction of the "Model Minority"

The eighth sections focus on the causes and consequences of the "model minority" stereotype. The publication of William Petersen's article on the virtues of Japanese Americans in the *New York Times Magazine*, in January 1966, marked a significant departure from the ways in which Asian immigrants and their descendants had traditionally been depicted in popular culture. Osajima's chapter is one of the few sources that analyzes the consistency of the "model minority" image over the course of several decades. He points out that, until the 1960s, the media had fed the fears of nativist groups by playing up the threat and the unassimilability of Asians into mainstream America, making life extremely difficult for Asian immigrants and their children and limiting their chances for mobility. The dramatic shift that occurred after World War II was by no means incidental, Osajima contends, but was deliberate, even orchestrated toward much larger ideological goals. On the surface, this new paradigm seems to praise Asian Americans for their achievements. In reality, however, it carried ramifications that extended well beyond the Chinatowns and Japantowns of America to criticize other racialized groups (specifically African Americans and Latinos) that had not achieved equal success in society. Osajima contends that the model minority image is insidious and destructive for the Asian American community. Not only is it used to pit one racial minority group against another, but it also places unreal expectations on the community by prioritizing certain avenues of success while downplaying others.

Cheng and Yang's chapter, based on analysis of the 1990 U.S. Census in the Los Angeles metropolitan region, empirically tests the model minority hypothesis. The authors trace the demographic changes within the Asian American community since the passage of the 1965 Immigration Act and question the viability of pan-Asian integration and the realization of an all-inclusive Asian American identity, an idea broached in the 1960s as a means of generating political unity among Asian Americans. They state that the diversity that underlies contemporary Asian American experiences undercuts the model minority stereotype, which blurs intragroup differences. They test the model minority hypothesis against several significant socioeconomic measures, including education, occupation, and income. They find that Asian Americans do show higher than average educational attainment. However, their occupational achievement is bifurcated, with significant variation by national origin groups and by place of birth, which raises questions about educational payoffs and implies possible obstacles in labor market entry and occupational mobility. In terms of economic standing, they contend that higher median household income level is deceptive as a way of measuring success. Using individual earnings measures, they show that Asian American men earn less than non-Hispanic white men of similar socioeconomic characteristics, despite their overall higher educational attainment and their comparable occupational achievement and higher median household income, and that there are significant differences by ethnicity and gender. Cheng and Yang also discuss the issue of pan-Asian identity and conclude that, in spite of the level of diversity within the contemporary Asian American community, a pan-Asian coalition or identity is important to the extent that it would be politically efficacious in effecting positive change for the community.

Few issues carried greater significance for Asian Americans in the 1980s than the admissions debate that unfolded at several of the most prestigious universities in the United States. Nakanishi enters this debate by stepping back and providing some context to the discussion. His chapter addresses three questions: What accounts for increased enrollment among Asian Americans at universities across the United States? Does evidence exist to support the charge that there exists an admissions bias against Asian Americans? How do we explain the political support enjoyed by Asian Americans from members of both major parties? Nakanishi rejects the cultural explanation for Asian Americans' educational achievement, noting that the socioeconomic diversity that characterizes contemporary immigration from Asia and Asian Americans' response to structural disadvantages play an important part. He shows that, despite their success, Asian Americans suffer from systematic bias in college admissions and that the situation will only worsen if action is not taken. He also shows that the growing political affluence of Asian Americans puts pressure on both parties to pay attention to Asian Americans as a voting bloc.

Confronting Adversity: Racism, Exclusion, and the Burden of Double Standards

The ninth section touches on several aspects of adversity that confront Asian Americans—racism, exclusion, and double standards. Misir's chapter aims at assessing the meaning of bigotry and violence directed against South Asian Americans in the small community of Jersey City over the span of about a decade, illustrating the difficulty involved in forging pan–Asian American unity on important issues like hate crime. She shows that from the time of their arrival in large numbers in Jersey City, South Asian immigrants were subjected to protracted campaigns of intolerance despite the fact that these immigrants were from middle-class backgrounds. Racial taunts, vandalism, anti-Indian graffiti, and intimidation all characterized the decade or so leading up to the 1987 murder of Navroze Modey. What is significant, according to Misir, is that the perpetrators of these crimes were not only white Americans but also included African Americans, Latinos, and other Asian Americans. Their participation in these crimes made the question of race problematic: How does one oppressed group inflict harm on another? Misir contends that the anti-Indian violence in Jersey City was done with an eye toward demarcating turf, with South Asian immigrants singled out as "the other," or "the alien." Misir posits that the black/white dyad along which race is usually understood cannot accurately account for the interminority tensions in Jersey City. She notes that the political maneuvering in response to the racialization of the South Asian Americans has important implications for the way in which communities organize themselves and highlights the obstacles facing the creation of pan-ethnic coalition.

Wang's chapter analyzes the hidden meaning of the 1996 campaign finance scandal that unfairly targeted the contributions of Asian American donors like John Huang and Charlie Trie. The racialization of the campaign served to reinforce the "foreignness" of Asian Americans while at the same time contributing to the historical legacy of political disenfranchisement that has characterized Asian Americans since they first reached American shores. Wang asserts that, from the start, both Democrats and Republicans "played the race card," manipulating Asian American political interests and ultimately denationalizing them, treating Asian Americans "as if they were strangers or worse—lepers, foreigners, criminals, and subversives." When it comes to political empowerment, he argues, the so-called model minority does not fare too well, as politicians must stoop to whatever means are available to them to exploit the weaknesses of their opponents. In light of the allegations and the controversy that the campaign scandal caused, one must question what concessions have been really won by Asian Americans.

Park's chapter speaks to the difficulties encountered by two sisters as they struggle to find their place in American life. Confronting her sister's suicide in a meaningful way forces the narrator to consider the emotional toll that societal double standards take on Asian Americans, especially those growing up in immigrant families. Park points out that racism, the perpetual drive to assimilate racial minorities to a white norm, the pressures placed on the family and the individual to live up to the model minority image, the family's frustration with downward mobility, and the community's reluctance to accept mental illness all played a part in her sister's suicide. She exposes the detrimental effects of the "model minority" stereotype—"Do you see what a lie it is and how it is used to reinforce the American Dream and punish those of us who don't 'succeed' or succeed 'too much'?" Park suggests that the model minority image not only places unrealistic and harmful expectations on Asian Americans who do not live up to its demands, but also extends to other racial minorities, specifically African Americans and Latino Americans, who are asked why they cannot do as well.

Queering Asian America

The tenth sections looks into an important subject area that has only recently begun to receive its due attention in Asian American Studies—the experiences of gay, lesbian, and transgendered Asian Americans. When Takagi's chapter first appeared in *Amerasia Journal* in 1994, it broke important ground, discussing the experiences of gays, lesbians, and transexuals in Asian America. Takagi argues that the consideration of sexuality in Asian American history is a critical part of expanding our narrow understandings of the range of experiences present in the Asian American community. For example, gay and lesbian Asian Americans experience double marginalization along racial and sexual lines, but there is a lack of a theoretical framework that facilitates our understanding and ways of understanding their experience. Takagi points out that "[m]arginalization is not as much about the *quantities* of experience as it is about the *qualities* of experience" and that identities are not "additive." Drawing on her own experiences as an activist, Asian American, lesbian woman, she finds that, while marginalized groups often collectively engage in their fight for equal rights, there are a number of tensions stemming from individual desires and histories that complicate this process. Where sexuality is concerned, Takagi suggests, an Asian American and a homosexual identity cannot necessarily be viewed as two parts of the same coin. One's sexual identity cannot be viewed as one more form of oppression subordinate to one's racial identity. It must be viewed as discrete to understand how sexuality is "troped in Asian America."

Hom's chapter brings new insight to the realm of the unspoken in Asian America—the response of Asian American parents to the sexual identities of their children. On the basis of personal interviews with fathers and mothers, Hom assesses the attitudes of parents toward gays and lesbians prior to knowing their children's sexual identities. She finds that, by and large, the response of these Asian American parents is contingent on their level of experience with gays and lesbians before their arrival in the United States. Most parents were aware of the gender role reversals in their children's growing up but tended to distance themselves from the phenomenon because it was "not your problem." On finding out that their own children were gay or lesbian, the parents experienced a number of different feelings: shame, guilt, surprise, shock, disbelief, and, in one common case, a sense of alienation from their children. Only one interviewee in Hom's study mentioned the loss of "Asian values," but for most there was a sense that in some manner they had failed their children. The road to acceptance was neither uniform nor without difficulties. In relating their children's sexualities to individuals within the ethnic community, the interviewees shared mixed feelings. A number of parents decided not to relate any information about their children to friends or to anyone else outside the immediate family, while others shared their feelings with friends in and out of the gay and lesbian community.

Manalansan's research focuses on immigrant lives in a community of gay Filipino Americans in New York City. Manalansan employs a fluid definition of community, which is both an "imagined" place where people organize around symbols and practices reminiscent of other symbolic communities and a place of dissent where forces of oppression also unite people toward common goals. The confluence of these seemingly contradictory definitions of community is critical to the way in which Filipino homosexuals, many of whom are recent immigrants to the United States, construct their own identities. According to the author, the differences among this group are substantial, and the kinds of homosexual traditions adopted by these men reflect their life circumstances and the contexts in which they grew up in the Philippines (for native-born Filipino Americans, whether or not they were exposed to these traditions at some point in their lives). Manalansan points to other elements that reflect the diversity of the Filipino gay community he surveys, such as social class and ethnic, racial, and national identities. Most of these gay Filipino immigrants possess a number of regional, ethnic, and linguistic differences that also makes a shared sense of community difficult to foster. In spite of these variances, Manalansan provides examples of certain events—the Broadway production of *Miss Saigon*; the Aids pandemic (Tita Aida); and the reproduction of Filipino cultural traditions in America—that have reduced barriers to group unity, while not necessarily galvanizing a shared sense of community. This chapter, in sum, is an early attempt to address both the obstacles that render community among gay Filipino Americans a seemingly impossible construction and the confluence of moments and events that fosters the shared sense of needing and the rearticulation of the community.

The Complexity of Ethnic Identity: Interracial Marriages and Multiethnic Asian Americans

The eleventh section delves into the phenomenon of intermarriages and multiracial and multiethnic ethnic identities. Fong and Yung provide new insight into the complexity of this phenomenon, challenging the traditional interpretations of out-marriage between racial minorities and whites as a natural progression toward full assimilation into American society. On the basis of findings from interviews with both men and women, the authors argue that, while assimilation has narrowed the gaps between the races and thus brought ethnic groups into closer proximity, factors explaining why individuals decide to out-marry are far more complicated. These reasons include the timing of relationships (a readiness to marry on the part of an individual weakens racial preferences), the relative lack of availability of Asian American partners in a specific geographic region, the existence of similar value and goals, which can supersede racial preferences (e.g., the proclivity of Asian Americans to marry Jewish partners), the propensity for Asian Americans from Hawaii to out-marry (partly because of the relative acceptance of out-marriage in Hawaii), an aversion to marrying partners from the same race, and a tendency to find fault with potential partners of the same race for not having qualities found in potential white partners, including the potential for upward mobility (hyperagamy). This work broadens the classical theoretical framework—assimilation—that has dominated the study of out-marriages.

Spickard's chapter addresses two crucial and interrelated questions: Why has Asian American Studies failed to include the life experiences of biracial Asian Americans, and how can the field make the subject relevant to the needs of this group? In answering the first question, Spickard maps out the complexity of identity formation and its evolution among biracial Asian Americans. According to Spickard, three trends are at work in the process of identity formation among multiracial Asian Americans. The first stems from the dominant society, which tends to categorize and identify multiracial Asian Americans as weak, inferior, promiscuous, and perverse. The net effect of this process is to demoralize these multicultural peoples, as well as to ostracize them from the white community proper. A second trend derives from the Asian American community's tendency, similar to that among the dominant society, to identify and categorize multiracial Asian Americans often in derogatory terms. It is only within the past three decades that a different trend has emerged in the identity formation process of multiracial Asian Americans, a trend that stems from these multiracial people themselves. Spickard's article raises the critical point: demographics no longer allow us to think of Asian American Studies as the realm of Japanese Americans, Chinese Americans, and Filipino Americans alone. Asian American communities throughout the United States are in a state of great transformation as new immigrants redefine the parameters of ethnicity and solidarity. The incorporation of diverse constituencies, among them multicultural Asians, will only enhance our understanding of Asian American history and the evolution of this community in the next millennium.

Visual Culture

The twelfth section looks into an exciting, yet underexplored area in Asian American Studies: visual culture. At a conference sponsored by the Asian American Arts Alliance and the Asian Pacific Student Alliance at Hunter College in New York, the panelists Alexander, Machida, Pfeiffer, Pekarik, and Tajima addressed a series of important questions attempting to come to some conclusions about the presence of an "Asian American Aesthetics." What qualities characterize Asian American artistic production? Who defines it? How important is visual culture to the manner in which the Asian American community approaches its own history, culture, and experiences? The variety of opinions provides an interesting first look into this critical debate.

Kondo's chapter deals with the critical linkage between artistic production and the deployment of interventions by Asian American artists and others from the community to disrupt the distorted representation of "other." Representations in popular culture—be it theater, literature, or film—while often masked in subtle or pleasant imagery, reinforce a power dynamic that oppresses racial and ethnic minority peoples, preventing them from representing their own interests and telling their own stories and experiences in a way that is meaningful, iconoclastic, and multidimensional. Kondo focuses her analysis on three contemporary events—the staging of *Miss Saigon* on Broadway, the production of Michael Crichton's *Rising Sun*, and a stage production of *The Mikado* at Claremont McKenna College (where Kondo was formerly a professor in the anthropology department). She examines the strategies utilized by Asian American artists and the community to interrogate racist and stereotyped images of Asian Americans. Kondo's chapter shows that artistic production and activism go hand in hand in reversing racialized images of Asian Americans as presented by the mainstream. Although the ability of these actions to effect change is debatable, it does raise the consciousness of Asian Americans to a new level, challenging them to critique racist imagery.

Mapping the Terrain: New Paradigms in Asian American Studies

The final section raises questions around the possibilities for the future of Asian American Studies. Hune's chapter was written for a special issue of the *Amerasia Journal* devoted to the topic of "thinking theory" in Asian American Studies. Hune assesses the importance of reconceptualizing theoretical paradigms by highlighting five paradigmatic shifts in recent years, which strike Hune as particularly relevant to Asian American Studies: (1) the shift from a dichotomous black-versus-white race relations model; (2) the shift from a static model that views race as a fixed category based on genetics and biological differences; (3) the shift from the model that reduces Asian American communities to victims of circumstance; (4) the shift from a model that treats the Asian American community as homogeneous, with all members having similar experiences and facing similar obstacles; and (5) the shift from a national model that looks at the Asian American community as a singularly Asian American experience within the confines of the nation-state to a transnational perspective. Hune asserts that emergent paradigms are better able to capture the present-day realities of life for minority peoples in the United States. These new paradigms, she argues, may not subvert the dominant paradigms in toto, but they nonetheless raise important questions that problematize the manner in which the dominant discourse analyzes issues and dictates policy.

Lowe's chapter is a challenging piece to read in its entirety, since it may be open to multiple interpretations. Her purpose is twofold: first, to disrupt the common tropes of generational conflict and filial relationships that permeate the Asian American experience, and, second, to reconceptualize Asian American identity as an entity in a continual state of flux. "Rather than considering 'Asian American identity' as a fixed, established 'given,'" Lowe writes, "perhaps we can consider instead 'Asian American cultural practices' that produce identity; the processes that produce such identity are never complete." The main point of her work is that Asian American culture is neither immutable nor vertically transmitted from one generation to the next. Asian American culture is as much a production of identities as it is a reception of traditions. As Lowe contends, "[t]he boundaries and definitions of Asian American culture are continually shifting and being contested from pressures both inside and outside the Asian-origin community." It is these shifting constructions of identity that constitute the heterogeneity, hybridity, and multiplicity of contemporary Asian American community.

These chapters, taken as a whole, illustrate some of the prospects, possibilities, and problems currently faced by Asian American Studies. It is our hope that readers will approach these issues in a critical and reflexive manner, one that draws heavily on their own experiences, histories, and interpretations. This anthology is by no means a definitive statement of the complexity and range of issues faced by Asian Americans today. In fact, it is only a start on raising questions that may not necessarily have clear or definitive answers. And it is these very questions with which Asian Americans are struggling at century's end. For some people, the resolution may be simple. For many others, however, the solution may require compromise. We are excited by the prospects for the future of Asian American Studies but offer a tone of caution, one that is cognizant of how far the field has come from those early days at San Francisco State College. Our greatest successes—legitimacy in the academy, recognition by mainstream departments at universities across the United States, and publication of works by major university presses—seem to have distanced us further from the original goals of the Asian American Movement. Nonetheless, we are moving forward as we enter the new millennium. There are no clear answers, only prospects and possibilities.

NOTES

1. Hong, 1998.

2. The author gained insight from Yuji Ichioka's comments. See also Yamamoto 1999 for details.

3. See the special issue (vol. 1, 2, 1995) of *Amerasia Journalo* and part II of Hirabayashi (1995) for details.

4. Indeed, all persons born in Asia, including those emanating from that area arbitrarily (and Euro-centrically) designated as the Middle East, were excluded from citizenship until the 1952 Immigration Act. For details, see Haney López 1996.

5. The number includes 1.6 million formerly unauthorized aliens and 1.1 million Special Agricultural Workers who were granted permanent resident status under the provisions of the Immigration Reform and Control Act of 1986 (Zhou 1998).

6. The number of Asian immigrants excludes those from Iran, Israel, and Turkey. The exception to the statement in the text is 1991 when the Asian share dropped to 18 percent because of the sudden increase in the number of legal immigrants, under the Immigration Reform and Control Act of 1986. Most of the legal immigrants in 1991 were Mexicans or Central Americans.

7. A small number of Asian Indians were present at the time. They were, however, classified as "Hindu" in the 1920, 1930, and 1940 censuses, as "white" in 1950 and 1960, and as "Asian or Pacific Islander" since 1970 (Nash 1997).

8. Originally quoted in Bernard Wong 1982, 33. Also cited in Morrison G. Wong 1995, 86.

9. Personal communication, retired Chinatown activist in New York.

10. The detail generation breakdown among Asian Americans is as follows: 62 percent belong to the first generation (foreign-born), 27 percent belong to the second generation (U.S.-born with foreign-born parentage); and 12 percent are part of the third or later generations (U.S.-born with U.S.-born parentage), compared to 9 percent, 11 percent, and 80 percent, respectively, for the general U.S. population. Figures are from the 1994–1997 Current Population Survey of the U.S. Census Bureau.

11. Class discussion on ethnic identity, UCLA, March 1999.

REFERENCES

Alba, Richard D. 1985. *Italian Americans: Into the Twilight of Ethnicity*. Englewood Cliffs, NJ: Prentice-Hall.

Barringer, Herbert, Robert B. Gardner, and Michael J. Levin. 1993. *Asians and Pacific Islanders in the United States* (p. 42, table 2.5). New York: Russell Sage Foundation.

Chan, Sucheng. 1994. *Hmong Means Free: Life in Laos and America*. Philadelphia: Temple University Press.

———. 1991. *Asian Americans: An Interpretive History*. New York: Twayne.

———. 1978. Contextual Frameworks for Reading *Counterpoint*. *Amerasia Journal* 5(1): 115–129.

De Crèvecoeur, J. Hector St. John. 1904 [1782]. *Letters from an American Farmer*. New York: Fox and Duffield.

Editors of the *Chronicle of Higher Education* 1995. *The Almanac of Higher Education, 1995*. Chicago: University of Chicago Press.

Endo, Russell, and William Wei. 1988. On the Development of Asian American Studies Programs. Pp. 5–15 in Gary Y. Okihiro, Shirley Hune, Arthur A. Hansen, and John M. Liu (eds.), *Reflection on Shattered Windows: Promises and Prospects for Asian American Studies*. Pullman: Washington State University Press.

Espiritu, Yen Le. 1992. *Asian American Panethnicity: Bridging Institutions and Identities*. Philadelphia: Temple University Press.

Fong, Timothy P. 1998. Reflections on Teaching about Asian American Communities. Pp. 143–159 in Lane Ryo Harabayashi (ed.), *Teaching Asian America: Diversity and the Problem of the Community*. Lanham, MD. Rowman Littlefield.

Gans, Herbert J. 1979. Symbolic Ethnicity: The Future of Ethnic Groups and Cultures in America. *Ethnic and Racial Studies* 2: 1–20.

Glazer, Nathan. 1993. Is Assimilation Dead? *Annals of the American Academy of Political and Social Sciences* 530: 122–136.

Gordon, Milton M. 1964. *Assimilation in American Life: The Role of Race, Religion, and National Origins*. New York: Oxford University Press.

Gupta, A., and J. Ferguson. 1992. Beyond "Culture": Space, Identity, and the Politics of Difference. *Cultural Anthropology* 7(1): 6–23.

Haney López, Ian F. 1996. *White by Law: The Legal Construction of Race*. New York: New York University Press.

Hirabayashi, Lane Ryo. 1995. Back to the Future: Re-Framing Community-Based Research. *Amerasia Journal* 21: 103–118.

Hong, Peter Y. 1998. The Changing Face of Higher Education; Trends: Asian Americans' Numbers and Influence Now Mark All Segments of College Life. *Los Angeles Times*, July 14, p. A1.

Jaynes, Gerald David, and Robin M. Williams, Jr. (eds.). 1989. *A Common Destiny: Blacks and American Society*. Washington, DC: National Academy Press.

Kang, Laura Hyun Yi. 1998. A Contending Pedagogy: Asian American Studies as Extracurricular Praxis. Pp. 123–141 in Lane Ryo Harabayashi (ed.), *Teaching Asian America: Diversity and the Problem of the Community*. Lanham, MD: Rowman Littlefield.

Kiang, Peter Nien-chu. 1995. The New Waves: Developing Asian American Studies on the East Coast. Pp. 305–314 in Gary Y. Okihiro, Marilyn Alquizola, Dorothy Fujita Rony, and K. Scott Wong (eds.), *Privileging Positions: The Sites of Asian American Studies*. Pullman: Washington State University Press.

Kim, Susan. 1999. Academic Achievement of Korean American Youths. Master's thesis, Department of Sociology, UCLA.

Kitano, Harry. 1969. *Japanese Americans: The Evolution of a Subculture*. Englewood Cliffs, NJ: Prentice-Hall.

Liu, John M., and Lucie Cheng. 1994. Pacific Rim Development and the Duality of Post-1965 Asian Immigration to the United States. Pp. 74–99 in Paul M. Ong, Edna Bonacich, and Lucie Cheng (eds.), *The New Asian Immigration in Los Angeles and Global Restructuring*. Philadelphia: Temple University Press.

Loo, Chalsa, and Don Mar. 1985–1986. Research and Asian Americans: Social Change or Empty Prize? *Amerasia Journal* 12(2): 85–93.

Lopez, David, and Yen Espiritu. 1990. Panethnicity in the United States: A Theoretical Framework. *Ethnic and Racial Studies* 13: 198–224.

Massey, Douglas S. 1995. The New Immigration and Ethnicity in the United States. *Population and Development Review* 21(3): 631–652.

Massey, Douglas S., Rafael Alarcon, Jorge Durand, and Humberto Gonzalez. 1987. *Return to Azlan: The Social Process of International Migration from Western Mexico*. Berkeley: University of California Press.

Massey, Douglas S., and Nancy A. Denton. 1987. Trends in the Residential Segregation of Blacks, Hispanics, and Asians. *American Sociological Review* 52: 802–825.

Matsumoto, Valerie J. 1993. *Farming the Homeplace*. Ithaca, NY: Cornell University Press.

Monaghan, Peter. 1999. A New Momentum in Asian-American Studies: Many Colleges Create New Programs; Many Programs Broaden Their Courses and Research. *Chronicle of Higher Education*, March 29.

Nakanishi, Don T., and Russell Leong. 1978. Toward the Second Decade: A National Survey of Asian American Studies Programs in 1978. *Amerasia Journal* 5(1): 1–19.

Nash, Philip Tajitsu. 1997. Will the Census Go Multiracial? *Amerasia Journal* 23(1): 17–27.

Nishi, Setsuko Matsunaga. 1995. Japanese Americans. Pp. 95–133 in Pyong Gap Min (ed.), *Asian Americans: Contemporary Trends and Issue*. Thousand Oaks, CA: Sage Publications.

Omi, Michael, and Dana Takagi. 1995. Thinking Theory in Asian American Studies. *Amerasia Journal* 21 (1, 2): xi–xv.

Ong, Paul M., Lucie Cheng, and Leslie Evans. 1992. Migration of Highly Educated Asians and Global Dynamics. *Asian and Pacific Migration Journal* 1(3–4): 543–567.

Oropesa, R. S., and N. S. Landale. 1997. Immigrant Legacies: Ethnicity, Generation and Children's Family and Economic Lives. *Social Science Quarterly* 78(2): 399–416.

Portes, Alejandro, and Rubén G. Rumbaut. 1996. *Immigrant America: A Portrait*, 2nd ed. Berkeley: University of California Press.

Portes, Alejandro, and Min Zhou. 1993. The New Second Generation: Segmented Assimilation and Its Variants Among Post-1965 Immigrant Youth. *Annals of the American Academy of Political and Social Science* 530: 74–98.

Rumbaut, Rubén G. 1995. Vietnamese, Laotian, and Cambodian Americans. Pp. 232–270 in Pyong Gap Min (ed.), *Asian Americans: Contemporary Trends and Issues*. Thousand Oaks, CA: Sage.

Sassen, Saskia. 1989. America's Immigration Problems. *World Policy Journal* 6(4).

Smith, James P., and Barry Edmonston (eds.). 1997. *The New Americans: Economic, Demographic and Fiscal Effects of Immigration*. Washington, DC: National Academy Press.

Sung, Betty Lee. 1987. *The Adjustment Experience of Chinese Immigrant Children in New York City*. Staten Island, NY: Center for Migration Studies.

Tachiki, Amy, Eddie Wong, and Franklin Odo, with Buck Wong (eds.). 1971. *Roots: An Asian American Studies Reader*. Los Angeles: UCLA Asian American Studies Center.

Takaki, Ronald 1989. *Strangers from a Different Shore: A History of Asian Americans*. New York: Penguin Books.

Tuan, Mia. 1999. *Forever Foreign or Honorary White? The Asian Ethnic Experience Today*. New Brunswick, NJ: Rutgers University Press.

U.S. Commission on Civil Rights. 1988. *The Economic Status of Americans of Asian Descent: An Exploratory Investigation*. Washington, DC: Clearing House Publications.

———. 1992. *Civil Rights Issues Facing Asian Americans in the 1990s: A Report*. Washington, DC: U.S. Government Printing Office.

U.S. Immigration and Naturalization Service (USINS). 1997. *Statistical Yearbook of the Immigration and Naturalization Service, 1995*. Washington, DC: U.S. Government Printing Office.

Wang, L. Ling-chi. 1995. The Structure of Dual Domination: Toward a Paradigm for the Study of the Chinese Diaspora in the United States. *Amerasia Journal* 12(1–2): 149–169.

Warner, W. Lloyd, and Leo Srole. 1945. *The Social Systems of American Ethnic Groups*. New Haven, CT: Yale University Press.

Wat, Eric C. 1998. Beyond the Missionary Position: Student Activism from the Bottom Up.

Pp. 161–174 in Lane Ryo Harabayashi (ed.), *Teaching Asian America: Diversity and the Problem of the Community*. Lanham, MD: Rowman Littlefield.

Waters, Mary C. 1990. *Ethnic Options: Choosing Identities in America*. Berkeley: University of California Press.

Wong, Bernard. 1982. *Chinatown: Economic Adaptation and Ethnic Identity of the Chinese*. New York: Holt, Rinehart, & Winston.

Wong, Morrison G. 1995. Chinese Americans. Pp. 58–94 in Pyong Gap Min (ed.), *Asian Americans: Contemporary Trends and Issues*. Thousand Oaks, CA: Sage.

Wong, Sau-Ling C. 1995. Denationalization Reconsidered: Asian American Cultural Criticism at a Theoretical Crossroads. *Amerasia Journal* 21(1–2): 1–27.

Yamamoto, Eric. 1999. *Interracial Justice: Conflict and Reconciliation in Post-Civil Rights in America*. New York: New York University Press.

Yanagisako, Sylvia. 1995. Transforming Orientalism: Gender, Nationality, and Class in Asian American Studies. Pp. 275–298 in Sylvia Yanagisako and Carol Delaney (eds.), *Naturalizing Power: Essays in Feminist Cultural Analysis*. New York: Routledge.

Yancey, William, Richard Juliani, and Eugene Erikson. 1976. Emergent Ethnicity: A Review and Reformulation. *American Sociological Review* 41(3): 391–403.

Yu, Henry. 1998. The "Oriental Problem" in America, 1920–1960: Linking the Identities of Chinese American and Japanese American Intellectuals. Pp. 191–214 in K. Scott Wong and Sucheng Chan (eds.), *Claiming America: Constructing Chinese American Identities during the Exclusion Era*. Philadelphia: Temple University Press.

Zangwill, Israel. 1914. *The Melting Pot: Drama in Four Acts*. New York: Macmillan.

Zhou, Min. 1999. Coming of Age: The Current Situation of Asian American Children. *Amerasia Journal* 25(1): 1–27.

———. 1998. American Becoming: Contemporary Immigration and the Dynamics of Race and Ethnicity. Paper presented at the *Conference on Racial Trends in the United States*, National Research Council, Washington, DC, October 15–16.

———. 1997. Employment Patterns of Immigrants in the U.S. Economy. Paper presented at the conference International Migration at Century's End: Trends and Issues. International Union for Scientific Study of the Population, Barcelona, Spain, May 7–10.

———. 1993. Underemployment and Economic Disparities Among Minority Groups. *Population Research and Policy Review* 12(2): 139–157.

———. 1992. *Chinatown: The Socioeconomic Potential of an Urban Enclave*. Philadelphia: Temple University Press.

Zhou, Min, and Carl L. Bankston. 1998. *Growing Up American: How Vietnamese Children Adapt to Life in the United States*. New York: Russell Sage Foundation.

Zhou, Min, and Yoshinori Kamo. 1994. An Analysis of Earnings Patterns for Chinese, Japanese and Non-Hispanic Whites in the United States. *Sociological Quarterly* 35(4): 581–602.

Part I

Claiming Visibility
The Asian American Movement

"On Strike!"
San Francisco State College Strike, 1968–1969:
The Role of Asian American Students

Karen Umemoto

The sixth of November, nineteen hundred and sixty-eight. Few thought this would mark the first day of the longest student strike in American history. Student leaders of the San Francisco State College Third World Liberation Front marched with their demands for an education more relevant and accessible to their communities. Their tenacity engaged the university, the police, and politicians in a five-month battle giving birth to the first School of Ethnic Studies in the nation. Batons were swung and blood was shed in the heat of conflict. But this violence was only symptomatic of the challenge made by activists to fundamental tenets of dominant culture as manifested in the university. African American, Asian American, Chicano, Latino, and Native American students called for ethnic studies and open admissions under the slogan of self-determination. They fought for the right to determine their own futures. They believed that they could shape the course of history and define a "new consciousness." For Asian American students in particular, this also marked a "shedding of silence" and an affirmation of identity.

The strike took place against the backdrop of nationwide Third World movements which had profound impact on the culture and ideology of America. Never before had a convergence of struggles—civil rights, antiwar, women, student and oppressed nationality—so sharply redefined the social norms of our society. Originating from the call for basic rights, protestors moved on to demand power and self-determination. When the State resisted, activists held to their convictions "by any means necessary." Though these movements did not produce major changes in the economic or political structure, they strongly affected popular ideology and social relations. They also resulted in the formation of mass organizations and produced a cadre of activists who would continue to pursue their ideals.

The San Francisco State strike was a microcosm of this struggle over cultural hegemony. The focus of the strike was a redefinition of education, which in turn was linked to a larger redefinition of American society. Activists believed that education should be "relevant" and serve the needs of their communities, not the corporations. The redefinition of education evolved from the early 1960s when students initiated programs to broaden the college curriculum and challenge admission standards. They supported the hiring and retention of minority faculty. They demanded power in the institution. When they were met with resistance, activists organized a campus-wide movement with community support for their demands. They built organizations, planned strategies and tactics, and published educational literature. Their activities were rooted in and also shaped more egalitarian relationships based on mutual respect. While this doctrine was not always fully understood nor always put into practice, it was the beginning of a new set of values and beliefs, a "New World Consciousness."

The emergence of this alternative vision is important to study today for several reasons. First, by understanding the beginnings of this vision, today's generation of students can revive certain "counterhegemonic" concepts that have been usurped and redefined by those in power. For example, campus administrators have re-vamped the concept of "self-determination" to the more benign ones of "diversity" and "cultural pluralism." Thus, the right of a group to decision-making power over institutions affecting their lives has been gutted to the level of "student input" by campus administrators.

Second, studying the strike can deepen our understanding of the process through which ideological currents develop among oppressed groups. Organizers are constantly trying to "raise political consciousness" among the people. But in what ways do the nature of the conflict, methods of organizing, strategy and tactics, propaganda and agitation, and historical factors influence mass consciousness within these movements?

This study will analyze the growth of political consciousness among Asian American students during the San Francisco State strike. I will analyze the development of the strike in four stages from 1964 to 1969, defined according to dominant concepts within the movement. They are: (1) 1964–66—end of the civil rights era marked by the ideals of "racial harmony" and "participatory democracy"; (2) 1966–67—implementation of programs under the banner of "serve the people" and "self-determination"; (3) Fall 1968/Winter 1969—struggle "by any means necessary"; and (4) Spring/Summer 1969—repression of protest and continued "commitment to the community." These concepts signify trends in ideological development and provide a means of understanding the strike as a seed of a revolutionary transformation in America.

1964–1966: "Racial Harmony" and "Participatory Democracy" and the Civil Rights Era

The civil rights era profoundly impacted the racial ideology of the nation, particularly Third World youth. The dreams of Martin Luther King, Jr., and unsung heroes inspired actions for equality, dignity, and self-respect. The African American movement clearly revealed the deep-rooted, institutionalized nature of racial oppression. Although protests resulted in reforms limited to the legal arena, their impact was felt in all other sectors of society.

Many Asian American students who were later to become active in the strike were moved by the protests. One Pilipino activist, R. Q., volunteered for a federal program on the East Coast:

When I was in VISTA and worked in a black neighborhood. . . . They had riots in New Haven. . . . I came back to State College in '67, and the black students were at the forefront in wanting programs. . . . I think the black students and the Black Movement of the sixties made a major impact. They laid the groundwork, which made it a lot easier for us.[1]

The civil rights movement reshaped popular thinking about one's role in society. One student, B. I., described the impact on him:

It had a very heavy impact because I found that to have anyone listen to you, you had to be forceful, expressing yourself, not being quiet. If you know you are in the right, you have every right to speak up and organize your people to a just cause. So that brought home to me the necessity of organized action, and to verbalize your feelings about what is going on.[2]

The protests forced President Kennedy to publicly support civil rights. His entrance into the historic March on Washington in 1963 lent federal legitimacy to the idea of racial harmony through integration. The enacting of legislation provided legal sanction for racial equality. Kennedy's slogan of a "New Frontier" also encouraged youth to participate in American democracy and transform society. This idealism contributed to formations of Students for a Democratic Society and Third World student organizations nationwide.[3] Faith in democracy led to initial acceptance of nonviolent protest and to the reform-oriented goals within mass movements.

This idealism manifested itself in experimentation in all aspects of life. What was called "counterculture" was indeed a reshaping of traditional goals, values, and behavior. One activist, I. C., explained this shift:

There was all this emphasis on doing things for other people, such as the Peace Corps. All those ideas were instilled in us . . . "doing something, giving back to society." You couldn't just live for yourself. And I think that influenced my participation in the strike more than anything."[4]

Prior to 1963, student activism at San Francisco State centered around these themes. Students joined a 1960 walk to San Quentin prison against capital punishment, protested at the 1960 House Un-American Activities Committee (HUAC) hearings, established an outdoor free speech area, joined the 1962 Freedom Rides, and organized lunch counter sit-ins at a local Mel's Drive-in. But 1963–64 also saw the assassination of Medgar Evers, the murder of four black children in an Alabama church bombing, the murder of three Student Nonviolent Coordinating Committee (SNCC) workers, and preparation for an escalation in the war in Vietnam. These and other conflicts provided the context for a growing student movement.

Meanwhile, the slogan of racial harmony clashed with the reality of racial conflict. Asian Americans faced discrimination, especially in the areas of education, employment and housing. A. S. described going to school in Stockton, California:

I went to Franklin because of where I lived. But Edison was . . . [a] minority school, our kissing cousin school—many Chinese, Japanese, Filipinos, Mexicans, and Blacks. Franklin had more poor Whites . . . You were told where to go. . . . There was a strict code that was enforced.[5]

For J. M., a growing awareness of racism caused conflicts within herself which altered life goals:

I was going with a white man whom I met at Berkeley, whom I eventually married. And so I don't know how to explain this to you, it seems very disorganized and very chaotic, but at the same time I was aspiring to be White, wanting a white child, wanting to marry a white man, I was simultaneously being impacted by all of these events that were challenging me as an Asian woman.[6]

B. I. was like the vast majority of students at San Francisco State who came from the ranks of the working class. He was a farmworker while in high school:

I spent some time in Fairfield, stoop labor, so I knew what they were saying about the low wages, and the twelve to fourteen-hour day. . . . I learned later on that Pilipinos were involved in organizing the first farmworkers' strike. And that made me very proud. . . . [7]

Several strike activists were with the U.S. armed forces in Asia and faced racial hostilities. E. D. C., who became involved with Pilipinos in the strike, described an instance where he was used to "play an agent enemy, in other words, a gook or whatever."[8]

Although it is difficult to determine if those who understood racism were more disposed to strike involvement or if their involvement sensitized them to racial issues or both, it is clear that racial cleavages were at the center of the Asian American experience.

Student-Initiated Programs

The period 1964–66 saw the development of student-run programs to address racial issues and other social concerns. These programs functioned within the university as alternative schools or "counterhegemonic sites" through which many students developed ideas running counter to prevailing paradigms.

The initial programs included the Fillmore Tutorial, [the] Community Involvement Program, the Experimental College, and the Work-Study Program. They were initiated with Associated Student government monies under its president, Tom Ramsey, a socialist, who wanted to use the $400,000 budget for community work.[9]

The Fillmore Tutorial was an African American–initiated program which tutored youth in the Fillmore District of San Francisco. The Community Involvement Program was an outgrowth of this. Students organized community activities including graphic arts workshops, a housing and job co-op, and support activities for the National Farmworkers Association and the Delano strike.[10]

The Experimental College offered alternative courses on topics including "Perspective on Revolution," "Urban Action," and "Competition and Violence." One outgrowth was the Work-Study Program, which was later renamed the Community Services Institute in 1968. A 1966 statement stated that education should be redefined to be relevant to community needs, to equip people to control their lives, and to teach that knowledge came from work in the community.[11]

These programs became increasingly popular. By fall 1966, the college had approximately fifteen courses with 300 students; by spring 1967, there were sixty courses with 800 students[12] and by fall 1968, nine experimental colleges existed in the eighteen-campus university system.[13]

A Master Plan for Future Confrontation

The foundation for growing contradictions between students and administrators was the 1960 Master Plan for Higher Education in California. The plan restructured education to meet the changing needs of industry and the growing student population. Projections estimated that by 1975, more than 1 million students would be enrolled in California higher education, nearly triple the full-time enrollment of 1958. Technically skilled and managerial workers were needed for developing high-tech and defense industries. The California Master Plan was preceded by the 1958 National Defense Education Act (NDEA), major federal legislation which provided aid to all levels of public and private education with particular support for the math, science, and foreign language fields. The linking of defense and education coincided with developments in the Cold War, including the 1957 Soviet lift-off of Sputnik, which launched the "space race."

The Master Plan established three tiers: University of California, California State College, and junior college systems, each with target student populations, specialized functions, and centralized governing boards. The UC system for the top 12.5 percent of high school graduates was provided "exclusive jurisdiction over training for professions and the sole authority in public higher education to award the doctor's degree."[14] The state college system was to provide "instruction in the liberal arts and sciences and in professions and applied fields . . . and teacher education." Previously open to 70 percent of high school graduates, it was now reserved for the top 33 percent.[15] The junior colleges were to provide vocational training, general liberal arts background, and preparation for transfer to a four-year institution.

The Master Plan's "solution" to the increasing numbers of students was the "diversion" of students from state colleges and UC campuses to junior colleges.[16] To improve the "quality" of students, the UC system and state colleges were directed to develop new admissions requirements for the fall 1962.[17] Thus, instead of expanding the four-year institutions, the Master Plan restricted admissions. The net result was the decline of minority enrollments. At San Francisco State, African American enrollment dropped from an estimated 11 percent in 1960 to 3.6 percent by 1968.[18]

The Master Plan centralized decision making in the hands of business and political figures. A twenty-one-member Board of Trustees was established to govern the state college system with the system-wide chancellor and board holding absolute control over all academic programs, distribution of allocated funds, and major personnel decisions.

Corporate spokespersons backed the Master Plan. In a 1969 speech entitled "Business and Campus Unrest" to the Education Section Meeting in Sacramento, E. Hornsby Wasson, the board chairman of the Pacific Telephone and Telegraph Company, stated:

> The best we in business can do is to try and work with you . . . furnishing the most clear-cut guidelines . . . to produce the type of young man and woman we need to keep our state and our national economy moving in the years ahead. The interest stems from what I already have expressed: business depends on education *to produce young men and women capable of meeting the demands of our free enterprise system and thus living full, economically independent life.* [Italics added][19]

Business concerns received strong political support with Ronald Reagan's rise to [the] governorship in 1966. Under his leadership, a collision course was set with growing student radicalism on the issues of university access, relevancy, and control.

1966–May 1968: "Serve the People" and "Self-Determination"

> As I got involved, I saw what happened [on campus] in terms of a microcosm . . . of what was going on in the city and the larger picture of inequality. You can stay neutral and let it slide by you, or you can walk away from it and deny those problems, or you can become a participant. To me, I was going to become a participant.[20]
> —B. L., student government and ICSA member

The process through which action gave rise to new ideas and new ideas shaped action was dialectical. For Asian American students, this process took many forms. Some were involved in the Experimental College, [the] Tutorial Program, and other Associated Student activities. Some became involved through friendships or contact with other activists. Others literally walked into the strike. Regardless of how they got involved, their actions led to greater questioning and understanding, which in turn shaped later actions.

International events had profound impact on the Third World movements in the United States. Anti-imperialist wars were raging in Asia, Africa, and Latin America. Works of revolutionary intellectuals like Frantz Fanon, Amilcar Cabral, Che Guevara, and Mao Zedong were studied by activists in the United States. The concept of "internal colonialism" became popular to depict the oppressed status of minorities in America. For those who used the colonial analogy, liberation movements abroad suggested that freedom also could be won at home. Anti-imperialism challenged fundamental tenets from the civil rights era. Instead of racial integration, anti-imperialist movements argued for national independence. Instead of nonviolence, they initiated armed struggle. And instead of shared power, they called for "self-determination."

Events abroad were coupled with a growing discontent at the limitations of civil rights programs. The discontent was felt most deeply by working class sectors of Third World communities, those least affected by legislation. An influential figure who clearly represented this sector was Malcolm X, who was killed in 1963 but whose message was popularized for years later. He called for African Americans to control the resources and institutions of their communities "by any means necessary" and to identify their primary enemies as established institutions and those who supported the status quo.[21] These themes are evident in the formation of Asian American organizations during this period. Although these groups were influenced by the African American movement, their development was unique to their cultures and respective experiences in the United States. These groups promoted pride in national heritage; they sought "self-determination" and "power to the people." These slogans captured the diverse life experiences of the activists who were conscious of racism and their lack of political power.

Intercollegiate Chinese for Social Action (ICSA)

ICSA was formed in October 1967 by Chinese students who were mainly interested in social, cultural, and community activities. They worked as volunteers for Chinatown social service agencies including the War on Poverty office, taught immigrant teenagers English language skills, and later solicited monies from the Associated Student government to expand the tutorial project and to study the Chinatown power structure.[22]

As campus conflicts intensified with a May 1968 sit-in, a new leadership arose and eventually steered ICSA toward the strike. By July 1968, the group established an office in Chinatown at 737 Clay Street. Though the organization was community-oriented from its founding, the new leadership was more militant. It immediately joined the Third World Liberation Front (TWLF). It also challenged the traditional Chinatown power brokers, particularly the Six Companies, over the use of Economic Opportunity Council monies and over problems of youth and working-class Chinese.

For the new ICSA leader, A. W., "power to the people" meant "a piece of the pie," since his experience showed him that poor people were rarely given anything. A. W. described himself as being a "playboy" and a "hippie." He accidentally walked into the May 1968 sit-in when he attempted to pay his fees in the administration building and "got busted" by the police.[23]

Following that incident, he and M. W were approached by a member of the Black Students Union (BSU). They were impressed by the his militancy and suggested joining forces, but A. W. initially saw it as benefiting only African Americans. He described his change of mind:

> And I said, "Okay fine, you Blacks need to go to school, so you guys fight it, and I won't go against it. But I'm not for it because what am I getting out of this?" And he said, "What about all your Chinese who can't get into school?." . . . And I said, "Okay you convince me what you can give me and my people." . . . And he said, "We've got counseling, tutoring service, we have special admission." . . . So I said, "All right, I'm in." That was the first time in my life that somebody, not Asian, was willing to share with me their pot of gold. So I had nothing to lose, and all to gain, and then I got involved.[24]

Other ICSA members got involved through community issues. I. C. worked in Chinatown and was aware of the difficulties of immigrant youth. She helped to coordinate ICSA's tutorial program. In reflecting on the reasons for her involvement, she discussed the strong influence of her family who "taught you that you had to do what was right, do what was fair. And when you would see things that were not right, were not fair, [it] just upsets you."[25]

Others like J. C., who came from a middle-class family and grew up for most of his life in a predominately white Bay Area suburb, experienced a cultural and political awakening through his participation in ICSA. His involvement in the strike "was the process of constructing an identity."[26] In high school, he felt competition between peers over "who was whiter than who." But the strike was different:

> We came together, I think, a little more comfortable with who we were. . . . We found issues we felt [were] lack[ing] in our lives. So we could organize ourselves. We could socialize with one another. We could actually sacrifice part of our egos. So we could join a movement towards some objective that we all thought was correct. I think the one thing you can't do when you are trying to melt into the white world is to complain about it. But if you join with others of your own kind, you have the opportunity to trade stories . . . and articulate your hostility.[27]

This quest to validate the ethnic experience fit squarely with the ICSA demand for Chinese American Studies under the authority of the people themselves.

M. W. and A. W. proceeded to involve the ICSA in the TWLF. M. W. described the conflict within ICSA:

> And so we had two factions. One faction that wanted to get more involved in the Third World group, because we figured that's where the power was. . . . There was another group that said, "No, we don't need that; we can go by ourselves" . . . and so we had elections, and all of a sudden I won . . . and we became part of the Third World Liberation Front, and became very active in the strike . . . which was radical for a lot of people at that time. They thought we were crazy.[28]

This was a major turning point for the organization and brought to power those who saw the importance of unity with other nationalities for the benefit of Chinese Americans.

Although joining with other Third World groups, the new ICSA leaders drew from figures in Chinese history, including Sun Tzu:[29]

> During the strike we read *The Art of War*. . . . All the Chinese in military history are raised on this . . . [which] says the main goal of war is to win . . . and the true leader doesn't lose lives. . . . The key to win victories is "know thyself."[30]

"Power to the people" for ICSA implicitly meant power to the working class of Chinatown. This is clear from their attacks on the landlords and power brokers, including the Six Companies. Frustrations had mounted over the latter's resistance to youth programs, including those of Leways and the Hwa Ching to develop jobs and programs. On 17 August 1968, ICSA members and community leaders including Reverends Larry Jack Wong, Ed Sue, and Harry Chuck led a peaceful march through Chinatown in support of "education, employment, health, housing, youth, senior citizens, and immigration."[31] ICSA members participated in a coalition called Concerned Chinese for Action and Change. The coalition held a press conference to present several demands, including those for a senior center, a full investigation of the Chinatown-North Beach Equal Opportunity Commission office, immediate action for a community youth center, and the future establishment of a multiservice center, educational program, and low cost housing.[32] Students also attended many of the EOC meetings to demand seats on the board and programs to serve youth and low-income residents.

A. W. sat on a community board to the police department. He joined discussions about youth "problems" in the public schools. He pointed to the need for institutions to speak to the needs of immigrant youth:

> At that time, I think that Galileo [High School] was about 80 percent Chinese and 50 percent were non-English speaking. I said, "You need bilingual classes, and you need to give the students some pride." Their argument was that [the students] didn't want to participate. I said "How do you expect them to participate? . . . Give them something to be proud of and they will, in turn, turn Galileo into a good school." They thought it was horse shit. . . . Now they have all those things.[33]

Just as ICSA participation in Chinatown helped build opposition to the Six Companies, their increased understanding of Chinatown's problems strengthened their resolve to fight for ethnic studies. In a position paper, the group stated:

> Chinatown is a GHETTO. In San Francisco there are approximately 80,000 Chinese of whom the vast majority live in Chinatown. It is an area of old buildings, narrow streets and alleys and the effluvia of a great deal of people packed into a very small space. . . . Tuberculosis is endemic, rents are high and constantly rising . . . and space is at such a premium as to resemble the Malthusian ratio at its most extreme conclusion.[34]

The position paper advocated ethnic studies. It stated, "There are not adequate courses in any department or school at San Francisco State that even begin to deal with problems of the Chinese people in this exclusionary and racist environment."[35]

Community efforts converged with that of students. For example, G. W., who worked with Hwa Ching youth, returned to school after the strike began. He and others initiated the Free University for Chinatown Kids, Unincorporated, "to find ways to merge the college students and street kids together and hopefully share the best of their experiences."[36] The acronym, F.U.C.K.U., was a statement: "You guys [the university] don't like us? Well, we don't like you either."[37] F.U.C.K.U. met for several sessions with films, speakers, and discussion on problems and solutions for Chinatown youth.

An organization which actively supported the strike was Leways. Short for "legitimate ways," it set up a pool hall and soda fountain at 615 Jackson Street called the "Fountain of Youth." Leways member Alex Hing wrote, "Because the strike was aimed precisely at giving oppressed Third World people access to college, Leways became the staunchest supporters of the TWLF in Chinatown."[38] Leways assisted in educational, fund-raising, and picket activity during the strike. Through the strike and community involvement, Leways became increasingly political, and later some members formed the revolutionary Red Guards.

Supporters came from many political persuasions. Despite differences, important alliances were built over strike demands. The Equal Opportunity Council board in Chinatown, dominated by members of the Six Companies, held more conservative views as compared with those of strike organizers. However, they shared concern over educational access. G. W. described an exchange which began as a board member responded to students' appeal for support:

> "How dare you people make such a racket! My grandson's trying to apply for the university and couldn't get in!" I said in Chinese to him. "Read our demand carefully. We're doing this for your grandson. It is precisely people like your grandson who feel that they have been kept out . . . and we want to get him in." And he said, "Oh, is that right? I'm for it!" And he turned around and looked at everybody. And since he's for it, the rest of the people said "for," and we got a majority. So we had EOC in Chinatown voting to support the San Francisco State Third World strike.[39]

Philippine-American Collegiate Endeavor (PACE)

PACE was established in spring 1968 by P. S. to organize and fight for the rights of Pilipino youth. He had learned about the efforts of Third World students through Professor Juan Martinez. PACE organized counseling programs, tutorial programs, tutor training, study centers, high school recruitment drives, newsletters, fund-raising dances, ethnic studies curricula, community outreach, and liaison with student government.

The backgrounds of PACE members were as diverse as those of other groups. However, most were foreign-born. A number came from military family backgrounds as well as farmworker families. A. S. remarked that "you had multidiverse types of Pilipinos who started PACE, which was really a miracle we even stuck together." But he added, "We had common backgrounds, we had common goals. And we really had a common thought . . . that there really had to be something better in life than what we were used to."[40]

PACE saw the inequality they faced as rooted in racism. It felt that uniting Third World people to create a new consciousness would enable them to control their own destinies. This viewpoint was expressed in the statement of goals and principles, which read:

> We seek . . . simply to function as human beings, to control our own lives. Initially, following the myth of the American Dream, we worked to attend predominantly white colleges, but we have learned through direct analysis that it is impossible for our people, so-called minorities, to function as human beings, in a racist society in which white always comes first . . . So we have decided to fuse ourselves with the masses of Third World people, which are the majority of the world's peoples, to create, through struggle, a new humanity, a new humanism, a New World Consciousness, and within that context collectively control our own destinies.[41]

One of the ways this "New World Consciousness" would develop was through ethnic studies. These courses would educate people to the Pilipino American experience, thus lessening racist attitudes.

Some PACE members organized support for their demands within the community through explaining the concept of "self-determination" with concrete illustrations. P. S. explained:

> Self-determination was probably the closest [term] to making other people understand what we were trying to express. Because when you had to explain self-determination, you had to explain the other side, against what? . . . So that buzzword was just convenient to open up . . . discussions . . . I thought it better to express how what we were doing was going to help. I would say it in different forms . . . how what we were doing would help kids get in school, get jobs . . . very visual things that they could relate to.[42]

Like ICSA members, PACE members saw "self-determination" as taking control over one's life. They initiated community programs through an off-campus office at 829 Cortland. The purpose was fourfold: to encourage and aid low-income Pilipino-American students in the Mission area to enter college; to establish communication channels between youth organizations in the Bay Area; to research socioeconomic problems and their solutions; and to serve as a referral agency for employment, medical, housing, recreation, and counseling services.[43]

PACE worked with youth groups at schools and churches like Mission High School and St. Patrick's. One focus was to recruit Pilipino high school youth to college through the Educational Opportunity Program. Once in college, PACE worked with students to "make sure they stayed on campus" and completed their education. E. I. helped to recruit students and described:

> Yeah, particularly on the south of Market . . . they played basketball to keep off the street. If they were out on the street, they would get busted . . . or they wound up in the Army. A lot of people got drafted. You know that the rank and file in the army was Third World. . . . So there was a better alternative: to get them onto campus.[44]

One issue in Manilatown and Chinatown concerned the eviction of elderly residents, community organizations, and small businesses from the International Hotel due to the encroaching financial district. Tenants and supporters resisted evictions for over ten years. Pilipino and other Asian students were active participants throughout the period of the campus strike. E. I. continued:

> Sometime in November, mid-December, there were eviction notices posted on the International Hotel door. It said, "You who live here are hereby notified . . . that the Hotel is going to be demolished and you have to leave." . . . And I enlisted the support of (M. W.) and (G. W. of ICSA) and they marched with us. And we had 120 Pilipinos out there, senior citizens, residents of that building. We picketed down Montgomery.. . . .These were elderly people, retired veterans. . . . I got appointed to the board of that association. And it was then becoming an issue that totally involved me, and I was a student.[45]

The community programs not only enabled a large number of students to participate in PACE, but it involved students in an implicit challenge to the individualistic pursuits promoted by the university. PACE's activities captured the sentiments of students to uplift their people. The membership roster included almost seventy out of an estimated 125 Pilipino students on campus.[46]

Asian American Political Alliance (AAPA)

AAPA was formed in late summer 1968 at San Francisco State College by mainly Japanese American women. It was a vehicle for students to share political concerns in a pan-Asian organization. One founder, P. N., had worked in the Experimental College and had participated in the May sit-in. During that summer, she met a woman whose brother was a member of AAPA at the University of California, Berkeley. She and others attended those meetings and by fall organized an AAPA at San Francisco State:

> I felt a lot of need to do something about racism. Also, there was a need to do something about the lack of political involvement of Asians.... [There] was also this amorphous sense of wanting to build a sense of Asian American identity and ... overcome what I saw as nationalistic kinds of trends. I wanted to see Asians from different ethnic backgrounds working together.[47]

The ideological development of San Francisco State AAPA was influenced by the movement at UC Berkeley. P. N. recalled that many of their concepts "were developed as a result of meetings and discussions, trying to get a sense of what AAPA should be and what its goals should be, what kinds of interests it should address."[48] In one of the first issues of the UC Berkeley AAPA newspaper in fall 1968, an article described the group as a "people's alliance to effect social and political changes."

> We believe that the American society is historically racist and is one which has systematically employed social discrimination and economic imperialism both domestically and internationally to exploit all people, but especially nonwhites.[49]

AAPA saw the problems facing Asian people as rooted in racism and imperialism; thus, it was important to build alliances based on race as well as common oppression; political organization should not only effect change but build new nonhierarchical social relationships; therefore, AAPA was only a transition to generate ideas "to effect fundamental social, economical, political changes." A parallel was drawn to the movements against imperialism in the Third World. "We Asian Americans support all oppressed peoples and their struggles for Liberation and believe that Third World People must have complete control over the political, economic, and educational institutions within their communities."[50]

At San Francisco State, AAPA attempted to organize political study which offered critical perspectives for its activity. One founding member stated that activists studied the "Red Book," which contained writings of Mao Zedong. They also read writings of Frantz Fanon and Black Power leaders, including the Black Panther Party newspaper. She described the impact of these readings:

> I think they helped to provide me with a conceptual framework within which I could look at how my involvement fit in with other events: the Vietnam war in particular and the connections between the strike, domestic issues, property, and international issues.[51]

Though AAPA did not have an off-campus office, there were informal gatherings at a house in the Richmond district, several miles west of Japantown. P. Y. explained how this house became a congregating point for AAPA activities, "like an extended family":

> Towards the end of the strike, they found us a big house on 4th and California, 4th and Cornwall actually . . . They got the whole house, it was three stories, two big flats. There were about eight people living there, seven of them were AAPA members. And it became the meeting place. There was a [mimeo] machine in there, and all of our stuff was printed out of there, all the meetings were held there, all the parties were held there. If anybody came in from out of town—a lot of people from L.A. used to come up—and that's where they would come. So that became a real home for AAPA.[52]

Cultural activities strengthened the closeness that P. Y. and many others spoke about during this period. One artist was Francis Oka, who was killed in an accident shortly after the strike. M. O. described his influence:

> We were like brother and sister. And he would always be the theoretical one; we kind of balanced each other off. And he was trying, struggling to be a writer and a poet and a songwriter. His idol was Dylan, Dylan Thomas. . . . because of our friendship, he always opened my mind up and made me read things . . . He was the foremost idealist in my life.[53]

The strike unleashed a creative spirit. AAPA member Janice Mirikitani became a leading figure in the Asian American arts movement. The strike provided a focus for her creative expression. She and others created the Third World Communications Collective, a Third World Women's Collective, and published one of the first Asian American journals, *Aion.*

The appointment in late 1968 of S. I. Hayakawa as San Francisco State College president stirred up controversy in the Japanese American community. Public protest against Hayakawa challenged social codes within the community which discouraged confrontation. However, a minority of Nisei publicly supported the students. The director of the YMCA office in Japantown, Y. W., explained this viewpoint:

> It could be that we had more contact with the younger generation in the course of our work. It could also be that we were far more interested in civil liberties, and in the question of freedom of speech, the freedom of assemblage . . . It could also be that we really didn't feel that restrained to rock the boat, to challenge the status quo. I think it might have been the lessons learned from the evacuation. If there is a wrong, you don't keep quiet about it . . . I think the evacuation was wrong, and this was one way to say so many years later.[54]

His sentiments may have been shared by some 100 Japanese Americans who expressed support and even pride for striking students at a community meeting at Christ United Presbyterian Church on 6 December 1968. The program consisted of student presentations followed by discussion. A statement by an elderly woman marked a turning point as she expressed her joy that young people were standing up for their rights.

On the evening of 21 February 1969, 125 Japanese Americans picketed a dinner featuring Hayakawa as a speaker. The dinner was sponsored by the Community Interest Committee of Nihonmachi, organized by several individuals affiliated with the Japanese American Citizen's League. AAPA members along with community leaders, including Yori Wada and Rev. Lloyd Wake of Glide Memorial Church, organized the protest and a press conference.

Third World Liberation Front (TWLF)

Closer relations among Third World students impacted the ideological development of Asian Americans by emphasizing the commonalities among "people of color" and creating a forum which facilitated a "cross-pollenization of ideas." The demands of the coalition set a foundation for unity and defined the political issues and struggles which occurred through the course of the strike. Due to the development of the African American movement and the participation of relatively experienced members of the BSU and Black Panther Party, African American students played an influential role in the TWLF.

One individual who was influential in the formation of the TWLF was Juan Martinez, a lecturer in the history department and the faculty advisor of the Mexican American Students Confederation (MASC). The TWLF coalition was formed with his encouragement in spring 1968. He had earlier encouraged P. S. to organize Pilipino students and when PACE was formed, it joined the TWLF. ICSA joined in spring. AAPA joined in summer 1968.

The themes of freedom and self-determination are evident in the "Third World Liberation Front Philosophy and Goals," which stated:

> The TWLF . . . has its purpose to aid in further developing politically, economically, and culturally the revolutionary Third World consciousness of racist oppressed peoples both on and off campus. As Third World students, as Third World people, as so-called minorities, we are being exploited to the fullest extent in this racist white America, and we are therefore preparing ourselves and our people for a prolonged struggle for freedom from this yoke of oppression.[55]

The TWLF saw immediate reforms in the context of radical, long-term change. A change in consciousness was seen as necessary to eliminate exploitation and racism.

Racism had been traditionally defined as a set of bigoted assumptions held by individuals. But in this period, racism was redefined as being "institutionalized" into all realms of society. The concept put emphasis on the structure of the economic and political system. Students began to deepen their analysis of society by merging this concept with their own life experiences.

In the immediate work, these ideas manifested themselves in three main demands made to the administration. First, the TWLF advocated the right of all Third World students to an education. They highlighted the existence of "institutionalized racism" as manifested in culturally biased "standardized" tests used as admissions criteria. They demanded open admissions and an expanded special admissions program.

In March and April 1968, TWLF members recruited many high school students to apply for admission to the university. On 30 April, they sponsored an orientation at which several hundred students presented their applications to President Summerskill's office. They later called for the college to use all special admissions slots for disadvantaged students. In 1966 and 1967, the state colleges had admitted only .27 and .85 percent "disadvantaged" respectively, even though 2 percent were allowed through the "exception rule."[56]

Second, the TWLF challenged the fundamental purpose of education by demanding a School of Ethnic Area Studies. This demand stressed that education should be relevant to their lives and communities. Relevancy in education was clarified by students in their stated purpose of a School of Ethnic Area Studies:

> The school clearly intends to be involved in confronting racism, poverty and misrepresentation imposed on minority peoples by the formally recognized institutions and organizations operating in the State of California.[57]

This perspective represented a fundamental challenge to the underpinnings of the Master Plan. While the Master Plan called for restructuring the university based largely upon the priorities of the corporate sector, students advocated a redefinition of education to serve their communities. I. C., who was tutoring in Chinatown, stated that "the community had so many needs, and there were so few people that participated. We always hoped that when these courses came about, more people would be encouraged to go back and help the community."[58] PACE member R. Q also stated, "I know nothing about my background, nothing historically about the people here in this country, and less about the Philippines."[59] Students wanted an education which would help them retrieve their historical legacy as well as contribute to social change in their communities.

Third, the TWLF demanded the right to have ethnic studies classes taught and run by Third World peoples. "Self-determination" meant that each nationality had the right to determine its own curriculum and hire its own faculty. Students argued that those who had lived a particular ethnic experience were best able to teach it to others. ICSA's M. W. added that "the winners are the ones who write the history books"[60] and that oppressed people had their own version of history. The TWLF also recognized that the existing criteria to evaluate ethnic studies and Third World faculty would be biased by racism. Thus, the TWLF demanded programmatic autonomy. The BSU had the most developed curricular philosophy. In their newspaper, *Black Fire*, they listed six goals for teaching:

> (1) a cultural identity, because we live in a society that is racist, that degrades and denies cultural heritage of Third World people, specifically black people; (2) to educate our people to understand that the only culture we can have is one that is revolutionary (directed toward our freedom and a complete change in our living conditions), and that this will never be endorsed by our enemy; (3) to build a revolutionary perspective and to understand the need for using the knowledge and skills we have and get only for our liberation and the destruction of all the oppressive conditions surrounding us; (4) to educate ourselves to the necessity of relating to the collective and not the individual; (5) to strive to build a socialist society; (6) to redistribute the wealth; the knowledge, the technology, the natural resources, the food, land, housing, and all of the material resources necessary for a society and its people to function.[61]

The politics of the TWLF were not as overtly revolutionary as those of the BSU but nonetheless were influenced by them. For example, in the TWLF's demand for a School for Ethnic Area Studies, a similar rationale was put forward:

> As assurance against the reoccurrence of education's traditional distortion and misrepresentation of Third World people's cultures and histories, the School of Ethnic Area Studies is to be developed, implemented, and controlled by Third World people. Whether an area study is at a developmental or a departmental level within the school, the people, of an area study will have sole responsibility and control for the staffing and curriculum of their ethnic area study.[62]

Resistance to the Challenge

DeVere Pentony, who had served as chairman of the Department of International Relations, dean of the School of Behavioral and Social Sciences, and deputy president at San Francisco State, wrote:

> The more promising the programs became in exploring and modifying basic assumptions, the more resistance grew. As student programs moved away from strictly academic problems toward direct action, problems of budget, propriety, the role of the university and the place of students in the scheme of things came sharply into view.[63]

As early as June 1967, students had pushed the Council of Academic Deans to authorize a special "task force" to establish Black Studies, but nothing had resulted from it. And by summer 1968, there was still no Black Studies program. When President John Summerskill resigned after the May sit-in, Robert Smith took over the presidency. In his co-authored book, he attributes the delays in the establishment of Black Studies to the fact that "the college did not sense the urgency of the demand; the black students did not trust the world of the honkies."[64] In his view, both sides were being unreasonable; the strike could have been avoided. But he fails to recognize the fundamental contradictions underlying the conflict: student demands ran totally contrary to those who held greatest power in the university and the state. Smith's position was eventually overridden by the trustees; he was forced to resign after the strike began.

Some trustees objected to Experimental College courses and ethnic studies on the grounds that they were not "objective" or had introduced politics into the curriculum. Chancellor Dumke opposed partisan stands of students and faculty on social issues. "If the campus enters politics no force under heaven can keep politics from entering campus ... the university must remain pure and unsullied and above the battle." Nor did Dumke believe there was a need to expand special admissions. In a letter of transmittal on the question of expanding the 2 percent special admit limit, he stated that "programs for the disadvantaged are a relatively recent development, and that the actual number of students admitted as exceptions ... is not at present sufficient in itself to justify either expansion or maintenance of present limitations."[65]

The resistance by administrators and trustees led students to use different tactics. In May 1968, Third World students and the Students for a Democratic Society (SDS) staged a sit-in at President Summerskill's office. This resulted in the granting of 412 slots for Third World students over the next two semesters, the creation of at least ten faculty positions for Third World professors with student voice in the hirings, and the rehiring of Juan Martinez in the history department.[66] SDS's demand for ROTC to be expelled from campus was the only demand denied. During the May sit-in, police responded with their first major act of violence against student protesters. One policeman charged a woman. Terrence Hallinan, an attorney, intervened. He was clubbed on the head. Ten were injured and taken to the hospital[67] and twenty-six were arrested. Conflicts heightened when Summerskill resigned a few months later without fulfilling the promises he had made in a signed agreement with the students.

P. N., who participated in this sit-in and later founded AAPA, felt that the administration's resistance to students' demands was rooted in a racially biased understanding of history. "The hardest thing for a lot of administrators to comprehend was the notion [that] there was an existing deficit in the way history brings us [knowledge]—there are subjects we weren't taught." Institutional racism, she continued, "was a very, very difficult thing for people to comprehend, and not just white people."[68]

The resistance of the administration, along with police violence, led greater numbers of students to challenge traditional protest channels. The sentiment to use more militant tactics rose as frustration and anger mounted.

Structure and Organization of the TWLF

During this period, there were many efforts to split the ranks of the student coalition by administrators, media, and others. There were also efforts to learn from these events. In one instance, the TWLF issued a leaflet summing up the major lessons from the 30 April 1968 high school orientation. This was precipitated by mischaracterizations of the event in several news articles. Excerpts from the leaflet read:

> Members of TWLF, beware. What resulted after the April 30 event is exactly what emasculates any effort, actions or programs within an organization when the constituents blame one another for what the outside sources of media . . . take to slander and falsify charges against whatever an organization, like TWLF, stands for or does.[69]

Disunity emerged during the May sit-in. According to one account, the BSU was granted some concessions preceding the sit-in. Several members were still on probation from an earlier confrontation between BSU members and the *Gator* campus newspaper staff. BSU decided not to join the sit-in, and their refusal caused mistrust among some in the TWLF. Also, MASC and PACE were reported to have set up the SDS-TWLF joint action without formal approval of the TWLF coordinators. This upset the Latin American Students Association (LASO), which reportedly pulled out of the action a few days before the sit-in.[70]

Conflicts with the white left on campus also shaped the functioning of the TWLF. Self-determination was applied to the movement itself; white students were expected to respect the right of Third World organizations to lead their respective movements. Nationalism, which deemed one nationality's struggle as important above all other causes, influenced some Third World activists. However, this viewpoint was distinct from sentiments for national pride, identity, and self-determination which were held by the majority of activists. Some sectors of the white left failed to distinguish between narrow nationalism and national self-determination. Additionally, members of the Progressive Labor Party considered all nationalism to be reactionary.

Nationalism was a point of conflict within the TWLF. While most activists were committed to improving the conditions of their people, there was a growing suspicion that some were looking out only for themselves. As the movement faced setbacks, the administration encouraged divisions by offering settlements to each group individually.

To counteract divisions and to insure internal accountability, the BSU developed an organizational structure which was to have great impact on the TWLF. BSU Central Committee member Terry Collins described this structure in a *Black Fire* article:

> In the spring of 1968 the Black Students Union saw that there was a need for democratic centralism. Before that time the Black Students Union had no formal structure. Dominant personalities of two or three people tyrannically reigned over the other students. Factionalism was rampant, potential revolutionary brothers were disillusioned, sisters were used and abused in the name of "blackness." It was the era of the bourgeois cultural nationalism, a stage of evolution that all black students involved in the movement move through, but must shake quickly. Bourgeois cultural nationalism is destructive to the individual and the organization because one uses "blackness" as a criterion and uses this rationale as an excuse not to fight the real enemy when the struggle becomes more intense. That is why we presented a new structure to the people in the spring of 1968 and called for the election of a central committee.[71]

In the TWLF structure, each of the six organizations[72] had two representatives to a Central Committee whose decisions were to be implemented by all groups. Chairpersons would be alternated every four months to provide training and to share responsibilities. No one was authorized to speak for the coalition, negotiate with the administration, make statements to the media without the sanction of the TWLF.[73] Democracy was to be promoted by input through the respective organizations around three principles : fight against racism, fight for self-determination for Third World peoples, and support the TWLF demands.[74]

Strategy and Tactics

The BSU's approach towards strategy also influenced the TWLF. BSU members popularized the concept of "heightening contradictions" in order to educate people. Black Studies professor Nathan Hare explained:

> For by heightening the contradictions, you prepare people for the confrontation which must come when they are fully sensitized to their condition. Rushing into confrontations without having heightened contradictions contrarily cripples the confrontation.[75]

Hare saw "heightening the contradictions" as a *strategy* to prepare people for confrontational *tactics*. The strategy was to educate the general student population about TWLF problems with the aim of involving them in confrontations to win demands. Violence was seen as a confrontational tactic rather than an organizing principle.

In contrast, P. N. of AAPA recalled a different interpretation:

> I guess the main reasons for using violent tactics . . . was . . . [to] heighten the contradictions, increase the level of confrontation. Because . . . the greater the amount of pressure, the more incentive there is to resolve it. So by heightening the contradictions, or by heightening the level of tensions . . . there may be a faster resolution than if things stayed at a lower level of activity.[76]

This interpretation defined "heightening the contradictions" as a tactic. P. N. also observed that "there was a certain amount of macho that was also involved, as distinguished from looking at violence in a more analytical perspective as a tactical movement."[77] The "macho" attitude may have reflected a larger difference; some students may have viewed violence as a *strategy* to win their demands.

The idea of exposing contradictions between students and the administration was based on the assumption that underlying the conflict was a fundamental difference in values, beliefs, and most of all, interests. Many students came to believe that racism, class, and political interests belied all rhetoric about the university as a neutral and objective entity.

1968–1969: "By Any Means Necessary"

> The trustees are worried about a Black Studies department having an all-black faculty. They didn't mention that there are departments with all-white faculties. These people are scared of giving black people control over their own destinies. Does the college plan to do something about institutional racism or is it just going to fire Black Power advocates? I haven't seen anybody fired for being a racist.[78]
>
> —Elmer Cooper, Dean of Student Activities

Students were angered by the refusal of the administration to act on their demands despite prior commitments. This period also saw police violence and political repression against mass movements, including the assassinations of Martin Luther King, Jr., and Robert Kennedy. Protesters at the Democratic National Convention were severely beaten. Many believed that substantive change would not be willingly given: it had to be won through force. Thus, they echoed the slogan of Malcolm X—"by any means necessary."

Many engaged in confrontational tactics after they had exhausted other channels. Some students had been seeking the expansion and institutionalization of ethnic studies and special admissions programs for four years. Promises had been made by Summerskill and others but were never implemented. Now, the administrators were using police to suppress student actions. Due to this repression, students began to understand that their demands represented a more fundamental challenge to the system. Although this understanding varied among students, it was widely shared and provided the basis for mobilizing hundreds in the confrontations with the administration. PACE's B. I. stated that Even "the silence on the part of the administration [told me] that our demands were not relevant, told me that our contributions were not anything. So that's what led me to get more involved."[79]

Firing of George Murray Heightens Confrontation

BSU central committee member George Murray was fired from the English department for his political beliefs and activism in November. He had been hired in May to teach Educational Opportunity Program (EOP) courses. The Board of Trustees opposed his hiring due to his public statements challenging the racism of the university. Murray was also Minister of Education of the Black Panther Party. The alternative campus newspaper, *Open Process*, summarized the reason for his termination:

> Institutionalized racism is embedded in the status quo of American society; to challenge it with that in mind is to challenge the very foundations of society. George Murray was suspended not because he is black, but because as a member of the Black Panther Party he has challenged the institutions which have always enslaved black people including the educational system.[80]

The controversy over Murray's case reflected a polarization within the administration and faculty. Smith, like other liberals, argued that "if we are to continue as a nation ruled by law, we must give all citizens the benefit of *due process* and the protection of the law."[81] Chancellor Dumke was less concerned with due process than with the problem of "certain tiny groups of students . . . who have lost faith in our system, and are simply interested in overthrowing the establishment." He expressed his determination to suppress any disruption with whatever force necessary.[82]

One month after the publication of Dumke's statements, George Murray gave a speech at a rally at a trustees board meeting in Fresno. In his speech, he spoke about the betrayal of America by politicians.

> So you get people deceiving college students, deceiving the general populace in the United States . . . to manipulate you to the extent that you'll die for some nonfreedom in Viet Nam, that you'll die for some nonfreedom throughout Asia, Africa, and Latin America fighting people of color who have never victimized any American persons.[83]

He discussed the demands of African Americans, including the right of self-determination and exemption from the draft. Murray pointed to the examples of revolutionary struggles to win demands.

> We understand that the only way that we're going to get them [is] the same way which folks got theirs in 1776, the same way black people in Cuba got theirs in the 1950s . . . that is with guns and force. We maintain that political power comes through the barrel of a gun.[84]

After the *San Francisco Chronicle* reported Murray advocating "guns on campus," trustee opposition to his appointment increased. On 1 November the administration announced his suspension. Murray was later arrested during the first week of Hayakawa's administration, suspended again, and jailed without parole.

War of the Flea

On 28 October, only days before Murray's suspension, the BSU called a rally to announce the strike and their demands.[85] In the following week, meetings were held by the BSU and TWLF, and the strike date was set as 6 November. On the day before the strike, the TWLF held a general meeting attended by nearly 700 Third World students and community supporters. SNCC representative Stokeley Carmichael delivered a speech which raised the level of analysis of many students. He warned against trying to solve institutional racism simply by replacing white administrators with Blacks. He said, "Now the way to insure that you get somebody . . . who has the same political ideology that you have is to make sure that you can choose or you have control over that person." He also urged them to take the struggle seriously, stating "do not start off with something you cannot maintain because in the long run you not only hurt yourself but movements to come." He concluded, "It is easier to die for one's people than it is to work and live for them, to kill for them, and to continue to live and kill for them."[86]

Following Carmichael, Benny Stewart presented the strategy of the "war of the flea." This strategy was adapted from the guerrilla war conditions facing many anticolonial movements in which the strength was based on mass support, familiarity with the terrain, and the advantage of elusivity. He pointed to the failure of other campus movements after leaders had been arrested and argued for a new strategy for a prolonged struggle:

> We call it the war of the flea. . . . What does the flea do? He bites, sucks blood from the dog, the dog bites. What happens when there are enough fleas on a dog? What will he do? He moves. He moves away. . . . We are the people. We are the majority and the pigs cannot be everywhere. . . . And where they are not, we are.[87]

One influential writer during this period was Frantz Fanon with his widely read book, *Wretched of the Earth*. He emphasized the role of revolutionary struggle by the oppressed to achieve liberation. Fanon and other Third World thinkers had great influence on student activists. At the same time, these ideas were integrated with the students' own experiences, both on campus and in American society. This period was marked by a rash of police incidents, including violence against the Panthers, assaults on Chicano youth in the Mission district, and the shooting of a Chinese woman in the eye by a drunk officer. Students also rallied at UC Santa Barbara, San Jose State, College of San Mateo, and throughout the nation. Student activity in Czechoslovakia, France, Italy, Spain, Japan, and China also received publicity. All of these events profoundly affected San Francisco State activists.

On 6 November, mobile teams of Third World students entered buildings, dismissed classes, set trash cans on fire, and otherwise disrupted campus operations. Meanwhile, 400 white students marched to President Smith's office in support of the TWLF demands. In contrast to characterizations of strikers as irrational youth, there was in fact a clear reasoning for actions based on a redefinition of violence.

Soon after the strike began, Smith called in the police and closed the campus. The next day, 600 persons marched on the administration building during a noon rally.

By the third day, the *Gator* reported a 50 percent drop in classroom attendance. By that time, students altered tactics and sent "educational teams" into classrooms to explain the strike issues.[88]

On 13 November, the San Francisco police Tactical Squad beat several TWLF members. A rally was called and 1,000 students gathered, ending in more police violence. By the end of the day, seven students had been arrested and eleven taken to the hospital for injuries.[89] Smith announced, "We'll keep classes closed until such time as we can reopen them on a rational basis."[90] The trustees gave Smith until 20 November to reopen the college. The faculty refused to resume classes and held "convocations" to try to resolve the problems. The BSU stated they would refuse to participate unless classes were canceled. When classes were not canceled on 21 November, 2,000 students rallied, and police again beat and arrested students. In the first two weeks of the strike, the police arrested 148 participants.[91] Though many Asian student activists participated in militant tactics, some were reluctant. AAPA member M. O. did not oppose the basic strategy because she believed that in order to gain ethnic studies, "the only answer at that time seemed to be: force them [administration]." However, she selectively chose not to participate in violent actions. "When I got to the point of throwing, I could pick it up, but I couldn't throw it. I thought, 'no, my involvement will have to be in other ways.' "[92] Another student opposed those tactics as he saw that the debris was cleaned up by Third World workers, including his father, who worked as a custodian on campus.

Winter–Spring 1968: Repression and Continued Community Commitment

On 26 November, President Smith resigned, explaining his failure "to get from the chancellor and the trustees the resources and kinds of decisions I felt we needed . . . Further, we could not get them to look past serious provocative acts to basic problems."[93] However, underneath the "problems" were basic differences, which the trustees and California Governor Ronald Reagan clearly understood.

The silencing of liberals matched the rise of conservative national and state political figures. Following the election of Reagan as governor in 1966, Nixon became President in 1968. Republicans won the majority in both houses of the California state legislature. Through appointments, Reagan gained control of the state college Board of Trustees.[94] The naming of faculty member S. I. Hayakawa as president of the college was part of this political realignment. Hayakawa and colleagues in the Faculty Renaissance organization had courted Chancellor Dumke. They proposed to deliver ultimatums, restrict due process, suspend students, and fire disobeying faculty.[95] Hayakawa was a perfect choice, being of Japanese descent. He took a hard line against the student movement and served as a public spectacle for media consumption.

On 2 December, 1,500 gathered after Hayakawa's ban on campus rallies. Hayakawa personally jumped onto the sound truck and ripped off the speaker cords. As the crowd was attempting to leave, several hundred police sealed off a section of campus and beat and arrested students, reporters, medics, and community support-ers.[96] Hayakawa stated at a press conference, "This has been the most exciting day of my life since my tenth birthday, when I rode on a roller coaster for the first time!"[97]

On the evening of 2 December, the American Federation of Teachers (AFT) held an emergency meeting and voted to request strike sanction from the San Francisco Central Labor Council. Their main concerns were faculty issues, including a nine-unit teaching requirement. On 4 December, 6,000 persons rallied on campus, and on 6 December a large rally was marked by police violence and arrests.[98] On 11 December, the AFT set up an informal picket line in front of the administration building. And on 13 December, Hayakawa announced an early Christmas recess.

TWLF leaders noted the tentativeness of their alliance with the AFT, whose strike began 6 January. "We view it as positive that the AFT has finally gone on strike. It must be clear, however, that the AFT is, by their own admission, striking primarily for their own demands and only secondarily, under pressure, for the fifteen demands of TWLF."[99]

As students, faculty, and community supporters gained strength, the university prepared to take more repressive measures. On 23 January, over 500 persons demonstrated on campus. Within five minutes, the police encircled the crowd and arrested 453 people.[100] Many spokespersons were incarcerated, leaving a void in the organized leadership. P. Y. of AAPA summarized this period:

> We just didn't have the money or the time to deal with 400 arrests at one time. At that point a lot of energy went preparing for trials. . . . From that point on, the strike went downhill. A lot of EOP students and people who weren't directly involved in the day to day organization just stopped showing up. . . . A large part of the white student popu-lation that had supported the strike stopped going to school. . . . And everybody's court dates were starting to come up. . . . Some people were being pulled in for probation violation, for previous arrests. That's what happened to me, all of February. I don't know what happened during the last part of the strike because I was in jail.[101]

For the following months, much time was consumed in legal support efforts. Most trials took between four and six weeks, and by the year's end, 109 persons were convicted, and many served jail sentences.[102] Statewide, over 900 students and faculty were arrested on the state college campuses between November 1968 and March 1969.[103] This repression severely crippled the movement.

State repression impacted Asian students' understanding of the police in several ways. For AAPA member P. Y., this experience reinforced his developing understand-ing of society:

> I think most kids have a real negative attitude [towards police]. What became clearer was that the political context they operated in . . . the role of the police [as] an internal army . . . against the working class and Third World people.[104]

P. Y. was indicted and served a jail sentence. In jail, he saw that the treatment in prison epitomized the status of poor and Third World people in society. From his four-month internment, he learned that "jail is like almost any other segment of society . . . class is such a determining thing on people's lives. For me that put into perspective a lot of the issues of the strike."[105] Meanwhile, Reagan, the trustees, and Hayakawa were able to distort the strike through the media and sway public support for their repressive measures. For example, Hayakawa described students as "a gang of goons, gangsters, con men, neo-Nazis, and common thieves."[106] Also, in a statement to the U.S. Congress on 3 February 1969, he boasted about the use of police repression:

> I believe that I have introduced something new to this business of preserving order on campuses. At most institutions the use of police is delayed as long as possible and when assistance is finally requested, the force is usually too small to handle the situation and new troubles develop. I went the other way. . . . The opposition has received my message. I think I have communicated successfully.[107]

B. L. stated his anger at the mischaracterization of the strike in the popular media:

> Their main focus points were probably on Hayakawa and the so-called violence. Like maybe you break a window. But what about the inequity, the psychological damage inflicted on an individual and [the destruction] of their history. What about that kind of violence?[108]

Negotiation and Evaluation

The internal weaknesses of the student movement and the external repression of the state forced students into a position of negotiating the "nonnegotiable" demands. Their negotiating power was weakened when the AFT returned to work on 5 March after voting 112–104 to end the strike, despite an unsatisfactory compromise.[109] Meanwhile, to prevent public questioning of their repressive strategy, Hayakawa and Reagan felt pressure to reopen the campus.

After several attempts, Hayakawa recognized a "Select Committee" of faculty which "expected to act with the full authority of the president" [110] and negotiate with the TWLF. However, this committee was more liberal than Hayakawa, and it negotiated a compromise to his objection. On 14 March, the committee met with Hayakawa to formalize the settlement. Since Hayakawa was to leave at 9 A.M. for a meeting with President Nixon, their meeting was set for 7:30 A.M., at which time he was quoted as saying, "I'll give you a month. . . . If all is quiet by April 11, I'll consider your recommendations. Now, if you'll excuse me, I have to catch my plane for Washington. Good morning."[111] Hayakawa never signed the negotiated resolution. TWLF members and faculty proceeded to implement the resolution.

It is important to note the BSU's reasons for entering negotiations with the administration. BSU Central Committee member Leroy Goodwin outlined "major contradictions" in a May 1969 *Black Fire* article. A major reason to enter negotiations was "the determination and support of the people rapidly decreasing due to a low political level, communication gaps, and paranoia or fear of the Central Committee." Also, he pointed to five classifications of opportunism which plagued the movement. They included: those who fronted as spokespersons and collected honorariums for themselves; those who left the struggle after the BSU secured their grades; spokespersons motivated by their personal prestige over the plight of the people; "shit slingers" who mainly criticized; and disruptiveness of the Progressive Labor Party.[112] He concluded, saying sarcastically, "But we came to grips with the reality that the struggle of oppressed people was more important than fourteen individuals walking around with the myth of the revolution going on in their minds. Imagine a flea worried about losing face."[113]

The BSU summation reflects demoralization and an emphasis on internal problems. Although there were internal contradictions, they existed within a context. This context included the alliance of conservative forces, popular sanction of police repression, racism in society including chauvinism in the white left, and the youthfulness of the movement, which, among other things, lacked more experience and theoretical grounding to sustain itself in an organized form.

Community Commitment

The lives of Asian student activists were changed in many ways. A common theme, however, voiced by all participants focused on a deep-rooted commitment to social change for the benefit of their communities. Some students stated that the strike may not have drastically altered their life. E. I., for example, felt he "would have wound up here anyway,"[114] working as a housing advocate and social worker. Others, like G. C., reflected upon the strike as a pivotal time in their lives:

I think it changed my life in terms of providing some focus to the extent that my career wasn't that important to me. . . . Take a look at the decisions people made back then. It was what the community needed first; and what you could contribute emanated from that.[115]

P. N. stated that her "what it means to be an Asian in American society" *[sic]*[116] shaped her view of legal work:

I don't think I would have gone to law school if it hadn't been for the strike. . . . The reason why I did go to law school was to get some skills . . . to practice law, and look at law as a vehicle for social change. [117]

Others, including A. S., stated that student activism led them to utilize their skills in channeling resources to their communities "to build low-income housing, parks for the people." [118] A. W. stated that though most of the leadership went into the community, he "chose to stay [to teach] in the university." [119]

Many activists expressed a feeling of personal liberation. Speaking out and taking stands to the point of facing serious consequences instilled a boldness of character. P. N. added that she became "more adventurous, less looking for the safe way to do thing," while at the same time "more cautious" in dealing with the complexities of human nature. [120]

M. W. discussed the political ramifications:

What it did is, I think, make me more politically conscious . . . when a person in administration, who is supposed to have authority, a title, . . . [you find that those] people use that [power] to put the pressure on you. Then after getting involved with bureaucrats and politicians, [you realize] that they are people like anyone else. I think that is one of the things I learned: not to be intimidated.[121]

Some activists left the campus with the view of reforming society. B. I. remarked, "I saw myself as a reformist working within the system, to try and get those things that would benefit poor people, regardless of whether you are Black, White or Asian."[122] However, others like P. N. added: "I'd always felt since the strike that what was necessary to eliminate or alleviate racism was a major restructing of our society, both economically and in eliminating barriers in terms of participation of Third World people in all walks of life." [123]

Conclusion: The Altered Terrain

Asian American students played a significant role in student movements of the sixties, as clearly demonstrated in the San Francisco State strike. The struggle was unique in that it was situated in an urban, multiethnic, liberal, working-class city. Perhaps that more closely tied the campus struggle to the respective national movements, while at the same time making bonds between them. In their challenge to the university, Asian students followed in the legacies of Pilipino farm labor organizers, International Hotel tenants, and concentration camp resisters. Their demand for a relevant and accessible education stemmed from the aspirations of peoples who had fought for justice and equality since their arrival in the United States. And, in many ways, it was this legacy which steeled the movement and today frames a context to understand the long-lasting significance of the strike.

The most obvious accomplishment was the establishment of the first School of Ethnic Studies in the nation. This school partially met the terms outlined in the TWLF demands, including the commitment of over twenty-two faculty positions, the establishment of a Black Studies department upon which the other ethnic studies departments were based, student participation in the committee to recommend the final plan for the school, and faculty power commensurate with that accorded other college departments. In addition, unused special admission slots were promised to be filled in spring 1969. Campus disciplinary action was recommended to be limited to suspension through fall semester 1969. Demands to retain or fire individual personnel were not met. Though negotiations fell short of meeting the demands in full, the school remains the largest national program in its faculty size and course offerings. The winning of these concessions set a precedent for other universities to follow. In fact, the organization and militancy shown by San Francisco State students led some administrators at other campuses to initiate minor concessions.

A less tangible, but equally significant, outcome of the strike was the emergence of a new generation of fighters who either remained on campus or entered their communities. Many took the concept of self-determination to establish self-help programs to continue political education and promote self-reliance. Many formed or joined organizations to define a collective approach to addressing problems. Some pursued advanced degrees to secure positions of influence within the system, while others concentrated on grassroots organizing to build progressive, community-based movements. Almost without exception, those interviewed affirmed a deep commitment to the basic values and beliefs forged during their days as students active in the strike; many traced their convictions to the period of the strike itself.

The legacy of the strike has also set the terrain for another generation of Asian students. Stemming from the post-1965 immigration, today's students have formed organizations based on the foundations set by an earlier generation. The institutionalization of ethnic studies and affirmative action programs has not only given students important support systems but has also led to greater political influence for Asians in higher education.

These gains, however, have been increasingly contested. Then-governor Reagan launched his political career to become President of the United States, marking the rise of the New Right. The U.S. economic decline has resulted in government cuts in education and social programs. Universities increasingly rely on private donations, defense-related contracts, and foundation grants, influencing the priorities of the university. Meanwhile, it is estimated that one-half of all ethnic studies programs have already been eliminated. Of those which remain, much of the emphasis has shifted away from the original intent for social change. Most programs have not enjoyed programmatic autonomy or student/community involvement in decision making, and many have lost relevance to community needs. Support for affirmative action has also waned. Since the landmark Bakke decision in 1978, minimum quotas for minority admissions have turned into invisible ceilings for Asians who are perceived as "overrepresented." The attention called to these unfair practices is now being used to question affirmative action for Chicanos, African Americans, and Native Americans. And Asians have been effectively eliminated from virtually all such programs. Tenure cases, particularly for minority faculty, have become battlegrounds over the definition of legitimate and relevant research. In short, the essence of the conflict in the San Francisco State strike remains central today.

The strike offers no blueprint for movements today. Its history, however, begins to reveal the nature of clashes between students and administrators. It reminds us that the existence of ethnic studies and special programs for oppressed groups has only been the result of hard-fought struggle. Students of today's movements can study this history as a benchmark to assess their own conditions. And, with that, democratic empowerment movements may set a new terrain for the next generation.

NOTES

1. R. Q., Interview, 11 September 1985, San Francisco.

2. B. I., Interview, 5 September 1985, San Francisco.

3. See also, Kirkpatrick Sale, *SDS* (New York, 1974) and Harry Edwards, *Black Students* (New York, 1970).

4. I. C., Interview, 13 September 1985, San Francisco.

5. A. S., Interview, 12 September 1985, Fremont, California.

6. J. M., Interview, 11 September 1985, San Francisco.

7. B. I., Interview, 5 September 1985, San Francisco.

8. E. D. C., Interview, 3 September 1985, San Francisco.

9. William Barlow and Peter Shapiro, *An End to Silence: The San Francisco State College Student Movement of the 60s* (New York, 1971), 49.

10. Ibid., 68.

11. Robert Smith, Richard Axen, and DeVere Pentony, *By Any Means Necessary: The Revolutionary Struggle at San Francisco State* (San Francisco, 1970), 39.

12. Ibid., 8.

13. DeVere Pentony, Robert Smith, and Richard Aven, *Unfinished Rebellions* (San Francisco, 1971), 25.

14. Master Plan Survey Team, *A Master Plan for Higher Education in California, 1960–75* (Sacramento, 1960), 43.

15. Ibid., 73.

16. Ibid., 60.

17. Ibid., 74.

18. Staff Report to the National Commission on the Causes and Prevention of Violence, prepared by William H. Orrick, Jr., *Shut It Down! A College in Crisis; San Francisco State College* (Washington, D.C., 1969), 75. Figures not available for other ethnic groups.

19. E. Hornsby Wasson, "Business and Campus Unrest" (Speech delivered 16 January 1969), *Vital Speeches* 35:11 (15 March 1969): 335.

20. B. I., Interview, 10 September 1985, San Francisco.

21. For a discussion on the influence of Malcolm X on the African American student movement, see Harry Edwards, *Black Students* (New York, 1970).

22. Compiled from William Barlow and Peter Shapiro, *An End to Silence*; Kuregiy Hekymara, "The Third World Movement and Its History in the San Francisco State College Strike of 1968–69" (Ph.D. diss., University of California, Berkeley, 1972).

23. A. W., Interview, September 1985, San Francisco.

24. Ibid.

25. I. C., Interview, 13 September 1985, San Francisco.

26. J. C., Interview, September 1985, San Francisco.

27. Ibid.

28. M. W., Interview, 13 September 1985, San Francisco.

29. See Sun Tzu, *The Art of War*, translated and with an introduction by Samuel Griffith (London, 1963).

30. M. W., Interview, 13 September 1985, San Francisco.

31. *East West*, 28 August 1968, 1, 4.

32. *East West*, 4 September 1968, 12.

33. A. W., Interview, September 1985.

34. ICSA Position Paper, mimeographed, Special Collections Library, San Francisco State University.

35. Ibid.

36. G. W., Interview, 21 March 1987, San Francisco.

37. Ibid.

38. Alex Hing, " 'On Strike, Shut It Down!': Reminiscences of the S. F. State Strike," *East Wind* 2:2 (Fall/Winter 1983):42.

39. G. W., Interview, 21 March 1987, San Francisco.

40. A. S., Interview, 12 September 1985.

41. "Statement of the Philippine-American Collegiate Endeavor (PACE) Philosophy and Goals" mimeograph.

42. P. S., Interviews, 14 May, 6 June 1986.

43. "PACE (Philippine-American Collegiate Endeavor) Program, S. F. State," mimeographed.

44. E. I., Interview, 13 September 1985, San Francisco.

45. Ibid.

46. Mimeographed roster of PACE members.

47. P. N., Interviews, 27 May 1984 and 11 September 1985.

48. Ibid.

49. "AAPA Is," *Asian American Political Alliance Newspaper* 1 (UC Berkeley, late 1968): 4.

50. "AAPA Perspectives," *Asian American Political Alliance Newspaper* 1:5 (UC Berkeley, fall 1969): 7.

51. P. N., Interviews, 27 May 1984 and 11 September 1985.

52. P. Y., Interviews, May 1984 and 9 September 1985.

53. M. O., Interview, 14 September 1985, San Francisco.

54. Y. W., Interview, 4 September 1985, San Francisco.

55. "Statement of the Third World Liberation Front Philosophy and Goals," undated mimeo.

56. Coordinating Council for Higher Education, *California Higher Education and the Disadvantaged: A Status Report* (Sacramento, March 1968), table v.

57. "Third World Liberation Front, School of Ethnic Area Studies," mimeographed packet, 2.

58. I. C., Interview, 13 September 1985.

59. R. Q., Interview, 11 September 1985.

60. M. W., Interview, 13 September 1985.

61. Smith et al., *By Any Means Necessary*, 332.

62. "School for Ethnic Area Studies."

63. Pentony et al., *Unfinished Rebellions*, 51.

64. Smith et al., *By Any Means Necessary*, 134.

65. Coordinating Council for Higher Education, *California Higher Education*, 53.

66. Barlow and Shapiro, *An End to Silence*, 167–170; "After the Strike: A Conference on Ethnic Studies Proceedings" (School of Ethnic Studies, San Francisco State University; Proceedings from 12, 13, 14 April 1984 Conference), 14; Smith et al., *By Any Means Necessary*, 58–59.

67. Smith et al., *By Any Means Necessary*, 50–51.

68. P. N., Interviews, 27 May 1984 and 11 September 1985.

69. *TWLF Newsletter*, n. d.

70. Barlow and Shapiro, *An End to Silence*.

71. Smith et al., *By Any Means Necessary*, 140–141.

72. The six organizations within the TWLF were the Mexican American Student Confederation (MASC), Intercollegiate Chinese for Social Action(ICSA), Philippine American College Endeavor (PACE), Asian American Political Alliance (AAPA), Latin American Student Organization (LASO), and Black Students Union (BSU).

73. "By the Direction of the Third World Liberation Front" (mimeographed TWLF leaflet, n. d.)

74. Ibid.

75. Nathan Hare, "Two Black Radicals Report on Their Campus Struggles," *Ramparts* 8 (July 1969):54.

76. P. N., Interviews, 27 May 1984 and 11 September 1985.

77. Ibid.

78. Staff report to the National Commission on the Causes and Prevention of Violence, prepared by William H. Orrick, 52.

79. B. I., Interview, 5 September 1985.

80. Quoted in Smith et al., *By Any Means Necessary*, 29.

81. Ibid., 113.

82. Campus Violence—Crackdown Coming: Interview with Glenn S. Dumke Leading College Official," U.S. *News and World Report* 65 (23 September 1968): 49.

83. Mimeographed copy of George Murray's speech, Fresno, California, n.d.

84. Ibid.

85. Barlow and Shapiro, *An End to Silence*, 213–17.

86. Dikran Karagueuzian, *Blow It Up! The Black Student Revolt at San Francisco State College and the Emergence of Dr. Hayakawa* (Boston, 1971), 100–102.

87. Quotes in Smith et al., *By Any Means Necessary*, 144–145.

88. Events compiled from Smith et al., *By Any Means Necessary*; Barlow and Shapiro, *An End to Silence*; Karagueuzian, *Blow It Up!*; and various chronologies.

89. Barlow and Shapiro, *An End to Silence*.

90. Smith et al., *By Any Means Necessary*, 166.

91. Ibid.

92. M. O., Interview, 14 September 1985.

93. Smith et al., *By Any Means Necessary*, 187.

94. Ibid., 90.

95. Ibid., 207–208.

96. Barlow and Shapiro, *An End to Silence*, 263–264.

97. Ibid., 264.

98. Ibid., 267–269 for a fuller account.

99. Quoted in Smith et al., 258–259.

100. Ibid.

101. P. Y., Interviews, May 1984 and 9 September 1985.

102. Smith et al., *By Any Means Necessary*, 282.

103. Glenn S. Dumke, "Controversy on Campus; Need for Peace and Order" (Speech delivered before the Town Hall of California, Los Angeles, 18 February 1969), *Vital Speeches* 35:11 (15 March 1969): 332–335.

104. P. Y., Interview, May 1984 and 9 September 1985.

105. Ibid.

106. S. I. Hayakawa, "Gangsters in Our Midst," in *Crisis at SF State*, edited by Howard Finberg (San Francisco, 1969), 11.

107. "Statement by President S. I. Hayakawa, of San Francisco State College: Order on Campuses," *Congressional Record* 115 (3 February 1969): 2462.

108. B. L., Interview, 10 September 1985.

109. Smith et al., 229.

110. Ibid., 311.

111. Ibid.

112. *Black Fire* [San Francisco] (May 1969).

113. Ibid.

114. E. I., Interview, 13 September 1985, San Francisco.

115. G. C., Interview, September 1985, San Francisco.

116. P. N., Interviews, 27 May 1984 and 11 September 1985, San Francisco.

117. Ibid.
118. A. S., Interview, 12 September 1985.
119. A. W., Interview, September 1985, San Francisco.
120. P. N., Interviews, 27 May 1984 and 11 September 1985, San Francisco.
121. M. W., Interview, 13 September 1985, San Francisco.
122. B. I., Interview, 5 September 1985, San Francisco.
123. P. N., Interviews, 27 May 1984 and 11 September 1985, San Francisco.

Chapter Two

The "Four Prisons" and the Movements of Liberation

Asian American Activism from the 1960s to the 1990s

Glenn Omatsu

According to Ali Shariati, an Iranian philosopher, each of us exists within four prisons.[1] First is the prison imposed on us by history and geography; from this confinement, we can escape only by gaining a knowledge of science and technology. Second is the prison of history; our freedom comes when we understand how historical forces operate. The third prison is our society's social and class structure; from this prison, only a revolutionary ideology can provide the way to liberation. The final prison is the self. Each of us is composed of good and evil elements, and we must each choose between them.

The analysis of our four prisons provides a way of understanding the movements that swept across America in the 1960s and molded the consciousness of one generation of Asian Americans. The movements were struggles for liberation from many prisons. They were struggles that confronted the historical forces of racism, poverty, war, and exploitation. They were struggles that generated new ideologies, based mainly on the teachings and actions of Third World leaders. And they were struggles that redefined human values—the values that shape how people live their daily lives and interact with each other. Above all, they were struggles that transformed the lives of "ordinary" people as they confronted the prisons around them.

For Asian Americans, these struggles profoundly changed our communities. They spawned numerous grassroots organizations. They created an extensive network of student organizations and Asian American Studies classes. They recovered buried cultural traditions as well as produced a new generation of writers, poets, and artists. But most importantly, the struggles deeply affected Asian American consciousness. They redefined racial and ethnic identity, promoted new ways of thinking about communities, and challenged prevailing notions of power and authority.

Yet, in the two decades that have followed, scholars have reinterpreted the movements in narrower ways. I learned about this reinterpretation when I attended a class recently in Asian American Studies at UCLA. The professor described the period from the late 1950s to the early 1970s as a single epoch involving the persistent efforts of racial minorities and their white supporters to secure civil rights. Young Asian

Americans, the professor stated, were swept into this campaign and by later antiwar protests to assert their own racial identity. The most important influence on Asian Americans during this period was Dr. Martin Luther King, Jr., who inspired them to demand access to policymakers and initiate advocacy programs for their own communities. Meanwhile, students and professors fought to legitimize Asian American Studies in college curricula and for representation of Asians in American society. The lecture was cogent, tightly organized, and well received by the audience of students—many of them new immigrants or the children of new immigrants. There was only one problem: the reinterpretation was wrong on every aspect.

Those who took part in the mass struggles of the 1960s and early 1970s will know that the birth of the Asian American movement coincided not with the initial campaign for civil rights but with the later demand for black liberation; that the leading influence was not Martin Luther King, Jr., but Malcolm X; that the focus of a generation of Asian American activists was not on asserting racial pride but reclaiming a tradition of militant struggle by earlier generations; that the movement was not centered on the aura of racial identity but embraced fundamental questions of oppression and power; that the movement consisted of not only college students but large numbers of community forces, including the elderly, workers, and high school youth; and that the main thrust was not one of seeking legitimacy and representation within American society but the larger goal of liberation.

It may be difficult for a new generation—raised on the Asian American codewords of the 1980s stressing "advocacy," "access," "legitimacy," "empowerment," and "assertiveness"—to understand the urgency of Malcolm X's demand for freedom "by any means necessary," Mao's challenge to "serve the people," the slogans of "power to the people" and "self-determination," the principles of "mass line" organizing and "united front" work, or the conviction that people—not elites—make history. But these ideas galvanized thousands of Asian Americans and reshaped our communities. And it is these concepts that we must grasp to understand the scope and intensity of our movement and what it created.

But are these concepts relevant to Asian Americans today? In our community—where new immigrants and refugees constitute the majority of Asian Americans—can we find a legacy from the struggles of two decades ago? Are the ideas of the movement alive today, or have they atrophied into relics—the curiosities of a bygone era of youthful and excessive idealism?

By asking these questions, we, as Asian Americans, participate in a larger national debate: the reevaluation of the impact of the 1960s on American society today. This debate is occurring all around us: in sharp exchanges over "family values" and the status of women and gays in American society; in clashes in schools over curricular reform and multiculturalism; in differences among policymakers over the urban crisis and approaches to rebuilding Los Angeles and other inner cities after the 1992 uprisings; and continuing reexaminations of U.S. involvement in Indochina more than two decades ago and the relevance of that war to U.S. military intervention in Iraq, Somalia, and Bosnia.

What happened in the 1960s that made such an impact on America? Why do discussions about that decade provoke so much emotion today? And do the movements of the 1960s serve as the same controversial reference point for Asian Americans?

The United States During the 1960s

In recent years, the movements of the 1960s have come under intense attack. One national bestseller, Allan Bloom's *Closing of the American Mind*, criticizes the movements for undermining the bedrock of Western thought.[2] According to Bloom, nothing positive resulted from the mass upheavals of the 1960s. He singles out black studies and affirmative-action programs and calls for eliminating them from universities.

Activists who have continued political work provide contrasting assessments. Their books include Todd Gitlin's *The Sixties: Years of Hope, Days of Rage*; James Miller's *"Democracy Is in the Streets": From Port Huron to the Siege of Chicago*; Ronald Fraser's *1968: A Student Generation in Revolt*; Tom Hayden's *Reunion: A Memoir*; Tariq Ali's *Street Fighting Years*; George Katsiaficas' *The Imagination of the New Left: A Global Analysis of 1968*, and special issues of various journals, including *Witness, Socialist Review*, and *Radical America*.

However, as Winifred Breines states in an interesting review essay titled "Whose New Left?," most of the retrospects have been written by white male activists from elite backgrounds and reproduce their relationship to these movements.[3] Their accounts tend to divide the period into two phases: the "good" phase of the early 1960s, characterized by participatory democracy, followed by the post-1968 phase, when movement politics "degenerated" into violence and sectarianism.

"Almost all books about the New Left note a turning point or an ending in 1968 when the leadership of the movement turned toward militancy and violence and SDS [Students for a Democratic Society] as an organization was collapsing," Breines observes. The retrospects commonly identify the key weaknesses of the movements as the absence of effective organization, the lack of discipline, and utopian thinking. Breines disagrees with these interpretations:

> The movement was not simply unruly and undisciplined; it was experimenting with antihierarchical organizational forms.... There were many centers of action in the movement, many actions, many interpretations, many visions, many experiences. There was no [organizational] unity because each group, region, campus, commune, collective, and demonstration developed differently, but all shared in a spontaneous opposition to racism and inequality, the war in Vietnam, and the repressiveness of American social norms and culture, including centralization and hierarchy.[4]

Breines believes that the most important contributions of activists were their moral urgency, their emphasis on direct action, their focus on community building, and their commitment to mass democracy.

Similarly, Sheila Collins in *The Rainbow Challenge*, a book focusing on the Jesse Jackson presidential campaign of 1984 and the formation of the National Rainbow Coalition, assesses the movements of the sixties very positively.[5] She contends that the Jackson campaign was built on the grassroots organizing experience of activists who emerged from the struggles for civil rights, women's liberation, peace and social justice, and community building during the sixties. Moreover, activists' participation in these movements shaped their vision of America, which, in turn, became the basis for the platform of the Rainbow Coalition twenty years later.

According to Collins, the movements that occurred in the United States in the sixties were also part of a worldwide trend, a trend Latin American theologians call the era of the "eruption of the poor" into history. In America, the revolt of the "politically submerged" and "economically marginalized" posed a major ideological challenge to ruling elites:

> The civil rights and black power movement exploded several dominant assumptions about the nature of American society, thus challenging the cultural hegemony of the white ruling elite and causing everyone else in the society to redefine their relationship to centers of power, creating a groundswell of support for radical democratic participation in every aspect of institutional life.[6]

Collins contends that the mass movements created a "crisis of legitimation" for ruling circles. This crisis, she believes, was "far more serious than most historians— even those of the left—have credited it with being."

Ronald Fraser also emphasizes the ideological challenge raised by the movements due to their mass, democratic character and their "disrespect for arbitrary and exploitative authority." In 1968: *A Student Generation in Revolt*, Fraser explains how these concepts influenced one generation of activists:

> [T]he anti-authoritarianism challenged almost every shibboleth of Western society. Parliamentary democracy, the authority of presidents . . . and [the policies of] governments to further racism, conduct imperialist wars or oppress sectors of the population at home, the rule of capital and the fiats of factory bosses, the dictates of university administrators, the sacredness of the family, sexuality, bourgeois culture—nothing was in principle sacrosanct. . . . Overall . . . [there was] a lack of deference towards institutions and values that demean[ed] people and a concomitant awareness of people's rights.[7]

The San Francisco State Strike's Legacy

The retrospects about the 1960s produced so far have ignored Asian Americans. Yet, the books cited above—plus the review essay by Winifred Breines—provide us with some interesting points to compare and contrast. For example, 1968 represented a turning point for Asian Americans and other sectors of American society. But while white male leaders saw the year as marking the decline of the movement, 1968 for Asian Americans was a year of birth. It marked the beginning of the San Francisco State strike and all that followed.

The strike, the longest student strike in U.S. history, was the first campus uprising involving Asian Americans as a collective force.[8] Under the Third World Liberation Front—a coalition of African American, Latino, American Indian, and Asian American campus groups—students "seized the time" to demand ethnic studies, open admissions, and a redefinition of the education system. Although their five-month strike was brutally repressed and resulted in only partial victories, students won the nation's first School of Ethnic Studies.

Yet, we cannot measure the legacy of the strike for Asian Americans only in the tangible items it achieved, such as new classes and new faculty; the strike also critically transformed the consciousness of its participants who, in turn, profoundly altered their communities' political landscape. Through their participation, a generation of Asian American student activists reclaimed a heritage of struggle—linking their lives to the tradition of militancy of earlier generations of Pilipino farmworkers, Chinese immigrant garment and restaurant workers, and Japanese American concentration camp resisters. Moreover, these Asian American students—and their community supporters—liberated themselves from the prisons surrounding their lives and forged a new vision for their communities, creating numerous grassroots projects and empowering previously ignored and disenfranchised sectors of society. The statement of goals and principles of one campus organization, Philippine-American Collegiate Endeavor (PACE), during the strike captures this new vision:

> We seek . . . simply to function as human beings, to control our own lives. Initially, following the myth of the American Dream, we worked to attend predominantly white colleges, but we have learned through direct analysis that it is impossible for our people, so-called minorities, to function as human beings, in a racist society in which white always comes first. . . . So we have decided to fuse ourselves with the masses of Third World people, which are the majority of the world's peoples, to create, through struggle, a new humanity, a new humanism, a New World Consciousness, and within that context collectively control our own destinies.[9]

The San Francisco State strike is important not only as a beginning point for the Asian American movement but also because it crystallizes several themes that would characterize Asian American struggles in the following decade. First, the strike occurred at a working-class campus and involved a coalition of Third World students linked to their communities. Second, students rooted their strike in the tradition of resistance by past generations of minority peoples in America. Third, strike leaders drew inspiration—as well as new ideology—from international Third World leaders and revolutions occurring in Asia, Africa, Latin America, and the Middle East. Fourth, the strike in its demands for open admissions, community control of education, ethnic studies, and self-determination confronted basic questions of power and oppression in America. Finally, strike participants raised their demands through a strategy of mass mobilizations and militant, direct action.

In the decade following the strike, several themes would reverberate in the struggles in Asian American communities across the nation. These included housing and anti-eviction campaigns, efforts to defend education rights, union organizing drives, campaigns for jobs and social services, and demands for democratic rights, equality, and justice. Mo Nishida, an organizer in Los Angeles, recalls the broad scope of movement activities in his city:

> Our movement flowered. At one time, we had active student organizations on every campus around Los Angeles, fought for ethnic studies, equal opportunity programs,

high potential programs at UCLA, and for students doing community work in "Serve the People" programs. In the community, we had, besides [Asian American] Hard Core, four area youth-oriented groups working against drugs (on the Westside, Eastside, Gardena, and the Virgil district). There were also parents' groups, which worked with parents of the youth and more.[10]

In Asian American communities in Los Angeles, San Francisco, Sacramento, Stockton, San Jose, Seattle, New York, and Honolulu, activists created "serve the people" organizations—mass networks built on the principles of "mass line" organizing. Youth initiated many of these organizations—some from college campuses and others from high schools and the streets—but other members of the community, including small-business people, workers, senior citizens, and new immigrants, soon joined.

The *mass* character of community struggles is the least appreciated aspect of our movement today. It is commonly believed that the movement involved only college students. In fact, a range of people, including high-school youth, tenants, small-business people, former prison inmates, former addicts, the elderly, and workers, embraced the struggles. But exactly who were these people, and what did their participation mean to the movement?

Historian George Lipsitz has studied similar, largely "anonymous" participants in civil rights campaigns in African American communities. He describes one such man, Ivory Perry of St. Louis:

> Ivory Perry led no important organizations, delivered no important speeches, and received no significant recognition or reward for his social activism. But for more than 30 years he had passed out leaflets, carried the picket signs, and planned the flamboyant confrontations that made the civil rights movements effective in St. Louis and across the nation. His continuous commitment at the local level had goaded others into action, kept alive hopes of eventual victory in the face of short-term defeats, and provided a relatively powerless community with an effective lever for social change. The anonymity of his activism suggests layers of social protest activity missing from most scholarly accounts, while the persistence of his involvement undermines prevailing academic judgments about mass protests as outbursts of immediate anger and spasmodic manifestations of hysteria.[11]

Those active in Asian American communities during the late 1960s and early 1970s know there were many Ivory Perrys. They were the people who demonstrated at eviction sites, packed City Hall hearing rooms, volunteered to staff health fairs, and helped with day-to-day operations of the first community drop-in centers, legal defense offices, and senior citizen projects. They were the women and men who took the concept of "serve the people" and turned it into a material force, transforming the political face of our communities.

The "Cultural Revolution" in Asian American Communities

But we would be wrong to describe this transformation of our communities as solely "political"—at least as our society narrowly defines the term today. The transformation also involved a cultural vitality that opened new ways of viewing the world. Unlike today—where Asian American communities categorize "culture" and "politics" into different spheres of professional activity—in the late 1960s they did not divide them so rigidly or hierarchically. Writers, artists, and musicians were "cultural workers" usually closely associated with communities, and saw their work as "serving the people." Like other community activists, cultural workers defined the period as a "decisive moment" for Asian Americans—a time for reclaiming the past and changing the future.

The "decisive moment" was also a time for questioning and transforming moral values. Through their political and cultural work, activists challenged systems of rank and privilege, structures of hierarchy and bureaucracy, forms of exploitation and inequality, and notions of selfishness and individualism. Through their activism in mass organizations, they promoted a new moral vision centered on democratic participation, cooperative work styles, and collective decision making. Pioneer poet Russell C. Leong describes the affinity between this new generation of cultural workers and their communities, focusing on the work of the Asian American Writers' Workshop, located in the basement of the International Hotel in San Francisco Chinatown/Manilatown:

> We were a post–World War II generation mostly in our twenties and thirties; in or out of local schools and colleges . . . [We] gravitated toward cities—San Francisco, Los Angeles, New York—where movements for ethnic studies and inner city blocks of Asian communities coincided. . . . We read as we wrote—not in isolation—but in the company of our neighbors in Manilatown pool halls, barrio parks, Chinatown basements. . . . Above all, we poets were a tribe of storytellers. . . . Storytellers live in communities where they write for family and friends. The relationship between the teller and listener is neighborly, because the teller of stories must also listen.[12]

But as storytellers, cultural workers did more than simply describe events around them. By witnessing and participating in the movement, they helped to shape community consciousness. San Francisco poet Al Robles focuses on this process of vision making:

> While living and working in our little, tiny communities, in the midst of towering highrises, we fought the oppressor, the landlord, the developer, the banks, City Hall. But most of all, we celebrated through our culture; music, dance, song and poetry—not only the best we knew but the best we had. The poets were and always have been an integral part of the community. It was through poetry—through a poetical vision to live out the ritual in dignity as human beings.[13]

The transformation of poets, writers, and artists into cultural workers and vision makers reflected larger changes occurring in every sector of the Asian American community. In education, teachers and students redefined the learning process, discovering new ways of sharing knowledge different from traditional, authoritarian, top-down approaches. In the social service sector, social workers and other professionals became "community workers" and under the slogan of "serve the people" redefined the traditional counselor/client relationship by stressing interaction, dialogue, and community building. Within community organizations, members experimented with new organizational structures and collective leadership styles, discarding hierarchical and bureaucratic forms where a handful of commanders made all the decisions. Everywhere, activists and ordinary people grappled with change.

Overall, this "cultural revolution" in the Asian American community echoes themes we have encountered earlier: Third World consciousness, participatory democracy, community building, historical rooting, liberation, and transformation. Why were these concepts so important to a generation of activists? What did they mean? And do they still have relevance for Asian American communities today?

Political analyst Raymond Williams and historian Warren Susman have suggested the use of "keywords" to study historical periods, especially times of great social change.[14] Keywords are terms, concepts, and ideas that emerge as themes of a period, reflecting vital concerns and changing values. For Asian Americans in the 1980s and 1990s, the keywords are "advocacy," "access," "legitimacy," "empowerment," and "assertiveness." These keywords tell us much about the shape of our community today, especially the growing role of young professionals and their aspirations in U.S. society. In contrast, the keywords of the late 1960s and early 1970s—"consciousness," "theory," "ideology," "participatory democracy," "community," and "liberation"— point to different concerns and values.

The keywords of two decades ago point to an approach to political work that activists widely shared, especially those working in grassroots struggles in Asian American neighborhoods, such as the Chinatowns, Little Tokyos, Manilatowns, and International Districts around the nation. This political approach focused on the relationship between political consciousness and social change and can be best summarized in a popular slogan of the period: "Theory becomes a material force when it is grasped by the masses." Asian American activists believed that they could promote political change through direct action and mass education that raised political consciousness in the community, especially among the unorganized—low-income workers, tenants, small-business people, high school youth, etc. Thus, activists saw political consciousness as rising not from study groups but from involving people in the process of social change—through their confronting the institutions of power around them and creating new visions of community life based on these struggles.

Generally, academics studying the movements of the 1960s—including academics in Asian American Studies—have dismissed the political theory of that time as murky and eclectic, characterized by ultra-leftism, shallow class analysis, and simplistic notions of Marxism and capitalism.[15] To a large extent, the thinking was eclectic; Asian American activists drew from Marx, Lenin, Stalin, and Mao—and also from Frantz Fanon, Malcolm X, Che Guevara, Kim Il-sung, and Amilcar Cabral, as well as Korean revolutionary Kim San, W. E. B. DuBois, Frederick Douglass, Paulo Freire, the Black Panther Party, the Young Lords, the women's liberation movement, and many other resistance struggles. But in their obsessive search for theoretical clarity and consistency, these academics miss the bigger picture. What is significant is not the *content* of ideas activists adopted but what activists *did* with the ideas. What Asian American activists *did* was to use the ideas drawn from many different movements to redefine the Asian American experience.

Central to this redefinition was a slogan that appeared at nearly every Asian American rally during that period: "The people, and the people alone, are the motive force in the making of world history." Originating in the Chinese revolution, Asian American activists adapted the slogan to the tasks of community building, historical rooting, and creating new values. Thus, the slogan came to capture six new ways of thinking about Asian Americans.

- Asian Americans became active participants in the making of history, reversing standard accounts that had treated Asian Americans as marginal objects.
- Activists saw history as created by large numbers of people acting together, not by elites.
- This view of history provided a new way of looking at our communities. Activists believed that ordinary people could make their own history by learning how historical forces operated and by transforming this knowledge into a material force to change their lives.
- This realization defined a political strategy: political power came from grassroots organizing, from the bottom up.
- This strategy required activists to develop a broad analysis of the Asian American condition—to uncover the interconnections in seemingly separate events, such as the war in Indochina, corporate redevelopment of Asian American communities, and the exploitation of Asian immigrants in garment shops. In their political analyses, activists linked the day-to-day struggles of Asian Americans to larger events and issues. The anti-eviction campaign of tenants in Chinatown and the International District against powerful corporations became one with the resistance movements of peasants in Vietnam, the Philippines, and Latin America—or, as summarized in a popular slogan of the period, there was "one struggle, [but] many fronts."
- This new understanding challenged activists to build mass, democratic organizations, especially within unorganized sectors of the community. Through these new organizations, Asian Americans expanded democracy for all sectors of the community and gained the power to participate in the broader movement for political change taking place throughout the world.

The redefinition of the Asian American experience stands as the most important legacy from this period. As described above, this legacy represents far more than an ethnic awakening. The redefinition began with an analysis of power and domination in American society. It provided a way for understanding the historical forces surrounding us. And, most importantly, it presented a strategy and challenge for changing our future. This challenge, I believe, still confronts us today.

The Late 1970s: Reversing Direction

As we continue to delve into the vitality of the movements of the 1960s, one question becomes more and more persistent: Why did these movements, possessing so much vigor and urgency, seem to disintegrate in the late 1970s and early 1980s? Why did a society in motion toward progressive change seem to suddenly reverse direction?

As in the larger left movement, Asian American activists heatedly debate this question.[16] Some mention the strategy of repression—including assassinations—U.S. ruling circles launched in response to the mass rebellions. Others cite the accompanying programs of cooptation that elites designed to channel mass discontent into traditional political arenas. Some focus on the New Right's rise, culminating in the Reagan presidency. Still others emphasize the sectarianism among political forces within the movement or target the inability of the movement as a whole to base itself more broadly within communities.

Each of these analyses provides a partial answer. But missing in most analyses by Asian American activists is the most critical factor: the devastating corporate offensive of the mid-1970s. We will remember the 1970s as a time of economic crisis and staggering inflation. Eventually, historians may more accurately describe it as the years of "one-sided class war." Transnational corporations based in the United States launched a broad attack on the American people, especially African American communities. Several books provide an excellent analysis of the corporate offensive. One of the best, most accessible accounts is *What's Wrong with the U.S. Economy?*, written in 1982 by the Institute for Labor Education and Research.[17] My analysis draws from that.

Corporate executives based their offensive on two conclusions: First, the economic crisis in the early 1970s—marked by declining corporate profits—occurred because American working people were earning too much; and second, the mass struggles of the previous decades had created "too much democracy" in America. The Trilateral Commission—headed by David Rockefeller and composed of corporate executives and politicians from the United States, Europe, and Japan—posed the problem starkly: Either people would have to accept less, or corporations would have to accept less. An article in *Business Week* identified the solution: "Some people will obviously have to do with less. . . . Yet it will be a hard pill for many Americans to swallow—the idea of doing with less so that big business can have more."

But in order for corporations to "have more," U.S. ruling circles had to deal with the widespread discontent that had erupted throughout America. We sometimes forget today that in the mid-1970s a large number of Americans had grown cynical about U.S. business and political leaders. People routinely called politicians—including President Nixon and Vice President Agnew—crooks, liars, and criminals. Increasingly, they began to blame the largest corporations for their economic problems. One poll showed that half the population believed that "big business is the source of most of what's wrong in this country today." A series of Harris polls found that those expressing "a great deal of confidence" in the heads of corporations had fallen from 55 percent in 1966 to only 15 percent in 1975. By the fall of 1975, public opinion analysts testifying before a congressional committee reported, according to the *New York Times*, "that public confidence in the government and in the country's economic future is probably lower than it has ever been since they began to measure such things scientifically." These developments stunned many corporate leaders.

"How did we let the educational system fail the free enterprise system?" one executive asked.

U.S. ruling elites realized that restoring faith in free enterprise could only be achieved through an intensive ideological assault on those challenging the system. The ideological campaign was combined with a political offensive, aimed at the broad gains in democratic rights that Americans, especially African Americans, had achieved through the mass struggles of previous decades. According to corporate leaders, there was "too much democracy" in America, which meant too little "governability." In a 1975 Trilateral Commission report, Harvard political scientist Samuel Huntington analyzed the problem caused by "previously passive or unorganized groups in the population [which were] now engaged in concerted efforts to establish their claims to opportunities, positions, rewards, and privileges which they had not considered themselves entitled to before." According to Huntington, this upsurge in "democratic fervor" coincided with "markedly higher levels of self-consciousness on the part of blacks, Indians, Chicanos, white ethnic groups, students, and women, all of whom became mobilized and organized in new ways." Huntington saw these developments as creating a crisis for those in power:

> The essence of the democratic surge of the 1960s was a general challenge to existing systems of authority, public and private. In one form or another, the challenge manifested itself in the family, the university, business, public and private associations, politics, the government bureaucracy, and the military service. People no longer felt the same obligation to obey those whom they had previously considered superior to themselves in age, rank, status, expertise, character, or talents.[18]

The mass pressures, Huntington contended, had "produced problems for the governability of democracy in the 1970s." The government, he concluded, must find a way to exercise more control. And that meant curtailing the rights of "major economic groups."

The ensuing corporate campaign was a "one-sided class war": plant closures in U.S. industries and transfer of production overseas, massive layoffs in remaining industries, shifts of capital investment from one region of the country to other regions and other parts of the globe, and demands by corporations for concessions in wages and benefits from workers in nearly every sector of the economy.

The Reagan presidency culminated and institutionalized this offensive. The Reagan platform called for restoring "traditional" American values, especially faith in the system of free enterprise. Reaganomics promoted economic recovery by getting government "off the backs" of business people, reducing taxation of the rich, and cutting social programs for the poor. Meanwhile, racism and exploitation became respectable under the new mantle of patriotism and economic recovery.

The Winter of Civil Rights

The corporate assault ravaged many American neighborhoods, but African American communities absorbed its harshest impact. A study by the Center on Budget and Policy Priorities measures the national impact:

- Between 1970 and 1980, the number of poor African Americans rose by 24 percent, from 1.4 million to 1.8 million.
- In the 1980s, the overall African American median income was 57 percent that of whites, a decline of nearly four percentage points from the early 1970s.
- In 1986, females headed 42 percent of all African American families, the majority of which lived below the poverty line.
- In 1978, 8.4 percent of African American families had incomes under $5,000 a year. By 1987, that figure had grown to 13.5 percent. In that year, a third of all African Americans were poor.[19]
- By 1990, nearly half of all African American children grew up in poverty. [20]

Manning Marable provides a stark assessment of this devastation in *How Capitalism Underdeveloped Black America*:

> What is qualitatively *new* about the current period is that the racist/capitalist state under Reagan has proceeded down a public policy road which could inevitably involve the complete obliteration of the entire Black reserve army of labor and sections of the Black working class. The decision to save capitalism at all costs, to provide adequate capital for restructuring of the private sector, fundamentally conflicts with the survival of millions of people who are now permanently outside the workplace. Reaganomics must, if it intends to succeed, place the onerous burden of unemployment on the shoulders of the poor (Blacks, Latinos and even whites) so securely that middle to upper income Americans will not protest in the vicious suppression of this stratum.[21]

The corporate offensive, combined with widespread government repression, brutally destroyed grassroots groups in the African American community. This war against the poor ripped apart the social fabric of neighborhoods across America, leaving them vulnerable to drugs and gang violence. The inner cities became the home of the "underclass" and a new politics of inner-directed violence and despair.

Historian Vincent Harding, in *The Other American Revolution*, summarizes the 1970s as the "winter" of civil rights, a period in which there was "a dangerous loss of hope among black people, hope in ourselves, hope in the possibility of any real change, hope in any moral, creative force beyond the flatness of our lives."[22]

In summary, the corporate offensive—especially its devastation of the African American community—provides the necessary backdrop for understanding why the mass movements of the 1960s seemed to disintegrate. Liberation movements, especially in the African American community, did not disappear, but a major focus of their activity shifted to issues of day-to-day survival.

The 1980s: An Ambiguous Period for Asian American Empowerment

For African Americans and many other people of color, the period from the mid-1970s through the Reagan and Bush presidencies became a winter of civil rights, a time of corporate assault on their livelihoods and an erosion of hard-won rights. But for Asian Americans, the meaning of this period is much more ambiguous. On the one hand, great suffering marked the period: growing poverty for increasing numbers of Asian Americans—especially refugees from Southeast Asia; a rising trend of racist hate crimes directed toward Asian Americans of all ethnicities and income levels; and sharpening class polarization within our communities—with a widening gap between the very rich and the very poor. But advances also characterized the period. With the reform of U.S. immigration laws in 1965, the Asian American population grew dramatically, creating new enclaves—including suburban settlements—and revitalizing more established communities, such as Chinatowns, around the nation. Some recent immigrant businesspeople, with small capital holdings, found economic opportunities in inner-city neighborhoods. Meanwhile, Asian American youth enrolled in record numbers in colleges and universities across the United States. Asian American families moved into suburbs, crashing previously lily-white neighborhoods. And a small but significant group of Asian American politicians, such as Mike Woo and Warren Furutani, scored important electoral victories in the mainstream political arena, taking the concept of political empowerment to a new level of achievement.

During the winter of civil rights, Asian American activists also launched several impressive political campaigns at the grassroots level. Japanese Americans joined together to win redress and reparations. Pilipino Americans rallied in solidarity with the "People's Power" movement in the Philippines to topple the powerful Marcos dictatorship. Chinese Americans created new political alignments and mobilized community support for the pro-democracy struggle in China. Korean Americans responded to the massacre of civilians by the South Korean dictatorship in Kwangju with massive demonstrations and relief efforts and established an important network of organizations in America, including Young Koreans United. Samoan Americans rose up against police abuse in Los Angeles; Pacific Islanders demanded removal of nuclear weapons and wastes from their homelands; and Hawaiians fought for the right of self-determination and recovery of their lands. And large numbers of Asian Americans and Pacific Islanders worked actively in the 1984 and 1988 presidential campaigns of Jesse Jackson, helping to build the Rainbow Coalition.

Significantly, these accomplishments occurred in the midst of the Reagan presidency and U.S. politics' turn to the right. How did certain sectors of the Asian American community achieve these gains amidst conservatism?

There is no simple answer. Mainstream analysts and some Asian Americans have stressed the "model minority" concept. According to this analysis, Asian Americans— in contrast to other people of color in America—have survived adversity and advanced because of their emphasis on education and family values, their community cohesion, and other aspects of their cultural heritage. Other scholars have severely criticized this viewpoint, stressing instead structural changes in the global economy and shifts in U.S. government policy since the 1960s. According to their analysis, the reform of U.S. immigration laws and sweeping economic changes in advanced capitalist nations, such as deindustrialization and the development of new technologies, brought an influx of highly educated new Asian immigrants to America. The characteristics of these new immigrants stand in sharp contrast to those of past generations and provide a broader social and economic base for developing our communities. Still other political thinkers have emphasized the key role played by political expatriates—both right-wing and left-wing—in various communities, but most especially in the Vietnamese, Pilipino, and Korean communities. These expatriates brought political resources from their homelands—e.g., political networks, organizing experience, and, in a few cases, access to large amounts of funds—and have used these resources to change the political landscape of ethnic enclaves. Still other analysts have examined the growing economic and political power of nations of the Asia Pacific and its impact on Asians in America. According to these analysts, we can link the advances of Asian Americans during this period to the rising influence of their former homelands and the dawning of what some call "the Pacific Century." Finally, some academics have focused on the significance of small-business activities of new Asian immigrants, arguing that this sector is most responsible for the changing status of Asian Americans in the 1980s. According to their analysis, Asian immigrant entrepreneurs secured an economic niche in inner-city neighborhoods because they had access to start-up capital (through rotating credit associations or from family members) and they filled a vacuum created when white businesses fled.[23]

Thus, we have multitiple interpretations for why some sectors of the Asian American community advanced economically and politically during the winter of civil rights. But two critical factors are missing from the analyses that can help us better understand the peculiar shape of our community in the 1980s and its ambiguous character when compared to other communities of color. First is the legacy of grassroots organizing from the Asian American movement, and second is the dramatic rise of young professionals as a significant force in the community.

A stereotype about the movements of the 1960s is that they produced nothing enduring—they flared brightly for an instant and then quickly died. However, evidence from the Asian American movement contradicts this commonly held belief. Through meticulous organizing campaigns, Asian American activists created an extensive network of grassroots formations. Unlike similar groups in African American communities—which government repression targeted and brutally destroyed—a significant number of Asian American groups survived the 1980s. Thus far, no researcher has analyzed the impact of the corporate offensive and government repression on grassroots organizations in different communities of color during the late 1970s. When this research is done, I think it will show that U.S. ruling elites viewed the movement in the African American community as a major threat due to its power and influence over other communities. In contrast, the movement in the Asian American community received much less attention due to its much smaller size and influence. As a result, Asian American grassroots formations during the 1970s escaped decimation and gained the time and space to survive, grow, and adapt to changing politics.

The survival of grassroots organizations is significant because it helped to cushion the impact of the war against the poor in Asian American communities. More important, the grassroots formations provided the foundation for many of the successful empowerment campaigns occurring in the 1980s. For example, Japanese Americans built their national effort to win reparations for their internment during World War II on the experiences of grassroots neighborhood organizations' housing and anti-eviction struggles of the early 1970s. Movement activists learned from their confrontations with systems of power and applied these lessons to the more difficult political fights of the 1980s. Thus, a direct link exists between the mass struggles of activists in the late 1960s and the "empowerment" approach of Asian Americans in the 1980s and 1990s.

But while similarities exist in political organizing of the late 1960s and the 1980s, there is one crucial difference: Who is being empowered? In the late 1960s and 1970s, activists focused on bringing "power to the people"—the most disenfranchised of the community, such as low-income workers, youth, former prisoners and addicts, senior citizens, tenants, and small-business people. In contrast, the "empowerment" of young professionals in Asian American communities marks the decade of the 1980s. The professionals—children of the civil rights struggles of the 1950s and 1960s—directly benefited from the campaigns for desegregation, especially in the suburbs; the removal of quotas in colleges and professional schools; and the expansion of job opportunities for middle-class people of color in fields such as law, medicine, and education.

During the 1980s, young professionals altered the political terrain in our communities.[24] They created countless new groups in nearly every profession: law, medicine, social work, psychology, education, journalism, business, and arts and culture. They initiated new political advocacy groups, leadership training projects, and various national coalitions and consortiums. They organized political caucuses in the Democratic and Republican parties. And they joined the governing boards of many community agencies. Thus, young professionals—through their sheer numbers, their penchant for self-organization, and their high level of activity—defined the Asian American community of the 1980s, shaping it in ways very different from other communities of color.

The emergence of young professionals as community leaders also aided mass political mobilizations. By combining with grassroots forces from the Asian American movement, young professionals advanced struggles against racism and discrimination. In fact, many of the successful Asian American battles of the past decade resulted from this strategic alignment.

The growing power of young professionals has also brought a diversification of political viewpoints to our communities. While many professionals embrace concerns originally raised by movement activists, a surprisingly large number have moved toward neoconservatism. The emergence of neoconservatism in our community is a fascinating phenomenon, one we should analyze and appreciate. Perhaps more than any other phenomenon, it helps to explain the political ambiguity of Asian American empowerment in the decade of the 1980s.

Strange and New Political Animals: Asian American Neoconservatives

Item: At many universities in recent years, some of the harshest opponents of affirmative action have been Chinese Americans and Korean Americans who define themselves as political conservatives. This, in and of itself, is not new or significant. We have always had Asian American conservatives who have spoken out against affirmative action. But what is new is their affiliation. Many participate actively in Asian American student organizations traditionally associated with campus activism.

Item: In the San Francisco newspaper *Asian Week*, one of the most interesting columnists is Arthur Hu, who writes about antiAsian quotas in universities, political empowerment, and other issues relating to our communities. He also regularly chastises those he terms "liberals, progressives, Marxists, and activists." In a recent column, he wrote: "The left today has the nerve to blame AIDS, drugs, the dissolution of the family, welfare dependency, gang violence, and educational failure on Ronald Reagan's conservatism." Hu, in turn, criticizes the left for "tearing down religion, family, structure, and authority; promoting drugs, promiscuity, and abdication of personal responsibility."[25]

Item: During the militant, three-year campaign to win tenure for UCLA Professor Don Nakanishi, one of the key student leaders was a Japanese American Republican, Matthew J. Endo. Aside from joining the campus-community steering committee, he also mobilized support from fraternities, something that progressive activists could not do. Matt prides himself on being a Republican and a life member of the National Rifle Association. He aspires to become a CEO in a corporation but worries about the upsurge in racism against Asian Pacific peoples and the failure of both Republicans and Democrats to address this issue.

The Asian American neoconservatives are a new and interesting political phenomenon. They are new because they are creatures born from the Reagan-Bush era of supply-side economics, class and racial polarization, and the emphasis on elitism and individual advancement. And they are interesting because they also represent a legacy from the civil rights struggles, especially the Asian American movement. The neoconservatives embody these seemingly contradictory origins.

- They are proud to be Asian American. But they denounce the Asian American movement of the late 1960s and early 1970s as destructive.
- They speak out against racism against Asian Americans. But they believe that only by ending affirmative-action programs and breaking with prevailing civil rights thinking of the past four decades can we end racism.
- They express concern for Asian American community issues. But they contend that the agenda set by the "liberal Asian American establishment" ignores community needs.
- They vehemently oppose quotas blocking admissions of Asian Americans at colleges and universities. But they link anti-Asian quotas to affirmative-actions programs for "less qualified" African Americans, Latinos, and American Indians.
- They acknowledge the continuing discrimination against African Americans, Latinos, and American Indians in U.S. society. But they believe that the main barrier blocking advancement for other people of color is "cultural"—that, unlike Asians, these groups supposedly come from cultures that do not sufficiently emphasize education, family cohesion, and traditional values.

Where did these neoconservatives come from? What do they represent? And why is it important for progressive peoples to understand their presence?

Progressives cannot dismiss Asian American neoconservatives as simple-minded Republicans. Although they hold views similar at times to Patrick Buchanan and William Buckley, they are not clones of white conservatives. Nor are they racists, fellow travelers of the Ku Klux Klan, or ideologues attached to Reagan and Bush. Perhaps the group that they most resemble are the African American neoconservatives: the Shelby Steeles, Clarence Thomases, and Tony Browns of this period. Like these men, they are professionals and feel little kinship for people of lower classes. Like these men, they oppose prevailing civil rights thinking, emphasizing reliance on government intervention and social programs. And, like these men, they have gained from affirmative action, but they now believe that America has somehow become a society where other people of color can advance through their own "qualifications."

Neoconservative people of color have embraced thinkers such as the late Martin Luther King, Jr., but have appropriated his message to fit their own ideology. In his speeches and writings, King dreamed of the day when racism would be eliminated— when African Americans would be recognized in U.S. society for the "content of our character, not the color of our skin." He called upon all in America to wage militant struggle to achieve this dream. Today, neoconservatives have subverted his message. They believe that racism in U.S. society has declined in significance and that people of color can now abandon mass militancy and advance individually by cultivating the content of their character through self-help programs and educational attainment and retrieving traditional family values. They criticize prevailing "civil rights thinking" as overemphasizing the barriers of racism and relying on "external forces" (i.e., government intervention through social programs) to address the problem.

Asian American neoconservatives closely resemble their African American counterparts in their criticism of government "entitlement" programs and their defense of traditional culture and family values. But Asian American neoconservatives are not exactly the same as their African American counterparts. The growth of neoconservative thinking among Asian Americans during the past twenty-five years reflects the peculiar conditions in our community, notably the emerging power of young professionals. Thus, to truly understand Asian American neoconservatives, we need to look at their evolution through the prism of Asian American politics from the late 1960s to the early 1990s.

Twenty-five years ago, Asian American neoconservatives did not exist. Our community then had only traditional conservatives—those who opposed ethnic studies, the antiwar movement, and other militant grassroots struggles. The traditional conservatives denounced Asian American concerns as "special interest politics" and labeled the assertion of Asian American ethnic identity as "separatist" thinking. For the traditional conservative, a basic contradiction existed in identifying oneself as Asian American and conservative.

Ironically, the liberation struggles of the 1960s—and the accompanying Asian American movement—spawned a new conservative thinker. The movement partially transformed the educational curriculum through ethnic studies, enabling all Asian Americans to assert pride in their ethnic heritage. The movement accelerated the desegregation of suburbs, enabling middle-class Asian Americans to move into all-white neighborhoods. Today, the neoconservatives are mostly young, middle-class professionals who grew up in white suburbs apart from the poor and people of color. As students, they attended the elite universities. Their only experience with racism is name-calling or "glass ceilings" blocking personal career advancement—and not poverty and violence.

It is due to their professional status and their roots in the Asian American movement that the neoconservatives exist in uneasy alliance with traditional conservatives in our community. Neoconservatives are appalled by the violence and rabid anticommunism of reactionary sectors of the Vietnamese community, Chinese from Taiwan tied to the oppressive ruling Kuomintang party, and Korean expatriates attached to the Korean Central Intelligence Agency. They are also uncomfortable with older conservatives, those coming from small-business backgrounds who warily eye the neoconservatives, considering them as political opportunists.

Neoconservatives differ from traditional conservatives not only because of their youth and their professional status but, most important of all, their political coming of age in the Reagan era. Like their African American counterparts, they are children of the corporate offensive against workers, the massive transfer of resources from the poor to the rich, and the rebirth of so-called traditional values.

It is their schooling in Reaganomics and their willingness to defend the current structure of power and privilege in America that gives neoconservative people of color value in today's political landscape. Thus, Manning Marable describes the key role played by African American neoconservatives:

> The singular service that [they] . . . provide is a new and more accurate understanding of what exactly constitutes conservatism within the Black experience . . . Black conservatives are traditionally hostile to Black participation in trade unions, and urge a close cooperation with white business leaders. Hostile to the welfare state, they call for increased "self-help" programs run by Blacks at local and community levels. Conservatives often accept the institutionalized forms of patriarchy, acknowledging a secondary role for Black women within economics, political life, and intellectual work. They usually have a pronounced bias towards organizational authoritarianism and theoretical rigidity.[26]

Marable's analysis points to the basic contradiction for African American neoconservatives. They are unable to address fundamental problems facing their community: racist violence, grinding poverty, and the unwillingness of corporate and government policymakers to deal with these issues.

Asian American neoconservatives face similar difficulties when confronted by the stark realities of the post-Reagan period:

- The neoconservatives acknowledge continuing discrimination in U.S. society but deny the existence of institutional racism and structural inequality. For them, racism lies in the realm of attitudes and "culture" and not institutions of power. Thus, they emphasize individual advancement as the way to overcome racism. They believe that people of color can rise through merit, which they contend can be measured objectively through tests, grades, and educational attainment.
- The neoconservatives ignore questions of wealth and privilege in American

society. In their obsession with "merit," "qualifications," and "objective" criteria, they lose sight of power and oppression in America. Their focus is on dismantling affirmative-action programs and "government entitlements" from the civil rights era. But poverty and racism existed long before the civil rights movement. They are embedded in the system of inequality that has long characterized U.S. society.

- The neoconservatives are essentially elitists who fear expansion of democracy at the grassroots level. They speak a language of individual advancement, not mass empowerment. They propose a strategy of alignment with existing centers of power and not the creation of new power bases among the disenfranchised sectors of society. Their message is directed to professionals much like themselves. They have nothing to offer to immigrant workers in sweatshops, the homeless, Cambodian youth in street gangs, or community college youth.
- As relative newcomers to Asian American issues, the neoconservatives lack understanding of history, especially how concerns in the community have developed over time. Although they aggressively speak out about issues, they lack experience in organizing around these issues. The neoconservatives function best in the realm of ideas; they have difficulty dealing with concrete situations.

However, by stimulating discussion over how Asian American define community problems, the neoconservatives bring a vibrancy to community issues by contributing a different viewpoint. Thus, the debate between Asian American neoconservatives and progressives is positive because it clarifies issues and enables both groups to reach constituencies that each could not otherwise reach.

Unfortunately, this debate is also occurring in a larger and more dangerous context: the campaign by mainstream conservatives to redefine civil rights in America. As part of their strategy, conservatives in the national political arena have targeted our communities. There are high stakes here, and conservatives regard the Asian American neoconservatives as small players to be sacrificed.

The high stakes are evident in an article by William McGurn entitled "The Silent Minority," appearing in the conservative digest *National Review*.[27] In his essay, he urges Republicans to actively recruit and incorporate Asian Americans into party activities. According to McGurn, a basic affinity exists between Republican values and Asian American values: Many Asian immigrants own small businesses; they oppose communism; they are fiercely prodefense; they boast strong families; they value freedom; and in their approach to civil rights, they stress opportunities, not government "set-asides." McGurn then chastises fellow Republicans for their "crushing indifference" to Asian American issues. He laments how Republicans have lost opportunities by not speaking out on key issues such as the conflict between Korean immigrant merchants and African Americans, the controversy over anti-Asian quotas in universities, and the upsurge in anti-Asian violence.

McGurn sees Republican intervention on these issues strategically—as a way of redefining the race question in American society and shifting the debate on civil rights away from reliance on "an increasingly narrow band of black and liberal interest groups." According to McGurn:

> Precisely because Asian Americans are making it in their adoptive land, they hold the potential not only to add to Republican rolls but to define a bona-fide American language of civil rights. Today we have only one language of civil rights, and it is inextricably linked to government intervention, from racial quotas to setaside government contracts. It is also an exclusively black-establishment language, where America's myriad other minorities are relegated to second-class citizenship.[28]

McGurn's article presages a period of intense and unprecedented conservative interest in Asian American issues. We can expect conservative commentaries to intensify black-Asian conflicts in inner cities, the controversy over affirmative action, and the internal community debate over designating Asian Americans as a "model minority."

Thus, in the coming period, Asian American communities are likely to become crowded places. Unlike the late 1960s, issues affecting our communities will no longer be the domain of progressive forces only. Increasingly, we will hear viewpoints from Asian American neoconservatives as well as mainstream conservatives. How well will activists meet this new challenge?

Grassroots Organizing in the 1990s: The Challenge of Expanding Democracy

> Time would pass, old empires would fall and new ones take their place, the relations of countries and the relations of classes had to change, before I discovered if, that it is not quality of goods and utility which matter, but movement; not where you are or what you have but where you have come from, where you are going and the rate at which you are getting there.[29]
>
> —C. L. R. James

On the eve of the twenty-first century, the Asian American community is vastly different from that of the late 1960s. The community has grown dramatically. In 1970, there were only 1.5 million Asian Americans, almost entirely concentrated in Hawaii and California. By 1980, there were 3.7 million, and in 1990, 7.9 million—with major Asian communities in New York, Minnesota, Pennsylvania, and Texas. According to census projections, the Asian American population should exceed 10 million by the year 2000 and will reach 20 million by the year 2020.[30]

Moreover, in contrast to the late 1960s—when Chinese and Japanese Americans comprised the majority of Asian Americans—today's community is ethnically diverse—consisting of nearly thirty major ethnic groups, each with a distinct culture. Today's community is also economically different from the 1960s. Compared to other sectors of the U.S. population, there are higher proportions of Asian Americans who are very rich and very poor. This gap between wealth and poverty has created a sharp class polarization in our community, a phenomenon yet to be studied.

But the changes for Asian Americans during the past twenty-five years have not been simply demographic. The political landscape has also changed due to new immigrants and refugees, the polarization between rich and poor, and the emergence of young professionals as a vital new force. Following the approach of C. L. R. James, we have traced the origins of these changes. We now need to analyze where these changes will take us in the decade ahead.

Ideologically and politically, activists confront a new and interesting paradox in the Asian American community of the 1990s. On the one hand, there is a great upsurge of interest in the community and all things Asian American. Almost daily, we hear about new groups forming across the country. In contrast to twenty-five years ago, when interest in the community was minimal and when only progressive activists joined Asian American organizations, we now find a situation where many different groups—including conservatives and neoconservatives, bankers and business executives, and young professionals in all fields—have taken up the banner of Asian American identity.

On the other hand, we have not seen a corresponding growth in consciousness—of what it means to be Asian American as we approach the the twenty-first century. Unlike African Americans, most Asian Americans today have yet to articulate the "particularities" of issues affecting our community, whether these be the debate over affirmative action, the controversy regarding multiculturalism, or the very definition of empowerment. We have an ideological vacuum, and activists will compete with neoconservatives, mainstream conservatives, and others to fill it.

We have a political vacuum as well. In recent years, growing numbers of Asian Americans have become involved in community issues. But almost all have come from middle-class and professional backgrounds. Meanwhile, vast segments of our community are not coming forward. In fact, during the past decade the fundamental weakness for activists has been the lack of grassroots organizing among the disenfranchised sectors of our community: youth outside of colleges and universities, the poor, and new immigrant workers. Twenty-five years ago, the greatest strength of the Asian American movement was the ability of activists to organize the unorganized and to bring new political players into community politics. Activists targeted high-school youth, tenants, small-business people, former prison inmates, gang members, the elderly, and workers. Activists helped them build new grassroots organizations, expanding power and democracy in our communities. Can a new generation of activists do the same?

To respond to this challenge, activists will need both a political strategy and a new ideological vision. Politically, activists must find ways to expand democracy by creating new grassroots formations, activating new political players, and building new coalitions. Ideologically, activists must forge a new moral vision, reclaiming the militancy and moral urgency of past generations and reaffirming the commitment to participatory democracy, community building, and collective styles of leadership.

Where will this political strategy and new consciousness come from? More than fifty years ago, revolutionary leader Mao Zedong asked a similar question:

Where do correct ideas come from? Do they drop from the skies? No. Are they innate in the mind? No. They come from social practice, and from it alone. . . . In their social practice, people engage in various kinds of struggle and gain rich experience, both from their successes and their failures.[31]

In the current "social practice" of Asian American activists across the nation, several grassroots organizing projects can serve as the basis for a political strategy and new moral vision for the 1990s. I will focus on three projects that are concentrating on the growing numbers of poor and working poor in our community. Through their grassroots efforts, these three groups are demonstrating how collective power can expand democracy, and how, in the process, activists can forge a new moral vision.

The three groups—the Chinese Progressive Association (CPA) Workers Center in Boston, Asian Immigrant Women Advocates (AIWA) in Oakland, and Korean Immigrant Worker Advocates (KIWA) in Los Angeles—address local needs. Although each organization works with different ethnic groups, their history of organizing has remarkable similarities. Each organization is composed of low-income immigrant workers. Each has taken up more than "labor" issues. And each group has fashioned very effective "united front" campaigns involving other sectors of the community. Thus, although each project is relatively small, collectively their accomplishments illustrate the power of grassroots organizing, the creativity and talents of "ordinary" people in taking up difficult issues, and the ability of grassroots forces to alter the political landscape of their community. Significantly, the focus of each group is working people in the Asian American community—a sector that is numerically large and growing larger. However, despite their numbers, workers in the Asian American community during the past decade have become voiceless and silent. Today, in discussions about community issues, no one places garment workers, nurses' aides, waiters, and secretaries at the forefront of the debate to define priorities. And no one thinks about the working class as the cutting edge of the Asian American experience. Yet, if we begin to list the basic questions now confronting Asian Americans—racism and sexism, economic justice and human rights, coalition building, and community empowerment—we would find that it is the working class, of all sectors in our community, that is making the most interesting breakthroughs on these questions. They are doing this through groups such as KIWA, AIWA, and the CPA Workers Center. Why, then, are the voices of workers submerged in our community? Why has the working class become silent?

Three trends have pushed labor issues in our community into the background during the past two decades: the rising power of young professionals in our community; the influx of new immigrants and refugees and the fascination of social scientists and policy institutes with the phenomenon of immigrant entrepreneurship; and the lack of grassroots organizing by activists among new immigrant workers.

Thus, although the majority of Asian Americans work for a living, we have relatively little understanding about the central place of work in the lives of Asian Americans, especially in low-income industries such as garment work, restaurant work, clerical and office work, and other service occupations. Moreover, we are ignorant about the role that labor struggles have played in shaping our history.[32] This labor history is part of the legacy that activists must reclaim.

In contrast to the lack of knowledge about Asian American workers, we have a much greater understanding about the role of young professionals, students, and, most of all, small-business people. In fact, immigrant entrepreneurs, especially Korean immigrants, are perhaps the most studied people of our community. However, as sociologist Edna Bonacich notes, the profile of most Asian immigrant entrepreneurs closely resembles that of workers, due to their low earning power, their long work hours, and their lack of job-related benefits. Thus, Bonacich suggests that while the world outlook of Asian immigrant entrepreneurs may be petit bourgeoisie, their life conditions are those of the working class and might better be studied as a "labor" question. Asian immigrant small businesses, she contends, play the role of "cheap labor in American capitalism."[33]

Other researchers have only begun to investigate the extent of poverty among Asian Americans and the meaning of poverty for our community. In California, the rate of poverty for Asian Americans rose from about 10 percent in 1980 to 18 percent in 1990. But, more important, researchers found that there are higher numbers of "working poor" (as opposed to "jobless poor") in the Asian American community than for other ethnic groups. Thus, in contrast to other Americans, Asian Americans are poor not because they lack jobs but because the jobs they have pay very low wages. According to researchers Dean Toji and James Jonhson, Jr., "Perhaps contrary to common belief, about half of the poor work—including about a quarter of poor adults who work full-time and year-round. Poverty, then, is a labor question."[34]

Activists in groups such as KIWA, AIWA, and the CPA Workers Center are strategically focusing on the "working poor" in the Asian American community. KIWA—which was founded in 1992—is working with low-income Korean immigrants in Los Angeles Koreatown, including garment workers and employees in small businesses. AIWA—founded in 1983—organizes Chinese garment workers, Vietnamese garment and electronics workers, and Korean hotel maids and electronics assemblers. And the CPA Workers Center—which traces its roots to the landmark struggle of Chinese garment workers in Boston in 1985—is composed primarily of Chinese immigrant women. Although their main focus is on workers, each group has also mobilized students and social service providers to support their campaigns. Through these alliances, each group has carried out successful community organizing strategies.

The focus of the three groups on community-based organizing distinguishes them from traditional unions. Miriam Ching Louie of AIWA explains this distinction:

> AIWA's base is simultaneously worker, female, Asian, and immigrant, and the organization has developed by blending together several different organizing techniques. As compared to the traditional union organizing strategy, AIWA's approach focuses on the needs of its constituency. *Popular literacy/conscientization/transformation* [based on the teachings of Paulo Freire] is a learning and teaching method which taps into people's life experiences as part of a broader reality, source of knowledge, and guide to action. *Community-based organizing* takes a holistic view of racial/ethnic people and organizes for social change, not only so that the people can win immediate improvements in their

lives, but so that they can also develop their own power in the course of waging the fight.[35]

AIWA's focus on grassroots organizing is illustrated by its "Garment Workers' Justice Campaign," launched in late 1992 to assist Chinese immigrant women who were denied pay by a garment contractor. AIWA organizers shaped the campaign to respond to the peculiar features of the garment industry. The industry in the San Francisco Bay Area is the nation's third largest—following New York and Los Angeles—and employs some 20,000 seamstresses, 85 percent of them Asian immigrant women. The structure of the industry is a pyramid with retailers and manufacturers at the top, contractors in the middle, and immigrant women working at the bottom. Manufacturers make the main share of profits in the industry; they set the price for contractors. Meanwhile, immigrant women work under sweatshop conditions.

In their campaign, AIWA and the workers initially confronted the contractor for the workers' back pay. When they discovered that the contractor owed a number of creditors, they took the unusual step of holding the garment manufacturer, Jessica McClintock, accountable for the unpaid wages. McClintock operates ten boutiques and sells dresses through department stores. The dresses—which garment workers are paid $5 to make—retail in stores for $175. AIWA and the workers conducted their campaign through a series of high-profile demonstrations at McClintock boutiques, including picket lines and rallies in ten cities by supporters. AIWA designed these demonstrations not only to put pressure on McClintock and educate others in the community about inequities in the structure of the garment industry but also to serve as vehicles for empowerment for the immigrant women participating the campaign. Through this campaign, the women workers learned how to confront institutional power, how to forge alliances with other groups in the community, and how to carry out effective tactics based on their collective power.[36]

Thus, through its activities promoting immigrant women's rights, AIWA is expanding democracy in the community. It is bringing labor issues to the forefront of community dicussions. It is creating new grassroots caucuses among previously unorganized sectors of the community and forming new political alignments with supporters, such as students, young professionals, labor unions, and social service providers. Finally, AIWA is developing a cadre of politically sophisticated immigrant women and promoting a new leadership style based on popular literacy, community building, and collective power.

Similarly, in Boston, the CPA Workers Center is expanding democracy through its grassroots efforts around worker rights. The Center emerged out of the Chinese immigrant women's campaign to deal with the closing of a large garment factory in Boston in 1985.[37] The shutdown displaced 350 workers and severely impacted the local Chinese community due to the community's high concentration of jobs in the garment industry. However, with the assistance of the Chinese Progressive Alliance, the workers formed a labor-community-student coalition and waged an eighteen-month campaign to win job retraining and job replacement. Lydia Lowe, director of the CPA Workers Center, describes how the victory of Chinese immigrant women led to creation of the Workers Center, which, in turn, has helped other work place campaigns in the Chinese community:

> This core of women activated through the campaign joined with community supporters from the CPA to found a community-based workers' mutual aid and resource center, based at CPA. . . . Through the Workers Center, immigrant workers share their experience, collectively sum up lessons learned, find out about their rights, and develop mutual support and organizing strategies. Today, the Workers Center involves immigrant workers from each of its successive organizing efforts, and is a unique place in the community where ordinary workers can walk in and participate as activists and decision-makers.[38]

Moreover, forming the Workers Center reshaped politics in the local Chinese community, turning garment workers and other immigrant laborers into active political players. "Previously the silent majority, immigrant workers are gaining increasing respect as a force to be reckoned with in the local Chinese community," states Lowe.

In Los Angeles, the formation of KIWA in March 1992—only a month before the uprisings—has had a similar impact. Through its programs, KIWA is bringing labor issues to the forefront of the Asian American community, educating labor unions about the needs of Asian American workers, and forming coalitions with other grassroots forces in the city to deal with interethnic tensions. KIWA is uniquely positioned to take up these tasks. Out of the multitude of Asian American organizations in Los Angeles, KIWA distinguishes itself as the only organization governed by a board of directors of mainly workers.

KIWA's key role in the labor movement and community politics is evident in the recent controversy involving the Koreana Wilshire Hotel.[39] The controversy began in late 1991 when Koreana Hotel Co. Ltd., a South Korean corporation, bought the Wilshire Hyatt in Los Angeles. The change in ownership meant that 175 unionized members, predominantly Latino immigrants, were out of jobs. Meanwhile, the new hotel management hired a new work force, paying them an average of $1.50 per hour less than the former unionized work force. The former workers, represented by Hotel Employees and Restaurant Employees (HERE) Local 11, called upon labor unions and groups from the Asian American, African American, and Latino communities to protest Koreana's union-busting efforts. Local 11 defined the dispute as not only a labor issue but a civil rights issue. With the help of groups such as KIWA and the Asian Pacific American Labor Alliance, Local 11 initiated a letter-writing campaign against Koreana, began a community boycott of the hotel, and organized militant actions outside the hotel, including rallies, marches, and a picket line, as well as civil disobedience at the nearby Korean consulate. In each of these actions, Local 11 worked closely with KIWA and members of the Asian American community. Due to the mass pressure, in late 1992 the Koreana management agreed to negotiate with Local 11 to end the controversy and rehire the union members.

Throughout the campaign, KIWA played a pivotal role by assisting Local 11 build alliances with the Asian American community. In addition, KIWA members promoted labor consciousness in the Korean community by urging the community to boycott the hotel. KIWA members also spoke at Local 11 rallies, mobilized for picket lines, and worked with the union in its efforts to put pressure on the South Korean government. By taking these steps, KIWA prevented the controversy from pitting the Korean community against Latinos and further enflaming interethnic tensions in Los Angeles.

Also, through campaigns such as this one, KIWA is educating Asian immigrants about unions; training workers around the tasks of political leadership; and creating new centers of power in the community by combining the resources of workers, young professionals, and social service providers.

Thus, through grassroots organizing, KIWA—like AIWA and the CPA Workers Center—is expanding democracy in the Asian American community. Moreover, the three groups collectively are reshaping community consciousness. They are sharpening debate and dialogue around issues and redefining such important concepts as empowerment. What is their vision of empowerment, and how does it differ from prevailing definitions?

The Twenty-first Century: Building an Asian American Movement

[A] movement is an idea, a philosophy. . . . Leadership, I feel, is only incidental to the movement. The movement should be the most important thing. The movement must go beyond its leaders. It must be something that is continuous, with goals and ideas that the leadership can then build on.[40]

—Philip Vera Cruz

In the late 1960s, Asian American activists sought to forge a new approach to leadership that would not replicate traditional Eurocentric models—i.e., rigid hierarchies with a single executive at the top, invariably a white male, who commanded an endless chain of assistants. In their search for alternatives, activists experimented with various ideas borrowed from other movements, but most of all, activists benefited from the advice and guidance of "elders" within the Asian American community—women and men with years of grassroots organizing experience in the community, the work place, and the progressive political movement. One such "elder" was Pilipino immigrant labor leader Philip Vera Cruz, then in his sixties. Vera Cruz represented the *manong* generation—the first wave of Pilipinos who came to the United States in the early twentieth century and worked in agricultural fields, canneries, hotels, and restaurants.

Now eighty-eight years old, Vera Cruz continues to educate a new generation of activists. His lifetime of experience in grassroots organizing embodies the historic themes of Asian American activism: devotion to the rights of working people, commitment to democracy and liberation, steadfast solidarity with all who face oppression throughout the world, and the courage to challenge existing institutions of power and to create new institutions as the need arises. These themes have defined his life and shaped his approach to the question of empowerment—an approach that is different from standard definitions in our community today.

Vera Cruz is best known for his role in building the United Farm Workers (UFW), a culmination of his many years of organizing in agricultural fields. In 1965, he was working with the Agricultural Workers Organizing Committee, AFL-CIO, when Pilipino farmworkers sat-down in the Coachella vineyards of central California. This sit-down launched the famous grape strike and boycott, eventually leading to the formation of the UFW. Many books and articles have told the story of the UFW and its leader Cesar Chavez. But, until recently, no one has focused on the historic role of Pilipinos in building this movement. Craig Scharlin and Lilia Villanueva have filled that vacuum with their new publication about Vera Cruz's life.

Following the successful grape boycott, Vera Cruz became a UFW vice president and remained with the union until 1977, when he left due to political differences with the leadership. He was critical of the lack of rank-and-file democracy in the union and the leadership's embrace of the Marcos dictatorship in the Philippines. Since 1979, Vera Cruz has lived in Bakersfield, California, and has continued to devote his life to unionism and social justice and to the education of a new generation of Asian American youth.

Vera Cruz's life experiences have shaped a broad view of empowerment. For Vera Cruz, empowerment is grassroots power: the expansion of democracy for the many. Becoming empowered means gaining the capacity to advocate not only for one's own concerns but for the liberation of all oppressed peoples. Becoming empowered means being able to fundamentally change the relationship of power and oppression in society. Thus, Vera Cruz's vision is very different from that of today's young professionals. For them, empowerment is leadership development for an elite. Becoming empowered means gaining the skills to advocate for the community by gaining access to decision makers. Thus, for young professionals, the key leadership quality to develop is assertiveness. Through assertiveness, leaders gain access to policymakers as well as the power to mobilize their followers. In contrast, Vera Cruz stresses the leadership trait of humility. For him, leaders are "only incidental to the movement"— the movement is "the most important thing." For Vera Cruz, empowerment is a process where people join to develop goals and ideas to create a larger movement— a movement "that the leadership can then build on."

Vera Cruz's understanding of empowerment has evolved from his own social practice. Through his experiences in the UFW and the AFL-CIO, Vera Cruz learned about the empty democracy of bureaucratic unions and the limitations of the charismatic leadership style of Cesar Chavez. Through his years of toil as a farmworker, he recognized the importance of worker solidarity and militancy and the capacity of common people to create alternative institutions of grassroots power. Through his work with Pilipino and Mexican immigrants, he saw the necessity of coalition building and worker unity that crossed ethnic and racial boundaries. He has shared these lessons with several generations of Asian American activists.

But aside from sharing a concept of empowerment, Vera Cruz has also promoted a larger moral vision, placing his lifetime of political struggle in the framework of the movement for liberation. Three keywords distinguish his moral vision: "compassion," "solidarity," and "commitment." Vera Cruz's lifetime of action represents compassion for all victims of oppression, solidarity with all fighting for liberation, and commitment to the ideals of democracy and social justice.

Activists today need to learn from Vera Cruz's compassion, solidarity, commitment, and humility to create a new moral vision for our community. In our grassroots organizing, we need a vision that can redefine empowerment—that can bring questions of power, domination, and liberation to the forefront of our work. We need a vision that can help us respond to the challenge of conservatives and neoconservatives, and sharpen dialogue with young professionals. We need a new moral vision that can help fill the ideological vacuum in today's community.

Nowhere is this ideological challenge greater than in the current debate over the model minority stereotype. The stereotype has become the dominant image of Asian Americans for mainstream society, and has generated intense debate among all sectors of our community. This debate provides an opportunity for activists to expand political awareness and, in the process, redefine the Asian American experience for the 1990s.

In the current controversy, however, activists criticize the model minority stereotype politically but not ideologically. Activists correctly target how the concept fails to deal with Asian American realities: the growing population of poor and working poor, the large numbers of youth who are not excelling in school, and the hardships and family problems of small-business people who are not "making it" in U.S. society. Activists also correctly point out the political ramifications of the model minority stereotype: the pitting of minority groups against each other and growing interethnic tensions in U.S. society. In contrast, conservative and neoconservative proponents of the model minority concept argue from the standpoint of both political realities and a larger moral vision. They highlight Asian American accomplishments: "whiz kids" in elementary schools; growing numbers of Asian Americans in business, politics, and the professions; and the record enrollment of youth in colleges and universities. Conservatives and neoconservatives attribute these accomplishments to Asian culture and tradition, respect for authority, family cohesion, sacrifice and toil, rugged individualism, and self-reliance—moral values that they root in conservative thinking. Conservatives and neoconservatives recognize that "facts" gain power from attachment to ideologies. As a result, they appropriate Asian culture and values to promote their arguments.

But is Asian culture inherently conservative—or does it also have a tradition of militancy and liberation? Do sacrifice, toil, and family values comprise a conservative moral vision only—or do these qualities also constitute the core of radical and revolutionary thinking? By asking these questions, activists can push the debate over the model minority concept to a new, ideological level. Moreover, by focusing on ideology, activists can delve into the stereotype's deeper meaning. They can help others understand the stereotype's origins and why it has become the dominant image for Asian Americans today.

Historically, the model minority stereotype first arose in the late 1950s—the creation of sociologists attempting to explain low levels of juvenile delinquency among Chinese and Japanese Americans.[41] The stereotype remained a social-science construct until the 1960s, when a few conservative political commentators began to use it to contrast Asian Americans' "respect for law and order" to African Americans' involvement in civil rights marches, rallies, and sit-ins. By the late 1970s, the stereotype moved into the political mainstream, coinciding with the influx of new Asian immigrants into all parts of the United States. But the widespread acceptance of the stereotype was not simply due to the increase in the Asian American population or the new attention focused on our community from mainstream institutions. More importantly, it coincided with the rise of the New Right and the corporate offensive against the poor. As discussed earlier, this offensive economically devastated poor communities and stripped away hard-won political gains. This offensive also included an ideological campaign designed to restore trust in capitalism and values associated with free enterprise. Meanwhile, conservatives and neoconservatives fought to redefine the language of civil rights by attacking federal government "entitlement" programs while criticizing the African American "liberal establishment."

In this political climate, the model minority stereotype flourished. It symbolized the moral vision of capitalism in the 1980s: a celebration of traditional values, an emphasis on hard work and self-reliance, a respect for authority, and an attack on prevailing civil rights thinking associated with the African American community. Thus, the stereotype took on an ideological importance above and beyond the Asian American community. The hard-working immigrant merchant and the refugee student winning the local spelling bee have become the symbols for the resurrection of capitalist values in the last part of the twentieth century.

Yet, we know a gap exists between symbol and reality. Today, capitalism in America is not about small-business activities; it is about powerful transnational corporations and their intricate links to nation-states and the world capitalist system. Capitalist values no longer revolve around hard work and self-reliance; they deal with wealth and assets and the capacity of the rich to invest, speculate, and obtain government contracts. And the fruits of capitalism in the last part of the twentieth century are not immigrant entrepreneurship and the revival of urban areas; they are more likely to be low-paying jobs, unemployment, bankruptcies, and homelessness.

However, as corporations, banks, and other institutions abandon the inner city, the immigrant merchant—especially the Korean small business—emerges as the main symbol of capitalism in these neighborhoods. For inner-city residents, the Asian immigrant becomes the target for their wrath against corporate devastation of their neighborhoods. Moreover, as this symbol merges with other historical stereotypes of Asians, the result is highly charged imagery, which perhaps underlies the ferocity of anti-Asian violence in this period, such as the destruction of Korean small businesses during the Los Angeles uprisings. The Asian immigrant becomes a symbol of wealth—and also greed; a symbol of hard work—and also materialism; a symbol of intelligence—and also arrogance; a symbol of self-reliance—and also selfishness and lack of community concern. Thus, today the model minority stereotype has become a complex symbol through the confluence of many images imposed on us by social scientists, the New Right, and the urban policies of corporate and political elites.

Pioneer Korean immigrant journalist K. W. Lee—another of our Asian American "elders"—worries about how the melding of symbols, images, and stereotypes is shaping the perception of our community, especially among other people of color. "We are not seen as a compassionate people," states Lee. "Others see us as smart, hard-working, and good at making money—but not as sharing with others. We are not seen as a people who march at the forefront of the struggle for civil rights or the campaign to end poverty."[42] Like Philip Vera Cruz, Lee believes that Asian Americans must retrieve a heritage of compassion and solidarity from our past and use these values to construct a new moral vision for our future. Asian Americans must cast off the images imposed on us by others.

Thus, as we approach the end of the twentieth century, activists are confronted with a task similar to that confronting activists in the late 1960s: the need to redefine the Asian American experience. And, as an earlier generation discovered, redefining means more than ethnic awakening. It means confronting the fundamental questions of power and domination in U.S. society. It means expanding democracy and community consciousness. It means liberating ourselves from the prisons still surrounding our lives.

In our efforts to redefine the Asian American experience, activists will have the guidance and help of elders like K. W. Lee and Philip Vera Cruz. And we can also draw from the rich legacy of struggle of other liberation movements.

Thus, in closing this chapter, I want to quote from two great teachers from the 1960s: Malcolm X and Martin Luther King, Jr. Their words and actions galvanized the consciousness of one generation of youth, and their message of compassion continues to speak to a new generations in the 1990s.

Since their assassinations in the mid-1960s, however, mainstream commentators have stereotyped the two men and often pitted one against the other. They portray Malcolm X as the angry black separatist who advocated violence and hatred against white people. Meanwhile, they make Martin Luther King, Jr., the messenger of love and nonviolence. In the minds of most Americans, both men—in the words of historian Manning Marable—are "frozen in time."[43]

But, as Marable and other African American historians note, both King and Malcolm evolved and became very different men in the years before their assassinations. Both men came to see the African American struggle in the United States in a worldwide context, as part of the revolutionary stirrings and mass uprisings happening across the globe. Both men became internationalists, strongly condemning U.S. exploitation of Third World nations and urging solidarity among all oppressed peoples. Finally, both men called for a redefinition of human values; they believed that people in the United States, especially, needed to move away from materialism and embrace a more compassionate worldview.

If we, too, as Asian Americans, are to evolve in our political and ideological understanding, we need to learn from the wisdom of both men. As we work for our own empowerment, we must ask ourselves a series of questions. Will we fight only for ourselves, or will we embrace the concerns of all oppressed peoples? Will we overcome our own oppression and help to create a new society, or will we become a new exploiter group in the present American hierarchy of inequality? Will we define our goal of empowerment solely in terms of individual advancement for a few, or as the collective liberation for all peoples?

> These are revolutionary times. All over the globe men are revolting against old systems of exploitation and oppression, and, out of the wombs of a frail world, new systems of justice and equality are being born. The shirtless and barefoot people of the land are

rising up as never before. "The people who sat in the darkness have seen a great light." We in the West must support these revolutions. It is a sad fact that, because of comfort, complacency, a morbid fear of communism, and our proneness to adjust to injustice, the Western nations that initiated so much of the revolutionary spirit of the modern world have now become the arch antirevolutionaries. . . . Our only hope today lies in our ability to recapture the revolutionary spirit and go out into a sometimes hostile world declaring eternal hostility to poverty, racism, and militarism.[44]

—Martin Luther King, Jr.

I believe that there will ultimately be a clash between the oppressed and those who do the oppressing. I believe that there will be a clash between those who want freedom, justice, and equality for everyone and those who want to continue the system of exploitation. I believe that there will be that kind of clash, but I don't think it will be based on the color of the skin.[45]

—Malcolm X

NOTES

1. Iranian philosopher Ali Shariati's four-prisons analysis was shared with me by a member of the Iranian Students Union, Confederation of Iranian Students, San Francisco, 1977.

2. Allan Bloom, *The Closing of the American Mind*, New York: Simon and Schuster, 1987.

3. Winifred Breines, "Whose New Left?" *Journal of American History*, vol. 75, no.2, September 1988.

4. Ibid., p. 543.

5. Sheila D. Collins, *The Rainbow Challenge: The Jackson Campaign and the Future of U.S. Politics*, New York: Monthly Review Press, 1986.

6. Ibid., p. 16.

7. Ronald Fraser, 1968: A *Student Generation in Revolt*, New York: Pantheon Books, pp. 354–355.

8. Karen Umemoto, " 'On Strike!' San Francisco State College Strike, 1968–69: The Role of Asian American Students," *Amerasia Journal*, vol. 15, no. 1, 1989.

9. "Statement of the Philippine-American Collegiate Endeavor (PACE) Philosophy and Goals," mimeograph: quoted in Umemoto, p. 15.

10. Mo Nishida, "A Revolutionary Nationalist Perspective of the San Francisco State Strike," *Amerasia Journal*, vol. 15, no. 1, 1989, p. 75.

11. George Lipsitz, "Grassroots Activists and Social Change: The Story of Ivory Perry," *CAAS Newsletter*, UCLA Center for Afro-American Studies, 1986. See also George Lipsitz, *A Life in the Struggle: Ivory Perry and the Culture of Opposition*, Philadelphia: Temple University Press, 1988.

12. Russell C. Leong, "Poetry within Earshot: Notes of an Asian American Generation, 1968–1978," *Amerasia Journal*, vol. 15, no. 1, 1989, pp. 166–167.

13. Al Robles, "Hanging on to the Carabao's Tail," *Amerasia Journal*, vol. 15, no. 1, 1989, p. 205.

14. Warren J. Susman, *Culture as History: The Transformation of American Society in the Twentieth Century*, New York: Pantheon Books, 1973; and Raymond Williams, *Keywords: A Vocabulary of Culture and Society*, revised edition, New York: Oxford University Press, 1976.

15. John M. Liu and Lucie Cheng, "A Dialogue on Race and Class: Asian American Studies

and Marxism," *The Left Academy*, vol.3, eds. Bertell Ollman and Edward Vernoff, Westport, CT: Praeger, 1986.

16. See Mary Kao, compiler, "Public Record, 1989: What Have We Learned from the 60s and 70s?" *Amerasia Journal*, vol. 15, no. 1, 1989, pp. 95–158.

17. Institute for Labor Education and Research, *What's Wrong with the U.S. Economy? A Popular Guide for the Rest of Us*, Boston: South End Press, 1982. See especially chapters 1 and 19.

18. Samuel Huntington, "The United States," *The Crisis of Democracy: Report on the Governability of Democracies to the Trilateral Commission*, ed. Michel Crozier, New York: New York University Press, 1975.

19. Center on Budget and Policy Priorities, *Still Far from the Dream: Recent Developments in Black Income, Employment and Poverty*, Washington, D.C., 1988.

20. Center for the Study of Social Policy, *Kids Count: State Profiles of Child Well-Being*, Washington, D.C., 1992.

21. Manning Marable, *How Capitalism Underdeveloped Black America*, Boston: South End Press, 1983, pp. 252–253.

22. Vincent Harding, *The Other American Revolution*, Los Angeles: UCLA Center for Afro-American Studies, and Atlanta: Institute of the Black World, 1980, p. 224.

23. For analyses of the changing status of Asian Americans, see Lucie Cheng and Edna Bonacich, eds., *Labor Immigration under Capitalism: Asian Workers in the United States before World War II*, Berkeley: University of California Press, 1984; Paul Ong, Edna Bonacich, and Lucie Cheng, *Struggles for a Place: The New Asian Immigrants in the Restructuring Political Economy*, Philadelphia: Temple University Press, 1993; and Sucheng Chan, *Asian Americans: An Interpretive History*, Boston: Twayne, 1991.

24. For an analysis of the growing power of Asian American young professionals, see Yen Espiritu and Paul Ong, "Class Constraints on Racial Solidarity among Asian Americans," *Struggles for a Place*, Philadelphia: Temple University Press, 1993.

25. Arthur Hu, "AIDS and Race," *Asian Week*, December 13, 1991.

26. Marable, *How Capitalism Underdeveloped Black America*, p. 182.

27. William McGurn, "The Silent Minority," *National Review*, June 24, 1991.

28. Ibid., p. 19.

29. C. L. R. James, *Beyond a Boundary*, New York: Pantheon Books, 1983, pp. 116–117.

30. LEAP Asian Pacific American Public Policy Institute and UCLA Asian American Studies Center, *The State of Asian Pacific America: Policy Issues to the Year 2020*, Los Angeles: LEAP and UCLA Asian American Studies Center, 1993.

31. Mao Zedong, "Where Do Correct Ideas Come From?" *Four Essays on Philosophy*, Beijing: Foreign Languages Press, 1966, p. 134.

32. See "Asian Pacific American Workers: Contemporary Issues in the Labor Movement," eds. Glenn Omatsu and Edna Bonacich, *Amerasia Journal*, vol. 18. no.1, 1992.

33. Edna Bonacich, "The Social Costs of Immigrant Entrepreneurship," *Amerasia Journal*, vol. 14, no. 1, 1988.

34. Dean S. Toji and James H. Johnson, Jr., "Asian and Pacific Islander American Poverty: The Working Poor and the Jobless Poor," *Amerasia Journal*, vol. 18, no. 1, 1992, p. 85.

35. Miriam Ching Louie, "Immigrant Asian Women in Bay Area Garment Sweatshops: 'After Sewing, Laundry, Cleaning and Cooking, I Have No Breath Left to Sing,' " *Amerasia Journal*, vol. 18, no. 1, p. 12.

36. Miriam Ching Louie, "Asian and Latina Women Take on the Garment Giants," *CrossRoads*, March 1993.

37. Peter N. Kiang and Man Chak Ng, "Through Strength and Struggle: Boston's Asian American Student/Community/Labor Solidarity," *Amerasia Journal*, vol. 15, no. 1, 1989.

38. Lydia Lowe, "Paving the Way: Chinese Immigrant Workers and Community-based Labor Organizing in Boston," *Amerasia Journal*, vol. 18, no. 1, 1992, p. 41.

39. Namju Cho, "Check Out, Not In: Koreana Wilshire/Hyatt Take-over and the Los Angeles Korean Community," *Amerasia Journal*, vol. 18, no. 1, 1992.

40. Craig Scharlin and Lilia V. Villanueva, *Philip Vera Cruz: A Personal History of Filipino Immigrants and the Farmworkers Movement*, Los Angeles: UCLA Labor Center and UCLA Asian American Studies Center, 1992, p. 104.

41. For an overview of the evolution of the "model minority" stereotype in the social sciences, see Shirley Hune, *Pacific Migration to the United States: Trends and Themes in Historical and Sociological Literature*, New York: Research Institute on Immigration and Ethnic Studies of the Smithsonian Institution, 1977 (reprinted in *Asian American Studies: An Annotated Bibliography and Research Guide*, ed. Hyung-chan Kim, Westport, CT: Greenwood Press, 1989). For comparisons of the "model minority" stereotype in two different decades, see "Success Story of One Minority Group in U.S.," *U.S. News and World Report*, December 26, 1966 (reprinted in *Roots: An Asian American Reader*, ed. Amy Tachiki et al., Los Angeles: UCLA Asian American Studies Center, 1971), and the essay by William McGurn, "The Silent Minority," *National Review*, June 24, 1991.

42. Author's interview with K. W. Lee, Los Angeles, California, October 1991.

43. Manning Marable, "On Malcolm X: His Message & Meaning," Westfield, NJ: Open Magazine Pamphlet Series, 1992.

44. Martin Luther King, Jr., "Beyond Vietnam" speech, Riverside Church, New York, April 1967.

45. Malcolm X, interview on Pierre Breton Show, January 19, 1965, in *Malcolm X Speaks*, ed. George Breitman, New York: Grove Press, 1966, p. 216.

1. Trace the evolution of the San Francisco State College Strike outlined by Umemoto. What motivated the strike? Who was involved? In what ways did the strike transform the consciousness of its participants? What other struggles evolved out of the strike? What were the significant effects of the strike, and what legacy did it leave behind for Asian Americans?

2. Omatsu contends that the 1970s signaled the ultimate disintegration of the social movements founded in the 1960s, specifically those movements centered on the liberation of racial and ethnic minorities. How did this process of disintegration contribute to what Omatsu calls "the winter of civil rights"? What implications were there for Asian American Studies?

3. How did the political landscape change for Asian America in the 1980s? Why were the 1980s an ambiguous period for Asian American empowerment? How does this period compare with the 1960s and with the 1990s? Are the concepts developed during the Asian American movement—self-determination, liberation, militant struggle—meaningful and relevant to Asian Americans today? Are the ideas of the movement alive today, or have they atrophied into relics—the curiosities of a bygone era of youthful and excessive idealism?

SUGGESTED READINGS

Aguilar-San Juan, Karin (ed.). 1994. *The State of Asian America: Activism and Resistance in the 1990s.* Boston: South End Press.

Gee, Emma, et al. (eds). 1976. *Counterpoint: Perspectives on Asian America.* Los Angeles: Asian American Studies Center, University of California.

Ichioka, Yuji. 1974. *A Buried Past: An Annotated Bibliography of the Japanese American Research Project Collection.* Berkeley: University of California Press.

Hune, Shirley. 1989. Opening the American Mind and Body: The Role of Asian American Studies. *Change.* November/December.

Kiang, P. N. 1994. When Know-Nothings Speak English Only: Analyzing Irish and Cambodian Struggles for Community Development and Educational Equity. Pp. 125–145 in Karin Aguilar-San Juan (ed.)., *The State of Asian America: Activism and Resistance in the 1990s.* Boston: South End Press.

Kibria, Nazli. 1998. The Racial Gap: South Asian American Racial Identity and the Asian American Movement. Pp. 69–78 in Lavina Dhingra Shankar and Rajini Srikanth (eds.), *A Part Yet Apart: South Asians in Asian America.* Philadelphia: Temple University Press.

Ling, Susie. 1989. The Mountain Movers: Asian American Women's Movement in Los Angeles. *Amerasia Journal* 15(1): 51–67.

Nakanishi, Don. 1995/96. Linkages and Boundaries: Twenty-Five Years of Asian American Studies. *Amerasia Journal* 21(3): xvii–xxv.

Quinsaat, Jesse, et al. (eds.). 1976. *Letters in Exile: An Introductory Reader on the History of Pilipinos in America.* Los Angeles: Asian American Studies Center, University of California.

Tachiki, Amy, Eddie Wong, and Franklin Odo, with Buck Wong (eds.). 1971. *Roots: An Asian American Reader.* Los Angeles: UCLA Asian American Studies Center.

Takezawa, Yasuko. 1995. *Breaking the Silence: The Redress Movement in Seattle.* Ithaca, NY: Cornell University Press.

Woo, Merle. 1989. What Have We Accomplished: From the Third-World Strike Through the Conservative Eighties. *Amerasia Journal* 15(1): 81–89.

FILMS

Choy, Curtis (producer/director). 1993. *The Fall of the I-Hotel* (58-minute documentary).
Dong, Arthur, (producer/director). 1991. *The Visual Communications Story.*
Tajiri, Rea, and Pat Saunders (directors/producers). 1993. *Yuri Kochiyama: Passion for Justice.* (57-minute documentary).

Part II

Making History
The Asian American Experience

Chapter Three

From a Different Shore
Their History Bursts with Telling

Ronald Takaki

In Palolo Valley on the island of Oahu, Hawaii, where I lived as a child, my neighbors had names like Hamamoto, Kauhane, Wong, and Camara. Nearby, across the stream where we caught crayfish and roasted them over an open fire, there were Filipino and Puerto Rican families. Behind my house, Mrs. Alice Liu and her friends played mah-jongg late into the night, the clicking of the tiles lulling me to sleep. Next door to us the Miuras flew billowing and colorful carp kites on Japanese boys' day. I heard voices with different accents, different languages, and saw children of different colors. Together we went barefoot to school and played games like baseball and *jan ken po*. We spoke pidgin English. "Hey, da kind tako ono, you know," we would say, combining English, Japanese, and Hawaiian: "This octopus is delicious." As I grew up, I did not know why families representing such an array of nationalities from different shores were living together and sharing their cultures and a common language. My teachers and textbooks did not explain the diversity of our community or the sources of our unity. After graduation from high school, I attended a college in a midwestern town where I found myself invited to "dinners for foreign students" sponsored by local churches and clubs like the Rotary. I politely tried to explain to my kind hosts that I was not a "foreign student." My fellow students and even my professors would ask me how long I had been in America and where I had learned to speak English. "In this country," I would reply. And sometimes I would add: "I was born in America, and my family has been here for three generations."

Indeed, Asian Americans have been here for over 150 years. Resting on benches in Portsmouth Square in San Francisco's Chinatown, old men know their presence in America reaches far into the past. Wearing fedora hats, they wait for the chilly morning fog to lift; asked how long they have been in this country, they say: "Me longtime Californ'." Nearby, elderly Filipinos—*manongs*—point to the vacant lot where the aging International Hotel had once offered these retired farm workers a place to live out the rest of their lives. They remember the night the police came to evict them and the morning the bulldozers obliterated a part of their history. In the California desert town of El Centro, bearded and gray-haired men wearing turbans sit among the fallen leaves on the grounds of the Sikh temple. One of them describes

117

what life was like in California decades ago: "In the early days it was hard. We had a hell of a time. We had to face a lot of narrow-mindedness."[1]

Asian Americans are diverse, their roots reaching back to China, Japan, Korea, the Philippines, India, Vietnam, Laos, and Cambodia. Many of them live in Chinatowns, the colorful streets filled with sidewalk vegetable stands and crowds of people carrying shopping bags; their communities are also called Little Tokyo, Koreatown, and Little Saigon. Asian Americans work in hot kitchens and bus tables in restaurants with elegant names like Jade Pagoda and Bombay Spice. In garment factories, Chinese and Korean women hunch over whirling sewing machines, their babies sleeping nearby on blankets. In the Silicon Valley of California, rows and rows of Vietnamese and Laotian women serve as the eyes and hands of production assembly lines for computer chips. Tough Chinese gang members strut on Grant Avenue in San Francisco and Canal Street in New York's Chinatown. In La Crosse, Wisconsin, welfare-dependent Hmong sit and stare at the snowdrifts outside their windows. Holders of Ph.D.s, Asian American engineers do complex research in the laboratories of the high-technology industries along Route 128 in Massachusetts. Asian Americans seem to be ubiquitous on university campuses: they represent 11 percent of the students at Harvard, 10 percent at Princeton, 16 percent at Stanford, 21 percent at MIT, and 25 percent at the University of California at Berkeley. From Scarsdale to the Pacific Palisades, "Yappies"—"young Asian professionals"—drive BMWs, wear designer clothes, and congregate at continental restaurants; they read slick magazines like *AsiAm* and *Rice*. "I am Chinese," remarks Chester in David Hwang's play *Family Devotions*. "I live in Bel Air. I drive a Mercedes. I go to a private prep school. I must be Chinese."[2]

Recently Asian Americans have become very visible. While Asians have constituted a majority of Hawaii's people for nearly a century, they have become populous elsewhere in the country. Three hundred thousand Chinese live in New York City—the largest Chinese community outside of China. Describing the recent grows of New York's Chinatown, the *New York Times* observed in 1986: "With new arrivals squeezing in at a rate of nearly 2,000 a month, the district spread north through what was once a Jewish section on the Lower East Side and west across Little Italy, turning Yiddish into Mandarin and fettucine into won tons." Meanwhile, Flushing in Queens has become a "suburban" Chinatown, the home of 60,000 Chinese; resident Eileen Loh observed: "We are changing the face of Flushing." On the other side of the continent, Monterey Park in southern California has come to be called the "Chinese Beverly Hills." About a fourth of San Francisco's population is Asian, and Asians represent over 50 percent of the city's public school students. In Los Angeles, there are 150,000 Koreans, and the Olympic Boulevard area between Crenshaw and Hoover has been designated Koreatown. Nearby, in an adjacent county, a new Vietnamese community has also suddenly appeared. "Along Garden Grove Boulevard in Orange County," the *New York Times* reported in 1986, "it is easier to lunch on pho, a Vietnamese noodle soup with beef, than on a hamburger." In California, Asian Americans represent nearly 9 percent of the state's population, surpassing blacks in number.[3]

Today Asian Americans belong to the fastest-growing ethnic minority group in the United States. In percentage, they are increasing more rapidly than Hispanics (between 1970 and 1980 the Hispanic population increased by 38 percent, compared to 143 percent for the Asian population). The target of immigration exclusion laws in the nineteenth and early twentieth centuries, Asians have recently been coming again to America. The Immigration Act of 1965 reopened the gates to immigrants from Asia, allowing a quota of 20,000 immigrants for each country and also the entry of family members on a nonquota basis. Currently half of all immigrants entering annually are Asian. The recent growth of the Asian American population has been dramatic: in 1960, there were only 877,934 Asians in the United States, representing a mere one half of one percent of the country's population. Twenty-five years later, they numbered over 5 million, or 2.1 percent of the population, an increase of 577 percent (compared to 34 percent for the general population). They included 1,079,000 Chinese, 1,052,000 Filipinos, 766,000 Japanese, 634,000 Vietnamese, 542,000 Koreans, 526,000 Asian Indians, 70,000 Laotians, 10,000 Mien, 60,000 Hmong, 161,000 Cambodians, and 169,000 other Asians. By the year 2000, Asian Americans are projected to represent 4 percent of the total U.S. population.[4]

Yet very little is known about Asian Americans and their history. In fact, stereotypes and myths of Asians as aliens and foreigners are pervasive in American society. During Lieutenant Colonel Oliver North's testimony before the joint House-Senate committee investigating the Iran-Contra scandal in 1987, cochair Senator Daniel Inouye became the target of racial slurs: some of the telegrams and phone calls received by the committee told the senator he should "go home to Japan where he belonged." But Senator Inouye was born in the United States and had been awarded a Distinguished Service Cross for his valor as an American soldier during World War II. The belief that Americans do not include people with Asian ancestries is usually expressed more innocently, more casually. A white woman from New Jersey, for example, once raved to William Wong of the *Oakland Tribune* about a wonderful new Vietnamese restaurant in her town: "We were there the other night and we were the only Americans there." Wong noted with regret: "She probably meant the only white people."[5]

But her remark reveals a widely shared assumption in American culture—one that reflects and is reinforced by a narrow view of American history. Many existing history books give Asian Americans only passing notice or overlook them altogether. "When one hears Americans tell of the immigrants who built this nation," Congressman Norman Mineta of California recently observed, "one is often led to believe that all our forebearers came from Europe. When one hears stories about the pioneers going West to shape the land, the Asian immigrant is rarely mentioned."[6]

Sometimes Asian pioneers are even excluded from history. In 1987, the editor of *The Californians*, a popular history magazine published in San Francisco, announced the "Pioneer Prize" for the best essay submitted on the "California pioneers." "By 'pioneers,'" the editor explained, "we mean those Americans and Europeans who settled permanently in California between 1823 and 1869 (the year the transcontinental Central Pacific was completed)." But actually, the "pioneers" also included Asians: thousands of them helped to build the very transcontinental railroad referred to in the magazine's announcement, and many settled permanently in California. Many classics in the field of American history have also equated "American" with "white" or "European" in origin. In his prize-winning study, *The Uprooted*, Harvard historian Oscar Handlin presented—to use the book's subtitle—"the Epic Story of the Great Migrations That Made the American People." But Handlin's "epic story" completely left out the "uprooted" from lands across the Pacific Ocean and the "great migrations" from Asia that also helped to make "the American people." Eurocentric history serves no one. It only shrouds the pluralism that is America and that makes our nation so unique, and thus the possibility of appreciating our rich racial and cultural diversity remains a dream deferred. Actually, as Americans, we come originally from many different shores—Europe, the Americas, Africa, and also Asia.[7]

We need to "re-vision" history to include Asians in the history of America, and to do so in a broad and comparative way. How and why, we must ask, were the experiences of the various Asian groups—Chinese, Japanese, Korean, Filipino, Asian Indian, and Southeast Asian—similar to and different from one another? Cross-national comparisons can help us to identify the experiences particular to a group and to highlight the experiences common to all of them. Why did Asian immigrants leave everything they knew and loved to come to a strange world so far away? They were "pushed" by hardships in the homelands and "pulled" here by America's demand for their labor. But what were their own fierce dreams—from the first enterprising Chinese miners of the 1850s in search of "Gold Mountain" to the recent refugees fleeing frantically on helicopters and leaking boats from the ravages of war in Vietnam? Besides their points of origin, we need to examine the experiences of Asian Americans in different geographical regions, especially in Hawaii as compared to the mainland. Time of arrival has also shaped the lives and communities of Asian Americans. About 1 million people entered between the California gold rush of 1849 and the Immigration Act of 1924, which cut off immigration from Asian countries, and, after a hiatus of some forty years, a second group numbering about three and a half million came between 1965 and 1985. How do we compare the two waves of Asian immigration?

To answer our questions, we must not study Asian Americans primarily in terms of statistics and what was done to them. They are entitled to be viewed as subjects—as men and women with minds, wills, and voices. By "voices" we mean their own words and stories as told in their oral histories, conversations, speeches, soliloquies, and songs, as well as in their own writings—diaries, letters, newspapers, magazines, pamphlets, placards, posters, flyers, court petitions, autobiographies, short stories, novels, and poems. Their voices contain particular expressions and phrases with their own meanings and nuances, the cuttings from the cloth of languages.

For a long time, Asians in this country were not allowed to tell their stories, sometimes even to talk. In Maxine Hong Kingston's novel *China Men*, Bak Goong goes to Hawaii, where he is told by a foreman that laborers are not permitted to talk while working. "If I knew I had to take a vow of silence," he says to himself, "I would have shaved off my hair and become a monk." In the cane fields, he hears the boss shout: "Shut up. Go work. Chinaman, go work. You stay go work. Shut up." He is not even supposed to scream when he feels the sting of the whip on his shoulder. After work, resting in the camp away from the ears of the foreman, Bak Goong tells his fellow workers: "I will talk again. Listen for me." Among themselves they curse the white man on horseback: "Take—that—white—demon. Take—that. Fall—to—the—ground—demon. Cut—you—into—pieces. Chop—off—your—legs. Die—snake." Then, one day, the workers dig a wide hole, and they flop on the ground "with their faces over the edge of the hole and their legs like wheel spokes." Suddenly their words come tumbling out: "Hello down there in China!" "Hello, Mother!" "I've been working hard for you, and I hate it." "I've become an opium addict." "I don't even look Chinese anymore." "I'm coming home by and by." "I'm not coming home." The men had, Kingston writes, "dug an ear into the world, and were telling their secrets."[8]

Today we need to fill the shouting holes, to listen to the Bak Goongs of the past and learn their secrets. Their stories can enable us to understand Asians as actors in the making of history and can give us a view from below—the subjective world of the immigrant experience. Detained at the Angel Island Immigration Station in San Francisco Bay, Chinese immigrants carved over a hundred poems on the walls of the barracks. One of them wrote:

> I used to admire the land of the Flowery
>   Flag as a country of abundance.
> I immediately raised money and started
>   my journey.
> For over a month, I have experienced enough
>   wind and waves. . . .
> I look up and see Oakland so close by. . . .
> Discontent fills my belly and it is difficult
>   for me to sleep.
> I just write these few lines to express what is
>   on my mind.[9]

We need to know what was on the "minds" of the people. As scholars of a new social history have noted recently, so much of history has been the story of kings and elites, rendering invisible and silent the "little people." An Asian American told an interviewer: "I am a second-generation Korean American without any achievements in life, and I have no education. What is it you want to hear from me? My life is not worth telling to anyone." Similarly, a Chinese immigrant said: "You know, it seems to me there's no use in me telling you all this! I was just a simple worker, a farmworker around here. My story is not going to interest anybody." But others realize they are worthy of scholarly attention. "What is it you want to know?" an old Filipino immigrant asked a researcher. "Talk about history. What's that . . . ah, the story of my life . . . and how people lived with each other in my time."

> Ay, manong
> your old brown hands
> hold life, many lives
> within each crack
> a story.[10]

When the people recount what happened, they become animated and their stories—to use Joy Kogawa's wonderful phrase—"burst with telling." They understand why their stories need to be shared. "I hope this survey do a lot of good for Chinese people," a Chinese man told an interviewer from Stanford University in the 1920s. "Make American people realize that Chinese people are humans. I think very few American people really know anything about Chinese." Remembering the discrimination he experienced, an old manong explained: "You cannot avoid racism, it is hanging over every Filipino-American. There are still too many ignorant people." In the telling and retelling of their stories, the elderly immigrants reclaim the authorship of their own history. They want the younger generations to know about their experiences. "Our stories should be listened to by many young people," said a ninety-one-year-old retired Japanese plantation laborer. "It's for their sake. We really had a hard time, you know." And when the listeners learn about their roots, they feel enriched—members of a "community of memory":

> Your intimate life,
> The story of your fight,
> Though not recorded
> In any history book,
> Yet lives engraved on my heart.[11]

Their stories belong to our country's history and need to be recorded in our history books, for they reflect the making of America as a nation of immigrants, as a place where men and women came to find a new beginning. Initially, many Asian immigrants, probably most of them, saw themselves as sojourners. But so did European immigrants. The view of Asian immigrants as "sojourners" and European immigrants as "settlers" is both a mistaken notion and a widely held myth. Large numbers of newcomers from both Asia and Europe, in the beginning at least, planned to stay here only temporarily; many sojourning laborers had left their wives and children behind in their homelands, intending to work in America for a few years and then return to their families. Chinese women staying behind in Guangdong sang lyrics of loss:

> Dear husband, ever since you sojourned
>   in a foreign land.
> I've lost interest in all matters.
> All day long, I stay inside the bedroom, my
>   brows knitted;
> Ten thousand thoughts bring me endless remorse.
> In grief, in silence.
> I cannot fall asleep on my lonely pillow.

Migratory Polish men also sang about the experience of separation from their families:

> When I journeyed from Amer'ca,
> And the foundry where I labored. . . .
> Soon I came to New York City,

To the agent for my passage. . . .
Then I left Berlin for Krakow;
There my wife was waiting for me.
And my children did not know me,
For they fled from me, a stranger.

"My dear children, I'm your papa;
Three long years I have not seen you."[12]

Actually, migrants from Europe returned to their homelands in sizable numbers. Between 1895 and 1918, according to historian Rowland Berthoff, 55 percent as many Englishmen returned home as left for the United States; the proportion was 46 percent for the Scots and 42 percent for the Irish. The rate of return migration was very high for many groups of European sojourners—40 percent for Polish and 50 percent for Italians. In "Home-Going Italians," published in *Survey* in 1912, Victor Von Borosini reported: "Most Italians remain in the United States from two to five years." Greek migration reflected a similar return pattern. Of the 366,454 Greeks who arrived in America between 1908 and 1923, 46 percent returned to Greece. "A very small percentage of the Greek emigrants go to foreign countries with the intention of remaining there," reported the U.S. consul in Athens in 1903. "They all go abroad with the intention to return to their native land sooner or later." But many Greeks eventually stayed. "It came gradually," said a Greek who became a settler. "I got married, began to raise a family and was immobilized." For this Greek immigrant and thousands of compatriots like him, explained historian Theodore Saloutos, the decision to remain in the United States permanently came as "an afterthought." Similarly, 55 percent of the 200,000 Japanese who went to Hawaii between 1886 and 1924 returned to Japan. Most of them had left Japan as *dekaseginin*, intending to work only for a few years in Hawaii. But significantly, almost half of the Japanese stayed, becoming *imin*, or people moving permanently to another country.[13]

But, coming here from Asia, many of America's immigrants found they were not allowed to feel at home in the United States, and even their grandchildren and great-grandchildren still find they are not viewed and accepted as Americans. "We feel that we're a guest in someone else's house," said third-generation Ron Wakabayashi, National Director of the Japanese American Citizens League, "that we can never really relax and put our feet on the table."[14]

Behind Wakabayashi's complaint is the question, Why have Asian Americans been viewed and treated as outsiders? In his essay "The Stranger," sociologist Georg Simmel develops a theory, based on the experiences of Jews, to explain the discrimination and estrangement experienced by a group entering another society. Not belonging in the new place initially, the intruders bring qualities that are not indigenous. Not bound by roots to the new place, they are in a state of detachment, viewed as clannish, rigidly attached to their old country and their old culture. Their "strangeness" stands out more sharply as they settle down in the new land and become traders and merchants, for they still lack organic and established ties of kinship and locality. What is stressed in the host society is not the individuality of the newcomers but their alien origin, the qualities they share with one another as "strangers."[15]

While Simmel's theory is heuristic and insightful for the study of Asian Americans, it needs to be grounded in history—the particularities of time and place. What transformed Asians into "strangers" in America was not simply their migration to a foreign land and their lack of indigenous and organic ties to American society but also their point of origin and their specific reception. Their experiences here, as they turned out in historical reality, were profoundly different from the experiences of European immigrants. To be sure, the immigrants who crossed the Atlantic Ocean suffered hardships and anguish. As historian John Higham has described so powerfully in *Strangers in the Land*, the Italians, Jews, Irish, and other European immigrant groups were victims of labor exploitation, social ostracism, and the sharp barbs of intolerant American nativism. Nevertheless, immigrants of European ancestry had certain advantages in America. The promise of this new world for them, as F. Scott Fitzgerald portrayed it, was mythic: here an individual could remake himself—Gatz could become Gatsby. They could give themselves new identities by changing their names as did Doris Kapplehoff to Doris Day, Bernie Schwartz to Tony Curtis, Issur Danielovitch to Kirk Douglas, and Edmund Marcizewski to Ed Muskie. "America represented a new life, new hope, new perspective," observed J. N. Hook in his book *Family Names*. "Why not enter it with a new name, an 'American' name that would have no association with the life forever left behind." A new "American" name also opened the way for economic opportunities. "Some immigrants believed, rightly in some instances, that their chances for material success would be improved if their name did not betray their origins." Others became "Americans" mainly by shedding their past, their ethnicity—the language, customs, dress, and culture of the old country. Physically indistinguishable from old-stock whites in America, they were able to blend into the society of their adopted country.[16]

Asian immigrants could not transform themselves as felicitously, for they had come "from a different shore." In the present study, the term "shore" has multiple meanings. These men and women came from Asia across the Pacific rather than from Europe across the Atlantic. They brought Asian cultures rather than the traditions and ideas originating in the Greco-Roman world. Moreover, they had qualities they could not change or hide—the shape of their eyes, the color of their hair, the complexion of their skin. They were subjected not only to cultural prejudice, or ethnocentrism, but also racism. They wore what University of Chicago sociologist Robert E. Park termed a "racial uniform." Unlike the Irish and other groups from Europe, Asian immigrants could not become "mere individuals, indistinguishable in the cosmopolitan mass of the population." Regardless of their personal merits, they sadly discovered, they could not gain acceptance in the larger society. They were judged not by the content of their character but by their complexion. "The trouble is not with the Japanese mind but with the Japanese skin," wrote Park as he observed American-white attitudes in 1913. "The Jap is not the right color."[17]

"Color" in America operated within an economic context. Asian immigrants came here to meet demands for labor—plantation workers, railroad crews, miners, factory operatives, cannery workers, and farm laborers. Employers developed a dual-wage system to pay Asian laborers less than white workers and pitted the groups against each other in order to depress wages for both. "Ethnic antagonism"—to use Edna

Bonacich's phrase—led white laborers to demand the restriction of Asian workers already here in a segregated labor market of low-wage jobs and the exclusion of future Asian immigrants. Thus, the class interests of white capital as well as white labor needed Asians as "strangers."[18]

Pushed out of competition for employment by racial discrimination and white working-class hostility, many Asian immigrants became shopkeepers, merchants, and small businessmen. "There wasn't any other opportunity open to the Chinese," explained the son of a Chinese storekeeper. "Probably opening a store was one of the few things that they could do other than opening a laundry." Self-employment was not an Asian "cultural trait" or an occupation peculiar to "strangers" but a means of survival, a response to racial discrimination and exclusion in the labor market. The early Chinese and Japanese immigrants had been peasants in their home countries. Excluded from employment in the general economy, they *became* shopkeepers and ethnic enterprisers. They also developed their own separate commercial enclaves, which served as an economic basis for ethnic solidarity, and their business and cultural separateness in turn reinforced both their image and condition as "strangers."[19]

Unlike European immigrants, Asians were also victimized by the institutionalized racial discrimination of public policies. The Chinese Exclusion Act of 1882 singled out the Chinese on a racial basis, and the National Origins Act of 1924 totally prohibited Japanese immigration while permitting the annual entry of 17,853 from Ireland, 5,802 from Italy, and 6,524 from Poland. Furthermore, the 1924 law supported the formation of families in European immigrant communities, allowing European immigrant men to return to their homelands and bring wives back to the United States. Their wives were accorded nonquota status, that is, there were no limits to the number of European women who could come here as wives. The law had the very opposite effect on Asian immigrant communities. Seeking to prevent the development of Asian families here, it barred the entry of women from China, Japan, Korea, and India. Even U.S. citizens could not bring Asian wives into the country, for the latter were classified as "aliens ineligible to citizenship" and hence inadmissible. While the 1924 law did not apply to Filipino immigration (because the Philippines was a territory of the United States), the Tydings-McDuffie Act of 1934 provided for the independence of the Philippines and limited Filipino immigration to fifty persons a year.[20]

The laws not only determined who could come to the United States but also who could become citizens. Decades before Asian immigration had even begun, this country had already defined by law the complexion of its citizens. The Naturalization Law of 1790 had specified that naturalized citizenship was to be reserved for "whites." This law remained in effect until 1952. Though immigrants from countries like Ireland and Italy experienced discrimination and nativist reactions, they nonetheless could become citizens of the United States. Citizenship is a prerequisite for suffrage—political power essential for groups to defend and advance their rights and interests. Unlike their European counterparts, Asian immigrants were not permitted to exercise power through the ballot and their own Tammany Halls. As "aliens ineligible to citizenship," they were also prohibited by the laws of many states from land ownership—the condition Frederick Jackson Turner celebrated as the foundation of democracy in America. One of the laws went even further. The 1922 Cable Act provided that any American woman who married "an alien ineligible to citizenship shall cease to be a citizen of the United States."[21]

During a revealing moment in the history of American citizenship, the line between white and nonwhite blurred briefly. Fleeing from genocide in their homelands, 50,000 Armenians had come to America in the early twentieth century. In 1909 federal authorities classified Armenians as "Asiatics" and denied naturalized citizenship to Armenian immigrants. But shortly afterward, in the *Halladjian* decision, a U.S. circuit court of appeals ruled that Armenians were Caucasian because of their ethnography, history, and appearance. Four years later California passed its alien land law, but the restriction did not apply to Armenians. By 1930, some 18,000 Armenians lived in the state; their access to landownership enabled many Armenians to become farmers in Fresno County. They became wealthy farmers—owners of vast acreage and leading producers of raisins. "The Armenians, they like the Japanese," recalled a Japanese farmer of Fresno. "Lots speak only Armenian—just like Issei [immigrant Japanese]. They came about the same time too. But I think they learned a little bit more English than the Japanese did and they looked more American and I think it helped them a lot." The experience of the Armenians illustrated the immense difference it made to be Caucasian and not "Asiatic."[22]

But the most terrible and tragic instance of this difference occurred during World War II. Setting aside the Constitution of the United States, President Franklin D. Roosevelt issued Executive Order 9066, which targeted Japanese Americans for special persecution and deprived them of their rights of due process and equal protection of the law. Unlike German Americans and Italian Americans, Japanese Americans were incarcerated in internment camps by the federal government. Even possession of U.S. citizenship did not protect rights and liberties guaranteed by the Constitution: two-thirds of the 120,000 internees were American citizens by birth.[23]

Behind state policy lay a powerful traditional vision of America as a "homogeneous" nation. In a sermon given aboard the *Arbella*, John Winthrop told his fellow Puritans as they sailed to America in 1630 that they would be establishing a "city upon a hill," with the "eyes of the world" upon them. Their colony was to be a "new" England. This conception of the character and purpose of the English "errand" to the New World embraced a racial identity. "In the settlement of this country," historian Winthrop Jordan noted, "the red and black peoples served white men as aids to navigation by which they would find their safe positions as they ventured into America." The question of the relationship between race and nationality became immensely important as the colonies struggled for independence and transformed themselves into a new nation. In 1751 Benjamin Franklin offered his thoughts on the future complexion of American society in his essay *Observations Concerning the Increase of Mankind*. All Africa was black or "tawney," he noted, and Asia was chiefly "tawney." The English were the "principle Body of white People," and Franklin wished there were more of them in America. Why should we, he asked, "darken" the people of America: "Why increase the Sons of Africa, by Planting them in America, where we have so fair an opportunity, by excluding all Blacks and Tawneys, of increasing the lovely White?" After independence, one of the *Federalist Papers* announced: "Providence [had] been pleased to give this one connected country to one united people—a people descended from the same ancestors, speaking the same language, professing the same religion, attached to the same principles of government, very similar in their manners and customs." In a letter to James Monroe, President Thomas Jefferson wrote that he looked forward to distant times when the American continent would be covered with such a people. Earlier, in his *Notes on the State of Virginia*, Jefferson had identified the particular people who should occupy the new continent, saying he recoiled with horror from the possibility of "either blot or mixture on that surface" and advocating the removal of blacks from the United States. America, for Jefferson, was to be a "sanctuary" where immigrants from Europe would establish a new society for themselves and their progeny. Jefferson's hope for America was articulated over a hundred years later by the United States Supreme Court in the 1923 decision of *U.S. v. Bhagat Singh Thind*. Denying naturalized citizenship to Asian Indians because they were not "white," the Court noted the assimilability of European immigrants: "The children of English, French, German, Italian, Scandinavian, and other European parentage quickly merge into the mass of our population and lose the distinctive hallmarks of their European origin."[24]

But America also had a countertradition and vision, springing from the reality of racial and cultural diversity. It had been, as Walt Whitman celebrated so lyrically, "a teeming Nation of nations" composed of a "vast, surging, hopeful army of workers," a new society where all should be welcomed, "Chinese, Irish, German—all, all, without exceptions."

> Passage O soul to India! . . .
> Tying the Eastern to the Western sea,
> The road between Europe and Asia . . .
> Lands found and nations born, thou born America,
> For purpose vast, man's long probation fill'd,
> Thou rondure of the world at last accomplish'd . . .
> Europe to Asia, Africa join'd, and they to the New
>   World.

The new society's diversity was portrayed by Herman Melville in his novel about the chase for the great white whale. The crew of the *Pequod* is composed of whites, blacks, Indians, Pacific Islanders, and Asians. As they work together, they are integrated in the labor process and united in a relationship of dependency, mutual survival, and cooperation. Nowhere is this connectedness more graphically illustrated than in the "monkey-rope," which is fastened to both Ishmael and Queequeg. Lowered down to the water to secure the blubber hook onto the dead whale, with vicious sharks swirling around it, Queequeg is held by a rope tied to Ishmael. The process is perilous for both men. "We two, for the time," Ishmael tells us, "were wedded; and should poor Queequeg sink to rise no more, then both usage and honor

demanded, that instead of cutting the cord, it should drag me down in his wake."
There is a noble class unity among the crew, and the working class aboard the *Pequod*
is saluted. An "ethereal light" shines on the "workman's arm," and the laborers are
ascribed "high qualities" and "democratic dignity." In the early twentieth century, a
Japanese immigrant described in poetry a lesson that had been learned by farm
laborers of different nationalities—Japanese, Filipino, Mexican, and Asian Indian:

> People harvesting
> Work together unaware
> Of racial problems.

A Filipino immigrant laborer in California expressed a similar hope and understanding. America was, Macario Bulosan told his brother Carlos, "not a land of one race
or one class of men" but "a new world" of respect and unconditional opportunities
for all who toiled and suffered from oppression, from "the first Indian that offered
peace in Manhattan to the last Filipino pea pickers."[25]

Asians migrated east to America. For them, the first glimpse of what F. Scott
Fitzgerald poetically described as this "fresh, green breast of the new world" was not
the Statue of Liberty but the ancient volcanoes of Hawaii reaching from the ocean
toward the sky, Mount Rainier rising majestically behind the port city of Seattle, and
the brown hills of California sloping gently toward the sea touching Asia. For these
arriving men and women, the immigration station was not on Ellis Island but Oahu,
Hawaii, and Angel Island in San Francisco Bay. But, like Fitzgerald's Dutch sailors
seeing the new land for the first time in the seventeenth century, Asian immigrants,
too, must have held their breath in the presence of this continent.[26]

America represented liminality, and the Asian immigrants' actions enabled them
to make history even in conditions they did not choose. In their trans-Pacific odyssey,
they "crossed boundaries not delineated in space." Their migration broke the "cake
of custom" and placed them within a new dynamic and transitional context, an
ambiguous situation "betwixt and between all fixed points of classification." They
reached a kind of geographical and cultural margin where old norms became de-
tached, and they found themselves free for new associations and new enterprises. In
America, Asian immigrants encountered long hours of labor and racial discrimination, but they did not permit exterior demands to determine wholly the direction
and quality of their lives. Energies, pent up in the old countries, were unleashed, and
they found themselves pursuing urges and doing things they had thought beyond
their capabilities. They had not read John Locke, but they, too, believed that "in the
beginning, all the world was America." Like the immigrants from Europe, many
Asians saw America as a place for a fresh start. They came here, as Filipino immigrant
Carlos Bulosan expressed it, searching for "a door into America" and seeking "to
build a new life with untried materials." "Would it be possible," he asked, "for an
immigrant like me to become a part of the American dream?" The hopeful question
also contained deep doubt, for Bulosan and his fellow Asian immigrants knew they
were "strangers from a different shore."[27]

NOTES

1. Leonard Greenwood, "El Centro's Community of Sikhs Dying Out," *Los Angeles Times*, December 28, 1966.

2. West Coast premiere of David Hwang's *Family Devotions*, San Francisco State University, February 1987.

3. Albert Scardino, "Commercial Rents in Chinatown Soar as Hong Kong Exodus Grows," *New York Times*, December 25, 1986; Douglas Martin, "Living in Two Worlds: Chinese of New York City," *New York Times*, February 19, 1988; Mark Arax, "Asian Influx Alters Life in Suburbia," *Los Angeles Times*, April 5, 1987; Robert Reinhold, "Flow of 3d World Immigrants Alters Weave of U.S. Society," *New York Times*, June 30, 1986.

4. Data from Cary Davis, Carl Haub, and JoAnne Willette, *U.S. Hispanics: Changing the Face of America*, a publication of the Population Reference Bureau, vol. 38, no. 3 (June 1983), p. 8; Robert W. Gardner, Bryant Robey, and Peter C. Smith, *Asian Americans: Growth, Change, and Diversity*, a publication of the Population Reference Bureau, vol. 40, no. 4 (October 1985), pp. 2, 3, 5, 7, 8.

5. William Wong, "Racial Taunts of Inouye Are a Chilling Reminder," *East/West*, July 23, 1987.

6. Congressman Norman Mineta, from the Foreword, in Timothy J. Lukes and Gary Y. Okihiro, *Japanese Legacy: Farming and Community Life in California's Santa Clara Valley* (Cupertino, Calif., 1985).

7. *The Californians*, May/June 1987, p. 5; Oscar Handlin, *The Uprooted: The Epic Story of the Great Migrations That Made the American People* (New York, 1951).

8. Maxine Hong Kingston, *China Men* (New York, 1980), pp. 100, 101, 102, 114, 117.

9. Mr. Yip, in Him Mark Lai, Genny Lim, Judy Yung (eds.), *Island: Poetry and History of Chinese Immigrants on Angel Island*, 1910–1940 (San Francisco, 1980), p. 136; poem, ibid., p. 40. "Flowery Flag" is a reference to the United States. For the need to study the excluded as well as the excluders, see Roger Daniels, "Westerners from the East: Oriental Immigrants Reappraised," *Pacific Historical Review*, vol. 35 (1966), pp. 373–383, and "American Historians and East Asian Immigrants," *Pacific Historical Review*, vol. 43 (1974), pp. 449–472.

10. Interview with Jean Park (pseudonym), Prologue of "The Autobiography of a Second Generation Korean American," in Christopher Kim, "Three Generations of Koreans in America," Asian American Studies 199 paper, University of California, Berkeley, 1976, pp. 42–44; interview with Suen Hoon Sum, in Jeff Gillenkirk and James Matlow, *Bitter Melon: Stories from the Last Rural Chinese Town in America* (Seattle, 1987), p. 56; interview with Filipino immigrant in Virgilio Menor Felipe, "Hawaii: A Pilipino Dream," M.A. thesis, University of Hawaii, 1972, Prologue, p. iii; Virginia Cerenio, "you lovely people," in Joseph Bruche, *Breaking Silence: An Anthology of Contemporary Asian American Poets* (Greenfield Center, N.Y., 1983), p. 11.

11. My thanks to Joy Kogawa for this phrase, in Joy Kogawa, *Obasan* (Boston, 1982), opening page; "Social Document of Pany Lowe, Interviewed by C. H. Burnett, Seattle, July 5, 1924," p. 6, Survey of Race Relations, Stanford University, Hoover Institution Archives; Dennis Akizuki, "Low-Cost Housing for Elderly Pilipinos Delayed," *Daily Californian*, November 1, 1974; interview with Toden Higa, in Ethnic Studies Oral History Project, *Uchinanchu: A History of Okinawans in Hawaii* (Honolulu, 1981), p. 520; Keiko Teshirogi, poem, in Kazuo Ito, *Issei: A History of Japanese Immigrants in North America* (Seattle, 1973), p. 480; Robert Bellah et al., *Habits of the Heart: Individualism and Commitment in American Life* (Berkeley, 1985), p. 153.

12. Folk song, translation, in Marlon K. Hom (ed. and trans.), *Songs of Gold Mountain:*

Cantonese Rhymes from San Francisco Chinatown (Berkeley, 1987), p. 134; "When I Journeyed from America," in Harriet M. Pawlowska (ed.), *Merrily We Sing: One Hundred Five Polish Folk Songs* (Detroit, 1961), pp. 154–155.

13. Rowland Berthoff, *British Immigrants in Industrial America, 1750–1950* (Cambridge, Mass., 1953), p. 10; Frances Kraljic, *Croatian Migration to and from the United States, 1900–1914* (Palo Alto, 1978), pp. 29, 46; Caroline Golab, *Immigrant Destinations* (Philadelphia, 1977), pp. 48, 58; Victor Von Borosini, "Home-Going Italians," *Survey*, September 28, 1912, p. 792; Theodore Saloutos, *They Remember America: The Story of the Repatriated Greek-Americans* (Berkeley, 1956), p. 50; Theodore Saloutos, "Causes and Patterns of Greek Emigration to the United States," *Perspectives in American History*, vol. 7 (1973), pp. 411, 417, 421, 423, and 436; Thomas J. Archdeacon, *Becoming American: An Ethnic History* (New York, 1983), pp. 138–139.

14. Michael Moore, "Pride and Prejudice," *Image: The Magazine of Northern California*, in *San Francisco Examiner*, November 15, 1987, p. 17.

15. Georg Simmel, "Der Fremde" or "The Stranger," in Simmel, *On Individuality and Social Forms*, edited by Donald N. Levine (Chicago, 1971), pp. 143–149. For suggestive discussions of Simmel, see Franklin Ng, "The Sojourner, Return Migration, and Immigration History," in Chinese Historical Society of America, *Chinese America: History and Perspectives*, 1987 (San Francisco, 1987), pp. 53–72; Stanford M. Lyman, "The Chinese Diaspora in America, 1850–1943," in Chinese Historical Society of America, *The Life, Influence and Role of the Chinese in the United States, 1776–1960* (San Francisco, 1976), pp. 131–134.

16. John Higham, *Strangers in the Land: Patterns of American Nativism, 1860–1925* (New York, 1966); F. Scott Fitzgerald, *The Great Gatsby* (rpt. New York, 1953); Stanley Lieberson, *A Piece of the Pie: Blacks and White Immigrants since 1880* (Berkeley, 1980), p. 33; J. N. Hook, *Family Names: How Our Surnames Came to America* (New York, 1982), pp. 351, 322–325. It would be difficult to count the number of people who changed their family names, but it may have been extensive. In western Pennsylvania, for example, 76 percent of Ukrainian names were changed by the third generation. Ibid., p. 322.

17. Robert E. Park, "Human Migration and the Marginal Man," *American Journal of Sociology*, vol. 33, no. 6 (May 1928), p. 890; Robert E. Park, "Racial Assimilation in Secondary Groups with Particular Reference to the Negro," *Papers and Proceedings, Eighth Annual Meeting of the American Sociological Society*, 1913, vol. 8 (Chicago, 1914), p. 71.

18. Robert Blauner, "Colonized and Immigrant Minorities," in Ronald Takaki (ed.), *From Different Shores: Perspectives on Race and Ethnicity in America* (New York, 1987), pp. 149–160; Edna Bonacich, "A Theory of Ethnic Antagonism: The Split Labor Market," *American Sociological Review*, vol. 37, no. 5 (October 1972), pp. 547–559. For the concept of the industrial reserve army, see Karl Marx, *Capital: A Critique of Political Economy* (New York, 1906), pp. 689–703; I have expanded this concept to include the racial and transnational dimensions of this labor reserve.

19. Victor and Bret de Bary Nee, "Growing Up in a Chinatown Grocery Store: Interview with Frank Ng," in Emma Gee (ed.), *Counterpoint: Perspectives on Asian America* (Los Angeles, 1978), p. 346; Edna Bonacich and John Modell, *The Economic Basis of Ethnic Solidarity: Small Business in the Japanese American Community* (Berkeley, 1980).

20. For quotas, see Proclamation 2283 of President Franklin D. Roosevelt, *Code of Federal Regulations* (Title 3—The President, 1936–38 Compilation), pp. 140–141; 1924 Immigration Act, section 13, reprinted in Eliot G. Mears, *Resident Orientals on the American Pacific Coast: Their Legal and Economic Status* (New York, 1927), appendix, p. 515. The 1924 law was amended in 1930 to allow the entry of Asian wives of American citizens married after June 1930.

21. *Debates and Proceedings in the Congress of the United States, 1789–1791*, 2 vols. (Wash-

ington, D.C., 1834), vol. 1, pp. 998, 1284; vol. 2, pp. 1148–1156, 1162, 2264; Cable Act, 42 U.S. *Stat* 1021; Yamato Ichihashi, *Japanese in the United States* (Stanford, 1932), pp. 324–325. The Cable Act was amended in 1931, permitting an American woman who married an alien ineligible to citizenship to retain her U.S. citizenship.

22. Robert Mirak, "Armenians," in Stephan Thernstrom, *Harvard Encyclopedia of American Ethnic Groups* (Cambridge, Mass., 1980), pp. 139, 141, 143; Mr. G. Sato, in David Mas Masumoto, *Country Voices: The Oral History of a Japanese American Family Farm Community* (Del Ray, Calif.' 1987), p. 13.

23. Roger Daniels, *Concentration Camps USA: Japanese Americans and World War II* (New York, 1971); Peter Irons, *Justice At War: The Story of the Japanese American Internment Cases* (New York, 1983).

24. Perry Miller, *Errand into the Wilderness* (New York, 1956); John Winthrop, in Ronald Takaki, *Iron Cages: Race and Culture in Nineteenth-Century America* (New York, 1979), p. 21; Winthrop Jordan, *White over Black: American Attitudes Toward the Negro, 1550–1812* (Chapel Hill, N.C., 1968), p. xiv; Benjamin Franklin, *Observations Concerning the Increase of Mankind* (1751), in Leonard W. Labaree (ed.), *The Papers of Benjamin Franklin* (New Haven, 1959–), vol. 4, p. 234; *Federalist Papers,* in Stephen Steinberg, *The Ethnic Myth* (New York, 1981), p. 9; Jefferson to Monroe, November 24, 1801, in Paul L. Ford (ed.), *The Works of Thomas Jefferson* (New York, 1892–1899), vol. 9, p .317; Jefferson, *Notes on the State of Virginia* (rpt. New York, 1964, originally published in 1781), p. 119; Jefferson to George Flower, September 12, 1817, in H. A. Washington (ed.), *The Writings of Thomas Jefferson* (Washington, D.C., 1853–1854) vol. 7, p. 84; U.S. v. Bhagat Singh Thind, 261 U.S. 215 (1923).

25. Walt Whitman, "By Blue Ontario's Shore" and "Passage to India," in Whitman, *Leaves of Grass* (rpt. New York, 1958), pp. 284, 40–343; Walt Whitman, in Horace Traubel, *With Walt Whitman in Canada,* 2 vols. (New York, 1915), vol. 2, pp. 34–35; Herman Melville, *Moby-Dick* (rpt. Boston, 1956), pp. 105, 182, 253, 322–323; Ito, *Issei,* p. 497; Carlos Bulosan, *America Is in the Heart: A Personal History* (rpt. Seattle, 1981, originally published in 1946), pp. 188–189.

26. Fitzgerald, *The Great Gatsby,* p. 182.

27. Maxine Hong Kingston, *The Woman Warrior: Memoirs of a Girlhood Among Ghosts* (New York, 1976), p. 9; Park, "Human Migration and the Marginal Man," pp. 881–893; Victor Turner, *Dramas, Fields, and Metaphors: Symbolic Action in Human Society* (Ithaca, N.Y., 1974), pp. 232, 237; Arnold Van Gennep, *The Rites of Passage* (rpt. Chicago, 1960); John Locke, *Of Civil Government: Second Treatise* (rpt. Chicago, 1955), p. 39; Bulosan, *America Is in the Heart,* pp. 104, 66, 251.

Chapter Four

When and Where I Enter

Gary Y. Okihiro

A solitary figure defies a tank, insofar as a solitary figure can defy a tank. A "goddess of liberty" in the image of the Statue of Liberty arises from the midst of a vast throng gathered in Beijing's Tiananmen Square. The November 1, 1991, issue of *Asiaweek* carries the caption "Welcoming Asians" under a picture of the Statue of Liberty in New York Harbor awash in the light of fireworks.[1] Contained within those images— vivid and memorable—is what Swedish social scientist Gunnar Myrdal called the American creed. Democracy, equality, and liberty form the core of that creed, and the "mighty woman with a torch" has come to symbolize those ideals to, in the words of the poet Emma Lazarus, the tired, the poor, the huddled masses "yearning to breathe free."

On another island, on the other coast, stands not a statue but a wooden barrack. Solitary figures hunch over to carve poems on the walls.[2]

> The sea-scape resembles lichen twisting and
> turning for a thousand li.
> There is no shore to land and it is difficult to
> walk.
> With a gentle breeze I arrived at the city thinking
> all would be so.
> At ease, how was one to know he was to live in a
> wooden building?
>
> In the quiet of night, I heard, faintly, the whistling
> of wind.
> The forms and shadows saddened me; upon
> seeing the landscape, I composed a poem.
> The floating clouds, the fog, darken the sky.
> The moon shines faintly as the insects chirp.
> Grief and bitterness entwined are heaven sent.
> The sad person sits alone, leaning by a window.

Angel Island, not Ellis Island, was the main port of entry for Chinese migrants "yearning to breathe free" from 1910 to 1940.[3] There, separated by cold currents from the golden shore, the migrants were carefully screened by U.S. Immigration officials and held for days, weeks, and months to determine their fitness for America. The

1882 Chinese Exclusion Act had prohibited entry to Chinese workers, indicative of a race- *and* class-based politics, because according to the act, "in the opinion of the Government of the United States, the coming of Chinese laborers to this country endangers the good order of certain localities within the territory thereof."[4]

In New York City, a year after passage of the Chinese Exclusion Act, Emma Lazarus wrote the poem that now graces the base of the Statue of Liberty. But the statue had not been envisioned as a symbol of welcome to the world's "wretched refuse" by its maker, French sculptor Frederic Auguste Batholdi, and at its unveiling in 1886, President Grover Cleveland proclaimed that the statue's light would radiate outward into "the darkness of ignorance and man's oppression until Liberty enlightens the world."[5] In other words, the statue commemorated republican stability, and according to the October 29, 1886, *New York World*, it stood forever as a warning against lawlessness and anarchy and as a pledge of friendship with nations that "dare strike for freedom." That meaning was changed by European immigrants, who saw the statue as welcoming them, and by Americanizers, who, during the 1920s and 1930s, after the 1924 Immigration Act restricting mass immigration, sought a symbol to instill within the children of immigrants patriotism and a love for country.[6]

The tale of those two islands, separated by the vast interior and lapped by different waters, comprises a metaphor of America and the Asian American experience. America was not always a nation of immigrants, nor was America unfailingly a land of democracy, equality, and liberty. The romantic sentiment of the American identity, "this new man," expressed by French immigrant J. Hector St. John de Crèvecoeur was probably not the dominant view, nor did it apply to all of America's people. Writing in 1782, Crèvecoeur exclaimed: "What then is the American, this new man? . . . I could point out to you a family whose grandfather was an Englishman, whose wife was Dutch, whose son married a French woman, and whose present four sons have now four wives of different nations. *He* is an American, who leaving behind him all his ancient prejudices and manners, receives new ones from the new mode of life he has embraced, the new government he obeys, and the new rank he holds. He becomes an American by being received in the broad lap of our great *Alma Mater*. Here individuals of all nations are melted into a new race of men."[7]

Instead, the prevailing view was a narrower construction that distinguished "settler," or original colonist, from "immigrant," and that required a single origin and common culture. Americans, John Jay wrote in the *Federalist* papers, were "one united people—a people descended from the same ancestors, speaking the same language, professing the same religion, attached to the same principles of government, very similar in their manners and customs."[8] That eighteenth-century discrimination between settler and immigrant proved inadequate for the building of a new republic during the nineteenth century. The quest for a unifying national identity, conceived along the lines of Crèvecoeur's notion whereby "individuals of all nations are melted into a new race of men," an idea later called the "melting pot," paralleled the building of networks of roads, railroads, and communications links that unified and bound the nation.[9]

Although Asians helped to construct those iron links that connected East to West, they, along with other peoples of color, were excluded from the industrial, masculine, destroying melting pot. Ellis Island was not their port of entry; its statue was not their goddess of liberty. Instead, the square-jawed, androgynous visage of the "Mother of Exiles" turned outward to instruct, to warn, and to repel those who would endanger the good order of America's shores, both at home and abroad. The indigenous inhabitants of Africa, Asia, and the Americas were not members of the community but were more akin to the wilderness, which required penetration and domestication. Three years after the Constitution was ratified, the first Congress met and restricted admission into the American community to "free white persons" through the Naturalization Act of 1790. Although the act was modified to include "persons of African nativity or descent" in 1870 and Chinese nationals in 1943, the racial criterion for citizenship was eliminated completely only in 1952, 162 years after the original delineation of the Republic's members, or, according to the Naturalization Act, the "worthy part of mankind."

In 1886, African American educator Anna Julia Cooper told a group of African American ministers: "Only the BLACK WOMAN can say 'when and where I enter . . . then and there the whole *Negro race enters with me.*' "[10] Cooper's confident declaration held profound meaning. African American men bore the stigma of race, but African American women bore the stigmata of race and gender. Her liberation, her access to the full promise of America, embraced the admission of the entire race. The matter of "when and where," accordingly, is an engendered, enabling moment. The matter of "when and where," in addition, is a generative, transformative moment. The matter of "when and where," finally, is an extravagant, expansive moment. That entry into the American community, however enfeebled by barriers to full membership, parallels the earlier entry into historical consciousness, and the "when and where" of both moments are engendered/enabling, generative/transformative, extravagant/expansive.

Asians entered into the European American historical consciousness long before the mid-nineteenth-century Chinese migration to "Gold Mountain" and, I believe, even before Yankee traders and American diplomats and missionaries traveled to China in the late eighteenth century. The "when and where" of the Asian American experience can be found within the European imagination and construction of Asians and Asia and within their expansion eastward and westward to Asia for conquest and trade.

Writing in the fifth or fourth century B.C.E., Hippocrates, Greek physician and "father of medicine," offered a "scientific" view of Asia and its people.[11] Asia, Hippocrates held, differed "in every respect" and "very widely" from Europe. He attributed those contrasts to the environment, which shaped the peoples' bodily conformations and their characters. Asia's mild, uniform climate supported lush vegetation and plentiful harvests, but under those conditions "courage, endurance, industry and high spirit could not arise" and "pleasure must be supreme." Asians reflected the seasons in their natures, exhibiting a "monotonous sameness" and "stagnation," and their form of government, led by kings who ruled as "despots," enfeebled Asians even more. Among Asians, Hippocrates reported, were "Long-heads" and "Phasians." The latter had yellowish complexions "as though they suffered from jaundice." Because of the differing environments in which they lived, Hippocrates concluded that Europeans had a wider variety of physical types and were more courageous and energetic than Asians, "for uniformity engenders slackness, while variation fosters endurance in both body and soul; rest and slackness are food for cowardice, endurance and exertion for bravery."[12]

Aristotle mirrored Hippocrates' views of Asia during the fourth century B.C.E. In his *Politics*, Aristotle observed that northern Europeans were "full of spirit, but wanting in intelligence and skill," whereas Asians were "intelligent and inventive" but lacked spirit and were therefore "always in a state of subjection and slavery." The Greeks, in contrast, lived between those two groups and thus were both "high-spirited and also intelligent." Further, argued Aristotle, barbarians were by nature "more servile in character" than Greeks, and he reported that some Asians practiced cannibalism.[13] The fourth-century B.C.E conflict between Persia and Greece, between barbarism and civilization, between inferior and superior, tested the "great chain of being" idea propounded by Plato and Aristotle. Alexander the Great's thrust into India, to "the ends of the world," was a one-sided affair, according to the Roman historian Arrian, a chronicler of the expedition. Using contemporary accounts but writing some four hundred years after Alexander's death in 323 B.C.E., Arrian contrasted Alexander's ingenuity and dauntless spirit—"he could not endure to think of putting an end to the war so long as he could find enemies"—with the cowardice of the barbarian hordes, who fled pellmell at the sight of the conqueror.[14] In a speech to his officers, as recorded by Arrian, Alexander reminded them that they were "ever conquerors" and their enemies were "always beaten," that the Greeks were "a free people" and the Asians, "a nation of slaves." He praised the strength and valor of the Greeks, who were "inured to warlike toils," and he declared that their enemies had been "enervated by long ease and effeminacy" and called them "the wanton, the luxurious, and effeminate Asiatics."[15]

Such accounts of Asia, based upon the belief in a generative relationship between the environment and race and culture, enabled an exotic, alienating construction of Asians, whether witnessed or simply imagined. Literary critics Edward W. Said and Mary B. Campbell have characterized that European conception of Asia and Asians— "the Other"—as "almost a European invention," according to Said, a place of "romance, exotic beings, haunting memories and landscapes, remarkable experiences," and for Campbell, that conception was "the ground for dynamic struggles between the powers of language and the facts of life."[16] Accordingly, the Greek historian Ctesias, writing probably in the fifth century B.C.E., reveled in the accounts of "dog-faced creatures" and "creatures without heads" that supposedly inhabited Africa, and he peopled his Asia with those same monstrous beasts. Likewise, the author of the early medieval account *Wonders of the East* described Asian women "who have boars' tusks and hair down to their heels and oxen's tails growing out of their loins. These women are thirteen feet tall, and their bodies have the whiteness of marble, and they have camels' feet and donkeys' teeth." Alexander the Great, hero of *Wonders of the East*, kills those giant, tusked, and tailed women "because of their obscenity" and thereby eliminates strangeness and makes the world sane and safe again. Asia in *Wonders of the East*, writes Campbell, "stands in opposition to the world we know and the laws that govern it" and thus was beyond and outside the realm of order and sensibility.[17]

That otherworldliness, that flight from reality, pervades the earliest Christian European text to define Europe in opposition to Asia, the *Peregrinatio ad terram sanctam* by Egeria, probably written during the late fourth century C.E. Although her account of her journey to the Holy Land contained "moments of awe, reverence, wonder, or gratitude," it described an exotic Asia that served to highlight the positive, the real, the substantial Europe. *De locis sanctis*, written during the late seventh century C.E. by Adamnan, abbot at Iona's monastery, recounted a similar Asia from the travels of Bishop Arculf to the Holy Land. Asia, according to *De locis sanctis*, was a strange, even demonic place, where people exhibited grotesque inversions and perversions of human nature and where a prerational, stagnant configuration existed, "a world stripped of spirit and past."[18]

Asia, according to Campbell and Said, was Europe's Other.[19] Asia was the location of Europe's oldest, greatest, and richest colonies, the source of its civilization and languages, its cultural contestant, and the wellspring of one of its most persistent images of the Other. At the same time, cautions Said, the assumptions of Orientalism were not merely abstractions and figments of the European imagination but composed a system of thought that supported a "Western style for dominating, restructuring, and having authority over" Asia. Within Orientalism's lexicon, Asians were inferior to and deformations of Europeans, and Orientalism's purpose was to stir an inert people, raise them to their former greatness, shape them and give them an identity, and subdue and domesticate them. That colonization, wrote Said, was an engendered subordination, by which European men aroused, penetrated, and possessed a passive, dark, and vacuous "Eastern bride," imposing movement and giving definition to the "inscrutable Orient," full of secrecy and sexual promise.[20] The feminization of Asia was well under way before the colonization of Asia by Europe in the sixteenth century, as evident in the accounts of Hippocrates, Herodotus,[21] Aristotle, Arrian, Egeria, and Adamnan.

Arrian's account of Alexander's effortless victory over "effeminate" Asian men, for example, parallels his discussion of Greek men's easy conquest of erotic Asian women. Indian women, wrote the Roman historian, "who will suffer themselves to be deflowered for no other gift, will easily condescend, when an elephant is promised as the purchase," thinking it "an honour to have their beauty valued at so high a rate."[22] The conqueror took for himself several Asian wives, he "bestowed the daughters of the most illustrious" Persians on his friends, and more than 10,000 of his soldiers married Asian women. Further, commented Arrian, despite being "in the very heat of youth," Alexander curbed his sexual desires and thereby displayed the triumph of mind over body, rationality over sensuality, Greek over Asian. "The daughter of Oxyartes was named Roxana, a virgin, but very marriageable, and, by the general consent of writers, the most beautiful of all the Asiatic women, Darius's wife excepted," wrote Arrian. "Alexander was struck with surprise at the sight of her beauty; nevertheless, being fully resolved not to offer violence to a captive, he forbore to gratify his desires till he took her, afterwards, to wife . . . and herein showed himself no less a pattern of true continency, than he had before done of heroic fortitude." "As to those pleasures which regarded the body," wrote Arrian in eulogizing Alexander, "he shewed himself indifferent; as to the desires of the mind, insatiable."[23]

The Greek representation of Asia yielded not only soft men and erotic women but also hard, cruel men and virile, martial women. Fifth-century B.C.E. polarities of Greek/barbarian, male/female, and human/animal helped to define the citizens of the *polis*—Greek men—as the negation of their Other—barbarian, female, animal— who were linked by analogy such that barbarian was like female was like animal.[24] Athenian patriarchy held that men were the norm, were superior, and brought order, whereas women were abnormal, inferior, and brought chaos. Marriage domesticated women, civilizing their wild, untamed sexuality and disciplining them for admittance into the city. Amazons reversed the gender relations of the *polis* and stood in opposition to its androcentrism by being members of a society of women who refused to marry and become mothers to sons and who assumed the preeminent male characteristics of aggressiveness, leadership, and strength. Although the myth of Amazons originated before the Persian wars, the Greeks considered Asia to be the Amazons' homeland, and they equated Persians with Amazons, in that both Persians and Amazons were barbarians and, according to Isocrates in 380 B.C.E., Amazons "hated the whole Greek race" and sought "to gain mastery over all." Athenians, explained Isocrates, defended themselves against Amazon expansion, defeated them, and destroyed them "just as if they had waged war against all mankind."[25] Besides posing a political threat, Asia served as an object lesson of how, when men ceased to act as men, order and normalcy vanished, resulting in the topsy-turvy world of the Amazons.[26]

The Mongol invasions of the thirteenth century not only breached Alexander's wall but also made palpable a hitherto distant, alien people and culture. "Swarming like locusts over the face of the earth," Friar William of Rubruck wrote in 1255, the Mongols "have brought terrible devastation to the eastern parts [of Europe], laying waste with fire and carnage . . . it seemed that God did not wish them to come out; nevertheless it is written in sacred history that they shall come out toward the end of the world, and shall make a great slaughter of men."[27] The Mongols, of whom the Tatars were the most prominent group, appeared as avenging angels from hell, "Tartarus," and hence the corruption of their name to "Tartars."[28] Although in awe of the Mongols' military prowess and strength, Friar William saw little to admire in their filth and barbarism: "the poor provide for themselves by trading sheep and skins; and the slaves fill their bellies with dirty water and are content with this. They also catch mice, of which many kinds abound there; mice with long tails they do not eat but give to their birds; they eat doormice and all kinds of mice with short tails."[29]

The late-thirteenth-century account of Asia by the Venetian Marco Polo contains both feminine and masculine attributions, chaste women and diabolical men, and grotesque and wondrous objects and people, including unicorns, Amazons, dog-headed creatures, mountain streams flowing with diamonds, and deserts full of ghouls. His narrative is a distillation of the brew that had preceded him. John Masefield, in his introduction to the 1908 edition of Polo's *Travels*, wrote that "his picture of the East is the picture which we all make in our minds when we repeat to ourselves those two strange words, 'the East,' and give ourselves up to the image which that symbol evokes."[30] A prominent part of that image was the exotic and the erotic, highlighted in Polo's ample accounts of prostitutes, sex, and women, leading Henry Hart to speculate: "One may surmise that the numerous references to women—the intimate descriptions of their persons, their various aptitudes in sex relations and many other details not usually related even by hardy travelers of that or a later day . . . were largely, if not entirely, called forth by the frank curiosity and continual questionings of the stay-at-home Westerners for whom his tale was told and written." Polo wrote of the Chinese that "their ladies and wives are also most delicate and angelique things, and raised gently, and with great delicacy, and they clothe themselves with so many ornaments and of silk and of jewels, that the value of them cannot be estimated."[31]

In Europe, *The Travels of Sir John Mandeville* was the most influential book about Asia from 1356, when it was first published, to the eighteenth century. "Mandeville" was a pseudonym for perhaps a number of authors, who claimed to have traveled from England to the Holy Land, Egypt, Arabia, and even to the court of the Great Khan in Cathay. Like Polo, Mandeville described the marvels and monsters of the East, from the bounties of gold, silver, precious stones, cloves, nutmeg, and ginger to the horrors of one-eyed and headless beasts, giants, pygmies, and cannibals. In a single passage, Mandeville poses an apparently curious juxtaposition of sexuality and war, but, upon reflection, the feminine (sexuality) and masculine (war) so constructed are really two sides of the same coin: the dominance of men over women and territory, achieved through heterosexual sex and war, and, by extension, under imperialism, European men's superiority over Asian women and men and their control of reproduction and the state. On the island of "Calonak" near Java, wrote Mandeville, the king "hath as many wives as he will. For he maketh search all the country to get him the fairest maidens that may be found, and maketh them to be brought before him. And he taketh one one night, and another another night, and so forth continually suing; so that he hath a thousand wives or more. And he lieth never but one night with one of them, and another night with another; but if that one happen to be more lusty to his pleasance than another. And therefore the king getteth full many children, some-time an hundred, some-time a two-hundred, and some-time more." Without a paragraph break, Mandeville continued: "And he hath also into a 14,000 elephants or more that he maketh for to be brought up amongst his villains by all his towns. For in case that he had any war against any other king about him, then [he] maketh certain men of arms for to go up into the castles of tree made for the war, that craftily be set upon the elephants' backs, for to fight against their enemies."[32]

Christopher Columbus was a great admirer of "Mandeville" and, along with English explorers Martin Frobisher and Walter Raleigh and Flemish cartographer Gerhardus Mercator, read and believed Mandeville's account of Asia and his idea of a circumnavigable and universally inhabited world.[33] The fabulous East, the earthly paradise "discovered" and described by Columbus, was to him and his contemporaries Asia—the "Indies"—and its peoples were Asians—the "Indians." They were just as surely Asian as the lands and peoples in Polo's and Mandeville's travelogues. As Columbus noted in the preface to his ship's daily log, the expedition's purpose was to go "to the regions of India, to see the Princes there and the peoples and the lands, and to learn of their disposition, and of everything, and the measures which could be taken for their conversion to our Holy Faith."[34] Columbus compared the new lands to the virtuous Garden before the Fall, where people were like children, innocent and unself-conscious in their nakedness, and where the feminized land invited conquest. His log entry for October 12, 1492, reported: "At dawn we saw naked people, and I went ashore in the ship's boat, armed. . . . I unfurled the royal banner. . . . after a prayer of thanksgiving I ordered the captains of the Pinta and Niña . . . to bear faith and witness that I was taking possession of this island for the King and Queen."[35] Much of the land was bountiful and laden with fruit, and on his third voyage, Columbus described the mouth of the Orinoco River as shaped "like a woman's nipple," from whence issued the waters of paradise into the sea.[36]

Some islanders, reported Columbus, were friendly, domestic, tractable, and even cowardly, but others were warlike, monstrous, and evil, even cannibalistic (a word derived from the name "Carib" Indians). "I also understand that, a long distance from here," wrote Columbus on November 4, 1492, "there are men with one eye and others with dogs' snouts who eat men. On taking a man they behead him and drink his blood and cut off his genitals."[37] The timid Indians were eager to submit to Europeans, being "utterly convinced that I and all my people came from Heaven," according to Columbus, whereas the fearless ones required discipline. Both kinds of Indians, "feminine" and "masculine," were fair game for capture, or, in Columbus's euphemism, "I would like to take some of them with me."[38] That, in fact, was what the admiral did, as easily as plucking leaves from the lush, tropical vegetation, to serve as guides, servants, and specimens. Columbus's text and others like it helped to justify a "Christian imperialism" and were the means by which the invaders "communicated—and helped control—a suddenly larger world."[39]

That world grew even larger in about 1510, when a few Europeans questioned Columbus's "India" and proposed the existence of a new continent that stood between Europe and Asia, although cartographers continued to append American discoveries to the Asian coast until the late sixteenth century. Accompanying and justifying their expanded physical world was an ideology, articulated in texts, of a growing racial and cultural distance between Europeans and the peoples of Asia, Africa, and the Americas. The first cracks had appeared, in the perceptions of Asians by Europeans, in the fifth-century B.C.E. works of Hippocrates, who had posited "very wide" differences "in every respect" between Europeans and Asians. The fissures continued to widen thereafter to the degree that Asia, Africa, and the Americas became antipodes of Europe, the habitations of monstrous beasts and perversions of nature itself. That world, it seemed, needed to be appropriated, worked over, and tamed.

The process of colonization and the relationship between colonizer and colonized were incisively described by Albert Memmi, the twentieth-century Tunisian philosopher and author. "The colonialist stresses those things which keep him separate, rather than emphasizing that which might contribute to the foundation of a joint community." That focus on difference is not of itself racist, but it takes on a particular meaning and function within a racist context. According to Memmi: "In those differences, the colonized is always degraded and the colonialist finds justification for rejecting his subject. . . . The colonialist removes the factor [the colonized] from history, time, and therefore possible evolution. What is actually a sociological point becomes labeled as being biological or, preferably, metaphysical. It is attached to the colonized's basic nature."[40] Whether because of race or culture, of biology or behavior, of physical appearance or social construct, Asians appeared immutable, engendered, and inferior. These differences not only served to set Asians apart from the "joint community" but also helped to define the European identity as a negation of its Other.

Reflecting on works published on the five-hundredth anniversary of Columbus's "discovery," anthropologist Wilcomb E. Washburn, noted interpreter of American Indian culture and director of the Office of American Studies at the Smithsonian Institution, reminded his readers that the initiative for discovery came from the West and not the East, and thus "Asia was more sharply etched on the European mind than on the Asian mind. . . . Both America and Asia were relatively stagnant," he explained, "being more wedded to their traditions than was the West, which found the novelty of other climes and other cultures stimulating. While the Western mind did not always move in directions that we would now applaud, it moved—indeed, darted here and there—as the Asian mind too often did not."[41]

Following Columbus's "great enterprise" and his "taking possession" of "Asia," the penetration of Asia proper began with the Portuguese, who seized parts of India and Southeast Asia during the early sixteenth century, established a colony at Macao in 1557, and controlled much of the trade with China and Japan. Despite Portugal's presumed sole possession of the hemisphere east of the 1493 papal line of demarcation, Spain, the Netherlands, France, and Britain also participated in the trade with and colonization of Asia. The conquest and colonization of the Americas was, of course, a product of that global expansion of Europeans, and the "when and where" of the Asian American experience must be similarly situated. I do not claim, however, that Orientalism's restructuring and domination of Asia simply migrated with Europeans to America, nor am I arguing a necessary relationship between European and European American perceptions of Asians. My contention is that there is a remarkable familiarity to Orientalism's face on both shores of the Atlantic and that its resemblance extends to European constructions of American Indians and Africans.[42]

Historian Stuart Creighton Miller, in his 1969 book, *The Unwelcome Immigrant: The American Image of the Chinese, 1785–1882*, argued that although it was sensible to assume that American attitudes toward Asians were rooted in the European heritage, he could find no direct connection between those views. Neither the writings nor the libraries of America's leading figures during the colonial period showed an interest in or even curiosity about Asians. Miller characterized that lacuna as indicative of an "innocent, unstructured perception of China in the American mind" and, as proof, pointed to George Washington, who was surprised to learn in 1785 that the Chinese were nonwhites. Further, Miller noted that the English failed to share the Continent's enthusiasm for Chinese government and law and for Confucian philosophy made popular by Jesuit missionaries and by the iconoclasts of the Age of Reason. In fact, in Britain, Sinophobes such as Daniel Defoe, Samuel Johnson, Jonathan Swift, and Adam Smith launched a vitriolic attack against the Chinese. The American image of Asians, Miller concluded, took shape only after direct American trade with China began with the departure of the *Empress of China* from New York Harbor in 1784.[43]

Miller underestimates the malleability and mobility of racial attitudes and notions of the Other, characteristics that have been amply demonstrated by scholars. Europeans, as noted by historian Dwight W. Hoover, "did not approach new lands and new people devoid of preconceptions. Instead, they brought with them a whole set of ideas concerning both the natural and historical worlds."[44] Some of those preconceptions included the idea of a biological chain of being that evolved from ape to wild man to man and the biblical notion of postdiluvian degeneration and diversity originating with the Tower of Babel.[45] Despite their manifest variety, ideas of race distinguished Europeans from their shadow—non-Europeans—and claimed superiority for the civilized, Christian portion of humankind.

William Shakespeare's *The Tempest*, first performed in 1611, was likely set in Bermuda but might just as well have been an allegory of race relations during the age of European overseas expansion and colonization, or perhaps even an account of the sugar plantation system that was installed along the European Mediterranean coast and on islands like Cyprus and Crete and that was driven mainly by Asian and African slave labor by the late fourteenth century.[46] Prospero, "a prince of power" and lover of books, is set adrift with his daughter, Miranda, and lands on an enchanted island which he takes from Caliban, whom he enslaves and banishes to the island's wasteland. Caliban (anagram of the word "cannibal") is everything Prospero is not; he is dark and physically deformed; he is "poisonous," "lying," "filth," "capable of all ill," and begotten of "the devil himself." He is both African and Indian; his mother was from Algiers, and he is descended from Brazilians, Patagonians, and Bermudans but is also part fish, part beast. Caliban's mother, Prospero said, was a "damn'd witch," a "hag," who had given birth to Caliban like an animal—"she did litter here" her son, who was "not honour'd with a human shape." Despite being excluded from their company and despite Miranda's abhorrence of him, Caliban is indispensable to Prospero and Miranda, because he "does make our fire, fetch in our wood; and serves in offices that profit us." Prospero pities Caliban, tutors him, and takes "pains to make [him] speak"; Prospero gives meaning to Caliban's "gabble." Instruction, however, proves insufficient. The wild man is driven by savage lust and tries to kill Prospero and rape the virginal Miranda, but he is repulsed by Prospero's magic.[47]

Caliban, the "savage man of Inde," was African and Indian, but he was also Asian insofar as Indians came from Asia, as was contended by Samuel Purchas, scholar and chaplain to the archbishop of Canterbury, in his widely read book *Purchas his Pilgrimage*, published in 1613, and seconded by the astronomer Edward Brerewood in his 1614 book, *Enquiries touching the diversity of languages, and religions through the chiefe parts of the world*, and by Walter Raleigh in his 1614 *History of the World*. The fact that Indians were once Asians accounted for their barbarism, according to these English writers.[48] Thus, although a separate race, Indians were still Asians, both groups having descended from the biblical Shem; and Asians, Indians, and Africans all belonged to the darker races of men, the Calibans of the earth, who were ruled by beastly passions, sought to impregnate white women (to people "this isle with Calibans"), and, although given a language and trained in useful labor, still turned against their benefactors and had to be subdued.[49] Perhaps influenced by those European views, Thomas Jefferson hypothesized the kinship of Asians and America's Indians: "the resemblance between the Indians of America and the eastern inhabitants of Asia would induce us to conjecture that the former are descendants of the latter, or the latter of the former."[50]

Although they arrived in the New World carrying the baggage of the Old World, Americans developed their own projections and invented their own mythologies, peering from their "clearing" into the "wilderness." George Washington may have been reflecting the light of European ideology bent by the prism of American experience when he declared that "being upon good terms with the Indians" was based upon economy and expediency, and instead of driving them "by force of arms out of their Country; which . . . is like driving the wild Beasts of ye forest . . . the gradual extension of our settlements will as certainly cause the savage, as the wolf, to retire; both being beasts of prey, tho' they differ in shape."[51] And Jefferson might have defended Indians as "a degraded yet basically noble brand of white man," but he was also defending the American environment and its quadrupeds, those "other animals of America," against French naturalist Georges Buffon's claim of American inferiority. Having failed to assimilate and civilize the savage and childish Indians, Jefferson argued for their extermination, made "necessary to secure ourselves against the future effects of their savage and ruthless warfare."[52] Jefferson, having reached that conclusion about Indians, linked America's determination to clear the forests with a New World version of British expansion and colonization and predicted that the "confirmed brutalization, if not extermination of this race in our America is . . . to form an additional chapter in the English history of [oppression of] the same colored man in Asia, and of the brethren of their own color in Ireland."[53]

When Yankee traders arrived in China during the late eighteenth century, they saw the Chinese through lenses that had already been ground with the grit of European views of Asia and Asians and the rub of historical and contemporary relations between European Americans and American Indians and Africans. The traders' diaries, journals, and letters were mostly free of racial prejudice, reports Miller, and the negative images of the Chinese that did appear concerned China's government and the officials with whom the traders dealt, whom they saw as despotic, corrupt, barbarous, begging, and cowardly. But traders' accounts also revealed extreme ethnocentrism. According to a trader, the Chinese were "the most vile, the most cowardly and submissive of slaves," and whites could bully even Chinese soldiers, whose "silly grunts and menaces mean nothing and are to be disregarded," wrote another.[54] A prominent theme was the bizarre and peculiar nature of the Chinese in their alleged taste for dogs, cats, and rats, in their music, which was a "mass of detestible discord," and in their theater, which was "ridiculous or disgracefully obscene." The records, wrote Miller, "portrayed him [the Chinese] as a ludicrous specimen of the human race and [were] not designed to evoke the admiration and respect for Chinese culture." The focus on the exotic, on "strange and curious objects," was complemented by a featuring of vice—gambling and prostitution— and practices showing the "moral debasement" of the people, including idolatry, polygamy, and infanticide. The Chinese, wrote a trader contemptuously, are "grossly superstitious . . . most depraved and vicious: gambling is universal . . . ; they use pernicious drugs, . . . are gross gluttons," and are "a people refined in cruelty, bloodthirsty, and inhuman."[55]

The journey begun in New England and continuing around South America's Cape Horn was just the start of America's masculine thrust westward toward Asia's open shores.[56] Like those Yankee China trade vessels, the Conestoga wagons and prairie schooners pushed their way through "vacant, virgin" land to the Pacific and in the process built a continental empire that stretched "from sea to shining sea." In 1879, Robert Louis Stevenson rode the iron rails that bound the nation together, and his account, "Across the Plains: Leaves from the Notebook of an Emigrant between New York and San Francisco," might be read as the great American epic. America was "a sort of promised land" for Americans, like Stevenson, who were immigrants from Europe and who found themselves among a diverse lot of fellow passengers, "a babel of bewildered men, women, and children." As the train carried them westward, Stevenson described, like Crèvecoeur, the beauties of the land, where "all times, races, and languages have brought their contribution." That equality, that melting pot, however, was broken at Chicago, at the frontier of civilization, where the travelers were placed on an "emigrant train" that consisted of segregated coaches: one for white men, another for white women and children, and yet another for Chinese. Stevenson reflected upon the hatreds that had prompted that racial, gender, and age segregation as the train "pushed through this unwatered wilderness and haunt of savage tribes." America, he wrote, was the meeting ground, where "hungry Europe and hungry China, each pouring from their gates in search of provender, had here come face to face," and where Europeans had come with preconceived hatreds of the Chinese that had moved them from one field of conflict to another. "They [Europeans] seemed never to have looked at them [Chinese], listened to them, or thought of them, but hated them *a priori*," observed Stevenson. "The Mongols were their enemies in that cruel and treacherous battle-field of money."[57]

Despite his contempt for those "stupid," albeit modified, Old World prejudices, prejudices given further license once having left civilization for the "unwatered wilderness" of the frontier, Stevenson son was not entirely free of those same perceptions of the Chinese. His fellow Europeans, reported Stevenson, saw the Chinese as physically repulsive, such that the mere sight of them caused "a kind of choking in the throat." "Now, as a matter of fact," admitted the observant Scotsman, "the young Chinese man is so like a large class of European women, that on raising my head and suddenly catching sight of one at a considerable distance, I have for an instant been deceived by the resemblance"—although, he offered, "I do not say it is the most attractive class of our women." And while looking upon the Chinese with "wonder and respect," Stevenson saw them as creatures from "the other" world: "They [the Chinese] walk the earth with us, but it seems they must be of different clay." "They hear the clock strike the same hour, yet surely of a different epoch.

They travel by steam conveyance, yet with such a baggage of old Asiatic thoughts and superstitions as might check the locomotive in its course.... Heaven knows if we had one common thought or fancy all that way, or whether our eyes, which yet were formed upon the same design, beheld the same world out of the railway windows."[58]

Stevenson's view of the Chinese as "different clay" might have been conditioned by his European origins, but Herman Melville, surely no stranger to the American metaphysics of race relations, cannot be similarly dismissed. His retelling of a story by James Hall, "Indian hating.—Some of the sources of this animosity.—Brief account of Col. Moredock," not only offered a stinging critique of inhumanity masked as morality, embodied in the "confidence-man" and Indian hater John Moredock, but also foresaw, according to Richard Drinnon, that "when the metaphysics of Indian-hating hit salt water it more clearly became the metaphysics of empire-building." Although believed to be a barbarian, predicted Melville, "the backwoodsman would seem to America what Alexander was to Asia—captain in the vanguard of conquering civilization." Melville, Drinnon points out, correctly saw that the relentless westward advance of the Indian hater would, after reaching the Pacific Ocean, continue on to Asia, and in Melville's words, his hatreds would ride "upon the advance as the Polynesian upon the comb of the surf."[59] And like Alexander, who had sought to conquer all of India, the "backwoodsman," the "barbarian," "could not endure to think of putting an end to the war so long as he could find enemies."

In truth, America's manifest destiny was "an additional chapter" in the Orientalist text of Europe's "dominating, restructuring, and having authority over" Asia. In July 1853, Commodore Matthew C. Perry pushed into Tokyo Bay carrying a letter from the U.S. president demanding the opening of trade relations. That "opening" of Japan was accomplished, like the "opening" of the American West, with the iron fist of industry and the might of military arms; Perry's "black ships" under full steam power and with matchless guns were complements of the iron horses and Kentucky rifles of the backwoodsmen, who were simultaneously taming the wilderness. Reflecting on the second period of America's manifest destiny, after the annexation of the Philippines and Hawaii in 1898 and after Secretary of State John Hay's pronouncement of an "Open Door" with China, Theodore Roosevelt declared: "Of course our whole national history has been one of expansion.... That the barbarians recede or are conquered, with the attendant fact that peace follows their retrogression or conquest, is due solely to the power of the mighty civilized races which have not lost the fighting instinct, and which by their expansion are gradually bringing peace into the red wastes where the barbarian peoples of the world hold sway."[60]

The filling of those "red wastes," those empty spaces, was, of course, the white man's burden. John Hay, a son of the frontier of sorts, sought "to draw close the bonds" that united "the two Anglo-Saxon peoples" of Britain and America in a common destiny and mission: "All of us who think cannot but see that there is a sanction like that of religion which binds us to a sort of partnership in the beneficent work of the world. Whether we will it or not, we are associated in that work by the very nature of things, and no man and no group of men can prevent it. We are bound by a tie which we did not forge and which we cannot break; we are the joint ministers of the same sacred mission of liberty and progress, charged with duties which we cannot evade by the imposition of irresistible hands."[61] China's "Open Door" and America's "splendid little war" with Spain, observed Hay, were of that beneficent quality. "We have done the Chinks a great service," wrote Hay of his policy, "which they don't seem inclined to recognize," and he admonished the next generation of backwoodsmen, "as the children of Israel encamping by the sea were bidden, to Go Forward." Indeed, noted Hay, America had gone forward and had charted a "general plan of opening a field of enterprise in those distant regions where the Far West becomes the Far East."[62] In becoming a Pacific power, America had fulfilled a European people's destiny and, like Columbus, had gone ashore, unfurled the royal banner, offered a prayer of thanksgiving, and taken possession of the land. America's Far West had become the Far East, where Indian fighters became "goo-goo" fighters in the Philippines and Indian savages became Filipino "niggers," and where a war of extermination was pursued with no less determination than the chastising of the Iroquois urged by George Washington in 1779 when he instructed Major General John Sullivan: "but you will not by any means, listen to any overture of peace before the total ruin of their settlement is effected.... Our future security will be in their inability to injure us ... and in the terror with which the severity of the chastisement they receive will inspire them."[63]

Asians, it must be remembered, did not come to America; Americans went to Asia. Asians, it must be remembered, did not come to take the wealth of America; Americans went to take the wealth of Asia. Asians, it must be remembered, did not come to conquer and colonize America; Americans went to conquer and colonize Asia. And the matter of the "when and where" of Asian American history is located therein, in Europe's eastward and westward thrusts, engendered, transformative, expansive. But another context of the "when and where" is the historical moment in America, where Prospero ruled over the hideous, the imperative Caliban. Asia not only provided markets for goods and outposts for military and naval bases but also supplied pools of cheap labor for the development of America's "plantations" along its southern and western frontiers. In 1848, Aaron H. Palmer, a counselor to the U.S. Supreme Court, anticipated the nation's destiny in the American Southwest and Asia when he predicted that San Francisco would become "the great emporium of our commerce on the Pacific; and so soon as it is connected by a railroad with the Atlantic States, will become the most eligible point of departure for steamers to ... China." To build that rail link and to bring the fertile valleys of California under cultivation, Palmer favored the importation of Chinese workers, explaining that "no people in all the East are so well adapted for clearing wild lands and raising every species of agricultural product ... as the Chinese."[64]

It was within those American "plantations" that Asians joined Africans, Indians, and Latinos in labor, making Prospero's fire, fetching his wood, and serving in offices that profited him. It was within those "plantations" that Europeans tutored Asians, Africans, Indians, and Latinos and gave meaning to their gabble. And it was within those "plantations" that Asians, Africans, Indians, and Latinos rose up in rebellion against their bondage and struck for their freedom.

In 1885, a Chinese American described his reaction to being solicited for funds for erecting the Statue of Liberty. He felt honored to be counted among "citizens in the cause of liberty," he wrote, "but the word liberty makes me think of the fact that this country is the land of liberty for men of all nations except the Chinese. I consider it an insult to us Chinese to call on us to contribute toward the building in this land a pedestal for a statue of liberty. That statue represents liberty holding a torch which lights the passage of those of all nations who come into this country. But are the Chinese allowed to come? As for the Chinese who are here, are they allowed to enjoy liberty as men of all other nationalities enjoy it?"[65] For China's prodemocracy students in 1989 and for Asians in America, the "goddess of liberty," featured so prominently by the American news media, situated squarely within the mainstream, and lifting up her torch above the masses in Tiananmen Square, was not their symbol of liberation. Instead, their true symbol, relegated to the background as the camera panned the crowd, situated inconspicuously along the margins, was the declaration emblazoned by the Chinese students on the banners they waved, the shirts they wore, and the fliers they distributed: the words were "We Shall Overcome."

NOTES

1. I have taken the title of this chapter from a narrative history of African American women by Paula Giddings, *When and Where I Enter: The Impact of Black Women on Race and Sex in America* (New York: William Morrow, 1984).

2. Poems published in Him Mark Lai, Genny Lim, and Judy Yung, *Island: Poetry and History of Chinese Immigrants on Angel Island, 1910–1940* (Seattle: University of Washington Press, 1991), pp. 34, 52.

3. A third island, Sullivan's Island, was the point of entry for many African slaves during the eighteenth century. "Sullivan's Island," wrote historian Peter H. Wood, "the sandy spit on the northeast edge of Charlestown harbor where incoming slaves were briefly quarantined, might well be viewed as the Ellis Island of black Americans" (*Black Majority: Negroes in Colonial South Carolina from 1670 Through the Stono Rebellion* [New York: Alfred A. Knopf, 1975], p. xiv).

4. The text of the 1882 Chinese Exclusion Act is quoted in Cheng-Tsu Wu, ed, *"Chink!" A Documentary History of Anti-Chinese Prejudice in America* (New York: World Publishing, 1972), pp. 70–75.

5. John Higham, *Send These to Me: Jews and Other Immigrants in Urban America* (New York: Atheneum, 1975), pp. 71–72, 74, 75.

6. Ibid., pp. 75, 77, 79.

7. J. Hector St. John de Crèvecoeur, *Letters from an American Farmer* (New York: Fox, Duffield & Co., 1904), pp. 54–55.

8. Higham, *Send These to Me*, p. 3.

9. Ibid., p. 199.

10. Giddings, *When and Where I Enter*, pp. 81–82.

11. For Hippocrates, Asia meant Asia Minor, or the area between the Mediterranean and Black seas. Depending upon who was writing and when, Asia meant variously Asia Minor (or Anatolia), the Levant, Southwest Asia, Central Asia, or India. Generally, during the fifth and fourth centuries B.C.E. the Greeks called the Persians "Asians."

12. *Hippocrates*, trans. W. H. S. Jones (Cambridge: Harvard University Press, 1923), I:105–33.

13. *The Politics of Aristotle*, trans. Benjamin Jowett (Oxford: Clarendon Press, 1885), pp. 96, 218, 248. "Barbarians," it should be noted, could refer to Europeans, such as Thracians and Illyrians, as well as to Asians.

14. *Arrian's History of the Expedition of Alexander the Great, and Conquest of Persia*, trans. John Rooke (London: W. McDowall, 1813), pp. 112, 117, 123, 146.

15. Ibid., p. 42. Arrian was an Asian from Nicomedia in northern Turkey and wrote in Greek, despite serving as a Roman governor. See also Alexander's contrast of intelligent Greeks with Persian and Indian hordes in the influential work of late Greek literature *The Greek Alexander Romance*, trans. Richard Stoneman (London: Penguin Books, 1991), pp. 105, 128, 181, and a similar representation of Persians by Romans during the third century C.E. in Michael H. Dodgeon and Samuel N. C. Lieu, comps. and eds., *The Roman Eastern Frontier and the Persian Wars* (A.D. 226–363): *A Documentary History* (London: Routledge, 1991), pp. 19, 26.

16. Edward W. Said, *Orientalism* (New York: Random House, 1978), p. 1; and Mary B. Campbell, *The Witness and the Other World: Exotic European Travel Writing, 400–1600* (Ithaca: Cornell University Press, 1988), p. 3.

17. Campbell, *Witness*, pp. 51, 63–65, 68–69, 84. See also *Greek Alexander Romance*, p. 124.

18. Campbell, *Witness*, pp. 7–8 21, 26, 44–45.

19. Ibid., p. 3; and Said, *Orientalism*, p. I. See also Christopher Miller, *Blank Darkness: Africanist Discourse in French* (Chicago: University of Chicago Press, 1985), who contends that Africa was Europe's Other.

20. Said, *Orientalism*, pp. I, 59, 62, 72, 74, 86, 207–8, 211, 222. For a cautionary critique of Said, see Lisa Lowe, *Critical Terrains: French and British Orientalisms* (Ithaca: Cornell University Press, 1991).

21. The contest between Greece and Asia was a major theme in ancient Greek literature, as seen in the writings of Homer, Aeschylus, Euripides, Xenophon, and many others. The work of Herodotus, written in the fifth century B.C.E., is perhaps the best known example of this genre. I simply present a selection of the evidence.

22. *Arrian's History*, p. 220.

23. Ibid., pp. 112–13, 181, 205. Arrian was a Stoic philosopher, accounting for his stress on mind over body.

24. Page duBois, *Centaurs and Amazons: Women and the Pre-history of the Great Chain of Being* (Ann Arbor: University of Michigan Press, 1982), pp. 4–5.

25. Quoted in W. Blake Tyrrell, *Amazons: A Study in Athenian Mythmaking* (Baltimore: Johns Hopkins University Press, 1984), pp. 15–16. For another view of Amazons and their relation to Greek patriarchy, see duBois, *Centaurs and Amazons*, pp. 4–5, 34, 70.

26. On the ambiguities of Greek attributions of male and female and the rhetoric of discourse and reality of practice, see John J. Winkler, *The Constraints of Desire: The Anthropology of Sex and Gender in Ancient Greece* (New York: Routledge, 1990).

27. Campbell, *Witness*, pp. 88–89.

28. David Morgan, *The Mongols* (London: Basil Blackwell, 1986), pp. 56–57.

29. Campbell, *Witness*, p. 114.

30. *The Travels of Marco Polo the Venetian* (London: J. M. Dent, 1908), p. xi

31. Henry Hart, *Marco Polo: Venetian Adventure* (Norman: University of Oklahoma Press, 1967), pp. 117,135.

32. *The Travels of Sir John Mandeville* (London: Macmillan, 1900), pp. 127–28.

33. Campbell, *Witness*, pp. 10, 161; and *The Log of Christopher Columbus*, trans. Robert H., Fuson (Camden, Maine: International Marine Publishing, 1987), p. 25.

34. *Log of Christopher Columbus*, p. 51.

35. Ibid., pp. 75–76.

36. Campbell, *Witness*, pp. 171, 247. Walter Raleigh also believed the Orinoco led to paradise (ibid., pp. 246–47).

37. *Log of Christopher Columbus*, p. 102

38. Ibid., pp. 145, 173; and "Letter of Columbus," in *The Four Voyages of Columbus*, ed. and trans. Cecil Jane (New York: Dover Publications, 1988), p. 10.

39. Campbell, *Witness*, p. 166.

40. Albert Memi, *The Colonizer and the Colonized* (Boston: Beacon Press, 1967), p. 71.

41. Wilcomb E. Washburn, "Columbus: On and Off the Reservation," *National Review*, October 5, 1992, pp. 57–58.

42. See chapter 5, Gary Y. Okihero, *Margins and Mainstreams* (Washington University Press, 1994) for an elaboration of this theme.

43. Stuart Creighton Miller, *The Unwelcome Immigrants: The American Image of the Chinese, 1785–1882* (Berkeley and Los Angeles: University of California Press, 1969), pp. 11–14.

44. Dwight W. Hoover, *The Red and the Black* (Chicago: Rand McNally, 1976), p. 4.

45. I merely allude to the vast literature on the history of racism and racist thought and cite as particularly helpful Arthur O. Lovejoy, *The Great Chain of Being: A Study of the History of an Idea* (Cambridge: Harvard University Press, 1936); and George L. Mosse, *Toward the Final Solution: A History of European Racism* (New York: Howard Fertig, 1978).

46. Hoover, *Red and Black*, pp. 1–3; and David Brion Davis, *Slavery and Human Progress* (New York: Oxford University Press, 1984), pp. 52–57.

47. *The Complete Works of William Shakespeare* (New York: Walter J. Black, 1937), pp. 2–6; Ronald T. Takaki, *Iron Cages: Race and Culture in Nineteenth-Century American* (New York: Alfred A. Knopf, 1979), pp. 11–12; and Leslie A. Fiedler, *The Return of the Vanishing American* (New York: Stein & Day, 1968), pp. 42–49. See O. Mannoni, *Prospero and Caliban: The Psychology of Colonization*, trans. Pamela Powesland (London: Methuen, 1956), for a more complex reading of the play, esp. pp. 105–6.

48. Hoover, *Red and Black*, pp. 35–37.

49. See Winthrop Jordan, *White over Black* (Chapel Hill: University of North Carolina Press, 1968), for British and American racial attitudes toward Indians and Africans from 1550 to 1812.

50. Frederick M. Binder, *The Color Problem in Early National America as Viewed by John Adams, Jefferson and Jackson* (The Hague: Mouton, 1968), p. 83.

51. Quoted in Richard Drinnon, *Facing West: The Metaphysics of Indian-Hating and Empire-Building* (New York: New American Library, 1980), p. 65.

52. Ibid., pp. 80–81, 98; and Jordan, *White over Black*, pp. 475–81.

53. Drinnon, *Facing West*, p. 81.

54. Miller, *Unwelcome Immigrant*, pp. 21, 25–27, 34.

55. Ibid., pp. 27–32, 35.

56. The phrase "masculine thrust toward Asia" is from the title of chapter II of Takaki's *Iron Cages*, p. 253.

57. Robert Louis Stevenson, *Across the Plains, with Other Memories and Essays* (New York: Charles Scribner's Sons, 1900), pp. I, II, 26–27, 48, 60, 62; and Drinnon, *Facing West*, pp. 219–21.

58. Stevenson, *Across the Plains*, pp. 65–66.

59. Herman Melville, *The Confidence-Man: His Masquerade*, ed. Elizabeth S. Foster (New York: Hendricks House, 1954), pp. lxv–lxx, 164, 334–41; and Drinnon, *Facing West*, pp. 214–15.

60. Quoted in Drinnon, *Facing West*, p. 232.

61. Ibid., p. 267.

62. Ibid., pp. 277, 278.

63. Ibid., p. 331.

64. Takaki, *Iron Cages*, p. 229.

65. Renqiu Yu, *To Save China, To Save Ourselves: The Chinese Hand Laundry Alliance of New York* (Philadelphia: Temple University Press, 1992), pp. 199–200.

1. One of the underlying goals of Takaki's article is to "re-vision Asian American history." What does Takaki mean by this? Why is it important for Takaki to listen to the voices of his research subjects? What accounts for the fact that "Asian Americans belong to the fastest-growing ethnic minority in the United States"? Compare and contrast the experiences of early Asian immigrants with those of immigrants who arrived after 1965, and explain why this date is significant.

2. Provide examples of how the first wave of Asian immigrants was subject to discrimination legislated by the local, state, and federal governments of the United States. Under what conditions did anti-Asian legislation come about? What were the philosophical basis and the practical purposes for Asian exclusion?

3. How did early Western colonists perceive Asians as they reached the territories of Asia? How did Western perceptions of Asian peoples color the interactions between early European Americans and Asian immigrants in the United States? Does Okihiro seem to suggest that European images of Asians migrated with them when they first arrived in the United States? How are these images linked with the colonization of Asia, and of Asian America?

SUGGESTED READINGS

Chan, Sucheng. 1991. *Asian Americans: An Interpretive History*. Boston: Twayne.

Chang, Gordon. 1997. *Morning Glory, Evening Shadow: Yamato Ichihashi and His Internment Writings, 1942–1945*. Palo Alto, CA: Stanford University Press.

Cordova, Fred. 1983. *Filipinos: Forgotten Asian Americans*. Dubuque, Iowa: Kendall/Hunt Publishing.

Daniels, Roger. 1988. *Asian America: Chinese and Japanese in the United States since 1850*. Seattle: University of Washington Press.

Friday, Chris. 1994. *Organizing Asian American Labor: The Pacific Coast Canned Salmon Industry*. Philadelphia: Temple University Press.

Hess, Gary R. 1974. The Forgotten Asian Americans: The East Indian Community in the United States. *Pacific Historical Review* 43: 576–596.

Ichioka, Yuji. 1988. *Issei: The World of the First-Generation Japanese Immigrants*. New York: Free Press.

Lee, Mary Paik. 1990. *A Quiet Odyssey: A Pioneer Korean Woman in America*. Seattle: University of Washington Press.

Leonard, Karen. 1991. *Making Ethnic Choices: California's Punjabi-Mexican Americans, 1910–1980*. Philadelphia: Temple University Press.

Mazumdar, Sucheta. 1989. A Woman-Centered Perspective on Asian American History. Pp.1–22 in Asian American Women United of California (eds.), *Making Waves: An Anthology of Writings by and about Asian American Women*. Boston: Beacon Press.

Okihiro, Gary Y. 1994. *Margins and Mainstreams: Asians in American History and Culture*. Seattle: University of Washington Press.

Patterson, Wayne K. 1988. *The Korean Frontier in America: Immigration to Hawaii, 1896–1910*. Honolulu: University of Hawaii Press.

Salyer, Lucy E. 1995. *Law Harsh as Tigers: Chinese Immigrants and the Shaping of Modern Immigration Law*. Chapel Hill: University of North Carolina Press.

Sawada, Mitziko. 1996. *Tokyo Life, New York Dreams: Urban Japanese Visions of America.* Berkeley: University of California Press.

Sumida, Stephen H. 1991. *And the View from the Shore: Literary Traditions of Hawaii.* Seattle: University of Washington Press.

Takaki, Ron. 1983. *Pau Hana: Plantation Life and Labor in Hawaii, 1835–1920.* Honolulu: University of Hawaii Press.

Weglyn, Michi. 1976. *Years of Infamy: The Untold Story of America's Concentration Camps.* New York: Morrow.

Wong, K. Scott, and Sucheng Chan (eds.). 1998. *Claiming America: Constructing Chinese American Identities during the Exclusion Era.* Philadelphia: Temple University Press.

Yamamoto, Eric. 1999. *Interracial Justice: Conflict and Reconciliation in Post–Civil Rights America.* New York: New York University Press.

FILMS

Ding, Loni (producer/director). 1998. *Chinese in the Frontier West: An American Story* (60-minute documentary).

———. *The Color of Honor: The Japanese-American Soldier in World War II.*

Dong, Arthur. 1989. *Forbidden City, U.S.A.*

Ishizuka, Karen (producer), and Bob Nakamura (director). 1996. *Looking Like the Enemy.*

Kelly, Nancy, and Kenji Yamamoto. 1991. *Thousand Pieces of Gold.*

Lowe, Felicia (producer/director). 1988. *Carved in Silence* (45-minute docudrama).

Ohama, Corey (producer/director). 1997. *Double Solitaire* (20-minute documentary).

Wehman, John (producer/director). 1994. *Filipino Americans: Discovering Their Past for the Future* (54-minute documentary).

Part III

Traversing Borders

Contemporary Asian Immigration to the United States

Chapter Five

U.S. Immigration Policies and Asian Migration

Paul Ong and John M. Liu

In the fifty years preceding the landmark 1965 Immigration Act, Europe was the main origin of people permanently settling in the United States. After 1965, Asia became a major source of immigration. Constituting less than 4 percent of total U.S. immigration between 1921 and 1960, Asians comprised 35 percent of legal immigration from 1971 to 1980 and 42 percent from 1981 to 1989 (Bouvier and Gardner, 1986, 8, 17; Papademetriou, 1991, 48). From 1971 to 1989, more than 4 million Asians immigrated to the United States, primarily from China (including Hong Kong and Taiwan), India, Korea, the Philippines, and Vietnam.

Understanding the larger societal changes that produced this radical immigration shift is not simple. Disparate forces, opposing ideologies, and conflicting political-economic objectives have prevented the formulation of a logically coherent set of policies. The laws that were enacted were the products of compromise among competing goals articulated by various segments of U.S. society, divided along class and social lines. The United States has never had a consensus regarding immigration. For instance, opinion polls consistently show public opposition to expanding immigration, yet legislation often disregards this sentiment (Morris, 1985). Even when there has been a consensus, the high degree of uncertainty over the consequences of any law or regulation has compounded the difficulty of devising policies that optimally realize any given underlying goal. Often the unanticipated outcomes have differed greatly from the ones intended.

Despite the complexity and uncertainties, it is possible to detect the logic of U.S. immigration policy formation within the larger political economy. U.S. immigration policy objectives have fluctuated because the factors shaping both racial and labor issues have changed continuously. In the post–World War II era, global and domestic forces moved the nation toward liberalizing its immigration laws. Internally, the civil rights movement made state-supported racism less tenable than before. While this movement fought for the extension of political rights and later economic rights, the attack on de jure discrimination logically extended to the immigration arena. It would have been inconsistent and dangerous to allow racism to persist in the immigration laws.

Global forces were perhaps even more important than domestic ones. As the United States became inextricably drawn into the world system, it adopted policies intended to legitimize and protect its hegemony against the Soviet Union in an increasingly integrated but restive world. In terms of immigration, this meant formulating policies that preserved U.S. dominance and promoted its image as leader of the "free world," while maintaining the right to set numerical limits. Eliminating racial barriers, accepting large numbers of political refugees, and encouraging the immigration of highly educated individuals under a preferred occupational category were policies that arose from these strategic concerns.

After 1965, changing economic and political conditions led to several revisions that affected immigration from Asia. Declining job opportunities and lobbying by special interest groups brought about a restriction of occupational immigration in 1976. Economic forces later worked to loosen immigration constraints. In the face of a severe shortage of highly educated labor in the late 1980s, the Immigration Nursing Relief Act of 1989 and the Immigration Act of 1990 again turned to foreign sources to address the country's labor and economic shortfalls by providing special preference to immigrants that met requisite human and financial capital standards.

The Dismantling of Racial Restrictions

In the last one hundred years, U.S. immigration laws have treated Asians equivocally. No group encountered more discriminatory immigration legislation than Asians in the pre–World War II period (Konvitz, 1946). Yet, beginning during the war and continuing through the postwar period, a sudden and extraordinary reversal occurred as Asians became a major beneficiary of revised immigration policies.

Congress first levied restrictions against Asians in the Chinese Exclusion Act of 1882. Before the 1880s, the United States loosely regulated the number and types of people permitted to enter the country. Capitalists generally supported the unrestricted migration of able-bodied labor, especially after the Civil War, when the United States began an industrial ascendancy that would make it the leading industrial power by the turn of the century (Calavita, 1984). A newly emerging organized labor movement opposed capitalist support of unfettered immigration and was a major force in obtaining passage of the Exclusion Act, which prohibited the admission of unskilled Chinese workers (Saxton, 1971).

Nearly all subsequent immigration legislation regarding Asians in the pre–World War II period either iterated or extended the racial exclusions first inflicted on the Chinese. The Gentlemen's Agreement of 1907–1908 cast Japanese and Koreans into this exclusionary net, and the 1917 Immigration Act denied entry to Asian Indians. A provision in the 1924 Immigration Act reaffirmed these prohibitions by banning the admission of persons ineligible for citizenship, a category that included all Chinese, Japanese, Koreans, and Asian Indians. The Tydings-McDuffie Act in 1934 added Filipinos to the list of excludables. Although the primary purpose of this legislation was to grant independence to the Philippines by 1946, it also declared Filipinos to be aliens and limited their immigration to fifty persons per year.

Given this history, a waning of racial discrimination in World War II and its aftermath seemed unlikely, but fundamental internal and international changes chipped away at the racial hierarchy. Domestically, wartime exigencies required the hiring of nonwhites in industries previously closed to them. Expanded minority participation in industry and in the military unleashed demands for greater equity, a process encouraged by the federal government. In 1941, President Franklin Roosevelt signed Executive Order 8802, ending employment discrimination in defense industries and federal agencies.

International acceptance of the United States as wartime leader of the free world added pressure to abolish all racially discriminatory policies and to adopt immigration policies congruous with democracy's fight against fascism. President Roosevelt and his administration saw repeal of racially proscriptive laws as a particularly vital step in refuting Japanese propaganda condemning the United States for its anti-Asian immigration policies.

Ironically, the easing of bias against Asian immigration coincided with the United States' most devastating anti-Asian action, the incarceration of nearly 110,000 U.S. residents and citizens of Japanese descent in 1942. The following year, the discriminatory immigration walls began to crack with the lifting of restrictions against the Chinese, a wartime ally (Riggs, 1950). This time, organized labor no longer uniformly or adamantly fought for continued Chinese exclusion. Though the American Federation of Labor (AFL) favored the status quo, the Congress for Industrial Organization (CIO) advocated strongly for its termination. Roosevelt placated domestic fears by noting that the repeal of exclusion gave China an annual quota of only 105 persons. In exchange, the nation would gain an important symbolic victory in the international arena.

Quotas based on national origins persisted as a problem after the war. Emergence as a global power mandated additional social change if the United States was to preserve its international image and leadership. Decolonization, rising nationalism in Third World nations, and Communist expansion forced the nation to broaden the bases of its legitimacy. Its dominance as a world leader depended on more than possessing the most powerful military. The ability of the United States to enhance its political position hinged also on the eradication of the most blatant forms of racism, which many Asian and African countries regarded as an abominable colonial legacy. The Truman administration maintained, for example, that "the Chinese Communists will continue to exploit the xenophobia latent in most of Southeastern Asia for decades, implanted there in some part by the Oriental exclusion features of past American immigration law" (U.S. Congress, House, President's Commission on Immigration and Naturalization, 1952, 52).

Presidential urging alone was insufficient to eliminate racial inequality. Previous presidents had worried about the international repercussions of exclusionary immigration laws (Coolidge, 1909; Neu, 1967), but domestic racism generally had prevailed over foreign affairs. The anti-Chinese movement had forced President Rutherford Hayes to renegotiate the 1868 Burlingame Treaty with China to create a legal foundation for passage of the Chinese Exclusion Act. Two decades later, the anti-Japanese movement pushed President Theodore Roosevelt to negotiate the Gentlemen's Agreement with Japan. In the post–World War II period, a new global role meant the United States could no longer afford the international cost of domestic racism.

Congress soon repealed remaining constraints on immigration from India, the Philippines, Korea, and Japan.

These changes were possible because domestic racism was not as rabid as before. Economic growth in the postwar period allowed minorities to make political and economic gains that did not threaten whites. Employment and income advances translated into political improvements as racial minorities struggled for their civil rights, culminating in the passage of the 1964 Civil Rights Act and the 1965 Voting Rights Act (Burstein, 1985). The drive for racial justice created a sociopolitical context conducive to the obliteration of de jure discrimination in immigration laws.

Another important domestic development was the convergence of interests between capital and labor. Expanding productive activities placed capital in the forefront of promoting U.S. hegemony. Unlike the case in the pre–World War II period, organized labor now shared this national goal. Labor bolstered the status of the United States as a world leader by exporting its own brand of unionism to developing countries. At home the major unions relaxed their insistence on racial exclusion in immigration and later supported the end of racial quotas, a position compatible with their pro–civil rights stance. Nevertheless, labor refused to abandon its position that numerical limits were a necessary safeguard to keep immigration in line with the economy's absorptive capacity.

A coalescence of these diverse forces formed the background for the enactment of the new basic immigration law in 1952. Congress readily discarded the concept of Nordic superiority used to justify the discriminatory elements of the 1924 act. It canceled the general interdiction toward Asian immigration, thus completing the piecemeal repeals of earlier years (U.S. Congress, Senate, Committee on the Judiciary, 1950, 455, 458). Yet it was still unwilling to eliminate completely ethnic and racially biased quotas. Instead of placing Asians on an equal footing with other immigrants, Congress devised the Asia-Pacific Triangle, which roughly comprised all Asian countries from India to Japan and the Pacific Islands north of Australia and New Zealand. Nations falling within this area received an annual quota of only 100, with a ceiling of 2,000 for the entire region. Any person at least one-half Asian by ancestry would be charged against this Asian quota, even if that individual had been born in a nation outside the triangle. The determination of quota chargeability by blood rather than country of birth applied only to Asians.

Key members of Congress justified retaining the regional limitation because the act was more generous to Asians than was the national-origins formula used in the 1924 Immigration Act (Bennett, 1963). This contention was undeniably true, since there were no quotas for Asian nations in the 1924 act! Congress's argument additionally ignored the racial bias inherent in using the census to calculate the annual national-origin quotas. Because of earlier anti-Asian legislation, the Asian population was minuscule. Use of the census as the basis for national quotas merely perpetuated past discrimination toward Asians.

President Truman vetoed the 1952 Immigration Act, but Congress overrode him. In his veto message, Truman stated tersely that unjust treatment of Asians in the new law would damage foreign policy by hampering "the efforts we are making to rally the men of the east and west alike to the cause of freedom" (U.S. Congress,

House, President's Commission on Immigration and Naturalization, 1952, 276). In spite of Truman's concerns, the removal of biased quotas had to wait for more than another decade. As with civil rights legislation, progress was slow.

In the decade following the 1952 enactment, U.S. immigration law became a statutory maze as Congress haphazardly added amendments, primarily in relation to the admission of political refugees. In the early 1960s, both the executive branch and Congress initiated efforts to rationalize the 1952 act.

A concerted effort to abrogate all remaining discriminatory immigration laws and regulations emerged in the 1960 presidential election. The Democratic Party opposed the use of the 1920 national-origin quotas in its national party platform, a position John Kennedy, the Democratic candidate, actively supported throughout the campaign (Bennett, 1963, 265). On assuming power, Kennedy, and later Lyndon Johnson, worked to expunge all extant prejudicial provisions.

In contrast to the case in earlier decades, little organized resistance developed (Reimers, 1985, 67–69). Three factors explain the absence of a strong opposition. One was a favorable economic environment. The United States was in the midst of its longest sustained economic expansion. Unemployment in 1965 stood at 4.5 percent and was reaching the full-employment level. A second factor was the success of the civil rights movement. The struggle for voting and employment equality and the drive to end discriminatory immigration laws were mutually reinforcing. Finally, the perception that abolition of the Asia-Pacific Triangle was unlikely to lead to a huge ingress of Asians eased the fears of many interest groups. This combination of factors led to the 1965 Immigration Act, which overhauled previous immigration legislation, including removal of the national-origins quotas and the Asia-Pacific Triangle concept. The act brought an end to systematic discrimination against Asian immigrants.

The 1965 law reorganized the immigration system to favor family reunification in two ways. First, it instituted a new preference system that eventually allocated 80 percent of available visas to extended family relatives of U.S. citizens and to immediate family members of permanent residents. Second, it extended nonquota status to the parents of U.S. citizens, exempting them from any numerical limitations, a privilege already enjoyed by spouses and children of U.S. citizens.

Initially, the preference system applied only to the Eastern Hemisphere, that is, all countries and colonies other than those in the Caribbean and North and South America. Each nation had a maximum annual quota of 20,000 persons. In 1971, legislation removed all hemispheric distinctions to establish a single worldwide ceiling of 290,000 people. A reduction to 270,000 occurred in 1980 (Levine, Hill, and Warren, 1985, 20). These revisions placed Asians on an equal footing with immigrants from the Americas. Most of the parties concerned with immigration issues—the administration, Congress, and organizations favoring or fearing the nullification of racial bias—believed the new preference system would not result in large-scale immigration from Asia (Reimers, 1985, 75–77).

Despite perceptions at the time of passage, Asians gained much from the 1965 Immigration Act. Whereas they accounted for less than 7 percent of total immigration in 1965, their share increased to nearly 25 percent five years later. By the mid-1970s, Asians constituted well over one-third of all immigrants. In the first decade after the 1965 act, Asians entered primarily under the family reunification provisions, with a sizable number also admitted through occupational preferences (discussed in the next section).

The admission of refugees substantially increased the number of Asians during the late 1970s and early 1980s. Growing involvement, especially military involvement, by the United States in Third World nations such as Vietnam had produced new potential sources of immigration. With the fall of its political allies in the mid-1970s, the United States accepted thousands of Southeast Asian refugees, for both political and humanitarian reasons.[1] Asians, who were only 9 percent of the nearly 213,000 refugees in the 1960s, comprised 39 percent of 539,000 refugees in the 1970s. From 1981 to 1988, 70 percent of the 867,000 refugees came from Asia. The combined effect of family reunification, occupational entries, and refugees was to push the Asian share of total immigration to greater than 43 percent between 1975 and 1984 (U.S. Immigration and Naturalization Service, 1987, vii).

By 1989, however, the Asian share of legal immigration had dipped to 29 percent because of the increase of Latino immigration following passage of the 1986 Immigration Reform and Control Act (IRCA). IRCA attempted to control undocumented immigration by imposing sanctions on employers who continued to hire illegal migrant workers. It additionally offered amnesty to undocumented migrants who either had lived in the United States a specified amount of time or had worked as agricultural laborers. Of the nearly 3 million people applying for amnesty, the overwhelming majority was of Mexican ancestry. Only about 5 percent of the applicants were Asians (Bean, Vernez, and Keely, 1989, 69). Still, Asian immigration in absolute terms remained extremely high, totaling more than a quarter million per fiscal year during the latter half of the 1980s.

The Development of Occupational Preferences

The economic objectives and the political conflicts that arose over them are nowhere more apparent than in the debates surrounding the use of occupational preferences in the immigration laws. Because of the occupational quotas in the 1965 act, a major feature of contemporary migration has been the movement of professionals and other highly trained Asians to the United States. The origin of occupational preferences dates from the 1924 Immigration Act, which allocated the first 50 percent of visas to certain relatives of U.S. citizens, to skilled agricultural workers, and to the dependents of both groups. Inclusion of skilled workers resulted from the shortage of laborers in U.S. agriculture during the early 1920s. Thereafter, the use of occupational preferences was a permanent feature of U.S. immigration law.

After World War II, Congress redefined the occupational preference to favor individuals in technical fields such as engineering, science, and health. The desire for highly skilled labor reflected the growing technological complexity in production. Work became more fragmented and specialized, encouraging the emergence of a large technologically based and university-trained professional class. Military and industrial considerations also induced a shift in occupational needs.

The United States faced a potential shortage of manpower, a condition the Joint Congressional Committee on Atomic Energy believed would allow the Soviet Union to surpass the United States in military technology (U.S. Congress, Joint Committee on Atomic Energy, 1956, iii). There was reason for concern. In the mid-1950s, the United States fell behind the USSR in the number of students graduating in scientific and engineering fields (U.S. Congress, Joint Committee on Atomic Energy, 1956, 483). For many, the launching of Sputnik in 1957 was a sign of Soviet scientific superiority. The immediate U.S. response was to focus on improving its educational system. Immigration clearly had a central role in the long-range effort to catch the Soviets. The contributions of foreign scientists to the construction of the atomic bomb and later to the development of rocketry proved that highly educated immigrants were crucial to building a technological lead in military weapons.

Industry shared the need for highly educated labor. Reinforced by the founding of engineering departments at prestigious universities, formally educated engineers gained prominence as an essential component for continued industrial growth (Ahlstrom, 1982). The major problem facing industry in the first two decades of the postwar period was the scarcity of engineering personnel in the face of rising demand. A similar problem existed in the health field. The proliferation of private health insurance and the establishment of public health coverage generated an enormous demand for health practitioners.

An early attempt to fulfill these emerging needs through immigration came with passage of the Displaced Persons Act of 1948. Scientists and people with specialized technical skills were among the groups receiving the first 30 percent of visas allocated under the act (Hutchinson, 1981, 497). When Congress revamped the 1924 Immigration Act in 1952, it again gave first preference to the highly educated. In hearings conducted over the bill, officials from the Immigration and Naturalization Service proposed giving preferential treatment to persons who "would be of most value to the United States," because "industrial expansion would be facilitated if desirable specialists could be obtained from oversubscribed countries" (U.S. Congress, Senate, Committee on the Judiciary, 1950, 450–451). Although President Truman disagreed strongly with other provisions of the bill, he concurred with the request for skilled labor. His commission on immigration stated that the law "should encourage entry in the United States of persons whose skills, aptitudes, knowledge or experience are necessary or desirable for our economy, culture, defense, or security" (U.S. Congress, House, President's Commission on Immigration and Naturalization, 1952, 119–120).

One subcommittee recommended giving 30 percent of the quota and first preferential status to aliens and their families "whose services are urgently needed in the United States" (U.S. Congress, House, President's Commission on Immigration and Naturalization, 1952, 457). The final bill later raised this figure to 50 percent, with skilled workers defined as persons possessing "education, technical training, specialized experience, or exceptional ability" (Bennett, 1963, 141). In practice, scientists, engineers, and health practitioners dominated the list of qualified occupations. The

1952 act also left the door open for the admission of less skilled persons through a lower, nonpreference category, which received any unused quotas. These individuals could enter only when the Department of Labor certified that they were not taking jobs from U.S. workers.

Despite the favorable status accorded professionals and the highly educated, they comprised less than 6 percent of quota immigrants and only 2 percent of total immigration from 1954 to 1964. The United States failed to attract the targeted group of highly educated Europeans, because Europe enjoyed an economic boom in the postwar period, a prosperity ironically underwritten by the U.S. Marshall Plan. Since preferential treatment of the highly skilled and the highly educated continued to be oriented toward Europe and other developed nations, the numerical objectives established in the law represented what the United States desired rather than what was attainable. Continued low utilization of this category by Europeans led the National Commission for Manpower Policy to conclude that the labor certification program was largely ineffective (U.S. National Commission for Manpower Policy, 1978, 33, 56).

Although the 1952 act yielded little in the way of immediate results, it did have a delayed effect on the migration of highly educated labor. The law facilitated the admission of exchange students from developing countries who came here to acquire the technical skills necessary for economic growth in their home nations. When these students returned home, they brought back with them Western technical skills as well as the English language and U.S. values. Acquisition of these skills and cultural attributes created an international pool of highly educated labor that was, and is, highly substitutable. Possession of these qualities underlaid the future migration and integration of highly educated foreign workers into the U.S. economy.

Efforts to rewrite the immigration laws in the early 1960s led again to debates over the treatment of the highly educated. President Kennedy's administration favored retaining, as a first preference, half the quotas for "persons with special skills, training, or education advantageous to the United States." The Johnson administration kept this recommendation when it resumed negotiations around revising the law (Reimers, 1985, 66, 72). Congressional proposals differed from that of the executive. They sought to reserve 30 percent of the quota for occupational immigrants. The final bill retained only 20 percent of the quota for these workers because of the extreme underutilization of the 1952 provisions for qualified professionals and because of efforts to minimize changes in the ethnic composition of future immigration.

The 1965 act downgraded preferential treatment of highly educated persons by equally dividing the 20 percent of visas into a third and sixth preference. More than 20 percent could enter if quotas under the family preferences went unused. The third preference applied to qualified professionals. Individuals eligible for this preference required the sponsorship of neither a relative nor an employer because they held occupations on the Department of Labor's Schedule A, a list of jobs for which qualified U.S. workers were hard to find. Before the mid-1970s, the list included three groups: those with advanced degrees in particular fields, including the scientific fields; those with a bachelor's degree in eighteen academic specializations, primarily in engineering and the health fields; and the clergy. The sixth preference pertained to other skilled and unskilled workers employed in jobs where there was a domestic labor shortage.

Even with the downgrading of occupational preferences, there was an ironical increase in the total flows of the highly educated. The elimination of racial barriers combined with the continuation of occupation preferences, albeit at only 20 percent of the allocated quotas, created a window of opportunity for highly educated Asians and enabled the United States to reach its goal of acquiring needed workers through immigration. The potential for large-scale movement of highly educated Asians was considerable.

A ready pool of labor had already developed through the educational exchange programs discussed earlier. In the decades after World War II, the number of South and East Asian foreign students in U.S. colleges and universities grew impressively, from 10,000 in the mid-1950s to about 142,000 in the mid-1980s, with a disproportionate share studying in the technical fields (Institute of International Education, various years). The potential pool of immigrants expanded with the global spread of academic programs based on Western, primarily U.S., curricula. As foreign graduate students returned to professorships in their home countries, they introduced Western material and technology into their educational systems (Portes and Walton, 1981). Many Asian nations embraced Western-oriented systems of higher education to achieve international prestige and to reinforce internal class distinctions.

A second condition that prompted migration of highly educated Asians was an international disparity in the rewards to labor. Greater availability of high wages and professional opportunities in the United States than in the periphery provided material incentives for Asians to migrate. The discrepancy in rewards between Asia and the United States was not entirely due to happenstance. It was a historical product of the unequal relationship between developed and developing nations within the world system. The willingness of U.S. firms to hire highly educated immigrants provided the "pull." The fact that Asians who found employment as engineers experienced no discernible wage discrimination is one indication of how well the U.S. economy absorbed Asian professionals (Finn, 1985). Even among those unable to practice their profession, the benefits of working in a less prestigious job provided enough incentive for many to relocate in the United States.

The corresponding "push" arose from the inability of Asian countries to absorb their highly educated persons. Many sending Asian countries adopted an economic strategy—export-driven industrialization—that relied on labor-intensive economic development with minimal opportunities for highly educated labor. Even when developing countries pursued technical training as a developmental strategy, human resources often became available before they could be fully used by the economy.

With the relaxation of racial barriers, a significant migration of highly educated Asians began almost immediately after the enactment of the 1965 act. Many Asian physicians, nurses, engineers, and scientists entered without first obtaining individual clearance from the Department of Labor because their occupations were on Schedule A. Not all highly educated Asians came directly as immigrants. Nurses frequently entered the United States first as nonimmigrants on temporary visas, while engineers and scientists were often students. Once in the country, many readjusted their legal status to permanent residency.

The post-1965 entry procedures had a stunning impact on the size and ethnic composition of highly educated workers in the United States. In 1964, out of 5,762 immigrant scientists and engineers, only 14 percent came from Asia (National Science Foundation, 1972, 26). By 1970, the absolute number had increased to 13,337, with Asians comprising 62 percent of the total (National Science Foundation, 1972, 3). The increase among Asian immigrants was more than eightfold, while migration from the rest of the world remained stable. A similar change occurred in medicine. Of the 2,012 foreign medical graduates (FMGS) entering as permanent residents in 1965, 10 percent came from Asia, compared to 28 percent from Europe and 42 percent from North and Central America. FMGS admitted as permanent residents more than tripled to 7,144 by 1972, with Asians accounting for 70 percent of the total FMG population and just under one-quarter of all physicians available to enter the labor market (Interstudy, 1974, 660; Lee, 1975, 408–409). Among nurses, Asians accounted for 327 of the 3,430 immigrants in 1966. Nine years later, 4,183 of the 6,131 immigrant nurses were from Asia (U.S. Immigration and Naturalization Service, 1991).

Although these increases were sharp, the 20 percent allocation reserved for the third and sixth preferences still constrained the movement of highly educated Asians. Unlike their European counterparts, Asians overused the two occupational preferences. From 1965 to 1976, nearly 30 percent of the Asian immigrants, representing more than 185,000 persons, entered as occupational immigrants.

Economic Restructuring and Policy Revisions

. . . Economic restructuring . . . had a noticeable though inconsistent impact on immigration policies. Changes that centered on occupational preferences most overtly reflected the shifts in economic trends. Just as broader societal developments engendered interests that moved in diverse directions, immigration policies swung like a pendulum, first toward greater restriction and then toward relative relaxation.

Beginning in the early 1970s, the immigration of highly educated Asians diminished. In part, this downturn was due to greater reliance on family reunification preferences, which cut into the number of unused quotas that could be reassigned to the occupational categories. There was also an economic factor: declining job opportunities and increasing global competition. In the early 1970s, the United States underwent a period of protracted economic stagnation. The annual unemployment rate, which stood at 4.5 percent in 1965, climbed to 8.5 percent in 1975. By the 1982 recession, unemployment peaked at 9.7 percent, the highest level since the Great Depression. Average wages and salaries remained correspondingly stagnant, although some workers suffered more than others (Harrison and Bluestone, 1988).

The economic stagnation of the 1970s combined with the slowdown in military spending after the end of the Vietnam War to affect adversely the industries that employed highly educated workers. The High Technology Recruitment Index, which measures the demand for scientists and engineers, hit two deep troughs in 1971 and 1975 (*Manpower Comments*, 1987, 1). This period saw a noticeable decrease in the number of engineers who immigrated to the United States. Depressed economic conditions undermined the desirability of high levels of immigration and augmented efforts to modify the immigration laws.

Concurrently, efforts were made to rewrite the regulations governing highly educated persons. Congress amended the 1965 Immigration Act in 1976 to tighten entry requirements for third-preference professionals. The 1976 amendment required professionals to have "prearranged employment in order to acquire third preference status." Moreover, it was now the employer's responsibility to show that U.S. workers were negatively unaffected before a third-preference applicant could receive a labor certificate (Bodin, 1977, 39–41; Yochum and Agarwal, 1988, 266–67). These legislative changes, together with administrative rulings that drastically reduced the occupations receiving blanket certification, considerably slowed the entry of professionals. By the late 1970s, only dieticians with an advanced degree, physical therapists with a bachelor's degree, and those with exceptional abilities in the sciences still received blanket certification.

The Health Professions Educational Assistance Act of 1976 added qualitative barriers to the 1965 act. To gain admission as medical professionals, alien physicians and surgeons first had to pass the National Board of Medical Examiners' Examination or its equivalent, the Visa Qualifying Exam. They needed also to demonstrate a competency in oral and written English. The joint effect of the 1976 amendment and the Health Professions Act was to reduce significantly the total applications for labor certificates, from 24,857 in 1976 to 9,581 two years later. Over the next four years, applications never exceeded 65 percent of the peak year total in 1976 (Yochum and Agarwal, 1988, 270).

Nowhere was the role of interest groups more apparent than in medicine, where the number of FMGs had grown remarkably since the 1965 act. Asian FMGs represented one-fifth of all practicing physicians as well as one-third of the interns and residents in graduate training programs by the mid-1970s (Stevens, Goodman, and Mick, 1978, 1). Their sizable presence inevitably raised the issue of whether the United Stated required any more FMGS.

The U.S. Department of Health, Education, and Welfare (HEW) argued for continued use of FMGS (Fink, 1976, 2261–2265; Weinberger, 1975, 308–325). It contended that any growth in the output capacity of health professional schools ran the danger of producing a glut of physicians. From the government's perspective, FMGS offered more flexible control over the supply of physicians than did the continued expansion of medical schools (Interstudy, 1974).

The medical profession, working through its various associations, publications, and membership in public and quasi-public organizations, strove to convince Congress that there was no longer a doctor shortage. It argued that the supply of U.S. medical graduates (USMGS) more than adequately met the health needs of the U.S. public, especially if the federal government financed the opening of new medical schools (de Vise, 1974; Interstudy, 1974; U.S. Department of Health, Education, and

Welfare, 1975, 5467–5468). Physician lobbyists acknowledged that certain geographic areas faced a shortage of doctors. They attributed this fact to the uneven regional distribution of U.S. physicians, not to any absolute scarcity of doctors.

The medical profession buttressed its position with two additional arguments. It contended that, contrary to the original intent of the 1965 act, preferential treatment of FMGS contributed to the "brain drain" of developing nations. This position mirrored the accusation of some developing countries that easy entry into the United States robbed those nations of potentially valuable talent and of resources already invested in the training of nonreturning doctors. A second tack questioned the care provided by FMGS because of their high failure rates on the Educational Council for Foreign Medical Graduates exam and the Federal Licensure Examination.

The medical profession carried the day when it persuaded Congress to declare in the 1976 Health Professions Educational Act that a shortage of physicians no longer existed. This proclamation disqualified foreign doctors from the Department of Labor's list of needed occupations (Schedule A). Of course, curtailing the inflow of FMGS had its cost. Hospitals lacking the financial ability or prestige to attract large numbers of interns, residents, and staff physicians of U.S. citizenry had been a primary employer of FMGS. Yet the American Hospital Association (AHA) did not oppose efforts to have doctors removed from Schedule A or to stiffen entry requirements. Instead, the AHA worked quietly for the inclusion of waivers that ensured hospitals access to FMGS and foreign-trained nurses (Gehrig, 1975, 487–490).

Efforts to obstruct the migration of the highly educated extended to the engineering field in the early 1980s. In 1982, Congress debated a proposed law requiring foreign students to leave the country after graduation for at least two years before applying for admission to the United States (Scully, 1983). Had this regulation passed, it would have seriously interrupted the flow of Asian scientists and engineers by eliminating the possibility of their adjusting from student to permanent resident status. Employers, such as universities and high-tech firms dependent on foreign-born personnel, successfully lobbied against the proposal. The debates continued within the engineering profession. Some citizens pressed their complaints that the "illegal recruitment of foreign engineers poses a significant threat to the employment of U.S. engineers" (Shulman, 1987, 15). The Institute of Electrical and Electronic Engineers argued that if employers used existing workers more efficiently, the apparent shortage of engineers would disappear (Watanabe, 1989).

The tightening of occupational preferences slowed but did not halt the movement of highly educated Asians. A sizable number found alternate modes of entry by coming to the United States as visitors. Once in the country, they looked for firms willing to sponsor them for employment and permanent residency. Through this means, employers traditionally dependent on highly educated immigrant labor, such as electronic, chemical, and pharmaceutical firms, research and development companies, and other businesses requiring advanced degrees, partially avoided critical labor shortages (National Science Foundation, 1986). The other avenue of entry was through the more available family preferences. Highly educated persons entering during the late 1960s and early 1970s became eligible to sponsor relatives, many of whom were also professionals (Liu, Ong, and Rosenstein, 1991; Stevens, Goodman, and Mick, 1978). Through these various means of entry, professional and technical workers comprised 30 percent of the Asian immigrants who entered during the 1989 fiscal year and reported a prior occupation; Asian immigrants comprised 52 percent of professional and technical workers from throughout the world.

Whereas the economic stagnation of the 1970s produced greater restrictions on immigration, the economic recovery of the late 1980s had the opposite effect. The necessity for and dependence on foreign-born labor persisted even though the United States had overcome many of the macro restructuring problems that appeared in the 1970s. Alarming projections about the growing skills gap in the current and projected U.S. labor pool accompanied the intractable labor shortages. For example, the Hudson Institute, in a report prepared for the Department of Labor, indicated that the U.S. labor force at the turn of the century would be incapable of meeting the rising need for highly skilled, specially trained personnel in the increasingly sophisticated economy (*U.S. Code Congressional and Administrative News*, 1990, 6721).

Existing labor shortages and projections of continued shortages of skilled workers added momentum for passage of new immigration legislation. Because it was unlikely that sufficient U.S. workers could be trained quickly enough to meet legitimate employment needs, organizations such as the President's Council of Economic Advisors advocated assigning immigration a greater role in closing this gap:

> Immigration policy can also contribute to the smooth operation of the U.S. labor market in the 1990s. While continuing the humanitarian principles that have shaped immigration policies in the past, the Federal Government can encourage the immigration of workers with skills important to the economy, both by increasing the number of visas for workers with a job in hand and by increasing quota levels for potential immigrants with higher levels of basic and specific skills. (*U.S. Code Congressional and Administrative News*, 1990, 6721)

Despite the demand for foreign-born labor, the waiting period for immigrants of exceptional ability (third preference) was eighteen months, and applicants in the other employment category (sixth preference) faced a thirty-month wait (*U.S. Code Congressional and Administrative News*, 1990, 6722).

Responding to this situation, Congress initially resorted to piecemeal measures. It approved legislation in 1989 allowing 16,000 foreign nurses holding temporary work visas to become permanent residents (*Interpreter Releases*, 1989, 1316). A majority of those who qualified were Asians, primarily Filipinas. The law also streamlined the process to recruit new temporary foreign nurses and created a visa category (H-1A) for these workers.

The incessant need for highly educated personnel eventually led to a major revision of the immigration laws in the 1990 Immigration Act. This act instituted a new preference system based on three tracks, one each for family-sponsored, employment-based, and diversity immigrants. Highly educated immigrants benefited in several ways. First, segregating the employment-based preferences meant that the availability of occupational visas was no longer directly dependent on the number of people admitted as family immigrants. Second, the act more than doubled the allocated visas for occupational immigrants and their families, from 54,000 to

120,000, with 80,000 for high-level professionals and their families. Members of professions with advanced degrees or aliens of exceptional ability received 40,000 visas, as did skilled and unskilled workers (with a cap of 10,000 for the latter). Congress intended this new track to increase the percentage of employment-based immigrants within the total immigration (*U.S. Code Congressional and Administrative News*, 1990, 6716).

Highly educated persons also could gain admission through the diversity preference track if they came from countries that had sent fewer than 50,000 immigrants in the five years preceding 1990. Although this new track primarily favors immigrants from Europe (up to 40 percent of the initial 55,000 allocated visas in this category were for Ireland), certain Asian nations such as Indonesia and Malaysia are also potential beneficiaries.

Passage of the 1990 act elated employers that had become dependent on immigrant and temporary foreign labor, particularly hospitals, research universities, and high-tech firms. These few sectors of the U.S. economy cannot solely decide the future trajectory of immigration policy, however, as resistance from other interest groups remains formidable. The employment of Asian and other highly educated immigrants still leaves many unanswered questions about economic development in the United States.

While skilled labor was the primary economic target of the act, the law also eased the entry for capitalists by allocating 10,000 visas to employment-creating investors. This provision has placed the United States in direct competition with other advanced economies, such as Australia and Canada, for Asian capitalists. One group particularly sought after are persons from Hong Kong who are seeking haven before the 1997 political reabsorption of the colony by the People's Republic of China. Although family reunification has remained at the heart of the United States's immigration policy, attracting both human and financial capital has resurfaced as a major economic consideration in this period of economic restructuring.

Future Prospects

Countervailing forces make it difficult to project the rate of Asian immigration for the rest of the 1990s. For example, we will not likely witness a new wave of Asian refugees to match that of the late 1970s and early 1980s, because the administration is now more concerned with refugees from eastern Europe and the former Soviet Union. On the other hand, some factors encourage continued large-scale Asian immigration. As argued above, highly educated and capital-rich Asians stand to benefit from the 1990 act. The major effect of the relevant provisions will be to alter the composition of the class background of Asian immigrants rather than to increase the inflow dramatically.

The most potent source of growth lies in another element of the immigration law. Under both the 1965 and 1990 immigration acts, parents, spouses, and children of citizens are exempt from the quota limits. This exemption could lead to a chain immigration that greatly exceeds the limits established under the 1990 Immigration

Act. If individuals admitted through the exempted categories become citizens and then sponsor other family members through the nonquota provisions of the act, the multiplier effect could be quite large. Asian immigrants have been a major utilizer of the exempt categories. For the 1989 fiscal year, 125,000 immigrated from Asia under the quota provisions while another 86,000 gained admission as exempt immediate relatives (U.S. Immigration and Naturalization Service, 1990). Fourteen thousand of the latter were from the People's Republic of China, 15,000 were from Korea, and 11,000 were from India. The number of exempt immediate relatives from the Philippines (about 27,000) nearly equaled the European total of 29,000.

Over time, the use of the immediate-relative avenue of entry is likely to grow. A study by the U.S. General Accounting Office concluded:

> The Asian countries we studied, especially China, exhibited some of the characteristics anticipated to occur during extensive chain migration (for example, a high percentage of naturalized petitioners and relatively short times before the arrival of exempt-immediate relatives). (1988, 61)

Without new restrictions, it is likely that exempted immediate relative immigrants from Asia will outnumber those admitted through the quotas by the end of the century.

The one factor that may stem future Asian immigration is racism. Asians have not escaped the reemergence of overt racial discrimination in the United States. They have been the scapegoats for widespread anti-Japan sentiment and victims of hate crimes (California Attorney General's Asian/Pacific Advisory Committee, 1988; U.S. Commission on Civil Rights, 1986). Fortunately, race has yet to become a prominent issue in the immigration debates. This is not to deny that the narrowing of occupational preferences and the cap on immediate-relative immigration have had a disproportionately adverse impact on Asians. But the executive branch has enforced these restrictions without retracting its policy of eliminating racial barriers to immigration. Nonetheless, rising racial prejudices and hostilities threaten to contaminate the debate over immigration policies. An opinion poll conducted by the Roper organization indicates that most respondents believed that Europeans have on balance contributed positively to the United States. Under 50 percent held a similar view toward Asians (Roper Public Opinion Research Center, 1982). The decade-long congressional debates leading to the enactment of the 1990 act also evidenced uneasiness with the high levels of Asian immigration and a desire to increase immigration from Europe (Bean, Vernez, and Keely, 1989, 101).

Even in an era when defense spending may decline because of the political reforms and revolutions in the former USSR and eastern Europe, there is an enduring sentiment that dependency on highly educated Asians represents a threat in a world where economic competition between the United States and Asian newly industrialized countries (NICS) is intensifying. With economic growth and better research facilities, many Asian NICS are now in a stronger position to retain their highly educated labor and to recruit their compatriots working in the United States (Gittlesohn, 1989). Although return migration to the countries of origin has been small, the returnees possess technological knowledge that will enable the NICS to develop high-tech industries (Watanabe, 1989). If the United States loses more of its technological lead and its ability to control high-tech markets, there will be greater cries for a closing of its borders both to market competition from Asia and to the movement of Asians, particularly the highly educated.

The disquietude with Asian immigration hardly portends a return to the racist policies that existed before World War II. Two decades of Asian immigration have led to the formation of new advocacy groups among the immigrant population. They have become an important part of the political scene, within both the civil rights movement and mainstream electoral politics as voters, politicians, and sources of campaign funds. Asian American political strength helped counter congressional attempts to curtail drastically the family-sponsored preferences that had revitalized the Asian population in the United States. This political muscle also may prevent a renewal of blatant discrimination against Asians. But whether Asian Americans alone can completely contain those interest groups desiring to make U.S. immigration policy Eurocentric again is questionable.

It is unclear how the United States will weigh its competing domestic economic and political interests. Ambiguity about the U.S. role in the evolving global economy adds to the uncertainty about the direction immigration policy will take. Future changes are likely to be protracted processes, particularly if Asian Americans transfer their economic clout to both the domestic and international political arenas.

NOTE

1. The 1965 act included provisions for political refugees. Passage of the Refugee Act in 1980 removed refugees from the quota system and brought U.S. policy into conformity with the 1967 United Nations Protocol on Refugees. A refugee is defined as "any person who is outside his or her country of nationality and who is unable or unwilling to return to that country because of persecution or a well-founded fear of persecution." The president, in consultation with Congress, annually establishes the number of refugees that the United States will accept from different regions of the world.

REFERENCES

Ahlstrom, Goran. 1982. *Engineers and Industrial Growth.* London: Croom Helm.

Awasthi, Shri. 1968. *Migration of Indian Engineers, Scientists, Physicians to the United States.* IAMR Report no. 2/1968. New Delhi: Institute of Applied Manpower Research.

Baker, Lyle, and Paul Miller, eds. 1987. *The Economics of Immigration.* Proceedings of a conference at the Australian National University, 22–23 April 1987. Canberra: Australian Government Publishing Service.

Bean, Frank, Georges, Vernez, and Charles Keely. 1989. *Opening and Closing the Doors: Evaluating Immigration Reform and Control.* Lanham, Md.: University Press of America.

Bennett, Marion T. 1963. *American Immigration Policies: A History.* Washington, D.C.: Public Affairs Press.

Bhagwati, Jagdish N. 1976. *The Brain Drain and Taxation II: Theory and Empirical Analysis.* Amsterdam: North Holland; New York: American Elsevier.

Bodin, Aaron. 1977. "Labor Certification Programs." In *Tenth Annual Immigration and Naturalization Institute*, ed. Austin Fragomen, pp. 27–43. New York: Practicing Law Institute.

Bouvier, Leon F., and Robert W. Gardner. 1986. "Immigration to the U.S.: The Unfinished Story." *Population Bulletin* 41(4):1–50.

Briggs, Vernon M., Jr. 1984. *Immigration Policy and the American Labor Force.* Baltimore: Johns Hopkins University Press.

Burstein, Paul. 1985. *Discrimination, Jobs, and Politics: The Struggle for Equal Employment Opportunity in the United States since the New Deal.* Chicago: University of Chicago Press.

Calavita, Kitty. 1984. U.S. *Immigration Law and the Control of Labor, 1820–1924.* London: Academic Press.

California Attorney General's Asian/Pacific Advisory Committee. 1988. *Final Report.* Sacramento: Office of the Attorney General.

Coolidge, Mary R. 1909. *Chinese Immigration.* Reprint. New York: Arno Press, 1969.

de Vise, Pierre. 1974. "The Changing Supply of Physicians in California, Illinois, New York, and Ohio: Redistribution of Physicians since 1960 and Projections to 1990." In U.S. Congress, Senate, Committee on Labor and Public Welfare, *Health Manpower*, 1974, Part 2, Hearings before the Senate Committee on Labor and Public Welfare, 93d Cong., 2d sess., pp. 421–448. Washington, D.C.: Government Printing Office.

Engineers Joint Council. 1969. *Foreign-Born and Educated Engineering Manpower in the United States.* New York: Engineering Joint Council.

Fink, Paul. 1976. "Memo from E. Fuller Torrey, Presented to the Subcommittee on Health, November 18, 1975." In *Health Manpower Legislation*, 1975, Part 4, Hearings before the Senate Committee on Labor and Public Welfare, 94th Cong., 1st sess., pp. 2261–2265. Washington, D.C.: Government Printing Office.

Finn, Michael. 1985. *Foreign-National Scientists and Engineers in the U.S. Labor Force, 1972–1982.* Oak Ridge, Tenn.: Oak Ridge Associated Universities.

Gehrig, Leo J. 1975. "Statement before the Subcommittee on Health and the Environment, February 21, 1975." *In Health Manpower Programs*, Hearings before the House Committee on Interstate and Foreign Commerce, 94th Cong., 1st sess., pp. 487–499. Washington, D.C.: Government Printing Office.

Ghosh, B. N., and Roma Ghosh. 1982. *Economics of Brain Migration.* New Delhi: Deep and Deep Publications.

Gillette, Robert. 1989. "Threat to Security Cited in Rise of Foreign Engineers." *Los Angeles Times*, 20 January, pp. 8, 14.

Gittlesohn, John. 1989. "Surging Economy Spurs Many Asians to Return Home." *Chronicle of Higher Education*, 15 November, pp. A45–46.

Harper, Elizabeth J. 1979. *Immigration Laws of the United States.* 1978 Supplement. Indianapolis: Bobbs-Merrill.

Harrison, Bennett, and Barry Bluestone. 1988. *The Great U-Turn: Corporate Restructuring and the Polarizing of America.* New York: Basic Books.

Hutchinson, Edward P. 1981. *Legislative History of American Immigration Policy, 1798–1965.* Philadelphia: University of Pennsylvania Press.

Institute for International Education. Various years. *Open Doors: Report on International Exchange.* New York: Institute for International Education.

Interpreter Releases: Report and Analysis of Immigration and Nationality Law. 1989. 66 (4 December): 1316.

Interstudy. 1974. "Information Regarding Foreign Medical Graduates in the United States." In *Health Manpower, 1974,* Part 2, Hearings before the Senate Committee on Labor and Public Welfare, 93d Cong., 2d sess., pp. 648–730. Washington, D.C.: Government Printing Office.

Jasso, Guillermina, and Mark R. Rosenzweig. 1982. "Family Reunification and the Immigration Multiplier: U.S. Immigration Law, Origin-Country Conditions, and the Reproduction of Immigrants." *Demography* 23(3):291–312.

Konvitz, Milton. 1946. *The Alien and the Asiatic in American Law.* Ithaca, N.Y.: Cornell University Press.

Lee, Philip R. 1975. "Statement before the Subcommittee on Health and the Environment, February 20, 1975." In *Health Manpower Programs,* Hearings before the House Committee on Interstate and Foreign Commerce, 94th Cong., 1st sess., pp. 387–430. Washington, D.C.: Government Printing Office.

LeMay, Michael C. 1987. *From Open Door to Dutch Door: An Analysis of U.S. Immigration Policy since 1820.* New York: Praeger.

Levine, Daniel B., Kenneth Hill, and Robert Warren, eds. 1985. *Immigration Statistics: A Story of Neglect.* Washington, D.C.: National Academy Press.

Liu, John M., Paul M. Ong, and Carolyn Rosenstein. 1991. "Dual Chain Migration: Post-1965 Filipino Immigration to the United States." *International Migration Review* 25(3):487–513.

Mann, Arthur. 1979. *The One and the Many: Reflections on the American Identity.* Chicago: University of Chicago Press.

Manpower Comments. April 1987. Washington, D.C.: Scientific Manpower Commission.

Mink, Gwendolyn Rachel. 1982. "The Alien Nation of American Labor: Immigration, Nativism, and the Logic of Labor Politics in the United States, 1870–1925." Ph.D. dissertation, Cornell University, Ithaca, N.Y.

Morris, Milton D. 1985. *Immigration: The Beleaguered Bureaucracy.* Washington, D.C.: Brookings Institution.

National Research Council. 1988. *Foreign and Foreign-Born Engineers in the United States: Infusing Talent, Raising Issues.* Washington, D.C.: National Academy Press.

National Science Foundation. 1972. *Scientists, Engineers, and Physicians from Abroad: Trends through Fiscal Year 1970.* Washington, D.C.: Government Printing Office.

———. 1985. *Immigrant Scientists and Engineers, 1982–84.* Washington, D.C.: Government Printing Office.

———. 1986. "Survey of 300 U.S. Firms Finds One-Half Employ Foreign Scientists and Engineers." *Highlights, Science Resource Studies,* 28 February, pp. 1–4.

Neu, Charles. 1967. *An Uncertain Friendship: Theodore Roosevelt and Japan, 1906–1909.* Cambridge: Harvard University Press.

Niland, John. 1970. *The Asian Engineering Brain Drain.* Lexington, Mass.: Heath Lexington Books.

Papademetriou, Demetrios G. 1991. "Temporary Migration to the United States: Composition, Issues, Policies." Paper presented at the Joint East-West Center and University Research Center of Nihon University Conference, "International Manpower Flows and Foreign Investment in the Asia/Pacific Region," Tokyo, 8–13 September.

Papademetriou, Demetrios G., and Mark J. Miller, eds. 1983. *The Unavoidable Issue: U.S. Immigration Policy in the 1980s.* Philadelphia: Institute for the Study of Human Issues.

Portes, Alejandro, and John Walton. 1981. *Labor, Class, and the International System.* New York: Academic Press.

Reimers, David M. 1985. *Still the Golden Door: The Third World Comes to America.* New York: Columbia University Press.

Riggs, Fred W. 1950. *Pressures on Congress: A Study of the Repeal of Chinese Exclusion.* Reprint. Westport, Conn.: Greenwood Press, 1972.

Roper Public Opinion Research Center. 1982. *A Guide to Roper Center Resources for the Study of American Race Relations.* Storrs, Conn.: Ropert Public Opinion Research Center.

Rosenberg, Nathan. 1972. *Technology and American Economic Growth.* New York: Harper and Row.

Saxton, Alexander. 1971. *The Indispensable Enemy: Labor and the Anti-Chinese Movement in California.* Berkeley: University of California Press.

Scully, Malcolm G. 1983. "Senate Eases '2 year' Rule on Foreigners at U.S. Colleges." *Chronicle of Higher Education* 26(May 25): 18.

Shulman, Seth. 1987. "Engineers and Immigration." *Technology Review* 90(January): 15.

Smith, James, and Finis Welch. 1986. *Closing the Gap: Forty Years of Economic Progress for Blacks.* Santa Monica, Calif.: Rand Corporation.

Stevens, Rosemary, Louis W. Goodman, and Stephen S. Mick. 1978. *The Alien Doctors: Foreign Medical Graduates in American Hospitals.* New York: Wiley.

U.S. *Code Congressional and Administrative News.* 1990. "Legislative History of the Immigration Act of 1990." 8:6710–6801.

U.S. Commission on Civil Rights. 1986. *Recent Activities against Citizens and Residents of Asian Descent.* Clearinghouse Publication no. 88. Washington, D.C.: Government Printing Office.

U.S. Congress. House. Committee on Foreign Affairs. 1974. *Brain Drain: A Study of the Persistent Issue of International Scientific Mobility.* Prepared for the Subcommittee on National Security Policy and Scientific Developments. Washington, D.C.: Government Printing Office.

———. Committee on Government Operations. 1968. *The Brain Drain of Scientists, Engineers, and Physicians from the Developing Countries in the United States.* Hearing before a Subcommittee. 90th Cong., 2d sess. Washington, D.C.: Government Printing Office.

———. Committee on the Judiciary. 1977. *Foreign Medical Graduates.* Hearings before the Subcommittee on Immigration, Citizenship, and International Law. 95th Cong., 1st sess. Washington, D.C.: Government Printing Office.

———. President's Commission on Immigration and Naturalization. 1952. Hearings. Washington, D.C.: Government Printing Office.

U.S. Congress. Joint Committee on Atomic Energy. 1956. *Engineering and Scientific Manpower in the United States, Western Europe, and Soviet Russia.* Washington, D.C.: Government Printing Office.

U.S. Congress. Senate. Committee on the Judiciary. 1950. *The Immigration and Naturalization Systems of the United States.* Senate Report 1515. 80th Cong., 1st sess. Washington, D.C.: Government Printing Office.

U.S. Department of Health, Education, and Welfare. 1975. " 'H' Manpower Legislative Proposal." *Congressional Record* 121(March 6): 5467–5468.

U.S. General Accounting Office. 1988. *Immigration: The Future Flow of Legal Immigration to the United States.* Report to the Chairman, Subcommittee on Immigration and Refugee Affairs, Committee on the Judiciary, U.S. Senate. Washington, D.C.: Government Printing Office.

U.S. Immigration and Naturalization Service. 1987, 1989. *Statistical Yearbook of the Immigration and Naturalization Service.* Washington, D.C.: Government Printing Office.

———. 1990. *Immigration Statistics: FY89, Advance Report.* Washington, D.C.: Government Printing Office.

————. 1991. *Immigrants Admitted to the U.S., 1972–1991* [Computer file]. Washington, D.C.: Immigration and Naturalization Service [producer].

U.S. National Commission for Manpower Policy. 1978. *Manpower and Immigration Policies in the United States.* Special Report no. 20. Washington, D.C.: Government Printing Office.

U.S. President. 1989. *The President's Comprehensive Triennial Report on Immigration, 1989.* Washington, D.C.: Government Printing Office.

Watanabe, Teresa. 1989. "Taiwanese 'Brains' Leave U.S.," *Los Angeles Times,* 29 December, pp. A1, A26–27.

Weinberger, Caspar. 1975. "Statement before the Subcommittee on Health and the Environment, February 20, 1975." In *Health Manpower Programs,* Hearings before the House Committee on Interstate and Foreign Commerce, 94th Cong., 1st sess., pp. 308–326. Washington, D.C.: Government Printing Office.

Yochum, Gilbert, and Vinod Agarwal. 1988. "Permanent Labor Certifications for Alien Professionals, 1975–1982." *International Migration Review* 22(2):265–281.

Chapter Six

Vietnamese, Laotian, and Cambodian Americans

Rubén G. Rumbaut

In the years following the end of the Indochina War in 1975, over 1 million refugees and immigrants from Vietnam, Cambodia, and Laos arrived in the United States. Together with their American-born children, by 1990 they already represented more than one out of every seven Asian Americans, adding significantly not only to the size but to the diversity of the Asian-origin population in the United States. They are the newest Asian Americans, and the story of their migration and incorporation in America differs fundamentally in various ways from that of other Asian American ethnic groups.

To be sure, except for persons of Japanese descent, the overwhelming majority of Asian Americans today are foreign born, reflecting the central role of contemporary immigration in the formation of these ethnic groups. But unlike other Asians, most Indochinese[1] have come as refugees rather than as immigrants. Unlike post-1965 immigrants from the Philippines, South Korea, China, India, and elsewhere in Asia whose large-scale immigration was influenced by the abolition of racist quotas in U.S. immigration law, the Indochinese have entered outside of regular immigration channels as part of the largest refugee resettlement program in U.S. history, peaking in 1980 and continuing ever since. As refugees from three countries devastated by war and internecine conflicts, they have experienced contexts of exit far more traumatic than practically any other newcomers in recent times, and they have had no realistic prospect of return to their homelands. Moreover, their reception as refugees reflects a different legal-political entry status conferred by the U.S. government, a status that among other things facilitates access to a variety of public assistance programs to which other immigrants are not equally entitled. The American welfare state has shaped their incorporation far more than any other immigrant group in U.S. history, even as their exodus and resettlement were complex, unintended consequences of the intervention and ultimate failure of U.S. foreign policies and of the American warfare state. Indeed, the Indochinese case underscores the need to attend carefully to historical contexts, and particularly to the role of the state and of war itself, in explaining specific types of migrations and ethnic group formations.

Unlike the Chinese and Japanese, the Vietnamese, Laotians, and Cambodians do not share a history of several generations in America, a history marked early on by harsh discriminatory treatment and official exclusion. Unlike the Filipinos, they are not veterans of a half-century of direct U.S. colonization. At first the Indochinese could not be resettled into coethnic communities previously established by earlier immigration, because such communities were essentially nonexistent prior to 1975; in the resettlement process, they were more likely to be dispersed throughout the country than other large immigrant groups. Unlike recent Asian immigrant flows, most notably those from India, which have been characterized by large proportions of highly educated professionals and managers, the Indochinese flows, with the notable exception of the "first wave" of 1975 evacuees from South Vietnam, have been characterized by far larger proportions of rural, less educated people than any other Asian immigrant group in decades. There are also significant contrasts with other large refugee groups: for example, unlike refugees from Cuba and the former Soviet Union, who are among the oldest populations in the United States, the Indochinese are among the youngest, with median ages of less than twenty for all groups except the Vietnamese, partly a reflection of high levels of fertility. All of these particular sociodemographic characteristics and contexts of exit and reception have shaped their adaptation to the American economy and society.

As refugees of the Indochina War, they share a common history and experiences that distinguish them from other Asian American groups. However, the various Indochinese ethnic groups—Vietnamese, Khmer (Cambodian), lowland Lao, Hmong, Mien, and other Laotian and Vietnamese highlanders, and ethnic Chinese from all three countries—also differ from each other in fundamental ways. As we will see in this chapter, they have different social backgrounds, languages, cultures, and often adversarial histories, and they reflect different patterns of settlement and adaptation in America. They range from members of the elite of former U.S.-backed governments to Vietnamese and Chinese "boat people," survivors of the "killing fields" of Cambodia in the late 1970s, and preliterate swidden farmers from the highlands of northern Laos. And within each of these ethnic groups there are major differences, especially by social class, between different "waves" or cohorts of arrival and by gender and generation. Tens of thousands of Amerasians—children of Vietnamese mothers and American fathers who served in Vietnam during the war—have also been resettled in the United States under a special law enacted in 1987 (the Amerasian Homecoming Act); much discriminated against and stigmatized as *bui doi* (children of the "dust of life"), they too form yet another distinct and poignant legacy of the war.

Given its limitations, this chapter cannot consider each of these points in detail nor provide a comprehensive review of the large research literature that has accumulated on these topics over the past decade and a half; it will aim rather to provide an overview of the most salient patterns. The chapter will be organized in two main sections, moving from a review of the available data at the national level to more detailed survey and other comparative data collected in a major metropolitan area where Indochinese are concentrated. We begin, however, with a brief discussion of the war that led to the formation of Vietnamese, Cambodian, and Laotian communities in America. One of the ironies of the war that took America to Vietnam, and of the war's expansion into Cambodia and Laos, is that a sizable part of Vietnam, and also of Cambodia and Laos, has now come to America.

A Legacy of War: Indochinese Refugees in Historical Perspective

The Indochinese refugees are a product of the longest war in modern history—the thirty-year Vietnam War (1945–1975) and its metastasis into Laos and Cambodia in the 1960s and early 1970s. An immensely complex conflict that still creates bitter controversy and whose full significance will continue to be assessed and debated for years to come, the war was a tragedy of staggering proportions for Americans, Vietnamese, Cambodians, and Laotians alike. With the exception of the American Civil War a century earlier, the Vietnam War became the most divisive event in U.S. history. By war's end about 2.2 million American soldiers had served in Vietnam: their average age was nineteen, five to seven years younger than in other American wars—and almost 58,000 died there or were missing in action, their names memorialized on a wall of polished black granite dedicated in 1982 in the nation's capital. The war also cost the United States over $120 billion during 1965 to 1973 alone, triggering a postwar inflation and an economic chain reaction that shook the world economy. The war defined an entire generation of young people in the 1960s, polarized the American electorate into "hawks" and "doves," and led to President Lyndon Johnson's early retirement from politics in 1968 and ultimately to the Watergate scandals of the Nixon Administration in the early 1970s (Baskir & Strauss, 1978; Hess, 1990; Kolko, 1985; Young, 1991). "The first war that the United States ever lost" produced a "Vietnam syndrome" whose political ramifications still affect the formulation of American foreign policy—for example, President George Bush promised "no more Vietnams" before launching Operation Desert Storm in 1991. It also influences the trajectory of national elections—for example, the controversies over the Vietnam-era draft status of former Vice President Dan Quayle in 1988 and of President Bill Clinton in 1992.

The war also produced a massive refugee population for whom the United States assumed a historic responsibility. Not coincidentally, Vietnam represents at once the worst defeat of U.S. foreign policy in the Cold War era and the leading example (with Cuba) of the functions of U.S. refugee policy; Vietnamese (and Cubans) admitted as political refugees into the United States have served as potent symbols of the legitimacy of American power and global policy (cf. Pedraza-Bailey, 1985; Portes & Rumbaut, 1990). The circumstances of the U.S. withdrawal from Vietnam, the dramatic fall of Saigon, and its aftermath—and indeed, the extent to which such refugee flows have been a dialectical consequence of U.S. foreign policy in an era of East-West superpower rivalry (Gibney, 1991; Hein, 1993; Zolberg, Suhrke, & Aguayo, 1989; Zucker & Zucker, 1987)—also provided added moral and political justification for significantly expanded domestic refugee programs, which totaled some $5 billion in cash, medical assistance, and social services to primarily Indochinese refugees during 1975 to 1986 alone (Rumbaut, 1989b).

If the war divided America, it devastated Vietnam, Laos, and Cambodia. During the period of U.S. involvement, starting with the defeat of the French at Dien Bien Phu in 1954, it is estimated that over 4 million Vietnamese soldiers and civilians on both sides were killed or wounded—a casualty rate of nearly 10 percent of the total population. The total firepower used by the United States in Vietnam exceeded the amount used by the United States in all its previous wars combined, including both world wars. In South Vietnam alone, about a third of the population was internally displaced during the war, and over half of the total forest area and some 10 percent of the agricultural land was partially destroyed by aerial bombardment, tractor clearing, and chemical defoliation. (Research on the long-term health effects on the local population of the dumping of more than 11 million gallons of the toxic defoliant Agent Orange is still fragmentary.) In Laos the war exacted its greatest toll on the Hmong, an ethnic minority from the rural highlands who fought on the U.S. side against the Pathet Lao; before the fall of Vientiane about a third of the Hmong population had been uprooted by combat, and their casualty rates were proportionately ten times higher than those of American soldiers in Vietnam. In Cambodia, whose fate was sealed after the war expanded in 1970, as many as a quarter of its people may have died during the horror of the late 1970s. The war shattered the region's economy and traditional society. A tragedy of epic proportions, the "war that nobody won" left these three countries among the poorest in the world (Becker, 1986; Chanda, 1986; Isaacs, 1983; Karnow, 1991; Korn, 1991; Mason & Brown, 1983; Shawcross, 1984). By the mid-1980s, in an international economic ranking of 211 countries, Vietnam was ranked 202nd (with an estimated per capita national annual income of $130), Laos 208th ($100 per capita), and Cambodia 211th (the world's poorest at $50 per capita) (Rumbaut, 1991b).

Since the war's end in 1975, over 2 million refugees are known to have fled Vietnam, Laos, and Cambodia. The refugee exodus was shaped by complex political and economic factors. As is true of refugee movements elsewhere, the first waves of Indochinese refugees were disproportionately composed of elites who left because of ideological and political opposition to the new regimes, whereas later flows included masses of people of more modest backgrounds fleeing continuing regional conflicts and deteriorating economic conditions (Portes & Rumbaut, 1990; Rumbaut, 1989b). Vietnamese professionals and former notables were greatly overrepresented among those who were evacuated to American bases in Guam and the Philippines under emergency conditions during the fall of Saigon. Lao and Cambodian elites, by contrast, were much more likely to go to France (the former colonial power in Indochina), where French-speaking Indochinese communities, particularly in Paris, had developed as a result of more than half a century of previous migration.

Among the first to flee on foot across the Mekong River into Thailand were the Hmong, but they were the least likely to be resettled by Western countries at the time. Most were to languish in Thai camps for years. In Vietnam and Laos, meanwhile, several hundred thousand persons with ties to the former regimes were interned in "reeducation camps." Beginning in 1989, over 50,000 of those former Vietnamese political detainees would be resettled in the United States under special legislation. In Cambodia the cities were deurbanized as the population was forced into labor camps in the countryside; the capital of Phnom Penh became a ghost town practically overnight. But the exodus of the 1975 refugees was only the beginning of an emigration that has not yet run its course.

A massive increase of refugees beginning in late 1978 was triggered by a series of events:

The Vietnamese invasion of Cambodia, which quickly ended three years of Khmer Rouge rule

The subsequent border war between Vietnam and China in early 1979, which accelerated the expulsion of the ethnic Chinese petit bourgeoisie from Vietnam

A new guerrilla war in the Cambodian countryside, already wracked by famine and the destruction of the country's infrastructure

The collapse of both the Chao Pa guerrilla resistance against the Pathet Lao and the new system of collective agriculture in Laos, compounded by mismanagement and natural catastrophes

Hundreds of thousands of Cambodian survivors of the Pol Pot labor camps fled to the Thai border, along with increased flows of Hmong and other refugees from Laos; about 250,000 ethnic Chinese from North Vietnam moved across the border into China; and tens of thousands of Chinese and Vietnamese boat people attempted to cross the South China Sea packed in rickety crafts suitable only for river travel, many of whom drowned or were assaulted by Thai pirates preying on refugee boats in the Gulf of Thailand. By spring 1979 nearly 60,000 boat people were arriving monthly in the countries of the region.

These events led to an international resettlement crisis later that year, when those "first asylum" countries (principally Thailand, Malaysia, and Indonesia) refused to accept more refugees into their already swollen camps, often pushing boat refugees back out to sea (Malaysia alone pushed some 40,000 out) or forcing land refugees at gunpoint back across border mine fields (U.S. Committee for Refugees, 1985, 1986, 1987). In response, under agreements reached at the Geneva Conference in July 1979, Western countries began to absorb significant numbers of the refugee camp population in Southeast Asia.

In total, just over 1 million had been resettled in the United States by 1992 and 750,000 in other Western countries (principally Canada, Australia, and France); many others still languished in refugee camps from the Thai-Cambodian border to Hong Kong. Harsh "humane deterrence" policies and occasional attempts at forced repatriation sought to brake the flow of refugees to first-asylum countries, with limited success. After 1979 the number of boat refugee arrivals declined, but it never dropped below 20,000 annually (until abruptly coming to a halt in 1992, when boat arrivals totaled a mere forty-one, exacting a horrific cost in human lives: it has been estimated that at least 100,000 boat people, and perhaps over twice that number, drowned in the South China Sea (U.S. Committee for Refugees, 1987).

Beginning in the 1980s, an Orderly Departure Program (ODP) allowed the controlled immigration of thousands of Vietnamese directly from Vietnam to the United States, most recently focusing on two groups with a unique tie to the war, Amerasians and former reeducation camp internees. By the end of 1992, over 300,000 Vietnamese had immigrated to the United States through the ODP, including 161,400 in the regular family reunification program, 81,500 Amerasians and their accompanying relatives, and 61,000 former political prisoners and their families (U.S. Committee for Refugees, 1993, p. 86; U.S. General Accounting Office, 1994). But the Amerasian program ended in 1994, and refugee processing for former political prisoners ended in 1995. In Laos and Cambodia, meanwhile, refugee flows had virtually ended by the early 1990s, with the focus shifting to the voluntary repatriation of refugees still in camps in Thailand and elsewhere.

Indeed, an entire era was coming to a close, while a new phase of the Indochinese diaspora was opening. The end of the Cold War in 1989, the collapse of the former Soviet Union in 1991, U.N.-supervised elections in Cambodia in 1993 that sought to end its long-running civil war, and the end of the U.S. trade embargo against Vietnam in February 1994 were but the most remarkable events of a compressed period of extraordinarily rapid and fundamental changes in international relations that is transforming the nature of Indochinese refugee resettlement in the United States. In this post–Cold War context, the U.N. High Commissioner for Refugees proclaimed the 1990s the "decade of repatriation." Already most of the ODP family reunification cases in the 1990s have been leaving Vietnam as regular immigrants, not as refugees, a pattern likely to become more pronounced over time.

The flows from Laos and Cambodia to the United States have been, respectively, sharply reduced and virtually terminated. For some first-generation Indochinese adults exiled in America, the new developments in their homelands may open the possibility of return or of establishing business and other linkages between their native and adoptive countries (Kotkin, 1994a; Lam, 1994); but for a sizable and rapidly growing second generation of young Vietnamese, Laotian, and Cambodian Americans now rooted in communities throughout the United States and speaking accentless English, a new era was dawning in which the legacy of war will likely recede in practical importance. Theirs is an American future.

The Indochinese in America: A National Perspective

The research literature which has accumulated on Indochinese Americans over the past decade or so is surprisingly large, especially when compared to that of larger groups with much longer histories in the United States. As state-sponsored immigrants, the refugee status of this population has not only provided them with greater eligibility for various forms of government assistance, but in some respects it may have also made them an "overdocumented" population in comparison with other immigrants. Indeed, the 1975 refugees in particular may be the most closely studied arrival cohort in U.S. history.

In this section we summarize available information from a variety of national data sources to ascertain the size of the distinct Indochinese populations and to describe their patterns of immigration, settlement, and socioeconomic progress. In addition to the U.S. Bureau of the Census, these national data sources include the U.S. State Department, Immigration and Naturalization Service (INS), Internal Revenue Service, and the Office of Refugee Resettlement (ORR), established by the Refugee Act of 1980, and its predecessor, the Indochinese Refugee Program. In a subsequent section we review a wide range of findings from local studies of Vietnamese, Chinese-

Vietnamese, Cambodian, Lao, and Hmong ethnic groups, to examine in more depth their adaptation processes, including such topics as mental health, pregnancy outcomes, and the educational progress of their children. There are a number of advantages and disadvantages to both the national and local studies and available data sets, and these will be pointed out in the course of the discussion.

Immigration History and Population Size

Among Asian Americans, the Indochinese constitute the most recently formed ethnic groups. According to the INS, the first recorded Vietnamese immigration to the United States occurred in 1952, when eight immigrants were admitted; the first Cambodian immigrant arrived in 1953, and the first Laotian in 1959 (Immigration and Naturalization Service, 1991). As late as 1969, fewer than 200 Cambodians and Laotians combined had immigrated to the United States, and the total from Vietnam amounted to little more than 3,000—mostly university students from elite families, as well as diplomats and war brides who had come in the late 1960s in the wake of the rapid expansion of U.S. involvement in Vietnam. As Table 6.1 shows, in the early 1970s the number of these pioneer immigrants quintupled to nearly 15,000 from Vietnam, whereas it increased only slightly to nearly 300 each from Cambodia and Laos. Thus, when Saigon fell in April 1975, the Vietnamese in America numbered about 20,000, whereas the number of Cambodians and Laotians was still negligible.

About 130,000 refugees, nearly all from South Vietnam, were resettled in the United States during 1975. A small number arrived during 1976 to 1978, bottoming out in 1977, but a massive new inflow began in late 1978 in the context of the international refugee crisis described earlier. As Table 6.1 shows, about 450,000 Indochinese refugees arrived en masse during 1979 to 1982 alone, peaking in 1980 (the record year in U.S. refugee resettlement history) when 167,000 were admitted. Since 1982, Indochinese arrivals have oscillated between 40,000 and 80,000 annually. Vietnamese refugee admissions, totaling over 650,000 from 1975 to 1992, have been supplemented by a substantial, if little noticed, flow of over 170,000 nonrefugee Vietnamese immigrants who arrived in the United States during the same period— the latter including persons coming to the United States from other countries and from Vietnam through the ODP, among them the young Amerasians and accompanying relatives mentioned earlier. By 1992, total Indochinese arrivals numbered 1,223,699: 147,850 Cambodians (12 percent), 230,385 Laotians (19 percent), and 845,464 Vietnamese (69 percent). Of that total, 86 percent entered as refugees (the remainder as immigrants), and four out of five arrived in the United States since 1980. U.S. government agencies collect these data only by nationality, not ethnicity, so it is not possible to determine the proportion of ethnic Chinese and other minority groups among them; however, ORR estimates that, of the 213,519 Laotian arrivals during 1975 to 1990, 92,700 were highlanders, primarily Hmong.

Immigration statistics do not include children born in the United States. A study of the newcomers' fertility patterns calculated this number at nearly 200,000 by 1985 (Rumbaut & Weeks, 1986). Allowing for natural increase, and adjusting for mortality (which is low because this is a very young population) and emigration (which is

TABLE 6.1

Arrivals in the United States from Cambodia, Laos, and Vietnam, 1952–1992: Refugees, 1975–1992; Nonrefugee Vietnamese Immigrants, 1975–1992; and Pre-1975 Immigrants

| Fiscal year | Post-1975 refugee arrivals | | | Nonrefugee immigrants Vietnam[a] | Total |
	Cambodia	Laos	Vietnam		
1992	193	7,272	26,841	45,580	79,886
1991	199	9,232	28,450	33,764	71,645
1990	2,323	8,719	27,714	28,271	67,027
1989	1,916	12,432	22,664	15,880	52,892
1988	2,805	14,556	17,654	4,391	39,406
1987	1,539	15,564	23,012	3,635	43,750
1986	9,789	12,869	22,796	6,068	51,522
1985	19,097	5,416	25,457	5,134	55,104
1984	19,851	7,291	24,818	5,244	57,204
1983	13,114	2,835	23,459	3,290	42,698
1982	20,234	9,437	43,656	3,083	76,410
1981	27,100	19,300	86,100	2,180	134,680
1980	16,000	55,500	95,200	1,986	168,686
1979	6,000	30,200	44,500	2,065	82,765
1978	1,300	8,000	11,100	2,892	23,292
1977	300	400	1,900	3,194	5,794
1976[b]	1,100	10,200	3,200	4,201	18,701
1975	4,600	800	125,000	3,038	133,438
Subtotal:	147,460	230,023	653,521	173,896	1,204,900

| Period | Pre-1975 immigrant arrivals | | | | Total |
	Cambodia	Laos	Vietnam		
1970–1974[c]	286	292	14,661		15,219
1960–1969	98	69	3,167		3,334
1952–1959	6	1	219		226
Subtotal	390	362	18,047		18,799
Total, 1952–1992	147,850	230,385	845,464		1,223,699

NOTE: Refugee arrivals from 1975 to 1981 are rounded to the nearest hundred.

   [a.] Totals include 55,985 Amerasians from Vietnam admitted as immigrants in fiscal year 1989–1992.

   [b.] The totals for 1976 include a transition quarter as a result of fiscal year changes.

   [c.] Totals include 98 Cambodians and 96 Laotians who entered as immigrants in fiscal year 1975.

SOURCE: Compiled from records maintained by the Statistics Division, U.S. Immigration and Naturalization Service; U.S. State Department; and U.S. Office of Refugee Resettlement.

negligible), Bouvier and Agresta (1987) projected a 1990 Indochinese population of over 1.3 million, including 859,600 Vietnamese, 259,700 Laotians, and 185,300 Cambodians. But the 1990 U.S. census counted only 614,547 Vietnamese (well below even the number of actual arrivals from Vietnam since 1975—see table 6.1); a Laotian population of 239,096 (including 90,082 Hmong); and a Cambodian population of 147,411. Taken together, the 1990 census count of these Indochinese groups totaled just over 1 million, well below all available projections.

What accounts for such a significant disparity, especially among the Vietnamese? The gap is too large to be explained by a census undercount, which probably did not exceed 5 percent among the Vietnamese in particular. One clue is that the 1990 census also counted a Chinese population of 1,645,472—well above what had been expected (e.g., Bouvier and Agresta had projected a 1990 Chinese population of 1,259,038). It appears that sizable numbers of ethnic Chinese from Vietnam, Laos, and Cambodia indicated their ethnicity as Chinese in response to the appropriate census question. Earlier research had estimated that ethnic Chinese from Vietnam accounted for up to 25 percent of total Vietnamese arrivals and up to 15 percent of total Cambodian arrivals (Rumbaut & Weeks, 1986; cf. Whitmore, 1985). Applying these proportions to the 1990 census figures would yield an additional 200,000 from Vietnam and 20,000 from Cambodia, bringing the total Indochinese population in the United States more closely in line with both immigration and natural increase data. Future research on Indochinese Americans based on 1990 census data should be cognizant of the ambiguity surrounding ethnicity, birthplace, and country of last residence (all of which may differ), and of the apparent exclusion of sizable numbers of these ethnic Chinese groups. It is also not clear how Amerasians from Vietnam may have responded to census questions on race and ethnicity, although most Amerasians arrived in the United States after the 1990 census was taken.

Patterns of Settlement

The 130,000 (mostly Vietnamese) refugees who arrived in the United States during 1975 were first sent to four government reception centers—at Camp Pendleton, California; Fort Indiantown Gap, Pennsylvania; Fort Chaffee, Arkansas; and Eglin Air Force Base, Florida—where they were interviewed by voluntary agencies and matched with sponsors throughout the country, including individuals, church groups, and other organizations (for studies of the refugees sent to Fort Indiantown Gap and Camp Pendleton, respectively, see Kelly, 1977, and Liu, Lamanna, & Murata, 1979). U.S. refugee placement policy aimed to disperse the refugee population to all fifty states in order to minimize any negative impacts on receiving communities ("to avoid another Miami," as one planner put it, referring to the huge concentration of Cuban refugees there), and indeed the 1975 Indochinese refugees were more significantly dispersed than other immigrant or refugee populations (Forbes, 1984).

One study (Baker & North, 1984) found that the refugees were initially placed in 813 separate zip code areas in every state, including Alaska, with about two-thirds settling in zip code areas that had fewer than 500 refugees and only 8.5 percent settling in places with more than 3,000 refugees. Less than half were sent to the state of their choice. Despite this general pattern of dispersal—shaped by government policy, the availability of sponsorships, and the relative absence of family ties and previously established ethnic communities in the United States—areas of Indochinese concentration nonetheless began to emerge, particularly in California, and to grow rapidly as a result of secondary migration from other states. Significantly, by 1980, 45 percent of the 1975 arrivals lived in a state other than the one where they had been originally sent; the proportion in zip code areas with fewer than 500 refugees had dropped to 40 percent, whereas those residing in places with more than 3,000 had more than doubled to 20 percent. The proportion of the refugee population living in California had doubled from about 20 percent to 40 percent; these were concentrated in Southern California metropolitan areas (Los Angeles, Orange, and San Diego counties) and, to the north, in the Silicon Valley city of San Jose.

As the much larger waves of Indochinese refugees began to arrive in the late 1970s and especially during the 1980s, their patterns of settlement continued to be shaped by the factors noted above, especially by the social networks that were becoming increasingly consolidated over time. Government policies and programs (such as the

Khmer Guided Placement Project—dubbed the "Khmer Refrigerator Project" by Cambodians because of its Frostbelt locations—and the Favorable Alternative Sites Project) sought the dispersal of refugees without family ties away from high-impact areas, whereas most others were reunited with family members already residing in areas of high concentration (Finnan & Cooperstein, 1983; Forbes, 1984, 1985). Remarkably, by the early 1980s about a third of arriving refugees already had close relatives in the United States who could serve as sponsors, and another third had more distant relatives, leaving only the remaining third without kinship ties subject to the dispersal policy (cf. Hein, 1993).

In addition, different localities of concentration emerged for the different ethnic groups, with the largest Cambodian community in the nation developing in the Long Beach area of Los Angeles County, the largest Lao enclave in San Diego, and the largest Hmong community around Fresno, in California's agricultural San Joaquin Valley (in the Fresno telephone directory, the Vangs—one of but two dozen Hmong clan names—are as numerous as the Joneses). By 1990 the largest Vietnamese concentration in the United States was found in Orange County, with its hub in the communities of Santa Ana and Westminster (Little Saigon); among recent Orange County home buyers, the Nguyens outnumbered the Smiths two to one (Kotkin, 1994b). Los Angeles, San Jose (where the Nguyens outnumbered the Joneses in the phone book fourteen columns to eight), San Diego, and Houston followed in rank order. But Indochinese Americans continue to reside in every state of the nation, as the 1990 census makes clear, and their patterns of settlement differ in some significant ways from those of other Asian Americans.

With the earlier caveat in mind about missing data for ethnic Chinese from the Indochinese totals, Table 6.2 breaks down 1990 census data by selected states of settlement of Vietnamese, Cambodian, Lao, and Hmong groups. Although California is home for 12 percent of the total U.S. population, 39 percent of the Lao—and of all Asian Americans, for that matter—live there; the degree of concentration in California is even greater for the Vietnamese (46 percent), the Cambodians (46 percent), and the Hmong (52 percent). By contrast, whereas over 20 percent of Asian Americans reside in New York/New Jersey and Hawaii (compared to 10 percent of the U.S. population), less than 4 percent of all Indochinese have settled in those states.

After California, the Vietnamese are most concentrated in Texas (11 percent), with sizable communities in Houston and Dallas (which began to be formed by the 1975 cohort, attracted by employment opportunities), and along the Gulf coast (especially of shrimp fishers). Remarkably, the Vietnamese are already the largest Asian-origin group in Texas and in the contiguous states of Louisiana, Mississippi, Arkansas, Kansas, and Oklahoma. After California, another 17 percent of all Cambodians are concentrated bicoastally in Massachusetts and Washington, and despite their comparatively small numbers they are the largest Asian-origin group in Rhode Island (see Martin, 1986). The Lao are the most dispersed among the Indochinese groups, and they do not predominate in any state; but the Hmong are the most concentrated, with another 37 percent located in the contiguous states of Minnesota and Wisconsin, where they are by far the largest Asian-origin group—an extraordinary development

TABLE 6.2

Selected States of Settlement of Vietnamese, Cambodian, and Laotian Groups in the United States, Compared to the Total U.S. Population and the Total Asian-Origin Population, 1990ᵃ

	Total population	Total Asian	Vietnamese	Cambodian	Lao	Hmong
Total U.S. (N)	248,709,873	6,908,638	614,547	147,411	149,014	90,082
(%)	100.0	100.0	100.0	100.0	100.0	100.0
Proportionately Above-Average States of Indochinese Settlement:						
California	29,760,021	2,735,060	280,223	68,190	58,058	46,892
	12.0	39.6	45.6	46.3	39.0	52.1
Texas	16,986,510	311,918	69,636	5,887	9,332	176
	6.8	4.5	11.3	4.0	6.3	0.2
Virginia	6,187,358	156,036	20,693	3,889	2,589	7
	2.5	2.3	3.4	2.6	1.7	0.0
Massachusetts	5,016,425	142,127	15,449	14,058	3,985	248
	2.4	2.1	2.5	9.5	2.7	0.3
Washington	4,866,692	195,918	18,696	11,096	6,191	741
	1.9	2.8	3.0	7.5	4.2	0.8
Wisconsin	4,891,769	52,782	2,494	521	3,622	16,373
	2.0	0.8	0.4	0.4	2.4	18.2
Minnesota	4,375,099	76,952	9,347	3,858	6,381	16,833
	1.8	1.1	1.5	2.6	4.3	18.7
Proportionately Below-Average States of Indochinese Settlement:						
New York	17,990,455	689,303	15,555	3,646	3,253	165
	7.2	10.0	2.5	2.5	2.2	0.2
Florida	12,937,926	149,856	16,346	1,617	2,423	7
	5.2	2.2	2.7	1.1	1.6	0.0
Pennsylvania	11,881,643	135,784	15,887	5,495	2,046	358
	4.8	2.0	2.6	3.7	1.4	0.4
Illinois	11,430,602	282,569	10,309	3,026	4,985	433
	4.6	4.1	1.7	2.1	3.3	0.5
Ohio	10,847,115	89,723	4,964	2,213	2,578	253
	4.4	1.3	0.8	1.5	1.7	0.3
Michigan	9,295,297	103,501	6,117	874	2,190	2,257
	3.7	1.5	1.0	0.6	1.5	2.5
New Jersey	7,730,188	270,839	7,330	475	478	25
	3.1	3.9	1.2	0.3	0.3	0.0

ᵃ These Indochinese population totals derive from the 1990 census question on race, which listed Vietnamese, Cambodian, Laos, Hmong, and Chinese among the available choices. As noted in the text, it appears that ethnic Chinese from Vietnam, Cambodia, and Laos indicated their ethnicity as Chinese in response to that census question, thereby significantly increasing the Chinese population counted by the 1990 census and decreasing that for the respective Indochinese groups. As many as 200,000 ethnic Chinese from Vietnam and 20,000 ethnic Chinese from Cambodia may be included among the 1,645,472 Chinese reported by the 1990 census.

SOURCE: Adapted from U.S. Bureau of the Census (1993a, Table 253). These data report the official census counts (100 percent tabulations); by contrast, because the data in Table 6.3 are based on a sample, group sizes may differ.

considering that prior to 1975 there had been virtually no immigration from Laos to America.

Social and Economic Characteristics

National data on social and economic characteristics of Vietnamese, Cambodian, and Laotian Americans are available from two main sources: the decennial census and annual government surveys of nationwide samples. Only the census reports data by ethnic groups (except, as noted, for the ethnic Chinese); data from the latter are reported only in aggregate form for the Indochinese as a whole. Here we discuss available information from both sources.

Table 6.3 presents a summary of socioeconomic characteristics from the 1990

TABLE 6.3

Social and Economic Characteristics of Vietnamese, Cambodian, and Laotian Groups in the United States, Compared to the Total U.S. Population and the Total Asian-Origin Population, 1990

	Total U.S.	Total Asian	Vietnamese	Cambodian	Laos	Hmong
Total persons	248,709,873	6,876,394	593,213	149,047	147,375	94,439
Nativity and immigration						
% born in the U.S.	92.1	34.4	20.1	20.9	20.6	34.8
% immigrated pre-1980	4.5	27.9	30.5	9.4	16.3	15.7
% immigrated 1980–1990	3.5	37.8	49.3	69.6	63.1	49.5
Age						
Median age	33.0	29.2	25.6	19.7	20.5	12.7
Median age (U.S. born)	32.5	14.7	6.7	4.7	5.4	5.2
Family contexts[a]						
Fertility per woman 35–44	2.0	1.9	2.5	3.4	3.5	6.1
% female householder	16.0	11.5	15.9	25.4	11.3	13.6
% with own children <18 years	48.2	59.2	69.0	83.8	82.8	90.1
% children <18 with 2 parents	73.0	84.6	76.6	71.0	82.6	86.2
English (persons over 5)[b]						
% speak English only	86.2	24.6	6.2	4.0	3.2	2.6
% does not speak "very well"	6.1	39.8	60.8	70.0	67.8	76.1
% linguistically isolated	3.5	25.1	42.1	54.7	51.5	59.8
Education (persons over 25)						
% less than 5th grade	2.7	7.1	11.4	40.7	33.9	54.9
% high school graduate	75.2	77.6	61.2	34.9	40.0	31.1
% college graduate	20.3	37.7	17.4	4.7	5.4	4.9
% postgraduate degree	7.2	14.4	4.4	1.6	1.5	1.5
Employment (persons over 16)[c]						
% in labor force	65.3	67.4	64.5	46.5	58.0	29.3
% unemployed	6.3	5.2	8.4	10.3	9.3	17.9
Of those employed						
% upper white-collar	26.4	31.2	17.6	9.8	5.0	12.8
% lower white-collar	31.7	33.3	29.5	23.3	15.2	18.9
% upper blue-collar	11.4	7.8	15.7	17.2	19.8	13.9
% lower blue-collar	14.9	11.9	20.9	30.0	43.9	32.1
Income						
Median family income ($)	35,225	41,583	30,550	18,126	23,101	14,327
Per capita income ($)	14,420	13,806	9,033	5,121	5,597	2,692
% below poverty	13.1	14.0	25.7	42.6	34.7	63.6
% receives public assistance	7.5	9.8	24.5	51.1	35.4	67.1
% own home	64.2	48.3	40.1	19.7	24.0	11.1

[a] Fertility is measured by: children ever born per woman aged 35–44.

[b] Linguistically isolated means a household in which no person age 14 or older speaks English only or very well.

[c] Upper white-collar are professionals, executives, managers; lower white-collar are clerical, sales; upper blue-collar are repair, craft; lower blue-collar are operators, fabricators, laborers.

SOURCE: U.S. Bureau of the Census (1993b). These data are based on a sample (not the 100 percent tabulations) and are subject to sample variability; group sizes may differ from Table 6.2.

census, comparing the main Indochinese ethnic groups to each other and to the total U.S. and Asian-origin populations. These data underscore the significant differences between the various Indochinese ethnic groups and between the Indochinese and other Asian Americans. All of the Indochinese groups are much younger than other Asians or the total U.S. population, reflecting their much higher levels of fertility. American and Asian American women average just under two children ever born per woman aged 35 to 44 (an approximate measure of completed fertility), compared to 2.5 for the Vietnamese, 3.5 for the Lao and Cambodians, and 6.1 per Hmong woman (possibly the highest in the country, confirming the results of earlier research; cf. Rumbaut & Weeks, 1986). Thus, despite the recency of their arrival, over a third of the Hmong (35 percent) were already U.S.-born in 1990; amazingly, their median age was under thirteen years (compared to thirty-three for the American population), and that of U.S.-born Hmong Americans was just five years.

These indicators vividly demonstrate the dynamics of new ethnic group formation through immigration and rapid natural increase and underscore the socioeconomic importance among the Indochinese of families with a high proportion of dependent children. Whereas less than half of American households have children under age 18, over two-thirds of the Vietnamese, over four-fifths of the Lao and Cambodian, and 90 percent of Hmong households consist of families with minor children. The structure of these families is a key social context shaping the adaptation of these recently resettled groups, including the tension over changing gender roles and intergenerational conflicts (cf. Kibria, 1993).

Indochinese groups and Asian Americans generally—who are preponderantly foreign born, as Table 6.3 shows—exhibit a smaller proportion of single-parent female-headed households than the U.S. norm; the main exception are Cambodian refugees, whose higher rate (25 percent) reflects in part the disproportionate presence of widows whose husbands were killed during the Pol Pot period of the late 1970s (one study in San Diego found that more than 20 percent of Cambodian women were widowed—see Rumbaut, 1989a). Among the Vietnamese, the proportion of children under eighteen living at home with both parents is slightly above the U.S. norm of 73 percent, but well below that of Asian Americans generally (85 percent)— partly a reflection of the sizable number of unaccompanied refugee children from Vietnam and of youths (disproportionately males) who escaped with other relatives or adult guardians.

As the most recently arrived Asian Americans, the substantial majority of the Vietnamese, Cambodians, and Laotians—not surprisingly—did not yet speak English "very well," as the 1990 census makes clear. In fact, about half of all Indochinese households were classified by the census as "linguistically isolated" (see Table 6.3 for a definition). Whereas 38 percent of all Asian American adults were college graduates and 14 percent also had postgraduate degrees—about double the respective levels of attainment of the U.S. population (20 percent and 7 percent)—all of the Indochinese groups were much less educated on average, particularly the non-Vietnamese groups, as detailed in Table 6.3. Only about a third of the refugees from Laos and Cambodia were high school graduates, and higher proportions had less than a fifth-grade education, underscoring the rural origins and severe social class disadvantages of many refugees in these ethnic groups.

Relative to the U.S. population, Asian Americans as a whole also showed higher rates of labor force participation, lower unemployment, and a greater percentage of professionals and managers among those employed; but the profile for each of the Indochinese groups was precisely the opposite on each of these indicators. Employed Indochinese were twice as likely to have jobs as operators and laborers (significant levels of downward occupational mobility have been noted among the earlier arrivals; cf. Haines, 1985, p. 39), and their levels of self-employment were significantly below those for other Asian Americans and the U.S. population, as were family and per capita incomes and rates of home ownership.

Moreover, as specified in Table 6.3, poverty rates for the Indochinese groups were two to five times higher than for the U.S. population, and the disparity in welfare dependency rates was even greater. Approximately one-fourth of the Vietnamese fell below the federal poverty line and received public assistance income, as did one-third of the Lao, about half of the Cambodians, and two-thirds of the Hmong (the latter are probably by far the highest rates in the country). By comparison, poverty rates for the U.S. and Asian American general populations were about the same (13–14 percent), with fewer than a tenth of households relying on public assistance. The diversity of these socioeconomic profiles underlines the widely different social class origins, age and family structures, and modes of incorporation of Asian-origin immigrants and refugees and the senselessness of "model minority" stereotypes. These census data, however, tell us little about the equally significant differences within ethnic groups, especially between different waves or cohorts of arrival, and of the dynamics of their socioeconomic progress over time. For that information we turn to available nationwide surveys.

Occupational and Economic Progress over Time

One useful longitudinal data source on the economic progress of the 1975 to 1979 refugees comes from their federal income tax returns—a data source unique among all immigrant groups in the United States. Indochinese refugees who arrived between 1975 and late 1979 were issued social security numbers in blocks through a special program in effect at the time, and as a result it is possible to obtain annual aggregate data from the Internal Revenue Service on incomes received and taxes paid by these cohorts (U.S. Office of Refugee Resettlement, 1991, pp. 98–102). Table 6.4 shows the median adjusted gross income they received annually from 1982 through 1988, comparing the 1975 cohort (who, as noted above, numbered 130,000, including 125,000 Vietnamese) to the 1976 to 1979 arrivals (a much more heterogeneous group of 118,000 persons—including about 60,000 Vietnamese, 49,000 Lao and Hmong, and 9,000 Cambodians—most of whom arrived in 1979 and were thus about four years

TABLE 6.4
Median Income of Indochinese Refugees (tax-filling units), 1982–1988, for Refugee Cohorts Arriving in the U.S. From 1975 to 1979

Tax Year	All cohorts (1975–1979)	1975 arrivals	1976–1979 arrivals	Ratio of 1975/76–79	All U.S. tax-filing units[a]
1982	12,192	14,232	8,803	1.62	14–15,000
1983	12,808	14,698	9,655	1.52	15–16,000
1984	14,377	16,377	11,105	1.47	16–17,000
1985	15,177	17,092	12,061	1.42	16–17,000
1986	16,021	17,861	12,907	1.38	17–18,000
1987	16,667	18,236	14,009	1.30	17–18,000
1988	17,560	18,963	15,261	1.24	18–19,000

[a] Comparative data provided by the Internal Revenue Service as a range
SOURCE: Internal Revenue Service summary data on incomes and taxes paid by Indochinese refugees who arrived in the United States from 1975 through late 1979, as reported by the U.S. Office of Refugee Resettlement (1991, p. 99).

behind the 1975 cohort). The data show clearly the economic progress of these groups over time; worth noting is the fact that since 1985 the median income of the 1975 refugees has surpassed that of all U.S. tax-filing units. As would be expected, as of 1988 the incomes of the 1976 to 1979 cohort still lagged noticeably behind the incomes of the 1975 cohort, but the gap between them was closing rapidly: the income ratio of the 1975 cohort to the 1976 to 1979 cohort was 1.62 in 1982 but had dropped to 1.24 by 1988. Between 1982 and 1988, their income from wages more than doubled; still, as late as 1988 over a quarter (28.6 percent) of individual W-2 forms were under $5,000, whereas less than a fifth (19.6 percent) of W-2 forms were over $25,000. In 1988, more than 10,700 tax returns reported income from self-employment, totaling over $103 million. All together, these Indochinese Americans reported more than $2.2 billion in annual income in 1988 and paid $218 million in federal income taxes (U.S. Office of Refugee Resettlement, 1991).

From the beginning of the Indochinese refugee resettlement program in 1975, the federal government has funded annual surveys of representative national samples of this population (conducted through telephone interviews in the respondent's native language). Reported each year by Office of Refugee Resettlement, in its *Annual Report to the Congress*, these are the only national survey data available that provide a comprehensive picture of the Indochinese occupational and economic adaptation over time (Bach, 1984; Bach & Carroll-Seguin, 1986; Gordon, 1989, U.S. Office of Refugee Resettlement, 1991, 1992). The results, however, are not broken down by ethnicity but are reported for the Indochinese refugee population as a whole (except for the first few surveys, which were limited to the Vietnamese; see Montero, 1979). Until 1983 the surveys were cross-sectional and based on random samples of refugees who had arrived since 1975; after 1983 the survey was redesigned into a panel study, following new arrival cohorts over a period of five years, and adding a sample of new arrivals every year. The new design has the advantage of a longitudinal study, but the disadvantage that it is restricted to refugees who have been in the United States five years or less; for example, the 1990 survey does not include any Indochinese refugees who arrived prior to 1986. In any case, Table 6.5 provides a summary of annual survey results on rates of labor force participation and unemployment during the 1980s for national samples of Indochinese who arrived in the United States between 1975 and 1989.

In general the data in Table 6.5 show increasing rates of labor force participation and, once in the labor force, decreasing unemployment rates over time in the United States. Arrival cohorts reflect very low rates of labor force participation and high rates of unemployment especially during their first year in the United States, when most refugees are enrolled in English as a Second Language (ESL) classes and job training programs while receiving cash and medical assistance. However, more recent cohorts show only small increases in labor force participation rates over time, staying in the 30 percent to 38 percent range (about half the U.S. rate of 66 percent), unlike earlier cohorts who moved from first-year rates in the 20 percent to 30 percent range to 40 percent to 50 percent by their second and third year in the United States. In particular, the 1975 to 1978 cohorts have shown the highest rates of labor force participation, exceeding the rate for the U.S. population within their first four years

TABLE 6.5

Percentage Employment Status for Indochinese Refugees in the United States, 1981–1989 (Data for all household members age 16 and over in national samples of refugee households)

Year of entry	Labor force participation				Unemployment rate			
	1986	1987	1988	1989	1986	1987	1988	1989
1989				21				27
1988			20	30			21	24
1987		22	30	35		32	11	10
1986	31	32	33	38	25	11	7	7
1985	25	32	32	37	20	9	5	12
1984	34	34	35	36	18	16	15	10
U.S. rates[a]	65	66	66	66	7	6	5	5

Year of entry	Labor force participation				Unemployment rate			
	1981	1982	1983	1984	1981	1982	1983	1984
1984				30				41
1983			21	42			55	36
1982		25	41	45		63	30	13
1981	23	42	47	51	45	41	17	16
1980	53	51	55	55	27	32	21	12
1979	49	60	61	60	8	19	18	10
1978	49	68	68	66	5	19	20	3
1976–1977	71	74	80	76	4	9	17	5
1975	76	72	70	67	6	13	12	6
U.S. rates[a]	64	64	64	65	8	10	8	7

[a] October unadjusted figures from the Bureau of Labor Statistics, U.S. Department of Labor, 1981–1989.
SOURCE: Annual surveys of national samples of Southeast Asian refugees reported by the U.S. Office of Refugee Resettlement (1982, p. 18; 1985, p. 91; 1991, p. 90). See also Gordon (1989, p. 30).

in the country. They also had lower unemployment rates than the U.S. average as of 1981, but the recession of 1981 to 1983 hit them much harder, with their unemployment rates doubling to quadrupling during those years (see Table 6.5). By 1984, however, their recovery was rapid, and their unemployment rates again fell below the U.S. average. In part, these patterns reflect the relative socioeconomic and other handicaps of different arrival cohorts. For example, the annual surveys have documented a decline in the educational levels of adult refugees over time: 1975 arrivals averaged 9.4 years of education, those arriving during 1976 to 1979 averaged 7.4 years; 1980 to 1984 arrivals averaged 6.8 years, and 1985 to 1989 arrivals about five years (Haines, 1989, p. 7). The 1990 to 1992 cohorts (which included many former reeducation camp internees from Vietnam) reversed this trend, however, averaging eight years of education (U.S. Office of Refugee Resettlement, 1985, 1991, 1992). Significantly an analysis of determinants of labor force participation based on the national data set (Bach & Carroll-Seguin, 1986) found that education was the strongest positive predictor.

The promotion of economic self-sufficiency is a principal goal of the U.S. refugee program, as enunciated by the Refugee Act of 1980; that is, to ensure early employment and minimal reliance on public assistance (such as Aid to Families with Dependent Children and Medicaid). Eligibility for the latter and levels of benefits vary widely among the states, however. For example, in 1982 monthly AFDC benefits for a family of four were $591 in California but $141 in Texas, the two largest states of Indochinese settlement; indigent two-parent families with dependent children were eligible for AFDC in California but not in Texas; and indigent adults without dependent children were eligible for local General Assistance in California but had no such "safety net" in Texas (Rumbaut, 1989b). A recent study of refugee use of public assistance based on the 1983 to 1988 national longitudinal survey data found that 18 percent of all Indochinese refugee households were economically self-sufficient after their first year in the United States, some of them never having used public assistance. Of those who did, 41 percent had left public assistance programs within their second year in the United States, as had 57 percent by their fifth year. However, there were significant differences between refugee households in California (home to over 40 percent of the total Indochinese population, as we saw earlier) and those in the rest of the country (the study grouped the other forty-nine states together, although there are major differences among them in their programs of public assistance). In California, only 7 percent of the Indochinese households were financially independent after their first year and only 18 percent had left public assistance by their second year, compared to 26 percent and 57 percent, respectively, outside California; by the end of five years, only one fourth (26 percent) of California refugee households had left public assistance, compared to three-fourths (75 percent) outside California (Bach & Argiros, 1991).

If California residence is significantly associated with a higher level of reliance on public assistance, what are the determinants of such reliance among refugees within California? A major study of welfare dependency among Indochinese groups in Southern California found that the strongest determinant was the number of dependent children in the family; the proportion of family income coming from public assistance grew by about 10 percent for each dependent child. Welfare dependency significantly decreased over time in the United States and increased with age and poor health status (Rumbaut, 1989b). Indeed, concern over medical care coverage is often a decisive consideration for large refugee families who continue to remain on public assistance (including Medicaid), although it keeps them below the poverty line, rather than risk low-wage jobs that provide no health care insurance at all (Forbes, 1985; Rumbaut, Chávez, Moser, Pickwell, & Wishik, 1988). Cambodian refugees we interviewed in San Diego in the 1980s, for example, referred to their MediCal stickers (as Medicaid is called in California) as being "more valuable than gold."

The Indochinese in America: A Local Perspective

Since the late 1970s, a large number of community surveys, ethnographies, and epidemiological or clinical studies by sociologists, anthropologists, psychologists, psychiatrists, and other researchers have reported on many aspects of the Indochinese refugee experience in settings throughout the United States. Although they lack the generalizability of national survey data and use different samples and methodologies that often preclude comparisons across studies, they nonetheless have greatly added to the richness and depth of our available knowledge for specific ethnic groups. It is well beyond our scope here to review this literature, but we can refer the reader to a few selected sources.

A central focus of the research has been on the social and economic adaptation of Indochinese groups, from the national surveys of the first waves (Montero, 1979) and other ORR-sponsored research to diverse studies such as those published in the 1981 and 1986 special issues of the *International Migration Review* on refugees, the 1982 special issue of *Anthropological Quarterly* on Southeast Asian refugees, and several major community surveys cited later (see also the recent review of research on socioeconomic mobility by Gold & Kibria, 1993). Another early focus, beginning with research done at Camp Pendleton and Seattle in 1975 (Lin, Tazuma, & Masuda, 1979; Liu, Lamanna, & Murata, 1979; Rahe, Looney, Ward, Tung, & Liu, 1978) concerned refugee mental health and the psychology of adaptation under conditions of severe stress; these have been followed by a wide range of research on this topic, from clinical studies to community mental health surveys (e.g., Meinhardt, Tom, Tse, & Yu, 1985–1986; Mollica & Lavelle, 1988; Owan, 1985; Rumbaut, 1985, 1991a, 1991b; Williams & Westermeyer, 1986). Ethnographic fieldwork includes research on Indochinese communities, neighborhoods, and families in California (Gold, 1992), Kansas (Benson, 1994), Chicago (Conquergood, 1992), and Philadelphia (Kibria, 1993, 1994); case histories of refugee adults (Freeman, 1989) and youth (Howard, 1990; Rumbaut & Ima, 1988); and edited collections of papers on each of the Indochinese ethnic groups (e.g., Haines, 1985; Hendricks, Downing, & Deinard, 1986).

The results of major community surveys have been collected by Haines (1989). They include:

A panel study of 1975 "first-wave" Vietnamese in nine cities in Northern California, Louisiana, Alabama, and Florida (Roberts & Starr, 1989)

A survey of a sample of Vietnamese in Los Angeles, Houston, and New Orleans stratified by year of entry, 1975 to 1979 (Dunning, 1982, 1989)

A survey of 1975 to 1979 arrivals in Illinois, including samples of Vietnamese, Cambodian, Lao, and Hmong refugees (Kim, 1989; Kim & Nicassio, 1980)

A 1981 survey of Vietnamese, Cambodian, Lao, and Hmong refugees in San Diego (Strand, 1989; Strand & Jones, 1985)

A survey of Vietnamese, Chinese-Vietnamese, and Lao 1978 to 1982 arrivals residing in Boston, Chicago, Houston, Seattle, and Orange County, plus a follow-up survey of a subsample of their school-age children (Caplan, Whitmore, & Choy, 1989; Whitmore, Trautmann, & Caplan, 1989)

The Indochinese Health and Adaptation Research Project (IHARP), a longitudinal study of Vietnamese, Chinese-Vietnamese, Cambodian, Lao, and Hmong adults and children in San Diego based on representative samples of 1975 to 1983 arrivals (Rumbaut, 1989a)

The latter two are among the few to focus specifically on the ethnic Chinese from Vietnam; another is the study by Desbarats (1986) of Sino-Vietnamese and Vietnamese in Chicago, Orange County, and San Francisco.

Some illustrative findings from the IHARP study in the San Diego metropolitan area are presented below, focusing on aspects of the experience of Vietnamese, Laotian, and Cambodian refugees that are almost completely missing from census and other national data sources. First, we will look briefly at prearrival characteristics, migration motives and events, and mental health outcomes among Indochinese adults and then touch on infant health outcomes and on the educational progress of their children. The respondents, ranging in age from eighteen to seventy-one, were interviewed at length in their native languages in 1983 and again a year later. Results are broken down by ethnic group and for three key cohorts of arrival (1975, 1976 to 1979, and 1980 to 1983, the latter being the most numerous). [2] We then conclude with a look at some intriguing comparative data for all racial-ethnic groups, including the Indochinese, drawn from the vital statistics for San Diego County (on infant health and mortality) and from the San Diego city schools (on the educational attainment of refugee children growing up in the United States).

Migration, Adaptation, and Mental Health

Who are they, why did they come, how did they leave? Table 6.6 summarizes information on the social background and migration process of the refugees. About 90 percent of the Hmong and 55 percent of the Cambodians came from rural areas, whereas the Chinese and Vietnamese were overwhelmingly from urban sectors in South Vietnam. These differences are reflected in their levels of premigration education: the Vietnamese were the most educated (9.8 years), followed by the Chinese (6.6), the Cambodians (4.9), and the Hmong (1.7). Two-thirds of Hmong adults had never attended school and were preliterate, their language lacking an alphabet until the 1950s, when missionaries in Laos developed a written notation for what had been until then only an oral tradition.

There were also very significant social-class differences by cohort of arrival. The 1975 refugees were much more likely to come from highly educated professional and managerial classes, whereas less educated farmers, fisherfolk, and manual laborers predominate among the more recently arrived. Vietnamese and Hmong men included high proportions of former military officers and soldiers. The ethnic Chinese—a largely segregated "middleman minority" of merchants from Saigon's *Cholon* (Large Market) area, which had been referred to as, "after Singapore, the largest Chinese city outside of China" (Whitmore, 1985, p. 65)—were least likely to have had any prior involvement with either the military (ARVN) or the South Vietnamese or American governments during the war. Indeed, very few Chinese-Vietnamese cited "past associations" in their motives to flee.

A distinction often made between refugees and other classes of immigrants revolves around their different motives for migration and the traumatic nature of their flight experiences (see Zolberg, Suhrke, & Aguayo, 1989). Refugees are said to be motivated to flee by fear of persecution (political motives), whereas immigrants are defined by their aspirations for better material opportunities and self-advancement (economic motives). IHARP respondents were asked to state all of their motives for leaving the homeland; over fifty different reasons were given, ranging from fear of repression or imprisonment in reeducation camps to past associations with the

TABLE 6.6

Social Background Characteristics and Contexts of Exit of Indochinese Refugees in San Diego County, by Ethnic Group and Time of Arrival in the United States (IHARP longitudinal adult sample, N = 500)

	Ethnic group				Time of arrival		
	Vietnamese	Chinese	Cambodian	Hmong	1975	1976–1979	1980–1983
Educational background							
Number of years of education	9.9	6.6	4.9	1.8	11.9	6.5	5.2
% high school graduate	47.1	19.3	13.3	2.8	74.4	23.8	15.6
% knew some English	39.5	13.2	5.8	1.8	66.7	12.8	13.1
% never attended school	1.9	12.3	23.3	67.9	2.6	19.2	29.4
% rural background	5.1	4.4	55.0	89.9	5.1	36.0	39.1
Occupational background							
% professional/managerial	25.6	11.2	5.3	3.0	38.7	15.4	7.3
% military	25.6	6.1	15.9	31.3	35.5	20.8	17.9
% clerical	7.5	1.0	1.8	2.0	9.7	4.0	2.3
% sales	18.8	38.8	14.2	2.0	6.5	20.1	18.6
% blue collar	10.5	27.6	8.0	2.0	3.2	7.4	15.2
% farmers, fishers	10.5	14.3	54.0	59.6	3.2	32.2	37.6
Motives for exit[a]							
Number of political motives	3.3	2.9	5.1	4.2	2.7	3.9	4.0
TARGETS	2.6	2.3	4.5	3.9	2.1	3.3	3.5
REBELS	0.7	0.6	0.5	0.3	0.6	0.6	0.5
Number of economic motives	0.5	0.7	2.1	0.4	0.2	0.6	1.1
VICTIMS	0.1	0.2	1.7	0.2	0.1	0.2	0.7
SEEKERS	0.4	0.5	0.4	0.2	0.1	0.4	0.4
Migration events							
% fled without family	13.4	11.4	29.2	19.3	25.6	19.8	15.9
% gave bribes to exit	32.7	71.7	19.3	21.3	13.2	35.7	39.0
% feared would be killed	73.2	73.7	80.7	92.7	18.4	86.6	83.0
% assaulted in escape	30.6	36.8	25.2	25.7	0.0	24.4	36.7
Number of violent events during exit	2.1	1.9	3.1	2.5	0.9	2.2	2.7
Number of years in refugee camps	0.6	0.9	2.1	2.9	0.2	1.2	1.9
Mental health status, 1984							
% sleep problems	21.7	23.9	55.8	61.5	23.1	36.6	42.7
% appetite problems	14.6	11.4	42.5	22.0	5.1	18.0	27.0
% positive well-being	50.6	31.0	15.0	35.5	56.4	35.1	30.8
% demoralization, moderate	28.8	43.4	46.7	34.6	30.8	35.7	39.8
% demoralization, severe	20.5	25.7	38.3	29.9	12.8	29.2	29.4

[a] Data refer to the number of migration motives reported by the respondent, classified as follows:

TARGETS: Forced relocation to new economic zone, into reeducation camp; imprisoned prior to exit; fear of arrest or harm from new regime; past policital involvement with old regime, armed forces; association with U.S. government, CIA, or military; drafted to fight in Cambodia; loss or confiscation of personal property or wealth; general harassment.

REBELS: Protest communism, lack of freedom; refusal to join cooperative; other political-ideological reasons.

VICTIMS: Starvation, famine, lack of health care, harsh or poor economic conditions, inability to make a living.

SEEKERS: Seeking better future, education, prospects for children; family reunification; other miscellaneous reasons.

former regime and ideological opposition to communism to desires for family reunification, better education for their children, and an improved standard of living. Some of these reasons may be defined as political in nature, others as economic or social. Often both kinds of reasons were cited by the same respondent, making the usual distinction between refugees and nonrefugees simplistic and misleading.

Their exit motives were classified into four main types, as shown in Table 6.6. Two involved more clearly political motivations:

1. Specific perceptions and experiences of fear or force, past political associations, and related motives (TARGETS)
2. Explicit forms of protest and ideological reasons (REBELS)

The other two types involved more clearly socioeconomic considerations:

3. Harsh material conditions of famine and other dismal economic conditions (VICTIMS)
4. Miscellaneous "pull" motives, such as seeking a better education for the children or family reunification (SEEKERS)

Cambodians reported by far the most TARGET and VICTIM reasons for flight (reflecting their life-threatening experiences during the holocaust of the late 1970s) and hence both more political and economic exit motives. The Hmong also reported many TARGET motives, the Vietnamese the most REBEL motives, and the Chinese the most SEEKER or economic-pull motives, as well as the fewest past associations with the former regime. Despite this diversity of motives in the refugees' decision to leave, by far more TARGET motives were reported overall (3.3 per person) than any of the other three motive types: REBELS (0.6), VICTIMS (0.5), and, lastly, SEEKERS (0.4). By this classification, far more political motives (3.8) than economic motives (0.9) were reported, underscoring the qualitative difference in modes of exit between refugees and conventional immigrants, but also the fact that economic and social as well as political factors were interwoven in the decision to flee. The effects of such different motives on subsequent psychological adjustment and mental health will be noted later.

Other aspects of the exit experiences of the refugee sample are broken down in Table 6.6 by ethnicity and cohort of arrival. Except for the 1975 refugees, most feared they would be killed during their escape. The Cambodians suffered the greatest number of family loss and violence events, followed by the Hmong and the Vietnamese. The Chinese—and more recent arrivals generally—were most likely to have left together as a family, to have given bribes to exit, and to have been assaulted during the escape (often by Thai pirates). Once they reached a country of first asylum, the Hmong stayed in refugee camps far longer than any other group before being resettled in the United States, followed by the Cambodians, the Chinese, and the Vietnamese. Taken together, such differences in the migration events experienced by these refugee groups may help explain why the Cambodians and the Hmong had a significantly higher number of chronic health problems (defined as existing physical symptoms or dysfunctions lasting six months or longer) whose onset occurred between their exit from their homeland and their arrival in the United States. By contrast, there were no significant differences by ethnicity or gender in chronic health problems whose onset occurred prior to migration.

Although not shown in Table 6.6, the refugees' social background characteristics were in turn reflected in their socioeconomic position in San Diego as they struggled to rebuild their lives. The same ethnic group rank order was mirrored in their levels of English literacy, employment and labor force participation in the local economy, income, and welfare dependency, although all groups were progressing gradually, if at different rates over time. English ability increases over time; it is primarily a function of level of prior education and secondarily of (younger) age and longer time of residence in the United States (Rumbaut, 1989a). The biggest differences in labor force participation and unemployment rates were seen between the 1975 first-wave refugees and later arrivals, reflecting the national survey data reviewed earlier. The most recently arrived refugee families reported very low annual incomes, and in 1984 about two-thirds of the 1976 to 1979 arrivals and over four-fifths of the 1980 to 1983 arrivals in the sample still had incomes that fell below the federal poverty line, compared to a poverty rate of about 15 percent for the general U.S. and local populations. One of the respondents in the IHARP study, a middle-aged Hmong refugee who had arrived in 1980 after spending five years in refugee camps in Thailand, had this to say about his situation, vividly and eloquently expressing the complexity of the economic and related psychosocial problems faced by these recently arrived groups:

> Any jobs they have require a literate person to get. We have the arms and legs but we can't see what they see, because everything is connected to letters and numbers. . . . When we were in our country we never ask anybody for help like this, [but] in this country everything is money first. You go to the hospital is money, you get medicine is money, you die is also money and even the plot to bury you also requires money. These days I only live day by day and share the $594 for the six of us for the whole month. Some months I have to borrow money from friends or relatives to buy food for the family. I'm very worried that maybe one day the welfare says you are no longer eligible for the program and at the same time the manager says that I need more money for the rent, then we will really starve. I've been trying very hard to learn English and at the same time looking for a job. No matter what kind of job, even the job to clean people's toilets; but still people don't even trust you or offer you such work. I'm looking at me that I'm not even worth as much as a dog's stool. Talking about this, I want to die right here so I won't see my future . . . How am I going to make my life better? To get a job, you have to have a car; to have a car you have to have money; and to have money you have to have a job, so what can you do? Language, jobs, money, living, and so on are always big problems to me and I don't think they can be solved in my generation. So I really don't know what to tell you. My life is only to live day by day until the last day I live, and maybe that is the time when my problems will be solved. (as translated and quoted in Rumbaut 1985, pp. 471–472).

The measure of mental health status shown in the bottom panel of Table 6.6 was based on a screening scale used by the National Center for Health Statistics in a major national survey of the general American adult population (Link & Dohren-wend, 1980). The results showed that 74 percent of Americans scored in the positive well-being range, 16 percent in the moderate demoralization range, and only 9.6 percent in the severe demoralization range (indicative of "clinically significant distress"). By contrast, in 1984 the respective prevalence rates for the Indochinese refugees were 34 percent positive well-being, 38 percent moderate demoralization, and 28 percent severe demoralization. That latter figure was three times the level of severe distress found for the general American population; a year before, in 1983, the corresponding refugee rate had been four times higher than the U.S. norm. These demoralization rates were highest for the Cambodians—who had experienced the most traumatic contexts of exit—followed by the Hmong, Chinese, and Vietnamese.

The process of psychological adaptation appears to be temporally as well as socially patterned. The first several months after arrival in the United States tend to be a relatively hopeful and even euphoric period, but during the second year, a period of "exile shock," depressive symptoms reach their highest levels, followed by a process of psychological recovery after the third year (see Portes & Rumbaut, 1990; Rumbaut, 1989a; Vega & Rumbaut, 1991). The general pattern is described succinctly by an elderly Cambodian widow:

> I was feeling great the first few months. But then, after that, I started to face all kinds of worries and sadness. I started to see the real thing of the United States, and I missed home more and more. I missed everything about our country; people, family, relatives and friends, way of life, everything. Then, my spirit started to go down; I lost sleep; my physical health weakened; and there started the stressful and depressing times. But now [almost three years after arrival] I feel kind of better, a lot better! Knowing my sons are in school as their father would have wanted, and doing well, makes me feel more secure. (quoted in Rumbaut, 1985, pp. 469–470)

What, then, among all of the stressors reviewed above, affects refugee mental health the most? Briefly stated, controlling for physical health status and for a wide range of socioeconomic and demographic variables, an analysis of the psychological distress scores among the refugees in San Diego found that in 1983, the principal predictors of demoralization were prearrival factors: the number of TARGET motives reported, an index of family loss and separation, and a rural background. A year later, however, the effect of these prearrival stressors had receded and current difficulties, primarily being unemployed, emerged as stronger predictors of depressive symptoms. In addition, by 1984 a significant predictor of lower distress and greater satisfaction was an attitudinal measure of biculturalism; measures of monocultural styles (whether of traditionalism or of assimilationism) showed no effect on psychological outcomes. That is, refugees who adopt an additive acculturative strategy, adapting to American ways while retaining ethnic attachments and identity, appear to reduce psychological distress over time. This finding points to the importance of creativity and flexibility in the acculturative process (Rumbaut, 1991a).

Infant Health, Children's Educational Progress, and Some Paradoxes of Acculturation

Another health-related dimension of the Indochinese adaptation process may be gleaned from a follow-up study of the infant mortality rates (IMR) of all ethnic groups in San Diego County, based on a linked data set of all live births and infant deaths recorded in the metropolitan area during 1978 to 1985 (Rumbaut & Weeks, 1989; Weeks & Rumbaut, 1991). The results are summarized in Table 6.7, along with selected risk factors of pregnancy. The various Indochinese ethnic groups appeared to be at high risk for poor infant health outcomes. After all, they had come from a background of high fertility and high infant mortality, often with preexisting health

TABLE 6.7
Infant Mortality Rates and Selected Risk Factors of Pregnancy by Ethnic Groups in San Diego County, 1978-1985

| Ethnic group | Total live births[a] | Infant mortality | | | Risk factors | | |
		Infant mortality rate	Early neonatal death rate	Post-early neonatal deaths	% Late or no prenatal care	% Teenage mothers	% Un-married mothers
Vietnamese	2,187	5.5	3.7	1.8	9.9	5.1	14.4
Cambodian	687	5.8	4.4	1.5	15.2	5.2	20.2
Laos	977	7.2	3.1	4.1	13.1	10.5	12.5
Hmong	990	9.1	3.0	6.1	20.3	16.5	11.4
All Indochinese	4,841	6.6	3.5	3.1	13.4	8.5	14.2
Japanese	2,253	6.2	3.1	3.1	2.4	8.7	11.5
Chinese	1,455	6.9	4.1	2.8	3.0	2.6	7.1
Filipino	12,445	7.2	4.2	3.0	3.4	5.6	7.9
Hispanic	71,641	7.3	4.1	3.2	6.6	15.4	23.5
White (non-Hispanic)	143,779	8.0	4.5	3.5	2.6	8.9	11.1
American Indian	5,714	9.6	4.4	5.3	4.2	16.4	28.3
Black (non-Hispanic)	22,080	16.3	8.9	7.4	4.6	19.0	45.8
Total county	269,252	8.5	4.7	3.7	4.2	11.6	18.0

NOTE: The number of live births = 269,252; the number of [linked] infant deaths = 2,281. Here is how the various factors were determined:
Infant Mortality Rate = number of (linked) deaths of infants under 1 year old per 1,000 live births.
Early Neonatal Mortality Rate = number of deaths of infants under 7 days old per 1,000 live births.
Postearly Neonatal Mortality Rate = number of deaths of infants 7 to 365 days old per 1,000 live births.
Late Prenatal Care = cases where prenatal care was begun in the third trimester (7th to 9th month), or not at all.
Teenage Mothers = cases where mother was 19 years old or younger at the time of the baby's birth.
Unmarried Mothers = cases where mother was single, separated, divorced, widowed, or of unknown marital status.
[a] N = number of live births in San diego County during 1978–1985, on which the infant mortality rates are based.

problems, and, as documented above, had levels of unemployment, poverty, welfare dependency, and depressive symptomatology that greatly exceeded U.S. norms. Lack of English proficiency limited their access to health care, and indeed Indochinese pregnant mothers exhibited the latest onset of prenatal care of all ethnic groups in San Diego.

Remarkably, however, the Indochinese overall were found to have much lower infant mortality rates (6.6 infant deaths per 1,000 live births) than the San Diego County average (8.5), and two refugee groups actually exhibited the lowest infant death rates: the Vietnamese (5.5) and the Cambodians (5.8). Only the Hmong (9.1) had a higher infant mortality rate than Hispanics (7.3) and non-Hispanic whites (8.0), although still much lower than blacks (16.3), and vastly lower than their own infant death rate prior to their arrival in the United States (104). The Lao and the Hmong, moreover, exhibited the unusual pattern of higher postearly neonatal death rates (deaths occurring to infants seven days and older) than early neonatal death rates (occurring during the first week of life, usually in the hospital), suggesting that infant death rates for these two groups could be reduced by paying more attention to the overall home environment to which the infants are taken after birth. Several behavioral factors were associated with these positive outcomes, particularly the nearly universal absence of tobacco, alcohol, and drug use among pregnant Indochinese women—and among most immigrant women in the groups listed in Table 6.7— in contrast to U.S.-born groups. One implication of these findings is that subtractive acculturation—that is, a process of Americanization that involves the learning bad habits in the U.S. milieu—may have negative consequences for infant health.

Other evidence bearing on the future prospects of the coming generation of Indochinese Americans comes from a study of their educational attainment in San Diego schools (Portes & Rumbaut, 1990, pp. 189–198; Rumbaut, 1990, 1994). Table 6.8 presents data on academic grade point averages for all high school seniors, juniors, and sophomores in the district, including nearly 2,400 Indochinese students, broken down by ethnic groups and English language status. The latter involves a classification of all students who speak a primary language other than English at home into two categories: fluent English proficient (FEP) and limited English proficient (LEP). Among all groups in the school district, the Indochinese have by far the highest proportion of LEP students, reflecting the fact that they are the most recently arrived immigrants. Despite the language handicap, however, their academic grade point averages (GPAs) (2.47) significantly exceed the district average (2.11) and that of white Anglos (2.24).

TABLE 6.8

Academic Grade Point Average (GPA)[a] of San Diego High School Students, in Rank Order, by Ethnolinguistic Groups and English Language Status, 1986

Ethnolinguistic Groups[b]	English[c] N	GPA	Non-English[d] FEP N	GPA	LEP N	GPA	Total N	GPA
East Asians	493	2.38	220	3.05	113	2.83	826	2.62
Chinese			98	3.40	68	2.94	166	3.21
Korean			33	3.00	23	2.76	56	2.90
Japanese			89	2.70	22	2.56	111	2.67
Southwest Asians	NA		127	2.67	106	2.42	233	2.56
Indian			16	3.11	3	2.62	19	3.04
Hebrew			20	3.18	17	2.50	37	2.85
Persian			49	2.70	68	2.46	117	2.56
Arab			42	2.21	18	2.21	60	2.21
Indochinese	140	2.66	607	2.88	1,641	2.30	2,388	2.47
Vietnamese			451	2.96	733	2.38	1,184	2.60
Cambodian			32	2.77	359	2.30	391	2.34
Hmong			30	2.66	83	2.27	113	2.37
Laos			94	2.63	466	2.18	560	2.26
Filipinos	794	2.33	1,034	2.53	236	2.02	2,064	2.39
Europeans	NA		308	2.39	103	2.24	411	2.36
German			58	2.73	16	2.54	74	2.69
French			28	2.70	13	1.71	41	2.39
Portuguese			74	2.17	32	2.23	106	2.19
Italian			66	2.11	16	1.83	82	2.05
Other Europe			82	2.48	26	2.59	108	2.51
White Anglos	19,796	2.24	NA		NA		19,796	2.24
Pacific Islanders	123	1.84	101	1.96	47	1.78	271	1.87
Guamanian			44	2.05	11	1.74	55	1.99
Samoan			51	1.80	13	1.51	64	1.74
Hispanics	2,296	1.81	2,631	1.85	2,080	1.71	7,007	1.79
Blacks	5,720	1.69	69	1.82	32	1.89	5,821	1.70
Totals	29,362	2.10	5,099	2.22	4,359	2.01	38,820	2.11

NOTE: *N* = 38,820 high school seniors, juniors, and sophomores in the San Diego Unified School District.

[a] GPA = Cumulative grade point average, excluding physical education courses; A = 4, B = 3, C = 2, D = 1, F = 0.

[b] Groups classified by ethnicity and (for mainly immigrant students) primary language spoken at home if other than English.

[c] Primary home language is English; speaks English only.

[d] Primary home language other than English; students' English proficiency is fluent (FEP) or limited (LEP).

Indeed, the latter is surpassed by most Asian and European language minorities; falling below the district norm are African Americans, Mexican Americans, and Pacific Islanders. At the top are Chinese, Asian Indian, and Korean students, with GPAs exceeding the norm by almost a full point. The highest GPAs among the Indochinese are found for the Vietnamese (2.60), Hmong (2.37), Cambodian (2.34), and Lao (2.26); within these groups they are significantly higher for FEP students. Remarkably, the GPAs of Cambodian and Hmong LEP students surpass the white Anglo average. Another noteworthy result is that for all ethnic groups without exception, English monolinguals (who tend to be U.S.-born) exhibit lower GPAs than their bilingual FEP coethnics (who tend to be foreign born); this is particularly clear among East Asians, Filipinos, and the Indochinese. One important implication of these findings is that educational achievement appears to decline from the first to the second and third generations. Another implication of these data is that they lend strong support to previous research noting a significant positive association between "true" bilingualism (most closely approximated by FEP students in Table 6.8) and educational achievement, in contrast to the lower GPAs registered by either of the essentially monolingual types (LEPs and English-only).

In a follow-up study using the 1983 IHARP sample of refugee parents (including the Lao), we identified all school-age children enrolled in the San Diego Unified School District (Rumbaut & Ima, 1988). Complete academic histories for this sub-sample of Indochinese students (including GPAs and standardized achievement test scores) were then obtained from the school district in 1986 and again in 1989 and matched with our 1983 data on their parents and households, producing an exceptionally in-depth data base on 340 secondary school students. Thus the design permitted, in a causally unambiguous way, the analysis of the effects of parental and family characteristics measured in 1983 on their children's academic achievement measured three and six years later. An analysis of the students' GPAs found that several student characteristics besides gender showed significant positive effects: the younger the students and the longer in U.S. schools, the higher their GPA; and FEP students (fluent bilinguals) clearly had an advantage over those classified as LEP (limited bilinguals). Objective family characteristics did not affect GPA directly, but two subjective variables did: (a) the level of psychological distress of the mother (the higher this score, the lower the student's GPA) and (b) the parents' score on an index measuring their sense of ethnic resilience and cultural reaffirmation (the higher this score, the higher the GPA of their children). The latter finding confirms similar results reported by Caplan, Whitmore, and Choy (1989) for Indochinese students in five other cities, but it runs counter to the conventional assumption that the more acculturated and Americanized immigrants become, the greater will be their success in the competitive worlds of school and work. Instead, it suggests an opposite proposition, parallel to the findings noted above with respect both to mental health and infant health: namely, that Americanization processes—all other things being equal and to the extent that they involve subtractive rather than additive forms of acculturation—may be counterproductive for educational attainment.

But all other things are never equal, except in mathematical models, and accultur-ative processes always unfold within concrete structural and historical contexts.

Exactly why and how the immigrant ethic—which appears to yield the positive outcomes reviewed earlier, often despite significant disadvantages—erodes over time in the United States remain at present unanswered questions. It is also unclear (if not unlikely) whether additive adaptations, such as fluent bilingualism, can be sustained beyond one generation in the United States. In the end, however, the complex processes of assimilation to different sectors of American society will vary for different types of second-generation Indochinese Americans located in different types of familial, school, and community contexts—from the inner cities to the suburbs to diverse ethnic enclaves—and exposed to different types of role models and forms of racial discrimination. Bilateral relations between the United States and the countries of origin are also likely to affect not only future immigration flows but also entrepreneurial opportunities and the very nature of institutional life within established refugee communities in areas of concentration. Many outcomes are possible: from a "lost generation" of Amerasian youth in Boston (Terris, 1987), to the reactive formation of Southeast Asian gangs in San Diego (Rumbaut & Ima, 1988), to Vietnamese "valedictorians and delinquents" in Philadelphia (Kibria, 1993), to the predominance in the electronics field of young Vietnamese technicians in Orange County (Kotkin, 1994b). The future of Vietnamese, Laotian, and Cambodian Americans will likely be as diverse as their past and will be reached by multiple paths.

Conclusion

Vietnamese, Laotian, and Cambodian Americans now form a sizable and diverse component of the Asian-origin population in the United States. They are the newest Asian Americans, most having arrived only after 1980; they are also among the fastest-growing populations in the country as a result of both the largest refugee resettlement program in American history—a legacy of the nation's bitterest and most divisive war—and of fertility rates that are among the highest of any ethnic group in the United States. They differ from other Asian Americans in significant ways, especially in the contexts of exit and reception that have shaped their refugee experience. They differ from each other in equally significant ways, and, if the research studies reviewed here are any indication, the Vietnamese, Cambodian, Lao, Hmong, and ethnic Chinese generations now coming of age in America will differ again from their parents. In their diversity they are writing yet another chapter in the history of the American population and society, and in the process they are becoming, quintessentially, Americans.

NOTES

1. "Southeast Asian" is sometimes preferred over "Indochinese," mainly to avoid any connection to the usage of the latter term during the period of French colonial rule. Southeast Asian, however, is a broad and imprecise term both geographically and historically, covering as it does a vast region and countries as diverse as Thailand, Burma, Malaysia, Indonesia, Brunei, Papua New Guinea, and the Philippines, none of whom share the fateful history of

U.S. involvement during the Indochina War, nor of special U.S. sponsorship of refugees who fled after the collapse in 1975 of U.S.-backed governments in Saigon, Vientiane, and Phnom Penh. To avoid the cumbersome repetition of each of the nationalities and ethnic groups being considered here while retaining those more precise geographic and historical meanings, Indochinese will be used in this chapter to refer collectively to refugees from the three countries of Vietnam, Laos, and Cambodia. In any case, it should be noted that persons from those countries do *not* identify ethnically either as Indochinese or Southeast Asian.

2. Because only cross-sectional data are available for the Lao, they are not included in Table 6.6; however, IHARP data on the Lao have been reported elsewhere (Rumbaut, 1985; Rumbaut, Chávez Moser, Pickwell, & Wishik, 1988; Rumbaut & Ima, 1988; Rumbaut & Weeks, 1986).

REFERENCES

Bach, R. L. (1984). *Labor force participation and employment of Southeast Asian refugees in the United States.* Washington, DC: U.S. Office of Refugee Resettlement.

Bach, R. L., & Argiros, R. (1991). Economic progress among Southeast Asian refugees in the United States. In H. Adelman (ed.), *Refugee policy: Canada and the United States* (pp. 322–343). Toronto: York Lanes.

Bach, R. L., & Carroll-Seguin, R. (1986). Labor force participation, household composition, and sponsorship among Southeast Asian refugees. *International Migration Review*, 20(2), 381–404.

Baker, R. P., & North, D. S. (1984). *The 1975 refugees: Their first five years in America.* Washington, DC: New TransCentury Foundation.

Baskir, L. M., & Strauss, W. A. (1978). *Chance and circumstance: The draft, the war, and the Vietnam generation.* New York: Knopf.

Becker, E. (1986). *When the war was over: Cambodia's revolution and the voices of its people.* New York: Simon & Schuster.

Benson, J. (1994). The effects of packinghouse work on Southeast Asian refugee families. In L. Lamphere, A. Stepick, & G. Grenier (eds.), *Newcomers in the workplace: Immigrants and the restructuring of the U.S. economy* (pp. 99–126). Philadelphia: Temple University Press.

Bouvier, L. F., & Agresta, A. J. (1987). The future Asian population of the United States. In J. T. Fawcett & B. V. Cariño (eds.), *Pacific bridges: The new immigration from Asia and the Pacific Islands* (pp. 285–301). Staten Island, NY: Center for Migration Studies.

Caplan, N., Whitmore, J. K., & Choy, M. H. (1989). *The boat people and achievement in America: A study of family life, hard work and cultural values.* Ann Arbor: University of Michigan Press.

Chanda, N. (1986). *Brother enemy: The war after the war—a history of Indochina since the fall of Saigon.* New York: Macmillan.

Conquergood, D. (1992). Life in the Big Red: Struggles and accommodations in a Chicago polyethnic tenement. In L. Lamphere (ed.), *Structuring diversity: Ethnographic perspectives on the new immigration* (pp. 95–144). Chicago: University of Chicago Press.

Desbarats, J. (1986). Ethnic differences in adaptation: Sino-Vietnamese refugees in the United States. *International Migration Review*, 20(2), 405–427.

Dunning, B. B. (1982). *A systematic survey of the social, psychological and economic adaptation of Vietnamese refugees representing five entry cohorts, 1975–1979.* Washington, DC: Bureau of Social Science Research, Inc.

Dunning, B. B. (1989). Vietnamese in America: The adaptation of the 1975–1979 arrivals. In D. W. Haines (ed.), *Refugees as immigrants: Cambodians, Laotians and Vietnamese in America* (pp. 55–84). Totowa, NJ: Rowman & Littlefield.

Finnan, C. R., & Cooperstein, R. A. (1983). *Southeast Asian refugee resettlement at the local level: The role of the ethnic community and the nature of refugee impact.* Menlo Park, CA: SRI International.

Forbes, S. S. (1984). *Residency patterns and secondary migration of refugees.* Washington, DC: Refugee Policy Group.

Forbes, S. S. (1985). *Adaptation and integration of recent refugees to the United States.* Washington, DC: Refugee Policy Group.

Freeman, J. M. (1989). *Hearts of sorrow: Vietnamese-American lives.* Stanford, CA: Stanford University Press.

Gibney, M. (1991). U.S. foreign policy and the creation of refugee flows. In H. Adelman (ed.), *Refugee policy: Canada and the United States* (pp. 81–111). Toronto: York Lanes.

Gold, S. J. (1992). Refugee communities: A comparative field study. Newbury Park, CA: Sage.

Gold, S. J., & Kibria, N. (1993). Vietnamese refugees and blocked mobility. *Asian and Pacific Migration Journal, 2*(1), 27–56.

Gordon, L. W. (1989). National surveys of Southeast Asian refugees. In D. W. Haines (ed.), *Refugees as immigrants: Cambodians, Laotians and Vietnamese in America* (pp. 24–39). Totowa, NJ: Rowman & Littlefield.

Haines, D. W. (ed.). (1985). *Refugees in the United States: A reference handbook.* Westport, CT: Greenwood Press.

Haines, D. W. (ed.). (1989). *Refugees as immigrants: Cambodians, Laotians and Vietnamese in America.* Totowa, NJ: Rowman & Littlefield.

Hein, J. (1993). *States and international migrants: The incorporation of Indochinese refugees in the United States and France.* Boulder, CO: Westview Press.

Hendricks, G. L., Downing, B. T., & Deinard, A. S. (eds.). (1986). *The Hmong in transition.* Staten Island, NY: Center for Migration Studies.

Hess, Gary R. (1990). *Vietnam and the United States: Origins and legacy of war.* Boston: Twayne.

Howard, K. K. (ed.). (1990). *Passages: An anthology of the Southeast Asian refugee experience.* Fresno: Southeast Asian Student Services, California State University.

Immigration and Naturalization Service. (1991). Immigrants admitted by country or region of birth, fiscal years 1925–1990 (unpublished data tables). Washington, DC: INS.

Isaacs, A. R. (1983). *Without honor: Defeat in Vietnam and Cambodia.* Baltimore: Johns Hopkins University Press.

Karnow, S. (1991). *Vietnam: A history* (rev. ed.). New York: Penguin Books.

Kelly, G. P. (1977). *From Vietnam to America: A chronicle of the Vietnamese immigration to the United States.* Boulder, CO: Westview Press.

Kibria, N. (1993). *Family tightrope: The changing lives of Vietnamese Americans.* Princeton, NJ: Princeton University Press.

Kibria, N. (1994). Household structure and family ideologies: The dynamics of immigrant economic adaptation among Vietnamese Americans. *Social Problems, 41*(1), 81–96.

Kim, Y. Y. (1989). Personal, social, and economic adaptation: 1975–1979 arrivals in Illinois. In D. W. Haines (ed.), *Refugees as immigrants: Cambodians, Laotians and Vietnamese in America* (pp. 86–104). Totowa, NJ: Rowman & Littlefield.

Kim, Y. Y., & Nicassio, P. M. (1980). *Psychological, social and cultural adjustment of Indochinese refugees.* Chicago: Travelers Aid Society of Metropolitan Chicago.

Kolko, G. (1985). *Anatomy of a war: Vietnam, the United States, and the modern historical experience.* New York: Pantheon.

Korn, P. (1991, April 8). Agent Orange in Vietnam: The persisting poison. *The Nation*, pp. 440–446.

Kotkin, J. (1994a, April 24). An emerging Asian tiger: The Vietnamese connection. *Los Angeles Times*, p. M1–6.

Kotkin, J. (1994b, April 22). Immigrants lead a recovery. *Wall Street Journal*, p. A10.

Lam, A. (1994, February 6). Vietnamese: Should we laugh or cry? *San Jose Mercury News*, pp. 1–3C.

Lin, K., Tazuma, L., & Masuda, M. (1979). Adaptational problems of Vietnamese refugees: 1. Health and Mental Health Status. *Archives of General Psychiatry*, 36, 955–961.

Link, B., & Dohrenwend, B. P. (1980). Formulation of hypotheses about the true prevalence of demoralization. In B. P. Dohrenwend (ed.), *Mental illness in the United States: Epidemiological estimates* (pp. 114–132). New York: Praeger.

Liu, W. T., Lamanna, M., & Murata, A. (1979). *Transition to nowhere: Vietnamese refugees in America.* Nashville: Charter House.

Martin, G. (1986, October). Phnom Penh, Rhode Island. *New England Monthly*, pp. 40–47, 105–111.

Mason, L., & Brown, R. (1983). *Rice, rivalry, and politics: Managing Cambodian relief.* Notre Dame, IN: University of Notre Dame Press.

Meinhardt, K., Tom, S., Tse, P., & Yu, C. Y. (1985–1986). Southeast Asian refugees in the "Silicon Valley": The Asian Health Assessment Project. *Amerasia*, 12(2), 43–65.

Mollica, R. F., & Lavelle, J. P. (1988). Southeast Asian refugees. In L. Comas-Díaz & E. E. H. Griffith (eds.), *Clinical guidelines in cross-cultural mental health* (pp. 262–302). New York: John Wiley.

Montero, D. (1979). *Vietnamese-Americans: Patterns of resettlement and socioeconomic adaptation in the United States.* Boulder, CO: Westview Press.

Owan, T. C. (Ed.). (1985). *Southeast Asian mental health: Treatment, prevention, services, training, and research*, Rockville, MD: National Institute of Mental Health.

Pedraza-Bailey, S. (1985). *Political and economic migrants in America: Cubans and Mexicans.* Austin: University of Texas Press.

Portes, A., & Rumbaut, R. G. (1990). *Immigrant America: A portrait.* Berkeley: University of California Press.

Rahe, R. H., Looney, J., Ward, H. W., Tung, T. M., & Liu, W. T. (1978). Psychiatric consultation in a Vietnamese refugee camp. *American Journal of Psychiatry*, 135, 185–190.

Roberts, A. E., & Starr, P. D. (1989). Differential reference group assimilation among Vietnamese refugees. In D. W. Haines (ed.), *Refugees as immigrants: Cambodians, Laotians and Vietnamese in America* (pp. 40–54). Totowa, NJ: Rowman & Littlefield.

Rumbaut, R. G. (1985). Mental health and the refugee experience: A comparative study of Southeast Asian refugees. In T. C. Owan (eds.), *Southeast Asian mental health* (pp. 433–486). Rockville, MD: National Institute of Mental Health.

Rumbaut, R. G. (1989a). Portraits, patterns and predictors of the refugee adaptation process. In D. W. Haines (Ed.), *Refugees as immigrants: Cambodians, Laotians and Vietnamese in America* (pp. 138–182). Totowa, NJ: Rowman & Littlefield.

Rumbaut, R. G. (1989b). The structure of refuge: Southeast Asian refugees in the United States, 1975–1985. *International Review of Comparative Public Policy*, 1, 97–129.

Rumbaut, R. G. (1990). *Immigrant students in California public schools: A summary of current knowledge* (CDS Report No. 11). Baltimore: Center for Research on Effective Schooling for Disadvantaged Students, The Johns Hopkins University.

Rumbaut, R. G. (1991a). Migration, adaptation, and mental health. In H. Adelman (ed.), *Refugee policy: Canada and the United States* (pp. 383–427). Toronto: York Lanes.

Rumbaut, R. G. (1991b). Passages to America: Perspectives on the new immigration. In A. Wolfe (ed.), *America at century's end* (pp. 208–244). Berkeley: University of California Press.

Rumbaut, R. G. (1994). The new Californians: Comparative research findings on the educational progress of immigrant children. In R. G. Rumbaut & W. A. Cornelius (eds.), *California's immigrant children: Theory, research, and implications for educational policy*. San Diego: Center for U.S.-Mexican Studies, University of California.

Rumbaut, R. G., Chávez, L. R., Moser, R. J., Pickwell, S. M., & Wishik, S. M. (1988). The politics of migrant health care: A comparative study of Mexican immigrants and Indochinese refugees. *Research in the Sociology of Health Care, 7,* 143–202.

Rumbaut, R. G., & Ima, K. (1988). *The adaptation of Southeast Asian refugee youth: A comparative study*. Washington, DC: U.S. Office of Refugee Resettlement.

Rumbaut, R. G., & Weeks, J. R. (1986). Fertility and adaptation: Indochinese refugees in the United States. *International Migration Review,* 20(2), 428–466.

Rumbaut, R. G., & Weeks, J. R. (1989). Infant health among Indochinese refugees: Patterns of infant mortality, birthweight, and prenatal care in comparative perspective. *Research in the Sociology of Health Care, 8,* 137–196.

Shawcross, W. (1984). *The quality of mercy: Cambodia, holocaust and modern conscience*. New York: Simon & Schuster.

Strand, P. J. (1989). The Indochinese refugee experience: The case of San Diego. In D. W. Haines (ed.), *Refugees as immigrants: Cambodians, Laotians and Vietnamese in America* (pp. 105–120). Totowa, NJ: Rowman & Littlefield.

Strand, P. J., & Jones, W., Jr. (1985). *Indochinese refugees in America*. Durham, NC: Duke University Press.

Terris, D. (1987, June 14). Kids in the middle: The lost generation of Southeast Asians. *The Boston Globe Magazine,* pp. 2–11.

U.S. Bureau of the Census. (1993a). *1990 census of the population, general population characteristics, the United States* (CP-1-1), Washington, DC: Government Printing Office.

U.S. Bureau of the Census. (1993b). *1990 census of the population, Asians and Pacific Islanders in the United States* (CP-3-5), Washington, DC: Government Printing Office.

U.S. Committee for Refugees. (1985). *Cambodians in Thailand: People on the edge*. Washington, DC: U.S. Committee for Refugees.

U.S. Committee for Refugees. (1986). *Refugees from Laos: In harm's way*. Washington, DC: U.S. Committee for Refugees.

U.S. Committee for Refugees. (1987). *Uncertain harbors: The plight of Vietnamese boat people*. Washington, DC: U.S. Committee for Refugees.

U.S. Committee for Refugees. (1993). *World refugee survey: 1993 in review*. Washington, DC: U.S. Committee for Refugees.

U.S. General Accounting Office. (1994). *Vietnamese Amerasian resettlement: Education, employment, and family outcomes in the United States* (GAO/PE114D-94-15). Washington, DC: U.S. General Accounting Office.

U.S. Office of Refugee Resettlement. (1982). *Annual report*. Washington, DC: U.S. Department of Health and Human Services.

U.S. Office of Refugee Resettlement. (1985). *Annual report.* Washington, DC: U.S. Department of Health and Human Services.

U.S. Office of Refugee Resettlement. (1991). *Annual report.* Washington, DC: U.S. Department of Health and Human Services.

U.S. Office of Refugee Resettlement. (1992). *Annual report.* Washington, DC: U.S. Department of Health and Human Services.

Vega, W. A., & Rumbaut, R. G. (1991). Ethnic minorities and mental health. *Annual Review of Sociology, 17,* 351–383.

Weeks, J. R., & Rumbaut, R. G. (1991). Infant mortality among ethnic immigrant groups. *Social Science and Medicine, 33*(3), 327–334.

Whitmore, J. K. (1985). Chinese from Southeast Asia. In D. W. Haines (ed.), *Refugees in the United States: A reference handbook* (pp. 59–76). Westport, CT: Greenwood Press.

Whitmore, J. K., Trautmann, M., & Caplan, N. (1989). The socio-cultural basis for the economic and educational success of Southeast Asian refugees (1978–1982 arrivals). In D. W. Haines (ed.), *Refugees as immigrants: Cambodians, Laotians and Vietnamese in America* (pp. 121–137). Totowa, NJ: Rowman & Littlefield.

Williams, C. L., & Westermeyer, J. (ed.) (1986). *Refugee mental health in resettlement countries.* New York: Hemisphere.

Young, M. B. (1991). *The Vietnam wars, 1945–1990.* New York: HarperCollins.

Zolberg, A. R., Suhrke, A., & Aguayo, S. (1989). *Escape from violence: Conflict and the refugee crisis in the developing world.* New York: Oxford University Press.

Zucker, N. L., & Zucker, N. F. (1987). *The guarded gate: The reality of American refugee policy.* New York: Harcourt Brace Jovanovitch.

Chapter Seven

The Social Construction of Gendered Migration from the Philippines

James A. Tyner

A growing, and too often neglected, global issue in migration studies is the exploitation of women overseas contract workers (OCWs). Considerable research has focused on contemporary Asian labor migration patterns (Arnold and Shah, 1986; Gunatilleke, 1986; Abella, 1992; Battistella and Paganoni, 1992; Huguet, 1992; Skeldon, 1992). Research has also examined the costs and benefits of labor migration for countries (Stahl, 1988; Agostinelli, 1991; Vasquez, 1992) as well as individuals and families (Cruz, 1987; Cruz and Paganoni, 1989). Decidedly less research has examined the vulnerability and exploitation of women overseas contract workers (Orozco, 1985; de Guzman, 1984; Sancho and Layador, 1993). Most information on the exploitation of migrants is scattered throughout the literature, found in social commentaries, journalistic reports or descriptive accounts of particular types of migrants such as domestic workers or entertainers (David, 1991; Palma-Beltran and de Dios, 1992; Sancho and Layador, 1993). Currently, there is no explicit attempt to provide a theoretical basis to our understanding of the vulnerability and exploitation of women overseas contract workers.

It is very difficult to provide a universal explanation for the variety of exploitative practices—double-charging of fees for labor contracts, false contracts, physical and sexual abuse—that are prevalent in the migratory process. Some practices are readily explainable and generalizable, e.g., the deception by illegal recruiters for quick and easy profit is made at the expense of unwary migrants. It is questionable, however, whether a holistic explanation for the exploitation of migrants exists (or is even desirable, given the place-specificity of many migration flows), since all types of workers are susceptible to various forms of exploitation. Some, however, are gender specific and, in fact, have important policy considerations.

The purpose of this chapter is to examine how the social construction of gender influences migration and how this contributes to the increased vulnerability and exploitation of women migrants. Building on recent developments in social construction theory (Ng, 1986; Aguilar, 1989; Jackson, 1994; Jackson and Penrose, 1989, 1993), my central thesis is that underlying social structures—while only partially responsible for migration[1]—play a significant role in shaping gender differences in international labor migration flows. Employment opportunities (i.e., "men's" work and "women's" work) are not biologically determined, but socially constructed. Specifically, women's labor in overseas contract work has been largely relegated to service sectors, such as domestic work and entertainment. These positions are usually independent, in the sense that workers often perform their duties alone and in private. Additionally, these positions place women in subservient roles, where the very job description is either to "serve" or to "entertain." Combined, these two conditions contribute to women's increased vulnerability and exploitation in overseas contract work. Empirically, this thesis is supported by a case study of contemporary Philippine international labor migration. Using interviews with government officials, private recruiters, and nongovernmental organizations, I document the causes (social construction of gendered migration) and consequences (increased vulnerability and exploitation) of this migration flow.

The intent is not to imply that only women, or Filipinas, are exploited as migrants, but rather to highlight how the social construction of gendered migration increases the vulnerability of many women migrants by confining these workers into more marginalized occupational niches. As Jackson and Penrose (1993: 2) attest, if we can learn how "specific constructions have empowered particular categories, we can disempower them or appropriate their intrinsic power, to achieve more equitable ends." And to this end, we may be in a better position to identify viable policies and programs for the protection of overseas contract workers (Tyner, forthcoming).

The Social Construction of Gender and Gendered Migration

Chant and Radcliffe (1992: 19) observe that "although sex has long been recognized as a variable in migrant selectivity, female migration has only recently been included within the rubric of general migration theories." Since the late 1970s, but especially in the late 1980s and early 1990s, there has been an increasing number of studies on gender and migration (Phizacklea, 1983; Fawcett, Khoo, and Smith, 1984; Orozco, 1985; Simon and Brettel, 1986; Radcliffe, 1990, 1991; Chant, 1992a; Palma-Beltran and de Dios, 1992; Sancho and Layador, 1993). In general, the study of women in migration has paralleled advances made within the larger field of women's studies, shifting from an emphasis on the documentation of patterns to the explanation of patterns (see Bowlby et al., 1989: 158). Early work identified biases in previous studies, such as methodological problems of interviewing only "male heads of households"; interviewing women when their spouses were present; discounting women's labor force participation, thus ignoring economic motives for female migration; and assumptions that women migrate predominantly with men (husbands) or to join husbands.

One area that is lacking in gender and migration research is theory building (Thadani and Todaro, 1984; Radcliffe, 1990; Chant, 1992a,b; Chant and Radcliffe, 1992). Some migration theories preclude a priori the study of women, while others are modified to explain the participation of women, albeit as a residual or aberrant phenomenon. Considerably fewer theories or models have directly addressed gender and migration simultaneously. This discussion contributes to theory building of gender and migration by adapting recent work in social construction theory to the study of gendered migration. This is parallel to developments in contemporary feminist scholarship, as McDowell (1992: 400) identifies:

> [T]he shift of emphasis in feminist scholarship away from women towards gender, allow[s] issues about the social construction of, and geographical variations in, masculinity as well as femininity to be raised.

The Social Construction of Gender

Social construction theory represents a fundamental attack on the imposition, and continuance, of social categories previously conceptualized as naturally occurring and immutable. It is a perspective which is "concerned with the ways in which we think about and use categories (e.g., class, gender, race) to structure our experiences and analysis of the world" (Jackson and Penrose, 1993: 2). Specifically, a social construction perspective challenges the sexist ideologies embedded within biological determinism. The basic premise of biological determinism, as it applies to occupational differences between the sexes, is that women and men perform different kinds of jobs because they have different biologically based abilities (Curthoys, 1986: 320). Thus, women are perceived to be naturally skilled at domestic work (e.g., child-rearing, cooking, and cleaning). In fact, most societies, across historical periods, have tended to assign females to infant care and to the duties associated with raising children because of their biological ability to bear children (Amott and Matthaei, 1991: 14).

Proponents of a social construction perspective, conversely, maintain that differences between women and men result from the development of sexist ideologies which confuse biological differences with sociological differences. In particular, the beliefs about "male" work and "female" work stem from a sexist ideology that is transmitted through a socialization process (Curthoys, 1986). Socialization refers to a lifelong process whereby children grow up and develop as socially defined men and women: the biological sexes are assigned distinct and often unequal work and political positions (Amott and Matthaei, 1991: 13). Support for this argument is well founded (Jackson and Penrose, 1989; Radcliffe, 1990, 1991). Radcliffe (1990, 1991), for example, finds that Peruvian women are socialized from an early age to perform domestic tasks. In fact, "patterns of gender subordination . . . influence the consolidation of a pool of domestically trained, undervalued peasant girls *before* their entry or supply to the labour market as domestic servants" (Radcliffe, 1990: 382). Ironically, the prevalence of women in the paid domestic sphere may even prevent the socialization of other members to perform household tasks. Duarte (1989: 199) argues that:

> the very presence of the domestic worker discourages the collaboration of male household members, children, and teenagers. The fact that domestic service is available, therefore, reaffirms machismo and patriarchy in the heart of the family.

This is correct—to a point. The fact that the domestic worker is presumed to be female reinforces patriarchy. The ability of a woman to hire a domestic worker to assume responsibilities for reproductive tasks may still be seen as liberating, in the sense that these women are able to enter the paid work force. However, since patriarchal structures relegate domestic work to the confines of other, often ethnically or racially different, women, this process does, in fact, reinforce existing social relations. Indeed, social constructions of gender cannot be considered separate from social constructions of class, race, or even nationality (Amott and Matthaei, 1991; Glenn, 1992; Jackson and Penrose, 1993). This is particularly evident when migration brings individuals from diverse cultures into contact. In Peru, migrant domestic workers are "looked upon by their employers as a homogeneous inferior group, because of their [the employees] peasant origins" (Radcliffe, 1990: 384). Glenn (1992: 33) demonstrates how "the racial division of labor [within the United States] bolstered the gender division of labor indirectly by offering white women a slightly more privileged position in exchange for accepting domesticity." Duarte (1989: 199) finds in the Dominican Republic that "the fact that [the female employer] is in a position to employ a domestic worker reinforces, rather than challenges, patriarchy and the subordination of women in society." At the international level it becomes clear that "ethnic" and "nationality" differences are equally privileging. For example, Filipina maids are looked down upon by Hong Kong or Singaporean employers (Tan and Devasahayam, 1987; Amarles, 1990). Indeed, the liberation of native women in developed countries frequently results from the oppression of migrant women, often of color.

The Social Construction of Gendered Migration

A social construction perspective has important implications for migration research. Through a sensitivity to how concepts of gender are socially constructed, it is possible to examine how these influence the migration, employment, and even exploitation of women and men. As Guest (1993: 224) writes, "to understand the determinants of gender differences in migration flows it is necessary to recognize that, within a society, sex roles, although not immutable, are historically determined." It should come as no surprise, therefore, that previous research found that women often did not migrate independently of men. In many cultures throughout history, socially constructed norms and values have impinged on the migration behavior of women. For example, the independent migration of women in Bangladesh has historically been constrained by patriarchal structures and purdah (Pryer, 1992: 141). Pittin (1984: 1321) likewise finds that the migration of Hausa women in Nigeria has been constrained by "social impediments designed to control women." Similar constraints are found through Latin America, Asia, and the Middle East (Wilkinson, 1987; Radcliffe, 1990, 1991).

The social construction of gender channels women into specific roles. First, because of direct socialization to perform household tasks, many women may genuinely be limited to domestic-service-oriented occupations; they may not have the skills required for other employment opportunities. Clearly, when women are precluded from obtaining higher education, or even vocational training, they are effectively prevented from higher-skilled and higher-paying occupations. In Peru, for example, "peasant families have tended to favour their sons' education and training, whereas daughters continue to face parental unwillingness to fund formal education or skills development" (Radcliffe, 1990: 382). In Thailand, as well, the son's education is commonly perceived as more important than the daughter's. In fact, the son's education is often supported not by his parents but by a daughter who had previously migrated (Singhanetra-Renard and Prabhudhanitisarn, 1992: 163).

Second, women may have greater opportunities for factory employment because of perceived benefits to employers. Women are specifically recruited because of sexist (and racist) stereotypes: these include dominant images of women as cheap, docile, temporary, and being predisposed to factory work, such as having nimble fingers and good eyesight (Floro, 1991; Eviota, 1992). Other times migrant women are in demand because indigenous women are not allowed to work. Women in some Middle Eastern countries, for example, are not allowed or encouraged to perform household tasks, thus creating a huge demand for domestic workers (Eelens and Speckmann, 1990). Moreover, as standards of living have risen in these countries, there has been a simultaneous increase in the demand for domestic work. The number of Sri Lankan domestic workers employed in the Gulf States, for example, increased from 4,898 to 41,912 during the period 1986–1991. In Hong Kong and Singapore also, the entry of indigenous women workers into waged labor has necessitated a rapid influx of domestic workers from less developed countries (Skeldon, 1992).

The Gendered Nature of Philippine Labor Migration

Despite early recognition that women predominate in flows of domestic workers and entertainers, migration research has neither adequately examined, nor critically questioned, this situation. Chiengkul (1986: 312), for example, discusses the labor migration of Thai workers to the Middle East and writes:

> Almost all Thai workers in the Middle East are male. The conditions in the labor-importing countries have discouraged the migration of female workers. *Most of the job opportunities for females are confined to domestic service.* (Emphasis added)

Within Sri Lanka, likewise, Eelens and Speckmann (1990: 300) note that it is becoming more difficult for men to find employment overseas:

> The reason for this sex discrepancy in migration opportunities is that the recruitment of male laborers, who are mainly active in development projects, is highly dependent on the economic trends in the Middle East, while that of housemaids relates to the living standards in Middle Eastern households.

These two statements vividly illustrate that international labor migration is not gender-free, but highly differentiated based on social constructions of gender. More important, however, they illustrate the uncritical acceptance of observed patterns, without addressing the causes or consequences of this imposed gendering of migration. In neither case is it questioned why job opportunities for females must be confined to domestic services. Have migrants been socialized into accepting certain roles? Are these sexual divisions of labor regulated by policy? What are the consequences of this gendered migration? To better address these questions, I provide an overview of the Philippine labor-export policy to examine how social constructions of gender contribute to: (1) patterns of gendered migration; (2) the social construction of gender in the Philippines; and (3) the social construction of Philippine labor migration. This is followed by an examination of the subsequent vulnerability and exploitation of Filipina overseas contract workers.

Trends in Philippine Overseas Labor Migration

Within overseas labor migration, men and women from the Philippines migrate in near equal numbers. In 1987, for example, of the 382,229 deployed Philippine contract workers, 47 percent were women.[2] However, occupational patterns reveal significant gender differences (Table 7.1).

Specifically, Filipinas are underrepreted in higher-level positions and over-represented in lower-level positions, as reflected by their dominance in both service and entertainment sectors. These do not, however, appear to be reflective of the skill levels of Philippine women in general. During the 1980s, for example, Filipinas made up 55 percent of all professional and technical positions in the Philippines, but only 44 percent of all professional and technical Philippine workers deployed overseas (Tables 7.1 and 7.2). Simultaneously, Filipinas comprised 44 percent of all sales and service workers in the Philippines, yet represented 82 percent of all Philippine sales and service workers deployed overseas. In fact, women comprised 98 percent of all domestic workers deployed, and these numbers are hidden in the general category of "services."

Because of the significant interrelation between occupation type and geographic destination, it is possible to further discuss gender differences exhibited in Philippine

TABLE 7.1

Deployed Philippine Overseas Contract Workers by Occupation and Sex, 1987

Occupation	Total	Male	Female
Professional, Technical	71,614	40,393 (56.4%)	31,221 (43.6%)
Entertainers	33,924	2,345 (6.9%)	31,579 (93.1%)
Administrative, Management	1,503	1,372 (91.3%)	131 (8.7%)
Clerical	13,694	9,888 (72.2%)	3,806 (27.8%)
Sales	3,722	1,773 (47.6%)	1,949 (52.4%)
Services	128,704	21,904 (17.0%)	106,800 (83.0%)
Agriculture	2,215	2,202 (99.4%)	13 (0.6%)
Production, Construction	126,853	121,911 (96.1%)	4,942 (3.9%)
TOTAL	382,229	201,788 (52.8%)	180,441 (47.2%)

SOURCE: Philippine Overseas Employment Administration (1987).

TABLE 7.2
Filipino Workers 15 Years and Over in the Philippines by Occupation and Sex,
1990

Occupation	Total	Male	Female
Professional, Technical	1,434,070	634,633	799,437
		(44.3%)	(55.7%)
Administrative, Management	920,493	549,951	370,542
		(59.8%)	(40.2%)
Clerical	763,048	298,013	465,035
		(39.1%)	(60.9%)
Sales & Services	954,647	537,025	427,622
		(56.3%)	(43.7%)
Agriculture	6,589,176	6,055,725	533,451
		(91.9%)	(8.10%)
Production, Construction	3,204,981	2,629,100	575,881
		(82.0%)	(18.0%)
Elementary Occupations[1]	3,765,793	2,144,271	1,621,522
		(56.9%)	(43.1%)
Non-Gainful[2]	15,474,331	3,442,305	12,032,026
		(22.3%)	(77.7%)
Unclassified	3,465,859	1,882,033	1,583,826
		(54.3%)	(45.7%)

1. Elementary occupations include market stall vendors, domestic helpers, caretakers, miscellaneous laborers, and so forth.
2. Nongainful occupations include housekeepers (own home), pensioners, and students.
SOURCE: National Statistics Office (1990: Table 16).

labor migration patterns based on major world regions. The Middle East region has continually received the largest proportion of Philippine OCWs since the late 1970s and into the early 1990s. In 1987, of 382,229 Philippine labor migrants deployed worldwide, 272,038 (71 percent) were deployed to this region. This migration system is composed primarily of men engaged in the production/construction sector. Of the total number of Philippine OCWs deployed to the Middle East, 68 percent were men. Women overwhelmingly found employment in two sectors: services (56 percent) and professionals (32 percent). The Asian region, as opposed to Middle Eastern destinations, is characterized by a predominance of female labor migrants: 92 percent of Philippine OCWs to this region are women. Within Asia there are distinct occupational patterns of Philippine OCWs. Both Hong Kong and Singapore import women domestic workers from the Philippines (Table 7.3), whereas Japan imports women to work in the entertainment industries. In 1987, of the 46,790 workers deployed to Hong Kong and Singapore, 99 percent were women, engaged primarily as maids and other servants. The phenomenal demand for Filipina domestic workers in Hong Kong and Singapore has been explained primarily by the large number of indigenous women entering the paid labor force, thus necessitating a demand for foreign maids to provide family care (Skeldon, 1992).

The predominance of women engaged in the entertainment industries in Japan is even more pronounced (Table 7.4). In particular, Japan accounts for the largest share of all deployed women migrant entertainers from the Philippines. In 1987, out of a total of 31,579 Filipina migrant entertainers deployed worldwide, 31,292 (99 percent) were destined for Japan. Viewed from another perspective, of the 33,791 deployed Philippine OCWs to Japan, 93 percent were Filipina entertainers. Bear in mind these numbers reflect only legally admitted labor migrants; when illegal entrants and

TABLE 7.3
*Top Ten Destinations of Legally Deployed Philippine Domestic
Workers by Sex, 1987*

Destination	Total	Male deployed	Female
Hong Kong	30,152	318 (1.1%)	29,834 (98.9%)
Singapore	16,638	26 (0.2%)	16,612 (99.8%)
Saudi Arabia	9,090	285 (3.1%)	8,805 (96.9%)
United Arab Emirates	8,561	132 (1.5%)	8,429 (98.5%)
Qatar	2,243	87 (3.9%)	2,156 (96.1%)
Malaysia	2,125	0 (0%)	2,125 (100.0%)
Brunei	2,067	62 (3.0%)	2,005 (97.0%)
Kuwait	1,683	10 (0.6%)	1,673 (99.4%)
Greece	1,679	33 (2.0%)	1,646 (98.0%)
Italy	1,668	168 (10.1%)	1,500 (89.9%)

SOURCE: Philippine Overseas Employment Administration (1987).

TABLE 7.4
*Top Five Destinations of Legally Deployed Philippine Entertainers
by Sex, 1987*

Destination	Total	Male deployed	Female
Japan	33,249	1,957 (5.9%)	31,292 (94.1%)
Hong Kong	254	197 (77.6%)	57 (22.4%)
Italy	99	6 (6.1%)	93 (93.9%)
United Arab Emirates	60	26 (43.3%)	34 (56.7%)
Korea	34	27 (79.4%)	7 (20.6%)

SOURCE: Philippine Overseas Employment Administration (1987).

overstayers are included, estimates of Filipinas working in the entertainment industries in Japan range from 60,000 to 150,000 (David, 1991; deDios, 1992).

Similar to the Asian region, labor-importing countries of Europe (e.g., Greece,
Italy, and Spain) and the Americas (e.g., Canada and the United States) predominantly employ women. Of the 5,643 workers deployed to Europe in 1987, nearly 83
percent were women; over 91 percent of the Filipina OCWs destined to Europe were
domestic workers. Occupational patterns to the Americas are comparable to Europe,
in the sense that a large proportion (31 percent) of all Philippine OCWs deployed are
female domestic workers. This situation is unlike Europe, however, in that both the
United States and Canada also import a large proportion of women (53 percent)
engaged in professional sectors (e.g., doctors, nurses).

Two final regions—Africa and the Pacific—reflect a predominance of male Filipino OCWs. The majority of these workers are engaged in production/construction occupations, reflecting an emphasis on the development of infrastructure throughout Africa and the Pacific. However, there is a smaller, but socially important, number of professionals deployed to these regions (especially in Nigeria; see Saliba, 1993).

To what extent are these observed patterns reflective of institutional regulations or underlying structural conditions that influence, but do not determine, deployment practices?

The Social Construction of Gender in the Philippines

The Filipino household is commonly viewed as egalitarian (Javillonar, 1979; Green, 1980) and the relatively high position of women in the Philippines is thought to date back to the precolonial era.[3] This social structure is evidenced by the many gender-neutral kinship terms in the Tagalog vocabulary (Medina, 1991: 23–24), including *asawa* (spouse), *anak* (son or daughter), *apo* (grandchild), *bata* (child), and *siya* (he or she). And even though men are generally recognized as the head of the household, women are thought to control the household through budget management and resource allocation. However, studies have increasingly indicated that the Filipino household is not as egalitarian as once thought (Aguilar-San Juan, 1982; Eviota, 1986, 1992; Aguilar, 1989; Floro, 1991). Indeed, the majority of Filipino couples follow the traditional division of labor or task allocation, with the husband as the breadwinner and the wife as the domestic (Medina, 1991: 123). Aguilar (1989: 543), for example, suggests that "egalitarianism is merely a tag that has been foisted upon a set of relations it really does not fit." Specifically, she argues that the wives' role as household manager does not translate into an increase in power or status within the household. Bulatao (1984: 352), in a survey of nearly 1,600 women, concludes that wives seldom make decisions by themselves in any region throughout the Philippines—a conclusion supported by Floro (1991: 109). Moreover, over 90 percent of the women in the Bulatao study indicated that they needed their husbands' permission to either go out with friends or to lend money to relatives. This latter finding, in particular, raises doubts as to Philippine women being in control of their households and household resources.

Philippine society thus reveals distinct gender roles, resulting from a lifelong socialization process. This process occurs in two different, yet simultaneously and mutually reinforcing guises: direct socialization and indirect socialization. Direct socialization results when the child is explicitly and directly taught standards, values, and proper behavior for boys and girls (Medina, 1991: 48). This form of socialization often results from family interactions and schooling. In Philippine society, for example:

> The *binatilyos* (adolescent males) participate in many affairs of the community with more freedom, tolerance and understanding from their parents, while the *dalagitas* (adolescent females) generally stay at home to take care of the siblings and other "womanly" chores like washing clothes, cooking the meals, and other work activities connected with the upkeep of the house (Medina, 1991: 123–124).

Although both parents play an active role in socialization, the mother assumes the bulk of childcare responsibility because it is she who spends more time at home and has a more intimate relationship with the child. This fact reinforces the Filipino stereotype of the woman playing the domestic role (Medina, 1991: 196).

In school, girls are often channelled into home economics courses (sewing, cooking, vegetable gardening), while boys learn woodworking, knot-tying, and agricultural techniques.[4] Textbooks also reflect gender biases. Aurora de Dios and her colleagues (1987) find, for example, that although negative images are not as prevalent as in the other media venues, women are still shown in very limited activities, mostly confined to domestic roles. Women are also defined, in general, by their relation to men (as wives, sisters, or mothers). The most prestigious roles for women found in the study were those of teachers and nurses. Moreover, not only are roles limited, but the behavior of women is conditioned to an inferior or dependent position. Women are routinely portrayed as passive, obedient, submissive, and docile (de Dios, et al., 1987), relying on the more successful or forceful male figurehead.

Indirect socialization, conversely, refers to the process whereby the child learns cultural values and norms from his or her observations and experiences (Medina, 1991: 48). Media, in particular, have been influential in reinforcing images of women and men. A five-month survey undertaken in the Philippines during 1985 revealed some particularly relevant results regarding the social construction of gender roles. Traditionally, the perceived role of Filipino wives, according to Sevilla (quoted in Medina, 1991) is that of "a loving and loyal mate to her husband"; one who is "responsible for keeping the marriage intact by her patience, submission, and virtues." Furthermore, she is a "diligent housekeeper" and the family treasurer who budgets the money for the various family needs (quoted in Medina, 1991:123). Azarcon-dela Cruz (1988) discusses how television shows reinforce these images of motherhood, beauty, docility, subservience to men. Women in radio serials are most often "portrayed as wife, mother, mistress or domestic helper" (p. 112). Indeed, television shows often portray men as "the main breadwinner who must support the family at all costs" (p. 95)

Radio and television ads likewise portray women as the epitome of beauty, docility, and household efficiency. Women are more likely to appear as mothers, wives and household help, while men are rarely present. These reinforce the image that home and household are solely a woman's domain. Other common images portrayed women as girlfriends, dates, and sex objects. Print ads as well "have persisted in reinforcing the stereotyped images of women as less important, less intelligent, of less consequence and weaker than men" (p. 38). Many advertisements also imply that women buy products, not so much for personal satisfaction but rather for male approval and acceptance. For impressionable children, these ads could easily be the source of role models and future expectations.

The Social Construction of Philippine Labor Migration

Historically, racial and sexual stereotypes have been institutionalized within labor markets (Glenn, 1992: Ng, 1986; Hossfield, 1994). Ng's (1986) study of an employment placement agency reveals the process by which immigrant women were commodified into specific locations in the Canadian labor market. Glenn (1992) likewise identifies the channelization of immigrant women into certain jobs, such as domestic work. Within the Philippine labor migration industry, however, there are no institutional or officially sanctioned policies restricting Filipinas to employment in domestic services and entertainment sectors. Neither are men or women specifically channelled or counselled into these sectors. Guidelines and regulations of the Philippines Overseas Employment Administration (POEA), for example, do not specify any distinction in employment contracts; thus (at least in the country of origin) there seem to be no restrictions on male/female employment. Additionally, an examination of Standard Employment Contracts provided by the POEA reveal no specificity regarding the sex of domestic workers. Indeed, some contracts repeatedly make reference to "he/she" and "his/her" when outlining employment parameters. In the case of Singapore, however, the contract only makes reference to women, as in:

> The worker is expected to commence her daily duties by ensuring that reasonable morning requirements of the Employer and his/her family are met and prepared on time and shall ensure that her day's chores are fulfilled before retiring to bed.

However, while not officially endorsing a gender-based policy, the marketing strategies of the POEA may unintentionally contribute to the social construction of gendered migration. The cover of a pamphlet lauding the virtues of "Filipino man-power"[5] distributed by the POEA, for example, reveals six Filipinos, dressed according to their job. Of the three women, one is dressed as a nurse, a second as a maid, and the third as an entertainer (wearing a miniskirt and holding a guitar). Of the three men, one is holding a t-square (an engineer perhaps?), a second is dressed as a construction worker, and the third as a ship-based officer. Inside, the text reveals that Filipinos are "properly educated and well-trained, proficient in English and of *sound temperament*" (emphasis added). This last statement might be read as implying the docility and subservience of all Filipino workers.

Although not officially sanctioned, underlying social constructions of gender are manifest within policies and programs of international labor migration. This manifestation is most evident in specific recruitment practices. When foreign principals submit "manpower" requests, they are required to specify the skills needed and qualifications desired. For many occupations, such as domestic services and entertainment work, employers often request potential employees based not on skill but rather personal characteristics (e.g., young, attractive, or happy). "Help-wanted" advertisements placed in various Hong Kong newspapers read: "Cheerful, live-in Filipina maid/cook wanted" or "Temporary Filipina maid wanted for month . . . clean, tidy appearance" (Mission for Filipino Migrant Workers, 1983).

In effect, women OCWs are commodified to fit preexisting and externally imposed images of what women/women-migrants should be and should perform. The social construction of *female maid*, in particular, reflects a mixture of gender and racial stereotypes. Moreover, hiring practices reveal the existence of racist hierarchies as to the most desirable, or acceptable, nationality. In Italy, for example, "Filipino women [as opposed to African women] . . . appear at the top of the hierarchy as determined by the preferences of Italian families for domestic workers" (Andall, 1992: 45). Hornziel (quoted in Andall, 1992: 45) states that "in middle-upper environments Filipino domestic workers, with their knowledge of the English language, also offer an element of cultural prestige."

In Jordan, also, maids are ranked according to skin color, communication abilities, beauty, and fashionable appearance (Humphrey, 1991: 56). Hierarchies such as these have translated into relatively higher wages for better-educated, light-skinned, English-speaking Filipinas, as opposed to poorly educated, dark-skinned, non-English speaking Sri Lankan women.

Women migrants are no longer viewed as individuals, but rather as products to be exported and imported. In Japan, Filipinas are often ordered through catalogues just as one might order office supplies. Tono (1986: 71) relates that in the Philippines:

> [A]fter a woman is targeted, her picture is taken and filed in a catalogue. Promoters exchange their catalogues and show them to customers, such as bar managers. "This girl is a 17-year-old high school student. She's got a terrific body, but is a drug addict," is a typical comment by the promoter when he shows the women's pictures in the catalogues.

Entertainers are doubly exploited because of race and sex. As Duenas (Philippines Free Press, April 4, 1987) writes of Filipinas:

> [She] is a downgraded woman in Japan. In that country where sex dominates the preoccupation of men and is a billion-dollar industry, the image of the Filipina is that of a shameless "Japayuki-san" whose only purpose in coming to Japan is to sell her body for Japanese yen. In the booming, countrywide sex trade, which in Japan is not looked down on as dirty business, the "Japayuki-san" is treated as merchandise, a commodity to be listed in the buy-and-sell catalogues.

In Hong Kong, Filipinas and domestic service have become so merged in the popular culture that a doll sold widely in Hong Kong is called simply "Filipina maid." Indeed, the word "Filipina" in Hong Kong has come to mean *amah*, a term for maidservant (Aguilar, 1989). A sample of advertisements placed by recruitment agencies in Hong Kong read: "Available with videotapes. Excellent Filipina babysitters, housekeepers," "A brand new selection! Filipina and Sri Lankan Maids," "A wide selection of Filipina maids with colour TV viewing" (Mission for Filipino Migrant Workers, 1983)

Notice also the selling points used by recruitment agencies to attract customers. They boldly proclaim "wide selections" to choose from. In fact, this preview is often vital. Within some labor-importing countries, the ability to employ a Filipina maid is seen as a status symbol. Similar to "owning the right car" and "living in the right area," it has become essential to employ the proper maid. Humphrey (1991: 56), for example, finds that in Jordan, "domestic servants are essentially an item of consumption with symbolic value."

The private sector is often compliant with these requests. When foreign employers specify "provincial girls," believing them to be better "trained" in domestic skills (i.e., cooking, cleaning, and childcare), labor recruiters continually leave the confines of Manila in search of better "products." Provincial girls, it is assumed, are less likely to be attracted by "bright lights" and thus more willing to remain isolated as live-in maids.

The recruitment of women in the provinces is, however, partially a response to supply. Some recruiters are finding that larger cities such as Manila are "tapped out." Many of the women residing in Manila, for example, have fallen prey regularly to illegal recruiters and have lost considerable sums of money; therefore they are less able to pay the processing fees for overseas employment.[6] Conversely, if recruitment is conducted in the provinces, recruiters often find pools of fresh applicants that potentially have the financial resources required for overseas employment.

Entertainers, likewise, are specifically recruited in provincial areas; this counters a common-sense assumption that entertainers are recruited in the entertainment districts of Manila. According to the recruiters, "once the girls work in [Philippine] nightclubs, they are hard to control." It is thought that these women have already been exposed to difficult and different situations; foreign employers, therefore, would no longer be able to impose discipline on the entertainers.

In short, employment opportunities are not deliberately or intentionally separated according to sex by the POEA and the private sector. Women can, and do, find employment as doctors, nurses, engineers, as well as domestic workers and entertainers. Men likewise find overseas employment as domestic workers and entertainers. However, global assumptions of men's work and women's work are manifest within the dominant flows of migrant workers from labor-exporting to labor-importing countries. Additionally, labor recruiters do employ social constructs about "provincial" girls when approaching applicants for overseas employment. Moreover, requests by foreign employers indicate that these constructs are widely known and accepted. Not only do these constructs influence the recruitment within the Philippines, but also the specific selection of "the Philippines" as opposed to other labor-exporting countries.

The Exploitation of Women Overseas Contract Workers

All labor migrants are susceptible to some forms of exploitation. Financial fraud is probably the most common, resultant from unscrupulous recruiters overcharging worker-applicants. However, I suggest that the imposed gendering (occupational channelization) of international labor migration has placed women in significantly more vulnerable positions, vis-à-vis their male counterparts. This is most evident in the domestic and entertainment sectors where job requirements have placed women in subservient positions, catering to domestic needs or sexual pleasures. The Standard Employment Contract for Filipino household workers in Singapore, for example, describes the employees' duties:

> The Worker undertakes to perform diligently and faithfully all duties of a domestic nature such as but not limited to laundry, cooking, child or baby care, general cleaning

and housekeeping of the residence of the employer and other relevant household chores which the Employer may from time to time require.

The Worker is expected at all times to observe proper decorum and shall be courteous, polite and respectful to her Employer and members of his/her family. She shall also observe the Code of Discipline for Filipino Workers and abide by the laws of Singapore and respect its customs and traditions.

Entertainers, especially, are in vulnerable positions; their very job description is to provide "entertainment." The Philippine Senate even recommended that Filipino entertainers be provided hazard pay! According to de Dios (1992: 49), these women are "selling a particular brand of female sexuality that caters to the needs and satisfaction of male clients and customers." Entertainers are thus simply sexual objects, or products, to be used at the convenience of customers.

> Why is this so? In 1990 the Philippine Senate questioned why are Filipino migrant women concentrated in the lowly-paid service sectors such as domestic helpers, chambermaids, entertainers, prostitutes, and nurses all over the world although most of them are in fact college graduates or professionals? (Philippine Senate, 1990: 37)

The previous section indicates that other overseas employment opportunities (e.g, professionals), according to the rules and regulations governing the deployment of Philippines OCWs, are open to women. However, the current global demand reflects a desire for Filipinas as servants. Their education and professional skills are not desired, but rather their "beauty, cheerfulness, and hospitality."

The commodification of women migrant workers has, in part, contributed to the widespread exploitation of overseas workers across cultures. Simply put, when migrants are not viewed as individuals but by the functions they perform, they become nonentities: products. Employers can select applicants through catalogues, order them through the mail (through the POEA), and have them delivered. Foreign workers arrive with a contract and instruction manual (job description). For some employers, their newly purchased workers represent a considerable investment. In Singapore, for example, employers are required to deposit a S$5,000 deposit to ensure the good behavior of foreign domestic workers (Tan and Devasahayam, 1987; Amarles, 1990). Good behavior means, in part, that domestic workers are not allowed to marry Singaporeans, get pregnant, or engage in any employment other than that contracted. Rather than risk losing this deposit, draconian measures are emplaced to provide for the "good" behavior of domestic workers. As a result, domestic workers are under constant surveillance.

Nevertheless, women still enter into overseas employment contracts; they are the ones who ultimately sign the contracts. Does this indicate that women willingly engage in these vulnerable occupations? Are they willing partners in a process of commodification? To answer these questions, we must look closer at the process of migration.

The act of migration may be seen as liberating: an exercise of free choice to escape a negative situation. According to African-American feminist bell hooks (1984: 5), however, being oppressed means the absence of choices. We can thus examine the gendering of migration, and the act of migration, from the standpoint of choices. Existing studies have consistently revealed that women (and men) undertake overseas work because of a lack of employment opportunities within the Philippines (Cruz and Paganoni, 1989; Ballescas, 1992; Palma-Beltran and de Dios, 1992). I contend that the reduction of choices to either service sector jobs or entertainment-related occupations represents an absence of choices: the lack of opportunities in the Philippines, coupled with limited opportunities based on subservience and sexuality, reflects an institutionalized system of oppression. This oppression is often exemplified by a private sector that claims they are providing a valuable service. According to members of the private sector, women "choose" to engage in occupations that native workers shun (e.g., those jobs which are dirty, dangerous, and demeaning) because no other job is available in the Philippines. But choice in this context is illusory. The acceptance of lower wages, the tolerance of contract violations, the threat of physical and sexual abuse—these are not conditions which migrants willingly accept. Rather, oppression within the Philippines, combined with global demands for housemaids and dancers, is why women are "willing" to leave their families while caring for other people's families in foreign countries. In short, when migration becomes the only option, it is no longer a choice. Orozco (1985) refers to these women as economic refugees.

Conclusions

Current patterns of international migration, especially contract labor migration, are changing. The rapid industrialization of capital-rich but labor-short countries of the Middle East (notably Saudi Arabia and Kuwait) and Asia (Hong Kong, Japan, and Singapore) stimulated new and major flows of temporary labor migration. Concomitantly, the origins of temporary contract workers shifted from predominantly Mediterranean and European countries toward South and Southeast Asia (e.g., Indonesia, the Philippines, Sri Lanka, and Thailand). Linkages between labor-sending and labor-receiving countries are now more likely to reflect capital linkages rather than colonial or postcolonial linkages.

Coincident with changes in international migration patterns have been significant theoretical advances in migration research, especially in consideration of women migrants (Radcliffe, 1990, 1991; Chant, 1992a,b; Chant and Radcliffe, 1992). Previous work has shown that women do not migrate predominantly in association or in conjunction with men. Nonetheless, many aspects of gendered migration, such as exploitation, remain unexplored. Indeed, current migration research reflects an uncritical acceptance of the sexual division of labor of overseas contract work. When gender differences are discussed, aggregate patterns are revealed at best, thus contributing little to our understanding of the conditions leading to these patterns, and outcomes resultant from these flows.

In part, this lack of awareness mirrors the "invisibility" of female migration. In countries such as Italy and Japan, for example, female migrants had been arriving in large numbers before any significant inflows of male migrants. However, it was not until the latter began to arrive that the "migrant invasion" generated any public response. On one hand, this is a reflection that women are not perceived as a threat, which according to Andall (1992: 42) "suggests that a paternalistic form of sexism may [be] at play." Women migrants also predominantly find employment in the domestic sphere, previously vacated by indigenous women workers. Thus, in the example of Italy, women migrants "have not essentially been perceived as representing a threat on the labour market, but rather are seen as filling a vacuum left by Italian women" (Andall, 1992: 43). In Japan, also, migrant women are seen as filling voids created by the occupational advancement of Japanese women. Indigenous women are less willing to work in the domestic services or entertainment sectors. These changes have created "labor" shortages, thus necessitating large influxes of foreign women. On the other hand, the lack of concern surrounding the import of women workers is related to their employment niches. As Andall (1992: 42) correctly observes, the concentration of women in the domestic sphere has meant that they "have literally been hidden from view."

Drawing on recent developments in social construction theory, I have examined how the social construction of gender and gendered migration channels women toward selected occupations within the international division of labor: domestic workers and entertainers. These occupational niches, in turn, place women in far more vulnerable positions, thus exacerbating exploitative practices.

Two findings are particularly relevant. First, the social construction of women in the Philippines may predispose women to take the roles of domestic helpers or entertainers. Early socialization processes reinforce the expectation that women are to excel in reproductive tasks. However, while occupational roles are significantly influenced by the social construction of women's roles, these roles are neither deterministic nor immutable, and should not be viewed as such. Further research is clearly needed. Are women socialized into the belief that they are only qualified to perform service-oriented functions? Are women more likely to comply with abuses because of continued messages of docility, subservience, and maintaining their proper place?

Second, gendered migration is not formally instituted within Philippine labor-export policy; rather, patterns of gendered migration reflect the acquiescence to global demands predicated on racist and sexist assumptions. Although regularly criticized for the deployment of women in both domestic services and entertainment sectors, the POEA maintains that they are merely responding to the global demands for labor, demands which currently reveal a shift from a predominance of construction and production to that of services. These trends are evidenced by data obtained from the Client Referral Assistance (CRA) system of the POEA. Beginning in 1985 the POEA established this system to facilitate and assist new foreign employers (principals) hiring Filipino workers by locating reputable private recruitment agencies in the Philippines. As such, the CRA system provides a unique glimpse into current demands and future trends of global labor requests. In 1991 skills in high demand included medical workers (47 percent of new job orders); service workers (23 percent); operation and maintenance workers (18 percent); and entertainers (11 percent). For 1992, 82 percent of new employers requested domestic helpers. Private recruiters also have also been continuously criticized for preying on women. And, like the POEA, the private sector maintains that they are simply responding to market demands. Moreover, the private sector sincerely believes that it is providing a much-needed service to an ailing country; through recruiters' efforts, employment is provided to hundreds of thousands of individuals, something the government has not been able to do. However, the acquiescence on the part of the POEA and the private sector does, in fact, indicate that these institutions are willing cater to an international and sexual division of labor which confines women to vulnerable occupations.

In all fairness, the POEA does go to great lengths in an attempt to protect Filipino overseas contract workers. These attempts are primarily evidenced by the introduction of complex and highly regulated procedures for the deployment of workers (especially entertainers). Unfortunately, however, rules and regulations may lead to greater vulnerability. Recent guidelines pertaining to the deployment of entertainers, for example, are overly concerned with certifying that only "reputable" and "legitimate" entertainers are deployed (see Tyner, forthcoming). These policies represent a faulty identification of the problem: that only illegal or nonskilled entertainers are subject to abuse. The newly implemented solution, therefore, is to increase the number of testing and training requirements for potential migrant entertainers. These guidelines, however, overlook the observation that all Filipinas engaged in the entertainment sectors, legal or illegal, trained or untrained, are employed in a vulnerable occupational niche. Moreover, increased costs accrued by potential migrant entertainers may ultimately place these individuals in a greater position of debt-bondage; research on the conditions of Filipina migrant entertainers reveal that many women, legal or otherwise, are coerced into illegal and dehumanizing acts because of debt-bondage (Iyori, 1987; de Dios, 1992; Ballescas, 1992). The POEA also routinely sends Marketing Missions overseas; often the function of these meetings is not marketing per se, but to address welfare problems. Admittedly, many of these missions and policy guidelines follow sensationalized reports of abuses overseas.[7] However, the POEA has responded to potential sites of exploitation. In 1992, for example, a Canadian club attempted to hire a group of Filipina entertainers; however, deployment was denied when the POEA found out that the dancers would be required to dance nude on table tops. The POEA would also like to deploy a higher percentage of skilled professionals, and not just domestic workers and entertainers. This is evidenced by long-range agendas. However, the POEA must also simultaneously respond to both global market demand and domestic considerations in the Philippines. The Department of Health, for example, informally reminds the POEA that rural areas are suffering from a lack of qualified health-care workers. Thus, while there is no official policy or memorandum on the deployment of skilled professionals, the POEA is acutely aware of internal pressures.

The messages embedded within this chapter are not to imply passive acceptance of exploitation on the part of women migrants, nor to deny the autonomy of these women. And, though the literature reveals examples of resistance on the part of abused women (Ballescas, 1992), there is also evidence that these women may more likely defer to the demands of their employers (de Guzman, 1984; Tan and Devasahayam, 1987; Amarles, 1990; Ballescas, 1992; Battistella and Paganoni, 1992). In Japan, for example, entertainers who have been physically abused by customers often tolerate their plight in silence; managers do not want to antagonize future customers (de Dios 1992: 49) and risk losing business. Live-in domestic workers are often isolated, indeed held prisoner, and are thus unable to find assistance (Amarles, 1990; Battistella, 1992). Further research is clearly needed on the response and resistance of migrant workers. Insights derived from this understanding of the social construction of migration patterns may, however, better lead to actual policy considerations. As Glenn (1992: 35) observes, "If race and gender are socially constructed rather than being real referents in the material world, then they can be deconstructed and challenged." To accomplish this, additional research is also required to understand how institutions translate underlying structural conditions to influence the "gendering" and even "racialization," of migration flows.

NOTES

1. The literature reflects an effort to move away from traditional determinants of labor export (e.g., poverty, overpopulation) to more institutional considerations such as labor recruitment mechanisms, policies, and capital investment. See Shah and Arnold (1986); Abella (1992, 1993); Alegado (1992).

2. Throughout this article I primarily utilize 1987 data. These data are the most complete and recent data supplied by the POEA during the writing of this article.

3. More detailed accounts of the social construction of gender in the Philippines are found in Aguilar-San Juan (1982); Aguilar (1989); Medina (1991); and Eviota (1992).

4. Gender biases in education are being challenged, albeit slowly. Home economics classes are now referred to as "Home Technology and Livelihood Education," with both boys and girls participating in these classes.

5. Official terminology used by government and private agencies for labor export is "manpower." While recognizing the sexism inherent in this term, I nevertheless have chosen to retain usage according to Philippine practice.

6. This is not to imply that prospective labor migrants who have lost considerable sums of money to fraudulent recruiters cease in the attempt for overseas employment. Indeed, worker-applicants often go into debt, borrowing from families, friends, and loan sharks to pay recruitment fees (see Lindquist, 1993).

7. Many policies were formulated and implemented following the highly publicized death of Maricris Sioson, an entertainer deployed to Japan, in 1991.

REFERENCES

Abella, Manolo. 1993. Role of Formal Labour Schemes in the Development of Third World Countries. *International Migration* 31 (2/3): 389–402.
———. 1992. International Migration and Development. In *Philippine Labour Migration: Impact and Policy*. Edited by Graziano Battistella and Anthony Paganoni. Quezon City: Scalabrini Migration Center.
Agostinelli, Gianni. 1991. Migration-development Interrelationships: The Case of the Philippines. *Occasional Papers and Documentation*. New York: Center for Migration Studies.
Aguilar, Delia D. 1989. The Social Construction of the Filipino Woman. *International Journal of Intercultural Relations* 13: 527–551.

Aguilar-San Juan, Delia D. 1982. Feminism and the National Liberation Struggle in the Philippines. *Women's Studies International Forum* 5(3–4): 253–261.

Alegado, Dean. T. 1992. *The Political Economy of International Labor Migration from the Philippines.* Ph.D. dissertation, Department of Political Science, University of Hawaii.

Amarles, Bienvendia M. 1990. "Female Migrant Labor: Domestic Helpers in Singapore." *Philippine Journal of Public Administration* 34(4): 365–387.

Amott, Teresa, and Julie Matthaei. 1991. "Race, Class, Gender, and Women's Work: A Conceptual Framework." In *Race, Gender and Work: A Multicultural Economic History of Women in the United States.* Edited by Teresa Amott and Julie Matthaei. Boston: South End Press.

Andall, Jacqueline. 1992. "Women Migrant Workers in Italy." *Women's Studies International Forum* 15(1): 41–48.

Arcinas, Fred R. 1986. "The Philippines." In *Migration of Asian Workers to the Arab World.* Edited by Godfrey Gunatilleke. Tokyo: United Nations University.

Arnold, Fred, and Nasra Shah, eds. 1986. *Asian Labour Migration: Pipeline to the Middle East.* Boulder, CO: Westview Press.

Azarcon-dela Cruz, Pennie S. 1988. *From Virgin to Vamp: Images of Women in Philippine Media.* Manila: Asian Social Institute.

Ballescas, Ma. Rosario P. 1992. *Filipina Entertainers in Japan: An Introduction.* Manila: Foundation for Nationalist Studies.

Battistella, Graziano. 1992. "Filipino Domestic Workers in Italy." In *Filipino Women Overseas Contract Workers . . . at What Cost?* Edited by Mary R. Palma-Beltran and Aurora Javate de Dios. Manila: Goodwill Trading Co.

Battistella, Graziano, and Anthony Paganoni, eds. 1992. *Philippine Labor Migration: Impact and Policy.* Quezon City: Scalabrini Migration Center.

Bowlby, Sophie, et al. 1989. "The Geography of Gender." In *New Models in Geography*, vol. 2. Edited by Richard Peet and Nigel Thrift. London: Unwin Hyman.

Bulatao, Rudolfo A. 1984. "Philippine Urbanism and the Status of Women." In *Women in the Cities of Asia: Migration and Urban Adaptation.* Edited by James T. Fawcett, Siew Khoo, and Peter C. Smith. Boulder, CO: Westview Press.

Chant, Sylvia (ed.). 1992a. *Gender and Migration in Developing Countries.* New York: Belhaven Press.

———. 1992b. "Conclusion: Towards a Framework for the Analysis of Gender-selective Migration." In *Gender and Migration in Developing Countries.* Edited by Sylvia Chant. New York: Belhaven Press.

Chant, Sylvia, and Sarah A. Radcliffe. 1992. "Migration and Development: the Importance of Gender." In *Gender and Migration in Developing Countries.* Edited by Sylvia Chant. New York: Belhaven Press.

Chiengkul, Witayakorn. 1986. "Thailand." In *Migration of Asian Workers to the Arab World.* Edited by Godfrey Gunatilleke. New York: United Nations Press.

Cruz, Victoria P. 1987. *Seasonal Orphans and Solo Parents: The Impact of Overseas Migration.* Quezon City: Scalabrini Migration Center.

Cruz, Victoria P. and Anthony Paganoni. 1989. *Filipinas in Migration: Big Bills and Small Change.* Quezon City: Scalabrini Migration Center.

Curthoys, Ann. 1986. The Sexual Division of Labour: Theoretical Arguments. In *Australian Women New Feminist Perspectives.* Edited by Norma Grieve and Ailsa Burns. Melbourne: Oxford University Press.

David, Randolf S. 1991. "Filipino Workers in Japan: Vulnerability and Survival." *Kasarinlan* 6(3): 8–23.

de Dios, Aurora J. 1992. "Japayuki-san: Filipinas at Risk." In *Filipino Women Overseas Contract Workers... at What Cost?* Edited by Mary R. Palma-Beltran and Aurora Javate de Dios. Manila, Goodwill Trading Co.

de Dios, Aurora J., Anita Obispo, and Manette Antoja. 1987. "Gender Roles in Elementary Textbooks: A Preliminary Analysis." In *Seminar 1: Images and Emerging Lifestyles of the Filipina*. Edited by Josefa S. Francisco. Manila: Women's Resource and Research Center, Maryknoll College Foundation.

de Guzman, Arnel. 1984. "Filipino Overseas Contract Workers: Problems and Prospects." In *Migration from the Philippines*. Edited by Anthony Paganoni. Quezon City: Scalabrini Migration Center.

Duarte, Isis. 1989. "Household Workers in the Dominican Republic: A Question for the Feminist Movement." In *Muchachas No More: Household Workers in Latin America and the Caribbean*. Edited by Elsa M. Chaney and Mary Garcia Castro. Philadelphia: Temple University Press.

Eelens, Frank, and J. D. Speckmann. 1990. "Recruitment of Labor Migrants for the Middle East: The Sri Lankan Case." *International Migration Review* 24(2): 297–322.

Eviota, Elizabeth U. 1992. *The Political Economy of Gender: Women and the Sexual Division of Labour in the Philippines*. London: Zed Books, Ltd.

———. 1986. "The Articulation of Gender and Class in the Philippines." In *Women's Work: Development and the Division of Labor by Gender*. Edited by Eleanor Leacock and Helen I. Safa. South Hadley, MA: Bergin and Garvey Publishers.

Fawcett, James T., Siew-Ean Khoo, and Peter C. Smith, eds. 1984. *Women in the Cities of Asia: Migration and Urban Adaptation*. Boulder, CO: Westview Press.

Floro, Maria Sagrario. 1991. "Market Orientation and the Reconstitution of Women's Role in Philippine Agriculture." *Review of Radical Political Economics* 23(3–4): 106–128.

Glenn, Evelyn Nakano. 1992. "From Servitude to Service Work: Historical Continuities in the Racial Division of Paid Reproductive Labor." *Signs: Journal of Women in Culture and Society* 18(1): 1–43.

Green, Justin. 1980. "Are Filipinas 'More Equal' than Western Women?" *ASIA*, pp. 34–37, 44.

Guest, Philip. 1993. "The Determinants of Female Migration from a Multilevel Perspective." In *Internal Migration of Women in Developing Countries*. New York: United Nations.

Gunatilleke, Godfrey (ed.). 1986. *Migration of Asian Workers to the Arab World*. Tokyo: United Nations University.

hooks, bell 1992. *Black Looks: Race and Representation*. Boston: South End Press.

———. 1984. *Feminist Theory from Margin to Center*. Boston: South End Press.

Hossfield, Karen J. 1994. "Hiring Immigrant Women: Silicon Valley's "Simple Formula." In *Women of Color in U.S. Society*. Edited by Maxine Baca Zinn and Bonnie T. Dill. Philadelphia: Temple University Press.

Huguet, Jerrold W. 1992. "The Future of International Migration within Asia." *Asian and Pacific Migration Journal* 1(2): 250–277.

Humphrey, Michael. 1991. "Asian Women Workers in the Middle East: Domestic Servants in Jordan." *Asian Migrant* 4(2):53–60.

Iyori, Naoko. 1990. "Exploitation by Any Name: The Human Cost of the Pacific Sex Industry." *Katipunan* 3 (10):7,10.

———. 1987. "The Traffic in Japayuki-san." *Japan Quarterly* 34 (1):84–88.

Jackson, Peter. 1994 "Black Male: Advertising and the Cultural Politics of Masculinity." *Gender, Place and Culture* 1(1): 49–59.

Jackson, Peter, and Jan Penrose (eds.). 1993. *Constructions of Race, Place and Nation*. Minneapolis: University of Minnesota Press.

———. 1989. "Geography, Race, and Racism." In *New Models in Geography*, volume 2. Edited by Richard Peet and Nigel Thrift. London: Unwin Hyman.

Javillonar, Gloria V. 1979. "The Filipino Family." In *The Family in Asia*. Edited by Man Singh Das and Panos D. Bardis. London: Allen and Unwin.

Lindquist, Bruce A. 1993. "Migration Networks: A Case Study in the Philippines." *Asian and Pacific Migration Journal* 2(1): 75–104.

McDowell, Linda. 1992. "Doing Gender: Feminism, Feminists and Research Methods in Human Geography." *Transactions, Institute of British Geographers* 17: 399–416.

Medina, Belen T. G. 1991. *The Filipino Family*. Manila: University of the Philippines Press.

Mission for Filipino Migrant Workers. 1983. "A Situationer on Filipino Migrant Workers." Unpublished paper.

Morokvasic, Mirjana. 1983. "Women in Migration: Beyond the Reductionist Outlook." In *One Way Ticket: Migration and Female Labour*. Edited by Annie Phizacklea. London: Routledge and Kegan Paul.

National Statistics Office. 1990. *Census of Population and Housing, Philippines*. Manila: National Statistics Office.

Ng, Roxana. 1986. "The Social construction of Immigrant Women in Canada." In *The Politics of Diversity*. Edited by M Barnett and R. Hamilton. London: Verso.

Orozco, Wilhemina S. 1985. *Economic Refugees: Voyage of the Commoditized: An Alternative Philippine Report on Migrant Women Workers*. Manila: Philippine Women's Research Collective.

Palma-Beltran, Mary R., and Aurora Javate de Dios (eds.). 1992. *Filipino Women Overseas Contract Workers . . . at What Cost?* Manila: Goodwill Trading Co.

Philippine Overseas Employment Administration. 1987. *Statistical Yearbook*. Manila: POEA.

Philippine Senate. 1990. "The Flight of Filipinas Working Overseas." Senate Committee Report No. 1033. Manila: Senate Archives.

Phizacklea, Annie (ed.). 1983. *One Way Ticket: Migration and Female Labour*. London: Routledge and Kegan Paul.

Pittin, Renee. 1984. "Migration of Women in Nigeria: The Hausa Case." *International Migration Review* 18(4): 1293–1314.

Pryer, Jane. 1992. "Purdah, Patriarchy and Population Movement: Perspectives from Bangladesh." In *Gender and Migration in Developing Countries*. Edited by Sylvia Chant. New York: Belhaven Press.

Radcliffe, Sarah A. 1991. "The Role of Gender in Peasant Migration: Conceptual Issues from the Peruvian Andes." *Review of Radical Political Economies* 23(3–4): 129–147.

———. 1990. "Ethnicity, Patriarchy, and Incorporation into the Nation: Female Migrants as Domestic Servants in Peru." *Environment and Planning D: Society and Space* 8: 379–393.

Saliba, James. 1993. "Filipino Overseas Contract Workers in Nigeria." *Asian Migrant* 6(2): 53–56.

Sancho, Nelia, and Layador, Ma. Angelica G. (eds.). 1993. *Traffic in Women: Violation of Women's Dignity and Fundamental Human Rights*. Manila: Asian Women Human Rights Council.

Sayer, Andrew, and Richard Walker. 1992. *The New Social Economy: Reworking the Division of Labor*. Cambridge, MA: Blackwell.

Shah, Nasra M., and Fred Arnold. 1986. "Government Policies and Programs Regulating Labor Migration." In *Asian Labor Migration: Pipeline to the Middle East*. Edited by Fred Arnold and Nasra Shah. Boulder, CO: Westview Press.

Simon, Rita James, and Caroline B. Brettel (eds.). 1986. *International Migration: The Female Experience*. Toyawa, NJ: Rowman and Allanheld.

Singhanetra-Renard, Anchalee, and Nitaya Prabhudhanitisarn. 1992. "Changing Socio-Economic Roles of Thai Women and Their Migration." In *Gender and Migration in Developing Countries*. Edited by Sylvia Chant. New York: Belhaven Press.

Skeldon, Ronald. 1992. "International Migration within and from the East and Southeast Asian Region: A Review Essay." *Asian and Pacific Migration Journal* 1(1): 19–63.

Stahl, Charles W. 1988. "Manpower Export and Economic Development: Evidence from the Philippines." *International Migration* 26(2): 147–168.

Tan, Thomas T. W., and Devasahayam, Theresa W. 1987. "Opposition and Interdependence: The Dialectics of Maid and Employer Relationships in Singapore," *Philippine Sociological Review* 35(3–4): 34–41.

Thadani, Veena, and Michael P. Todaro. 1984. "Female Migration: A Conceptual Framework." In *Women in the Cities of Asia: Migration and Urban Adaptation*. Edited by James T. Fawcett, Siew-Ean Khoo, and Peter C. Smith. Boulder, CO: Westview Press.

Tono, Haruhi. 1986. "The Japanese Sex Industry: A Heightening Appetite for Asian Women," *AMPO Japan-Quarterly Review* 18(2): 70–76.

Tyner, James A. Forthcoming. "Bound to Perform: The Deployment of Filipina Performing Artists." Paper for presentation to the Association of American Geographers, Chicago, IL.

Vasquez, Noel D. 1992. "Economic and Social Impact of Labor Migration." In *Philippine Labor Migration: Impact and Policy*. Edited by Graziano Battistella and Anthony Paganoni. Quezon City: Scalabrini Migration Center.

Wilkinson, Clive. 1987. "Women, Migration and Work in Lesotho." In *Geography of Gender in the Third World*. Edited by Janet H. Momsen and Janet G. Townsend. New York: State University of New York Press.

1. The end of World War II brought a sense of urgency to immigration reform. Why did Congress make even greater concessions in immigration policy after World War II than during the war? What domestic changes enabled Congress to effect immigration reform? What were the provisions of the 1952 McCarran-Walter Act? In what ways did the passage of this immigration law remedy the litany of anti-Asian immigration acts passed in the years leading up to World War II? How did the 1965 Immigration Act alter the preference system? Why have so many well-educated Asian immigrants immigrated into the United States in the wake of the passage of this act? What impact does Asian immigration have on the ethnic composition of the U.S. labor force?

2. Rumbaut notes that diversity is the hallmark of Vietnamese, Laotian, and Cambodian refugees coming to the United States. How are the groups similar or different from one another? What factors have shaped the patterns of settlement and secondary migration that later emerged? What occupational and economic progress has been made by the refugee population? To what extent have members of this population made use of public assistance programs? How do Southeast Asian refugees differ from refugees from Cuba and from the former Soviet Union? From other Asian immigrants?

3. What kinds of constraints are imposed on Filipino women migrants as a result of the social construction of gender? What are some examples provided by Tyner to illustrate how the demand for migrants in industrialized and postindustrialized economies hinges on constructions of gendered employment? Are male and female migrants socialized into accepting these roles? What are the effects of gendered migration on developing countries, as well as on countries that already have advanced economies? What are the implications of social construction of gender for our understanding of international migration, both historically and in the present day?

4. To what extent will Asian immigrants continue to enter the United States in the twenty-first century? Drawing on evidence presented by the authors, make a case that Asian immigration to the United States will continue at a steady rate, slow down significantly, or halt altogether. What factors might promote Asian immigration in the next decade or two, and what factors might stem its tide?

SUGGESTING READINGS

Alexander, Meena. 1989. Poem by the Wellside. Pp. 27–29 in Asian Women United of California (ed.), *Making Waves: An Anthology by and about Asian American Women*. Boston: Beacon Press.
Bulosan, Carlos. 1974. *America Is in the Heart*. Seattle: University of Washington Press.
Butler, Robert Olen. 1992. *A Good Scent from a Strange Mountain: Stories*. New York: Penguin.
Chan, Sucheng. 1990. European and Asian Immigration into the United States in Comparative Perspective, 1820s–1920s. Pp. 37–75 in Virginia Yans-Mclaughlin (ed.), *Immigration Reconsidered: History, Sociology, and Politics*. New York: Oxford University Press.
Daniels, Roger. 1997. United States Policy towards Asian Immigrants: Comparative Developments in Historical Perspective. Pp. 73–89 in Darrell Y. Hamamoto and Rudolfo D. Torres

(eds.), *New American Destinies: A Reader in Contemporary Asian and Latino Immigration.* New York: Routledge.

Dirlik, Arif. 1996. Asians on the Rim: Transnational Capital and Local Community in the Making of Contemporary Asian America. *Amerasia Journal* 22(3): 1–24.

Fong, Timothy. 1994. *The First Suburban Chinatown: The Remaking of Monterey Park, California.* Philadelphia: Temple University Press.

Gosha, Joseph D. 1993. Perilous Journey: 1979. Pp. 320–335 in James Freeman, ed., *Hearts of Sorrow: Vietnamese American Lives.* Stanford: Stanford University Press.

Hing, Bill Ong. 1993. *Making and Remaking of Asian America Through Immigration Policy.* Stanford: Stanford University Press.

Jensen, Joan. 1988. *Passage from India: Asian Indian Immigrants in North America.* New Haven: Yale University Press.

Lee, Chang-Rae. 1995. *Native Speaker.* New York: Riverhead Books.

Liu, J., P. Ong, and C. Rosenstein. 1991. Filipino Immigration to the United States. *International Migration Review* 25: 487–513.

Ma, Sheng-mei. 1998. *Immigrant Subjectivities in Asian American and Asian Diaspora Literatures.* Albany: State University of New York Press.

Ong, Paul, and Tania Azores. 1994. The Migration and Incorporation of Filipino Nurses. Pp. 164–198 in Paul Ong, Edna Bonacich, and Lucie Cheng (ed.), *The New Asian Immigration in Los Angeles and Global Restructuring.* Philadelphia: Temple University Press.

Smith-Hefner, Nancy J. 1998. *Khmer American: Identity and Moral Education in a Disaporic Community.* Berkeley: University of California Press.

Verghese, Abraham. 1997. The Cowpath to America. *The New Yorker* (June 23 and 30): 70–88.

FILMS

Nair, Mira (producer/director). 1991. *Mississippi Masala.*

Nakasako, Spenser, and Vincent Digiriolamo. 1982. *Monterey's Boat People.*

Wang, Wayne. 1989. *Eat a Bowl of Tea.*

Yonemoto, Bruce. 1982. *Green Card: An American Romance.*

Part IV

Struggling to get Ahead
Life and Work in Asian America

Chapter Eight

Life and Work in the Inner City

Paul Ong and Karen Umemoto

Asian Pacific Americans play an increasingly significant role in the economy of America's inner cities. For many Americans living in suburbs and small cities, the inner city has become synonymous with a multitude of social and economic problems plaguing this nation—poverty, drug abuse, crime, welfare dependency, and physical blight. These problems are the products of a cumulative process of abandonment that marginalizes and alienates an ever increasing number of people. A disproportionately large number of inner-city residents are African American, a testimony to the powerful and pervasive role of racism. However, America's older urban areas and their problems should not be seen as endemic to only one racial group. The particular hardships of inner-city life affect others, including Asian Pacific Americans.

Asian Pacific Americans play multiple roles in the economy of the urban core—as residents, workers and entrepreneurs. Residents live in neighborhoods populated largely by immigrants or refugees. A high poverty rate is common, despite the fact that a high employment rate is the norm in many of these neighborhoods. In others, a high rate of joblessness prevails. Many are part of the working poor or find employment in an ethnically defined subeconomy. Ethnic entrepreneurs play a strong role in the enclave economy but have also emerged as prominent "middleman" merchants in other low-income neighborhoods. They fill a void created by the absence of mainstream retailers and producers. At the same time, their presence has generated new sources of interracial tensions.

Asian Pacific Americans will influence the way this nation pursues urban revitalization. Certainly, low-income Asian Pacific neighborhoods share many of the problems facing other inner-city neighborhoods; consequently, the corresponding urban policies and programs must involve Asian Pacific Americans along with other groups. At the same time, there are features unique to the development of Asian Pacific enclaves in the inner city. These bring with them specific sets of problems as well as potential contributions that Asian Pacific Americans can offer under informed public policy.

We begin this chapter by first discussing the larger process of urban decline and how it has created communities of high poverty. We place the general development of Asian Pacific inner-city neighborhoods in this historical context and profile several communities for illustrative purposes.[1] We have selected four urban neighborhoods, two that are older enclaves and two that have emerged with the arrival of post-1965 immigrants and refugees from Asia. The neighborhoods are: San Francisco and New York Chinatowns, Los Angeles Koreatown, and the Cambodian community in Long Beach, also known as New Phnom Penh. We then look at the role of Asian Pacific entrepreneurs in non-Asian Pacific inner-city communities. We conclude by summarizing the problems facing Asian Pacific Americans in the inner city and the prospects concerning their role in urban revitalization.

Inner-City Communities and Urban Decline

Inner-city neighborhoods are not new to this nation. Immigrant tenements existed in the great industrial cities of the manufacturing belt that stretched from the Northeast to the Midwest around the turn of the century. Employment, health, and housing problems in these slums were horrendous. In later decades, minorities and African Americans, in particular, became a growing share of the population in aging inner-city areas. Today, America's racial ghettos have been characterized by the social ills associated with being economically marginalized, such as high rates of crime, substance abuse, teen pregnancy, welfare dependency, school drop-out, and long-term unemployment.

These problems have grown in severity as poverty has become more concentrated in major urban centers. Between 1959 and 1985, the percentage of the nation's poor residing in metropolitan central cities grew from 27 percent to 43 percent (Kasarda, 1993). This increased concentration has transformed the neighborhoods. Between 1970 and 1990, the total number of persons living in a metropolitan census tract in which the poverty rate was greater than 40 percent increased steadily from less than four million to nine million (Mincy and Wiener, 1993, Table 1; Tobin, 1993, Table 5.2).

The residents of extremely poor inner-city neighborhoods are predominantly nonwhite. In the largest metropolitan areas, non-Hispanic blacks comprised 52 percent of the 1990 population residing in concentrated poverty areas (tracts where the poverty level was at least 40 percent); they were followed by Hispanics (36 percent), non-Hispanic whites (9 percent), and "others" (3 percent) (Mincy, 1993, Table 3c). An increasing percentage of those living in poverty are immigrants. In 1990, foreign-born residents constituted 10 percent of all those living in concentrated poverty areas, up from 3.5 percent two decades earlier (Mincy and Wiener, 1993, Table 6).

The growth of inner-city poverty can be traced to an exodus of jobs driven by three phenomena: 1) suburbanization, 2) regional realignment, and 3) global competition. Suburbanization, which dates back to at least the last century, occurs as firms relocate to the outer edges of the city in response to rising land costs within the urban center and to changes in the cost of transportation and public services. Firms also take advantage of prior suburbanization by following the labor force and consumers outwards (Mills 1989; Mieszkowski and Mills, 1993). The building of efficient transportation systems accelerates suburbanization, as the cost and time required to transport goods declines. Federal government policies after World War

II contributed to the process by subsidizing highway construction and homeowner-ship. Race plays a role in suburbanization, as studies indicate that the presence of a large minority population in the central city, relative to the number of minorities in the suburbs, accelerates the exodus of both white residents and jobs.

The flight of jobs from the urban center is not solely a result of suburbanization. During the late 1960s and through most of the 1970s, the shift in production and jobs from the older industrial "frost belt" of the Midwest and Northeast to the "sunbelt" of the South and Southwest has also contributed to employment losses (Harrison and Bluestone, 1988). The rise of the sunbelt took place gradually, but several factors accelerated its emergence. Public policy, particularly in the form of defense spending, facilitated the industrial development of this region (Markusen, 1984). Rising oil prices during this period favored firm relocation to the sunbelt, where energy costs and energy requirements were lower. Lower labor costs and weaker unions also attracted established firms and new capital investments. More-over, a more moderate climate, a lower cost of living, and lower land prices lulled residents, insuring a growing labor pool for expanding businesses (Sawers and Tabb, 1984). The net result of the regional shift was the disappearance of hundreds of thousands of manufacturing jobs from the older industrial cities.

International competition is a third factor. Over the last two decades, U.S. manu-facturers have increasingly found themselves competing against both developed and developing nations which are able to produce and sell goods at lower prices. The significance of imports can be traced to the late 1960s, but the effects became pronounced in later years. Imports as a percentage of the gross domestic product grew modestly in the 1970s, from 7 percent in 1969 to 8 percent in 1979, but jumped to 11 percent by the end of the 1980s. One reaction to competition has been to cut labor costs through layoffs, wage and benefit reductions, and the relocation of production to low-wage areas both within the United States and abroad (Sassen-Koob, 1988; Mollenkopf and Castells, 1991). These changes have been supported by deregulation and federal tax laws which favor corporate restructuring and speculative strategies (Goldsmith and Blakely, 1992).

In urban centers, the above three phenomena have transformed the composition of employment. Higher-paying jobs in manufacturing have been replaced by lower-paying jobs in services and retailing. At the same time, the demand for the highly educated and highly skilled expanded in finance, insurance, and real estate (FIRE), and in professional services, which together created a new class of well-paid urban workers. Consequently, urban labor markets across metropolitan regions have sharply divided, with increasing disparity between high-paying, upwardly mobile, stable jobs and jobs which are low-paying, unstable, with little job mobility (Sessen-Koob, 1988; Goldsmith and Blakely, 1992; Harrison and Bluestone, 1988).

The economic transformation had a devastating effect on African Americans. Blacks held a disproportionate share of the jobs that were lost, with many of those displaced unable to find equivalent employment. Discrimination and lack of afford-able housing in many suburban areas prevented many from following the outmigra-tion of jobs (Massey and Denton, 1993). Additionally, the lack of education and training created a "mismatch" between the skills possessed by inner-city residents and those required for emerging jobs (Kain, 1968; Kasarda, 1989). The employment problems created by the mismatch were aggravated by racial discrimination in hiring by employers (Moss and Tilly, 1993a, 1993b). Some employers drew a "redline" around inner-city areas which they identified as undesirable places from which to recruit (Kirschenman and Neckerman, 1991).

In some African American neighborhoods, the structural changes and resulting joblessness led to a cumulative decline that undermined social and community institutions, leaving behind what William Julius Wilson labeled the urban underclass (1987). The "concentration effects" of poverty resulted in alienation and behavioral patterns which, in turn, reinforced their economic marginalization.[2] Although the size of the urban underclass is small, approximately 2.7 million according to one estimate (Mincy and Wiener, 1993, Table 1), its existence reveals the ultimate tragedy produced by contemporary racism.

The economic transformation also led to the growth of Latino inner-city neighborhoods. Latinos account for over one-fifth of those residing in concentrated poverty areas nationwide and one-third of those in concentrated poverty areas in the largest metropolitan cities. The poverty rates in many Latino barrios match those of the most depressed African American ghettos. The major source of poverty, however, is different. Many Latinos are immigrants or migrants who have been absorbed into the expanding low-skilled sector where poverty arises from the low level of wages as opposed to widespread joblessness (Morales and Ong, 1993; Betancur, Cordova, and Torres, 1993). With the exception of some Puerto Rican neighborhoods, there is not yet a clear emergence of a Latino urban underclass (Moore, 1989).

Latinos and African Americans, however, were not the only minority groups to be incorporated into the inner-city segment of the urban economy. Asian Pacific Americans have built an economic and residential niche. In the following sections, we discuss the economic characteristics of Asian Pacific communities in several inner-city metropolitan areas.[3]

Asian Pacific Urban Settlements

Asian immigrants formed some of the earliest racially defined communities in urban America. Long before the establishment of black ghettos in New York's Harlem and Chicago's South Side,[4] the Chinese were forced by racial violence and legal restrictions to retreat into Chinatowns throughout the West. The origins of land-use control and restrictive covenants, which had been the legal basis for housing segregation, can be traced to the effort to isolate the Chinese (Ong, 1981; Vose, 1959). Subsequent waves of Asian immigrants led to the formation of enclaves such as Little Tokyo in Los Angeles, Manilatown in San Francisco, and the International District in Seattle.

Many of the older Asian communities went into decline during World War II and the first two decades following the war. Japanese American enclaves were destroyed by the mass and illegal internment of this population during the war. Although some residents did return to their prewar neighborhoods, most dispersed throughout the nation. Urban renewal programs destroyed other residential communities, further dispersing the population.[5] With new immigration restricted by a racially biased national-origins quota and with a waning of overt state-sponsored racism, other Asian enclaves lost population. Many completely disappeared by the early 1960s.[6]

A major exception to the post–World War II decline was San Francisco's Chinatown,[7] which, as the largest and oldest Asian enclave at that time, received a large share of the limited number of new arrivals. Between 1940 and 1960, the Chinese population increased from about 16,000 to over 28,000.[8] However, this community was not destined to grow much more despite the reemergence of large-scale immigration from Asia following the enactment of the 1965 Immigration Act. This community grew slightly during the 1970s, from about 28,000 Chinese in 1960 to about 32,000 in 1970.[9] Since then, Census data indicate that the number has remained stable. This lack of a net growth is due to a limited ability to expand into adjacent neighborhoods, for Chinatown is surrounded by the financial district, Union Square (the city's major retailing district), Fisherman's Wharf, and high-income neighborhoods such as Nob Hill. Developments in these neighborhoods, along with other problems,[10] continue to threaten the future vitality of Chinatown.

Though the absolute number of residents in San Francisco Chinatown remained fairly stable over the past two decades, there is a high rate of turnover in residence. Chinatown still serves as a point of entry for new immigrants, as two-fifths (44 percent) of Chinese in Chinatown arrived between 1980 and 1990.[11] Many families have moved to more spacious quarters in less densely populated areas once they could afford to do so. San Francisco's Richmond district, which is located several miles to the west, has challenged the preeminence of Chinatown as the commercial and residential center of the Chinese population in that city. At the same time, there remains a stable core of elderly residents in Chinatown.[12]

Post-1965 immigration has had a far more profound impact on New York City's Chinatown, whose growth has made it the largest Chinese enclave in the United States. By 1970, its population of nearly 27,000 Chinese was nearly as large as that of San Francisco's Chinatown.[13] Unlike its West Coast counterpart, the enclave in New York is geographically less constricted. By 1990, the number of Chinese had grown to about 50,000,[14] and larger if one considers that the census enumeration missed many immigrants. The growth is driven by recent immigrants, who comprised 43 percent of the Chinese population in 1990. It is questionable whether this enclave can continue to expand at a phenomenal rate. Though less constricted than San Francisco, New York's Chinatown is similarly adjacent to financial centers and residential areas where housing prices are expensive. Already, "new Chinatowns" have emerged or expanded throughout the New York area—Sunset Park in Brooklyn, Canal Street in Manhattan, and Main Street in Queen's Flushing district.

The older Asian urban enclaves have been joined by new ones, such as Koreatown in Los Angeles. Prior to post-1965 immigration, Koreans were concentrated in parts of South Central.[15] Today's Koreatown is located north of the original enclave centered at Western Avenue and Olympic Boulevard. This community lies within an older and centrally located section of the city but is not directly adjacent to the downtown commercial district. In contrast to the older Chinatowns, Koreatown and

TABLE 8.1
1990 Population Characteristics Asian Pacific Americans in Selected Urban Neighborhoods

	N.Y. Chinatown	S.F. Chinatown	L.A. Koreatown	L.B. New Phnom Penh
Age				
Youth (age <15)	15%	14%	20%	46%
Elderly (age 65+)	14%	23%	8%	3%
Nativity				
U.S.-born	17%	23%	12%	22%
Recent immigrant	43%	44%	67%	71%
Below Poverty	25%	17%	26%	50%
Median HH Income	$18,200	$20,000	$20,000	$17,000
Mean HH Size	3.1	2.6	3.0	5.7
Homeowners	8%	18%	11%	8%

NOTE: Statistics for New York and San Francisco Chinatowns, Los Angeles Koreatown, and Long Beach New Phnom Penh include values for Chinese, Koreans, and Cambodians, respectively. "Recent immigrant" includes those entering the U.S. between 1980 and 1990.
SOURCE: U.S. Bureau of the Census, Public Use Microdata Sample, 1990

other recently emerged enclaves do not have an ethnically homogeneous core. Koreans comprise only one-third of the total population in Koreatown and live alongside Latinos, who comprise the majority. The Korean population in Koreatown has rapidly grown, however, from less than 1,200 in 1970 to over 30,000 today.[16]

Los Angeles Koreatown has served as a point of entry for many who arrive to the U.S. and remains a predominantly immigrant community. Approximately two-thirds (67 percent) of its Korean residents are recent arrivals, having immigrated after 1980. Despite the low unemployment rate among Koreans living in Koreatown (4 percent), there is a high level of poverty. Over one-quarter (26 percent) of Korean residents live below the poverty level. It is also a fairly youthful population, with 20 percent under the age of 15 and only 8 percent who are age 65 and over.

The Cambodian community in Long Beach, a city located in the southern part of the Los Angeles metropolitan area, is another example of the new Asian Pacific urban enclave. As late as the spring of 1975, there were only seven Cambodian families who were reported living in Long Beach.[17] That changed rapidly with the fall of the Lon Nol government in 1975 and the subsequent mass exodus of refugees. The movement started with the assistance of several exchange students who aided the relocation of refugees from Camp Pendleton military facility to this city. In five short years, the Cambodian community expanded to over 8,000.[18] Ethnic and kinship ties and later the establishment of mutual aid organizations, churches, and services such as ESL classes attracted more residents, including "second migrants" from other parts of the country. By 1990, over 15,000 Cambodians lived in New Phnom Penh. The population is very young with an extremely high proportion of recent arrivals; 71 percent arrived to the U.S. between 1980 and 1990 and 46 percent are under 15 years of age.

The Cambodian population is distinct from the other communities profiled in this section, as it is a refugee rather than an immigrant population. Like other Southeast Asian refugee communities, the socioeconomic conditions facing Cambodians are more severe than those facing other ethnic and racial groups. This is certainly true in the case of the Long Beach enclave, where half of all Cambodians live below the poverty line. Households often include the extended family, and it is not uncommon for more than one nuclear family to share housing. An average of about six persons live in each Cambodian household in the Long Beach enclave, nearly twice that of the other selected neighborhoods. Table 8.1 provides selected characteristics of these neighborhoods.

These profiles do not represent the wide range of inner-city Asian Pacific communities, but they illustrate their diversity and common characteristics. First, their growth is driven by immigration, and as immigration continues these communities will remain important points of entry. Second, these communities are culturally and socially unique, providing a comfortable home for ethnic minorities and adding to the diversity of the urban milieu. And, third, these communities face serious social and economic problems. These include the strains of cultural adjustment among new arrivals, economic poverty, deteriorating housing conditions, overcrowding, and special problems facing elderly, youth, and refugee populations. These communities are growing at a rapid rate during a time of fierce economic competition and global recession.

Employment of Enclave Residents

With the exception of New Phnom Penh in Long Beach, the three enclaves—San Francisco Chinatown, New York Chinatown and Los Angeles Koreatown—are characterized by a high level of economic activity among the working-age population (see Table 8.2). As a community of refugees, the residents of New Phnom Penh suffer from a multitude of personal and social problems that limits employment opportunities and forces many to rely on public assistance . . . In the other three enclaves, the labor force participation rates range from slightly below to well above the national rate. This has occurred despite the presence of severe deficiencies in human capital. A majority of the working-age population (61 percent) either do not speak English or speak it poorly, and nearly half (48 percent) have less than a high school level education. There are also significant differences across communities, with Koreatown having the smallest proportion of disadvantaged workers and New York's Chinatown having the largest proportion. There is not, however, a corresponding difference in

TABLE 8.2
Economic Characteristics of Working-Age Population

	N.Y. Chinatown	S.F. Chinatown	L.A. Koreatown	L.B. New Phnom Penh
Limited English proficiency	65%	58%	56%	69%
Limited education	61%	50%	24%	68%
Labor force participation	81%	76%	69%	28%
Unemployment rate	6%	6%	4%	21%
Median earnings	$9,000	$11,000	$15,000	$12,000
Self-employed	7%	7%	27%	6%

NOTES: Prime working-age population includes those between the ages of 24 and 64.
See Table 8.1 for definition of ethnic groups included.
The category of limited-English-speaking ability includes those who indicated they speak English "not well" or "not at all."
SOURCE: U.S. Bureau of the Census, Public Use Microdata Sample, 1990

the labor force participation rates. For example, despite the astonishingly high pro-portions of adults with limited English ability and limited education in New York Chinatown, the labor force participation rate ranks first. Clearly, factors other than the observed measures of human capital influence whether or not a person works.

One explanation is that many residents, particularly those with limited skills, are immigrants with a strong work ethic that is reinforced by social pressure. For example, the typical Chinatown resident in San Francisco feels compelled to work to avoid "tarnishing his public image and, perhaps more importantly, to avoid bringing shame upon the family" (Ong, 1984, p. 50). This behavior is so strong that a large number of individuals are willing to accept very low wages rather than remain jobless. Over one-quarter of the employed in the four communities work for less than $4.00 (1989$) per hour.[19] Low wages, in fact, can have the effect of increasing the number who work because they force households to send two or more workers into the labor market in order to meet their financial needs.

The high participation rates are by no means due solely to individual characteris-tics. Employment occurs when there is also a demand for the workers' labor. Al-though many enclave residents find employment in mainstream firms, frequently in clerical and janitorial positions in adjacent retailing and office centers, others work in what is known as the ethnic economy.[20] This subeconomy can be defined by its reliance on ethnic capital and labor; ethnicity serves as a basis for pooling resources and defining employer-employee relations.[21] . . . [T]hese resources help some Asian Pacific Americans to establish and operate businesses. While the contribution of ethnic resources to Asian Pacific entrepreneurship as a whole is limited, they can play a significant role for firms within the ethnic economy. Ethnic solidarity also supports economic functions in relation to labor. Social networks and community institutions facilitate job searches by individuals and recruitment by firms. Moreover, a common language and a shared set of values facilitate the coordination of produc-tion.

A significant segment of the ethnic economy is concentrated in the ethnic enclave. Many of these firms exist through agglomeration effects created by the presence of a multitude of economic and cultural activities. Collectively, these activities are able to draw in outside dollars by attracting co-ethnics from throughout the region, tourists looking for "exotic" sights, and non-Asian Pacific workers from adjacent employ-ment centers.[22] The firms rely on a local, ethnically bounded labor pool of low-wage workers who are limited by a lack of transportation, low skills, and low English-language proficiency. Because of limited capital and the nature of the client base, the "export" sector of the ethnic economy is often limited to activities such as curio and novelty shops, ethnic-oriented groceries, restaurants, garment assembly plants, and menial services. There is also an economic sector that caters to "domestic" needs of local residents. This sector is comprised of banks, real estate and insurance offices, health and legal services, and a variety of establishments that meet social and cultural needs. The "export" and "domestic" sectors are interlinked. The income generated from the former enlarges the latter, and the existence of "ethnically" looking estab-lishments on the "domestic" side contributes to the ambiance that attracts outsiders. Moreover, many enclave firms actually serve both local residents and outsiders.[23]

While many residents find employment in the enclave segment of the ethnic economy, it is not a self-enclosed system. Even in San Francisco's Chinatown, which has one of the most developed enclave economies, there is considerable movement into and out of this unit. Roughly half of those working in the enclave commute from other parts of the region, while roughly half of the working residents find work outside the enclave, in both ethnic and nonethnic firms. Nonetheless, the ethnic economy and its enclave segment play an important role in absorbing what would otherwise be excess and unemployable labor.

Although the Census does not provide information on the ethnicity of employers, which would indicate the level of employment within the ethnic economy, we can use industrial distributions of workers and other variables to estimate the relative importance of the ethnic economy. Among the working residents in the four enclaves, 15 percent are in apparel manufacturing and another 16 percent are in restaurants, two industries that are closely identified with the ethnic economy. The combined percentages vary by community, ranging from 50 percent in New York's Chinatown to only 18 percent in Koreatown. The low percentage in Koreatown is offset by an unusually high self-employment rate (27 percent), which is another economic activity that is largely based within the ethnic economy. A broader, but more ambiguous measure is employment in wholesale and retailing. Roughly one-quarter of the employed work in this sector.

A survey of Asian Pacific households in low-income Asian Pacific communities in Los Angeles found that 40 percent of the employed respondents either had a co-ethnic employer or supervisor (Ong, Park, and Tong, 1993, p. 54). These numbers suggest that at least one-third of enclave workers depend on the ethnic economy. Without this internally generated demand for co-ethnic workers, it is unlikely that the labor force participation rates would be as high as observed.[24]

Ethnic economies generate benefits, but not without liabilities. These subeconomies provide employment opportunities not available elsewhere and can provide a preferable alternative to employment in the secondary labor market.[25] The ethnically bounded labor markets shelter ethnic group members from direct interethnic and interracial competition for the same jobs. In some cases, the ethnic economy reproduces many of the desirable features of the primary labor market such as higher returns to human capital. This is possible when ethnic firms exercise monopolistic control and provide informal training which leads to greater opportunities for self employment. Finally, there are nonmonetary benefits, such as the chance to work among co-ethnics and shelter from racial subordination in the workplace.

But there is an underside. Although the enclave economy may bring comparable returns to human capital for business owners, the same is not always true for their employees. Enclave businesses have a narrow economic base, face harsh competition, suffer high turnover, and earn low profits. They consequently create undesirable labor conditions. The isolation of workers often leaves workers vulnerable to unfair labor practices. Ethnic solidarity can facilitate the exploitative nature of the relationship between owner and worker, leading to harsh conditions. Wages tend to be low, and benefits such as health insurance are often absent. Unfair labor practices are not uncommon, including unpaid wages, violation of worker health and safety regulations, unpaid workers' compensation, and violation of minimum wage laws.[26] Additionally, the utilization of unpaid family labor is more frequent among ethnic small businesses.

The relative balance of the positive and negative employment outcomes for enclave residents hinges on the interplay of supply and demand in the labor and product markets. The degree of competition, the supply of cheap labor, the growth of firms, and the final demand for their goods and services are key variables. Outcomes are partly dependent on market forces within the ethnic/enclave economy. The isolation of its labor market can concentrate the adverse effects of a growing supply of immigrant labor, which tends to push down wages in the absence of a concomitant growth in businesses. However, merely expanding the current set of business activities would not necessarily raise wages beyond current levels because of the pressures on firms to keep prices down.

These pressures are formed by market forces beyond the ethnic/enclave economy. Although Asian Pacific workers may not be in direct competition with other minority workers for the same jobs, there is indirect competition because the ultimate buyers have the option of purchasing from other sources. This is true in the garment industry, for example, where the extent of garment production within the Asian Pacific community is determined by the availability of non-Asian Pacific subcontractors who rely on low-wage Latino workers. Restaurants and curio shops, heavily dependent on tourism and on nearby office workers, are also sensitive to the business cycle. When the economy goes into recession, both industries take a dive.

Despite these limitations, ethnic/enclave economies are nevertheless a key factor that explains why employment outcomes differ among minority neighborhoods in the inner city. Moreover, there are many noneconomic dimensions of ethnic-based development that affect the quality of life in the inner city. Enclaves serve as a spatial center from which members organize to facilitate social relations, promote cultural activities, and increase political leverage. Subsequently, many community-based institutions and associations play a role in local politics and have the potential to play a greater role in revitalization efforts. One segment of the community which has a large influence not only on the ethnic enclave economy but on the economy of the inner city at large are small business owners.

Middleman Minority

Asian Pacific entrepreneurship in the inner city is not limited to Asian Pacific enclaves. Throughout recent American history, Asian Pacific–owned businesses could be found in various urban neighborhoods, including communities of color. Paul C. P. Siu (1987), for example, traces the existence of Chinese laundries in urban centers to the late 19th and early 20th centuries. Chinese, Japanese, and Korean Americans operated retailing businesses in African American communities such as South Central Los Angeles prior to the 1960s. A few are still in business, but it is more common to find recent immigrants from the countries or from other parts of

Asia—such as South Asia, Hong Kong, Taiwan, and Vietnam—running neighborhood grocery stores and restaurants, gas stations, clothing and wig boutiques, stalls in "swap" meets, and small hotels. In addition to businesses in retail and service sectors, Asian Pacific Americans are also involved, though to lesser degrees, in small-scale manufacturing, international trading, and professional services in the urban core.

The presence of Asian Pacific businesses in minority neighborhoods is a result of various factors, including their entrepreneurial drive, barriers to their employment in the mainstream labor market, barriers to entrepreneurship faced by other minority groups, and the commercial void created by the absence of mainstream firms in inner-city neighborhoods. Asian Pacific entrepreneurs have overcome some of the barriers to business ownership through such strategies as the mobilization of ethnic and family resources. Additionally, the oversaturation of businesses in many of their respective ethnic enclaves, especially in retail and service industries, has prompted entrepreneurs to venture outside of their ethnic market niche. Some, particularly those with limited funds, have opted to run businesses in low-income minority communities where the startup costs are relatively low. Most of these businesses are mom-and-pop operations, but there are also larger firms ranging from small supermarkets and retail chains to import wholesalers and medium-scale assembly or production plants.

Asian Pacific entrepreneurs have been said to fill the function of "middleman minority," which refers to their position as brokers between a racial minority clientele and nonminority business elites (Bonacich, 1973). Asian Pacific Americans are not the first to play this role and have often followed in a succession of ethnic business owners. For example, the urban riots of the 1960s prompted many Jewish merchants to sell their stores, many to newly arrived Asian Pacific immigrants whose populations were rapidly growing during that period.[27]

At the same time, business practices among some recent Asian Pacific groups have changed the definition of the middleman. The original concept was developed when production and wholesale distribution were controlled by a white elite. Although this pattern still persists, the global economy has added new complexity. Today, retail trade in some sectors involves ethnic wholesalers who do business directly with producers in their country of origin. Moreover, Asian Pacific entrepreneurs are not limited to retailing. Some have established production facilities that rely on minority labor. This is particularly true in labor intensive industries as in the case of garment work, where Asian Pacific immigrants act as labor contractors for U.S. producers (Bonacich, 1993). "Middleman" in reference to Asian Pacific Americans now characterizes businesses in minority neighborhoods regardless of the sources of capital, goods, or services (Ong, Park, and Tong, 1993).

Although it is impossible to quantify the size of this phenomenon, we can identify issues pertinent to public policy concerning community economic development. The experiences of these entrepreneurs can be described as a bittersweet endeavor. On the one hand, operating businesses has provided Asian Pacific Americans with a means of economic survival and, in some cases, an avenue for upward mobility. At the same time, their presence in economically distressed areas has generated resentment among other racial and ethnic groups. While intergroup antagonism is not present in all situations, reports of conflict have become commonplace.[28]

Racial antagonisms often begin with complaints directed by customers towards individual merchants. At least four complaints have been repeatedly aired: 1) merchants exhibit racist attitudes and rudeness; 2) there is an inability to communicate due to language and cultural differences; 3) merchants do not hire local residents; and 4) merchants do not "give back" to the community in the form of economic or civic participation outside of profit making. Although individual members of the various Asian Pacific groups do business with local clientele or hire local workers, the publicity over racial conflict has centered on Korean merchants. This may be due to the high proportion of Korean businesses which serve non-Korean clientele.[29]

While ethnic and racial antagonism has its economic roots, the resentments among residents are shaped by broader historical forces. Longstanding grievances against discriminatory practices on the part of financial institutions, for example, set the stage for racially based resentment by African Americans against newly arrived immigrants who were able to establish businesses. The emergence of Asian Pacific merchants is perceived by some groups as another mechanism in a long history of racial oppression which contributes to their subordinate status in the U.S. Meanwhile, some Asian Pacific immigrant entrepreneurs hold negative stereotypes acquired in their home countries, either through the media or through limited contact with U.S. military personnel. The high crime rate in many inner-city neighborhoods has served to reinforce negative images of other minority groups and has fostered a defensive posture among Asian Pacific entrepreneurs (Ong, Park, and Tong, 1993; Kim 1981). Misunderstandings as a result of language and cultural differences have often exacerbated antagonisms and hindered conflict mediation.

Interracial tensions not only fester between merchants and customers but often involve employers and employees. In Los Angeles, for example, racial tensions have arisen in the garment industry between Asian Pacific contractors and Latino workers. In this highly competitive and exploitative industry, conflict between owners and workers is endemic. Where class positions are defined along ethnic categories, the clashes are often transformed into ethnic antagonism (Bonacich, 1993).

Though ethnic and racial conflicts do not occur between all merchants and their patrons or between all employers and those they employ, conflicts between individuals can feed into intergroup tensions, transcending class and geographic boundaries. This has taken place among Korean Americans and African Americans in sections of New York, Chicago, and Los Angeles. Complaints against individual merchants have become political rallying points for boycotts and demonstrations, becoming embroiled in a wider movement for racial justice and community control. Korean merchants have taken collective action to protect their economic interests in their quest to attain the "American dream." Ironically, this group solidarity has further emphasized the racial dimension of the conflict, fueling intergroup antagonism.

The escalation of tension is an interactive process involving direct participants but is often affected by government. The widely publicized conflicts in Los Angeles illustrate this process. One case which heightened tensions between the African

American and Korean American communities involved the fatal shooting of an African American girl, Latasha Harlins, by liquor store owner Soon Ja Du. The guilty verdict with the absence of a prison sentence enraged many in the African American community who saw the judicial system as valuing Korean American life over that of African Americans. The judge's action confirmed in the minds of many African Americans a prevalent view that Korean Americans are collaborating with the very system that historically victimized them.[30]

The tensions between African Americans, Latinos, and Korean Americans further escalated in the wake of the April-May 1992 civil unrest. In addition to 43 deaths, 2,383 injuries, over 16,000 arrests, and $1 billion in property losses, over 2,000 Korean-owned stores were damaged or looted, representing over $400 million in monetary losses. Many of those businesses lost were located in South Central Los Angeles (Ong and Hee, 1993). Koreans felt betrayed both by the police department which did not respond to their calls as well as by those who looted and vandalized their stores. As rebuilding proceeded, residents objected to the city permitting the reopening of liquor stores, the majority of which were owned by Korean Americans. Organizers saw these outlets as contributing to substance abuse, the deterioration of the social environment, and the lack of neighborhood control.[31] Though individual leaders within the Korean and African American communities made efforts to prevent the racialization of this controversy, the politics of the issue was racially tinged, since the majority of closed outlets were owned by Korean Americans and protestors were predominantly African American.

This controversy illuminates a dilemma facing Asian Pacific Americans operating businesses in low-income minority communities. Although Asian Pacific Americans are not the cause of poverty and discrimination, they have become a part, albeit a relatively powerless part, of an economic system that drains meager resources from these neighborhoods. One could argue that many of the desired services would not be provided were it not for Asian Pacific entrepreneurs. But this does not negate the daily hardships faced by local residents, nor does it justify the presence of undesired businesses. Occupying the middleman-minority position, many Asian Pacific merchants have become the target of rage and resentment held by those who are frustrated with the treatment received in an economically and racially polarized society.

Concluding Remarks

Asian Pacific Americans have historically been an integral part of inner-city life and continue to play an increasing role today. They occupy the roles of worker, resident, and entrepreneur. Each position is accompanied by a set of issues and concerns which have implications for urban policy. The conditions facing Asian Pacific Americans in the inner city are important to address and provide insight into the problem of economic revitalization.

One lesson is the importance of the ethnic enclave economy in the absorption of ethnic immigrant labor. The evidence shows that the ethnic economy provides employment opportunities, but working conditions are often harsh, wages low, and benefits nonexistent. For immigrants who are most disadvantaged, there is some improvement over time, but not enough to lift them into the middle class. . . . The challenge is to support the economic viability of urban ethnic enclaves in such a way as to take the particular needs and concerns of all parties into consideration.

The experience of Asian Pacific entrepreneurs in other low-income minority communities raises serious policy questions concerning the role of entrepreneurial development in inner-city revitalization. How does business development in the inner city benefit those who live there? Who should be given public support to do business in the inner city? What type of business development is desirable or undesirable and from whose perspective? How should state and local government regulate business development in the inner city in order to reach the related but distinct goals of commercial revitalization and poverty alleviation? And how can urban revitalization policies address the problem of interracial conflict?

Clearly, the root causes of poverty and inequality must be eliminated in order to fully alleviate racial group tensions.[32] However, to the extent that Asian Pacific entrepreneurs play a role in economic revitalization, there are areas in which business owners can exercise choice to maximize their contributions and minimize unnecessary intergroup conflict. The choice of business type, the employment of local residents, attention to wage scales and working conditions, investment into the overall life of the communities in which they conduct business, and the improvement of interpersonal skills and business practices are several ways that Asian Pacific business owners can affect economic and social outcomes. Entrepreneurial development is one area in which members of some Asian Pacific groups have extensive experience, expertise, and support networks. However, the potential they possess in playing a more productive role in urban revitalization has yet to be tapped by public policy instruments.

The development of small businesses, however, represents only one of a variety of ways to revitalize the economy of the inner city. While ethnic enclave development has provided an economic livelihood for some residents, the experience of Asian Pacific Americans shows that other measures are still needed to overcome the numerous barriers to better employment. Additionally, other forms of economic development, including cooperatives, nonprofit business training projects, and alternative vehicles for economic activity, merit consideration. And, lastly, as changes in the global economy focus greater attention on the importance of human capital for economic survival, the education and training which inner-city residents receive is of utmost importance.

Appendix—Asian Pacific Suburban Enclaves

Not all Asian Pacific urban communities are located in the inner-city. New York's Jackson Heights/East Elmhurst area (in Queens), San Francisco's Sunset District (on the western edge and south of Golden Gate Park), and the City of Cerritos (southeast

TABLE 8.3
*1990 Population Characteristics Asian Pacific Americans in Selected
Suburban Neighborhoods*

	Jackson Heights	Cerritos	S.F. Sunset District
Age			
Youth (age <15)	19%	23%	19%
Elderly (age 65+)	5%	5%	9%
Nativity			
U.S.-born	14%	29%	34%
Recent immigrant	61%	38%	28%
Below Poverty	16%	8%	9%
Median HH Income	$33,000	$55,460	$46,250
Mean HH Size	3.4	4.0	3.5
Homeowners	27%	78%	64%

NOTE: "Recent immigrant" includes those entering the U.S. between 1980 and 1990.
SOURCE: U.S. Bureau of the Census, Public Use Microdata Sample, 1990.

of the City of Los Angeles) are examples of newer Asian Pacific enclaves. These communities tend to be ethnically diverse. The Asian Pacific population in these areas is comprised of Chinese (40 percent), Korean (20 percent), Indian (12 percent), Filipino (15 percent), and others (13 percent) including those of Japanese, Southeast Asian, and Pacific Islander ancestries. Like other recently emerging and rapidly growing communities, a large proportion of residents (45 percent) are recent immigrants.

Located in less densely populated areas where land values are lower as compared to inner-city Asian Pacific enclaves, these areas have attracted a number of residents who can afford to purchase homes. While the home ownership rate ranges between 8 to 18 percent for the other selected neighborhoods, the home ownership rate among Asian Pacific Americans in suburban-urban areas ranges from 27 percent in Jackson Heights/East Elmhurst to 78 percent in Cerritos, as shown in table 8.3. Similarly, while the median household income for the other selected neighborhoods ranged from $17,000 to $20,000 in 1990, the median annual household income for Asian Pacific Americans in these three suburbs ranged from $33,000 to $55,460. While the median income is higher in comparison to the other four selected neighborhoods profiled in this chapter, poverty may still remain a problem. For example, approximately 16 percent of Asian Pacific Americans in Jackson Heights/East Elmhurst live below the poverty level.

NOTES

1. We view these inner-city communities in contrast to other Asian Pacific communities in large metropolitan areas, many of which remain in urban core areas but do not exhibit the same degree of economic hardship as do those highlighted in the body of this chapter. See Appendix for economic and employment data for a sampling of cities which do not fit the more commonly known characteristics of the inner-city but which are located in large metropolitan areas.

2. According to Wilson (1987), the underclass is defined by a lack of attachment to the labor force among adults, the prevalence of female-headed families with children and correspondingly high welfare usage rates, high crime rates, and a youth population alienated from schools and other traditional social institutions.

3. There are other social indicators which can be used to measure the well-being of these communities. These include measures of welfare dependency, school drop-out, involvement in criminal activity, and the breakup of the nuclear family. However, due to a lack of systematic data on Asian Pacific American ethnic groups, this chapter will rely on economic indicators.

4. See Osofsky (1971) for discussion of blacks in New York City and Spear (1967) for discussion of blacks in Chicago. Both authors date the formation of the black urban ghetto in the two respective cities to the period around the turn of the century.

5. See Okamoto, 1991; and Tatsuno, 1971.

6. See Lee (1960) regarding this process for Chinatowns.

7. Urban decline did not affect Asian Pacific Americans in Honolulu in the same way due to differences in historical conditions and population ratios.

8. In 1969, the San Francisco Chinese Community Citizens' Survey & Fact Finding Committee listed a total of 28,578 persons who were neither white nor black residing in three areas: Hard-Core Chinatown, Residential Chinatown, and Potential Chinatown. There was no separate count for Asian Pacific Americans or Chinese, but the Committee stated that nearly all of the nonwhite/nonblack population were Chinese. This area also contained some Filipinos, who lived in the eastern portion of greater Chinatown, which was also know as Manilatown. The 1940 figure is from Loo (1991, p. 50).

9. The latter figure is reported in Loo (1991, p. 50).

10. Past redevelopment projects and the encroachment of the financial district have reduced the size of Chinatown and pushed up rents. Other factors also threaten the economic viability of Chinatown businesses, including the closing of the Embarcadero Freeway damaged during the 1989 earthquake and declines in the tourist trade.

11. The data describing the population characteristics of the Asian Pacific populations have been tabulated from the 1990 U.S. Census Public Use Microdata Sample (PUMS), a sample of 5 percent of the population. We use PUMS areas, submetropolitan areas of at least 100,000 persons, to define our sample. The boundaries for the PUMS samples do not necessarily correspond to the boundaries of the residential ethnic enclave for each of the communities profiled in this section. Therefore, the numbers and percentages may vary slightly and are presented as approximate rather than exact totals and proportions. The use of the term "recent immigrants" refers to those entering the U.S. between 1980 and 1990.

12. San Francisco Chinatown has a more stable residential core in comparison to New York Chinatown. This is indicated by a higher proportion of elderly (23 percent as compared to 17 percent), a slightly higher median annual household income ($20,000 compared to $18,200), and a higher rate of home ownership (18 percent as compared to 8 percent) among Chinese residents in San Francisco Chinatown as compared to their cohorts in New York Chinatown.

13. 1970 and 1980 statistics are listed in Zhou (1992, p. 187, Table 8-1).

14. Using the geographic definition of what had been considered greater Chinatown in 1970, the 1990 Census listed 50,309 Asian Pacific Americans and 49,020 Chinese. However, the 1990 Census shows adjacent census tracts that contain over 1,000 additional Chinese.

15. According to Givens (1939, pp. 31–32), this settlement began with the establishment of the first Korean church in 1905. The Korean community in Los Angeles in the late 1930s was

concentrated in the area between Vermont and Western Avenues and between Adams Boulevard and Slauson Avenue. These were older neighborhoods with families from a mix of racial and ethnic backgrounds who located where racial housing covenants were not strictly enforced.

16. As of 1990, there were 28,000 Koreans residing in Koreatown. With the recent growth, the number has reached an estimated 30,000. U.S. Bureau of the Census, Census of the Population, 1970 and 1990.

17. The history of this community is based on Trounson (1981); Holley (1986); and Ong, Park, and Tong (1993).

18. At that time it was bounded by 7th Street on the south, Pacific Coast Highway on the north, California Avenue on the west, and Freeman Avenue on the east.

19. The hourly rate at the 25 percentile was $3.91. The minimum wage in 1989 was $3.35 per hour and moved up to $3.80 per hour in 1990.

20. Ethnic economies are not unique to Asian Pacific Americans but also exist in other immigrant populations. For example, see Portes and Bach (1985) for a discussion on Cuban enclave economies.

21. The literature on enclave economies and working conditions in these subeconomies has grown considerably over the last few years. The following discussion is based on Zhou (1992), Light (1972), Light and Bonacich (1988), Light and Bhachu (1993), Portes and Wilson (1980), Portes and Bach (1985), Wong (1987), Portes and Jensen (1987), Zhou and Logan (1991), Mar (1991), Kim (1981), Bonacich (1987), Kwong (1987), Ong (1984), Sanders and Nee (1987), Ong, Park, and Tong (1993).

22. Another way of defining the enclave economy is as one part of a sequence of stages of ethnically defined business development proposed by Waldinger, Aldrich, and Ward (1990). In the first stage, a limited number of very small businesses arises to serve a small population of immigrant workers. As the population grows, the community undergoes a qualitative change that marks the second stage with a much broader set of social, cultural, and economic activities. This describes the ethnic enclave. The third stage involves ethnic entrepreneurial activity in communities other than their own, including the role of middleman merchants. In the last stage of this sequence, immigrant entrepreneurs assimilate and disperse over the wide range of industrial activity and become closer to the characteristics of white-owned businesses.

23. In many cases, owners themselves live outside of the inner-city enclave in which their businesses are located.

24. The low labor force participation rate of adults in New Phnom Penh may be partly explained by the lesser degree of enclave economic development within the Cambodian community relative to the other three communities.

25. Jobs in the secondary labor market, in contrast to those in the primary labor market, according to dual labor market theory, are characterized by low-skill work, low wages and fringe benefits, poor working conditions, job instability, high rates of labor turnover, and little chance of upward job mobility. See the following for discussions of labor market segmentation theories: Gordon, Edwards, and Reich, 1982; Doeringer and Piore, 1971, Chapter 8.

26. For example, a recent crackdown by the U.S. Department of Labor on a random sample of restaurants in San Francisco found violations of federal minimum wage and hour, overtime, and wage reporting laws, particularly in ethnic restaurants. See *San Francisco Chronicle*, December 17, 1993.

27. Many store owners doing business in the Watts area of south central Los Angeles prior to the 1970s were Jewish, along with early Asian immigrant groups, primarily Japanese and Chinese. Following the Watts rebellions of the late 1960s, however, many closed their busi-

nesses or relocated to other areas. This period coincided with the period of increased immigration from Asia following the 1965 Immigration Act. Many new Asian Pacific immigrants took over small businesses from established Jewish, Chinese, and Japanese merchants who were leaving the south central area.

28. Data and analyses on the conflict are drawn from Ong, Park, and Tong (1993), Umemoto (1994), and Freer (1994), unless otherwise noted. There are also numerous accounts of tensions between Asian Pacific merchants and non-Asian Pacific residents in the popular media. For examples, see: *New York Times*, November 25, 1990, and July 30, 1990.

29. Waldinger and Aldrich, 1990. They refer to Illsoo Kim's findings (1981) to note that the distinguishing mark of Korean business in America, as compared to other immigrant groups, is the fact that business growth has occurred by selling nonethnic products in the general market.

30. For example, collaboration was suggested by a reporter of the *Los Angeles Sentinel*, the largest West Coast African American vernacular, in an interview with Judge Karlin, who presided over the trial of Soon Ja Du. The reporter asked how the Korean community views her after the sentencing, referring to a donation reportedly made by the Korean American Grocer's Association to Karlin's reelection campaign. See *Los Angeles Sentinel*, March 18, 1992.

31. The campaign to lower the density of liquor stores had begun over nine years prior to the civil unrest. With weak and largely ineffective regulations by the alcohol and beverage control board, the relative numbers of liquor outlets flourished in neighborhoods with little political power to control zoning commission decisions and with low-income populations vulnerable to substance abuse and addiction.

32. For example, the implementation of the Community Reinvestment Act increasing capital to inner-city borrowers, ending redlining practices discriminating against inner-city economic development on the part of banks and insurance companies, implementing effective employment and training programs, ending employment and housing discrimination, improving the educational infrastructure, and other more fundamental steps need to be taken.

REFERENCES

Betancur, J. Cordova, T., and Torres, M. (1993). "Economic Restructuring and the Process of Incorporation of Latinos into the Chicago Economy." In R. Morales and F. Bonilla (eds.), *Latinos in a Changing U.S. Economy* (pp. 109–132). Newbury Park, Calif.: Sage.

Bonacich, E. (1973). "A Theory of Middlemen Minorities." *American Sociological Review* 35: 583–594.

———. (1987). " 'Making It in America A Social Evaluation of the Ethics of Immigrant Entrepreneurship." *Sociological Perspective* 30:446–466.

———. (1993). "Asians in the Los Angeles Garment Industry." Unpublished manuscript, University of California, Riverside.

Doeringer, P., and Piore, M. (1971). *Internal Labor Markets and Manpower Analysis*. Lexington, Mass.: Heath.

Freer, R. (1994). "Black-Korean Conflict." In M. Baldassare (ed.), *The Los Angeles Riots: Lessons for the Urban Future* (pp. 175–203). Boulder, Colo.: Westview Press.

Givens, H. (1939). "The Korean Community in Los Angeles County." M.A. thesis, University of Southern California.

Goldsmith, W., and Blakely, E. (1992). *Separate Societies: Poverty and Inequality in U.S. Cities*. Philadelphia: Temple University Press.

Gordon, D., Edwards, R., and Reich, M. (1982). *Segmented Work, Divided Workers: The Historical Transformation of Labor in the United States*. Cambridge: Cambridge University Press.

Harrison, B., and Bluestone, B. (1988). *The Great U-Turn: Corporate Restructuring and the Polarizing of America*. New York: Basic Books.

Holley, D. (1986, October 27). "Refugees Build a Haven in Long Beach." *Los Angeles Times*, pp. B1, B3.

Kain, J. (1968). "Residential Segregation, Negro Employment, and Metropolitan Decentralization." *Quarterly Journal of Economics* 82: 175–197.

Kasarda, J. (1989). "Urban Industrial Transition and the Underclass." *Annals of the American Academy of Political and Social Sciences* 501: 26–47.

———. (1993). "Inner-City Poverty and Economic Access." In J. Sommer and D. A. Hicks (eds.), *America: Perspectives Rediscovering Urban America: Perspectives on the 1980s*. U.S. Department of Housing and Urban Development, Office of Policy Development and Research. Washington, D.C.: U.S. Government Printing Office.

Kim, I. (1981). *New Urban Immigrants: The Korean Community in New York*. Princeton, N.J.: Princeton University Press.

Kirschenman, J., and Neckerman, K. (1991). "We'd Love to Hire You, But . . . : The Meaning of Race for Employers." In C. Jencks and P. Peterson (eds.), *The Urban Underclass*. Washington, D.C.: Brookings Institution.

Kwong, P. (1987). *The New Chinatown*. New York: Hill and Wang.

Light, I. (1972). *Ethnic Enterprise in America*. Berkeley: University of California Press.

Light, I., and Bhachu, P. (1993). *Immigration and Entrepreneurship: Culture, Capital, and Ethnic Networks*. New Brunswick, N.J.: Transaction.

Light, I., and Bonacich, E. (1988). *Immigrant Entrepreneurs: Koreans in Los Angeles, 1975–1982*. Berkeley: University of California Press.

Lee, R. (1960). *The Chinese in the United States of America*. Hong Kong: Hong Kong University Press.

Loo, M. L. (1991). *Chinatown: Most Time, Hard Time*. New York: Praeger.

Mar, D. (1991). "Another Look at the Enclave Economy Thesis: Chinese Immigrants in the Ethnic Labor Market." *Amerasia Journal* 17:5–21.

Markusen, A. (1984). *Military Spending and Urban Development in California*. Berkeley: Institute of Urban and Regional Development.

Massey, D., and Denton, N. (1993). *American Apartheid: Segregation and the Making of the Underclass*. Cambridge, Mass.: Harvard University Press.

Mieszkowski, P., and Mills, E. (1993). The Causes of Metropolitan Suburbanization." *Journal of Economic Perspectives* 7(3): 135–148.

Mills, E. (1989). *Urban Economics*. Glenview, Ill.: Scott, Foresman.

Mincy, R. (1993). *Reforming Services for High Risk Youth*. Washington, D.C.: Urban Institute.

Mincy, R., and Wiener, S. (1993). "The Under Class in the 1980s: Changing Concept, Constant Reality." Working paper, The Urban Institute. Washington, D.C.: Urban Institute. Unpublished manuscript.

Mollenkopf, J., and Castells, M. (eds.). (1991). *Dual City: Restructuring New York*. New York: Russell Sage Foundation.

Moore, J. (1989). "Is There an Hispanic Underclass?" *Social Science Quarterly* 70(2): 265–284.

Morales, R., and Ong, P. (1993). "The Illusion of Progress: Latinos in Los Angeles." In R. Morales and F. Bonilla (eds.), *Latinos in a Changing U.S. Economy* (pp. 55–84). Newbury Park, Calif.: Sage.

Moss, P., and Tilly, C. (1993a). "Race Hurdles for Black Men: Evidence from Interviews with Employers." Unpublished manuscript, Department of Policy and Planning, University of Massachusetts, Lowell.

———. (1993b). " 'Soft' Skills and Race: An Investigation of Black Men's Employment Problems." Unpublished manuscript, Department of Policy and Planning, University of Massachusetts, Lowell.

Okamoto, Phillip M. (1991). "Evolution of a Japanese American Enclave: Gardena, California—A Case Study of Ethnic Community Change and Continuity." M.A. thesis, University of California, Los Angeles.

Ong, P. (1981, Winter). "An Ethnic Trade: The Chinese Laundries in Early California." *Journal of Ethnic Studies* 8(4): 95–113.

———. (1984). "Chinatown Unemployment and Ethnic Labor Markets." *Amerasia Journal* 11(1): 35–54.

Ong, P., and Hee, S. (1993). "Korean Merchants and the L.A. Riot/Rebellion." In Center for Pacific Rim Studies (ed.), *Losses in the Los Angeles Civil Unrest*. Los Angeles: University of California, Los Angeles.

Ong, P., Park, K., and Tong, J. (1993). "The Korean-Black Conflict and the State." Unpublished manuscript, University of California, Los Angeles.

Osofsky, G. (1971). *Harlem: The Making of a Ghetto; Negro New York, 1890–1930*. New York: Harper and Row.

Portes, A., and Bach, R. (1985). *Latin Journey: Cuba and Mexican Immigrants in the U.S.* Berkeley: University of California Press.

Portes, A., and Jensen, L. (1987). "What's an Ethnic Enclave? The Case for Conceptual Clarity." *American Sociological Review* 52: 768–770.

Portes, A., and Wilson, K. (1980). "Immigrant Enclaves: An Analysis of the Labor Market Experiences of Cubans in Miami." *American Journal of Sociology* 86: 295–319.

Sanders, J., and Nee., V. (1987). "Limits of Ethnic Solidarity in the Enclave Economy." *American Sociological Review* 52: 745–767.

Sassen-Koob, S. (1988). *The Mobility of Labor and Capital: A Study of International Investment and Labor Flow*. Cambridge: Cambridge University Press.

———. (1993). "Urban Transformation and Employment." In R. Morales and F. Bonilla (eds.), *Latinos in a Changing U.S. Economy*. Newbury Park, Calif.: Sage.

Sawers, L., and Tabb, W. (eds.). (1984). *Sunbelt/Snowbelt: Urban Development and Regional Restructuring*. New York: Oxford University Press.

Siu, C. P. (1987). *The Chinese Laundryman: A Study of Social Isolation*. New York: New York University Press.

Spear, A. (1967). *Black Chicago; The Making of a Black Ghetto, 1890–1920*. Chicago: University of Chicago Press.

Tatsuno, Sheridan. (1971). "The Political and Economic Effects of Urban Renewal on Ethnic Communities: A Case Study of San Francisco's Japantown." *Amerasia Journal* 1 (1): 33–51.

Tobin, M. (1993). "Sensitivity Analyses of the Growth and Composition of the Underclass and Concentrated Poverty. Unpublished manuscript, The Urban Institute, Washington, D.C.

Trounson, R. (1981, December 26 and 27). "8,000 Refugees Make Long Beach Cambodian Capital of U.S." *Los Angeles Times*, Long Beach edition, p. B1.

Umemoto, K. (1994). "Blacks and Koreans in Los Angeles: The Case of Latasha Harlins and Soon Ja Du." In J. Jennings (ed). *Blacks, Latinos, and Asians in Urban America: Status and Prospects for Politics and Activism*. Westport, Conn.: Praeger.

Vose, C. (1959). *Caucasians Only*. Berkeley: University of California Press.

Ward, D. (1971). *Cities and Immigrants*. New York: Oxford University Press.

Wilson, W. (1987). *The Truly Disadvantaged: The Inner City, the Underclass, and Public Policy*. Chicago: University of Chicago Press.

Waldinger, R., and Aldrich, H. (1990). "Ethnicity and Entrepreneurship." *Annual Review of Sociology* 16: 111–135.

Waldinger, R., Aldrich, H., and Ward, R. (1990). *Immigrant Entrepreneurship Immigrant and Ethnic Business in Western Industrial Societies*. Beverly Hills, Calif.: Sage.

Wong, B. (1987). "The Role of Ethnicity in Enclave Enterprises: A Study of the Chinese Garment Factories in New York City." *Human Organization* 46 (2):120–130.

Zhou, M. (1992). *Chinatown: The Socioeconomic Potential of an Urban Enclave*. Philadelphia: Temple University Press.

Zhou, M., and Logan, J. (1991). "Returns on Human Capital in Ethnic Enclaves: New York City's Chinatown." *American Sociological Review* 54: 809–820.

Chapter Nine

Work and Its Place in the Lives of Immigrant Women
Garment Workers in New York City's Chinatown

Min Zhou and Regina Nordquist

Ah Mei, a trans-Pacific bride, was pregnant with her first child. Her husband expected her to rest at home to take care of their unborn baby. She wandered around Chinatown and walked up to a garment shop. She tried for a couple of days and took the job, making $200 the first week. That was a half year's pay in China! Besides, she had her own money.[1]

Liu had never touched a sewing machine, nor had she planned to be a "super sewer" before she came to the United States. She had dreams a lot fancier. After seven years in the apparel trade, she became one of the most skilled sewing women in Chinatown, so good that she could even "fire" her boss if she chose to. With substantial savings from her garment work, Liu's family had just moved from a tiny little apartment in Chinatown to their new home in Flushing, Queens. She continued to work in Chinatown full-time. Her family had a big mortgage note to pay . . .[2]

Chen was 16 and had been here for eleven months. She worked in a garment factory because she felt obliged to help her family. Chen worked from three to seven everyday and all day Saturday and Sunday in the same factory as her mother. She didn't really know how much she made because the boss gave the money to her mother . . .[3]

In New York City's Chinatown, three out of five women work in the garment industry, a backbone industry of the growing ethnic enclave economy. Most of these working women are new immigrants, married, and with school-aged and younger children. Day in and day out, they bend over row after row of sewing machines; they are surrounded by piles of fabric scraps; and they are sometimes with children, including toddlers and infants, clustered at their skirts. But the garment factory only reflects one side of their lives. The other side is the home front. They are expected to care for their children, nurture their husbands, and attend to a long list of household chores, including cooking, cleaning, laundering, grocery shopping, paying bills, and so on.

In this article, we examine how immigrant Chinese women juggle multiple roles as wives, mothers, and wage workers and how their experience between home and the workplace contributes to the survival of their immigrant families.

Theoretical Considerations

Women working outside the home is not a phenomenon unique to immigrants in the United States. There has been a dramatic change nationwide in the size and composition of women's labor force participation (LFP) over the last few decades. Women of all ages, marital and maternal statuses have entered the labor market, seeking paid employment (Stromberg & Harkess 1978, p. 5). Regardless of race/ethnicity and national origins, they share some common labor market experiences.

Working women are generally viewed by our society as supplementary or secondary wage earners, and hence their newly assumed role as wage workers is not automatically accompanied by changes in household behavior and norms (Huber & Spitze 1981; Morokvasic 1983, p. 13). Their traditional roles as wives and mothers continue to influence their work experience as paid employees, creating pressures as women juggle the workplace and home (Stromberg & Harkess 1978, p. 6; Huber & Spitze 1988). As a result, working women are disproportionately concentrated in low-ranking and low-wage occupations and uniformly receive less earnings than their male counterparts with similar levels of educational and occupational attainments (Becker 1957; England & Norris 1985).

The situation for immigrant women at work is worse than U.S.-born working women. Not only are they doubly burdened with household responsibilities and paid work, but they also suffer from additional disadvantages as immigrants. Lack of English language ability, transferable education and skills, and knowledge about the larger economy render them more vulnerable and less competitive in the job market than their U.S.-born counterparts. In the face of limited opportunities and discrimination in the larger economy, immigrant women are often confined to their ethnic enclaves, taking jobs that are highly exploitative and offer little social mobility (Bonacich 1992).

To develop our framework of analysis in this study, we draw on three theoretical approaches, which are relevant to the study of labor market experience of immigrant women: the neo-Marxist approach, the sociocultural-context approach, and the reference-group approach.

The Neo-Marxist Approach to Women's Work

The neo-Marxist approach views the inferior status of working women as intrinsically rooted in capitalist exploitation (Ward 1990; Ollenburger & Moore 1992; Bonacich 1992, 1993). Neo-Marxists argue that women's work, in both a wage and a nonwage sense, functions to maintain capitalism. In the context of postindustrial capitalism, which is characterized by global economic restructuring, working women have become the world's new industrial proletariat—a critical element in the global economy and a key resource for expanding multinational corporations (Ehrenreich & Fuentes 1981). Take garment manufacturing in the United States as an example. Industrial globalization has shifted the center of garment manufacturing to less developed countries to take advantage of low-wage female labor and has informalized the production process through subcontracted piecework at home (Tiana 1990). In New York City, apparel employment dropped from 360,000 following World War II to under 150,000 workers in 1975 (Waldinger 1986, p. 56). Paradoxically, while low-wage jobs in garment manufacturing are moved across the southern border to Mexico or cross the Pacific Ocean to Hong Kong, Taiwan, and China and other developing nations, the typical Third World informal economy is emerging in immigrant enclaves in America's major urban centers. During the period of economic restructuring, immigrant entrepreneurs are able to expand sweatshops and other informal or subcontracted operations precisely because they have access to low-cost immigrant labor, especially female labor.

Neo-Marxists maintain that the globalization of manufacturing industries and the increasing use of female immigrant labor is a common strategy employed by the capitalist class against organized domestic workers (Bernard 1987; Fernandez-Kelly & Garcia 1989; Ward 1990). Hence, benefits brought about by international and immigrant workers in the workplace accrue not to all members of the dominant group, but only to the capitalist class. Such benefits are extracted precisely against the interests of the domestic working class (Portes & Bach 1985). As a reserve pool of potential workers, women can be easily manipulated by the capitalist class. In the labor market, immigrant women are in a particularly weak position to resist capitalist exploitation and employer discrimination. This is not only because they are socially, linguistically, and culturally separated from the domestic working class but also because they are subject to legal constraints such as exclusion or deportation. Thus, even though organizational efforts or protests among immigrants are occasionally made, they rarely involve legitimate class revindications (Castells 1975). Consequently, immigrant working women, as well as their Third World counterparts, remain the most impoverished segment of the working class.

The neo-Marxist approach is generally correct about the possible outcomes of low-wage labor under capitalism, and it captures certain economic realities affecting working women. However, it treats all women as members of the exploited or oppressed class and overlooks the differences in employment conditions and sociocultural contexts among working women. In the case of immigrant working women, for example, their low-wage labor may not necessarily lead to working-class impoverishment as expected by neo-Marxists. Although many immigrant workers are being disproportionately absorbed by low-wage, "degraded" industries composed of sweat-shops and other informal operations, they do not seem to be unduly disadvantaged and impoverished. Instead, some immigrant groups are found to be able to translate their low-wage work and hard-earned dollars into business ownership, home ownership, and suburban residence within only one generation (Fenandez-Kelly & Garcia 1989; Zhou 1992).

The Sociocultural Context of Work among Immigrant Women

While the neo-Marxist approach emphasizes the exploitative aspect of employment under capitalism, the sociocultural-context approach emphasizes the "embeddedness" of women's work. The sociocultural-context approach maintains that women's work takes on different meanings in different sociocultural contexts. Central to its argument is the notion of "embeddedness." Women enter the labor market with expectations and goals different from those of men. These expectations and goals are not only class specific but also cultural specific. In the United States, the norm of female labor force participation is specified on the basis of the middle class. That is, women enter the labor force to help maintain a comfortable standard of living for the family, on the one hand, and to gain certain level of economic independence from men, on the other hand (Spitze 1988). Their paid work is considered secondary or supplementary in an economic sense. Immigrant women, in contrast, work in a situation unique to immigration. Their primary concern is survival. They cannot afford to make decisions to work on the basis of rational cost/benefit calculation between home and paid work, nor can they set priority of work for the purpose of establishing economic independence. Many of them simply have to work, while at the same time managing child-care and major household responsibilities, to survive in an unfamiliar and often hostile environment (Perez 1986; Fernandez-Kelly & Garcia 1989; Zhou & Logan 1989; Zhou 1992). They are not unconcerned about their own rights but simply set priorities for their families in the early stages of economic adaptation.

Previous research has found that, in many cases, immigrants are incorporated into a specific social and structural context in which socioeconomic gains for immigrant men are backed by the close association of women (their wives) and kinship ties linking them to the labor market (Ferree 1979; Fernandez-Kelly & Garcia 1989; Perez 1986; Zhou & Logan 1989). Perez (1986) reported results suggesting that economic assimilation of immigrant groups is largely a family phenomenon rather than a process of individualistic status attainment. Zhou and Logan (1989) argued that the primary purpose of work for women is not to develop a working career but rather to contribute immediately to the household income for the benefit of younger members and for the upward social mobility of the family as a whole. Fernandez-Kelly and Garcia (1989) further contended that while individual characteristics may be important in the status-attainment process, economic adjustment of immigrants is largely a family affair. Female involvement in the labor market, whether as paid or unpaid labor, is a necessary means to protect the living standards of the family. Research on Cuban women in Miami revealed that most of the married Cuban immigrant women entered the labor force out of the economic necessity in a situation of downward mobility upon arrival in the United States. Their employment served as a continuation of cultural patterns—an obligation to the family (Ferree 1979, p. 36). Once their families moved upward, these women tended to withdraw from the labor force (Fernandez-Kelly & Garcia 1989).

The Reference Group for Immigrant Women at Work

The reference-group approach explains how women react to their relatively disadvantaged social and labor market positions. This approach does not contradict in any observable way either the neo-Marxist approach or the sociocultural-context approach. The neo-Marxist discourse often centers around equity and labor rights issues, such as gender discrimination and exploitation (Mincer & Polacheck 1974; Almquist & Wehrle-Einhorn 1978; Bonacich 1980, 1992, Cooney & Ortiz 1983). In contrast, the reference group approach puts an individual working woman in a comparative framework with other working women, emphasizing that women usually react to their disadvantages on the basis of their gender-group membership (Form & Geschwender 1962; Loscocco & Spitze 1991). Past studies on pay satisfaction emphasize the importance of comparative context in which job satisfaction is assessed. Women seem satisfied with low pay because they use other women as referents (England, Farkas, Kilbourne, & Dou 1988).

However, while making a gender distinction in selection of a reference group, previous studies have often applied an American middle-class standard to women at work (see Spitze 1988 for details), and hence have insufficiently explained the subjective responses to work conditions of women from different racial/ethnic backgrounds. Relatively little research has directly utilized the reference-group approach to explain the situation of immigrant women. In dealing with their labor market disadvantages, immigrant women also have a reference group. Their choice of reference group, however, is not merely based on the comparison of other women within their own or a different group. Rather, the choice is a result of the specific conditions under which these women form their expectations. Frequently, they compare their current situation with their own past, perceiving immigration into the United States as a process of long-term upward social mobility for their families, children, and themselves.

Immigrant minority women suffer from a double disadvantage associated with their status as both women and immigrant minority group members (Almquist & Wehrle-Einhorn 1978, p. 63). The effects of this dual status are reflected in patterns of their labor market incorporation; they are concentrated in worse jobs at lower pay than U.S.-born non-Hispanic white women. However, their disadvantaged position does not seem to discourage them from participating in paid work. Immigrant women generally show higher rates of labor force participation (LFP) than do U.S.-born non-Hispanic white women, and their LFP is often related strongly to the successful economic adaptation of many immigrant groups (Perez 1986; Stier 1991). For example, close to 60 percent of the Chinese female population in New York were in the labor force as compared to 45 percent for non-Hispanic white women in 1980.

Many immigrant women are apparently willing to accept low-pay, menial jobs, not just because other immigrant women have held similar jobs but because they have a different orientation toward work. When it comes to assessing satisfaction of paid work and wages, they appear to be more concerned with what is best for their families than with what is fair for themselves as individuals, a phenomenon unique to immigrant women at work. In the case of Chinese women, they compare themselves with the reference group from which them have emigrated and consider themselves fortunate to be in the United States (Sung 1987, p. 93).

In sum, immigrant workers often justify their employment from the framework of their original culture. When they evaluate themselves and their labor market behavior, they refer to the standards of the culture from which they emigrate rather than American standards. However, as they become more and more assimilated into American ways, they have a tendency to change their frame of reference.

Work and Its Place in the Lives of Immigrant Women: A Framework for Analysis

Drawing on the neo-Marxist approach, the sociocultural-context approach, and the reference-group approach, we propose a framework for understanding work and its place in the lives of immigrant women and illustrate it through the example of garment workers in New York City's Chinatown. We argue that immigrant women's work is an intrinsic part of a family strategy to survive and eventually adapt to U.S. society and that the adoption of such a strategy depends on specific sociocultural contexts from which immigrant women came and into which these women immigrated upon arrival in the United States. Our task is not to refute the neo-Marxist approach but rather to demonstrate contrasts in the meaning of women's work under unique sociocultural circumstances. We attempt to reconcile seemingly contradictory elements of work and experience of immigrant women and to shed light on how cultural components interplay with economic factors to affect the lives of immigrant women in U.S. society.

Survival versus Career Attainment

Labor force participation of immigrant women generally involves two analytically distinct dimensions: survival and career attainment. Each contains a different set of strategies and goals. Survival refers to settling down and securing from an unfamiliar and often hostile environment the necessary means of livelihood. Career attainment involves the socialization of women into the normative structure of the economy traditionally dominated by men, equal occupational mobility to that of men, and economic independence from men (Mueller & Campbell 1977; Philliber & Hiller 1978; Van Velsor & Beeghley 1979). More often than not, newly arrived immigrants are busy surviving and striving toward economic stability. Certain segments of the immigrant population may quickly bypass mere survival because they bring with them strong human capital and economic resources (Borjas 1990). However, a disproportionate number of immigrants have first to secure a means of livelihood—food, clothing, and shelter—in order to proceed to their American dream after arrival in the United States. The survival strategies of many immigrant families entail not only employment of men but also the economic participation of women in paid work. Therefore, the work of immigrant women may not be secondary but necessary in the struggle for survival.

Immigrant Workers versus U.S.-Born Workers

Immigrant workers are analytically and socially distinguishable from U.S.-born workers. On the one hand, immigrants are often perceived as aliens threatening job securities and labor rights of U.S. workers. Historically and routinely, immigrants have been excluded as "the indispensable enemy" from the working class of the host society (Saxton 1971). A 1992 *Business Week* poll revealed that more than 60 percent of U.S. residents interviewed believed that new immigrants took jobs away from U.S. workers and that immigrants drove wages down. Even descendants of immigrants who were born in the United States and have been fully assimilated suffer from certain immigrant disadvantages merely because they look foreign (U.S. Commission on Civil Rights 1992).

On the other hand, immigrants are handicapped by initial disadvantages associated with immigration. They lack English language ability, economic resources, transferable skills, and legal protection to compete on equal terms with U.S. workers. Moreover, because of their foreign status, immigrant workers lack political muscle and economic resources to consciously fight for labor rights and social equality. They tend to distance themselves from the politics of the American labor force and to focus on their struggle for survival. Thus, they appear to willingly take "bad" or "abandoned" jobs and accept substandard wages. However, the notion of "willingness" is misleading. Immigrants are not cheap labor by nature. Rather, they see low-wage jobs as the best option to meet their survival needs and to facilitate social mobility.

Immigrant Enclave Economies versus the Larger Economy

Finally, we analytically distinguish between the capital/labor relationship in the context of an immigrant enclave economy and such a relationship in the context of the larger political economy of capitalism. Within the Marxist framework, the relationship between labor and capital is inherently conflictual. The employer class exploits the working class. It extracts surplus values from the workers, establishes its dominance over the workers, and consolidates its privileges by politically suppressing the workers.

However, this line of argument does not seem to hold well within the context of an immigrant enclave economy. In ethnic enclaves, ethnic entrepreneurs enter self-employment as an alternative way to low-wage menial work or unemployment. They are workers themselves. They routinely work in their own shops over ten hours a day and at least six days a week. Moreover, they depend their business operation on the availability of reliable family labor and the ethnically committed labor force whose human capital characteristics are lower than the minimum requirements for entry to the larger labor market (Zhou & Bankston 1993).

From the point of view of ethnic workers, enclave economies offer material and symbolic compensations, such as a familiar cultural environment in which workers can interact in their own language, flexible work hours, and training, that escape a gross accounting of benefits based exclusively on wages. More important, ethnic culture creates a common bond between employers and workers, making for a more personalized work environment than the highly alienating working conditions in comparable employment in the larger economy (Portes & Zhou 1992). Therefore, the close association between class status and ethnicity within a unique cultural context makes possible an alternative path to social mobility, one that effectively shields immigrant workers from initial immigrant disadvantages and racial discrimination.

In the following section, we present a case study on Chinatown's garment workers, which is based on the 1980 census data and field observations in Chinatown. The census data provide detailed demographic and socioeconomic information about immigrant Chinese women in the garment trade and allow for a refined analysis of patterns and determinants of labor market participation and poverty to produce more generalizable and more representative results (U.S. Bureau of the Census 1983). The analysis of the census data will be supplemented with fieldwork data collected by the authors through personal interviews and participant observations in New York City's Chinatown from 1988 to 1990 and a follow-up field study between spring of 1991 and spring of 1992.[4]

Chinatown's Garment Workers: An Example

The Impact of Female Immigration on Chinatown's Garment Industry

New York City's garment industry has been an immigrant trade since the early 1800s. The earliest garment workers were German and Irish immigrants, followed by Polish and Russian Jews, Italians, and Eastern European Jews. The garment industry was able to grow because of the availability of a large pool of low-wage and mostly female immigrant labor. After World War II, however, New York lost its place of predominance in garment manufacturing due to standardization for economies of scale and the internationalization of capital and labor. Only a small portion of the industry has remained to respond to a fluctuating demands susceptible to nonstandardized and quickly changing fashion/style garments, which has created a niche for small garment shops.

Despite overall industry decline, where growth exists in New York City's garment industry, it continues to be predicated on low-cost immigrant labor. Between 1975 and 1980, the number of Chinese-owned garment factories grew by an average of thirty-six a year, reaching a peak of 430 in 1980. In 1980, Chinatown contained one-third of all the jobs in Manhattan's women's outerwear industry (ILGWU 1983, p. 44).

The most important factor in the growth of Chinatown's garment industry has been the surge of female Chinese immigration, a recent phenomenon. During the period of Chinese exclusion in the late nineteenth century and the first half of this century, few Chinese women were allowed to enter the country, not even to join their families. Reflecting earlier migration patterns, New York's Chinatown was a bachelor's society for many years. In the 1940s, there were six times as many Chinese men as women in New York. Even after the passage of the War Brides Act in 1945,[5] which allowed Chinese women to join their husbands in the United States, Chinese men still outnumbered women by nearly 300 percent in New York City. It was not until after 1965, when U.S. immigration policies were revised to favor family reunification, that Chinese women began to pour into New York City. By 1970, the sex ratio for New York City's Chinese population decreased to 117 men per 100 women; and a decade later, this ratio was further reduced to 106 men per 100 women (Sung 1987; Zhou 1992).

Recent immigration of Chinese women reflects a predominant pattern of family migration. The primary motive has been family reunification. Immigrants from mainland China, Hong Kong, and Taiwan have fully utilized their quotas (Sung 1987, pp. 15–22). In fact, migration from each area has been greater than that allowed by the quota, indicating that many arrived as nonquota immigrants (i.e., immediate family members of U.S. citizens).[6] According to immigration statistics, Chinese women have outnumbered men entering the U.S. every year since the mid-1970s. In 1980, family unification was responsible for 85 percent of all Chinese immigration (Sung 1987, p. 20). Immigrant Chinese women have constituted more than half of the total Chinese influx in recent years, and this trend will continue in the near future. Not only have women dominated the immigration trend, they were disproportionately (65 percent) in working ages between 20 to 59 (Zhou 1992).

The arrival of female Chinese immigrants has dramatically altered the social fabric of New York City's Chinatown. As more and more women have immigrated, many coming to join their families, the once exclusive male character of Chinatown's demography has been transformed into a community bustling with young families. The 1980 Census shows that some 80 percent of the Chinese households in New York are family-type households, and 87 percent of the Chinese families are married-couple families (10 percent higher that the average numbers for New York State). Further, large-scale immigration of women has stimulated economic development in Chinatown. On the one hand, the sheer numbers of immigrants and the shift to a family-centered community has expanded the market for Chinese goods and services inaccessible in the larger society, creating opportunities for ethnic entrepreneurship. On the other hand, the availability of a large pool of low-skilled female labor at a critical time in the City's overall economic restructuring has promoted the rapid growth of informal or subcontracted operations in New York's garment industry (Waldinger 1986).

Immigrant Chinese women's concentration in the garment industry is extraordinary: while over half of all Chinese working women aged 16 to 64 in New York City were garment workers, 85 percent of the work force in the garment industry in

Chinatown were immigrant women (Zhou 1992). In 1983, 70 percent of garments produced in New York City were sewn by Chinese immigrant women.[7]

Characteristics of Immigrant Chinese Women

Table 9.1 illustrates major characteristics of Chinese women. In terms of family situation, foreign-born Chinese women share many characteristics similar to those of their U.S.-born counterparts and non-Hispanic women in general, except that they tend to have lower rate of divorce or separation and are more likely to live with school-aged children. However, foreign-born Chinese women show severe human capital deficiency. They have the lowest level of educational attainment and poorest English proficiency. Less than half of them have finished high school, and only 42 percent of them speak English well.

Chinese women are traditionally regarded as temporary members of their birth families, who make little effort to educate or train them. A fifty-eight-year-old Taiwanese immigrant we interviewed in 1990 explained that she had no schooling at all because it wasn't considered appropriate for girls. Her brothers, however, went to school and received additional tutoring at home.[8] The lack of emphasis on women's

TABLE 9.1

Major Characteristics of Females Aged 16 to 64 from Family Households in New York City by Race and Place of Birth: 1980

Characteristics	Chinese		Non-Hispanic white	
	Foreign born	U.S. born	Foreign born	U.S. born
Median Age	39.0	30.0	40.0	41.0
Marital Status				
Currently married (%)	85.0	69.2	87.2	73.3
Divorced or separated (%)	1.5	2.5	4.2	7.5
Single or widowed (%)	15.5	28.3	8.6	19.2
Household Types				
Married-couple families (%)	90.5	88.0	90.0	82.5
Single-female-headed households (%)	9.1	11.1	9.5	16.7
Single-male-headed households (%)	.4	.9	.5	.8
Relationship to Household Heads				
As household heads (%)	10.6	11.1	11.8	17.2
As spouses (%)	80.0	61.5	82.7	67.7
As children (%)	9.5	27.4	5.5	15.1
Presence of Children				
With own children under 6 (%)	21.8	20.6	20.1	15.1
With own children 6 to 17 (%)	35.5	25.6	29.0	25.9
Without own children (%)	42.8	53.8	50.9	59.0
Fertility				
Number of children ever born	2.2	1.1	2.0	1.6
Human Capital				
Mean years of school completed	9.1	13.0	10.6	12.6
High school graduates (%)	45.2	78.6	56.1	79.3
English proficiency (%)	41.8	92.3	79.9	99.6
Labor Market Status				
In the garment industry	40.2	6.8	7.9	1.9
In other industries	32.7	65.0	41.2	55.3
Not in the labor force	27.2	28.2	50.9	42.8
Total Number of Cases	1,307	117	8,194	32,253

SOURCE: U.S. Bureau of the Census, 1983.

education and training results in serious human capital deficiencies in women upon immigration.

Despite their lack of human capital, Chinese women immigrants display a particularly low rate of labor force nonparticipation. Inversely, the labor force participation rate of immigrant Chinese women is 73 percent, 24 percentage points higher than that of immigrant white women and 16 percentage points higher than U.S.-born white women. Over 40 percent of immigrant Chinese women are found employment in the garment industry, which suggests that Chinatown indeed provides job opportunities for immigrant women who would have had a hard time finding work in the larger economy because of the human capital deficiency.

Table 9.2 presents demographic characteristics of working women by industrial sectors. Overall, more than half of Chinese women found jobs in the garment industry, compared to only 6 percent of white women. Chinese garment workers are generally younger than white garment workers but older than workers in other industries. Compared to Chinese workers in other industries and all white workers, Chinese garment workers are more likely to be married, to live in married-couple families as wives, to live with school-aged children, and to have a higher fertility rate. These intra- and inter-racial group differences highlight a unique context: most Chinese garment workers are married and have young children.

Table 9.3 further reveals selected socioeconomic characteristics of working women by industrial sectors. Compared to other Chinese workers and white workers, Chinese garment workers show several marked differences. First, Chinese garment workers are extremely poor in human capital. They have only an average of 6.5 years of

TABLE 9.2

Demographic Characteristics of Females Aged 16 to 64 from Family Households in New York City by Race: Garment Workers versus Other Workers, 1980

Characteristics	Chinese		Non-Hispanic white	
	Garment workers	All other workers	Garment workers	All other workers
Percent group total N	51.4	48.6	5.6	94.4
Median Age	44.0	34.0	49.0	40.0
Marital Status				
Currently married (%)	87.4	74.0	77.7	67.7
Divorced or separated (%)	1.0	3.1	5.0	8.5
Single or widowed (%)	11.6	22.9	17.3	23.8
Household Types				
Married-couple families (%)	91.7	85.9	83.8	80.3
Single-female-headed households (%)	8.3	13.3	15.6	18.7
Single-male-headed households (%)	—	.8	.6	1.0
Relationship to Household Heads				
As household heads (%)	9.8	14.3	15.3	19.4
As spouses (%)	82.9	67.0	73.2	61.3
As children (%)	7.3	18.7	11.5	19.3
Presence of Children				
With own children under 6 (%)	14.4	17.7	5.3	8.1
With own children 6 to 17 (%)	43.5	31.6	26.7	27.4
Without own children (%)	42.1	50.7	68.0	64.5
Fertility				
Number of children ever born	2.7	1.5	1.7	1.4
Total Number of Cases	533	503	1,264	21,211

SOURCE: U.S. Bureau of the Census, 1983.

TABLE 9.3
Socioeconomic Characteristics of Females Aged 16 to 64 from Family Households in New York City
by Race: Garment Workers versus Other Workers, 1980

Characteristics	Chinese		Non-Hispanic white	
	Garment workers	All other workers	Garment workers	All other workers
Human Capital				
Mean years of school completed	6.5	12.5	9.6	13.0
High school graduates (%)	22.0	74.8	43.0	84.1
English proficiency (%)	15.4	74.4	79.1	97.6
Immigrant Status				
Foreign born (%)	98.5	74.9	51.1	15.9
Immigrated after 1975 (%)[a]	32.2	18.5	9.3	13.4
Occupational Status				
Executive/profession occupations (%)	.4	26.2	6.5	25.9
Operator/laborer occupations (%)	94.0	10.7	64.8	3.6
Other occupations (%)	5.6	63.1	28.7	70.5
Work Status				
Mean usual hours worked per week	37.5	36.6	34.2	32.6
Full-time, year-round employment (%)[b]	45.2	59.8	40.7	55.2
Unemployment (%)	1.7	3.8	13.8	5.5
Economic Status				
Mean earnings[c]	$5,207	$10,480	$7,789	$10,887
Working at minimum wages or lower (%)	52.3	15.9	18.0	9.8
Earnings as a percentage of dual earnings[d]	44.8	47.3	40.0	40.3
Median household income	$14,130	$23,108	$22,325	$28,225
Households below 1.00 poverty level (%)	12.0	6.0	3.7	2.9
Characteristics of Household Heads				
Male (%)	88.9	81.9	80.1	75.2
Mean years of school completed	7.8	11.8	9.6	12.6
At work (%)	75.2	74.4	61.8	63.8
Mean income from all sources	$7,242	$13,269	$14,164	$18,537
Total Number of Cases	533	503	1,264	21,211

NOTES: [a] Of all foreign-born persons.
 [b] Employed 35 hours a week and 48 weeks a year.
 [c] The sum of wages and farm or nonfarm self-employment incomes.
 [d] Own earnings divided by the sum of household head and own earnings, limited to married-couple families only.
SOURCE: U.S. Bureau of the Census, 1983.

schooling; only 22 percent of them have finished high school; and they speak little English. Second, they are mostly immigrants, a third of whom arrived after 1975. Third, Chinese garment workers disproportionately occupy the lowest occupational rank as operators. Compared to other workers, they general work longer hours per week, and their unemployment rate is much lower, though their rate of full-time, year-round employment is lower than that of other workers (but higher than that of white garment workers). Fourth, Chinese garment workers have the lowest earnings compared to other groups, and over half of them work at minimum or lower wages, but their contribution to the family is quite substantial. Their household incomes are the lowest, and the poverty rate the highest. Finally, Chinese garment workers come from households where household heads, mostly males, also have poor education and work at low wages.

In sum, immigrant Chinese working women display the following disadvantages. They lack human capital and English language ability. They are disproportionately recent arrivals. They are low-wage workers at the bottom of the occupational hierarchy. They are mostly wives of low-wage workers and mothers of school-age children. They are concentrated in low-income households. Given these disadvantages, immigrant Chinese women are in a situation where they face few options, and most of them are limited to working in Chinatown, which is to say to low-wage menial jobs in Chinatown's garment industry. The alternative to not working in the garment shops is not working anywhere at all. Because their husbands make low wages and because they are at the stage of survival, the latter is not feasible. Questions are thus raised: How does immigrant Chinese women's paid work relate to the family? How do they juggle paid work and home work? How do they perceive low-wage work in the garment industry? How does this perception affect their orientation toward work? What have they achieved through this line of work? Next, we explore these issues through our field observations.

Immigrant Women's Paid Work and the Family

Traditionally, a Chinese woman's tangible value lies in her ability to provide support to both her birth family and her husband's family upon marriage through unpaid or paid labor and in her ability to produce sons for her husband's family. She is expected to be responsible for all domestic work and work outside the home. Her life is tied to the family to which she belongs and her own self is buried in her family. Women's subordinate status is reflected in a popular Chinese folk song:

> Marry a rooster, follow a rooster.
> Marry a dog, follow a dog.
> Marry to a cudgel, married to a pestle,
> Be faithful to it. Follow it. (Kingston 1975, p. 193)

For Chinese women, the family comes first. This cultural value persists not just symbolically but realistically after immigration to the United States. Many Chinese women have come to the United States to join their families in search of an American dream. Once settled, they are expected (and expect themselves) to help their families adjust to the new environment, to sponsor other family members to immigrate, or to make regular remittances to their families in their countries of origin. For most immigrant women, the only way to meet these goals and expectations is to work to make money. Some of our interviews are illustrative:

Ah Mei only had four years of formal schooling in rural China. She was one of the trans-Pacific brides in Chinatown. She came join her husband, who worked in a Chinatown grocery store. Her husband did not want his new bride to work outside the home because she was pregnant. Ah Mei found a job in a garment factory. She made about $200 a week in the first few months. Eventually her weekly wages rose to $350, and she was able to take some of her garment work home. She said:

> Nobody I know comes here just to sit around at home. Everybody works. My husband is not rich. If I don't work, I don't see how we can save money. Besides, I need money to send home to my parents. I can't just ask my husband for money.[9]

Mrs. Li was in her early fifties. She and her husband were very well established in China. She was qualified for immigration into the United States under the fourth preference category because her mother was a U.S. citizen. Mrs. Li and her husband did not want to emigrate initially. However, because it was the only way they could help their three adult unmarried children immigrate, they came. Mrs. Li recalled:

> I came only for my children. Because, under the immigration law, my mother could only sponsor me, but not her grandchildren. I came so that I could send for my adult children. What else is in it for myself? Not much. My husband, a college professor, returned to China shortly because he could not stand working in a tofu shop. I had to stay around to take care of my children. I am still working in a garment shop to help pay some of the bills. My children are attending college while working part-time. Once they graduate from college, I will return to China too.[10]

These interviews suggest that immigrant Chinese women's economic contribution to the family is crucial for survival, especially during early stages of immigration. These women seem to be more concerned about their families, which are extended beyond the nuclear family, than about their own individual needs. However, through our observations of and interviews with garment workers, we found that their paid work has not only contributed to their families' economic well-being but also created a sense of confidence and self-fulfillment which they may never have experienced in traditional Chinese society. Some garment workers interviewed made the following remarks without hesitation: "My husband dares not look down on me; he knows he can't provide for the family by himself"; "I do not have to ask my husband for money, I make my own"; and "I help pay for the house."[11]

Women's Triple Role

While a woman's paid employment is regarded as an obligation for her family's welfare, she is still bound by her role as wife and/or mother, whether or not she works outside the home. Even though their employment becomes necessary in Chinatown, immigrant Chinese women are not expected to develop careers as their primary concern. Rather, they are expected, and expect themselves, to earn wages in ways that do not conflict with their traditional roles as wives and/or mothers.

Chinatown's garment industry provides unique opportunities to integrate employment with traditional role expectations for Chinese women. First, the garment industry offers both full-time and part-time jobs to women, regardless of their prior labor market experience. Although most of the women have not worked in the job before immigration, they learn as they work because the required skills are minimal. Within a short period of time, many become experienced sewing machine operators. Moreover, the garment industry is easily accessible and does not require a strong commitment to work. Immigrant Chinese women are expected to act in the best interests of the family. Even though they work outside the home, they are still expected to carry major household responsibilities at home. Working wives or mothers prefer jobs that leave them flexibility and time for taking care of their children and home work. Garment work does not need to be done on a fixed schedule, and many Chinese garment contractors offer flexible work hours and favorable locations to their workers, in part to compensate for low wages.

The majority of the Chinatown garment workers are mothers of small children. They juggle everything—working, arranging baby-sitters, grocery shopping, cooking, and household chores. They frequently rely on ethnic relations and family members for support. Workers bargain with their co-ethnic bosses to take time off during the day to drop off and pick up their children at school or to nurse their babies. Bosses allow children to come to the garment shop and wait for their mothers. Working mothers usually take their children to school before they go to work. If school is in Chinatown, children simply walk to the garment shops after school and wait for their mothers to finish work. Some grade-school youths help their mothers in the garment shops by hanging up finished garments, turning belts, or preparing garments for sewing (Sung 1987, p. 86). But if children are not in Chinatown schools, mothers have to arrange pickup and extended daycare for their children. Whether a woman is working or not, she is expected to do most of the housework and child care. The following story reflects the busy life of these garment workers.

Mrs. Chow was a recent immigrant with a four-year-old daughter and an eighteen-month-old son. She lived in Woodside, Queens, and worked in a garment factory in Manhattan's Chinatown. She and her husband, who works in a restaurant in Bronx, were on different work schedules, and they rarely had time together.

Every day, Mrs. Chow got up at 5:00 in the morning to prepare breakfast for the children. She left the house with her two children at 6:30 A.M. while her husband was still sleeping. She fed the children on the subway train. Getting off the subway, she dropped the older child off at the Chinatown Daycare Center and left the smaller one at her baby-sitter's home not far from her factory. She started work at 8:00 A.M. and got off at 5:00 P.M. She went to see her baby during the midday break. After work, she hurried to pick up some ready-made food and groceries nearby. Then she picked up her kids. The three arrived home around 7:00 P.M. Then she prepared dinner for the children and herself. She bathed the children and put them to bed at 8:30 P.M. She went to bed around 9:30, while her husband was still at work.

Mrs. Chow worked about thirty-five to forty hours a week but was laid off about three months a year when there was not enough work at the factory. She was able to take the time off during the day to go to the babysitter's house to see her baby. When the children were sick she could take a day or two off or take the garment work home. She wanted to work as much as she could so that her family could save money to open up a small family business. With two young children and her husband's long working hours, she could only manage a job with a flexible schedule.[12]

Some garment workers rely on kinship networks and family members for child-care support. In Chinatown, many older retired women take care of their grandchildren as older women are traditionally expected to. Private day care in individual homes is another alternative. Some mothers choose not to work and stay home with their children. They usually babysit two or three more children in addition to their own in order to make some extra money and find playmates for their own children. The costs range from $14.00 to $20.00 per day, and the services are reliable and flexible. It has become an effective means to solve the child-care problem. Working mothers usually spend half of their wages on child care.

Perception of Low-Wage Work

Although immigrant Chinese women have particularly high labor force participation rates, they are disproportionately concentrated in the low-wage garment industry in Chinatown. As our data suggest, the average annual wage in 1979 was a little over $5,000, and the median hourly wage was only $2.90, lower than the minimum wage of $3.10 at the time.

Are immigrant Chinese women willing to accept substandard wages? The answer is that they are not. Then, why are they overrepresented in the low-wage work force in the garment industry? Part of the reason is that immigrant Chinese women do not generally rely on the American frame of reference in their perception of their work and their evaluation of their behavior. As recent arrivals, they tend to translate American wages in absolute terms into Chinese wages. Thus, they consider low wages in the United States to be invariably higher than wages they earned in China.

Moreover, many Chinese women are accustomed to working outside the home. Low-wage jobs and long working hours do not seem to create new pressures on them since these women, most of whom are from the rural areas, are used to doing back-breaking farm work and menial factory work. Long before immigration they knew that the material standard of living in America is better than that in China and that, if they were willing to work just as hard as in China, they could make a lot more money and become much "richer." So they are ready and eager to work, either to help bring in additional income to for their own families or to save money to remit to their birth families in China.

Further, most garment workers are uneducated, unskilled, and lack English language ability. Their options are limited to working in garment shops in Chinatown or staying home. Few are able to take even the same type of jobs beyond Chinatown. Moreover, in the garment industry, they can quickly learn the minimum skills required to operate a sewing machine. Thus, they perceive the availability of garment work in Chinatown as an opportunity. Holding a job helps them to withstand social and psychological pressures associated with immigrant status rather than creating pressures relating to their own perceptions about themselves. The following examples illustrate how women perceive their work and their wages.

When in China, Mrs. Cheng, a former garment worker in Chinatown, quit school in the fourth grade to work with other women in the fields to help support her family, making less than $125 a year. Regarding garment work, she said:

> I was paid by the piece. On average, I probably made about $4.50 an hour. My weekly wages were a lot more than my annual wages in China.[13]

Mrs. Wu, a recent immigrant who came from one of the villages in Taishan to join her husband, had a similar story. Wu had only three years of schooling, did not know a single word of English, and had few occupational skills; yet she was more than willing to work and make money. The second week after she arrived, she got a job in a garment factory through a relative who was also a sewing machine operator. When asked whether the low wages and long working schedule had been a problem, she said:

I never thought of it as a problem. I am a semi-illiterate country girl. I know nothing but work. As long as I have a job, I am happy. I have a chance to make money. Here I am paid by the piece, and I can make an average of $3.00 per hour. A lot of my coworkers can make more than this; some make $5.00 per hour. By the end of the week I can bring home about $180 to $200 dollars [for a sixty-hour work week]. If I work for lo-fan (referring to Americans), my take-home money would be less because of tax deductions and shorter working hours. I like to be able to work extra hours and over the weekend. That's what I was used to when I was in China.[14]

Mrs. Liang remarks also reflect the perception of low wages among the garment workers. She said:

If you are a new hand, you do not demand higher wages. All you want is some sort of job, and wages do not seem too bad to you even at $2.50 an hour. You tend compare this rate to the rate in China which equaled to a week's pay at the time I left. Thus, getting a job is only lucky for you. If you complain, you are simply out of work. The boss can easily get a replacement by firing you. But if you are really good and quick-handed, the boss tends to keep you by offering higher wages, or you can 'fire' him.[15]

Mrs. Zhao added:

Some girls can make as much as $400 a week. That's hard-earned money from back-breaking jobs, of course, but it's more than two years' pay in China. At whatever wages, most of us just want to work. Also, we are used to hard work and long hours. In China, working six days a week is routine, and working overtime without pay is encouraged as some sort of moral obligation to socialism. Here, if you work harder, you make more. You can't compare with lo-fan. If you don't accept the wage, you will have no job at all.[16]

In sum, immigrant Chinese women in Chinatown are extremely low paid. Three out of five women are low-wage garment workers. Based on interviews with garment workers, most of the factories set the hourly rate according to experience. For new hands, it is below or at the minimum wage rate. For more skilled workers, the rate varies from $4.25 to $5.50. However, older women who do miscellaneous work in the factory (e.g., cleaning, cutting thread, and wrappings) are paid $2.50 to $3.00 per hour.

They are aware that owners can and do take advantage of workers. Despite open acknowledgment of "exploitation" in Chinatown, however, they do not seem to feel themselves unduly disadvantaged, nor do most knowledgeable observers we have interviewed perceive them that way. Rather, they are hard workers, matter-of-fact about their employment conditions but purposeful and determined to do the best they can in a very difficult transitional situation (Sung 1987:197). From the point of view of these women workers, the garment industry is their only opportunity. As Mrs. Chen put it, "I would have to go back to China if there wasn't a garment industry in Chinatown."[17] Besides, they are skewed to less educated and less skilled workers unable to speak English. Under these constraints, immigrant workers have overcrowded the industry, leading to depression of wages and declines in working conditions.

The willingness of immigrant Chinese women to accept substandard working conditions and wages is certainly a problem because it can create pressure on other enclave workers to reduce what they are willing to work for. However, getting a job and being paid fairly remain two separate issues for many immigrant Chinese women.

In Chinatown, most immigrant families cannot possibly survive with only one income. Women's paid work is an economic necessity to maintain daily household life. It was estimated that Chinatown's garment workers made a total of $105 million in wages in 1981. Most of the income was spent on food, housing, clothing, and shelter (ILGWU 1983). Women are well aware of this reality because they are the ones who handle the rent, bills, and everyday expenses, and they are the ones who know exactly how much is required to meet the basic household needs. Women have to worry how to make ends meet daily. Thus, they are more concerned about having a job of some sort to help their families to get settled and move ahead than they are about their own rights, particularly during the earlier stages of immigrant adaptation.

The Prospect of Social Mobility

The strong desire of immigrant Chinese women to work and their acceptance of low wages and unpopular labor practices, which may be considered abusive and/or illegal by U.S. standards, cannot simply be understood as an individualist drive for social mobility. In the eyes of immigrant Chinese women, emigration is a form of upward social mobility, and they often base their value judgments on comparisons with their past experience. Moreover, social mobility is an important part of the collective effort to fulfill family obligations, helping the family to move ahead in the U.S. society. Thus, women's low-wage labor in Chinatown's garment industry facilitates upward social mobility of the family.

But beyond survival, immigrant Chinese families have their notion of the American Dream—home ownership or business ownership. To realize the dream, women's contribution is indispensable. With women's wages to help pay for household expenses, many immigrant families are able to save money. As Mrs. Zhao said:

> The worst thing of not working is that you can't even survive. Even if you can afford to stay home, you won't be able to save much money. Every immigrant family here dreams to buy a home. If you don't start working and saving, you can never make things happen.[18]

Mrs. Cheng, the garment worker we had interviewed earlier, and her husband, a former restaurant worker, had just started a fast-food takeout restaurant in Brooklyn. With savings from her garment work, she not only helped build her family business but also paid all traveling and settlement expenses for her mother and brother to immigrate. Mrs. Cheng was satisfied and felt her hard work paid off. She said:

> Now my husband and I are working for our own business. I work more hours than I did in the garment shop. Neither of us gets paid regularly. If business goes well, we both make money; otherwise, we both lose money. The difference is that the restaurant is ours.[19]

When families open up small businesses, women frequently quit their garment jobs and became unpaid family labor. When the primary goal is to own a house, women's cash contribution is equally important to that of men.

Mrs. Chang was an experienced seamstress and had been in the Chinatown garment industry for quite some time. When she was first interviewed in 1988, she and her husband were making plans to buy a small business and to move out of their one-bedroom apartment in Chinatown. Mrs. Chang's income contributed substantially to her family's savings. In the spring of 1992, she was interviewed in her new home in Brooklyn. The family owned a home—a step closer to their dream. But Mrs. Chang continued to commute to Chinatown to work. She told us why:

> You can never afford not to work. We used to pay only $75 for the rent-controlled apartment in Chinatown. Now we have a big mortgage note to pay each month. My husband does not have a stable job. So my family depends on me, especially when he gets laid off. You just have to keep on working.[20]

Discussion and Conclusions

Working wives and mothers are traditionally considered secondary wage earners, and employment is not automatically accompanied by occupational attainment of individual workers. For immigrant women, the double burden is compounded by lack of English, transferable education and skills, and knowledge of the larger economy. In this article, we have illustrated the special meanings of immigrant women's work in the context of ethnic enclave employment and family responsibility, based on the experience of garment workers in New York's Chinatown. Our findings from census data and fieldwork suggest that the particularly high rate of immigrant Chinese women's labor market participation is largely accounted for by the availability of jobs provided by the ethnic enclave economy, that those women are overrepresented in low-wage menial jobs mostly concentrated in Chinatown, and that they tend to perceive their work as meaningful, despite low wages, long working hours and poor working conditions. Although their labor practices may not be compatible with American middle-class values and norms and they are poor by American standard, Chinese garment workers do not seem to feel exploited and hopeless. These findings suggest that immigrant Chinese women's positions are embedded in ethnic social networks which are built into the structure of social relations and cultural values. Their work is crucial to status attainment for their families.

Our research provides several tentative conclusions that support the sociocultural-context approach and the reference-group approach. First, working outside the home is an economic necessity. For immigrant Chinese women, participation in paid work is nothing new since it was part of their everyday life before immigration. After entering the United States, social and economic adaptation became a family affair for immigrant Chinese, both men and women. Because of disadvantages associated with immigrant status, the chance of individual achievement is slim. It becomes necessary that all adult family members work together to conquer difficulties in getting settled down and save money for future plans. Although incomes contributed by women may still be considered secondary, they are in fact indispensable.

Second, Chinese culture gives priority not to individual achievement but to the welfare of the family and the community. As part of cultural expectations, women's lives are tied to their families. When families are in difficult economic situations during transition from one country to another, it is women's obligation to work outside of the home. However, their employment does not mean that they neglect their primary responsibilities in the home such as housework and child rearing. Sewing at piecework rates is a good fit for these expectations: working hours are flexible; and a higher income can be gained by working faster and longer, even if the pay per piece is low. Many middle-aged women, those who immigrated at age forty or fifty, accept a short-term orientation toward work; their purpose is not to develop a working career (this applies to many who had professional occupations in China) but to contribute immediately to the household income for the benefit of younger members. Thus, they are usually content with what they have in Chinatown.

Third, immigration and employment in Chinatown creates a specific sociocultural situation in which low-wage work does not spontaneously exploit and impoverish workers. Rather, it is considered a time-honored path to social mobility. In Chinatown, there is a consensus that low wages are compensated for by the savings of time and effort involving in finding "good" jobs in the larger labor market, by the choice of working longer hours and more days, by a familiar work environment where English is not required, and by the prospect of learning the skills of a trade and accumulating capital for eventual transition to business or home ownership (Zhou 1992).

However, acceptance of substandard wages and labor practices does not necessarily suggest that immigrant Chinese women are docile and retiring. Rather, they use their past work experience as a point of reference in evaluating their current position in Chinatown and perceive their struggle between home and the workplace as part of the struggle to achieve the American Dream. For these women, immigration is a process, and, in the earlier stages of immigrant adaptation at least, survival is more important to them than their own rights in the workplace.

Our analysis has produced results implying that immigrant incorporation is not a simple unilateral process from community to individuality. We believe that menial, low-wage work in Chinatown's garment factories cannot be viewed solely from a frame of analysis which treats men as women's reference group, nor can it be understood from a frame of analysis which compares immigrant working women with American middle-class women. For immigrant women, the choice of reference group is a result of the specific sociocultural conditions which brought them to the United States; and many compare their current situation to their own past, perceiving immigration to the United States as a process of long-term social mobility for their families.

Our study raises some questions about the role of ethnic enclave economies in facilitating, or impeding, long-term economic mobility. Do ethnic economies benefit from purposely keeping their co-ethnic members from adapting to American society, or do they provide their co-ethnic members with an alternative to compensate for lingering labor market disadvantages? Is low-wage employment in ethnic economies an effective strategy for co-ethnic members to fight poverty, or is it a "trap" in a dead-end situation? Should public policy be directed in discouraging or promoting ethnic economies? In our opinion, the key issue is less what kind of jobs ethnic economies offer but whether ethnic economies open employment or self-employment opportunities otherwise unavailable for co-ethnic members. In China-town, the availability of jobs enables immigrant women to become major players in the struggle for survival and adaptation to American society. Their wage labor is an indispensable part of the collective family effort for social mobility, and the payoff for earlier stints of low-wage work contributes to the socioeconomic gains of the family, as commonly seen in entrepreneurship, home ownership, and, for many, educational and occupational attainments of their children. The work experience of immigrant Chinese women suggests that, for socioeconomically disadvantaged groups, it is difficult to achieve long-term social mobility merely through individual efforts. The ethnic community, the family, ethnic networks, and ethnic normative structures function to support or constrain individual economic behavior to facilitate economic success. Therefore, policies dealing with those groups mired in poverty and confined to survival at the margins of society should put more emphasis on community development in connection to the promotion of individual education and job training.

NOTES

An earlier version of this manuscript was presented at the 54th Annual Meeting of the Southern Sociological Society, Atlanta, April 1991. The authors wish to thank Sucheta Mazumdar, John R. Logan, Lynn Newhart Smith, Glenna Spitze for their helpful comments and suggestions.

1. Personal interview with Ah Mei, September 1988.

2. Field interview, April 1991.

3. Wendy Lau. 1990. "Children at a Sewing Machine: Grim Choice for Immigrants." In Chinese Staff and Worker Association, *CSWA News: The Voice of Chinese American Workers* 2(1), 8.

4. Fieldwork data were collected by periodic observations in Chinatown and through extensive interviews with garment workers and entrepreneurs. We also interviewed community leaders, community organizers and union activists, investors, bankers, real estate agents, and long-time residents. The snowball sampling method was used in selecting about 60 informants. The authors (one of whom is a native from Canton), conducted all of the face-to-face interviews and telephone interviews with informants during the 1988–1989 period. Follow-up field observations and some six follow-up interviews were conducted between 1991 and 1992. For the sake of confidentiality, only pseudo-names of the interviewees are used.

5. The War Brides Act was passed on December 28 1945 to allow wives of members of the American armed forces to enter the United States. The following year fiances of American soldiers were allowed to immigrate. Public Law 271. United States Statutes at Large: 1945. Vol. 59, Part II, Public Laws, p. 659.

6. The six preference categories specified in the 1965 Immigration Law are: (1) unmarried

sons and daughters of U.S. citizens; (2) spouses and unmarried sons and daughters of U.S. permanent residents; (3) professionals and persons of exceptional ability in science and arts; (4) married sons and daughters of U.S. citizens; (5) brothers and sisters of U.S. citizens; (6) skilled and needed workers. Public Law 89–236, United States Statutes at Large: 1965. U.S. Government Printing Office: Washington D.C. 1967: 911–22. The Immigration Act of 1990 regrouped the former six preference categories into family-sponsored preferences and employment-based preferences.

7. *New York Times*, May 10 1986.
8. Personal interview, June 1990.
9. Personal interview with Ah Mei, April 1988.
10. Personal interview with Mrs. Li, September 1987 and March 1992.
11. Field interviews March 1992.
12. Personal interview with Mrs. Chow, May 1988. Also see Zhou 1992, Chapter 7.
13. Personal interview with Mrs. Cheng, May 1988.
14. Personal interview with Mrs. Wu, April 1988.
15. Personal interview with Mrs. Liang, January 1989.
16. Personal interview with Mrs. Zhao, January 1989.
17. Personal interview with Mrs. Chen, May 1988.
18. Follow-up interview with Mrs. Zhao, March 1992.
19. Follow-up interview with Mrs. Cheng, March 1992.
20. Follow-up interview with Mrs. Chang, March 1992.

REFERENCES

Almquist, Elizabeth M., and Wehrle-Einhorn, Juanita L. (1978). The doubly disadvantaged: Minority women in the labor force. Pp. 63–88 in Ann H. Stromberg and Shirley Harkess (eds.), *Women working: Theories and facts in perspective*. Palo Alto, CA: Mayfield.

Becker, G. (1957). *The economics of discrimination*. Chicago: University of Chicago Press.

Bernard, J. (1987). *The female world from a global perspective*. Indiana: Indiana University Press.

Bonacich, Edna. 1980. Class approaches to ethnicity and race. *Insurgent Sociologist* 10, 2.

———. (1992). Reflection on Asian American labor. *Amerasian Journal* 18(1), xxi–xxvii.

———. (1993). The other side of ethnic entrepreneurship: A dialogue with Waldinger, Aldrich, Ward and Associates. *International Migration Review* 27(3), 685–692.

Borjas, J. George. (1990). *Friends or strangers: The impact of immigrants on the U.S. economy*. New York: Basic Books.

Business Week. (1992). The immigrants: How they are helping to revitalize the U.S. economy? July 13.

Castells, Manuel. (1975). Immigrant workers and class struggles in advanced capitalism: The Western European experience. *Politics and Society* 5, 33–66.

Cooney, Rosemary, and Ortiz, Vilma. (1983). Nativity, national origin and Hispanic female labor force participation. *Social Science Quarterly* 64, 510–523.

Ehrenreich, Barbara, and Fuentes, Annette. (1981). Life on the global assembly line. *Ms. Magazine*, January.

England, Paula, Farkas, George, Kilbourne, Barbara, and Dou, Thomas. (1988). Sex, segregation and wages. *American Sociological Review* 53, 544–558.

England, Paula, and Norris, Bahar. (1985). Comparable worth: A new doctrine of sex discrimination. *Social Science Quarterly* 66, 627–643.

Fernandez-Kelly, M. P., and Garcia, A. M. (1989). Power surrendered, power restored: The politics of home and work among Hispanic women in southern California and southern Florida. In Louise Tilly and Patricia Guerin (eds.), *Women and politics in America*. New York: Russel Sage Foundation.

Ferree, Myra Marx. (1979). Employment without liberation: Cuban women in the United States. *Social Science Quarterly* 60, 35–50.

Form, William H., and Geschwender, James A. (1962). Social reference basis of job satisfaction: The case of manual workers. *American Sociological Review* 27, 228–237.

Huber, Joan, and Spitze, Glenna. (1981). Wives' employment, household behaviors and sex-role attitudes. *Social Forces* 60, 151–169.

———. (1988). Trends in family sociology. In Neil J. Smelser (ed.), *Handbook of sociology*. Beverly Hills, CA: Sage.

ILGWU-Local 23–25 (International Ladies' Garment Workers' Union). (1983). *The Chinatown garment industry study*. New York: Abeles, Schwartz, Haeckel & Silverblatt, Inc.

Kingston, Maxine H. (1975). *The woman warrior: Memoirs of a girlhood among ghosts*. Vintage International Edition, April 1989. New York: Random House.

Loscocco, Karyn, and Spitze, Glenna. (1991). The organizational context of women's and men's pay satisfaction. *Social Science Quarterly* 72(1), 1–19.

Mincer, Jacob, and Polacheck, Solomon. (1974). Family investment in human capital: Earnings of women. *Journal of Political Economy* 82(2), S76–S108.

Morokvasic, Mirjana. (1983). Women in migration: Beyond the reductionist outlook. In Annie Phizacklea (ed.), *One way ticket: Migration and female labor*. London: Routledge & Kegan Paul.

Mueller, Charles, W. & Campbell, Blair G. (1977). Female occupational achievement and marital status: A research note. *Journal of Marriage and the Family* 39, 587–593.

Ollenburger, Jane C., and Moore, Helen A. (1992). *A sociology of women: The intersection of patriarchy, capitalism, and colonization*. Englewood Cliffs, NJ: Prentice-Hall.

Perez, Lisandro. (1986). Immigrant economic adjustment and family organization: The Cuban success story reexamined. *International Migration Review* 20(1), 4–20.

Philliber, William W., and Hiller, Dana V. (1978). The implication of wife's occupational attainment for husband's class identification. *Sociological Quarterly* 19, 450–458.

Portes, Alejandro, and Bach, Robert. (1985). *The Latin journey: Cuban and Mexican immigrants in the United States*. Berkeley: University of California Press.

Portes, Alejandro, and Zhou, Min. (1992). Gaining the upper hand: Economic mobility among immigrant and domestic minorities. *Ethnic and Racial Studies* 15(4), 491–522.

Saxton, Alexander. (1971). *The indispensable enemy: Labor and the anti-Chinese movement in California*. Berkeley: University of California Press.

Spitze, Glenna. (1988). Women's employment and family relations: A review. *Journal of Marriage and the Family* 50, 595–618.

Stier, Haya. (1991). Immigrant women go to work: Analysis of immigrant wives's labor supply for six Asian groups. *Social Science Quarterly* 97, 67–82.

Stromberg, Ann H., and Harkess, Shirley. (1978). *Women working: Theories and facts in perspective*. Palo Alto, CA: Mayfield.

Sung, Betty Lee. (1987). *The adjustment experience of Chinese immigrant children in New York City*. New York: Center for Migration Studies.

Tiana, S. (1990). Maquiladora women: A new category of workers? Pp. 193–224 in Kathryn Ward (ed.), *Women workers and global restructuring*. Ithaca, NY: Cornell University Press.

U.S. Bureau of the Census. (1983). *Census of population and housing 1980: Public-Use microdata samples [A]* [MRDF]. Washington, DC: U.S. Bureau of the Census [producer and distributor].

U.S. Commission on Civil Rights. (1992). *Civil rights issues facing Asian Americans in the 1990s: A report.* Washington, DC: U.S. Government Printing Office.

Van Velsor, Ellen, and Beeghley, Leonard. (1979). The process of class identification among employed married women: A replication and reanalysis. *Journal of Marriage and the Family* 41, 771–778.

Waldinger, Roger. (1986). *Through the eye of the needle: Immigrants and enterprise in New York's garment trades.* New York: New York University Press.

Ward, Kathryn. (1990). *Women workers and global restructuring.* Ithaca, NY: Cornell University Press.

Zhou, Min. (1992). *Chinatown: The socioeconomic potential of an urban enclave.* Philadelphia: Temple University Press.

Zhou, Min, and Bankston, Carl L. III. (1993). Variations in economic adaptation: The case of post-1965 Chinese, Koreans, and Vietnamese immigrants. *National Journal of Sociology* 6(2), 105–140.

Zhou, Min, and Logan, John R. (1989). Returns of human capital in ethnic enclaves: New York City's Chinatown." *American Sociological Review* 54(October), 809–820.

Chapter Ten

Striving for the American Dream
Struggle, Success, and Intergroup Conflict among Korean Immigrant Entrepreneurs

Jennifer Lee

> It takes intellectual sophistication to resist blaming the economic ills of the ghetto on the immediate agents of exploitation, whether Jewish or not, and to see these ills as products of impersonal social and economic forces that transcend the responsibility of particular individuals.[1]

Introduction

The immigrant ethnic group with the highest rate of self-employment in the United States, Korean immigrants have changed the commercial landscape of today's cities. Greengrocers neatly displaying fruit and fresh-cut flowers, nail salons, dry cleaners, and fish stores are ubiquitous symbols of Korean immigrant entrepreneurship. Koreans offer their services not only to fellow ethnics but to the white and minority populations alike. Studies estimate that approximately one-third of Korean immigrant families are engaged in small business, figures paralleling the staggering self-employment rate of Jewish immigrants in the early twentieth century. Following in the footsteps of Jewish immigrants, Koreans are experiencing rapid economic mobility through self-employment. The second- and third-generation Jewish immigrants have largely moved into the primary labor market, with substantial portions in professional and white-collar occupations, and today's second-generation Korean immigrants are following close behind.

From the outside, Korean immigrant entrepreneurs seem to have "made it." Touted as "model minorities," Koreans have become symbols that the American dream is still alive—if an individual works hard enough, delays gratification, makes sacrifices, and, most of all perseveres, he or she can make it, too. The opportunity structure is equal and the path open to anyone who wants to follow it (Bonacich 1987).

However, Koreans' relatively rapid economic success has come with social costs. Black nationalists have charged Korean merchants with disrespectful treatment toward their customers, prejudice, and exploitation of the black community. They have also accused Korean merchants of buying all the stores in black neighborhoods, draining the communities of its resources, and failing to "give back" by hiring local residents (Lee 1993; Min 1993). Labeled "absentee owners," Korean storeowners are accused of owning businesses in poor black neighborhoods yet not living in the communities in which they serve (Reiss and Aldrich 1971).

The tension between Korean merchants and black customers crystallized in 1990 with an eighteen-month-long boycott of a fruit and vegetable store in the Flatbush section of Brooklyn, New York (Lee 1993).[2] Much of the media coverage focused on the individual-level differences between the Korean merchant and his black customers, pointing to the cultural and linguistic misunderstandings between two minority groups while ignoring the structural conditions under which intergroup conflict emerges. The friction mounted on March 16, 1991, when a Korean storeowner, Soon Ja Du, shot and killed an African American teenager, Latasha Harlins, in South Central Los Angeles. The tension climaxed on April 29, 1992, after four white police officers were acquitted of beating a twenty-five-year-old African American motorist, Rodney King. The nation remained paralyzed as it watched buildings in South Central and Koreatown aflame while inner-city residents looted stores, taking everything from televisions and VCRs to food and diapers. The worst domestic uprising in the twentieth century ended with a toll of 16,291 arrested, 2,383 injured, 500 fires, and fifty-two dead (Njeri 1996). Korean merchants suffered almost half the property damage, which amounted to more than $400 million and affected more than 2,300 Korean-owned businesses in Los Angeles (Ong and Hee 1993). The nation was left stunned.

This article addresses four main questions. The first examines why Korean immigrants enter self-employment at such high rates, especially compared to native-born Americans. The second focuses on the resources that these immigrants utilize in starting and maintaining their businesses. Third, the article explores the "retail niches" that Korean immigrants dominate and also studies the reasons why they choose to locate in inner-city neighborhoods. Last, this article enlarges our understanding of intergroup relations between Koreans and blacks by examining the structural conditions under which tension between merchants and customers becomes racially coded and explodes into conflict.

The study is based on thirty face-to-face, in-depth interviews with Korean merchants in five predominantly black neighborhoods in New York City and Philadelphia.[3] Each of these neighborhoods has a bustling commercial strip lined with small businesses that offer a variety of merchandise, some of which is geared specifically to a black clientele, including wigs, ethnic beauty supplies, and inner-city sportswear, and there are beauty salons and barber shops that service black customers. The data also include seventy-five in-depth interviews with black customers from each of these research sites. African American research assistants conducted face-to-face, open-ended interviews with local residents from these communities who were asked about their shopping experiences in Korean-owned stores and about their opinions of

Korean merchants more generally.[4] Unlike previous studies on black-Korean conflict that include interviews of only the Korean merchants, this study allows us to understand intergroup conflict from both perspectives.

Choosing Self-Employment as a Means to Upward Mobility

Post-1965 Korean immigrants come to the United States with relatively high levels of "human capital," measured by educational attainment and occupational skills. Thirty percent of Korean immigrants age 25 and over have completed four years of college— about twice the rate for the U.S. native-born population—and a large proportion held white-collar and professional positions in Korea. These measures indicate that Korean immigrants are largely from middle-class backgrounds (Hurh and Kim 1980; Yoon 1997). With relatively high levels of education and skills, why have Korean immigrants been unable to transfer their "human capital" into commensurate professional occupations in the United States, instead turning to self-employment?

Social scientists have argued that certain ethnic groups, particularly when they are immigrants, turn to small business to overcome disadvantages in the American labor market (Light 1972; Light and Bonacich 1988; Min 1984; Yoon 1997). A language barrier, unfamiliarity with American customs and culture, the inability to transfer educational and occupational capital, and discrimination leave immigrants severely disadvantaged to compete with the native-born in the primary labor market. For example, U.S. companies have little understanding of credentials obtained outside of the country. Whereas a degree from Seoul National, Yonsei, or Ewha universities immediately connotes academic rigor and high status in Korea, companies in the United States have difficulty translating and measuring these credentials. Furthermore, like many first-generation immigrants, Koreans have difficulty mastering a new language, making their transition into an English-speaking workforce extremely difficult.

Compared to the native-born, immigrants have fewer "high-priced salable skills" (Light 1972) and therefore turn to self-employment as an alternative to entering the secondary labor market where they would receive relatively low wages in unskilled or low-skilled occupations. In fact, many Korean entrepreneurs previously worked in low-paying jobs with little room for advancement prior to opening their own business. Korean immigrants opt to open small businesses not because self-employment is their primary occupational choice but because their alternatives in the U.S. labor market are less lucrative. Self-employment becomes a means to relatively quick upward mobility in the face of severe handicaps and obstacles in the primary labor market.

However, disadvantages in the labor market alone cannot explain why Korean immigrants enter self-employment at such high rates, since ethnic groups that find themselves similarly disadvantaged in the labor market, such as Laotians and Malaysians, have self-employment rates of less than 3 percent (Yoon 1997). To explain the variance in the rates of self-employment, social scientists have focused on the importance of class and ethnic resources and social capital in the development and success of small businesses among immigrant groups such as Cubans, Israelis, and Koreans.

Resources Used in Business

Class and Ethnic Resources

Class resources are characterized as human capital, economic capital, and wealth, and ethnic resources are defined as "forms of aid preferentially available from one's own ethnic group."[5] Social capital, in the form of rotating credit associations, has also contributed to the survival of Korean-owned businesses. These resources are invaluable to business success and are used not only at the initial stages of capitalization but also throughout business ownership. Access to class and ethnic resources and the utilization of social capital are crucial in understanding how Korean immigrants are able to open small businesses at such high rates.

Korean business owners use a variety of class and ethnic resources such as personal savings, loans from family and co-ethnic friends, and advertising in Korean-language newspapers to purchase their businesses. But, unlike previous literature that stresses the significance of rotating credit associations (kye) in the formation of businesses (Light 1972; Light and Bonacich 1988), my research indicates the majority of Korean immigrant merchants do not use this resource at the start-up phase. Table 10.1 indicates that only 7% percent acquired capital to open their business through funds from a rotating credit association. By contrast, 76 percent bought their businesses using a combination of other resources: personal savings, loans from family and co-ethnic friends, and credit from the previous co-ethnic storeowner. The remaining 17 percent bought their businesses from a family owner—usually a brother, sister, or in-laws who immigrated several years before them.

When co-ethnics purchase businesses from one another, rather than going through a financial third party like a bank, the new Korean owner will normally pay the previous owner one-third of the business's value as a down payment and the remaining two-thirds in monthly installments over a period of a few years. Bates (1994) notes that Koreans use this debt source more frequently than other groups since Koreans are more likely to purchase retail firms that are already in business.

Social Capital–The Rotating Credit Association

Although the use of rotating credit associations may not be as prevalent at the start-up phase, this resource is highly utilized at the later stages of business. Rotating credit associations range in both membership size and value, with participation extending from only a few people to more than thirty, and value ranging anywhere from $100 to more than $100,000. Korean merchants report that the average kye ranges from ten to twenty people, with each member contributing between $1,000 to $2,000 into a pot totaling $10,000 to $40,000. Each member contributes to the fund, and every member takes turns in receiving the lump sum of money. For example, a

TABLE 10.1
Resources Used by Korean Merchants in Starting Their Businesses

Means of establishing business ownership	Number of businesses	Percentage
Savings + loans from family/friends + credit from previous co-ethnic storeowner	23	76
Bought from a family member	5	17
Rotating credit association (kye)	2	7
Total	30	100

Korean merchant explained that she belonged to a rotating credit association with twenty members. Each member contributed $2,700 per month, and the first member who received the pot received $51,300 ($2,700 × 19). The pot rotated according to a predetermined schedule until each member had received his or her share. After receiving the pool of money, each individual was obligated to contribute $3,100 until the rotation was complete. Therefore, the member who received the money first got only $51,300, while the one who received the pot last was rewarded with $58,900— the surplus from interest and appreciation for those at the tail end of the rotation. Implicit in such a system is a high degree of mutual trust, obligation, and expectation among its members.

Rotating credit associations are less important when Korean merchants purchase their first businesses but become very significant after they have already established their businesses for various purposes such as buying new merchandise or equipment, remodeling, or purchasing their second businesses. Kyes also serve as a crucial economic resource when merchants have little cash flow or in case of unforeseen emergencies such as break-ins or fires, which are not uncommon in low-income neighborhoods. Even though the use of kye varies among Korean merchants, all have admitted that the rotating credit association is a resource they *could* draw upon if they needed to quickly accumulate capital. The facility with which Korean immigrants can draw upon such ethnic resources attests to their easy access to social and economic capital.

The sociologist James Coleman explains the value of social capital:

> Social capital is defined by its function. It is not a single entity but a variety of different entities, with two elements in common: they all consist of some aspect of social structures, and they facilitate certain actions of actors—whether persons or corporate actors—within the structure. Like other forms of capital, social capital is productive, making possible the achievement of certain ends that in its absence would not be possible. Like physical and human capital, social capital is not completely fungible but may be specific to certain activities. A given form of social capital that is valuable in facilitating certain actions may be useless or even harmful to others (1988, S98).

Central to Coleman's concept of social capital is the role of closure in the social structure; closure facilitates the trust needed to allow actions such as exchange, lending, and borrowing from members within the social structure. Also essential is the degree to which these relations are indispensable, or the extent to which members within the social structure depend on one another. Coleman offers the rotating credit association as a prime example by which social capital is manifested among members as a form of obligation, trust, and expectation, the absence of which would render such a system unable to function.

Social capital differs from economic or human capital in that it is not a tangible resource but, instead, is the capacity of individuals to command and mobilize resources by virtue of membership in networks (Portes 1995). But it must be pointed out that without a group's economic capital, a high degree of social capital would not be nearly as beneficial for that group. For example, Stack (1974) and Liebow (1967) illustrate that informal networks of exchange exist among poor African Americans in urban communities, but poor blacks "swap" resources that are significantly smaller in scale, such as food stamps, a few dollars, food, or child care. The high degree of social capital among Korean immigrant entrepreneurs, coupled with their wealth of economic resources, gives them a distinct advantage in business over other ethnic groups.

Koreans are not the only ethnic group to benefit from social capital. In fact, first-generation immigrants of many different ethnic groups use rotating credit associations. However, as these groups acculturate into the American social structure, they utilize this resource far less frequently. For example, whereas first-generation Jewish immigrant entrepreneurs used mutual loan associations (Katz and Bender 1976; Ellison and Jaffe 1994; Morawska 1996), later generations have long abandoned this tradition. Today, not only Korean but also West Indian and Asian Indian immigrants draw upon their versions of rotating credit associations. Furthermore, second-generation Korean immigrants, like the second- and third-generation Jewish immigrants, have already abandoned this practice.

As instrumental as kyes may be, some Korean merchants have become wary of using rotation credit associations, since they realize the inordinate amount of trust required for such a system to operate. Many have heard of kye failures where one person takes the lump sum of money and leaves the country. For instance, a Korean merchant who has used kye a few times illustrates the risks involved and the difficulty in holding someone legally responsible for defaulting:

> Some people, they don't do kye because no matter what they don't trust because it could happen too. When a guy gets $40,000, after a couple of months, you don't see him anymore. Then where are you going to go get him? You cannot tell anybody what happened. It's no protection. . . . So let's say you owe a big company, you don't pay enough on your credit card. They're going to send you a thousand letters. They going to send you [to a] collection [agency], but those big companies can afford it, but a lot of people, you want to get $10,000 from that guy who run away. You want to hire a lawyer, you want to go to court, this and that, time and money, headache. Forget about it. They know what is the risk, so they don't even want to [get] involved.

Although Korean merchants explain that there are no legal ramifications to defaulting since none of these agreements are written, the social sanctions—such as loss of standing in the immigrant community and exclusion from it—are strong enough to prevent losses on a regular basis.

Korean merchants not only complain of the risks; they also mention the costly interest payments, which can be as high as 30 percent surpassing the legal limit in New York state, for instance, which is 25 percent. Although rotating credit associations may be helpful to those who need cash very quickly, they also function as financial investments for more affluent co-ethnics who benefit from the high interest payments.

Even though not all Korean merchants have participated in kye, all have admitted to borrowing funds from their family or co-ethnic friends at one point, either at the start-up phase or while in business. Koreans often borrow tens of thousands of dollars from other family members or co-ethnic friends. That the high degree of social and economic capital remains the most valuable resource for these immigrant entrepreneurs cannot be overemphasized, since the availability of cash resources can determine whether small businesses will be able to withstand emergencies such as break-ins or slow periods when cash flow is extremely tight.

Ethnic Succession and Vacant Niches

"By the last quarter of the twentieth century, the once ubiquitous Jewish shopkeeper had faded from the scene: the storekeepers' sons and daughters had better things to do than mind a shop; and their parents, old, tired, and scared of crime, were eager to sell out to new groups of immigrant entrepreneurs . . . the Jewish withdrawal from New York's traditional small business sectors provided a chance for a legion of immigrants, and not just Koreans" (Waldinger 1996, 100–101). The Jewish exodus from the inner cities left a vacant niche for Korean immigrants to succeed them as ethnic owners of small business.

Entering the Inner City

Immigrant entrepreneurs such as Koreans open businesses in black neighborhoods largely because there is little competition from the larger, chain corporations that predominate in white middle-class neighborhoods and suburban malls. Considered high-risk and high-crime neighborhoods, poor black communities are largely ignored by larger corporations, leaving a vacant niche for Koreans to set up shop. And, because the market is less saturated in low-income neighborhoods, rent is relatively cheaper. Korean immigrants also claim that running a business in a middle-class, white neighborhood is more difficult because they do not have the language fluency and middle-class mannerisms to deal with a more educated clientele. For example, when asked why she opened a business in a low-income, black neighborhood as opposed to a middle-income, white neighborhood, a Korean storeowner in Harlem replied:

> Because easier. First of all, you don't have to have that much money to open up the store. And, second of all, easier because you don't need to that much complicate. White people is very classy and choosy, and especially white people location is not like this, mostly they go to mall. Here they don't have many car, so easier, cheaper rent. When

you go to white location, Second Avenue, Third Avenue, rent is already cost $20,000, you know, and they don't have any room for us. But black people area, other people hesitate to come in because they worry about crime and something like that, so they got a lot of room for Koreans.

After gathering experience and accumulating capital running businesses in low-income neighborhoods, some Korean storeowners leave the inner city and open stores in safer, middle-income white neighborhoods.

Immigrant entrepreneurs also cluster in particular "retail niches" (Lee 1999). The newest immigrant storeowners find themselves in the most physically exhausting, labor-intensive businesses that require relatively little capital and have low profit margins, such as greengroceries, take-out restaurants, and fresh fish stores (Light and Bonacich 1988). The extremely long hours and the physically demanding labor often ensure that first-generation immigrants will be the ones to occupy these lines of business. Accordingly, Korean immigrants presently dominate these niches, but they are merely the successors in a line of immigrant ethnic groups who occupied these business lines before them. Immigrant entrepreneurs will continue to succeed one another and flourish in low-income black neighborhoods because they bring products and services to an underserviced population by taking advantage of previously unfilled niches. As long as second-and third-generation immigrants find better opportunities in the mainstream labor market, retail businesses, particularly those catering to a low-income clientele, will remain a protected niche among immigrant communities, who will continue to succeed one another in these businesses.

"Mass Marketing" a Once Exclusive Product

Evaluating the industries in which immigrant entrepreneurs concentrate, we can see that some succeed in those areas in which they are able to "mass market" a once exclusive product. In other words, they take a luxury product and make it cheaper, thereby making it more accessible for a wider population. For instance, before Korean-owned manicure salons opened on virtually every block in New York City, manicures used to be available only in full-service beauty salons. In upscale salons, manicures would cost about $20, making them accessible only to an elite group of people, namely upper- and upper-middle-class white women. Koreans took this luxury service out of the beauty salon and mass-marketed the manicure. They made it cheaper by charging women only $7, thereby making manicures more widely available to a greater population (Kang 1996). Koreans have used the same strategy in selling fresh flowers, once only available at florist shops, now readily available at corner delis.

These business owners have successfully adapted to the changing demands of the service economy by bringing small, full-service retail shops close to both high- and low-income consumers (Sassen 1991). Korean-owned manicures shops and delis have become a ubiquitous symbol of New York City, as evidenced from an article in the *New York Times* in which a woman who had moved out of the city complains, "There are no Koreans. Which explains why you can never find flowers and why manicures cost $15." [6] This strategy of "mass marketing" transcends industries and also explains immigrants' success in selling ethnic beauty supplies (which includes both hair and skin care products for an ethnic clientele) and ethnic urban sportswear. Since low-income blacks cannot afford to purchase designer clothing, Korean-owned businesses that sell designer knock-offs for the urban teenage market prosper in poor neighborhoods.

Interethnic Conflict—Korean Merchants and Black Customers

The tension between blacks and Koreans has been popularized and exploited by the media. Newspaper headings such as "Will Black Merchants Drive Koreans from Harlem?" (Noel 1981), "Blacks, Koreans Struggle to Grasp Thread of Unity" (Jones 1986), "Cultural Conflict" (Njeri 1989), and "Scapegoating New York's Koreans"[7] have become common in both mainstream and ethnic presses. Spike Lee's poignant film *Do the Right Thing* and Ice Cube's controversial lyrics in the rap song "Black Korea" brought black-Korean tension and conflict to the fore in both communities. The shooting of an African American teenager, Latasha Harlins, by a Korean storeowner, Soon Ja Du, on March 16, 1991, in South Central Los Angeles intensified tensions between these minority communities. And, finally, the innocent verdict rendered by a Simi Valley jury in the Rodney King case, on April 29, 1992, sparked riots in Los Angeles, the first multiethnic riot in U.S. history. Although many ethnic groups were involved, the riot was framed as the culmination of black-Korean conflict—an oversimplified and misleading framework that failed to capture the depth and complexity of the issues at hand. This section of the chapter examines both the daily encounters between Korean merchants and black customers and the larger structural processes under which simple economic arguments turn into racialized anger.

Dispelling the Myths—The Intersection of Race, Class, and Experience

To be a Korean merchant in an inner-city neighborhood such as New York's Harlem or in South Central Los Angeles is a mixture of prosaic routine and explosive tension, of affectionate customers and racial anger. Despite the violent media portrayal of Korean merchants arming themselves with nine-millimeter handguns and black customers looting stores during the Los Angeles riots, most striking is the sheer ordinariness of most merchant-customer relationships. In fact, for most merchants and customers, their everyday shopping experiences boil down to a simple formula: "business as usual" (Lee 1996). However, there is a considerable amount of variation within the merchant-customer relationship, and there are two important factors that shape the daily encounters between Korean business owners and their black clientele: (1) the merchants' experience and (2) the class composition of the customer population.

Korean merchants who have been in business for many years have far better relations with their black customers than newer merchants who have little experience dealing with a minority clientele. With time, merchants come to realize that, contrary to the dominant stereotypes, the inner-city residents are not all welfare queens, drug addicts, or criminals; experience teaches Korean storeowners that even the poorest neighborhoods are economically diverse and culturally rich. Merchants who have been in business for ten or fifteen years know and recognize their customers, speak with them more frequently than newer merchants, and generally feel more comfortable doing business in low-income black neighborhoods. They see their customers as a diverse population, recognizing differences in ethnicity, class, and character. Years of experience have taught veteran business owners that negative experiences—no matter how traumatic—come few and far between.

Class differences also matter. Running a small business in a low-income, urban neighborhood is not easy, especially for new immigrants who come from an ethnically homogeneous country and therefore have little understanding of the nuances of America's pluralistic society. Without prior business experience and a solid command of the English language, they set up shop in inner cities, where they are exposed to persistent poverty and its resultant consequences—welfare dependency, teenage pregnancy, single motherhood, unemployment, and drugs (Wilson 1987). Most consequential for these merchants is the relatively high level of customer theft and robberies. In response, merchants often perch themselves behind unusually high counters or behind bulletproof glass in order to minimize shoplifting and the risk of harm. They may follow customers, especially teenagers, as they browse, making some customers feel unwelcome in these stores.

In the context of poverty, Korean merchants seem to appear successful. Poor black customers often assume that new immigrants such as Koreans take away opportunities for blacks. Even though immigrant merchants may not directly compete with black merchants or black residents for jobs, low-income residents are more likely to *perceive* these immigrant newcomers as outside competitors who take opportunities away from them. Frustrated by the infusion of immigrant newcomers who barely speak English yet are able to open up shops so easily in their communities, they often direct their resentment toward the immediate agents of exploitation (Rieder 1990). Poor black customers often question what U.S. government agency helped them out and also wonder why aid has not come their way. It is a common misperception among low-income black customers that immigrants, especially Korean immigrants, receive special loans from the government to help them open businesses. Although this is a fallacious rumor, low-income residents are quick to embrace it because they cannot otherwise explain how these "foreigners" are able to accumulate the mass amounts of capital and "take over" the businesses in their communities.

However, the scenario is very different in middle-class black communities. When Korean merchants serve middle-class black customers, there is little sign of tension between these groups. Korean merchants claim that middle-class customers are far less likely to steal merchandise than those in low-income neighborhoods, giving storeowners little reason to feel threatened. Furthermore, middle-class customers do not perceive Korean merchants in their communities as economic competitors who take opportunities away from them, since most middle-class blacks have jobs, are economically stable, and therefore do not express feelings of economic and ethnic antagonism. Instead, they view merchants as businessmen and women who provide services for the community and have the right to open a business wherever they choose. Economic security affords this opinion. The stark differences in low- and middle-income black neighborhoods reveals that class, rather than race or ethnicity, is more important in determining the level of tension or conflict between blacks and Koreans.

Racially Coding Economic Arguments

Writing about the black-Jewish relationship of the 1960s, Gans (1969, 10) explains, "When Negroes express their anger in anti-Semitic terms, it is only because many of the whites who affect their lives are Jewish; if the ghetto storeowners, landlords and teachers were Chinese, Negro hostility would surely be anti-Chinese." Although most merchant-customer encounters in black neighborhoods may be quite ordinary, when tensions rise, both merchants and customers tend to lose cognitive control, and even those who do not normally engage in stereotypes may do so under strained conditions. Seemingly trivial economic arguments between black customers and out-group merchants such as Koreans can quickly turn racial. In this tricky area of merchant-customer conflict, Robert K. Merton's concept of "in-group virtues" and "out-group vices" is particularly useful. Merton (1968) demonstrates that similar patterns of behavior by in-group and out-group members are differently perceived and evaluated. Yet, because the most apparent distinction between Korean merchants and their black customers is race, the economic relationship is often overlooked by customers as a source of tension in favor of racial or ethnic explanations.

As racially distinct immigrant newcomers who are not part of the dominant white racial hierarchy, Korean merchants are vulnerable to racial and ethnic taunts by angry customers. All of the Korean merchants I interviewed have admitted that, at some point while doing business, particularly at the beginning, economic arguments have become racially or ethnically coded. For example, a furniture storeowner in West Philadelphia explains that, when customers become very angry over economic disputes, "the argument always does down to race." Accusations such as, "You damn Orientals are coming into our neighborhoods taking over every fucking store!" are not uncommon when merchants and customers disagree over exchanges or refunds.

When a Korean storeowner refused to take back the floor display furniture model that he had recently sold to a woman at a discount, she immediately uttered to her mother, "He's just a chink and a gook." Incensed by the racial insult, the Korean merchant retorted, "Now wait a minute, what would happen if I called you a nigger? What would happen then? You're sitting here calling me these names; what if I did that to you?" Infuriated by the hint of a racial epithet, the woman threatened to start picketing outside his store. Realizing the problems that he could incur from this incident, the Korean merchant immediately called the Philadelphia Commission on Human Relations to intervene, which later proved to be unnecessary since the woman did not carry out her threat. The Korean furniture storeowner comments about the situation:

I called up City Hall because I thought it was going to be a problem, but it wasn't. The next day they were gone, but it just shows that it's totally backwards. It's reverse racism is what it is. And anytime there's an argument about anything, it always comes down to, "You damn Orientals are taking over all the businesses in the neighborhood!" or "You Koreans are doing it!"

This isn't all the time, but every once in a while you get a customer who's totally unreasonable, and if things don't go their way, they pull that old card out of their pocket, the race card, and throw it down. And it's a shame that they got to stoop to that level just to get what they want. I mean if they were to talk to me reasonable, without yelling and ranting and raving, we probably would have got things worked out more to their liking. But you can't come in here and yell at somebody and expect to get what you want.

Even Korean merchants who are veterans of the black communities they serve—who know most of their customers—fully realize that their nonblack status can easily make them targets for hostile customers and boycotters. For example, a Korean carry-out restaurant owner who has been in the Harlem community for thirteen years explains that racial tension is a fact of life in Harlem. She is a mainstay in West Harlem's community and has many customers who frequent her eating establishment on a daily basis. Yet even she understands that as a nonblack merchant on 125th Street in New York's Harlem, she is always at risk of potential conflict such as a boycott, regardless of how many people in the community support her:

> We always feel like a boycott could happen no matter how you famous on 125th Street, no matter how much they like you, no matter how you good to this community. Always one bum or one knucklehead hates you. He can bring you a ton of problem. So far, people support me but some people against me too.

When asked whether this insecurity stems from the simple fact that she is not black, she immediately confirms:

> That's right. And they can put me as Korean merchant coming here to make money out of this community. So I got a thousand of them full of respect, it don't mean anything. Something happen, a thousand people I don't know them, they can against me, coming here for protesting, hollering, shut down business. It could happen, you know. Some person get mad at me, so I argue, and he could start picket outside. Maybe some other people say, "You crazy, why you do that to this store?" But few people going to do that.
>
> And a lot of those protesters, they don't know me, they could stay there shouting and give me a lot of trouble because it always could happen no matter how much you are good to this community or something like that. And that kind of crazy thing can happen, and nobody can stop it. . . . Nobody can move those protesters out in front of my door. They got a right to stand there and shouting. And the ones who shouting, I don't know them, and they don't know me. They just want to be here. They angry because I'm Korean. But they not get mad at me, they get mad some place else.

When customers engage in stereotypes, they may not necessarily be reacting to the objective features of the situation but may be reacting instead to the symbolism that the situation represents. For instance, when merchants refuse a customer's request for a refund or an exchange, the refusal becomes symbolic of stingy, cheap commercial outsiders who exploit the community in which they serve. And similarly, when black customers become angry and yell at merchants, storeowners may quickly engage in stereotypes about blacks—that they are violent, ignorant, and lazy.

In order to defuse tensions in poor, black communities, Korean merchants hire black employees and managers to act as "cultural brokers" between them and their predominantly black clientele (Lee, 1998a). Black employees serve as bridges who link the linguistic and cultural differences; they also serve as visible symbols that merchants are "giving back" to the low-income communities in which they serve. Most critical, black employees act as conflict resolvers who can quickly deracialize rising tensions between merchants and customers.

Placing Black-Korean Conflict in the Context of Urban Poverty

In the context of urban poverty, small arguments can explode into racial conflict. This heightened tension can result from the daily strains and frustrations of inner-city life—joblessness, persistent poverty, and despair—leading customers to racially code economic arguments. An African American customer in Philadelphia explains the complexities of the merchant-customer relationship and offers insights about the tension and frustration resulting from life in the inner city:

> Well, there is a certain amount of sensitivity here because black folks, living the way we do, we have a certain amount of cynicism, so when we go into these stores, we're like angry, cursing them out and everything, and they're like, "You come in my store and you're cursing at me! You get out my store!" And a lot of people around here, they're stealing, they're strung out on something, don't know no better, trying to be cool. It's a whole myriad of things. That's why when I walk into a store, they're watching me. I haven't stole a thing in my life, too scared. I'm not going to say I never had a thought, but I'm just too scared, and I'm not going to do it. And there's a certain amount of despair, which is why they don't care if they get caught.

The media often depict merchant-customer relations in poor, inner-city neighborhoods as the principle source of black-Korean tensions. However, the source of this tension is in the nature of the economics of poverty and its resultant pattern of dominant-subordinate contact between merchants and customers. These tensions are symptoms of larger circumstances in which both the merchants and the customers are victims. As Caplovitz (1967, 192) stated in his classic work, *The Poor Pay More*, "the consumer problems of low-income families cannot be divorced from the other problems facing them. Until society can find ways of raising their educational level, improving their occupational opportunities, increasing their income, and reducing the discrimination against them—only limited solutions to their problems as consumers can be found." This was true in the 1960s when Jewish merchants predominated in poor, black neighborhoods, and it still holds true today as a new legion of immigrants enters these communities.

Conclusion

Immigrant entrepreneurs have made distinct inroads in many large U.S. cities. Approximately one-third of Korean families are engaged in small business, representing the highest rate of self-employment among all U.S. ethnic groups. Their access to class and ethnic resources, coupled with their utilization of social capital, contributes to the extraordinary rate of entrepreneurship. Once a nucleus of entrepreneurs becomes established, ethnic networks have a "fateful effect," paving the path for other family members and co-ethnic friends to follow suit.

Running a small business in an inner-city neighborhood is not what Korean immigrants had in mind when they immigrated to the United States. Educated and trained as white-collar professionals, they see self-employment as a symbol of downward mobility for the many Korean immigrants who find themselves extremely underemployed. Korean immigrant entrepreneurs work twelve to sixteen hours a day, six to seven days a week, in physically demanding and routine work. To succeed in a competitive market, they exploit themselves, their family members, and fellow ethnics. However, given the obstacles they face in the primary labor market and their inability to transfer their education and preimmigrant skills, Koreans turn to self-employment as an alternative to working in relatively low-wage salaried jobs. Entrepreneurship becomes the ladder to reaching the American dream of upward mobility.

This dream was shattered on April 29, 1992—the first day of the Los Angeles riots—when Korean shopowners suffered devastating losses totaling $400 million in property damage. Koreans now refer to this unforgettable turning point as *Sai-I-Gu*, simply referring to the first day of the riots. The worst domestic uprising of the century placed black-Korean conflict in the fore. However, this dyadic relationship fails to capture the depth and complexities facing the nation's inner-city communities. Placing black-Korean conflict at the core of the Los Angeles riots also distorts the nature of most merchant-customer encounters. Most day-to-day encounters are not fraught with racial animosity but characterized by customary civility.

Against the backdrop of inner-city poverty, heightened tension can transform small economic arguments into racialized conflict. A Korean merchant's refusal to give a cash refund for a defective beeper or an already worn dress may become symbolic of cheap, exploitative "out-group" business owners who make money from the community and drain it of its resources. The irate customer who is not given the refund may react not necessarily to the objective features of the situation but to the symbolism that the situation represents, leading him or her to racially code an economic argument. Even though civility may characterize the daily lives of both merchants and customers, the normalcy of everyday encounters does not preclude the possibility of interethnic conflict such as boycotts or urban riots.

In speaking of black-Jewish relations, Gans (1969, 3) explains that "it is more useful to look at the Negro-Jewish relationship from a longer sociological perspective. From that perspective, the recent incidents are only more visible instances in a long series of primarily economic conflicts between blacks, Jews (and other ethnic groups) which are endemic to New York and to several other large American cities, and which can only be dealt with through economic solutions." Korean merchants are not the first group to experience conflict with the black customers in poor neighborhoods, and they will undoubtedly not be the last, unless the structural problems that plague the inner city—poverty and unemployment—are confronted.

NOTES

The author wishes to thank Herbert Gans, Kathryn Neckerman, Katherine Newman, John Skrentny, Rob Smith, Roger Waldinger, and Rhacel Parreñas for helpful comments on an earlier version of this paper. The author gratefully thanks the International Migration Program of the Social Science Research Council, the Andrew W. Mellon Foundation, and the National Science Foundation SBR-9633345 for research support on which this paper is based. The University of California President's Office provided research support during the writing of this paper. This article is based on the author's Ph.D. dissertation, "Immigrant Entrepreneurs: Opportunity Structure and Intergroup Relations," Columbia University.

1. Quoted from Selznick and Steinberg 1969, 130.

2. "Black" refers to a generic category that includes African Americans, West Indians, and Africans.

3. The research sites include three low-income and two middle-income black communities. The three low-income neighborhoods are West Harlem, New York; East Harlem, New York; and West Philadelphia, and the two middle-income communities are Jamaica, Queens, New York, and East Mount Airy, Philadelphia.

4. The customers were paid $10 to thank them for taking the time to participate in the study. The funds were provided by a Dissertation Improvement Grant from the National Science Foundation, SBR-9633345.

5. Pyong Gap Min and Charles Jaret, "Ethnic Business Success: The Case of Korean Small Business in Atlanta," *Sociology and Social Research* 69 (1984): 432.

6. Laura Zigman, "Living Off-Center on Purpose," *New York Times*, December 12, 1996, C6.

7. "Scapegoating New York's Koreans," *New York Post*, January 25, 1990.

REFERENCES

Abelmann, Nancy, and John Lie. 1995. *Blue Dreams: Korean Americans and the Los Angeles Riots.* Cambridge, MA: Harvard University Press.

Bates, Timothy. 1994. An Analysis of Korean-Immigrant-Owned Small-Business Start-Ups with Comparisons to African-American-and Non-Minority-Owned Firms. *Urban Affairs Quarterly* 30: 227–248.

Bonacich, Edna. 1987. 'Making It' in America, a Sociological Evaluation of the Ethics of Immigrant Entrepreneurship. *Sociological Perspectives* 30: 446–466.

Caplovitz, David. 1967. *The Poor Pay More: Consumer Practices of Low-Income Families.* New York: Free Press.

Coleman, James S. 1988. Social Capital in the Creation of Human Capital. *American Journal of Sociology* 94: S95–S121.

Ellison, Elaine Krasnow, and Elaine Mark Jaffe. 1994. *Voices from Marshall Street: Jewish Life in a Philadelphia Neighborhood, 1920–1960.* Philadelphia: Camiko Books.

Gans, Herbert J. 1969. Negro-Jewish Conflict in New York City. *Midstream* 15: 3–15.

Hurh, Won Moo, and Kwang Chung Kim. 1980. *Korean Immigrants in America.* Macomb: Western Illinois University.

Jo, Moon H. 1992. Korean Merchants in the Black Community: Prejudice Among the Victims of Prejudice. *Ethnic and Racial Studies* 15: 395–410.

Jones, Von. 1986. Blacks, Koreans Struggle to Grasp Thread of Unity. *Los Angeles Sentinel.* May 1, p. A-1.

Kang, Miliann. 1996. Korean-owned Nail Salons in New York City: Gender, Race, and Class in the New Service Economy. Paper presented at the Annual Meeting of the Association for Asian American Studies, May, Washington, DC.

Katz, Alfred H., and Eugene I. Bender. 1976. *The Strength in Us.* New York: New Viewpoints.

Kim, Illsoo. 1981. *The New Urban Immigrants: The Korean Community in New York.* Princeton, NJ: Princeton University Press.

Lee, Heon Cheol. 1993. Black-Korean Conflict in New York City: A Sociological Analysis. Ph.D. dissertation, Columbia University.

Lee, Jennifer. 1999. Retail Niche Domination Among African American, Jewish, and Korean Entrepreneurs: Competition, Coethnic Advantage, and Disadvantage. *American Behavioral Scientist* 42: 1398–1416.

———. 1998a. Cultural Brokers: Race-based Hiring in Inner-City Neighborhoods. *American Behavioral Scientist* 41: 927–937.

———. 1998b. Immigrant Entrepreneurs: Opportunity Structure and Intergroup Relations. Ph.D. dissertation, Columbia University.

———. 1996. Business as Usual. *Common Quest: The Magazine of Black-Jewish Relations* 1:35–38.

Liebow, Elliot. 1967. *Tally's Corner.* Boston: Little, Brown.

Light, Ivan H. 1972. *Ethnic Enterprise in America.* Berkeley: University of California Press.

Light, Ivan, and Edna Bonacich. 1988. *Immigrant Entrepreneurs.* Berkeley: University of California Press.

Light, Ivan, and Angel A. Sanchez. 1987. Immigrant Entrepreneurs in 272 SMSA's. *Sociological Perspectives* 30: 373–399.

Merton, Robert K. 1968. Self-fulfilling Prophecy. *Social Theory and Social Structure.* New York: Free Press.

Min, Pyong Gap. 1996. *Caught in the Middle: Korean Merchants in America's Multiethnic Cities.* Berkeley: University of California Press.

———. 1993. The Prevalence and Causes of Blacks' Rejection of Korean Merchants. Paper presented at the Annual Meeting of the Association for Asian-American Studies, June, Ithaca, NY.

———. 1984. From White-Collar Occupations to Small Business: Korean Immigrants' Occupational Adjustment. *Sociological Quarterly* 25: 333–352.

Morawska, Ewa. 1996. *Insecure Prosperity: Small-Town Jews in Industrial America, 1890–1940.* Princeton, NJ: Princeton University Press.

Njeri, Itabari. 1996. Kimchee and Grits. *Common Quest: The Magazine of Black-Jewish Relations* 1:39–45.

———. 1989. Cultural Conflict. *Los Angeles Times,* November 8, p. E1.

Noel, Peter. 1981. Koreans Vie For Harlem Dollars. *New York Amsterdam News.* July 4, p. 26.

Ong, Paul, and Suzanne Hee. 1993. *Losses in the Los Angeles Civil Unrest, April 29–May 1, 1992.* Los Angeles: University of California, Los Angeles, Center for Pacific Rim Studies.

Park, Kyeyoung. 1997. *The Korean American Dream.* Ithaca, NY: Cornell University Press.

———. 1996. Use and Abuse of Race and Culture: Black-Korean Tension in America. *American Anthropologist* 98: 492–499.

Portes, Alejandro, ed. 1995. *The Economic Sociology of Immigration: Essays on Networks, Ethnicity, and Entrepreneurship*. New York: Russell Sage Foundation.

Reiss, Albert, and Howard Aldrich. 1971. Absentee Ownership and Management in the Black Ghetto: Social and Economic Consequences. *Social Problems* 18: 319–339.

Rieder, Jonathan. 1990. Trouble in Store. *New Republic* 203: 16–22.

Sassen, Saskia. 1991. The Informal Economy. In John Mollenkopf and Manuel Castells (eds.), *Dual City: Restructuring New York.* (79–101). New York: Russell Sage Foundation.

Selznick, Gertrude J., and Stephen Steinberg. 1969. *The Tenacity of Prejudice*. New York: Harper and Row.

Stack, Carol B. 1974. *All Our Kin: Strategies for Survival in a Black Community*. New York: Harper and Row.

Waldinger, Roger. 1996. *Still the Promised City? African Americans and New Immigrants in Postindustrial New York*. Cambridge, MA: Harvard University Press.

Wilson, William Julius. 1987. *The Truly Disadvantaged*. Chicago: University of Chicago Press.

Yoon, In-Jin. 1997. *On My Own: Korean Businesses and Race Relations in America*. Chicago: University of Chicago Press.

1. Ong and Umemoto suggest, in their chapter, that the increase in inner-city poverty is directly linked to the decline in available employment opportunities in the manufacturing sector. What factors do the authors provide to account for this phenomenon? How did these same factors shape the changing nature of available employment? Why were African Americans disproportionately affected by these changes? Latinos also experienced poverty rates similar to those of their African American counterparts, yet the authors contend that the nature of their poverty is different. How is this the case? What are the origins of inner-city neighborhoods in the United States, and how have they changed in composition and demographically in the past fifty years?

2. Zhou and Nordquist view the high labor force participation of immigrant Chinese women as an inseparable part of a family strategy for upward social mobility under extremely difficult circumstances. Why are women so overrepresented in Chinatown's low-wage garment industry? Why do they seem to be "willing" to take low-wage jobs, unconscious of their labor rights, unaware of their exploitation, and pressured to conform to traditional roles? What other options do they have should they reject employment in the garment industry?

3. Lee argues that Korean immigrants possess certain resources that give them a distinct advantage when entering into self-employment. What are these resources? Give examples for each. How do Korean immigrants mobilize these resources when beginning a business? When sustaining their businesses? What role do *kyes* (rotating credit associations) play in supporting these business ventures? Why, according to Lee, have some Korean immigrants become wary of relying on such capital?

4. The articles by Ong and Umemoto and by Lee both suggest that the presence of Asian Americans in inner-city neighborhoods as entrepreneurs, occupying a position as "middleman minorities," has often sparked intergroup tensions. What are the sources of these antagonisms? Can you think of any additional factors that might affect interethnic tensions between Korean merchants and African American customers? How might these factors be altered in when relationships between Korean American merchants and Latino American customers? When tensions develop between Korean American merchants and their African American customers, what mechanisms are employed by both groups to diffuse tensions? How do interethnic conflicts become racially coded? Why is this significant to the nature of African American and Korean American relations? To what extent are these animosities displaced on the Asian American entrepreneurs?

SUGGESTED READINGS

Agbayani-Siewert, P., and L. Jones. 1997. Filipino American Work, and Family. *International Social Work* 40(4): 407–424.

Bonacich, Edna, and John Modell. 1980. *The Economic Basis of Ethnic Solidarity: Small Business in the Japanese American Community*. Berkeley: University of California Press.

Bankston, Carl L., and Min Zhou. 1996. Go Fish: The Louisiana Vietnamese and Ethnic Entrepreneurship in an Extractive Industry. *National Journal of Sociology* 10(1): 1–18.

Bulosan, Carlos. 1974. *America Is in the Heart.* Seattle: University of Washington Press.

Glenn, Evelyn Nakano. 1986. *Issei, Nisei, Warbride: Three Generations of Japanese American Women in Domestic Service.* Philadelphia: Temple University Press.

Faderman, Lillian, with Ghia Xiong. 1998. *I Begin My Life All Over: The Hmong and the American Immigrant Experience.* Boston: Beacon Press.

Gibson, M. A. 1988. *Accommodation Without Assimilation: Sikh Immigrants in an American High School.* Ithaca, NY: Cornell University Press.

Kim, Elaine, and Eui-Young Yu. 1996. *East to America: Korean American Life Stories.* New York: New Press.

Lee, Gen Leigh. 1996. Chinese Cambodian Donut Makers in Orange County: Case Studies of Family Labor and Socioeconomic Adaptations. Pp. 208–219 in *The State of Asian Pacific America: Reframing the Immigration Debate: A Public Policy Report.* Los Angeles: LEAP Asian Pacific American Public Policy Report and UCLA Asian American Studies Center.

Leonard, Karen, and Chandra S. Tibrewal. 1993. Asian Indians in Southern California: Occupations and Ethnicity. In Ivan Light and Parminder Bhachu (eds.), *Immigration and Entrepreneurship: Culture, Capital, and Ethnic Networks.* New Brunswick, NJ: Transaction.

Min, Pyong Gap. 1996. *Caught in the Middle: Korean Merchants in America's Multiethnic Cities.* Berkeley: University of California Press.

Saito, Leland. 1993. Contrasting Patterns of Adaptation: Japanese Americans and Chinese Immigrants in Monterey Park. Pp. 33–43 in L. Revilla, G. Nomura, S. Wong, and S. Hune (eds.), *Bearing Dreams, Shaping Visions: Asian Pacific American Perspective.* Pullman: Washington State University Press.

Shin, E. H., and K. S. Chang. 1988. Peripherization of Immigrant Professionals: Korean Physicians in the United States. *International Migration Review* 22: 609–626.

Welaratna, Usha. 1993. *Beyond the Killing Fields.* Stanford: Stanford University Press.

Zhou, Min. 1992. *Chinatown: The Socioeconomic Potential of an Urban Enclave.* Philadelphia: Temple University Press.

FILMS

Mishan, Ahrin, and Nick Rothenberg (producers). 1994. *Bui Doi: Like Dust* (28-minute documentary).

Nakasako, Spencer, and Sokly Ny (directors). 1995. *a.k.a. Don Bonus* (55-minute documentary).

Young, Donald (director). 1994. *Chrysanthemums and Salt* (25-minute documentary).

Part V

Ties That Bind
The Asian American Family and Community

Children of Inmates

The Effects of the Redress Movement among Third-Generation Japanese Americans

Yasuko I. Takezawa

During the 1950s, it was predicted that Japanese American communities would eventually disappear. American society praised their "success story";[1] and their social and economic mobility, as well as their assimilation into the mainstream of society proceeded remarkably. The ethnic boundary of Japanese Americans appeared to have become blurred after World War II. Over the past decade, however, an ethnic identity has been reconfirmed and a sense of community has been revived amongst Japanese Americans. Such a reaffirmation of ethnic identity seems to be derived largely from the reconceptualization of their wartime internment brought about by the redress movement and its recent success in forcing the United States Government to acknowledge its own misconduct.

It is now no longer a secret in American history that by Executive Order 9066 Japanese Americans living on the West Coast were uprooted from their homes to live in internment camps surrounded by barbed wire during the Second World War. Over 110,000 people of Japanese descent, including American citizens who constituted nearly two-thirds of all the victims, were deprived of their constitutional rights and subjected to this evacuation and internment merely because of their Japanese ancestry. Not only did the short-notice evacuation order cause their total economic ruin, but a maximum of three and a half years of imprisonment left deep psychological scars among the internees, which subsequently kept them silent for decades after the war.

It was only after the redress campaign began in the early 1970s that former internees broke their silence to start talking about their experiences. After nearly two decades of long, difficult struggle, Japanese Americans finally won the redress legislation in August 1988 and the guarantee of individual payments by the Entitlement Program[2] enacted in November 1989. Letters of apology signed by President Bush, together with monetary compensation, began to be distributed to senior former internees in October 1990. Most of the recipients of redress are the Nisei (the second-generation Japanese Americans), since a majority of the Issei (the first generation) have already died and only a handful of the Sansei (the third generation) experienced internment.

It has been pointed out that their imprisonment during the Second World War has had psychological effects on the Nisei (Morishima 1973; Kashima 1980; Mass 1986) and even on the Sansei (Nagata 1989). Internment decisively gave a psychological blow to Japanese Americans, but another major turning point came with the redress movement. Through the movement, Japanese Americans have come to recognize the unique reality of being Japanese Americans. I have discussed elsewhere the transformation of ethnicity among Japanese Americans (Takezawa 1989a) and the impact of interment and redress upon the Nisei (Takezawa 1989b). How, then, has the wartime internment and the subsequent redress movement affected children of inmates, the Sansei? This chapter will examine, from an anthropological viewpoint, the social and psychological effects of the internment and the subsequent redress movement upon the ethnic identity of the third generation Japanese Americans. Before developing my thesis in detail, however, I will briefly review the current theoretical concerns on ethnicity in cultural anthropology.

Recent years have witnessed remarkable advances in the study of ethnicity as ethnic tensions and ethnic identity have become more prominent in complex societies. While the dichotomy between the primordialists (e.g., Geertz 1963; Isaacs 1975) and the instrumentalists (e.g., Despres 1967; Cohen 1969) has dominated the theoretical issues of ethnicity within anthropology, attention amongst anthropologists has moved slowly towards the question of whether ethnicity is mutable and nonpermanent, and if so, of how ethnic identity is constituted and maintained. Some students of ethnicity place special importance on the historical continuity of an ethnic group as a factor in explaining the persistence of an ethnic identity (e.g., Spicer 1971; De Vos 1975). These scholars are concerned with a sense of shared history and the symbolic interpretations of that history. George De Vos (1975:17) contends that "Ethnicity . . . is in its narrowest sense a feeling of continuity with the past, a feeling that is maintained as an essential part of one's self-definition," stressing additionally the individual's needs for "collective continuity" and survival as the essence of ethnicity at the deepest psychological level: "If one's group survives, one is assured of survival, even if not in a personal sense." Charles Keyes, developing this notion, suggests that an intense suffering experience of the ancestors of a people provides the experimental foundation for ethnic identity (1981:9–10).

In line with this view emphasizing the interpretation of historical experience amongst members of an ethnic group, this chapter will argue that the ethnicity of the Sansei today is constructed not merely from racial and cultural markers of prewar days but from a sense of suffering of their forebears who experienced internment. In the process, I will argue that the more recent reaffirmation of ethnic identity and sense of community among the Sansei, in spite of acculturation and a high degree of interracial marriage, is a cultural product of their reconceptualization of their forebears' suffering and the subsequent victory in acknowledgement of this from the Government.

The chapter is based primarily on participant observation, in-depth personal interviews,[3] and archive research,[4] which was carried out in the Japanese American community in Seattle, Washington, during a period of fieldwork undertaken between 1986 and 1989.[5] The Sansei subjects were not interned.[6] The selection of subjects was not random. However, a great effort was made to assemble a wide range of individuals with varying experiences of acculturation. For example, some were actively involved in community organizations, others were entirely uninterested. Again, some had strong ethnic ties, others' were much looser.

Childhood and Adolescence of the Sansei

The majority of the Sansei were born between the late 1940s and the early 1960s, and the social environment of their childhood and adolescence differed sharply form that of the Nisei in prewar years. In general, the Sansei enjoyed affluence, high educational opportunities, and the reputation of being a "model minority." Moreover, due to the lack of a segregated geographical community, the ethnic solidarity of the kind possessed by the Nisei did not develop among the Sansei. Instead, the Sansei had more open social associations than their parents' generation with other ethnic groups, such as White, Black, Chinese, and Filipino Americans, encountered very largely by racially mixed schools and neighborhood environments. Consequently, the Sansei came to adopt American values and mores to a much greater extent than the Nisei.

Maykovich (1972:59) points out the Nisei's aspiration for Americanization, stating, "Anything that identified him as Japanese became taboo to the Nisei, simply because it was detrimental to his attempts to establish himself as an American." In fact, many Nisei suffered from shame due to the imprisonment, which occurred on the basis of their ethic origin. The Sansei characterize the Nisei as Maykovich does, saying that the Nisei Neisi tried to Americanize 200 percent at the expense of their Japanese heritage. Carol Namiki, an older Sansei, expresses her view of the Nisei's assimilation:

> If you had any ties with Japan it was considered negative so that there was this—in some Niseis there was this thing to be accepted by the White community. If you were accepted by the White community, that erased the discrimination of the war and so then they felt good. And so there were a lot of families who tended to bring up their children so they would be accepted in the mainstream. (Carol Namiki)[7]

Thus, unlike their Issei parents, the Nisei did not teach Japanese to their children. Nor did they emphasize many of the cultural values or being of Japanese descent, although some behavioral patterns were passed on to the Sansei without verbal socialization. The Sansei's experience as ethnic Japanese resulted in an ethnic identity that was not as strong or exclusive as that of the Nisei.

During the 1950s and 1960s, the Nisei report, they were busy raising their children and working hard, and they did not have time to look back to their past. Many of the Nisei also acknowledge that they evaded discussion of "camp," an issue too painful for them to discuss. The Sansei who overheard parents' conversation about "camp" in their early childhood, although small in percentage, thought that it referred to a summer camp. Many Sansei, however, often learned about internment, or realized the true meaning of "camp," from books, films, or Asian American courses in college. Being middle class and, in most cases, being a socially accepted minority by the time they reached adolescence, the Sansei felt anger and shock upon learning about the internment. Kathy Hashimoto recalls her anger at having not been informed earlier about camp when she first learned about the history of internment:[8]

> I was about 15, I was at a friend's house, looking at his parents' library. I found a book. It was called "Citizen 13660" . . . I remember coming home very angry about it, angry because what happened, but also with my parents for never telling me. . . . I said to my mother, "How could you have just allow 120,000 of you to just go into these camps? Why didn't you tell me before?" She said because she thought I couldn't understand what it was like because the time has changed and it wasn't easy. (Kathy Hashimoto)

One of the questions common among the Sansei is why the Nisei obeyed the evacuation order in the first place. Some Sansei directed their anger not only at the Government but also at their parents for not resisting the evacuation order.[9] It puzzled the Sansei, whose values and behavior pattern are more acculturated than those of the Nisei and whose experience as a minority differs sharply from them.

> Since I was born here, I would have at least tried to protest. I would not have become violent, but I would have at least tried to say, "Hey, there's a book of rules here in the Constitution." I would have tried to be a little bit more active, rather than submitting without any effort. . . . I believe that they should have acted differently, but knowing what I know now, I can understand how they acted. (Steve Kondo)

To the Nisei, on the other hand, the Sansei's questioning of such matters itself appears to demonstrate their lack of understanding of the Nisei's position in the context of the evacuation. The Nisei retort, "What can you do when you have soldiers with guns behind your back?" Today, exposed to more information about the time of the evacuation, many Sansei understand the historical circumstances surrounding the Nisei and their limited options available in 1942.

One example of the failure in mutual understanding between the two generations is how the Sansei perceive the Nisei camp experience. The Nisei often complain that the Sansei have little or no interest in camp, saying, "They don't ask questions (about camp)." The Sansei, however, did not feel free to ask their parents such sensitive issues:

> I think, on one level, I was pretty upset because I felt like they owed it to me to tell me what that experience was, so I could understand them and understand myself better. But I also realized that it was very painful to them. So, while I did ask a question, I really didn't press very hard because I didn't think it was my right, I guess. (Dan Hayashi)

As mentioned earlier, the Nisei experienced feelings of shame deriving from their imprisonment during the war. To some extent, the shame has been passed on to some Sansei as well. To them, such as Gary Tanaka, the internment has been a stigma attached to their entire ethnic community, including his own generation, children of inmates:

It's an embarrassing blotch on the community. It's also true for Sansei. White Americans would say, "Were your parents in camp?" Then they ask questions, "How was it?" I start feeling this is kind of personal, I don't want to talk about it. Parents being thrown into a prison—it is almost as bad as saying "My parents were in jail: one was for robbery and the other one was for murder." It's the same type of process you have to go through in explaining why your parents and relatives had to go to camp. It is the same kind of stigma. What makes this magnified is, it wasn't only your parents, but your grandparents, uncles, aunts, your friends, everybody was there. And it wasn't just a day or two, but it was for years. (Gary Tanaka)

While the feeling of shame described above was shared among some Sansei, to the majority of the Sansei such a feeling is remote. Instead, they feel more anger than embarrassment—anger at the injustice of the U.S., Government and at the racial discrimination prevalent within American society.

Other Sansei show only a limited interest in camp and redress. In Bruce Akimoto's case, his discussion with his father about internment calmed his anger.

Their attitude about camp was that it happened and there's not much that I, my generation, can do about it. It's just something that happened in history, and . . . they wanted me to concentrate on my life, rather than worry about what happened to them. (Bruce Akimoto)

The Akimoto family represents one type of family in the community which attached weak emotional feelings to the internment and a minimum interest in redress.

While admitting a significant difference from the prewar discrimination experienced by their parents, most of the Sansei have memories of occasional racial discrimination or prejudice directed against themselves in their childhood, especially around the critical anniversary date: Pearl Harbor Day. Many recall verbal and, in some cases, physical attacks.

I remember year after year hating to go to school because of December 7th. That was real horrible. But I think that's typical for almost all Japanese. That's a real bad time of the year to go out of the house. I think the first time that I noticed was one day walking to grammar school and getting rocks thrown at me and people chasing me and calling me, "Jap, Jap, Jap." (Jenni Miyagawa)

Some Sansei, however, assert that they have never experienced any discrimination based on their ethnicity at an individual level. Still, they acknowledge existing discrimination and prejudice against other Japanese Americans, Asian Americans, and other ethnic minorities.

During the late 1960s and the early 1970s, the repercussions of the nationwide Asian American movement stimulated the Sansei as well as other Asian Americans in Seattle. Following African Americans' examination of slavery and the effects of other African American experience to redefine their own identity, young Japanese Americans became increasingly conscious of discrimination against Asian Americans generally. In this movement, Sansei's ethnic awareness of and interest in their cultural heritage and history grew, resulting in the subsequent rise in ethnic consciousness on the part of Japanese American communities across the nation. The Seattle Japanese American community was not an exception.

The Redress Movement and Its Effects on the Sansei

In 1970, Edison Uno (real name) of San Francisco introduced a resolution at the national convention of the Japanese American Citizens League (JACL) in Chicago, calling for redress for internment to be adopted as an official policy of the League (cf. Tateishi 1986:191). At that time, Uno offered no specific plan, however.[10] In Seattle in 1972, without knowledge of Uno's resolution, Henry Miyatake (real name), a Nisei, started research on the possibility of reparations for Japanese Americans. He soon joined the Seattle chapter of the JACL, when the chapter was looking for volunteers to look into reparations. With several other Nisei and Issei, Miyatake's group, representing the Seattle chapter of the JACL, advanced the idea of redress with a concrete individual payment plan at the national level. During the early and mid-1970s, nonetheless, the redress campaign made little progress, mostly because of ideological differences amongst national Japanese American political leaders and the resistance of many Nisei to the idea. Recollection of internment reopens old wounds, and since the Nisei were attempting to reestablish themselves through hard work, the idea of monetary redress gained little support. "Don't rock the boat" was a typical reaction among the Nisei at that time.

A breakthrough came in 1978, when the nation's first Day of Remembrance was held at the Puyallup fairgrounds in Western Washington, a former temporary camp ("assembly center") where the internees in the Seattle area spent three months before being transferred to a more permanent camp in Minidoka. Since the purpose of the event was to commemorate the evacuation and internment, the evacuation process was dramatically recreated in this program, with people forming a car caravan and wearing replicas of numbered name tags and with former internees giving speeches. A part of the flyer distributed prior to the event read "Remember the Concentration Camps," apparently countering "Remember Pearl Harbor."

This program was soon followed by other major Japanese American communities and became a nationwide event in Japanese America. The program had been organized by a Chinese American playwright and several Sansei, who approached the redress leaders in Seattle showing a keen interest in camp and redress. Joe Fukiai, one of the key Sansei involved in this program, recalls the time of organizing this first Day of Remembrance event:

> He[the Chinese American playwright] pitched me and said, "There would be no Japanese American art if we don't say about Japanese American history. If we lose redress, we lose history. If these people in Seattle fail to win some kind of recognition for the injustice in the camps and to get some token payment for it as a symbol of the recognition that it was wrong, then the myth that camps were justified, that Nisei willingly cooperated with them, would stand. Then, no artist can create plays, books, or stories from the truth, because no one would believe them." Then I thought, "Gee! This is much bigger than me. I have to devote my entire soul to this." (Joe Fukiai)

The event turned out to be a large success. Over 2,000 Japanese Americans with their friends participated in the program. The Issei and the Nisei recaptured their past experiences with vivid memories of three and a half decades before.

The participants included a large number of the Sansei as well, and the whole event provided them with the first opportunity to grasp visually the idea of evacuation and the condition of the camps through experiencing the recreated evacuation process and observing the exhibition with their parents and other Japanese Americans.

> When it really hit me was at the Puyallup fairgrounds, they had some kind of—it was some display, and they actually showed the living modules. They had set up models, living areas, and stuff like that. And the space that a family had to live in was just like— I couldn't comprehend that: it's like a small, small living area. To hear people talk about it is one thing, but to see some physical display of the thing was kind of unreal. That's when it started to really hit me. (Paul Takei)

The Day of Remembrance set a trend, which was followed by several programs during subsequent years. These include the Day of Remembrance 1983, which was observed as a "Fun-Run" at a local park. The participants ran 9,066 feet, the number standing for Executive Order 9066. All participants, after completing the run, were awarded a T-shirt which read on the back, "I survived 9066" with a design of barbed wire. The T-shirt was designed by a Sansei redress activist.

The next large event, perhaps the largest in the whole redress movement in terms of its penetration to the wider population of Japanese Americans, occurred in 1981, when hearings of the Commission on Wartime Relocation and Internment of Civilians were held in Seattle as well as in other major Japanese American communities across the nation. In Seattle alone, over 150 people gave testimonies at the hearings.[11] After a series of hearings, the Report of the Commission concluded that internment was based on "racial prejudice, wartime hysteria and a failure of political leadership." The Commission went on to recommend individual payments of $20,000, a formal government apology, and the establishment of an educational fund (Commission on Wartime Relocation and Internment of Civilians 1983:24).

The Commission hearings directed the whole Japanese American community's attention to their recent past because of the recollections presented by former internees.

> I was very moved by the testimony that I heard when people would tell their stories because it was obvious that they hadn't really told their stories. It was like the first time a lot of those people were really talking about it. . . . It was part of their catharsis of forgetting about it by talking about it. So I felt kind of like I was taking part in this catharsis. And it was kind of an honor to be able to hear people's stories like that, that they were brave enough to get up and talk about it. And it was very painful for them, and it was private, but they still did it. And I was very moved by that experience. (Susan Ochiai)

Excepting political activists, most Japanese Americans were skeptical about gaining redress. The federal budget deficit and mistrust of government among some Nisei intensified the mood of pessimism. When the redress bill passed, therefore, Japanese Americans felt great relief, happiness, and pride.

> I was extremely happy because I felt that now in some ways it took a lot of pressure off, it brought the whole issue out into the open for people to acknowledge. And I think there's just been so much guilt and repression around the whole issue within the community and really was just kind of a big sigh of relief, I think as much as anything else, but also a feeling that we were now really righted and everybody acknowledged the fact that we were wronged as a community. (Dan Hayashi, Sansei)

The overwhelming majority of the Nisei and Sansei, including some Nisei who were opposed at the beginning, now support redress. Even after the passage of the bill, however, some are uncomfortable with monetary redress. Scott Iizuka, an older Sansei, considers that accepting money as compensation demeans the experience of internment for the Nisei.

> I guess I was not supportive because I don't think that something like that should be— You can't undo what was done with money. To me . . . it's almost like America is trying to buy out, or sell out their guilty conscience, or try to relieve themselves of the guilt by giving money away. It's really cheap . . . and I know a lot of people don't feel that way, but that's how I feel. (Scott Iizuka)

However, the monetary redress attached to a government apology is now widely supported within the community as the most effective way to prevent the U.S. Government from repeating the same mistake with other minorities, if not with themselves again. They deem verbal apologies alone to be insufficient to prevent a recurrence of a similar mistake by the Government.

Japanese Americans assert today that, although nothing can compensate for the loss of three and half years in prison and the prolonged pain caused by the injustice, it is the American way to sue and claim monetary compensation for damage. Monetary redress, in that sense, is a symbol of the official apology.

The redress campaign and related cultural events have triggered many feelings about identity, sense of community, and other aspects of Sansei life. Many Sansei reveal their respect to the community for its achievement and attribute their sense of ethnic pride to the redress movement and the passage of the bill. Redress has generally served to reinforce the ethnic identity of the Sansei. Gary Tanaka, a politically active Sansei, says:

> It reinforced my identity with *Nikkei* [Japanese American community]. Up until redress, my ethnic identity was things like the food I ate, people I like to be friends with, interests, things Japanese. With redress, I found a much newer, different, and also very important strong identification with my cultural, historical background, the history of my community. My parents went to the camp, that affected me indirectly. Now I have become closer to the Japanese American community, whereas originally before the redress, I wouldn't say that I was very much close to the community. (Gary Tanaka)

While other Sansei did not report as overt an identity shift as Tanaka, some indicated how learning about camp helped them understand and define who they are.

From that, I learned why it is that I act the way I act. Or I have a better idea of why I behave the way I do. . . . When I was growing up, you always try to act like regular people, regular Americans. . . . I never made any effort to emphasize my difference from everybody else. . . . And now I know why, the way they acted in camp explains to me why I act the way I do often times, which is to—you're always kind of hesitant to promote your culture among other people. If they're interested in talking to you about it, I'm more than happy to talk about it, but I never try to promote it. Kind of a humility. (Steve Kondo)

Some Sansei claim that although redress is a victory, there are more important issues to be dealt with, such as racial discrimination.[12] It seems, however directly or indirectly, redress has made them aware, or more aware, of existing discrimination as well. Susan Ochiai, a Sansei who grew up in a White environment, had mostly White American friends throughout her life and little contact with the Japanese American community. Her sensitivity to discrimination increased:

What happened is early, early on, when I was younger, I was aware of it [discrimination]. And then I think when I got older I was less aware of it than when the whole redress issue came up again, I think. I started reading more books, and then I also talked to more people about their experience. I think I realized, okay it hasn't disappeared, it may have just gone underground. I think there is still a great deal of discrimination and prejudice against Japanese, and Asians, and other minorities. . . . And that's just made me aware that by learning more about the redress and what happened during World War II, made me aware that it still does exist. (Susan Ochiai)

Thus, internment, although an experience unique to Japanese Americans, has aroused their consciousness of discrimination in American society as a whole. Such sensitivity to discrimination, together with their upbringing in multiethnic neighborhoods, has generated amongst the Sansei emotional affinities with other Asian Americans and minorities. They feel the closest intimacy with Chinese Americans, another major group from Asia who have been in the U.S. over three generations:

We certainly share a history, certainly in terms of how we've been treated by this country, in terms of exclusionary acts, discrimination, process of migration. We share that broader community base. We're both Asians. And in some ways culturally, I certainly know that the two cultures are very close in terms of where their roots are. Their art forms, their writings. I mean there's a difference. It's kind of like Chinese, to an extent, are a generation behind, in a lot of ways. But I feel very closely akin to what their experiences are. (Dan Hayashi)

Further, more Sansei than Nisei mention other minority groups when discussing the needs of redress, although both generations regard redress as a constitutional issue.

On an absolute scale, any American could expect if he or she as an individual were wrongfully imprisoned and stripped of their rights for that period of time, it [monetary payment] is a drop in the bucket. But I think as a political thing, and as a symbolic thing, it was a real milestone in our history in this country, not just for Japanese Americans but for Asian Americans, Americans of different colors, particularly, though, for the Japanese American community; because for so long we had been stereotyped as the silent Americans who accept anything that is dealt to our community, who strive only to better our economic conditions and to get along in society, and not depicted as a people who care deeply about our rights and the rights of other people. This organizing of the movement was a real statement the community made about who we really are and what our values are as Americans.(Alice Segawa)

The redress movement has also contributed to strengthening intergenerational ties in the community. It is of interest that not a few Nisei and Sansei mention their feeling of gratitude to their parents. Most Sansei, including even the ones most disinterested in redress, wish to see payment given to their parents while the parents are still alive. Kathy Hashimoto, whose parents and sisters were interned, describes her feeling:

> I kept saying, the only thing I prayed for all the time was that if it happened, it would happen while my parents are alive, because it wouldn't mean the same thing. Even if the rest of my family can get the money, it would mean nothing. Really it would mean nothing if my parents couldn't see that something was going to happen. I wouldn't even want it. We weren't the ones that had to suffer. (Kathy Hashimoto)

It would not be wrong to say that the Sansei have a lower emotional attachment to redress than the Nisei. Nonetheless, the "suffering" of their parents and relatives from the evacuation and internment make them relate to redress emotionally as well as intellectually, with particularist, as well as universalist concerns:

> I support it on different levels. I think it's very personal because my parents and my grandparents went through that experience. In that sense I support it because they're my relatives, and I'm close to that experience. In the bigger picture, I support it so that it won't happen to other people, not necessarily other Japanese again. It was like with the Iranian [hostage crisis] those people were saying, "Let's send those people back to Iran." (Susan Ochiai)

In fact, the belief that it was the Nisei who suffered, and not the Sansei, and therefore that the Nisei deserve redress more than those who only experienced camp as small children—this belief is widely shared among the Sansei:[13]

> Most of the Sansei who are getting the money, almost all of them, don't even remember the camps. They don't remember the camps. They didn't suffer. They really didn't suffer. And that's my opinion. I don't think they suffered. For them to put some of it back into the community would not be such a bad thing. (Jenni Miyagawa)

> It was perhaps good for Sansei to be involved in that, to understand what that meant for their parents, and again many great sacrifices and injustices that they suffered because of that. (David Hayama)

People in the community also agree that redress has strengthened community ties. The following is an opinion by a Sansei who grew up in a suburban White American neighborhood:

> I think it brought the Japanese community close nationally, everybody close together. . . . I supported it because it brought people closer. For Sansei there hasn't been an issue like redress that bound us together. . . . The issue is not an emotional issue, but it makes

us feel like something we have to fight for, something we get excited about. (Cynthia Ube)

This sense of community has become more intense over discussion as to which organizations should receive all or part of the individual redress payment. Various community organizations, some of which have critical financial difficulties, are hoping for donations to expand their services for the community.

> I guess I don't feel as community oriented as a lot of people do, but it has a lot to do with the way I get along with people. I get along individually with people more than community oriented. But I still think the community has helped us a lot, helped us make it through, made everything easier for us. And the community somehow should get some of it back. (Jenni Miyagawa)

The perception that it is the ethnic community organizations that mounted the long and extensive redress campaign, without which redress would never have happened, has motivated donations of redress money to community organizations among many recipients-to-be. Others say that they are fully entitled to spend the money, perhaps on a trip to Japan or buying a car. However, most of the Sansei interviewed, all of whom are nonrecipients, show rather less interest in how their parents spend the money, saying "It's their money."

The ways in which the Sansei have increased their interest, involvement, and ties with the community vary. Whatever their level of contact, for the majority of the Sansei, the redress movement has played a vital role in strengthening their ethnic identity and their ties to the community.

Theoretical Considerations

I have shown that the internment of Japanese Americans during the Second World War and the redress campaign affected the ethnic identity among the third-generation Japanese Americans, despite the fact that they themselves were, except for a small number, not direct victims of "camp." Learning about the missing segment of their ethnic group's history, observing the community tied together to work for one goal, and seeing the rectification made by the Government have made the Sansei realize the uniqueness of being Japanese Americans.

There are, in particular, several aspects in which the redress movement has crystallized or reshaped the ethnic identity of the Sansei. One such aspect involves the Sansei's renewed recognition of racial discrimination against Japanese Americans and other Asian Americans. As Ochiai described, their memories of receiving verbal racial abuses in their childhood faded as they later enjoyed the general reputation of being a model minority and good performers in school. By recognizing internment as an ultimate form of racial discrimination against Japanese Americans, however, the Sansei's jigsaw pieces of memories of discrimination they had suffered in childhood resurfaced as a whole picture.

Although the discrimination they received is less institutionalized and harsh than that endured by the Nisei, the Sansei also have constantly encountered remarks about

Pearl Harbor and even more naive but routine questions and comments such as where they are from and how "good" their command of English is. These remarks indicate, at least to Japanese Americans, many Americans' ignorance of the difference between Americans of Japanese descent and Japanese nationals and their "alien" status in America even after more than three generations. Now with redress, the Sansei realize that it was this very confusion between the two different nationality groups that caused the misfortune of evacuation and internment for their parents during the Second World War. This point is supported by the following testimony given by one Sansei at the Commission hearings in 1981.

> I am a Sansei . . . born 13 years after the implementation of Executive Order 9066. But that order, with its far reaching consequences has touched my life and the impression it has left with me is what I want to share with you.
>
> . . . from the time I was old enough to attend school, people have asked me what I was. Classmates asked: "Are you Chinese? Or, are you Japanese?" Strange kids I'd never see again asked. And the answer "American" never seemed to satisfy. . . .
>
> Occasionally I've been complimented on my good command of English language. . . .
>
> As I see it, this is very like the problem we face with Executive Order 9066. It seems we have been content to accept just the fact that it happened and some of us haven't even got that far. (Jane A. Yambe, real name)[14]

Mary Waters (1990:160) points out how Asian Americans are disturbed when they are asked about their ancestry. She goes on to argue, "all ethnicities are not equal, all are not symbolic, costless, and voluntary"; Asian Americans, thus, do not have an "option" to "have a symbolic ethnicity" as White Americans do (1990:151). In encountering questions about their ancestry, the Sansei realize that outside society labels them as "Japanese" merely because of their physical differences, no matter how "American" they may behave and identify themselves as. Because of this discrepancy in reality between their own identity and outsiders' perception of them, the Sansei can relate to the racism that caused internment during the Second World War and become keenly aware of the existing racial prejudice and discrimination against their own group and other minorities in American society.

Through the redress movement, political Sansei stood up against the label of "Japs" who "bombed Pearl Harbor." Examples can be found in phrases such as "Day of Remembrance," "Remember the concentration camps" in the flyer for the 1978 Day of Remembrance event, and "I survived 9066" on T-shirts given to participants on the 1983 Day of Remembrance. The repudiation of the accusation concerning Pearl Harbor against Japanese Americans is also shown in the following testimony at the Commission hearings.

> In July 1981, John Miller of Seattle's KING-TV reported that he was flooded with responses after his commentary on the World War II internment of Japanese Americans. . . .He said that typical of the more restrained responses was the man who indignantly asked whether Japanese Americans thought that "true Americans" had forgotten Pearl Harbor. I do not know about others, but Japanese Americans have not forgotten that "day of infamy." Neither have we forgotten the years of infamy that followed Pearl

Harbor; the years when our government drove out families from their homes to concentration camps for an average term of three and half years. . . . It greeted our pioneer forebears when they immigrated to this country, and it continues, as Miller's responses indicate, to be an ugly reality for us today. (Diane Narasaki, real name)[15]

Citing the internment of United States citizens to balance the rhetoric surrounding Pearl Harbor is itself an active response to social prejudice against Japanese Americans. Through redress, pieces of their childhood memories of racial remarks and the suffering of their imprisoned forebears came to be linked together and synchronized.

The redress movement has also served to lead the Sansei to appreciate their ethnic history. The Sansei had been previously exposed to little knowledge about their ethnic history because of the Nisei's long silence and the Sansei's inability to communicate with their grandparents, most of whom spoke only Japanese with a poor command of English. Through learning about camp and observing and participating in the redress movement, they have come to understand the struggles and hardships that their forebears endured and the latter's significant achievements even after their total economic ruin due to evacuation.

Furthermore, the Sansei's perceptions of their parents and other Nisei seem to have undergone a transformation. As described earlier, the majority of the Sansei initially questioned why the Nisei "cooperated" with the evacuation order, which appears to them to be an un-American response. On the other hand, they designate the Nisei in the postwar period as 200 percent American, which implies, in a sense, that the Nisei are not typically "American" either. It is in the drive for redress that the Nisei spoke out to the public and demanded apology and monetary compensation from their own government, all which is in the tradition of American political practice. This is also true of the increased level in the Nisei's consciousness of the civil rights of other minorities, as well as their own. Furthermore, the Government's acknowledgement of its injustice to all Japanese American internees makes clear the Government's official commitment to the view that Japanese Americans should possess and enjoy United States Citizenship in the full and entire sense. For the Sansei, this acknowledgement means that, at last, their parents' generation too could be considered truly "American," morally as well as legally.

Internment and the consequent redress movement opened a new phase in the evolution of the Japanese American identity. Internment itself was an experience unique to Japanese Americans, and so was redress. Yet the process itself and means used in the quest for redress were as much symbolically American as the Government's recognition of its past inequity. In this process, pride gradually replaced past shame of the Nisei; just as the shame of the Nisei was once passed onto the Sansei, the pride of the Nisei has now been passed on to the Sansei.

While the experiences of internment and redress are unique to Japanese Americans, the process in which their ethnic identity was reformulated is not an isolated case. This empirical study of the ethnicity of the third-generation Japanese Americans has wider implications for our understanding of ethnicity and ethnic change in general. I have shown, among other things, that the feelings associated with the historical experiences of members of an ethnic group is critical for the formation of ethnicity. What De Vos calls "sense of survival" (1975) and Keyes calls "intense suffering experience of the ancestors of a people" (1981) often provide the experiential foundation for ethnic identity. These concepts serve as heuristic devices to explain the reassertion of ethnicity among Japanese Americans, as well. Among the Sansei, a history of past suffering, a shared group history that the Issei and the Nisei suffered unreasonably as "martyrs" due to the Government's injustice, has been constructed. One Sansei said that, to the Nisei, camp means "shame," and to the Sansei, it means "guilt." The belief that the Sansei's educational and economic opportunities and social status are based on their forebears' suffering, struggles, and efforts and, hence, that they owe much to their parents and grandparents has brought greater unity both to the community at large and between different generations. The formation of the history of past suffering is not unique to Japanese Americans. It is certainly true for African Americans in their slavery and for Jews with the Holocaust. In each case, affective bonds that bind the group together are based on the sense of past suffering.

This chapter has focused on the third-generation Japanese Americans. How, then, will the ethnic identity be maintained among the fourth, fifth, and forthcoming generations? It may be predictable that the ethnic history discussed here will be cherished with pride among these descendants. The degree of their continued identification with this story may depend on how strongly they feel about racial discrimination and prejudice they encounter in their own times. We will have to wait another decade or two to examine this question.

NOTES

1. Cf. William Peterson (1966). Recently, however, criticism of the "myth" of the "success story" and the idea of a "model minority" of Japanese Americans has been presented by Asian American scholars and political activists. See, for example, Bob Suzuki (1980).

2. The program automatically funds the amounts due to individual Japanese American without the yearly process of appropriation approval.

3. An average of four to five hours per person of personal interviews was conducted from 1987 to 1989 with about fifty Japanese Americans (split almost equally between the Nisei and the Sansei) in the greater Seattle area.

4. Archive materials included testimonies at the hearings conducted by the Commission on Wartime Relocation and Internment and various documents, records, and community newsletters pertinent to redress.

5. This research was funded by the Toyota Foundation from 1988 to 1989.

6. The Sansei subjects were raised and have, for most of their lives, continued to live in the greater Seattle area. They are between their late 20s and early 40s, which automatically excludes them from receiving individual payments.

7. All names, unless indicated as real names, are pseudonyms. Save for omissions, as shown with . . . , all quotations from interviews are rendered in the original.

8. According to Nagata's survey research (in press), when her respondents were asked to identify the manner in which their parents had discussed the internment, approximately 50% answered that it was mentioned as an incidental topic in passing; an additional 20% stated that it appeared in a conversation as a reference point in time; and only 30% reported that their parents discussed camp as a central topic in itself.

9. There were three Nisei men who challenged the evacuation order: Min Yasui of Port-

land, Oregon, Fred Korematsu of San Francisco, and Gordon Hirabayashi of Seattle. All three were convicted of violating the evacuation and/or curfew orders in 1942 and imprisoned.

They were finally vindicated in 1986 after disclosure of the War Department's suppression of pertinent documents at the original trials.

10. Also from personal interviews with redress leaders.

11. In July of 1981, hearings by the Commission on Wartime Relocation and Internment of Civilians started in Washington, D.C., followed in Los Angeles, San Francisco, Seattle, Unalaska, Chicago, New York, Cambridge, and then again Washington, D.C. Over 750 people, including Aleut victims of evacuation, Japanese Americans, former government officials, interested citizens, and scholars who studied the subject matter of the Commission's inquiry testified before the Commission.

12. In survey research, O'Brien and Fugita (1983) reported that 74.3% of the Sansei respondents either strongly agreed or agreed with the statement, "currently, Japanese experience discrimination in social situations."

13. On the other hand, a similar view of the Issei—that the Issei suffered more than anybody including the Nisei—is shared among the Nisei.

14. A written testimony submitted to the Commission hearings in Seattle in 1981.

15. A written testimony submitted to the Commission hearings in Seattle in 1981.

REFERENCES

Cohen, Abner (1969). *Custom and Politics in Urban Africa: Hausa Migrants in Yoruba Towns.* Berkeley: University of California Press.

Commission on Wartime Relocation and Internment of Civilians (1983). *Personal Justice Denied: Summary and Recommendations of the Commission on Wartime Relocation and Internment of Civilians.* San Francisco: Japanese American Citizens League.

De Vos, George (1975). Ethnic Pluralism: Conflict and Accommodation. Pp. 5–41 in *Ethnic Identity: Cultural Continuities and Change*, George De Vos and Lola Romanucci-Ross (eds.). Chicago: University of Chicago Press.

Despres, Leo (1967). *Cultural Pluralism and Nationalist Politics in British Guiana.* Chicago: Rand McNally.

Geertz, Clifford (1963). The Integrative Revolution: Primordial Sentiments and Civil Politics in the New States. Pp. 105–57 in *Old Societies and New States*, Clifford Geertz (ed.). New York: Free Press.

Isaacs, Harold (1975). *Idols of the Tribe, Group Identity and Political Change.* New York: Harper and Row.

Kashima, Tetsuden (1980). Japanese American Internees Return, 1945 to 1955: Readjustment and Social Amnesia. *Phylon* 41:2: 107–115.

Keyes, Charles F. (1981). The Dialectics of Ethnic Change. Pp. 4–30 in *Ethnic Change*, Charles F. Keyes (ed.). Seattle: University of Washington Press.

Maykovich, Minake K. (1972). *Japanese American Identity Dilemma.* Tokyo: Waseda University Press.

Mass, Amy Iwasaki (1986). Psychological Effects of the Camps on the Japanese Americans. Pp. 159–162 in *Japanese Americans: From Relocation to Redress*, Roger Daniels, Sandra C. Taylor, and Harry H. L. Kitano (eds.). Salt Lake City: University of Utah Press.

Morishima, James (1973). The Evacuation: Impact on the Family. Pp. 13–19 in *Asian-Americans: Psychological Perspectives*, Stanley Sue and Nathaniel Wagner (eds.). Palo Alto: Science and Behavior Books.

Nagata, Donna K. (1989). Long-term Effects of the Japanese American Internment Camps: Impact upon the Children of the Internees. *Journal of Asian American Psychological Association* 13: 48–55.

O'Brien, David J., and Stephen S. Fugita (1983). Generational Differences in Japanese Americans' Perceptions and Feelings about Social Relationships between Themselves and Caucasian Americans. Pp. 223–240 in *Culture, Ethnicity, and Identity*, William C. McCready (ed.). New York: Academic Press.

Peterson, William (1966). Success Story, Japanese-American Style. *New York Times*, January 9, 1966.

Spicer, Edward (1971). Persistent Cultural Systems: A Comparative Study of Identity Systems That Can Adapt to Contrasting Environments. *Science* 174: 795–800.

Suzuki, Bob (1980). Education and Socialization of Asian Americans: A Revisionist Analysis of the Model Minority Thesis. Pp. 155–175 in *Asian-Americans: Social and Psychological Perspectives Vol. II*. Russell Endo, Stanley Sue, and Nathaniel Wagner (eds.). Palo Alto: Science and Behavior Books.

Takezawa, Yasuko, I. (1989a). *"Breaking the Silence": Ethnicity and the Quest for Redress Among Japanese Americans*. Unpublished dissertation. Seattle: University of Washington.

Takezawa, Yasuko, I. (1989b). *Nikkei Amerika-jin ni okeru Dento no Soshutsu to Ethnicity* ("The Invention of Tradition" and Ethnicity Among Japanese Americans.) *Shikyo* (En Marge de l'Histoire) 19: 53–66, 98–99. Tsukuba, Japan.

Tateishi, John (1986). The Japanese American Citizens League and the Struggle for Redress. Pp. 191–195 in *Japanese Americans: From Relocation to Redress*; Roger Daniels, Sandra C. Taylor and Harry H. L. Kitano (eds.). Salt Lake City: University of Utah Press.

Waters, Mary C. (1990). *Ethnic Options*. Berkeley: University of California Press.

Chapter Twelve

Social Capital in Chinatown
The Role of Community-Based Organizations and Families in the Adaptation of the Younger Generation

Min Zhou

Chinese Americans are by far the largest subgroup of Asian Americans. As a direct result of the liberalization of the U.S. immigration law in 1965, which abolished the national quotas system, they have become one of the fastest-growing minority groups in the United States. Over the past fifty years, their numbers have increased fifteen times. Between 1970 and 1990, in particular, the number of Chinese Americans more than tripled, from 435,062 to 1,645,472. Much of this growth has been attributed to immigration. According to the U.S. Immigration and Naturalization Service (1991), a total number of 682,755 immigrants were admitted to the United States from China, Hong Kong, and Taiwan as permanent residents between 1971 and 1990. The 1990 U.S. Census also attests to the big part played by immigration: foreign-born persons account for 69.8 percent of Chinese Americans nationwide and 78.7 percent in New York City.

Parallel to the rapid growth in sheer numbers is the extraordinarily high educational achievement of immigrant Chinese and their offspring. In recent years, Chinese American children have scored exceptionally high in standardized tests, have been overrepresented in the nation's most prestigious high schools and universities, and have disproportionately made the top lists of many national or regional academic contests. They have, for example, appeared repeatedly in the top-ten award winners' list of the Westinghouse Science Talent Search, one of the country's most prestigious high school academic contests. In 1991, four of the top ten winners were Chinese Americans. Although fewer than a third of Chinese American school-aged children were born outside the United States, a majority of them grew up in immigrant households. Why are younger-generation Chinese Americans so well adapted to U.S. society? Into what specific social contexts are they adapting? How do their community and families affect their adaptational experience? This chapter attempts to address these questions by focusing on the role of community-based organizations and families in New York City's Chinatown.

Chinatown: The Basis of Social Capital

Adaptation to the U.S. society is a complex process depending not only upon individual motivation and abilities but also upon specific contexts of reception. Preexisting ethnic communities represent the most immediate dimension of the context of reception (Portes and Rumbaut 1990), serving as the basis of a unique form of social capital to facilitate immigrant adaptation. This social capital is defined as "expectations for action within a collectivity that affect the economic goals and goal-seeking behavior of its members, even if these expectations are not oriented toward the economic sphere" (Portes and Sensenbrenner 1993), or as closed systems of social networks in a community, which allow parents to "establish norms and reinforce each other's sanctioning of the children" (Coleman 1990). In fact, the social capital thesis touches on one of the oldest sociological theories, Durkheim's theory of social integration. Durkheim maintains that individual behavior should be seen as the product of the degree of integration of individuals in their society (Durkheim 1951). The greater the integration of individuals into a social group, the greater the control of the group over the individual. In the context of immigrant adaptation, children who are more highly integrated into their ethnic group are likely to follow the forms of behavior prescribed by the group, such as studying or working hard, and to avoid the forms of behavior proscribed by the group.

If ethnic communities are interpreted in terms of social capital, it becomes possible to suggest a mechanism by which the adherence to community-based support systems and positive cultural orientations can provide an adaptive advantage for immigrants and their offspring in their strive to achieve their goals in American society. However, this mechanism is never stagnant; it constantly accommodates changes in the process of immigration. Social capital should thus be treated as "a process," rather than as a concrete object, that facilitates access to benefits and resources (Fernandez-Kelly 1995) that best suit the goals of specific immigrant groups. Chinatown, with its networks of support and social control mechanisms, serves as a prime example for understanding the meaning of social capital.

New York City's Chinatown started as a bachelors' society at the turn of the century. By the 1940s, Chinatown, still a bachelors' shelter with a sex ratio of 603 men per 100 women, had grown into a ten-block enclave, accommodating almost all Chinese immigrants in the city. The old-timers were motivated by a sojourning goal of making a fortune in America and returning home with "gold." They left their families behind in China and were drawn to this community by extensive kinship networks. During the time when legal and institutional exclusion set barriers and American society made available few options of life to these Chinese sojourners, they had to isolate themselves socially in Chinatown and to work at odd jobs that few Americans wanted. Since they had no families with them and had no intention to stay for a long time, they built Chinatown initially as a place of refuge that resembled home. In Old Chinatown, immigrant workers could speak their own language, eat their own food, play their own games, exchange news from home, and share common experiences with fellow countrymen day in and day out. The level of social interaction was fairly high through various tongs (merchants' associations) and kinship or family associations (Kuo 1977; Wong 1979).

After World War II, the bachelors' society began to dissolve when Chinese women were allowed into the United States to join their husbands and families. Resulting from the repeal of the Chinese Exclusion Act and passage of the War Bride Act, immigrant Chinese women composed more than half of the postwar arrivals from China. However, the number of Chinese immigrants entering the United States each year was quite small because the annual quota was set at 105 (Sung 1987). After 1965, when Congress amended the immigration law abolishing the national origins quota system, the number of Chinese in New York City increased rapidly, from 33,000 in 1960 to 240,014 in 1990.

As Chinese immigrants and their families pour into New York City, Old Chinatown has undergone a series of dramatic transformations. These transformations have been physical, social, and economic. Once confined to a ten-block area in Lower East Manhattan, Chinatown has expanded in all directions beyond its traditional boundaries, taking over decaying neighborhoods and giving rise to "satellite" Chinatowns in Queens and Brooklyn (Zhou 1992). Unlike the old-timers who were predominantly from rural Canton, immigrant Chinese in recent years have come from other parts of mainland China, Hong Kong, Taiwan, and elsewhere in Asia and Latin America. Upon arrival, they have tended to bypass Old Chinatown in Manhattan to settle in outer boroughs. Immigrants from mainland China have been fairly evenly distributed across Manhattan, Queens, and Brooklyn; those from Hong Kong have tended to reside in Queens or Brooklyn; and those from Taiwan have overwhelmingly concentrated in Queens. Cantonese is no longer the sole language spoken in Chinatowns. In newly established Chinatowns such as the one in Flushing, Queens, Mandarin is now the most commonly used language among immigrant Chinese.

Today's Chinese Americans in New York City have become more diverse in their socioeconomic backgrounds than the earlier arrivals, who were uniformly unskilled laborers. According to the 1990 U.S. Census, immigrant Chinese born in Taiwan displayed the highest proportion of college graduates (four times as high as the U.S. average), the highest proportion of workers in professional specialty occupations, and the highest median household income compared to those born in mainland China, Hong Kong, and other countries. Mainland-born Chinese were the most disadvantaged, except for their citizenship status. Fewer than half of them showed proficiency in English; fewer than half had completed high school; and only 13.8 percent held professional occupations. Their median household income was at least $7,000 less than that of their counterparts born elsewhere. In contrast, U.S.-born Chinese showed exceptionally high levels of educational and occupational achievements. However, regardless of differences in socioeconomic status, over 80 percent of Chinese spoke a language other than English at home, indicating that not only immigrants but also the younger generation lived in a bilingual environment.

Recent immigrant Chinese are not only more diverse than earlier arrivals, they also come with goals that are vastly different from those of the old-timers, who were here to sojourn rather than to settle and assimilate. They are characterized by their strong desire to become integrated into the mainstream society and to make America their new home. Many of them have immigrated to the United States to secure their already well-established lives and, more importantly, to provide their children with a future without fear and uncertainty, in which the children can realize their full potential. The demands of immigrant Chinese for speeding up the process of assimilation have brought about important changes in the economic and social structures of Chinatown.

Since 1965, the stereotypical Chinatown has been withering away, and a full-fledged family community with a strong ethnic economy has gradually and steadily taken its place. During the 1930s and 1940s, Chinatown's ethnic economy was highly concentrated in restaurant and laundry businesses. By the 1970s, the laundry business had shrunk substantially and had been replaced by the garment industry, which has become one of the backbone industries in Chinatown. Today, the garment industry, estimated at over 500 factories run by Chinese entrepreneurs, provides jobs for more than 20,000 immigrant Chinese, mostly women. It is estimated that three out of five immigrant Chinese women in Chinatown work in the garment industry. The restaurant business, another backbone industry in Chinatown, has continued to grow and prosper. Listed restaurants run by Chinese grew from 304 in 1958 to 781 in 1988, employing at least 15,000 immigrant Chinese workers (Kwong 1987; Zhou and Logan 1989). In addition to garment and restaurant businesses, various industries, ranging from grocery stores, import/export companies, barber shops, and beauty salons to such professional services as banks, law firms, financial, insurance, and real estate agencies, and doctors' and herbalists' clinics also experienced tremendous growth. These ethnic economies have created ample job opportunities for immigrant Chinese and have provided convenient and easy alternatives to meet ethnically specific consumer demands.

Changes in Chinatown's economic structure have had a lasting impact on the adaptation of the younger generation. On the one hand, jobs made available in ethnic economies and goods and services provided by the community tend to tie immigrant Chinese and their offspring to Chinatown despite spatial dispersion. These ties have directly or indirectly broadened the base of ethnic interaction and thus increased the degree of ethnic cohesion, which in turn sustains a sense of identity, community, and ethnic solidarity. On the other hand, despite the low wages and long working hours typical of many jobs in Chinatown, immigrants take pride in being able to work for and support their families. The work ethic and the capacity for delayed gratification in parents is explicitly or implicitly passed on to children, who are expected by their parents to appreciate the value of schooling as a means to move out of Chinatown. Moreover, the prosperity of ethnic economies in Chinatown offers material support for the establishment and operation of many community-based voluntary organizations. These community-based organizations, in turn, furnish a protective social environment, which shields off adversaries, such as drugs, crime, teenage pregnancies, prevalent in inner-city poor neighborhoods where immigrants tend to concentrate, and provides them with access to resources that can help them move ahead in mainstream American society.

The Changing Role of Community-Based Organizations

The transformation of Chinatown from a bachelors' society into a family-oriented community has increased the number and broadened the role of community organizations. The rapid change in the nature of Chinese immigration has created pressing demands for services associated with resettlement and adjustment problems which have overwhelmed the ability of the existing traditional organizations (Sung 1987). To accommodate these changes, traditional organizations have been pressured to redefine their role, and various new organizations have been established in Chinatown. By glancing at one of the Chinese business directories, for example, one can easily come up with a list of over 100 voluntary associations, sixty-one community service organizations, forty-one community-based employment agencies, sixteen daycare centers, twenty-seven career training schools, twenty-eight Chinese and English language schools, and nine dancing and music schools (Chinatown Today Publishing 1993—note that the actual number of community organizations in Chinatown was approximately twice as many as this list because many were not listed in this particular directory). Most of these organizations are located in Manhattan's Chinatown; some are located in new satellite Chinatowns in Flushing and Sunset Park.

In Old Chinatown, family or clan associations and merchants' associations (tongs) were the major community-based organizations. These organizations functioned primarily to meet the basic needs of fellow countrymen, such as helping workers obtain employment and offering different levels of social support, and to organize economic activities. Powerful tongs controlled most of the economic resources in the community and were oriented toward shielding Chinatown from outsiders and preserving the status quo within the community (Kuo 1977). Some of the tongs capitalized on the demands of the sojourning Chinese, mostly males, by running brothels, opium dens, and gambling parlors. Because of the illicit nature of some of the tongs' operations, Chinatown was often stereotyped as an unruly den of vice and co-ethnic exploitation, and immigrant Chinese as inassimilable aliens with an imputed "filthy" and "immoral" second nature.

The single most important social organization was the Chinese Consolidated Benevolent Association (CCBA). The CCBA was established as an apex group representing some sixty organizations in Chinatown, including different family and district associations, the guilds, the tongs, the Chamber of Commerce, and the Nationalist Party, and it operated as an unofficial government in Chinatown (Sung 1987, 42–46). The CCBA was mainly controlled by tongs but cooperated with all voluntary association (Kuo 1977).

While traditional organizations functioned to secure the standing of Chinatown in the larger society and to provide a refuge for sojourning laborers, some of them formed underground societies to profit from such illicit activities as partitioning territories, extortion for business protection, gambling, prostitution, and drugs (Dillon 1962; Kuo 1977; Sung 1987). Tong wars were frequent, and youth gangs, consisting almost entirely of immigrants, arose as tongs needed lookouts for raids, guards, escorts, and debt collectors (Sung 1987). Although youth gangs come and go, they have formed a disruptive segment of the community to which new immigrant youth, mainly boys, are extremely vulnerable.

Since the 1960s, as the community has become more and more family oriented, the concerns and needs of community members have broadened and diversified. Not only do the immigrants themselves have strong desires to integrate into American society, they overwhelmingly expect their children to become successful. Many immigrants have experienced considerable downward mobility, but they accept the sacrifices to win better futures for their children. The more diversified resettlement concerns and needs of newcomers have pressured Chinatown's traditional social organizations to change and expand. To appeal to new immigrants and their families, the CCBA has established a Chinese language school, an adult English evening school, and a career training center and has instituted a variety of social service programs, including employment referral and job training services.

The CCBA-operated New York Chinese School is perhaps the largest children- and youth-oriented organization in Chinatown. The school has annually (not including summer) enrolled about 4,000 Chinese children, from preschool to 12th grade, in their 137 Chinese language classes and over ten specialty classes (e.g., band, choir, piano, cello, violin, T'ai chi, *ikebana*, dancing, and Chinese painting). The Chinese language classes run from 3:00 to 6:30 P.M. daily after regular school hours. Students usually spend one hour on regular school homework and two hours on Chinese language or other selected specialties. The school also has English classes for immigrant youth and adult immigrant workers.

The Chinese-American Planning Council (CPC) is another important organization that has been established since the late 1960s in Chinatown. Although not as influential and deeply rooted in Chinatown as the CCBA, the CPC has utilized a grass-root community effort and has managed to draw upon government funds to provide services to immigrant Chinese. The CPC's mission is to provide "access to services, skills and resources toward the goal of economic self sufficiency and integration into the American mainstream" (CPC 1993).

During the 1970s, the CPC, then the Chinatown Planning Council, initiated a number of youth-targeted programs, such as drug-prevention, outreach, and various recreational programs to help immigrant children and youth to adapt to their new environment. These programs targeted high-risk youth not only by offering counseling and opportunities for young people to voice their concerns and problems but also by providing recreational activities, such as renting places where they could read, party, and play pool, video or ballgames and furnishing free field trips, shows, and museum visits (Kuo 1977). Most of these programs have continued, expanded, and diversified into the 1990s.

In 1995, the CPC has three branch offices in the Lower East Side of Manhattan, Sunset Park, Brooklyn, and Flushing, Queens. It is operating over forty programs, including twelve daycare services, eight youth programs, and seventeen multiservice programs associated with youth. Within each of the programs, there are various subprograms. For example, the Manhattan branch of the CPC-Youth Program offers five specific services to young people, especially those from low-income families, including the career educational program, after-school ESL classes, the theater workshop, and in-school counseling. The main purpose of the CPC's youth-oriented programs is to enhance new immigrant students' well-being, class attendance, and academic performance and, in turn, to prevent students from dropping out of school and to help them become aware of future educational opportunities and career options.

In addition to large, well-established organizations such as the CCBA and the CPC, many smaller voluntary organizations have been established to address concerns and demands of new immigrants and their children. The Chinatown History Museum (CHM), a community-based, member-supported organization, was established in 1980 primarily as a history project for reclaiming, preserving, and sharing Chinese American history and culture with a broad audience. The museum offers historical walking tours, lectures, readings, symposia, workshops, and family events year-round, not only to Chinese Americans but also to the general public. The museum also provides school programs for grades K to 12, guided and self-guided visits for college-level students, and a variety of videotapes, slide presentations, and exhibits.

Recently, the CHM has formed the Exhibition Planning Student Committee, depending mainly on voluntary efforts of Chinese American students, to create a permanent exhibition entitled "Who's Chinese American?" The purpose of the museum in mobilizing student volunteers is to stimulate input from the second generation and to incorporate the experiences of children of immigrants, in addition to the more widely recognized experiences of the old-timers, into Chinese American history. The Student Committee has attracted an increasing number of concerned Chinese American youth. For example, at their first meeting, organizers only expected a handful of students, but some forty students showed up despite a citywide social event, a dance party for high school students, happening the same evening.

Ethnic religious institutions have also played an important role in helping immigrants adjust to life in the United States. In the larger Chinese community in New York City, the number of churches or temples has doubled since 1965 including over eighty churches and eighteen Buddhist and Taoist temples, about three-quarters of which are located in Manhattan's Chinatown. While Buddhist and Taoist temples tend to attract adults, including some college students and the elderly, Christian churches generally have well-established after-school youth programs, in addition to their regular Sunday Bible classes. The Youth Center of the Chinese Christian Herald Crusade, for example, has established an after-school program and an ongoing intensive program for high-risk youth. Located conveniently across from a public high school in Chinatown, the Youth Center annually provides services to about 200 high school students, most of whom are immigrant youth. The center's after-school program, which is preventive in orientation, offers tutoring, counseling, and language aid to students whose major adjustment problem is English.

Since 1992, the center has started a small, intensive, crisis-oriented program for high-risk youth, referred to or sent to the center either by parents or by social workers. This crisis-oriented program is aimed at youth who frequently play truant and "hang out" with other truants on streets or in video game shops. According to the center director, "these kids have serious adjustment problems besides language.

Since they are not interested in school, we have to approach them differently. Our purpose is not to brainwash them but to influence them with compassion, sympathy, and understanding, and to help them find their own selves." The crisis-oriented program offers daily escorts to participants from home to school, organizes basketball games on Saturdays, and arranges weekend overnight trips.

The center also runs a summer camp in upstate New York, where "problem" youth are offered a free four-week camp in exchange for their help with maintenance, cleanup, and landscaping work in the camp. During their stay at the summer camp, youth are also given the opportunity to voice their concerns and feelings in voluntary study groups. "It is very important to allow youth to express themselves in their own terms without parental pressures. Chinese parents usually have very high expectations of their children. When children find it difficult to meet these expectations and do not have an outlet for their frustration and anxiety, they tend to become alienated and lost on streets." The center director estimated that over half of these participants had shown improvement in their school attendance and that at least half of them had become Christian after a two-year intensive involvement in the program.

Social organizations in Chinatown, whether they are formal or informal, government funded or community rooted, have played a vital role in meeting the social and economic needs of the Chinese community. Interviews with community leaders, organizers, and activists indicate that the functions of new community organizations specific to the younger generation are many-fold. Instrumentally, community organizations provide a safe, healthy, and stimulating environment where youngsters, especially those whose parents are at work, can go after school. The after-school programs not only ensure the time spent on homework or on other constructive activities but also help to keep children off the streets and to reduce the anxieties and worries of working parents.

These organizations also serve as bridges between a closed immigrant community and the mainstream society. Immigrant children and youth growing up in Chinatown are relatively isolated. Their daily exposure to the larger American society is limited; they generally come from low-income families, live in crowded housing, attend inner-city public schools, walk on streets surrounding primarily by small, family-based businesses, and are vulnerable to ghetto youth subcultures. Their parents, usually too busy working just to make ends meet, tend to expect their children to do well in school and to have successful careers in the future, but the parents are unable to give specific directions to their children's educational and career plans, leaving a gap between high expectations and realistically feasible means of meeting these expectations. Community-based organizations fill this gap in helping young people to become more aware of their choices and potentials and to find realistic means of moving up socioeconomically into mainstream society instead of being stuck in Chinatown.

Culturally, these organizations function as ethnic centers, where Chinese traditional values and a sense of ethnic identity are nurtured. Students participating in the after-school programs, especially the U.S.-born and-reared, often speak English to one another in their Chinese classes, and they actually learn a limited number of Chinese words each day. However, they are exposed to something which is quite different from what they learn in school and are able to relate to Chinese "stuff" without being teased about it. They also listen to stories and sing songs in Chinese, which reveal different aspects of Chinese history and culture. Children and youth learn to write in Chinese such phrases as "I am Chinese," "My home country is in China" and to recite classical Chinese poems and Confucius sayings about family values, behavioral and moral guidelines, and the importance of schooling. A Chinese school principal made it clear that "these kids are here because their parents sent them. They are usually not very motivated in learning Chinese per se, and we do not push them too hard. Language teaching is only part of our mission. An essential part of our mission is to enlighten these kids about their own cultural heritage, so that they show respect for their parents and feel proud of being Chinese."

A latent function of these community organizations is that they create a common bond between immigrants, their children, and the community at large. Participation in after-school programs enables not only children but also their parents to directly interact with each other and with the community. The increasing contact among co-ethnic members and with the community can strengthen the social networks in a community. The involvement in the community-based organizations not only enables parents to establish norms and reinforce each other's sanctioning of the children but also provides some space where children and youth can express themselves, easing intergenerational conflicts. In this sense, community organizations furnish resources of support and direction that promote value consensus and behavioral conformity among individual families and build bridges between immigrant, often non-English-speaking, parents and their U.S.-born or-reared children. Next, we discuss the role of the family in the adaptation of second-generation immigrants.

The Family: Values, Behavioral Standards, and Expectations

The 1965 amendment to the U.S. Immigration and Naturalization Act, which emphasizes family reunification, has provided the end link to a system of chain migration. Because 80 percent of the quota is allocated to relatives, post-1965 Chinese immigrants are not only vertically (spouses, parents, and children) but also horizontally (brothers and sisters and their immediate families) related to their sponsors within an extended family network. This family-chain migration suggests that, unlike the old-timers who intended to return to China, the newcomers are here to stay and to assimilate (although much of the assimilation may take place through the children) into U.S. society. As a result, the base of the kinship structure in Chinatown has been broadened (Sung 1987).

Chinese immigrants arriving after 1965 have mostly been family-sponsored immigrants, about 75 percent of whom were admitted as immediate family members (spouses, unmarried children, and parents) or as close relatives (married children, brothers, or sisters of U.S. citizens). Some 20 percent have been employment-based immigrants (whose admission was sponsored by a U.S. employer). Consequently, about 80 percent of the Chinese in New York City live in married-couple households, and only 5 percent live in female-headed households. The family has stabilized the community and become the most important institution, furnishing an immediate source of social capital for facilitating the adaptation of immigrant children to American society in a unique way.

In New York City, as in other parts of the United States, the majority of Chinese American youngsters grow up in intact families. However, the socioeconomic status of Chinese families varies by length of stay since immigration. Based on the 1990 U.S. Census, only 15 percent of the children had parents who were U.S.-born or immigrated before 1965, about 40 percent of them had parents who immigrated between 1965 and 1979, and 46 percent of them had parents who immigrated after 1980. Among these three groups, children of post-1980 immigrant parents were more likely to reside in Brooklyn, children of immigrant parents arriving between 1965 and 1979 disproportionately resided in Queens, and children of U.S.-born or pre-1965 immigrant parents were geographically dispersed throughout the city. The proportion of female-headed households was generally low for all three groups. Children of post-1980 immigrant parents tended to live in the homes where Chinese was spoken, and most lived in linguistically isolated neighborhoods. This residential pattern implied that children from post-1980 immigrant families were the most isolated group and had the least exposure [to] the larger society.

The economic gap between the three groups was fairly large. Close to two-thirds of the children of most recent immigrant parents lived in rental housing, whereas almost two-thirds of the children of U.S.-born or pre-1965 immigrant parents lived in owner-occupied housing. Moreover, children of post-1980 immigrant parents were most economically disadvantaged, with a poverty rate of 27 percent, more than four times as high as that among children of U.S.-born or pre-1965 immigrant parents. Furthermore, parents who immigrated after 1980 had much lower levels of education, were less likely to be in executive or professional occupations, and had much lower average earnings comparing to parents who immigrated earlier or who were U.S.-born. However, regardless of the length of stay since immigration, most of these parents were married and stayed married and were employed full time. Dependence on public assistance was uncommon among them.

Despite socioeconomic variations, Chinese American families, no matter how integrated they may be into the larger society, do not function in isolation. They are embedded in a long-standing cultural tradition and in the social structure of the larger Chinese American community. Comparing the Chinese American family to the traditional Chinese family, Betty Lee Sung (1987, chapter 7) has specified several distinctive characteristics of the Chinese American family. First, the Chinese family in the United States carries a long history of dismemberment, where immigrant men crossed the Pacific to seek fortunes, leaving their parents, wives, and children behind in China. After 1965, family reunification has been in relays, generally with the men arriving much earlier and wives and children arriving at later times. Consequently, many immigrant families have suffered varied length of family separation, and, once reunited, they have to adapt to the norm of the nuclear family. Second, women in Chinese American families have taken a more independent role than they did in the traditional family; working outside the home has become a norm and an economic necessity for women in Chinatown. The work role gives women some measures of power and makes them less exclusively dependent upon their husbands. Third, the size of a Chinese American family is generally much smaller, with an age gap between children and with older children who are foreign-born. Fourth, kinship or clan ties become weakened in the process of migration, and face-to-face interaction among family members decreases as both men and women are out working for long hours.

However, the Chinese American family remains culturally distinct from the mainstream American family despite the alterations specified above. The Chinese American family has not simply retained its "Chineseness" but has also incorporated a set of characteristics associated with adaptational strategies for coping with uprooting and assimilation. While assimilation is the ultimate goal for the Chinese American family, parents are constantly caught in the conflict between maintenance of cultural identity in children and the adoption of desirable mainstream cultural ways.

In general, the Chinese American family has continued to be influenced by Confucianism. Confucianism emphasizes traditional values, such as ancestor worship, a respect for authority (e.g., the ruler, the elder, the parent, and the teacher), a belief in consensus, a willingness to put society's or the family's interests before the individual's interest, an emphasis on education as a means of mobility, clear rules of conduct, constant self-examination, and the importance of face saving. These values have been carried over to America with few modifications and have been essential for the Chinese American family to socialize the younger generation.

For the younger generation, obedience, hard work, and success in school are matter-of-fact expectations. These values and family expectations are not only instilled in individual families but also reinforced in the Chinese community. Illustrative are some of the most common adult-child greetings observed in the homes, streets, and restaurants in Chinatown. Parents frequently greet children with, "How was school?" "Did you behave in school today?" "Have you got your grades yet? How good are they?" or "Have you done your homework?" Relatives or adult family friends often greet children with, "Have you been obeying your parents?" "Have you been good?" "Have you been working hard in school?" "Have you been making good grades?" These simple everyday adult-child greetings reflect the Chinese values of obedience, respect, hard work, and education, and children are expected to give positive answers. As a continuation of the long-standing Chinese tradition, Confucius values have been transplanted to America and become the normative behavioral standards in Chinese American families. Deviation from these standards is considered shameful or "face lost" and thus sanctioned by the family and the community.

Specifically, we can summarize the following distinctive characteristics of the Chinese American family. First, Chinese parents believe that discipline and hard work, rather than natural ability or innate intelligence, are the keys to educational success. Regardless of socioeconomic backgrounds, they tend to think (also tend to make their children believe) that their children can all get A's in their tests in school if they are disciplined and hard working. Many folk tales make the point that diligence can achieve any goal, such as the tale of a woman who ground a piece of iron by hand into a needle and that of an old man who removed a mountain with just a hoe. There is also a saying that dullness can be overcome by industriousness.

Because of the cultural influence, Chinese children are pushed to work at least twice as hard as their American counterparts, which has indeed brought about remarkable results. A downside of this cultural emphasis, however, is that Chinese parents tend to be less sensitive than American parents to individual ability of their children, such as varied degrees in their ability to master English, to adjust to the new school and social environments, and to interact effectively with teachers and fellow students. Children fear their parents and are hesitant to discuss these problems with them. Even if they do, they may be misunderstood as "finding excuses for being lazy."

Second, unlike the American family, which emphasizes individual responsibilities, the Chinese American family values collective responsibilities. The success of children in school is very much tied to face saving for the family. Parents themselves are expected to bring up their children in ways that honor the family. In Chinatown, one frequently hears parents brag about their children's success but seldom hears them talk about problems. Children are constantly reminded that if they fail, they will bring shame to the family. According to several school counselors, this collective orientation works both ways. On the one hand, children's education is given priority with social and material support from their family and community, and children are pushed to their full potential, which contribute to their success. On the other hand, however, children act like "little adults," sacrificing the opportunities of being children, exploring and developing their own selves (Sung 1987, 91).

Third, the parent-child relationship in Chinese American families tends to be more formal and rigid and less emotionally expressive than the mainstream family. Chinese culture emphasizes submission to authority. The parent is the authority in the home, as is the teacher in the school. The parent, often the father, is not supposed to show too much affection, to play with children, or to treat children as equals. The stone-faced authoritative image of the parent often inhibits children from questioning, much less challenging, their parents. Moreover, there is a general lack of demonstrative affection in the Chinese American family, which applies not only to children but to the spouse and friends as well. Chinese parents are not expected to show emotions or express love in a direct way. Children rarely hear their parents say, "I love you." They seldom receive kisses or hugs from their parents in public. In a culture where physical intimacy and affection are publicly displayed, children tend to feel deprived and to interpret the lack of demonstrative affection as, "My parents don't love me" (Sung 1987, 116). Therefore, while parental authority effectively reinforces behavioral standards, which are constructive to the adaptation of children to school, it intensifies cultural conflicts and thus increases the level of anxiety in children.

Fourth, most of the Chinese American families have both parents working. Working parents, particularly those in immigrant families, tend to work long hours each day, six days a week. Although parents are very concerned about their children's schooling, they have very little time to be physically involved, to help their children with their homework, much less to talk with them or play with them. Moreover, the contact between school and parents is minimal, not because parents do not want to get involved but because they can't find time and their English is not proficient enough for such contact. Some children do not even bother to pass teachers' notes to their parents about conference arrangements or participation in school events. Or they simply pass the notes to their parents and then say, "Never mind. I know you can't go."

Many immigrant parents are struggling for survival in the hope that their children will appreciate their hard work and repay them by doing well in school. Many children do understand the pain and struggle their parents have had to endure. One teenager wrote in her essay at school,

> [Our] ancestors came to this country hoping to make a better life for themselves and generations thereafter. Although they did not find much gold or money in the "Gold Mountain" at first, they succeeded in staying together and making their children's lives and grand-children's lives a much easier one to endure.[1]

Still, long working hours and exhaustion from work make some parents overlook the specific needs of their children. When serious problems occur, they are surprised and puzzled. A parent reacted with shock and disappointment after learning that his child had been absent from school for more than a week, "I don't understand why this has happened. He never mentioned to me that he didn't like school. I work, and work, and work. For what? Isn't it just for my boy to be able to finish high school and to go to college? I have given him everything I can possibly afford. What else does he want?" The bilingual counselor in school explained, "This parent apparently did not understand what his child really wanted." According to this counselor, many Chinatown children are aware of their parents' expectations and try to meet them.[2] However, they encounter a lot of adjustment problems daily in school, such as language difficulties, inability to express themselves, frequent teasing or harassment by other students because of their different look, accent, and dress, misunderstanding by the teacher or fellow students, and they fear to bring these problems up at the dinner table for fear that their parents will get upset or blame them. When their problems are unaddressed, they become discouraged, and discouragement is sometimes followed by loss of interest, dropping grades, and dropping out of school.

In sum, the Chinese culture in which the family is embedded is a double-edged sword. While it provides specific goals, behavioral guidelines, and a social basis of support to facilitate adaptation of immigrant children to school and the society, it does not always deal adequately with the problems facing the younger generation. In Chinatown, however, voluntary organizations have started to address the new challenges by initiating family-oriented programs. The CPC, for example, has several ongoing programs, providing services to immigrant families, including crisis-prevention, parental skills, counseling, referral, and family recreational activities. In this sense, the community and the families are connected to establish a unique social context in which the younger generation is brought up. Next, we take a close look at this younger generation.

The Young Generation: The Process of Becoming American

Although Chinese American children are generally considered by public school teachers to be well adjusted, motivated, hard working, disciplined, and respectful, they are burdened with a number of bicultural and adjustment problems, including issues of identity, perceptions of parental affection, conflicting values and behavioral standards, the gang subculture, and the problem of achieving. The question of "Who am I?" or "Who's Chinese American?" is sometimes ambiguous among children of Chinese immigrants. The following is an excerpt from a student paper that reflects the feelings of many Chinese American children:

> His ten minute long speech [at a family dinner table] was apparently comprehensible to all but my parents and me. I watched my cousins' attentive faces with interest as my great uncle spoke. I know that to them, what I spoke was the foreign language. I was amazed that I was in a room with twenty-five relatives, and felt like such an outsider. When my uncle was finished and dared to release his grasp of the table to fall quite gracefully back into his seat, everyone exchanged cheers in Chinese. I just smiled back at every one as they addressed me, and for the first time, I saw myself through their eyes. I saw an Americanized teenager who had casted off her Chinese identity in order to conform more to American ways. Suddenly, I became aware of overwhelming feelings of guilt, anger and confusion ... These conflicting emotions threw me into a state of confusion and wonder, a confusion and wonder I have yet to figure out.[3]

Apparently, growing up in America is a difficult process for children of immigrants, as they are constantly torn between conflicting cultural goals and demands at home and in the larger society. An immediate bicultural conflict in the Chinese American family is the difference in the perception of affection between parents and children. As discussed in the previous section, parent-child relationships in immigrant Chinese families are not as emotionally expressive as those in American families. In the countries of origin, Chinese children are socialized into this pattern of relationships and seldom feel deprived. Since immigrant children, even those who are isolated in the enclave, are increasingly exposed to the television, movies, magazines, books, and the popular culture, they become aware of the different ways of expressing affection in different families and tend to interpret their parents' way as insufficient (Sung 1987). A Chinatown teenager recalled, "My mom never kissed me 'good night' or said 'I love you.' When I told her what American moms did, she answered, 'We Chinese don't do it this way.' For a long time, I felt that I was not loved." While this particular pattern of parent-child interaction may help maintain parental authority, the cost is often an emotional detachment from parents and a reduction of communication with parents on the part of the children.

Another cultural dilemma in which immigrant Chinese children often find themselves is that of conflicting values and behavioral standards. First, immigrant Chinese families tend to rely on the value of thrift as an important means of achieving future goals. In immigrant Chinese families, where parents are struggling to make ends meet and to attempt to save as much money as possible for the future—buying a home, opening up a small business, and sending children to college—children are taught the values of thrift and the importance of saving. However, influenced by the mass media and the larger consumer market, immigrant children tend to pick up quickly what is "in," or what is "cool," which is unquestionably at odds with the Chinese cultural value of thrift.

Parents bluntly reject material possessions and conspicuous consumption on the part of children and perceive spending money on name brand clothes, luxurious accessories, and fashionable hairstyles as a sign of corruption, which they often term as becoming "too American." Commonly heard from parents are, "You shouldn't have spent $35 on this stupid haircut when you can spend $5 on a much nicer cut"; "How can you spend like this when you don't even know how to make money?" "What if you had a family to feed?" When they do work, immigrant Chinese children are expected to hand over the wages to their parents.

In an interview with a group of eighth and ninth graders who participated in one of the youth programs in Chinatown, the young people indicated that their major concerns were the lack of spending money and the lack of understanding from their parents. "My mother didn't care what people think of me," said a fourteen-year-old boy. "She used to force me to wear a jacket, which she bought two years ago from China and which had become too small for me, not to mention the outdated style and the kiddy patterns. She would say to me, 'It still fits and you can wear it for another spring.' I was so embarrassed that I took it off and packed it in my book sack the minute I got out of the house." Another boy said, "My mother never bought me clothes from Gap or Levi's. I had to save my meager allowance for months to buy what I want and then told her that I bought it cheap from a street vendor." An immigrant girl echoed, "My mother did not know what I have to go through in school everyday. I was made fun of or looked down on by my peers because I couldn't speak English well, had a strange haircut, and wore weird and cheap clothes. I used to be called 'nerdy' and 'boring.' I was so ashamed." When children complain, parents simply reply, "Just ignore them and concentrate on your study. When you make good grades, make it to an elite college, and eventually get a good job, you can afford whatever you want."

While immigrant parents value thrift and denounce luxurious consumption, they never hesitate spending on whatever they consider good for their children, such as books, after-school programs, Chinese lessons, private tutors, private lessons on the violin or the piano, and other educational-oriented activities. At a family counseling session, a mother puzzled at why her daughter would insist on going to a party instead of going to a scheduled piano lesson, "I only make $5 an hour, but pay $20 an hour for my daughter's piano lessons. I do this for her own good. Can't she understand?" This is a common parent-child problem in immigrant Chinese families, where parents are too driven by the mentality of "turning sons into dragons" and do what they think is good for their children but tend to ignore what their children think is good for themselves.

The American cultural values of individualism and personal freedom are also downplayed in immigrant Chinese families. Chinese culture gives priority to the family as a whole rather than individual self-gratification. Parents fear that too much individualism would undermine their authority and the moral basis of their families. They consistently remind their children that achievement is a duty and an obligation to the family rather than to the individual. Moreover, they expect their children to respect authority, to be polite and modest, to refrain from aggression, and to stay away from trouble. Chinese children are generally stereotyped as hardworking, respectful, and well disciplined. In terms of parent-child interaction, this stereotype works to ensure effective control and sanctioning of children. In terms of student-teacher interaction, the stereotype can also work as an advantage, for high teacher expectations generally result in high student performance (Sung 1987). The major drawbacks, however, are children's reluctance to express their own views in class or at home, a lack of creative and independent thinking, and the "little adult" syndrome (accepting too much responsibility and acting like an adult).

A third major problem immigrant Chinese children are facing is the fear and the appeal of the gang subculture. Street gangs have been a common problem in many immigrant and minority neighborhoods since the nineteenth century. In Chinatown, gangs were formed for the same reasons as other gangs in Little Italy, Little Saigon, Mexican American *barrios*, or South Central Los Angeles (Kuo 1977; Sung 1987; Vigil 1990; Vigil and Yun 1990). Kuo (1977) points out some of the mains reasons why immigrant youth join gangs: the lack of a sense of home because parents are too busy working or are unemployed, overcrowded housing, language deficiency, the lack of recreational facilities, the existence of gambling houses offering "easy money" and status, ghetto segregation, peer pressure for recognition, searching for identity and self-esteem, and the need for self-protection. Immigrant children, especially boys, are extremely vulnerable to the gang subculture in Chinatown.

On the one hand, many immigrant children fear being involved in gangs because of the stigma and the rule of conduct prescribed by the community. A Chinatown teenage boy said, "I am afraid of walking on certain streets by myself because people tend to identify boys hanging out there as gangsters and I don't want to be so identified. On the other hand, the real gangsters would approach you, put their arms around you, check you out, and try to kick you in." On the pressure of gang subculture, a community organizer commented,

> Youngsters have to spend a lot of energy trying to interpret whom other people think they are. They have to constantly prove certain things and unprove certain things. A student volunteer was once asked to take some fliers to streets that were gang dominated. He had to go with some girls because he was afraid of being identified as gang or being approached by gangsters. The pressure of coming to Chinatown is certainly real. But young people still come to Chinatown to see families and friends, to eat at the restaurants, and to do other things.[4]

On the other hand, street gangs are appealing to some immigrant youth in that they correspond to the desire for affiliation and achievement (Vigil 1990). In Chinatown, new gang recruits are typically those immigrant youth having severe adjustment problems, especially problems due to English language deficiency, which makes adaptation to school extremely difficult, resulting in frequent truancy and high dropout. This community organizer also pointed out another dimension of the problem: "It is sometimes easier to be a gangster. These kids were generally considered 'losers' by their teachers, parents, and peers in school. In school or at home, they feel uncomfortable, isolated, and rejected, which fosters a sense of hopelessness and powerlessness and a yearning for recognition. In the streets, they feel free from all the normative pressures. It is out there that they feel free to be themselves and to do things wherever and whenever they want, giving them a sort of identity and a sense of power."

While youth gangs continue to be a major concern in Chinatown, there are conscious and grass-roots effects to redirect them to more productive activities. Since the early 1970s, many community-based organizations, such as the CCBA, the CPC, and the Chinese Christian Herald Crusade, established various types of high-risk youth rehabilitation or prevention programs. Drawing on government and private funds and community resources, these programs have met with considerable success. Some gangs have agreed to make peace; some members of the gangs were provided with jobs or enrolled in English language and other job training classes by the CCBA; and still others reformed and enrolled in a preparatory school in Chinatown aiming at preparing high school dropouts and ex-gang members to enter college (Kuo 1977).

Although youth gangs are still a threatening force in the streets of Chinatown that is not going to go away in the near future, community organizers have been persistent and optimistic in their efforts to run and expand the existing preventive and targeted youth programs. "We can't reform them all, but we can do something good for these youngsters in ways that can be accepted by them. Most of the gangsters have a lot of energy and a strong desire to get recognized. Our goal is to redirect their energy to more productive activities," said the director of the Youth Center of the Chinese Christian Herald Crusade.

Finally, the problem of achieving is perhaps the most profound conflict confronting immigrant Chinese children. In recent years, the emphasis on education has paid off. Even though they are a small fraction of the total population (less than 1 percent) in the United States, Chinese Americans, many of whom are immigrants themselves or the children of immigrants, have surpassed other ethnic minorities in school attendance, grades, conduct, high school graduation rates, standardized tests, college admission rates, and other major indicators of academic achievement. In New York City, Chinese make up only 3 percent of the city's population, but in the city's most prestigious public high schools, such as the Hunter College High School, the Stuyvesant High School, and the Bronx High School of Science, where admission is based on standardized tests, Chinese American children are disproportionately represented.[5]

The academic achievement of Chinese American children has gained public attention, resulting in a positive stereotype as a model minority (Bell 1985; Kasindorf 1982). A school administrator commented,

> This positive stereotype has both positive and negative impacts. On the positive side, it helps develop a favorable attitude of the public and school teachers toward Chinese American children, leading to expected results like what is predicted by the self-fulfilling prophecy. On the negative side, it creates tremendous pressures for achieving both on parents and on children, leading to withdrawal from school and rebellious behavior, especially among those who have adjustment problems.[6]

The pressure for achieving also comes from within the community. "The pressure comes from the mothers and from those whom their mothers work with," said a community organizer. "When a mother hears that other mothers are sending their sons or daughters to the Hunter College High School, or to the Stuyvesant High School, or to the Bronx High School of Science, she would naturally think, 'Why shouldn't my child go to that school?' It's the peer pressure of the parents."[7]

Immigrant mothers, most of whom work in garment shops or other ethnic economies in Chinatown, are very aware which public high school is the best in the city. At work, if a mother hears that another's child is going to one of the best schools, she will go home and tell her children to prepare for that school. Many working mothers work all day and are isolated in Chinatown, and all they see is that many of the graduates at the public elementary school in Chinatown (with 90 percent of the students being Chinese) go to the Hunter College High School each year. This information is circulated among mothers, and going to Hunter becomes a standard. "My mother used to scold me and called me a dummy because I couldn't get into Hunter. She didn't have a clue how hard it was to get in these elite schools," said a college freshman who grew up in Chinatown.

Parental pressure is combined with accessible ethnic resources in Chinatown to push children to move ahead in school. After-school programs, tutor services, and test preparation programs are run by Chinese parents or entrepreneurs and are readily available in the community. School after school has become an accepted norm. An educator said, "when you think of how much time these Chinese kids put in their studies after regular school, you won't be surprised why they succeed in such a high rate."

From the children's perspective, they are motivated to learn and do well in school because they believe that education is their only way to get out of their parents' status. Also, many children do well in school hoping to make their parents happy and proud. "But that never happens. My mother is never satisfied no matter what you do and how well you do it," said a student, echoing a frustration felt by many other Chinese youth, who voiced how much they wish not to be compared with other children and how much they wish to rebel. Following success, however, many Chinese American youth return to or go to Chinatown to find their paths and identities. Some of them have become actively involved in the community to help another generation of immigrant youth in their struggle to become "Chinese American." As one youngster from Brooklyn remarked, "I am certainly Chinese American, because I feel that, being exposed to Chinese and American cultures, I have the best of both worlds."[8]

Conclusion

This chapter examines how the process of adaptation of young Chinese Americans is affected by tangible forms of social relations between the community, immigrant families, and the younger generation. We have shown that Chinatown serves as the basis of social capital that facilitates, rather than inhibits, the assimilation of immigrant children in the expected directions. Although today's immigrant Chinese overwhelmingly desire to ultimately assimilate into the mainstream society, the majority of them have only limited resources and face structural barriers, making assimilation an extremely difficult and lengthy process. In order to prevent immigrants and their children from assimilating into the margins of the American society, Chinatown has broadened its economic and social bases and has established various economic and social organizations to provide jobs, job referral services, career training, language learning facilities, child care, after-school programs, family counseling, and various youth-oriented crisis-prevention and rehabilitation programs. Because many parents and children are involved, in one way or another, in these intense ethnic networks in Chinatown, it becomes possible for the community to reinforce norms and to promote a high level of communication among group members and a high level of consistency among standards. In this sense, the community, as an important source of social capital, not only makes resources available to parents and children but serves to direct children's behavior. This type of social capital helps many of Chinatown's children to overcome intense adjustment difficulties and unfavorable conditions, such as linguistic and social isolation, bicultural conflicts, poverty, gang subculture, and close proximity to other underprivileged minority neighborhoods and to ensure successful adaptation.

This case study provides useful insight into the role of community-based organizations and families in promoting adjustment and success of immigrant children and offers a point of departure for studying the process of adaptation for the second and later generations. The generalizability of our findings, however, may be limited since we have focused only on children in Chinatown. Because different social contexts and different dynamics may affect different sets of immigrants and their offspring, the theoretical issues of social capital and social integration will require more elaboration and refinement than we have been able to give in this case study of a specific social setting. It will be necessary, also, to delve in greater detail into how and under what circumstances our findings may be generalized to other situations. Therefore, additional research is needed to examine in greater detail the ways in which children and their families are connected to one another by ethnically concentrated communities and how these connections between families and community-based organizations facilitate the adaptation of young people.

NOTES

The study relied on the 1980 and 1990 U.S. Census data and fieldwork in New York City's Chinatowns in Lower East Manhattan, Flushing, and Sunset Park. The field observations were conducted by the author sporadically in selected homes, streets, community-based organizations, restaurants, and garment factories during the months of September and October in 1994. Face-to-face or telephone interviews (lasting half an hour to an hour) were conducted by the author in English or in Chinese on a convenient sample of four community-based Chinese schools, six youth-oriented programs run by various organizations, three family associations, two Christian churches, and two Buddhist temples, in addition to Chinese Consolidated Benevolent Association, Chinese American Planning Council, and Chinatown History Museum. Pseudonyms are used when individuals' names were mentioned. The author wish to thank all informants who provided generous help in this study. This chapter was written while the author was in residence at the Russell Sage Foundation, whose support is also gratefully acknowledged. The author is exclusively responsible for the contents of the chapter.

1. Excerpt from "Yellow Discrimination" written in 1994 by Eunyang Theresa Oh, a member of the Student Committee of the Chinatown History Museum, as part of the exhibition entitled "Who's Chinese American?"

2. Recorded from one of the parent-counselor conferences and a conversation with the counselor at a public high school in Chinatown, October 1994.

3. Excerpt from "The Smell of the Wet Grass" written in 1994 by Carla Shen, a member of the Student Committee of the Chinatown History Museum, as part of the exhibition entitled "Who's Chinese American?"

4. Personal interview with a community organizer at the Chinatown History Museum, September 1994.

5. Telephone inquiries of the staff of the schools mentioned, October 1994.

6. Personal interview with an administrator of a public high school in Chinatown, September 1994.

7. Personal interview, September 1994.

8. Recorded from a discussion at one of the youth sessions, October 1994.

REFERENCES

Bell, D. A. 1985. "An American Success Story: The Triumph of Asian Americans." *New Republic* 3677 (July 15): 24–31.

Chinese-American Planning Council (CPC). 1993 (October). *Chinese-American Planning Council: Program List.* New York: CPC.

Chinatown Today Publishing. 1993. *Chinese-American Life Guide.* Hong Kong: Chinatown Today Publishing.

Coleman, James. 1990. *Foundations of Social Theory.* Cambridge, Mass.: Belknap Press of the Harvard University Press.

Dillon, R. H. 1962. *The Hatchetmen: Tong Wars in San Francisco.* New York: Coward McCann.

Durkheim, É. 1951 [1897]. *Suicide: A Study in Sociology.* John A. Spaulding and George Simpson, tr., G. Simpson, ed. New York: Free Press.

Fernandez-Kelly, M. Patricia. 1995. "Social Capital and Cultural Capital in the Urban Ghetto: Implications for the Economic Sociology and Immigration." In Alejandro Portes (ed.), *Economic Sociology.* New York: Russell Sage Foundation.

Immigration and Naturalization Service. 1991. *Statistical Yearbook of the Immigration and Naturalization Service 1990.* Washington, D.C.: U.S. Government Printing Office.

Kasindorf, Martin. 1982. "Asian Americans: A Model Minority." *Newsweek* (December 6): 39–51.

Kuo, Chia-Ling. 1977. *Social and Political Change in New York's Chinatown: The Role of Voluntary Associations.* New York: Praeger.

Kwong, Peter. 1987. *The New Chinatown.* New York: Hill and Wang.

Portes, Alejandro, and Rubén G. Rumbaut. 1990. *Immigrant America: A Portrait.* Berkeley: University of California Press.

Portes, Alejandro, and Julia Sensenbrenner. 1993. "Embeddedness and Immigration: Notes on the Social Determinants of Economic Action." *American Journal of Sociology* 98: 1320–50.

Sung, Betty Lee. 1987. *The Adjustment Experience of Chinese Immigrant Children in New York City.* New York: Center for Migration Studies.

Vigil, James Diego. 1990. "Gangs, Social Control, and Ethnicity: Ways to Redirect." In Shirley Brice Heath and Milbrey W. McLaughlin (eds.), *Identity and Inner-City Youth: Beyond Ethnicity and Gender*, 94–119. New York: Teachers College Press.

Vigil, James Diego, and S. Yun. 1990. "Vietnamese Youth Gangs in Southern California." In R. Huff, ed., *Gangs in America: Diffusion, Diversity, and Public Policy*, 146–62. Beverly Hills, CA: Sage.

Wong, Bernard P. 1979. *A Chinese American Community: Ethnicity and Survival Strategies*. Singapore: Chopmen Enterprise.

Zhou, Min. 1992. *Chinatown: The Socioeconomic Potential of an Urban Enclave*. Philadelphia: Temple University Press.

Zhou, Min, and John R. Logan. 1989. "Returns on Human Capital in Ethnic Enclaves: New York City's Chinatown." *American Sociological Review* 54: 809–20.

Chapter Thirteen

New Household Forms, Old Family Values

*The Formation and Reproduction of the Filipino Transnational
Family in Los Angeles*

Rhacel Salazar Parreñas

Much like other immigrant groups in the United States, Filipino migrants turn to the family for support against the social and economic pressures that they encounter upon settlement. They use the family in myriad ways. For example, Filipino migrants are known to have preserved various cultural practices to secure the use of the family as a source of support in settlement. They create fictive kinship, enforce a keen sense of obligation among kin, and use an extended as opposed to a nuclear base for the family (Almirol 1982; Agbayani-Siewart and Revilla 1995). In general, Filipino migrants preserve various cultural practices so as to secure from the community mutual support for the economic mobility of the family and assistance in difficult periods of adjustment in settlement.

In my own observations, Filipinos use the family in other ways. The family is a social institution that adapts strategies variably in response to structural, cultural, and ideological forces in society. Concomitantly, Filipinos have taken advantage of this flexibility by incorporating various strategies of household maintenance. For example, multiple nuclear families may reside in one household so as to decrease expenses and in some cases may go as far as to purchase a house collectively. They also share tasks such as child care across households. These examples show that Filipino families are neither monolithic nor static but instead consist of diverse household forms.

This chapter presents one strategy of household maintenance utilized by Filipino migrants for easing their settlement into the United States. In particular, I document the formation and reproduction of the Filipino transnational household. By transnational family or household, I refer to a family whose core members are located in at least two or more nation-states. In such a family, a migrant settles in the host society, while his or her family—spouse, children, and/or parents—stays in the Philippines. The purpose is to explain how and why transnational households form and reproduce among contemporary Filipino migrants in Los Angeles. Thus, I elaborate on the *structural factors* propelling Filipinos into transnational households as well as the *cultural factors* to which Filipinos turn in order to form such households.

Background

The data are derived from a comparative study of migrant Filipina domestic workers in Rome and Los Angeles. I rely primarily on interviews conducted with twenty-six Filipina domestic workers in Los Angeles. I supplement this data with interviews that I had gathered with fifty-six domestic workers in Rome and ten children who had grown up in transnational households. Transnational households are in fact the dominant strategy of household maintenance for migrant Filipina domestic workers. Of the twenty-six women interviewed in Los Angeles, twenty maintain transnational households. Of these twenty women, fourteen have dependent children living in the Philippines, one lives apart from her husband in the Philippines, and five are single women whose monthly remittances sustain the day-to-day living expenses of their families.

Before I proceed with my discussion of the transnational household, I need to first acknowledge the limitation in my data. The sample of domestic workers does not represent the wide range of occupations held by Filipino migrants in the United States and correspondingly does not reflect the varying demands imposed on the family by different work routines. Because live-in work arrangements are still common among Filipina domestic workers, they can more or less be expected to turn to transnational household structures. Responsibilities for the families of employers prevent them from meeting the demands of child care and other reproductive labor in their own families. As a result, they send their children to the Philippines or leave them there, where a wide kin network inclusive of blood and affinal relations may provide care for dependents.

However, professional Filipino women such as nurses are also known to maintain transnational households in the community. They do so to balance their work inside and outside the home. Immigrant Filipinas have one of the highest rate of labor force participation, reaching 83 percent in 1980 among married immigrant women (Espiritu 1997). In 1990, immigrant Filipino women also held the highest employment ratio among women in Los Angeles, with 83 percent of the working age population gainfully employed (Ong and Azores 1994a). Confronted with a wage gap, Filipina immigrants often maximize their earnings by working extended hours (Yamanaka and McClelland 1994; Espiritu 1997). For example, it is common for Filipina nurses in Los Angeles to hold two full-time jobs (Ong and Azores 1994b). Despite their high rate of labor force participation, Filipina women are still expected to do most of the housework and child care in their families. Consequently, long hours at work coupled with their continued responsibility for domestic chores may lead even professional women to send their children back to the Philippines. They usually do so only for a short period of time, during infancy, when child care demands are greatest. They also usually do so because of their preference for child care to be provided by kin instead of strangers in child care facilities in the United States.

Notably, the formation of transnational households is not exclusive to Filipino labor migrants. Various studies document its formation among contemporary migrants from the traditional sending countries of Haiti and Mexico.[1] Transnational families are also not particular to present-day migrants. They have historically been a common form of household maintenance for temporary labor migrants in various regions of the world. The earliest Chinese migrant workers in the United States, "guest workers" in Western Europe, and Mexican *braceros* in the Southwestern United States, to name a few examples, adapted "split households" because of the disparate levels of economic development in the sending and the receiving countries and the legal barriers to the integration of migrants in the United States (Glenn 1983); these conditions continue today.

We can also speculate that it was not uncommon for Filipino migrants in the pre–World War II period to adopt such households. Prior to World War II, the Filipino community was composed mostly of single men. The cost of bringing women to the United States, coupled with the uncertainty of life for migrant farm workers, discouraged the migration of women. In 1930, women composed only 16.6 percent of the population (Espiritu 1995). Yet, this skewed gender composition does not reflect the distribution of marital status in the community. In 1930, the number of married Filipino men (7,409) far exceeded the number of Filipino women (1,640) on the U.S. mainland (Parreñas 1998b). This strongly suggests that Filipino migrants, as they were subject to anti-miscegenation laws, adapted transnational households when wives could not join them because of either economic uncertainties or legal restrictions barring the entry of Filipinos into the United Status.[2]

Yet, while split households in earlier migrant communities were homogeneous and composed primarily of a male income producer living apart from female and young dependents in the sending country, contemporary split households, for example, those from the Philippines and the Caribbean (Basch et al. 1994), include income-producing female migrants. Unlike in the past, with the split households of male migrants, traditional gender roles are contested in today's transnational families of female migrants, with women acting as the breadwinner of the family.

How and why do transnational households form among contemporary Filipino migrants? This is the question I answer in this chapter. My discussion of the transnational household is divided into three sections. In the first section, I describe the structural forces propelling the formation of transnational households. Then, in the second section, I enumerate the cultural practices enabling the formation of such households. The third and final section proceeds to describe the Filipino transnational family. In this section, I present two vignettes that illustrate the difficulties and sacrifice entailed in the reproduction of the transnational family.

Global Capitalism: Structural Factors of Transnational Household Formation

Global capitalism and its resulting processes within sending and receiving communities of migration propel the formation of transnational households. Migrants form transnational households to mediate the following structural forces: the unequal level of economic development in sending and receiving nations; legal barriers that restrict their full incorporation into the host society and polity; and the rise of anti-immigrant sentiments. Transnational households result from a conglomeration of contemporary social realities. However, these constitutive features are not particular to global capitalism. Instead, they are old practices—long-standing realities—that are merely being redeployed with greater speed and force with the advent of globalization.

As structural forces in society spur the formation of transnational households, they are not uncommon strategies of household maintenance for low-wage migrant workers, such as Filipina domestic workers. While affording their families a comfortable, middle-class lifestyle in the sending country, the meager wages of low-paid migrant workers do not provide a comparable lifestyle in receiving countries. The lesser costs of reproduction in sending countries such as the Philippines enable migrant laborers to provide greater material benefits for their children, including comfortable housing, as opposed to the cramped living quarters imposed on migrants by high rents in "global cities," burgeoning economic centers that rely on the "routine" services of low-wage immigrant laborers (Sassen 1988, 1994). Finally, the family can expedite the achievement of its goals of accumulating savings and property by forming transnational households. Thus, migrants create transnational households as a strategy to maximize resources and opportunities in the global economy. The migrant family transcends borders and the spatial boundaries of nation-states to take advantage of the lower costs of reproducing—feeding, housing, clothing, and educating—the family in the "third world." Its spatial organization is in direct response to the forces of global capitalism as the geographical split of the family coincides with the uneven development of regions and the unequal relations between states in the global economy.

Restrictions against the integration of immigrants in postindustrial nations today also fuel the formation of transnational families. The displacement of workers and loss of stable employment for middle-income "native" workers have led to the scapegoating of immigrants, particularly Latinos in the United States (Perea 1997; Feagin 1997). The resulting enforcement of barriers against the integration of migrant laborers and especially their families promotes the maintenance of transnational households. In the United States, lawmakers are entertaining the promotion of temporary labor migration and the elimination of certain preference categories for family reunification, including the preference categories for adult children and parents of U.S. citizens and permanent residents—the trend being to preserve the labor provided by migrants but to discontinue support for their reproduction (Chavez 1997). Moreover, nativist grassroots organizations (e.g., Americans for Immigration Control, Stop the Out-of-Control Problems of Immigration Today) aimed at the further restriction and exclusion of immigration have sprouted throughout the United States.[3] With anti-immigrant sentiments brewing in the United States, migrant parents may not want to expose their children to the racial tensions and anti-immigrant sentiments fostered by the social and cultural construction of low-wage migrants as undesirable citizens (Basch et al. 1994; Ong 1996). Yet, among my interviewees, many had been caught in the legal bind of being either undocumented or obtaining their legal status only after their children had reached adult age, when children are no longer eligible for immediate family reunification. Hence, while they may have wanted to sponsor the migration of their children to the United States, they have legally been unable to do so.

"Receiving" societies such as the United States most likely support the formation of transnational households. This is because such households guarantee them the low-wage labor of migrants without forcing them to accept responsibility for their reproduction. By containing the costs of reproduction in sending countries, receiving countries can keep to a minimum the wages of immigrant workers. Thus, while receiving countries need the low-wage labor of migrants, they want neither the responsibilities nor the costs of the reproduction of these workers. This is particularly shown by the passage of Proposition 187, the 1995 California state referendum that bars undocumented immigrants from receiving any tax-supported benefits, including education, health, and social services (Martin 1995). Thus, the formation of transnational households, though a strategy of resistance in globalization, maintains the inequalities of globalization. Receiving countries benefit from the minimized wage demands of a substantial proportion of their workforce. Such economic benefits translate to increased production activities, leading to growth and profits for the higher-tier workers of receiving countries.

The formation of transnational households further enforces the limited integration of low-wage migrant workers. The separation of the migrant family stunts the incorporation of the migrant into the host society, since it is often the children whose greater ability to acculturate paves the way of integration in settlement (Portes and Rumbaut 1996). The consideration of the workings of border politics in transnational households also illustrates the enforcement of limited integration in this process of household formation. On the one hand, the operation of transnational households transcends territorial borders, with the family acting as a conduit between localized communities in separate nation-states. Transcendence, however, does not signify elimination of barriers (i.e., borders). Transnational households should not be praised as a small-scale symbol of the migrant's agency against the larger forces of globalization, because the formation of transnational households marks an enforcement of "border control" on migrant workers. If transnational households can be seen as representing transcendence, they also signify segregation. Transnational households form from the segregation of the families of immigrant workers in sending countries. Thus, they form from the successful implementation of border control, which makes families unable to reunite. Border control further aggravates the experience of transnational families by making return migration difficult for undocumented workers. In turn, family separation is often prolonged and may even extend to a span of a life cycle. Among my interviewees, for example, the length of separation between mothers and their now adult children in transnational families is as long as sixteen years.

The Persistence of Familism: Cultural Factors of Transnational Household Formation

Transnational households emerge in response to the global labor market but also form because of strong kinship ties (Basch et al. 1994). However, in the Philippines, transnational households have come to signify the decline and disintegration of family values and consequently "the destruction of the moral fabric" of society (Tadiar 1997, 171). Because they fail to fulfill the ideological notion of a traditional Filipino family, transnational households are considered "broken homes."

Filipino families are traditionally nuclear in structure. Members carry a strong sense of solidarity and obligation to members of their nuclear family and, to a lesser extent, to their larger kin group inclusive of consanguineal (i.e., parent and sibling), affinal, and fictive kin (Medina 1991). The kinship base on which Filipinos may rely is extended by the multilineal and bilateral descent system in the Philippines. Filipinos maintain an equal sense of allegiance to maternal and paternal kin. Moreover, they extend their kinship network by including in their families fictive kin, kin obtained spiritually (e.g., *compadrazgo* system), and cross-generational and cousin ties.

Transnational households are considered "broken" for a number of reasons. First, the maintenance of this household form diverges from traditional expectations of cohabitation among spouses and children. Second, transnational households do not meet the traditional division of labor in the family, as transnational mothers do not maintain the social expectation that women to perform domestic chores. Notably, this expectation still stands despite the high labor force participation of women in the Philippines (Medina 1991). Third, they diverge from traditional practices of socialization in the family. While the socialization of children is expected to come from direct supervision and interaction with parents as well as other adults, the geographic distance in transnational households inhibits the ability of mothers to provide direct supervision to their children.

Yet, the formation of these households depends on the persisting cultural value of *pakikisama*, meaning mutual cooperation or familism, that is, sentiments of collectivism and mutual obligation among kin. Transnational households would not be able to form and reproduce without the cultural value of *pakikisama*, and the mechanisms strengthening such an allegiance including (1) mutual assistance, (2) consanguineal responsibility, (3) "generalized family exchange networks" (Peterson 1993), and (4) fosterage. Transnational households have come to show the resilience of the Filipino family in the advent of globalization.

The operation of transnational households rests on the strength of mutual assistance among extended kin in the Philippines. In transnational households, the migrant shoulders the responsibility of providing for primary and extended kin by remitting funds regularly. In fact, not one of my interviewees has failed to provide consistent financial assistance to her family. Notably, most single migrants send remittances to elderly parents on a monthly basis. Only those with relatives (e.g., brothers and sisters) working outside the Philippines do not send money regularly since they are able to share the responsibility of financial support.

Another mechanism on which transnational families rely is consanguineal responsibility, that is, the extension of responsibility to parents, siblings, and even nieces and nephews for those without children. The high level of interdependency in extended families of Filipina domestic workers is first illustrated by the tremendous responsibility women have for their extended kin in the Philippines. Many single domestic workers shoulder the financial costs of reproduction of the extended family by investing in the education of younger generations. While married domestic work-ers with children usually cover the schooling only of their own children, those who migrated as single women support extended kin prior to marriage. Besides sending remittances to cover the day-to-day living expenses of their parents and other rela-tives, Pacita Areza and Letty Xavier, for example, covered the costs of the college education of at least four nieces and nephews before getting married in the United States.

> I sent my sisters to school. . . . One finished a degree in education and the other one in commerce. One only finished high school. . . . Until now, I still help my nieces and nephews. I am sending them to school. With one of my brothers, I am helping him send his two children to college. One just graduated last March and one has two more years to go. With one of my sisters, she has two children and she does not have a job and she is separated from her husband. I help her out—I am helping by paying for their schooling. Once all my nieces and nephews are done with their schooling, I can go back to the Philippines. [Pacita Domingo Areza, married with no children, domestic worker in Los Angeles]

> From the start, when I started working in the Philippines, I have helped my family significantly. My nieces and nephews, I sent them to school. . . . One of the first nephews I sent to school is a civil engineer. . . . The second one is a midwife, and the third one is a teacher. The next two sisters are also in education, and they are all board passers. My dreams have come true through them. Right now, one is in nautical school, and he is going overseas soon. Right now, I have stopped supporting them. Those I sent to school, I want them to be the ones supporting their younger brothers and sisters. They are their responsibilities already. I think I have done my part. (Letty Xavier, married, domestic worker in Los Angeles)

Of thirteen migrant workers who at one point had been single women in Los Angeles, five women sent at least three or more nieces and nephews to college. Others provided valuable financial support to their families. Besides subsidizing the everyday living expenses of elderly parents, some purchased the house where their parents and siblings, including those with children, now live and sent at least one younger relative to college. As Gloria Diaz, a domestic worker in Rome with a sister in the United States, explains, they would feel guilty if they did not provide for their relatives in need: "When I don't send money, I feel guilty because my mother is alone, and it is my obligation to help."

Often, the primary contribution of migrant domestic workers to the "kin work" of the extended family is the education of younger generations. In acknowledgment of their extensive support, younger members of their extended family often consider the migrants second mothers. Nieces and nephews refer to them as "Mama" or "Nanay" (Mom) as opposed to just the customary reference of "Tita" (Aunt). For domestic workers, their financial assistance to the family provides them the most tangible reward for their labor. Because of a cultural system based on an economy of gratitude, the immense generosity of migrant workers, especially adult single mi-grants, guarantees them a well-established kinship base if they choose to return to the Philippines. This economy of gratitude is premised on the value of *utang na loob*, literally, debt of the soul, in which favors are returned with lifelong debt.

The cooperation of sending younger members of the extended family to college also operates on the system of generalized family exchange among kin (Peterson 1993). In such a system, the success of one member of the family represents the success of the family as a collective unit. Peterson defines this family exchange system as entailing an open reciprocal exchange: "Generalized exchanges are those in which A gives to B, B gives to C, C gives to a D, and D gives to an A" (1993, 572). By sending one or more persons to college, domestic workers assume that those that they send to school will reciprocate by later supporting their younger siblings and relatives through school. These younger relatives are then culturally expected to provide care and support for the domestic worker once she chooses to return and retire in the Philippines.

The high level of interdependency among extended families is also reflected in the reliance of migrant parents on grandparents, aunts, and other relatives for the care of dependents left in the Philippines. In the Philippines, it is not uncommon for families to take in extended family members whose own immediate families may not be able to provide as much material or emotional security. Fosterage of children is in fact a common practice among extended kin in the Philippines (Peterson 1993). For example, Cecilia Impelido, a street vendor in Rome, was raised by her grandmother for fourteen years. The arrangement, she claims, strengthened kinship ties to her maternal grandmother in the province even as it eased the financial costs of reproduction for her parents in Manila. Transnational families are embedded in the cultural practice of fosterage. Parents outside the Philippines rely on other relatives to act as "guardians" of their children. In exchange, the remittances sent by parents to dependents in the Philippines benefit the "guardians." The reciprocal bond of dependency between migrant parents and guardians keeps the family intact: migrant parents usually rely on female kin—grandmothers, aunts, and other relatives—to care for the children they have left behind in the Philippines, while caregiving relatives are more than likely ensured a secure flow of monthly remittances.

Inasmuch as their maintenance is aided by relations with extended kin, transnational households strengthen extended family kinship, with children (and also elderly parents) acting as the enduring embodiment of the bond of interdependency. Migrants rely on extended kin to care for their dependents, while extended kin raise their standard of living with the financial support provided by migrant workers. The extended family bolsters the option of migration for individuals otherwise bound by duties and responsibilities to dependents in the Philippines. Thus, transnational households depend on the resilience of extended family bonds in the Philippines. They form not solely from the limits imposed by the structures of globalization and the manipulation of these structures by migrants. The persisting cultural value of familism assists with the formation of transnational households as much as the structural forces of globalization.

A Description of the Filipino Transnational Family

In this section, I describe the Filipino transnational family by presenting vignettes of the two most common forms of transnational households in the Filipino diaspora. Transnational households can be divided into three subcategories: one-parent-abroad transnational households, two-parent-abroad transnational households, and adult-child(ren)-abroad transnational households. One-parent-abroad transnational households are families with one parent—a mother or a father—producing income abroad as other members carry out the functions of reproduction, socialization, and the rest of consumption in the Philippines. In two-parent-abroad transnational households, both the mother and the father are migrant laborers, while the children usually reside together in the Philippines under the care of other relatives. Finally, adult-children-abroad transnational households are families in which the earnings of adult children as migrant laborers provide necessary or additional financial support to relatives (e.g., parents, brothers and sisters) in the Philippines.

The two most common forms of transnational households are one-parent-abroad and adult-children-abroad households. Among my interviewees in Los Angeles, twelve of twenty married domestic workers maintain one-parent-abroad transnational households. Only three married women maintain two-parent-abroad transnational households, which suggests that parents are hard pressed to leave children behind without any direct parental supervision. Finally, five of six single women maintain adult-children-abroad transnational households.[4]

The two vignettes that follow place a microscope in the migrant family to interrogate its transformations, household dynamics, and the meanings and consequences of migration to family relations. Recognizing and examining the various ways and means by which migrants maintain their families illustrate the social process of transnational household formation. Hence, analyzing migrant households reveals the structures that mold and influence the family life of migrants and the resources that families in turn utilize to perform essential tasks in household maintenance.

Vicky Diaz: An Example of a One-Parent-Abroad Transnational Family

In 1988, Vicky Diaz, a thirty-four-year-old mother of five children between the ages of ten and two years old, left the Philippines for Taiwan. Lured by the financial rewards of employment outside the Philippines, Vicky Diaz had not been content with her salary as a public school teacher in the Philippines, nor had she been comfortable with the insecurities of running a travel agency in Manila. Although made more lucrative by the greater demand for employment outside the Philippines in the preceding ten years, the business of travel agencies had not been as profitable in the late 1980s. And so Vicky decided to move to Taiwan, because there the wages of a domestic worker would give her a more secure income.

In Taiwan, Vicky worked as a housekeeper and a factory worker but mostly as a janitor, for which she earned a salary of approximately $1,000 a month. Vicky, who speaks English very well, also subsidized her earnings by teaching English part-time at nights:

In Taiwan, darling, what I mopped everyday would be five floors. If you put them all together, it would be around five miles. I surely learned how to use the floor polisher and mop the whole day. I would have to clean thirty bathrooms and thirty toilets, that much. I was able to work part-time in the evenings. At night, I got my chance to teach. I taught English grammar. I made good money doing that because per head it is ten dollars an hour. And I had five students who would pay me and so that is $50 an hour. That is how I made good money. Every other day, I would teach them English. That was my additional income.

Although satisfied with her earnings in Taiwan, Vicky found that the situation of illegal workers like herself became more tenuous with the greater enforcement of restrictive polices against migrants in the early 1990s. She decided to leave Taiwan and return to the Philippines in 1992.

Yet, her return to the Philippines after five years in Taiwan turned out to be just a "stopover" on her way to the United States:

From Taiwan, I only stayed in the Philippines for three months. I used this time to fix my papers to come here. After Taiwan, my real target was the United States. It was because I knew that America is the land of promises and the land of opportunities. I had several friends who went to America and never went back to the Philippines. I figured it was because life was wonderful in the United States. . . . So, why not give myself the same opportunity?

Although geographically distanced from her children for at least five years, Vicky did not seem at all concerned about or interested in spending "quality" time with them. The prolonged distance from her family seemed to have fostered feelings of emotional distance in Vicky. Only a few months after her return to the Philippines, Vicky used her savings from Taiwan to pay a travel agency 160,000 pesos (approximately $8,000) for the use of another woman's passport to enter the United States. As Vicky herself states, "You know, in the Philippines, nothing is impossible if you have the money."

Considering her middle-class status after running a travel agency in the Philippines and her ability to raise such a huge sum of money for her trip to the United States, one can easily wonder why Vicky risked such a prolonged separation from her family. Over a span of nine years, Vicky spent only three months with her husband and children in the Philippines. Clearly an absentee mother for most of her children's adolescence, Vicky explained that it was for her family's benefit that she came in the United States:

They were saddened by my departure. Even until now my children are trying to convince me to go home. . . . The children were not angry when I left because they were still very young when I left them. My husband could not get angry either because he knew that was the only way I could seriously help him raise our children, so that our children could be sent to school.

When assessing the effects of separation to her family, Vicky downplayed the emotional strains engendered by separation by highlighting its material rewards. Neither her marriage nor her relations with her children were of great concern to her. Clearly, her family's desire for her to return to the Philippines was not given much consideration. Instead, Vicky insisted that her family needed her higher earnings outside the Philippines. Although aware of her children's persistent requests for her return to the Philippines, Vicky was not convinced that her family could sustain its middle-class status without her earnings outside the country.

In the United States, Vicky initially worked as a domestic worker, primarily caring for a two-year-old boy for a wealthy family in Beverly Hills. As the mother "would just be sitting around, smoking and making a mess," Vicky cleaned, cooked, and cared for the boy for $400 a week, clearly a sharp contrast to the $40 she pays her own family's live-in domestic worker in the Philippines. Vicky did not like being a housekeeper for two main reasons: the physically demanding load and the excruciating loneliness, heightened by the contradiction of caring for someone else's children while not caring for her own.

> Even though it paid well, you are sinking in the amount of your work. Even while you are ironing the clothes, they can still call you to the kitchen to wash the plates. It was also very depressing. The only thing you can do is give all your love to the child. In my absence from my children, the most I could do with my situation is give all my love to that child.

Not completely indifferent about the separation her family has endured for almost ten years, Vicky did entertain feelings of regret over missing the formative years of her children's adolescence:

> What saddens me the most about my situation is that during the formative years of their childhood, I was not there for them. That is the time when children really need their mother, and I was not there for them.

Yet for Vicky, the economic rewards of separation softened its emotional costs:

> In my one year in the US, I was able to invest on a jitney. I wanted to do that so that no matter what happens with me, my husband does not have a hard time financially. . . . *Of course, I have neglected them and the least I could do to make up for this is to make their lives a little bit easier. I could ease their lives for them materially.* That's how I console myself. . . . Besides the jitney, there's the washing machine and TV. In the Philippines, it is hard to get to buy these things, right? At least they are not desolate and are at least provided for well.

To overcome the emotional gaps in her family, Vicky relied on "commodifying her love" and compensated for her absence with material goods. Yet while Vicky claimed that she works outside the Philippines so that her family would not "starve," it is actually more accurate to say that Vicky worked in the United States to sustain a comfortable middle-class life for her family in the Philippines.

Vicky hoped that her family would eventually reunite in the United States, because she was convinced that there are few opportunities available for her family in the Philippines. Yet without legal documents, she was unable to sponsor the migration of her family. Obtaining legal status continues to be the biggest challenge for Vicky and has been the main obstacle blocking the reunification of her family. Yet, while Vicky hopes for the relocation of her entire family to the United States, her children ironically prefer to witness the reunification of their family much sooner and would rather have Vicky return to the Philippines.

Maria Batung: An Example of a Children-Abroad Transnational Household in Los Angeles

A single domestic worker in Los Angeles, Maria Batung has been working for a Filipino family for more than twelve years and supports her family in the Philippines with her earnings in the United States.

In the Philippines, Maria also worked as a domestic worker—a nanny—because without a college degree or appropriate networks she did not have access to other types of employment in Manila. Maria had been attending college prior to entering domestic work, but she had to give up her aspirations for a college degree because her parents, whose sole income had been her father's sporadic earnings as a carpenter, could not afford to send her or any of her five brothers and sisters to school.

In Manila, she usually worked for foreigners, mostly diplomats and businessmen. In 1980, ten years after she started working as a domestic helper, Maria accepted the offer of a former employer to move to London with them. Although she could have continued working for the English family, Maria decided, after four years in London, to take up the offer of another former employer, a Filipino family, but this time for a job in the United States. These employers were migrating to the United States to establish an import-export rattan furniture business in Southern California and, by investing capital in the United States, qualified to bring a small number of employees with them, including their former domestic worker, Maria. They covered all of her travel expenses and the costs of obtaining legal papers to work in the United States. With their sponsorship, Maria was able to obtain a green card to stay in the United States permanently.

Maria has been very satisfied with her work, earning far more than she ever did in London ($150 per month), always having a manageable workload, and not having to deal with demanding or strict employers.

> I earn enough so that I could help my family in the Philippines. I get more than $1,000 a month, and everything is free. They pay for my Social Security, and they handled my papers. They pay for my ticket home every year. When I go, they also give me vacation pay for two months. That is why I don't have a problem here. Everything is free and they also cover my insurance. . . . It is OK. Anytime I want to leave I can. . . . That is why I lasted long with this family. If that were not the case, I would have probably returned to the Philippines a long time ago.

Of all the employment benefits she receives, the one Maria appreciates the most is her annual vacation—a two-month paid vacation and a round-trip ticket to the Philippines—for it affords her time to spend with her father. Very satisfied with her job, Maria plans to work for them until she is old herself.

Without personal expenses to cover, Maria invests all of her earnings in her family in the Philippines. She has sent numerous relatives to college, wanting to ensure that no one else in her family has to abandon his or her studies and settle for domestic work as she was forced to do almost thirty years ago. When asked whether she had sent her relatives money, she replied:

> I send my father money and my nieces and nephews I equally sent to school. For every single sibling of mine, I sent one of their children to school. So there is no jealousy. The rest they could send to school on their own, but each one of them I sent at least one of their children to school. It was equal so there were no bad feelings. . . .

> So, I am very happy. Although I was not able to finish school, these are the ones that I was able to ensure finished their education. It is hard when you don't finish. I told them that they would have a hard time if they did not have a degree and that it was necessary that they finish school. Thank God they were able to finish school.

Because Maria sends most of her earnings to the Philippines, she has not been able to accumulate any savings after many years of domestic work, a fact that is not of concern for Maria. With her legal status in the United States, she is secure that she will qualify to receive government aid such as Social Security once she retires.

Maria's earnings do not cover only the college education of younger relatives but also assist her family with day-to-day living expenses.

> The last time I sent money it was for $500. That is the lowest. It is mostly $1,000 or $600 or $700. So I have no savings. My bank is with all those that I sent to school. I also had a house built in the Philippines where my father lives right now. I had that house remodeled and everything. My father was telling me that maybe when I get older I would regret what I did because they would no longer recognize me. But I told him that they can do what they want to do, but I am happy that I was able to help them.

The generosity of Maria is voluntary, and for it her most satisfying rewards have been the love of her family and their appreciation for her tremendous financial support. While very appreciative of the money and material goods Maria provides them, Maria's relatives also hope that she will soon return and settle down in the Philippines so that they may have the opportunity to transform their relationship to one that is more intimate than the monthly remittances she sends them. A single adult migrant in a transnational family, Maria Batung works in Los Angeles to sustain her family in the Philippines.

Conclusion

The formation of transnational families is a creative response to and an adaptive strategy against the economic challenges and legal barriers faced by migrant workers. It has been adapted as a household form by members of numerous migrant groups in the United States, including those from the Philippines. By structurally reconstituting their family form from a nuclear to a transnational household, Filipino migrants, like other migrants, increase the material benefits afforded by their wages; maintain a family despite the legal restrictions constraining the migration of dependents; and, in many cases, reconstitute the traditional gender roles in the family. However, the formation of transnational households does more than reveal the creativity, agency, and resistance of migrants facing structural barriers in society. To some extent, it unavoidably causes emotional distance and strains among members of transnational families.

The challenge for members of transnational families is to confront and negotiate the emotional costs imposed by geographic distance. They do so in various ways. Like the Latina transnational mothers interviewed by Hondagneu-Sotelo and Avila (1997) in Los Angeles, Filipina transnational mothers and daughters rationalize distance by taking advantage of the communication technology in this age of late capitalism. They increase their familiarity with members of their families located thousands of miles away by using the telephone frequently and by writing letters at least once a week.

The familiarity allowed by the rationalization of distance is, however, limited and cannot replace fully the intimacy of daily interactions. Mothers such as Vicky Diaz and daughters such as Maria Batung are aware of this fact, but they reason that the financial gains afforded by the maintenance of transnational families is worth its emotional costs. Thus, adult children such as Maria generally do not see an end to their separation from their families in the near future as they plan to maximize their earnings and work until they are no longer able bodied. Similarly, mothers such as Vicky Diaz extend the duration of separation in their families so as to maximize the financial gains of migration. Lured by the greater income available in the United States, most of them plan to stay indefinitely. In the process, they have to put emotional tensions in their families aside for the sake of financial security.

The priority given to material rewards in the family results in the temporal extension of transnational households. Parents in Los Angeles do wish for their children to somehow join them in the United States so as to take advantage of the greater opportunities in this country (especially education, as is recognized universally). Yet, in Los Angeles, many transnational mothers, like Vicky, are undocumented. If not undocumented, they have been caught in the legal bind of obtaining their legal status only after their children reach adult age, when children are no longer eligible for immediate family reunification. Hence, family reunification for U.S. migrants may be possible only with their return to the Philippines. This may explain why the dependents of migrants such as Vicky and Maria strongly prefer to see their families reunify via return migration.

The emotional difficulties wrought in the maintenance of transnational households remain a continuous challenge for migrants and the relatives they have left behind in the Philippines. Interestingly, members of transnational households have varying opinions regarding this problem. Migrants tend to see the material gains of transnational households as being worth their emotional costs. This reasoning enables them to prolong the geographic separation of the family. In contrast, family members in the Philippines consider the material gains not worth the emotional costs. As a result, they prefer to see the immediate reunification of their families in the Philippines. This cross-national difference in opinion shows that, just like other family forms, the reproduction of the transnational household entails varying and sometimes conflicting experiences, concerns, and priorities for different members of the family.

NOTES

This chapter is an abridged version of Chapter 4 of my doctoral dissertation *The Global Servants: (Im)Migrant Filipina Domestic Workers in Rome and Los Angeles*, University of California at Berkeley. I would like to thank Evelyn Nakano Glenn, Arlie Hochschild, Michael Omi, and Raka Ray for their helpful comments and suggestions. I would also like to thank Charlotte Chiu, Angela Gallegos, Mimi Motoyoshi, and Jennifer Lee for their support through the completion of this chapter.

1. See Basch et al. 1994; Chavez 1992; Curry 1988; Hondagneu-Sotelo 1994; Laguerre 1994; Massey et al. 1987; Paz-Cruz 1987.

2. In 1934, the Tydings-Mcduffie Act limited the migration of Filipinos into the United States to an annual quota of fifty (Takaki 1989).

3. See the recent anthology by Perea, *Immigrants Out!* (1997).

4. Only one single woman does not send remittances to her family in the Philippines regularly, because her parents and all of her siblings also live in Los Angeles. She therefore falls under the category of single householder.

REFERENCES

Agbayani-Siewart, Pauline, and Linda Revilla. 1995. Filipino Americans. Pp. 134–168 in Pyong Gap Min (ed.), *Asian Americans: Contemporary Trends and Issues*. Thousand Oaks, CA: Sage.

Almirol, Edwin. 1982. Rights and Obligations in Filipino American Families. *Journal of Comparative Family Studies* 3(3): 291–306.

Basch, Linda, Nina Glick Schiller, and Cristina Szanton Blanc. 1994. *Nations Unbound: Transnational Projects, Postcolonial Predicaments, and Deterritorialized Nation States*. Langhorne, PA: Gordon and Breach Science Publishers.

Chavez, Leo. 1997. Immigration Reform and Nativism: The Nationalist Response to the Transnationalist Challenge. Pp. 61–77 in Juan F. Perea (ed.), *Immigrants Out! The New Nativism and the Anti-Immigrant Impulse in the United States*. New York: New York University Press.

———. 1992. *Shadowed Lives: Undocumented Immigrants in American Society*. Fort Worth: Harcourt Brace.

Curry, Julia. 1988. Labor Migration and Familial Responsibilities: Experiences of Mexican Women. Pp. 47–63 in Margarita Melville (ed.), *Mexicanas at Work in the United States*. Houston: Mexican American Studies Program, University of Houston.

Espiritu, Yen Le. 1997. *Asian American Women and Men*. Thousand Oaks, CA: Sage.

———. 1995. *Filipino American Lives*. Philadelphia: Temple University Press.

Feagin, Joe. 1997. Old Poison in New Bottles: The Deep Roots of Modern Nativism. Pp. 13–43 in Juan F. Perea (ed.), *Immigrants Out! The New Nativism and the Anti-Immigrant Impulse in the United States*. New York: New York University Press.

Glenn, Evelyn Nakano. 1983 (February). Split Household, Small Producer and Dual Wage Earner: An Analysis of Chinese-American Family Strategies. *Journal of Marriage and the Family* 45: 35–46.

Hondagneu-Sotelo, Pierrette. 1994. *Gendered Transitions: Mexican Experiences of Migration*. Berkeley: University of California Press.

Hondagneu-Sotelo, Pierrette, and Ernistine Avila. 1997. "I'm Here, but I'm There": The Meanings of Latina Transnational Motherhood. *Gender and Society* 11(5): 548–71.

Laguerre, Michel. 1994. Headquarters and Subsidiaries: Haitian Immigrant Family Households in New York City. Pp. 47–61 in Ronald Taylor (ed.), *Minority Families in the United States.* Englewood Cliffs, NJ: Prentice-Hall.

Martin, Philip. 1995. Proposition 187 in California. *International Migration Review* 29(1): 255–263.

Massey, Douglas et al. 1987. *Return to Aztlan: The Social Process of International Migration from Western Mexico.* Berkeley: University of California Press.

Medina, Belinda T. G. 1991. *The Filipino Family: A Text with Selected Readings.* Quezon City: University of the Philippines Press.

Ong, Aihwa. 1996. Cultural Citizenship as Subject-Making: Immigrants Negotiate Racial and Cultural Boundaries in the United States. *Contemporary Anthropology* 37(5): 737–762.

Ong, Paul, and Tania Azores. 1994a. Asian Immigrants in Los Angeles: Diversity and Divisions. Pp. 100–129 in Paul Ong et al. (eds.), *The New Asian Immigration in Los Angeles and Global Restructuring.* Philadelphia: Temple University Press.

———. 1994b. The Migration and Incorporation of Filipino Nurses. Pp. 164–195 in Paul Ong et al. (eds.), *The New Asian Immigration in Los Angeles and Global Restructuring.* Philadelphia: Temple University Press.

Parreñas, Rhacel Salazar. 1998a. "White Trash" Meets the "Little Brown Monkeys": The Taxi Dance Hall as a Site of Interracial and Gender Alliances Between White Working Class Women and Filipino Immigrant Men in the 1920s and 30s. *Amerasia Journal* 24(2): 115–134.

———. 1998b. *The Global Servants: (Im)Migrant Filipina Domestic Workers in Rome and Los Angeles.* Ph.D. dissertation, University of California, Berkeley.

Paz-Cruz, Victoria. 1987. *Seasonal Orphans and Solo Parents: The Impacts of Overseas Migration.* Quezon City: Scalabrini Migration Center.

Perea, Juan, ed. 1997. *Immigrants Out! The New Nativism and the Anti-Immigrant Impulse in the United States.* New York: New York University Press.

Peterson, Jean Treloggen. 1993 (August). Generalized Extended Family Exchange: A Case from the Philippines. *Journal of Marriage and the Family* 55: 570–584

Portes, Alejandro, and Rubén Rumbaut. 1996. *Immigrant America: A Portrait* (2d ed.). Berkeley: University of California Press.

Sassen, Saskia. 1994. *Cities in a World Economy.* Thousand Oaks CA: Pine Forge Press.

———. 1988. *The Mobility of Labor and Capital: A Study in International Investment and Labor.* New York: Cambridge University Press.

Tadiar, Neferti Xina. 1997. Domestic Bodies of the Philippines. *Sojourn* 12(2): 153–191.

Takaki, Ronald. 1989. *Strangers in a Different Shore.* Boston: Little, Brown.

Yamanaka, Keiko, and Kent McClelland. 1994. Earning the model-minority image: diverse strategies of economic adaptation by Asian American women. *Ethnic and Racial Studies* 17(1): 79–114.

1. Takezawa argues that both the wartime incarceration of Japanese Americans and the redress movement of the 1980s were experiences not only unique in American history but of singular importance to informing the distinct ethnic identies of this population. At the same time, she asserts that the evolution of ethnic identification among the Nikkei has implications for our understanding of ethnicity generally. How is this the case? To what extent will the "collective suffering" of Japanese Americans impact the process through which the yonsei (fourth), gosei (fifth), and subsequent generations assert their ethnic identities?

2. Compare and contrast the kinds of community-based organizations that functioned in "old Chinatown" with those utilized by contemporary Chinese immigrants and their families. What were the functions of both kinds of organizations? What are their similarities and differences? How does Zhou account for the evolution of such organizations?

3. Describe the family structure of contemporary Chinese immigrants and their socioeconomic backgrounds. How do Chinese American families compare with their counterparts in China in terms of the transmission of cultural ideals onto the children? What are some of the distinctive characteristics of a Chinese American family? How does the Chinese American family promote adaptation among the second generation? How might community-based organizations and families that facilitate adaptation to mainstream American life prevent youths from aligning themselves with gangs? Consider some concrete ways in which youths might be encouraged to stay away from such activities.

4. How does transnationalism truly affect what we consider to be an Asian American identity? To what extent would such a household promote or retard adaptation to an American or Asian American cultural identity? Will Asian Americans whose families have been in the United States for several generations distance themselves from these newcomers, from individuals with stronger ties to the homeland countries? How different may contemporary transnational households shared by Filipino, Chinese, Koreans, Japanese, and Asian Indians differ from those sustained by the first wave of pre–World War II immigrants from these countries?

SUGGESTED READINGS

Almirol, Edwin B. 1985. *Ethnic Identity and Social Negotiation: A Study of a Filipino Community in California.* New York: AMS Press.

Cimmarusti, R. A. 1996. Exploring Aspects of Filipino-American Families. *Journal of Marital and Family Therapy* 22(2): 205–217.

Espiritu, Yen. 1995. *Filipino American Lives.* Philadelphia: Temple University Press.

Gill, Dhara S., and Bennett Matthews. 1995. Changes in the Breadwinner Role: Punjabi Families in Transition. *Journal of Comparative Family Studies* 26(2): 255–264.

Glenn, Evelyn Nakano, and Rhacel Salazar Parreñas. 1996. The Other Issei: Japanese Immigrant Women in the Pre–World War II Period. Pp. 124–140 in Silvia Pedraza and Rubén G. Rumbaut (eds.), *Origins and Destinies: Immigration, Race and Ethnicity in America.* Belmont, CA: Wadsworth.

Jen, Gish. 1991. *Typical American*. New York: Penguin.

Hope, Trina L., and Cardell K. Jacobson. 1995. Japanese American Families: Assimilation over Time. In Cardell K. Jacobson (ed.), *American Families: Issues in Race and Ethnicity*. New York: Garland.

Kang, K. Connie. 1995. *Home Was the Land of the Morning Calm*. New York: Addison-Wesley.

Kibria, Nazli. 1993. *Family Tightrope: The Changing Lives of Vietnamese Americans*. Princeton, NJ: Princeton University Press.

Kogawa, Joy. 1984. *Obasan*. Boston: David R. Godine.

Lee, Mary Paik. 1990. Oahu and Riverside. Chapter 2 in S. Chan (ed.), *Quiet Odyssey: A Pioneer Korean Woman in America*. Seattle: University of Washington Press.

Lessinger, Johanna. 1995. *From the Ganges to the Hudson: Indian Immigrants in New York City*. Boston: Allyn and Bacon

Matsumoto, Valerie. 1993. *Farming the Homeplace: A Japanese American Community in California, 1919–1982*. Ithaca, NY: Cornell University Press.

Santos, R. 1983. The Social and Emotional Development of Filipino American Children. Pp. 131–146 in G. Powell (ed.), *The Psychological Development of Minority Group Children*. New York: Brunner/Mazel.

Sung, Betty Lee. 1987. *The Adjustment Experience of Chinese Immigrant Children in New York City*. New York: Center for Migration Studies.

Tamura, Eileen. 1994. *Americanization, Acculturation, and Ethnic Identity: The Nisei Generation in Hawaii*. Urbana: University of Illinois Press.

Tan, Amy. 1989. *The Joy Luck Club*. New York: Ivy Books.

Tran, T. V. 1988. The Vietnamese American Family. Pp. 276–302 in C. Mindel, R. Habenstein, and R. Wright Jr. (eds.), *Ethnic Families in America: Patterns and Variations*, 3d ed. New York: Elsevier.

Yanagisako, S. J. 1985. *Transforming the Past: Tradition and Kinship Among Japanese Americans*. Palo Alto: Stanford University Press.

Ying, Yu-Wen, and Chua Chiem Chao. 1996. Intergenerational Relationship in Iu Mien American Families. *Amerasia Journal* 22(3): 47–64.

Zhou, Min, and Carl L. Bankston III. 1998. *Growing Up American: How Vietnamese Children Adapt to Life in the United States*. New York: Russell Sage Foundation.

FILMS

Chien, Windy (producer/director). 1992. Assimilation/A Simulation (14-minute experimental).

Cho, Michael (producer/director). 1996. *Another America* (56-minute documentary).

Uno, Michael (producer/director). 1988. *The Wash*.

Yasui, Lise (producer/director). 1988. *Family Gathering* (30 minutes).

Part VI

Keeping the Faith
Spiritual Practices among Asian Americans

Sangha of the South
Laotian Buddhism and Social Adaptation in Rural Louisiana

Carl L. Bankston III

Every migrant faces the challenge of finding a meaningful moral order and a meaningful personal identity in a new environment. The further the migrant has traveled, in both the geographic and cultural senses, the greater this challenge is likely to be. The refugees of Southeast Asia who have resettled in the United States since 1975 may have faced some of the greatest normative and epistemological challenges encountered by any immigrant.

In 1990, according to the U.S. Census, there were about 172,000 refugees in the United States from the country of Laos alone (U.S. Bureau of the Census 1991). This number, which includes close to 90,000 Hmong from the mountains of Laos, may have been a drastic undercount, since the substantial and continuing secondary migration of Laotians within the United States has made it difficult to keep accurate records (Bankston 1995a, 1995b). The Laotians have, perhaps, traveled as great a cultural distance as any migrants in history. They come to postindustrial America from a largely subsistence economy, based heavily on the cultivation of rice by hand and water buffalo. They have left small villages organized by interlocking kinship ties for a mobile, urban/suburban civilization. Overwhelmingly Buddhist in their original homeland, they now live in a nation heavily influenced by Christian traditions and beliefs.

Laotian Buddhism is a part of the new diversity in American religion identified by R. Stephen Warner (Warner 1998a, 1998b). As Warner notes, the literature on the new religious diversity is "mostly nonexistent" (Warner 1998a, p. 193). The post-1965 wave of immigrants from Asia and Latin America has resulted in the rise of new congregations, many of which were previously unknown in the regions where the immigrants have settled (see the accounts in Warner and Wittner 1998). Overlooking these new ethnic congregations is a serious problem because they have become part of the social landscape in many areas of the United States and because these religious groups are frequently central to the adaptation of their members to life in the new homeland.

This chapter looks at the role of Theravada Buddhism in the construction of moral order and identity among ethnic Laotians. Although it does rest on empirical data from observations and interviews, it is primarily an attempt at interpretive, rather than empirical, sociology. Immigrant adaptation is, I suggest, greatly shaped by the systems of meaning that immigrants bring with them and draw on to understand their new environment. To establish this point, I use qualitative data from participant observation and interviews. This makes it possible to provide a substantive picture of the meaning system of a particular group of immigrants, and it makes it possible to show how these immigrants use a conceptual framework from a previous life to fashion a way of being in a new life.

The Sociology of Religion and Cultural Analysis

A substantial body of literature supports the view that religion is an important source of psychological adjustment (Witter, Stock, Okun, and Haring 1985; Antonovsky 1987: Ellison, Gay, and Glass 1989; Pollner 1989; Ellison 1991; Stack 1983; Ellison 1994). A number of researchers have found, further, that religious involvement contributes specifically to the psychological adjustment of immigrants to their new homelands (Haddad and Lummis 1987; Hurh and Kim 1990; Kivisto 1993). Those who have studied the religions of the traumatically resettled Southeast Asian refugees have found that these religions are often central in promoting adjustment (Bankston and Zhou 1995a, 1995b; Zhou and Bankston 1994; Nash 1992; Rutledge 1985). The studies, however, generally lack specificity on how religions contribute to immigrant adaptation. I believe we can obtain some insight into this question by considering religion as the key cultural institution for addressing the problem of meaning in human life and by looking at some of the ways in which religious beliefs persist and change in the process of resettlement.

Wuthnow (1987) has suggested that classical and neoclassical approaches to culture have been overwhelmingly concerned with the problem of meaning. This tendency has, perhaps, been clearest in classical and neoclassical approaches to the sociology of religion. Durkheim's collective representations, for example, are not simply a collection of beliefs but beliefs that provide an ordered basis of social life. The social control aspect of this ordering has been heavily emphasized in objective analyses of human behavior, particularly in the literature on deviance. However, ordered systems of beliefs provide interpretive frameworks for understanding the world and one's place in it, as well as mechanisms of control.

According to Wuthnow (1987, pp. 36–37), neoclassical theorists of religion, such as Berger, Bellah, and Geertz, have emphasized this last aspect of Durkheimian theory. Geertz (1973) sees religion as a central part of a cultural web of meanings used to comprehend the nonhuman world. Berger (1969, p. 23) describes the *nomos* of religion as "an area of meaning carved out of a vast mass of meaninglessness." In making the world meaningful, Bellah (1970) argues, religion provides identity and motivation to groups and to individuals as members of groups.

Swidler (1986) raises the important question of how culture is related to action and, in raising this question, creates a means of conceptualizing the role of cultural tradition in social change. Swidler argues that, rather than seeing culture as a set of values that shape behavior, we should understand culture as a " 'tool kit' " of symbols, stories, and worldviews, which people may use in varying configurations to solve different kinds of problems" (p. 273). Thus, actors can draw on different aspects of their cultural equipage to deal with the new situations presented by social change. This is a helpful way of thinking about culture, and religion as an element of culture, but the metaphor of the toolbox may be a little misleading. As images of dominant social themes, cultural components form not loose assemblages of tools but dramatic depictions for thinking about the problems to be solved. These depictions shift, some parts are erased, some magnified, and some moved about as the problems to be solved change.

Swidler maintains that ideological aspects of culture are particularly important when people's lives are unsettled: "when people are learning new ways of organizing individual and collective action, practicing unfamiliar habits until they have become familiar, then doctrine, symbol, and ritual directly shape action" (p. 278). In other words, the kinds of interpretive frameworks provided by religion, as a central source of cultural components, become particularly important when people are coping with changing environments.

Culture, I suggest, is shaped by the kinds of problems it solves. If a culture is to render comprehensible the relations of an agricultural society, it will reproduce and represent the forms of agricultural relations. A radical social change may make a religion, as a system of cultural representations, inadequate for carving out Berger's "area of meaning," since the change presents an entirely new set of environmental challenges. At the same time, though, religion acquires even greater importance as a means of coping with the environment, since change presents new situations that demand interpretation. A social group can resolve this tension by drawing at once heavily and selectively on a religious heritage to construct a moral order in which the old symbolic elements are reoriented to a new environment.

I argue here that Laotian Buddhism developed as an expression of social relations within highly interdependent rice-growing rural villages. In the American community studied here, resettled Laotians live in an urban/suburban environment and engage in industrial economic activities. They make sense out of their new environment by utilizing cultural components from traditional religion, but these are subtly altered and rearranged to reflect the demands of the new environment.

Methods and Data

This study is based on participant observation data, collected over a period of several years in Southeast Asia and in the United States, and on interviews conducted during the summer of 1996 with members of a particular Laotian community.

Participant Observation

I assembled the background information and formed a grasp of the conceptual context of this study during three periods of participant observation. First, from the beginning of 1983 until the middle of 1985, I lived in a small village in the ethnic

Laotian part of Thailand, near the Thai-Lao border, while serving as a U.S. Peace Corps volunteer. Living with an ethnic Laotian family, I learned to speak Lao at this time, and I participated regularly in religious ceremonies. Second, from the middle of 1985 until the end of 1989, I worked with the U.S. Refugee Program in a camp in the Philippines for refugees from Southeast Asia. There, I had daily contact with Laotian refugees and spent a great deal of time at the Laotian Buddhist temple in the camp. My discussion of Lao religion in a village social context is based heavily on participant observation in an ethnic Lao village in Thailand and in the refugee camp, but I also rely on written sources, which are cited. Third, during the summer of 1996, I conducted a study of a Laotian community in southwestern Louisiana. This involved visiting homes, eating meals with members of the community, and participating in rituals. I wrote down notes each evening on observations during each day.

Interviews

In addition to information collected during the course of daily interaction, I also conducted, sixty-three unstructured interviews with members of the Laotian community. All of the interviewees arrived in the United States between 1980 and 1986, and all arrived in this particular community before 1989. Some interviews were conducted in English, some in Lao, and some interviews involved shifting back and forth between languages. All of the Laotians that I interviewed were Buddhists, as are well over 90 percent of the Laotians in Laos. These interviews concentrated on experiences during the resettlement process, adjustment difficulties in the United States, and respondents' views on American society and their places in it. I carried out further interviews with non-Laotian neighbors, local policemen, and employers of Laotians.

In the following analysis, I draw on my observations of Laotian Buddhism in Southeast Asia to offer, first, a brief description of how Laotian Buddhism functions as a system of meaning in the rural village context. Then, I describe the development of a particular Laotian American Buddhist community in the United States in order to show how a group of refugees adapted their traditional religious society to changed circumstances. Finally, I use both observations and interviews to describe how adherents use concepts from an adapted traditional religion to make sense out of a new and strange environment and to define their own identities in this environment. I quote responses that represented themes that emerged repeatedly in our talks and that appeared to be matters of general consensus.

Findings

Laotian Buddhism as a Village Moral Order

Laotian Buddhism incorporates both canonical Buddhism and elements of pre-Buddhist animism (LeBar and Suddard 1960; Tambiah 1976). Since most of the religion's practitioners do not distinguish doctrinal Buddhism from "folk Buddhism," it seems best to treat both the historically "orthodox" aspects of the religion and its adoptions from other belief systems as parts of a single set of religious beliefs and practices.

For the most part, Laotian Buddhism is virtually identical to the form of the faith found in Thailand, and it belongs to the Theravada school that also predominates in Cambodia, Burma, and Sri Lanka. One of the central philosophical differences between Theravada Buddhism and the Mahayana version found in Vietnam, China, Japan, and Korea has to do with the role of the *Bodhisattva* (literally, "enlightened being"). To simplify a complex doctrinal issue, *Bodhisattvas*, in Mahayana Buddhism, are individuals who have achieved enlightenment but delay passing over into Nirvana in order to help with the salvation of others. The position of Theravada Buddhism is that each individual must achieve enlightenment and salvation by his or her own efforts.

The three central concepts of Buddhism may be identified as *dharma (dhamma,* in Pali, *Tham* in Lao), karma (*kamma* in Pali, *kam* in Lao), and sangha (*sang* in Lao). The first term may be translated as "law," but it refers more broadly to the order of the universe and the Buddha's teachings on right order and belief. In the present context, it may be interesting to note that it is similar in meaning to the ancient Greek *nomos* adopted by sociologists. *Karma* refers to the retribution for actions and to the responsibility of individuals for their actions in prior incarnations and for all actions in the present life. It thus presupposes reincarnation. The *sangha* is the monastic community within which people can improve their own positions.

The best way to improve one's position is by becoming a monk. Indeed, it is traditional for Laotian men to try to be ordained for a period, either in youth before marriage and family or in old age. Even in Laos, however, this may not be possible for all men, and it is impossible for women. Therefore, in addition to become a part of the *sangha*, Laotian villagers may improve their lots through their relations to the monastic community (Halpern 1958; Archimbault 1973).

The chief mechanisms for influencing one's own destiny, in the present life or in the future, are *bun* (usually translated as "merit") and *baab* (which may be cautiously translated as "sin"). Any type of meritorious action may "make merit," but the primary source of merit is the temple. Nearly every Laotian village has a temple at its geographic and cultural center. Villagers make merit by feeding monks, by donating robes, and by contributing labor. This emphasis on external activity contrasts with the emphasis of textual Buddhism on meditation and internal states (Conze 1972; Tambiah 1984).

Temples are gathering places, and virtually all ceremonies, which are timed according to the agricultural cycle of seasons, are held at temples. Thus, in a Durkheimian sense, we can see the temples and the monks in them as expressions of communal existence. Making merit through temples can be interpreted as expressing commitment to the sacralized collectivity of the village.

One pre-Buddhist ritual, perhaps the key ritual for Laotians that has become a part of the national Buddhist belief system, is the ritual of the *baci* or *soukhouan*, or "invitation of the soul." The *khouan* might be described as a "mobile soul": the soul can wander away, causing an individual to become ill or even die. When people are parting, especially, a soul may go off with the other to whom one is attached.

The *baci* or *soukhouan* ceremony is one that should delight sociologists and anthropologists everywhere, since it involves explicit symbolic expressions of individuation and social bonding. The ceremony is usually preceded by the chanting of scriptures in the Pali language by a group of monks. Then, participants take bits of white cotton string as an elder layman calls on the *khouan* to reenter the bodies of those present. The celebrants tie the cloths around one another's wrists. If one of those present is being especially honored, or has just returned from a journey, or is about to set out on a journey, or has experienced the death of a family member, those present will concentrate on tying the bits of cloth around this person's wrist, binding the soul to the individual.

Before tying the knot, celebrants often place hard-boiled eggs or rice, symbols of fertility, into the palms of those whose wrists are being encircled. While tying, they make wishes for those being honored, most often wishing them long life, good luck, and many children (on this ceremony, see also Rajadhon 1988; Ngaosyvathn 1989; Bankston 1996).

The ceremony lends itself readily to interpretation as an expression of finding an individual identity (represented through the *khouan*) through group membership: one's soul is bound to one by other members of the community. It is revealing that those in liminal situations such as grief or preparation for travel receive special attention: these are the ones who particularly need to have their identities bound to them by the group.

Laotian Buddhism, then, can be taken as portraying the village as a meaningful social universe. The center of this universe, its Mount Meru, is the temple, where the development of individuals proceeds through their contributions to an expression of community. At the temple, also, explicit ritual metaphors of the relationship between individual and collectivity, such as the *soukhouan* ceremony, occur. What lies beyond this microcosm, though?

The nonhuman world is haunted. Laotian Buddhism has inherited from its pre-Buddhist past the cult of spirits, or *phi*. The jungles and forests, outside the village pales, are inhabited by these spirits, and wild or unknown places are described as fearsome by Laotians because they are home to spirits.

Phi may also be spirits in the sense of spirits of the dead, or ghosts. The dead are those who have passed beyond the known, social, collectively represented universe. When an individual dies, after funeral rituals, during which monks recite prayers for the deceased, the body is taken away from the village to a field or riverbank. Following festivities, the body is cremated, and the ashes are taken even further from the village and buried in the forest. It is hoped that all signs of the grave will disappear quickly; otherwise the spirit of the deceased may join a particularly evil set of *phi*, who bring sickness and misfortune to villages.

If religion is, as the Durkheimian tradition maintains, an expression of social relations, then we can interpret many characteristics of Laotian Theravada Buddhism as symbolic affirmations of village social relationships. In the system of wet rice farming that prevails in the lowlands inhabited by the ethnic Lao, villages lie at the center of fields owned by individual families. Despite individual ownership, farmers require continual help from friends and neighbors in the cultivation of this labor-intensive crop. While each person is expected to take responsibility for his or her own sustenance, this is possible only through shared contributions to a collective existence. The contributions people make to shared efforts result in obligations from others so that, in the profane as in the sacred sphere, individual benefits flow from donations of time and energy to a central collective.

These benefits are products of a form of moral causation that shapes both present and future lives. As Orru and Wang (1992) recognize, in canonical Buddhism we find little of the strict sacred-profane dichotomy proposed by Durkheim. Buddhists move toward the ultimate resolution of suffering and temporality by following the teachings of the Buddha. They also achieve "better" rebirths, in the sense of lives that are closer to the ultimate resolution of Nirvana, by the same moral process. Thus, in a sense, moral and psychological improvement is a matter of worldly progression.

In popular Laotian Buddhism, making merit does lead to better future lives in the sense of lives that are more advanced spiritually, but it also leads to better future lives in the sense of lives that are more materially rewarding. The present life is simply one part of this progression, and a believer influences material destiny in this life by the same moral means that he or she can influence destiny through a series of lives.

Laotian Resettlement and the Problem of Meaning

Bar-Yosef (1968, p. 27) has described immigration as "a type of social situation characterized by the disintegration of the person's role system and the loss of social identity." Successful immigrant adaptation, she suggests, consists of constructing a new role system and adopting a new social identity. The Laotian cultural constellation described in the previous section consists of a village-based cultural system in which a form of Buddhism establishes the identity of each individual and establishes the relations among individuals.

When I asked my interviewees about their initial problems in adapting to life in America, they did frequently mention issues such as worries about finding jobs, concerns with money, and difficulties with the English language. They also, however, described a social-psychological difficulty that was even more basic than these specific cares: life in the new world did not make sense to them. One of them put this reaction into words:

> At first, I didn't want to go anywhere or do anything. I was afraid of everything around me, because it was all so different. Even the sky and the earth were different. I thought that everything that was right in Laos might be wrong in America.

The fundamental social-psychological problem for these refugees from a vastly different society was one of establishing a means of interpreting life in the new country. In the following sections, I describe how a Laotian American community based on Buddhist beliefs and practices has enabled a group of Laotians to translate a preexisting moral order into an American social context.

Construction of a Laotian American Buddhist Community

The peak of resettlement of Laotian refugees in the United States occurred in the years 1979 through 1981, when about 105,000 people from Laos (including both Hmong and ethnic Laotians) came from Thailand, their country of first asylum (Rumbaut 1995, p. 239). The creation of a large Laotian community in Iberia Parish, Louisiana, in the early 1980s, and the growth of other Southeast Asian communities outside the New Orleans area, emerged from new job opportunities produced by the Louisiana oil boom of that period and by federal funding for job training. In Iberia, in 1980, Redfox Industries began training unemployed Vietnamese to do welding, pipe fitting, and other forms of skilled labor. The funds for this training were made available under the federal Comprehensive Training and Employment Act (CETA) (Bankston 1995a).

Laotians who had been settled elsewhere in the United States heard from Vietnamese contacts that training and jobs were becoming available in southwestern Louisiana, and Laotians began moving to the area in order to be placed in these programs. Laotians quickly became known for their welding skills and for their eagerness to learn and train one another. In 1998, the human resources director at one of the largest oil field fabrication companies at the Port of Iberia estimated that Laotians made up 15 percent of his workforce of 500 men and that their efficiency was so great that the company would lose 25 percent of its revenue if it were to lose the Laotian workers (personal communication, human resources director, Unifab Inc., July 14, 1998).

Since kinship networks directed the flow of secondary migration, the new Laotian arrivals in Iberia Parish tended to reconstitute a small set of homeland villages, and they tended to settle in ethnic concentrations. The first such concentration took root in a complex of federally subsidized, low-income apartments on the western edge of the city of New Iberia. The neighborhood surrounding the apartments is rough: one of the New Iberia policemen I interviewed, who wished to remain anonymous, referred to it as "Dodge City" because of the frequent drug-related shootings.

Southwestern Louisiana has a textile industry, as well as an oil industry. Laotian women began finding work just north of New Iberia, at a factory in St. Martinville. Thus, by the mid-1980s, almost all of the women were commuting to jobs in the north every day, while their husbands were commuting south to the Port of New Iberia.

Reliable data on the Laotian population are difficult to obtain, since their numbers have grown so rapidly and since they tend not to respond to official inquiries. The 1990 U.S. Census reports only 688 Laotians in Iberia Parish (U.S. Bureau of the Census 1991), but this appears to be a drastic undercount. Moreover, the number of Laotians has been growing rapidly since 1990. Police, community leaders, and Laotian proprietors of stores selling ethnic goods estimate the actual numbers at roughly

3,000 in 1996. The majority of adults are first-generation immigrants, who come from rural, village backgrounds in Laos. Few of these first-generation adults completed high school in their native country. Most men over the age of forty were soldiers, which is commonly the case for Laotian men, given the country's history of internecine warfare prior to 1975.

The original apartment complex and its surrounding area have continued to provide homes for large numbers of the Southeast Asian settlers. However, the incomes provided by having at least two wage-earners in most homes made it possible for many to move away from this low-income, high-crime neighborhood. They began to purchase homes in other, more suburban, parts of New Iberia and its environs. Instead of dispersing, however, they formed a number of ethnic pockets, with individuals attempting to buy or build homes close to friends and kin.

The availability of land and housing meant that they could not establish a single ethnic enclave. Driving, however, is nearly universal among adult and adolescent members of this group, since many had driven to Louisiana from other parts of the United States, and most commute daily to jobs at the port or the mill. Therefore, there is a single Laotian community in this area, consisting of scattered clusters of homes joined by the automobile.

In the mid-1980s, community members began to talk of building a cultural and religious center. In 1986, a number of men generally recognized as leaders formed the Temple Corporation, an association dedicated to building a Lao-style Buddhist temple that would be surrounded by an ethnic residential enclave. They found a tract of land in a semirural area on the northern edge of Iberia Parish, near the boundary of Lafayette Parish. The tract was relatively inexpensive, as it was outside established residential, commercial, and industrial zones, and it was at that time unused for farming.

In 1987, the temple was completed, and streets named after provinces in Laos were laid out in from of it. The little settlement was named Lane Xang ("Million Elephants") Village, after the historic Laotian kingdom of Lane Xang. Initially, most of the homes were trailers, but members of the community set a rule that any settlers would have to build a permanent home within five years of moving into the neighborhood. There has been some flexibility in the enforcement of this rule, and new people have moved to the area; by 1996 approximately one-quarter of the homes were still trailers, but about three-quarters were permanent buildings. In 1996, approximately 400 people resided in Lane Xang Village, and the temple itself served as a religious and cultural center for all of the Laotians in Southwest Louisiana. Through contacts with Laotian communities elsewhere in the United States, the community leaders found a Buddhist monk, who took up residence in the temple (see the discussion later in this chapter).

Moral Order and Identity in a Laotian American Buddhist Community

Monasticism and Moral Order. In Laos, as I have mentioned, the ideal is for every male to serve some time in a monastery. The Louisiana Laotians, however, all agreed that this ideal was unrealistic under the conditions of American society. None of my interviewees planned to become a monk, even for a short period of time. As one explained:

> We have jobs that we have to go to every day. Everybody has to work to get by. So we can't take time out to go into the temple. But we still hold Buddhism. We want to make merit, so we give to the monk who's there, and we can make merit through him.

The function of monk and temple as focal points, in other words, has been intensified and altered by the demands of the American working environment. Monasticism is no longer seen as a status into which many, if not most, male community members will enter at some point. Thus, while the single monk in the Louisiana temple remains a center of religious attention, monasticism is no longer as deeply intertwined with laity. It has, in a word, become a matter of professional specialization.

When I asked my interviewees what they would do if the single monk currently at the temple moved to another temple, they all had the same answer: they would seek to bring in another lifelong monk from another Laotian American community. The monastic order continues to lie at the heart of social relations, and it continues to be the chief mechanism for individual moral advancement, but monasticism has become a specialized job, rather than a stage of life.

Redefining monasticism as a specialized job serves as a means of mediating between the centrality of monasticism to traditional Laotian Buddhism and the demands of the contemporary American social and economic structure. In social-psychological terms, monasticism enables Laotian Buddhists to establish a sense of worth by making merit. Previously, in Laos, this was done both by active participation as monks and by contributions to monks. Active participation in monasticism is no longer possible for most. Having one individual take on monasticism as a full-time job, then, serves as one means of translating the preexisting moral order into an American social context.

Temple Participation and Ethnic Identity. While they are focal points of village identity in Laos, in America temples have become a focus of a minority ethnic identification. Temples in Laos are found in the centers of tightly clustered settlements, but the temple of the Louisiana Laotians serves the needs both of those residing in its immediate vicinity and of those who live in the small suburban pockets radiating around it. Living surrounded by non-Laotians, they come to see religious participation as an affirmation of ethnic identity. Another interviewee observed:

> In Laos, my religion was Buddhism. My religion taught me to be a good person, but I never thought my religion made me Lao. In America, Buddhism is a Lao religion, and that makes me Lao. The ones who become Christian—they are still Lao, but it isn't the same.

Religious and cultural events are held at the temple, as in Laos, but they are, by the very nature of the scattered settlement of Laotians, occasions in which people leave their American-style homes, after their American-style jobs, to celebrate ethnic events. The biggest event of the year is the "Water Festival," or Lunar New Year's

Celebration, held each year about the time of Easter. It is worth noting that the timing of this festival, which is held at the full moon of the fifth month in Laos, has been set to coincide with Easter holidays, so that people can get away from their jobs to participate.

The Louisiana Laotians engage in many of the same activities that characterize the Water Festival in Laos. There are parades with young women performing traditional dances, the *baci* or *soukhouan* ceremonies are held, and believers build sand *stupas* in the temples. But the festival is increasingly seen as a means of rejuvenating and perpetuating an imperiled ethnic identity. "It is a chance for my children to learn how we do things in my country and to bring something of my country to America," one middle-aged man observed of this occasion.

Ceremonies and festivals are more than occasions for nostalgia. They help to translate older role systems and identities as members of a village society into newer roles and identities as members of an American ethnic minority. "Of course, America is our home now," one of my interviewees reflected, "but when we have a *baci* here, in our own temple, in America. I feel like we are bringing Laos to America. It makes me feel like we can be Laotian and American." This is a revealing statement, because in Laos, religious ceremonies and festivals serve to bind people together as members of villages or family groups but not as members of an ethnicity. It is precisely the resettlement in a non-Laotian setting that makes ethnicity the basis of a new social identity, and the transplanted religious practices serve to express this identity.

From Village Community to Suburban Community. The temple continues to function as a community center, then, but it is a center for a vastly different sort of community. Although it is situated in an entirely Laotian settlement, the homes are all either newly built suburban-style houses or trailers serving as temporary homes before the owners can afford to put up permanent structures. Those living in the settlement drive daily to jobs at the port or in the mill; they do not walk to surrounding fields. Beyond the settlement are other small clusters of Laotians who must drive to the temple for their religious practices.

At noon each day, one can find small numbers of older men and women having lunch in the temple. It is really only on weekends, though, that large numbers of people, especially people living outside Lane Xang Village itself, gather at the temple. The American workweek has reorganized the use of time. "Before [in Laos]," remarked one of my interviewees, "we were together all the time. Now, we have to come together. The temple gives us a place to be together."

The religious institution no longer lies at the heart of a small knot of tightly intertwined social relations. Instead, the little clusters of Laotians that have settled in the area of Iberia Parish are tethered to one another by weekend trips.

Moral Causation and Immigrant Adaptation. As noted in the discussion of Swidler (1986), ideologies can be particularly important for guiding behavior in situations of rapid social change. Ironically, this means that the belief systems that are used to adapt to a new situation are developed as responses to the old situation. An important part of adaptation, then, may be the establishment of continuity between the old and the new so that a dramatic representation of social reality is shifted without being abandoned.

Baci ceremonies continue to be held at the temple on all major occasions. People may be living in vastly different circumstances, but they still feel the need for this symbolism of social binding and self-definition. They also like to include outsiders in these ceremonies as a way of creating connections between themselves and the non-Lao world in which they now live. "It is an occasion when we can welcome our American friends and treat them as our guests, since they brought us as guests to this country," a woman in her mid-thirties told me.

The *phi*, the spirits ubiquitous in Laos, seem to have somewhat of an attenuated existence in America. "I think I still believe in *phi*," one man told me, "but I don't feel them here in America. Maybe it's like the AM-FM radio. I could feel the *phi* in my own country, but here I'm an AM radio trying to pick up an FM station." Many others reported a similar insensitivity to the spirit world. Some said that they could sometimes feel that *phi* were present but that the spirits were much weaker and much less concentrated in particular places than in Laos.

If I am correct that the *phi* symbolize the nonhuman realm that surrounds the little intelligible universe of the Laotian village, then the decline in the detectable presence of these beings may be a result of the lack of strict separation between the human and the nonhuman in the urban/suburban settings of Laotian Americans. They no longer live in village islands of humanity, surrounded by forests. Although most people reported that they still believed in the existence of spirits, they generally said that they now feared the spirits much less than they did in the old homeland. One woman, who lived in the low-income neighborhood in New Iberia where the Lao first settled, told me, "I used to be afraid of *phi*. But now I'm more afraid of the people around me."

While the *phi* have diminished as a part of the Louisiana Laotian cultural depiction, the idea of life as part of a morally shaped sequence of births and rebirths remains strong. My interviewees often described their "new life" in America in terms of a rebirth. Several were even explicit about reincarnation as a paradigm for thinking about starting over in America. "We are always starting new lives," one observed, "before we die, and after we die. We always change."

Conceiving of life in a strange and new country in cosmological terms, as part of an ongoing universal cycle, helps to establish continuity between the familiar and the unfamiliar. Understanding this universal cycle as a moral process helps to humanize it. "My religion teaches me," said a woman in her mid-thirties, "that we make the world around us by our actions. It is our world."

It is true that this kind of moral interpretation of events can, in some cases, lead to "blaming the victim." It also, however, provides a *nomos*, in Berger's usage of the word, an "area of meaning." One of the dangers faced by immigrants, and especially by refugees, is that of finding themselves in a world that simply makes no sense: the occurrences around them are random and without normative form. The Buddhist chain of causation places actors in a universe in which their own thoughts and actions are linked to events outside themselves so that they can avoid falling into the anomie that threatens the uprooted and dislocated.

Conclusion

This study has attempted to offer a cultural analysis of Laotian-American Buddhism in three parts. First, it has offered an interpretive discussion of Theravada Buddhism in the social context of Laotian village society. Second, it has described how a particular community of Laotians, resettled in the United States, came to construct a temple and to re-construct their religious practices in America. Third, it has used interviews with members of this community to suggest how the religion has been subtly reshaped by the American social context and to describe how this reshaped religion supplies the resettled refugees with ethnic identities and with a comprehensible moral order.

My research indicates that religion affects adaptation to social change by cultural means: religious beliefs provide an interpretive framework that enables individuals to make sense of their world and to establish their own place in this world. This interpretative framework undergoes a subtle shift as social surroundings change, but the persistence and continuity of beliefs enables individuals to comprehend new situations through traditional worldviews. The ways in which groups adapt to change, therefore, depend both on the nature of the older situation, in which beliefs and practices are formed, and on how beliefs and practices are reshaped to address questions of moral order and identity in the new situation.

I have looked at one group: the Laotians of southwestern Louisiana. In order to comprehend variations among groups, it is important that future research look at how other religious traditions that have taken shape in differing social and historical circumstances may be related to adaptation to social change. I have also concentrated here on members of a moral community who retain and modify their religion as their environment changes. These ideas may also, however, be fruitfully applied to the phenomenon of religious conversion. For example, in Steltenkamp's (1993) excellent study of the later years of the famed Oglala Lakota medicine man Black Elk, when Black Elk had converted to Catholicism and become a catechist, it seems evident that the former medicine man and his fellow converts were translating many of their older beliefs into the new language of Christianity and adjusting to social change by reshaping, rather than discarding, their traditional representations of reality.

REFERENCES

Antonovsky, Aaron. 1987. *Unravelling the Mystery of Health.* San Francisco: Jossey-Bass.

Archimbault, Charles. 1973. *Structures Religieuses Lao.* Vientiane: Vigna.

Bankston, Carl L. III. 1995a. Southeast Asians in Louisiana. Pp. 661–677 in Carl Brasseaux (ed.), *A Refuge for All Ages: Immigration in Louisiana History.* Lafayette: Center for Louisiana Studies.

———. 1995b. Who Are the Laotian Americans? Pp. 131–142 in Susan Gall and Irene Natividad (eds.), *The Asian-American Almanac.* Detroit: Gale Research.

———. 1996. Refuge. *Sycamore Review* 8(1): 54–66.

Bankston, Carl L. III, and Min Zhou. 1995a. The Ethnic Church, Ethnic Identification, and the Social Adjustment of Vietnamese Adolescents. *Review of Religious Research* 38: 18–37.

———. 1995b. Religious Participation, Ethnic Identification, and the Adaptation of Vietnamese Adolescents in an Immigrant Community. *Sociological Quarterly* 36: 523–534.

Bar-Yosef, Rivka-Weiss. 1968. Desocialization and Resocialization: The Adjustment Process of Immigrants. *International Migration Review* 2: 27–45.

Bellah, Robert N. 1970. *Beyond Belief: Essays on Religion in a Post-Traditional World*. New York: Harper & Row.

Berger, Peter L. 1969. *The Sacred Canopy: Elements of a Sociological Theory of Religion*. New York: Doubleday.

Conze, Edward. 1972. *Buddhist Meditation*. London: Unwin.

Durkheim, Emile. [1915] 1965. *The Elementary Forms of Religious Life*. Trans. J. W. Swain. New York: Free Press.

Ellison, Christopher G. 1991. Religion and Subjective Well-Being. *Journal of Health and Social Behavior* 32: 80–99.

———. 1994. Religion, the Life Stress Paradigm, and the Study of Depression. Pp. 78–121 in J. S. Levin (ed.), *Religion in Aging and Health*. Thousand Oaks, CA: Sage.

Ellison, Christopher G., David A. Gay, and Thomas A. Glass. 1989. Does Religious Commitment Contribute to Individual Life Satisfaction? *Social Forces* 68: 100–123.

Geertz, Clifford. 1973. *The Interpretation of Cultures*. New York: Basic Books.

Haddad, Yvonne Y., and Adair T. Lummis. 1987. *Islamic Values in the United States: A Comparative Study*. New York: Oxford University Press.

Halpern, Joel Martin. 1958. *Aspects of Village Life and Culture Change in Laos*. New York: Council on Economic and Cultural Affairs.

Hurh, Won Moo, and Kwang Chung Kim. 1990. Religious Participation of Korean Immigrants in the United States. *Journal for the Scientific Study of Religion* 29: 19–34.

Kivisto, Peter. 1993. Religion and the New Immigrants. Pp. 75–96 in W. J. Swatos (ed.), *A Future for Religion: New Paradigms for Social Analysis*. Newbury Park, CA: Sage.

LeBar, Frank M., and Adrienne Suddard. 1960. *Laos: Its People, Its Society, Its Culture*. New Haven: Hraf Press.

Nash, Jesse W. 1992. *Vietnamese Catholicism*. Harvey, LA: Art Review Press.

Ngaosyvathn, Mayoury. 1989. *Individual Soul, National Identity: The Baci-Sou Kh'uan of the Lao*. M.A. thesis, Cornell University.

Orru, Marco, and Amy Wang. 1992. Durkheim, Religion, and Buddhism. *Journal for the Scientific Study of Religion* 31: 47–61.

Pollner, Melvin. 1989. Divine Relations, Social Relations, and Well-Being. *Journal of Health and Social Behavior* 30: 92–104.

Rajadhon, Anuman. 1988. *Essays on Thai Folklore*. Bangkok: The Intra-Religious Commission for Development and Sathirakoses Nagapradipa Foundation.

Rumbaut, Rubén G. 1995. Vietnamese, Laotian, and Cambodian Americans. Pp. 230–267 in Pyong Gap Min (ed.), *Asian Americans: Contemporary Trends and Issues*. Thousand Oaks, CA: Sage.

Rutledge, Paul D. 1985. *The Role of Religion in Ethnic Self-Identity: A Vietnamese Community*. Lanham, MD: University Press of America.

Stack, Steven. 1983. The Effect of Religious Commitment on Suicide: A Cross-National Analysis. *Journal of Mental Health and Social Behavior* 24: 362–474.

Steltenkamp, Michael F. 1993. *Black Elk: Holy Man of the Oglala*. Norman: University of Oklahoma Press.

Swidler, Ann. 1986. Culture in Action: Symbols and Strategies. *American Sociological Review* 51: 273–86.

Tambiah, Stanley J. 1976. *Buddhism and the Spirit Cults.* New York: Cambridge University Press.

———. 1984. *The Buddhist Saints of the Forest and the Cult of Amulets: A Study in Charisma, Hagiography, and Millennial Buddhism.* New York: Cambridge University Press.

U.S. Bureau of the Census. 1991. *Census of Population and Housing, 1990: Summary Tape File 3 (U.S.).* Washington, DC: U.S. Bureau of the Census.

Warner, R. Stephen. 1998a. Approaching Religious Diversity: Barriers, Byways, and Beginnings. *Sociology of Religion* 59: 193–215.

———. 1998b. Introduction: Immigration and Religious Communities in the United States. Pp. 3–34 in R. Stephen Warner and Judith G. Wittner (eds.), *Gatherings in Diaspora: Religious Communities and the New Immigration.* Philadelphia: Temple University Press.

Warner, R. Stephen, and Judith G. Wittner. 1998. *Gatherings in Diaspora: Religious Communities and the New Immigration.* Philadelphia: Temple University Press.

Witter, Robert A., William A. Stock, Morris A. Okun, and Marilyn J. Haring. 1985. Religion and Subjective Well-Being in Adulthood: A Quantitative Synthesis. *Review of Religious Research* 26: 332–342.

Wuthnow, Robert. 1987. *Meaning and Moral Order: Explorations in Cultural Analysis.* Berkeley: University of California Press.

Zhou, Min, and Carl L. Bankston III. 1994. Social Capital and the Adaptation of the Second Generation. *International Migration Review* 28: 821–845.

Chapter Fifteen

The Structure and Social Functions of Korean Immigrant Churches in the United States

Pyong Gap Min

Although Korea has never been a major Protestant country, Christians have constituted a large proportion of Korean immigrants to the United States. Historical studies (Choy, 1979; Paterson, 1988) suggest that approximately 40 percent of the pioneer immigrants to Hawaii at the turn of the century were Christians prior to immigration and that the majority of them attended ethnic churches in the United States. The same studies emphasize that ethnic churches became the most important ethnic organizations for Korean immigrants, which helped them to maintain social interactions and cultural traditions. In addition, Korean ethnic churches became centers of the Korean independence movement against Japan (Lyu, 1977).

A larger proportion of post-1965 Korean immigrants are affiliated with ethnic churches than are earlier Korean immigrants. Case studies in Los Angeles, Chicago, and Atlanta indicate that approximately 70 percent of Korean immigrants regularly attend ethnic churches (Hurh and Kim, 1984, 1988, P. Min, 1988, 1989). As will be elaborated, a large proportion of Korean immigrant church attendants were not Christians in Korea. Many probably began attending the ethnic church primarily because it met their practical needs associated with immigrant adjustment. Religious services may be the primary motive for attending the ethnic church for many other Korean immigrants. However, various social functions that Korean immigrant churches serve seem to be important for all Korean immigrant church participants.

Although several articles on Korean immigrant churches are available (Dearman, 1982; Hurh and Kim, 1990; I. Kim, 1981, 1985; Shin and Park, 1988), none has systematically examined the structure and social functions of Korean immigrant churches. A recent article by Hurh and Kim (1990) analyzes the religious participation patterns of Korean immigrants in considerable detail. However, the study, based on interviews of Korean immigrants, does not shed light on the structure of Korean immigrant churches. Kim's study of the New York Korean community (I. Kim, 1981), which devotes an entire chapter to ethnic churches, provides rich descriptive information on fellowship and social service functions of Korean immigrant churches. However, the chapter, largely based on the author's participant observation, lacks statistical data. In addition, New York and other Korean communities in the United States have achieved a phenomenal increase in population size since the mid-1970s, when data for Kim's book were collected. As the Korean population has increased in each Korean community, the number of Korean immigrant churches has also increased. Moreover, as each Korean community has achieved transition from an immigrant community to an immigrant-ethnic community, secular functions of Korean churches also have undergone changes. In the 1970s, when each Korean immigrant community was in its early stage of development, providing new Korean immigrants with fellowship and various services associated with immigrant adjustment may have been major practical functions of the Korean immigrant church. However, offering the Korean language and cultural education for second-generation children and providing social status for Korean adult immigrants seem to be increasingly important for the Korean immigrant church at present.

This chapter has two major objectives. First, it provides descriptive information on the structure of Korean immigrant churches. Second, it systematically analyzes social functions of Korean immigrant churches. Based on the theoretical discussion in the next section, it focuses on four major functions: (1) providing fellowship for Korean immigrants, (2) maintaining the Korean cultural tradition, (3) providing social services for church members and the Korean community as a whole, and (4) providing social status and social positions for adult immigrants. Interviews with 131 Korean head pastors in New York City provide the main data source for this chapter.

Overview of the Literature

Max Weber (1978) viewed religion mainly as a response to the basic needs of human beings. For him, any religious institution cannot be properly understood when isolated from the role it plays in meeting human needs. Social functions of religious institutions can probably be observed most clearly in ethnic churches in the United States. In the course of American history, ethnic churches have served a number of important nonreligious social functions for the minority and immigrant communities. Although no theory has been developed on social functions of ethnic churches or ethnic churches themselves, there is a plethora of literature touching on social functions or roles of minority and immigrant churches. For the purpose of clarity, these social functions associated with ethnic churches can be classified into four main types: fellowship; maintenance of ethnic identity and ethnic subculture; social services; and social status and social positions.

Fellowship

Many people are affiliated with religious institutions to meet their need for comfort, fellowship, and a sense of belonging. This function of satisfying the need for primary social interactions was important particularly for Afro-Americans before emancipation, when they were completely alienated from the white society. The black church for them was the family and community center. As W. E. B. Dubois put it in *The Philadelphia Negro* (1967:201), "its family functions are shown by the fact that the church is center of social life and intercourse; acts as newspaper and intelligence bureau, is the center of amusements—indeed is the world in which the Negro moves and acts." Meeting the need for primordial ties is also important for immigrants who are separated from their relatives and friends with whom they maintained closest ties. As one of the Hebrew words for synagogue, *Beth Haknesseth* (place of gathering), denotes, the Jewish synagogue has probably played the most important role in providing communal ties for Jews settled in the United States, as well as in other parts of the world. Although contemporary American Jews have been much secularized, many attend synagogue to be involved in the Jewish network. It is also a well-known fact that Catholic parishes constituted territorial enclaves for many European immigrants in the latter half of the nineteenth and the early twentieth centuries (Linkh, 1975).

Maintenance of the Native Tradition

Another important social function of the ethnic church, closely related to the function of meeting the need for primordial ties, is the maintenance of ethnic identity and the native cultural tradition of a minority/immigrant group. European immigrant groups, threatened with the loss of ethnic identity, have turned to their ethnic churches to preserve their identity and cultural traditions. Thus, "the church was the first line of defense behind which these immigrants could organize themselves and with which they could preserve their group, i.e., system, identity" (Warner and Srole, 1945:160). The Italian Catholic parishes "functioned to maintain the ethnic personality by organizing the group around the familiar religious and cultural symbols and behavioral modes of the fatherland" (Tomasi and Engel, 1970:186). The same is true of other white Catholic immigrant groups. Thus, different Catholic ethnic groups in the United States—French, Irish, Italian, and Polish Catholics—modified the Catholic religion in such a way that religious life fits into each ethnic subculture. That is why Greeley argued that "the various nationality groups were, at least to some extent, quasi-denominations within American Catholicism" (Greeley, 1972:119). The synagogue has been essential to maintaining Jewish ethnicity and identity in the long history of Jewish diaspora (Rosenberg, 1985). Starting with Sephardic Jews in the seventeenth century, the synagogue has been the center of Jewish cultural activities for different waves of Jewish immigrants in the United States.

Although assimilation and intermarriage have diminished primordial loyalties and the significance of nationalistic denominationalism during recent years (Wuthnow, 1988), the ethnic church still plays the central role in providing the language and cultural education for such white ethnic groups as Italian, Polish, and Greek Americans. Moreover, some recent nonwhite immigrant groups also try to preserve ethnic identity and ethnic subculture mainly through their religious organizations (Fenton, 1988; Rutledge, 1985; Seller, 1988; Williams, 1988).

Social Services

Religious institutions have been the major social service organizations in the modern world. Churches have played crucial roles, particularly in meeting the service needs of new immigrants. Many settlement houses were established in Chicago and other American cities in the late nineteenth and the early twentieth centuries to provide a variety of services for new immigrants, and religious organizations were actively involved in the settlement movement during the period. A number of Catholic fraternity organizations of diverse nationalities were created in the early twentieth century to help the influx of new immigrants from Catholic countries (Linkh, 1975:49–75). The synagogue played a central role in providing services for Jewish immigrants from Eastern European countries at the turn of the twentieth century (Rosenberg, 1985). Although ethnic social service organizations are more diverse in the current Jewish American community than before, the synagogue still plays an important role in providing social services for Jewish Americans. In addition, Catholic religious organizations as well as government agencies have been actively involved in assisting recent refugees in the United States (Jenkins, 1988; Nichols, 1988).

Social Status and Social Positions

Ethnic churches have provided immigrant/minority members not only with fellowship, ethnic identity, and social services but also with social status. This social status function of ethnic churches may be best illustrated by Afro-American churches. Deprived of status and power in the larger society, Afro-Americans aspired to achieve leadership in the black church hierarchy. This aspiration was strong particularly for Afro-American males who had never been able to take the dominant male role. As Frazier (1963:43) puts it:

> The church was the main arena of social life in which Negroes could aspire to become the leaders of men. It was the area of social life where ambitious individuals could achieve distinction and the symbols of status. The church was the arena in which the struggle for power and the thirst for power could be satisfied. This was especially important for Negro men who had never been able to assert themselves and assume the dominant male role, even in family relations, as defined by American culture.

In her study of the Polish American community, Lopata (1979) also observes that the quest for social status motivated many Polish Americans to establish ethnic organizations such as the ethnic church.

Data Sources

The Council of Korean Churches in Greater New York was established in 1976. The association has annually published the Korean Churches Directory of New York. The directory published in 1988, the most recent one available at the time of data collection, provided information on the name and address of each Korean church in the New York metropolitan area. It also included names of the head pastor, associate pastors, education pastors, and elders, if any, serving each church. New York, the city with the second largest Korean population, is the home of approximately 100,000

Koreans. The church directory listed 290 Korean ethnic churches in the New York metropolitan area, including Long Island, northern New York State, and parts of New Jersey and Connecticut. One hundred sixty-five of the 290 Korean churches listed in the directory were located in the five New York City Boroughs.

To obtain information on social functions of Korean immigrant churches, we tried to interview by telephone the head pastor for each of these 165 Korean churches in New York City. This investigator and two Korean bilingual students successfully interviewed 131 of the New York City pastors between February and March 1989. Only five pastors declined to be interviewed, and the listed telephone numbers were disconnected for seven churches. For the remaining churches not included in the interviews, pastors were not available—some were out of town, and others were away from home until late at night. Almost all pastors were interested in our research project and very cooperative, more cooperative than any other sample of Korean immigrants studied by this investigator. It also was very convenient to interview Korea pastors because most were available for the interview at home during the day as well as at night.

The interview schedule included fifty-two closed-ended and open-ended items. Each of the questionnaire items is related to one of the following areas: general characteristics of the church; social interactions and friendship networks; maintenance of the Korean cultural tradition; social services; and social status and positions. It took an average of twenty minutes to complete one telephone interview.

This investigator has participated in Sunday services at ten Korean churches in New York City, including the one with which he is formally affiliated. Participation in religious and fellowship services given by these ten Korean ethnic churches provides additional information for this study.

Korean Immigrants' Church Affiliation

In Korea, Christians constitute approximately 21 percent of the population, and the vast majority of Korean Christians (76 percent) are Protestants (Korean National Bureau of Statistics, 1987). Protestants and Catholics combined make up the second largest religious group, next to Buddhists (24.4 percent). Although Christianity is a minority religion in Korea in terms of number of adherents, it is more active than Buddhism in social, political, and educational activities and services (Dearman, 1982). American Christian missionaries established modern schools and hospitals in Korea at the turn of the century. Korean Christian churches and Christian organizations have been engaged in a number of social service activities (K. Min, 1981).

Although only a little more than 20 percent of Koreans are affiliated with Christian churches in Korea, the majority of Korean immigrants in the United States have had a Christian background in their home country. For example, in a survey of the 1986 cohort of Korean immigrants conducted in Seoul before emigration (Park et al., 1989:60), 54 percent of the respondents reported that they were affiliated with Protestant (41.6 percent) or Catholic (12.3 percent) churches. A survey in Chicago also indicates that 52.6 percent of Korean immigrants were Christians in their country of origin (Hurh and Kim, 1990).

Three major factors seem to have contributed to the overrepresentation of Christians among Korean immigrants. First, the Christian religion is very strong among urban, middle-class Koreans, and Korean immigrants have largely drawn from this segment of the population. The 1986 predeparture survey indicates that 58.6 percent of the 1986 Korean immigrants lived in Seoul and that 71 percent lived in the four largest metropolitan cities in South Korea (Park et al., 1989:31–32). Second, many Christians fled from North Korea to South Korea before and during the Korean War, and North Korean refugees, who have no strong kin and regional ties in South Korea, have immigrated to the United States in a greater proportion than the general population in South Korea (I. Kim, 1981). Third, Korean Christians, who are more Westernized and more modernized than other Koreans, are more likely to choose immigration to the United States than Korean Buddhists, Confucians, or those not affiliated with a religion.

Case studies of Korean immigrants indicate that approximately 70 percent of Korean immigrants regularly attend Christian churches and that almost all of them attend Korean ethnic churches (Hurh and Kim, 1988; P. Min, 1989). By contrast, Buddhists constitute a very small fraction of Korean immigrants. The 1986 Chicago survey shows that only 4.2 percent of the respondents were affiliated with Buddhist temples (Hurh and Kim, 1990). The increase in the proportion of Christians among Korean immigrants from approximately 50 percent in Korea to 70 percent in the United States indicates that roughly 40 percent of non-Christian Korean immigrants have become Christians since their immigration. The Korean group seems to show a higher level of affiliation with ethnic churches than any other ethnic group in the United States. Much smaller proportions of Chinese and Japanese Americans are Christians (B. Kim, 1978). Although approximately 85 percent of Filipino Americans are Catholics (Pido, 1986), most Filipino American Catholics attend American churches. One study (Mangiafico, 1988:174) indicates that only 17 percent of Filipino Americans are affiliated with ethnic churches. Judaism has played a significant role in uniting Jewish Americans, but less than half of the Jewish Americans are affiliated with synagogues. A survey conducted in Boston, for example, shows that only 38 percent of Jewish Americans are affiliated with synagogues (Cohen, 1985:56).

The Structure of Korean Immigrant Churches

Before discussing their social functions, data reflecting the structure of Korean immigrant churches may be useful to those unfamiliar with the Korean immigrant community. Table 15.1 shows the year each Korean church surveyed was established. Only four Korean churches under consideration were established before 1970, and only 11 percent existed before 1975. Data reveal that 70 percent of the Korean churches in New York City have opened since 1985. Starting years suggest that the vast majority of Korean residents in New York consist of the post-1965 immigrants. The oldest

Korean church in New York was established in 1921 by Korean students attending Columbia University, and the church is still located on 115th Street, just across from Columbia University.

Another useful data set concerning Korean churches in New York is denominational distribution. Denominations were identified not only for the 131 Korean churches located in New York City whose head pastors were interviewed but also for other Korean churches in the New York metropolitan area based on the church directory. The results are presented in Table 15.2. Presbyterian churches account for 49 percent of the total Korean churches in New York. This proportion is a little smaller than that of Presbyterian churches in Korea. The 1980 survey reported that Presbyterian churches accounted for 56 percent of total churches in Korea (Korean Christian Institute for the Study of Justice and Development, 1982:163). The prevalence of the Presbyterian denomination in Korea stems from the introduction by American Presbyterian missionaries of Protestantism in Korea at the turn of the twentieth century. Korean churches of the Methodist denomination, which is the second largest denomination in Korea, make up 15 percent of Korean churches in New York. Eight percent of New York Korean churches are nondenominational independent churches. Nondenominational churches are popular in the Korean community because Korean immigrant churches very often are established based on personal ties rather than religious doctrines.

Table 15.3 classifies Korean churches by congregation size, another important structural aspect of churches. Korean churches are characterized by a small size. Churches with fifty or fewer members (including children) constitute 30 percent of

TABLE 15.1
Establishment Years of Korean Churches in New York City

Established	Number	%
Before 1970	4	3.1
1970–74	10	7.6
1975–79	25	19.1
1980–84	46	35.1
1985–88	46	35.1
Total	131	100.0

TABLE 15.2
Denominational Distribution of Korean Churches in New York City

Denomination	N	%
Presbyterian	91	49.2
Methodist	27	14.6
Baptist	16	8.6
The Assembly of God	8	4.3
Holiness	8	4.3
Full Gospel	5	2.7
Catholic	5	2.7
Nondenominational	15	8.1
Others	10	5.4
Total	185	99.9

TABLE 15.3
Congregation Size of Korean Churches in New York City

Size	N	%
50 or Below	39	30.2
51–100	37	28.7
101–500	46	35.7
More than 500	7	5.4
Total	129	100.0
Mean	214	
Median	82	

the total churches in New York City, and only seven of the 129 surveyed churches have more than 500 members. Korean churches in New York City have, on the average, 214 members. The mean number of church members is inflated because of several large churches. The median number of members is only eighty-two. Full Gospel and Catholic churches are found to be much larger than other churches in congregational size. The small congregational size of Korean immigrant churches, which is not unique to the New York Korean community, can be largely explained by the need of Korean immigrants for small-group, primary social interactions.

Most Korean churches in the United States do not have their own buildings. Instead, they usually have service and fellowship meetings in American churches. Our New York City survey reveals that 24 percent have their own buildings and that the rest either use American churches (59 percent) or rent private buildings (17 percent). When they use American churches, they usually use predominantly white churches of the same denomination free of charge. Some Korean churches which hold service at American churches start services at the same time the main white congregation starts (usually at 11:00 A.M.) but in a separate hall. Others have service in the afternoon after that of the main white congregation. All New York Korean churches using physical facilities owned by white congregations, with the exception of one, are financially and operationally independent. They usually hold service together with the white congregation twice or three times a year.

Those Korean churches with their own buildings provide many services through formal and informal programs for church members, such as the Korean language school, a full Korean lunch after service, and seminars. They attract a large number of Korean immigrants, sometimes more than their buildings can accommodate, because of these practical functions. Several New York Korean churches with their own church buildings provide religious services three or four times consecutively on Sundays to accommodate an increasing number of members. Many of the New York Korean churches who do not have their church building have been raising a fund for construction of a church building from church members in the form of contributions. This raised fund has been a source of conflict for some churches.

Most Christians in Korea attend church two or three times a week, and some attend church every morning for prayer. The 1979 survey shows that 85 percent of Korean Protestants go to church twice or more per week (Korean Christian Institute for the Study of Justice and Development, 1982:67). Have Korean immigrants reduced the frequency of church participation to adapt themselves to American modernity?

Results of our survey indicate that they have reduced it significantly but that a significant proportion of them go to church more than once a week. More than 83 percent of the New York City Korean churches are found to provide one or more additional religious services, in addition to the regular service on Sunday. They usually hold extra services on Wednesday and/or Friday. For the majority of those churches which provide extra religious services, 20–30 percent of church members are found to participate in weekday services.

Korean is used exclusively as the medium of language for religious services for adult immigrants, whereas the bilingual service is common for second-generation Koreans. Results from this survey indicate that approximately 80 percent of Korean churches provide religious services separately for children and that 58 percent of those churches with separate services offer bilingual services. Twenty-three percent are found to provide services for children in Korean alone, whereas 19 percent use English exclusively for children's services. Those Korean churches located in suburban areas and thus serving more "old timers" tend to provide English services for children. By contrast, those located in Flushing, Woodside, and Elmhurst, where new Korean immigrants concentrate, tend to use the Korean language for both children's and adults' religious services. A few Korean churches located in suburban areas provide English language services even for college students.

The Christian religion has contributed to the modernization and Westernization of Korea by establishing American-style modern schools and introducing American customs. To that extent, it has helped to moderate sexual inequality deeply rooted in the ideology of Confucianism. However, Christian churches are probably more sexist than any other social institutions in Korea, at least in terms of their hierarchical structure. The Korean Catholic Church and most Korean Protestant denominations do not allow women to be ordained as minister, and few women hold important positions in Korean churches. A survey indicates that only 2.4 percent of head pastors and 24.6 percent of evangelical pastors in Korea in 1979 were women, although women accounted for 63.5 percent of church members (Korean Christian Institute for the Study of Justice and Development, 1982:29).

The Korean Churches Directory of New York includes the names of head pastors for all Korean churches in the New York metropolitan area with their pictures. Thus, the sex of each pastor is known. It shows only four female head pastors, who account for only 1.4 percent of 290 head pastors in the New York metropolitan area. The 131 churches whose head pastors were interviewed had 381 head pastors, associate pastors, and unordained evangelical pastors. Sixty-four of these 381 clerical leaders were women, making up only 17 percent of the total. Almost all sixty-four female clerical leaders were serving as (unordained) evangelical pastors. Thus, women are underrepresented among clerical leaders to a greater extent in Korean churches in the United States than those in Korea. This suggests that the immigration of Koreans to the United States has not led to a significant change in sexism practiced in Christian churches in Korea.

Social Functions of Korean Immigrant Churches

We previously noted that approximately 40 percent of those immigrants who were non-Christians in Korea attend the Korean ethnic church in the United States. Some Korean immigrants may have decided to participate in the ethnic church for religious purposes. Others may have done so for practical purposes such as meeting with other Koreans, acquiring information useful for immigrant adjustment, and teaching children the Korean language and customs. This section analyzes four major social functions of Korean immigrant churches in detail.

Fellowship

Meeting the need of immigrants for maintenance of social interactions and friendship networks with fellow Koreans may be the most important social function of Korean ethnic churches. Separated from their relatives and friends with whom they maintained primary social interactions in Korea, most new immigrants feel a sense of alienation in a foreign environment. Association with co-ethnic members may be essential for coping with this alienation, and the Korean ethnic church is an ideal place for association with co-ethnic members.

Approximately one fourth of Korean immigrants are affiliated with one or more ethnic associations other than ethnic churches, such as alumni and occupational associations (Hurh and Kim, 1987:61). However, nonreligious ethnic organizations are less effective than ethnic churches for helping to maintain social interactions and friendship networks with fellow Koreans because they do not have frequent meetings.

All Korean immigrant churches have a fellowship hour after the Sunday service. During the fellowship hour, church members exchange greetings and enjoy informal talks with fellow church members. Almost all Korean head pastors interviewed in New York City (129 out of 131) reported that their churches provide refreshments during the fellowship hour. Twenty-eight percent of the Korean churches in New York City provide a full lunch or dinner after Sunday service. Korean meals are usually prepared by each church member on a rotating basis. Almost all Korean churches surveyed also have parties after services to celebrate important Korean traditional and religious holidays. In addition, most small-scale Korean churches have birthday parties after Sunday service for children and elderly people, with cakes, food, and gifts.

As previously noted, Korean immigrant churches are usually small. This seems to have a lot to do with the practical needs of Korean immigrants for fellowship and a sense of belonging. Small Korean congregations do not provide many of the social service programs for church members that are available in large congregations. However, many Korean immigrants want to be affiliated with small congregations mainly because of the advantage of primary social interactions, which are possible only in small-group settings. As Kim (1981:199) rightly points out, the ethnic church plays the role of "a pseudo-extended family" for many Korean immigrants.

Korean immigrants attending a small church enjoy intimate friendship networks with church members not only inside the church but also outside of it. In this connection, it is important to note that 45 percent of those Korean immigrants in Chicago with one or more intimate Korean friend in the same city made friends in the ethnic church (Hurh and Kim, 1987).

A large Korean church is less effective than a small church for meeting the need of immigrants for an intimate social environment. However, even large Korean immigrant churches have made adjustments to facilitate the immigrants' primary social interactions. Korean immigrant churches usually divide church members into several different groups by the area of residence and help each group to hold regular district meetings called *Kuyok Yebae*. A district meeting combines a religious service and a dinner party at a member's private home, which provides district members with ample opportunity for informal social interactions. Church members belonging to the same district rotate hosting the meeting.

Nearly 80 percent of the Korean churches in New York City under consideration were found to have district groups. Some small churches have divided members into only two district groups, but 31 percent have ten or more district groups. The percentage of church members who regularly participate in district meetings differs for different churches, ranging from 10 percent to 90 percent with an average of 54 percent. Approximately half (51 percent) of the churches that have district groups hold district meetings once a month, and the other half hold meetings twice a month or more often. It is surprising that more than half of the Korean churchgoers, most of whom work long hours, participate in a district meeting biweekly or monthly, in addition to attending regular services. Korean immigrants seem to actively participate in district meetings in spite of their busy work schedules because they serve as a medium for friendship ties and mutual assistance.

Korean immigrant churches provide members with an outlet for relieving tensions and alienation not only through fellowship services and district meetings but also through other recreational activities. The vast majority of Korean churches organize various sports activities, outdoor services, and retreats. The majority of Korean churches in New York City (51 percent) hold at least one athletic meeting per year for all church members, and more than 30 percent hold one or more sports meetings particularly for children. Volleyball, table tennis, and fishing are major annual events. Ninety-two percent of the New York Korean churches also hold at least one outdoor service per year, and nearly 70 percent hold two or more such services. At an outdoor service, church members eat Korean food and enjoy different kinds of recreational activities after a short religious service. Eighty-five percent of Korean churches in New York City also go on at least one retreat per year, which usually lasts two to seven days, and 70 percent take two or more retreats per year. Korean church retreats include not only Bible studies, but also many recreational activities such as swimming, fishing, singing, and playing sports and games.

Maintenance of the Korean Cultural Tradition

Another major social function of Korean immigrant churches is to help immigrants maintain their cultural traditions. The churches help to preserve Korean culture in several ways. First, the Korean language and customs are more strictly observed inside the church than outside of it. Immigrants give sermons in Korean for almost all adult worship services. As previously noted, even children's services are provided bilingually or in Korean far more often than in English. Many Korean children practice the language at home to attend a Korean-language or bilingual service.

Moreover, Korean immigrant churches help to maintain culture by providing Korean language programs for children, which is vital to language retention. Nearly half of the Korean churches in New York City have established a Korean language program. Most (67 percent) have a one-hour class before or after the Sunday service, but others provide a three-hour class Saturday mornings. Several Korean churches in New York City provide summer schools ranging from one week to two months, focusing on teaching the Korean language and customs. They offer the summer cultural program not only for church members but also for other Korean children. The church language school also teaches Korean history, folk dance, games, and etiquette. Thus, it plays an important role in passing on the Korean cultural traditions to second generation Koreans. Contributions that church language schools make to maintaining the language and culture are significant, particularly because there are only a few community-wide Korean language schools not affiliated with the church and because most Korean parents have no time to teach their children the language at home.

Exposure to Korean culture at church is not limited to the Korean language. All Korean immigrant churches celebrate religious and traditional holidays by serving a variety of Korean traditional food. Many churchgoers also wear Korean traditional dresses on important Korean holidays. Moreover, churches teach children traditional values such as filial piety by preparing gifts for parents on Mother's and Father's Day. In addition, church members usually play traditional games and sports during picnics. Almost all Korean churches celebrate the year-end party at a member's private home on New Year's Eve, and church members usually play a traditional game called yoot at the party.

Pastors very often emphasize Korean values in their sermons, and this is another way ethnic churches contribute to maintaining culture and identity. Korean pastors as a group seem to be more conservative than other college-educated Koreans in their attitudes toward American mass culture in general and adolescent subculture in particular. Many Korean pastors tend to think that American society, which originated from the Christian background, is turning against the Christian ideology. They argue that Korean traditional values such as respecting adult members are more consistent with Christian values than "American individualism." They frequently tie certain Korean traditional values to a paragraph from the Bible and preach church members to preserve those Korean values to live as sincere Christians. Finally, Korean immigrant churches contribute to maintaining ethnic identity by bringing church members' attentions to their homeland in many different ways. One way is through their sermons and prayers. They very often pray for the democratization of South Korea, the unification of the two Koreas, the elimination of corruption on the part of government officials, a quick recovery from flood damages in a certain area of Korea, and so forth. Pastors tie their sermons to Korea on Korean national holidays such as the March First Independence Movement Day and the Independence Day. Many Korean churches prepare special commemoratory services to mark these politically important holidays. In addition, Korean immigrant churches help members remember their homeland and Korean identity by inviting ministers and professors from Korea to give sermons or lectures. Our survey reveals that 78 percent of the New York City Korean churches have had at least one visiting preacher or lecturer from Korea over the last year and that they have invited, on the average, four visiting speakers from Korea.

Social Services

Another major social function of Korean immigrant churches is to provide a variety of services for church members. New immigrants need different kinds of information and services for the initial immigration orientation and successful adjustment in the United States. There are, however, few formal social service agencies in the Korean immigrant community that new immigrants can depend upon for assistance. The Korean ethnic church seems to be the only social institution that most immigrants turn to for useful information and services.

The Korean church provides social services for church members in two ways. First, the head pastor and other religious leaders help church members informally on an individual basis by providing information and counseling on employment, business, housing, health care, social security, children's education, and so forth. They also help by visiting hospitalized members, interpreting and filling out application forms for those with serious language difficulty, going to court as a witness for members with legal problems, etc. Second, the Korean immigrant church provides services for church members through a number of formal programs such as the Korean language school, the Bible school, seminars, and conferences.

To determine the extent to which Korean pastors provide services to church members, we asked our respondents to indicate how many times they had helped church members over the last year in several specified areas. Their responses are analyzed in Table 15.4. All 129 head pastors who responded to this question have provided service for at least one church member over the last year. Each pastor has helped church members with problems on the average fifty times over the last year. Seventy percent of the churches surveyed have two or more pastors, and only the head pastor was interviewed. Since associate and education pastors also help church members, the extent to which Korean religious leaders provide services for church members is greater than the statistics included in Table 15.4 might suggest.

Table 15.4 also gives clues to the common problems faced by immigrants that Korean pastors usually help to solve. Two major problems that new immigrants of any nationality face are the language barrier and the difficulty of finding a job. Thus, Korean pastors are deeply involved in helping church members with these two problems. However, Korean pastors are greatly involved also in helping church members with children's and other family problems.

Korean community social workers in the New York metropolitan area and ethnic newspaper articles suggest that many Korean immigrant families have marital con-

TABLE 15.4
Services Provided by the Korean Head Pastor to Church Members for One Year

Category of service	N of pastors who ever provided service	Number as % of total pastors interviewed	Mean number of services
Family Counseling (Marital)	107	82.8	8.2
Help with Language Problem	87	69.1	8.4
Help with Other Adjustment Problems	88	70.1	7.1
Counseling for Children's Problems	80	63.0	6.3
Job Information & Job Referral	82	64.2	8.3
Help with Legal Problems	78	61.0	3.5
Help with Housing Problems	67	53.0	4.3
Help with Businesses	53	40.5	2.3
Help with Other Problems	17	12.5	0.9
Total	129	100.0	49.3

flicts and difficulty handling adolescents. In the New York City survey, head pastors were asked to indicate four major problems of Korean immigrants in the order of importance, based on their personal experiences with church members. Their responses also indicate that the above-mentioned family problems are the most serious problems for many Korean immigrant families. Pastors' comments, conversations with Korean social workers, and ethnic newspaper articles lead to the conclusion that physical fatigue, mental weariness, and the lack of companionship due to both partners' long hours of work and the wife's increased economic role contribute to Korean immigrants' marital conflicts. Korean parents' lack of time for children and their inability to understand Americanized children's psychology also seem to contribute to parent-child tensions and juvenile delinquency.

The majority of our respondents provide family counseling to church members. Moreover, many Korean immigrant churches hire young education pastors especially to help families with children's problems. Table 15.4 reveals that 63 percent of the respondents have helped at least one family with children's problems over the last year and that each respondent has taken care of six or seven cases on the average. Since the education pastor, who was not interviewed, specializes in family problems with children in many Korean immigrant churches, the involvement of Korean religious leaders in helping to solve children's problems is much greater than what the table suggests.

As previously indicated, Korean immigrant churches provide services for church members not only through the pastor's direct contact with each member or family but also through formal programs on a group basis. Each head pastor was asked to indicate what kinds of programs his/her church provides for church members. Small churches are disadvantaged in establishing formal programs in terms of financial resources and manpower, and thus they focus on the pastor's direct help of church members on an individual basis. By contrast, the majority of large churches have group activities and formal programs to help Koreans adjust to American society effectively. In fact, more than half of the respondents reported that their churches have provided at least one seminar, lecture, and/or health clinic for educational purposes.

A variety of topics, including health, insurance, U.S. laws, income taxes, marital adjustment, American educational system, and small business, have been covered by seminars and lectures provided by Korean immigrant churches. However, children's education and educational problems are found to have been covered more often by church-sponsored seminars and lectures than any other topic. Approximately one-third of the churches represented by the respondents have done something to educate parents about solving juvenile problems. Several churches regularly hold the "union hour" for an effective dialogue between parents and children. Moreover, approximately 70 percent of the New York Korean churches surveyed offer education for children at least once a week, teaching the Korean language and culture, the Bible, Korean dancing, and/or Tae Kwon Do. They usually provide educational services on Saturday and/or Sunday. Two churches offer after-school services on weekdays, helping with homework, English, and math and teaching the Korean language and customs. Several churches regularly teach children special talents such as Korean ballet, singing, and skiing. In addition, many Korean churches have special programs during summer vacation, such as the Korean language school, the Bible study program, summer camps, and retreats.

While Bible school, Korean language school, the chorus, etc. were supposed to teach children the Bible, the Korean language, or singing, these church programs were created in Korean churches for other practical purposes. Most Korean parents do not know how to handle their adolescent children, who are vulnerable to juvenile delinquency in a large city like New York City. Furthermore, most Korean parents with adolescents do not have time to supervise their children, especially on weekends or holidays when children do not go to school. These parents seem to mainly depend upon the Korean churches for education and child custody on holidays. Several Korean pastors told this investigator that parents' repeated requests had led to the establishment of Bible study and Korean language programs and that church membership had increased since the establishment of these children's programs.

Korean Catholic Apostolate Church of Queens has operated a credit union effectively. The church is the second largest Korean Christian church and the largest Korean Catholic church in the New York metropolitan area, with approximately 2,500 members. The credit union started in 1979 as a self-help financial organization with voluntary services by a number of church members. It has now turned into a large banking system with seven full-time workers and an asset of 7 million dollars. Both members of the church and those attending the other five Korean Catholic churches in the New York metropolitan area can belong to the credit union, whose membership has increased to 3,000. Members can take a loan from the union with a lower interest rate than they can get from commercial banks and without going through a complicated credit check. The credit union currently provides not only loans but all other banking services, including personal checking accounts, for its members. As a nonprofit organization it distributes all profits to its members.

However, for the most part, while Korean immigrant churches have been active in providing services for their own church members, they have neglected to respond to the welfare needs of the Korean community as a whole. The New York City survey indicates that 60 percent of Korean churches have not helped the Korean community with financial contributions at all over the last year, and 66 percent have not provided any nonmonetary service for the Korean community at large.

Most Korean immigrant churches which provided monetary or nonmonetary services to the Korean community are large churches with financial and manpower resources. In an effort to solve Korean youth gang and other juvenile problems, the council of Korean churches in New York raised $300,000 and established a youth center in 1991 in Flushing, which has provided Korean young people with counseling, seminars, education, and recreational and cultural activities. Most of the churches in New York that made monetary contributions for the Korean community contributed to this fund for the Korean youth center. Most of those churches which provided nonmonetary services did so mainly through educational programs. Several Korean churches in New York offered the Korean language program and/or the summer school not only for their own church members but also for other Korean children regardless of church affiliations. Several Korean churches sent volunteers to help Koreans to complete the 1990 census form.

Social Status and Positions

Another important social function of Korean immigrant churches is to provide social status and social positions for Korean immigrants. The majority of Korean immigrants held satisfactory professional, managerial, and administrative positions in Korea. However, most Korean immigrants cannot maintain the same levels of occupation in this country because of the language barrier and other disadvantages. Thus, most Korean immigrants experience downward mobility (Hurh and Kim, 1984; I. Kim, 1981; P. Min, 1984; Yu, 1983). Although many Korean immigrants achieve economic mobility through self-employment in small businesses, blue-collar small businesses do not help them enhance their social status (P. Min, 1984, 1988). Some American natives who hold low-status jobs may enjoy relatively high status by playing leadership roles in voluntary associations. However, few Korean immigrants have found leadership positions in American voluntary organizations. Accordingly, dissatisfaction with low social status and position is a major problem of Korean immigrants' adjustment.

Therefore, most Korean immigrants need to find meaningful positions in the Korean community. They seem to meet their status needs mainly in the Korean ethnic church. Each Korean ethnic church provides a number of religious and nonreligious positions. First, Korean churches provide professional occupations for Korean ministers. The surveyed churches in New York City provide professional occupations either as head pastors, associate pastors, education pastors, or unordained evangelists for 381 people, almost all of whom are Korean. Ministers are the only group of Korean nonscience professional immigrants, most of whom can maintain their preimmigrant professional occupations in the United States. Moreover, it is noteworthy that Korean immigrant churches offer lay leaders many religious positions as elders, exhorters, and deacons, whereas American churches are not so hierarchical among lay members. Table 15.5 shows the number of adult church members and lay position holders for fifty-four Korean churches in New York City. Each church provides nearly eighty lay positions, which account for 32 percent of total adult church members. Koreans who hold these lay positions usually are not paid, although they contribute more money and spend more time for services than other church members. However, these ethnic church positions meet their needs for social status, which cannot be met in the larger society. The title indicating a church position as an elder, an exhorter, or a deacon is carried not only inside the church but also outside of it. That is, Elder Kim is called as such not only by church members but also by other Koreans, unless he possesses a better title associated with his occupation or a voluntary organization.

Korean immigrant churches also provide a number of nonreligious administrative and organizational positions. Church members are divided into a number of groups based on ages and districts of residence, and each age/district group has an elected president and vice-president. Each church also has a number of task-oriented special committees, such as the Publication Committee, Fellowship Committee, Education Committee, Committee for Social Concern, and Financial Committee, each with elected chairpersons. In addition, each church has several specialized organizations, such as the choir, the Korean language school, and the children's Bible school, which require the services of many administrators and professionals.

The social status function of Korean immigrant churches is a typical example of what Merton (1957) called "latent functions." Latent functions are those functions "unintended and unrecognized." Korean pastors probably do not intend to enhance Korean immigrants' social status by creating many religious and nonreligious positions in their churches, and many Koreans may not recognize the social status function of Korean immigrant churches. However, church staff positions, created largely for the smooth operation of the church, help many Korean immigrants to enhance social status. A survey of Korean immigrants in Chicago indicates that Korean male immigrants who hold staff positions in the ethnic church show a lower level of depression and a higher level of life satisfaction than those who do not (Hurh and Kim, 1990). This finding comes as no surprise, considering the fact that most Korean adult immigrants have lost their relatively high social positions associated with their preimmigrant occupation. There is strong competition for staff positions in the immigrant churches, which is one of the major reasons for schisms within Korean immigrant churches (Shin and Park, 1988). A few Korean pastors admitted that they created more staff positions than necessary to meet Korean immigrants' social and psychological needs. High social status is not attached to a Korean language school teacher. However, the role is meaningful to many Korean women who

TABLE 15.5
Number of Lay Religious Positions

Mean number of adult members	Mean number of elders	Mean number of exhorters	Mean number of deacons	Total position holders
246	5.1	8.6	64.8	78.5 (31.9%)

used to teach in Korea but who cannot continue their preimmigrant occupation because of the language difficulty.

Conclusion

The extent to which members of an ethnic/immigrant group maintain their native cultural tradition and social interactions with co-ethnic members is referred to as "ethnic attachment" or "ethnicity" (Hurh and Kim, 1984; Reitz, 1980; Yinger, 1980). Korean immigrant churches help Koreans maintain social interactions with co-ethnic members and the Korean cultural tradition. Thus, Koreans in the United States maintain a high level of ethnicity, probably higher than any other Asian ethnic group, partly because the vast majority are affiliated with ethnic churches (Mangiafico, 1988: 174; P. Min, 1991).

European white ethnic groups tried to preserve ethnic identity and ethnic subculture largely through participation in ethnic churches. However, the role of Korean ethnic churches in sustaining Korean ethnicity is interesting, particularly because Protestantism is not a Korean national religion, such as Catholicism was for earlier Italian and Polish immigrants. In their effort to preserve the Korean subculture and identity through Christian churches, Korean immigrants have significantly "Koreanized" Christianity.

The role of Korean ethnic churches in providing a number of social services for Korean immigrants is not surprising. However, social services provided by Korean ethnic churches are of interest because they are somewhat different in nature from those provided for the earlier white immigrants by churches and synagogues. Korean ethnic churches focus on counseling and educational services for Korean families with marital and juvenile problems, whereas synagogues and Catholic churches seem to have helped earlier European immigrants meet their economic needs, helping to obtain housing and jobs. This difference in the nature of social services provided by ethnic churches indicates an important difference between recent Korean immigrants and the earlier European immigrants. The earlier European immigrants, who were predominantly of low economic class origin, usually came without personal resources, and thus meeting basic economic needs was very important for their adjustment. By contrast, family and other noneconomic adjustment problems are more serious than economic problems for middle-class Korean immigrants, the vast majority of whom have brought a moderate or significant amount of money and belongings from Korea.

We have noted that Korean ethnic churches help Korean immigrants with their status problems by providing a number of clerical and lay positions for church members. This function has not been discussed much in connection with white immigrant churches. This may also suggest an important difference between recent Korean immigrants and the earlier white immigrants. Recent Korean immigrants of middle-class background experience severe downward mobility in their occupational adjustment, and thus status inconsistency is a major problem for most Korean male immigrants. Status inconsistency, however, seems to have been a less serious problem for the earlier European immigrants. These differences reflect the ways in which ethnic churches have helped meet the pressing needs of different immigrant groups.

REFERENCES

Choy, B. Y. 1979. *Koreans in America*. Chicago: Neilson Hall.

Cohen, S. 1985. *American Modernity and Jewish Identity*. New York: Tavistock Publications.

Council of Korean Churches of Greater New York. 1988. *The Korean Churches Directory of New York 1988*. New York: Council of Korean Churches of Greater New York.

Dearman, M. 1982. "Structure and Function of Religion in the Los Angeles Korean Community: Some Aspects." In *Koreans in Los Angeles: Prospects and Promises*. Edited by E. Y. Yu, E. H. Phillips and E. S. Yang. Los Angeles: Center for Korean and Korean-American Studies, California State University. Pp. 165–183.

Du Bois, W. E. B. 1967. *The Philadelphia Negro*. New York: Schocken Books.

Fenton, J. Y. 1988. *Transplanting Religious Traditions: Asian Indians in America*. New York: Praeger.

Frazier, E. F. 1963. *The Negro Church in America*. New York: Schocken Books.

Greeley, A. 1972. *The Denominational Society: A Sociological Approach to Religion*. Glenview, IL: Scott, Foresman.

Hurh, W. M., and K. C. Kim. 1990. Religious Participation of Korean Immigrants in the United States," *Journal of the Scientific Study of Religion* 19:19–34.

———. 1988. "Uprooting and Adjustment: A Sociological Study of Korean Immigrants' Mental Health." Final report submitted to National Institute of Mental Health, U.S. Department of Health and Human Services.

———. 1987. "Korean Immigrants in the Chicago Area: A Sociological Study of Migration and Mental Health." Interim descriptive report submitted to National Institute of Mental Health, U.S. Department of Health and Human Services.

———. 1984. *Korean Immigrants in America: A Structural Analysis of Ethnic Confinement and Adhesive Adaptation*. Madison, NJ: Fairleigh Dickinson University Press.

Jenkins, S. 1988. *Ethnic Associations and the Welfare States: Services to Immigrants in Five Countries*. New York: Columbia University Press.

Kim, B. L. 1978. *The Asian Americans: Changing Patterns, Changing Needs*. Montclair, NJ.: Association for Korean Christian Scholars in North America.

Kim, I. S. 1985. "Organizational Patterns of Korean-American Methodist Churches: Denominationalism and Personal Community." In *Rethinking Methodist History*. Edited by R. Richey and K. Rowe. Tennessee: United Methodist Publishing House.

———. 1981. *New Urban Immigrants: The Korean Community in New York*. Princeton: Princeton University Press.

Korean Christian Institute for the Study of Justice and Development. 1982. *A Comprehensive Research Report on Korean Churches in Commemoration of the One Hundred Years' Anniversary*. Seoul: Korean Christian Institute for the Study of Justice and Development.

Korean National Bureau of Statistics. 1987. *1985 Population and Housing Census*. Seoul: Economic Planning Board, Korean Government.

Linkh, R. M. 1975. *American Catholicism and European Immigrants*. Staten Island, NY: Center for Migration Studies.

Lopata, H. Z. 1979. *Polish Americans: Status Competition in an Ethnic Community*. Englewood Cliffs, NJ: Prentice-Hall.

Lyu, K. 1977. "Korean Nationalist Activities in Hawaii and the Continental United States, 1900–1919," *Amerasia Journal* 1:23–90.

Mangiafico, L. 1988. *Contemporary American Immigrants: Patterns of Filipino, Korean, and Chinese Settlement in the United States.* New York: Praeger.

Merton, R. K. 1957. *Social Theory and Social Structure.* New York: Free Press.

Min, K. B. 1981. *The History of Korean Christian Churches* (in Korean). Seoul: Korean Christian Publishing Company.

Min, P. G. 1991. "Cultural and Economic Boundaries of Korean Ethnicity: A Comparative Analysis," *Ethnic and Racial Studies* 14:225–241.

———. 1989. "Some Positive Effects of Ethnic Business for an Immigrant Community: Koreans in Los Angeles." Final report submitted to the National Science Foundation.

———. 1988. *Ethnic Business Enterprise: Korean Small Business in Atlanta.* Staten Island, NY: Center for Migration Studies.

———. 1984. "From White-Collar Occupations to Small Business: Korean Immigrants' Occupational Adjustment," *Sociological Quarterly* 25:333–352.

Nichols, B. 1988. *Religion, Refugee Work, and Foreign Policy.* New York: Oxford University Press.

Park, I. S., J. Fawcett, F. Arnold, and R. Gardner. 1989. "Koreans Immigrating to the United States: A Pre-Departure Analysis." Paper No. 114. Hawaii: Population Institute, East-West Center.

Patterson, W. 1988. *Korean Frontier in America: Immigration to Hawaii, 1886–1910.* Honolulu: University of Hawaii Press.

Pido, A. J. A. 1986. *The Pilipinos in America.* Staten Island, NY: Center for Migration Studies.

Reitz, J. 1980. *The Survival of Ethnic Groups.* Toronto: McGraw-Hill.

Rosenberg, S. 1985. *The New Jewish Identity in America.* New York: Hippocrene Books.

Rutledge, P. 1985. *The Role of Religion in Ethnic Self-Identity: A Vietnamese Community.* Lanham, MD: University Press of America.

Seller, M. S. 1988. *To Seek America: A History of Ethnic Life in the United States.* Englewood, NJ: Jerome S. Ozer.

Shin, E. H., and H. Park. 1988. "An Analysis of Causes of Schisms in Ethnic Churches: The Case of Korean-American Churches." In *Koreans in North America.* Edited by Seung Hyung Lee and Tai Hwan Kwak. Seoul: Kyung Nam University Press. Pp. 231–252.

Tomasi, S. M., and M. H. Engel. 1970. *The Italian Experience in the United States.* Staten Island, NY: Center for Migration Studies.

Warner, W. L., and L. Srole. 1945. *The Social System of American Ethnic Groups.* New Haven: Yale University Press.

Weber, M. 1978. *Economy and Society: Guenther Roth and Claus Wittich,* vol. I. Berkeley: University of California Press.

Williams, R. B. 1988. *Religions of Immigrants from India and Pakistan: New Threads in the American Tapestry.* New York: Cambridge University Press.

Wuthnow, R. 1988. *The Restructuring of American Religion: Society and Faith Since World War II.* Princeton: Princeton University Press.

Yinger, M. 1980. "Toward a Theory of Assimilation and Dissimilation," *Ethnic and Racial Studies,* 4:249–264.

Yu, E. Y. 1983. "Korean Communities in America: Past, Present, and Future," *Amerasia Journal* 10:23–52.

Chapter Sixteen

Asian Indian and Pakistani Religions in the United States

Raymond Brady Williams

India and the United States share some characteristics that provide the environment for the flowering of religious faith and devotion. India and the United States are the world's largest democracies, in which religious freedom is a part of basic civil rights. The constitution of each establishes a secular government that permits religions to develop as they will within the restraints of civic order. Both countries incorporate a large number of ethnic, social, and religious groups for whom religion is an important and primary marker of individual and group identity. The constellation of characteristics combined with contemporary migrations of peoples provides the framework for the development of modern multicultural and multireligious societies in both India and the United States—and a set of transnational religious networks between them.

India and the United States are, by some measures, the most religious countries in the world, which is surprising. Citizens of these countries share high levels of various markers of religiosity: self-identification with religious groups, participation in individual and group religious activities, and affirmations of belief in God. Religions shape much of the calendar, cultural affairs, and negotiations of political power in both countries. Difference extends beyond dichotomies of First World, of which the United States is exemplary, and developing world, in which the Indian subcontinent has been a prominent member since independence. The majority religion in India is an indigenous religion—or constellation of religious systems—that was designated as Hinduism, whereas adherents of indigenous religious systems in the United States form a small minority. The Indian subcontinent is a mother of religions—as is the Middle East, which gave birth to the Abrahamic religions of Judaism, Christianity, and Islam—but the Indian subcontinent conceived a family of religions significantly different from the Abrahamic tradition: Buddhism, Hinduism, Sikhism, and Jainism. Through the centuries, other religions entered India with conquerors and migrants, including those with missionary zeal, such as Muslims and Christians, but these religions did not displace the indigenous ones. The United States is the primary receiver of the people and religions of the world, at first various forms of Christianity and, more recently, most of the other religions of the world, and all these virtually replaced indigenous religions.

The United States is permanently and firmly linked with the countries of the Indian subcontinent by the new immigrants who accepted the opportunities provided by the changes in immigration laws since 1965 to establish their families and their religions in a new land. In the new transnational context, South Asian religions are becoming world religions in new ways, resulting in significant changes in India and Pakistan. More important, however, is the fact that new religions are finding their place in the United States with increasing numbers of adherents, thereby changing the American religious landscape.

Immigration from India and Pakistan to the United States

A commonly told story of American immigration is about the open door to European peoples that resulted in the designation of the United States as the country of immigrants symbolized by the Statue of Liberty. Not all peoples of the world participated in these early migrations, however, and the history has been like a swinging door as people from the Indian subcontinent and other Asian countries have ventured toward America. Although the first immigrants from the Indian subcontinent entered in 1820, it was not until the beginning of this century that more than 275 persons immigrated from South Asia in a single decade (INS 1982, 2–1). Punjabi farmers moved from western Canada into Washington, Oregon, and California to escape the aftermath of an anti-Oriental riot in Vancouver on 7 September 1907, eventually establishing a thriving farming community in California. They were denied the opportunity for citizenship in 1923 by a decision of the U.S. Supreme Court that South Asians, who had previously been treated as Caucasians, were not "free white persons" under the law. They were defined as Asian under immigration and naturalization procedures.

As Asians, they were excluded by a series of laws culminating in the Immigration Act of 1924, which codified the "Asiatic Barred Zone," placed the first permanent limitation on immigration, and established a "national origins" quota system. The door was effectively closed to Asians. From 1820 to 1960, a total of only 13,607 persons emigrated from the Indian subcontinent, and an unrecorded number of these departed (INS 1982, 2–4). The 1924 act had the effect of dramatically reducing the total number of immigrants from all countries, so that the previous levels of immigration were not reached again until 1989.

The years between 1925 and 1965 were a peculiar period of American history when there was a major lull in immigration. Because of a variety of special circumstances during that period, which included the passage of restrictive laws, the Great Depression, and World War II, many fewer people immigrated to the United States than before or since. Indeed, in some years during the lull, more people left the United States than entered as immigrants. This lull had profound effects on developments in American culture and religion. A rather homogenized religious-cultural synthesis of Christianity, Judaism, and Enlightenment deism shaped what was called the Judeo-Christian tradition that underlay much of mid-century educational, political, and religious rhetoric. Ecumenical movements of all sorts thrived during this period,

when successive generations of immigrant families passed through a common experience of Americanization undisturbed by the arrival of new immigrants on the
scene. The growth and influence of the ecumenical movement among Protestants,
the homogenization of ethnic groups, the shape of American general education, and
the general placidity of the 1950s could be attributed, in part, to the lull in immigration. Second and third generations of immigrant families were learning to get along,
after a fashion, and the results of their negotiation provided the context for the
development of the civil rights movement in which African Americans demanded
their place at the negotiating table.

All that dramatically changed when the Immigration and Nationality Act of 1965
was passed in the emotional aftermath of the assassination of President John F.
Kennedy, along with several other bills that he had proposed to the Congress. By
setting a nondiscriminatory quota for immigrants from every country, the act reopened the doors to immigrants, especially those from Asia and from other places
who had previously been systematically excluded. The number of immigrants increased rapidly. In 1991, some 1.8 million persons were granted permanent resident
status, the highest total ever recorded (INS 1991, 12, 18). The places of origin of
immigrants shifted from Europe to Asia, so that, for the period of 1981–90, nearly 50
percent of those naturalized as citizens had been born in Asia. Those born in South
Asia contribute to the growth in immigration, with 57,448 gaining admission in 1993
(India 44,121; Pakistan 8927; Bangladesh 3291; and Sri Lanka 1109). The number from
India has dropped slightly (40,121 in 1993; 34,921 in 1994; and 34,748 in 1995), and the
number from Pakistan has grown slightly, to 9774 in 1995 (INS 1995, tab. 5).

Those arriving in the first decade after passage of the 1965 law were part of the
brain drain, not "Your tired, your poor/Your huddled masses yearning to breathe
free," as earlier immigrants were described by words enshrined on the Statue of
Liberty. Rather, they were the physicians, engineers, scientists, nurses, and computer
specialists needed in the growing American economy.

South Asian immigrants in the 1970s were among the best educated, most professionally advanced, and most successful of any immigrant group, and the income of
Asian Indians recorded in the 1980 census ranked second highest among ethnic
groups in the country. However, a major shift has taken place from the 1970s and
early 1980s, when a majority of immigrants qualified by meeting professional and
educational criteria, to the current situation, in which a large majority qualify on the
basis of family reunification.

The growth of the South Asian community in the United States has been dramatic,
up from 371,630 persons, as recorded in the 1980 census, to 919,626 in 1990. Specifically, those from India increased by 815,447, or 125.6 percent, in the decade; those
from Pakistan, by 81,371, or 415.3 percent; those from Bangladesh, by 11,838, or 800.9
percent; and those from Sri Lanka, by 10,970, or 275.3 percent. These percentages
reflect the fact that Pakistanis and Bangladeshis were relatively slower at moving
through the open door in the 1970s but arrived in somewhat greater numbers in the
1980s.

The most important fact about the new immigration is that it continues unabated.
Even though the number of immigrants changes year by year and new regulations

revise the preference categories slightly, the door remains open, and new immigrants from South Asia arrive every year in large numbers both to join the established communities and religious groups and to transform them. They will continue to do so for the foreseeable future, reinforcing the special defining characteristic of the United States as a country of immigrants.

Immigrant Religions and Religious Pluralism in the United States

Because the Indian subcontinent is such a fertile place for religions, immigrants bring and establish several religions and regional forms of religions from India and Pakistan previously relatively absent from the American religious landscape: for example, Hinduism in several regional forms, Sikhism, Jainism, Syro-Malabar Catholicism, Orthodox Christianity, and both Sunni and Shi'a forms of South Asian Islam. Together immigrants from India and Pakistan introduce the most diverse and active new ingredients into American religious pluralism of any immigrant group. Since 1957 the U.S. government has observed a congressional prohibition against maintaining records of religious affiliation on immigrants and American citizens, so reliable governmental statistics on the number of adherents of these religions are lacking. Nevertheless, their presence is revealed by the many temples, gurdwaras, mosques, and churches they have constructed and by the many new religious festivals and rituals they have introduced. Diana Eck's Pluralism Project at Harvard University demonstrates that one can study the world's religions in any major U.S. metropolitan area; it is certainly the case that one can study in America all the major religions of the Indian subcontinent, without traveling to South Asia.

Hindus

The survival of Hinduism in India through the turmoil of several invasions and conquests results in part from its strong links to the home, where both mothers and fathers are religious specialists for the family. Home shrines are more central to the lives of most Hindus than temples are, and life-cycle and other family-based rituals are fundamental to personal identity. This home-based strategy serves Hindus well in India, where Hindus form the religious majority, and it proves effective also in the United States, where Hindus are a very small minority. The new immigrants of the brain drain came to the United States as individuals, brought personal ritual objects for home shrines, and practiced privately at home. Then they engaged in more elaborate religious activities after bringing spouses and families to join them. As they became financially secure, they established homes throughout metropolitan areas and in many towns and cities throughout the country, not in ghettos. Settlement pattern affects the development of religious organizations. One can trace several stages of growth beyond the home influenced by the length of residence of the South Asians in a given location and by the size of the community there.

Cultural and religious organizations came into existence when children of the early immigrants reached an age to be socialized outside the home, and parents looked for help in raising their children. The first organizations created were national in character, gathering Asian Indians (and even Pakistanis) into social and cultural organizations such as India cultural centers. Because Hindus constituted a large majority of the members, the religious ethos of many of these organizations was Hindu: the organizations observed Hindu holidays and welcomed Hindu religious leaders as guests. Out of these organizations developed the Hindu temple societies, which raised funds and built Hindu temples in most major American cities. These are as elaborate as the Meenakshi Temple near Houston or the Rama Temple near Chicago and as modest as a residential house converted for use as a temple. Ecumenical Hindu temples attempt to serve Hindus from all regions of India. Images of many deities are placed in shrines in a single ecumenical temple, although some of these deities would not be found in the same temple in India. In the larger metropolitan areas, Gujarati, Tamil, Telugu, Hindi, and other regional groups establish separate organizations and temples where the language, ethos, form of deity, rituals, cuisine, and leaders from a particular region of India are prominent. Another constellation of groups comprises devotees of gurus, living or dead, and the hierarchy of religious leaders who preserve and transmit their teachings. As in India, the Hindu organizations in any major American metropolitan area create a complex network of organizations, temples, leaders, calendars, and rituals on a grid of national, ecumenical, regional-linguistic, and sectarian identity markers. These are the forms shaping the Hindu community at the end of the century and that provide the ingredients for an American Hinduism for the new century.

Jains

In India, Jains form a very small minority closely allied with Hindus, and they are renegotiating that relationship in the United States. Initially, Jains met regularly with Hindus at India cultural centers and observed special Jain festivals and rituals at home. They joined in building some ecumenical Hindu temples and established small Jain shrines in the temples, as, for example, in the Hindu temple in Monroeville, Pennsylvania. A majority of Jains in the United States have family origins in Gujarat, even though many of them migrated from Bombay or other cities of India. The Jain community is so small in the United States that only more recently and in large cities have they amassed sufficient resources, both human and financial, to establish separate Jain temples like the one in Bartlett, a suburb of Chicago.

Jains share with other Asian Indian religious groups the striking characteristic that they are organized and led by lay people who were part of the brain drain because, with the exception of the Christians, South Asian religious specialists were not among the first group of South Asian immigrants. Traditional rules for Jain monks and nuns prohibited them from traveling abroad, so fewer Jain religious specialists have been available in the United States to assist in the establishment of institutions. Two Jain monks did travel to the United States. One of them, Chitrabanu Muni, came in 1971, first to lecture as a visiting scholar at Harvard. Sushil Kumar Muni came to establish a series of teaching centers, the most important of which is Siddhachalam in the

Pocono Mountains of Pennsylvania. Siddhachalam has become an important center for retreats and national conferences. Jains created two national organizations: the Jain Study Circle, which publishes a magazine that contains essays explaining Jain doctrine and practice, especially nonviolence and vegetarianism; and the Jain Association in North America, which engages in activities for the affiliated organizations, including a biennial convention. (Note that it is common for South Asian organizations and annual meetings to include membership from both Canada and the United States.)

Sikhs

Sikhs have roots in the Punjab region of India and occupy a space—both geographic and religious—between Hindus and Muslims, and they maintain an intricate amalgam of Sikh religious practice and Punjabi ethos. Sikhs established themselves in the United States earlier than other South Asian groups, having migrated from British Columbia into California to escape the 1907 anti-Oriental riots. They soon became isolated by restrictive immigration laws that prevented them from bringing brides or relatives from the Punjab to join them. Nevertheless, they pursued their traditional occupation as farmers and established a prosperous Sikh farming community and the first Sikh institutions. They were joined after 1965 by young professionals and their families, coming directly from the Punjab and the cities of India and representing different class, regional, and religious characteristics. The newer immigrants quickly established organizations and gurdwaras throughout the country. Gurdwaras are centers of instruction in the Sikh religion and Punjabi language and culture. There are thirty gurdwaras in California alone and approximately eighty in the United States overall.

The negotiations between the older and newer Sikh immigrant communities and the development of Sikh institutions were rudely interrupted by conflict between Sikhs and the Indian government over demands for an independent Sikh state in the Punjab to be called Khalistan. The complex issues of the dispute, involving preservation of Punjabi cultural and political identity and Sikh religious rights, deteriorated into an Indian army exercise in 1984, called Blue Star, in which the army occupied the most sacred Sikh shrine at Amritsar, which Sikhs often refer to as their Vatican. The conflict in India both galvanized and divided the Sikh community in the United States. The emotion was strong because threats to Punjabi identity and the Sikh religion in India are mirrored by less visible threats to both in America. Annual elections of officers for Sikh organizations became occasions for conflict and division, and fund drives were for a period more often directed to support for Khalistan independence than for establishing gurdwaras and other Sikh institutions in America. As political turmoil has subsided in the Punjab, American Sikhs have learned that their influence has diminished in India and are therefore free to return to negotiations between themselves and with other South Asian religious groups regarding the distinct Sikh identity they will create in the United States.

Muslims

Pakistan was created as an independent Muslim state in 1947, at the same time that India was also granted independence by the British. Subsequently, in a civil war, Pakistan divided into two Muslim countries: Pakistan and Bangladesh. Over 80 million Muslims are Indian citizens, however, so Muslims in the three countries of the Indian subcontinent constitute one of the largest concentrations of Muslims in the world. South Asian Muslims migrate from all three countries to join Muslims from over sixty nations who are now establishing themselves in the United States. Islam claims to establish one brotherhood of people from all national and ethnic groups, and nowhere outside of Mecca during the hajj pilgrimage would one find more national and ethnic groups exhibiting that brotherhood than in a mosque in an American metropolitan area. Muslims are a minority in India, although they hold significant political power there, and they form large majorities in Pakistan and Bangladesh; in the United States, South Asian Muslims form a minority within a minority.

Muslims share with others the tension between universality and particularity. Mosques must be open to all Muslims, and some are inclusive by necessity, as in communities with small immigrant populations, or by design, as in Houston, where decentralization from an inclusive central mosque led to the establishment of inclusive mosques throughout the area. In some metropolitan areas, such as Chicago, however, mosques serve distinct national or ethnic groups and are known as Asian, African, European, or Arab. The regional identity of the mosque is revealed by the native place of the governing boards, the training of the imams, the language of instruction and social intercourse, the modes of dress, and the cuisine at mosque functions. Over 1,250 mosques and Islamic centers serve a growing American Islam that includes a significant Asian Indian and Pakistani component. National organizations like the Muslim Student Association and the Islamic Society of North America direct a wide array of educational, religious, and social welfare activities. New Muslim immigrants continue to arrive from all sixty countries, so Muslims from the Indian subcontinent are negotiating within a multicultural and multigenerational Islam what the shape of American Islam will be.

Christians

Christians come from where they are very small minorities among Hindus in India and Muslims in Pakistan to a context where they become part of a putative majority-Christian population. Christianity has a long history in India, claiming a tradition about the arrival of the Apostle Thomas as a missionary in A.D. 52 and another tradition about the coming of a different Thomas with a group of Syrian Christians in the fourth century. Although the accuracy of these traditions is questioned, Indian Christianity contains several strands reaching back to the earliest centuries: (1) St. Thomas Christians (also called Syrian Christians) preserve ancient oriental rites of Syrian Orthodox Christianity; (2) St. Xavier, the most important of the Roman Catholic missionaries in the sixteenth century, converted Christians from the lower castes and attempted to bring St. Thomas Christians into communion with Rome, thereby eventually creating Indian Christianity in three rites (Syro-Malabar, Syro-Malankara, and Latin); (3) Protestant missionaries established denominational churches and institutions throughout the Indian subcontinent during British colonial rule; (4) Pentecostal missionaries and indigenous leaders encourage a lively evangelistic effort; and (5) the Church of South India (1947) and the Church of North India (1970) united several denominations following Indian independence.

All these streams of Indian Christianity are now flowing into American Christianity with the immigrants and are expanding in most major metropolitan areas. Christian immigrants from India are unique in two ways. First, they immigrated on the shoulders of the women because Christian families and institutions in India produced a surplus of nurses who were admitted under interpretations of immigration regulations as part of the brain drain. The nurses were needed in inner-city American hospitals in the 1970s. The second difference is that they brought their priests and pastors with them, many of whom were spouses or siblings of nurses.

Indian Christian immigrants have followed several adaptive strategies. Many joined churches that are in communion with their churches in India. Although the bishops of the Mar Thoma church and the Church of South India at first actively discouraged the establishment of Indian churches in America, the attraction of Indian languages, rituals, and customs was enormously strong. Immigrants gathered in congregations where they could sing the songs of Zion, first in English in all-India Christian fellowships and then in Malayalam, Gujarati, Tamil, Telugu, Hindi, or one of the other regional languages. During the late 1980s and the 1990s, congregations and parishes established their own American dioceses, synods, judicatories, and national fellowship groups and affiliated with churches in India: the Mar Thoma church, the Malankara Syrian Orthodox church, various Pentecostal groups, the Brethren Assemblies, Syro-Malabar and Syro-Malankara Catholics, the Knanaya parishes (an endogamous castelike association), the Church of South India, and the Southern Asia Caucus of the United Methodist Church.

The highlights of church life for many Indian Christians are the annual family conferences that many of these churches hold over summer weekends, some of which attract several thousand Indian Christians. Some Indian pastors affiliate with American denominations, especially the Methodist, Episcopalian, and Catholic denominations, and serve as pastors of parishes or chaplains in hospitals. As individuals and congregations, these Christians are finding their place in American Christianity, and the process is fraught with complexity, disappointment, misunderstanding, hope, and potential. They add new ingredients to Christian pluralism in America.

Parsis

Parsis are a small and diminishing group in India, primarily centered in Bombay, who come to America to be reunited with fellow Zoroastrians who fled from persecution in Iran following the revolution under Ayatollah Khomeini. Parsis are descendants of migrants escaping Muslim persecution in Persia in the tenth century who found safe landing in Gujarat and then prosperity in Bombay. Now approximately

6,500 Zoroastrians and Parsis from India and Iran reunite two strands of the religion in American cities, already with four Zoroastrian buildings: one each in Chicago and New York, and two in California. The Federation of Zoroastrian Associations of North America has a membership of seventeen associations in the United States and four in Canada that sponsor publications, conferences, and youth activities. These immigrants from India and Iran speak different languages and preserve two distinct cultures and two interpretations of Zoroastrianism. Zoroastrians are unique among religious groups in rejecting converts not born into the religion; offspring of marriages of people outside the community are not eligible for membership. They often interpret their experience as immigrants to America as a second migration like that of their ancestors from Persia to India in the tenth century and say that American Zoroastrianism will constitute a vital and reformed form of the religion.

Their American Cousins

Even before South Asian immigrants arrived, some Americans responded positively to their religions. The most notable example was the effects of the preaching of Swami Vivekenanda at the world's fair in Chicago in 1893. Indeed, immigrants arrived after 1965 to encounter people claiming to be converts to their religions, sometimes a form of religion very different from their own. Young members of the International Society of Krishna Consciousness (ISKCON), sometimes called the Hari Krishnas because of their devotion to Krishna and their public chanting of a Krishna mantra, were often dancing in the airport terminals when Hindu immigrants arrived, and their Krishna temples welcomed early immigrants. The Nation of Islam intrigued immigrants with a race-based interpretation of Islam and a set of rituals foreign to their experience of Islam. The white Sikhs were converts of Harbhajan Singh Puri, a teacher who linked Hatha yoga with religious aspects of Sikhism to attract a number of American converts.

The negotiations between these groups and their effects have been diverse. ISKCON attempted to attract the allegiance of Hindu immigrants, and for a brief period it appeared that ISKCON members, who had renounced the world, might become the primary religious specialists for Hindu immigrants, who were part of the brain drain engaged in gaining the world. However, the arrival of an array of religious specialists from India to serve institutions founded by immigrants and the turmoil and schisms within ISKCON have greatly reduced its size and influence. The so-called ghora ("white") Sikhs became almost irrelevant during the Khalistan controversies that racked the Sikh community. The Nation of Islam went through a metamorphosis to emerge as a much more orthodox form of Islam under the inspiration of Malcolm X and the subsequent leadership of Wallace Muhammad in the American Muslim Mission. Immigrant Muslims influenced this transformation by providing examples of traditional forms of Islam and by funding new, more orthodox initiatives. The interaction between these groups of Hindus, Muslims, and Sikhs regarding identity, activities, and new directions foreshadow the negotiations between these and other religions of immigrants regarding their place in American religion.

Recent immigration from most countries of the world is adding new religions and new forms of old religions to the complex tapestry woven by previous immigrants that is American religion. Immigrants from India and Pakistan add some of the most colorful and distinctive textures to the work—and some significant design challenges. The tapestry is still on the loom, so the work of weaving involves the many colors of the issues these immigrants share, the texture of their effect on American religions, and the shape of the reverse effects they have on the religions in the Indian subcontinent.

Experiences of Recent Immigrants: The Power of Religion

In responses to questionnaires, immigrants commonly indicate that they are more religiously active in the United States than they were in India or Pakistan. The relative low level of involvement prior to migration is not so surprising because many of them came as young adults directly from university studies in the sciences, but the higher level of commitment in the United States is striking. It reflects the power inherent in religion to provide a transcendent foundation for personal and group identity in the midst of the enormous transitions that migration entails. The conjunction of that power with the special requirement that immigrants reformulate personal and group identities in new contexts helps to account for the fact that, as a country of immigrants, the United States is by many measures the most religious of the Western industrialized countries. Each new immigrant group, including new immigrants from India or Pakistan, turns to religion to shape and strengthen identity. Increasing secularization in the third quarter of the twentieth century may be the lingering result of the lull in immigration in the second quarter, and some revival of religion at the turn of the century, especially in conservative forms, may be due in part to the resurgence of immigration.

Plausibility Structures

Migration results in threats to all sorts of plausibility structures that undergird individual and social knowledge and support civic order and personal health. A Christian from a small village of Kerala reported that the only familiar parts of the landscape when he arrived in New York were the church towers, and he took great comfort in their shadows. That is a symbol of the absence of many plausibility structures that had undergirded knowledge, morals, customs, leadership styles, and commitments. Immigrants gravitate to both religious and social organizations not in the first instance to keep themselves separate from the settled society but to gain a breathing space within recognized plausibility structures in order to establish new plausibility structures that will be effective for themselves and their children in their new homes. Even groups that form small minorities in India or Pakistan rely nonetheless on the structures that assign to them a place within a diverse society. Such social location is the result of long and intricate negotiations between social and religious groups that, to a large extent, are insecure in the United States. The new relation between various Asian Indian and Pakistani social and religious groups requires the introduction or revision of plausibility structures for both the immigrants and those in the receiving society that will support the new social reality. American religion is in the midst of such negotiations between religious groups and between them and other social groups.

Family and Children

A marker for the establishment of immigrant religious organizations and buildings is the point at which children of the second generation reach the age when they are socialized outside the home. Parents are able to transmit whole cloth the plausibility structures that establish family identity and loyalty until that point. Thereupon, parents seek the assistance of other like-minded people in raising their children, often through the establishment of religious study groups and organizations. Sunday schools, summer camps, youth groups, and annual national conferences are adaptations to the American scene that help parents maintain some continuity of culture and religion with their children.

When asked what their major contribution to America might be, immigrants from India and Pakistan often reply, "Our close family ties." Family values are topics of many South Asian religious conferences and meetings. Immigrants from the Indian subcontinent have relatively few friends from the receiving society—in part because the primary channel for social intercourse in India and Pakistan is family, not friendship—so they are suspicious of American family life and fearful of bad influences from their children's peers. Many believe that American children do not care for their parents and will desert them in their old age and that American families fail to inculcate morals in the children. The greatest perceived threat to the integrity of the family is marriage to a person distant from the family by race, ethnic group, caste, religion, country of family origin, or social class. Parents' preferences for marriage partners reflect this list. Because arranged marriages are the traditional pattern in India and Pakistan, the American pattern of young people's searching for partners and even living together prior to marriage is very threatening to the immigrant families. Friendships and dating between boys and girls in a multicultural and multireligious society are occasions for great tension between parents and children. Religious groups often provide safe locations for intergenerational discussions of these issues and of the future of Asian Indian and Pakistani families. Religious leaders mediate such negotiations between the generations.

Strangers in a Strange Land

Immigrants find themselves to be strangers in a strange land. Even though most South Asian immigrants are fluent in English as a legacy of British influence in the Indian subcontinent, the use of their native languages is a powerful attraction for first-generation immigrants. As one immigrant remarked, "If I am going to sing the hymns of my childhood, I want to sing them in Malayalam" (and others would say "Gujarati" or "Tamil" or "Bengali"). Religious meetings are one of the few places where immigrants can feel at home outside their homes. There they can speak in their birth language; enjoy the ethos of their native place; participate in Indian or Pakistani music, drama, and other arts; taste traditional cuisine; and exercise leadership skills that involve oratory in the birth language and manipulation of other symbols. Religious organizations also provide the primary network connecting the immigrant with institutions and events in the Indian subcontinent.

A great sadness is that children of the second generation are losing love for and facility in the use of the family language and in the manipulation of other symbols. Indian languages are becoming sacred languages as they are used in temples, gurdwaras, and mosques. Sporadic attempts are made to hold language classes for the children, but many leaders realize that they are waging a losing battle and that the third generation will be alienated from their past. The older children often resist visits back to the family home and find themselves strangers in the strange land of the Indian subcontinent. How the religious organizations adapt to these realities is the most important challenge that they face. Have the parents gained the whole world but lost their children in the bargain? That is the awful question.

Effects on American Religion and Society: The Future of the Judeo-Christian Synthesis

Recent immigrants witness the diminishing power of the Judeo-Christian synthesis in American civic, religious, and educational arenas. The Judeo-Christian tradition is a fairly recent creation resulting from the negotiations of nineteenth- and early-twentieth-century immigrants who developed the "Protestant-Catholic-Jew" ethos of mid-twentieth-century America. The political ethos of Enlightenment values provided a civic framework that both empowered the Judeo-Christian tradition and preserved the religious freedom cherished by many immigrants. The new social reality that involves the presence of many different religions and intellectual traditions that have no clear place in the earlier synthesis engenders a reformulation, a revision, or perhaps a negotiation of a new synthesis that some claim will be more adequate. A host of religions from many countries are involved in this negotiation, but Hindus, Muslims, and others from India and Pakistan are prominent participants.

Negotiations have begun regarding the integration of Islam into a new synthesis. Including Muslims is in some ways easier than involving Hindus, Jains, Sikhs, or Parsis because Islam is a part of the Abrahamic tradition, sharing some of the same religious syntax, stories, and heroes. It is also more difficult in some ways because of the suspicion of Islam and discrimination against Muslims common among Americans. Regardless of the difficulties, the negotiation is essential because of the size and growth of the Muslim community. The recognition of that growth is shown by the inclusion of Muslim imams in the schedule of opening prayers for the U.S. Congress, provision of Muslim chaplains in prisons and other governmental institutions, and the invitations to Muslims to have the Id celebration in the White House. Muslims often claim that, sometime near the turn of the millennium, Islam will surpass Judaism to become the religion with the second-largest number of adherents in the

United States. Internally, South Asian Muslims have been influential in moving African American Muslims toward more orthodox forms of Islam. That creates a four-way tension: between African American Muslims and immigrant Muslims, between African American Muslims and Jews, between African American Muslims and the black church, and between all these and the majority population. The results of the competition of black masjid and the black church for the lives and souls of African Americans may well be the most important development in American culture in the first decades of the new century. Externally, that has profound implications both for the relative levels of influence of American Jews and Muslims in U.S. foreign policy and for political negotiations in the Middle East and with other countries that have large Muslim populations.

Public negotiations with Hindus, Jains, or Sikhs often involve zoning codes and building regulations for religious structures or regulations about dress codes that conflict with religious sensibilities or rules. Mediating institutions, such as councils of churches or interfaith organizations, are now skeletons of their former selves and have been thus far ineffective in providing venues for effective negotiation. The promise of the open door of immigration to America is that the nation will be able to welcome, absorb, and protect the civil rights and freedoms of both new and old immigrants and their descendants. The reality in the new century could become levels of turmoil and conflict that characterized earlier periods of large immigration and threatened to destroy individual dreams and the civic order. Alternatively, *inshallah* ("if Allah wills"), as some new immigrants say, negotiations could result in the creation of a new synthesis that will provide a broad civic umbrella for the renewal and preservation of the American dream.

The United States as a Missionary Territory

Christian immigrants from many countries, including India and Pakistan, are disappointed when they reach the United States and discover that it is not "the shining city set on the hill." Indeed, many immigrants feel that America is in need of missionaries and a revival of religious and moral values cherished in their churches, mosques, gurdwaras, and temples. Although some elements of religions of the Indian subcontinent have gained allegiance of Americans in the past, the vitality of the new immigrant communities confronts Americans with new, permanent, self-renewing alternatives. Strong opposition to the proselytizing activities of some groups (ISKCON in the 1970s, for example) led some Hindu, Jain, and Sikh leaders to forswear any attempts to make converts. It was almost as if the terms of compromise between old and new immigrants was the agreement, "Don't touch our children, and we won't touch yours."

The primary outreach—beyond their own children—for most immigrant religious groups has been the unchurched, unmosqued, or unaffiliated compatriots. Strategies that have been used extend from a simple notice posted in South Asian grocery stores to elaborate advertising and public relations campaigns associated with religious festivals. Some Hindus, some Jains, and the Parsis think that conversion to their religions is impossible. South Asian Muslims have been active in establishing institutions that propagate Islam among immigrants, in the African American community, and in the wider society. Marriage with persons outside the religious group that involves the conversion of the partner is an early extension of immigrant religions into the receiving society. (Marriage to an American citizen is one of the easiest and quickest ways to gain permanent resident status.) Development of resident religious leaders, sophisticated communication networks, elaborate organizations, and impressive facilities attracts the interest and allegiance of people beyond the immigrant group. Hence, they provide new resources for the American marketplace of ideas and religious alternatives for seekers. The situation evolves quickly, but it is still too soon to determine how successful the newly introduced forms of religion will be either in preserving the allegiance of the second and third generations or in attracting converts.

Education for the New Religious Reality

The public educational system from kindergarten through university and religious education in the United States produced curricula and resources for incorporating people from many lands into a common civic and religious structure. Those curricula were based on the earlier synthesis. They were enshrined in the basic canons of the liberal arts and then summarized in various types of Western civilization courses.

Following World War II, revised thinking introduced forms of area studies to take account of the new global responsibilities assumed by the United States. Considerable turmoil in education and curriculum development results from responses to and attacks on the earlier canons and curricula under the banners of multiculturalism and postmodernism. The presence of vital immigrant communities and their customs, ideologies, and religions also fuels controversy about the adequacy of earlier models and current proposals for reform. In some instances, curricula that were intended to teach students about other parts of the world now function to teach students about their neighbors across the street. Indeed, college courses on the religions of India now enroll significant numbers of children of immigrants from India and Pakistan who are seeking to learn about their own ancestral religions. Colleges and universities are responding by hiring specialists who institute courses on Islam and other religions of the Indian subcontinent. South Asian immigrants are part of the brain drain who quickly established financial security for themselves, their families, and their communities. They have begun to raise money for endowed chairs and research centers in Indian studies, Sikh studies, and Jain studies in American universities. Hindus are establishing a Hindu university in Florida, and Muslims are developing a religious school network and an Islamic university. These educational initiatives will help shape American education into the new century.

Transnationalism

Migration from India and Pakistan takes place in a radically different context of rapid mobility and communication that brings profound changes to the experience of both the immigrants and other citizens. Asian Indian and Pakistani families maintain almost immediate contact with family members and institutions in several countries, including in East Africa, the gulf states, the United Kingdom, Canada, and the United States. It is a new transnational reality in which individuals and families occupy and are intimately influenced by social locations in two or more countries. In this transnational context, religions of the Indian sub-continent have become world religions in new ways that call into question rubrics of analyses developed in relation to earlier immigrant groups. "Ethnicity" and "nationality" are categories of social description that require some revision to account for the current transnational reality; it is not just that new ethnic groups can be added to any list but that the category of ethnicity could be misleading. Both the earlier immigration and the midcentury lull in immigration were accompanied by difficulties of communication so that immigrants had difficulty communicating with relatives and institutions in their homelands or in other countries and, in relative isolation, formed ethnic groups on American models. Now travel and communication are rapid so that immigrants are more directly shaped by contacts abroad. In this regard, computer-assisted communication on the Internet is significant. Religious groups increasingly use the Internet to transmit information and define their religions.

Transnational networks make it increasingly possible for the United States to receive religious leaders and religious messages from India and Pakistan. They also enhance the capability of the new immigrants in the United States to exercise influence and authority in the Indian subcontinent. The effects that new immigrants are having on American society and religion are becoming clearer, but the effects that immigrants have on religious and social institutions back home are often overlooked. The United States has become an important funding source for religious leaders and institutions there. Families remit funds to relatives, a portion of which are donated to religious causes. Hindu, Jain, Sikh, Muslim, and Christian religious specialists come from India and Pakistan each summer to visit disciples and followers and to collect gifts for their activities. Although remittances of nonresident Indians and Pakistanis are important sources of hard currency for those countries, it is impossible to trace or estimate how much is donated. The networks handle not just money but also ideas, modes of behavior, and styles of leadership that have enormous potential for shaping religion in India and Pakistan at the same time that immigrants are affecting American religion.

Conclusion

Few people recognized the profound effects that post-1965 immigration would have on American religion and society. Those effects are permanent, but the exact shape of future developments is dependent upon the vagaries of revisions in the immigration laws and changes in administrative regulations, the results of which are incalculable. Nevertheless, it seems safe to make a few predictions. Immigration from India and Pakistan will continue for the foreseeable future, primarily under the family reunification provisions of the immigration law, which will constitute a constant transfusion for the nascent religious organizations. Asian Indians and Pakistanis will continue to establish religious organizations and to build temples, mosques, gurd-waras, and churches. Their religions will gain increasing visibility, and some will become more active in attracting participation and support from the society at large. If the analysis of the effects of the mid-century lull [is] close to accurate, it seems likely that portions of American society will become more religious as we move into the new century and people turn to a variety of forms of religion both new and old to create, preserve, and transmit elements of personal and group identity. The crystal ball does not reveal whether the result will ultimately be a breakdown in the civic order that provided the foundation for religious freedom and economic opportunity or a renewal in the American experiment, which is unique in human annals, in preserving freedom and democracy that has attracted immigrants and sheltered our common life. One best faces the nagging fear of the former with fervent prayers for the latter and all sorts of good work to enhance its likelihood.

REFERENCES

US Immigration and Naturalization Service (INS). 1982. *Statistical Yearbook of the Immigration and Naturalization Service.* Washington, DC: INS.

———. 1991. *Statistical Yearbook of the Immigration and Naturalization Service.* Washington, DC: INS.

———. 1995. *Statistical Yearbook of the Immigration and Naturalization Service.* Washington, DC: INS.

1. What role do Buddhist temples play in Laotian villages? How do community members interact with this institution? How is a standard code of conduct, a "village moral order," reestablished through the Buddhist religion? What are the implications of this order for those who leave Laos?

2. Assess the varying social, cultural, and economic forces that have reconstituted the Laotian interpretation of Buddhism in the United States. Which forces have had the most significant effect in shaping the Buddhist religion as one of the primary means of ethnic identification among Laotian refugees? Consider the implications of this meaning to second- and third-generation Laotian Americans. How might ethnic identification be complicated along generational lines?

3. According to Min, "[a]lthough only a little more than 20 percent of Koreans are affiliated with Christian churches in Korea, the majority of Korean immigrants in the United States have had a Christian background in their home country." What factors explain the overrepresentation of Christians among Korean immigrants to the United States? To what extent are these individuals involved in Christian church life upon settling in the United States? How does this involvement compare with that of other Asian American groups?

4. Min contends that because Christianity (specifically Protestantism) is not the Korean national religion, Korean immigrants have had to "Koreanize" Christianity as a means of sustaining ethnic identity. How is the issue of ethnicity complicated by the burgeoning numbers of Korean American youth worshipping at these local churches? Do Korean immigrant churches provide the same services and functions in the same way for this subgroup as they do for their parents and grandparents? To what degree is the church an active force in helping these youth generate a specifically "Korean American" ethnic identity?

5. Williams contends that religious activity among South Asians within the United States is higher than that found in South Asia. Why is this the case? Why is it so pronounced? What are the most important social functions played by South Asian religions in the United States? How do these religious traditions cultivate a transnational network among South Asian immigrants?

6. What religious traditions have South Asians brought with them to the United States? What elements of each of these religions characterize their growth or continued presence within the United States? How does the practice of these religions within the United States compare with their practice in India, Pakistan, and Bangladesh? To what extent is the immigration of South Asians to the United States since 1965 rearticulating the Judeo-Christian ethos that has been central to our understanding of American religion since World War II? What are some factors that are forcing scholars of American religion to renegotiate this consciousness?

SUGGESTED READINGS

Buenaventura, Steffi San. 1999. Filipino Folk Spirituality and Immigration: From Mutual Aid to Religion. Pp. 52–86 in David K. Yoo (ed.), *New Spiritual Homes: Religion and Asian Americans*. Honolulu: University of Hawaii Press.

Canda, E. R., and T. Phabtong. 1992. Buddhism as a Support System for Southeast Asian Refugees. *Social Work* 37(1): 61–67.

Fadiman, Anne. 1997. *The Spirit Catches You and You Fall Down: A Hmong Child, Her American Doctors, and the Collision of Two Cultures*. New York: Farrar, Straus, and Giroux.

Fenton, John Y. 1988. *Transplanting Religious Traditions: Asian Indians in America*. Westport, CT: Praeger.

Hayashi, Brian. 1995. *"For the Sake of Our Japanese Brethren": Assimilation, Nationalism, and Protestantism Among the Japanese of Los Angeles, 1895–1942*. Stanford: Stanford University Press.

Hurh, Won Moo, and Kwang Hun Kim. 1990. Religious Participation of Korean Immigrants in the United States. *Journal for the Scientific Study of Religion* 29(1): 19–34.

Kashima, Tetsuden. *Buddhism in America: The Social Organization of an Ethnic Religious Institution*. Westport, CT: Greenwood Press, 1977

Kim, Jung Ha. 1997. *Bridge-Makers and Cross-Bearers: Korean-American Women and the Church*. Atlanta: Scholars Press.

Matsuoka, Fumitaka. 1995. *Out of Silence: Emerging Themes in Asian American Churches*. New York: Pilgrim Press.

Nash, Jesse W. 1992. *Vietnamese Catholicism*. Harvey, LA: Art Review Press.

Park, Andrew Sung. 1996. *Racial Conflict and Healing: An Asian-American Theological Perspective*. Maryknoll, NY: Orbis Books.

Rutledge, Paul. 1985. *The Role of Religion in Ethnic Self-Identity: A Vietnamese Community*. Lanham, MD: University Press of America.

Shinto, Bill. 1970. *Towards an Understanding of Asian American Theology*. Berkeley: PACTS, California.

Suzuki, Lester E. 1979. *Ministry in the Assembly and Relocation Centers of World War II*. Berkeley: Yardbird Publishing.

Versluis, Arthur. 1993. *American Transcendentalism and Asian Religions*. New York: Oxford University Press.

Williams, Raymond Brady. 1989. *Religions of Immigrants from India and Pakistan*. New York: Cambridge University Press.

Woo, Wesley. 1991. Chinese Protestants in the San Francisco Bay Area. Pp. 213–245 in Sucheng Chan (ed.), *Entry Denied: Exclusion and the Chinese Community in America, 1882–1943*. Philadelphia: Temple University Press.

Yang, Fenggang. 1998. Tenacious Unity in a Contentious Community: Cultural and Religious Dynamics in a Chinese Christian Church. Pp. 333–361 in R. Stephen Warner and Judith G. Wittner (eds.), *Gathers in Diaspora: Religious Communities and the New Immigration*. Philadelphia: Temple University Press.

Yep, Jeanette, and Peter Cha. 1998. *Following Jesus without Dishonoring Your Parents*. Downers Grobe, IL: Intervarsity Press.

Yoo, David. 1999. *New Spiritual Homes: Religion and Asian Americans*. Honolulu: University of Hawaii Press.

FILM

Sarin, Ritu, and Tenzing Sonam (producers/directors). 1985. *The New Puritans: The Sikhs of Yuba City* (27-minute documentary).

Part VII

Women in Asian America

Chapter Seventeen

Doing Gender with a Feminist Gaze
Toward a Historical Reconstruction of Asian America

Shirley Hune

Race and gender are sites of power relations as well as organizing principles in intellectual discourse. Historically interpreted as biologically based and fixed, race and gender are now viewed as hierarchically designated "spaces of difference" created and maintained by the dominant order to ensure its hegemony (Soja and Hooper 1993). As socially constructed categories, they are flexible and subject to change, in part, through the negotiation and contestation of subordinate groups seeking a more equitable social order (Omi and Winant 1986; Spain 1992).

The incorporation of race and gender in the study of American history is transforming what we know about the subject and how we historicize. Nonetheless, scholarship on race and gender has remained relatively distinct. Race is the dominant organizing category in Asian American history, and gender is too often treated as neutral or separate, at best. Consequently, Asian American women are rendered invisible, misrepresented, or subsumed in Asian American history as if their experiences were simply coequal to men's lives, which they are not. On the other hand, gender as a category of analysis has focused almost exclusively on females and on the forces that contribute to their low status and circumscribed activities, as if men were not gendered. New works on Asian American women are filling historical gaps, but women's perspectives, roles, and contributions are still marginalized in Asian American history. Moreover, Asian American women's history has not significantly changed women's studies, which views middle-class white women's experiences as normative and in which differences of women of color, especially related to power, are homogenized (Hune 1997, ch. 1).

Engendering history would entail a systematic and comprehensive reassessment of the lives of both women and men. It would also involve a reappraisal of the historical constructions of femininities and masculinities, the interactions of women and men in all aspects of public and private life, and the ideologies and institutional structures that contribute to gender formation in a given society (Anderson 1997, 1–4). Such an undertaking of American history is far from complete, given the present scholarship. The master narrative of Asian American history continues to center men's lives and to assume masculinist values and perspectives. It also privileges the Western region and has focused largely on working-class experiences to the neglect of different forms of work, including those identified with women. In short, a male-centered standpoint and agenda have dominated much of Asian American research, and teaching as well (Yanagisako 1995).

The purpose of this chapter is to provide a reinterpretation of aspects of Asian American history by foregrounding Asian American women, incorporating scholarship that uncovers hidden aspects of their history, and reassessing women's gendered lives. Within this limited space, I have selected facets of Asian American women's experiences—immigration, family, work, and community—to critique traditional understandings of Asian American history and to transform existing frameworks, especially gender relations, within the field. Scholars who deliberately look for women and see them as subjects and active agents of history present a more complex reading of gender roles and an alternative perspective to a male-centered history (Gabaccia 1994; Weinberg 1992). In doing gender with a feminist gaze, I seek to advance the engendering of Asian American history and its reconstruction.

Privileging women is a necessary corrective, a step toward but not a substitution for a new history. Nor is a feminist agenda static, having shifted from adding in women to centering women and, more recently, to revising concepts and theories involving gender relations (Espiritu 1997, 4). Furthermore, although Asian American women share commonalities, differences exist, such as ethnicity, class, sexuality, generation, and level of incorporation into U.S. society. A full reconstruction of Asian American history awaits studies on masculinities and femininities, homogeneity and heterogeneity, and a reanalysis of women and men's experiences in the intersections of race, gender, class, sexuality, nationality, and other hierarchies.

Reconstructing Asian Immigration

Histories of American immigration have yet to fully write in women, viewing male immigrants as representative of their communities' experiences. The commonplace interpretation of the centrality of male migration, with women simply accompanying the men or being sent for at a later time by spouses, intended spouses, or other family members, treats females as passive objects of social forces, especially patriarchy. Many Asian women fulfilled accepted gender roles, but their motivations to emigrate were complicated, often in defiance of limited life choices, and, like those of their male counterparts, influenced by economic and political conditions. In this section, I call attention to Asian women who actively negotiated their way into American immigration history, thereby extending traditional gender definitions.

At age nine, Mary Bong ran away from life on a Chinese riverboat. Hearing of fortunes to be gained across the Pacific and to avoid U.S. barriers against the entry of Chinese women, Mary purchased boat passage to Vancouver, Canada, with savings from years of manual labor. She arrived in Alaska in 1895 at age fifteen, having convinced Ah Bong, owner of a bakery and a restaurant in Sitka, to marry her. As "China Mary," she managed her husband's restaurant, learned the Tlinglit language, and on occasion served as midwife for the Indian community. With her second husband, she worked in the commercial fishing industry as Sitka's first woman troller, and as a fox farmer (McCunn 1988, 27–32).

"Adventurous" and eager "to see foreign countries," Michiko Sato opposed her parents and father-in-law and immigrated to the United States. As a member of a middle-class family, she had choices other than those afforded Mary Bong, including ownership of a noodle shop offered to her by her mother if she and her husband would stay in Japan. Saburo Tanaka lacked an education but had worked in the United States. Although she did not care for him much and could have married better, Michiko saw Saburo as a means to get to America. Michiko persuaded him to return to the United States in the early 1920s. Contrary to her expectations, life was hard, but she was a hard worker. Over the years, Michiko worked in fields, operated a restaurant, farmed leased land, and cleaned hotel rooms, while raising thirteen children and dealing with her husband's gambling (Kikumura 1981).

Other women did not leave their homeland with the original intent of coming to the United States. Myung-ja Sur was a schoolteacher and a patriotic Korean. Active in the March First Movement of 1919, which opposed Japanese colonialism, she fled to Shanghai to escape Japanese domination. Arrested by Japanese secret police and incarcerated for a month, she returned to Korea. Aware of being monitored daily by the Japanese, Myung-ja decided to leave her homeland. She chose America, intending to further her education, but not before arranging her own picture bride marriage to a Korean man in the United States (Takaki 1989, 54–55). The lives of women such as Mary Bong, Michiko Tanaka, and Myung-ja Sur clearly expanded the boundaries of Asian womanhood.

Women began to outnumber men as immigrants to the United States in 1930, yet the image of male immigrants prevails in popular culture and research. By the mid-1970s, more than half the emigrants from Burma, China, Indonesia, Japan, Korea, Malaysia, the Philippines, and Vietnam were female, in large part a result of U.S. military involvement in Asia and of the 1965 Immigration Act (Houstoun, Kramer, and Barrett 1984). Some came as wives of American servicemen and relatives of U.S. citizens, but other Asian women were immigrants in their own right, many specifically recruited for professional positions or to fill low-paying jobs unwanted by other Americans. Hence, the *centrality* of women in contemporary immigration without question requires a reevaluation of recent Asian immigration history.

Bending gender roles, many Asian female immigrants have taken on the role of principal breadwinner and are the first of their family to emigrate. They bear the responsibility of bringing husbands and other family members to America and often assist in obtaining jobs and housing. Luz Latus, for example, is one of many nurses who emigrated from the Philippines between the 1960s and the 1980s. She and other colleagues decided to fill out applications for nursing positions when U.S. hospitals came recruiting. Successful in the United States and a leader in organizing groups to protect Asian American nurses from discrimination, she also dreams of giving back to "her country" by returning to volunteer in health centers in her hometown (Espiritu 1995, 81–91).

Perceiving America as a place where women are treated better and can gain economic independence, many contemporary Korean women have urged husbands and families to emigrate. The tendency of daughters and younger sons to immigrate first and establish small businesses is also displacing the power and traditional respect held by first-born Korean males who stay behind to uphold family obligations and arrive later. The formation of women's groups to promote women's personal and professional goals and women's role in family businesses have given Korean American females more power to negotiate household decisions and to participate with confidence in the larger society. As their dependence on male kin lessens, many immigrant women are questioning the benefits of marriage and seeking divorces or remaining single in greater numbers, in contradiction to traditional values. This shift in gender ideology and relations has met resistance from some Korean American men and contributes to household tensions and domestic violence against women (Park 1997, and forthcoming).

Life histories and other women-centered research, whether on early or recent Asian immigrants, challenge dominant frameworks of the primacy of males in Asian immigration and the view of women as quiescent immigrants. A reconstruction of Asian immigration needs to include women as central figures, incorporate the complexities of their choices and lives more fully, and identify changes in gender perspectives and relations of both Asian American women and men.

Reconstructing Asian American Families and Households

Bachelor societies, prostitutes, and picture brides frame the historical construction of gender in the first decades of Asian American history. Racialized patriarchal conceptions of women's proper role as wives, mothers, and daughters, both in Asia and in the United States, have narrowly defined women's presence in early Asian American history as largely absent and their participation as filial, passive, and reactive. Such a narrow interpretation points to women's subordinate status and limited life choices and supports the masculinist agenda in the dominant narrative of Asian American history. A feminist viewpoint considers how Asian American women actively engaged in the creation of American households and the making of Asian America.

I explore here new ways of looking at Asian American family and household formation and argue that a central issue of Asian immigrants was the creation and maintenance of family life in conjunction with economic survival and mobility. Immigration restriction and other racist practices did make Asian family and community formation in the United States more difficult, but they could not prevent permanent settlement. Male-centered scholarship has neglected the family as a historical construction. Feminist scholars, on the other hand, have been critical of the nuclear family's role in women's subordination. Attention is being given to different family formations and ways to reorder the family to establish egalitarian relations rather than to simply discard it (Nelson 1997). New formations such as split households and picture bride marriages in early Asian America and the new Asian family in the United States are considered here.

Transpacific Families/Split Households

Feminist scholars (Weinberg 1992; Gabaccia 1994; Hondagneu-Sotelo 1994) find new evidence that immigrants do not give up their country of origin easily but maintain linkages between the homeland and America through transnational processes and institutions where women play a critical role. One outcome is the transnational family, a distinct household formation. The first and best-known form of the transnational family among Asian Americans is the Chinese American "split household." From the 1840s to the 1930s, many Chinese American men were denied families in the United States because of racist and anti-female immigration laws, but they were *not* lacking family. Wives in China and husbands in the United States functioned as interdependent but geographically separated households (Glenn 1983).

Class influenced family formation and gender roles, as well. Working-class Chinese were subject to exclusion laws and sustained long periods of family separation. To send money home, many men did heavy labor at low wages. Merchants, however, could bring families to America or establish families in China and the United States and prosper in two places. The first wife of a rich merchant might remain in China to watch over property and raise children with the help of kin and servants, while a second wife or concubine came to America, worked in the family business, and watched over American-born children (Liu 1992; See 1995). In men's absence, some women were neglected, but others had major household obligations and cared for in-laws and children. Many women had significant economic responsibilities, including the management of property, and a great deal of autonomy (Yung 1995). Consequently, to speak of "married" bachelors in North American Chinatowns and "widowed" wives in China offers an incomplete description of men and women's lives in transpacific households. The Chinese American transpacific family is also an adaptive strategy to ensure economic survival and to maintain family relations and a form of resistance against racist U.S. policies.

Including Asian American women as historical subjects shifts the focus from male communities to communities of women and men *cooperating* to maintain households. Bachelor societies are reinterpreted and situated within the larger context of transpacific families where women are not marginalized but actively involved in the making of early Asian America and central to the functioning of split households. Gender roles are changed in each other's absence. Considering how women and men negotiated transpacific relations and the ways in which both were "feminized" and "masculinized" in early Asian America contributes to a reconstruction of gender in Asian America. Studies of contemporary transnational households would also shed light on current gender dynamics.

Picture Brides

Relying on a photograph and perhaps some letters, many Japanese and Korean immigrant women came as "picture brides" to marry countrymen who had emigrated to the United States. Picture bride marriages were a modification of the traditional practice of arranged marriages by family members or professional go-betweens and were initiated to overcome the barrier and costs of transpacific migration (Gee 1976).

I view women's agreement to become picture brides as a strategy they adopted to make new lives for themselves and not simply as filial duty. Life histories of picture brides reveal their heterogeneity and their active participation in their life choices. Daughters of poor families hoped to provide support for parents. Some women were adventurous. Some desired an education. Others sought to escape the confines of Asian male privilege. Freedom from Japanese colonialism and the opportunity to practice Christianity compelled many Korean women to choose picture bride marriages (Gee 1976; Chai 1992).

In-Sook and Ok-Ja were among the first Koreans to settle in Oregon and Montana in the years between 1910 and 1924. At age ten, In-Sook decided a woman's life in feudal Korea was too regimented. She independently arranged to become a picture bride, expecting a life of freedom and comfort. Determined and only fifteen, she cared for her prospective in-laws in their home until she could join her husband in America, much to the astonishment of her parents. Ok-Ja sought travel and study and defied her father to visit Japan. Disowned, she agreed to a picture bride marriage in the hopes of fulfilling her goals in America (Sunoo 1978).

Japanese picture brides began negotiating new lives almost immediately. Upon their arrival at Pacific Northwest seaports and finding their intended husbands rather common, older, and often less attractive than their photographs, some women refused to marry them (Gee 1976; Chai 1992). Other women later left their husbands, sometimes running off with another man, at great risk. Japanese American men countered women's defiance. To regain their wives, they had photographs and descriptions of them and their new lovers printed in Japanese American newspapers. Consequently, women encountered obstacles in establishing new lives elsewhere (Ichioka 1980). Nonetheless, women's efforts to break away demonstrated their desire to define their own lives and their unwillingness to remain in an unacceptable marriage at any cost.

Most picture bride marriages endured, but not without Japanese and Korean women having their womanhood severely tested. They persisted in rural communities without the household comforts and social supports of their homelands and despite the harshness of the work on Hawaii's plantations and on Pacific Northwest farmlands. Many were widowed at a young age, having married older spouses, and raised children alone with limited resources (Chai 1992). Korean American women in Oregon and Montana spoke with pride of managing economic crises themselves and with satisfaction of personal freedom and good times with family and friends in their senior years (Sunoo 1978).

In their personal desires for greater freedom, economic security, and self-improvement, Asian women demonstrated a willingness to emigrate as picture brides that was critical to family and community formation in early Asian America. Picture brides in their activities inside and outside the home expanded the role traditionally assumed by women in Asian households. In America, many women realized traditional gender roles while simultaneously extending them; others contested their marriages and sought to make new choices.

The New Asian Family in America

The Asian American family that evolved in the first half of the twentieth century was different from that in Asia. The idealized multi-generational patriarchal Asian household generally did not take hold in the United States because the traditional authority held by men in Asia could not be replicated in the new country. Early Asian male immigrants were limited to low-wage work, sometimes in "feminized" occupations, such as laundry or domestic work, and were denied the civil and political rights to protect and enhance their family's welfare. Racist laws and practices emasculated Asian American men, while few Asian American women led lives of domesticity. Women frequently worked outside the home in agricultural fields, as domestics, in light industries, family businesses, and other arenas, often doing heavy "masculine" work (Espiritu 1997). In this context, the Asian American household became a refuge from racism, as well as a means of economic survival. Cut off from families in Asia and restricted from full participation in American society, women and men were more interdependent, and a new, more egalitarian marriage partnership could be negotiated. Child-rearing practices also changed, with attempts to combine Asian and American ways. There were tensions, as well, as many women and men sought to hold onto traditional roles, while at the same time adapting to forces that changed gender relations.

The American-born children of immigrants moved between an American world that extolled freedom and democracy but practiced racial segregation and ethnic communities that sought to protect them from racism and give them a sense of ethnic pride, yet reinforced their difference (Chan 1991, ch. 6). Racial beliefs and practices kept Chinese, Japanese, Filipino, Korean, and other Asian American families apart from the mainstream. Nonetheless, they engaged in mainstream American life from the 1920s through the 1950s, going to movies, parks, the beach, and sports events. Working-class daughters joined the workforce early, while many middle-class daughters were able to further their education. American-born women generally wanted more autonomy and opportunities. In addition to negotiating the racial order outside their communities, Asian American women confronted gender and generational hierarchies within their households. Second-generation Chinese American women, for example, resented the greater freedom and the educational opportunities given to privileged brothers (Chan 1998; Yung 1995). Although a traditional division of labor in the household persisted among the American-born, their marriages were noted for companionship, egalitarianism, and warm affection, in contrast to their parents' relationships (Cordova 1983; Matsumoto 1999; Yung 1995).

Family reunification and maintenance were important issues for early Asian American communities, as they are for recent groups. Many Vietnamese and other Southeast Asian households, for example, have sought to reconstruct their families in their own chosen locales in spite of government efforts to disperse them (Zhou and Bankston 1998, 45–48). A feminist perspective focuses attention on the significance of families and households in the making of Asian America and on how new family formations have altered traditional gender roles and contributed to new notions of womanhood and manhood. New interpretations of Asian American history need to consider families and households as agencies of adaptation and change as well as cultural preservation and as sites of refuge and solidarity and exploitation and conflict, with women as active and central actors.

Reconstructing Work

In contrast to the dominant culture's dual and conflicting racial construction of Asian American manhood as weak, subservient, and asexual and smart, cunning, and a threat to white womanhood (Espiritu 1997, 90–93), the master narrative of Asian American history has valorized the Asian American male as worker. The significance of Asian American men's labor in national development is noteworthy. It does not fully represent Asian American work, however. We know much about men's work in railroad construction, agriculture, and fisheries in the early decades and as small business owners in recent history, but less about the nature and types of work borne by women. Historically, Asian American women have not led protected lives of domesticity. Most have worked outside the home out of economic necessity, as do their contemporary counterparts. In many cases, women's economic role has been fundamental to a household's survival. To examine how women's work lives have contributed to a reconstruction of gender in Asian American history, I consider family businesses, the wage system, and the informal economy.

The Family Business as Women's Work

Faced with menial wages and unstable jobs, immigrants have adopted self-employment as strategy of economic advancement and have operated small family businesses heavily dependent on the unpaid labor of wives and, occasionally, children. Typical Asian American family businesses in the first half of the twentieth century were small farms, laundries, groceries, restaurants, and curio shops. They relied in part on the ethnic community as clientele. Ethnic enterprises in the post-1965 era are more diverse and include dry cleaners, liquor stores, fast food outlets, nail salons, motels, and newsstands, along with restaurants and greengroceries; these are frequently in non-Asian neighborhoods, including low-income minority communities.

For Alice Yun Chai (1987), the family business is a site of "intermediate public domain." It brings women into the public sphere but does not provide them an independent income. As unpaid labor, Asian American women enabled businesses to be economically competitive by lowering labor costs. Many have helped family enterprises prosper with their business and social skills. Throughout the day, women moved between public and private spheres, extending their workday and juggling work with child care and housekeeping, winning little recognition but feeling proud of their contribution to the household's survival. In spite of long hours and hard work, women expressed satisfaction at being able to carry out family responsibilities and to work alongside their husbands to achieve shared goals (Glenn 1983). Asian American women's dual workload has changed little over the decades, and working six and even seven days a week in family businesses is common.

The volume and variety of family businesses and the role of women as business operators increased with the post-1965 immigration. Middle-class Asian women joined working-class women as unpaid labor in family enterprises. To gain a separate or greater income, many became small business operators themselves, with their husbands employed elsewhere. The motives of Vietnamese American women in setting up nail salons, for example, are complex and intricately tied to their gendered lives. For Jasmine Trinh, who had been a schoolteacher in Vietnam, her nail salon has meant more time with family and a much larger income than that earned at the sewing factory. Lani Nguyen likes being able to "take my daughter to the shop and look after her while I work on my customers." Cam Van, who was going through a difficult divorce, wanted to be economically independent and to show her husband that she and her three children would not end up on welfare without his financial support (Huynh 1996, 198–200).

For the most part, Asian American women today, as in the past, view the family business as an extension of the appropriate boundaries of their domestic sphere, rather than as a new and autonomous activity. It is their way of fulfilling child care responsibilities and contributing to the household economy. Few anticipated that small businesses would involve long hours, small profits, contentious customers, safety concerns, and fierce competition from co-ethnics, along with economic failure, no matter how hard family members worked (Huynh 1996; Min 1995; Thaker 1982).

Women's Work in the Wage System

As many Asian American households required dual and sometimes multiple paid workers to survive, women have entered the wage system. Paid work is in the public sphere and has status and value. Consequently, feminist scholarship has viewed the wage system as emancipatory, with women gaining freedom from domesticity and subjugation by the family system. This interpretation of women's gendered lives as a public/private dichotomy is based on middle-class white women's experiences and their emphasis on personal freedom and self-fulfillment. The experiences of women of color and of immigrant and working-class women dispute the universality of this framework.

Employment as a domestic worker, for example, challenges notions of a public/private dichotomy. Here one woman's private sphere is another woman's place of employment. Domestic service meant downward mobility for many Japanese American women engaged in it from the 1920s to the 1940s, but racial discrimination restricted their options. While domestic work was within the female sphere, it still took women outside the family and loosened husbands' control. Some husbands opposed women's outside employment for fear of losing their authority. Women persisted in search of ways to increase their own income and to provide more for their children. Through work and interactions with middle-class white women, Japanese American women became more self-reliant and negotiated relations with the larger world for their own development and that of their children (Glenn 1986).

Paid work, regardless of its location, has provided a separate income and served as a vehicle for women's greater autonomy and social interaction. Punjabi American women employed as cannery workers in central California in the 1970s and 1980s detested their working conditions and discriminatory treatment but gained new friends and a break from cloistered domestic lives (Williams 1989). Chinese American garment workers compensate for their low wages by enjoying flexible work hours and proximity to friends, relatives, food shopping, and home (Wong 1989). Unlike family members who work together in the family business, members of dual-wage-earner families have led separate lives, and women have feared losing influence over their children's lives (Glenn 1983; Kibria 1993). In contrast to working-class women, who have been limited to low-wage, dead-end menial jobs, professional Asian American women have had wider opportunities but often hit a "glass ceiling." Their income and advancement have not been commensurate with their education and professional experience (Woo 1994).

Women in the Informal Economy

Asian American women have also turned to the informal economy to supplement a marginal family income. Generally, this has involved expanding their traditional gender roles. In the early decades of Asian America, for example, Japanese and Filipino American women took in laundry and boarders, prepared meals for single men, and babysat for others (Nomura 1989; Cordova 1983).

Global economic restructuring during the past three decades has led many Southeast Asian women into the informal economy. The growth of low-wage service work and the decline in the number of high-wage manufacturing jobs has favored women's employment and made it more difficult for Southeast Asian men whose livelihoods were destroyed by war to adequately support their families (Benson 1994). Women who lack English skills have innovated, turning their traditional roles in the household and as culture bearers into informal economic activities that have provided necessary family income. Vietnamese American women have patched together a family subsistence by preparing food for sale in shops or sewing clothes for others (Kibria 1993). Cambodian American women have done likewise. Some are small traders, bringing back market goods, such as fish and fruit, to be sold by the piece in their neighborhoods (Ui 1991). Hmong American women are selling needlework, which they formerly produced for home use and rituals (Donnelly 1994). Such activities have flexible work hours and can be carried out at home in conjunction with child care. The informal sector is labor intensive and unstable, however, and is not an economic solution to low wages. As a second job, it extends a woman's day.

Asian American women's work lives, whether they are unpaid labor, self-employed, or in the wage system or the informal economy, bring conflicts and opportunities. Women, especially the immigrant generation, have viewed work outside the home as a necessary extension of their domestic obligations to ensure the family's welfare and children's future (Pessar 1995). But as household and child care responsibilities have remained women's obligation, their double burden has been a mixed blessing, neither fully liberating nor fully oppressive. Although gendered and hierarchical, the home has served as a safe and nurturing place for Asian American women and men in a hostile racial environment. A feminist gaze views women's struggles to support their households economically as acts of resistance against a racial patriarchal order that diminished the lives of Asian American women, men, and children.

Nonetheless, Asian American women's work outside the home has affected gender roles. It has made women "co-providers" for the family, even if their earnings were small (Ling 1998, 85). It has altered women's self-worth, engaged them in the larger world, and enhanced their social capital. Women have used the knowledge and interactions they have gained to advance their interests, making them less dependent on men (Yanagisako 1985; Park 1997). Another outcome is their negotiation of new gender relations. Work has increased women's decision-making power in the family, especially where they have an independent income, and empowered them to voice their views and determine priorities, whether the subject is household purchases, social activities, or a child's future. Women have been known to set aside some of their earnings to use for household emergencies, their own needs, and special items for their children.

This shift in power relations is not always welcome. Some Asian American men, having lost their traditional status and authority in the larger society, have sought to affirm them within the family, leading to domestic conflict, divorce, and, occasionally, violence (Park forthcoming; Luu 1989). Many women, such as refugee Vietnamese women, have struggled against transforming gender relations and have sought to moderate their subordination to men in an effort to maintain family relationships that became severely strained in America (Kibria 1993). More attention to Asian American women's and men's work and its implications for gender dynamics within and outside of households would contribute to the historical reconstruction of Asian America.

Reconstructing Community

Ethnic communities are more than historical groupings of people or bounded geographic spaces. They are social-spatial-temporal formations of shared meaning that are dynamic and flexible and shaped and reshaped, largely from within, by members seeking to meet their changing needs. The larger society and its context of opportunities and constraints also help form ethnic communities. Communities can span social distances, including transnational space, as well as time, as in historical epochs and generations (Rouse 1991; Okamura 1995; Takahashi 1997). The concept of community and community participation are also gendered. Generally, men are identified with formal institutions and women with informal associations (Weinberg 1992), reinforcing the notion of distinct public/private spheres and males as community leaders.

A feminist view of Asian American community emphasizes women's active role in community building. By creating and sustaining webs of relations and organizations, women have connected Asian Americans beyond their families to realize community interests. A consideration of women's activities gives new attention to their leadership and situates community building within the domestic sphere and informal networks, as well as within the public sphere and formal associations. With the formation of communities, Asian American history made the transition from immigrant history to ethnic history, with women as active participants.

Building Community through Women's Informal Networks

Historically, Asian American women, like other women, have had limited access to formal power and the public sphere and have used informal power—kinship and friendship ties—to advance personal, family, and community interests. From the earliest days of Asian America, women have constructed and sustained community through social visits to relatives and friends and by holding gatherings to celebrate traditional festivals and family achievements. For example, at the turn of the twentieth century, immigrant Chinese women held New Year's celebrations, feasts to observe a new-born's one-month birthday, and other events, breaking down their isolation from one another and facilitating social interaction among the men (Ling 1998, 101–102). As households grew and stabilized after World War II, Filipinas ensured that birthdays, baptisms, weddings, graduations, housewarmings, promotions, and the arrivals of relatives, as well as deaths, were acknowledged with large gatherings and an abundance of home-cooked food (Cordova 1983, 188–189). Women's social activities honored cultural traditions and life passages, while providing Asian Americans a respite from their hard work and giving them opportunities to mix, exchange information, and develop contacts for community and personal needs. Through informal networks, Asian American women have built community.

Community has emerged out of the need for collective aid, as well. Women without kin in America pursued social relations for friendships and mutual assistance. In the first part of the twentieth century, Korean American women in Hawaii turned to women in their neighborhoods or church groups for help with births, deaths, and illnesses. Japanese and Korean American women came together to fund business and real estate ventures, as well as personal activities, by instituting female-based rotating credit associations, a form of mutual aid used in their homelands (Chai 1987, 1992). Towards the end of the twentieth century, Vietnamese American women developed informal affiliations to support their households, exchanging money, supplies, cooking, and child care, as well as information about jobs, housing, and social services (Kibria 1993). Out of everyday necessity for survival, women's friendships developed into social networks to address short-term emergencies and long-term plans. Through these activities and others, women created community among co-ethnics and others who had been strangers. Hence, women's informal networks are more than social activities, they are essential to family support and community formation.

Asian American women have also relied on kinship ties for mutual assistance. In their new homeland and in the absence of strong, male-dominated kinship systems, women and men have been innovative. For example, while the issei turned to conjugal families for community, and to Japan in the case of successor sons, nisei women looked to their siblings. Sisters and their families aided one another and reached outside their immediate families for support. Their women-centered kinship networks changed familial dynamics and reshaped the Japanese American community (Yanagisako 1985).

By creating alternative sources of aid that took them outside their traditional family system, Asian American women enhanced their support system for meeting household and other needs and became less dependent on their husbands' familial and social networks, as was customary in their homelands. These informal networks are a source of community building that has affected gender relations. Women's increased autonomy has contributed to a weakening of the hierarchical male-dominated household, with household activities oriented toward women's as well as men's kinfolk and interests. Asian American women have also used their informal power to establish women-centered formal associations, either within ethnic community-based organizations or distinct from them, to address women's issues. Male community leaders often resist women's activism in an effort to maintain patriarchy and a masculinist community agenda (Shah 1997b).

Building Community in the Public Sphere through Women's Formal Associations

Asian American women have been active in the public sphere in effecting social change. Their activities often joined the public sphere of their ethnic communities with that of the larger society. The exclusion of racial/ethnic communities from full participation in American mainstream life led Asian Americans to establish formal organizations to address community concerns. Asian Americans' activities included creating civic, cultural, and social institutions, providing social services, and opposing racism and other forms of oppression.

Asian American women initiated and participated in numerous gender and generation-based organizations. Beginning in the 1920s, for example, middle-class Chinese American women were visibly active in San Francisco's Chinatown, enhancing community services. Through the YWCA, they worked to improve housing, health care, child care, and job skills. Through church groups and women's clubs, they held American-style events such as raffles, musical performances, and fashion shows to raise funds for orphanages and hospitals. They also formed organizations to register voters, clean up Chinatown, and contest racist legislation directed at immigrants and noncitizens (Yung 1995).

Similarly, Filipinas in the 1930s began their tireless organization and governance of social clubs to raise funds for community affairs. They arranged dances, athletic events, beauty contests, and other functions to provide Filipino Americans, who were restricted from public places such as beaches, parks, and restaurants, with opportunities to socialize and to develop community. They also formed children's clubs to teach Philippine folk dance and other cultural activities to the American-born (Cordova 1983, 151–153). Hence, social and recreational activities served a political purpose of ameliorating racial segregation and preserving cultural forms and practices in an America that sought Asian American exclusion or assimilation.

Asian American women also extended their community participation into the larger society, often linking their subordination in America with injustice in Asia. In the first half of the twentieth century, for example, they supported Asian independence and nation-building struggles. Chinese American women raised funds, sewed garments, and made speeches in support of the 1911 Revolution against the Qing dynasty and its efforts to establish a republic. In the late 1930s and 1940s, they opposed Japan's aggression in China and Manchuria, actively marching and picketing American shipyards that transported materials to Japan (Yung 1995, 92–102). Korean American women in California and Hawaii formed patriotic and relief societies to raise funds for Korea's independence efforts in 1919 and afterward (Gabaccia 1994, 84). More recently, contemporary women from India, Pakistan, Nepal, Sri Lanka, and Bangladesh have come together to challenge the unequal status of South Asian American women in the United States and in their homelands. Their U.S.-based groups have joined global associations and South Asian women's groups to protest the dowry-related deaths of women in India (Vaid 1989).

Asian American women have also addressed issues of social justice. Their formal organizations can be ethnic-specific, pan-Asian, or issue-specific, and they sometimes work in coalition with other racial/ethnic groups. As part of their history of active participation in labor movements, women have protested working conditions and occupation segregation, not simply for themselves but for the welfare of their communities and for all workers. Others have established professional organizations to protect women and men from discrimination and to advance their career development and skills. Women's community-based organizations today provide counseling services to immigrant women on issues such as domestic violence and employment discrimination, improve women's health care, offer media and political representation, and fight environmental racism in Asian American communities (Asian Women United of California 1989, part 7; Shah 1997a). In their community activities for civil, political, and human rights, educational reform, women's equality, in political campaigns, and in their struggles against oppression globally, Asian American women seek to strengthen community and mediate with American institutions for inclusion and greater justice for all.

Stacey Yap (1989) suggests that women become involved in community work on at least four levels—as volunteers, professionals, officials, and activists—and that community work has at least three stages—pioneering, professional, and activist. In whatever capacity or stage, women's community-building efforts, like employment, take them outside the home. Asian American women often represent, speak for, and mediate for their community in the public sphere. Their community leadership and resources have challenged men's authority in public and private spheres, as well, and have sought to protect women from discriminatory treatment and to advance issues ignored by men. For example, Asian American women have formed groups against domestic violence to protest their communities' silence on women's exploitation and safety and have supported lesbians and gays, who remain invisible to many families and communities, and their concerns (Shah 1997a). Hence, women's organizing activities build community in ways that support and contest gendered priorities and leadership.

This chapter has focused on Asian American women's gendered lives from a feminist perspective. Asian American history's dominant narrative has centered men's lives, assumed masculinist values and perspectives, and viewed gender as neutral or separate at best, rendering gender relations invisible or inconsequential. Toward a reconstruction of Asian America, I have privileged women and analyzed their experiences in four areas—immigration, family, work, and community—to reconceptualize gender ideologies, roles, and relations. I have uncovered how some Asian women challenged traditional authority and chose to pursue personal goals and dreams to immigrate to the United States. Asian American women have been coparticipants in strategies to establish families and households in America in the face of racist laws and practices and male-dominated family systems. They have shared in the formation of new types of families and marriages. Asian American women's work lives have extended the boundaries of the domestic sphere and been crucial to the survival of households, although their contributions remain underrecognized. At the same time, their work lives have given women more power in the household and enhanced opportunities for social contacts to improve their lives and their families' lives. Work has also led them to seek more equitable treatment in both the private and the public spheres. An analysis of Asian American women's activities recovers their role in community building. Their informal and formal activities and networks have both supported and challenged community interests and contested inequities in the larger society. Their decision-making and new organizations also bring conflict and resistance, as many Asian American women and men seek to maintain cultural traditions in a sea of change.

Viewing Asian American women's lives as gendered reveals how they have actively negotiated and contested traditional hierarchical gender relations and flexed their gender roles to fulfill personal goals and to pursue household and community interests. Women have also changed their ideology of what constitutes womanhood as they have sought greater autonomy and ways to enhance the welfare of their families and communities, as well as their own personal and professional development. Asian American women have created new cultural forms to moderate patriarchal tendencies, enhance women's place and concerns, and affirm community in America even as that community is reshaped by changing gender and other relations. The exploration of Asian American women's gendered lives as fluid and flexible challenges the notion of a public/private dichotomy and of men's gender ideology and relations as stable. More attention to gender studies will contribute to the engendering and reconstruction of Asian American history.

NOTE

This paper was first conceptualized and presented in different form as "The Cultural Politics of Gender: The Space of Difference that Asian American Women Make," at the annual meeting of the Association for Asian American Studies, Washington, DC, May 31–June 2, 1996. A different version of parts of this paper appeared in chapter 2 of *Teaching Asian American Women's History*, published by the American Historical Association, 1997.

REFERENCES

Anderson, Karen. 1997. *Teaching gender in U.S. history*. Washington, DC: American Historical Association.

Asian Women United of California, ed. 1989. *Making waves*. Boston: Beacon Press.

Benson, Janet E. 1994. "The effects of packing house work on southeast Asian refugee families." In L. Lamphere, A. Stepick, and G. Grenier (eds.), *Newcomers in the workplace*, 99–126. Philadelphia: Temple University Press.

Chai, Alice Yun. 1992. "Picture brides: Feminist analysis of life histories of Hawai'i's early immigrant women from Japan, Okinawa, and Korea." In D. Gabaccia (ed.), *Seeking common ground*, 123–38. Westport, CT: Greenwood Publishing Group.

———. 1987. "Adaptive strategies of recent Korean immigrant women in Hawaii." In J. Sharistanian (ed.), *Beyond the public/domestic dichotomy*, 65–99. New York: Greenwood Press.

Chan, Sucheng. 1998. "Race, ethnic culture, and gender in the construction of identities among second-generation Chinese Americans, 1880s to 1930s." In K. S. Wong and S. Chan (eds.), *Claiming America*, 127–164. Philadelphia: Temple University Press.

———. 1991. *Asian Americans: An interpretive history*. Boston: Twayne.

Cordova, Fred. 1983. *Filipinos: Forgotten Asian Americans*. Dubuque, IA: Kendall/Hunt.

Donnelly, Nancy D. 1994. *The changing lives of refugee Hmong women*. Seattle: University of Washington Press.

Espiritu, Yen Le. 1997. *Asian American women and men*. Thousand Oaks, CA: Sage.

———. 1995. *Filipino American lives*. Philadelphia: Temple University Press.

Gabaccia, Donna. 1994. *From the other side: Women, gender, and immigrant life in the U.S. 1820–1990*. Bloomington: Indiana University Press.

Gee, Emma. 1976. "Issei women." In E. Gee (ed.), *Counterpoint: Perspectives on Asian America*, 58–59. Berkeley: University of California Press.

Glenn, Evelyn Nakano. 1986. *Issei, nisei, war bride*. Philadelphia: Temple University Press.

———. 1983. "Split household, small producer, and dual wage earner: An analysis of Chinese-American family strategies." *Journal of Marriage and the Family* 45 (February): 35–46.

Hondagneu-Sotelo, Pierrette. 1994. *Gendered transitions: Mexican experiences of immigration*. Berkeley: University of California Press.

Houstoun, Marion F., Roger G. Kramer, and Joan Mackin Barrett. 1984. "Female predominance of immigration to the United States since 1930: A first look." *International Migration Review* 28(4): 908–963.

Hune, Shirley. 1997. *Teaching Asian American women's history*. Washington, DC: American Historical Association.

Huynh, Craig. 1996. "Vietnamese-owned manicure businesses in Los Angeles." In B. Hing and R. Lee (eds.), *Reframing the immigration debate*, 195–203. Los Angeles: LEAP Asian Pacific American Public Policy Institute and UCLA Asian American Studies Center.

Ichioka, Yuji. 1980. " 'Amerika Nadeshiko': Japanese immigrant women in the United States, 1885–1924." *Pacific Historical Review* 44(2): 339–357.

Kibria, Nazli. 1993. *Family tightrope: The changing lives of Vietnamese Americans.* Princeton: Princeton University Press.

Kikumura, Akemi. 1981. *Through Harsh Winters.* Novato, CA: Chandler & Sharp.

Ling, Huping. 1998. *Surviving on the gold mountain.* Albany: State University of New York Press.

Liu, Haiming. 1992. "The trans-Pacific family: A case study of Sam Chang's family history." *Amerasia Journal* 18(2): 1–34.

Luu, Van. 1989. "The hardships of escape for Vietnamese women." In Asian Women United of California (ed.), *Making waves,* 66–69. Boston: Beacon Press.

Matsumoto, Valerie J. 1999. "Japanese American women and the creation of urban Nisei culture in the 1930s." In V. J. Matsumoto and B. Allmendinger (eds.), *Over the edge: Remapping the American West,* 291–306, Berkeley: University of California Press.

McCunn, Ruthanne Lum. 1988. *Chinese American portraits.* San Francisco: Chronicle Books.

Min, Pyong Gap. 1995. "Korean Americans." In P. G. Min (ed.), *Asian Americans: Contemporary trends and issues,* 199–231. Thousand Oaks, CA: Sage.

Nelson, Hilde Lindemann (ed.). 1997. *Feminism and families.* New York: Routledge.

Nomura, Gail. 1989. "Issei working women in Hawaii." In Asian Women United of California (ed.), *Making waves,* 135–148. Boston: Beacon Press.

Okamura, Jonathan Y. 1995. "The Filipino American diaspora: Sites of space, time, and ethnicity." In G. Okihiro et al. (eds.), *Privileging positions,* 387–400. Pullman: Washington State University Press.

Omi, Michael, and Howard Winant. 1986. *Racial formation in the United States.* New York: Routledge & Kegan Paul.

Park, Kyeyoung. Forthcoming. "Sudden and subtle challenge: Disparity in conception of marriage and gender in the Korean American community." In Martin Manalansan (ed.), *Cultural compass: Ethnographic explorations of Asian America.* Philadelphia: Temple University Press.

———. 1997. *The Korean American dream.* Ithaca, NY: Cornell University Press.

Pessar, Patricia R. 1995. "On the homefront and the workplace: Integrating immigrant women into feminist discourse." *Anthropological Quarterly* 68(1): 37–47.

Rouse, Roger. 1991. "Mexican migration and the social space of postmodernism." *Diaspora* (Spring): 8–23.

See, Lisa. 1995. *On gold mountain.* New York: St. Martin's Press.

Shah, Sonia, ed. 1997a. *Dragon ladies: Asian American feminists breathe fire.* Boston: South End Press.

Shah, Sonia. 1997b. "Redefining the home: How community elites silence feminist activism." In S. Shah (ed.), *Dragon ladies: Asian American feminists breathe fire,* 46–56. Boston: South End Press.

Soja, Edward, and Barbara Hooper. 1993. "The spaces that difference makes." In M. Keith and S. Pile (eds.), *Place and the politics of identity,* 183–205. London: Routledge.

Spain, Daphne. 1992. *Gendered spaces.* Chapel Hill: University of North Carolina Press.

Sunoo, Sonia S. 1978. "Korean women pioneers of the Pacific Northwest." *Oregon Historical Quarterly* 79(1): 51–64.

Takahashi, Jere. 1997. *Nisei/sansei: Shifting Japanese American identities and politics.* Philadelphia: Temple University Press.

Takaki, Ronald. 1989. *Strangers from a different shore.* Boston: Little, Brown.

Thaker, Suvarna. 1982. "The quality of life of Asian Indian women in the motel industry." *South Asia Bulletin* 2(1): 68–81.

Ui, Shiori. 1991. " 'Unlikely heroes': The evolution of female leadership in a Cambodian ethnic enclave." In M. Burawoy et al. (eds.), *Ethnography unbound*, 161–177. Berkeley: University of California Press.

Vaid, Jyotsna. 1989. "Seeking a voice: South Asian women's groups in North America." In Asian Women United of California (ed.), *Making waves*, 395–405. Boston: Beacon Press.

Weinberg, Sydney S. 1992. "The treatment of women in immigration history: A call for change." *Journal of American Ethnic History* (Summer): 25–46.

Williams, Marcelle. 1989. "Ladies on the line: Punjabi cannery workers in central California." In Asian Women United of California (ed.), *Making waves*, 148–159. Boston: Beacon Press.

Wong, Diane, with Dennis Hayashi. 1989. "Behind unmarked doors: Developments in the garment industry." In Asian Women United of California (ed.), *Making waves*, 159–171. Boston: Beacon Press.

Woo, Deborah. 1994. *The glass ceiling and Asian Americans*. Washington, DC: U.S. Department of Labor Glass Ceiling Commission.

Yanagisako, Sylvia. 1995. "Transforming orientalism: Gender, nationality, and class in Asian America studies." In S. Yanagisako and C. Delaney (eds.), *Naturalizing power: Essays in feminist cultural analysis*, 275–298. New York: Routledge.

———. 1985. *Transforming the past: Tradition and kinship among Japanese Americans*. Stanford: Stanford University Press.

Yap, Stacey. 1989. *Gather your strength, sisters*. New York: AMS Press.

Yung, Judy. 1995. *Unbound feet: A social history of Chinese women in San Francisco*. Berkeley: University of California Press.

Zhou, Min, and Carl L. Bankston III. 1998. *Growing up American: How Vietnamese children adapt to life in the United States*. New York: Russell Sage Foundation.

Chapter Eighteen

Power, Patriarchy, and Gender Conflict in the Vietnamese Immigrant Community

Nazli Kibria

Women maximize resources within patriarchal systems through various strategies (Collier 1974; di Leonardo 1987; Wolf 1972). Kandiyoti (1988) has suggested that women's strategies reveal the blueprint of what she calls the "patriarchal bargain," that is, the ways in which women and men negotiate and adapt to the set of rules that guide and constrain gender relations. The notion of "bargaining with patriarchy" suggests that both men and women possess resources with which they negotiate to maximize power and options within a patriarchal structure. The bargaining is asymmetric, for as long as patriarchy is maintained, women's power and options will be less than those of men in the same group.

The analysis of women's strategies, with its potential to reveal processes of negotiation between men and women, may also shed light on the dynamics of change in gender relations. Social transformations, such as those implied by modernization and migration, often entail important shifts in the nature and scope of resources available to women and men (Lamphere 1987; Pessar 1984). A period of intense renegotiation between women and men may thus ensue as new bargains based on new resources are struck. Indeed, the fundamental rules of the previous system of gender relations may come into question as the social worlds of men and women undergo change. However, when patriarchal structures remain in place despite certain changes, limited transformations in the relations between women and men may occur without deep shifts in men's power and authority.

This article examines the organization and activities of the informal community life of Vietnamese immigrant women in the United States. Data are drawn from an ethnographic study of a community of Vietnamese refugees in Philadelphia. Through research on the women's social groups and networks, I explored the effects of migration on women's roles in the family and community and the collective strategies forged by women to cope with male authority in the family.

Settlement in the United States has increased opportunities for the growth of Vietnamese women's power because their economic contributions to the family economy have grown while those of men have declined. Women use their new resources to cope more effectively with male authority in the family. However, male authority is not openly challenged. Because there are important advantages for women in maintaining the old "bargain" between men and women, the Vietnamese women have tried to maintain the patriarchal family structure.

Research Design

Using participant-observation and in-depth interviews, I studied twelve Vietnamese households located in a low-income, inner-city area of Philadelphia from 1983 to 1985 (Kibria 1986). Interviews were conducted with fifteen women and sixteen men, all of whom were members of the households composing the core sample.

The twelve households were located in close proximity to each other, within a radius of ten blocks. They ranged in size from three to nineteen members, with a median number of seven. Study participants had been in the United States for three to five years. Of the forty-six adults, thirty-two had lived in the urban areas of southern and central Vietnam prior to leaving the country. The men had often been in the South Vietnamese army or worked in small businesses and middle-level government administrative and clerical occupations. The women had engaged in farming and commercial activities or a variety of odd jobs in the informal urban economy, such as selling goods in the bazaar and working in restaurants and laundries.

All of the households had experienced a decline in their socioeconomic status with the move to the United States, especially when compared to their situation in Vietnam before the political changes of 1975. At the time of the study, the economic situation of the study participants was generally marginal and precarious, a finding that is supported by other studies of post-1978 Vietnamese arrivals to the United States (Gold and Kibria 1989; Haines 1987; Rumbaut 1989). In 1984, over 30 percent of the men in the households of the study were unemployed. Of the men who were employed, over half worked in low-paying, unskilled jobs in the urban service sector or in factories located in the outlying areas of the city. The women tended to work periodically at jobs in the informal economic sector as well as in the urban service economy. Eight of the households had members who collected public assistance payments (Kibria 1989).

The family economy or a system of pooling and exchanging material resources within family groups was an important strategy by which the Vietnamese households coped with these economic uncertainties and difficulties (Finnan and Cooperstein 1983; Gold 1989; Haines, Rutherford, and Thomas 1981).

Another important sphere of economic cooperation were the informal, women-centered social groups and networks in the community. I use the term *social group* to refer to clusters of people who gathered together on a regular, if not frequent, basis. These groups had a stable core membership that usually included kin but were by no means exclusive to family members. Over the course of a year, I attended and observed the informal gatherings of seven social groups in women's homes as well as in Vietnamese-owned service establishments (ethnic grocery stores, restaurants, hairdressers) where the women worked. I gained access to each of the seven groups through my relationships with members of the study households. The women's groups included members of these households and others in the community.

The study of the women's social groups revealed the complex and powerful role of the Vietnamese women in the ethnic community. The women's community was organized around two central activities: the distribution and regulation of the exchange of resources among households and the mediation of domestic tensions and disputes. Through these activities, the women's groups were an important source of collective power and support for women. However, the power of the women's groups was "unofficial" in nature and limited by the structural and ideological boundaries of the patriarchal family system. In their involvement in family conflicts, the women's groups often tried to protect the interests of individual women who were in conflict with male authority in the family. Yet they did so in ways that did not challenge, but rather reaffirmed, traditional Vietnamese ideology concerning the family and gender roles.

The Effects of Migration: Old Strategies and New Resources

The traditional Vietnamese family was modeled on Confucian principles. In the ideal model, households were extended, and the family was structured around the patrilineage or the ties of the male descent line (Keyes 1977; Marr 1976). Women were married at a young age and then entered the household of their husband's father. The young bride had minimal status and power in the household until she produced sons (Johnson 1983; Kandiyoti 1988; Lamphere 1974; Wolf 1972). The patriarchal bargain in this setting was one in which women expected significant rewards in their old age from allegiance and deference to the patrilineal family system. The power and resources of women in the patrilineal extended household tend to vary across the life cycle. While young brides are subservient to both men and older women in the household, older women hold a position of some power and status (cf. Wolf 1974).

There were also resources available to Vietnamese women in traditional rural society that could be used to cope with male authority in the family and community. According to recollections of my informants, in rural Vietnam, women's neighborhood groups were an important source of informal power. Women were able, through gossip, to affect the reputations of men and women in the community. However, in rural Vietnam, the influence of the women's groups was curbed and limited by powerful male organizations, such as village political and legal bodies, as well as the patrilineal descent group (Hendry 1954; Hickey 1964; Keyes 1977).

Women in rural Vietnam also had some access to economic resources through their involvement in village commerce and business. Women often sold food and other goods at the village market, and many played an important role in the family business (Hendry 1954; Hickey 1964; Nguyen Van Vinh 1949). But while such activities may have enhanced the resources and bargaining power of women in the family, there is little evidence that they weakened the fundamental economic subordination and dependence of women on men.

The social and economic bases of the traditional system of gender relations were deeply affected by the social turmoils in Vietnam of the 1950s and 1960s, which also transformed the lives of the participants of this study. War and urbanization eroded the structure of the patrilineal extended household. Within the cities, the households that survived retained their extended character, but they were less centered on patrilineal ties and incorporated a wider array of kin. For many Vietnamese, economic survival in the cities was precarious (Beresford 1988, 57). However, many Vietnamese from middle-class backgrounds, such as the participants in this study, were able to take advantage of the expansion of middle-level positions in the government bureaucracy and army. Such occupational opportunities were fewer for women; they engaged in informal income-generating activities or worked in low-level jobs in the growing war-generated service sector in the cities (Beresford 1988; Nyland 1981; Thrift and Forbes 1986). As in rural Vietnam, most women remained dependent on men for economic support.

War and migration to the cities thus served to weaken the patrilineal extended household—the structural core of the traditional patriarchal system. However, because the middle-class status of the families depended in large part on the incomes of the men, the threat of economic impoverishment sustained the ideals of the traditional family system and men's authority in the family. Women feared the economic consequences of male desertion, a not uncommon occurrence, especially when men were on military duty for extended periods. The "bargain" between women and men that emerged in this setting was one in which women deferred to men's authority in exchange for economic protection.

In the United States, the social context of gender relations was both similar to and different from that of modern, urban South Vietnam. The most important difference was that the relative economic resources of men and women had shifted. As in Vietnam, women continued to engage in a variety of income-generating activities, including employment in informal and low-level, urban, service-sector jobs. In contrast to Vietnam, however, the economic contributions of men had declined significantly. In Vietnam, the men held jobs that enabled them to maintain a middle-class standard of living for their families. In the United States, many Vietnamese men faced unemployment or had low-paying unstable jobs that did not usually enable them to support a family. Compounding the men's economic problems has been a widespread sense of powerlessness and alienation from the institutions of the dominant American society. The shifts in the resources of women and men that have accompanied the migration process have thus created the potential for a renegotiation of the patriarchal bargain.

The Women's Community: Strategies of Power and Responses to Change

The women's social groups were formed around household, family, and neighborhood ties. Groups had a stable set of regular members, ranging in size from six to ten women. The boundaries of groups were fluid and open, with participation in group activities generally unrestricted to women in the ethnic community. The groups had heterogeneous membership, including women of varied ages and social backgrounds, and the Vietnamese women in the community tended to participate in the gatherings and activities of several social groups. Such overlapping membership in the groups led to connections of both a direct and indirect nature among women across the community. The groups were thus at the core of social networks of women that extended throughout the area.

A woman's membership in a group, regardless of the extent of her involvement, signified an obligation to participate in exchange activities with others in the group and connecting network. Exchange was a central and perhaps the most visible activity of the women's community, in ways similar to those in low-income, urban, black communities (Martin and Martin 1978; Stack 1974). Women exchanged food and material goods of various sorts, as well as services and tasks such as child care and cooking. They exchanged information on such issues as where to get "good buys" on food and other items for the family. They also shared knowledge on available jobs and income-generating opportunities in the area, as well as how to cope with and maximize gains from various institutions (e.g., welfare and social service agencies, hospitals, and schools). For both men and women in the community, the exchange networks of the Vietnamese women represented a highly valued material and informational resource.

Besides their involvement in exchange activities, the women's groups also played an important part in strategies for coping with familial male authority, often playing a pivotal role in supporting and protecting women who were in conflict with the men in their family. In traditional Vietnamese society, the principle of male authority was expressed in the cultural and legal acceptance of wife beating (Marr 1976; Ta Van Tai 1981). In three of the study households, physical assaults by men on women in the family were a regular occurrence, thus suggesting that wife beating continues among the Vietnamese in the United States. However, in the United States, the Vietnamese women's groups play an important moderating role in situations of domestic violence, protecting women from the excesses of the patriarchal family system, as shown by the following:

> Several women were gathered at Dao's house. Dao brought up the situation of her older sister Thu. She said she hadn't wanted to talk about it before . . . but everyone here was family. Now it was so bad she had to talk about it. Thu's husband (Chau) was hitting her very much. The other day, Dao had to take Thu to the hospital, when Chau had hit Thu on the face. One of the women says, "What about Chau's brother? Does he say anything?"

> Dao replies that the brother had told Chau to stop it. But nobody really cared about what the brother said, certainly Chau didn't. The brother was very old. He did nothing but eat and sleep. And he hardly talked to anyone anymore, he was so sad to leave Vietnam. Dao starts crying, saying that if her parents were here, they could help Thu.

> Dao's neighbor says that maybe Thu should leave the husband. That wasn't a bad thing to do, when the husband was so bad, the woman should leave the husband. Chau didn't even take care of the children. He wasn't a good father. He also hit the children. Even the smallest one, who was only three years old. No good father would do that.

Dao says that yes, that was true, Chau wasn't a good father. He also didn't like to work and have a job. Thu talked about leaving Chau, but she was scared. She thought maybe Chau would come after her and the children and do something bad to them. One of the women says, "My brother, he's Chau's friend. I'll talk to my brother and he'll tell Chau to be good, and not make trouble for Thu." Several other women mention people they know who are in some way associated with Chau. They all say they will talk to these people about Chau. Someone says, "Thu is a good woman. She wants to take care of her children, her family. Chau, he's no good." (Fieldnotes)

Dao's social network was an important source of support for Thu. Largely through gossip, the women were able to bring pressures to bear on Thu's husband. Chau found his reputation throughout the community affected by the rapidly disseminated judgments of the women's group. In conversations with a number of men and women in the community, I found that Chau had been ostracized not only by the women but also by male friends and relatives. Chau left the city to join a cousin in California. There were no legal divorce proceedings, but the marriage had been dissolved in the eyes of the Vietnamese community. Thu and her children continued to live in the city, receiving help and support from family and friends. Chau, in contrast, severed almost all relationships in the area.

The example above shows how the women collectively helped to bring male authority back into its acceptable limits. The women's group supported Thu in breaking ties with the husband, a course of action that conflicted with the values and norms of family solidarity and female propriety. Marital separation or divorce is a stigma among the recently arrived Vietnamese in the United States, particularly for women. But in Thu's case, the women created an interpretation of the situation in which the man was at fault. The judgment or "message" of the women's group was that the principle of male authority had been abused, contradicting other central familial values. The women interpreted Thu's actions so that she was not seen as violating family and gender norms. Women emerged in this situation as both guardians of the family and as supporters of a particular woman's interests.

There were other instances in which women collectively stepped in to protect the interests of women who were in conflict with men in the family, most often husbands. These situations involved not only domestic violence but also disputes between women and men over various sorts of household decisions. In one case that I observed, a young woman named Lien was supported by female kin and friends in her decision to seek employment despite the objections of her husband. After completing six months of training in haircutting, Lien had had her second child. She planned to leave the baby in the care of her aunt while she worked as a hairdresser in Chinatown. Lien's husband objected to her plans, feeling that it was important for her to stay at home with the baby. While Lien agreed that it was preferable for her to remain at home, she argued that her husband's frequents bouts of unemployment made it necessary for her to go out and work.

With the support of other women in the community, Lien's aunt intervened in the couple's dispute in a powerful fashion. At a gathering of friends, Lien's aunt discussed how she had "had a talk" with Lien's husband in which she had emphasized that Lien was not deviating from traditional women's roles but merely adapting out of necessity to economic circumstances:

> I told him that Lien should take care of the baby, that is the right way. But this is America and we have a different kind of life now. If Lien doesn't work, then the children won't get good food, good clothes . . . the welfare money is not enough. I explained to him that she's not being a bad mother, she's working for the children.

The women at the gathering accepted the interpretation of the situation presented: that Lien was acting in conformity with the dictates of traditional gender roles. Because of the gossip that ensued, Lien's husband found himself under community pressure to accept Lien's decision to work outside the home.

In another case women mobilized community opinion against a man who forbade his wife to see her brother, whom he disliked. Ha, a woman in her early thirties, had been living in the city with her husband and their children. Some time ago, Ha's brother and his four children had arrived in the city from the refugee camp to join Ha. Ha described the household atmosphere as tense and uncomfortable during this time. Her husband, Le, was in "a bad mood," as he was not able to find a suitable job. Le and Ha's brother had been fighting constantly over small matters. Because of these problems, after a stay of two months, the brother and his children moved to another apartment in the area.

Ha went over to see her brother frequently, usually every other day. Ha often cooked for her brother's children, and she sometimes lent her brother small amounts of money. Le resented Ha's involvement in her brother's life and eventually told her to stop visiting them. Ha became incensed and told women kin and friends that she would divorce Le if he did not allow her to take care of her brother:

> I told my friends and Le's sister that I don't want to stay with Le. They said I must stay with Le because it's not good for me and my children to leave. They talked to me a lot about it. And then Le's sister said that Le was bad to tell me not to see my brother. All my friends said that was right, that my brother was like Le's brother, Le must understand that. Le changed after that. Because his sister talked to him, everyone talked to him. He knows that everyone will think he's bad if he tells me to not see my brother.

In this case the women's community "stepped in," both to discourage Ha from leaving the marriage and to change Le's behavior and attitude toward Ha's relationship with her brother. The women were able to muster considerable support for their position. Because of the women's actions, Le felt social pressures from both his family and the community to allow Ha to maintain her relationship with her brother. The women constructed an interpretation of the situation such that Le was seen to be violating the foremost value of family solidarity.

While extremely powerful, the women's groups were not always successful in their interventions in family disputes. In one such case, a women's group supported a member named Tuyet in her efforts to dissuade her husband from purchasing an expensive car with the family savings. Tuyet told women friends that the purchase of the car would significantly postpone their plans to buy a house. Despite the gossip that followed and the women's collective disapproval of his actions, Tuyet's husband went ahead with the purchase. His decision to ignore the women's community was influenced perhaps by his stable and favorable employment situation, which reduced his sense of economic dependency on the women's resources. However, while Tuyet's social group was unsuccessful in deterring the purchase of the car, their judgments did serve to cause Tuyet's husband to reconsider and delay his purchase.

In all of these cases, the process by which the women's community attempted to influence the outcome of the disputes was similar. The women's groups derived influence from their ability to interpret situations, define who was right or wrong, and impose these interpretations through gossip and the threat of ostracism. In the process of generating collective interpretations of situations, women drew on the symbols and values of the traditional family ideology to provide legitimacy for their actions and opinions. The judgments of the women were often effective sanctions, as both men and women in the ethnic community valued the economic and social resources available to them through the women's exchange networks.

The New Patriarchal Bargain

The collective strategies of the women for coping with male authority reveal some aspects of the new patriarchal bargain being generated by migration. The power exerted by the women's groups over the behavior of men and women in the Vietnamese immigrant community reflects the decline in men's social and economic resources. But, while the women's groups use their enhanced power to support the struggles of individual women with male authority in the family, they are careful not to disturb the traditional boundaries of family and gender relations.

In their activities, the women's groups constantly displayed concern for upholding and preserving elements of the relationship they had had with men and the family system prior to settlement in the United States. For example, the women's groups did not support women in their conflicts with men in the family when they had violated traditional sexual norms. In one case, a widow had developed a reputation for sexual promiscuity. In the second case, a woman had left her husband for a man with whom she had been having an affair for several months. In both cases, the women's groups disparaged and isolated the two women, and in the second case, provided support to the husband. In general, the women's groups judged harshly those women who failed to show a high degree of commitment to "keeping the family together" or to the norms of behavior appropriate to wives and mothers. The women would mobilize their community resources to sanction and enforce these normative codes by withholding resources from offenders.

Anything that threatened to disrupt the fundamental structure and ideological coherence of the family was unacceptable to the women's community. Repeatedly during my research, the Vietnamese women talked of the threat presented by the familial and sexual values of the dominant American culture to their family system. Thus, when asked about the greatest drawback of living in the United States, women often expressed fears concerning children's defection from the traditional family system:

> The biggest problem of living here is that it's difficult to teach your children how to be good and to have good behavior. The children learn how to be American from the schools, and then we don't understand them and they don't obey us. The customs here are so different from our culture. The children learn about sex from TV. Maybe American parents think that's OK but for me that's not OK because I know the children will learn bad behavior (*hu*) from watching TV. Also, I worry about when my children grow older they won't ask me my opinion about when they have girlfriends and they get married.

Another expression of the conflicts about the dominant American culture felt by the women was their ambivalence about the protection from domestic violence offered to them by the American legal system. While many women felt positively about the illegality of wife beating in American society, there was also widespread concern that intervention of the law into family life detracted from the authority and rights of parents to discipline their children.

Besides the decline of parental authority, there was another consequence of Vietnamese assimilation into American culture that women feared: the desertion of men from the family. Both the economic protection of men and the officially sanctioned authority of parents over children were aspects of the premigration patriarchal bargain that women viewed as attractive and beneficial for themselves, and they would often use the resources and power available to them through their community groups and networks in an attempt to preserve these aspects of the old "bargain," as illustrated by the following situation:

> Ly told me her sister-in-law Kim's daughter, fifteen-year-old Mai, was thought to be mixing with American boys at school. Ly thought Kim was "making too much fuss about it," as Mai was "really a good, smart girl who's not going to get into trouble." This afternoon, in the restaurant where Kim worked, the regular crowd of five or six women gathered around a couple of tables, chatting and drinking tea and bittersweet coffee. Kim, quite suddenly, started crying and dabbing her eyes with a napkin. Everyone's attention focused on Kim, who then talked of how she didn't know what to do with her children who were on the streets all the time, she couldn't keep her eye on them continually because she worked all the time. Especially Mai, who was growing up to be a woman now, she was always playing on the streets, sometimes until late at night. And she didn't take care of her younger brothers and sisters, and didn't do any of the housework, instead always wanting money to go and buy the latest fashions.
>
> An elderly white-haired women wearing traditional dress and seated at the next table piped in loudly about how this was what happened to all the children when they came here, they became like American children, selfish and not caring about their family. The other women then talked of how they all had similar problems, that children here just didn't listen to their parents and family. One said, "You should make her behave right, otherwise she'll be sorry later. She's not an American girl, she's Vietnamese." There were murmurs of agreement. (Fieldnotes)

In this case, a women's group supported a member's authority as a parent. In the process of doing so, the group upheld and affirmed traditional notions of appropriate female conduct. Following the incident described above, the women's group also carefully watched and supervised Mai's activities in an attempt to support her mother's concerns actively.

The new patriarchal bargain emerging in the United States is thus one in which women use their heightened resources to cope more effectively with male authority. But there is also a concern for maintaining the old modes of accommodation between women and men and the traditional ideological relationships within the family.

Conclusions

This study showed how the Vietnamese women's groups, using the resources that had become available to them as a result of migration and that were necessary to their families' survival, challenged male authority. But they did not use their newly acquired resources to forge a radical restructuring of the old patriarchal bargain. In many ways, the women remained attached to the old male-dominant family system that called for female deference and loyalty because it offered them economic protection and allowed them to continue their officially sanctioned authority over the younger generation.

The social losses incurred by the Vietnamese men with settlement in the United States have enhanced women's collective power. Their exchange networks have come to assume an important source of economic security and family survival. Moreover, the women's groups have become an important, if not the primary, agent of negotiation between the Vietnamese community and "outside" institutions, such as hospitals and welfare agencies. As a result, the men defer to the moral judgments of the women's community in part because many cannot afford to be cut off from these resources. In sum, the Vietnamese women's community in the United States is continuous with the past in its basic organization and activities, but it is now operating in a social context that enhances its status and power.

The women's status and power, however, are not great enough to transform gender relations in the Vietnamese immigrant community radically. While the economic resources of the women have risen, compared to those of the men, they are seen as too limited to sustain the economic independence of women from men, and so the women continue to value the promise of male economic protection. In short, the difficult economic environment and the continued material salience of family ties in the United States help preserve the attraction and meaning of the traditional patriarchal bargain for women, although in a tempered form.

Migration to the United States has thus had a complex, somewhat contradictory, impact on the status of Vietnamese immigrant women. On the one hand, migration has weakened men's control over economic and social resources and allowed women to exert greater informal family power. At the same time, the precarious economic environment has heightened the salience of the family system and constrained the possibilities for radical change in gender relations. For the moment, the patriarchal family system is too valuable to give up as it adds income earners and extends resources. Another appeal of the traditional family system for women is the status-related privileges that are promised to them—in particular, the authority to wield considerable influence over the lives of the young.

Thus, because they expected to gain important economic and status benefits from allegiance to the traditional family system, by and large, the Vietnamese women of the study were a conservative force in the community, deeply resistant to structural changes in family and gender relations. In this regard, the responses of the Vietnamese women are not unlike views expressed by many women supporters of the current antifeminist movement in the United States, who see shifts in gender relations as a threat to their economic security (Chafetz and Dworkin 1987; Ehrenreich 1982; Klatch 1987).

The experiences of these Vietnamese women also suggest that women may, in a selective manner, take advantage of the resources that have become available to them as a result of the very social transformations they resist. These new resources strengthen women's capacity to cope effectively with male authority; as long as the men need the women's economic and social resources, their ability to resist the collective interventions of women is limited. At the same time, the women themselves fight to hold back the social consequences of migration, in particular the cultural incursions into the family that cause the undermining of their own authority over their children.

The "bargain" between the Vietnamese women and men that has been described here is highly unstable and tenuous in quality. The ability of women collectively to sanction the behavior of men rests on the dependence of men on the economic and social resources of women. If there is little economic progress in the situation of the Vietnamese men in the future, then a fundamental appeal of the traditional patriarchal bargain for women, that is, the promise of men's economic protection may become far less compelling. Male authority may then be openly challenged, paving the way for a radical restructuring of gender relations. In such a situation, the traditional family structure may further erode—without the material support of men, women may find their traditional status and authority over the younger generation difficult to sustain.

Alternatively, the Vietnamese men may gain economic and social resources in the future, in which case they are likely to reinstate their authority over women. A rise in the economic status of these Vietnamese families has other implications as well. As I have described, the women's strategies for coping with male authority are collective in nature, closely tied to the presence of a distinct and highly connected ethnic community that allows for the growth of women's social networks. A rise in the economic status of the Vietnamese families may be accompanied by movement into the outlying areas of the city and the subsequent geographic dispersal of the Vietnamese ethnic community. Such changes would have serious implications for the ability of the Vietnamese women to forge the kind of powerful community life that I have described in this article. Thus, somewhat ironically, the assimilation of the Vietnamese into dominant American economic and social structures may indicate both a major shift from the traditional Vietnamese patriarchal family system and a reassertion of the economic and social bases of male authority in the family.

Recent scholarship on the effects of modernization and migration on women's lives has seriously questioned the prior assumption that these processes are uniformly liberating for women (Morokvasic 1984; Ybarra 1983). My research on Vietnamese immigrant women suggests that the effects of migration on gender relations must be understood as highly uneven and shifting in quality, often resulting in gains for women in certain spheres and losses in others.

REFERENCES

Beresford, M. 1988. *Vietnam: Politics, economics, society.* London: Pinter.

Chafetz, J., and A. Dworkin. 1987. In the face of threat: Organized antifeminism in comparative perspective. *Gender and Society* 1: 33–60.

Collier, J. 1974. Women in politics. In *Women, culture and society,* edited by M. Rosaldo and L. Lamphere. Palo Alto: Stanford University Press.

di Leonardo, M. 1987. The female world of cards and holidays: Women, families and the work of kinship. *Signs* 12: 440–454.

Ehrenreich, B. 1982. Defeating the ERA: A right-wing mobilization of women. *Journal of Sociology and Social Welfare* 9: 391–398.

Finnan, C. R., and R. A. Cooperstein. 1983. *Southeast Asian refugee resettlement at the local level.* Washington, DC: Office of Refugee Resettlement.

Gold, S. 1989. Differential adjustment among immigrant family members. *Journal of Contemporary Ethnography* 17: 408–434.

Gold, S., and N. Kibria. 1989. Vietnamese refugees in the U.S.: Model minority or new underclass? Paper presented at Annual Meetings, American Sociological Association, San Francisco.

Haines, D. 1987. Patterns in Southeast Asian refugee employment: A reappraisal of the existing research. *Ethnic Groups* 7: 39–63.

Haines, D., D. Rutherford, and P. Thomas. 1981. Family and community among Vietnamese refugees. *International Migration Review* 15: 310–319.

Hendry, J. B. 1954. *The small world of Khanh Hau.* Chicago: Aldine.

Hickey, G. C. 1964. *Village in Vietnam.* New Haven: Yale University Press.

Johnson, K. A. 1983. *Women, the family and peasant revolution in China.* Chicago: University of Chicago Press.

Kandiyoti, D. 1988. Bargaining with patriarchy. *Gender and Society* 2: 274–291.

Keyes, C. F. 1977. *The golden peninsula.* New York: Macmillan.

Kibria, N. 1989. Patterns of Vietnamese women's wagework in the U.S. *Ethnic Groups* 7: 297–323.

————. 1986. Adaptive and coping strategies of Vietnamese refugees: A study of family and gender. Ph.D. diss., University of Pennsylvania, Philadelphia.

Klatch, R. E. 1987. *Women of the new right.* Philadelphia: Temple University Press.

Lamphere, L. 1987. *From working daughters to working mothers.* Ithaca, NY: Cornell University Press.

————. 1974. Strategies, cooperation and conflict among women in domestic groups. In *Women, culture and society,* edited by M. R. Rosaldo and L. Lamphere. Stanford: Stanford University Press.

Marr, D. G. 1976. The 1920's women's rights debate in Vietnam. *Journal of Asian Studies* 35: 3.

Martin, E. P., and J. M. Martin. 1978. *The Black extended family*. Chicago: University of Chicago Press.

Morokvasic, M. 1984. Birds of passage are also women. *International Migration Review* 18: 886–907.

Nguyen Van Vinh. 1949. *Savings and mutual lending societies (ho)*. Southeast Asia Studies, Yale University.

Nyland, C. 1981. Vietnam, the plan/market contradiction and the transition to socialism. *Journal of Contemporary Asia* 11: 426–428.

Pessar, P. R. 1984. The linkage between the household and workplace in the experience of Dominican women in the U.S. *International Migration Review* 18: 1188–1212.

Pleck, E. H. 1983. Challenges to traditional authority in immigrant families. In *The American family in social-historical perspective*, edited by M. Gordon. New York: St. Martin's.

Rumbaut, R. G. 1989. Portraits, patterns and predictors of the refugee adaptation process: Results and reflections from the IHARP panel study. In *Refugees as immigrants: Cambodians, Laotians and Vietnamese in America*, edited by D. W. Haines. Totowa, NJ: Rowman and Littlefield.

Stack, C. 1974. *All our kin: Strategies for survival in a Black community*. New York: Harper and Row.

Ta Van Tai. 1981. The status of women in traditional Vietnam: A comparison of the Le dynasty (1428–1788) with the Chinese codes. *Journal of Asian History* 15: 97–145.

Thrift, N., and D. Forbes. 1986. *The price of war: Urbanization in Vietnam, 1954–1985*. London: Allen and Unwin.

Wolf, M. 1974. Chinese women: Old skills in a new context. In *Women, culture and society*, edited by M. Rosaldo and L. Lamphere. Palo Alto: Standford University Press.

———. 1972. *Women and the family in rural Taiwan*. Palo Alto: Stanford University Press.

Ybarra, L. 1983. Empirical and theoretical developments in studies of the Chicano family. In *The state of Chicano research on family, labor and migration studies*, edited by A. Valdez. Stanford: Stanford Center for Chicano Research.

1. In her reconstruction of Asian American women's history Hune explains the role that women play in international migration, the labor market, the family, and the community. In what ways are Asian American women active players in these social processes? Employing a feminist perspective on Asian American history, what other events or activities are spearheaded by Asian American women?

2. In what ways do Vietnamese women in the United States negotiate their positions relative to Vietnamese men? How do their situations in the United States differ from those of women in Vietnam? What are some possible outcomes predicted by Kibria with respect to the ways in which Vietnamese immigrant women negotiate their positions to men as men's economic fortunes improve? How might succeeding generations of Vietnamese Americans negotiate this delicate male-female relationship? Will the patriarchal relationship cease to exist in succeeding generations? If so, why?

SUGGESTED READINGS

Chow, Esther N. 1994. The Feminist Movement: Where Are All the Asian American Women? Pp. 184–191 in Ronald Takaki (ed.), *From Different Shores*. New York: Oxford University Press.

Donnelly, Nancy D. 1997. *Changing Lives of Refugee Hmong Women*. Seattle: University of Washington Press.

Espiritu, Yen Le. 1997. *Asian American Women and Men: Labor, Laws, and Love*. Thousand Oaks, CA: Sage.

Hune, Shirley. 1997. Higher Education as Gendered Space: Asian-American Women and Everyday Inequalities. Chapter 11 in Carol R. Ronai, Barbara A. Zsembik, and Joe R. Feagin (eds.), *Everyday Sexism in the Third Millennium*. New York: Routledge.

Hurh, Won Moo, and Kwang Chung Kim. 1988. The Burden of Double Roles: Korean Wives in the United States. *Ethnic and Racial Studies* 11:151–167.

Khare, Brij B. 1997. *Asian Indian Immigrants: Motifs and Ethnicity and Gender*. Dubuque: Kendall/Hunt.

Kibria, Nazli. 1990. Power, Patriarchy, and Gender Conflict in the Vietnamese Immigrant Community. *Gender and Society* 4 (1): 9–24.

Kim, Kwang Chung, and Won Moo Hurh. 1988. The Burden of Double Roles: Korean Wives in USA. *Racial and Ethnic Studies* 11(2): 151–167.

Kingston, Maxine Hong. 1989. *The Woman Warrior*. New York: Vintage International.

Leonard, Karen Isaksen. 1992. *Immigrant Punjabi Men and Their Spouses*. Philadelphia: Temple University Press.

Okihiro, Gary. 1994. Recentering Women. Pp. 64–92 in Gary Okihiro, *Margins and Mainstreams: Asians in American History and Culture*. Seattle: University of Washington Press.

Shah, Soniah (ed.). 1997. *Dragon Ladies: Asian American Feminists Breath Fire*. Boston: South End Press.

Wong, Sau-ling Cynthia. 1992. Ethnicizing Gender: An Exploration of Sexuality as Sign in Chinese Immigrant Literature. Chapter 6 in Shirley Geok-lin Lim and Amy Ling (eds.), *Reading Literature of Asian America*. Philadelphia: Temple University Press.

Yamada, Mitsuye. 1981. Invisibility Is an Unnatural Disaster: Reflection on Asian American

Women. Pp. 35–40 in *This Bridge Called My Back: Writings by Radical Women of Color.* New York: Kitchen Table.

Yung, Judy. 1995. *Unbound Feet: A Social History of Chinese Women in San Francisco.* Berkeley: University of California Press.

FILMS

Chow, Henry (producer/director). 1987. *Liru* (25-minute documentary).

Choy, Christine (producer). 1993. *Sa-I-Gu: From Korean Women's Perspective* (36-minute documentary).

Ding, Loni (producer/director). 1982. *Four Women* (30-minute documentary).

———. (producer/director). 1982. *Frankly Speaking* (30-minute documentary).

Part VIII

The Construction and Deconstruction of the "Model Minority"

Asian Americans as the Model Minority
An Analysis of the Popular Press Image in the 1960s and 1980s

Keith Osajima

The year 1986 marked an anniversary of sorts: twenty years earlier, the first articles proclaiming Asian Americans as the "model" minority appeared in the popular press. Since then, the model minority thesis has been the target of considerable criticism. Members of the Asian American community have argued that the image is racially stereotypic, empirically inaccurate, and no longer applicable to the changing Asian American population. Yet, in spite of these critiques, the image remains dominant in the 1980s, appearing in numerous popular press articles in recent years.

The analytic focus of this chapter is the persistence of the model minority image into the 1980s. It will examine how the image of Asian Americans as the successful minority has been able to withstand criticism and changing conditions, yet remain an important conceptual force in the popular press. It will compare the discursive construction of the model minority image as portrayed in the popular press during two historical periods—the 1960s and 1980s—and discuss how that discourse has been shaped by surrounding social and political conditions. The comparative analysis will reveal how changes in the discourse on Asian American success have enabled it to maintain relevance and explanatory power in the contemporary literature.

Elements of an Image—1960s

At the beginning of January 1966, William Petersen went to great lengths in a *New York Times Magazine* article to praise the efforts of Japanese Americans in their successful struggle to enter the mainstream of American life.[1] In December of that same year, the *U.S. News and World Report* also published a story lauding Chinese Americans for their remarkable achievements and praised Chinatowns as bastions of peace and prosperity.[2] As with the Japanese Americans, the article praised the Chinese for their ability to overcome years of racial discrimination.

The newfound "success" image for both groups rested upon a foundation of two basic elements. The first was the empirical evidence for success. Embedded in each story were a number of "facts" that substantiated Asian American success. Statistics on the educational achievements of Japanese and Chinese headed the list. Other evidence of success included movement into high-status occupations, rising incomes, and low rates of mental illness and crime.

Second, the articles offered an explicit theoretical explanation for why Asian Americans had succeeded. At the heart of this explanation was a direct link between traditional Asian cultural values and subsequent achievement in education and occupations. Petersen argued that Japanese Americans' adherence to values such as a deep respect for parents and authority, a reverence for learning, and a proclivity for hard work created a psychological achievement orientation that drove Japanese to do well in school. Similarly, the *U.S. News and World Report* article identified cultural emphases on hard work, thrift, and morality as factors that helped Chinese Americans to overcome obstacles and move up the socioeconomic ladder.

Asian American Success—Ideological and Political Implications

The 1966 articles marked a significant turning point in the public's perception of Asian Americans. After enduring a century of blatant racial discrimination and negative stereotypes, the Japanese and Chinese suddenly found themselves cast into a favorable light. In place of the unassimilable, inscrutable Fu Manchu and the vicious *kamikaze* pilot emerged the image of the high-achieving, successful minority.

This image of Asian American success did not appear in a vacuum. The definition of a new racial identity emerged at a moment of tremendous racial upheaval in America. The Civil Rights Movement, increased state intervention in race relations, urban riots, and black militancy collided in the mid-1960s, touching off intense debates on the direction of racial politics.[3]

In this context, the Asian American success story took on new meanings. The accomplishments of less than one million Asian Americans emerged as a model for how all minority groups could "make it" in society. The articulation of successful Asians in the popular press carried ramifications that extended well beyond the Chinatowns and Japantowns of America.

On the political level, Asian American success constituted a direct critique of Blacks who sought relief through federally supported social programs. Asian Americans, we were told, were able to make it on their own. Welfare programs were unnecessary. "At a time when it is being proposed that hundreds of billions be spent to uplift Negroes and other minorities, the nation's 300,000 Chinese Americans are moving ahead on their own, with no help from anyone else," declared the *U.S. News and World Report*,[4] and wrote Petersen: "By any criterion we choose, the Japanese Americans are better than any other group in our society, including native-born whites. They have established this remarkable record, moreover, by their own almost totally unaided effort."[5]

Asian American success also sent a distinct political message to the nascent Black Power Movement. The achievements of Asians diffused the black militants' claim that America was fundamentally a racist society, structured to keep minorities in a subordinate position. The Asian American experience identified cultural values and hard work as the keys to success. The political implication for those who had yet to make it was that their culture was not "good" enough. This delineation of good and bad culture deflected attention away from societal factors and placed the blame for racial inequality on minorities.[6]

Beyond these political implications, the model minority thesis presented a picture of American society that resonated with dominant ideological precepts.[7] Asian achievement confirmed that the United States was indeed the land of opportunity. It defined success in narrow, materialistic terms. The movement of Asians into the mainstream of American life affirmed the ideal that America was an open society, willing to accept and incorporate those minorities and immigrants who were willing to assimilate. Perhaps most importantly, the thesis upheld a fundamental meritocratic belief that America was a fair society.[8] Asian Americans had made it because America judged and rewarded people, not by the color of their skin, but on the basis of their qualifications, skills, attitudes, and behavior.

The model minority thesis, then, was far from a neutral construct. It was an image that carried political and ideological implications specific to the historical conditions of race relations in the mid-1960s. I now turn to the 1980s, where the nexus of political, racial, demographic, and economic conditions demarcates a historical context in sharp contrast to the 1960s. The following sections will look at how the changing context of the 1980s has altered the discourse on the Asian American experience.

Incorporating Change and Dissent—1980s

Between 1982 and 1986, ten articles on Asian American success appeared in major popular press publications.[9] Two changes in the focus and content of the discussion on Asian American success in the present period are immediately apparent. First, the articles all recognized the changing nature of the Asian American population. The focus of these articles was on Korean, Vietnamese, and other foreign-born Asians, rather than on Japanese and Chinese Americans. This modification is directly attributable to the tremendous demographic changes that have occurred over the past twenty years. Since the 1965 Immigration Act, Asians have become the fastest growing minority in the country. From 1970 to 1980, the Asian population grew from 1.4 to 3.5 million people. During this period, the Korean population increased 400 percent from 69,000 to over 350,000, while the Filipino population more than doubled from 340,000 to 780,000, and the Chinese population grew from 435,000 to 812,000.[10] In addition to these immigrants, the Asian American population has grown due to the influx of nearly a million Vietnamese and Southeast Asian refugees after the fall of Saigon in 1975.

Second, the articles displayed a greater recognition of the complexities and critiques associated with the model minority thesis. Three out of the ten articles presented substantial discussions on the negative impact that parental pressures have had on Asian American students.[11] Four articles acknowledged the stereotypic nature of the success image and noted the resentment that some Asians feel toward being considered the model minority.[12] In a related theme, six articles pointed out that Asians were entering arenas not previously associated with the quiet Asian image, such as politics, business management, art, fashion, and music.[13] Six articles mentioned that one of the indicators of success, median family income, was somewhat misleading because Asians tend to have more workers per family.[14]

That complex portrait of the Asian American experience reflects the recognition in the popular press that the Asian community has grown more diverse in the past fifteen years. In addition to the immigration that has brought highly skilled people into new occupational settings, the social movements of the late 1960s and 1970s, that included the Asian American Movement, heightened the political, social, and cultural consciousness of many Asian Americans. In this context, many Asians were encouraged to explore a broader range of political and cultural arenas.

The inclusion of potentially negative consequences in these articles also acknowledges a more comprehensive understanding of the model minority thesis that has been developed through scholarly research. The sensitivity to stereotyping and the pressures associated with success, for example, stems from the research on culture and identity that emerged in the early 1970s.[15] The critique of certain statistical indicators of success flows directly from the critical research on the Asian labor market experience.[16] These studies showed that median family income was not a good measure for success because it masked the fact that the per-worker income rates for Asian Americans fell significantly below that of comparably educated whites.

Consistency Amidst Change

The incorporation of new information and dissent is one way the discourse on Asian Americans has changed in the 1980s. The increased comprehensiveness of contemporary articles may lead one to conclude that the popular press is taking a more critical, fair, and balanced view of Asian Americans and that the articles are less political than similar stories in the 1960s. Further examination, however, reveals a certain consistency amidst change. The core elements of the original model minority thesis—the empirical evidence for success and a culturally based explanation for achievement—continue to be an integral part of the current discussion on Asian Americans.

The educational achievement of Asian Americans, for example, remained a critical indicator of success. In nine of the ten recent articles, the outstanding performance of Asian students in the Westinghouse Science Talent competition was cited as a measure of achievement. In seven of those articles, the high percentage of Asian students in universities was offered as proof of educational success. In seven stories, Asian student success was substantiated by their above-average SAT scores in math.

In explaining this success in school, the articles offered a theory that is consistent with the 1960s model minority thesis. At the heart of the explanations are familiar, culturally based attributes. In all ten articles, the Asian American family was mentioned as a key to educational success. Anecdotal stories of refugee parents working sixteen hours a day to pay for their children's education; of mothers insisting that their children study long hours; and of parents impressing upon their children the importance of education were offered to illustrate the influence of the family. Hard work and a reverence for learning also returned in the 1980s as vital to success. References to hard work appeared in five of the ten articles;[17] and the reverence for learning appeared in four stories.[18] In four articles, the reasons for Asian success were encompassed under the broader influence of Confucian ethics, where education was sacred and scholarly achievements were a way to express filial piety.[19]

The continued reliance on culturally based explanations for success mirror the same dominant ideological assumptions that articles from the 1960s rested upon. Asian American success once again reaffirms that America is a land of opportunity, where people are rewarded for their hard work and diligence. The rapid movement of Asian immigrants into the educational and economic mainstream proves that America is still open, fair, and able to incorporate industrious people. The stress on educational achievement and subsequent occupational mobility remains the main, albeit narrow, criteria for success.

Political Implications of the 1980s Image

In addition to maintaining the core elements of the original model minority thesis and conveying dominant ideological messages, contemporary articles continue to address political concerns. What must be noted, however, are changes in the form and content of those political messages that reflect changes in the surrounding racial and political climate. Borrowing from authors Michael Omi and Howard Winant, these discursive changes represent a "rearticulation" of Asian American success images in the 1980s, in which core elements of the discourse are infused "with a new political meaning and link(ed) with other key elements of conservative political ideology."[20] This rearticulation is achieved in three ways.

First, the overt racial comparisons between the success of Asians and the failures of other minorities are tempered and replaced in the current literature by a nonracial discourse that focuses primarily on differences between Asian American families and "American" families. In several articles, the authors suggest that Asian American families are "better," which accounts for their remarkable success. In "Why Asians Succeed Here," the author quotes a professor who says that "Asian families pay more attention to their children,"[21] and the *U.S. News and World Report* article cites the following observation: "If an American child isn't doing well in school, his parents think the teacher or school has failed or the student just doesn't have it. The Asian parents' view is that the student isn't trying hard enough."[22] In "Why Asians Are Going to the Head of the Class," the writer states that "Asian or Asian American parents are able to instill in their children a much greater motivation to work harder" and quotes conservative scholar Thomas Sowell's observation: "Asian parents are teaching a lesson that otherwise isn't being taught in America anymore. When you see a study that says Asian kids study harder than white and black kids and are getting better grades, it tells you something."[23]

While many of these comparisons are made in non-racial terms, they carry significant racial meaning in the conservative political action and discourse of the 1980s. Praise for the Asian American family is a consistent part of a broader conservative perspective that blames many of today's social problems on the deterioration of the family. President Reagan's attacks on abortion and school busing and his support for school prayer and tuition tax credits have been made in the name of restoring strength to the family and community. That many of these policies constitute direct attacks on programs originally designed to benefit racial minorities speaks to the subtle manner in which the elevation of family is actually a code word to disguise underlying racial concern.[24]

Second, the discussion on Asian American achievement is shaped by conservative educational reform proposals that have emerged from the recent national level debates on public schools. In the fervent debates following reports such as *A Nation at Risk*, many suggest that American education could be improved by lengthening the school year and increasing the amount of homework in school.[25] References to these conservative reforms infuse the dialogue on Asian Americans. Three articles argue that the longer school year in Asian countries, roughly 225 days compared to 180 in the United States, plays an important role in the educational success of Asian immigrants.[26] One of the articles attributes success to the work ethic of Asians and their willingness to do homework. It cites a study that found that American first grade students spent an average of fourteen minutes a night on homework and hated it, while Japanese first graders spent thirty-seven minutes and Chinese spent seventy-seven minutes on homework and loved it.[27]

Finally, the discourse on Asian American success, particularly in higher education, is linked to growing anti-Asian sentiments. "A Drive to Excel," for example, explicitly mentions that the growing number of Asian students in universities are resented by white students, who feel threatened. It reports stories of white students dropping courses if there were "too many Oriental faces." It also tells of jokes that MIT stood for "Made in Taiwan," and UCLA was "University of Caucasians Living Among Asians."[28] The controversy over admissions ceilings for Asian students is another arena where Asian American success appears to be the basis for discriminatory action.

The notion that Asian American success constitutes a potential threat is also expressed in subtle forms. A *New York Times Magazine* story exemplifies this in describing Asian Americans as *"surging* into the nation's best colleges like a *tidal wave"*[29] (emphasis added), and another author, in referring to the increase of Asians at Harvard, writes: "The figure is now 10%—five times their share of the population."[30] In both instances, Asian success is discussed in almost alarming tones, reminiscent of the "hordes" of Asians that threatened California in the late 1800s.

The irony that Asian American success has become a basis for discriminatory backlash is understandable in the context of growing anti-Asian sentiment in the 1980s. The decline of the American economy in the 1970s and the concomitant competition from Japan has given rise to increased tensions between Asians and Whites in the 1980s. These tensions have manifested themselves in numerous instances of violence against Asian Americans as exemplified by the 1982 murder of Vincent Chin. Discrimination and resentment in universities is another manifestation of those growing hostilities.

Tilting the Scale

Contemporary articles on Asian American success are remarkably pliable constructs. They have expanded to incorporate new information and critiques of the model minority thesis. At the same time, they maintain the core elements of the original model minority thesis, that continues to address political and ideological concerns. The question remains: what is the overriding message expressed in these articles? Does the incorporation of new information and critiques balance the image of Asian American success and create a fair picture of the Asian experience in the 1980s, or do the articles largely perpetuate a stereotypic view of Asians as the model minority?

I would argue that the portrayal of Asian Americans continues to be largely stereotypic. The dominant message conveyed is that Asian Americans are successful and have overcome discrimination with determination and hard work. This message is evident in the titles alone that grab the reader's attention and impart an initial image of Asian Americans as successful.

Beyond the titles, the image of Asian American success, and the explanatory emphasis on culture, family, and hard work, is constructed through a number of discursive mechanisms. First, the texts of articles invariably contain key sentences or passages that assign analytic *priority* to information that supports the model minority thesis. For example, the review of studies on the educational achievement of Asian Americans in the *New York Times Magazine* concludes with the sentence: "It is here [the family] that almost all the studies converge."[31] This simple sentence plays the critical role of identifying and prioritizing the family as the key to success, even though studies might suggest a range of explanations. Similarly, the essayist in the *New Republic* observes: "Social scientists wonder just how this success was possible. . . . There is no single answer, but all the various explanations of the Asian-Americans' success do tend to fall into one category: self-sufficiency."[32] These two passages provide an interpretive framework for the reader.

Second, the model minority thesis is upheld by passages that *minimize* the impact of contradictory information. This is most evident in the discussion on median Asian American family income. As mentioned earlier, six articles cite high median family incomes of Asian Americans as an indicator of success.[33] Five of the articles acknowledge that this measure is problematic because Asian American families tend to have more income earners than the norm or because there are large numbers of Asian Americans in poverty. The inclusion of this information, however, does not alter the dominant message that Asian Americans are economically successful. In four of the five articles, the authors minimize or discount the importance of the critiques.[34] One article discusses the critiques, then says, "Yet success stories abound. Even among recent Indo-Chinese refugees, large numbers have climbed out of poverty and found jobs."[35] Another article prefaces the critique of family income with the following line: "By at least one indicator, it seems hard to believe that Asian-Americans suffer greatly from discrimination."[36] These minimizing passages are important, for they enable authors to include potentially contradictory information yet still maintain the overall model minority thrust.

Finally, the articles promote the model minority thesis through the selective use of scholarly research. Research studies that support the notion that families are the key to Asian American success appear as authoritative evidence. For example, three articles cite Harold Stevenson's study of education in the United States, Japan, and Taiwan to substantiate their claim that Asian families instill a proclivity for hard work.[37] On the other hand, research that is critical of the model minority thesis never appears in the articles. This is particularly true in the discussion on median family income. There are no references to the extensive body of research that shows that Asians earn less than their educational levels would normally warrant.

Conclusion

I conclude this discussion with a simple but important image. Todd Gitlin, in describing how hegemonic ideologies operate, writes, they "stand still, in a sense, by moving."[38] This analysis of the treatment of Asian Americans by the popular press illustrates how this process works. There was significant movement in the discourse on Asian Americans in the 1980s. The articles have been updated through the incorporation of new information. They have withstood critiques, not by denying them, but by acknowledging them and then minimizing their power through a variety of discursive techniques. They have maintained relevance in the 1980s by changing to address contemporary political issues.

NOTES

1. William Peterson, "Success Story, Japanese-American Style," *New York Times Magazine*, January 9, 1966, 20–21, 33, 36, 38, 40–41, 43.

2. "Success Story of One Minority in the U.S.," *U.S. News and World Report*, December 26, 1966, 73–78.

3. Stokely Carmichael and Charles V. Hamilton, *Black Power: The Politics of Liberation in America* (New York: Vintage Books, 1967); and Frances Fox Piven and Richard Cloward, *Poor People's Movements* (New York: Vintage Books, 1977).

4. "Success Story," 73.

5. Peterson, "Success Story," 21.

6. William Ryan, *Blaming the Victim*, rev. ed. (New York: Vintage Books, 1976).

7. Ira Katzenelson and M. Kesselman, *The Politics of Power*, 2nd ed. (New York: Harcourt Brace Jovanovich, 1979).

8. Samuel Bowles and Herbert Gintis, *Schooling in Capitalist America: Educational Reform and the Contradictions of Economic Life* (New York: Basic Books, 1976).

9. The ten articles reviewed in this section, chronologically ordered, are: "Asian Americans: A 'Model Minority'," *Newsweek*, December 6, 1982, 39, 41–42, 51; "Confucian Work Ethic," *Time*, March 28, 1983, 52; "A Drive to Excel," *Newsweek-On Campus*, April 1984, 4–8, 12–13; "A Formula for Success," *Newsweek*, April 23, 1984, 77–78; Suzana McBee, "Asian Americans, Are They Making the Grade?" *U.S. News and World Report*, April 1984, 41–43, 46–47; "To America with Skills," *Time*, July 8, 1985, 42–44; David Bell, "The Triumph of Asian Ameri-

cans," *New Republic*, July 1985, 24–31; Fox Butterfield, "Why Asians Are Going to the Head of the Class," *New York Times Magazine*, August 3, 1986, 19–24; Robert Oxnam, "Why Asians Succeed Here," *New York Times Magazine*, November 30, 1986, 74–75, 89–90, 92; and Anthony Ramirez, "America's Super Minority," *Fortune Magazine*, November 24, 1986, 148–149, 152, 156, 160.

10. Robert Gardner, Bryant Robey, and Peter C. Smith, "Asian Americans: Growth, Change, and Diversity," *Population Bulletin* no. 40 (1985).

11. See "Confucian Work Ethic"; "A Drive to Excel"; and "A Formula for Success."

12. See "A Drive to Excel"; "A Formula for Success"; McBee, "Are They Making the Grade?"; and Oxnam, "Why Asians Succeed Here."

13. See "Asian Americans, a 'Model Minority' "; "A Drive to Excel"; "A Formula for Success"; McBee, "Are They Making the Grade?"; Bell, "The Triumph of Asian Americans"; and Oxnam, "Why Asians Succeed Here."

14. See "Asian Americans, A 'Model Minority' "; "A Formula for Success"; McBee, "Are They Making the Grade?"; "To America with Skills"; Bell, "The Triumph of Asian Americans"; and Oxnam, "Why Asians Succeed Here."

15. Ben Tong, "The Ghetto of the Mind," *Amerasia Journal* 1 (1971): 1–31; and Colin Watanabe, "Self-expression and the Asian American Experience," *Personnel and Guidance Journal* 51 (1973): 390–396.

16. Amado Cabezas, "The Asian American Today as an Economic Success Model" (Paper presented at Break the Silence: A Conference on Anti-Asian Violence, Berkeley, 1986); Kwang Chung Kim and W. M. Hurh, "Korean Americans and the 'Success' Image—A Critique," *Amerasia Journal* 10 (1983): 3–21; and Morrison Wong, "The Cost of Being Chinese, Japanese, and Filipino," *Pacific Sociological Review* 25 (1982): 59–78.

17. See "Asian Americans, A 'Model Minority' "; "A Drive to Excel"; "A Drive to Excel"; McBee, "Are They Making the Grade?"; Butterfield, "Going to the Head of the Class"; and Oxnam, "Why Asians Succeed Here."

18. See "Asian Americans, A 'Model Minority' "; "A Drive to Excel"; "A Formula for Success"; and Oxnam, "Why Asians Succeed Here."

19. See "Confucian Work Ethic"; McBee, "Are They Making the Grade?"; Butterfield, "Going to the Head of the Class"; and Oxnam, "Why Asians Succeed Here."

20. Michael Omi and Howard Winant, *Racial Formation in the United States: From the 1960s to the 1980s* (New York: Routledge & Kegan Paul, 1986), 114.

21. Oxnam, "Why Asians Succeed Here," 89.

22. McBee, "Are They Making the Grade?" 42.

23. Butterfield, "Going to the Head of the Class," 20, 21.

24. Omi and Winant, *Racial Formation*, 84.

25. National Commission on Excellence in Education, *A Nation at Risk* (Washington, D.C.: Government Printing Office, 1983).

26. See "Confucian Work Ethic"; "A Formula for Success"; and Butterfield, "Going to the Head of the Class," 21.

27. Butterfield, "Going to the Head of the Class," 21.

28. "A Drive to Excel," 8.

29. Butterfield, "Going to the Head of the Class," 21.

30. Bell, "The Triumph of Asian Americans," 26.

31. Butterfield, "Going to the Head of the Class," 24.

32. Bell, "The Triumph of Asian Americans," 26.

33. See "Asian Americans, A 'Model Minority' "; "A Drive to Excel"; "A Formula for

Success"; McBee, "Are They Making the Grade?"; "To America with Skills"; and Oxnam, "Why Asians Succeed Here."

34. See "A Formula for Success"; McBee, "Are They Making the Grade?"; "To America with Skills"; and Oxnam, "Why Asians Succeed Here."

35. McBee, "Are They Making the Grade?," 42.

36. Bell, "The Triumph of Asian Americans," 28.

37. See "A Drive to Excel"; McBee, "Are They Making the Grade?" and Butterfield, "Going to the Head of the Class."

38. Todd Gitlin, "Television's Screens: Hegemony in Transition," in *Cultural and Economic Reproduction in Education*, Michael Apple, ed. (London: Routledge & Kegan Paul, 1982), 210.

Chapter Twenty

The "Model Minority" Deconstructed

Lucie Cheng and Philip Q. Yang

Introduction

"I thought I would never say this. But these new immigrants are ruining things for us." Jim Yamada, a third-generation Japanese American, said in disgust. "Asian Americans fought for decades against discrimination and racial prejudice. We want to be treated just like everybody else, like Americans. You see, I get real angry when people come up to me and tell me how good my English is. They say: 'Oh, you have no accent. Where did you learn English?' Where did I learn English? Right here in America. I was born here like they were. We really hated it when people assume that just because Asian Americans look different we were foreigners. It took us a long time to get people to see this point, to be sensitized to it. Now the new immigrants are setting us back. People see me now and they automatically treat me as an immigrant. I really hate that. The worst thing is that these immigrants don't understand why I am angry."

"Am I an Asian American? No, I am Vietnamese," Le Tran asserted. "Actually, I am Vietnamese-Chinese. I came from Vietnam, but my ancestors were Chinese. Well, now maybe you can call me an Asian American. However, I don't usually identify myself that way." Her ethnic identity proves elusive. Some people tell her only those Asians born in the United States are Asian Americans; others say only Chinese, Japanese, Koreans, and Filipinos are Asian Americans because their ancestors came here long ago and shared a history of discrimination; still others say one has to have citizenship or at least a green card to be Asian American. "It's all so confusing! Does it matter?" she asked.

"My husband is a *kongzhong feiren* (spaceman or trapeze flier)," sighed Mrs. Li, the wife of a Chinese immigrant engineer turned entrepreneur: "There is no normal family life. But I am glad that he isn't like so many other 'trapeze fliers' who keep a 'wife' in every city." Dr. Li flies from Los Angeles to Taipei, Shenzhen, and Hong Kong every other month, managing a thriving garment manufacturing business. He anticipates tough competition from Taiwan entrepreneurs who are moving their plants to Indonesia to take advantage of cheap labor without the uncertain politics of the People's Republic of China.

These vignettes paint an initial portrait of Los Angeles's changing Asian American communities. For Americans of Asian descent, ethnicity seems to have undergone periodic reconstruction. From the early immigration of the nineteenth century to the end of World War II, Asians in America identified themselves as distinct ethnic groups: Chinese, Japanese, and Filipinos. Each group was brought to the United States to meet the specific labor needs of the time and suffered the somewhat similar fate of discrimination, restriction, and exclusion. These similar experiences gave rise to a new identity constructed during the civil rights era. In order to gain political access, Chinese, Japanese, and Filipinos became "Asian Americans" (Espiritu 1992). But no sooner was this new identity established than a new, post-1965 wave of immigrants from Asia coming from a wider range of countries called the concept of Asian American into question. Speaking different languages and engaging in distinct cultural practices, the new immigrants reversed, if only temporarily, the trajectory of pan-Asian integration. Their separate ethnic identities as Chinese, Japanese, Filipino, Indian, Korean, Vietnamese, Cambodian, and so forth strengthen—are strengthened by—international ties that bind the global political economy.

Between 1970 and 1990, two parallel migration streams from diverse Asian countries converged in Los Angeles (Liu and Cheng 1994). The first was made up of highly educated Asian immigrants who joined the local professional-managerial class, usually on the lower rungs of the ladder, and slowly worked their way up. As new members of this class, which is becoming increasingly international, these immigrants are supported by a large group of other Asian immigrants who fill the semiskilled and unskilled jobs in manufacturing and services. While Asian immigrant professionals serve as a link to the most advanced sectors of the world economy, the less-developed sectors are maintained by less-skilled immigrant labor.

Entrepreneurship is a common characteristic of Asian immigrants. Although traditional Mom-and-Pop stores are still significant in the ethnic economy, Asian businesses are increasingly diverse in size and scope. They not only fill niches in the local Los Angeles economy but create international business networks, as well. For example, Chinese immigrants and Vietnamese refugees have played a unique role in the development of bilateral trade between the United States and their countries of origin, contributing to the privatization of the economy in China and Vietnam as well as to the transformation of businesses in Los Angeles. The restructuring of the world political economy has created not only multinational corporations but also an emerging group of transnational residents whose activities and presence weave an international network of professional and business people. Asian participation in this network is gaining significance (Ong et al. 1992). Once limited to jobs as professionals, entrepreneurs, and low-skilled laborers, Asian immigrants now include a growing number of capitalists looking for investment opportunities in the United States. Not only do their occupations reinforce capitalism as an economic system, but at the same time their influx into the United States and their comparatively greater social mobility help strengthen the capitalist ideology of meritocracy and its ethno-racial variant, the "model minority" (Ong et al. 1992)

On the other hand, the conditions that Asian immigrants encounter may not long support the optimistism with which so many arrive. The visibility and the high profile of their residential enclaves and their occupational niches in particular have tapped into undercurrents of racism and nativism deep in the American psyche. Many Asian Americans maintain that a "glass ceiling" keeps them from getting ahead, and these charges of discrimination have increased over the last decade. Anti-Asian violence has erupted in several major American cities. Alarmed by the resurgence of anti-Asianism, federal and state agencies have begun to monitor racial crime. An upsurge in hostility and discrimination, coupled with the changing Asian demographics, has made pan-Asian solidarity an issue of necessity and urgency for all groups of Asian descent. Nevertheless, historical rifts and current relations among Asian groups also pose challenges to Asian American identity.

Asian immigrants are victims of racism in two ways. They suffer from discrimination from non-Asians, and, yet, at the same time, many Asians discriminate against other racial groups. Coming from very different national backgrounds, often also from more culturally homogeneous societies, some Asian immigrants seem less tolerant of diversity. Cultural conflict aggravates already strained economic relations between Asians and other disadvantaged minorities. As victims of racism in the first sense, Asians are a progressive force for change. But Asian racism itself threatens to push the community toward conservatism.

This chapter focuses on the diversity of Asian Americans. What significant changes have occurred in the Asian American population in the past three decades? How well do Asians fare, and how do they adapt to the changing social environment? Do Asian experiences challenge or reinforce common stereotypes and concepts, such as "model minority" and "glass ceiling," which are thought to be especially applicable to Asian Americans? Finally, what do the changing intergroup relations mean for Asian Americans, for the formation of a pan-Asian ethnicity or coalition, and for the needs and aspirations of the reconstituted Asian ethnic groups? These are the main questions addressed in the following sections.

Immigration and Changes in Ethnic Composition

The rapid restructuring of the Pacific Rim political economy, ushered in by a long-term crisis in advanced capitalism, the advent of the global economy, and the challenge of ascending East Asian states, has influenced profoundly the pattern of immigration to the United States in the last two and half decades (Ong et al. 1994). In 1965, less than 7 percent of all immigrants to the United States were from Asia. In 1970, the figure rose to 25 percent, and in 1980 to 44 percent. Although Asian immigration continues to rise in the 1990s, official statistics from the Immigration and Naturalization Service show that the Asian share of total immigration during the 1980s dropped to 22 percent. This decline is more illusory than real, however, largely reflecting the results of the 1986 Immigration Reform and Control Act (IRCA). This act legalized a largely Mexican and Latin American origin population, many of whom had arrived in the United States prior to 1982.[1]

Four general features distinguish the new wave of Asian immigration from the old: a larger size, a higher percentage of women, greater ethnic and socioeconomic diversity, and more extensive—as well as intensive—global linkages. These same features characterize Asian immigrants to Los Angeles. The Los Angeles region, a significant gateway of the Pacific Rim and an emerging "global city," is a favorite destination of post-1965 Asian immigration. In this multiethnic region, Asians have been the fastest-growing segment of the population over the past two and half decades, largely because of immigration. In 1970, 240,000 Asians lived in Los Angeles, about 2 percent of the total population. By 1990, with over 1.3 million Asians making up 9 percent of the total population, the Los Angeles region was home to the single largest Asian population in the nation, far surpassing other major Asian centers such as San Francisco-Oakland, Honolulu, and New York. Between 1970 and 1990, the region's Asian population increased by 451 percent, ten times the regional average population growth rate (46 percent) and significantly more than the runner-up, the Latino population, which shot up by 236 percent. In contrast, the black population barely increased (0.4 percent), and the white population declined.

While all Asian groups experienced large increases in absolute size and relative population share, rates varied considerably between 1970 and 1990. The Korean and Indian populations, each beginning with a small base, increased dramatically, by more than 1,000 percent, while the already established Chinese and Filipino groups showed impressive growth, 626 percent and 563 percent, respectively. The Vietnamese, who began to settle in southern California after North Vietnam's conquest of South Vietnam in 1975, increased from 48,320 to 142,890 between 1980 and 1990, a 196 percent growth rate in one decade (see Figure 20.1).

Vietnamese are the largest of several groups whose presence became visible after

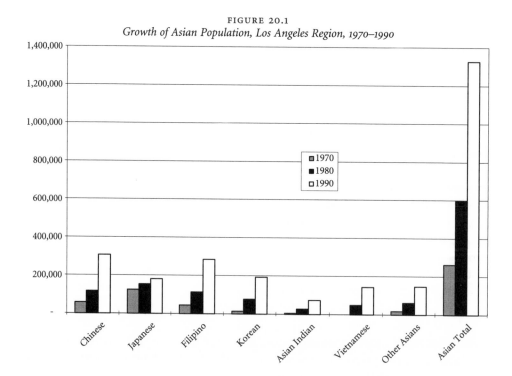

FIGURE 20.1
Growth of Asian Population, Los Angeles Region, 1970–1990

1970. Cambodians and Laotians were also absent from the region before the American involvement in the Vietnam War and internal strife on the Indochinese peninsula led to their arrival. Korean immigration began in the early twentieth century in small numbers and increased after the Korean War, as war brides and orphans adopted by Americans arrived. It was not until 1965, the year in which the discriminatory national origins quota system was abolished, that Koreans began moving to the United States in larger numbers. The change in immigration law also affected established groups such as Chinese, Japanese, and Filipinos, whose foreign-born populations consist mostly of post-1965 immigrants. Most of the foreign-born Asians came after the enactment of the 1965 Immigration and Nationality Act. In particular, almost all foreign-born Vietnamese, Koreans, and Asian Indians arrived after 1965.

The new immigration also ended the demographic predominance of the Japanese in transforming Asian American Los Angeles into a multiethnic community. In 1970, the Japanese, accounting for 51 percent of the region's Asian population, were the largest and dominant group. But, with fewer immigrants and a low fertility rate, the Japanese lost their top-ranking position; no single dominant group replaced them in the new mix of Asian groups that emerged over the next two decades. By 1990, the Japanese stood fourth (with 14 percent of the region's Asian population), following the Chinese, with 23 percent, the Filipinos, with 22 percent, and the Koreans, with about 15 percent. Vietnamese and other Asians each accounted for somewhat more than 10 percent of the total Asian population in 1990.

The influx of new immigrants also reversed the earlier demographic dominance of the U.S. born, as Figure 20.2 shows. In 1970, 57 percent of the Asian population in Los Angeles was made up of Americans by birth; twenty years later, they accounted for only 31 percent. From 1980 on, the foreign-born made up the majority of every Asian group except for the Japanese. For almost all groups, the proportion of the foreign-born significantly increased from 1970 to 1980, but the increase slowed in the next decade, and for the Vietnamese and Koreans the proportion declined. A relatively youthful female immigrant population and lower immigration rates may both have contributed to this change.

Although early Chinese, Japanese, Filipino, and Korean American communities were characterized as bachelor societies, the situation changed after 1965, when U.S. immigration policies were revised to favor of family reunification and large numbers of female immigrants from Asia came to Los Angeles. The large influx of Asian women immigrants generated balanced sex ratios for the major Asian communities, which now have slightly higher proportions of females than males. The future sizes and compositions of the Asian populations will surely reflect the current age compositions of women immigrants admitted during the past two decades.

The "Model Minority": Image and Reality

The phenomenal surge of Asian immigration and the resulting changes in ethnic composition have hardly tarnished the image of Asian Americans as a "model

FIGURE 20.2
Foreign-born Asian Population by Ethnicity, Los Angeles Region, 1970–1990

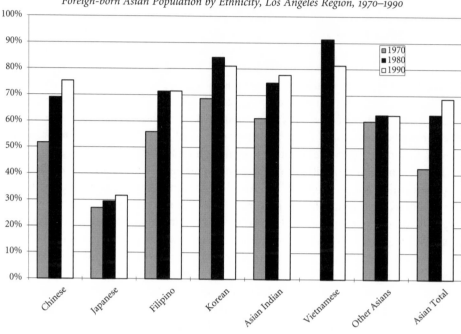

minority." This portrayal began in the mid-1960s at a time of massive racial upheaval; the term was first used by the press to depict Japanese Americans who struggled to enter the mainstream of American life and to laud Chinese Americans for their remarkable accomplishments.[2] These accounts conveyed the message that Japanese and Chinese Americans had achieved great success by overcoming discrimination with determination and hard work. Later extended to Asian Americans as a group,[3] the label filtered into college textbooks, where it further promoted the image of Asian Americans as minorities who "made it" in this "land of opportunity."

Ever since its inception, the model minority thesis has been a subject of considerable controversy, especially from critics who have argued that the image is racially stereotypic, empirically inaccurate, and no longer applicable to the changing Asian American population (Ong and Hee 1994; Takaki 1987). In their view, the model minority label is also objectionable for its political implications, which cast America as a fair, open society and a real land of opportunity, where minorities can make it as long as they work hard. The concept that some minorities could be a "model" thus counters the black militant claim that America is fundamentally a racist society, structured to keep minorities in a subordinate position. By extolling Asian Americans as a model minority, this critical literature asserts, the established world hopes to set a standard of behavior for other minorities.

Despite an unending barrage of attacks, the model minority image has persisted into the 1990s, quite alive if not entirely unscathed. The supporting literature often begins by citing the educational achievements of Asian Americans reported in data from the 1980 and earlier censuses (Hirschman and Wong 1986). Statistics for Los

Angeles confirm the pattern of high levels of education and disproportionate representation in universities and colleges but demonstrate significant variations across groups. Compared with U.S.-born non-Asian groups, U.S.-born Asians as a whole had higher levels of educational achievement in each census year. In 1990, for example, the average U.S.-born Asian adult reported 14.2 years of schooling, the highest among all broad ethnic groups. Not all groups of U.S.-born Asians were equally well educated, however. While Chinese, Japanese, Koreans, and Asian Indians ranked ahead of U.S.-born whites, Filipinos fell slightly behind and Vietnamese and other Asians fell substantially behind whites, with educational levels similar to or lower than those of U.S.-born blacks and Hispanics. As a whole, Asian immigrants were less well educated than their U.S.-born co-ethnics. Though relatively small at the beginning of 1970, the immigrant-native gap widened in successive years; by 1990, the average Asian immigrant was slightly less well schooled than the average native white, a reversal of the pattern from twenty years earlier. As average schooling levels for most Asian immigrant groups either improved or stayed the same between 1970 and 1990, the slight decline in average education for the entire Asian group seems largely due to two factors: the influx of poorly educated Vietnamese and other Indochinese in the 1980s and the arrival of female immigrants, whose educational levels were generally lower than those of their male counterparts (Filipinas excepted).

Data on the percentage distributions of educational level by ethnicity and nativity in 1990 (Table 20.1) further substantiate the phenomenal accomplishments of Asian Americans in higher education, but again with great variation. Among U.S.-born Asians every group outpaced native whites in completion of the college degree. Of particular note is the disparity between Chinese Americans, among whom 65 percent had finished college, and native whites, among whom 31 percent had finished college. Japanese Americans, the other large group of U.S.-born, also ranked well ahead of whites on this count, as did all the other smaller groups.

A similar pattern held up among immigrants, though with considerably greater variation. Once again, rates of college completion among all Asian groups Vietnamese excepted, substantially exceeded whites'; even among the Vietnamese, almost half reported some college or more. At the other end of the spectrum, the immigrants were also underrepresented among the ranks of the poorly schooled with a high school diploma or less, pointing to the continued selectivity of Asian immigration to Los Angeles; again, only the Vietnamese exceeded whites on this count.

While the schooling profile of adult Asian Americans shows some unevenness, a look at the educational performance of the younger generations erases any doubt. When it comes to school achievement and attainment, Asians leave all other groups far behind in the dust, and that generalization holds for all Asian ethnic groups, regardless of nativity and generational status, which we have broken down by adding a 1.5 generation to capture those immigrants who came as children under the age of ten. As Table 20.2 shows, Asian teenagers ages sixteen to nineteen drop out of high school at a rate that is either under or comparable to the rate for whites; only Vietnamese and Filipino immigrants, who lag behind whites on so many other indicators, do worse on this count, by exactly one percentage point. At a slightly older age, Asians of every group—Vietnamese immigrants excepted—are more

TABLE 20.1

Percentage Distribution of Educational Level by Ethnicity and Nativity, Persons Ages 25 and Over, Los Angeles Region, 1990

Education	Chinese FB	Chinese USB	Japanese FB	Japanese USB	Filipino FB	Filipino USB	Korean FB	Indian USB	Vietnamese FB	White USB	Black USB	Hispanics USB	Hispanics FB
No school/nursery	5.5	1.2	2.0	0.3	0.6	0.7	2.6	2.3	7.3	0.3	0.8	1.5	10.4
Elementary school	8.3	0.7	1.6	0.5	2.9	0.9	3.7	3.2	9.3	0.9	2.5	6.6	38.1
Some high school	9.5	2.0	6.1	3.1	3.8	7.3	6.8	8.1	19.4	8.1	16.6	23.2	20.8
High school graduate	14.1	7.5	26.7	17.1	10.6	19.3	23.8	12.2	15.4	22.0	24.8	27.9	13.5
Some college	2.4	23.2	28.5	35.1	28.2	39.4	25.0	19.0	30.3	37.9	39.6	30.7	12.4
College degree or more	40.2	65.4	35.1	43.9	53.9	32.4	38.1	55.2	18.4	30.8	15.8	10.0	4.8
Total	100.0	100.0	100.0	100.0	100.0	100.0	100.0	100.0	100.0	100.0	100.0	100	100.0

NOTES: Total may not add up to 100 percent due to rounding errors.
USB = U.S.-born; FB = Foreign-born.

TABLE 20.2
Educational Attendance and Completion Levels, Los Angeles Region, 1990

	Japenese	Chinese	Vietnamese	Filipino	Korean	Asian Indian	Mexican	White
High school dropouts, ages 16–19								
Foreign-born	3%	6%	9%	9%	6%	6%	58%	6%
1.5 generation	NA	2%	5%	4%	4%	5%	23%	6%
U.S.-born	3%	0%	5%	3%	3%	0%	15%	8%
High school dropouts, ages 18–24								
Foreign-born	5%	7%	16%	9%	6%	7%	64%	8%
1.5 generation	1%	4%	6%	4%	3%	3%	38%	9%
U.S.-born	4%	2%	9%	8%	3%	2%	25%	11%
College attendance, ages 18–24								
Foreign-born	64%	64%	49%	40%	52%	51%	8%	42%
1.5 generation	54%	60%	60%	61%	71%	69%	21%	40%
Native-born	59%	79%	53%	55%	71%	71%	28%	38%

NOTE: White foreign-born and 1.5 generation are immigrants born in Europe or Canada.

likely to complete high school than whites. As for college attendance, the Asian advantage is truly outstanding; every Asian ethnic and nativity group, with the exception of Filipino immigrants, surpasses whites in this respect. Chinese Americans attend college at twice the white rate, and U.S.-born Asian Indians and Koreans are not that far behind. Numbers like these account for the growing Asian presence in higher education, so easily seen on the campuses of the elite universities of the Los Angeles region. In 1993, for instance, Asians accounted for 32 percent of the undergraduate students at UCLA, 20 percent at USC, and 23 percent at Caltech—rates that pointed to two- to threefold Asian overrepresentation among elite undergraduate ranks.

Several theories have been offered to explain the success of Asians in school. One earlier explanation attributed this success to the Confucian culture that prevails in many Asian societies. This view emphasizes a cultural reverence for learning and scholarly achievements and its role in shaping parental behavior. Parents urge their children to study longer hours, reward them for doing well in school, and emphasize the importance of education for social mobility; consequently, Asian students are motivated or compelled to learn and succeed. A second explanation accentuates the role of stable Asian American families, which provide a good learning environment for educational success. The selectivity of highly educated Asian immigrants is also a factor (Barringer et al. 1993; Hirschman and Wong 1986). Although these explanations have merit, they do not capture all the important determinants. We argue that the social environment in the receiving country is an essential consideration. In a society dominated by whites, where racial minorities often must find their own special channels of social mobility, education has been a primary route for many minority groups. In other words, the reception context in the United States forces Asian immigrants and their U.S.-born children to pursue higher levels of education as a means of upward mobility. It is the combination of culture, family, selectivity of immigration, and the receiving context that determines the remarkable educational achievements of Asian Americans.

The occupational mobility of Asian Americans is another piece of evidence often cited in support of the model minority thesis. Historically, Asians tended to be clustered at physically difficult, low-prestige, and low-paying occupations; Chinese often worked as laundrymen or small restaurateurs, Japanese as gardeners and farmers. But after World War II, the occupational status of Asians gradually improved. Previous studies have shown Asians climbing the occupational ladder with such success that the U.S.-born Chinese and Japanese reached or almost achieved parity with whites (Barringer et al. 1990). The Los Angeles data shown in Table 20.3 demonstrate the significant progress that Asians have made over the past two decades.

Employment in high-skill occupations (HSOs)—here defined as professional, managerial, and technical occupations—went up significantly among U.S.-born Angelenos of all ethnic stripes between 1970 and 1990, reflecting the area's transition to a high-tech, high-information economy. But, even within this comparative frame, the performance of U.S.-born Asians remains impressive. Although the then small population of U.S.-born Asians held a lead over all other groups in 1970, it pulled farther ahead over the next decades until, by 1990, almost half the region's Asian Americans had moved into HSOs. As with the other indicators that we examine, the high overall average conceals considerable intra-Asian diversity. The Chinese American lead over whites opened up dramatically after 1970; Japanese American progress,

TABLE 20.3

Percentage Distribution of Employed Persons Ages 25–64 in High-Skill and Low-Skill Occupations by Nativity, Los Angeles Region, 1970–1990

	High-skill occupations			Low-skill occupations		
	1970	1980	1990	1970	1980	1990
U.S.-born						
Asians	36%	39%	50%	28%	20%	14%
Chinese	39%	58%	69%	23%	11%	7%
Japanese	36%	38%	51%	29%	21%	12%
Korean	35%	28%	50%	23%	25%	14%
Filipino	31%	30%	39%	36%	21%	20%
Asian India	NA	58%	50%	NA	21%	17%
Vietnamese	NA	NA	41%	NA	33%	39%
Other Asian	33%	24%	29%	33%	31%	25%
White	34%	39%	44%	23%	18%	15%
Black	16%	24%	31%	49%	36%	28%
Hispanics	13%	19%	25%	49%	40%	31%
Foreign-born						
Asians	35%	38%	39%	40%	25%	22%
Chinese	45%	47%	43%	41%	27%	21%
Japanese	22%	36%	41%	56%	33%	24%
Korean	NA	29%	31%	NA	33%	20%
Filipino	26%	39%	41%	34%	21%	20%
Asian India	NA	58%	52%	NA	12%	13%
Vietnamese	NA	30%	32%	NA	36%	33%
Other Asian	NA	27%	32%	NA	31%	25%
Hispanics	8%	9%	10%	66%	62%	59%

NOTE: High-skill occupations include managerial, professional, technical, and related workers, while low-skill occupations include private household workers, service workers, operatives, transportation workers, laborers, and farm workers.

also dramatic, pales only in comparison with the Chinese American record. On the other hand, Filipinos were doing somewhat worse than native whites in 1970 and lagged further behind in 1990, which meant that the intra-Asian disparity in HSO employment had widened still further.

A look at the bottom of the occupational spectrum shows that the Asian migration to the Los Angeles region does indeed contain a proletarian component, but one that has diminished in relative terms over time. In 1970, Asian immigrants in the Los Angeles region were a good deal more likely than native whites to be employed in low-skill occupations (LSOs, here defined as all blue-collar occupations, craft excepted, as well as service and farm jobs). By 1990, the proportion of Asian immigrants in LSOs was still larger than that of whites, but, the massive immigration notwithstanding, the gap was a good deal smaller than it had been two decades earlier. In fact, in 1990, the immigrant concentration in LSOs was modest not just in comparison with the overwhelmingly blue-collar Latino immigrants but in comparison with native African Americans and Latinos, as well.

Still, not every group of Asian immigrants was equally successful in escaping from the region's humbler jobs. As expected, Asian Indians were the least likely to work in LSOs; just as predictably, Vietnamese reported the largest concentration of LSO employment. Nonetheless, Vietnamese had managed to reduce their dependence on LSOs during the 1980s, even though this same period saw a large influx of Vietnamese newcomers who were less well qualified than those who had come before. And the 1990 rate of Vietnamese employment in LSOs made them more or less comparable with U.S.-native Hispanics and African Americans; since Vietnamese were the most disadvantaged of the region's Asian immigrant groups, this fact alone tells us something about how well the others were doing.

In explaining the occupational patterns of Asian Americans, researchers have pointed to cultural factors, such as an ethic of hard work (Kitano 1988). The current literature is critical of cultural explanations, emphasizing instead structural factors or socioeconomic characteristics of immigrants. More recent research shows that the occupational status of Asian Americans is associated with their human capital (for example, education), physical capital (e.g., money brought to the United States by immigrants from abroad), and social capital (such as ethnic networks, occupational niches, and ethnic enclaves). The social origins of contemporary Asian immigrants, most notably their tendency to come from better-educated and more urban segments of their home societies, may also contribute to their current occupational status (Barringer et al. 1990; Ong et al. 1992).

The high average income levels of Asian Americans provide the most powerful evidence for the model minority thesis. The past three censuses show that, for the country as a whole, Asians have significantly higher levels of median household income than all other broad ethnic groups. But median household income may be a misleading indicator, since Asian families have more workers per household than white families and since Asians tend to be concentrated in a few large metropolitan areas, where incomes, as well as costs of living, are higher than the national average (Takaki 1987). In an effort to control for regional location, Ong and Hee compared the 1989 median incomes of non-Hispanic whites with those of Asian and Pacific

TABLE 20.4

Median Household Income, Los Angeles Region, 1979–1989

Foreign-born

	All Asians	Chinese	Japanese	Korean	Filipino	Asian Indian	Vietnamese	Other Asian	Hispanics
1979	$33,302	$34,466	$27,574	$29,732	$41,366	$39,979	$21,553	$31,546	$23,277
1989	$40,449	$38,427	$38,677	$34,382	$50,056	$48,539	$35,564	$33,371	$26,494

U.S.-born

	All Asians	Chinese	Japanese	Korean	Filipino	Asian Indian	Vietnamese	Other Asian	Hispanics	Whites	Blacks
1979	$40,350	$40,315	$43,993	$35,451	$33,036	NA	NA	$31,546	$29,576	$35,000	$21,554
1989	$48,221	$49,146	$51,067	$37,871	$45,082	NA	NA	$40,197	$35,107	$43,220	$26,386

Islanders nationally and within the combined four metropolitan areas that have the largest Asian Pacific American populations (Los Angeles, San Francisco, Oakland, and New York) (Ong and Hee 1994). Asian Pacific Americans did have a higher level of average median household income ($36,000) than whites ($31,000) for the county as a whole, but the order was reversed ($40,000 for whites and $37,200 for Asian Pacific Americans) for the four metropolitan areas (Takaki 1987).

The evidence from Los Angeles—which eliminates the influence of differences in the regional distribution of Asians and whites and therefore makes our contrast groups directly comparable—yields a picture that differs from Ong and Hee's. In 1989, median family income among the U.S.-native Asians ($48,221) put them significantly ahead of U.S.-native whites ($43,220) and even further ahead of other U.S.-born groups (see Table 20.4). Disaggregation by ethnicity shows that U.S.-native Japanese, Chinese, and Filipinos, the numerically larger groups, fared much better than their white counterparts, while the much less numerous (and presumably younger) Koreans lagged behind. Asian immigrants as a whole fared much better than Hispanic immigrants and even U.S.-born Hispanics and blacks. Foreign-born Filipinos and Asian Indians especially outperformed other groups, since many of them were highly educated. Similar patterns obtained in 1979.

As we have noted, white/Asian differences in the number of adults working per family help explain why Asians tend to outrank whites in median family income. According to the 1990 census, U.S.-born Asian families contained an average of 1.5 adults who worked, as opposed to 1.2 persons for U.S.-born white families; similarly, foreign-born Asian families had an average of 1.6 working adults, compared with 1.1 working adults in foreign-born white families.

If the Asian lead in median family income is consistent with the model minority thesis, a look at personal earnings confounds it. Most groups of Asian men do worse than whites, a finding consistent with Ong and Hee's. But caution is needed before we decide that Asians have indeed fallen behind on the wage front, since the prevalence of newcomers, who undoubtedly need time to learn the ropes and to gain the specific skills needed by the region's employers, may well drag average earnings down. Untangling the question is complicated further by the diverse ethnic and nativity mix of the region's Asian groups, making it difficult to grasp the picture as a whole.

In effect, two competing hypotheses offer interpretations of the Asian wage lag. The discrimination hypothesis suggests that Asians, while often highly skilled, confront a structure of rewards different from that of their white counterparts, lagging behind comparable whites because employers treat the two groups differently. In contrast, the immigrant hypothesis suggests that for the foreign-born it is all a matter of adjustment; with time and the acquisition of better English skills and other proficiencies specific to the U.S. labor market, Asian immigrants eventually receive their just desserts.

We attempted to assess these hypotheses by adjusting for the labor market, family, and individual characteristics that affect earnings, giving Asians the average characteristics of native whites and then seeing how doing so affects the mean earnings of persons who made at least $1,000 in the year prior to the relevant census year. The answer, as one might expect, differs by nativity, ethnicity, and gender. Among men, U.S.-native Asians do worse than U.S.-native whites; adjustment has virtually no effect on Asian earnings, since for the most part U.S.-born Asian men possess the characteristics associated with higher earnings. The earnings of U.S. native Asian women in 1969 and 1979 surpassed those of U.S.-born whites; adjustment brings Asian earnings down to about parity with whites, suggesting some slight advantages of Asians over whites. The Asian advantage diminished over time, however, so that in 1989 the adjusted earnings of Asian women fell largely below those of whites. Thus, the situation among the those born in the United States, men in particular, generally supports the discrimination hypothesis, indicating the handicapped market position of Asians.

The immigrant story, however, reads differently and needs to be looked at in a somewhat different manner. On the basis of the raw data for all Asian groups combined, time, measured as length of settlement in the United States, clearly matters. The newest cohorts did much worse than native whites, and the earlier cohorts did better. To be sure, not every individual group experienced the beneficial effect of time in quite the same way; Filipinos, for example, registered modest progress, with men in the cohort of the 1960s still doing worse than whites in 1989, whereas Koreans of the same cohort charged ahead, greatly outdistancing whites in 1989.

But, time is not the only attribute that counts; immigrants' labor market and familial characteristics should make them better earners than whites; by giving the older cohorts of immigrants the characteristics of whites pushed immigrant earnings down, indicating that comparable immigrants and whites are not rewarded equally. Hence, immigrants have a double burden to bear: the time needed to learn the ropes and discriminatory treatment that persists even after they gain the skills and experience that employers want.

A similar view emerges when we trace cohorts over time, though the small size of the populations in place as of the 1960s prevents extensive disaggregations. In 1969, men in the 1960s cohort were doing a good deal worse than native whites; the adjustment procedure did little to alter earnings. While earnings for men in the 1960s cohort improved over the next two decades, with the result that Asians had outdistanced whites by 1989, the adjustment yields a continued lag, suggesting that Asian immigrant men were not rewarded for education and experience at the same rate as native whites. By 1989, however, the women of this cohort had surpassed their white counterparts, both before and after any adjustment, evidence of gender differences in the opportunity structures.

Generalizing from older to newer cohorts can be hazardous, since the newer cohorts may not resemble their predecessors and in any case move into a labor market transformed by the increased immigrant presence. The data provide some suggestion of erosion; compared with subsequent cohorts at comparable periods of time, the 1960s cohort seems to have done somewhat better in the first decade of residence, though small numbers make any such conclusion tentative. Moreover, the 1980s cohort seems to be doing worse than the 1970s cohort at the end of the first decade of residence—as one might have expected, given the tremendous expansion in immigrant numbers and the immigrant convergence on a limited number of occupations and industries.

It must be noted that reality is more complex than the simplifying metaphors that shape the public discourse about the Asian American experience. The model minority concept is not without its virtues; historically, it helped turn around the negative stereotypes of Asian Americans and enhanced the positive image of Asian Americans, and empirically it is consistent with Asian Americans, advantageous position, relative to other minorities if not always to native whites. On the other hand, discrimination still inhibits Asian American progress. Many Asian Americans could be doing even better were it not for the persistent effects of discrimination. Diversity further complicates the picture; newcomers abound among today's Asian Angelenos, and these new arrivals are paying a sizable penalty as they struggle to get ahead. But, perhaps the most fatal criticism is that the various ethnic groups do not seem to be progressing at comparable rates, no matter how hard they try. The variation suggests that there is no single model minority but rather an aggregate of groups undergoing very different fates.

Trajectories of Adaptation

Diversity is the hallmark of Asian American Los Angeles. In this section, we seek to account for that diversity and to identify its most important axes. As most Asian Angelenos are immigrants, their origins and the circumstances of their departure from their home countries are likely to explain a large part of the variation in their current status. Asians, especially Asian immigrants, fall into five main categories: professionals, entrepreneurs, capitalists, workers, and refugees. Each type has followed a distinct path of adaptation, and each ethnic group tends toward one or more of these categories. Some groups are relatively successful, while others are not. The varying experiences in initial immigration largely determine the paths and outcomes of adaptation and incorporation; we therefore focus on how Asians have adapted to the social environment under different patterns of initial entry.

Professionals

The large presence of professional workers does much to account for Asians' relative success. Not only do professionals raise the average socioeconomic status of their particular ethnic group, but they play an important role in the success of their children and communities as a whole. In 1990, 25 percent of Asians between the ages of twenty-five and sixty-four in the Los Angeles region were professionals, compared with 24 percent of whites, 19 percent of blacks, and 8 percent of Hispanics. Note that the number of Asians with professional training is doubtless even greater, since those who cannot find professional employment in the United States are excluded from the professional category in the census. In particular, professionals were overrepresented among Asian Indians (33.7 percent), Japanese (27.9 percent), Chinese (27.4 percent), and Filipinos (27.5 percent). Although some Asian professionals were U.S.-born (mainly Japanese, and some Chinese and Filipinos), the majority (76.8 percent) immigrated from abroad, primarily from the Philippines, India, mainland China, Taiwan, and Korea.

Studies of the "brain drain" have demonstrated the causal connections between this phenomenon and the differences between sending and receiving countries in terms of living standards, research conditions, and professional employment opportunities. Recent studies further pinpoint the important role of international economic interdependency and articulation of higher education in determining the flows of immigrant professionals (Cheng and Yang 1998; Ong et al. 1992). In the context of the immigration of Asian professionals, several factors may be important. The economic involvement of the United States in Asian Pacific countries has created opportunities for Asian professional migration. Furthermore, American influence on the education systems and curricula of Asian countries, along with the exchange of students and scholars, has forged a pool of professionals who are employable in the United States. The so-called educational surplus—that is, the production of college graduates in excess of demand for them—also motivates the migration of higher-skilled persons. The Philippines, for example, produces far more college graduates than its labor market can absorb, and with skills not entirely relevant to the needs of an agricultural economy; the same phenomenon occurs in the Indian subcontinent. In both instances, the result is the exodus of professionals. Changes in U.S. immigration policy that favor the immigration of professional and technical workers and allow foreign students to adjust their resident status upon finding a permanent job in the United States have also facilitated the immigration of Asian professionals.

The factors affecting the flow of professionals may not always remain the same, however. Prior to the 1980s, low income and living standards prompted most foreign students from Asia to remain in the United States permanently after the completion of their education. In recent years, economic and political conditions in Taiwan and Korea have greatly improved, leading Taiwanese and Korean graduates of U.S. universities to return to their homelands in increasing numbers.

We detect at least two patterns of adaptation among Asian immigrant professionals in the Los Angeles region. In one pattern, immigrants begin in lower-level slots somehow connected to their original specialization and gradually move up the occupational ladder and back into the profession for which they trained earlier. This tortured road to success reflects immigrant selectivity, since immigrant professionals come from the upper, not the lower, ranks of their peers back home. They immigrate to the United States not to escape unemployment and poverty but to improve their careers and well-being. In the first few years after their arrival, many experience downward occupational mobility, because they lack U.S. labor market experience and English-language competence. Scientists or researchers are relegated to jobs as lab technicians or assistants, university faculty become high school or elementary school teachers, and doctors work as nurses or assistants. Their salaries are not commensurate with their human capital. After a sufficient period of time, some

Asian professionals gain recognition and get established, while others achieve higher status through additional schooling and extraordinarily hard work.

A second pattern of integration involves a temporary or permanent shift out of the professions. Some professionals move to a new occupation because it is more profitable or enjoyable, but others do so because they cannot find jobs in their field, in some cases finding themselves forced to do menial work. For example, a volleyball coach at the provincial level in China became a cleanup man at the UCLA hospital, a senior doctor was a babysitter, an engineer watched the gate at a swap meet, and a university teacher became a waiter. In time, such downwardly mobile professionals move up, but many never return to their original occupations or positions.

Whether they move right into professions on arrival in the United States or do so after a detour into more menial jobs, Asian professionals follow the typical immigrant path of moving into ethnic concentrations or clusters. Asian niches abound throughout the region's various professional and semiprofessional occupations, with Asians often constituting a very significant proportion of the entire workforce. In their range and type, the Asian professional clusters are no different in terms of immigrant density from the traditional immigrant pursuits, but they are distinctive in the types of work and remuneration they involve. Thus, Asians make up more than one-third of the region's pharmacists and chemists, more than one-quarter of the dentists, and more than one-fifth of the physicians, accountants, computer programmers, electrical engineers, and civil engineers, to cite a few notable examples. Of course, not every Asian group moves into professional niches such as these. Filipinos are much more likely to concentrate in the health care sector and its semiprofessions; 16 percent of the region's nurses are of Filipino origin, as are 18 percent of its lab technicians. Those groups with origins in refugee flows are less likely to move into high-level clusters. Still, Vietnamese immigrants are considerably overrepresented among the ranks of computer programmers and electrical engineers, perhaps a sign of better things to come.

Movement into the professions brings its rewards. In 1989, the average Asian immigrant physician made over $100,000, the average dentist $58,000, and the average electrical engineer $43,000. Some occupations, like dentistry or medicine, allow for self-employment, but most professionals find themselves working as cogs in vast bureaucratic organizations, where they soon encounter the glass ceiling that prevents them from moving to the top rung of the job ladder, especially into management positions. As time passes, these immigrant professionals discover that America seemed to want them for their skills and work ethic as employees but not for their assertiveness and ambition as bosses. The land of opportunity is far more limited than they had expected, and, contrary to what they have been taught, meritocracy is not color blind. Many seek to compensate for their race by outperforming their peers. Working longer hours and carrying out jobs beyond the call of duty, they ironically provide support for the "model minority" stereotype and harden the glass ceiling. In so doing, they alienate their native-born sisters and brothers and drive a wedge between Asians and other minorities.

The problem of the glass ceiling is commonly perceived by Asian professionals.

Asian Americans for Community Involvement (AACI) surveyed more than 300 white-collar Asian American professionals in Silicon Valley and found that 80 percent believed Asian Americans to be underrepresented in upper management and that concerns about the glass ceiling increased with age and experience. The respondents felt that Equal Employment Opportunity (EEO) programs had very little effect at this level; among those whose employers had EEO programs in place, about two-thirds stated that Asian Americans were underrepresented in middle and upper management. Many respondents felt that their employers perceived them as "modern-day, high-tech coolies"—hardworking, diligent employees but not potential managers. The AACI report concluded, "Regrettably, Asian Americans are still a long way off from adequate management representation in corporate boardrooms and executive suites, in educational institutions, and in government agencies" (Asian Pacific American Coalition U.S.A. 1993). The analysis of census data discussed in the previous section provides considerable support for this point of view. Asian Americans still have a long way to go before they reach full socioeconomic, legal, and political equality in this country.

Entrepreneurs

Entrepreneurship, usually measured by self-employment, has been described as a characteristic avenue of adaptation and social mobility of Asian Americans. In the Los Angeles region, Asian immigrants are much more likely to be entrepreneurs than are their native-born counterparts; for most Asian immigrant groups, the trend in self-employment lies on an upward curve. Not all Asian groups are equally interested in running their own businesses, however. Small business tends not to engage Filipinos, in particular. By contrast, the Koreans' propensity for entrepreneurship is now well known (Light and Bonacich 1988; Min 1996). Almost a quarter of Korean immigrants were working for themselves in 1980, and more than a third in 1990, testifying to the ability of Koreans to expand their economic base through self-employment.

The firms run by Korean immigrant entrepreneurs in Los Angeles tend to be small, to use family members or a fewer employees, and to be concentrated in retail trade, manufacturing, and services (Light and Bonacich 1988; Min 1996). Like professionals, the self-employed establish niches. The liquor trade is prototypical, a site of extraordinary Korean overrepresentation (by a factor of twenty-three) and for that reason a particularly poignant point in the Koreans' troubled relationship with the blacks. All the leading Korean industrial niches provide extraordinary opportunities for self-employment, from the low point in apparel, where 22 percent of Koreans work for themselves, to the high point in laundering, where 74 percent of Koreans work on their own account. As these business lines suggest, self-employment is not easy work, and Korean immigrant business owners work long hours indeed. But Koreans earn a significant self-employment bonus; those who work for themselves do much better than their compatriots employed in wage and salary jobs, even after controlling for differences in human capital and hours spent on the job.

The Chinese, especially immigrants, also had relatively higher rates of self-employment than other groups in all three census years. Chinese-owned businesses are concentrated in Chinatown, Monterey Park, and the San Gabriel Valley, though Chinese restaurants are found throughout Los Angeles. Chinese firms vary in size, from husband-wife stores to businesses employing more than 100 workers. In addition to serving their local communities, Chinese immigrant entrepreneurs also play an active role in linking the United States, their home countries, and other Pacific Rim countries through import-export trade, remittances, and foreign investment. Although the Chinese persist in some of the traditional ethnic trades such as restaurants, there are new business specializations—for example, engineering, computers, and data processing—that stand out from the type of businesses that Koreans pursue. Overall, self-employment is a lucrative pursuit, giving Chinese entrepreneurs a substantial earnings advantage over their counterparts still working for others.

Capitalists

Capitalists are entrepreneurs with sizable capital. We single them out for analysis because of their growing significance. In the past, Asians seldom immigrated to the United States as investors or capitalists, but, as a result of the rapid economic growth in Japan, South Korea, Taiwan, and Hong Kong in the past three decades and more recently in mainland China, along with the passage of the 1990 Immigration Act, a new category of Asian immigrants—capitalists or investors—has emerged. Among this group are Japanese, Koreans, and Taiwanese who want to make a fortune in the United States and Hong Kong Chinese who are fearful of the colony's return to Chinese rule in 1997.

The Immigration Act of 1990 authorized the granting of permanent residency to foreign nationals who make a minimum $1 million investment in a business employing at least ten workers in the United States. In rural or high-unemployment areas, the investment can be as little as $500,000. The act took effect on October 1, 1991. As of September 30, 1992, seventy-three millionaire immigrants had been admitted, among whom fifty-eight, or 80 percent, were Asians, with thirty from Taiwan (the leading country), six from Pakistan, five from India, five from Macao, three from Hong Kong, one from South Korea, and the rest from other Asian countries. While the number of Asian millionaire immigrants is expected to grow in the foreseeable future, many other wealthy Asians, not quite in the millionaire category, have invested and settled in the Los Angeles region. For instance, Monterey Park, the first suburban Chinatown in the United States, has attracted a significant number of wealthy Chinese immigrants. According to Li-Pei Wu, chairman of General Bank, it is not unusual for families—mainly those from Taiwan—to bring $200,000 or more to southern California for investment. Indeed, the 1990 census showed that the Chinese have already established a concentration in security investments—perhaps the first instance of an immigrant niche in finance capitalism.

The adaptation pattern of this category of Asian immigrants is little known, although we may expect it to differ greatly from those of other immigrants. These immigrants are rich, resourceful, and self employed, but they may still lack knowledge of U.S. laws, market experience, and English ability and therefore may run the risk of losing money, going bankrupt, or becoming involved in legal troubles. An incident reported by the Los *Angeles Times* serves as an example.[4]

Taung Ming-Lin abandoned a lucrative career in Taiwan as an importer of U.S.-made products and immigrated with his family to this country in 1990. In addition to investing over $1 million in the United States, he paid $310,000 for 723 acres of land outside Bakersfield, California, on which to grow bamboo. Unfortunately, Taung did not know that the land held little agricultural promise, requiring years of irrigation to turn scrubland to farmland; nor did he realize that he had bought property in an area set aside for kangaroo rats and two other animals protected under the Endangered Species Act. Recently, his bookbinding shop in South El Monte was raided by the INS for allegedly employing undocumented workers from Mexico.

Workers

Workers are defined as persons employed in manual and low-paying jobs, that is, those positions that we earlier classified as low-skill occupations (LSOs). In absolute numbers, the Asian working class is not inconsiderable, but, contrary to common perception, currently most Asian Americans in the Los Angeles region are not proletarians. In 1990, for example, 41 percent of employed Asians worked in managerial, professional, and technical jobs, and another 39 percent worked in clerical, sales, and craft positions; only 20 percent were engaged in lower-level jobs. Since immigrants predominate among Asians, the class structure of the immigrant population does not differ much from that of the general Asian population. As Table 20.3 shows, in 1990 only about 22 percent of Asian immigrants belonged to the worker category, and the percentage of native-born Asian workers was even smaller (14 percent).

Asian workers adapt to the receptive environment via at least two avenues. The majority of Asian workers strive for survival in the secondary labor market, which is characterized by low pay, poor working conditions, high turnover rate, and lack of opportunities for promotion. Most of them do operative and service jobs; for instance, new Asian immigrants, many of them women, have been an important source of the cheap labor that has supported and revived the Los Angeles garment industry. Significant proportions of Chinese and Korean workers, however, work in ethnic enclaves such as Chinatown and Koreatown, where some expect a better chance of upward mobility than in the secondary labor market, although others may suffer exploitation by their coethnic employers.

Refugees

Among Asian immigrants, the Vietnamese, Laotians, and Cambodians are the least successful, because of their refugee experiences. The Vietnamese refugees began pouring into the Los Angeles area in 1975, when U.S. involvement in the Vietnam War ended abruptly. Since then, more than 600,000 have settled in the United States, with the heaviest concentration in the Los Angeles region, especially Orange County.

The 1978 Indochinese Refugee Act permitted them to become permanent residents. There have been two major waves of Vietnamese immigration to Los Angeles. The first wave, from 1975 to 1980, was made up of South Vietnam's elites, who were evacuated with the U.S. troops and citizens immediately following the collapse of Saigon. Over 166,000 Vietnamese entered the United States as refugees in this period. A later wave consisted of the "boat people" and others who escaped from concentration camps or economic hardship in search of survival and advancement.

The varying backgrounds of the Vietnamese have determined the heterogeneity of the Vietnamese community and the diverse paths of Vietnamese adaptation in the Los Angeles region. In 1990, for instance, about 49 percent of the Vietnamese in the region had some college or higher education, while about 36 percent had not finished high school, including 7 percent with no formal schooling. Significant proportions were found both in well-paid professional occupations (25 percent) and managerial careers (7 percent) and in low-paid menial or service work (31 percent). Entrepreneurship is also an option for some Vietnamese. In 1990, 11 percent of the Vietnamese were self-employed. The chief Vietnamese occupational niches—as assemblers, hairdressers, electrical technicians, and machinists—reflect the group's overall economic status: not at the very bottom, perhaps, but still several removes from the middle class.

High rates of unemployment are a final distinguishing factor. In 1990, the unemployment rate of Vietnamese was about 7 percent, much higher than the rates for Japanese (1.7 percent), Koreans (2.4 percent), Chinese (3.3 percent), and Filipinos (3.6 percent), and even slightly higher than the rates for Hispanics (5.8 percent) and blacks (5.9 percent). Such high levels of joblessness appear to be linked to the welfare provision of the 1980 Refugee Act, which made it possible for certain unemployed Vietnamese refugees to survive for relatively long periods of time without work. Vietnamese refugees who have little schooling and work skills are most likely to stay unemployed. In short, the Vietnamese are a bifurcated community, and their adaptation patterns are even more diverse than those of other immigrant groups.

Conclusion

Asian Americans in Los Angeles are an increasingly diverse population, differing in ethnic composition, nativity, socioeconomic status, and patterns of adaptation and incorporation. Whether one focuses on demography, culture, or class, treating Asian Americans as a group is likely to conceal more than it reveals.

The term "Asian American" was coined by second- and third-generation Americans of Asian descent during the civil rights era for political reasons and was accepted by the larger population for convenience. Throughout the 1960s and 1970s, Americans—Asians and others—deemphasized the separate identities of Asian groups and together, albeit with different motives, helped solidify an Asian American identity. Since the 1970s, however, the massive new immigration of Asians from diverse backgrounds has challenged the validity of this inclusive concept, and separate ethnic identities have gradually assumed more importance. Recognizing the growing diversity of the population, Asian Americans simultaneously began a process of "deconstruction" and "reconstruction." On the one hand, differences between Asian groups were emphasized and their needs distinguished. The individual group identities under construction today are, however, quite different from those in the past. They are more transnational than national. The Chinese, the Vietnamese, and many other Asian groups tend to see themselves not just as Chinese or Vietnamese Americans but as Chinese or Vietnamese transnationals who are not rooted in any specific country. Many immigrant families assume multiple national identities to take full advantage of the global economy and culture. On the other hand, a new Asian American identity dubbed "pan-Asian ethnicity" came into being and recently has gained more momentum. This new inclusive national identity, like its old counterpart, is more politically than culturally significant.

Using census data for the two decades, we have tried to unravel the demographic and socioeconomic basis for this identity transformation as it unfolded in Los Angeles. In addition to examining the internal dynamics of the Asian American population, we challenged the commonly held model minority concept of the group and analyzed some key relations between Asian Americans and other populations in the area. In a restricted sense, the model minority image is not farfetched for Asian Americans, if we must lump them together; taken together, they fare much better than other minorities, such as blacks and Hispanics, in terms of the major socioeconomic indicators of education, occupation, and income. The model minority image has been exaggerated and inflated, however; contrary to media reports that Asian Americans have even outperformed whites, we found that in personal income, Asians still lag behind, generally receiving lower earnings returns on their human capital than U.S.-born whites. More important, there are considerable differences across Asian American groups in almost every aspect of life. As groups, Japanese and Chinese fare relatively well, but Vietnamese and other Southeast Asians arc struggling for survival. Although the majority of Asians in the Los Angeles region are not poverty stricken, neither have they fully succeeded. Furthermore, even within each Asian group individual diversity is substantial. Given these great diversities, it is dangerous to lump Asians together for statistical convenience and to treat them as a monolithic whole in terms of socioeconomic policies. Disregarding the differences among Asian communities will lead to serious neglect of the needs of various segments of the Asian American population.

Massive immigration after 1965 has been the leading force of Asian diversification in the Los Angeles region. The largely different origins and experiences of Asian immigrants have led to diverse paths and outcomes of adaptation and incorporation. For instance, immigrant professionals from India, the Philippines, China, and Taiwan, like their counterparts from other countries, achieve some measure of success after first experiencing downward mobility and then slowly climbing up the occupational ladder; the difference seems to be how far these Asian professionals can go before they reach the glass ceiling. Immigrant entrepreneurs, exemplified by the Koreans and Chinese, manage to survive and, with time, prosper by running usually small, family-oriented businesses that serve either outsiders or their co-ethnics while bridging the United States and their native countries in trade. Increasingly, Asian immigrant capitalists come to settle in America, bringing significant investments. There is also the bifurcated refugee population from Vietnam, whose paths of adaptation are just as diverse as those of other immigrants.

Asian American groups, with their small numbers and their continuing disadvantageous position in American society, recognize the need for pan-Asian unity. Yet historical enmity, diverse group status and interests, and a lack of intergroup interaction make unity difficult. Should Asian immigration decline, the barriers to intra-Asian solidarity will gradually diminish. Whether immigrant numbers expand, decline, or remain stable, the ranks of the second generation will inevitably expand, and solidarity is likely to grow when this new generation of U.S.-born Asian Americans comes into its own. In the end, however, the emergence of a new pan-Asian ethnicity remains uncertain; its prospects hinge on the larger political and economic environment and, perhaps more important, on Asian Americans themselves and their conscious efforts at reconstruction.

NOTES

This chapter is an abridged version of "Asians: The 'Model Minority' Deconstructed," chapter 11 in Roger Waldinger and Mehdi Bozorgmehr (eds.), *Ethnic Los Angeles* (New York: Russell Sage Foundation, 1996).

1. Under IRCA, illegal immigrants who applied for amnesty were eligible for permanent resident status two years after the approval of their amnesty application. Since the INS fiscal year 1989, more than 3 million illegal immigrants (mainly from Mexico and other Latin American countries) have been granted permanent residency, leading to the relative decline of Asians' share of total immigration after 1989. However, the absolute number of Asian immigrants steadily increased from 236,097 in 1980 to 338,581 in 1990.

2. William Petersen, "Success Story, Japanese-American Style," *New York Times Magazine*, January 9, 1966, pp. 20–21, 33, 36, 38, 40–41, 43; William Petersen, "Success Story of One Minority in the U.S.," *U.S. News and World Report*, December 26, 1966, pp. 73–78.

3. See, for example, "Asian Americans: A Model Minority," *Newsweek*, December 6, 1982, pp. 39, 41–42, 51; David Bell, "The Triumph of Asian Americans," *New Republic*, July 1985, pp. 24–31.

4. Mark Arax, "INS Raids Firm of Farmer in Kangaroo Rat Case," *Los Angeles Times*, November 3, 1994.

REFERENCES

Asian Pacific American Coalition U.S.A. 1993. Glass Ceiling Report Published. *Alert* 13 (September/October): 2–4.

Barringer, Herbert, Robert W. Gardner, and Michael J. Levin. 1993. *Asians and Pacific Islanders in the United States*. New York: Russell Sage Foundation.

Barringer, Herbert, David T. Takeuchi, and Peter Xenos. 1990. Education, Occupational Prestige, and Income of Asian Americans. *Sociology of Education* 63: 27–43.

Cheng, Lucie, and Philip Q. Yang. 1998. Global Interaction, Global Inequality, and Professional Migration to the United States. *International Migration Review* 32(3): 626–653.

Espiritu, Yen. 1992. *Asian American Panethnicity*. Philadelphia: Temple University Press.

Hirschman, Charles, and Morrison G. Wong. 1986. The Extraordinary Educational Attainment of Asian Americans: A Search for Historical Evidence and Explanations. *Social Forces* 65: 1–27.

Kitano, Harry. 1988. *Japanese Americans: The Evolution of a Subculture*. Englewood Cliffs, NJ: Prentice-Hall.

Light, Ivan, and Edna Bonacich. 1988. *Immigrant Entrepreneurs*. Berkeley: University of California Press.

Liu, John, and Lucie Cheng. 1994. Pacific Rim Development and the Duality of Post-1965 Asia Immigration to the United States. Pp. 74–99 in Paul Ong, Edna Bonacich, and Lucie Cheng (eds.), *The New Asian Immigration in Los Angeles and Global Restructuring*. Philadelphia: Temple University Press.

Min, Pyong Gap. 1996. *Caught in the Middle: Korean Merchants in Multiethnic America*. Berkeley and Los Angeles: University of California Press.

Ong, Paul, Edna Bonacich, and Lucie Cheng. 1994. *The New Asian Immigration in Los Angeles and Global Restructuring*. Philadelphia: Temple University Press.

Ong, Paul, Lucie Cheng, and Leslie Evans. 1992. Migration of Highly Educated Asians and Global Dynamics. *Asian and Pacific Migration Journal* 1: 543–567.

Ong, Paul, and Suzanne J. Hee. 1994. Economic Diversity. Pp. 31–56 in Paul Ong (ed.), *Economic Diversity, Issues and Policies*. Los Angeles: LEAP Asian Pacific American Public Policy Institute and UCLA Asian American Studies Center.

Takaki, Ronald. 1987. *Strangers from a Different Shore: A History of Asian Americans*. Boston: Little, Brown.

Chapter Twenty-one

A Quota on Excellence?
The Asian American Admissions Debate

Don T. Nakanishi

Allegations of possible quotas or limitations in the admission and enrollment of Asian American applicants to some of the country's most selective public and private colleges are fueling one of the hottest educational policy controversies in recent years. From the White House to the California State House, from Berkeley to Cambridge, and from New York's Chinatown to Los Angeles's Koreatown, the so-called "Asian American admissions issue" has been the focus of extensive media scrutiny, unprecedented bipartisan political intervention, and prolonged protests by Asian American students, professors, and civil rights groups. And although some colleges have responded by formally apologizing to the Asian American community, by launching fact-finding studies, and by revising admissions procedures, it is highly likely that this issue will be with us for some time. The major competing social forces as well as perspectives of change and tradition that gave rise to this controversy still remain in an uneasy tug-of-war.

For over five years—beginning in 1983 at Brown and other private Ivy League colleges in the Northeast and shortly after at the Berkeley and Los Angeles campuses of the public, taxpayer-supported University of California system—this admissions controversy has placed Asian Americans on an unexpected collision course with their most prized vehicle for social mobility. Indeed, despite the growth and heterogeneity of the Asian American population during the past two decades—with respect to national origin, religion, social class, and generation—there is unmistakable unanimity in the belief that higher education is the sine qua non for individual and group survival and advancement in American society. Consequently, it is not surprising that the admissions debate has elicited powerful emotional responses from Asian American students and parents alike and has been an ongoing front-page news story in the Asian American ethnic press for several years. It also now occupies the top rung of the leadership agenda of Asian American civil rights and educational groups across the country.

However, probably not so obvious is why this admissions issue has escalated far beyond a simple tête-à-tête between Asian Americans and college administrators. Why, for example, have Presidents Reagan and Bush joined an unusually diverse group of liberals and conservatives from both political parties in Congress and in state legislatures—like Democratic U.S. Senators Paul Simon and Thomas Daschle, Republican U.S. Representatives Patricia Saiki and Dana Rohrabacher, and top Democratic California state legislators Tom Hayden, Willie Brown, David Roberti, and Art Torres—in embracing this admissions issue, denouncing "exclusionary racial quotas," and spearheading numerous hearings in Washington and across the country?

Why is the Office of Civil Rights of the Department of Education conducting full-scale Title VI anti-bias compliance investigations of potentially discriminatory admissions practices and policies toward Asian American applicants at UCLA and Harvard? And why is it highly likely that other colleges will be targeted in the future? Why has almost every major newspaper and magazine in the nation, many television news programs, as well as just about every syndicated columnist from left to right on the political spectrum—including Doonesbury—found this controversy to be so newsworthy and symptomatic of much of what is wrong with American education?

Above all, why does the Asian American admissions debate represent a serious challenge to a number of long-standing institutional goals and practices of American higher education, whether the goal is socially engineering a "diverse" or "balanced" undergraduate student body or seeking the meritocratic ideal of choosing the best of the brightest? And what, if anything, can be done to resolve this issue?

The answers to these questions, I believe, require an understanding of not only the specific points of contention regarding possible bias and unfairness in evaluating Asian American applicants but also the social and political context within which this controversy has emerged.

The Emergence of the Debate

The Asian American admissions debate probably could not have been foreseen. Until recently, the Asian American college-going population received little media, policy, or scholarly attention, because of their relatively small numbers nationally and their seemingly strong academic performance levels. In two of the more highly regarded comparative studies of minority students—Alexander Astin's *Minorities in Higher Education* (1982) and John Ogbu's *Minority Education and Caste* (1978)—Asian Americans were not included in the data collection and analysis because they were not considered to be "educationally disadvantaged" like other non-white minority groups. Indeed, there is much to suggest that the admissions debate might not have become so explosive if there had been a body of empirical knowledge that all parties to the dispute could have used to test or verify their largely unfounded assumptions and assertions about Asian American students. (One major point of contention has focused on the predictive value of admissions criteria—high school GPA, SAT verbal and math, and achievement tests—in explaining future college performance of Asian American and other groups of students. Contrary to conventional wisdom, a comparative study of University of California students found that the SAT math score was a better predictor of first-year grades than the SAT verbal for Asian Americans. For whites, the SAT verbal score remained the stronger predictor. Similarly, math achievement was a better predictor than English composition for Asian Americans, while the opposite was true for whites. The study served to challenge the common admissions practice of placing greater weight on verbal rather than math scores. See Stanley Sue and Jennifer Abe, "Predictors of Academic Achievement Among Asian American and White Students," *College Board Report*, No. 88–11, 1988.) Instead, much of this controversy has evolved in a virtual scholarly vacuum.

Beginning in the early 1980s, the national press became increasingly interested in the Asian American college-going population. They initially wrote stories touting the individual academic achievements of some of the most gifted Asian American students—such as the winners of the Westinghouse Talent Search—and what appeared to be their dramatic rise in enrollment at many of the country's most selective institutions. *U.S. News and World Report* wrote that "Asians are, in fact, flocking to top colleges. They make up about 10 percent of Harvard's freshman class and 20 percent of all students at the Juilliard School. In California, where Asians are 5.5 percent of the population, they total 23.5 percent of all Berkeley undergraduates." And *Newsweek* asked rhetorically: "Is it true what they say about Asian American students, or is it mythology? They say that Asian Americans are brilliant. They say that Asian Americans behave as a model minority, that they dominate mathematics, engineering, and science courses—that they are grinds who are so dedicated to getting ahead that they never have any fun."

Beginning in 1985, however, journalists and syndicated columnists began portraying Asian American undergraduates not only as "Whiz Kids," as *Time* magazine boldly proclaimed in a major cover story, but also as possible victims of racially discriminatory admissions practices. In a highly influential 1986 *Chronicle of Higher Education* article, Lawrence Biemiller wrote, "Charges that some elite colleges and universities may be purposefully limiting the admission of persons of Asian descent continue to worry students and parents. . . . The allegations come at a time when reports of racially motivated violence against Asians are increasing and talk of 'trade wars' with Asian countries continues, prompting concern about a possible resurgence of anti-Asian sentiment."

Historical analogies often were drawn to the situation facing American Jewish students before World War II when invidious, discriminatory policies and procedures officially were adopted to limit their access to many of the same selective institutions now concerning Asian/Pacific Americans. As *Los Angeles Times* reporter Linda Mathews wrote, "There may be a parallel between what is happening to Asian Americans now and what happened to Jews in the 1920s and 1930s at some Ivy League schools. . . . To keep a lid on the number of Jewish students—denounced as 'damned curve raisers' by less talented classmates—the universities imposed quotas, sometimes overt, sometimes covert. . . . Today's 'damned curve raisers' are Asian Americans, who are winning academic prizes and qualifying for prestigious universities in numbers out of proportion to their percentage of the population. And, like Jews before them, the members of the new model minority contend that they have begun to bump up against artificial barriers to their advancement."

Conservative and liberal commentators alike also joined the fray, linking the Asian American admissions issue to their ongoing ideological donneybrooks on a range of such unsettled policy topics as affirmative action programs, the nation's competitiveness with foreign economic powers, or recent educational reform measures. George F. Will, writing in April 1989, shortly after Berkeley Chancellor Ira Michael Heyman apologized to the Asian American community for his administration's past admissions policies that "indisputably had a disproportionate impact on Asian Americans," declared that liberalism was to blame for the admissions controversy. In echoing the highly controversial views expressed a few months earlier by former Assistant Attorney General William Bradford Reynolds, columnist Will argued that the discrimination that Asian American students encountered was due to affirmative action policies, one of the major cornerstones of the liberal social agenda. He wrote, "Affirmative action discriminated against Asian Americans by restricting the social rewards open to competition on the basis of merit. We may want a modified meritocracy, but it should not be modified by racism and the resentment of excellence. . . . At a time of high anxiety about declining educational standards and rising competition from abroad, and especially from the Pacific Rim, it is lunacy to punish Asian Americans— the nation's model minority—for their passion to excel."

Clarence Page was one of many liberal commentators, along with major Asian American community leaders, who denounced the conservatives' attack on affirmative action and their attempt to connect it with the situation facing Asian American students at Berkeley. As Page wrote, "Since this announcement offers ammunition in their relentless fight against affirmative action programs, some political conservatives applaud it. Conservatives often offer the success of Asian Americans as evidence that the American system is so fair to all that blacks and other minorities jolly well better look to themselves, not to the government or 'reverse discrimination,' for solutions to their problems. But the Berkeley problem was not reverse discrimination.' It was plain, old-fashioned discrimination of a sort affirmative action programs were intended to remedy, not create. The big difference this time is that it penalizes a people who have a reputation for overachievement."

During the past decade, the media's changing portrayal of Asian American college students may have appeared to reflect a zealous search for not only good but provocative news stories rather than focusing on policy. However, beyond the catchy headlines and one-line history lessons, a new and potentially far-reaching controversy about undergraduate admissions was gradually, and unexpectedly, unfolding. In many respects, the points of contention appeared quite familiar, and somehow *seemed* to be settled, especially in the aftermath of *Bakke*. Like other recent conflicts dealing with access and representation of women or historically underrepresented racial minorities in America's institutions of higher education, the Asian American admissions debate eventually focused on the potential bias and arbitrariness of selection criteria procedures and policies that might limit equal educational opportunities. Broad philosophical concepts (like meritocracy) and seemingly widely shared, long-standing institutional goals (like the deliberate social engineering of a "diverse" or "balanced" undergraduate student body) were again debated, and their procedural role in the admissions process was both questioned and justified.

And yet not anticipated was that this new admissions controversy would involve Asian Americans, a group that had not figured prominently in the earlier policy and legal disputes over admissions and a group that did not have a reputation for being particularly assertive, visible, or efficacious in the political or other decision-making arenas. However, during the 1980s, a new and different Asian American population emerged as a result of unprecedented demographic, economic, and political trends. Higher education officials, like others who were not population specialists, probably could not have foreseen the dramatic changes that were occurring among Asian Americans, nor could they have fully realized how these trends would seriously challenge their seemingly well-established institutional practices and policies.

Contrary to the media's interpretation, the extraordinary rise in Asian American enrollment in many of the country's most competitive institutions starting in the early 1980s probably had far less to do with Asian American students' suddenly becoming more academically motivated and qualified than it did with their phenomenal demographic growth. According to the 1980 U.S. Census, Asian Americans were America's fastest-growing group. Between 1970 and 1980, they increased nationally by 128 percent from 1.5 million to 3.5 million. Recent projections estimate that Asian Americans will again double in size to 7 million by 1990 because of the continued large influx of refugees and immigrants from East and Southeast Asia, along with the Pacific Islands.

By extension, Asian Americans also are the fastest-growing group in the American college-going population, and the large increases in enrollment that the media reported with such surprise and awe for the most competitive private colleges were simultaneously occurring at other, less selective institutions as well. In the fall of 1976, there were 150,000 Asian American undergraduates in American higher education nationwide. A decade later, in fall of 1986, there were almost three times as many—448,000 Asian Americans in colleges and universities across the country, with almost half enrolled in two-year institutions. All demographic projections of the Asian American college-age sector indicate that this exceptionally fast growth pattern will continue well into the next century.

Coinciding with this demographic upsurge during the '80s was the Asian American population's growing political maturity and influence at both the national and local levels. Perhaps at no other period in the over 150-year history of Asians in the United States have so many individuals and organizations participated in such a wide array of political and civil rights activities, not only in relation to the American political system but also to the affairs of their ancestral homelands in Asia. In traditional electoral politics, what had come to be taken as a common occurrence in Hawaii—namely the election of Asian Americans to public office—suddenly became a less than surprising novelty in the so-called mainland states with the election and appointment of Asian Americans to federal, state, and local positions in California, Washington, New York, and elsewhere. And, perhaps most significantly, the Asian American population came to demonstrate that it, too, had resources and talents—organizational, financial, or otherwise—to advance its specific concerns in a variety of political arenas and to confront political issues that potentially are damaging to its group interests. Two widely reported grassroots campaigns illustrate this new collective determination: the successful drive by Japanese Americans to gain redress and reparations for their World War II incarceration and the effective national movement to appeal and overturn the light sentences given to two unemployed Detroit auto workers who, in 1982, used a baseball bat to kill Chinese American Vincent Chin. (The two men mistook Chin for a Japanese and, therefore, someone who was viewed as having taken away their jobs).

The Asian American population's enhanced political participation during the '80s had several idiosyncratic features, with peculiar consequences for the Asian American admissions controversy. For example, other ethnic groups register and vote in overwhelming proportions for one or the other of the two major political parties—for example, blacks and American Jews for the Democratic party—which makes them largely beholden to the electoral success of that one party. Asian Americans, however, began during the '80s to exhibit a very different pattern of political affiliations at both the mass and elite levels. In numerous studies I conducted for the UCLA Asian/Pacific American Voter Registration Project, Asian Americans were almost evenly divided between Democrats and Republicans in their registration and voting behavior. Both political parties, especially the Republicans, have attempted to register the hundreds of thousands of recent Asian immigrants and refugees who annually become naturalized citizens—most notably in key electoral states like California. At the same time, Asian Americans have been cultivating a strong reputation as major financial contributors to Republican and Democratic candidates alike. Their estimated $10 million in contributions to the 1988 presidential election were divided almost equally between George Bush and Michael Dukakis. This 1980s pattern of supporting both parties at the voting and campaign fund-raising levels will likely continue. In turn, Democratic and Republican leaders, attempting to appeal to their growing and valued Asian American constituents, are addressing issues of special concern to them.

This unusual pattern of bipartisan affiliations among Asian Americans might well explain why the Asian American admissions issue is gaining the support of top leaders from both political parties. In California, for example, the state legislature's foremost liberal Democratic leaders—like Tom Hayden, Art Torres, David Roberti, and Willie Brown—have actively monitored the admissions controversy at the public University of California campuses for close to five years. They held numerous fact-finding hearings, intervened by bringing together university officials and Asian American community leaders, passed special resolutions on admissions, and had the state Auditor General undertake an unprecedented audit of admissions procedures at Berkeley. When addressing local Asian American communities, these politicians—along with other key municipal leaders like Mayor Tom Bradley of Los Angeles—have frequently spoken out against potentially discriminatory admissions practices. At the national level, in Washington, where politics often do make for very strange bedfellows, the issue has been championed by liberals like Senator Paul Simon and conservatives like Congressman Dana Rohrabacher. Simon and Rohrabacher, on separate occasions, both expressed a keen interest in the current Title VI compliance investigations by the Office of Civil Rights at UCLA and Harvard and indicated they may request that other institutions be formally reviewed in the future.

Rohrabacher, whose Southern California congressional district has a large number of Asian American voters, and Hawaiian representative Patricia Saiki, a Japanese American, introduced a bill in Congress last June dealing with bias against Asian American applicants. Hearings were held in cities across the nation. And although many Asian American liberals fear that conservative Republicans like Rohrabacher will attempt to use the Asian American issue to dismantle or discredit affirmative action programs and policies in higher education, it also is evident that Republican leaders are attempting to address one of the foremost concerns raised by their own constituents and the increasingly influential group of Asian American leaders in the Republican party.

For Asian Americans, then, the admissions controversy has gone beyond party or ideological differences, and has come to rest at the top of the leadership agenda for Asian Americans of all political persuasions. It is highly likely, therefore, that Republican and Democratic Asian American leaders, working together or independently, will continue pushing officials from both parties to resolve this issue.

The Asian American admissions controversy evolved out of the largely unexpected convergence of dramatic demographic and political changes among the Asian American population during the 1980s. Although higher education officials probably could not have anticipated these extraordinary social trends, it was their general reluctance and inability to fully and expeditiously address the complaints raised initially by Asian American students and professors on their own campuses that dramatically escalated this controversy.

Some commentators speculate that university administrators were fully convinced their customary policies and procedures were sound and fair and did not believe there were compelling reasons to change them. Writing in *The New Republic*, David Bell said, "The universities, however, consider their idea of the academic community to be liberal and sound. They are understandably hesitant to change it because of a demographic shift in the admissions pool."

Still others suggest that university administrators simply did not believe the admissions debate involving Asian Americans would get out of control or receive such prominent national media and political attention. These observers speculate that higher education officials were blinded by stereotypic images of Asian Americans as being politically passive and ineffectual, and did not anticipate how a new and more assertive Asian American population would use its many resources and alliances to confront a potentially discriminatory situation.

Whatever the case, the Asian American admissions controversy emerged and continues to be played out in this broader social context. Specific points of contention of the ongoing debate must be considered in terms of the interplay of these larger social forces and perspectives.

The Pros and Cons

All parties to the controversy—the critics as well as the admissions officers—agree that Asian American applicants to many of the nation's most selective undergraduate

Ivy League institutions, as well as Stanford and the flagship Berkeley and Los Angeles campuses of the UC system, now have lower rates of admission than other groups of applicants, including whites (see Tables 21.1 and 21.2 for Harvard and Berkeley).

Although disparities have existed and been acknowledged officially for several years, data for the fall 1985 entering class are illustrative. At Princeton, 17 percent of all applicants and 14 percent of the Asian American applicants were admitted. At Harvard, 15.9 percent of all applicants and 12.5 percent of the Asian Americans were accepted. And at Yale, 18 percent of all applicants and 16.7 percent of Asian Americans were admitted. Put another way, Asian American applicants to Princeton were admitted at a rate that was only 82.4 percent of that for other applicants; to Harvard at 78.6 percent; and to Yale at 92.6 percent. Likewise, a study undertaken by a Standard University Academic Senate committee found that, between 1982 and 1985, "Asian American applicants to Stanford had admission rates ranging between 66 percent and 70 percent of admission rates for whites."

Similarly, in perhaps the most exhaustive external investigation of the admissions controversy performed to date (at the time this article was being written, the Office of Civil Rights of the U.S. Department of Education had not completed its Title VI compliance investigations of potentially biased admissions practices toward Asian American applicants at Harvard and UCLA), the California State Auditor General, at the State Senate's request, conducted a full-scale audit of white and Asian/Pacific American freshman applicants to the UC-Berkeley campus. Academic records for applicants to Berkeley's seven different undergraduate colleges and programs from 1981 through 1987 were examined, producing a total of forty-nine different categories of comparison between Asian/Pacifics and whites. In thirty-seven of the forty-nine cases, whites had higher admission rates than Asian/Pacifics, even though Asian/Pacific applicants were found to have higher academic qualifications in practically all comparison groups.

Indeed, the academic qualifications of Asian American applicants have never been an issue, nor have they been used in rebuttal to explain lower admission rates. Every campus that launched its own ad hoc inquiry to examine and resolve this debate—Brown, Princeton, Harvard, Berkeley, and Stanford, among others—has found that Asian/Pacific applicants have stronger group-level academic profiles as measured by

TABLE 21.1
1978–87 Admission Rates at Harvard for Asian Americans and Whites

	1978	1979	1980	1981	1982	1983	1984	1985	1986	1987
Asian Americans	12%	15%	15%	14%	13%	14%	13%	12%	11%	12%
Whites	17%	16%	15%	16%	18%	19%	18%	17%	18%	16%

SOURCE: Harvard University, Office of Admissions.

TABLE 21.2
1981–87 Admission Rates at U.C. Berkeley for Asian Americans and Whites

	1981	1982	1983	1984	1985	1986	1987
Asian Americans	50.4%	60.3%	66.8%	45.0%	44.4%	28.4%	27.7%
Whites	54.3%	64.5%	70.5%	56.4%	52.3%	32.7%	31.4%

SOURCE: University of California, Berkeley, Chancellor's Report

high school grades and standardized tests and that those who are ultimately admitted usually have far stronger academic qualifications than other groups of admits.

Bunzel and Au wrote in *Public Interest* that, of the students who were admitted to Harvard in 1982, "Asian Americans had average verbal and math scores of 742 and 725, respectively, for an average combined score of 1467, while the scores for Caucasians were 666 and 689, for a total of 1355, or 112 points lower." An official letter sent by Harvard's admissions office to its alumni recruiters nationwide challenged these figures while acknowledging that Asian/Pacific admits usually had higher test scores than whites: "The actual difference for the year cited in the article was 50 points, and the typical difference in a given year is 40 points for the verbal and mathematics SATs combined."

The findings by these individual campuses are consistent with other formal studies. The California Postsecondary Education Commission's periodic investigations of eligibility rates for the UC system consistently show that Asian/Pacific Americans have the largest proportion of "academically eligible" students of any group and, thus, should have the highest admission rate if grades and test scores were the *only* selection criteria. In the most recent study, based on the state's 1986 high school graduating class, 32.8 percent of the Asian American graduates were found to be eligible for the University of California, in contrast to 15.8 percent for whites, 5 percent for Latinos, and 4.5 percent for blacks. Similar patterns of university eligibility by ethnic group have been found in previous years.

Several major explanations have been offered to account for these disparities in admission rates. Critics contend that admissions officers at both highly selective public and private institutions are engaging in intentionally discriminatory practices to limit the representation of Asian/Pacific students—who tend to be the fastest-growing group of applicants at these campuses. For example, over 20 percent of the fall 1987 entering class at Berkeley was Asian American. Given that Asian Americans make up approximately 2 percent of the nation's population and 6 percent of California's population, at first glance this figure might provide credence to the claim that Asian Americans were "over-represented." However, what is not apparent is that Asian/Pacific Americans now represent an increasingly sizeable proportion of the total applicant pools at these colleges. Of the 16,318 applicants who competed for regular admissions slots at Berkeley for the fall 1987 class, 5,032—or 30.8 percent—were Asian Americans.

Critics also contend that public institutions like the UC campuses have secretly, without adequate public and legislative discussion, deviated from their long-standing academic, merit-based admissions policies by giving weight to a variety of subjective criteria in the selection process. They also argue that Asian/Pacific American faculty and administrators at the institutions are systematically excluded from participating in decision-making committees and activities dealing with undergraduate selection policies and procedures.

Admissions officers, on the other hand, deny that quotas, informal or formal, exist for Asian/Pacific Americans or any other group, especially in the post-*Bakke* era. They contend that admission rates are simplistic indicators of discrimination and do not fully describe the highly professional, multilevel process of admissions review that all applicants receive. They further argue that privacy laws, like the so-called Buckley Amendment of 1974, prevent access to all the relevant materials that are reviewed in an applicant's file, especially personal essays and letters of recommendation that can play a far more decisive role in highly competitive admissions situations than is generally recognized.

Finally, admissions officers at private institutions, and increasingly at public colleges as well, have argued that their admissions policies are not entirely meritocratic but encompass other significant institutional goals and traditions. A common explanation offered to account for lower admission rates among Asian/Pacific American applicants is that they are less likely to be proportionately represented among a range of criteria that underlie a broad and flexible interpretation of the goal of seeking undergraduate diversity. Ironically, current officials at many of the nation's most prestigious research universities, like their predecessors who dealt with the upsurge in American Jewish applicants, have found themselves defending their institutional need to enroll good football players and the siblings of loyal and wealthy alumni rather than a meritocratic ideal of choosing the best of the brightest.

Geographic diversity, for example, is a well-established and widely accepted goal of private elite institutions, which is explicitly routinized in the admissions process. Recruiting in certain cities and states, specific admissions officers not only identify but are advocates for, the top students in admissions committee deliberations, which systematically reflect geographic considerations rather than a random review of the entire applicant pool. As a result, only a few of the many applicants from any particular geographic area can be admitted. Thus, the various talents and characteristics of student diversity, or other institutional priorities, must be encompassed within this formal geographic quota.

Admissions officers argue that Asian Americans are at a disadvantage because the vast majority of their applicants are from New York, California, or the western states, and, as a result, their representation in the entering class is a function of the size and strength of their local applicant pools. Ironically, this goal of geographic diversity was first instituted by many of these same undergraduate institutions to limit indirectly the enrollment of American Jews before World War II, who were concentrated mainly in New York and other parts of the Northeast.

However, the geographic skewing of the Asian Americans and American Jewish applicant pools may not be unique. Indeed, New York probably provides more applicants and matriculants overall to the Ivy colleges than any other state. California, the site of intensive recruiting campaigns by institutions from across the nation, usually ranks second or third in its overall representation of these student bodies. For example, during the 1985–86 academic year, there were 1,094 students from New York, 747 from Yale's home state of Connecticut, and 455 Californians among Yale's total undergraduate enrollment of 5,190. Together, these three three top feeder states accounted for 44.2 percent of Yale's undergraduate student body. Similarly, Harvard's entering class of 1985 had 290 students from New York, 279 from its home state of Massachusetts, and 168 from California. Although all fifty states were represented among the 1,525 domestic freshman students, Harvard's top three feeder states of

New York, Massachusetts, and California accounted for 48.3 percent of its entering class.

Admissions officers at the nation's selective institutions, public and private, also argue that Asian American applicants show a disproportionate interest in specific future college programs, especially premed studies, engineering, and the natural and physical sciences. For example, an official faculty and student committee investigating Asian American admissions at Princeton in 1985 argued that "Asian American applicants have not been strongly represented in those subgroups tending to have higher than average rates of admission (e.g., alumni children, athletes); on the other hand, Asian Americans are strongly represented in the one applicant group with a somewhat lower rate of admission (engineering school candidates)." Similarly, L. Fred Jewitt, former dean of admissions at Harvard, made an analogous assessment: "A terribly high proportion of Asian students are heading toward the sciences. In the interests of diversity, then, more of them must be left out."

Admissions to these majors, of course, tends to be extremely competitive because of the oversupply of highly qualified applicants and the formal and informal restrictions placed on the number of potential admits by specific departments. Thus, university administrators argue that the lower admission rate for Asian American applicants is due to their over-concentration in particular majors of choice that are designated when filing applications. Put another way, they believe that if Asian Americans were less homogeneous and were equally distributed among a range of majors, then there would be no disparities in admission rates.

A comparative analysis of data on the characteristics of California SAT test-takers in 1977 and 1985 tends to support the notion of "lack of diversity of major." Approximately 70 percent of the state's Asian/Pacific American males and over 50 percent of the females who took the test in 1985 indicated at the time that they intended to major in engineering, the sciences, or mathematics. For the males, interest in majoring specifically in engineering or computer science jumped from 26.1 percent to 46.1 percent from 1977 to 1985, while for females there was an increase from 5.3 percent to 15.8 percent. Interest in being a premed major declined slightly for Asian American males from 8.6 percent to 7.8 percent, and rose slightly for females from 6.2 percent to 8.6 percent (Table 21.3).

However, admissions data from UC's Los Angeles and Berkeley campuses, as well

TABLE 21.3
Changes in Intended Undergraduate Majors for Asian/Pacific American Students*

Intended Major	Males		Females	
	1977 N=3,699	1985 N=6,730	1977 N=3,738	1985 N=7,008
All sciences and engineering combined**	2,325 (62.9%)	4,672 (69.4%)	1,876 (50.2%)	3,590 (51.2%)
Engineering and computer science only	966 (26.1%)	3,104 (46.1%)	200 (5.3%)	1,106 (15.8%)

*Based on SAT data tapes for California test-takers, 1977 and 1985.
**Includes all test-takers who indicated a preference for majoring in the biological sciences, computer science, engineering, health and medicine, mathematics, physical sciences, and psychology.
SOURCE: UCLA Project on Asian/Pacific Americans in Higher Education.

as Stanford, empirically support the more important hypothesis that there are disparities in admit rates across fields. As Table 21.4 illustrates, Asian American applicants to UCLA from 1983–85 had lower overall admission rates than other applicants,
including white applicants, that cannot be explained by analyzing separate admissions
statistics for the institution's three undergraduate colleges. Aside from the College of
Fine Arts, which accounts for a small proportion of applicants and admits for all
groups, Asian Americans consistently had lower rates than whites and other applicants in engineering, as well as letters and science at UCLA. Similarly, as noted
earlier, the situation at the Berkeley campus for applicants to the seven different
undergraduate colleges and programs from 1981–87 demonstrated comparable differences in admission rates for Asian and white applicants in engineering, the sciences,
and the liberal arts. A Stanford University Academic Senate report found that for
every category of intended majors, Asian Americans had a lower admission rate than
whites.

Finally, another common argument for explaining away admission rate disparities
is that Asian Americans are less likely than whites to be among specific categories of
applicants who receive, by tradition or official decree, special consideration in the
admission process—alumni children and athletes. Applicants from these "special"
groups usually are admitted at twice or more the rate of other applicants and tend
to be largely white at Ivy League and other private elite institutions. For example, the
overall admission rate for Brown's entering class in fall of 1987 was an extremely
competitive 18.5 percent for all who applied. The admission rates, on the other hand,
for alumni legacies and athletes, were 46.1 percent and 56 percent, respectively. The
rationale for giving such added preference to special groups of applicants is usually
embedded in long-standing institutional policies and practices.

Admissions officers argue that differences in admit rates would not be apparent if

TABLE 21.4
1982–85 Applicants and Admits to the UCLA School of Engineering, College of Letters and Science,
and College of Fine Arts

	1983			1984			1985		
	Applicants	Admits	Admit rate	Applicants	Admits	Admit rate	Applicants	Admits	Admit rate
School of Engineering									
All Applicants	655	368	56.2%	1,665	596	35.8%	1,780	712	40.0%
Asian Americans	174	94	54.0%	617	145	23.5%	719	241	33.5%
Whites	350	161	46.0%	807	281	34.8%	860	319	37.0%
College of Letters and Science									
All Applicants	7,184	4,826	67.2%	8,271	4,787	57.9%	8,426	4,620	54.8%
Asian Americans	1,296	804	62.0%	1,356	647	47.7%	1,325	595	44.9%
Whites	3,903	2,480	63.5%	4,479	2,362	52.7%	4,496	2,137	47.5%
Colleges of Fine Arts									
All Applicants	514	231	45.0%	614	319	51.9%	680	299	44.0%
Asian Americans	63	25	40.0%	72	42	58.3	97	46	47.4%
Whites	374	165	44.1%	437	220	50.3%	478	211	44.1%
Combined Total									
All Applicants	8,852	5,508	63.2%	10,550	5,782	53.9%	10,889	5,631	51.7%
Asian Americans	1,533	923	60.2%	2,047	834	40.7%	2,141	882	41.2%
Whites	4,627	2,806	60.6%	5,727	2,863	50.0%	5,834	2,667	45.7%

SOURCE: UCLA Planning Office

Asian Americans were proportionately represented among applicants with alumni and athletic preferences. They also believe that such disparities will vanish in the future as those who are currently enrolled become alumni and urge their own siblings to apply to their alma maters. For example, as Harvard's admissions office wrote, "Today, relatively few Asian Americans are the children of alumni/ae, although the recent dramatic increases in the percentages of Asian Americans in the college will obviously change this significantly in the coming years."

Since the Asian American admissions issue evolved out of an extraordinary historical convergence of social, political, and demographic changes among the Asian American population—a pattern projected to continue for many more years— positive steps must be taken to resolve the major points of the dispute. If they are not resolved, it is highly likely we will witness further intervention by legislative bodies and governmental compliance agencies; more protests by Asian American students, professors, and civil rights leaders; and continued attention by the news media. There might also be an individual or class-action lawsuit. (In the January 1989 issue of the *Yale Law Journal*, attorney Grace Tsuang provided the necessary legal foundation for a possible future lawsuit, which might be filed by an Asian American who is denied admission to either a public or private college because of an upper-limit quota on Asian Americans.)

The Asian American admissions controversy represents only the most recent dispute focusing on issues of equal and fair access and representation in higher education. If the Asian American applicant pool continues to increase in the future, two complex policy issues will become increasingly significant and controversial. First, how large a difference in admission rates between Asian Americans and other groups of applicants will be tolerated by university administrators before they take, or are compelled by others to take, corrective measures? As indicated earlier, the present disparities in admission rates are not closely guarded secrets but rather are openly and publicly acknowledged facts. Although several campuses have initiated fact-finding studies, most admissions officers have only speculated on the causes of what they perceive to be less than compelling differences. What would be compelling? If Asian American applicants to a college were 75 percent, 50 percent, or 25 percent as likely as other applicants to gain admission, would this constitute sufficient cause for university administrators to address the issue more rigorously? Would such disparities lead to further external intervention or perhaps legal challenges?

The second issue relates directly to the first, and it deals with the broader issue of how much of an Asian American presence will be accepted and tolerated by institutions of higher learning. University officials usually do not maintain an inflexible and predetermined score card on how much varied representation they seek from different groups. However, they do not seem to have given sufficient thought and attention to relating institutional goals of academic-based meritocracy and valued diversity to the Asian American representation on their campuses. Indeed, it seems that Asian American applicants are evaluated exclusively with the nonminority, regular admission pool and tend to be strong candidates. Their presence in the pool, and ultimately in the college, strengthens the academic profile of the university's entering class. However, because Asian American applicants are counted as minorities, university officials also can boast about the racial diversity of their entering class. There is something at least peculiar, and perhaps insidious, about this relationship that demands closer and more serious attention.

The continuation of an adversarial relationship is not in the best interests of any of the parties involved in the Asian American admissions debate. There is definitely more to be gained by seeking a mutually advantageous partnership between the new and growing Asian American population and institutions of higher education. Berkeley Professor L. Ling-Chi Wang, a major national spokesperson for fair and equal admissions practices toward Asian Americans, best summarized what should be done. "Universities, public or private, should allow full access to their admissions policies and data to avoid suspicion and abuse of power. Asian Americans are not asking for numerical increases in their enrollments, nor are they challenging the merit of existing affirmative action programs. Not unlike whites, they are asking only for fair and equal treatment and demanding equal participation in decision-making processes. In other words, Asian Americans want only equality and justice, no more and no less."

1. What are the origins of the model minority thesis? How does this model compare with previous mainstream depictions of Asian Americans? What, if anything, is significant about the evolution of these images over time? What, in your opinion (and Osajima's), has prompted these changes in the model minority thesis? Is it still utilized with the same political agenda in mind?

2. What are some of the causes underlying the debate on Asian American admissions quotas? When did admissions quotas become a contested issue within the Asian American community, and when did the issue become national in terms of scope and recognition? Nakanishi asserts that members from both conservative and liberal political groups joined in the debate by adding their own opinions and commentaries. How did conservatives interpret the Asian American admissions debate? Conversely, how did liberals interpret these events? What policy topics served as the springboard for discussion on this topic?

3. Members of the Asian American community have been divided on the issue of affirmative action programs. Some argue that these programs have been detrimental to Asian American university students, while others contend that the programs have been beneficial to all racial and ethnic minorities generally. In your opinion, how may affirmative action programs benefit racial and ethnic minorities, and how would they affect Asian Americans? To what extent has the dismantling of such programs at universities in California impacted admissions demographies?

SUGGESTED READINGS

Espiritu, Yen Le. 1992. *Asian American Panethnicity: Bridging Institutions and Identities.* Philadelphia: Temple University Press.

Hing, Bill Ong. 1997. *To Be an American: Cultural Pluralism and the Rhetoric of Assimilation.* New York: New York University Press.

Hirschman, Charles, and Morrison G. Wong. 1986. The Extraordinary Educational Attainment of Asian Americans. *Social Forces* 65: 1–27.

Hurh, Won Moo, and Kwang Chung Kim. 1984. The Success Image of Asian Americans. *Ethnic and Racial Studies* 12: 512–538.

Ima, Kenji. 1995. Testing the American Dream: Case Studies of At-Risk Southeast Asian Refugee Students in Secondary Schools. Pp. 191–208 in Rubén G. Rumbaut and Wayne A. Cornelius (eds.), *California's Immigrant Children: Theory, Research, and Implications for Educational Policy.* San Diego: Center for U.S.-Mexican Studies.

Lee, Stacey J. 1996. *Unraveling the "Model Minority" Stereotype: Listening to Asian American Youth.* New York: Teachers College, Columbia University.

Petersen, William. 1966. Success Story: Japanese-American Style. *New York Times Magazine.* January 9, 1966.

Sue, Stanley, and Sumie Okazaki. 1990. Asian American Educational Achievement: A Phenomenon in Search of an Explanation. *American Psychologist* 45: 913–920.

Takagi, Dana Y. 1990. From Discrimination to Affirmative Action: Facts in the Asian American Admissions Controversy. *Social Problems* 37: 578–592.

Trueba, H. T., L. R. L. Cheng, and K. Ima. 1993. *Myth or Reality: Adaptive Strategies of Asian Americans in California.* London: Falmer Press.

Tuan, Mia. 1999. *Forever Foreign or Honorary White? The Asian Ethnic Experience Today*. New Brunswick, NJ: Rutgers University Press.

Walker-Moffat, Wendy. 1995. *The Other Side of the Asian American Success Story*. San Francisco: Jossey-Bass.

Wolf, Diane L. 1997. Family Secrets: Transnational Struggles Among Children of Filipino Immigrants. *Sociological Perspectives* 40(3): 457–482.

Wollenberg, Charles M. 1995. "Yellow Peril" in Schools (I & II). Pp. 3–29 in Don T. Nakanishi and Tina Yamano Nishida (eds), *The Asian American Educational Experience: A Source Book for Teachers and Students*. New York: Routledge.

Wu, William. 1982. *The Yellow Peril: Chinese Americans in American Fiction 1850–1940*. Hamden, CT: Archon Books.

Zhou, Min, and Yoshinori Kamo. 1994. An Analysis of Earnings Patterns for Chinese, Japanese and Non-Hispanic Whites in the United States. *Sociological Quarterly* 35(4): 581–602.

FILMS

Ding, Loni (Producer/director). 1982. *On New Ground* (30-minute documentary).

Nakasako, Spencer (producer/director). 1984. *Talking History* (30-minute documentary).

Part IX

Confronting Adversity
Racism, Exclusion, and the Burden of Double Standards

The Murder of Navroze Mody
Race, Violence, and the Search for Order

Deborah N. Misir

Shortly after 2 A.M. on September 24, 1987, Dr. Kaushal Sharan was attacked from behind and beaten unconscious with baseball bats by a group of white men on a street in Jersey City. Sharan fell into a weeklong coma that left him with partial brain damage. Three nights later on September 27, Navroze Mody was taunted and beaten to death by eleven Hispanic youths after he left a cafe in Hoboken. These two incidents were the most serious among a rash of anti-Indian violence that gripped the Jersey City area during 1987–1988. Indian Americans were terrorized by random physical and verbal attacks and by a letter sent to a local newspaper *The Jersey Journal*, in which a group calling themselves the "Dotbusters" wrote that they would go to any lengths to get Indians to move out of Jersey City.

This essay will briefly examine and analyze how these events were represented within the discourse of (1) the Dotbusters and those who supported them in northern New Jersey, (2) local politicians and public officials, and (3) the Indians and their supporters who mobilized in response to the attacks. Content analysis of these discourses is a means of narrowly contextualizing the racial attacks. In doing so, I use the approach of some recent scholarship on race which views racist discourse as a model, continually appropriated and utilized to frame social and economic disorder in our society. It follows that individual *racisms* must be studied within their specific sociological and historical conjunctions.[1]

I will argue that the racial violence of the Dotbusters and others with anti-Indian sentiments were public exhibitions of social dominance and belonging. Whites, African-Americans, Hispanics, and other Asians participated in racial attacks on Indians as a form of demarcating the Other, the Alien. The invention and construction of an Other, in this case Indian Americans, not only strengthened everyone else's sense of group solidarity and commonality but also provided a convenient scapegoat on which to vent out frustrations.

The Jersey City Dotbusters' rhetoric was clearly marked by a sense of precarious class position and discontent. These conditions provided fertile ground for the hatred of seemingly prosperous Indians. Jealousy of economic success, however, is not the whole story. The middle-to upper-middle-class Lost Boys also engaged in a variety of attacks and harassment of Indian residents. Their activities should be viewed in light of the *racialization* of Indians in northern New Jersey; Indians are no longer discursively anonymous or invisible. In local residents' "common-sense" about the societal groups around them, Indians have become intrinsically linked with certain qualities and behaviors, i.e. stereotypes. In particular, the line between being an Indian and adhering to a conceived "Indian culture" has become blurred. An example of this lies in the term "Dotbuster" itself. The *bindi*[2] has literally come to signify Indian-ness. The racialization of Indians meant that they were tempting targets for the unarticulated frustrations of the Dotbusters.

This racialization of Indians into a discrete, identifiable group highlights the larger theme of this essay, that the paradigm of pan-Asian American unity does not reflect political and social realities. While the state has characterized Indians as Asian Americans in the U.S. Census since 1980,[3] this attempted, forced reclassification "from above" by no means changes individuals' and groups' perceptions of themselves and others. The U.S. Census Bureau solicited suggestions from national Indian-American groups before implementing its classification changes in 1980. The India League of America noted, "It is clear that an overwhelming proportion of immigrants from India . . . regard themselves as racially different from White, Black and Oriental Americans."[4] The India League concluded that Indian Americans wished to be classified as a distinct and separate racial minority group. Fifteen years later, Indian Americans' racial self-perceptions are reflected in the empirical data collected in this project's research into Indian-American political activity. The data overwhelmingly points to the fact that Indians and other South Asian groups do not politically organize or vote as a bloc with Korean, Chinese, and other East Asian groups in this country.[5]

Indian American political participation is increasingly informed and shaped by a narrow ethnic identity. South Asian immigrants drawn from all parts of the subcontinent, Guyana, the West Indies, Fiji, and Malaysia organize politically along caste, regional, religious, and linguistic lines. First-generation political mobilization will continue to center around these ethnic subgroups with few exceptions. Their children—the second generation—appear to embrace a broader South Asian American identity, finding commonality with those who share a similar racial appearance and cultural values. Elite members of this second generation, who have attended private, exclusive colleges, have sought alliance with other Asian American groups. These South Asian elites have joined with other Asian Americans in campus protests against admissions quotas and hate crimes. However, these few examples are not proof that pan-Asian unity exists among the second generation but rather of class differences among the second generation. Second-generation elites turn to familiar, "natural" paradigms, of racial organization such as pan-Asian unity promulgated in college race relations classes, which have themselves grown out of racial categories stuffed by the state and other institutions down the throats of Indian Americans. To paraphrase Foucault, power creates: knowledge creates truth.[6] This essay suggests that we look beyond paradigms artificially created by the state to paradigms actually lived out in individuals' political behaviors.

Working-class or state-school-educated second-generation Indian Americans do not see a natural alliance or unity with other Asian American groups. They do know that when they are called "Dothead" the slur is meant for them, and others who look like them. These young Indian Americans are more inclined than their elite peers to socialize exclusively with each other at their universities' large Hindu youth, South Asian students, or Indian cultural groups. Their political identity, as well as that of the first generation, is drawn by their racial group identity.

The conflicts in New Jersey, between Whites and Indians, Blacks and Indians, Latinos and Indians, and finally between other Asians and Indians, are an example of new racial realities. Like the tensions between Koreans and African Americans in the 1992 L.A. riots and New York City, the Dotbuster incidents highlight increasing interminority confrontation and the failure of conventional black-white or pan-Asian paradigms to adequately address contemporary race issues. The irrelevance of the pan-Asian unity paradigm does not mean that South Asians and Asian Americans cannot cooperate for mutual political benefit *à la* African-Americans and Latinos on certain issues. Before this can happen however, we must reformulate our understanding of racial categories in America to reflect real political possibilities.

Theoretical Parameters

Two ideas are central to our discussion: first, that nationality is not an absolute or a priori; it is consciously constructed and shaped by the social system from which it arises. Second, race and racial representation are currently part of the discourse of American nationality.

Benedict Anderson provides an interesting discussion of the origins of national identity in *Imagined Communities*. In contrast to the rhetoric of nationalism which implies the absolute, historical origins of a nation in the distant past, he argues that nations are an imagined, created community. Anderson feels that nations grow out of preexisting sociocultural systems. Thus more akin to religion than political ideology, nationalism is not merely a way of organizing a political entity but also a meaning around which people shape their lives, identity, and orientation to the world.

Homi Bhabha draws on this notion of the constructed nation, or what Bhabha calls the "ambivalence" of the nation, to make a case for studying the nation and nationhood by examining the language of narrative address itself.[7] Bhabha sees two benefits to this. First, it delegitimizes traditional authoritative history that is often accepted unquestioningly, and, second, it highlights the fact that representations of the national culture and life are found in and spread through many mediums and mechanisms. Language and narration are the tools of national myth making and thus also construct the marginalized and the Other. Anderson's and Bhabha's ideas about a contested, constantly shifting construction of nationality and its relationship to language and narrative provide a context within which we can examine the place of racial discourse and representation in the United States.

Race has been part of the struggle to define who is an American and who is not in our national discourse. In *Racial Formation in the United States*, Michael Omi and Howard Winant argue that race should be viewed as the basic determinant in

American politics and society. While they accept some of the insights offered by competing theories such as the conventional ethnicity paradigm and radical class and nation-based theories,[8] Omi and Winant feel that these theories do not capture the full realities of race in the U.S. Their alternative approach, which they term "racial formation," rejects the notion of fixed absolute notions of race and argues that racial meaning systems and sociopolitical forces reify and in turn shape each other: "The effort must be made to understand race as *an unstable and 'decentered' complex of social meanings constantly being transformed by political struggle.*" Ultimately the process of racial formation discussed by Omi and Winant is an ongoing process of creating and assigning sociopolitical and economic order through a discourse of difference.

Two interesting examples of this form of analysis are Joel Williamson's *A Rage for Order*, and Lloyd and Susanne Rudolph's discussion of "Modern Hate."[9] *A Rage for Order* is an analysis of Southern black-white relations that incorporates many of the insights offered by Omi and Winant. Williamson provides a historical study of how mechanisms of racial violence including lynching, sexual roles, and racial identities have maintained a Southern hierarchy of white elites above separated black and white masses.

The Rudolphs observe that the end of the Cold War has seen the politics of identity and ethnicity, among others, filling the vacuum created by the collapse of political ideological difference. They argue that the seemingly "ancient," primordial hatreds between Hindus and Muslims in India, Serbs and Bosnians in the former Yugoslavia, and other ethnic and racial conflicts are very much modern reformulations, specific to contemporary social and economic anxieties. "Friendships are as 'ancient' as hatreds. The face we see depends on what human agents cause us to see." Actual or perceived difference does not automatically create tensions. What does create and legitimize them is the discourse and rhetoric of political leaders, writers, and the media—the public culture.

In terms of this case study of racism in Jersey City, these theoretical parameters about the sociopolitical manipulation of race suggest that the rhetoric of the Dotbusters and others with anti-Indian sentiments was not "just prejudice." It was also an attempt to make sense of perceived economic and social disorder. For the Dotbusters, focusing on race functioned as a means of creating order and reasserting their hierarchical dominance. The Dotbusters were architects of racial meaning systems about the place of Indians in American society.

"They Ain't Americans"[10]

Look! Let's cut the small talk. . . . we will go to any extreme to get Indians to move out of Jersey City. If I'm walking down the street and I see a Hindu and the setting is right, I will hit him or her. . . . We use the phone books and look up the name Patel. Have you seen how many of them there are? . . . Do you walk down Central avenue and experience what it's like to be near them: well we have and we just don't want it anymore.

—excerpts from the "Dotbuster" letter sent to *The Jersey Journal*[11]

Northern New Jersey residents discussed their Indian neighbors using two themes. The first was that Indian Americans are economically successful. Second, Indians were identified as a separate, alien group. These themes created a common language and framework for competing narratives about Indians in New Jersey. Specifically, the Dotbusters and their supporters used the notions of economic success and alienness to formulate an anti-Indian discourse, but these same attributes were also used by residents who asserted that Indians were desirable neighbors and by politicians eager to pay lip service to the Indian community's demands.

For anti-Indian residents, Indians' supposed economic success provided a central reason for hatred. A young woman interviewed on the streets of Jersey City noted: "We're just jealous because they [Indians] have more money than we do."[12] This perceived economic success was commonly explained by the government's supposed special treatment of Indians. Joe Dimick, another Jersey City resident, complained, "These people [Indians] come over here and get $10,000 to start a business.... That's not right. And we have to work and fight all our life."[13] Dimick was referring to the common belief that immigrants get Small Business Administration loans taxfree. In fact, neither Indians nor other immigrant groups receive such special loans.

This theme of privilege was employed most potently by lawyers for the men charged in beating Dr. Sharan. The defense repeatedly sought to characterize the federal government's case as a "witch-hunt" to appease Indian protests. Defense attorney Peter Willis argued: " 'The Asian-Indian-American community owns property and they are active. You can bet they brought pressure."[14] The defense was successful in obtaining an acquittal in part because local jurors could readily accept what was already "common-sensical" to them—the suggestion that Indians had a privileged relationship with the government.

The Dotbusters discredited Indians' financial success by portraying them as parsimonious. "You [*The Jersey Journal*] say that Indians are good business men. Well I suppose if I had fifteen people living in my apartment I'd be able to save money too."[15] The letter suggested that Indians live without dignity in subhuman conditions that moreover degrade others living in the neighborhood. The invocation of "quality of neighborhood" and importance of excluding undesirables was an important facet of anti-Indian rhetoric. In one embarrassing incident for the local Democratic party, Jed Colicchio, the former mayor of Wanaque and a candidate for a council seat, said he opposed new housing because it would bring in "dot-heads" from New Jersey's urban areas. He later amended his remarks by saying that he meant to describe "transients who 'bop' their way into town."[16]

Paradoxically, anti-Indian rhetoric assailed supposed Indian prosperity while deeming their presence detrimental to the quality of a neighborhood. Recent work on the significance of race over class in housing segregation rings true here.[17] Race is inextricably linked to dominant discourses of our social hierarchy. Anti-Indian residents' concern with the "quality" of their neighborhood was directly linked to the presence of nonwhites, regardless of their economic status. Within the context of local discourses of race and social position, Indians were a daily reminder to their white neighbors that the minority presence was growing and the social prestige of the area slipping. More crucially, the middle-class characteristics of many Indians outright challenged those very discourses of race and social order because the Whites most threatened perceived themselves to be less prosperous than their Indian neighbors.

The second theme of anti-Indian discourse centered on Indians' alienness, aloofness, and social difference from "real" Americans. Jersey City residents declared, "They [Indians] don't like us. I know for a fact. . . . they consider themselves higher than we are."[18] The maintenance of Indian customs and religion was portrayed as further evidence of condescension toward other groups. A resident named Dave told a reporter:

> . . . the Hindu people—they should live the way we live. You know they shouldn't have the smell they have, dress the way they do, dress in curtains and walk around in tribes. They should live in our culture the way we live.[19]

This man posited a normal American "we"—which was made clear during other parts of the interview included Blacks and Hispanics against an alien and abnormal "Hindu people."

The use of gendered imagery was used to further portray Indians as un-American and worthy of scorn. Indian males' perceived inability to conform to a masculine role confirmed their abnormality and alienness. "They [Indians] will never do anything. They are a weak race physically and mentally. We are going to continue our way. We will never be stopped."[20] The actual group beatings on lone Indians tell a very different story. Navroze Mody's attempts to defend himself against at least ten young men were later distorted into menacing martial arts moves by lawyers for his murderers. James Kerwin and Peter Jester carried out one of their self-described "Patel attacks" by breaking into Bharat Kanubhai Patel's apartment and beating him over the head with a baseball bat while he slept.

The lynching characteristic of these attacks points to the larger social significance of the racial violence. They were social exhibitions that reasserted, at least temporarily, dominance over Indians. The irony of proclaiming racial physical superiority while many people beat up one escaped the macho-conscious Dotbusters because it was not a mere physical confrontation but a symbolic enactment of putting *all* Indians in their place. Group identification and solidarity was an important factor in the decision to join in verbal and physical racial attacks on "alien" Indians on the streets. Leo Szymanski, a prosecution witness in the Sharan trials, admitted, " 'I would shout obscenities. . . . Everyone was doing it. It was the thing to do back then.' "[21]

The Dotbusters' emphasis on the alienness of Indians echoes a larger historical narrative of the Asian as unassimilable and un-American. Ronald Takaki and others have assailed these discourses by detailing the history of Asian Americans. His definition of Asian American includes Japanese, Chinese, Korean, Filipino, Indian, and Southeast Asian (Laotian, Vietnamese, etc.) immigrants. Takaki's notion of the Asian Other is certainly important to an analysis of the Dotbuster rhetoric against Indians, but it is not complete. How does one explain the anti-Indian, "Lost Boys" gang in the Edison-Iselin? The arrested members included ". . . one black, one Jew, several Greeks and Italians, three Filipinos, one half Filipino and half Indian, and several Anglos. . . ."[22] These multiracial gangs complicate the old paradigm of white vs. nonwhites and, in the case of Asian-on-Asian violence, shatter Takaki's inclusion of Indians into, and indeed the very existence of, a monolithic Asian Other.

Anti-Indian sentiment cut across the race and class spectrum, and the resulting narratives varied accordingly. But anti-Indian narratives did have one thing in common: the words of hatred centered on the Indian "self" as defined by the symbols of Indian culture. The Dotbusters and others disliked the "dot-heads" because among other things they dressed in "curtains," had that odor, and had "alien" religious principles." "Indian culture" has become not merely a reference to the traditional habits, customs, religion, food, and dress of Indians or other South Asians. It has become a loaded marker, fraught with racialized meaning. Being "Indian" is not defined as being a nonwhite minority or Asian. Rather, the notions of Indian-ness and a narrowly delineated Indian culture reify and define each other. Thus the meanings of the terms "Indian" and "Indian culture" have become inextricably linked and indeed interchangeable. The "dot-head" has become the "Indian," and "Indians" have become "dot-heads."

Racial Violence in the Public Space: The Official Response

Only a few cowardly people disgrace us. . . .
—New Jersey Gov. Thomas Kean[23]

The rhetoric of the Dotbusters and others with anti-Indian sentiments was of course not the only public discourse about racial violence in northern New Jersey. There were many competing narratives, including those of local and state politicians, religious leaders, the police, and the courts. Not surprisingly, these universally denounced racism and spouted the conventional rhetoric of equal civil rights for all. Public officials also seemed to celebrate racial and ethnic diversity. Referring to Indian immigrants, Wanaque Chief of Police Robert C. Kronyak noted that the borough "has seen more and more new faces coming here, people who have added to and strengthened the community."[24] In the case of the Dotbusters, the public question was not whether racially motivated violence against Indian Americans was bad; all agreed publicly that it was. The vital, contested issue became whether these incidents were in fact of a racial nature.

The official response also attempted to marginalize the perpetrators of racial crimes. This reflected the notion that the scourge of racism has been conquered in American society and therefore racial attacks are unusual and must be perpetrated by extremists. Thus, in New Jersey, racism against Indians was depicted as bizarre and sporadic, and definitely not part of conventional, mainstream life. At a rally, Governor Kean described the Dotbusters as people "who oozed from the gutters."[25] Kean's vivid allusion to class was one tactic in some efforts to marginalize the participants in racial attacks. Public officials also attempted to discredit and isolate the Dotbusters by asserting that their numbers were small and meaningless. After the arrests of James Kerwin, author of the Dotbuster letter, and Peter Jester, Hudson County Prosecutor Paul DePascale claimed that the Dotbusters had fewer than ten members. He added that "Kerwin was at the epicenter of the Dotbuster movement."[26] It later became well known that the police had not arrested Martin Riccardi for the Patel beating even though he too was linked to it. Kerwin and Jester became scapegoats, personifying the Dotbusters, just as the Dotbusters became a convenient symbol of racism against Indians. The trouble with this was that racial violence against Indians was not just perpetrated by the Dotbusters, just as Kerwin and Jester were not the only Dotbusters. The racial attacks did not occur in a social vacuum but were in fact applauded by some local residents. When racial incidents in the northern New Jersey area continued even after the supposed dismantling of the Dotbusters, local officials were forced to abandon their public claim that racial violence against Indians was an isolated, unusual occurrence.

Police hesitancy to label racial attacks as "racially motivated" was partially due to the fact that the attitudes of local police officers reflected the general attitudes of their community. Jersey City Sixth Precinct Captain James Galvin told *New York Newsday*, "that the Indians' growing protests, both of the racial hostility and the police department's apparent indifference, are '95 percent overreacting."' He further added, "They [Indians] get a snowball through the window and they want a [police] car there right away."[27] Here Galvin alluded to the local feeling that Indians get and expect privileged treatment from authorities.

These attitudes were not, however, the only reason for the lack of police sympathy. The local police did not speedily investigate Indian bias cases because suspects in the cases were linked to the police department. In the Sharan case, defendant Mark Evangelista was a Hudson County police officer, and his brother was a Jersey City police officer; codefendant Martin Riccardi was the son of the North District former chief of detectives. The police claim that the incidents were not racially motivated functioned as a means of stalling federal intervention and thereby protected the perpetrators.

Prosecutors and the local courts also sought to deny the bias basis of the cases for as long as possible. The local government, legal, and law enforcement establishment were tightly intertwined political allies, reluctant to rock the boat by fingering the suspects. They were unwilling to risk the political implications of revealing the embarrassing fact that the Dotbusters were not marginalized, isolated criminals but rather were tightly connected to the local police department. Hudson County Prosecutor Paul DePascale's concerted and deliberate attempt to dismiss the bias elements of anti-Indian attack cases often led him to make ludicrous contradictions. When it became known that two of the Mody defendants were responsible for a racial attack on a Pakistani and Indian student the week before Mody's death, DePascale still denied that the Mody attack was ethnically motivated but then added, "I think you can make the assumption that these two [the Mody defendants] didn't like Asian Indians."[28] The local police have to this day not completed their investigation into the Sharan case. During the federal trial against Riccardi, Evangelista, and Kozak, it was revealed that witness Leo Szymanski had had his life threatened by two Hudson County sheriff's officers after he agreed to testify. Local prosecutors never brought charges against Riccardi, Evangelista, and Kozak, even after federal investigators uncovered "new" evidence, and federal prosecutors indicted them [for] federal civil rights violations.

Paul DePascale was not only the Hudson County Prosecutor, he was also appointed acting Police Director of the Jersey City police department in March 1988 by Mayor Cucci. The defendants in the Mody case were arraigned in July 1988. DePascale's dual roles as a prosecutor and as head of the Jersey City police department would have conflicted if he had chosen to vigorously prosecute the Mody case as a racial incident because it was already known that Martin Riccardi, the son of the chief of detectives, was linked to the Dotbusters. Characterization of the Mody case as racially motivated would have created public pressure to get results on the Sharan case quickly and made it more difficult to stall the investigation. As part of the police department, he acted to protect the suspected Dotbusters by refusing to prosecute Mody's death as racially motivated. Finally, Cucci's appointment of DePascale indicates their close political relationship. Cucci also had strong ties to suspected Dotbuster Martin Riccardi's father, Ben Riccardi. Cucci, Riccardi, and DePascale were effectively the political and law enforcement establishment of Jersey City.

The strongest piece of evidence in the above claims against DePascale, the local police department, and Mayor Cucci is that they definitely knew that Martin Riccardi was linked to the Bharat Kanubhai Patel beating and the Dotbusters as early as February 1988—the same time that the Mody case was being put together. Martin Riccardi was linked to the beating of Patel on tapes of Peter Jester and James Kerwin. Incidentally, although Jester and Kerwin served time for that beating, Riccardi was never even indicted. In September 1988, Mayor Cucci proposed to appoint Ben Riccardi, Martin's father, Police Director of the Jersey City police department. Ben Riccardi declined the appointment after *The Jersey Journal* ran a story revealing that his son Martin's name was on the Jester and Kerwin tapes. At that time Mayor Cucci confirmed that he had been told in February 1988 that Riccardi's name was on the tapes. Additionally, *The Jersey Journal* revealed that, earlier, Ben Riccardi had asked Mayor Cucci to intervene when Martin failed his Fire Department entrance drug test.

The local authorities' collective effort to protect the Dotbusters was blatantly obvious to federal investigators and prosecutors, and the federal judge who presided over the Sharan case, U.S. District Judge Joseph Irenas, publicly chastised the police investigation:

> Drawing parallels with official tolerance of anti-Semitic violence in Nazi Germany Irenas said the department neglected to pursue obvious leads. . . . "I would be deaf, dumb and blind not to say that I am very disappointed in what at least appears to be what the Jersey City police did."[29]

The judge's harsh indictment of the actions of the police was singular. Federal prosecutors merely hinted at a police conspiracy—"a wall of silence"—in their closing arguments. Department of Justice attorney Gerard Hogan related to the jury how the woman who placed the 911 call the night of the beating refused to give her name. " 'She did not want to be a witness against these three men. . . . That was the beginning of the chorus of no's.' " He then detailed how the Jersey City police had not bothered to interview people who hung out in the area of the attack. Although federal investigators and prosecutors were aware of local authorities' activities, the Department of Justice did not directly accuse them of inappropriate and illegal behavior. This attitude remained controversial for Indian Americans, who sensed local authorities' stonewalling and were frustrated by a perceived lack of justice in the Mody and Sharan cases.

Public discourse by local politicians, prosecutors, and the courts generally gave lip service to the notions of racial tolerance, diversity, and a vigorous enforcement of equal civil rights—the rights of all citizens to equal protection and treatment by the government. However, in the case of Jersey City, Indian Americans had less than equal rights because of their attackers' close ties with the political and law enforcement establishment.

Don't You Want to Defend Yourselves?[30]

The explosion of racial violence in 1987–1988 was not a new phenomenon. Indian residents in Jersey City had long endured hostility and racial taunts. Mono Sen, the founder of the Indo-American Association (IAA) and a resident of downtown Jersey City for fifteen years, noted:

> Fifteen years ago there were only about 3,000 Indians in the city.... Some kids had never seen Indians before. They would shout things like, "Hey you Hindus." Then around 10 years ago, Indian stores on Central Avenue and homes of Indians in the Heights area were broken into with greater frequency.[31]

The Dotbusters' open hatred and war against Indian residents not only tapped into existing anti-Indian sentiment but also "legitimized" it in a sense. Physical assaults, verbal taunts, and attacks on Indian property jumped dramatically in the 1987–1988 period. Indians developed a siege-like mentality, living in constant fear of harassment and attack. As a result, they curtailed their activities and limited leaving their homes. Indian residents' perception of racial violence was far more important than the actual number of incidents. Reports of more and more attacks fed on the general climate of fear and further increased anxiety. Likewise, those with anti-Indian sentiments, sensing Indians' mounting apprehension, took the opportunity to engage in small acts of bigotry. In public places, eggs were thrown, and Indians were verbally taunted. One woman related how young men would harass Indian shoppers at supermarkets on Central Avenue by blocking their paths and shouting insults. They routinely received threatening anonymous phone calls after their names had been selected from the phone book. Minibombs were thrown at homes. Rocks were tossed into windows. Apartment buildings were defaced with graffiti spelling out racial slurs or messages such as "Go back to India." Youths would drive up to homes, throw beer bottles and other garbage, and then drive off. Not surprisingly, many Indian families moved out of Jersey City, just as the Dotbusters had hoped.

The various organizations that formed in reaction to the violence in northern

New Jersey held views about the role of Indian Americans in the political process and larger society that had been informed by varying discourses on multiculturalism, ethnicity, and race. With regard to multiculturalism vs. assimilation, it can be loosely generalized that Indian-American political organizations espoused a multicultural vision of society. The blatant attacks by the Dotbusters on the *sari, bindi,* and "Indian culture" guaranteed that they would be strongly and uniformly defended by Indians. Indeed, these symbols of Indian culture became a rallying point for many. Indian women, including Dr. Lalitha Masson, who founded and headed the National Organization for the Defense of Indian Americans (NODIA), wore *saris* as a sign of defiance at protests and rallies. Students at the University of Pennsylvania organized MASALA, Movement Advocating South Asian Links in America.

The political response was characterized by the use of Indian heritage as a rallying point around which to organize but was also a reflection of the ghosts and inner doubts of the collective Indian psyche. The Dotbusters hit a raw nerve among Indians when they wrote to *The Jersey Journal* that Indians were a physically and mentally weak race. Within the local context of Jersey City, the supposed cowardice of Indians marked them as alien and un-American. But for Indians, both first and second generation, reading these words invoked colonial memories of white domination, Indian weakness, and, ultimately, Gandhi's non-violent resistance to oppression. As a result, a pervasive theme of the Indian response to the crisis was an almost self-admonishment to stop being so passive, so cowardly perhaps, and start fighting back. For some, this meant physical retribution. Most responded with nonviolent protest and political pressure. However, the use of this collective cultural fear became central to the tactics of Indian-American political activists, who admonished, " 'The Indian community has been lily-livered too long.' "[32] Flyers quoting Gandhi called for the defense of women and places of worship.

Despite the general embrace of multiculturalism, there were vast differences among the various political groups as to what exactly multiculturalism meant. The local Indian-American political scene was characterized by in-fighting, shifting alliances, competition for political capital and influence, diverging strategies and goals, and a politics of personality. The lack of political unity within the community was partially a result of the highly different ways in which various groups perceived both the problem and their place in American society.

The Indian American political response was splintered by cleavages of class and age. These differences interacted to produce highly varying political ideologies and goals among the organizations that sprung up to deal with the racial violence. The most ideologically and strategically significant of these two was the gap between first- and second-generation Indian political activists. The first-generation group can be characterized as immigrant individuals who owned homes or businesses in the area. Second-generation activists were primarily college students and graduates who had either been born in the United States or were part of what has been called the one-and-a-half generation.[33] These two groups diverged most prominently on the issue of collective action and alliance building with other racial minority groups. First-generation political organizations were exclusively concerned with the racial violence against Indian Americans. They viewed the crisis in Jersey City to be an Indian-

American problem and did not seek to act with other minority groups. In contrast, second-generation groups viewed it as part of a larger historical continum of racism against all racial minority groups in the United States. They sought support and alliance with other minority groups and especially with Asian American organizations.

Class played an important role within both first- and second-generation responses to the Dotbusters. Indian immigrants in Jersey City tended to coalesce into political groups along class lines. Dr. Lalitha Masson and NODIA represented the interests of professional Indians. Hardyal Singh's group, the International Mahatma Gandhi Association (IMCA), was comprised of working-class Indians in the area. Although there were no competing class organizations among the second generation, many of them were drawn from elite universities and had solid middle-class backgrounds. This background in large part determined the ideological orientation of second-generation groups.

Dr. Masson and NODIA were loosely allied with the leaders of several other local Indian cultural, religious, and political groups, including Mono Sen and the IAA. It was commonly held within these first-generation professional organizations, and, indeed, among Indians across the class spectrum, that those with anti-Indian sentiments were simply jealous of their economic success. Masson relied on the notion of privileged ethnicity to press her demands. She described Indian immigrants as middle-class professionals who had arrived in the late 1970s and bought up real estate bargains along Jersey City and Hoboken streets deserted by whites. These residents, many of them the children of Irish and Italian immigrants, were moving out as the Latino and African American population increased. Masson noted, "We were the pioneers. . . . These streets were boarded up.'" She added, "'We came to this country, and the hospitals in this city were abandoned by white doctors. So for many years they were run by Pakistani and Indian doctors."[34] Masson painted a picture of a model minority—well educated, middle class, and hardworking. "We don't get into crime. Our children are getting top awards at schools. What more could you ask from a community?"[35] This self-image—NODIA's political identity—would have significant consequences on the shape of political strategies formulated in response to the Dotbusters. Specifically, this political identity led to the notion that Indians are faultless, tax-paying citizens entitled to state protection against hate crimes—entitled to protection because they pay their taxes, not because they are a racial minority group with moral claims upon society. Not only did these Indian Americans see themselves as distinct from other racial minorities; emphasizing their middle-class thrift and education was a subtle means of drawing a contrast with the many lower-middle-class white residents of Jersey City.

The first-generation professional groups were primarily concerned with self-protection, i.e., stopping the actual daily harassment and attacks. They did not regard themselves as part of a dramatic larger struggle against racism. Accordingly, they spoke not of broad societal racism against Indians but rather concentrated on the individuals who participated in the attacks and the local police and officials who had failed to forcefully prosecute and investigate the crimes. Despite their rhetoric of middle-class moderation, the obvious conspiracy of inaction surrounding the Sharan and Mody cases led NODIA to openly attack the integrity of the police and local politicians and [to] use radical tactics such as demanding a role in selecting prosecutors for the trials.

Hardyal Singh and IMGA vied with Masson and NODIA for political recognition and capital. The tension between the two can be attributed to a combination of personality and class differences. Both Singh and Masson enjoyed a lot of political and media attention because of their efforts. Their desire to maximize their own political power often seemed as important as furthering the goals of the "Indian community." Finally, these groups could not appeal to large cross-sections of Indians because they were *ad hoc* organizations, with their membership primarily drawn from informal acquaintance and family networks. As a result, they were self-segregated along class, regional, religious, language, and caste lines.

Perhaps the best example of the rivalry between NODIA and IMGA was the controversy over NODIA and IAA's meeting with New Jersey's Governor Kean at a school in Jersey City. The problem was that IMGA had also asked to meet with the Governor but never received a response to their requests. Before the meeting, NODIA and IAA got together to review group demands and also to explicitly distance themselves from Singh. At this meeting, a member "downplayed the significance of Singh's group, charging, 'the United Indian American Association[36] maybe represents 10 people' "[37] and that Singh's thinking was not typical of the majority of Indians. He further added that Singh and IAA had personal conflicts. Singh's public comment on the whole affair was that there was no split within the Indian community, but he also expressed anger at Kean's snub. Politicians and the media quickly learned that it was best to deal with both Singh and Masson. The two were usually asked for separate comments by reporters hip to the local political scene, and both were appointed to the Jersey City Human Rights Commission.

Singh and IMGA's rhetoric was marked by a type of chauvinist Indian nationalism that tapped into some Indians' ambivalence about perceived American cultural values. The implications of the name of Singh's group, the International Mahatma Gandhi Association, are obvious enough. He also donned the Gandhi cap and Nehru jacket for public appearances. At rallies, Singh spoke in Hindi. At one point he sought the intervention of the Indian government because, among other things, "Indian women are assaulted and spat upon."[38] Singh's perspective on the problems in Jersey City centered on appropriate gender roles, drinking and drugs, pitting narrowly defined good Indian family values against an immoral, pleasure-oriented American lifestyle. "You cannot say 'I saw one Indian girl with her boyfriend'. . . . You never see an Indian girl smoking, taking beer, or taking wine."[39] The result was a glorification of traditional Indian-ness. The use of Indian nationalist symbolism and rhetoric was a tangible means of conveying that traditionality.

The Indian nationalist approach taken by Singh was a comprehensible way for him and others to cope with the crisis in Jersey City. How effectively it engaged the local racism of the Dotbusters is uncertain. In East Brunswick, New Jersey, David Mortimer graffitied "Dots U Smell" on the garage door of the Khodbuis, a Pakistani-American family.[40] The Dotbusters and others with similar sentiments could not distinguish between Indians and Pakistanis and did not care if there was a difference—they were all "dot-heads" alike. The problem with Singh's appeals to Indian nationalism and use of traditional Indian political symbols and rhetoric lay in its exclusion of people like the Khodbuis and many second-generation Indians. Like Masson and NODIA, Singh's political strategies failed to confront the centrality of race and color to the discourse of the Dotbusters.

In stark contrast, second-generation groups contextualized the attacks within a larger U.S. history of racism and therefore sought to make alliances and act with other racial groups, employing a more panoramic rhetoric of fighting *all* racism. These differences were mainly at the product of each group's life experiences, and, to some extent, class. Having grown up in the U.S., the second generation was familiar with narratives of racial oppression against African Americans, Native Americans, Latinos, and Asians. They identified as Indian-American—their membership was, after all, primarily and specifically Indian, but they were also willing to assume an additional identity as "people of color." Their class backgrounds were also important in shaping their political agendas. All were college students or graduates at the time, often at elite, private universities. Their self-described "progressive" outlook was in tune with the liberal norms of many of their college peers.

In 1987 New York and New Jersey-area college students and graduates organized Indian Youth Against Racism (IYAR, which was later changed to Youth Against Racism, YAR) as a direct response to the Dotbusters' activity. Himanshu Shukla, an investment banker and member of IYAR, also created the Indian American Political Action Club of Hudson County (IMPACT). In addition, several nearby campuses had their own groups and organized protests. IYAR and IMPACT's activities emphasized continuous political mobilization and education through lobbying and rallies. Second-generation groups actively sought alliance with other minority political groups, especially Asian American groups such as the New York City–based Asian American Legal Defense and Education Fund.

Second-generation rhetoric also less successfully attempted to appropriate existing African American, Latino, and Native American narratives of societal oppression. Students protested "institutional racism in the U.S." For example, student leader Jaykumar Menon charged that U.S. immigration laws had only let in rich, professional people, resulting in a group ". . . artificially isolated from the struggle for voice that all minorities share."[41] Menon's lament that there was a nonexistent Indian American working class was, as we have seen, not exactly accurate. Right there in Jersey City, Hardyal Singh and IMGA were actively challenging Masson and NODIA for leadership of the Indian community. However Singh's rhetoric of good Indian values vs. bad American ones and use of nationalist symbolism was probably not the type of working-class Indian Menon had in mind.

Menon's romanticization of the working class reflected dominant U.S. race relations paradigms. These paradigms sometimes speak of race only in terms of economic inequality and class, while forgetting that middle-class minority individuals—Black, Asian, and Latino—are still subject to virulent racism. The progressive ideology of alliance and identification with other people of color espoused by student activists is in many ways itself an elite ideology. Working-class Indian immigrants are anxiously engaged in a daily struggle to improve their social and economic status.

They do not appear to be interested in identifying with African Americans and Latinos; rather, they often emphasize their differences with these groups.

The real story in the Dotbuster case may lie in the emergence of Singh. He and IMGA provided a possible model of future political participation by working-class Indian Americans, who until now have been much less active than middle-class and affluent Indians. If this group becomes politically mobilized in the future, it is unlikely that it will embrace an ideology of multiracial alliance and identify with other racial minorities. An ideology along the lines of Singh's is far more possible.

Conclusion

The events in Jersey City indicate, more than anything else, that Indian Americans have been narratively racialized by others. However, the notion of an "Indian culture" was not just the racializing tool of the Dotbusters but also the symbol around which all Indians rallied to some extent. In other Indian immigrant contexts—the United Kingdom, Kenya, South Africa, the West Indies, and Guyana—the historical conditions have been different, but all are marked by a cross-generational maintenance of an "Indian" identity. Likewise, Indian Americans have and in the future are likely to maintain a distinct racial and cultural group identity that will inevitably limit the efficacy of pan-Asian unity paradigms. While recognition of this may mean an end to the notion of a monolithic Asian American political force, it opens the door to the building of relationships between South Asians and Asian Americans that may yet have a meaningful impact on the political scene.

NOTES

1. See David Theo Goldberg, ed., *Anatomy of Racism* (Minneapolis: University of Minnesota Press, 1990), and Toni Morrison, ed., *Race-ing Justice, En-gendering Power* (New York: Random House, 1992). These narrative analyses draw out the racial and gender imagery of racist discourse.

2. The traditional red dot worn by some Hindu married women.

3. Prior to 1980, Indian-Americans were counted into the "White" category by the U.S. Census. See Hekmat Elkhanialy and Ralph W. Nicholas, *Immigrants from the Indian Subcontinent in the U.S.A.: Problems and Prospects* (Chicago: India League of America, 1976). The same problem is faced today by other, small "racially marginal" groups such as Arab Americans and other Middle Easterners. Some Arab American students have called for the inclusion of Arab Americans into the Asian American category, citing the need for protection from hate crimes and racial discrimination. A scheduled topic at the 1994 Association of Asian American Studies National Conference addressed this very issue, "Is There an 'A' in Asian American for Arabs?" The scheduled speaker was Moustafa Bayoumi.

4. Hekmat Elkhanialy and Ralph W. Nicholas, *Immigrants from the Indian Subcontinent in the U.S.A.: Problems and Prospects* (Chicago: India League of America, 1976), 6.

5. Other studies supporting this conclusion abound. For example, an analysis of Asian American voter participation in the 1993 New York City Mayoral election conducted by the

Asian American Legal Defense and Education Fund found that Korean and Chinese voters prefered Rudolph Giuliani over David Dinkins by a margin of 71 percent to 22 percent and 70 percent to 23 percent. South Asian voters (Indian, Pakistani, and Bangladeshi) were the only group studied who favored Dinkins over Giuliani, by a margin of 48 percent to 36 percent. While 62 percent of South Asian voters were registered as Democrats, only 38 percent of Chinese, 24 percent of Filipino, and 30 percent of Korean voters were. See Sumantra Tito Sinha, "Asian American Voter Participation in the 1993 New York City Elections," Voting Rights Project, Asian American Legal Defense and Education Fund (1994). Courtesy of Sumantra Tito Sinha.

6. Foucault theorized that the relationship between power, knowledge, and truth could be viewed in terms of a triangle. Power, delineated by right, creates truth. In turn, truth—that society's version of it—legitimates right: "We are subjected to the production of truth through power and we cannot exercise power except through the production of truth." Michel Foucault, "Lecture Two: January 14, 1976," in *Power/Knowledge*, ed. Colin Gordon (New York: Pantheon Books, 1980), 93.

7. See Benedict Anderson, *Imagined Communities* (New York: Verso, 1983), and Homi K. Bhabha, *Nation and Narration* (New York: Routledge, 1990).

8. See Michael Omi and Howard Winant, *Racial Formation in the United States: From the 1960s to the 1980s* (New York: Routledge, 1986), 68. Omi and Winant describe the ethnicity paradigm as "the mainstream of the modern sociology of race." They critique it for reducing racially defined minorities to ethnically defined minorities, thus neglecting race. Class-based theories include: the market relations approach, which explains race within market-based economic models, stratification theory exemplified by William J. Wilson's *The Declining Significance of Race* (1978) (the movement of middle-class blacks out of the community has created an underclass devoid of job networks and strong family models), and class conflict theory, situating race within class models based on the notion of exploitation. Omi and Winant describe nation-based theory as a model in which racial conflict is the outcome of colonialism and imperialism.

9. See Joel Williamson, *A Rage for Order* (New York: Oxford University Press, 1986), and Susanne Hoeber and Lloyd I. Rudolph, "Modern Hate," *The New Republic*, March 22, 1993, 24–29.

10. Tom Kozak, later tried for the beating attack on Dr. Sharan, during an informal street interview. Transcript of "Eye on Asia" videotape. Interviews with Jersey City residents. Conducted two weeks after the beating of Dr. Sharan in 1987. Courtesy of Asian American Legal Defense and Education Fund.

11. Letter to *The Jersey Journal*, September 2, 1987. Courtesy of Rita Sethi, Youth Against Racism.

12. Transcript of "Eye on Asia" videotape.

13. Michel Marriott, "In Jersey City, Indians Protest Violence," *The New York Times*, October 12, 1987, B1.

14. Joseph D. McCaffrey, "Jury Told of Resistance to Indian Beating Probe," *The Star Ledger*, February 5, 1993, 14.

15. Letter to *The Jersey Journal*, September 2, 1987.

16. Albert J. Parisi, "A Remark Enrages the Indian Community," *The New York Times*, October 30, 1988.

17. See Douglas S. Massey and Nancy A. Denton, *American Apartheid* (Cambridge: Harvard University Press, 1993). Massey and Denton argue that racial segregation in the form of the inner-city ghetto is the primary factor for the continuation of black poverty in the U.S.

18. Transcript of "Eye on Asia" videotape.

19. Ibid.

20. Letter to *The Jersey Journal*, September 2, 1987.

21. Kirsten Danis, "Witness in Bias Case Tells of Death Threat," *The Jersey Journal*, January 26, 1993, 8.

22. Al Kamen, "After Immigration, An Unexpected Fear," *The Washington Post*, November 16, 1991, A6.

23. R. Clinton Taplin, "Indians Rally for Probe," *The Record*, April 5, 1988, B-5.

24. Parisi.

25. Taplin, B-1 and B-5.

26. Raul Vicente Jr., "Cops Arrest Two As 'Dotbusters,' " *Gold Coast*, March 24–31, 1988, 4.

27. Vivienne Walt, "A New Racism Gets Violent in New Jersey," *New York Newsday*, April 6, 1988, Part II 5.

28. Rekha Borsellino, "Tougher Law Asked in Attacks on Indians," *The New York Times*, July 10, 1988, 1 [sect. 12].

29. Deborah Yaffe, "Judge Rips Local Probe of Beating," *The Jersey Journal*, June 19, 1993.

30. Indian Youth Against Racism flyer, 1988. Courtesy of Rita Sethi.

31. Helen Zia, "Jersey City Jags," *The New Asian Times*, December 1988, 3.

32. Chris Mitchel, "Lily-livered No Longer," *The Hoboken Reporter*, February 28, 1988, 10.

33. The 1.5 generation, meaning individuals who immigrated as children. This term has been used most prominently in work by Korean-Americans. See Charles Ryu, "1.5 Generation," in Joann Faung Jean Lee's *Asian Americans Oral Histories* (New York: New Press, 1992).

34. Walt, 5.

35. Ibid.

36. Apart from being president of IMGA, Singh was also president of the United Indian American Association, which was said to be an umbrella group representing six Hudson County Indian-American organizations.

37. Jeffrey Hoff, "Indians Adamant on Trials," *The Hudson Dispatch*, April 4, 1988, 8.

38. Savyasaachi Jian, "Consulate Criticized on Jersey Attacks," *India Abroad*, October 23, 1987.

39. Lee, 114.

40. He also sprayed "Die Jew" on a car outside of a Jewish family's home.

41. Mitchell, 10.

Chapter Twenty-three

Race, Class, Citizenship, and Extraterritoriality
Asian Americans and the 1996 Campaign Finance Scandal

L. Ling-chi Wang

Not since the protracted national debate over whether the Chinese should be excluded from the U.S. in the 1870s and early 1880s have we seen more sustained media coverage and acrimonious debate on the so-called Asian connection in the campaign finance scandal of 1996. Based on my own collection and estimate, no less than 4,000 articles have been published on the subject (newspapers and magazines) between September 1996 and February 1998. As of this writing, no end is in sight for this long-running media obsession and partisan brawl among the political elite.

At the eye of the storm are two key figures, John Huang and Charlie Yah-lin Trie, two Asian American donors/fundraisers for Clinton's reelection and the Democratic National Committee (DNC). They are joined by "a supporting cast" which includes Johnny Chung, Maria Hsia, Eugene and Nora Lum, Yogesh Gandhi, Congressman Jay Kim, and Chong Lo, and a cast of "extras," made up of business executives from Asia countries, like James Riady of Indonesia, Pauline Kanchanalak of Thailand, Liu Tai-ying of Taiwan, Wang Jun of China, Johnny Lee of South Korea, among others. The two central figures have become household names, as well known as world-class Asian American figure skaters Kristi Yamaguchi and Michelle Kwan, even if the donors' notoriety is achieved through adverse publicity. What's more, not since the advent of the Asian American movement in the late 1960s have Asian Americans experienced a more significant civil rights setback than the one resulting from the deluge of negative, and at times racist, coverage of the scandal, as outlined in the Asian American petition to the U.S. Commission on Civil Rights.[1] Not surprisingly, Asian Americans across the nation were stunned by the unwanted national attention, and many felt outraged, betrayed, ashamed, violated, discouraged, injured, or insulted, depending on their perspectives on the scandal and their class positions within the Asian American communities and in society at large.

How do we sort through and interpret the daily barrage of sensational disclosures, media spins and counterspins? How do we begin to analyze and understand what has been happening to Asian Americans in general and to the leaders and organizations implicated, directly and indirectly, in the scandal in particular? Are they representative of what Asian America has become in an age dominated by transnational capital? Are Asian Americans simply innocent victims of political drive-by shooting, as some have alleged? Or, are they being singled out by the media, Republican leaders, and the law-enforcement agencies in the U.S. Department of Justice because they are Asians? Are they an integral part of what has seriously gone wrong with the post-Watergate campaign finance reform law? Exactly whose interests do these Asian Americans represent? What are the implications for Asian American community development and political empowerment in the long run?

These are some of the complex questions that must be addressed by scholars in Asian American Studies and community activists concerned about the political development of Asian American communities, if we are to learn anything from the scandal and the racially charged political discourse surrounding the scandal. Even more important is what appropriate trajectory Asian Americans must pursue to achieve political empowerment if they possess neither the numerical strength of Euro-Americans, African Americans, and Latino Americans, nor the solidarity and financial clout of Jewish Americans.

Racialization of the Scandal

First, there is obviously a racial dimension to the entire scandal, as documented in the Asian American petition filed before the U.S. Commission on Civil Rights. Indeed, the media and partisan power struggle played a decisive role in racializing the scandal and political corruption. For example, two months before the 1996 presidential election, Bill Clinton's two challengers, Republican Bob Dole and Independent Ross Perot, had already tried every conceivable political strategy and arsenal at their disposal to try to seize political power from the Democratic incumbent. But they failed to make a dent into Clinton's commanding lead at the poll. Perhaps out of desperation, and with the help of columnists like William Safire of the *New York Times* and the editorial writers of the *Wall Street Journal*, they decided to dip into the well-entrenched, rich national reservoir of anti-Asian sentiment: they launched an all-out attack on Clinton and the DNC for using John Huang to raise money from illegal foreign Asian sources, most notably James Riady, owner of the Indonesia-based, multinational Lippo Group.[2] Their intention was to incite voter anger against an alleged foreign Asian plot to buy influence in Washington, D.C., and to undermine voters' trust in Clinton. Before long, the foreign "Asian connection" and "Asian Americans" became synonymous with political corruption and foreign subversion, even though Huang and Trie raised about $4.5 million out of the total of $2.2 billion raised and spent in the 1996 federal elections.[3] In fact, Dole, Perot, and the national media went out of their way to "Asianize" or "Orientalize" the political corruption and to lay the problem of corruption squarely on several Asian Americans and their so-called foreign connections in several Asian countries, not the least of which was "communist" China.[4] (The China connection was established initially by the fact that the Lippo Group had investments in China, just as it had investments in the U.S. and several countries throughout the world). Instantly, James Riady, John Huang, Charlie Yahlin Trie, and others became household names, and the mysteries around them deepened with each new disclosure or leak.

In essence, Asian Americans became the menacing "new yellow peril," and worse yet, the "new yellow peril" also happened to be the "Red peril." Clinton, Gore, and the DNC were indirectly accused of selling out the presidency and national interests and of compromising even our national security by accepting money from foreigners and by having "foreign Asian guests" in several events in the White House. This line of nationalist thinking and argument persisted throughout 1997 with Safire insinuating regularly in his *New York Times* columns that several Asian Americans, including John Huang and Charlie Trie, were "Red Chinese" spies. The China conspiracy took on a life of its own in the media and a favorite pastime among the China-bashers from the Left and the Right when Bob Woodward of the Watergate fame reported similar allegations in a sensational "exclusive" in February 1996 in the *Washington Post*.[5] The Woodward article was based on leaks supposedly from counterintelligence sources in the FBI. Since there has been no independent confirmation of the allegation, the leaks could have been politically calculated disinformation campaign, either to discredit Clinton or to make him look like an innocent victim of some vicious "communist plot." Led by Sen. Fred Thompson, Republican chairman of the Senate Governmental Affairs Committee, several committees of both houses also pursued the same line of investigation, aimed at times to discredit Clinton and the DNC and at other times to incite fear of and hostility toward "Red" China. The Thompson Committee conducted four months of highly publicized public hearings, from July to October 1997, aimed at proving two theses: 1) "Red China" laundered money to influence Clinton and subvert American democracy and 2) John Huang and Charlie Trie were Red China's spies.[6] However, the Senate hearings ended abruptly in disarray in November 1997, failing to incite public outrage against Clinton and produce any credible evidence in support of its two theses.[7] The hearings also raised disturbing questions about the GOP strategy of concentrating primarily on alleged Asian American wrong-doings and demonizing China on the one hand and ignoring the central issue of campaign finance reform on the other hand. The Thompson Committee succeeded in using the media to discredit Clinton, the DNC, and China and to divert public attention from the need for campaign finance reform. It also succeeded in racializing the political scandal and demonizing China in the service of American xenophobic nationalism or nativism. The 1977 Congress recessed in December with no findings on the scandal and no legislative measures to reform campaign finance system. As soon as the Monica Lewinsky scandal erupted, both politicians and the media found a new distraction.

Playing the Race Card

But to stop at the superficial level of the partisan power struggle and media sensationalism is to overlook the cynical playing of the race card by the leaders of both political parties and the media. From the start, both Democrats and Republicans played it. The latest round had its origin in the Clinton presidential campaign. Under chairman Ron Brown, the DNC quietly reinstated what his predecessor, Paul Kirk, had eliminated in 1985, the constituent and ethnic caucuses, and developed a racial strategy in an attempt to expand the party's political mobilization and fundraising capability in various constituencies including minority communities across the nation. John Huang, a former executive of the Indonesian Lippo Group, was recruited to work under then Secretary Ron Brown in the U.S. Commerce Department after the Clinton victory in 1992. He was brought into the DNC in December 1995 specifically to raise "soft money," $7 million to be exact, from Asian American communities to help jumpstart Clinton's 1996 reelection campaign.[8] Since Asian American communities had neither the deep pockets nor the tradition of big-time political giving, Huang, Trie, and others turned to transnational Asian sources in Indonesia, Thailand, Taiwan, Hong Kong, South Korea, Japan, etc. (It is unclear if Huang, Trie, and the DNC knowingly conflated Asian Americans and foreign Asians when they decided to solicit political donations from these transnational sources.) The rapid integration of global economy after the Cold War, especially in the growing ties between the U.S. and dynamic East and Southeast Asian economies and in increasing Asian investment in the Asian American communities, made their fundraising strategy easy. Besides, Huang had the necessary credentials and connections to accept the DNC assignment and to exploit the transnational connections.

However, Dole, Perot, and anti-Clinton forces in the media saw the role of John Huang quite differently: they detected his vulnerability and decided to exploit the racist sentiment against Asians and Asian Americans, as has been done repeatedly throughout the history of the U.S. They accused Clinton and the DNC of selling the presidency to foreign Asians and Asian Americans, deliberately conflating the two and treating both as foreigners. Overnight, the scandal was racialized and Asian Americans were collectively and effectively *de-naturalized* in the eyes of the public. In addition to putting Clinton and Democrats on the defensive, the perception that all Asians were foreigners or noncitizens had the immediate effect of rendering them convenient targets for public suspicion, resentment, and outrage.

Sensing their vulnerability, Clinton and the DNC decided to play the same race card, but to turn it on the Republicans. At the suggestion of Sen. Christopher Dodd, the general chair of the DNC, several Asian American national leaders and organizations called a series of coordinated preelection national press conferences before the November presidential election, in which they angrily accused Dole, Perot, and the media of being racist toward Asian Americans for depicting Asian Americans indiscriminately as foreigners and characterizing Asian contributions as "foreigners buying up America."[9] Suddenly, Huang became a victim of Republican and media racism and a symbol of oppressed Asian America. "The Huang matter has become much more than an issue of partisan politics. It has turned from a question of one person's dealings into scapegoating of a racial minority group," wrote press conference participants Stewart Kwoh of Los Angeles and Frank Wu of Washington, D.C., in an op-ed column in the *Los Angeles Times* October 24, 1996. The strategy would have been effective if many of the big donations had not come from questionable if not illegal foreign sources, as postelection investigations soon uncovered. The DNC was forced to return several million dollars to the original donors. It also made several national Asian American organizations vulnerable to editorial ridicule, e.g., the *Boston Globe*, January 21, 1997, and the *Washington Post* on July 10, 1997, and attacks by Asian American Republicans, most notably Susan Au Allen of the U.S. Pan Asian American Chamber of Commerce. She openly accused Asian American leaders and organizations of defending inappropriate fundraising or wrongdoings by John Huang and others at a public briefing at the U.S. Commission on Civil Rights in December 1997.

Unfortunately for Asian Americans, the Clinton victory did not bring an end to the playing of the race card. Immediately after the election, as Republican leaders and national media pressed U.S. Attorney General Janet Reno for the appointment of an Independent Counsel to investigate Clinton, Gore, and the DNC in the scandal, the Democrats quickly dumped Huang on November 17 and began to treat Asian Americans, including some big donors, as if they were strangers or worse—lepers, foreigners, criminals, and subversives. Under mounting pressure, the Democrats played the race card in two different ways. First, the DNC decided after the November election to conduct its own inhouse investigation. The primary political objectives were to do some internal housecleaning and, above all, to demonstrate its commitment to "clean money, including an announcement that it would, hence forth," accept money from *citizens only*, not permanent residents and American subsidiaries of foreign corporations. It hired an army of private auditors and investigators to look for donors of "dirty money," which turned out to mean mostly Asian and Asian American donations. Suddenly, all major Asian donors became targets of overzealous investigation, harrassment, and intimidation. The tactic backfired: many Asian Americans felt harrassed, criminalized, or insulted and they protested loudly and rightly accused the DNC of trying to sanitize its image at the expense of Asian Americans.[10]

Secondly, the Clinton administration decided to also distance itself from Asian Americans in the appointment of high-ranking officials, reneging, thus, on a Clinton promise to have his cabinet reflect the diversity of America. In spite of intense lobbying under the leadership of the Asian Pacific American Coalition for Presidential Appointments, Clinton failed to name any Asian American to both cabinet-level and subcabinet positions. (A belated attempt to appoint Bill Lann Lee to the position of the U.S. Assistant Attorney General for civil rights toward the end of 1997 ended in failure.) Asian Americans became the "collateral casualties," to borrow a military jargon, in the racialized scandal and partisan power struggle. Former chancellor of UC Berkeley Chang-lin Tien was among the first casualties, and even invited Asian American guests of the White House were subjected to humiliation and harassment.[11] In short, both Democrats and Republicans treated Asian Americans as pawns!

Class and Money Politics in the Communities

The most direct benefit from racializing political corruption by both political parties is the diversion of public attention from the crisis facing American democracy. Instead of addressing the systemic problem of money corruption in politics, politicians discovered the perfect distraction: blame the problem on Asian Americans and the unscrupulous "spies" or "agents" of "communist" China. Since the money raised by John Huang, Charlie Trie, and other Asian Americans represents only a tiny fraction of what both parties raised and spent in 1996 and since no evidence has been uncovered on the alleged role of China in trying to subvert American democracy, we must conclude that the racialization of corruption and the subplot of "communist subversion" are calculated attempts by both parties to divert public attention from the real issue, campaign finance reform. Little wonder, both parties have expressed no interest in passing even the toothless McCain-Feingold campaign finance reform bill.[12] Money has effectively become the lifeline of, and prerequisite for, participating in American democracy. Americans have become increasingly alienated from the electoral process. No wonder the fastest-growing and by far the largest political party in the U.S. today is neither Republican nor Democrat but the party of nonvoters. Money has made a mockery of American democracy! The U.S. may be the oldest democracy on earth, in terms of voter participation and access to government, but it has become the most undemocratic country in substance among all the democracies in the world today.

Missing also in this highly racialized political discourse over the role of John Huang, Charlie Trie, and other Asian Americans in the campaign finance scandal is what or whose interests these Asian American leaders really represent. John Huang himself has steadfastly insisted that his sole motive in going into the DNC to do fundraising is to help empower and to represent the interests of Asian Americans across the nation.[13] To him, the only way for the Asian American minority to gain political power and to make its voice heard in the U.S. is to make significant contributions to politicians. Many Asian American political leaders shared this view. In a comprehensive defense of John Huang, for example, Keith Umemoto wrote,

> The relatively low numbers of APA voters compared with other groups and our scarcity of APA representatives holding elected offices accounted for our lack of political influence. One of the ways we have begun to generate success in gaining access and recognition has been through financial contributions. . . . John left the private sector to devote his energy to public service and to help elevate the power of our community by serving as *a bridge* between the influential Asian donors he had access to and the APA community in general.[14]

Yet, when we examine the various fundraising schemes Huang and others had devised and examine the class background of the big Asian donors, it becomes very clear that they represent the interests of a very small class of people within the Asian American communities: a handful of the rich business entrepreneurs and professionals and, above all, persons with extensive connections to transnational Asian capital and multinational corporations based in places like Indonesia, Thailand, Hong Kong, Taiwan, South Korea, and Japan.[15] This is hardly surprising: the overwhelming majority of Asian Americans do not have available cash to make the kind of political donations John Huang and others demanded and brought in. In fact, the majority of Asian Americans fall within the lower and middle classes, desiring only to work hard to make ends meet and, above all, to put their children through schools. Their idea of making it, in other words, is not making huge donations to politicians of either party.

The class-based donations generated by Huang, Trie, and others have their roots in the transformation of Asian economies and the expansion of transnationalism since early 1970s. The geopolitical realignment in Asia following the U.S.-China detente in 1972 and the ensuing influx of Asian immigrants, refugees, and capital to the U.S. inaugurated several new trends in the development of the Asian American communities, not the least of which was increasing demographic, linguistic, and cultural diversity among Asian Americans and growing division and conflict along class and national origin lines within each of the Asian American communities. An example of this conflict is the struggle since 1968 over the International Hotel. The conflict became a housing struggle between a Chinese Thai tycoon, Supasit Mahaguna, and the poor Chinese and Filipino elderly at the International Hotel in San Francisco Chinatown.[16] Owned by San Francisco real estate magnate Walter Schorenstein of Milton Meyer Co., the hotel was sold to Mahaguna in the midst of a political upheaval in Thailand in 1973. The real Asian American victims of transnational capital, as Peter Kwong's study on New York City's Chinatown since the 1970s demonstrates, are the poor and disadvantaged working class. The Riady's investment in the U.S. through the Lippo Group likewise reflects the pattern of flight capital since the early 1970s. John Huang and Charlie Trie, in fact, represent a similar convergence of newly emergent class interests, transnational capital, and, not infrequently, foreign political interests in the Asian American communities, hitherto ignored by the mainstream media and perhaps forgotten by many Asian Americans as well.[17]

From the perspective of Asian American history, persons like John Huang, Johnny Chung, and Charlie Trie are not totally unknown or without their predecessors. Among the earlier big donors, fundraisers, power brokers, or influence peddlers are figures including Eddie Chin of New York and Pius Lee of San Francisco of the 1980s, Tongsun Park and Susie Park Thompson of Washington, D.C., in the so-called Koreagate in 1970s, Anna Chennault of Washington, D.C., of the 1960s, a key figure on the Finance Committee of the National Republican Committee, and H. H. Kung of New York and Albert Chow and Doon Yen Wong of San Francisco in the 1950s.[18] Instead of representing the interests and rights of lower- and middle-class Asian Americans in the communities, they represented primarily the interests of transnational political and economic elite in their insatiable pursuit of profit, market penetration, and political influence. In this sense, what these prominent figures have done does not differ much from what all foreign CEOs, corporations, and governments do routinely in the U.S. to protect their interests by buying political access and influence and extracting economic favors for themselves, whether they are the Riadys of Indonesia, the Bronfmans of Canada, the Rothchilds of France, the Murdochs of Australia, or Bill Gates of the U.S. They represent class and transnational capital interests, competing for resource, market share, profit, and, ultimately, access to political power.

Citizenship and Extraterritoriality

Two other neglected issues of importance in the scandal are citizenship and extraterritoriality, both of which have been largely overlooked by both scholars and the media. Citizenship is the creation and legacy of the modern European nation-state and nationalism and, by definition, a legal and political device designed to convey privileges to some and to exclude others. Thus, Asian immigrants were denied citizenship before World War II, and, since then, Asian Americans have continued to be seen and treated as if they were foreigners, even though, since the late 1960s, the Asian American movement has been doing its utmost to debunk the stereotype and to assert Asian American citizenship. It is this racist legacy or nativism that the Republicans and media sought to reignite and incite and to broadly represent Asian Americans as untrustworthy and unscrupulous aliens eager to buy influence into the Clinton administration and to subvert American democracy and national security. The strategy succeeded in "denaturalizing" Asian Americans and in compelling the Clinton administration to treat Asian Americans as political untouchable, as we saw above. In the context of a partisan political power struggle, Asian Americans were considered weak and expendable, whether they were citizens or not and whether their rights as citizens had been compromised or not. The inevitable outcome was political exclusion.

However, traditional nationalist notions of citizenship, nation-state, sovereignty, national borders, and political loyalty have been called into question and have been undergoing rapid transformation in the age of transnationalism, aided in no small measure by the U.S. and its multinational and transnational corporations. American transnational corporations and their subsidiaries of foreign-owned corporations in the U.S. are treated as U.S. corporations and, under the laws of the U.S., as persons with the same rights and privileges protected by the Constitution, including the right to contribute huge amounts of money, though not the right to vote. The Lippo Group of Indonesia, along with thousands of foreign corporations with registered branch offices and subsidiaries in the U.S., [is] entitled to make legitimate political contributions with virtually no legal restriction and to use [its] contributions to help elect politicians and influence legislation. Many of the executives of these foreign subsidiaries are permanent residents who can also make generous political contributions, even if they have no right to vote. This, of course, is how wealthy business executives routinely gain more effective access to elected officials than American citizens in the U.S. In this regard, the campaign finance scandal has raised important questions about citizenship and the role of transnational corporations and permanent residents in U.S. politics. This issue should have placed the status of foreign subsidiaries, permanent residents, and persons with dual citizenship at the center of campaign finance reform. Incredibly, none of these have been given public attention, not even in the Senate hearings.

Lastly, an integral component of transnationalism is extraterritoriality, an idea deeply imbedded in the history of Western colonialism and imperialism in Asia, in particular, in the infamous unequal treaties imposed by Western imperialist powers on China between 1842, at the end of the Opium War, and 1949. Under the unequal treaty system, China was forced to surrender significant sectors of its sovereign power to the Western imperialists, including customs duties in treaty ports, immunity from Chinese legal jurisdiction, foreign concessions or privileged zones, special treatment of foreign business and Christian missions, and free military access to Chinese ports. This type of extraterritorial power undermined the Chinese sovereign state and inspired Chinese nationalism at home and abroad. Not quite as harsh as what the U.S. and other countries had imposed on China under the unequal treaties, the U.S. government, businesses, and the so-called nongovernmental organizations (NGOs) have, since the Cold War began, routinely carried out this tradition by interfering both covertly and overtly with other countries' political and economic affairs, including massive use of public money to influence elections in well over one hundred countries, the most recent of which was in the Boris Yeltsin's presidential campaign.[19] In fact, our long-standing practice of intervening in the political affairs of other countries has severely undermined the credibility of our claim of Chinese or Indonesian interference with the 1996 presidential election. Worse yet, even as politicians and newspapers conducted their investigation into and denounced claims of Chinese interference in the electoral process, at no time did they mention, much less show any interest in investigating, what the U.S. government, transnational corporations, and NGOs have been doing in influencing and manipulating the internal affairs of countries worldwide.

Within the Asian American communities, there is also a perverse reciprocity in the exercise of extraterritorial domination. Historically, due to racist and exclusionary policies toward Asian immigrants, Asian American ghettoes were established and community affairs were left largely to the control of the business elite and, above all, to agents of foreign Asian governments. Throughout their histories, Asian Americans were discriminated against by the mainstream, and their community affairs were dominated and manipulated by the business and political interests of their homeland countries, giving rise to the highly institutionalized extraterritorial domination of Asian governments. For example, the Chinese American and Korean American communities were used by Taiwan and South Korea to support their respective military dictatorships throughout the Cold War and to lobby the interests of the two governments.[20] Community dissidents or critics were invariably intimidated, harassed, and sometimes subjected to physical violence, including murder. Since the early 1970s, foreign Asian businesses have frequently used Asian American communities for their investment and as their covers or beachheads for launching their penetration into the American market.[21] These investments have had a profound impact on the lives and businesses in the Asian American communities, especially in terms of class relations and political development. The influx of transnational capital in the past twenty-five years has brought mixed blessings into the communities and has effectively marginalized the original vision and mission of the Asian American movement, replacing grassroots political mobilization for community improvement and empowerment with money-influence politics. Some of the most important fundraising activities of John Huang, in fact, fit into this historical pattern.[22] If Asian Americans are to achieve full freedom and citizenship in the U.S., they must be liberated from the new forms of racial oppression and extraterritorial domination as manifested through the campaign finance scandal.

Conclusion

One of the most remarkable things about the so-called Asian connection in the 1996 campaign finance scandal was how a molehill was transformed into a mountain by the media; the Republican leaders, a few right-wing columnists, and the Thompson Committee succeeded in portraying China as the No. 1 villain without a shred of evidence. John Huang was personally responsible for raising about $3.5 million out of a total of $2.2 billion raised and spent in just the 1996 federal elections, excluding money raised and spent in state and local elections. Yet, he and other Asian American fundraisers received at least 90 percent of media coverage. In the process, they became the obsession of Republican-controlled congressional hearings and the targets of endless investigation by the operatives of both parties and by the U.S. Department of Justice. (The obsession was finally eclipsed by the Monica Lewinsky/Paula Jones story in late 1997.) By indiscriminately mingling reporting with opinion and speculation, the media and Republicans deliberately conflated Asian Americans with foreign Asians and fabricated an imagined connection and conspiracy between Asian contributors with "Red" China, already being vilified and demonized by both the Right (antiabortion, Christian Right, pro-Taiwan, isolationists, Patrick Buchanan, Jesse Helm, etc.) and the Left (human rights groups, AFL-CIO, pro-Tibet, environmentalists, Richard Gephardt, Nancy Pelosi, etc.) in the post–Cold War era.

Both Democrats and Republicans in the political elite generously exploited the race card for their respective advantages and against each other as they had done routinely. Since the arrival of the Chinese during the Gold Rush and succeeding Asian immigrants were repeatedly used by political parties to incite nativism and racism and to garner populist votes. In the 1996 election, the Democrats targeted Asian Americans and foreign Asians to raise some "soft money" to jump-start the Clinton reelection campaign while the Republicans seized upon the vulnerability of the Democrats by exploiting the anti-Asian and anti-foreign sentiment with the so-called foreign Asian connection to discredit Clinton and the Democrats. Sensing their vulnerability, the Democrats advanced the anti-Asian thesis before the November election, only to distance and abandon Asian Americans after the election in order to protect the Clinton presidency and to demonstrate their commitment to the so-called clean money and politics. In short, both parties unscrupulously used Asian Americans to racialize the issue of political corruption and in the process, to divert public demand for campaign finance reform.

Racialization of the campaign finance scandal seriously challenged Asian Americans across the nation, especially the political and intellectual leadership of the communities. The major questions were how Asian Americans should correctly analyze and understand the issue and how best to respond to the issue. Certainly, it was important for Asian American community leaders and activists to meet the challenge head-on. Before the November 1996 election, one strategy was to view it solely as an issue of identity politics and incorporation within the existing campaign finance political patronage system and to mobilize the communities accordingly to fight media and Republican racism. Were community leaders being victimized by racism. This analysis and strategy assumed his innocence and, above all, homogeneity within the Asian American communities. The same perspective saw no flaw in the campaign finance system and the political institution. If everyone was doing it, why couldn't the Asians do it as well! This, in fact, was the dominant perspective. It is, in my opinion, short-sighted and wrong. As more and more disclosures of wrongdoing came to light after the election, the position rapidly lost its credibility.

Another scenario was to view John Huang and his collaborators as representatives of an increasingly fragmented Asian American community, separated by national origin, generation, linguistic and cultural differences, and, above all, class distinctions and to see Huang as a representative of a growing transnational business and professional elite in the Asian American communities. This elite, according to this analysis, is fully integrated with transnational and, at times, flight Asian capital which needs to establish a beachhead in the U.S. Asian American communities come in handy, and they become the vehicle used to penetrate the U.S. market and politics for its own interests. Accordingly, the Asian American communities become a convenient shelter for investment and extraterritorial economic and political domination and penetration. The interests of transnational capital is incompatible with the interests of the communities. Contradiction between these interests in the Asian American communities becomes inevitable, and, as a consequence, community development and welfare are rendered secondary or subordinate to the interests of transnational capital. From the vantage of transnational capital, conflation of Asian Americans and foreign Asians or obfuscation of citizens and aliens is strategically necessary and expedient if the elite [are] to dominate the communities and move smoothly and swiftly into the world of corporate America and be competitive in both politics and economics. From the point of view of the American corporate elite, Asian Americans provided also an effective bridge for American penetration into the emerging Asian economies.

Still another perspective on the Asian entanglement in the campaign finance scandal is to see John Huang and other Asian Americans as symptomatic of a larger problem in American democracy. From this point of view, Asian Americans embroiled in the scandal represent the tip of an iceberg called political corruption. Money, according this view, has become the prerequisite for democratic participation and the only means toward gaining both access and influence in politics. This is the cancer in American democracy. From this perspective, Asian Americans have been dealt a severe blow and setback because of the racialization of the scandal. They have become "denaturalized" and effectively linked to an alleged Chinese conspiracy. By viewing the John Huang case as a symptom of a larger problem and racialization as a pretext to divert public attention from the need for campaign finance reform, Asian Americans can treat the setback as a rare opportunity to clarify many key issues in both the communities and the nation, to deal effectively and unapologetically against racism. Asian Americans can join forces with other public interest and community groups in a nationwide movement to achieve substantive, not superficial or procedural, campaign finance reform. Such efforts would help revive and restore democracy in the U.S. As long as money is inextricably tied to the electoral process, more and more Americans, including Asian Americans, will be alienated from and drop out of the political process. Public financing of elections appears to be the only viable remedy to remove the cancer and to restore faith in democracy.

NOTES

1. "In the U.S. Commission on Civil Rights: Petition for Hearing," a twenty-three-page petition submitted by attorneys Edward M. Chen and Dale Minami on behalf of several Asian American individuals and organizations, September 10, 1997. K. Connie Kang and Robert L. Jackson, "Asian Americans Charge Fund-Raising Scandal Bias," *The Los Angeles Times*, September 12, 1997; Steven A. Holmes, "Asian American Groups File a Complaint of Bias in Inquiries and Coverage," *The New York Times*, September 12, 1997. In response to the petition, the U.S. Commission on Civil Rights prepared a forty-three-page briefing paper, "Asian Pacific American Petition: Brief Paper," and conducted a public briefing session on December 5, 1997 in which several witnesses, including this writer, presented evidence of civil rights violations to the commission. See Wendy Koch, "Asian Groups Protest Probe,"*San Francisco Examiner*, December 6, 1997; Helen Zia, "Can Asian Americans Turn the Media Tide?" *The Nation* 265:21, December 22, 1997, 10.

2. In rapid succession, William Safire wrote several columns on the so-called Asian Connection: "The Asian Connection," "Get Raidy, Get Set . . ." "Absence of Outrage," "Lippo Suction," "Huang Huang Blues," and "Helping Janet Reno," *The New York Times*, October 7, 10, 21, 28, November 4, December 5, 1996; "Wealthy Indonesian Businessman Has Strong Ties to Clinton" and "Family Tied to Democratic Party Gifts Built an Indonesian Empire," *The New York Times*, October 11 and 20, 1996; "Soft Money, Easy Access," *Newsweek*, October 13, 1997; Peter Waldman, "East Meets West: By Courting Clinton, Lippo Gains Stature," *The Wall Street Journal*, October 16, 1996; "Candidates for Sale: Clinton's Asia Connection," a cover story of *Newsweek*, October 28, 1996; Kevin Merida and Serge F. Kovaleski, "Mysteries Arise All Along the Asian Money Trail," *The Washington Post*, November 1, 1996; John Greenwald, "The Cash Machine: Was Huang a Maverick or Part of a Scheme to Shake Down Foreign Tycoons?" *Time*, November 11, 1996; Sara Fritz, "Huang, Riady Paths Crossed at Commerce," *The Los Angeles Times*, December 4, 1996. For a summary of the unfolding scandal at the end of 1996, see, "Column One: How DNC Got Caught in a Donor Dilemma," *The Los Angeles Times*, December 23, 1996; David E. Rosenbaum, "In Political Money Game, The Year of Big Loopholes," *The New York Times*, December 26, 1996; Ruth Marcus and Charles R. Babcock, "The System Cracks Under the Weight of Cash," *The Washington Post*, February 9, 1997.

3. The $2.2 billion figure comes from a report published by the Center for Responsive Politics, a public interest research organization based in Washington, D.C. The report, entitled *The Big Picture: Money Follows Power Shift on Capital Hill*, was released on November 25, 1997. "Cost of '96 Campaigns Sets Record at $2.2 Billion," *The New York Times*, November 25, 1997. The complete report can be read on the internet at the Center's webpage at www.crp.org. See also Ellen Miller and Randy Kehlen, "Mischievous Myths about Money in Politics," *Dollars and Sense*, July/August 1996, 22–27 and Anthony Corrado, "Campaign '96: Money Talks," *In These Times* 20:26, November 11, 1996, 18–21.

4. The so-called China connection of money raised by Huang, Trie, and others did not

surface until *The New York Times* columnist William Safire first constructed the link in his article "I Remember Larry," *The New York Times*, January 2, 1997; "Beware the Princelings (of China)," *The New York Times*, February 13, 1997. Before that January 2 date, most of the allegations of wrongdoing were based on money raised from the Riadys and the Lippo Group of Indonesia. A possible source of this thesis may be found in a rightwing publication, *The American Spectator*, which published two articles by James Ring Adams, "What's Up in Jakarta?" and John Huang's Bamboo Network," respectively, in September 1995 and December 1996. The China connection was given a new boost when the press reported that Wang Jun, Chairman of the Poly Technologies group, the Chinese army's arms exporting company, was among the guests in one of the many coffee gatherings at the White House on February 6, 1996. See Michael Weisskopf and Lena H. Sun, "Trie Gained Entree for Chinese Official," *The Washington Post*, December 20, 1996; David E. Sanger, "Businessman at White House Social Has Close Ties to China's Military Power," *The New York Times*, December 21, 1996; Steven Mufson, "Chinese Denies Seeking White House Visit," *The Washington Post*, March 16, 1997.

5. Bob Woodward and Brian Duffy, "Chinese Embassy Role in Fund-Raising Probed," *The Washington Post*, February 13, 1997. See also Mark Hosenball and Evan Thomas, "White House: A China Connection?" and "A Break in the Case," *Newsweek*, February 24 and May 19, 1997 Silverstein, "The New China Hands: How the Fortune 500 Is China's Strongest Lobby," *The Nation*, February 17, 1997, 11–16; Nigel Holloway, "The China Connection," *The Far Eastern Economic Review* (Hong Kong), February 27, 1997, 16; David Johnston, "U.S. Agency Secretly Monitored Chinese in '96 on Political Gifts," *The New York Times*, March 13, 1997; "The China Connection," *The Economist* (London), March 15, 1997; Kenneth R. Timmerman, "All Roads Lead to China" and "China's 22nd Province (California)," *The American Spectator*, March 1997, 30–38, and October 1997; Marcus W. Brauchli, Phil Kuntz, and Leslie Chang, "Vying for Influence: Fund-Raising Flap Has Roots in Bitter Rivalry between China, Taiwan," *The Wall Street Journal*, April 4, 1997. Among the most sensational reports is the cover story "Selling Out? China Syndrome" by Rich Lowry, in *The National Review* 49:5, March 24, 1997, 38–40; Phil Kuntz, "Asian Tycoon with Ties to China Visited White House," *The Wall Street Journal*, July 31, 1997; Christopher Matthews, "Clinton's Open-door Policy with China," *The San Francisco Examiner*, July 13, 1997. Even after the failure of the Senate committee to substantiate the original points raised by his article, Woodward continued to press his points based on leaks, "FBI Had Overlooked Key Files in Probe Chinese Influence," *The Washington Post*, November 14, 1997. For a different take on this point, see David Sanger, " 'Asian Money,' American Fears," *The New York Times*, January 5, 1997; Joel Kotkin, "Asian Americans Left Holding the Bay," *The Wall Street Journal*, January 23, 1997; Franklin Foer, "The Chinese Connection," *Slate*, March 15, 1997; "America's Dose of Sinophobia," *The Economist*, March 29, 1997, 35–36.

6. David E. Rosenbaum, "Huang May Yet Testify to Senate Panel: As Hearings Open, Chairman Alleges a Chinese Plot," *The New York Times*, July 9, 1997. Sen. Thompson's opening statement can be found in *The New York Times*, July 9, 1997, A–11; Lance Gay, "Foreign Influence—Lifting the Veil," *The San Francisco Examiner*, July 6, 1997. Even as the Republicans on the Thompson Committee were publicly advancing the Chinese conspiracy theory, Sheila Kaplan of MS-NBC reported July 21, 1997, that no one on the committee subscribed to the theory. Sheila Kaplan, "GOP Backpedals on Huang Accusation So Far; Hearings Are Leaving Republicans Dissatisfied."

7. Francis X. Clines, "Campaign Panel to End Hearings on Fund-Raising," and David E. Rosenbaum "News Analysis: Senate Committee Failed to Zero in on the Verities of Campaign Finance" in the *The New York Times*, November 1, 1997. In its 1,500-page draft final report,

the Thompson Committee blamed Clinton, Gore, and the DNC for widespread improper fundraising, but it failed to substantiate the two primary theses of the Republicans. See Jill Abramson and Don Van Natta, Jr., "Draft of Report for G.O.P. Attacks Clinton Campaign" and David E. Sanger and Don Van Natta, Jr., " 'China Area' Tied to 'Illegal' Gifts: Senate Republicans Can't Link the Contributions to Beijing," *The New York Times*, February 8 and 11, 1998. The draft report is so vague that the editorials of the *The New York Times* and the *The Washington Post* could not agree on its findings of the China connection. *The New York Times* saw credibility in the China thesis, but not *The Washington Post*. "The Prince of Scandal Fatigue," *The New York Times*, February 12, 1998, and "The China Connection," *The Washington Post*, February 12, 1998.

8. The DNC Plan for the Asian American fundraising drive is entitled "National Asian Pacific American Campaign Plan," code name "Constituency Outreach Plan." The plan was drawn up in April 1996 by the Asian Pacific American Working Group, formed in February 1996, which included several prominent Asian American political insiders in the beltway. Tim Weiner and David E. Sanger, "Democrats Hoped to Raise \$7 Million from Asians in the U.S.," *The New York Times*, December 28, 1996; Ruth Marcus, "Oval Office Meeting Set DNC Asian Funds Network in Motion," *The Washington Post*, December 29, 1996.

9. The role of Sen. Dodd in instigating the strategy and press conferences was not known until after the election. His role was discovered among the DNC documents subpoenaed by the Justice Department. See Jill Zuckman, "DNC Stumbles on Asian Issue," *The Boston Globe*, January 19, 1997. The four press conferences were held in New York, Los Angeles, Chicago, and Washington, D.C. The press conference in Washington, D.C, included representatives from the Congressional Asian Pacific American Caucus Institute (CAPACI), the Organization of Chinese Americans (OCA), the Japanese American Citizens League (JACL), Filipino American Civil Rights Advocates (FACRA), National Conference of Korean American Leaders (NCKAL), India Abroad Center for Political Awareness, and the American Association for Physicians from India. See Michael Fletcher, "Coalition Says DNC Fundraising Flap Generating 'Asian-Bashing,' " *The Washington Post*, October 23, 1996; K. Connie Kang, "Asian Gifts Coverage Called Stereotyping," *The Los Angeles Times*, October 23, 1996; Frank H. Wu, "The John Huang Affair: The Controversy Involves Much More than Dollars for the DNC," *Asianweek*, November 1, 1997. Two of the participants at the press conferences, Stewart Kwoh and Frank Wu, also coauthored an op-ed piece, "Don't Build Reform on a Scapegoat," *The Los Angeles Times*, October 24, 1996.

10. On February 28, 1997, the DNC announced the results of its audit and its decision not to accept "any contribution from any individual who is not a U.S. citizen," meaning "contributions from legal permanent residents" and "contribution from a U.S. subsidiary of a foreign company or any other corporation which is majority-owned by non-U.S. citizens" are no longer lawful and acceptable. Alison Mitchell, "Democrats Say They Will Return More Money with Murky Sources," *The New York Times*, February 22, 1997; K. Connie Kang, "Asian Americans Bristle at Democrats' 'Interrogation,' " *The Los Angeles Times*, February 27, 1997; "Thanked with an Insult: Asian Americans Are Right to Be Offended by Democrats' Inquiries—An Editorial," *Los Angeles Times*, March 3, 1997.

11. Seth Rosenfeld, "Tien Ties to Asia Money May Have Cost Him Job: Source Says Clinton Leery of Hearings for a Cabinet Post," *The San Francisco Examiner*, December 22, 1996; Lena Sun, "Asian Names Scrutinized at White House; Guards Stopped Citizens Who Looked 'Foreign,' " *The Washington Post*, September 11, 1997.

12. The McCain-Feingold bill (S. 25, 105th Congress, 1st Session, January 21, 1997) is designed to ban the "soft money" contributions and to advance several incremental reforms,

among which are more stringent disclosure requirements, strong regulatory power for the Federal Election Commission, and restrictions on the so-called issue advertisements. Examples of bipartisan opposition to the McCain-Feingold bill and any kind of campaign finance reform can be seen from the following sample headlines from *The New York Times* in 1997: "GOP Panel See No Major Flaw in Fund-Raising Rules," July 19, 1997; "Despite Controversy, Money Continues to Pour into Party Coffers," August 6, 1997; "The Talk in Washington: With Eyes on 2000, the Big Issue Is Money," September 3, 1997; "Campaign Finance Measure Blocked in Senate Votes," October 8, 1997; and "After 1996, Campaign Finance Laws in Shreds," November 2, 1997; Doug Ireland, "Thompson's Supporting Role: The Senator Follows the Script to Preserve Corrupt Campaign Financing," *The Nation*, July 21, 1997, 21–24, For a debate on campaign finance reform issues, see the special issue of the *American Prospect: A Journal for the Liberal Imagination* 36, January/February 1998; "Money and Politics: Politicians for Rent," *The Economist*, February 8, 1997, 23–25.

13. Ying Chan, "Assailed Dem; Cash Man Talks," *The New York Daily News*, June 16, 1997, and "Huang: Fund-Raising Charges Biased," an exclusive interview of John Huang with the *Zhongguo Shibao (The China Times* of Taiwan), translated by the Associated Press, December 3, 1997. "I only hoped to try my utmost to help Asian Americans exercise some strength," he said in the interview. He also blamed "muckraking by the media" for what he called "unfair allegations against Asian Americans." See also, "From Hero to Political Hot Potato: John Huang Brought in Millions for Democrats While Working to Give Asian Americans Clout" and "John Huang: Man in Middle of Political Storm," *The Los Angeles Times*, October 19 and 23, 1996; K. Connie Kang, David Rosenzweig, and Alan Miller, "John Huang, A Changed Lifestyle, Friends Say," *The Los Angeles Times*, August 3, 1997; Michael Isikoff and Mark Hosenball, "Scandal: Calling All Lawyers," *Newsweek*, November 11, 1996; Stephen Labaton, "Democrats Urged Huang to Raise More Money," *The New York Times*, December 22, 1996; Leslie Wayne, "Huang Donated Thousands to Congressional Contests," *The New York Times*, March 2, 1997; Brian Duffy, "A Fund-Raiser's Rise and Fall," *The Washington Post*, May 13, 1997.

14. Keith Umemoto, "In Defense of John Huang," *Asian Week*, November 29, 1996, 7. This article is representative of the view of most of the Asian American political insiders.

15. For a highly Orientalized depiction of the major Asian figures involved in the scandal, see Lena Sun and J. Pomfret, "The Curious Cast of Asian Donors; Some Sought Access to Clinton, Others' Motives Remain Murky," *The Washington Post*, January 27, 1997. For the various schemes used to raise political donations from Asian and Asian American sources, see "South Korean's Firms (Cheong Am America Inc.); Democrats Reimburse Temple for Fund-Raiser" and "Principals Say (Hsi Lai) Temple Event Was Explicit Fund-Raiser," *The Los Angeles Times*, October 19 and November 3, 1996; "Vanish After Gift to Democrats," *The Los Angeles Times*, October 17, 1996; "Controversy Swirling around (Yogesh) Gandhi Donation Grows," *The Los Angeles Times*, October 24, 1996; "Democrats Return $324,000 Gift from Gandhi Relative," *The Los Angeles Times*, November 7, 1996; Glenn F. Bunting, "Democrats Return $253,500 to Thai Businesswoman (Pauline Kanchanalak)," *The Los Angeles Times*, November 21, 1997; Alan C. Miller, "Democrats Give Back More Disputed Money (from Indonesian Couple)," *Los Angeles Times*, November 23, 1996; Jonathan Peterson and Sara Fritz, "Clinton Legal Team Returns $600,000 in Contributions," *The Los Angeles Times*, December 17, 1996; Christopher Drew, "Asian Links of a Donor Put Gifts to Democrats in Doubt," *The New York Times*, February 22, 1997; Judy Keen, Judi Hasson, and Tom Squitieri, "Dinner Raised $488,000 — And Questions," *USA Today*, February 7, 1997; Nancy Gibbs, "Cash-and-Carry Diplomacy,"*Time*, February 24, 1997, 22–25; Michael Duffy and Michael

Weisskopf, "Johnny Come Often," *Newsweek*, March 3, 1997, 24–28; Eyal Press, "The Suharto Lobby," *The Progressive* 61:5, May 1997, 19–31; D. Van Natta, "Donations to Democrats Traced to Phony Firms and Dead Person," *The New York Times*, July 6, 1997. Thus far, three Asian Americans have been convicted of illegal activities in connection with campaign fund-raising. Nora T. and Gene K. J. Lum, wife and husband, were convicted and sentenced to ten-month imprisonment for funneling illegal contributions to several politicians. See George Lardner, Jr., "Two Donors Agree to Plead Guilty" and "Judge Sets 10-Month Term in Political Donations Case," *The Washington Post*, May 22 and September 10, 1997. The couple was also the focus of a special *Frontline* report, "The *Fixers*," produced by Michael Kirk and Kenneth Levis, aired April 14, 1997, and a long article, "American Guanxi" by Peter J. Boyer in *The New Yorker* 72:8, April 14, 1997, 48–61. Republican Congressman Jay Kim pleaded guilty to illegal fundraising and misuse of campaign money. See David Rosensweig, "Rep. Kim, Wife to Plead Guilty to Misdemeanors," *The Los Angeles Times*, August 1, 1997; Walter Pincus, "Kim Probe Found Wide Variety of Campaign Violations," *The Washington Post*, August 19, 1997. Charlie Yah-lin Trie, a key figure in the scandal, surrendered himself to law enforcement authorities on February 3, 1998. See David Johnston, "Key Figure in Campaign Fundraising Inquiry Surrenders to Federal Authorities," *The New York Times*, February 4, 1998. For a case study on how the Chinese American community in San Francisco became fragmented by class and politics, see L. Ling-chi Wang, "Exclusion and Fragmentation in Ethnic Politics: Chinese Americans in Urban Politics," in *The Politics of Minority Coalitions: Race, Ethnicity, and Shared Uncertainties*," edited by Wilbur C. Rich, 129–142 (Westport, Connecticut: Praeger, 1996).

16. Beatrice Dong, "An Analysis of the International Hotel Struggle," a Senior Honors Thesis, Department of Ethnic Studies, University of California, Berkeley, November 22, 1994.

17. Peter Kwong, *The New Chinatown* (New York: Wang and Hill, 1987). For articles on foreign government interests in U.S. politics and government, see Jill Abramson, "Taiwan Won Platform Terms with Democrats," *The Wall Street Journal*, October 25, 1996; "Taiwan Political Donations Implicated in the U.S. Presidential Election (in Chinese)," in the *Yazhou Zhoukan* (Hong Kong), October 15, 1996; Paul Jacob, "In Jakarta: Riady's Actions Benefited Indonesia, Says Suharto's Son," *The Strait Times* (Singapore), October 20, 1996; Sara Fritz and Rone Tempest, "Ex-Clinton Aide Arranged for Taiwan Connection," *The Los Angeles Times*, October 30, 1996; Keith Richburg and Dan Morgan, "Taiwanese: Ex-Clinton Aide Said He Was Raising Money," *The Washington Post*, October 30, 1996; John M. Broder, "Taiwan Lobbying in U.S. Gets Results," *The Los Angeles Times*, November 4, 1996; Michael Isidoff and Melinda Liu, "Scandal: Now, The Taiwan Axis," *The Newsweek*, November 4, 1996; Maggie Farley, "Claim of Campaign Offer Clouds Taiwan Diplomacy" and "Clinton Met Foreign Donor to Discuss U.S.-China Trade," *The Los Angeles Times*, November 9 and 16, 1996; "Indonesian Fulfills Aim for Firm, Nation," *The Los Angeles Times*, October 16, 1996; Stephen Labaton, "Indonesian Magnate and Clinton Talked Policy, White House Says," *The New York Times*, November 5, 1996; Sharon LaFraniere and Susan Schmidt, "NSC Gave Warnings about Asian Donors," *The Washington Post*, February 15, 1997.

18. No systematic study has been done of the ways foreign Asian governments have tried to buy political and foreign policy influence in the U.S. through the various Asian American communities. The following articles provide a glimpse into how Asian governments extended their extraterritorial domination in the Asian American communities to interfere with American politics: Alejandro A. Esclamado, "The Story of the Marcos Coercion;" Woon-Ha Kim, "The Activities of the South Korean Central Intelligence Agency in the U.S.;" Brett de Bary and Victor Nee, "The Kuomintang in Chinatown;" H. Mark Lai, "China Politics and the U.S. Chinese Communities." All these studies are found in *Counterpoint: Perspectives on Asian*

America, edited by Emma Gee and published by the Asian American Studies Center of the University of California, Los Angeles, 1976. For more general studies see Ross Y. Koen, *The China Lobby in American Politics* (New York: Harper, 1974); Stanley D. Bachrack, *The Committee of One Million: 'China Lobby Politics, 1953–1971* (New York: Columbia University Press, 1976); and Robert Boettcher, *Gifts of Deceit: Sun Myung Moon, Tongsun Park and the Korean Scandal* (New York: Holt, Rinehart and Winston, 1980). For a recent example, see Laurence Zuckerman, "Taiwan Keeps a Step Ahead of China in U.S. Lobbying," *The New York Times*, March 14, 1997. For a more theoretical treatment of the subject of extraterritoriality in the Chinese American experience, see L. Ling-chi Wang, "The Structure of Dual Domination: Toward a Paradigm for the Study of the Chinese Diaspora in the United States," *Amerasia Journal*, 21:1 & 2 (1995), 149–170.

19. Norman Solomon, "Money Scandals: 'Mr. Smith' Goes to Washington," *The Minneapolis Star-Tribune*, March 16, 1997; Wendy Koch, "US helps Sway Vote in Foreign Countries; Taxpayers Bankroll Overseas Programs," *The San Francisco Examiner*, October 24, 1997; John Broder, "Foreign Taint on National Election? A Boomerang for U.S.," *The New York Times*, March 31, 1997; James Risen, Alan Miller, "DNC Donor's Offer of Funds to Yeltsin Told," *The Los Angeles Times*, September 10, 1997.

20. Illsoo Kim, *New Urban Immigrants: The Korean Community in New York* (Princeton: Princeton University Press, 1981), 225–241; L. Ling-chi Wang, *Politics of Assimilation and Repression: A History of the Chinese in the U.S. since World War II*, 1981, Chapter 8, an unpublished manuscript, Ethnic Studies Library, University of California, Berkeley. See also, L. Ling-chi Wang, "The Structure of Dual Domination," 149–170.

21. For a general discussion on the transformation of the Asian American communities since the 1970s, see L. Ling-chi Wang, "The Politics of Ethnic Identity and Empowerment: The Asian American community since the 1960s," *Asian American Policy Review*, 2 (Spring 1991), 51–55. The most famous example of extraterritorial domination and repression by a foreign Asian government is the political assassination of Chinese American journalist Henry Liu by hired agents of the Taiwan government on October 15, 1994, in his home in Daly City, California, because he had written articles and books critical of Taiwan's president, Chiang Ching-kuo. For a detailed account of this case, see David Kaplan, *Fire of the Dragon: Politics, Murder, and the Kuomintang* (New York Atheneum, 1992). See also "Henry Liu: Justice Is Stonewalled," by L. Ling-chi Wang, in *Silenced: The Unsolved Murders of Immigrant Journalists in the United State*, edited by Juan Gonzalez (New York: Committee to Protect Journalists), 47–56. Only very preliminary studies have been made on the foreign Asian investments in the Asian American communities. Among them are: Peter Kwong, *The New Chinatown* (New York: Hill and Wang, 1987); Paul Ong, Edna Bonacich, and Lucie Cheng, *The New Asian Immigration in Los Angeles and Global Restructuring* (Philadelphia: Temple University Press, 1994), Timothy Fong, *The First Suburban Chinatown: The Remaking of Monterey Park, California* (Philadelphia: Temple University Press, 1994).

22. This conclusion is based on my own review of Asian American contributions through John Huang in the 1996–96 cycle. The big contributors, those contributing more than $5,000, made up a lion's share of the $3.5 million he raised for the DNC and the Clinton reelection campaign. Most of the biggest donors have extensive foreign connections.

Chapter Twenty-four

A Letter to My Sister

Lisa Park

It's been almost six years since your suicide. Now when I think about you (and I think about you often), I feel you are somehow with me. My dreams of us together are as vivid and life-composing as any conscious, waking moment. Some like to think that our waking lives are more real, because we believe we can determine them through the choices we make, and that our dreams are merely their epiphenomenal reflections or, worse, expressions of unfulfilled desires. Your presence is more than a memory or a wish. My dreams are ghostly impressions of our collective past, as well as a spontaneous living of experiences I know we never shared before you died, like the dream I had of you and me walking arm in arm. I remembered it as if it was a lost memory, even though I know it never "really happened." I am sometimes grateful for this, because your phantom presence helps me to continue remembering, which I know is important even though it almost rips me apart. No matter how hard I try to subdue, through forgetting, the pain that came with the destruction of our lives, I must bear witness to the crimes committed against you (and against us) that led to your suicide. Conscious memories require constant attention, or else history will erase what happened, and you will disappear as if you had never existed at all. Isn't this why you haunt me to this day, to inscribe what you had learned from living under siege?

I remember the first time, when I found you after you had cut your wrists with a kitchen knife, and later when our father, using his deft surgical skills, sewed you back up in his office. For a while after you had cut your wrists, you undertook to "better" your life and attitude, even though it inevitably meant reinserting yourself into the old vise of conformity. One of the ways you tried to affirm your "new" resolve was to change your physical appearance through plastic surgery, for which our parents willingly put up the money in an effort to keep you happy. They were at their wits' end trying to appease you, but their efforts to pacify you pushed you further into self-hatred. (The annihilation of uniqueness and self-worth is indeed the pacifying aim.) Your obsession with plastic surgery exposed the myth of the whole beauty industry, which portrays plastic surgery as a beautifying, renewing experience, "something special you do just for you." It began with your eyes and nose, and you continued to go back for more. You tried to box yourself into a preconditioned, Euroamerican ideal and literally excised the parts that would not fit. But plastic surgery is irreversible, and so were the twenty-one years of assimilation. You told the doctors in the psychiatric ward, where they placed you just after your second suicide attempt, the reason you took all those pills (which your psychiatrist had given you) was because the plastic surgeons had "ruined" your face. Did you come to a realization (under the advice of your doctors) that you were obsessed with changing your looks, which could only dishearten you further because it medically legitimated your neurosis? Or did you think that the surgery botched up your corporeal plan, which you realized you would have had to live with for the rest of your life? The plastic surgeon referred you to a psychiatrist to help you "work out" your obsession. Help is a four-letter word. You decided death was your only alternative to being stuck with an inescapable body. As soon as you were released from the hospital, you committed yourself to finding a way to kill yourself. Now, on top of what you considered a mistake of a body, you wanted to avoid being thrown into a mental institution, where you were sure you were headed as a consequence of being found out by the psychiatrists.

The first time was different in many ways. First of all, no professional psychologists or mental health experts knew about it. Everyone in our family kept your suicide attempt secret and normalized it as if it had never happened. Secondly, I know you did not want to die, but to get our attention. I remember coming home and discovering you in bed with your wrists bandaged and the bathtub full of blood and water. You thrust your limp arms into the air and cried, pleading for my help. I was devastated, broken-hearted, sickened, and bizarrely nervous all the while about what our parents would do if they had to be interrupted at work! I looked to our brothers for direction, but they acted as if there was no big emergency. I convinced myself that you were not dying, that your slashed wrists were not much worse than a cut finger. When our parents finally discovered you, they became hysterical and burst into wails of anguish—I was so taken aback by their rare show of sympathy that I began crying myself, throwing my body onto yours, because only then did I feel safe enough to reach out to you. Once our mother wondered aloud why I had not told them right away about your suicide attempt. I did not explain myself to her, but it was because all the violence in our lives, both physical and emotional, made your suicide attempt seem normal, everyday. It was not that I was unaware of what a crisis looked like, but that I was used to having to assimilate them into quotidian experience. I was more worried about controlling the "disruption" than about what was actually happening to you. That was the extent of our spiritual and emotional isolation. Do you see how our culture of pain worked? I knew there was an emergency, I was ready to do something! But then I felt I was supposed to walk away, like all the other times when one of us was in distress. Silence was disciplined into us. How did we get to be so utterly ruined? How did we get to the point where we turned our backs on one another?

I feel comfortable placing blame on everyone, and some more than others. We have taken in the values that ultimately hurt and divide us, while some benefit from the suffering of "others." We were too stupid (not innocently, but the result of engineered ignorance) to see it happening to us. Even when it was clear, oftentimes all I could bear was to take care of myself, for my own survival. Most of all, I blame dominant institutions and mainstream society, because of the impossible alternatives they set up for us. They set up what is "good," what is "normal"—everything else is secondary, the "other." And they are very clever about it—they fix it so that the suicide looks like an individual problem, not a social or political matter. Labels of "mental illness" and "madness" are ways of silencing difference and shifting blame from the social to the individual. The social stigma of "dysfunctionality" kept our family secret and prevented us from seeking assistance from those who could offer it. For a long time, I felt we were atypically and inherently flawed, as individuals and as a family, but later learned from other Asian women that our experiences were neither unusual nor indicative of an intrinsic, Asian cultural pathology. However, regardless of any real possibility for collectivity, we had few means for support outside the family. We distrusted social workers and counselors, who had little insight into what we were experiencing.

The Asian "model minority" is not doing well. Do you see what a lie it is and how it is used to reinforce the American Dream and punish those of us who don't "succeed," or who succeed "too much"? It is making me mad knowing the truth of this culture, which is so obvious and yet so strategically dissimulated in the everyday that it becomes invisible, and nothing is left but the violence that results from its disappearance. How do you point out the horror of something that is so fundamentally banal and routine that it ceases to appear traumatic? And when you do point out the lie that is the truth, you feel (and usually are) alone in seeing this and wanting to root it out. It's enough to make you paranoid, because it is such a thorough conspiracy—how can you reform something that is so structural, so absolutely essential to the constitution of this society? Therapy and social work are out of the question, because the point is not to heal or to cope—no token of change can rectify our injury. Why would you want to place yourself into the hands of an institution that seeks to resocialize you into the environment that made a mess of you in the first place? Our inclusion into the American process turned out to be our worst form of oppression. Most people are proud to call themselves Americans, but why would you want to become a productive, well-adjusted citizen when the primary requisite of American-ness is racism? Isn't our madness often the only evidence we have at all to show for this civilizing terror?

I remember when you got arrested for stealing a car in order to escape the nearly all-white university you were attending. A white woman social worker ordered by the courts came to check up on you at home, where you were remanded for probation. Even though you had locked yourself in your bedroom, the social worker tried to break down the door when you refused to see her, despite all of our protests. I was desperate for you to break out of our circle of torment, but I knew my familial and social duty was to defuse the awkwardness and shame of divulging our "personal" problems. As far as our family was concerned, the state was the last place we would look for help, and, according to standards of social acceptability, there was no such thing as a family problem that could not be solved within the family. So I put on a calm, diplomatic facade for the social worker, who had finally given up on making you understand that she was only there to help and decided to interview me instead about our family situation, which her limited thinking deduced to be the problem. I assured her she was wasting her time and that everything was fine. That was enough to satisfy the social worker, and she never came back.

It is a very insidious process that starts when we are young. One of my first memories of the "weeding out" was when we visited our father's place of work. When we were introduced to his co-workers, one of them looked at me and said to our father, "Oh, this one has big eyes." Pretty/normal = big eyes, white. And I at least had relatively "big" eyes. So, did I pass? Can my brothers and sister come, too? Racial passing was impossible for us, even though we were continually pitted against each other according to their racial fantasies.

Another memory: we were on a school bus; our brother broke an implicit rule and occupied one of the rear seats, which one white boy decided he wanted. I burned with rage and humiliation, not knowing what to do, as I watched the white boy repeatedly bang our brother's head against the bus window. (Our brother remembers it a different way, but for a long time I could only recall the young thug's taunting laughter.) Although I pleaded with the bus driver to intervene, which he did only too slowly, I felt helpless. I was afraid to call attention to myself and my already awkward difference. This was only the beginning of our conditioning by their divide-and-conquer strategy.

We became pathetic victims of whiteness. We permed our hair and could afford to buy trendy clothes. Money, at least, gave us some material status. But we knew we could never become "popular," in other words, accepted. It had something to do with our "almond-shaped" eyes, but we never called it racism. You once asked, "What's wrong with trying to be white?" You said your way of dealing with racism was not to let them know it bothered you. But they don't *want* it to bother us. If it did, they would have a revolution on their hands. The "just-convince-them-they-should-be-like-us" tactic. It is so important for the American racial hierarchy to keep us consuming its ideals so that we attack ourselves instead of the racial neuroses it manufactures.

I feel disgusted and angry and so, so sorry when I think of how I participated in the self-hatred that helped to kill you. I did not like to be reminded of my own "Orientalness," and I could not be satisfied with our failure to fit into the white American mold. Our parents were accomplices and victims, too. I remember when our mother once criticized you for cutting off your long, straight, black hair (in your effort to appear less "exotic"). Insulting you, she said, "You have such a round, flat face." She always told us, "You not American. Why you try to be American?" Our father could not understand our dilemma, either: "Your only job is study—Be number one—Do what your father tell you and you never go wrong." When he was challenged, which was usually by you, the one-who-paved-the-way-for-the-rest-of-us, he became a frustrated madman and abuser. We interpreted this as a failure in communication, a clash of cultural values, but the conflict ran deeper than a matter of individual understanding or cultural sensitivity. We did not believe in the possibility of surviving as an Oriental in an American society. Oriental/American. Our only choices. This is what we call a serious identity crisis.

I know people thought they could pick on you because you wore pink Laura Ashley dresses and glasses. Racists think "Oriental" girls never fight back. You told me some white girl, backed by her white thug friends, was threatening to beat the shit out of you. But you were more than this Laura Ashley reflection. The white girl was in for a big shock the day you put on your fighting gear and confronted her in the girls' restroom. You had to "toughen up" just to survive. (What does that entail, what price did you pay?) Our schizophrenia was a conditioned disease. You always and never had a grip on who you were.

You could draw a picture of a tiger springing to attack, frontal view, at the age of nine, and it would be good enough to pass for a *National Geographic* illustration. You were the fastest runner in elementary school and broke the school record for the fifty-yard dash. You made the junior high school track team, but our mother forbade you to run because she thought it would make your legs big and ugly. When our mother told your track coach, you were so embarrassed and humiliated that you never tried to run again. You stopped drawing, too, because you were being groomed by our father to become a doctor. You used to sell your drawings for twenty-five cents each to other classmates in elementary school but soon learned you had no time for art (or "fooling around," as our father would say) because you had to study hard. You broke down one day after having received a B on an exam, because you were afraid it would ruin your straight-A record. Our father told me you had asked your white, male professor to reconsider the grade, but he told you he never gave *foreign* students A's! The real irony was that you were always a capable student, and, more important, an insightful, critical thinker.

I had a desperate feeling something very bad was going to happen. So I wrote a letter to you a week before your second suicide attempt, warning you about my premonition, but the letter never got to you. I wrote that I wanted you to take care of yourself and that, like you, I was barely getting by. (You once wrote a goodbye note to me before you ran away—or was it meant to be read after your death?— that read, "I still don't know how you do it.") I wrote that I would be there for you and to have faith, because no one else was going to do it for us. But mostly, I expressed a deep sense of urgency. I sensed that if you did not do something about the crisis you were living, you would explode.

We spoke on the phone two nights before you took the pills. I was worried and impatient with you, because I wanted you to reassure me that you would not do anything self-destructive, so you told me you were not feeling suicidal. You even said you thought you were "probably the most fucked-up person on this planet" but you felt "good" about how you were going to handle it. I got off the phone feeling relieved, for the moment. Handle it? Was it supposed to be a hint (but I couldn't get it)? Our mother told me you cried, "Mommy, I'm sorry," which she believed signaled your regret for the "mistakes" you had made. "If you can't do anything good for society, you might as well kill yourself." Still, she told me your death took an important part of her, a connection she felt most strongly with you because you had her face. The same face she insulted and helped you to "reconstruct." Our father laughed when you told him the reason you wanted the plastic surgery was because you did not want to look like our mother.

In some ways, your death has shocked this family out of denial. For the first time, our parents owned up to the abuse they inflicted, as well as the suffering they endured from their own social alienation. Imagine how hard it was to maintain their dignity, having to work three times as hard as their white colleagues, who turned up their noses at broken English, and their own kids thinking they were stupid. Our brothers began to rely on me for support they used to get from you. You once told me what our lives would be like if you died. I realize now all the things you told me are true. But without these traumatic changes, I never would have appreciated your wisdom. I wonder if your vision was part of a plan. Did you know what you had to do?

I think you left because you could not live in the world that you knew. It hurts (so much) to imagine your pain and loneliness, . . . but I also know of your courage. You told me you were not afraid to die. *How much you must have known to feel so comfortable with death.* You weren't just a victim. However compromised, your suicide was also a form of resistance, a refusal to carry on under such brutal conditions.

I still have some of your old belongings, including some postsurgery photos that were hidden in a box. I didn't recognize you in the pictures at first. *My* sister is the girl I joked around with, shared a bed with and respected, who cut my hair, let me tag along, took some beatings for me, tolerated my impatience, envied me (too much) and was sometimes proud of me, saved animals with me, spoke Korean more fluently than the rest of us, was the dependable one, the pride of our father, the closest to our mother, the one with the "good heart," the confidant of our grandmother, the toughest one, who could beat us up and occasionally did, our younger brother's favorite sister, the only one who could really talk to our older brother, the one to have my teachers first, and the smart one. My perceptions of you. You said later, "I always feel obligated." Mired in my own worldview, I refused to believe you had it so hard. Your suicide was finally something that belonged to *you*.

I pieced together the events of your suicide through stories told by our family. You pawned a TV set and bought a .38 Magnum. Put blank cartridges into where the bullets should be and sat in bed with the gun hidden underneath the covers. Our mother had spent the day tailing your car around the city, following you from one pawnshop to the next, begging the dealers not to sell you a gun. Eventually she found you at home safely in bed and reassured you that everything was going to be fine. You asked her if you would have to go back there, to the psychiatric place. Our mother tried to comfort you and then left to get you a glass of orange juice, but she had walked no further than the bathroom down the hall when she heard an explosion. You were declared "dead" a few hours later.

So, why am I writing to you, dearest sister? It would be nice to extract an ultimate meaning from all this, to acquire some comfort from analysis, but I am still confronted with the abysmal magnitude of my soullessness. (That is what it feels like, the utter uprootedness of living in this lobotomizing culture.) I cannot hope to achieve a level of wholeness, because my soullessness refuses to be quiescent under this civilizing regime. I am writing to let you know that I still remember, and I will live to tell it regardless of my state of ruin, which means I think it is possible to militate against violence and loss without buying into civility and unity. I am not even calling for anarchy; I cannot allow myself that luxury because we already live in a (nation-)state of organized chaos. Your presence haunts and compels me to recount your death. Maybe my story will be useful in some way—to galvanize a historical or political consciousness—who knows? Maybe through remembering I will even find a patchwork place for myself to take root, just as we do in my dreams.

1. Misir notes that the racial antipathy and violence directed against the Indian American community in Jersey City were not always the acts of white racists but also involved people from a number of different ethnic groups, including African Americans, Latinos, and other Asian Americans. What explanations does Misir provide for this phenomenon? What other factors might have been important contributing factors? Are there any other examples that you can think of where Asian Americans have had conflicts with other nonwhite ethnic groups? What are the sources of intergroup tensions that involved oppressed groups, and how might they be overcome?

2. Misir notes that a number of Asian Indian Americans "do not see a natural alliance or unity with other Asian American groups." On such an important issue as hate crimes, there are still a significant number of Indian Americans who have expressed opposition to creating unity along pan–Asian American lines. Why might this be the case? How does Misir account for this opposition? What opposition might other Asian American groups/individuals experience in incorporating Indian Americans into their organizations? To what degree do generation and class affect the outcome of such linkages?

3. What is the basis of allegations made by Ross Perot, Bob Dole, and anti-Clinton forces about the presidential campaign fund-raising during the President's 1996 bid for a second term in office? Wang asserts that, from the start, both Democrats and Republicans "played the race card," manipulating Asian American political interests, and ultimately denationalized Asian Americans, treating them "as if they were strangers or worse—lepers, foreigners, criminals, and subversives." Explain how the race card was played along partisan lines. How did Republican treatment of the Asian American community differ from its treatment by their Democratic counterparts? In short, what steps did the Clinton campaign ultimately take to distance itself from its Asian American donors? Why is this significant? What benefits do these political parties derive from linking this political corruption to Asian American donors? What long-term effects does this have on coalition building with these communities?

4. Park illustrates, through a letter to her sister, how the model minority myth is a destructive force in the Asian American community today. She poses a dismal view of mental health and its relationship to the community, even asking, at one point, "Why would you want to place yourself in the hands of an institution that seeks to resocialize you into the environment that made a mess of you in the first place?" What are the social forces in the larger society and within the community that pushed her sister toward multiple suicide attempts? What obstacles prevented her sister and her family from seeking mental health counseling? To what extent does her sister's tragic experiences mirror the experience of young people growing up in the Asian American community? What lessons can we draw from this tragedy?

SUGGESTED READINGS

Ancheta, Angelo N. 1998. *Race, Rights, and the Asian American Experience*. New Brunswick, NJ: Rutgers University Press.

Anderson, Benedict. 1991. *Imagined Communities: Reflections on the Origin and Spread of Nationalism*. New York: Verso.

Du, Phuoc Long, and Laura Ricard. 1996. *The Dream Shattered: Vietnamese Gangs in America*. Boston : Northeastern University Press.

Kagiwada, G. 1989. The Killing of Thong Hy Huynh: Implications of a Rashomon Perspective. Pp. 253–265 in G. Nomura et al. (eds.) *Frontiers of Asian American Studies*. Pullman: Washington State University Press.

Law-Yone, Wendy. 1983. *The Coffin Tree*. Boston: Beacon Press.

Lien, Pei-te. 1997. *The Political Participation of Asian Americans: Voting Behavior in Southern California*. New York: Garland.

McClain, Charles J. 1996. *In Search of Equality: The Chinese Struggle Against Discrimination in Nineteenth-Century America*. Berkeley: University of California Press.

National Asian Pacific American Legal Consortium. 1993. *Selected Incidents of Anti-Asian Violence in 1993*. Washington, DC: National Asian Pacific American Legal Consortium.

Reynold, W. B. 1988. *Discrimination Against Asian Americans in Higher Education: Evidence, Causes, and Cures*. Washington, DC: Civil Rights Division.

Saxton, Alexander. 1971. *The Indispensable Enemy: Labor and the Anti-Chinese Movement in California*. Berkeley: University of California Press.

Sethi, Rita C. 1994. Smells Like Racism: A Plan for Mobilizing Against Anti-Asian Bias. Pp. 235–250 in Karin Guillar-San Juan (ed.), *The State of Asian America: Activism and Resistance in the 1990s*. Boston: South End Press.

Takagi, Dana Y. 1992. *Retreat from Race: Asian-American Admissions Policies and Racial Politics*. New Brunswick, NJ: Rutgers University Press.

US Commission on Civil Rights. 1992. *Civil Rights Issues Facing Asian Americans in the 1990s*. Washington DC: US Government Printing Office.

———. 1986. *Recent Activities Against Citizens and Residents of Asian Descents*. Washington, DC: US Government Printing Office.

US Congress (House Committee on the Judiciary, Subcommittee on Civil and Constitutional Rights). 1989. Anti-Asian Violence: Oversight Hearing Before the Subcommittee on Civil and Constitutional Rights of the Committee on the Judiciary, House of Representatives, One Hundredth Congress (first session, November 10, 1987). Washington, DC: US Government Printing Office.

Watanabe, M. E. 1995. Asian American Investigators Decry Glass Ceiling in Academic Administration. *Scientist* 9 (11, May 29):1.

Yamanaka, Lois-Ann. 1998. *Blue's Hanging*. New York: Avon Books.

FILMS

Choy, Christine, and Renee Tajima (producers/directors). 1988. *Who Killed Vincent Chin* (87–minute documentary).

Okazaki, Steven. 1995. *American Sons* (41-minute docudrama).

Siegel, Taggart (director). 1988. *Blue Collar and Buddha* (57-minute documentary).

Soe, Valerie (producer/director). 1986. *All Orientals Look the Same* (1½-minute experimental).

Vu, Trac Minh (producer/director). 1997. *Letters to Thien* (57-minute documentary).

Part X

Queering Asian America

Maiden Voyage
Excursion into Sexuality and Identity Politics in Asian America

Dana Y. Takagi

The topic of sexualities—in particular, lesbian, gay, and bisexual identities—is an important and timely issue in that place we imagine as Asian America. *All of us* in Asian American Studies ought to be thinking about sexuality and Asian American history for at least two compelling reasons.

One, while there has been a good deal of talk about the "diversity" of Asian American communities, we are relatively uninformed about Asian American sub-cultures organized specifically around sexuality. There are Asian American gay and lesbian social organizations, gay bars that are known for Asian clientele, conferences that have focused on Asian American lesbian and gay experiences, and electronic bulletin boards catering primarily to gay Asians, their friends, and their lovers. I use the term "subcultures" here rather loosely and not in the classic sociological sense, mindful that the term is somewhat inaccurate since gay Asian organizations are not likely to view themselves as a gay subculture within Asian America any more than they are likely to think of themselves as an Asian American subculture within gay America. If anything, I expect that many of us view ourselves as on the margins of both communities. That state of marginalization in both communities is what prompts this essay and makes the issues raised in it all the more urgent for all of us—gay, straight, somewhere-in-between. For, as Haraway has suggested, the view is often clearest from the margins where "The split and contradictory self is the one who can interrogate positionings and be accountable, the one who can construct and join rational conversations and fantastic imaginings that change history."[1]

To be honest, it is not clear to me exactly *how* we ought to be thinking about these organizations, places, and activities. On the one hand, I would argue that an organization like the Association of Lesbians and Gay Asians (ALGA) ought to be catalogued in the annals of Asian American history. But on the other hand, having noted that ALGA is as Asian American as Sansei Live! or the National Coalition for Redress and Reparation, the very act of including lesbian and gay experiences in Asian American history, which seems important in a symbolic sense, produces in me a moment of hesitation. Not because I do not think that lesbian and gay sexualities are not deserving of a place in Asian American history, but rather, because the inscription of nonstraight sexualities in Asian American history immediately casts theoretical doubt about how to do it. As I will suggest, the recognition of different sexual practices and identities that also claim the label *Asian American* presents a useful opportunity for rethinking and reevaluating notions of identity that have been used, for the most part, unproblematically and uncritically in Asian American Studies.

The second reason, then, that we ought to be thinking about gay and lesbian sexuality and Asian American Studies is for the theoretical trouble we encounter in our attempts to situate and think about sexual identity *and* racial identity. Our attempts to locate gay Asian experiences in Asian American history render us "uninformed" in an ironic double sense. On the one hand, the field of Asian American Studies is mostly ignorant about the multiple ways that gay identities are often hidden or invisible within Asian American communities. But the irony is that the more we know, the less we know about the ways of knowing. On the other hand, just at the moment that we attempt to rectify our ignorance by adding say, the lesbian, to Asian American history, we arrive at a stumbling block, an ignorance of how to add her. Surely the quickest and simplest way to add her is to think of lesbianism as a kind of ad hoc subject-position, a minority within a minority. But efforts to think of sexuality in the same terms that we think of race, yet simultaneously different from race in certain ways, and, therefore, the inevitable "revelation" that gays/lesbians/bisexuals are like minorities but also different too, is often inconclusive, frequently ending in "counting" practice. While many minority women speak of "triple jeopardy" oppression—as if class, race, and gender could be disentangled into discrete additive parts—some Asian American lesbians could rightfully claim quadruple jeopardy oppression—class, race, gender, and sexuality. Enough counting. Marginalization is not as much about the *quantities* of experiences as it is about *qualities* of experience. And, as many writers, most notably feminists, have argued, identities whether sourced from sexual desire, racial origins, languages of gender, or class roots, are simply not additive.[2]

Not Counting

A discussion of sexualities is fraught with all sorts of definition conundrums. What exactly does it mean, sexualities? The plurality of the term may be unsettling to some who recognize three (or two, or one) forms of sexual identity: gay, straight, bisexual. But there are those who identify as straight but regularly indulge in homoeroticism, and, of course, there are those who claim the identity gay/lesbian but engage in heterosexual sex. In addition, some people identify themselves sexually but do not actually have sex, and, there are those who claim celibacy as a sexual practice. For those who profess a form of sexual identity that is, at some point, at odds with their sexual practice or sexual desire, the idea of a single, permanent, or even stable sexual identity is confining and inaccurate. Therefore, in an effort to capture the widest possible range of human sexual practices, I use the term sexualities to refer to the variety of practices and identities that range from homoerotic to heterosexual desire. In this essay, I am concerned mainly with homosexual desire and the question of what happens when we try to locate homosexual identities in Asian American history.

Writing, speaking, acting queer. Against a backdrop of lotus leaves, sliding *shoji* panels, and the mountains of Guilin. Amid the bustling enclaves of Little Saigon, Koreatown, Chinatown, and Little Tokyo. Sexual identity, like racial identity, is one of many types of recognized "difference." If marginalization is a qualitative state of being and not simply a quantitative one, then what is it about being "gay" that is different from "Asian American"?

The terms "lesbian" and "gay," like "Third World," "woman," and "Asian American," are political categories that serve as rallying calls and personal affirmations. In concatenating these identities we create and locate ourselves in phrases that seem a familiar fit: black gay man, third world woman, working-class Chicana lesbian, Asian American bisexual, etc. But is it possible to write these identities—like Asian American gay—without writing oneself into the corners that are either gay and only gay, or Asian American and only Asian American? Or, as Trinh T. Minh-ha put it, "How do you inscribe difference without bursting into a series of euphoric narcissistic accounts of yourself and your own kind?"[3]

It is vogue these days to celebrate difference. But underlying much contemporary talk about difference is the assumption that differences are comparable things. For example, many new social movements activists, including those in the gay and lesbian movement, think of themselves as patterned on the "ethnic model."[4] And for many ethnic minorities, the belief that "gays are oppressed too" is a reminder of a sameness, a common political project in moving margin to center, that unites race-based movements with gays, feminists, and greens. The notion that our differences are "separate but equal" can be used to call attention to the specificity of experiences or to rally the troops under a collective banner. Thus, the concept of difference espoused in identity politics may be articulated in moments of what Spivak refers to as "strategic essentialism" or in what Hall coins "positionalities." But in the heat of local political struggles and coalition building, it turns out that not all differences are created equally. For example, Ellsworth recounts how differences of race, nationality, and gender, unfolded in the context of a relatively safe environment, the university classroom:

> Women found it difficult to prioritize expressions of racial privilege and oppression when such prioritizing threatened to perpetuate their gender oppression. Among international students, both those who were of color and those who were White found it difficult to join their voices with those of U.S. students of color when it meant a subordination of their oppressions as people living under U.S. imperialist policies and as students for whom English was a second language. Asian American women found it difficult to join their voices with other students of color when it meant subordinating their specific oppressions as Asian Americans. I found it difficult to speak as a White woman about gender oppression when I occupied positions of institutional power relative to all students in the class, men and women, but positions of gender oppression relative to students who were White men, and in different terms, relative to students who were men of color.[5]

The above example demonstrates the tensions between sameness and difference that haunt identity politics. Referring to race and sexuality, Cohen suggests that the "sameness" that underlies difference may be more fiction than fact:

> ... the implied isomorphism between the "arbitrariness of racial categorizations" and the "sexual order" elides the complex processes of social differentiation that assign, legitimate, and enforce qualitative distinctions between different types of individuals. Here the explicit parallel drawn between "race" and "sexuality," familiar to so many polemical affirmations of (non-racial) identity politics, is meant to evoke an underlying and apparently indisputable common sense that naturalizes this particular choice of political strategy almost as if the "naturalness" of racial "identity" could confer a corollary stability on the less "visible" dynamics of sexuality.[6]

There are numerous ways that being "gay" is not like being "Asian." Two broad distinctions are worth noting. The first, mentioned by Cohen above, is the relative invisibility of sexual identity compared with racial identity. While both can be said to be socially constructed, the former are performed, acted out, and produced, often in individual routines, whereas the latter tends to be more obviously "written" on the body and negotiated by political groups.[7] Put another way, there is a quality of voluntarism in being gay/lesbian that is usually not possible as an Asian American. One has the option to present oneself as "gay" or "lesbian" or, alternatively, to attempt to "pass" or to stay in "the closet," that is, to hide one's sexual preference.[8] However, these same options are not available to most racial minorities in face-to-face interactions with others.

As Asian Americans, we do not think in advance about whether or not to present ourselves as "Asian American," rather, that is an identification that is worn by us, whether we like it or not, and which is easily read off of us by others.

A second major reason that the category "gay" ought to be distinguished from the category "Asian American" is for the very different histories of each group. Studying the politics of being "gay" entails on the one hand, an analysis of discursive fields, ideologies, and rhetoric about sexual identity, and on the other hand, knowledge of the history of gays/lesbians as subordinated minorities relative to heterosexuals. . . . Similarly, studying "Asian America" requires analysis of semantic and rhetorical discourse in its variegated forms, racist, apologist, and paternalist, and requires in addition, an understanding of the specific histories of the peoples who recognize themselves as Asian or Asian American. But the specific discourses and histories in each case are quite different. Even though we make the same intellectual moves to approach each form of identity, that is, a two-tracked study of ideology on the one hand, and history on the other, the particular ideologies and histories of each are very different.[9]

In other words, many of us experience the worlds of Asian America and gay America as separate places—emotionally, physically, intellectually. We sustain the separation of these worlds with our folk knowledge about the family-centeredness and supra-homophobic beliefs of ethnic communities. Moreover, it is not just that these communities know so little of one another, but we frequently take great care to keep those worlds distant from each other. What could be more different than the scene at gay bars like "The End Up" in San Francisco, or "Faces" in Hollywood, and, on the other hand, the annual Buddhist church bazaars in the Japanese American community or Filipino revivalist meetings?[10] These disparate worlds occasionally collide through individuals who manage to move, for the most part stealthily, between these spaces. But it is the act of deliberately bringing these worlds closer together that seems unthinkable. Imagining your parents, clutching bento box lunches, thrust into the smoky haze of a South of Market leather bar in San Francisco is no less strange a vision than the idea of Lowie taking Ishi, the last of his tribe, for a cruise on Lucas' Star Tours at Disneyland. "Cultural strain," the anthropologists would say. Or, as Wynn Young, laughing at the prospect of mixing his family with his boyfriend, said, "Somehow I just can't picture this conversation at the dinner table, over my mother's homemade barbecued pork: 'Hey, Ma. I'm sleeping with a sixty-year-old white guy who's got three kids, and would you please pass the soy sauce?' "[11]

Thus, "not counting" is a warning about the ways to think about the relationship of lesbian/gay identities to Asian American history. While it may seem politically efficacious to toss the lesbian onto the diversity pile, adding one more form of subordination to the heap of inequalities, such a strategy glosses over the particular or distinctive ways sexuality is troped in Asian America. Before examining the possibilities for theorizing "gay" and "Asian American" as nonmutually exclusive identities, I turn first to a fuller description of the chasm of silence that separates them.

Silences

The concept of silence is a doggedly familiar one in Asian American history. For example, Hosokawa characterized the Nisei as "Quiet Americans," and popular media discussions of the "model minority" typically describe Asian American students as "quiet" along with "hardworking" and "successful." In the popular dressing of Asian American identity, silence has functioned as a metaphor for the assimilative and positive imagery of the "good" minorities. More recently, analysis of popular imagery of the "model minority" suggests that silence ought to be understood as an adaptive mechanism to a racially discriminatory society rather than as an intrinsic part of Asian American culture.[12]

If silence has been a powerful metaphor in Asian American history, it is also a crucial element of discussions of gay/lesbian identity, albeit in a somewhat different way. In both cases, silence may be viewed as the oppressive cost of a racially biased or heterosexist society. For gays and lesbians, the act of coming out takes on symbolic importance, not just as a personal affirmation of "this is who I am," but additionally as a critique of expected norms in society, "we are everywhere." While "breaking the silence" about Asian Americans refers to crashing popular stereotypes about them and shares with the gay act of "coming out" the desire to define oneself rather than be defined by others, there remains an important difference between the two.

The relative invisibility of homosexuality compared with Asian American identity means that silence and its corollary space, the closet, are more ephemeral, appear less fixed as boundaries of social identities, less likely to be taken for granted than markers of race, and, consequently, more likely to be problematized and theorized in discussions that have as yet barely begun on racial identity. Put another way, homosexuality is more clearly seen as *constructed* than racial identity.[13] Theoretically speaking, homosexual identity does not enjoy the same privileged stability as racial identity. The borders that separate gay from straight, and "in" from "out," are so fluid that in the final moment we can only be sure that sexual identities are, as Diana Fuss notes, "in Foucaldian terms, less a matter of final discovery than a matter of perpetual invention."[14]

Thus, while silence is a central piece of theoretical discussions of homosexuality, it is viewed primarily as a negative stereotype in the case of Asian Americans. What seems at first a simple question in gay identity of being "in" or "out" is actually laced in epistemological knots.

For example, a common question asked of gays and lesbians by one another, or by straights, is, "Are you out?" The answer to that question (yes and no) is typically followed by a list of who knows and who does not (e.g., my coworkers know, but my family doesn't . . .). But the question of who knows or how many people know about one's gayness raises yet another question, "How many, or which, people need to know one is gay before one qualifies as "out?" Or, as Fuss says, "To be out, in common gay parlance, is precisely to be no longer out; to be out is to be finally outside of exteriority and all the exclusions and deprivations such outsider-hood imposes. Or, put another way, to be out is really to be in—inside the realm of the visible, the speakable, the culturally intelligible."[15]

Returning to the issue of silence and homosexuality in Asian America, it seems that topics of sex, sexuality, and gender are *already* diffused through discussions of Asian America.[16] For example, numerous writers have disclosed, and challenged, the panoply of contradictory sexually charged images of Asian American women as docile and subservient on the one hand and as ruthless Mata-Hari, dragon-lady aggressors on the other. And, of course, Frank Chin's tirades against the feminization of Asian American men has been one reaction to the particular way in which Asian Americans have been historically (de)sexualized as racial subjects. Moving from popular imagery of Asian Americans, *the people*, to Asia, *the nation*, Chow uses Bertolucci's blockbuster film, *The Last Emperor*, to illustrate what she calls "the metaphysics of feminizing the other (culture)" wherein China is predictably cast as a "feminized, eroticized, space."[17]

That the topic of *homo*-sexuality in Asian American studies is often treated in whispers, if mentioned at all, should be some indication of trouble. It is noteworthy, I think, that in the last major anthology on Asian American women, *Making Waves*, the author of the essay on Asian American lesbians was the only contributor who did not wish her last name to be published.[18] Of course, as we all know, a chorus of sympathetic bystanders is chanting about homophobia, saying, "she was worried about her job, her family, her community. . . ." Therefore, perhaps a good starting point to consider lesbian and gay identities in Asian American studies is by problematizing the silences surrounding homosexuality in Asian America.

It would be easy enough for me to say that I often feel a part of me is "silenced" in Asian American Studies. But I can hardly place all of the blame on my colleagues. Sometimes I silence myself as much as I feel silenced by them. And my silencing act is a blaring welter of false starts, uncertainties, and anxieties. For example, on the one hand, an omnipresent little voice tells me that visibility is better than invisibility, and, therefore, coming out is an affirming social act. On the other hand, I fear the awkward silences and struggle for conversation that sometimes follow the business of coming out. One has to think about when and where to time the act, since virtually no one has ever asked me, "Are you a lesbian?" Another voice reminds me that the act of coming out, once accomplished, almost always leaves me wondering whether I did it for myself or them. Not only that, but at the moment that I have come out, relief that is born of honesty and integrity quickly turns to new uncertainty. This time, my worry is that someone will think that in my coming out, they will now have a ready-made label for me, lesbian. The prospect that someone may think that they know *me* because they comprehend the category *lesbian* fills me with stubborn resistance. The category lesbian calls up so many different images of women who love other women that I do not think that any one—gay or straight—could possibly know or find me through that category alone. No wonder that I mostly find it easier to completely avoid the whole issue of sexual identity in discussions with colleagues.

There are so many different and subtle ways to come out. I am not much of a queer nation type, an "in your face" queer—I catalogue my own brand of lesbian identity as a kind of Asian American "take" on gay identity. I do not wear pink triangles, have photos of girls kissing in my living room, or make a point of bringing up my girlfriend in conversation. In effect, my sexual identity is often backgrounded or stored somewhere in between domains of public and private. I used to think that my style of being gay was dignified and polite—sophisticated, civilized, and genteel. Work was work and home was home. The separation of work and home has been an easy gulf to maintain, less simple to bridge. However, recently, I have come to think otherwise.

But all this talk about me is getting away from my point, which is that while it would be easy enough for me to say many of us feel "silenced," which alone might argue for inclusion of gay sexualities in discourse about the Asian American experience, that is not enough. Technically speaking, then, the terms "addition" and "inclusion" are misleading. I'm afraid that in using such terms, the reader will assume that by adding gay/lesbian experiences to the last week's topics in a course on Asian American contemporary issues, or by including lesbians in a discussion of Asian women, the deed is done. Instead, I want to suggest that the task is better thought of as just begun, that the topic of sexualities ought to be envisioned as a means, not an end, to theorizing about the Asian American experience.

For example, one way that homosexuality may be seen as a vehicle for theorizing identity in Asian America is for the missteps, questions, and silences that are often clearest in collisions at the margins (identities as opposed to people). In the following discussion, I describe two such confrontations—the coming out of a white student in an Asian American Studies class and the problem of authenticity in gay/lesbian Asian American writing. Each tells in its own way the awkward limits of ethnic-based models of identity.

The Coming-Out Incident

Once, when I was a teaching assistant in Asian American Studies at Berkeley during the early 1980s, a lesbian, one of only two white students in my section, decided to come out during the first section meeting. I had asked each student to explain their interest, personal and intellectual, in Asian American Studies. Many students mentioned wanting to know "more about their heritage" and "knowing the past in order to understand the present." The lesbian was nearly last to speak. After explaining that she wanted to understand the heritage of a friend who was Asian American, her final words came out tentatively, as if she had been deliberating about whether or not to say them, "And, I guess I also want you all to know that I am a lesbian." In the silence that followed I quickly surveyed the room. A dozen or so Asian American students whom I had forced into a semicircular seating arrangement stared glumly at their shoes. The two white students, both of whom were lesbians, as I recall, sat together, at one end of the semicircle. They glanced expectantly around the circle, and then they, too, looked at the ground. I felt as though my own world had split apart, and the two pieces were in front of me, drifting, surrounding, and, at that moment, both silent.

I knew both parts well. On the one side, I imagined that the Asian American students in the class recoiled in private horror at the lesbian, not so much because she was a lesbian or white but because she insisted on publicly baring her soul in front of them. I empathized with the Asian American students because they reminded me of myself as an undergraduate. I rarely spoke in class or section, unless, of course, I was asked a direct question. While my fellow white students, most often the males, chatted effortlessly in section about readings or lectures, I was almost always mute. I marveled at the ease with which questions, thoughts, answers, and even half-baked ideas rolled off their tongues and floated discussion. For them, it all seemed so easy.

As for me, I struggled with the act of talking in class. Occasionally, I managed to add a question to the discussion, but more often I found that, after silently practicing my entry into a fast-moving exchange, the discussion had moved on. In my silence, I chastised myself for moving too slowly, for hesitating where others did not, and, alternately, chastised the other students for their bull-dozing, loose lips. I valorized and resented the verbal abilities of my fellow classmates. And I imagined how the Asian American students who sat in my class the day the lesbian decided to come out, like me, named the ability to bare one's soul through words "white." On the other side, I empathized as well with the lesbian. I identified with what I imagined as her compelling need to claim her identity, to be like the others in the class, indeed to be an "other" at all in a class where a majority of the students were in search of their "roots." I figured that being a lesbian, while not quite like being Asian American, must have seemed to the intrepid student as close to the ethnic model as she could get. Finally, I thought she represented a side of me that always wanted, but never could quite manage, to drop the coming-out bomb in groups that did not expect it. Part of the pleasure in being an "outsider" can be in the affirmation of the identity abhorred by "insiders." I imagined that she and her friend had signed up for my section because they *knew* I too was a lesbian, and I worried that they assumed that I might be able to protect them from the silence of the closet.

In the silence that followed the act of coming out, and, indeed, in the ten weeks of class in which no one spoke of it again, I felt an awkwardness settle over our discussions in section. I was never sure exactly how the Asian American students perceived the lesbian—as a wannabe "minority," as a comrade in marginality, as any White Other, or, perhaps, they did not think of it at all. Nor did I ever know if the lesbian found what she was looking for, a better understanding of the Asian American experience, in the silence that greeted her coming out.

The silences I have described here dramatize how dialogue between identities is hampered by the assumption of what Wittig calls the "discourses of heterosexuality." She says:

> These discourses of heterosexuality oppress us in the sense that they prevent us from speaking unless we speak in their terms. Everything which puts them into question is at once disregarded as elementary. Our refusal of the totalizing interpretation of psychoanalysis makes the theoreticians say that we neglect the symbolic dimension. These discourses deny us every possibility of creating our own categories. But their most ferocious action is the unrelenting tyranny that they exert upon our physical and mental selves.[19]

More important, the coming-out incident suggests that marginalization is no guarantee for dialogue. If there is to be an interconnectedness between different vantage points, we will need to establish an art of political conversation that allows for affirmation of difference without choking secularization. The construction of such a politics is based implicitly on our vision of what happens, or what ought to happen, when difference meets itself—queer meets Asian, black meets Korean, feminist meets Greens, etc., at times, all in one person.[20] What exactly must we know about these other identities in order to engage in dialogue?

The Question of Authenticity

What we do know about Asian American gays and lesbians must be gleaned from personal narratives, literature, poetry, short stories, and essays. But, first, what falls under the mantle Asian American gay and lesbian writings? Clearly, lesbians and gays whose writings are self-conscious reflections on Asian American identity and sexual identity ought to be categorized as Asian American gay/lesbian writers. For example, Kitty Tsui, Barbara Noda, and Merle Woo are individuals who have identified themselves, and are identified by others, as Asian American lesbian voices. Similarly, in a recent collection of essays from a special issue of *Amerasia,* "Burning Cane," Alice Hom ruminates on how an assortment of Others—white dykes, Asian dykes, family, and communities—react to her as butchy/androgynous, as Asian American, as a lesbian. These writers are lesbians, and they write about themselves as lesbians, which grants them authorial voice as a lesbian. But they also identify as Asian American and are concerned with the ways in which these different sources of community—lesbian and Asian American—function in their everyday lives.

But what then about those who do not write explicitly or self-consciously about their sexuality or racial identity? For example, an essay on AIDS and mourning by Jeff Nunokawa, while written by a Japanese-American English professor, does not focus on issues of racial and sexual identity and, as such, is neither self-consciously gay nor Asian American.[21] What are we to make of such work? On the one hand, we might wish to categorize the author as a gay Asian American writer, whether he wishes to take this sign or not, presuming, of course, that he is gay, since his essay appears in an anthology subtitled "gay theories," and, in addition, presuming that he is Asian American, or at least identifies as such, given his last name. On the other hand, we might instead argue that it is the author's work, his subject matter, and not the status of the author, that marks the work as gay, Asian American, or both . . . In this case, we might infer that since the topic of the essay is AIDS and men, the work is best categorized as "gay," but not Asian American.

This may seem a mundane example, but it illustrates well how authorial voice and subject matter enter into our deliberations of what counts and what does not as Asian American gay/lesbian writings. . . . The university is filled with those of us who, while we live under signs like gay, Asian, feminist, ecologist, middle-class, etc., do not make such signs the central subject of our research. And what about those individuals who write about gays/lesbians but who identify themselves as heterosexual? In the same way that colonizers write about the colonized, and, more recently, the colonized write back, blacks write about whites and vice versa, "we" write about "them," and so on.

I want to be clear, here. I am not suggesting that we try to locate Asian American gay/lesbian sensibilities as if they exist in some pure form and are waiting to be discovered. Rather, I think we ought to take seriously Trinh T. Minh-ha's warning that "Trying to find the other by defining otherness or by explaining the other through laws and generalities is, as Zen says, like beating the moon with a pole or scratching an itching foot from the outside of a shoe."[22] My concern here is to turn the question from one about a particular identity to the more general question of the way in which the concept of identity is deployed in Asian American history.

Thus, not only is marginalization no guarantee for dialogue, but the state of being marginalized itself may not be capturable as a fixed, coherent, and holistic identity. Our attempts to define categories like "Asian American" or "gay" are necessarily incomplete. For example, as Judith Butler has noted:

> To write or speak as a lesbian appears a paradoxical appearance of this "I," one which feels neither true nor false. For it is a production, usually in response to a request, to come out or write in the name of an identity which, once produced, sometimes functions as a politically efficacious phantasm.
>
> ... This is not to say that I will not appear at political occasions under the sign of the lesbian, but that I would like to have it permanently unclear what precisely that sign signifies.[23]

A politics of identity and whatever kind of politics ensues from that project— multiculturalism, feminism, and gay movements—is first of all a politics about identity. That is, about the lack of a wholistic and "coherent narrative" derived from race, class, gender, and sexuality. . . . Because no sooner do we define, for example, "Japanese American" as a person of Japanese ancestry when we are forced back to the drawing board by the biracial child of Japanese American and an African American who thinks of herself as "black" or "feminist."

Rethinking Identity Politics

Lisa Lowe in her discussion of identity politics affirms the articulation of "Asian American" identity while simultaneously warning us of its overarching, consuming, and essentializing dangers. She (Lowe) closes her discussion saying:

> I want simply to remark that in the 1990s, we can afford to rethink the notion of ethnic identity in terms of cultural, class, and gender differences, rather than presuming similarities and making the erasure of particularity the basis of unity. In the 1990s, we can diversify our political practices to include a more heterogeneous group and to enable crucial alliances with other groups—ethnicity-based, class-based, and sexuality-based—in the ongoing work of transforming hegemony. [24]

I have intended this essay, in part, as an answer to Lowe's call to broaden the scope of Asian American discourse about identity. But there is a caveat. The gist of this essay has been to insist that our valuation of heterogeneity not be ad hoc and that we seize the opportunity to recognize nonethnic based differences—like homosexuality—as an occasion to critique the tendency toward essentialist currents in ethnic-based narratives and disciplines. In short, the practice of including gayness in Asian America rebounds into a reconsideration of the theoretical status of the concept of "Asian American" identity. The interior of the category "Asian American" ought not be viewed as a hierarchy of identities led by ethnic-based narratives but rather, the complicated interplay and collision of different identities.

At the heart of Lowe's argument for recognizing diversity within Asian American, generational, national, gender, and class, as well as my insistence in this essay on a qualitative, not quantitative, view of difference, is a particular notion of subjectivity. That notion of the subject as nonunitary stands in sharp contrast to the wholistic and coherent identities that find expression in much contemporary talk and writing about Asian Americans. At times, our need to "reclaim history" has been bluntly translated into a possessiveness about the Asian American experience (politics, history, literature) or perspectives as if such experiences or perspectives were not diffuse, shifting, and often contradictory. Feminists and gay writers, animated by poststructuralism's decentering practices, offer an alternative, to theorize the subject rather than assume its truth or, worse yet, assign to it a truth.

Concretely, to theorize the subject means to uncover in magnificent detail the "situatedness"[25] of perspectives or identities as knowledge which, even as it pleads for an elusive common language or claims to establish truth, cannot guarantee a genuine politics of diversity, that is, political conversation *and* argument, between the margins.[26] Such a politics will be marked by moments of frustration and tension because the participants will be pulling and pushing one another with statements such as "I am like you" and "I am not like you." But the rewards for an identity politics that is not primarily ethnic-based or essentialist along some other axis will be that conversations like the one which never took place in my Asian American Studies section many years ago will finally begin. Moreover, our search for authencity of voice—whether in gay/lesbian Asian American writing or in some other identity string—will be tempered by the realization that in spite of our impulse to clearly (de)limit them, there is perpetual uncertainty and flux governing the construction and expression of identities.

NOTES

My special thanks to Russell Leong for his encouragement and commentary on this essay.

1. See Donna Haraway, "Situated Knowledges: The Science Question in Feminism and the Privilege of Partial Perspective," *Feminist Studies* 14:3 (1988): 575–599.

2. See Teresa de Lauretis, "Feminist Studies/Critical Studies: Issues, Terms, and Contexts," in *Feminist Studies/Critical Studies*, edited by Teresa de Lauretis (Bloomington: Indiana University Press, 1986), 1–19; bell hooks, *Yearning: Race, Gender and Cultural Politics* (Boston: South End Press, 1990); Trinh T. Minh-ha, *Woman, Native, Other* (Bloomington: Indiana University Press, 1989); Chandra Talpade Mohanty, "Under Western Eyes: Feminist Scholarship and Colonialist Discourses," in *Third World Women and the Politics of Feminism*, edited by Chandra Talpade Mohanty, Ann Russo, and Lourdes Torres (Bloomington: Indiana University Press, 1991), 52–80; Linda Alcoff, "Cultural Feminism versus Post-Structuralism: The Identity Crisis in Feminist Theory," *Signs* 13:3 (1988): 405–437.

3. Trinh T. Minh-ha, 28.

4. Epstein (1987). Jeffrey Escoffier, editor of *Outlook* magazine, made this point in a speech at the American Educational Research Association meetings in San Francisco, April 24, 1992.

5. See Elizabeth Ellsworth, "Why Doesn't This Feel Empowering? Working Through the Repressive Myths of Critical Pedagogy," *Harvard Education Review* 59:3 (1989): 297–324.

6. Ed Cohen, "Who Are We"? Gay 'Identity' as Political (E)motion," in *inside/out*, edited by Diana Fuss, (New York and London: Routledge, 1991), 71–92.

7. Of course, there are exceptions, for example, blacks that "pass," and perhaps this is where homosexuality and racial identity come closest to one another, amongst those minorities who "pass" and gays who can also "pass."

8. I do not mean to suggest that there is only one presentation of self as lesbian. For example, one development recently featured in the *Los Angeles Times* is the evolution of "lipstick lesbians" (Van Gelder, 1991). The fashion issue has also been discussed in gay/lesbian publications. For example, Stein (1988), writing for *Outlook*, has commented on the lack of correspondence between fashion and sexual identity, "For many, you can dress as femme one day and a butch the next. . . ."

9. Compare for example the histories Takaki's *Strangers from a Different Shore*, Sucheng Chan's *Asian Americans*, and Roger Daniels' *Chinese and Japanese in America* with Jonathan Katz's *Gay American History*, Jeffrey Week's *The History of Sexuality*, Michel Foucault's *The History of Sexuality*, and David Greenberg's *The Construction of Homosexuality*.

10. See Steffi San Buenaventura, "The Master and the Federation: A Filipino-American Social Movement in California and Hawaii," *Social Process in Hawaii* 33 (1991): 169–193.

11. Wynn Young, "Poor Butterfly" *Amerasia Journal* 17:2 (1991): 118.

12. See Keith Osajima, "Asian Americans as the Model Minority: An Analysis of the Popular Press Image in the 1960s and 1980s," in *Reflections on Shattered Windows: Promises and Prospects for Asian American Studies*, edited by Gary Y. Okihiro, Shirley Hune, Arthur A. Hansen, and John M. Liu (Pullman: Washington State University Press, 1988), 165–174.

13. See Judith Butler, *Gender Trouble* (New York: Routledge 1990); Michel Foucault, *The History of Sexuality, Volume 1: An Introduction*, trans. Robert Hurley (New York: Vintage, 1980); Monique Wittig, *The Straight Mind and Other Essays* (Boston: Beacon 1992); Greenberg, *The Construction of Homosexuality*.

14. Diana Fuss, "Inside/Out," in *inside/out*, edited by Diana Fuss (New York: Routledge, 1991), 1–10.

15. Ibid.

16. Consider, for example, debates in recent times over intermarriage patterns, the controversy over Asian Americans dating white men, the Asian Men's calendar, and the continuation of discussions started over a decade ago about gender, assimilation, and nativism in Asian American literature.

17. See Rey Chow, *Woman and Chinese Modernity* (Minneapolis: University of Minnesota Press, 1991).

18. See Asian Women United, *Making Waves* (Boston: Beacon Press, 1989).

19. Monique Wittig, "The Straight Mind," in *The Straight Mind and Other Essays* (Boston: Beacon Press, 1992), 25.

20. All too often we conceptualize different identities as separate, discrete, and given (as opposed to continually constructed and shifting). For an example of how "identity" might be conceptualized as contradictory and shifting moments rather than discrete and warring "homes," see Minnie Bruce Pratt, "Identity: Skin Blood Heart" and commentary by Biddy Martin and Chandra Talpade Mohanty, "Feminist Politics: What's Home Got to Do with It?"

21. See Jeff Nunokawa, " 'All the Sad Young Men' Aids and the Work of Mourning," in *inside/out*, edited by Diana Fuss (New York: Routledge, 1991), 311–323.

22. Trinh T. Minh-ha, 76.

23. Judith Butler, "Imitation and Gender Subordination," in *inside/out*, edited by Diana Fuss (New York: Routledge, 1991), 13–31.

24. Lisa Lowe, "Heterogeneity, Hybridity and Multiplicity: Marking Asian American Differences," *Diaspora* (Spring 1991): 24–44.

25. Haraway.

26. I am indebted to Wendy Brown for this point. See Wendy Brown, "Feminist Hesitations, Postmodern Exposures," *Differences* 2:1 (1991).

Chapter Twenty-six

Stories from the Homefront

Perspectives of Asian American Parents with Lesbian Daughters and Gay Sons

Alice Y. Hom

> Having been a classroom teacher since 1963, I have new knowledge that ten percent of all the students who came through my classroom have grown up and are gay and lesbian. . . . Because I cannot undo the past, I want to teach people the truth about homosexuality so people will not abandon these children.[1]

These are stories from the homefront; the emotions, responses, and attitudes of Asian American parents about their lesbian daughters or gay sons. The stories attempt to shed some light on parents' attitudes and inform lesbians and gay men various ways parents may react and respond to their coming out.

I focus on four themes that illustrate important concepts around understanding Asian American parents and their views on homosexuality. These themes emerged from the interviews: (1) the attitudes of parents before disclosure/discovery; (2) the attitudes and reactions of parents after disclosure/discovery; (3) disclosure to friends and their communities; and (4) advice for other parents.

Sexuality is an issue rarely or never discussed amongst Asian families, yet it remains a vital aspect of one's life. What are the implications of alternative sexualities in family situations? Coming out stories and experiences of Asian American lesbians and gay men have had some exposure and publication,[2] however the voices of the parents are rarely presented or known.

I found the majority of interviewees through personal contacts with individuals in organizations such as Asian Pacifica Sisters in San Francisco, Mahu Sisters and Brothers Alliance at UCLA and Gay Asian Pacific Alliance Community HIV Project in San Francisco. I met one set of parents through the Parents and Friends of Lesbians and Gays group in Los Angeles. Obviously, this select group of people, who were willing to talk about their child, might represent only certain perspectives. Nonetheless, I managed to pool a diverse set of parents despite the small size in terms of disclosing time and time lapse—some parents have known for years, and a few have recently found out. I did receive some "no" answers to my request. I also offered complete anonymity in the interviews; most preferred pseudonyms. Names with an asterisk sign denote pseudonyms.

I interviewed thirteen parents altogether, all mothers except for two fathers.[3] The interviewee pool consisted of four single mothers by divorce, a widower, two couples, and four married mothers. The ethnicities included four Chinese, four Japanese, three Pilipinas, one Vietnamese, and one Korean. Most live in California, with one in Portland and another in Hawaii. All of the interviews occurred in English with the exception of one interview conducted in Japanese with the lesbian daughter as translator. Ten out of the thirteen interviewees are first-generation immigrants. The other three are third-generation Japanese American. I interviewed four mothers of gay sons, including one mother with two gay sons. The rest had lesbian daughters, including one mother with two lesbian daughters. Six were told and seven inadvertently discovered about their children's sexual orientation.[4]

Most books on the topic of parents of lesbian and gay children report mainly on white middle-class families.[5] *Beyond Acceptance: Parents of Lesbians and Gays Talk about Their Experiences*, by Carolyn W. Griffin, Marian J. Wirth, and Arthur G. Wirth, discusses the experiences of twenty-three white middle-class parents from a Midwestern metropolitan city involved with Parents and Friends of Lesbians and Gays (PFLAG).[6] Another book, titled *Parents Matter: Parents' Relationships with Lesbian Daughters and Gay Sons*, by Ann Muller, relates the perspectives of lesbian and gay children with a few stories by the parents. Seventeen percent of the seventy-one people interviewed were black.[7] These examples present mainly an Anglo picture and fail to account for the diversity of lesbian and gay communities as well as different experiences of parents of color.

Attitudes of Parents toward Gays and Lesbians Predisclosure

The knowledge of lesbians and gay men in their native countries and in their communities in the United States serves as an important factor in dismantling the oft-used phrase that a son or daughter is gay or lesbian because of assimilation and acculturation in a Western context. The parents interviewed did not utter "it's a white disease," a phrase often heard and used when discussing coming out in an Asian American community and context. Connie S. Chan in her essay, "Issues of Identity Development among Asian American Lesbians and Gay Men," found in her study that nine out of ninety-five respondents were out to their parents. Chan suggested that this low number might be related to "... specific cultural values defining the traditional roles, which help to explain the reluctance of Asian-American lesbians and gay men to 'come out' to their parents and families."[8]

Nonetheless, the parents interviewed recounted incidents of being aware of lesbians and or gays while they were growing up and did not blame assimilation and Anglo American culture for their children's sexual orientation. One quote by Lucy Nguyen, a fifty-three year old Vietnamese immigrant who has two gay sons, does however, imply that the environment and attitudes of the United States allowed for her sons to express their gay identity. She stated

> I think all the gay activities and if I live at this time, environment like this, I think I'm lesbian. You know, be honest. When I was young, the society in—Vietnam is so strict—I have a really close friend, I love her, but just a friendship nothing else. In my mind, I say, well in this country it's free. They have no restraint, so that's why I accept it, whatever they are.[9]

This revealing remark assumes that an open environment allows for freedom of sexual expression. Nevertheless, it does not necessarily suggest lesbians and gay men exist solely because of a nurturing environment. Rather, lesbians and gay men must live and survive in different ways and/or make choices depending on the climate of the society at the time.

Midori Asakura,* a sixty-three-year-old Japanese immigrant with a lesbian daughter, related an example of lesbianism in Japan. She remembered, while studying to be a nurse, talk in the dorm rooms about "S," which denotes women who had really close friendships with one another.[10] She recalled,

> One day you'd see one woman with a certain blouse and the next day, you'd see the other woman with the same blouse. They would always sit together, they went everywhere together. There was talk that they were having sex, but I didn't think they were. . . . People used to say they felt each other out. I thought, "Nah, they're not having sex, why would they?" Everyone thought it was strange but no one really got into it.[11]

When asked what she thought of the "S" women, Midori replied, "I didn't think much of it, although I thought one was man-like, Kato-san, and the other, Fukuchi-san, who was very beautiful and sharp-minded was the woman."[12]

Another parent, George Tanaka,* a fifty-three-year-old Japanese American who grew up in Hawaii and has a lesbian daughter, remembers a particular person known as *mahu*.[13] Toni Barraquiel, a fifty-four-year-old Pilipina single mother with a gay son, commented on gay men in Manila because of their effeminacy and admission of being gay. Toni asserted these men would be in certain careers such as manicurists and hairdressers. When asked of the people's attitudes toward them, she replied,

> that they look down on those gays and lesbians, they make fun of them. . . . It seems as if it is an abnormal thing. The lesbian is not as prominent as the gays. They call her a tomboy because she's very athletic and well built.[14]

Maria Santos,* a fifty-four-year-old Pilipina immigrant with two lesbian daughters, spoke of gays and lesbians in Luzon. She said, "There were negative attitudes about them. 'Bakla' and 'Tomboy'—it was gay-bashing in words not in physical terms. There was name-calling that I did not participate in."[15]

Lucy Nguyen* had lesbian classmates in her all-girls high school. She said, "They were looked down upon, because this isn't normal. They were called 'homo'."[16] A common thread throughout the observations of the parents about gays and lesbians lies in stereotypical gender role associations. For example, Margaret Tsang,* a sixty-

*Names followed by asterisks are pseudonyms.

year-old Chinese single parent who has a gay son, recalled a family member who might possibly be gay, although there was not a name for it. She observed, "He was slanted toward nail polish and make-ups and all kinds of things. And he liked Chinese opera. He behaved in a very feminine fashion."[17]

Similarly, Liz Lee, a forty-two-year old Korean single parent with a lesbian daughter, clearly remembered lesbians in Seoul. "My mother's friend was always dressed like man in suit. She always had mousse or grease on her hair and she dressed like a man. She had five or six girlfriends always come over."[18] Liz related that she did not think anything about it and said they were respected.[19] When asked of people's attitudes toward these women, Liz responded, "They say nature made a mistake. They didn't think it was anybody's choice or anybody's preference."[20]

For the most part, the interviewees, aware of gays and lesbians during their growing-up years, associated gender-role reversals with gays and lesbians. The men were feminine and the women looked male or tomboy, with the women couples in a butch-femme type relationship. The belief and experiences with lesbians and gay men who dress and act in opposite gender roles serve as the backdrop of what to compare their children with when faced with their coming out. Most of what these parents see is a part of homosexuality, the dress or behavior. They have not seen the whole range of affectional, emotional, intellectual, and sexual components of a person. Although I asked the interviewees if they had any thoughts or attitudes about lesbians or gay men, most said they did not think about them and did not participate in the name calling or bashing. This might not be necessarily true because they were able to relate quite a few incidents of homophobic opinions which might have been internalized. Moreover, once they know they have a lesbian or gay child, that distance or non-judgmental attitude radically changes. As one mother remarked, "the fire is on the other side of the river bank. The matter is taking place somewhere else, it's not your problem."[21]

Disclosure or Discovery

For the most part, parents experience a wide range of emotions, feelings, and attitudes when they find out they have a lesbian daughter or gay son. Parents find out through a variety of ways, ranging from a direct disclosure by the child themselves, discovering the fact from a journal, confronting the child because of suspicions, or by walking in on them.

For example, Liz Lee, who walked in on her daughter Sandy, said, "[it was] the end of the world. Still today I can't relate to anything that's going on with my daughter, but I'm accepting."[22] She found out in 1990 and said,

> I was hoping it was a stage she's going through and that she could change. I didn't accept for a long time. I didn't think she would come out in the open like this. I thought she would just keep it and later on get married. That's what I thought but she's really out and open. . . . I said to myself I accept it because she is going to live that way.[23]

Because Sandy serves as the cochair of the Gay, Lesbian, and Bisexual Association at school, her mother sees Sandy as happy and politically fulfilled from this position, which assists her process in accepting Sandy's sexual orientation. However, like many of the parents interviewed, she initially thought she had done something wrong. "I didn't lead a normal life at the time either. But Sandy always accept me as I was and she was always happy when I was happy and I think that's love. As long as Sandy's happy."[24]

Toni Barraquiel responded differently when Joel told her at an early age of thirteen or fourteen that he was gay back in the mid-1980s. She plainly asked him if he felt happy, which he replied affirmatively. Thus her response, "well, if you're happy I'll support you, I'll be happy for you."[25] Their relationship as a single mother and only child has always been one of closeness and open communication, so problems did not arise in terms of disclosing his sexual orientation. Toni Barraquiel experienced confusion because at the time he had girlfriends and she did not think of him as a typical feminine gay man, since he looked macho. She also wondered if her single-mother role had anything to do with Joel's gay orientation:

> Maybe because I raised him by myself, it was a matriarchal thing. I have read now that these gays, there is something in the anatomy of their bodies that affect the way they are. So it is not because I raised him alone, maybe it's in the anatomy of the body. Even if I think that because I raised him alone as a mother, even if he came out to be gay, he was raised as a good person. No matter what I would say I'm still lucky he came out to be like that.[26]

In the end she accepted Joel no matter what caused his sexual orientation.

Katherine Tanaka,* a fifty-three-year-old Japanese American from Hawaii, found out about Melissa's lesbianism through an indirect family conversation. George Tanaka* brought up the issue of sexuality and asked Melissa* if she was a lesbian. He suspected after reading her work on the computer. Katherine* remembered her response:

> I was in a state of shock. I didn't expect it, so I didn't know how to react. It was the thing of disbelief, horror and shame and the whole thing. I guess I felt the Asian values I was taught surface in the sense that something was wrong. That she didn't turn out the way we had raised her to be.[27]

George Tanaka* recalled, "After we hugged, she went off to her bedroom. As she was walking away from us, all of a sudden I felt like she was a stranger. I thought I knew [her]. Here was a very important part of her and I didn't know anything about it."[28] The idea of not knowing one's children anymore after discovering their sexual orientation remains a common initial response from the interviewees. Because of this one aspect, parents believe their child has changed and is no longer the person they thought they knew. For example, one parent said:

> The grieving process took a long time. Especially the thing about not being a bride. Not having her be a bride was a very devastating change of plans for her life. I thought I was in her life and it made me feel when she said she was a lesbian that there was no

place for me in her life. I didn't know how I could fit into her life because I didn't know how to be the mother of a lesbian.[29]

Upon finding out, the parents interviewed spoke of common responses and questions they had. What did I do wrong? Was I responsible for my child's lesbian or gay identity? What will others think? How do I relate to my child? What role do I have now that I know my child is a lesbian or gay man? The emotions a parent has ranged from the loss of a dream they had for their child to a fear of what is in store for them as a gay or lesbian person in this society.

Nancy Shigekawa,* a third-generation Japanese American born and residing in Hawaii, recalled her reaction:

> I had come home one night and they were in the bedroom. Then I knew it wasn't just being in the room. My reaction was outrage, to say the least. I was so angry. I told them to come out . . . and I said [to her girlfriend], "I'm going to kill you if you ever come back." That's how I was feeling. I look back now and think I must have been like a crazy lady.[30]

Maria Santos* remembered her discovery.

> I found out through a phone call from the parents of [her] best friend. They [Cecilia* and her friend] were trying to sneak out, and they had a relationship. I thought it would go away. Let her see a psychiatrist. But she fooled me. In her second year at college she told me she was a lesbian. It broke my heart. That was the first time I heard the word lesbian, but I knew what it meant. Like the tomboy.[31]

She also had a feeling about her youngest daughter, Paulette:*

> At Cecilia's graduation I saw them talking secretly and I saw the pink triangle on her backpack. I can't explain it. It's a mother's instinct. I prayed that it would not be so[starts to cry]. Paulette told me in a letter that she was a lesbian and that Cecilia had nothing to do with it. I wanted it to change. I had the dream, that kids go to college, get married, and have kids.[32]

Maria Santos* did not talk to anyone about her daughters. She grew up having to face the world on her own without talking to others. However, she said, "But I read books, articles all about gays and lesbians as members of the community. They are normal people. I did not read negative things about them."[33]

In this sense, parents also have a coming-out process that they go through. They must deal with internalized homophobia and re-evaluate their beliefs and feelings about lesbians and gay men. One method in this process includes reading about and listening to gay men and lesbians talk about their lives. Having personal contact or at least information on lesbian and gay life takes the mystery out of the stereotypes and misconceptions that parents might have of lesbian and gay people. What helped some women was the personal interaction and reading about lesbian and gay men's lives. They had more information with which to contrast, contradict, and support their previous notions of lesbians and gay men.

Yet, sometimes some parents interviewed have not yet read or do not seek outside help or information. Some of the parents did not talk to others and have remained alone in their thinking. This does not necessarily have negative effects. Liz Lee said, "Still today I don't think I can discuss with her in this matter because I can't relate. . . . I can't handle it. I wouldn't know how to talk to her about this subject. I just let her be happy."[34]

MG Espiritu,* a sixty-year-old Pilipina immigrant, believes her daughter's lesbianism stems from environmental causes such as being with other lesbians. Nonetheless, less than a couple of years after finding out about her daughter Michelle, she went with her daughter to an Asian Pacific lesbian Lunar New Year banquet. MG* did so because her daughter wanted it and she wanted to please her. When asked how she felt at the event, MG* replied, "Oh, it's normal. It's just like my little girls' parties that they go to."[35] She speaks of little by little trying to accept Michelle's lesbianism.

Parents, Friends, and Their Ethnic Communities

For some parents, having a lesbian or gay child brings up the issue of their status and reputation in the community and family network. Questions such as: What is society going to think of me? Will the neighbors know and what will it reflect upon us? Did they raise a bad child?

> I told her we would have to move away from this house. I felt strongly neighbors and friends in the community would not want to associate with us if they knew we had a child who had chosen to be homosexual.[36]

The above quote reflected one parent's original reaction. Now she feels differently but is still not quite out to her family in Hawaii.

Some parents have told their siblings or friends. Others do not talk to relatives or friends at all because of fear they will not understand.

The following quote highlighted a typical anxiety of parents:

> I was ashamed. I felt I had a lot to do with it too. In my mind I'm not stupid, I'm telling myself, I know I didn't do it to her. I don't know if it's only because I'm Japanese . . . that's the way I saw it. I felt a sense of shame, that something was wrong with my family. I would look at Debbie* and just feel so guilty that I have these thoughts that something's wrong with her. But mostly I was selfish. I felt more for myself, what I am going to say? How am I going to react to people when they find out?[37]

Despite her apprehension in the beginning, she did disclose Debbie's lesbianism to a close friend:

> I have a dear friend who I finally told because she was telling me about these different friends who had gay children. I couldn't stand it, I said, "You know, Bea, I have to tell you my daughter is gay." She was dumfounded. I'm starting to cheer her up and all that. That was a big step for me to come out.

Nancy Shigekawa's* quote emphasizes the complexity of feelings that parents have when adjusting to their children's sexual orientation.

If parents are not close to their immediate family, they might not have told them.

Others have not spoken because they do not care whether or not their family knows. Some parents do not disclose the fact of their gay son or lesbian daughter to protect them from facing unnecessary problems.

When asked how their respective ethnic communities feel about lesbians and gay men, some parents responded with firm conviction. Liz Lee, who spoke about the Korean community, said, "As long as they're not in their house, not in their life, they accept it perfectly."[38] She mentioned her daughter's lesbianism to a nephew but not to others in her family. "I'm sure in the future I have to tell them, but right now nobody has asked me and I don't particularly like to volunteer."[39] Jack Chan,* a sixty-one-year-old Chinese immigrant, claimed, "Shame, that's a big factor. Shame brought upon the family. You have to remember the Chinese, the name, the face of the family is everything. I don't know how to overcome that."[40]

Lucy Nguyen* gave this answer about the Vietnamese community, "They won't accept it. Because for a long, long time they say they [gays and lesbians] are not good people, that's why."[41] Lucy felt that by talking about it would help and teach the community to open their minds. The frankness and openness of speaking out about gay and lesbians will inform people of our existence and force the issue in the open. In this way having parents come out will make others understand their experiences and allow for their validation and affirmation as well.

Although most of these parents have negative views about the acceptance level of friends and particularly with ethnic communities, some have taken steps to confide in people. One must also realize their opinion reflects their current situation and opinion which might change over time. Three of the parents have participated in panels and discussions on Asian American parents with lesbian and gay kids.

Advice to Other Parents

In many ways the mere fact these parents agreed to the interview has much to say about their feelings or attitudes toward lesbian and gay sexuality and their kids. Although some parents might feel some unease and reservations, they had enough courage to speak to me and voice their opinions. Many of the parents did so out of love and concern for their children. A few thought that they did not have anything to say but agreed to talk to me. In the process of these interviews, some parents expressed appreciation and comfort in talking to someone about their experiences. Their struggle of coming to terms with their lesbian daughters and gay sons merits notice.

One of my last questions related to helping other parents. While some did not have an answer to the question, "What advice do you have for other parents with lesbian and gay kids?" a few responded with the following suggestions. For example,

> Love them like a normal individual. Give all the compassion and understanding. Don't treat your child differently because the person is gay, because this is an individual. . . . I cannot understand why it is so hard for these parents to accept their child is gay. What makes them so different, because they are gay? The more you should support your kid, because as it is in society, it has not been accepted one hundred percent.[42]

I cannot throw them out. I love them so much. Even more now because they are more of a minority. They are American Asian, women and lesbian. Triple minority. I have to help fight for them. . . . Accept them as they are. Love them more. They will encounter problems. It will take years and years to overcome homophobia. Make them ambitious, well educated, better than others so they can succeed.[43]

Tina Chan,* a fifty-eight-year-old Chinese immigrant, offers similar advice. Other parents concurred:

My advice is to accept them. They haven't changed at all. They're still the same person. The only thing different is their sexual orientation. They should really have the support from the family, so they would not have this battle like they're not even being accepted in the family. They should look at them like they have not changed. Parents can't do it. They think the whole person has changed, and I think that's terrible because they haven't. I mean it's so stupid.[44]

Jack Chan* also leaves us with advice to take to heart:

Don't feel depressed that their parent[is] coming around so slow or not coming around at all. Remember when you come out to them, the parent generally go[es] into the closet themselves. However long it take you to come out, it'll probably take them longer to accept. It's a slow process. Don't give up.[45]

Concluding Remarks

George Tanaka* relates an incident where he and his wife told their coming out process in front of ten Asian American gay men and in the end found some of the men crying. "The tears surprised me. . . . We were representing the sadness that there could not be loving parents. Representing some hope their parents would likewise be able to become loving about it."[46] The belief that parents can change and go through a process where eventual acceptance and supportiveness appear to have a basis in reality, although a happy ending might not always be the case.

From these interviews one can sense some of the thoughts, actions, and experiences of Asian American parents. These stories are not the last word but signal the beginning of a more informed dialogue.

What would the stories of their daughters and sons look like against their parents' perceptions? It would be helpful to have the stories side by side to evaluate the differences. Moreover, gay and lesbian children might have perspectives that inform parents. Other issues such as socialization processes, religious, language, and cultural issues, and spouses' opinions need further exploration. I did not include a discussion on the origins of lesbian and gay sexual identity. I hope these stories from the homefront can serve as an initial mapping of a complex sexual territory that is part of Asian American family dynamics.

NOTES

The desire to work on this project came after listening to two Japanese American parents, George and Katherine Tanaka, talk about their lesbian daughter. They revealed a painful process of going through their own coming out while grappling with their daughter's sexual identity and their own values and beliefs. As members of Parents and Friends of Lesbians and Gays (PFLAG), they mentioned they were the only Asian Americans, the only parents of color, for that matter, in this organization. Despite being the Asian American contact, Katherine has received less than ten calls during a two year time span, and not one Asian American parent has ever come to PFLAG. She recounted her feelings and belief of being the only Asian parent with a gay child. That feeling of loneliness and alienation struck me deeply because as an Asian American lesbian I could identify with her feelings.

1. Interview with Katherine Tanaka. Los Angeles, California, February 21, 1993.

2. See Kitty Tsui, *the words of a woman who breathes fire* (San Francisco: Spinsters Ink, 1983). C. Chung, Alison Kim, and A. K. Lemshewsky eds., *Between the Lines: An Anthology by Pacific/Asian Lesbians* (Santa Cruz: Dancing Bird Press, 1987). Rakesh Ratti, ed., *A Lotus of Another Color: The Unfolding of the South Asian Gay and Lesbian Experience* (Boston: Alyson Press, 1993). Silvera Makeda, ed., *A Piece of My Heart: A Lesbian of Colour Anthology* (Toronto: Sister Vision Press, 1993).

3. Mothers comprise the majority of the parents interviewed. Perhaps mothers are more apt to talk about their feelings and emotions about having a gay son or lesbian daughter than the father. Mothers might be more understanding and willing to discuss their emotions and experiences than the fathers who also know.

4. I did not interview parents who had a bisexual child. I believe a son or daughter who comes out as bisexual might encounter a different set of questions and reactions. Especially since the parent might hope and persuade the daughter or son to "choose" heterosexuality instead of homosexuality.

5. See Carolyn W. Griffin, Marian J. Wirth, and Arthur G. Wirth, *Beyond Acceptance: Parents of Lesbians and Gays Talk about Their Experiences* (New York: St. Martin's Press, 1986).

6. Parents and Friends of Lesbians and Gays (PFlag) has chapters all around the United States. One couple and a father interviewed are involved with PFlag in their respective locales.

7. Ann Muller, *Parents Matter: Parents' Relationships with Lesbian Daughters and Gay Sons* (Tallahassee: Naiad Press, 1987), 197.

8. Connie S. Chan, "Issues of Identity Development Among Asian-American Lesbians and Gay Men." *Journal of Counseling and Development*, 68 (September/October, 1989), 19.

9. Interview with Lucy Nguyen. Los Angeles, California, February 20, 1993.

10. Interview with Midori Asakura. Los Angeles, California, April 18, 1993.

11. Midori Asakura.

12. Ibid.

13. *Mahu* does not necessarily mean gay but defines a man who dresses and acts feminine. However, it's common usage does denote a gay man.

14. Interview with Toni Barraquiel. Los Angeles, California, April 18, 1993.

15. Telephone interview Maria Santos. Portland, Oregon, May 9, 1993.

16. Lucy Nguyen.

17. Interview with Margaret Tsang. San Francisco, California, February 5, 1993.

18. Interview with Liz Lee. Los Angeles, California, May 11, 1993.

19. Liz based this respect on this particular woman's election to something similar to a city council and her standing in the community.

20. Liz Lee.

21. Midori Asakura.

22. Liz Lee.

23. Ibid.
24. Ibid.
25. Toni Barraquiel.
26. Ibid.
27. Katherine Tanaka.
28. Interview with George Tanaka. Los Angeles, California, February 21, 1993.
29. Katherine Tanaka.
30. Telephone interview with Nancy Shigekawa. Kaneohe, Hawaii, March 20, 1993.
31. Maria Santos.
32. Ibid.
33. Ibid.
34. Liz Lee.
35. Interview with MG Espiritu. Northern California, July 20, 1993.
36. Katherine Tanaka.
37. Nancy Shigekawa.
38. Liz Lee.
39. Ibid.
40. Interview with Jack Chan. Northern California, July 18, 1993.
41. Lucy Nguyen.
42. Toni Barraquiel.
43. Maria Santos.
44. Interview with Tina Chan. Northern California, July 18, 1993.
45. Jack Chan.
46. George Tanaka.

Chapter Twenty-seven

Searching for Community
Filipino Gay Men in New York City

Martin F. Manalansan IV

Introduction

In 1987, a Filipino gay man named Exotica was crowned Miss Fire Island. The Miss Fire Island beauty contest is an annual drag event in Fire Island (located off the coast of Long Island) and is considered to be the premier gay summer mecca in America. It was interesting to note that a considerable number of the contestants who were not Caucasian were Filipinos. Furthermore, Exotica was not the first Filipino recipient of the crown; another Filipino was crowned earlier in the seventies. In 1992, a Filipino gay and lesbian group called *Kambal sa Lusog* marched in two parades in New York City, Gay Pride Day and Philippine Independence Day. These iconic events suggest the strong presence of Filipinos in the American gay scene, particularly in New York City.

This paper delineates this presence by analyzing the issues of identity and community among fifty gay Filipino men in the city in their attempts to institutionalize or organize themselves. Through excerpts from life history interviews and field observations, I explore the ways in which being "gay" and being "Filipino" are continually being shaped by historical events.

I use the term "community" not as a static, closed, and unified system. Rather, I use the term strategically and conceptualize it as a fluid movement between subjectivity/identity and collective action.[1] Therefore, intrinsic to this use of the term "community" is a sense of dissent and contestation along with a sense of belonging to a group or cause. I also use Benedict Anderson's notion of community as "imagined,"[2] which means symbols, language, and other cultural practices and products, from songs to books, are sites where people articulate their sense of belonging. The concept of identity is not a series or stages of development or as a given category but a dynamic package of meanings contingent upon practices that are both individually and collectively reconfigured.[3]

The first section briefly explores the cleavages that gave rise to a diversity of voices and outlines differences such as class, attitudes toward various homosexual practices, and ethnic/racial identity. In the next two sections, two pivotal moments, the *Miss Saigon* controversy and the AIDS pandemic, are discussed in terms of the patterns of cultural actions and countereactions. I focus on new or reconfigured collective discourses, specifically language and ritual. I also emphasize the organizing efforts of Filipinos to create a gay and lesbian group (*Kambal sa Lusog*) and an AIDS advocacy group. A specific activity called the *Santacruzan* by *Kambal sa Lusog* incorporates symbols from different national traditions and provides an example of the collective representation of community.

Divergent Voices

Ang sabi nila, iba't iba daw ang bakla, mayroon cheap, may pa-class, nandito yoong malandi at saka ang mayumi—kuno! [They say there are different kinds of *bakla*, those who are tacky, those who pretend they have class, then there are the whorish and the virginal—not!]

We are all gay. We are all Filipinos. We need to empower ourselves as a group.

Tigilan ako ng mga tsismosang bakla, wiz ko type maki-beso-beso sa mga baklang Pilipino— puro mga intrigera! [Get me away from those gossipy *bakla*, I don't want to socialize with those Filipino *bakla*, they are all gossip mongers!]

If we take these voices as indices of the opinions and stances of Filipino gay men, we will find a spectrum of similarities and divergences. Most Filipino gay men consider place of birth as an important gauge of the attitudes and ideas of a gay individual. The dichotomy between U.S.-born versus Philippine- or native-born Filipino gay men is actually used by many informants I have interviewed. This simplistic dichotomy is inadequate and erroneous. It does not begin to address the diversity among Filipino gay men.

Attitudes toward Homosexual Practices

In a group discussion I lead with a group of Filipino gay men and lesbians, one gay man pointed out that the culture in which one was raised in and, more importantly, where one was socialized into a particular homosexual tradition mattered more than place of birth. This is particularly true in many of my informants who immigrated as young children or in their early teens. Many of them explored their sexual identities under the symbols and practices of American culture. Many of them were not exposed to the *bakla* traditions[4] and more frequently followed the idioms and practices of American gay culture. These men were usually concerned with issues of coming out and identified more with a hypermasculine gay culture.

While almost all of my informants identified as gay, many of those who immigrated as adults and had some encounters in *bakla* practices and traditions were emphatic in delineating major difference between American gay and Philippine *bakla* culture. Most of these differences centered on the issue of cross-dressing and effeminacy.

However, there were some informants, including two American-born Filipinos, who through frequent visits to the Philippines as well as extended stays as students in Philippine schools were exposed to and involved in the *bakla* tradition. This group of men were more familiar with the cross-dressing traditions of homosexuality in the Philippines and usually spoke versions of Filipino swardspeak (a kind of gay argot).[5]

A case illustrates this point. One informant who was born and raised in California said that a turning point in his life was when he went to the Philippines at the age of sixteen and his uncle introduced him to cross-dressing and other practices among homosexuals. That brief (month and a half) visit was to become an important element in the way he now socialized in the gay community. He seeks cross-dressing opportunities not only with other transvestites but with other Filipinos. He said that Filipino gay men did not cross-dress for shock value but for realness. He further mentioned that he was unlike those gay men who were into queer androgyny, consciously looking midway between male and female. He and other gay men who cross-dressed attempted to look like real women. More important, despite the fact that he was raised speaking English at home, his friendships with other Philippine-born gay men has encouraged him to attempt to speak at least some smattering of the Filipino gay argot.

Some informants felt that Filipino cross-dressers had illusions (*ilusyonada*) and were internally homophobic or self-hating. These same informants were the ones who reported that they were part of the mainstream gay community. Some of them go to gyms and assume masculine ("straight-acting") mannerisms. They saw the cross-dressing practices of other Filipinos to be either low-class, archaic/anachronous (meaning cross-dressing belonged in the Philippines and not here in America).

On the other hand, the cross-dressers would call these guys *pamacho* (acting macho) or *pa-min* (acting like men). Filipino gay cross-dressers accused these "masculine" men of mimicking white Americans and of having illusions of being "real" men. Exotica,[6] one of my informants, said that cross-dressing for him was a way of getting men. He liked assuming more exotic identities and *nom de plumes* such as "Suzie Wong" or "Nancy Kwan." In the Philippines, he said he was able to get men for sex, but he had to pay them. In America, he said there was a "market" for his cross-dressing talent and exotic beauty. He said that he could not compete in the hypermasculine, gym-oriented world of mainstream gay life in New York. He said, "With my slight build, who would even give me a second look if I was wearing a T-shirt." However, he said that there were men, particularly those who were not gay-identified, who were attracted to "beautiful," "oriental" cross-dressers. He said that here in America, he did not have to pay the man to have sex with him, it was the other way around. He said, "Sometimes I feel so cheap because the man will insist on paying for everything including the pleasure of having sex with you. It is like everything goes on an opposite current here in America. I like it."

Conflicts between Filipino gay cross-dressers and non-cross-dressers are not dramatically played out in violent confrontations, but rather in avoidance. Furthermore, the differences are usually played down with a "live and let live" or "*yun ang type niya*" (that is his/her choice) attitude.

Social Class

Class is a more implicit boundary marker among gay Filipinos. Many of my informants denied noting any difference between themselves and other gay Filipinos. However, upon further probing, several of them (mostly those who were born and raised
in the Philippines) will say, "Well, there are those who gossip a lot and just make
bitchy remarks," or "Other Filipino gays are so tacky." Some Filipino gay men
actually used terms as *baklang talipapa* (the *bakla* of the wet market), *baklang cheap*
(tacky *bakla*), and *baklang kalye* (*bakla* of the streets), to designate gay Filipinos who
they think are of a lower class standing or of lower "breeding." The indices of "low
breeding" are myriad, but some informants agree that fluency in the English language, styles of dress, schools attended, and "bearing" or how a gay Filipino carries
himself.

Family roots are said to be another marker of class. *De buena familia* (from a
good family) is a term used by gay men to portray how someone has class and social
standing. Another word used to describe somebody who has a lot of money as
datungera (*datung* is swardspeak for money, and the noun is given the feminine
form). In most conversations between Filipinos that I have heard and observed, the
typical insult hurled at other gay men apart from physical traits were the idioms
derived from class or the lack thereof.

Despite these occurrences, many still assert that America has leveled off some of
these distinctions. An informant said, "There are some Filipinos I would normally
not have contact with back home in the Philippines, but here in America we are
thrown together in the bars, in the streets, some neighborhoods . . . you know."

The case of David, a gay Filipino in his forties, is particularly instructive. He was
very proud of his aristocratic background in the Philippines. He said America was
very funny because he was able to maintain relationships with people who were not
of his class. Coming from a landed family in the Philippines, he said that he tried to
create some distance from people who were not his equal. But this was not true in
America. For a long time, his lover was a telephone linesman with a high school
degree. He said there were times when the class disparity showed. For example,
conflicts occurred in situations when their tastes for particular leisure activities
were divided into, in his mind, the classy and the tasteless, between a concert and
bowling.

He further reported that his first ten years of living in America were spent as an
illegal alien. Despite having money and a good education, he started as a janitor or a
busboy due to lack of legal papers. He said, "I guess living during those years and
doing those kinds of jobs were exciting in a way . . . a different way of experiencing
America." Indeed, David's own class-conscious ways have been tempered to a large
extent by the immigration experience. He now has contacts with several Filipino gay
men, many of whom were of lower class origins.

Most of those who were born in America did not report any class distinctions
among Filipinos. They were, however, more up front about their class origins. Two
of my informants who were born and raised in California prefaced their stories about
childhood by stating that they were from working-class families in the U.S. army.

Ethnic/Racial Identity

Most articles on Asian American gay men regard identity as a static given and construct ethnic identity as a polar opposite of gay identity.[7] Among the questions I asked my fifty Filipino informants was how they identified ethnically or racially. All but one said that they identified as Filipino or Filipino American. When I asked about the category Asian/Pacific Islander, most of them said that while they assumed this category in official papers and functions, they perceived Asia or Asian only in geographic terms. When I asked the Filipino gay men how they differed from Asian gay men, many Filipino informants said that they did not have the same kind of issues such as coming out and homophobia.

A majority of informants, mostly immigrants, felt that Philippine society was relatively tolerant of homosexuality. Some informants reported very good responses from families when they did "come out." Others felt that they didn't have to come out about being gay because they thought that their families knew about their identity without their having to verbally acknowledge it. Filipino informants felt that other Asian men, particularly those who have just immigrated to America, did not speak English as well as they did. Important cultural differences, such as religion, were cited by informants as significant. Many felt that they had a closer cultural affinity with Latinos.

Among those who were born in the Philippines, regional ethnolinguistic differences became apparent in relation to other Filipinos. Some of the informants did not speak Pilipino or Tagalog and instead spoke a regional language such as Bisaya or Ilongo. However, differences in languages and region were usually displaced by the use of English or Filipino swardspeak by many of the informants.

What I have presented above is a broad outline of the differences and similarities among Filipino gay men. This is to provide a kind of foundation in which to situate the succeeding discussions of Filipino men coming together and acting in a more collective manner. This section has shown how there are pivotal points that act as markers of difference such as class, cultural traditions, and practices of homosexuality.

The Miss Saigon Interlude: Irony of a Different Kind

In the first full length article on Asian gays and lesbians in the now-defunct magazine Outweek,[8] Nina Reyes (a Filipino American lesbian) wrote how the controversy surrounding the Broadway show Miss Saigon acted as a catalyst in bringing together many Asian gay and straight political activists to the forefront. According to Reyes, apart from the controversy around hiring (specifically, the use of a Caucasian, Jonathan Price, to play a Eurasian pimp) and the allegedly racist Madame Butterfly–inspired storyline, the opening night of Miss Saigon was the venue of protests by Asian gay and lesbian groups.

It is ironic that in the same article, Miss Reyes quoted a Filipino gay man who pointed out that not all Filipinos agreed with the protests since, after all, the star of the show, Lea Salonga, was a Filipina. Indeed, many of my informants have seen the show and have reported how relatives and Filipino friends (both gay and straight), particularly those from other states and the Philippines, would include seeing the show as the highlight of their visits to the Big Apple. The issue here was not just a matter of taste but had important political underpinnings. Many Filipinos felt that their sentiments and thoughts about the show were not represented in the mass media.

This was not to be the end of this controversy. The Gay Asian Pacific Islander Men of New York (GAPIMNY), one of the most vociferous groups in the *Miss Saigon* protest, celebrated its anniversary with a variety show and dance at the Lesbian and Gay Community Center in Manhattan in the summer of 1992. One of the drag performers, a Filipino gay man, decided to participate with a lipsync performance of one of Lea Salonga's songs in *Miss Saigon*. This caused a lot of ruckus. Before the performance, attempts were made by certain non-Filipinos to dissuade the drag performer from going though his intended repertoire even while the emcee was reading a disclaimer by GAPIMNY that stated that the group disavows any connection with the Broadway show. Furthermore, the disclaimer also stated that the audience should enjoy the performance and at the same time remember the racist underpinnings of the show's storyline and production practices.

It is important to note not only the effects of the *Miss Saigon* controversy on Asian American gay politics but also how the representations and characters of this Broadway show have become icons of Filipino gay men. After each show, many Filipinos gathered backstage to talk to the actors and actresses (many of whom are Filipino or Filipino American). A good number of these fans are gay men.

Filipino gay men have appropriated many of the symbols and figures of this Broadway play. For Halloween in 1991, Leilani, a Filipino cross-dresser, bought a *cheongsam* in Chinatown, had a friend pull his hair back into a bun, and paraded around Greenwich Village with just a small woolen scarf to protect him from the blustery cold weather. He was extremely delighted to hear people scream "Miss Saigon" at him.

Several cross-dressing Filipinos I interviewed have admitted to using either Kim (the main character in *Miss Saigon*) or Lea Salonga as drag names. In fact, they said that when they talk about another gay Filipino who is either in a moody sad state or is extremely despondent, they say that he is doing a *Miss Saigon* or he is playing the role of Kim (*nagmi—Miss Saigon* or *Kim ang drama niya ngayon*).

The issues surrounding the controversy and the reaction of Filipinos, particularly gay men, have to do with several factors. The first is that of immigration and the American dream. For many of these gay Filipinos, Lea Salonga represented their own aspirations regarding America. She initially had to be certified by Actor's Equity to enable her to work on Broadway since she was neither an American citizen/resident nor a member of the group. Her success in winning the Tony Award and her receiving the green card (permanent resident status) was very much seen as a collective triumph. An informant pointed to Miss Salonga's Tony acceptance speech as particularly meaningful. After receiving the award, she said, "Your dreams can come true."

Indeed, for many Filipinos, gay or straight, these words seemed to be directed at them. Since a large number of my informants are immigrants, some of whom are illegal, the play provided an alternative narrative to the frustrations of daily life as foreigner trying to attain the American dream. As one informant said, "*Mahirap dito sa Amerika pero kaunting tiyaga . . . byuti ka na.*" [It is hard here in America, but with a little perseverance, you will succeed (beauty here is used as part of swardspeak, and connotes good luck or fate.)]

Race and racism, which were the central issues of the controversy, were less significant for many of my informants. Those who saw the play talked about the singing abilities of the actors and the magnificent stage design. When queried about the themes of the show, they said that the bar scenes reminded them of Olongapo and Angeles cities in the Philippines. These cities were sites of the two biggest U.S. military installations outside America. In these places, bars, prostitutes and American servicemen were everyday scenes.

The discourse of race was not particularly meaningful for many of my informants, a majority of whom have immigrated in their twenties. Out of the fifty informants, four reported an incident of racial discrimination. Most reported never encountering it. This was not entirely fortuitous. These men may have encountered some kind of discriminatory practices but interpreted it as part of the hardships of being an immigrant in America.

While many of them did not pick up on the Orientalist symbolisms of *Miss Saigon*, this should not be interpreted as a case of false consciousness, rather this kind of reaction is symptomatic in immigrant cultures. Immigrants constantly negotiate both dominant/hegemonic and subordinate (minority) cultural products and practices into meaningful arrangements that inform their lives.[9] In the case of *Miss Saigon*, the racial stereotypes are subsumed, and instead, the play is interpreted as a symbolic and literal vehicle for attaining success in America. Many of my informants felt that the crucial element of the play was that of getting to America and attaining the American dream.

In sum, with the *Miss Saigon* controversy, we have a historical moment which provided Filipinos in the U.S. a pool of collective symbols from which they could create discursive practices from cross-dressing to swardspeak. For many gay Filipino men in New York City, *Miss Saigon* was the impetus for the generation of camp symbols and discourses about some kind of national/ethnic and immigrant identities and aspirations.

AIDS: Or the Aunt That Pulled Us Together

I remember that around 1986, I began to hear about some Filipino *bakla* dying of AIDS in the West Coast. Then soon after that I heard about a Filipino who died in New York City. Then, I heard about this famous Filipino hairdresser who died. Afterwards the first of my friends came down with pneumonia. It was of course, Tita Aida. She struck again and again.

Tita Aida or Auntie/Aunt Aida is the name Filipino gay men have coined for AIDS. I have explored this unique construction of AIDS by this group of men in an earlier paper,[10] but it is necessary to note that this construction is not idiosyncratic. It emanates from Philippine concepts of illness, gender, and sexuality. The personification of the disease by gay Filipinos reflects the growing number of AIDS cases among Filipino gay men in America.[11] During the period from 1986 to 1988, the rise of AIDS cases among Asians in San Francisco was first documented.[12]

It was the same period of time when many of my informants started to become aware of the devastation of the disease. Most of them thought that the disease only affected white men. One informant said, "I thought that only white men, *yung mga byuti* (the beautiful ones) who were having sex constantly, were the only ones getting it." Before 1986, there were rumors as well as some published articles both in Filipino publications here and back in the Philippines which talked about the natural immunity of Filipinos against the disease. Some articles talked about the diet (such as eating *bagoong* or salted shrimp paste) as the reason why there were no Filipinos with AIDS.

This was soon dispelled by the sudden onslaught of Filipino cases during the late eighties. An informant remembered how he took care of about five friends. He said,

> *Ang hirap . . . manash* [it was hard sister] I had to massage, clean, shop, and do so many things. It was a horror watching them die slowly and painfully. And when they died. . . . My friends and I realized that there was no money for a burial or to send the bodies back to the Philippines. That was when we had some fundraising dinners. We just had dinner, not the *siyam-siyam* (traditional Filipino prayer ritual held several days after a burial), but just a simple get-together at somebody's place and a hat is passed to get some money to defray some expenses.

Many of the informants who have had friends die of AIDS reported similar themes and situations. Many of their friends were alone and without family because they were the first in their families to settle here or because their families refused to have anything to do with them after the truth came out. Some families took these ailing gay Filipinos back and refused to acknowledge both these men's disease and sexual orientation. However, there were also a number of families who accepted them, their gay friends, and lovers. In cases where there was a lover (usually Caucasian), it was he who oftentimes took care of the ailing Filipino.

In cases when the Filipino was alone, going back home to the Philippines was not seen as a viable option. First, because there were no adequate medical facilities that could take care of a patient with AIDS. Second, there were horror stories going around about how some Filipinos with AIDS were deported from the Philippines. Third, coming down with the disease was seen by some as a failure on their part of attaining the American dream, particularly those who found out as part of their naturalization (citizenship) process. American immigration laws prohibit (despite high hopes for changes in the new Clinton administration) the immigration of people who either have AIDS or are HIV seropositive.

AIDS has created a common experience from which gay Filipinos in New York build and create new discourses and practices. *Abuloy* or alms for the dead have become institutionalized and have acquired a new dimension. Gay Filipinos put up fashion shows and drag parties to help defray the burial or medical expenses of friends who have died. These collective efforts have become a regular occurrence.

Other collective efforts (most of whom are by gay and lesbian) include symposiums about AIDS in the Filipino community in New York. A group of gay Filipino men was formed to institutionalize efforts to help Filipinos with AIDS. This group, the Advocacy Group, got Filipinos with HIV/AIDS and formed to provide support services. There are still problems. Some Filipino gay men with AIDS are wary of other Filipino gay men helping them because of the interlocking network of gay Filipinos. There is a real possibility coming into contact with other Filipinos whom one knows. Other problems include Filipinos' inadequate access to services due to fear and lack of information.

Notwithstanding these difficulties, AIDS has provided a way of pulling Filipinos into some kind of collective action. While there are still sporadic attempts at solving some of the issues and problems many Filipino gay men face in the pandemic, there is a growing systematization of efforts.

Coming Together: Some Voices and (Re) Visions

In March 1991, an organization of Filipino gay men and lesbians called *Kambal sa Lusog* (which literally means "twins in health" but is interpreted to be "comrades in the struggle") was formed. Some informants who were members of this organization said that one of the impetuses for the formation of this group was the *Miss Saigon* controversy. However, after talking to one of the founders of the group, he said that there has been talk about such a group even before the *Miss Saigon* controversy. A large factor was that many Filipinos do not relate to other Asians or to an Asian identity.

This statement had been confirmed by my interviews with Filipino gay men. Many perceived Asia only in terms of geography; significant differences existed between other Asians and themselves. Furthermore, there was also a perception that Asian meant East Asians such as Japanese and Chinese. Due to these views, many felt that their interests as gay men would not be served by a group like GAPIMNY.

Kambal sa Lusog is a unique group because it includes gay men, lesbians, and bisexuals. It has a newsletter that usually comes out monthly. The group meets almost every month at the Lesbian and Gay Community Center in Manhattan. They have had numerous fundraisers and other group activities.

Among such fundraising activities was the *Santacruzan*. It was not only successful in attracting other Filipino gay men who were not members but more importantly, this particular production of the traditional Filipino ritual is perhaps the most evocative example of the kind of community and identity formation that Filipino gay men in New York are struggling to achieve.

The *Santacruzan* is an important traditional Catholic celebration in the Philippines held every May. It is a street procession that begins and ends in the church. The procession is essentially a symbolic reenactment of the finding of the cross of Christ by Queen Helena or Reyna Elena, the mother of Emperor Constantine of the Holy Roman Empire. The procession usually includes female personages, both mythical and historical. Among the usual figures are: *Reyna Sentenciada* (Justice), the three Virtues (*Fe, Esperanza,* and *Caridad* or Faith, Hope and Charity), *Reina Banderada* or Motherland (Queen of the Flag), Reina Elena, Rosa Mistica, Constantino (the young Emperor Constantine), and biblical characters such as Judith and Mary Magdalene.

In the Philippines, the important figures in the processions are usually portrayed by women with male escorts. Constantino is the only named male figure and is usually played by a child. However, in some areas, there have been cases when crossdressing men have participated in these processions. In fact one of these kinds of *Santacruzans* in Pasay City (one of the cities in the metropolitan Manila area) is famous for its cross-dressing procession.

Kambal sa Lusog's Santacruzan is significant not only for its cross-dressing personages, but because of the reconfiguration of the whole structure of the ritual. By describing the procession staged at the Lesbian and Gay Community Center in Manhattan in August, 1992, I am presenting what can be interpreted as a collective representation of identity and community. It is in this ritual where idioms of American and Philippine social symbolisms are selectively fused to provide structure to an implicit and subtle narrative of a community as well as a common cache of meanings and sentiments. This specific event locates the efforts of the organization at establishing a sense of collectivity.

First of all, this *Santacruzan* was not presented as a procession but as a fashion show. The focal point of the show was the stage with a fashion runway. In the center of the stage, before the runway began, was a floral arch which is reminiscent of the mobile arches of flowers that are carried in the procession for each mythical or historical personages.

The personages or figures were a combination of traditional Santacruzan figures as well as configurations of traditional figures and personages together with the creation of new ones. For example, while *Reyna Sentenciada*, who is usually portrayed like the figure of Justice, carrying scales and in a blindfold, the "gay" *Reyna Sentenciada* is dressed in a leather (S & M) dominatrix garb. During the presentation, before he left the stage, *Reyna Sentenciada*, lifted his wig to show his bald pate. *Reyna Libertad* or Liberty was dressed also in a dominatrix garb complete with a whip. Liberty in this instance was construed to be sexual freedom. The three Virtues were the only figures who were portrayed by women (lesbians) dressed in denim shorts, combat boots, and *barong tagalog* (the traditional Filipino male formal attire). Constantino, who is usually portrayed by a child, was a muscular Filipino in brief swimming trunks.

Other bolder representations were *Reyna Banderada*, who usually carried the Philippine flag incorporated the symbols of the flag such as the stars and the red and blue strips in a slinky outfit. The three stars of the flag were strategically placed in each nipple and in the crotch area. A mask of the sun was carried by this new version of the motherland. Infanta Judith came out as a Greek goddess, and, instead of the head of Holofernes, the gay Judith revealed the head of George Bush. A new kind of queen was created for this presentation, *Reyna Chismosa* or Queen of Gossip. This queen came out in a tacky dressing gown, hair curlers screaming on a cordless phone.

However, the finale was a return to tradition as *Reyna Elena* and the Emperatriz were dressed in traditional gowns and tiaras. The *Reyna Elena* carried an antique cross and flowers as all *Reyna Elenas* have done in the past.

The combination of secular/profane and religious imagery as well as Filipino and American gay icons provided an arena where symbols from the two countries were contested, dismantled, and reassembled in a dazzling series of statements. This *Santacruzan* therefore was built on shared experiences that juxtaposed such practices such as S & M and cross-dressing with androgyny (the pulling off of the wig) with traditional Filipino ones like the *bakla* notion of drag.

Filipino gay men who participated in this presentation operated within the contours of the *Santacruzan* ritual while at the same time transgressing long-held beliefs and practices by injecting the culture and politics of the adopted country (i.e., George Bush's head). The *Santacruzan* can be seen as "a style of imagining" a community. In other words, the presentation can be seen as an attempt by Filipino gay men to negotiate and represent their collectivity to themselves and to others.

The Future of a Filipino Gay Community

The edges or borders of a Filipino gay community cannot be clearly demarcated as they traverse the edges of other communities of this diasporic world. However, despite the cleavages that run accross individuals and group interests, Filipino gay men, as I have shown, respond to various historical instances, such as the AIDS pandemic, anchored to shared cultural traditions that are continually renewed and reassembled. This kind of anchoring is never complete or final. There will always be oscillations between attachments or allegiances to particular groups, be it the Filipino gay community, the Asian gay community, or even the so-called American gay community.

While many observers and theorists of Asian American political movements see both the political necessity as historical inevitability of pan-Asian ethnic groupings, I argue that the path of the political evolution of Filipino gay men in America will not be unilinear. Filipinos as a group will not "mature" into a monolithic pan-Asian stage of development. Rather, there will emerge a multiplicity of identities and groupings.[13] Sentiments and allegiances to cultural traditions are continually strengthened and reshaped by the circular pattern of diasporas and migrations. The Filipino diaspora is continually replenished and altered by the sentiments and allegiances of its migrants and exiles.

Such responses are reflected nationally in Filipino gay men's reactions to the *Miss Saigon* controversy and the AIDS pandemic. Especially with the *Santacruzan*, we find a vigorous and continued creation and reconstitution of cultural symbols and practices that go hand in hand with the revivification of a sense of belonging. These discourses will pave the way for a stronger future of a Filipino gay community in New York.

NOTES

1. Terralee Bensinger, "Lesbian Pornography: The Re/Making of (a) Community." *Discourse* 15:1 (1992): 69–93.

2. Benedict Anderson, *Imagined Communities: Reflections on the Origin and Spread of Nationalism* (London: Verso, 1983).

3. See Gillian Bottomley, *From Another Place: Migration and the Politics of Culture* (Melbourne: Cambridge University Press, 1992).

4. See William Whitam and Robin Mathy, *Homosexuality in Four Societies* (New York: Praeger, 1986), as well as my paper "Tolerance or Struggle: Male Homosexuality in the Philippines," which explored the tolerant and seemingly benign attitude of Filipinos as well as the cultural practices towards that *bakla*.

I do not use the term *bakla* as the equivalent of gay. Rather, I juxtapose the native term for homosexual/faggot as a way of portraying the different homosexual traditions, U.S. and Philippines. *Bakla* is socially constructed as a transvestic and/or effeminized being that occupies an interstitial position between men and women. In this paper, therefore, I use the term gay only as a provisional term and do not imply a totally "gay"-identified population. I also do not want to portray *bakla* traditions as static and unchanging, rather, as specifically demarcated practices continually being shaped and reshaped by both local and global influences and processes.

5. See Donn Hart and Harriet Hart, "Visayan Swardspeak: The Language of a Gay Community in the Philippines." *Crossroads* 5:2 (1990): 27–49; and M. F. Manalansan, "Speaking of AIDS: Language and the Filipino Gay An Experience in America" (in press).

6. All names of informants and other identifying statements have been changed to protect their identities.

7. Examples include Connie S. Chan, "Issues of Identity Development Among Asian-American Lesbians and Gay Men," *Journal of Counseling & Development* 68 (1989): 16–20; and Terry Gock, "Asian Pacific Islander Identity Issues: Identity Integration and Pride," in Betty Berzon (ed.), *Positively Gay* (Los Angeles: Mediamix Association, 1984).

8. Nina Reyes, "Common Ground: Asians and Pacific Islanders Look for Unity in a Queer World," *Outweek* 99 (1990).

9. See Bottomley, chapter 6.

10. Manalansan, ibid.

11. While more than 85 percent of Filipino AIDS cases in America are gay and bisexual men, the opposite is true in the Philippines, where more than half of the cases are women.

12. Jean M. Woo, George W. Rutherford, Susan F. Payne, J. Lowell Barnhardt, and George F. Lemp, "The Epidemiology of AIDS in the Asian and Pacific Islander Population in San Francisco," *AIDS* 2 (1988): 473–475.

13. See Yen Le Espiritu, *Asian American Panethnicity* (Philadelphia: Temple University Press, 1992), ch. 7.

1. Why, according to Takagi, is it important to interrogate the role that sexuality plays in informing Asian American identity? What reasons does Takagi give for linking the gay and lesbian experience to a larger interpretation of Asian American history? Why has it been difficult to incorporate the experiences of gays and lesbians into the Asian American Studies curriculum? What are the dangers that arise in trying to be inclusive of these experiences? How is a gay/lesbian/transsexual identity different from an Asian American identity in the face of societal treatment and oppression?

2. What are the general attitudes adopted by parents interviewed about gays and lesbians prior to learning about their own children's sexual identities? How have these attitudes changed once they learn about their children's coming out?

3. The majority of the parents interviewed by Hom are immigrants and women. How may homeland cultures and cultural exposure in the host society affect the acceptance process of Asian American parents? How does gender affect this process? What are the common trends that these parents experienced in their own "coming out" process? Why are Asian American parents reluctant to confide in their friends and family within the ethnic community? To what degree do you think that ethnicity played a role in their hesitation to share their feelings with others?

4. One of the things that comes out of Manalansan's study is the number of obstacles that have prevented gay Filipino Americans from buttressing solidarity within their "community." Explain what these obstacles are and how they might be overcome. What obstacles have prevented gay and lesbian Filipinos from forging ties within pan-Asian gay and lesbian organizations? With other Filipino Americans?

SUGGESTED READINGS

Cheung, King-Kok. 1998. Of Men and Men: Reconstructing Chinese American Masculinity. Pp. 173–199 in Sandra Stanley (ed.), *Other Sisterhoods: Literary Theory and U.S. Women of Color*. Urbana: University of Illinois Press.

Eng, David, and Alice Hom (eds.). 1998. *Q&A: Queer in Asian America*. Philadelphia: Temple University Press.

Fung, Richard. 1998. Looking for My Penis: The Eroticized Asian in Gay Porn. Pp. 115–134 in David Eng and Alice Hom (eds.), *Q&A: Queer in Asian America*. Philadelphia: Temple University Press.

Fuss, Diana. 1991. Inside/Out. Pp. 1–10 in Diana Fuss (ed.), *inside/out*. New York: Routledge.

Kim, Daniel. 1998. The Strange Love of Frank Chin. Pp. 270–303 in David Eng and Alice Hom (eds.), *Q&A: Queer in Asian America*. Philadelphia: Temple University Press.

Kudaka, Geraldine (ed.). 1995. *On a Bed of Rice: An Asian American Erotic Feast*. New York: Doubleday/Anchor Books.

Leong, Russell (ed.). 1996. *Asian American Sexualities: Dimensions of the Gay and Lesbian Experience*. New York: Routledge.

Lim-Hing, Shirley (ed.). 1994. *The Very Inside: An Anthology of Writing by Asian and Pacific Island Lesbian and Bisexual Women*. Toronto: Sister Vision Press.

Mura, David. 1996. *Where the Body Meets Memory: An Odyssey of Race, Sexuality, and Identity.* New York: Anchor Books.

Roy, Sandip. 1998. The Call of Rice: (South) Asian American Queer Communities. Pp. 168–185 in Lavina Dhingra Shankar and Rajini Srikanth (eds.), *A Part Yet Apart: South Asians in Asian America.* Philadelphia: Temple University Press.

Tajima, Renee. 1996. Site-Seeing Through Asian America. Pp. 263–294 in Avery Gordon and Chris Newfield (eds.), *Mapping Multiculturalism.* Minneapolis: University of Minnesota Press.

Wat, Eric C. 1994. Preserving the Paradox: Stories from a Gay-Loh. *Amerasia Journal* 20 (1): 149–160.

FILMS

Bautista, Pablo (producer). 1992. *Fated to Be Queer* (25-minute documentary).

Choy, Christine (producer/director). 1994. *Out in Silence: AIDS in the Pacific American Community.* (37-minute documentary).

Fung, Richard (producer/director). 1982. *Orientations.*

Lee, Ang (producer/director). 1993. *The Wedding Banquet.*

Lee, Quentin (producer/director). 1995. *Flow.* (80-minutes experimental).

Ganatra, Nisha (producer/director). 1997. *Junky Punky Girlz.* (12-minute experimental).

Part XI

The Complexity of Ethnic Identity
Interracial Marriage and Multiethnic Asian Americans

In Search of the Right Spouse
Interracial Marriage among Chinese and Japanese Americans

Colleen Fong and Judy Yung

Through in-depth interviews with Chinese and Japanese American women and men who are or have been married to Whites, this study examines factors involved in contemporary Asian-white heterosexual marriages. We[1] chose to focus on Chinese and Japanese because they have a long presence in the United States and were the first Asian Americans to out-marry, usually to Whites, in the largest numbers.[2] Specifically, we wanted to find out what factors were involved in their decision to out-marry—which factors were shared by both the women and the men and which were unique—and why a higher proportion of women than men out-married.

This research broadens the parameters of existing work on Asian American out-marriage in several ways. First, it is gender-comparative, looking at both Asian American women and men who have out-married. Much of the recent interest in Asian intermarriage focuses only on the pairing of Asian women and white men. While this can be explained in part because higher proportions of contemporary Asian American women than men have out-married, the gap is closing.[3] Further-more, the focus on women has at times been divisive, racist, and sexist, as indicated by the record number of letters sent to the editor following the publication of one such article.[4] Second, our research draws from qualitative interview data and fleshes out the demographic profiles of out-married Asian Americans provided by most other studies on the topic.[5] Finally, our work goes beyond the assimilationist inter-pretation of out-marriage, which posits that once the physical and social distance between members of different racial groups is minimized, romantic love and mar-riage will follow.[6] While our findings support the view that intermarriage is facilitated by the dismantling of racial barriers and the assimilation process, they also indicate other factors are involved, such as: aversion to Asian patriarchy; overbearing Asian mothers; cultural and economic compatibility, particularly with Jewish Americans; upward mobility; and media representations of beauty and power. Thus, intermar-riage may be tied to racial and gender power relations in our society.

Interracial marriage, as we know it today, is a relatively recent phenomenon. Antimiscegenation laws, which date back to the 1660s, were an outgrowth of slavery that reinforced a racial/class/gender hierarchy with white, male property holders at the top.[7] In California, marriage between Chinese and whites was deemed illegal in

1880. By 1933 the statute had been amended to include all other "Mongolians" (namely Japanese, Koreans, and Indians—predominantly Sikhs) and "Malays" (namely Filipinos). In 1948, California repealed its antmiscegenation law, after Congress amended the War Bride's Act of 1945, which permitted the entry of Japanese brides married to American soldiers. But it was not until 1967, at the height of the civil rights movement, that the U.S. Supreme Court declared all antimiscegenation laws unconstitutional.[8] As a result of these legal actions and improved racial relations in this country, marriages between Asian and white Americans first occurred in noticeable numbers during the post–World War II period and increased dramatically in the post–civil rights era.[9] In 1980, the majority of Asian Americans in the state of California were married within their own ethnic groups; however, 25 percent of married Asian American women and 14.4 percent of married Asian American men were intermarried, compared to 8.2 percent for other racial/ethnic groups. Of the Asian American wives, 73 percent had white spouses compared to 54 percent of Asian American husbands.[10]

Many studies have explained the increasing rate of interracial marriage among Asian Americans since World War II. Utilizing demographic profiles based on marriage license applications or census data, most support the assimilationist interpretation epitomized in the works of Emory Bogardus and Milton Gordon. While Bogardus regards intermarriage as the pinnacle of racial acceptance and toleration on the part of the dominant group in his Social Distance Scale,[11] Gordon defines it as the step toward the final stages of assimilation where a sense of peoplehood is established in the absence of prejudice, discrimination, and value or power conflicts. According to Gordon, "If children of different ethnic backgrounds belong to the same playgroup, later the same adolescent cliques, and at college the same fraternities and sororities; if the parents belong to the same country club and invite each other to their homes for dinner; it is completely unrealistic not to expect these children, now grown, to love and to marry each other."[12] Given that proximity is at the heart of the assimilation theory, it is not surprising that, despite differences in theoretical orientation, the findings of most studies on Asian American intermarriages can be used to support an assimilationist interpretation. Implicit in these studies is that increased contact between Asian Americans and Whites leads to increased intermarriage with Whites.[13]

A few studies go beyond the theoretical interpretation that Asian American interracial marriage represents little more than the natural outcome of the assimilation process. In *Mixed Blood*, Paul Spickard chooses to look at both changing social structural factors and racial/gender images. He points out, "As more Japanese Americans become middle class, their outmarriage rate has shot up. But intermarriage patterns, particularly gender patterns, are not just functions of social structure. They depend in large part on the images that people of the various ethnic groups have of each other and of themselves."[14] In a study based on the 1980 California census data, Larry Shinagawa and Gin Yong Pang use the theory of hypergamy to explain why Asian Americans, especially women of high socioeconomic class background, are marrying Whites. As they conclude, "Intermarriage is not distributed proportionately throughout the classes, but is concentrated disproportionately among the higher classes of Asian Americans, who marry the more advantaged members of the white population. . . . Asian Americans outmarry to individuals who are more advantaged than they are, and who enjoy a better socioeconomic and racial status than potential Asian American mates."[15] Betty Lee Sung's study of intermarriage among Chinese Americans in New York can be said to support the assimilation theory in that she points to the large Chinese immigrant population there as the cause of their low intermarriage rate. However, her interviews with fifty intermarried couples reveal other factors were involved in their decisions to out-marry, including psychological motives, political ideology, Asian patriarchy, and racial/gender images.[16] Our findings complement these studies in showing that interracial marriage is a complex phenomenon—the result of assimilation factors to be sure, but, more importantly, additional factors intimately related to issues of racial and gender power relations.

Methodology

A total of nineteen women and twenty-four men were interviewed for this study. Most of the interviewees were born in the 1940s or 1950s, representing the generation most affected by the repeal of antimiscegenation laws and the civil rights movement. Most interviewees live in the greater San Francisco Bay Area, where Chinese Americans and Japanese Americans have consistently resided since the beginning of their immigration in the mid-nineteenth century. Among the women are thirteen of Chinese descent (six foreign-born) and six of Japanese descent (all U.S.born). Among the men are thirteen of Chinese descent (six foreign-born) and eleven of Japanese descent (three foreign-born). All except one has attended college and most hold professional occupations, thus corresponding to the middle-class background of Asian Americans who have outmarried, according to statistical studies.

Interviewees were obtained from four sources: (1) a snowball sample beginning with our Asian American acquaintances; (2) responses to one of several classified ads which appeared in Asian American and Chinese-language newspapers; (3) responses to one of several classified ads which appeared in a San Francisco Bay Area free weekly newspaper; and (4) responses to letters requesting an interview sent to interracial couples who had filed for marriage licenses at the Alameda County Courthouse in 1986.

The interviews were usually conducted in the homes of the subjects and averaged two hours in length. Asian American female interviewers were used to interview the women and Asian American male interviewers for the men. Interviewees were assured that their confidentiality would be protected, and all names used here are pseudonyms. Open-ended questions were asked about family background, childhood, education, and social life prior to marriage, and, most important, interviewees were asked to describe their lives at the time they met their partners and decided to marry. Finally, interviewees were asked about their married lives, children (if applicable), in-laws, and so forth.

Proximity: A Precondition for Marrying for Love and Compatibility

Most men and women interviewed met their spouses at school or at work and described their marriages as the outgrowth of compatibility, love, and trust—factors which are based primarily on romantic love.[17] Chinese American Byron Woo and his wife met in college in the 1970s through mutual friends. They started dating and after a year or so moved in together. Upon graduation, they purchased a house together. Once co-owners of a house, Byron says, "In essence we were married." A few years after buying the house, they decided to get married. The marriage appears to be the culmination of a long-term relationship. They had been a couple for so long the wedding ceremony itself was, in Byron's words, "no big deal." They went to Reno to get married.

Third-generation Japanese American Kevin Osuga met his wife, Susan, at an academic conference while they were both graduate students in the early 1980s. After an intellectually stimulating plenary session, Kevin and Susan went out with a large group of people. The next day they attended a number of sessions together and continued their intellectual conversation. At the end of the conference, he headed back to the Eest Coast and she to the South. Even though they were both involved with other people at the time, they broke off these relationships, and Susan arranged to study on the East Coast. Kevin comments on the strength of their relationship, "We're both academics. We're both interested in the same kinds of things—theoretical stuff, political things, involved in the same kind of work. We share those kinds of struggles in terms of understanding the nature of the pressure [of academic work]. We laugh because in the first part of our relationship it was fun to go to a bookstore and browse for hours. That was a cheap date!"

These are examples of interracial marriages that seem to have grown out of mutual attraction and love. As third-generation Chinese American Daniel Chan comments, "I meet who I meet. I get along with who I get along with. The cards fell where they did." Born in 1954 in Hawaii, Daniel's comment reflects his age cohort in that when he began dating in the early 1970s, legalized segregation had been outlawed and antimiscegenation laws had been repealed. In this sense these interviews can be used as evidence of the assimilationist understanding of out-marriage in that without prior "contact" between members of different races, these love relationships could not have developed. While this is a legitimate explanation for the increasing rate of out-marriage among Asian Americans, responses in our interviews indicate that other factors are also involved.

Timing and Unavailability of Asian American Partners

Timing is an important factor in the decision to marry. Some interviewees were more cognizant of this than others. Third-generation Chinese American Marcia Ong was in her late thirties when she was interviewed. She said she finally felt ready to commit herself to marriage after "pretty much" accomplishing what she wanted professionally and personally. No doubt she would have married an Asian American in the 1970s because, being a part of the Ethnic Studies movement then, that was all she dated. But she had "outgrown" that "antiwhite" phase and was now dating a "Jewish, white guy." Women in particular mentioned they were getting older and felt the time was right. Whom they married sometimes seemed less significant than their readiness. These women believed that if they did not marry soon, they would "lose" the opportunity. In 1976 Chinese American Diana Prentice was twenty-eight and still living with her immigrant parents close to San Francisco Chinatown when she met Dan at work. She admits she was not attracted to him at all because he had "long hair, a beard, and always wore sandals." But after he showed interest in her and other coworkers told her he was "nice," she accepted a date with him. She says, "I was feeling kind of bad that I was getting so old and I hadn't really dated and been around men much. That [her inexperience] really bothered me." Dating Dan prompted Diana to move out of her parents' home. They dated for seven years and then married.

Some Asian American men and women married Whites because Asian American partners were not available in the geographic areas in which they grew up or in their places of work or professional fields. Wes Gin, born in 1943, grew up in a small, coastal California town where he had little contact with other Chinese Americans. The pool of women from which he dated were white, and it is no surprise that both his first and present wife are white. Lorelei Fong was born and raised in a large metropolitan area full of other Chinese Americans, but she found herself having less contact with Chinese American men as she became more involved in her field as a performing artist. Although she went to a college with many other Chinese Americans, she says they were not in her field and, "I just wasn't interested in dating Chinese engineering students at that time in my life—I was into the arts!" At age twenty-eight, when she met her future Jewish-American husband, she had not had an Asian American boyfriend for a number of years. "The kinds of things I was doing [professionally] just didn't expose me to Asian American men . . . you can look at the field today and see how many Asian American men are there and of the ones who are there, they're usually married to white women."

Cultural Affinity: The Jewish Connection; The Hawaiian Propensity

Although Lorelei married a white man, she married a white, Jewish man, and it appears that there is a propensity for our interviewees to meet and date Jews in college or in their professional fields and marry them. Eighteen percent of the Chinese and Japanese American women and men we interviewed were married to Jewish partners. Five described how they shared a cultural affinity with their Jewish spouses; most often they mentioned how both cultures valued strong family ties and educational achievement. Interviewees also described their Jewish spouses as having a sense of "ethnic tradition" and an immigrant legacy found lacking in non-Jewish whites they had known or dated. Calvin Jung pointed out that both he and his wife were third generation and how her grandfather, an immigrant from Russia, enjoyed trading stories with Calvin about his Chinese immigrant grandparents. Similarly,

Nellie Tsui, born in Boston in 1950, reported she and her Jewish husband often joke about possibly being "related" since his grandfather traded on the Chinese silk road. Marcia Ong says her husband, who is aware of the history of anti-Semitism, understands her sense of racial justice. "I don't have to explain it," she says. In all of these cases, there is also the added factor of economic compatibility in that both spouses shared similar middle-class values and socialized in the same professional circles.

There also seems to be a propensity for individuals who grew up in Hawaii to out-marry. Unlike the mainland, Hawaii has a long history of marital mixing.[18] Japanese American Mary Fujimoto, who lived in Hawaii from age fifteen to twenty-five, said she was used to being around people of all different backgrounds and in fact always considered "hapa [racially mixed] children cuter." She dated Asians and Whites before marrying her white college sweetheart. Third-generation Chinese American Timothy Tom grew up in a multiracial Hawaiian neighborhood of Japanese, Portuguese, Hawaiian, Puerto Rican, and other Chinese. He believes it was this environment that provided him with an openness to other groups and, most importantly, an openness to Whites, who do not occupy the same dominant position as they do on the mainland. He later chose to marry a white classmate he met and dated while attending college on the mainland.

Aversion to Marrying Within the Same Race

Even when potential Asian American spouses were available, many of the Asian American men and women we interviewed found them "less attractive" than the white partners they eventually chose. Analysis of these interviews reveals both men and women had formed negative opinions and feelings about Asian Americans of the opposite sex. On the one hand, cultural attributes such as a patriarchal family structure, an overbearing mother, or growing up in an ethnically insulated neighborhood turned them away from seeking Asian American partners. On the other hand, the media promotion of white beauty and power encouraged them to date and marry white Americans.

A number of our interviewees grew up in repressive family situations where one or both parents were unbearably domineering and manipulative and where negative reinforcement and strict discipline were practiced. They said this resulted in views of their parents as anti-role models and an aversion to marrying within the same race. "I knew I didn't want to marry someone like my father [or mother]" was one of the more common responses from women who described their fathers as too patriarchal, insensitive, and nonexpressive and from men who characterized their mothers as manipulative and complaining. Hoping to escape what they perceived to be unhappy marriages of their parents', interviewees placed great emphasis on marriages based on romantic love and grounded in mutual respect and equality.

The Women's Perspective

Mimi Kato, a third-generation Japanese American woman born in the early 1940s, was very aware of both the patriarchal oppression in her mother's two in-marriages and the status mobility to be gained by marrying someone white. Mimi's father walked out on the family when she was five, and her stepfather was physically abusive to both her and her mother. She knew at an early age that she did not want to end up victimized like her mother and powerless to resist the abuse. Mimi dated Japanese American men but found them too protective and the relationships "suffocating." While most of the interviewees' parents had strong objections to interracial dating and marriage, Mimi's mother encouraged her in that direction for reasons of class mobility. Media messages that "white is right, beautiful, and acceptable" also encouraged Mimi to date white men who shared her interest in art and literature. In searching for her "white knight," someone who would be the kind father she never had, she settled upon Dave, her Teaching Assistant in a literature class. As she admitted some twenty years after their divorce:

> He was very sensitive, very bright, very very good as a writer, and he was really kind and very tolerant. He was the kind of person that I would really want to be the father of my child. I think I had decided at that time that I wanted a child that was half-white [because] . . . I was raised with all the values that white was infinitely more attractive, infinitely more acceptable, infinitely more powerful. And I wanted my child to have half the power, to have all that that dream represented, all that that program represented.

However, as with a number of other interviewees, when Mimi became politicized by the Third World strike at San Francisco State University,[19] she reassessed her motivations for marriage, and the marriage ended in divorce.

The women interviewed reported that Asian American men tended not to treat them as equals. This they learned from either observing real situations in their own families or through firsthand dating experiences. Born in Hong Kong in 1950, Nellie Tsui came from a well-to-do family. She remembers that, while her brother was groomed to follow in the footsteps of their father, a successful businessman with a Harvard degree, she was expected to marry and become a housewife like her mother. When she immigrated to the United States after high school, Nellie's parents expected her to date and marry Chinese. She consciously dated Chinese American men in college with that in mind but found them unattractive or thought they found her unattractive because she was tall, dark, and had a tendency to be outspoken. In the end, she married a white, Jewish colleague who offered her what she found lacking in Chinese men like her own father. "Bill was very feminine, very caring, and very verbal," she says. "He's a great cook, and he's always done the dishes no matter who cooks." As she told her mother right after she met Bill, "I said I think I met the man I'm going to marry, and I said jokingly, 'he has my martini ready for me when I come home from work.' And that was the kind of person he was. There's no way my father would do that. You know, it's too demeaning." Upon further analysis, Nellie realized that her father's cultural upbringing and insecurities—which stemmed from his awareness of his racial minority status—prevented him from being more giving and encouraging. Whereas her father had devalued her, Bill always made her feel good about being an Asian woman.

We found that Asian American interviewees who identified as feminists had the hardest time accepting sexist attitudes and behavior. Their coming to a new sense of consciousness as a result of the growing women's liberation movement of the 1970s no doubt contributed to the increased rate of intermarriage among these women. As feminists, they were much more aware of patriarchy and less willing to tolerate it. Alice Stein, who grew up in China after the 1949 Revolution, had feminist beliefs even before she came to the United States. Upon arrival as a foreign student in 1980, she was immediately struck by the sexism that pervaded American culture and the attitudes of the Chinese American men she met:

> I guess growing up in a Communist society, at least the Communist Party advocates equality a lot between men and women. That's one thing that I was hit [with] the minute I got here. Everything is so sexually oriented, putting women on such a degrading [level]. All the selling of cars and everything has a woman perched on it. I felt it very strong among Chinese American men, not only among the two that I met but even with other Chinese American men that I talked to. So I sort of got turned off real fast.

Having experienced an unhappy marriage in China, Alice was determined not to marry until the right person came along however badly she needed a green card to stay in the United States. What drew her to marry Joseph—a white, Jewish man— was his nonsexist attitude. He had an appreciation for Chinese culture and for her as a person. "He was very open, very equal, and communication with him was very easy," she says.

While the women recognized certain positive characteristics in Asian American men—well educated, stable, reliable—these qualities were evidently not enough for them. As Marcia Ong says of Terrence, her Asian American boyfriend of many years, "He was the kind an Asian woman would really like. He's educated, polite, generous, kind, and tall. My mother really loved him." But, like her father, he was not expressive or nurturing enough. According to Marcia:

> I would say, "I need to hear from you. I know you care, but you're just like my Dad." He would show me by being reliable and doing things for me, but I would say, "You have to TELL me. I need to hear it. I need more. Do you care about me? How do you feel about me?" It was not okay because I had to ask. I wanted him to volunteer to talk about it. It was difficult. As I have become better at expressing myself, I've expected my partners to be good at expressing themselves.

What Marcia found lacking in Terrence she found in Clarence and John, her African American and white, Jewish boyfriends, respectively. Both were good about expressing their appreciation of her, their feelings about what they liked or disliked, and, unlike Terrence, they had a sense of humor. Also unlike most Asian American men she had known, neither Clarence or John were threatened by her tough personality and her outspokenness. Both men saw and appreciated what she called her "compliant" self underneath her "tough" exterior. "With Asian guys, I would have to pursue them," says Marcia. "Black and white men take the chance. They are persistent. John said if we hadn't been introduced he would have found a way to meet me." This difference in courtship patterns can be deemed an indication of where the racial power lies in our society because like their male counterparts, white women were reportedly more aggressive than Asian American women in pursuing men—four of the male interviewees admitted to being pursued or "pushed into marriage" by their white girlfriends.

The Men's Perspective

The male interviewees talked in similar ways about Asian cultural attributes in women they wanted to avoid in a marital relationship. Although they may have been favored as sons, they too found their family environments oppressive, with one or both parents too domineering and manipulative. While the Asian patriarchy no doubt benefited them in some ways, they wanted no part in it. At all costs, they did not want their marriages to end up like their parents', and so they consciously looked for partners whom they felt were kind, sensitive, and egalitarian. These spouses turned out to be white women.

Third-generation Japanese American Vincent Kaneko describes his father as "abusive, dominating, and cheap" and his mother as "very shy, giving, loving, and tolerant." It was an unhappy marriage that lasted fifty-two years "only because my mother was the most tolerant person in the world." He admired and loved his mother as much as he despised his father. Knowing that his mother did not approve of interracial dating or marriage, he chose to date and marry a Japanese American woman whom he thought would be like his mother. Vincent was eighteen years old at the time; the year was 1963. But his wife turned out to be more like his father, "the grouchiest Japanese woman I've ever known in my whole life." They divorced eleven years later, and he swore he would never date another Japanese American woman as long as he lived. To get himself out of what he called "the syndrome of marrying [his] father," Vincent turned to dating white women. As he admits, he had been conditioned by television and magazines to regard "the white female body as the best overall." What surprised and pleased him, because he had been teased as a youngster about being short and nerdy, was that white women found him sexually attractive. This boosted his self-esteem and male confidence. After a number of relationships, Vincent married again. His second wife was a white, Jewish woman who proved to be very unlike the mother figure he was searching for. Not only was she aggressive and outspoken, but she was in his words a "confirmed lesbian." At the time of the interview, they had just divorced after a stormy marriage, and he was engaged to a Chicana he had met at work.

Born in 1960, fifth-generation Chinese American Winston Fong cites his troubled family background as a factor contributing to his out-marriage. In his words, his father was a "spoiled, rotten brat" who was used to having his way. He controlled his wife and children "out of fear, not out of respect or love or anything like that." He had violent fits and would not think twice about hitting his children at the dinner table if he felt like it. His mother "was pretty screwed up" too, often lying to the children in order to manipulate them. Pressured to date and marry Chinese, Winston's first serious relationship was with Pearl, a Chinese American classmate from high school. But she was too much like his father. "I was not about to go through life with someone who throws tantrums and calls everyone stupid," says Winston.

"She was a pretty spoiled kid, fairly well taken care of throughout life." Although he dated other Chinese American women and had every intention of finding one who was soft, outgoing, energetic, and family oriented, he ended up marrying his colleague Betty, who was white. They lived together for five years before the wedding. He reported that, unlike his parents, they had an equal relationship and hardly fought despite their differences; they could communicate well and had common interests and goals.

In at least two cases, Chinese American men reported they could not consider dating or marrying a Chinese American woman because it would be like marrying their own sister—incestuous. Wes Gin, born in 1943, grew up in a tight-knit Chinese American family in a predominantly white community. In high school Wes dated Japanese American women. After college, as soon as antimiscegenation attitudes began to change in the mid-1960s, he dated white women. Wes married twice, both times to white women. He said his first wife, Grace, resembled the media stereotype of feminine beauty. After nine years of marriage, they divorced. His second wife, Leah, was "calm, intelligent, dependable," and Jewish—someone who shared his values and goals in life. "It seems like I'm enough different from Leah where it doesn't feel like it's hugging my sister or myself," he replied when asked why he married her.

Although Calvin Jung spent his childhood years in San Francisco Chinatown, he shared Wes Gin's sentiments about not wanting to marry someone who was Chinese American like him:

> The Chinese [American] women that I knew growing up I knew all my life, sort of like your sisters—[beginning in] first grade. And I keep running into these people now, you don't really think of them as marriage partners. They're too close. They remind you of your mother—voice, intonation, and the ease in which they operate in Chinatown. All the things I was running from. They were just what I was trying to escape. Also, you were so familiar with them, it was almost like incest.

His family was the first Chinese American family to move into a white suburb outside of San Francisco. It was 1950, and his parents wanted their children to assimilate and lose their Chinatown accents but not to go so far as to risk eliciting white racism by dating or marrying a white woman. So Calvin went steady with a Japanese American classmate throughout high school:

> Anyway, we looked right. We were the cute couple and all that. She was bright and we were all headed for [the University of California at] Berkeley. She was going to be an English teacher and I was going to be the dentist. And everything was going to work out just fine.

By the time Calvin attended college in the early 1960s, he discovered that white attitudes had changed, and he began to date white women. Also, living in Europe for a year opened up doors to him in terms of interracial romance. "Gee, you got to know [white] girls and go out and be civilized and all that," said Calvin. "So by the time I got back to school again, I had finally outgrown my insularity."[20] Calvin was also aware of the empowerment resulting from relationships with white women. As he says,

You have more access in the society if you're connected with the majority. I realized that very early on. I don't think it was any conscious thing that I was only going to date white in order to get into these places, but in fact, you operate in a fashion where you take chances you wouldn't take. I don't have to protect, be in a position of being responsible for my Chinese [American] wife if someone calls her a Chink or [threatens] to beat her up. You're connected to the majority. That dynamic is very real.

As it turned out, Calvin married Jean—a white, Jewish woman who shared his interest in the fine arts. Although Calvin's sense of ethnic pride and solidarity was awakened by the Third World strikes at San Francisco State and the University of California at Berkeley in 1968–69, he did not abandon his marriage as a result. His wife, Jean, was supportive and encouraged his political activism while she went off to pursue her own interests in theater.

Power Relations Behind the Stated Motivations

Both female and male interviewees shared a common complaint about the Asian Americans they dated—they were disinterested in or ignorant of the popular youth culture of the period. This limitation spilled over to other areas, namely their dates' inabilities to meet Western standards of attractiveness or to fit into mainstream society. Women reported they found Asian American men physically unattractive, conservative, and boring. They claimed the men weren't into exciting things like parachute jumping, camping, motorcycle rides, and Bob Dylan. Male interviewees complained that Asian American women were workaholics and too serious about relationships. They claimed the women weren't vivacious and were too laden with Asian cultural baggage. Unlike white women they dated, Asian women were reportedly too introverted and not into fishing, partying, and backpacking. In other words, both women and men faulted the opposite sex for the same weaknesses: being overly serious, having pragmatic occupations or narrow interests, being rather lackluster and not a part of the dominant or counterculture.

Such complaints are remiscent of two pieces published in an early Asian American anthology, Roots: *An Asian American Reader.* In "White Male Qualities," an anonymous third-generation Japanese American woman explains why she intends to marry a white man. She describes Asian American men as "short, ugly, unconfident, clumsy, [and] arrogant." In contrast, she describes her white fiance as "tall, handsome, manly, self-confident and well-poised" and someone who, because he doesn't have any "hangups about proving his masculinity," treats women with respect. She believes that "Sanseis [third-generation Japanese Americans] marrying other Sanseis will grow up to be exactly like their parents." She faults Asian American men for having cultural "hangups" about sex. She writes, "After an Oriental boy has seduced his girl friend, she will expect to marry him, and he begins to take her for granted." She says she aspires to something better—something which she can obtain from a relationship with a white man.[21]

Similarly, in the poem, "I Hate My Wife for Her Flat Yellow Face," Japanese American author Ron Tanaka describes how his Japanese American wife pales in comparison to a white (presumably) Jewish woman named Judith Gluck. Tanaka explains how his marriage was one of convenience and how he initially had hoped that he could learn to love his wife and that she, steeped in traditional Japanese ways, could save him from "bopping round L.A. ghettos, western civilization and the playmate of the month." Finding he could not love her, he faulted her for "her lack of elegance and lack of intelligence compared to judith gluck." Tanaka goes on to describe his wife as a "stupid water buffalo from the old country" who knows nothing "about Warhol, Ginsberg or Viet Nam."[22]

The question arises, If the anonymous author of "White Male Qualities" and Ron Tanaka met, would they find each other attractive? Interviewee Calvin Jung specifically addressed this issue when he remarked:

> I did date other Asian [American] women at UC Berkeley. The reason why I was attracted to them was because they were like me; but like me, they were also looking elsewhere. The reason why I was charming and appealing [to them] was because I was conversant in American society.

Calvin, who also mentioned the feelings of incest when he dated Chinese women, went on to say that all the Asian American women he found attractive and dated ended up like him—marrying Whites. As he concluded, "Why pick an imitation if you can get a real one?" In a similar vein, Ben Fong-Torres laments the fact that his former Chinese American girlfriend is now dating a white man:

> Michelle had said she could relate to me because I was a Chinese guy who knew about rock-and-roll and the arts. Now, she'd found a [white] guy who played music, who could write songs, and perform with her. With me she'd gone from Chinatown Chinese to an Americanized Chinese. Now, at my expense, she was graduating.[23]

In both of these cases, white American culture is regarded as superior. Asian Americans like Calvin and Michelle are attracted to those who are part of the dominant culture; but, if given two equally acculturated Americans, they will choose the "real" American who is white over the "imitation" who is Asian American.

While the attraction to the "real" is an important factor in Asian American interracial marriages, it does not explain why higher proportions of Asian American women than Asian American men have married Whites—which departs significantly from patterns of other groups (for example, African American and Jewish men tend to out-marry more than their female counterparts). Our findings indicate that the dominant U.S. racial and gender hierarchy and its concomitant stereotypes play a crucial role. On the one hand, the mass media portrays Asian American women as petite, submissive, and sexually desirable, which departs little from the mainstream image of what constitutes an attractive, feminine woman. This image, combined with notions of the "exotic," may make Asian American women attractive to white men. At the same time, white men may be gravitating to Asian women because they perceive white American women as too liberated, career-minded, and demanding. On the other hand, popular images of Asian American men as small and socially inept depart significantly from what is considered to be an attractive masculine man. Based on these images, white and Asian American women would most likely not be attracted to Asian American men. These negative images combined with the psychological needs of men to be "taller" and "stronger" than their female partners led someone like Nellie Tsui, who is five feet nine inches tall and muscular, to difficulties when it came to finding Asian American dating partners. She said Asian American men were just not attracted to her. She ended up marrying a white man who was over six feet tall.

However, these negative images and psychological needs are changing. There may be a correlation between the increasing rate of out-marriages among Asian American men and three recent trends: (1) *macho* and romantic images of Asian American men are appearing in movies (Bruce Lee, Jason Scott Lee, Russell Wong) and in calendars like the *Asian Pacific Islander Men, 1991*;[24] (2) Asian American men are perceived as more economically stable and supportive than men of other races (vis-à-vis the "model minority" stereotype); and (3) the definition of an "ideal man" is moving beyond physical stature to include qualities such as expressiveness and nurturing—qualities previously used only to describe women.[25] Thus, we can make sense of Chinese American Lance Jue, who is five feet four inches tall, when he reports that a white female friend told him, "You're a very big little man, Lance," and Wayne Fong's comment that his white wife didn't initially consider him "attractive" but told him, "I got past the look and got to your soul."

Conclusions

Our data indicate that Asian American out-marriage is not simply the "natural" outcome of more contact with white Americans, as assimilationists would have us believe, but also the result of a number of complex factors, some of which have been raised by Spickard, Shinagawa and Pang, and Sung. While proximity is a necessary precondition to interracial marriage, other factors intimately tied to issues of race and gender power relations are also involved. Interviewees who grew up in Hawaii, where interracial marriage was not as negatively sanctioned as on the mainland, seemed to be more open to out-marriage in general. Other interviewees were attracted to Jewish Americans because they shared certain middle-class values and traditions. A few admitted they married Whites for some measure of upward mobility—clear cases of hypergamy. Both male and female interviewees stated outright that they had an aversion to marrying a member of their own group because they wanted to avoid replicating their parents' marriages. Finally, both men and women complained that their Asian American dates were too out of touch with the popular youth culture of the time—music, literature, fashion—and overburdened with the protocol dictated by traditional Chinese or Japanese culture. Aware of the race/class/gender hierarchy in American society, they opted to marry white Americans over Asian Americans who were equally acculturated into the dominant lifestyle. Likewise, they chose Whites over other groups such as Hispanic or African Americans because of the racial hierarchy of preference ingrained in them through their parents and popular media.[26]

Despite the overwhelming overlap in motivation shared by the women and men, some differences do stand out. Asian American women, in particular, seemed to have out-married in part to escape from what they perceived as Asian patriarchy. These women reported that Asian American men treated them in less egalitarian ways than men of other races, and they wanted equal partners in a marriage. This combined with the fact that Asian American women have been "positively" depicted in the mass media while Asian American men have been "negatively" depicted, provides some insight into why Asian American women out-marry at higher proportions than men. Timing also played a more crucial role for women who out-married than men. Women more often felt they were running out of time or getting too old to be considered marriageable. Asian American men reported that white women appreciated their economic stability and emotional support. They also said that dating and marrying white women, upon which standards of beauty are based, boosted their self-esteem. Some who grew up in predominately white areas discussed their aversion to marrying Asian American women as rooted in the incest taboo. Dating other Asian American members of the community—families that had considered themselves like fictive kin for decades—seemed incestuous.

Clearly, the complexity of the factors involved in outmarriage uncovered by this study indicates that beyond simply proximity lies a whole host of factors. Future research in this area might explore some of the more interesting findings of this project such as: the cultural affinity and economic compatibility between Asian and Jewish Americans; Asian American aversion to Asian patriarchy and matriarchy; the perception of in-marriage as a violation of the incest taboo; and the impact of political activism and ethnic consciousness on marital choice in the 1960s, particularly between the various Asian groups and between Asians and other groups of color. Other topics we hope to explore in future studies include: war brides and military wives; foreign students; mail-order brides; those who married during the antimiscegenation era; views of white partners married to Asian Americans; the current generation of marriage-age Asian Americans; gay/lesbian couples; and racially mixed Asian Americans.

NOTES

1. Both authors contributed equally to this work; the order of the authors is alphabetical. We wish to acknowledge Elaine Kim for initiating this research project, the CSUH Affirmative Action Faculty Development Program for partial funding, and Pat Guthrie, Rivka Polatnick, Ann Lane, Warren Lane, Deborah Woo, Rudy Busto, and Peggy Pascoe for their helpful comments. We are also grateful to the interviewees who took part in this study.

2. Our larger sample of interviewees includes Korean American women and "mail-order brides," mostly from the Philippines. We plan to treat these populations separately in future writings. In this paper, White is used to denote the race of spouses as reported to us by the interviewees.

3. See Larry Shinagawa and Gin Yong Pang, "Intraethnic, Interethnic, and Interracial Marriages Among Asian Americans in California, 1980," *Berkeley Journal of Sociology* 33 (1986), 95–114; and Betty Lee Sung, *Chinese American Intermarriage* (Staten Island, N.Y.: Center for Migration Studies, 1990).

4. See reaction to Joan Walsh, "Asian Women, Caucasian Men: The New Demographics of Love," *Image, San Francisco Examiner/Chronicle*, December 2, 1990, in the January 6 and 13, 1991, issues.

5. See Sharon M. Lee and Keiko Yamanaka, "Patterns of Asian American Intermarriage and Marital Assimilation," *Journal of Comparative Family Studies* 21:2 (1990), 287–305; Shinagawa and Pang, "Intraethnic, Interethnic, and Interracial Marriages"; Akemi Kikumura and Harry H. L. Kitano, "Interracial Marriage: A Picture of the Japanese Americans," *Journal of Social Issues* 29:2 (1973), 67–81; Harry H. L. Kitano and Lynn Chai, "Korean Interracial Marriage," *Marriage and Family Review* 5 (1982), 75–89; Harry H. L. Kitano and Wai-tsang Yeung, "Chinese Interracial Marriage," *Marriage and Family Review* 5 (1982), 35–48; and Harry H. L. Kitano, Waitsang Yeung, Lynn Chai, and Herbert Hatanaka, "Asian-American Interracial Marriage," *Journal of Marriage and the Family* 46 (1984), 179–190.

6. See D. Yuan, "Significant Demographic Characteristics of Chinese Who Intermarry in the United States," *California Sociologist* 3 (Summer 1980), 184–96; John N. Tinker, "Intermarriage and Ethnic Boundaries: The Japanese American Case," *Journal of Social Issues* 29 (1973), 49–66; Donna Lockwood Leonetti and Laura Newell-Morris, "Exogamy and Change in the Biosocial Structure of a Modern Urban Population," *American Anthropologist* 84 (1982), 19–36; C. K. Cheng and Douglas S. Yamamura, "Interracial Marriage and Divorce in Hawaii," *Social Forces* 36:1 (1957), 77–84; John Burma, "Interethnic Marriage in Los Angeles, 1948–1959," *Social Forces* 42:2 (1963), 156–165; Che-Fu Lee, Raymond H. Potvin, and Mary J. Verdieck, "Interethnic Marriage as an Index of Assimilation: The Case of Singapore," *Social Forces* 53:1 (1974), 112–119; Joseph J. Leon, "Sex Ethnic Marriage in Hawaii: A Nonmetric Multidimensional Analysis," *Journal of Marriage and the Family* 34 (1975), 775–781; Larry D. Barnett, "Interracial Marriage in California," *Marriage and Family Living* 25:4 (1963), 424–427; and Teresa Labov and Jerry A. Jacobs, "Intermarriage in Hawaii, 1950–1983," *Journal of Marriage and the Family* 48 (1986), 79–88.

7. The first antimiscegenation law was passed in the colony of Maryland in 1664. Some forty states and colonies did likewise, sixteen of which still had antimiscegenation laws in force when the U.S. Supreme Court ruled them unconstitutional in 1967. See David Fowler, *Northern Attitudes toward Interracial Marriage* (Garland, 1987), xi. For a discussion of interracial marriage as an issue of both race and gender relations, see Peggy Pascoe, "Race, Gender, and Intercultural Relations: The Case of Interracial Marriage," *Frontiers: A Journal of Women Studies* 12:1 (1991), 5–18.

8. See *Loving v. Virginia* 388 U.S. 1 (1967); Megumi Dick Osumi, "Asians and California's Anti-Miscegenation Laws," in *Asian and Pacific American Experiences: Women's Perspectives*, edited by Nobuya Tsuchida (Minneapolis: Asian/Pacific American Learning Resource Center and General College, University of Minnesota, 1982), 1–37; and Anselm Strauss, "Strain and Harmony in American-Japanese War-Marriages," *Marriage and Family Living* 16 (1954), 99–106. Strauss estimates that between 1947 and 1952, 10,517 U.S. citizens, mostly white military personnel, married Japanese women.

9. For studies of increased out-marriages among Chinese Americans and Japanese Americans during the 1960s and 1970s, see D. Yuan, "Significant Demographic Characteristics of Chinese Who Intermarry in the United States"; Tinker, "Intermarriage and Ethnic Boundaries: The Japanese American Case"; Russell Endo and Dale Hirokawa, "Japanese American Intermarriage," *Free Inquiry in Creative Sociology* 11:2 (1983), 159–162, 166; and Leonetti and Newell-Morris, "Exogamy and Change in the Biosocial Structure of a Modern Urban Population."

10. Shinagawa and Pang, "Intraethnic, Interethnic, and Interracial Marriages," 103. National statistics drawn from the 1980 U.S. Census, as presented in Lee and Yamanaka, "Patterns

of Asian American Intermarriage and Marital Assimilation," gave a comparable picture: 25.4 percent of Asian Americans were intermarried (31.5 percent among Asian American women and 16.6 percent among Asian American men); 76 percent of them to white spouses (290, 294).

11. See Emory Bogardus, *A Forty Year Racial Distance Study* (Los Angeles: University of Southern California, 1967).

12. Milton Gordon, *Assimilation in American Life* (New York: Oxford University Press, 1964), 80.

13. See Kitano, Yeung, Chai, and Hatanaka, "Asian-American Interracial Marriage," *Journal of Marriage and the Family* 46 (1984), 179–190; C. K. Cheng and Douglas S. Yamamura, "Interracial Marriage and Divorce in Hawaii," *Social Forces* 36:1 (1957), 77–84; John Burma, "Interethnic Marriage in Los Angeles, 1948–1959," *Social Forces* 42:2 (1963), 156–165; Yuan, "Significant Demographic Characteristics of Chinese Who Intermarry in the United States;" and Tinker, "Intermarriage and Ethnic Boundaries."

14. Paul R. Spickard, *Mixed Blood: Intermarriage and Ethnic Identity in Twentieth-Century America* (Madison: University of Wisconsin Press, 1989), 19.

15. Shinagawa and Pang, 109.

16. Betty Lee Sung, *Chinese American Intermarriage*.

17. A few interviewees mentioned other factors in the decision to marry: pregnancy, leaving for the armed services, and a strong taboo against "living together" among both sets of parents.

18. But, as Spickard points out in *Mixed Blood*, the intermarriage rate among Japanese Americans in Hawaii is lower than that of the mainland because the large Japanese community in Hawaii works to discourage outmarriage (73–84). For a discussion of intermarriage patterns in Hawaii, see also Labov and Jacobs, "Intermarriage in Hawaii, 1950–1983."

19. In November 1968, students of color at San Francisco State University, inspired by the civil rights movement, went on strike to demand the establishment of an autonomous Ethnic Studies program. See Karen Umemoto, " 'On Strike!' San Francisco State College Strike, 1968–69: The Role of Asian American Students," *Amerasia Journal* 51:1 (1989), 3–41; and William Wei, *The Asian American Movement* (Philadelphia: Temple University Press, 1993), 15–24.

20. In another case, Wayne Fong, who was expected to marry another Chinese American in particular because he was the only son in a family of five children, found that being away from the social pressures of home afforded him opportunities to date outside his group. His decision to marry a white American woman he met while serving in the Peace Corps would not have been as possible if he were home in the United States.

21. "White Male Qualities," in *Roots: An Asian American Reader*, edited by Amy Tachiki, Eddie Wong, Franklin Odo, and Buck Wong (Los Angeles: Asian American Research Center, University of California, 1971), 44–45. This article was originally published in *Gidra*, an Asian American periodical, in January 1970.

22. Ron Tanaka, "I Hate My Wife for Her Flat Yellow Face," *Roots*, 47–48. This poem was originally published in *Girda*, September 1969.

23. Ben Fong-Torres, *The Rice Room* (New York: Hyperion, 1994), 137.

24. This calendar featured six Asian American men fully clothed and then in "beefcake" poses. For a discussion of how this calendar can be viewed as both subversive of and subverted by hegemonic culture, see Sau-ling Cynthia Wong, "Subverting Desire: Reading the Body in the 1991 Asian Pacific Islander Men's Calendar," *Critical Mass: A Journal of Asian American Cultural Criticism* 1:1 (Fall 1993), 63–74.

25. See Marie Richmond Abbott, *Masculine and Feminine* (New York: McGraw-Hill, 1992),

and Michael S. Kimmel and Michael A. Messner, eds., *Men's Lives* (New York: Macmillan, 1992).

26. Statistics for California and the United States indicate that Asian Americans also marry interethnically (for example, Chinese Americans to Japanese Americans) and interracially to other groups of color (for example, Japanese Americans to African Americans) but not to the same extent as to Whites. Lee and Yamanaka found that among Asian Americans who were intermarried in 1980, 76.6 percent had white spouses, 10.7 percent Asian spouses, 5.2 percent black spouses, 3.3 percent Hawaiian and Pacific Islander spouses, 2.5 percent Hispanic, and 1.7 percent American Indian, Eskimo, Aleutian, and other spouses ("Patterns of Asian American Intermarriage," 291). Responses from our interviewees about their racial preferences in spouses prior to their marriages concur with the aggregate findings in Shinagawa and Pang that was based on a cross-tabulation of actual and expected frequencies of marriages between certain racial/ethnic groups ("Intraethnic, Interethnic, and Interracial Marriages Among Asian Americans in California, 1980," 101–103). Asian Americans' first choice of spouse was a member of their own ethnic group; second choice, other Asian/Pacific Islanders; third choice, Whites; and fourth choice, Hispanic and African Americans. In anticipation as well as in actuality, there appears to be a low incidence of intermarriage between Asian Americans and other groups of color. We attribute this to proximity and assimilation; but more important, the low socioeconomic status of a high proportion of Hispanic, African, and Native Americans.

Chapter Twenty-nine

What Must I Be?

Asian Americans and the Question of Multiethnic Identity

Paul R. Spickard

In 1968, Asian American Studies was born out of the Third World Strike at San Francisco State; in 1995, Stanford announced it would finally join the rest of West Coast higher education by offering a major in Asian American Studies. Times and institutions change, as has the definition of what is an Asian American.

When I took the first Asian American Studies class at the University of Washington in 1970, "Asian American" meant primarily Japanese and Chinese Americans, with a few Filipinos allowed a place on the margin. Now "Asian American" includes Koreans, Vietnamese, Thais, Burmese, Laotians, Cambodians, Hmong, Asian Indians, and other Asians and Pacific Islanders. The multiplication of significant Asian and Pacific American populations, and their relative inclusion or lack of inclusion in the pan-Asian group, is the subject of another essay.[1] The topic here is more elusive and perhaps more subtle: the inclusion or lack of inclusion of people of multiple ancestries who are, as some would say, "part Asian," in Asian American Studies.

The Identity Question

Is it possible to have more than one ethnic identity? In *Hunger of Memory*, Richard Rodriguez asserts that members of ethnic minority groups must choose between private and public identities. By this he means that, in order to make satisfactory places for themselves in American society, minorities must either retain the ethnic culture of their youth, family, and community, or they must eschew their ethnicity and adopt the culture, values, and viewpoints of the dominant Anglo-American group. The ethnic, or "private," identity Rodriguez regards as inferior and limiting; the dominant group, or "public," identity he finds superior and liberating, even as he recounts the emotional costs of choosing to flee his own ethnicity.[2] According to Rodriguez and Pat Buchanan and Malcolm X, to name just three examples, a person can have only one ethnic identity and cannot live in more than one community simultaneously. One cannot be Black *and* White, Asian *and* American.[3]

W. E. B. Du Bois had a different view. He contended that every African American possessed and was possessed by a double consciousness, two identities in dialectical conversation. In an *Atlantic Monthly* essay, Du Bois wrote in 1897:

> [T]he Negro is a sort of seventh son, born with a veil, and gifted with second-sight in this American world,—a world which yields him no self-consciousness, but only lets him see himself through the revelation of the other world. It is a peculiar sensation, this double-consciousness, this sense of always looking at one's self through the eyes of others, of measuring one's soul by the tape of a world that looks on in amused contempt and pity. One ever feels his two-ness, an American, a Negro; two souls, two thoughts, two unreconciled strivings; two warring ideals in one dark body, whose dogged strength alone keeps it from being torn asunder.[4]

Such questions of double identity—of ethnicity and nationality—are issues for nearly all people of color in the United States. For no group of people is the dilemma of double identity more pointed than for people of multiple ancestry. They find themselves continually defined by people other than themselves. Regardless of how they construct their own identities, they always find themselves in dialogue with others who would define them from the outside.

Amerasian Santa Cruz poet Douglas Easterly rebels against being defined by Whites, in this excerpt from "Guessing Game":

> Five seconds and they've gotta have you figured
> or it gnaws at them all night in a tiny
> part of their brain till they come up and ask you
> what *are* you?
> like you're from another planet
> *   *   *
> . . . Leaving you
> a footnote
> in race relation theory
> a symbol
> for the intersection of two worlds,
> one foot in each of them
> so you can be dissected
> stuffed into labeled boxes—
> What *are* you?[5]

Cindy Cordes, a woman of Caucasian and Filipino ancestry raised in Hawaii, puts it this way:

> I have a *hapa* [multiple-identity] mentality. I look white but I don't identify with white culture. I grew up with a Filipino mother in an Asian household. We ate Asian food, had Filipino relationships, Filipino holidays, with Filipino values of family. In Hawaii, I always felt comfortable, so much of our culture is a conglomeration of cultures.

But then she went to Columbia University and found that other Asian Americans "look at me as white." When she went to a meeting of an Asian American student group, "They asked me, 'Why are you here?' "[6]

For multiracial Asians like Cordes and Easterly, one task is to defend themselves against the dominant discourse imposed by White America, in order to establish control of their own identity. But there is a second task that Cordes sees as equally important: to defend herself against the subdominant discourse imposed by Asian Americans. Throughout their history, Asian Americans have also defined people of part-Asian descent,[7] without regard to their actual life-situations or wishes. In thus specifying identities for mixed people of Asian ancestry, some Asian Americans have been as guilty of stereotyping and oppressing, of mythologizing and dominating, as have Whites. Throughout their history, however, multiracial Asian Americans have also chosen identities for themselves. They have created patterns of choosing identities which are the portents for the future.

The Dominant and Subdominant Discourses: Pre-1960s

For most of the history of mixing between Asians and non-Asians in the United States, people of part-Asian ancestry have not had much choice about how to identify themselves. Either the Asian minority or the white majority told them what they must be.

Prior to the 1960s, most Asian American peoples were so opposed to intermarriage that they shunned not only the intermarried couples but also their mixed children. That is in marked contrast to the situation for multiracial people of African American descent, who found at least a grudging welcome among African Americans and who were in any case forced by White Americans to identify as Black. Chinese-Hawaiians in the 1930s, by far the largest group of Amerasians in that era, were far more readily accepted in the Hawaiian community than in the Chinese community.[8] In that same period, Japanese Americans thrust out of their midst most mixed people. The Los Angeles Japanese community ordinarily took care of any of its members who were in need. One result was that only 101 orphans had to be taken care of by the Japanese American Children's Village in 1942. But nineteen of them were people of mixed ancestry. That was far more than their percentage in the Japanese American child population at large. Most of them, probably, were children who had been abandoned and whom no Japanese family would adopt.

White Americans also opposed intermarriage with Asians, and they were not inclined to celebrate the presence in their midst of multiracial people of Asian descent. But the number of Amerasians was so small that whites could ignore such individuals and let them slide by on the margins of white society.

Strange and vicious ideas about multiracial people of Asian descent have emerged historically from white racism. Those ideas are important because they shaped people's life chances then and now. The fullest exploration of this topic is in a recent essay by Cynthia Nakashima.[9] White ideas about mixed-race people proceeded from biological ideas propounded by pseudoscientific racists in the late nineteenth and early twentieth centuries.[10] Reasoning from the physical properties of plants and animals to the physical and moral qualities of human beings, pseudoscientific racists put on the American intellectual agenda a set of assumptions about multiracial people that still plague mixed people today. Cynthia Nakashima summarizes these ideas:

[T]hat it is "unnatural" to "mix the races"; that multiracial people are physically, morally, and mentally weak; that multiracial people are tormented by their genetically divided selves; and that intermarriage "lowers" the biologically superior White race . . . that people of mixed race are socially and culturally marginal, doomed to a life of conflicting cultures and unfulfilled desire to be "one or the other," neither fitting in nor gaining acceptance in any group, thus leading lives of confused loneliness and despair.[11]

Most dominant discourse about Amerasians has been in terms of these myths of degeneracy, confusion, conflict, and despair. Edward Byron Reuter, the foremost academic authority on racial mixing in his day, had this to say in 1918:

Physically the Eurasians are slight and weak. Their personal appearance is subject to the greatest variations. In skin color, for example, they are often darker even than the Asiatic parent. They are naturally indolent and will enter into no employment requiring exertion or labor. This lack of energy is correlated with an incapacity for organization. They will not assume burdensome responsibilities, but they make passable clerks where only routine labor is required.[12]

About the same time, a white California journalist wrote that: "The offspring are neither Japanese nor American, but half-breed weaklings, who doctors declare have neither the intelligence nor healthfulness of either race, in conformity with the teaching of biology, that the mating of extreme types produces deficient offspring."[13] Even Whites who fancied themselves defenders of Asians found themselves debating in terms set by the pseudobiological argument. Sidney L. Gulick, who opposed Japanese exclusion, felt compelled to give evidence that (1) unlike mules, Amerasians were not sterile, and (2) far from being weak and imbecilic, they were stout and smart.[14]

Within popular culture, Amerasians are perceived as sexual enthusiasts. This is related to a mechanism of dominance that attributes lack of sexual control to dominated peoples—women especially—as a way to excuse white male abuses of women.[15] This dynamic, the

myth of the erotic exotic," is compounded for women of mixed race.[16] Speaking of Amerasians, Nakashima writes, "The mixed-race person is seen as the product of an immoral union between immoral people, and is thus expected to be immoral him- or herself. . . . [M]ultiracial females are especially likely targets for sexual objectification because of their real and perceived vulnerability as a group. . . . [17]

During World War II, when Japanese Americans were placed into concentration camps on account of their ancestry, a small but significant number of mixed-race people—perhaps 700 Amerasians—also shared that experience. The army and the War Relocation Authority (WRA) ruled that all persons of full Japanese ancestry living on the West Coast had to be imprisoned. Some had non-Japanese spouses; the spouses could choose whether or not to go to the government's prison camps. Amerasians presented a special problem. Were they more Japanese, in which case they should be required to go to prison camp? Or were they more American, in which case they might remain at liberty with their non-Japanese parent? First the government incarcerated all the multiracial people of Japanese ancestry, then they tried to figure out what to do with them.

The WRA eventually made a judgment about each Amerasian's prewar environment. This judgment was made on the basis of the gender of the non-Japanese parent. Amerasian children who had White fathers and Japanese mothers could leave the camps and return to their presumably "Caucasian" (the army's term) prewar homes. Amerasian children who had Japanese fathers and non-Japanese mothers were presumed to have been dominated by their fathers, so while they could leave the prison camp, they were not allowed to return to the West Coast until late in the war. Adult Amerasians could leave the camps, but only if they had "fifty per cent, or less, Japanese blood," and could demonstrate that their prewar environment had been "Caucasian."[18]

Whites were confused about Amerasians and uncertain exactly where to place them. They had a number of stereotypes of multiracial people (Amerasians especially) that were perverse and demeaning. Asians were less confused than whites: generally speaking, they did not want multiracial people of Asian ancestry, and they told them they could not be Asians.[19]

This made life problematic for many multiracial people of Asian descent. Take the case of Kathleen Tamagawa. Born at the turn of the century, she did not like being an Amerasian. She opened her autobiography with the words: "The trouble with me is my ancestry. I really should not have been born." There follows a tale of tortured passage through her young life in America and Japan, undermined rather than supported by parents who had problems of their own. She was, by her own reckoning, a "citizen of nowhere," but by that she meant that she could find no place for herself in Japan. In time, in fact, she married a nondescript, middle-class White American and faded into White suburban life.[20]

Peter, a Japanese-Mexican boy, had a tougher time of it in Los Angeles in the 1920s. His Mexican mother died when he was very young, and he never established ties to any Chicanos. His father remarried, this time to a Japanese woman who did not like Peter. She beat him, ridiculed him, refused to feed him, and finally threw him out of the house. School authorities found him running unsupervised in the streets at age seven. Peter's father told him that "he wished that I had never been born; and at times I have even wished that myself. I have often wished that I were an American and not a Japanese or Mexican." Juvenile court authorities found Peter "an outcast" from both Japanese and Chicano communities. They tried to find a foster home for Peter, but no one would take him because of his mixed ancestry. He finally was sent to the state reformatory.[21]

For every Kathleen or Peter who suffered for their mixed raciality, however, there were others much happier. Kiyoshi Karl Kawakami, a prominent writer and interpreter of Japan to America and America to Japan, married Mildred Clark of Illinois and had two children, Clarke and Yuri. The younger Kawakamis spoke positively of their Eurasianness when interviewed in 1968. They grew up from the 1910s to the 1930s, mainly in the Midwest, well educated and insulated from life's blows by their father's money and status. They had almost nothing to do with Japanese Americans except their father, and in fact looked down on Nisei as people suffering from an "inferiority complex."[22] The common thread is that nearly all mixed racial people of Asian descent prior to the 1960s had to make their way outside of Asian American communities, for Asian communities would not have them.

This was true even for the great Asian American writer Sui Sin Far. Born Edith Maud Eaton in 1865, daughter of an English father and a Chinese mother, she was raised and lived her adult life in several parts of Canada and the United States. She chose to identify with Chinese people to the extent of choosing Chinese themes and a Chinese pseudonym, and she wrote prose sympathetic to the sufferings, fears, and hopes of Chinese North Americans. But she was nonetheless always more on the white side than the Chinese, in relation to where she lived and worked, who were her friends, and the point of view from which she wrote. In Sui Sin Far's writing, there were always people and Chinese. Partly it was because her literary aspirations demanded her work be intelligible to a White audience, partly because Chinese people treated her as an outsider, albeit a friendly one. For example,

> Some little Chinese women whom I interview are very anxious to know whether I would marry a Chinaman. I do not answer No. They clap their hands delightedly, and assure me that the Chinese are much the finest and best of all men. They are, however, a little doubtful as to whether one could be persuaded to care for me, full-blooded Chinese people having a prejudice against the half-white.[23]

Like other part-Asians before the 1960s, Sui Sin Far spent her life racially on the White side.

Winds of Change: Post-1960s

Substantial numbers of Asian Americans began to marry non-Asians in the 1960s. By the 1970s, the numbers of Chinese and Japanese who married outside their respective groups and then had children were so large that Asian American communities were forced to begin to come to terms and accept the existence of mixed people. There were some limitations on this acceptance, however. Those involved in the Asian American movement of the sixties and seventies seldom had a place for people of multiple ancestry or their distinctive issues. Stephen Murphy-Shigematsu describes the dynamic:

> [I]t has been difficult to include biracial Asian Americans in Asian American communities.
>
> The subject of biracial Asian Americans relates directly to interracial couples—an issue that is often seen as threatening to Asian American communities and individuals. There is a feeling that openly discussing this topic amounts to sanctioning interracial marriage and endorsing the death of Asian American ethnic groups."[24]

Today multiracial people of Asian descent take a number of paths to ethnic identity. Very few are inclined or able to identify solely with one part of their inheritance. Many adopt what Amy Iwasaki Mass calls "situational ethnicity." They feel mainly White or Black or Latino (according to their mix) when among White or Black or Latino relatives and friends and act mainly Asian when among Asians.[25]

Joy Nakamura (pseudonym) grew up in Brooklyn. She was in most respects a normal, Jewish girl in a Jewish neighborhood, except that her father was Japanese. Her Nisei father seldom talked about his childhood in California, her Japanese American relatives were far away, and although she felt somehow connected to Japan, she never had an opportunity to explore the connection until she entered a large eastern university. "I met more Asians my first year [in college] than I had ever known. When one Japanese American called me on the phone to invite me to join a Japanese American discussion group, I was very excited. I went to the group meetings a few times, but my 'white-half' began to feel uncomfortable when the others began putting down Whites," so she stopped going. She took classes on Japanese language and culture and enrolled in a seminar on Asian Americans. "I was desperately trying to find myself as an Asian-American woman, but I was not succeeding." She had clashes with her white boyfriend over racial issues, and she tried to ignore her Jewishness. Pressure from an African American activist friend helped Nakamura clarify her feelings. He said,

> "You must decide if you are yellow, or if you are White. Are you part of the Third World, or are you against it?" I laughed at his question. How could I possibly be one and not the other? I was born half-yellow and half-white. I could not be one and not the other anymore than I could cut myself in half and still exist as a human being.

At length she decided, "I do not feel guilty about not recognizing my Asianness. I have already done so. I have just readjusted by guilt feelings about ignoring my Jewish half. . . . My Jewishness is something that can be easily hidden. I do not want to hide that fact. I want to tell the world that I am a Jew and a Japanese American."[26]

When I told Joy Nakamura's story at a conference on Jewish history and identity, one member of the audience—a distinguished Jewish scholar—snorted loudly that Nakamura was obviously a sick person. On the contrary, she is healthy and whole. Her choice to embrace both halves of her identity in the mid-1970s is a point of self-understanding to which increasing numbers of multiracial people have reached in the two decades since. There is no question that to embrace both (or all) parts of one's identity is a healthier situation than to cling to one and pretend that the other does not exist. The general thinking here is to overturn the idea of a tortured "half-breed," torn between two unreconcilable identities. One has, not a split consciousness, but an integrated identity fused from two—"I am a whole from two wholes," is the way one Japanese-Caucasian man put it.[27]

In recent years a number of organizations of multiracial Asian Americans have sprung up around the country—the Amerasian League in West Los Angeles is an outstanding example—where people can come to explore their multiraciality. There has also grown up a veritable cottage industry of scholarly studies by and about multiracial people of Asian descent.[28]

Asian American Responses

Many mainstream Asian American groups still do not know quite what to do with multiracial Asians. Until very recently, there has been no place for them in Asian American Studies curricula.[29]

Asian Americans have, until recently, merely adopted the biases and boundaries set by White America. In so doing, they internalize the oppression that circumscribes their lives and project that oppressive vision on Amerasians. The 1990–91 controversy over the Broadway version of the hit musical *Miss Saigon* illustrates this point. The play's lead character was a Eurasian pimp. The play's producer and director chose a White person for the role. Asian American actors and community activists protested bitterly, saying the role should go to an Asian. Lost in the shuffle was the fact that, if ethnicity were the casting criterion, the only appropriate actor would be neither a Caucasian nor an Asian, but a person of mixed ancestry.[30] Multiracial Asian Americans exist (and in large numbers), and no amount of ignoring them will cause them to go away.

Increasing numbers of Amerasians are inclined to regard themselves as a variety of Asian Americans, and increasingly they find that Asians of unmixed ancestry will accept them as fellow ethnics. Across the country, it is hard to find a Japanese American or Chinese American church that does not have interracial couples and biracial children; there are even a few biracial adults. Sometimes, as Nakamura complained, Asian groups will accept Amerasians only if they renounce their non-Asian background. But with increasing frequency Asian American institutions, from athletic leagues to community newspapers to social welfare organizations, seem inclined to admit Amerasians as something like full participants.

Creating Amerasian Culture

In this new era, most Amerasians do not link up primarily with other Amerasians. But in some cultural respects they nonetheless constitute a distinct group. Those who grew up in Japan, for example, the children of American soldiers and Japanese women, have created a social world of their own, different from but not walled off from the Japanese or the Americans around them. They socialize more with each other than with non-Amerasians and have begun to form a third culture that mixes the languages, values, and symbol systems of their two parental cultures.[31]

Intra-Asian Ethnic Variations

In all this, one must remember that there are large differences among multiracial Asians. No one has yet studied the meaning of multiethnicity for multiracial Asians of differing derivations.

A few observations can be made. The community acceptance level for Filipino Amerasians has long been much higher than for other groups. This is because the

Filipino immigrant population was so heavily male that, until after World War II, almost any Filipino man who married had to find a non-Filipina mate. The majority of the American-born generation was multiracial.[32]

The situation for multiracial Japanese Americans differs from that of multiracial Chinese Americans, who are fewer in number. The difference has to do not only with the relatively greater numbers of Japanese Amerasians but also with structural differences in the two communities. Japanese Americans are an almost entirely American-born ethnic group. The bulk of the adult population are members of the third or fourth generation. By contrast, over half the current Chinese American population is made up of immigrants. The unmixed Japanese Americans are, as a group, much more assimilated to American society and culture at large, and somewhat more accepting of intermarriage and multiracial people.[33]

A third example of difference is between Korean and Vietnamese Amerasians, on the one hand, and Amerasians whose Asian ancestry is from the other countries mentioned above. Most Amerasians are American-born and-raised, the children of Asian Americans and other sorts of Americans. Nearly all Korean and Vietnamese Amerasians, however, were born in Asia, the children of American GIs and Asian women. Many of the Korean Amerasians were given up for adoption and came to the United States at a very young age. They were raised by people with names like Lund and Anderson in the Midwest. Their life trajectories and their identity issues are quite different from other sorts of Amerasians. These frequently revolve around how to connect with their Korean background when they grew up in rural Minnesota knowing only Swedish American culture. Most of the Vietnamese Amerasians, like the Koreans, were born in Asia. But the Vietnamese typically came to the United States only recently, in their teens and twenties. Generally speaking, the Korean and Vietnamese communities have been less eager to include Amerasians than have other Asian groups.[34]

Geographical Differences

If there are intra-Asian ethnic differences, there are also substantial differences depending on one's geographical location. Ethnic dynamics in Hawaii, for example, are quite different from those on the mainland. For over a century, there has been a great deal of intermarriage in Hawaii, and therefore a large number of Hapas, or people of mixed ancestry.

To some extent, in Hawaii the mainland patterns of ethnic acceptance are inverted. Island Chinese these days seem more accepting of multiracial Asians than do island Japanese communities. Hawaii's Chinese community may once have shunned people of mixed parentage, but in the last several decades that community has learned to make room for part-Chinese. One finds people in Chinese churches with Chinese names who look Hawaiian and went to the Kamehameha Schools, which are reserved for people of Hawaiian ancestry. By comparison, island Japanese communities and institutions have less room for multiracial Japanese Americans. There is a substantial number of Japanese Amerasians in Hawaii, but generally they are not tightly connected to Japanese community institutions. They find places in the social system, but usually in a wider, mixed sector that includes Whites, various Asians, some Polynesians, and other mixed people. To be Hapa among Chinese in Hawaii is more acceptable; to be Hapa among Japanese in Hawaii is less acceptable. A Japanese-Caucasian woman recently reported from Hawaii that a Japanese relative twirled the Hapa woman's red hair in her finger and snorted, "What part of you is Japanese—your big toe?"[35]

The reverse is true for most West Coast cities. There, intermarriage by Japanese Americans is more frequent than in Hawaii, and mixed people are more likely to be included in Japanese American communities. By contrast, multiracial Chinese Americans in cities like San Francisco and Seattle are more likely to be treated with suspicion and are less likely to be included in Chinese community institutional life.[36]

Perhaps the biggest difference, however, is between the Pacific states, where there are large Asian communities, and most of the rest of the country, where Asians are more of a novelty. Those large communities keep down the rate of Asian out-marriage.[37] But they also encourage non-Asians to regard Asian Americans as ordinary parts of the social fabric. That acceptance of Asians extends to Amerasians: Amerasians (like unmixed Asians) are less likely to be harassed by Whites in Monterey Park, California, than they are in Columbus, Birmingham, or Boston.[38]

Physical Appearance

Another way in which the experiences of multiracial people of Asian descent vary has to do with their physical appearance. University of Washington professor Jim Morishima tells the story of Kimiko Johnson (pseudonym), whom on the basis of her last name and appearance he took to be a Japanese American married to a Caucasian. When Morishima asked her about her husband, she replied cryptically that she was not married and had never been married but would show him his mistake. Soon she reappeared with an African American youth whom she introduced as her brother. The brother spoke Black English and identified himself as Black. The two Johnsons had the same set of parents—an African American father and a Japanese American mother—yet they identified themselves differently, one as Japanese, one as Black, because that is the way they looked, and therefore the way other people treated them.[39]

Physical appearance, however, does not completely determine one's identity. Christine Hall, Michael Thornton, and Teresa Williams, in studying children of Japanese-American intermarriages, all found some people whose features appeared to favor the Japanese side but who nonetheless identified more strongly with their American heritage (White or Black). Conversely, they found others who appeared physically more American but who for reasons of their upbringing felt more attached to their Japanese identities. Williams found that

> Darker-skinned Afroasians did not automatically relate to African Americans, nor did lighter-skinned Afroasians necessarily identify with their Japanese parentage. Eurasians

who appeared more Caucasian did not always blend in naturally with Euro-Americans; those who looked relatively more Asian did not always accept their Japanese background willingly and readily.[40]

Only in instances of conspicuous achievement are Asian communities willing to treat mixed people of African American parentage as insiders. This is related to what Cynthia Naka-shima calls the "claim-us-if-we're-famous syndrome."[41] It is not likely that many San Francisco Japanese Americans thought of attorney Camille Hamilton as one of their own until she was named by *Ebony* magazine as one of "Fifty Black Leaders of the Future" in 1990. By then *Hokubei Mainichi* was quick to feature her accomplishments.[42]

Implications of Multiple Identities

An increasing number of people who are of mixed ancestry are choosing to embrace multiple identities. Psychological studies by Amy Iwasaki Mass, George Kitahara Kich, and others suggest that a choice of a biracial identity is, for most mixed people, a healthier one than being forced to make an artificial choice.[43] In helping individuals make their way to identity choices, family support is crucial. One must add here, however, that since the pull of the dominant Anglo-American culture is so strong in America, if a child is of mixed Asian and White descent, it is prudent to emphasize the Asian heritage.[44]

In addressing multiracial people of Asian descent, the task for the dominant group in America is to rearrange its understandings to accommodate the reality of biracial identity. Asian Americans must also rearrange their understandings. This means redefining in more inclusive terms what it means to be an Asian American. In the case of some Asian groups—certainly Japanese Americans, and probably Chinese, Koreans, and Filipinos before long—their very survival in an era of high intermarriage depends on coming to terms with and incorporating multiracial Asians.

Asian American Studies programs, to take just one example, ought to do more to include Amerasians. Stephen Murphy-Shigematsu states:

> When biracial people see their concerns expressed as legitimate within the context of Asian American issues, there is a greater opportunity for continued interest and involvement and less chance of alienation. When they are free to acknowledge their non-Asian heritage as an integral part of who they are as a people, without fear of rejection, then their ability to study and work among other Asian Americans will grow.[45]

The good news is that a growing number of Asian American Studies programs—and many other Asian institutions—are doing just that: changing to include issues and persons of multiracial people of Asian descent.

NOTES

1. See Yen Le Espiritu, *Asian American Panethnicity* (Philadelphia: Temple University Press, 1992); William Wei, *The Asian American Movement* (Philadelphia: Temple University Press, 1993).

2. Richard Rodriguez, *Hunger of Memory: The Education of Richard Rodriguez* (New York: Godine, 1982).

3. Buchanan's sentiments on the necessity of obliteration of ethnic differences, and the need to put strict limits on non-northwest European immigrants because they are, in his view, harder to "assimilate," were much in the news during his 1992 run for the U.S. presidency, and they threaten to appear again. See, for example, DeWayne Wickham, "Buchanan Is Mounting a Racist Campaign," *Honolulu Star Bulletin* (December 16, 1991). Malcolm X called on African Americans, most of whom shared his mixed ancestry, to denounce their White background and embrace the Black. In his autobiography he recounted how "I learned to hate every drop of that white rapist's blood that is in me." When he came to self-consciousness as a member of the Nation of Islam, he changed his name: "For me, my 'X' replaced the white slave-master name of 'Little' which some blue-eyed devil named Little had imposed upon my paternal forbears." *The Autobiography of Malcolm X* (New York: Grove, 1965), 2, 199.

4. W. E. Burghardt Du Bois, "Strivings of the Negro People," *Atlantic Monthly* 80 (August 1897), 194–195.

5. Douglas P. Easterly, "Guessing Game," in Asian/Pacific Islander Student Alliance, *Seaweed Soup*, vol. 2 (Santa Cruz, Calif.: University of California, Santa Cruz, Pickled Plum Press, 1990), 26–27.

6. Susan Yim, "Growing Up 'Hapa'," *Honolulu Star-Bulletin and Advertiser* (January 5, 1992).

7. Terminology for mixed-descent people is problematic and cumbersome, and there is no standard. In this paper, I use the term "Amerasian" most frequently, as a label for people who have Asian ancestry on one side and American (White, Black, Native American, etc.) on the other. "Eurasian" refers specifically to people whose non-Asian heritage is European. I also use a number of descriptions, such as "multiracial Asians," "mixed people of Asian ancestry," and "people of part-Asian ancestry," more or less interchangeably. I do not wish here to enter into a discussion of the difference or nondifference between "race" and "ethnicity" (see Paul R. Spickard, *Mixed Blood: Intermarriage and Ethnic Identity in Twentieth-Century America* [Madison: University of Wisconsin Press, 1989], 9–10, for that discussion). Here I use "multiethnic" and "multiracial" interchangeably. By describing a person as having "part-Asian ancestry" I specifically do *not* mean to imply that she is less than a fully integrated personality, nor that she is less than fully entitled to membership in an Asian American community. If in any of this I offend a reader, I can only apologize, plead that the offense is unintentional, and ask that the reader attend to the argument and evidence presented here rather than to taxonomy.

8. Doris M. Lorden, "The Chinese-Hawaiian Family," *American Journal of Sociology* 40 (1935), 453–463; Everett V. Stonequist, *The Marginal Man* (New York: Russell and Russell, 1965; orig. New York: Scribner's, 1937), 41.

9. Cynthia L. Nakashima, "An Invisible Monster: The Creation and Denial of Mixed-Race People in America," in Maria P. P. Root, ed., *Racially Mixed People in America* (Beverly Hills: Sage, 1991), 162–178. Nakashima writes about the images of all sorts of mixed-race people, but her findings apply particularly well to the Amerasian case.

10. On American ideas about race, see Paul R. Spickard, "The Illogic of American Racial Categories," in Root, *Racially Mixed People*, 12–23; James C. King, *The Biology of Race* (Berkeley: University of California Press, 1981).

11. Nakashima, "Invisible Monster," 165.

12. Edward Byron Reuter, *The Mulatto in the United States* (New York: Negro Universities

Press, 1969; orig. Ph.D. dissertation, University of Chicago, 1918), 29. See also E. B. Reuter, "The Personality of Mixed Bloods," in Reuter, *Race Mixture* (New York: Negro Universities Press, 1969; orig. New York: Whittlesey House, 1931), 205–216.

13. Quoted in Kiyoshi K. Kawakami, *Asia at the Door* (New York: Revell, 1914), 71.

14. Sidney L. Gulick, *The American Japanese Problem* (New York: Scribner's, 1914), 153–157.

15. For fuller treatment of this theme, see Spickard, *Mixed Blood*, 35–42, 252–259; Calvin Hernton, *Sex and Racism* (New York: Grove, 1965); Winthrop D. Jordan, *White over Black* (Chapel Hill: University of North Carolina Press, 1968), 154.

16. Elaine Louie speaks of Asian women in general, not specifically of Amerasians, in "The Myth of the Erotic Exotic," *Bridge* 2 (April 1973), 19–20.

17. Nakashima, "Invisible Monster," 168–169.

18. Paul R. Spickard, "Injustice Compounded: Amerasians and Non-Japanese Americans in World War II Concentration Camps," *Journal of American Ethnic History* 5:2 (Spring 1986), 5–22.

19. Rejection of multiracial people of Asian descent was common in China and Japan as well as among Chinese and Japanese Americans. Filipino communities were an exception to this rule of rejection (see below).

20. Kathleen Tamagawa Eldridge, *Holy Prayers in a Horse's Ear* (New York: Long and Smith, 1932), 1, 220.

21. William C. Smith, "Life History of Peter," Survey of Race Relations Papers, Hoover Institution Archives, Stanford University, Major Document 251-A; William C. Smith, "Adjutant M. Kobayashi on the Second Generation," Survey of Race Relations Papers, Major Document 236.

22. Clarke Kawakami and Yuri Morris, interviewed by Joe Grant Masaoka and Lillian Takeshita, May 22, 1968, Bancroft Library, Berkeley, Calif., Phonotape 1050B:10. Other elite Eurasian children inhabited similarly comfortable positions, aware of the Asian aspect to their identities–even trading on it in their careers—but essentially White in outlook and connections. See, for example, the autobiographical portions of Isamu Noguchi, *Isamu Noguchi: A Sculptor World* (Tokyo: Thames and Hudson, 1967); *The Life and Times of Sadakichi Hartmann* (Riverside, Calif.: Rubidoux, 1970); and (also on Hartmann) Gene Fowler, *Minutes of the Last Meeting* (New York: Viking, 1954). Others in less comfortable circumstances had to struggle — psychically, interpersonally, and financially—to make places for themselves. See, for example, Sui Sin Far, "Leaves from the Mental Portfolio of an Eurasian," *The Independent*, 66:3136 (January 7, 1909), 125–132.

23. Sui Sin Far, *Mrs. Spring Fragrance and Other Writings*, Amy Ling and Annette White-Parks, eds. (Urbana: University of Illinois Press, 1995), 223. The essay is titled, "Leaves from the Mental Portfolio of an Eurasian." See also Paul Spickard and Laurie Mengel, "Deconstructing Race: The Multi-ethnicity of Sui Sin Far," *Books and Culture*, November, 1996.

24. Stephen Murphy-Shigematsu, "Addressing Issues of Biracial/Bicultural Asian Americans," in Gary Y. Okihiro et al., eds., *Reflections on Shattered Windows* (Pullman: Washington State University Press, 1988), 111.

25. Amy Iwasaki Mass, "Interracial Japanese Americans: The Best of Both Worlds or the End of the Japanese American Community?" in Root, *Racially Mixed People*, 265–279. See also Maria P. P. Root, "Resolving 'Other' Status: Identity Development of Biracial Individuals," in L. Brown and M. P. P. Root, eds., *Complexity and Diversity in Feminist Theory and Therapy* (New York: Haworth, 1990), 185–205.

26. Joy Nakamura (pseud.), letter to the author, May 22, 1974.

27. Jean Y. S. Wu, "Breaking Silence and Finding Voice: The Emergence of Meaning in

Asian American Inner Dialogue and a Critique of Some Current Psychological Literature" (Ed.D. dissertation, Harvard University, 1984), 173–182.

28. See, for example, Nakashima, "Invisible Monster"; Cynthia Nakashima, "Research Notes on Nikkei Hapa Identity," in Okihiro, *Reflections on Shattered Windows*, 206–213; Barbara Posadas, "Mestiza Girlhood: Interracial Families in Chicago's Filipino American Community Since 1925," in Asian Women United of California, eds., *Making Waves* (Boston: Beacon Press, 1989), 273–282; Murphy-Shigematsu, "Biracial/Bicultural Asian Americans"; Stephen Murphy-Shigematsu, "The Voices of Amerasians: Ethnicity, Identity, and Empowerment in Interracial Japanese Americans," (Ed.D. dissertation, Harvard University, 1986); Christine C. I. Hall, "Please Choose One: Ethnic Identity Choice of Biracial Individuals," in Root, *Racially Mixed People*, 250–265; Christine C. I. Hall, "The Ethnic Identity of Racially Mixed People: A Study of Black-Japanese" (Ph.D. dissertation, UCLA, 1980; Nathan D. Strong, "Patterns of Social Interaction and Psychological Accommodations among Japan's Konketsuji Population" (Ph.D. dissertation, University of California, Berkeley, 1978); Teresa Kay Williams, "Prism Lives: Identity of Binational Amerasians," in Root, *Racially Mixed People*, 280–303; Mass, "Interracial Japanese American"; George Kitahara Kich, "The Developmental Process of Asserting a Biracial, Bicultural Identity," in Root, *Racially Mixed People*, 304–317; George Kitahara Kich, "Eurasians: Ethnic/Racial Identity Development of Biracial Japanese/White Adults," (Ph.D dissertation, Wright Institute, 1982); George Kitahara Kich, "The Developmental Process of Asserting a Biracial, Bicultural Identity," in Root, *Racially Mixed People*, 304–317; Michael C. Thornton, "A Social History of a Multiethnic Identity: The Case of Black Japanese Americans" (Ph.D. dissertation, University of Michigan, 1983); Kieu-Linh Caroline Valverde and Chung Hoang Chuong, "From Dust to Gold: The Vietnamese Amerasian Experience," in Root, *Racially Mixed People*, 144–161; Ana Mari Cauce et al., "Between a Rock and a Hard Place: Social Adjustment of Biracial Youth," in Root, *Racially Mixed People*, 207–222; Ronald C. Johnson, "Offspring of Cross-Race and Cross-Ethnic Marriages in Hawaii," in Root, *Racially Mixed People*, 239–249; Cookie White Stephan and Walter G. Stephan, "After Intermarriage: Ethnic Identity Among Mixed Heritage Japanese-Americans and Hispanics," *Journal of Marriage and the Family* 51 (1989), 507–519; Ronald C. Johnson and Craig T. Nagoshi, "The Adjustment of Offspring of Within-Group and Interracial/Intercultural Marriages: A Comparison of Personality Factor Scores," *Journal of Marriage and the Family* 48 (1986), 279–284; Lorraine K. Duffy, "The Interracial Individual: Self-Concept, Parental Interaction, and Ethnic Identity" (M.A. thesis, University of Hawaii, 1978).

29. In just the past few years, Asian American studies programs at the University of California campuses at Berkeley and Santa Barbara have begun to teach about Amerasian issues.

30. It has been asserted by some that the part was originally written for an Asian pimp and then transformed into a Eurasian so that a Caucasian could play the part. If that be true, then the situation is similar to the controversy over the *Kung-Fu* television series of the early 1970s, where an originally Chinese leading character was rewritten as a Eurasian so that a White actor could play the part. If that is the situation here, then my analysis must be revised. However, to my knowledge this assertion has never been supported by any hard evidence.

31. Williams, "Prism Live"; Strong, Social Interaction and Psychological Accommodation among "Japan's Konketsuji Population."

32. Posadas, "Mestiza Girlhood."

33. Spickard, *Mixed Blood*, 61–70; Betty Lee Sung, *Chinese American Intermarriage* (New York: Center for Migration Studies, 1990), 74–86.

34. Kieu-Linh Caroline Valverde and Chung Hoang Chuong, "From Dust to Gold: The

Vietnamese Amerasian Experience," in Root, *Racially Mixed People*, 144–161; Nancy Cooper, " 'Go Back to Your Country': Amerasians Head for Their Fathers' Homeland," *Newsweek* (March 18, 1988), 34–35; K. W. Lee, "Korean War Legacy," *Boston Herald Advertiser* (March 24, 1974).

35. Private communication with the author.

36. A unique transition occurred for one group of Amerasians during the period 1930–1960. These were the children of mixed Chinese-Black families in the Delta region of Mississippi. During that period, according to sociologist James W. Loewen, Chinese gradually made a climb in status, from being segregated along with African Americans into the bottom layer of Mississippi life to being granted a kind of acceptance at the lower margin of the White group. In the decades before that transition, quite a few Chinese immigrant men had married African American women. Those mixed couples and their offspring, according to Loewen, were left behind by the unmixed Chinese as they made their ascent; Loewen, *The Mississippi Chinese: Between Black and White* (Cambridge, Massachusetts: Harvard University Press, 1971), 135–153.

37. Spickard, *Mixed Blood*, 73–84.

38. There is also, of course, the enormous difference between the ways multiracial Asians are perceived and treated in the United States and the ways they are treated in various Asian countries. See, for example, Strong, "Social Interaction and Psychological Accommodation among Japan's Konketsuji population"; Williams, "Prism Lives"; "Court Rejects Japan Nationality for Children of U.S. Fathers," *Japan Times Weekly* (April 4, 1981); Elizabeth Anne Hemphill, *The Least of These* (New York, 1980); Valverde and Chuong, "From Dust to Gold." There is another difference in harassment that is very difficult to express clearly. Insofar as Asians or Whites may be bothered by the presence of multiracial people of Asian descent, Whites are more likely than Asians to be open about their opposition. Whites are more likely to use a racist epithet in public or to snub a person openly. Some of that may be because Asians are more likely to be indirect, even passive-aggressive, in the ways they express disapproval. But also the characteristic—the Asianness of the Amerasian—that sets off a White bigot is perceived by the White to be a disempowering thing. The White person's sense of advantage over the Amerasian may encourage the White bigot to express openly her or his hostility. By contrast, the distinct characteristic—the Americanness of the Amerasian—that sets off the Asian bigot is perceived by the Asian to be an empowering thing. The Asian's sense of threat or disadvantage relative to the Amerasian may encourage the Asian bigot to keep quiet about her or his hostility.

39. James Morishima, "Interracial Issues among Asian Americans" (Panel discussion before the Association for Asian/Pacific American Studies, Seattle, November 1, 1980).

40. Christine Hall finds that Whites and people of color emphasize different characteristics when they consider the physical aspects of racial identity: "It seems that Whites concentrate primarily on skin color, while people of color (who vary tremendously in skin color and ancestry) attend to other features, such as eyes, hair, nose, body build, and stature." Hall, "Please Choose One"; Williams, "Prism Lives"; Thornton, "Multiethnic Identity"; Mass, "Interracial Japanese Americans."

41. Nakashima, "Invisible Monster."

42. That a Japanese American community newspaper would claim a Black Japanese American as one of their own was in itself a remarkable step forward ; it could not have happened a decade earlier; *Hokubei Mainichi* (April 1990). Rex Walters, a Eurasian from San Jose, is also an object of the claim-us-if-we're-famous syndrome, on the basis of his basketball exploits for

the University of Kansas and National Basketball Association; "Japanese American Athletes," *Hokubei Mainichi* (January 1, 1992).

43. Mass, "Interracial Japanese Americans"; Kich, "Eurasians"; Hall, "Ethnic Identity of Racially Mixed People."

44. Mass, "Interracial Japanese Americans."

45. Murphy-Shigematsu, "Biracial/Bicultural Asian Americans."

1. Fong and Yung contend that out-marriage, on a large scale, between Asian Americans and other ethnic groups has taken place only within recent decades. What factors prevented Asian Americans from out-marrying prior to World War II?

2. One of the traditional interpretations of out-marriage among Asian Americans is that this process is a natural progression toward the full assimilation of this group into mainstream society. According to Fong and Yung, what contributes to out-marriage? Why is there a greater propensity for Asian Americans from their sample to marry Jewish Americans? How might their findings have been different had they focused on intermarriage between Asian Americans and nonwhites or non-co-ethnic Asian Americans? To what degree does race factor into one's dating experience? Why may one choose to date one race over another? Why do some whites actively seek out Asian American women and men and vice versa? What obstacles exist today in dating outside one's race?

3. What are the obstacles encountered by multicultural Asian Americans in identifying with the Asian American community or the ethnic community into which they marry? How does acceptance of multicultural Asian Americans into the Asian American community differ along ethnic and racial lines, according to Spickard? How has this changed over time? What is situational ethnicity? How does this relate to the experiences of multicultural Asian Americans?

4. Until quite recently, the history of multicultural Asian Americans has been excluded not only from the larger discourse in American history, but also from Asian American Studies. Why do you think this is the case? How might this situation be remedied to bring the field of this group into the curriculum? According to Spickard, there are multiple ways in which the identities of multicultural Asian Americans have been historically constructed. Explain.

SUGGESTED READINGS

Daniel, G. Reginald. 1992. Passers and Pluralists: Subverting the Racial Divide. Pp. 91–107 in Maria P. P. Root (ed.), *Racially Mixed People in America*. Thousand Oaks, CA: Sage.

Kitano, Harry H., Diane C. Fujino, and Jane Takahashi Sato. 1998. Interracial Marriages: Where Are the Asian Americans and Where Are They Going? Pp. 233–260 in Lee C. Lee and Nolan W. S. Zane (eds.), *Handbook of Asian American Psychology*. Thousand Oaks, CA: Sage.

Labov, T., and J. Jacobs. 1986. Intermarriage in Hawaii, 1950–1983. *Journal of Marriage and the Family* 48: 79–88.

Lee, S. M., and K. Yamanaka. 1990. Patterns of Asian American Intermarriages and Marital Assimilation. *Journal of Comparative Family Studies* 21: 287–305.

Spickard, Paul R. 1989. *Mixed Blood: Intermarriage and Ethnic Identity in Twentieth-Century America*. Madison: University of Wisconsin Press.

Stephan, C., and Stephan W. 1989. After Intermarriage: Ethnic Identity Among Mixed Heritage Japanese Americans and Hispanics. *Journal of Marriage and the Family* 51: 507–519.

Sung, Betty Lee. 1990. *Chinese American Intermarriage*. Staten Island, NY: Center for Migration Studies.

Waters, Mary. 1990. *Ethnic Options: Choosing Identities in America*. Berkeley: University of California Press.

Wong, Morrison G. 1989. A Look at Intermarriage Among the Chinese in the United States. *Sociological Perspective* 32(1): 87–107.

FILMS

Fulbeck, Kip (producer/director). 1990. *Banana Split*. (37-minute experimental).

Hwang, Jason (producer/director). 1982. *Afterbirth* (34-minute documentary).

Soe, Valerie (producer/director). 1992. *Mixed Blood* (20-minute documentary).

Part XII

Visual Culture

Chapter Thirty

Is There An Asian American Aesthetics?

Transcribed by Gargi Chatterjee and edited by Augie Tam

This was the question addressed in the opening plenary session of a conference titled "Defining Our Culture(s), Our Selves" on June 8, 1991, at Hunter College in New York City. The conference was spearheaded by the Asian American Arts Alliance in collaboration with the Asian Pacific Student Alliance at Hunter College and with other representatives from the Asian American arts community. Five panel speakers, namely Meena Alexander, Margo Machida, Paul Pfeiffer, Andrew Pekarik, and Renee Tajima, participated in the discussion on Asian American aesthetics, which was moderated by Vishakha Desai from The Asia Society. They addressed questions like "What is Asian American art?," "Who defines Asian American art?," and "What is the importance of Asian American art to the community?" The panel speakers represented a wide range of perspectives from different arts fields; the following are their often divergent responses to these questions.

MEENA ALEXANDER *is a writer and poet. She also teaches English literature and writing at Hunter College and at Columbia University. She is the author of* Women in Romanticism: Mary Wollstonecraft, Dorothy Wordsworth, and Mary Shelley *(Macmillan, 1989),* Truth Tales *(Feminist Press, 1990), and* Nampally Road *(Mercury House, 1991).*

Is there an Asian American aesthetics? I would resolutely say "yes." There is the work of art, but there is also the people who look at it. We have a great multiplicity, and this multiplicity is the most exciting thing about being Asian American. It is the most exciting element of the Asian American aesthetics, because a large part of the current debate in the critical field has to do with trying to splinter the holism, the Eurocentric point of view that has been imposed upon us who have been defined as "the other." Though you must go beyond "the other" when you construct a work of art, it also gets inculcated somehow into the structure of the work. For me, an "aesthetics of dislocation" is one component of an Asian American aesthetics. The other is that we have all come under the sign of America. In India, no one would ask me if I were Asian American or Asian. Here we are part of a minority, and the vision of being "unselved" comes into our consciousness. It is from this consciousness that I create my work of art. Because of this dialectical element there is a "violence" involved for me even in the production of the work or art, which is perhaps the most intimate thing which I do as a person—apart from bearing children, making love, or occasionally cooking.

I wrote a few lines as a reflection on what it means to be a poet in the United States, for someone like myself as opposed to someone who looks different but is of European origin:

> As much as anything else, I am a poet writing in America. But American poet? What sort? Surely not of the Robert Frost or Wallace Stevens variety. An Asian American poet then? Clearly that sounds better. Poet, *tout court*, just poet? Will that fit? Not at all. There is very little that I can be *tout court* just by itself in America, except perhaps woman-mother. But even there I wonder. Everything that comes to me is hyphenated: a woman-poet, a women-poet of color, a South Indian woman-poet who makes up lines in English, a postcolonial language, as she waits for the red light to change on Broadway, a third world woman-poet, who takes as her right the inner city of Manhattan, making up poems about the hellhole of the subway lines, the burntout blocks so close to home on the Upper West Side. Oh confusions of the heart, thicknesses of the soul, the borders we cross tattooing us all over! Is there any here beyond the skin-flicking thing where we can breath and sing? Yet our song must also be of politics, a perilous thing, crying out for a place where a head is held high in sunlight, so that one is not merely a walking wound, a demilitarized zone, a raw sodden trench.

I allude to Frantz Fanon, who speaks of the dividing line, the barracks, the barbed wire that exists in a colonized state. What he says is applicable to Asian American art. He speaks of that "zone of occult instability" which we must come to in our art, in our culture of decolonization. I use that word "decolonization" advisably, because we bear within us histories which are not visible in the world around us. For me, in the United States the barbed wire is taken into the heart, and the art of an Asian American grapples with the disorder in society, with violence. And in our writing we need to evoke a chaos, a power equal to the injustices that surround us. So, for me, art is always political, even if it is most abstract, even if it is a simple visual image of a leaf falling from a tree. It is the way that the work of art stands appropriate for us.

This new emerging art, without even knowing that we are buying in and are bought in, consists of images magnified, bartered in the high places of capitalist chic. I think of Carlos Bulosan's *America Is in the Heart* when I think that one of the things that is incumbent upon us as artists is to create works which, even as they take this phase within the social world, are in some way recalcitrant to it. The power of the media is so enormous. The public language in relation to which our work stands is extremely important. And it is painful because there is an extraordinary intimacy about the work which we are sharing with the public world.

The notion of ethnicity is exciting because already we are making alliances, and therefore our works will be refracted against that of each other. A life in art requires a resolute fracturing of sense, a splintering of older ways of being, ways of holding that might have made the mind think of itself as intact and innocent. Now the talk of wholeness and innocence doesn't really make sense except as a trope for the mind which cuts back wherever and whenever it is for a beforeness that is integral in precisely the ways that only a past can be. I want to find a way that we can make a durable and usable past that is not just nostalgic but exists in the present. The present for me is the present of "multiple anchorages." It is these multiple anchorages that an ethnicity of Asian American provides for me, learning from Japanese Americans, Chinese Americans, African Americans, Indian Americans, and everyone, juggling, jostling, shifting, and sliding the symbols that come out of my own mind.

However, it is a fiction, a very dangerous one, to think that we can play endlessly in the postmodernist fashion, because our ethnicity is located in our bodies and comes in as a pressure to resist this sort of fracturing. I thus end with a paradox that this pressure is and is not fictive, and it rests on this unknown that seizes you from behind in darkness. We have an ethnicity that breeds in the perpetual present and I think this is our great enticement and our challenge as Asian American artists.

MARGO MACHIDA *is an artist, independent curator, and writer specializing in contemporary Asian American visual art. Most recently, she wrote* "Seeing Yellow: Asians and the American Mirror," *a catalog essay for* The Decade Show *(1990). She has curated a number of exhibitions, including* Street of Gold *at the Jamaica Arts Center (1990),* Cross Cultures: Three Japanese Sculptors *at the Rotunda Gallery (1989), and* Invented Selves: Images of Asian American Identity *at the Asian American Arts Centre (1988).*

No, there is not an Asian American aesthetics. Though there is a desire of cultural activists to establish a position of strength and unity based on identifying qualities that can be considered unique to Asian Americans, there are a number of underlying assumptions to be considered when raising this question of an Asian American aesthetics. Aesthetics in the broad sense refers to the philosophical study of art, its meanings, and its functions; it is often primarily associated with concepts of beauty, truth, quality, and moral and social value. Yet, the nature of these assumptions is not universal but relative and subjective. It reflects bodies of opinion and preferences that originate in the traditions of local culture. Therefore, the desire to have any simple, overarching, or definitive aesthetics is both limiting and prescriptive. It is imposing the judgements of a few on what should or should not be considered legitimate, authentic artistic expression. So the major problem of this desire for a singular aesthetics is in this baggage of essentialist expectation, as if an artist's race or ethnicity would automatically be manifest in his/her work, transcending national and generational difference, cultural upbringing, and education. The fact is that the work of contemporary Asian American visual artists runs the gamut from traditional Asian and folk art to a full range of Western idioms, much of which is uninvolved in the consideration of race.

I pose the question whether it is really useful to seek a unique Asian American aesthetics or whether we should go on with investigating and promoting the broad range of contributions that Asian American artists are making to the American cultural scene. In fact, with the arrival of new immigrants from all parts of Asia, Asian American communities are undergoing continuous change through its rapid expansion. The key to understanding the many art forms that are emerging in this atmosphere is in accepting this diversity within Asian generational and national voices, a "multiplicity of voices." Although the pursuit of any singular definition of an Asian American aesthetics is clearly problematic, it is important that the issues raised by the work of artists, specifically dealing with being Asian in America, be investigated.

There is frequently a relationship between generational status and the issues with which Asian American artists choose to contend. For recent Asian immigrants, framing and asserting continuity with their national identity remains primary. They experience the United States with their cultural sensibilities acquired in Asia. They seek to continue aspects of such practices and attitudes in their new life in the United States. For others, separated from their homeland for political or economic reasons, themes of longing, loss, and the need to speak to and of their cultural origins are often emphasized. Among the first-generation immigrants there are also those who are defined as the one-point-five generation, a distinct subgroup. They came to the United States as children, and although born and partially acculturated in Asia, their years here have given them a uniquely bicultural perspective. Many of them see their relationship to both cultures as ambivalent and some as having a "double vision." Such feelings often lead to work that contain political or sociological elements. This sense of divided identity is also seen among many in the second generation, where individuals are often torn between traditional familial expectations and a desire to be integrated into the larger American society. By the third generation, artists often look back to an idealized heritage which they can claim as their cultural legacy. Others try to construct new images of uniquely Asian American or pan-Asian identity emerging in the United States. Some of them consciously combine imagery derived from different nationality groups in order to evoke the sense of unity based on common experiences in Asian American immigrant history. Ironically, members of this generation often experience the most frustration because, as American as they may feel, the majority culture continues to look on them as aliens and foreigners.

In addition, a number of issues that cross generational lines have emerged. In struggling against being defined by others, many artists are actively critiquing American cultural stereotypes of Asians, especially in the mass media and in popular culture, and are inventing alternative signs and symbols of their presence. With increasing anti-Asian violence, some artists are inspired to confront explosive tensions between Asians and other racial groups by initiating collaborative projects to foster interracial dialogues.

Finally, images investigating sexuality and gender roles, highly controversial in the Asian American community, have also begun to appear, signaling a new willingness to approach subjects which were formally taboo and which take on a great urgency with the current AIDS crisis.

Despite the established and rapidly growing presence of Asians in the United States, it is striking that Asian American expression seldom finds its way to a larger public consciousness, which is informed by stereotypes mostly originating from the legacy of European Orientalism and from popular media. In the visual arts, Asian American contributions are rarely being recognized as distinct, in ways that African American or Latino art forms, for example, are.

While interest expressed by institutions like [The] Asia Society or The Asian Art Museum indicate that prevalent attitudes are beginning to change, without institutions specifically devoted to the serious study, documentation, and preservation of Asian American art, the mechanisms for verification and consistent attention will not exist. Thus, the major impetus for change and development has to come from within the Asian American arts community. In addition to vital community arts organizations, we are beginning to see involvement of young Asian art professionals, writers, and curators interested in focusing on Asian American artists. The emergence of strong Asian American art networks to build a strong national presence has begun. This is a very exciting time for all of us to be part of the Asian American art scene.

PAUL PFEIFFER *is a graduate art student at Hunter College as well as an activist with groups such as the Asian/Pacific Islander Caucus of ACT-UP NY and Youth for Filipino Action.*

To me the answer is plain. Yes, there is an Asian American aesthetics, and it is crucial for us to continue to develop our discussion along those lines, because, given the immense contributions that we have made to the history and culture of North America, we are sorely lacking in any adequate structure for revealing and recognizing those contributions. And this is a major obstacle to the healthy development of our identities as important players in twentieth- and twenty-first-century American culture. It is also a major obstacle to the full development of any understanding of the United States as a truly diverse nation. I think of Asian American aesthetics as a framework or established level of discussion in the form of all different kinds of scholarship, including criticism, exhibitions, art history, etc.—as a defining of terms to aid in the recognition of those contributions that we're talking about. In an ideal world this may not be necessary. However, given the obvious Eurocentric bias of current American scholarship and the invisibility of Asian American artists within that, we must maintain and develop our discussion on Asian American aesthetics, until such time as the American record can be set straight.

I would like to mention two of the most often repeated arguments questioning the validity of an Asian American aesthetics. The first asks, "How can there be an Asian American aesthetics, when Asia is made up of so many different countries and so many different cultures, some of which have been warring with each other for centuries?" It is most interesting that those people who are the quickest to question the validity of a unifying Asian American aesthetics on the basis of the diversity within the term "Asian American" would never think to question "Western" (meaning Euro-American) aesthetics, which is based on an equally diverse area with an equally turbulent history. When we speak of Euro-American aesthetics, there is room for diversity and a myriad of cultural influences, many of which come from Asia and other parts of the world. But suddenly when we speak of the possibility of an Asian American aesthetics, it must either be monolithic or not viable. Our diversity, our myriad of influences, and our history of cultural interactions are problematic only when discussing Asian American aesthetics, which serves as a direct assault on the one-dimensional and caricaturized terms in which the United States is accustomed to thinking of Asian and Asian American culture. It is exactly to counteract these stereotypes that we need to continue expanding the ground on which the complexity of Asian American culture can be revealed.

The second question often heard asks, "Doesn't recognition of an Asian American aesthetics act as an artificial barrier which destructively separates Asian American artists from their peers in the American art scene?" To answer the question, we begin by defining more precisely what constitutes an Asian American aesthetics. An Asian American aesthetics cannot be defined by an emphasis on race consciousness alone. We cannot define Asian American as completely distinct from the rest of American culture. Doing so would imply a complete isolation of cultures, which in this day would be completely ludicrous. There is no longer the naive myth that Asian Americans are totally alienated from the rest of America.

The discussion of an Asian American aesthetics is viable only if we are truly committed to revealing the complexity of Asian American experiences. We cannot limit our attention only to those expressions that are by separatist standards more pure, more Asian. As artist, we must not be afraid to draw from the full range of resources at our disposal, since in doing so we would limit our chances of achieving an expression that adequately reflects the complexity and richness of Asian American aesthetics.

Finally, discussion of Asian American aesthetics is important because of its increasing role as a direct challenge to the notion of a monolithic mainstream of American art, which claims to represent the highest in American aesthetic achievement but in reality represents a thoroughly Eurocentric, patriarchal, and thus lopsided vision of art. In a time when Asian Americans constitute a faction of our fastest-growing population and when it is predicted that Anglos will be a minority by the middle of the next century, the notion of a monolithic mainstream of culture is already obsolete. Continued discussion on Asian American aesthetics is one more step toward the replacement of that obsolete vision with a more pluralistic and inclusive one—one which is more appropriate for describing the complex reality of American culture.

ANDREW PEKARIK *was formerly Director of The Asia Society Galleries and is currently serving as a consultant to museums and arts organizations. He received a Ph.D. in Japanese Literature from Columbia University and has written books on Japanese art and literature.*

No, there isn't an Asian American aesthetics, but I'd like to qualify this a little because we are all talking about different things here.

If an Asian American aesthetics is simply an aesthetics of dislocation, my answer is that every artist is dislocated. If an Asian American aesthetics is a process of defining terms, then I say that the process of defining terms goes on all the time, whether or not we apply the term "aesthetics." To me "aesthetics" means some sort of graspable, holistic view that you can associate with a set of characteristics or qualities, and if that is what is meant by "aesthetics," then it cannot be applied to anyone. In the modern world where cultures increasingly intermix and where change has become increasingly rapid, there is no aesthetics for anyone. There is no American aesthetics, no Japanese aesthetics. The artist creates the aesthetics, and each one is creating an aesthetics of his/her own.

To deal with the practical rather than the philosophical issues of aesthetics, I will address the question "Who defines Asian American art?" I'd say that the experience of the visual artist is much more mediated than that of the writer or performer, because the visual work of art is by definition ambiguous, difficult, private, personal, and often impenetrable. Interpretation of that work is therefore critical, and interpretation is constructed in the larger world by a discourse that is held within what I call "the art system." It is the art system that defines the terms, that defines the process of aesthetics, that allows and disallows, that recognizes and rejects artists, and that is done to a certain extent without regard for their ethnic origin, without regard for sense, without regard for quality. "The system" consists of a series of functions: the artist who makes the art, the collector who patronizes the artist, the dealer who profits from finding the market for the art, the museum which is often supported by the collector to show the art, and then along with the museum the curator, the scholar, and the critic. It is a complex system, analagous to the stock market, in which many people make independent decisions on the basis of private standards with some overlapping public discussion but which somehow moves in an unpredictable way, which none of the participants are fully able to understand.

The system is controlled by a group of people whom we can call the "gatekeepers." These are the people who let things out, let things in, and keep things out. If one wishes to change the existing system one must infiltrate it and become a gatekeeper. The Asian American community has not been bad at putting together some good gatekeepers, particularly in the areas of criticism and administration. But there are a couple of areas in this system where there are big holes. One, no one has infiltrated the collectors. Where are the collectors of Asian American art? And why aren't they bringing dealers into being, by their visible support for this art? Once you have collectors and dealers, your circuit will be complete, because you have plenty of artists, a fair number of critics, some administrators, and others in the chain. So I would say, talk to a rich friend and encourage them to collect Asian American art, and it might be one of the most important things you can do for the field.

RENEE TAJIMA *is an Oscar-nominated filmmaker* (Who Killed Vincent Chin?) *as well as a film critic for National Public Radio and* The Village Voice. *She is currently a Fellow in Documentary Film at the Rockefeller Foundation.*

I will talk very specifically about Asian American movies and their history. An interesting problem about Asian American film today is that it has begun to achieve the quality of the so-called Western or white filmmakers, and it has become something of a "model minority" of American cinema in certain limited fields, particularly in public television. In the earlier years, we were not heading in that direction. In the 1960s and 1970, Asian American filmmakers were definitely developing an Asian American aesthetics, and to a certain extent we have lost that, partly due to history.

I would say Asian American cinema is separated into two major periods. First, in the sixties and seventies, the work was very urgent, idealistic, political, largely directed to an Asian American audience. Then in the eighties, the works were very institutionalized; we built institutions, Asian American cinema institutions. The films were very pragmatic, there was a focus on skills attainment, and our direct concern was the mass audience. The ideal combination of the two periods would be like filmmaking in the tone of Spike Lee's films, with our command of the craft plus our passion for social change. That, unfortunately, has not happened. We should try to regain what we began to develop in the sixties and seventies, when there was much more daring and more of an effort to develop a unique Asian American voice.

On the question of an Asian American cinema aesthetics, all I can say is that Asian American filmmaking is very eclectic, and that's true for Asian American arts as a whole. Wang's *Chan Is Missing*, on the surface, seems like a cultural hodgepodge, with traces of film noir, Italian neorealism, with languages of English, Mandarin, Cantonese being spoken, with the title song from Rodgers and Hammerstein. It is eclectic, and it is essentially Asian American.

On the positive side, this eclecticism makes us a part of the future, because the future is plural or "multicultural" (for a lack of a better word). Asian Americans do not necessarily deal with dual cultures, which is the cultural wisdom, because Asian American culture really is multicultural. I grew up a Japanese American in a culturally black neighborhood in white America. The plurality of cultural influences has always defined the Asian American experience, shaped as it is by a core of ethnic traditions, whether transmitted by family, community, or intellectual affinity. Tomas Ybarra-Frausto described this aesthetic development, "Rather than flowing from a monolithic, unifying aesthetic, our art forms arise from strategic necessities, what the Mexican writer Carlos Monsivais has called *la cultura de la necesidad*—the culture of necessity. This implies fluid, multivocal exchangers between cultural traditions."

The negative side of this eclecticism is in the identity crisis. For years and years, Asian American works searched for Asian American soul. In Maxine Hong Kingston's *Tripmaster Monkey*, the character Wittman Ah Sing, who is supposedly based on Frank Chin, says, "Where's our jazz? Where's our blues? Where's our ain't-taking-no-shit-from-nobody street-strutting language?" Asian American artists have scrambled for an Asian equivalent to African American and Latino cultural forms, themselves hybridizations. In an interesting way, that is why Asian American features have never really found a mass market, because we have no pop cultural equivalent. Successful African American or Latino filmmakers have been able to crossover hip hop culture or la bamba, music or dance, which has a mass audience. This has not happened with Asian American filmmakers. This has hobbled them, because we draw from the cultural forms of Asian Americans.

There was a definable Asian American cultural form which was beginning to develop, for good and for bad. In the Asian American film of the sixties and seventies, there was the ideal of "antislick." The form, the technical and artistic mastery, was considered reactionary; the message was very important—art for the people. This is evident in Asian American poster art of that time and in the music of that time. When the band Hiroshima played in my high school in L.A., they were loud and crazy—they were hip. Now they are mellow, laid back, and easy listening.

The works were largely documentary, and this is true in the beginnings of many cinemas of liberation and of radical filmmaking. They were mostly documentary and experimental. Films had guts, passion, and very strong messages. They had something uniquely Asian American about them. They also reflected a third world unity, were influenced by Black and Latino cultures, and included black, Latino, and Asian political sensibilities. The problem with these films, because of the "antislick" and liberal ideals, was that they were often very didactic and that they denigrated experiments with form and denigrated artistic bearing. This had a negative impact on Asian American film in those early days. Many of them were very raw, incoherent, and some just unwatchable.

In the 1980s, things changed, for many reasons. One, of course, was the Reagan era. But even within the independent filmmaking world and the Asian American movement, people got involved in electoral politics, becoming more assimilated into the American political scene. Asian American film became much more professionalized. There was more narrative and more feature films. And the marketplace began to determine the work, and the marketplace was public television. There was greater formal and technical improvement, and at the same time Asian American film became safer for public consumption. Because of the new interest in dramatic film and the greater technical expertise there was more narrative coherence.

One interesting motif which continued from the sixties was the building of an insular Asian world in the art fields. We wanted to convey the oral histories and life experiences of Asian Americans. In films about internment camps by Japanese American directors, for example, people speak about their years of victimization and struggle, but there are never any white characters. One of the main failures of Japanese American filmmaking is that we have not documented the whites who put Japanese Americans in the camps or who supported the policy. So there is this fear of direct confrontation with white America that has been conveyed in the film and has made it safe for public television and for a larger audience.

In the 1990s, there are some interesting things that will happen. One, there will be more participation by Asians of other nationalities besides Chinese and Japanese. The Asian American media community as a whole has failed to involve the participation of these other groups. There is also a third generation of film school trained directors who are not necessarily making films about Asian American characters. I do not regard them as Asian American films, since we must define Asian American film as something that deals with our themes and our realities. Otherwise, we are just directors and filmmakers making films in the larger world, rather than making Asian American cinema, which is what we need.

Chapter Thirty-one

Art, Activism, Asia, and Asian Americans

Dorinne Kondo

I [have] argued [elsewhere] that we must take . . . a politics [of pleasure] seriously in order to appreciate its power even as we interrogate its effects. These modes of appreciation and critique are essential when we analyze racial representation in popular culture. The pleasure we experience in images, spectacle, and narrative can be simultaneously seductive, insidious, empowering, life giving. A strategically deployed critical consciousness would require a sensitivity to this complexity. Such a pursuit would comprise at least two general forms of subversion.[1] When we speak of an oppressive politics of representation in film, theater, and television, the dominant minimizes oppositional critique through the pleasures of narrative ("It's such a beautiful story"), of the visual (spectacle, cinematography), and through a sharp distinction between fiction and fact ("It's just a story"; "It's just a satire"). One tactic depends on deconstructing the dominant and exposing these ruses of power. Another tactic could be called a strategic deployment of authenticity that would create alternative visions to oppressive representations: spaces where those of us on the margins could "write our faces." Here, the pleasures for Asian American audiences would be those of self-recognition and empowerment. Though radical separation from the dominant is impossible, these faces might be ones we could at last recognize as ours. Both tactics and their myriad context-specific variations must be part of a repertoire of activist strategies.

Whatever the risks, we must continue to explore those strategies in the face of continuing racism, for to remain silent ensures a smooth, seamless reproduction of power relations. For Asian Americans, this includes deconstructing hegemonic representations of Asia that—like it or not—make a profound impact on Asian American lives. Such elisions abound. Cambodian children are shot in Stockton; Asian American women pushed in front of subway trains by Vietnam vets with posttraumatic stress disorder; Asian Americans meet up with everyday racisms, from outright racial epithets to the well-intentioned racisms of "You speak English so well"; white Asianophiles, whatever their sexual persuasion, fetishize Asian Americans in terms of sexuality and submissiveness. The ineffable "foreignness" of Asian Americans continues to bristle with life-determining significance, and as long as that is so, we must continue to interrupt the reproduction of structures of racial domination reflected in the reproduction of whiteness as universal norm and the specific, phantasmatic constructions of its various colored Others.

Such interruptions require outspoken critique and organized efforts to effect social transformation, exemplified in three interventions in which Asian American artists, activists, and academics have been prominently involved. The *Miss Saigon* controversy and its aftermath engage multiple modes of political/artistic intervention, including organized protest, educational efforts, satire, and counterhegemonic cultural production. Perhaps this elaboration indexes the undying persistence of the *Madame Butterfly* trope recirculated in *Miss Saigon*. The second involves the latest incarnation of Japanese male stereotypes—the businessman as corporate soldier—in Michael Crichton's novel and film *Rising Sun*. Mobilizing martial metaphors alive with historical resonances from the Pacific War, *Rising Sun* creates a sinister Japanese threat that skillfully, seductively draws upon a venerable Orientalist tradition. Finally, we turn to local institutional interventions that have made a difference, through the case of an organized teach-in/protest that occurred around a performance of Gilbert and Sullivan's *The Mikado* at the Claremont Colleges, where a concerted organizational effort linking Asian American faculty with other faculty of color and with other campus progressives—including Women's Studies and gay/lesbian groups—was one pivotal step in bringing about the establishment of a fledgling Asian American Resource Center and a still nascent Asian American Studies program.

The continuing need for actions such as those I describe might seem discouraging, a Sisyphean task of battling the "changing same." Yet, . . . I would also argue that these interventions illustrate useful, sometimes even life-giving, strategies. None is perfect or beyond complicity or recuperation, yet all are interventions that have made a difference.

Dead Butterflies

Perhaps no recent debate over Asian American representation has galvanized Asian American artistic communities or captured the attention of mainstream media as has the casting controversy over *Miss Saigon*. It remains for Asian American theater artists a historical and political watershed that forced the mobilization of actors and community, spawning numerous artistic and political interventions that represent an array of tactical possibilities.

The controversy began when producer Cameron Mackintosh designated Jonathan Pryce, a white actor who had played the Engineer in the London production, to repeat the role in *Miss Saigon's* Broadway premiere. In response to pressures from Asian American activists and actors, Mackintosh reportedly "looked under every rock" for an Asian or Asian American for the part, but he claimed to have failed in his quest. With the deadline looming, Actors' Equity refused to grant the card Pryce needed to work in the United States. Their decision recognized the objections raised by Asian American actors that Asian or Eurasian parts should be cast with Asian Americans, since historically, both Asians *and* Eurasians had been played by whites. Indeed, the category Eurasian was often deployed precisely in order to hire white actors: David Carradine in *Kung Fu* is but one example. Asian American artists like Dom Magwili and Ping Wu argued that Mackintosh had in fact used this tactic, since the libretto makes no reference to the Engineer as a person of mixed race (Cf. "Fallout over *Miss Saigon*" 1990). Mackintosh subsequently revoked his decision to bring *Miss Saigon* to Broadway. This spelled the loss of millions of dollars of revenue and a substantial number of jobs for the theater world. Succumbing to Mackintosh and to protests from some of its members, Equity reversed their initial decision. *Miss Saigon* opened on Broadway in February 1991 with Jonathan Pryce as the Engineer.

The parameters of the debate expose the assumptions and limitations of liberal humanist ideologies. *The Los Angeles Times* devoted a special page to the controversy immediately following the Equity decision to refuse Pryce his card. On the Right, Charlton Heston called the decision "racist" and declared his shame to be a member of Equity. Fueling his indignant reaction were his claims that actors as a group are more discriminated against than are people of color. Two producer-directors, one Asian American and one white, read the issue as one of artistic freedom, since directors and producers should be able to cast whomever they choose, race notwithstanding. Here, the argument was that "the best person" should get the part. Velina Hasu Houston raised the issue of multiracials. In her view, neither side was in fact right, for Eurasians are neither white nor "pure-blooded" Asian Americans. Finally, actor/writer/director Dom Magwili noted the political and historical forces involved. He argued that casting a white actor as an Asian *or* Eurasian is *traditional casting* that gives whites license to portray people of color, while people of color cannot even play themselves. This traditional casting, he argued, is racist casting.

With the exception of Magwili, most writers subscribed to the common liberal humanist assumption that the individuals involved are shorn of history and beyond or outside power relations. Heston ignores the racial stratifications and divisions within the category "actor"; certainly, Heston himself enjoys wealth and celebrity. He erases the historically constructed power relations that allow whites to play Asians and Asian Americans, while the reverse has never been the case. His cry of "racism" (or its cousin, "reverse racism") assumes that any critical discussion of race by people of color is racist. Such a view mistakes hurt feelings or individual inconvenience for systematic historical domination. Similarly, the producers' invocations of artistic freedom mobilize a liberal individualism that authorizes us to do what we please, without regard for the consequences. Their fear of censorship arises from a faulty analysis of power relations. Asian American activists and Equity are hardly in a position to dictate or silence; rather, they were attempting to compel Mackintosh to take seriously the issue of historical inequality and to search more assiduously for a talented Asian American actor—of whom there are many—to fill the role. Here, as often happens, who counts as the best is racially marked, where supposedly objective standards are in fact imbued with power relations. Defining the parameters of debate solely in terms of artistic freedom fails to give equal weight to artistic *responsibility* to various communities. Velina Hasu Houston's poignant argument about the specificity of Eurasians and the ways people of mixed race are often marginalized by members of all their constituent racial groups, is at one level indisputable. However, like most of the other writers, she fails to account for the historical overdetermination of the decision to allow a white actor to play Asian *and* Eurasian. In this case, the "white" and "Asian" halves are not equally weighted in political terms. A clear analysis of the issues must take into account the historically constructed, *systemic* power relations that informed Mackintosh's casting decision. In short, it matters who is doing the casting, for whom, for what purposes, and where those subjects and institutions are located in larger matrices of power.

In the mainstream media, focus on the casting controversy served to obscure other protests and other issues. Ultimately, the casting controversy is—or should be— a relatively minor aspect of the *Miss Saigon* story, for the striking feature here is the problematic politics of representation. *Miss Saigon* is a "colored museum" of Asian stereotypes, including the tenacious trope of Asian women's sacrifice and death. Asian American groups vociferously denounced the oppressiveness of these images, picketing *Miss Saigon* on its opening night on Broadway; gay Asian Pacific American groups made similar interventions when the Lambda Legal Defense Fund used *Miss Saigon* as a fundraiser for the Fund. Yet by that time, the story of *Miss Saigon* was old news, and the protests scarcely garnered media attention. When *Miss Saigon* opened in Los Angeles in late January 1995, I submitted the following piece to The *Los Angeles Times*, which was published after almost a month had elapsed and at less than half its original length.[2] Given that the longer piece deals substantively with the politics of representation and issues of institutional complicity, I reproduce it here:

> *Miss Saigon* opened on January 25 as the inaugural production of the newly renovated Ahmanson Theater. The blockbuster musical was the subject of live TV coverage, a cover story in the *Times Calendar* section, and extensive advertising hype. We have all heard about the controversy surrounding the Broadway production: should Jonathan Pryce, a white actor, play the Eurasian engineer or should the role go to an Asian American actor? However, reportage in both New York and Los Angeles has erased a far more urgent issue, the focus of protests among Asian Americans on both coasts: *For what kinds of Asian roles are we competing?* In New York, Asian American groups asking such questions picketed at opening night; in Los Angeles, many Asian Americans actively object to the stereotypes staged in *Miss Saigon*. Yet, aside from two letters published in the *Times Calendar* section, coverage of this side of the story has been conspicuously absent.
>
> What are our objections to *Miss Saigon?* In the play Kim, a Vietnamese bar girl and prostitute, falls in love with Chris, an American G.I. in Vietnam. He returns to the U.S. as Saigon falls, and in his absence she bears him a son. In the meantime, Chris marries a white woman, but when he discovers Kim to be alive in Thailand, he returns with his American bride to search for his son. Ultimately, Kim kills herself to ensure her son's "escape" to a "better life" with his father. An update of the opera *Madama Butterfly*, *Miss Saigon* admittedly seems a mild improvement over the Puccini warhorse: the U.S. soldier, Chris, feels sorrow upon abandoning his Asian paramour; a song, "Bui-Doi," decries the plight of Amerasian children. Deploying deeply problematic narratives of East-West relations, *Miss Saigon* restages and conveniently expiates American guilt over Vietnam.
>
> This expiation occurs through the recirculation of all-too-familiar Asian stereotypes: *extremes of sexuality*, represented in the *prostitute and the pimp*, the shy *lotus blossom*,

and *asexual, faceless peasants and cadres; Oriental despotism* in the statue of Ho Chi Minh and in Kim's Vietnamese suitor, and its inverse, *Oriental subservience*, in the phalanxes of soldier hordes; *the sleazy, sneaky Oriental*, in the person of the Engineer, and familiar paternalistic narratives, such as *White man saves Asian woman from Asian man*, and *Asian woman dies for white man*. However updated, *Miss Saigon* is simply a case of "the changing same."

So what of the many Asian American jobs that *Miss Saigon* represents? Having had the misfortune of seeing *Miss Saigon* on Broadway for the book I'm writing, it is difficult for me to imagine a more disempowering, heartbreaking spectacle than the sight of gifted Asian American actors displaying their creative talents as pimps, prostitutes, lotus blossoms, and faceless Orientals. Equally disturbing is the fact that Cameron Mackintosh has apparently established schools to train Asian American theater professionals to populate further productions of *Miss Saigon*. Presumably we are to be grateful, even happy, for these opportunities. True, *Miss Saigon* gives Asian American actors jobs: jobs fleshing out the white man's fantasy, jobs that allow us to participate enthusiastically in our own oppression. Too often, artists of color are still the hired help, recruited to fill out the vision of a white playwright or director. In the name of empowerment through employment, *Miss Saigon* instead secures Asian American subordination.

There are, of course, notable exceptions in the work of artists of color. I was part of the creative team on Anna Deavere Smith's play *Twilight: Los Angeles 1992* at the Mark Taper Forum, part of the Center Theater Group that is also sponsoring *Miss Saigon*. In *Twilight*, Smith took on the bristling tensions around race and the historical oppressions that led to the L.A. uprisings. Given the Taper's putative commitment to racial diversity, it is particularly disappointing that *Miss Saigon* arrives in L.A. under the aegis of the Center Theater Group as the Ahmanson's inaugural production. I hope that progressive people of all races will think twice before spending $65 on this multimillion-dollar celebration of racial stereotypes. Let us register our protests. Boycott *Miss Saigon*. No matter how seductive the spectacle, racism is still racism.

Concerted forms of political activity around *Miss Saigon* arose across the country.[3] in the Twin Cities, for instance, the Pan Asian Voices for Equality (PAVE) organized a protest of *Miss Saigon* that embraced a coalition of African Americans, Native Americans, Asian Americans, feminists, and gays and lesbians. Widely covered in the local media, the demonstrations, pamphlets, articles, and teach-ins aimed to encourage debate and to draw attention to the depiction of Asians. As part of their intervention, Asian American Renaissance staged a counterperformance called *Missed Saigon* that dealt with stereotypes perpetuated in the play and the larger issues of power and culture it raises.[4]

What were the effects? Though the theater did not cancel performances or alter their performance schedules, they did make some concessions. Fifteen thousand complimentary tickets originally designated for schoolchildren were withdrawn in light of PAVE's objections that the musical presented stereotypical images to young children without a dissenting point of view. The theater also agreed to provide an insert with each playbill, written by an Asian American woman who specializes in media portrayals of Asian Americans (*Asian American Press*, December 3, 1993, 2). Moreover, the protest committee sent me Xeroxes of numerous letters from people

I assume to be white, attesting to the value of the interventions. A few people sent in donations, some in the amount of the ticket price ($50.00). One canceled her subscription to the Ordway Theater performance series. Asian Pacific community organizations also solicited information and presentations from people on the committee, which were positively received. These small but significant signifiers of the protest's impact deserve to be marked. Yet, given the unequal distribution of resources, it is unrealistic at best to expect a small group—or even a major Broadway production like *M. Butterfly*—to derail permanently the circulation of persistent hegemonic fantasies like the Butterfly trope, for one cannot at one stroke eliminate the geopolitical relations, the masses of capital, and the overdetermined histories that create and perpetuate these insidious ideologemes.

So stated, the Gramscian "wars of position" seem bleak. But perhaps we should mark an equally important effect of the protests and the organizing: an enactment of political identity and "community."[5] In such instances, this enactment is part of the intervention, giving Asian Americans the occasion to grapple with critical issues and to make alliances amongst the various Asian Pacific groups and with other subaltern groups. Perhaps this outcome is as important as subverting the dominant. David Mura puts it this way:

> Whatever the effect of the anti-*Miss Saigon* activities on people outside the community, it's clear that the protests are part of a larger sea change occurring in the consciousness of Asian Americans and other people of color throughout this country. That sea change is something neither the Ordway nor *Miss Saigon* nor its mainly white middle-class patrons can stop. Increasingly, Asian Americans and other people of color are demanding that we be able to present our own images, to tell others how we see ourselves (*City Pages*, February 9, 1994).

Telling others how we see ourselves can sometimes involve the use of theatrical hyperbole as political strategy. Performance artist and playwright Ken Choy and performance artist Juliana Pegues, both members of the artistic organization Asian American Renaissance, staged a "die-in" at Minneapolis' Ordway Theater at a performance of the opera *Madama Butterfly*. Standing up in the midst of the proceedings, they screamed, "No more Butterfly!" and fell down repeatedly to simulate their deaths. Choy was tackled, Pegues manhandled, as both were forcibly removed and charged with disorderly conduct.[6] Notable here is the theatricality of their challenge, reminiscent of ACT UP and its deployment of hyperbole. Equally important are the stakes as performers these artists have in *Madama Butterfly*. Their artistic life is constricted by the limitations described by Butterfly and other Oriental stereotypes, for unless Asian American artists write our own roles, there will be few alternatives to a life of playing lotus blossoms, dragon ladies, pimps, rapacious businessmen, or, as actor/director François Chau wryly stated, "druglords, bodyguards to the druglord, druglords on the run." Dramatically focusing attention on the paucity and the oppressiveness of roles for people of color in mainstream productions, Pegues and Choy, in concert with other members of Asian American Renaissance, mounted a critical and theatrical statement of protest.[7] In short, Asian American artist/activists have, through conventional and unconventional means of political mobilization, interrupted the smooth recirculation of hegemonic racial representations.

Rewriting Our Faces: *Face Value* and Buzz Off, Butterfly

To subvert the dominant can involve recognizable forms of political activity. But cultural production is always already political, and performance can enact its subversions textually and on stage. Satire and parody are valuable tools for politically committed artists, providing ways to subvert oppressive representations through performing their absurdity. Deconstructive readings depend upon invoking and then deconstructing or subverting the dominant; David Henry Hwang's *M. Butterfly* does precisely this. Hwang transposes his deconstructive critique into the register of farce with his first full-length play to follow *M. Butterfly: Face Value*, his satire of the *Miss Saigon* controversy. Hwang knows the controversy from the inside, as one of the original instigators of the *Miss Saigon* protest; along with actor B. D. Wong, he served as one of the spokespersons for the movement.

The version of *Face Value* that played on Broadway is a farce of mistaken racial identities in a physically comic style. It brings to mind comedies such as *Much Ado about Nothing*, as well as farces that pivot around mistaken gender identity, such as *Twelfth Night* and Marivaux's *The Triumph of Love*. In *Face Value*, a white actor in yellowface is set to star on Broadway in a musical called *The Real Manchu*. Two Asian American activists dressed in whiteface are planning to disrupt the opening night performance from the audience. Two white supremacists, mistakenly believing *The Real Manchu* to be about "real Orientals" and believing the lead actor to be Asian, lurk in the wings, ready to hold up the proceedings. There begins the comedy of mistaken racial identities. By the last scene, all the characters except for the white supremacists are coupled with someone of another race: the male Asian American activist/actor with a young white actress who had been the white actor's mistress; the white actor with the Asian American woman activist/actress; the white producer with the African American stage manager. A white supremacist conveniently named Pastor (he is one) has a change of heart and marries them all, in a wedding scene à la *Much Ado about Nothing*. Whatever one may make of the politics of this narrative closure (for example, why must the people of color all be heterosexually coupled with white people?), *Face Value* offers an intriguing proposition: that race is a mask that is in some sense performative.

A complex politics of reception was at work during the production of the play. *Face Value* was slated to open on Broadway in March 1993. Producers took it on the road to Boston, where it opened in February to dismal reviews and small houses (due no doubt to the combination of the reviews and winter storms). The play went into previews on Broadway in March, and—in view of audience reaction, poor box-office performance, and the artistic and production team's assessments—*Face Value* closed before it officially opened. Whatever one makes of the success of the production as a theatrical/artistic endeavor (since I did not see the production, my remarks are based on a reading of the text alone) the politics of this chilly reception suggest that Hwang had touched a nerve about race.

The Boston press coverage confirms this suspicion. Kevin Kelly of the *Boston Globe* wrote, "*Face Value* illuminates very little. It proves as *shrill as its real-life stimulus* [my emphasis]. Worse, for all the intensity of its message, it's labored and unfunny" (1993). Whether or not the play was "labored and unfunny," the phrase that resonates with political significance is "shrill." For those whose stake is continued oppressive racial representation, both the *Miss Saigon* protests and Hwang's play were forms of political critique. One wonders whether the critic's less than complimentary appraisal of the *Miss Saigon* disputes affected his reading of *Face Value*. Furthermore, audience nervousness around race may indicate that a farce about race, especially by a person of color, may be too unsettling at this historical juncture. Hwang opined that audiences, both in Boston and on Broadway, were unsure whether or not it was all right to laugh. This nervousness and uncertainty are not uncommon in the mainstream reception of work by people of color: Jessica Hagedorn and Han Ong's collaborative work *Airport Music* at the Berkeley Repertory Theater is one recent example that comes to mind.[8] In such instances, racial critique from people of color can provoke guilt. Perhaps it is especially disturbing when that critique comes from Asian Americans. Hwang tells of a white woman in the audience who proclaimed her shock that *Asian Americans* were raising issues of racism (1994). She clearly viewed Asian Americans as model minorities, assuming that racism for us is no longer an issue. Her anger/guilt/doubt/surprise may have been shared by many members of the audience.

Hwang stated that he intends to rework the play as a comedy of manners in the style of Molière, rather than its present incarnation as a physical farce. The delicacy and nuance of comedies of manners may yield more fruitful ways of coming to terms with the prickly issues of race. However, the broad parody of the lyrics to *The Real Manchu* also allows us to see the absurdity of hackneyed anti-Asian tropes:

JESSICA AND CHORUS
Don't get sentimental
he's a crafty Oriental
he's inscrutable
CHORUS
(You know his conscience is gone)
JESSICA
He's inscrutable
CHORUS
'Cuz he comes from Canton
JESSICA
He's inscrutable
CHORUS
(And he hates women's rights)
He's Fu-u-u—
ALL
Cruel yet transcendental
He's a crafty Oriental
CHORUS
He's a crafty Oriental
CHORUS
He's inscrutable

JESSICA
(You know, he's greedy and brown)
CHORUS
He's inscrutable
JESSICA
And he's bound for your town
CHORUS
He's inscrutable
JESSICA
(You can't read him at all)
CHORUS
He's inscrutable
JESSICA
'Cuz his eyes are so small
ALL
He's Fu
Fu Manchu
JESSICA
Gesundheit!
CHORUS
Fu Manchu!
JESSICA
God bless you!
. . . .
BERNARD
Ni hao mah
I come from land so far
I'm Fu
That's spelled F-U to you . . .
Those foolish whites don't know . . .
I will soon rule their land . . .
I'll buy Miss USA
And ship her to Japan (Act I, Scene 4)

Here, Hwang lampoons a panoply of pernicious stereotypes of Asians, particularly Asian and Asian American men: Oriental despotism and its correlative, Oriental patriarchy; inscrutability; lust for white women; and stereotypical characteristics, such as slanted eyes and unpronounceable or nonsensical names. The Yellow Peril, Japanese invasion, and Fu Manchu's will to world domination are invoked and rearticulated in the register of parody. Taken to an extreme, the stereotypes seem at once ludicrous and hilarious. Here, farce works as a tool of deconstructive critique.

Finally, *Face Value* elaborates the leitmotiv of Hwang's work: the fluidity of identity. While *F.O.B.* treats the shift from the mythic to the mundane and *M. Butterfly* thematizes shifting gender and sexual identities, in *Face Value* and Hwang's one-act, *Bondage*, it is race that shifts and changes. These later plays suggest that race, too, is performative, but there are limits to its fluidity. For example, in the last three plays, a dramatic unmasking occurs, revealing a truer self whose vulnerabilities are thereby exposed. This suggests that shifting identity is not simply a free play; rather, certain identities are socially and culturally constructed and their borders patrolled. They cannot simply be jettisoned. Though Hwang's ideas are still in formation as *Face Value* is rewritten, his interventions around race are provocative and invite further reflection on performances of race and on race as a performative.

Chinese-Hawaiian gay performance artist Ken Choy takes up the battle with dominant cultural representations on multiple levels. He deploys satire as a political tool in his performance art, and he was among the organizers of the *Miss Saigon* interventions in the Twin Cities. Trained at the University of California at Irvine and performing in Los Angeles out of Highways Performance Space, Choy lived in Minneapolis after winning a Jerome Playwriting Fellowship and stayed some two years before returning to Los Angeles. His performance piece *Buzz Off, Butterfly*, is a series of vignettes loosely connected by a narrative about the plight of performance artist Ken Chow, who shuttles between unsupportive parents and uncomprehending grant agencies. Many episodes articulate the poignancy of self-Orientalizing Asian Americans who engage in versions of Bhabha's "mimicry," including a young Asian American who wants to be Chuck Norris's son, or "Ken Markewitz," an Asian American who thinks [he] is Jewish, or, in "Ode to a Butterfly," an Asian American gay man who literally becomes a butterfly, wings and all. Choy begins cocooned in diaphanous white, complaining about his Midwestern, beer-guzzling, chest-haired, dominatrix white male lover, to whom Ken must play Butterfly. "Why," Choy asks, "have I become a classified ad?" adding, "Subservience . . . Ain't it grand." As the piece progresses, the character becomes more and more defensive of that subservience, acquiring first one wing, then another.

Buzz Off, Butterfly thematizes the colonizing of the minds, bodies, and lives of Asian Americans. Choy quite clearly stated to me his intentions in the piece; he means to depict someone who is deluded and who through that delusion becomes in fact insane. The last word is eloquent here. *Buzz Off, Butterfly* ends with a spectacular display of Choy's wacky performative energy in a hilarious and disturbing explosion of epithets entitled "The Angriest Asian in the World." The "angriest Asian" represents for me the inevitable outcome when subaltern people succumb to the seductions of mimicking the dominant. Indeed, Choy has explicitly invoked his anger as a source of creative inspiration: "I'm very issue-oriented so issues make me angry. So, I find something I'm very angry about and that stirs something inside me and I try to think of an unusual and unique way of presenting that" (Sigmund 1992).

Choy's work leads us outside the text, to consider issues beyond the levels of representation, including venue and the genre of performance art as a contestatory practice. My intent is not to erect a binarism between performance art and "conventional" theater; rather, I want to point out the different levels at which these genres can operate and at which they can be appraised. Choy premiered these pieces at Highways, a gay/lesbian and multiracial performance space founded by Tim Miller (one of the "NEA Four"), among others. His work highlights the importance of venue; for example, Highways has fostered senses of community for gays and lesbians and people of color, nurturing a host of young artists, including Choy. Equally pivotal, Highways-sponsored performances give space, time, and voice to different racial and sexual communities; for instance, *Buzz Off, Butterfly* was part of an annual series of Asian American performance and visual art, "Treasure in the House," curated by Dan Kwong and Dylan Tranh.

In formal terms, work like *Buzz Off, Butterfly* operates against naturalistic conventions. For example, the genre often depends upon an episodic structure that disrupts notions of the well-made play and linear narrative. Moreover, there is for the performer an accessibility to performance art that refuses the requirements of spectacular theatricality—or overproduction, depending on one's perspective. The material requirements are minimal: a body; a voice; perhaps a few clothes—or none; a few lights; perhaps some music, perhaps not; and stories based on personal experiences. The result can be an intimacy of theme, form, and practice that allows access to many who might otherwise be prevented from telling their stories. Similarly, for an audience a smaller venue like Highways is a far more intimate experience of spectatorship than witnessing the proscenium stage at a Broadway theater. There can be a kind of empowering accessibility about a piece like *Buzz Off, Butterfly* in such a setting.

The interventions I have described use different genres—mainstream theater and drama, on the one hand, performance art, on the other—and are directed at somewhat different audiences. Broadway's overwhelmingly white, mainstream, and upper-middle-class clientele constitutes one key site of intervention. The presence in mainstream venues of work by people on the margins is crucial in terms of interrupting the pleasures of spectacle, of the familiar (and often racist or sexist) revival, of uncontested racial stereotypes, of easily digestible entertainment that serves only to confirm the audience's prejudices. Performance art like the Ken Choy piece and the series of which it was a part occurs in smaller, more intimate venues offering accessibility to artists and to educated, middle-class audiences, including gays, lesbians, and people of color. Whatever the venue, these productions must be set within an increasingly vibrant Asian American performance scene, the national sea change David Mura invokes. Creating Asian American culture becomes a way to write our faces and, in the process, to rewrite the contemporary meanings of race.

Trade Wars and Corporate Soldiers

If the *Madama Butterfly* trope in its many guises continues to circulate as a mechanism for the continued oppression of Asian American women and gay men, then the contemporary straight male counterpart is the Japanese businessman. He is a corporate soldier, an automaton whose polite demeanor conceals a samurai spirit devoted to the company and to the nation. Feeding fears of a "Japanese invasion" and "takeover," he is among the most salient Orientalist stereotypes in the contemporary American imaginary. Nowhere was this trope more visibly circulated than in the novel and the film *Rising Sun*. Both have provoked considerable controversy among Asian American communities and caused consternation among progressive American scholars of Asia.

Rising Sun imparts an ominous sense of the impending threat to American autonomy posed by Japanese business. From the outset, it establishes familiar terms of
discourse rooted in essentialist national identities: the U.S. and Japan as two separate
and distinct nations/races, whose ways of life are opposed and mutually hostile. The
specter of "trade wars" so familiar from the American news media looms in the
book from the opening aphorisms. The first is attributed to an American, Phillip
Sanders, who is allowed a proper name: "We are entering a world where the old
rules no longer apply." Underneath we read, "Business is war," a "Japanese motto."
Note that no specificity or individuality is allowed the Japanese characters. Is this a
particular company? An individual? Or is it, as the attribution suggests, a motto
familiar to all Japanese, a clarion call to which an entire nation responds? These
epigrams introduce the tone and the themes of the book: the word of individual
American warning precedes the bald statement of collective Japanese martial intentions.

Set in Los Angeles, *Rising Sun* introduces us to narrator/protagonist Smith, a
special-services liaison officer and a police lieutenant who is called upon to investigate
a murder in the new headquarters of the Nakamoto Corporation on the gala open-
ing-night festivities. Veteran John Connor, an "expert on Japanese culture," acts as
Smith's adviser on "Japanese customs," in the manner of a hunter instructing a
neophyte on how to deal with wild animals: "Control your gestures. Keep your hands
at your sides. The Japanese find big arm movements threatening. Speak slowly. Keep
your voice calm and even" (Crichton 1992, 15). Such passages have the effect of
creating Connor's authoritative voice—the we-know-them-better-than-they-know-
themselves Orientalism is striking here—and solidifies the impression of Japan as an
alien Other, imbued with an unfamiliar essence that can be comprehended only
through professional translation and mediation.

Rising Sun trumpets a wake-up call to Americans, alerting them to the pervasive-
ness of the Japanese threat and advocating a response in kind, lest America "turn
Japanese." Indeed, the book represents the U.S. as engaged in a battle for its very
existence as an autonomous nation. To fend off this enemy, the first step is precisely
to recognize Japanese efficiency. For example, a Black man who works monitoring
the security cameras in the Nakamoto Towers describes his family's experiences
working in Japanese auto factories and in the old GM plant. American practices were
slipshod and inefficient; overpaid, arrogant, and ignorant management imperiously
gave nonsensical orders to production workers, while "the Japanese" collaborated
with line workers to solve problems. "I tell you: *these people pay attention*" (Crichton
1992, 45).[9]

The Japanese threat to American autonomy is all the more formidable because—
in addition to their efficiency—they are ineffably strange, engaging in practices "we"
would label unethical or inconsistent. Here Connor patrols the borders of essentialized cultural and racial difference. His pseudosocial scientific pronouncements about
Japanese behavior attest to the deeply alien nature of the economic enemy. (This
passage might have been based in part on my own *Crafting Selves*, which discusses,
among other things, shifting and contextually constructed identity in Japan.) Crichton embellishes this notion to create a transposed version of the sneaky, crafty

Oriental through the term "inconsistency," though this is not a term used in my book. The Japanese of *Rising Sun* seem all the more dangerous because their inconsistency—hence inscrutability—is located in cultural norms.

> "It's annoying," Connor said. "But you see, Ishigura takes a different view. Now that he is beside the mayor, he sees himself in another context, with another set of obligations and requirements for his behavior. Since he is sensitive to context, he's able to act differently, with no reference to his earlier behavior. To us, he seems like a different person. But Ishigura feels he's just being appropriate....
>
> Because for a Japanese, consistent behavior is not possible. A Japanese becomes a different person around people of different rank. He becomes a different person when he moves through different rooms of his own house."
>
> "Yeah," I said. "That's fine, but the fact is he's a lying son of a bitch."
>
> Connor looked at me. "Would you talk that way to your mother?"
>
> "Of course not."
>
> "So you change according to context, too," Connor said. "The fact is that we all do. It's just that Americans believe that there is some core of individuality that doesn't change from one moment to the next. And the Japanese believe context rules everything." (Crichton, 1992, 54)

Perhaps Crichton, himself the possessor of an anthropology degree, wanted to render this "social scientific" analysis in an evenhanded way. But the passage describes "the Japanese" as a monolithic whole, incapable of consistency, prone to lie in American terms. This "the Japanese" may do not out of pernicious individual intent but because their "culture" deems such behavior to be normative. Blame here then rests at the level of culture. The subtle implication is that such cultural norms could be even more insidious precisely because they shape the behavior of individual Japanese, imbuing Japan as a whole with a proclivity for what we would, at best, call inconsistency, and which would strike most of "us" as "lying." And because it is posited as an immutable cultural essence, such behavior is by implication virtually incorrigible.

"The Japanese" become even more deeply, ineffably Other as we make further discoveries about "their" sexual practices. The dead blonde is the mistress of playboy Eddie Sakamura, who kept her in an apartment complex with other call girls. The specter of Japanese conquest through the seduction of white women looms here. One of them invokes the well-worn stereotype of bizarre sexuality as the flip side of the "polite" Japanese veneer:

> "And to them," she said, "their wishes, their desires, it's just as natural as leaving the tip.... I mean, I don't mind a little golden shower or whatever, handcuffs, you know. Maybe a little spanking if I like the guy. But I won't let anybody cut me. I don't care how much money. *None of those things with knives or swords* [my emphasis]. A lot of them, they are so polite, so correct, but then they get turned on, they have this . . . this *way . . .*" She broke off, shaking her head. "They're strange people." (Crichton 1992, 64)

Rising Sun thus recirculates the hackneyed trope of the polite, conventional, repressed Japanese businessman, who conceals a penchant for the sadistic, a notion I have criticized elsewhere (1986). The reference to swords, laughable were it not invoked so seriously, signals a transhistorical Oriental despotism emergent in "their" conquest of "our" women and metaphorically, "our" country. Surely, Crichton suggests, this same cruelty fuels Japanese dedication to the economic wars.

This crafty Other has succeeded in infiltrating the top echelons of "our" government and business. Geopolitical intrigue heightens through a plot element introducing trade negotiations between the Nakamoto Corporation and a U.S. firm. The Senate Finance Committee is holding hearings on the issue, and its chair, we discover, made love with the dead call girl on the boardroom table before her murder. Clearly, Crichton is drawing a picture of a Senate and government riddled by politicians beholden to the Japanese, who are figured as the foreign presence that has penetrated the national body on multiple levels.

Such a penetration is particularly degrading and to be feared when it involves races like "the Japanese," who are troped as alien and as fundamentally less worthy than "we." Connor's authoritative pronouncements explicitly thematize race; here he puts the Japanese in their place while attributing racism to *their* cultural proclivities, not to his own characterizations.

> "The Japanese think everybody who is not Japanese is a barbarian.... They're polite about it, because they know you can't help the misfortune of not being born Japanese. But they still think it.... The Japanese are extremely successful, but they are not daring. They are plotters and plodders." (Crichton 1992, 196)

Uttered in Connor's voice, these derogatory statements have an authoritative ring. The Japanese may have the upper hand now, but clearly all is not lost. "They" are, after all, merely "plodders"—hardworking but uncreative, successful only because of their dedication to work and their devious business practices. Representing "them" as clannish and endowed with a racist superiority complex, Connor not so subtly allows us to counter by asserting "our" own superiority.[10]

Racial discourses are amplified with the introduction of Smith's romantic interest: the beautiful, half-Black, half-Japanese computer whiz, Theresa Asakuma, who simultaneously embodies the exotic-erotic and the computer-nerd stereotypes. She analyzes the doctored tapes that erroneously depict the murderer as playboy Eddie Sakamura; her zeal is driven by revenge for the discrimination she experienced while growing up in Japan, both as someone of mixed race and as someone with a physical disability. Again, Japanese racism makes American racism pale in comparison:

> You Americans do not know in what grace your land exists. What freedom you enjoy in your hearts. You cannot imagine the harshness of life in Japan, if you are excluded from the group. But I know it very well. And I do not mind if the Japanese suffer a little now, from my efforts with my *one good hand* (Crichton 1992, 261).

Though one could hardly make an argument for Japan as a multiracial utopia, and though oppressive forms of racial, caste, and other forms of discrimination undeniably exist, the matter is considerably more complex. For example, John Russell writes eloquently on the racial formations shaping various Japanese responses and tropings of African Americans, which he argues were mediated through the West (1991). This level of complexity never enters Connor's analysis.

Connor neatly preempts any attempt to problematize American racism when he invokes the Chrysanthemum Kissers, academics who kowtow to Japanese contacts lest their sources of information disappear. "Anybody who criticizes Japan is a racist" (Crichton 1992, 204). In *any* fieldwork situation—no matter where it might be— relationships are crucial, but the assertions Connor makes are simply unfounded. Criticizing Japan is not the problem—no nation is beyond criticism—but those criticisms must always be appraised on multiple levels: the tropes they engage, the analyst's positioning in a geopolitical matrix, and subject's stake in that critique. Rather than coming to terms with his own positioning, Crichton's character merely provides a convenient justification for American racisms. For Connor, racism lies at the level of individual prejudice, rather than with larger systemic inequality.[11] He fails to recognize that his experiences of "racism" reflect partial—and only partial— loss of white male privilege. As Said would argue, he confronts Japan as first and foremost a white male citizen of a country accustomed to dominating world geopolitics in this century, and that legacy endures, despite a changing geopolitical/economic order.

At stake throughout *Rising Sun* is a white *masculine* subjectivity that must preserve its boundaries at all costs. Threats to the dominance and to the integrity of the boundaries of such an identity proliferate, and in the face of such threats, this subjectivity must eschew an infantilizing, feminizing dependence on others. For example, according to Connor, America has gone wrong by underestimating the formidable Japanese threat to "our" autonomy through "our" debilitating dependence on Japanese capital. This theme is transposed into the "drunken uncle" metaphor when he tells Smith of meetings various Japanese industrialists held in Los Angeles, ostensibly to determine the fate of the U.S. Smith is indignant, but Connor replies:

> Do you want to take over Japan? Do you want to run their country? Of course not. No sensible country wants to take over another country. Do business, yes. Have a relationship, yes. But not take over. Nobody wants the responsibility. Nobody wants to be bothered. Just like with the drunken uncle—you only have those meetings when you're forced to. It's a last resort. (Crichton 1992, 193)

On the one hand, this passage supports Connor's own self-presentation as eschewing Japan-bashing for an approach that is critical of the U.S. Yet this seeming evenhandedness cannot mask a preoccupation with restoring American masculinity to its "rightful" dominance. The drunken uncle is an adult who should be authoritative, responsible, and in control—but his lack of control elicits caretaking efforts from, presumably, a nephew (the subjects presumed in the book are always already masculine). The uncle is lacking in masculine authority and ideally must be restored to his proper, responsible, *senior* position. The desire to reinstate white American men as global leaders animates the allegory.

The novel closes in a symphonic orchestration of stereotypes, with "business-as-war" the leitmotiv. And the viciousness of the war exacts many casualties. Internally, competition among *keiretsu* is associated with the torture and the death of Eddie Sakamura, whose father's company belongs to a rival of the Nakamoto *keiretsu*. The merciless Ishigura is revealed as the killer of the blonde woman, for she is merely a pawn in the plot to blackmail Senator Morton into changing his views on the MicroCon sale. Like a good corporate samurai, Ishigura then jumps off the terrace to his death in order to spare himself and his company the shame of his crime. With heavy-handed symbolism, he is engulfed in cement, immolated in the foundations of the building owned by the company to which he had devoted his life. Predictably, Orientalist stereotypes and the demands of narrative closure dictate that he will commit suicide.

This very predictability becomes the source of our pleasure as readers, and here the politics of pleasure must be interrogated. Crichton is a master of his genre. It is no surprise that *Rising Sun* was a bestseller. He adeptly deploys the techniques of the whodunit to keep the reader turning the pages: breathless pacing, cliffhanger chapter endings, clever plot twists. Even readers like myself who were predisposed to be critical can be drawn in—for we want to know *who committed the murder*. Here, genre conventions create suspense, providing the seductive tease and the satisfying resolution. Mainstream audiences can pleasurably encounter Orientalist stereotypes that are sufficiently attentive to historical context to be familiar yet different. The Orientalist stereotypes have the ring of authenticity, rearticulating all-too-familiar martial metaphors extant since before the Pacific War.[12] Crichton masterfully orchestrates these pleasures in a riveting narrative—hence its heightened insidiousness.

How more precisely does that insidiousness operate? First, the book firmly reinscribes national, racial, and cultural essentialisms; such processes have never been more problematic than in this era of transnational capitalism. Certainly, the suggestion that the U.S.—or any other major economic power—has been an innocent in geopolitical terms seems disingenuous at best. The presumption of a nation-state-based form of capitalism fails to account for the presence of multinational capital and for the economic interpenetrations of the economies of multiple nation-states. In an era of global flows of information, technology, and capital, where does the Japanese economy end, where does the American one begin? What does the invocation of these national essences reveal and obscure? And what is at stake in this essence fabrication?

Second, because *Rising Sun* is written from a site of embattled U.S. white masculinity, Crichton's characters' aggressive reassertion of national, cultural, and racial essence occurs at a moment when that identity is on the verge of being deposed from its accustomed site of privilege. Inevitably, the threat to masculine dominance is sexualized and gendered. In *Rising Sun*, the transgressive threat of penetration comes from an alien and formerly "inferior" feminized Other. In the novel and film *Disclosure*, Crichton writes a similar scenario, but this time the threat is the femme fatale: the sexually voracious, power-hungry woman executive who uses every conceivable strategy, including accusations of sexual harassment, to "fuck" both literally and figuratively the male protagonist. In the film, Michael Douglas adds to his body of work performing threatened white masculinity, this time fending off the advances of, and finally outwitting, his former lover/boss/corporate adversary Demi Moore. In *Rising Sun* and in *Disclosure*, Crichton articulates the anxieties of white men who must patrol the boundaries of their essential identities to remain on top, for above all, they must *avoid being fucked*—by women, by the Japanese. In this way, Crichton brilliantly captures the sense of white male outrage and loss represented in the recent attacks on affirmative action and the anti-immigrant sentiment of California's Proposition 187. Riding the Zeitgeist, he has created seductive blockbuster entertainment that clearly touches a national nerve at a moment of historical transition.

The publication of *Rising Sun* raised consternation and protest among Asian Americans and scholars of Asia, who raised the kinds of arguments I have outlined here. Crichton staunchly denied allegations of Japan-bashing, arguing that he was, if anything, "America-bashing." Though the book is indeed critical of present American business practices, one could hardly label Crichton a basher. Further, his presumed bashing is deployed in order to resecure the dominance of white masculinity as it confronts the threat of infantilization, penetration, and feminization. The criticisms of the U.S. aim to restore us to "our rightful position" of global leadership, while criticisms of Japan construct an alien, hostile enemy through the circulation of numbingly familiar racial images of despotism, bizarre sexuality, cruelty, inconsistency, inscrutability, and a self-immolating devotion to work.

Critical reaction among American scholars of Japan and among Asian Americans was immediate. Crichton, a Harvard alumnus, was a member of the Visiting Committee for the Department of Social Anthropology at Harvard and is a member of the Harvard Board of Overseers. Robert J. Smith of Cornell, an eminent anthropologist of Japan, resigned his position from the Visiting Committee when he read *Rising Sun* and distributed the letter of resignation to scholars of Japan, including myself. In it, Smith decried the racist representations of Japan in the book, saying that he had dedicated his life to combatting these very stereotypes. Among the local interventions in Los Angeles, historian of Japan Miriam Silverberg gathered scholars of Japan to critique the book. Asian American groups across the country gathered to protest the racist depictions of Japan represented in the novel.

Responding to criticisms from Asian Americans, several changes were incorporated when the book was made into a film. The most obvious is the race of the perpetrator: the murderer in the film is a white Nakamoto employee. However, the racial alteration from Japanese to white is only marginally better. Indeed, it appears at least equally insidious, for the Japanese thereby prove successful in infiltrating, even "brainwashing," Americans who will collaborate with them. The language of war is inescapable.

Further, the casting of actor Wesley Snipes, an African American actor, as Smith sets up a complex discourse around race given the media attention accorded to Black/Asian, and specifically, Black/Korean, tensions. (In the novel, Smith is racially unmarked.) It shows the inadvertent naiveté or the calculating cynicism of the filmmakers around race, for selecting Snipes has a divide-and-conquer function: the filmmakers can claim they are not racist because they have introduced an African American character; this in turn gives them license to reproduce various pernicious Asian stereotypes. Yet Snipes is not allowed to escape his position of subordination as a man of color; he is allowed to challenge Connery's veneer of authority, but he cannot go too far. For example, at one point, Snipes jokes defiantly that Connery is acting like a "massa," which is indeed accurate. Yet the filmmakers fail to recognize that simply calling attention to the authority of the white man over people and cultures of color does not depose that authority. Snipes is still junior to Connery; Connery provides the brains, while Snipes is there mostly for the ride.

Given the plot changes and the change in the race of the perpetrator, several well-known Asian American scholars with whom I spoke considered the film version of *Rising Sun* to be far more innocuous than the novel. With this expectation in mind, I went to the movie and found myself reeling in horror. It took me some time to recover from what I found to be a highly disturbing experience. Cinema's powerful materiality, the use of image and sound, created the palpable presence of an ominous Japanese threat that begins from the first frames. A red rising sun flashes onto screen to the refrain of insistent, relentless drumming, much like the relentless Japanese threat the film will present to us. The dark cinematography, the sleek, monolithic black tower, the images of Los Angeles in the rain, create a high-tech vision reminiscent of *Blade Runner* and *Black Rain*. The director creates a cold, cruel, hyperefficient Japanese world that evoked for me Vincent Chin and Japanese American internment.

The film vividly recirculates other stereotypes not present in the book. Oriental decadence and the colonizing of the white female body by the alien other is depicted on screen through Eddie's use of a nude blonde woman's body as a table laden with sushi, which he picks from her stomach as he reclines with his harem on a large bed. Stan Egi portrays Ishigura, but the costumers and makeup artists have dressed him in an ill-fitting, cheap-looking suit, with slicked-down hair. An unflattering picture to say the least, this costuming choice contributes to the sleazy Oriental stereotype and would hardly be appropriate in a high-powered Japanese corporate setting. Furthermore, Egi is clearly directed to play the character as unappetizingly obsequious; though his actions are far too exaggerated for an actual Japanese, he apparently fits the director's notion of a Japanese corporate soldier.

When the film opened, a public outcry arose. Media Action Network for Asian Americans (MANAA), among other organizations, and Asian American journals and newspapers decried the politics of representation in the film. MANAA had attempted to discuss the issues with Twentieth Century Fox, but "after eight months of failed negotiations, including three months of meetings canceled by Fox" (Chung 1993, 4), they decided to go public with their concerns. MANAA President Guy Aoki stressed that the organization "took the high ground," never calling for a boycott of the film. Instead, they concentrated their efforts on an educational campaign (personal interview). Picketers greeted the opening of the film in San Francisco and New York, representing coalitions of numerous Asian American political organizations (Chouy 1993, 6). According to some Asian American analysts, Twentieth Century Fox deployed divide-and-conquer tactics in their dealings with Asian Americans. On the one hand, the studio attempted to win over some Asian American journalists with all-expense-paid trips to a preview of the film and used the participation of some Asian American actors as "proof" that the film was not racist. Simultaneously, people with Asian American names were excluded from attending Los Angeles-based previews of film; when they called back with other surnames, they were admitted to the screenings (Muto 1993, 9). The protests led to a delay in the film's release in Japan, where it lost revenue. Though Twentieth Century Fox never made an effort to work with Asian American groups on the issue of representation, the activism and educational efforts of Asian Americans meant that the pernicious racialisms did not go uncontested, and that Asian American organizations joined together in coalition, in an important enactment of solidarity.[13]

Finally, it seems appropriate to clarify my stakes in this critique of *Rising Sun*. At the end of his book, Crichton appends a bibliography, citing works that he found helpful and consulted while he wrote the novel. My book *Crafting Selves* is on this list. Paradoxically, my aims were antithetical to his: to deploy a strategic humanism that would involve in part the fundamental problematizing of the term "the Japanese." After deliberating on the matter, however, one could attribute such a reading to the strategic essentialisms common in interpretivist and other strains of cultural anthropology that invoke "culture" at the level of language, custom, practice. These strategic essentialisms can be deployed for various ends. In my case, the aim was critique of dominant American concepts—in particular, the monadic, bounded "self" or "whole subject"—in order to further antiracist and feminist struggle in the United States. For Crichton, descriptions of language and cultural practice can be appropriated for different ends: to further buttress American superiority. On the one hand, this misappropriation could be seen as a risk inherent in any form of explanation that invokes "culture." Armed with a degree in anthropology, Crichton can convincingly exaggerate the boundedness of "culture" for his novelistic ends.

Yet perhaps the issue of appropriation is more general. As I learned during my stint as a dramaturge for Anna Deavere Smith's *Twilight: Los Angeles 1992*, based on the bristling histories and tensions that fueled the L.A. uprisings/riots/civil unrest, the work of critics or artists is inevitably interpreted in unanticipated ways. Despite our best dramaturgical efforts to anticipate audience readings of the politics of racial representation, someone always came up with a completely surprising reaction. *Twilight* foregrounded for me the salience of the intentional fallacy, for authorial/ dramaturgical intention could never guarantee meaning. In the case of Crichton's reading of my book, the intentional fallacy seems all the more fallacious, for authorial intention not only failed to guarantee meaning, but the text generated meanings antithetical to authorial intent. Once released in language, the subject-positions, histories, and (structurally overdetermined) interpretive schemas of readers and audiences shape reception. We can but do our best to anticipate certain overdetermined misreadings and preempt them, taking seriously authorial responsibility and attempting to do battle with the misappropriations of our work. In the case of a highly popular film and novel such as *Rising Sun*, the stakes are even more urgent. We must continue to challenge the highly resilient structures of racism and male dominance that fuel the recirculation of subjugating discourses such as Orientalism.

The Mikado and Institutional Intervention

The material effects of critiques of representation might seem to be distant from our everyday lives, especially for those of us in the academy. Most obviously, the politics of representation reverberate in the entertainment and culture industries, and on intangible levels we would call psychological. I contend, however, that taking the politics of representation seriously can have *institutional* impact—even in the academy. I [have] argued [elsewhere] for the profound and potentially transformative effects of feminist and minority discourse. I end this discussion of art and politics with an account of a local intervention around a performance of Gilbert and Sullivan's *The Mikado* at the Claremont Colleges. My narrative figures the *Mikado* protest as a pivotal event within a history of activism and protest that led to greater institutional recognition of Asian Americans at the Colleges. It serves to instantiate successful attempts at political coalition. My perspective is that of a central organizer of the protest; hence, it is both partial and inevitably celebratory. It is a story that will no doubt always remain beyond the bounds of official institutional history.

In September 1990 I had just arrived at Pomona as a newly tenured faculty member and was busily trying to acquaint myself with the new campus. While going through my mail one day, I noticed a listing of coming events at our large auditorium, which we call "Big Bridges." The season was to commence with a performance of Gilbert and Sullivan's *The Mikado*. I groaned inwardly as I looked at the listing. Not again. The last production of *The Mikado* I remembered was in Boston, where the Emperor's Court had metamorphosed into a Japanese company populated by Japanese businessmen, conjoining the Oriental despot trope with that of the corporate soldier. Not again—facing the situation that women, people of color, gays, and lesbians face all too often when oppressive stereotypes recirculate in forms that the dominant considers harmless fun. And as in all such occasions, one must decide what to do. Make a fuss? So much effort, and I just got here. Let it go? Then I would hate myself for being the "silent Asian" who allows an egregious event to slip by without a whisper of protest.

Supportive colleagues and allies eased my dilemma. Historian Samuel Yamashita intended that his students write a critique of the event. But after speaking with Yamashita and other colleagues of color, including Deena González, Sid Lemelle, Ray Buriel, Ruth Gilmore, Lynne Miyake, and Sue Houchins, the possibility of larger collective action emerged. The faculty and staff of color organized ourselves into a consortium-wide "Coalition of the International Majority/National Minority," which rallied around *The Mikado* issue and provided a forum to deal with issues of significance for the faculty, staff, and students of color. The coalition deemed the politics of representation in *The Mikado* to be highly offensive, and its selection as an appropriate form of entertainment at our major auditorium signified the systematic marginalization of Asian American issues at the Claremont Colleges. Despite yearly proposals from Asian American students for an Asian American Studies program and an Asian American Resource Center, and despite the precedent of Chicano Studies and Black Studies programs dating from the 1960s, comprising both academic and student services branches, Pomona College and the other Claremont Colleges continued to ignore the needs of Asian American students. During the graduation ceremony just before my arrival, faculty, students, and the one Asian American trustee sympathetic to Asian American issues had worn yellow armbands in protest and provoked the wrath of the administration, but this had elicited no concrete response. Many of us thought this marginalization of Asian American issues to be linked with the "model minority" stereotype: that Asian Americans are quiet and docile, and hence will not cause trouble; that we don't need "special programs" because we've "made it"; that racism has no bearing on our lives. Given the years of administrative nonresponse, it seemed high time to forego politeness and make some noise.

For *The Mikado*'s opening night, the Coalition of the International Majority decided to hold a demonstration outside the auditorium. Once the performance began, we would conduct a teach-in and counterperformance at the student ball-room. We mobilized student groups of color, Women's Studies, the gay and lesbian organizations, and sympathetic groups of faculty and staff. Outside the campus, we contacted members of the Asian American artist/activist organization APACE (Asian Pacific Alliance for Creative Equality) that had formed around the *Miss Saigon* controversy. We alerted the media, distributed flyers, and prepared presentations.

I wrote an analysis of the politics of representation of the play, which we then circulated to the faculty and staff of color and to other potentially sympathetic colleagues, giving versions at the teach-in preceding opening night and at the teach-in/counterperformance. The piece singled out the problematic Orientalist tropes that permeate the text: nonsensical and offensive renderings of Chinese (not Japanese) names, Oriental exoticism and despotism, Oriental proclivities for suicide, and Oriental women as either submissive lotus blossoms or witch-like dragon ladies. Anticipating objections, I took issue with predictable responses to our critique: that *The Mikado* is a cultural classic; that it is simply a satire; that Gilbert and Sullivan were "really" writing about England. I argued that in the light of work by feminist scholars of music and opera such as Catherine Clément, we must ask: for whom is *The Mikado* a cultural classic? Further, in this instance "satire" merely excuses the continued circulation of racist and sexist tropes. In this regard, the choice of Japan as the setting for this satire was overdetermined given the contemporary discourses of Orientalism and Britain's imperialist project. Finally, the choice to stage *The Mikado* at the Colleges effectively preempted the performances of Asian American plays written and performed by Asian Americans, echoing an institutional history that had failed to confront Asian American issues.

Several other faculty provided their cogent perspectives at a teach-in preceding the protest. Samuel Yamashita described Britain's imperialist project at the moment Gilbert and Sullivan penned *The Mikado*. Jennifer Rycenga, a feminist scholar of religion and music, analyzed the Orientalist motifs of the music itself. Theater professor Leonard Pronko presented another point of view, raising the anticipated objections.

The evening of the performance became an emblematic, inspirational moment when coalition politics appeared to fulfill its promise. Hundreds of faculty and students assembled at the Office of Black Student Affairs. From there we walked, phalanxes of people of many colors, to the auditorium, shouting and chanting all the while. One phrase was especially memorable: "El Mikado *es un pecado*," "*The Mikado* is a sin." The demonstration continued in front of the auditorium while we picketed, passed out leaflets, and chanted our protests. When the performance began, we adjourned to the student ballroom.

The teach-in continued for three hours. The faculty repeated and embellished their remarks from the previous teach-in. Samuel Yamashita retold a poignant story starkly revealing the links between Orientalist representations of Asia and Asian American lives. When he taught at a small liberal arts college in upstate New York, each December 7 (Pearl Harbor Day) his car would be trashed—probably by members of the fraternity that held an annual "kamikaze" party every year on that date. Eventually, Yamashita took to hiding his car in the yard of a Jewish colleague.

A group of actors from APACE had driven from Los Angeles to the Colleges to lend their support. Their presence linked our local intervention larger issues of Asian American representation, and a buzz of excitement accompanied their arrival. Representations of Asians and Asian Americans are clearly of critical salience to actors, who must decide whether or not they can in good conscience play certain kinds of roles. In particular, artists Kim Miyori, Natsuko Ohama, Steve Park, Tzi Ma, and Rosalind Chao spoke of the *Miss Saigon* casting controversy and the importance of continued activism on the part of Asian Americans around issues of representation. Their presence highlighted for us *The Mikado*'s exclusionary gesture that constituted effective silencing of three-dimensional Asian American portrayals in works authored by Asian Americans.

Alliance across different groups, then, became a critically important consequence of the protest. APACE extended our struggle beyond the Colleges, but equally important were local solidarities among people of color and campus progressives. The support of the Office of Black Student Affairs and the Black Studies faculty, the Chicano Studies faculty, and students and staff of color was indispensable to our efforts. Indeed, at the close of the teach-in, the president of the Pan African Student Association rousingly invoked our common struggles around race, culminating in a scathing satire of the Claremont University Center administration. I ended the teach-in with a call-response with the audience, the power of coalition vibrant and alive as we joined together to denounce racist representation and to work for institutional change.

I can venture only an educated guess as to the real impact of *The Mikado* protest. The Deans subsequently began discussions with the Asian American faculty about establishing an Asian American Resource Center. We advertised and interviewed candidates for Director during the spring, and by the following year a fledgling center was inaugurated. Though others might tell a different story, I see the *The Mikado* protest as a critical event that, in combination with years of proposals, petitionings, and graduation protests, helped pave the way for a still fledgling Asian American Resource Center, discussions with Asian American and Asianist faculty around Asian American Studies, and funding for an Asian American Performance Art series. More hires at Pomona and at other colleges are continuing in the Asian American fields, and we hope to establish a Five-College Asian American Studies Department.

From the point of view of official history, though, *The Mikado* protest never happened. At the official opening of the Asian American Resource Center, the establishment of the Center was instead attributed to "student efforts" and to the foresight of the College. These might indeed be key factors. But I would argue that the groundswell of support—especially from other faculty, staff, and students of color, and from other progressive groups on campus such as Women's Studies, gay and lesbian groups, and the differently abled—created a daunting coalition that could no longer be ignored.

My tale of *The Mikado*, then, is a guardedly optimistic narrative of a local intervention that speaks to the power of political alliance. Though the institutional gains seem modest—in our especially busy moments some of the Asian American faculty laugh wryly that now it means yet another committee assignment—even these modest gains might never have occurred had faculty and students not researched, lobbied, protested, and raised our voices. *The Mikado* protest foregrounds the power of political coalition and the profound stakes that Asian Americans inevitably have in representations of Asia. Local institutional interventions are one site of political change, where hegemonic representations can be contested.

For all disenfranchised people, these struggles continue daily, urgently, in multiple registers.[14] Local interventions can shift discourses, interrupting a smooth reproduction of dominant imaginaries. When we think about a cultural politics that makes a difference, we must examine their workings on multiple levels. I have suggested that Asian American artists, activists and academics have pursued different strategies of subversion, challenging the seductive pleasures of dominant narratives and using those challenges to shape institutions, hiring practices, and the production of images in the culture industries. When analyzing particular interventions, critics should take into account a multiplicity of factors. For theater and performance, these include: (1) different genres, such as mainstream theater, performance art, and conventional political action; (2) formal interventions in text, thematics, and structure; (3) the ways production and performance can generate and alter textual meaning; (4) venue; (5) audience and reception (critical, academic, mainstream, community); (6) accessibility in form, content, and price, for both the audience and the performer; (7) processes of production (rehearsal and collaboration); (8) grants and funding;[15] (9) institutional structures, as in the case of *The Mikado* and the Asian American Resource Center; (10) the formation of community and political identity.

A cultural politics that makes a difference must be animated by a willingness to locate these and other levels at which any cultural work may simultaneously reinscribe and contest. I would further argue that we must speak of opposition with precision: oppositional for whom, in what ways, under what circumstances. Equally important, these tactics of intervention must engage a notion of critical positionality, for the binaristic notion of cultural politics—resistance OR accommodation—is invariably associated with the assumption that the critic inhabits an inviolable moral space.[16] This Manichean view is better supplanted by a notion of a cultural politics that makes a difference, realizing all the while that interventions are always partial and positioned, and pristine separation or liberation from the dominant is illusory at best.

However, this should not mean that significant intervention is impossible. Far from it. For example, in theater and performance—despite the carefully controlled and limited visibility for artists from disenfranchised groups—it is nonetheless remarkable that even mainstream regional theater has become a site where, increasingly, "others" are "talking back," and that so many of the fine plays of the past few years have been written by people "on the margins," asserting the need for hope and vibrantly affirming life in the midst of daily oppression. I think of Tony Kushner's luminous *Angels in America*, José Rivera's *Marisol* and his witty, lyrical love letter to L.A., *The Street of the Sun*, or, on a more interested note, Anna Deavere Smith's *Twilight: Los Angeles 1992*, where our process of multiracial collaboration recapitulated the tensions, contradictions, and utopian possibilities of life in a multiracial society. Given such interventions, I passionately resist a view that consigns all efforts at contestation to the junkheap of recuperation. Though inevitably compromised, spectacularized, and tokenized, some interventions matter.

Such interventions at all levels continue to vibrate with urgency in an historical moment marked by the resurgence of radical conservatism in its many guises. To see culture as a transcendent domain apart from the messy politics of everyday life has become a politically dangerous assumption: it leads to elitism and Eurocentric universalism, while simultaneously justifying Republican budget cuts of a domain deemed to be extraneous to the practicalities of everyday life. On the contrary, the realms of cultural production are constituted through forces such as gender, race, class, economics, politics, even as the sites of performance problematize and enact those larger abstractions. In the face of the attacks on the arts and what may be the imminent demise of affirmative action, cultural production by people on the margins becomes even more potentially contestatory and valuable. Theater, performance, and design have created spaces where Asians and Asian Americans can "write our faces," mount institutional interventions, enact emergent identities, refigure utopian possibilities, and construct political subjectivities that might enable us to effect political change.

Performing alternative visions of cultural possibility on stage, on the runway, or on the streets may not in itself force an about-face of the advancing conservative tide or thoroughly transform the political/discursive structures that shape our lives. But the work of the artists and designers I have discussed in these pages sketches out and performs for us utopian wish-images for gender, race, sexuality, and other dynamic forces. Perhaps they introduce us to new forms of possibility and new forms of intellectual and political intervention. For without the refiguration of the possible, there can be no social transformation; there can be no "about-face."

NOTES

1. Unlike DeCerteau, I make no distinction between "strategy" and "tactics."

2. Initially submitted this version to the Editorials division at *The Los Angeles Times*, which sent it to their Counterpunch section, devoted to opinions and reactions to stories about the arts. The editor there kept my piece and apparently had decided against publishing it after two letters of protest on the opening of *Miss Saigon* appeared in the Sunday *Calendar* section. Eventually, after many delays, the essay was published at less than half its length in a section called Voices, opinions and writings from "the community," under the title "Gripe." Nothing that remotely resembled a call to action made it to print. The label "Gripe" undercut the message by individualizing and trivializing a serious *position* on an issue that was shared by many members of a community. The label casts the critical voices of people of color in terms

of sheer negativity, rather than seeing the call to action and the positive political solidarity in such a critique.

3. Locally, Asian American student groups at the Claremont Colleges organized a teach-in around *Miss Saigon*, responding in part to the Colleges' use of the play as a "student activity" sponsored by various student governments. Actors Tzi Ma (who was present at the *Mikado* protest), Ping Wu, and Ken Choy participated. Larger protests in Los Angeles were muted; some leafleting occurred on opening night, but the unfortunate timing of opening night immediately after Christmas vacation and technical difficulties meant that highly visible collective action did not occur.

4. Choy has created another piece entitled *Miss Appropriated*, a collection of performances by various artists, many of whom were involved in protests around *Miss Saigon* and the performance of Puccini's *Madama Butterfly*. The program suggests a similar strategy of wild satire and subversion of stereotypes, including "Death Is Our Way," lampooning the supposed Asian proclivities for suicide and brutality.

5. About a similar protest in New York, Yoko Yoshikawa describes eloquently the heady atmosphere animating the work of Asian Pacific gays and lesbians who sought to disrupt the Lambda Legal Defense Fund's use of *Miss Saigon* as a fundraiser. She revels in the gay and pan-Asian character of their coalition—loving descriptions of the different kinds of food, the open physicality—that were part of their meetings, and soberly discusses their multiple marginalization in a gay community dominated by whites and a largely heterosexual Asian American community, as well as a mainstream press which never really understood what queer Asians were doing at this protest.

6. The two were arraigned and fined $25, after charges were lowered to a petty misdemeanor.

7. There was yet another twist to the controversy. The Opera cast Geraldine McMillan, an African American, to sing the role of Cio-Cio-san, in recognition of opera's "tradition of colorblind casting," in the words of the Opera manager. Choy noted, "It seems like a technique of pitting minority against minority." He went on to observe the desirability of colorblind casting "in a perfect world, but the reality is that only Caucasians, and sometimes non-Asians, are allowed to play Asians, and not the other way around."

8. The evening I attended, the handful of Asian Americans in the audience was in gales of laughter while the white audience was utterly silent.

9. For Crichton, the invasion is occurring on multiple fronts. America appears to be losing in the halls of academe as well as in the corporate towers and on the production line. Knowledge of the Other is a tactical necessity during a state of war, and the Japanese have responded with a vengeance. When Smith meets Ishigura, the Nakamoto representative, Ishigura's perfect English is striking. Connor responds, "He must have gone to school here. One of the thousands of Japanese who studied in America in the seventies. When they were sending 150,000 students a year to America, to learn about our country. And we were sending 200 American students a year to Japan" (23). The suggestion here is that acknowledgment of Japanese tactical advantage must be followed by an adoption of their practices in order to restore America's (presumably rightful) economic and political preeminence.

10. Indeed, "we" will learn that our sense of superiority is justified, for "our" racism is deemed to be innocuous compared to that of the Japanese. Later, when discussing the case of a "turncoat" who went from a leading position in the U.S. trade negotiator's office to work with the Japanese, Connor replies to the man's allegations that the Congressional scrutiny of the proposed purchase of Fairchild Corporation by Fujitsu was fueled by racism.

"This racist stuff. He knows better. Richmond knows exactly what happened with the

Fairchild sale. And it had nothing to do with racism."

"No?"

"And there's another thing Richmond knows: the Japanese are the most racist people on earth." (Crichton 1992, 219)

Here, the authoritative voice of the "expert" on Japan rings eloquently. Connor's definitive pronouncements provide a condemnation of Japan that can be used to justify all manner of retaliatory practice for, after all, the Japanese are even more racist than we.

11. This racial discourse provides a rationale for American response in kind—or worse. The martial imagery is deployed with full force when Connor and Smith confront the Senator who chairs the Finance Committee deciding on the MicroCon case. The Senator, speaking about his fears of Japanese takeover, ends his speech ominously.

He dropped his voice, becoming one of the boys. "You know, I have colleagues who say sooner or later we're going to have to drop another bomb. They think it'll come to that." He smiled. "But I don't feel that way. Usually." (Crichton 1992, 230)

This, I would suggest, is one extreme Final Solution that Crichton invokes as a possible strategy in the economic wars.

12. See John Dower's important book, *War without Mercy: Race and Power in the Pacific War*.

13. Though the battles over racial representation in Hollywood film seem endless, activism laid the groundwork for meetings in 1994 between MANAA and executives at Warner Brothers, which released *Falling Down*, another film with a problematic politics of racial representation much decried by Asian American artists and activists. High-ranking studio executives, including Rob Friedman, president of Worldwide Advertising and Publicity, and director Joel Schumacher met with representatives from MANAA, the Korean-American Grocers' Association, and other Asian American organizations. Though the studio refused to disclaim the racial representations circulated in *Falling Down*, they did agree to produce a public-service announcement about racial tolerance directed by Schumacher, that was shown with film trailers (Guy Aoki, interview).

14. They can be subtle, but they are still battles. Recently I attended a moving performance by Dan Kwong that used the relentlessly cheerful letters of Kwong's mother and uncles while they were in relocation camps as the basis for a piece centered on his grandfather's life and the ravages of internment. During the question and answer session, whites dominated the space of the Japanese American Community and Cultural Center. One woman, obviously wanting to be the "good white woman," tried to differentiate the "evil" stereotypes from what her father had taught her, as though a wide gulf existed between the two, and as though any of us—especially whites—can completely escape the influence of such stereotypes. Another asked questions that betrayed both ignorance of cultural conventions and asserted the I-know-you-better-than-you-know-yourselves strain of Orientalism. Capping off the evening, a white man stood up, called the artist "Dan," as though they were intimates, and pontificated on the necessity for us to tell the stories of "great men"—such as his own grandfather. After the performance, it was clear that the dominant must try to appropriate and domesticate even this, the mournful reference point that touches the lives of mainland Issei, Nisei, Sansei, and Yonsei (first-, second-, third-, and fourth-generation Japanese Americans). Even this experience cannot "belong" to us as such; it cannot be treated with respect. Rather, the dominant appropriates the oppression in which it is centrally implicated in its attempts to allay its own guilt and to prove its own good intentions.

15. E.g., *Miss Saigon*, in Minneapolis, cost $41 million and was funded by the established Ordway Theater and by the city.

16. This failure to problematize one's own position rests in part on monolithic, essentialist notions of identity and subjecthood; for example, the first-world, middle-class, heterosexual male critic of color who takes his position to be coextensive with "the race," or white female critics who colonize the category "woman," who is assumed to be always already white.

REFERENCES

Chung, Phillip. "Clouds Hover over Rising Sun." *Asian Week* 14:4 (June 4, 1993).

Chouy, Lee San. "The Land of the Rising Voices." *The Straits Times*, August 11, 1993.

"The Fallout over *Miss Saigon*." *Los Angeles Times*, August 13, 1990: F3.

Hwang, David Henry. "Foreword." In *The State of Asian America*, edited by Karin Aguilar-San Juan. Boston: South End Press, 1994.

Kelly, Kevin. *Boston Globe*, February 17, 1993, Living Section: 25.

Kondo, D. "Dissolution and Reconstruction of Self: Implications for Anthrological Epistemology." *Cultural Anthropology* 1:1 (1986): 74–88.

Muto, Sheila. "APA Activists Say 20 Century Fox Trying to Divide APA Community." *Asian Week* 15:1 (August 27, 1993).

Russell, John. "Race and Reflexivity: The Black Other in Contemporary Japanese Mass Culture." *Cultural Anthropology* 6:1 (1991): 3–25.

Sigmund, Suzanne. "Chinese-Hawaiian Performance Artist Enlivens Local Arts Scene." *Asian Pages* 3:3 (October 1–14, 1992): 13.

1. Survey the range of opinions held by the panelists on the existence of an "Asian American aesthetics." How does each panelist define these aesthetics, and what evidence does each utilize to support his or her arguments?

2. What does Alexander mean when she refers to the "multiplicity" of Asian American visual culture and its production? What objections does Machida raise about focusing too intently on an "Asian American aesthetic?" How does Pfeiffer attempt to discount the criticisms of those arguing against an "Asian American aesthetics"? Pekarik poses the important question "who defines Asian American art?" Explain the way in which Pekarik's "art system" helps resolve this question. How does Tajima characterize the role played by film in developing an "Asian American aesthetic?" How has "eclecticism" come to characterize the genre of film we have defined as "Asian American"?

3. According to Kondo, what strategies have Asian American artists deployed to subvert representations of Asian Americans that serve to objectify, stereotype, and ultimately oppress? Kondo contends that the issue around the *Miss Saigon* controversy and the mainstream media's representation served "to obscure other protests and other issues," with profound implications for Asian American autonomy. To what is Kondo referring? How do these issues reflect Asian American interests in the politics of their representation?

4. What forms of protests emerged around the *Miss Saigon* controversy and what effects did these protests have upon the staging of the show at different sites? Compare Hwang's subversion techniques with those presented by the performance artist Kim Choy. How are the two styles different, and what effects did Hwang's and Choy's performances have on the Asian American community?

5. How did Crichton construct "Other" in his book *Rising Sun*? Provide examples from the text to illustrate the kinds of stereotypes that were being promoted. Kondo writes that the central issue in *Rising Sun* is the challenge posed to "white masculine subjectivity" as it tried to preserve its boundaries. To what is Kondo referring? How is it manifest in Crichton's work and in the film adaptation?

SUGGESTED READINGS

Ding, Loni. 1991. Strategies of an Asian American Filmmaker. Pp. 46–59 in Russell Leung (ed.), *Moving the Image: Independent Asian Pacific American Media Arts*. Los Angeles: UCLA Asian American Studies Center and Visual Communications, Southern California Asian American Studies Central.

Fung, Richard. 1994. Seeing Yellow: Asian Identity in Film and Video. In Karin Aguilar-San Juan (ed.), *The State of Asian America: Activism and Resistance in the 1990s*. Boston: South End Press.

Gong, Stephen. 1991. A History in Progress: Asian American Media Arts Centers, 1970–1990. Pp. 1–9 in Russell Leong (ed.), *Moving the Image: Independent Asian Pacific American Media Arts*. Los Angeles: UCLA Asian American Studies Center.

Hamamoto, Darrell Y. 1994. *Monitored Peril: Asian Americans and the Politics of TV Representation*. Minneapolis: University of Minnesota Press.

Higa, Karin M. 1992. *The View from Within: Japanese American Art from the Internment Camps, 1942–1945: Wight Art Gallery October 13 through December 6, 1992*. Los Angeles: Japanese American National Museum.

Houston, Velina Hasu (ed.). *But Still, Like Air, I'll Rise*. Philadelphia. Temple University Press.

Krieger, Lois L. 1992. Miss Saigon and Missed Opportunity: Artistic Freedom, Employment Discrimination, and Casting for Cultural Identity in the Theater. *Syracuse Law Review* 43: 839–866.

Kurahashi, Yuko. 1998. *Asian American Culture on Stage: The History of East-West Players*. New York: Garland.

Marchetti, Gina. 1994. *Romance and the "Yellow Peril."* Berkeley: University of California Press.

Moy, James S. 1993. *Staging the Chinese in America*. Iowa City: University of Iowa Press.

Mura, Dave. 1994. A Shift in Power, a Sea Change in the Arts: Asian American Constructions. In Karin Aguilar-San Juan (ed.), *The State of Asian America: Activism and Resistance in the 1990s*. Boston: South End Press.

Lee, Josephine. 1998. *Performing Asian America: Race and Ethnicity on the Contemporary Stage*. Philadelphia: Temple University Press.

Lee, Robert. 1999. *Orientals: Asian Americans in Popular Culture*. Philadelphia: Temple University Press.

Tsutakawa, Mayumi. 1994. *They Painted from Their Hearts: Pioneer Asian American Artists Directory and Asian American Artists Directory*. Seattle: Wing Luke Museum and University of Washington Press.

Wechsler, Jeffrey. 1997. *Asian Traditions, Modern Expressions: Asian American Artists and Abstraction, 1945–1970*. New Brunswick, NJ: Rutgers University Press.

Yoshikawa, Yoko. 1994. The Heat Is on *Miss Saigon* Coalition. In Karin Aguilar-San Juan (ed.), *The State of Asian America: Activism and Resistance in the 1990s*. Boston: South End Press.

FILMS

Berges, Paul Mayeda (producer/director). 1991. *En Ryo Identity* (23-minute documentary).

Gee, Deborah (producer/director). 1988. *Slaying the Dragon* (60-minute documentary).

Minh-ha, Triah T. (director). 1995. *A Tale of Love*.

Soe, Valerie. (director). 1992. *Picturing Oriental Girls* (15-minute experimental).

———. (director). 1993. *Art to Art: Expressions of Asian American Women*.

Part XIII

Mapping the Terrain
New Paradigms in Asian American Studies

Rethinking Race
Paradigms and Policy Formation

Shirley Hune

Thomas Kuhn has defined paradigms as worldviews, values, and techniques held in common by members of a given community. Paradigms in the scientific community often become simplified as models or examples that govern its practitioners more than the subject matter itself. As "exemplary past achievements," paradigms are difficult to change.[1] More important, paradigms endure outside of the scientific community and reflect the dominant belief system of the general society.

Race relations models or theories are outgrowths of paradigms. They become habits of mind and patterns of behavior taught to subsequent generations of scholars. Racial paradigms are also embedded in ideologies, policies, and practices and are integrated into the formal structures and institutions of U.S. society as well as our everyday lives.[2] People who benefit from existing racial paradigms have a vested interest in maintaining them and tend to resist innovation. But sometimes paradigms shift as new models emerge to challenge traditional ways of defining problems and, in some cases, begin to replace existing models. As Kuhn has observed, paradigm shifts are begun typically by newcomers to the field who are less encumbered by existing approaches.[3] I would add that paradigm shifts are also initiated by outsiders to a particular community whose experiences offer alternative views to established ways of explaining the same phenomena. It is not surprising then that Ethnic Studies as a new field would begin to transform existing modes of thought and contribute to recent shifts in theoretical orientation.

I employ the term rethinking here to refer to new directions in race relations that are both being conceived and in need of development given the current social realities. I frame this rethinking within the concept of *shifting paradigms*, which I have utilized elsewhere,[4] and highlight below in five racial paradigms. While in my view these racial paradigms have not shifted in the sense that they have replaced traditional frameworks, they are beginning to change how problems and policies are perceived and developed. The results are what I call here *emergent paradigms*. I will focus my comments on the implications of dominant and emergent racial paradigms on policy formation and their significance for Asian American Studies.

From Black/White Paradigm or Vertical Dynamics and Integration to the Multiplicity of Racial Dynamics

For decades, research agendas have analyzed racial interactions in the U.S. almost exclusively as Black/White relations. As the predominant racial model, the individual and community development of African Americans is viewed within a vertical dynamic with Whites at the apex. All power and race relations have come to be seen within this framework of subordinate/majority dynamics.

Black/White relations is *the* model for Asian American/White, Latino/White, and Native American/White relations. Studies of separate and distinct vertical dynamics and integration of each group with the dominant white group prevail. Hence Asian American Studies is replete with examinations of each Asian American ethnic group's relations with Whites. Furthermore, Asian American struggles for justice and their strategies of resistance, conflict resolution, cooperation, and empowerment are measured primarily against African Americans. Gary Okihiro has asked, "Is Yellow Black or White?" He suggests that the Black/White paradigm marginalizes Asian Americans along a continuum where they are seen by the dominant culture "as Blacks" or as "near-Whites" depending upon the historical situation.[5] In rethinking racial paradigms, we need to go beyond binary and vertical relations and to consider standpoints other than that of Whites and of being subordinate. The well-being and daily interactions of Asian Americans are not determined solely within Asian American/White vertical dynamics. Our past, present, and certainly future power relations have been and will continue to be interlinked both horizontally and vertically with other subordinate racial groups as well as vertically with the dominant majority. The relations between Asian American small business owners and their non-Asian American employees and clientele, new multiracial and multiethnic residential patterns, biracial families, the growing class disparities within racial/ethnic groups, the shift in party affiliation and voting preferences of racial groups from Democrats to Republicans, and other indicators give rise to rethinking race relations.

The emergent paradigm gives greater attention to the multiplicity of racial dynamics. It considers race relations in their complexities with the intersection of multiple racial groups and class differentiations along with gender, immigrant generation, and age as a more accurate portrayal of the nation's race realities.[6] Changing majority/minority and minority/minority perspectives are evident in two recent hotly contested issues in California.

First, Proposition 187, which denies most social services, medical benefits, and public education to illegal immigrants, was approved by 53 percent of the voters in November 1994, with racial groups holding different views. Exit polls differed somewhat. About 70 percent of Latinos opposed 187, while white voters favored it by over 60 percent and blacks and Asians were split. Similarly, the debates over a proposed California Civil Rights Initiative that would eliminate the use of race, sex, color, ethnicity, or national origin as a criterion for either discriminating against or granting preferential treatment to any individual or group in public employment, public education, or public contracting, indicate changes in majority and minority views toward affirmative action. With the proposed Initiative likely to appear on the

California state ballot in November 1996, a March 1995 *Los Angeles Times* poll found that 48 percent of African Americans oppose the Initiative and 71 percent of Whites, 54 percent of Asians, and 52 percent of Latinos support it.[7] Both proposals have become politicized and expose splits within racial groups, possible divisions between minority groups, and suggest the potential for new alliances.

A binary paradigm is inadequate in a multiracial context. What is needed is a framework that incorporates multiple racial groups and explores the complexity of current and future intergroup dynamics. Furthermore, the dominant Black/White paradigm reinforces the exclusion of Asian Americans and others from public and private agendas because they are viewed as being neither Black nor White. In contrast, a multiplicity paradigm will contribute to the inclusion of Asian Americans in American public policy.

From Race and Racism as Static Concepts and One Aspect of American Life and Politics to Racial Formation and Racism as Dynamic, Expansive and at the Center of American Life and Politics

Intertwined with the Black/White paradigm is another long-standing racial model that presumes race in America to be a relatively unchanging set of categories, experiences, and outcomes governed largely by biology.[8] In turn, the paradigm of racism has focused on laws that discriminate and privilege civil and political rights in achieving equality. The assumption is that social and economic justice will follow once legal discrimination is abolished.

Current rethinking, notably the writings of Omi and Winant, views race as a historical process and a social construction whose meaning is contested collectively and individually and whose practice is embedded in all aspects of American life.[9] The emergent paradigm extends the struggle against racism beyond civil and political rights to broad issues of economic, social, and cultural rights. It also views race relations as a dynamic that is continuously being redefined. For example, the study of race relations is expanding to incorporate the environmental justice movement. Policies and programs in support of Asian Pacific Americans, therefore, need to be active, view race as central, and connect race with the overall quality of life of the community.[10]

From Asian Pacific American Communities as Victim Paradigm to Differential Power and Agency

Much of race relations literature and analysis has placed communities of color in the victim mode. Communities and researchers of color sometimes assume this position. While this may have held some truth in the past, current and future race realities suggest that this depiction is limited. For example, the concept of internal colonialism as a descriptor of residential and commercial social and spatial relations ignores class differences within Asian American communities and between Asian American employers and their co-ethnic and non-co-ethnic employees and clientele. Similarly, while noting the bifurcated educational achievement of Asian Americans, the differential attainments of various Asian American ethnic groups and the high educational accomplishments of many low-income Asian Americans cannot be ignored.

The emergent paradigm considers that Asian American communities, like other communities of color, have differential power. The old model of passive objects is being replaced with analyses of subject and agency. Those involved in policy studies are redefining community development and challenging the top-down approach. Where communities once waited for those with political and economic resources to define solutions and develop appropriate public and private policies, the shift in thinking is to view communities as agents of change who can plan and develop for themselves, from their own perspectives, and not always to the wide acceptance of other residents.[11] Community empowerment, particularly of low-income members, gives greater attention to a bottom-up, community-based approach appropriate to the needs of a specific community, its size, strengths, and resources.[12] Hence, Asian American community development, how growth, preservation, and conservation are defined, and the use and allocation of resources by whom and for whom become central issues of empowerment. This paradigm also acknowledges that Asian Americans have a social responsibility to address the needs and concerns of disadvantaged peoples within and outside their own communities.

From Ethnic-Specific and Homogenous Studies to Heterogenous, Comparative, and Panethnic Studies

A traditional paradigm in immigration studies and race relations is to treat each ethnic group linearly and as a separate and relatively homogenous entity. Hence, we find studies on individual Asian American communities—the Chinese, Japanese, Filipinos, and now Koreans, Vietnamese, Asian Indians, Cambodians, Thais, and so forth—from their first years in the U.S. to the present. The lives of first-generation immigrant males are privileged, and the experiences of the first wave of Asian immigrant groups dominate the scholarship. This approach was a necessary beginning for Asian American Studies as it sought to reclaim its historic place in American history and culture. However, this paradigm results in descriptions of ethnic-specific experiences that are circumscribed, while assumed to be representative of the entire community. Consequently, policy recommendations that address the needs of a particular Asian American ethnic group or Asian Americans in general presume a one-size-fits-all solution that does not meet the range and complexity of contemporary communities.

The emergent paradigm recognizes the heterogeneity of Asian America and of each Asian American group. For example, recent studies that focus on gender and generation as variables in the work world and family politics of Japanese and Vietnamese Americans disclose the rich and intricate interplay of sharing and tensions that abounds within these communities.[13] Other studies remind us that Asian Americans are not defined by urban and working-class experiences alone but are also rural or suburban and middle class.[14]

The new thinking needs to discern the role of social class, gender, ethnicity, sexual orientation, the perspectives and experiences of different generations, political and economic dynamics, specific historical situations, political affiliations, regionality, nationality, and other dimensions that challenge the limitations of the existing homogenous ethnic-specific paradigm. The emergent heterogeneity paradigm may finally give attention to neglected areas of research within our communities, to comparative studies between ethnic groups and panethnic studies of Asian Pacific American communities. It also suggests that public policies need to be refined if they are to adequately meet the needs of our communities and their many segments.

The emphasis on creating a homogeneous Asian American experience in Asian American Studies has caused us to overlook variations and distinctions. The shift to incorporating diversity carries with it a rebalancing of ethnic group realities, such as recognizing the implications of different political and economic eras. Asian Americans who have dissimilar political and economic experiences often possess different worldviews. At the same time, it highlights the need to appraise the strengths and weaknesses of Asian American panethnicity as a political strategy and an ethnic identity.[15]

From Asian Pacific American Communities as an American Experience to Global and Diasporic Studies

Asian Pacific immigration as a racial paradigm in the U.S. is predominantly viewed as a phenomenon of American exceptionalism. Once more the dynamic is primarily linear—one leaves the Pacific Rim, settles in the U.S., works, establishes a family, and a community emerges. The emphasis is on intergroup dynamics in the receiving society, the adaptation of newcomers, and the uniqueness of the United States as an immigrant nation.[16]

The emerging paradigm views the immigrant experience as circular and global. It recognizes that Asian emigration is diasporic and that Asians in the United States is only one part of the story.[17] The Asian experience abroad has historically been global, but the new realities of contemporary international migration have contributed to its recent (re) "discovery." There is new recognition that the transnational flow of capital, labor, technology, information, cultural motifs, and consumer habits are not simply one-way, but circular.[18] Consequently, there is a need to address families, economic enterprises, community formation, political and social movements, and other aspects of the Asian American experience as transnational and global.

Asian American Studies had its historic origins in the demand for ethnic studies in the late 1960s. As a mass-based curriculum and research agenda, it challenged American higher education as an elite and Eurocentric institution. It has also been in direct tension with the more established and largely state-sponsored Asian Studies programs. If racial paradigms have dominated ethnic studies, area studies programs have been driven by the Cold War paradigm and U.S. hegemonic interests. Given their different beginnings, missions, and frameworks of analysis, Asian American Studies sought to forge its own identity distinct from Asian Studies. In so doing, it attracted many scholars originally trained in area studies who favored the democratizing tendencies of Asian American Studies. At the same time given their divergent intellectual and political interests, Asian Studies kept its distance from Asian American Studies, while university administrators tried to figure out the difference between the two fields.[19] This form of academic labor market segmentation, however, has contributed to the narrowing of the intellectual boundaries of Asian American Studies. For example, we know little about the impact of Asian emigration on the sending states or of the relations between communities of origin and communities of settlement.

The end of the Cold War era and the rise of globalization are leading to new academic pursuits, such as global and diasporic studies. Diasporic studies can expand the parameters of the Asian experience abroad from a largely American experience to a global one and serve as a bridge between ethnic studies and area studies. It can link Asian American scholars with those studying Asian Pacific experiences in Asia itself, Europe, the Americas, Africa, and the Middle East. The internationalization of Asian American Studies can contribute to the decentering of Asian Studies from a paradigm of regionality and one of importance when it is of national interest to the West. The linkage is a potential for intellectual exchange. However, it will continue to be problematic as long as area studies are privileged in the academy and Asian Studies retains its Cold War paradigm. New linkages do not replace or take away from Asian American Studies developing as a field in its own right. Nonetheless, global forces are transforming all aspects of our lives. Hence, policy studies directed at Asian Pacific Americans cannot be limited by concepts of national borders and American exceptionalism.

Conclusions

I have confined my discussion to five shifting racial paradigms to suggest what researchers are thinking about today. Emerging paradigms, however, do not negate the persistence of dominant race relations models. The most important distinction of these emerging paradigms is that they are being formulated largely by scholars and practitioners pushing at the margins of traditional disciplines, many of whom are people of color and women. They are the newcomers to academic disciplines and outsiders to the academy that Kuhn identifies as less fearful of novelty and open to changing paradigms.

The theoretical repositioning on race and its impact on Asian American Studies raise some concerns. First, the rethinking is part of a resurgence of interest in race-specific theories to explain inequality in America and reflects the debates over race-specific policies to redress injustice.[20] Race matters to and for Asian Pacific Americans. But so do class and gender. Race matters differently depending on one's social class and gender.[21] Race itself can become a dominant paradigm contributing to a serious lack of attention to other factors. Asian Americanists cannot afford to neglect such factors as class, gender, generation, and others in rethinking race theory.

The new multiracial realities have been part of our landscape for some time. The changing demographics, the Los Angeles uprising of 1992 and the resurgence of anti-immigration activities have led researchers to give them new attention. Secondly, the rethinking of racial paradigms is just that—*rethinking*. The *doing* of new kinds of research in race relations is still in the making. Replication is easier than innovation. Institutional barriers, including surmounting the zealously guarded boundaries of academic units and disciplines, also complicate the conduct and implementation of interdisciplinary studies. However, when new forms of research are not carried out, old paradigms predominate.

Finally, what is the relationship between theory and practice? When Asian American Studies was founded, it represented a new paradigm that challenged the existing academic elite and traditional scholarship. Participants saw themselves as part of a different way of thinking, being, and doing in the academy that included new forms of scholarship, pedagogy, and research. Asian American faculty and students also saw themselves as a bridge between campus and community. Underlying this original mission was the notion that the privilege of education would contribute to the liberation of the less privileged and the increased democratization of U.S. society.[22] It has been said that each generation rewrites history in its own image. Similarly, social movements and organizations often revise their mission to reflect the context of their times. In striving for legitimacy in the academy, much of current theory and scholarship, especially in the area of cultural studies, is remotely connected to and often incomprehensible to those whom Asian American Studies is said to represent. We need to consider whether the paradigm of Asian American Studies is shifting from its original mission and links with community and the less privileged to one in which our practice is centered exclusively in the university. If the primary engagement of Asian American Studies is with and for other academicians and if the new theoretical positioning maintains the status quo rather than changes it, we are moving in the direction of becoming another elite.

In summary, old racial paradigms are limited in explaining existing conditions but persist. In rethinking race, new paradigms are emerging that speak to the multiplicity of racial dynamics, the ever-changing but centrality of race and racism in America, the differential power and agency of communities, the increased attention to heterogeneous, comparative, and panethnic studies as well as viewing Asian Pacific American communities in the context of global and diasporic studies. Each of these emergent paradigms, in turn, impacts on policy formation.

Rethinking race also has implications for Asian American Studies. One consideration is that race-specific paradigms will contribute to the neglect of other factors, such as class, gender, and generation. Another is that when the conduct of research is not commensurate with theoretical developments and new empirical studies are not forthcoming, old racial paradigms will continue to determine Asian Pacific American research. Finally, and most important, the relationship between current theoretical repositioning and the practice of Asian American Studies is not clear.

New paradigms are not necessarily transformative. Furthermore, current practices that disconnect Asian American Studies from community and place the academy at its center shift the paradigm of Asian American Studies from social transformation to the production of a new academic elite. In rethinking race, we also need to reexamine our practices. It is my hope that the new theoretical repositioning will not neglect the links to community but reinforce and further the historic mission of Asian American Studies.

NOTES

1. Thomas Kuhn, *The Structure of Scientific Revolutions* (Chicago: University of Chicago Press, 1970. Second edition, enlarged), 171–194.

2. The October-November 1994 alleged hoax concocted by Susan Smith of a black man stealing her car with her two sons in it when she had drowned her children in the car in a lake near Union, South Carolina, is only the most recent dramatic incident of a well-established racial paradigm to blame black males for individual or societal wrongs. "Woman's False Charge Revives Hurt for Blacks," *New York Times*, November 6, 1994.

3. Kuhn, 144–159.

4. Shirley Hune, "An Overview of Asian Pacific American Futures: Shifting Paradigms." In *The State of Asian Pacific America: Policy Issues to the Year 2020* (Los Angeles: LEAP Asian Pacific American Public Policy Institute and UCLA Asian American Studies Center, 1993), 1–9.

5. Gary Y. Okihiro, *Margins and Mainstreams* (Seattle: University of Washington Press, 1994), 31–63.

6. For examples of multiracial economic relations, see James W. Loewen, *The Mississippi Chinese: Between Black and White*, second edition (Prospect Heights, Illinois: Waveland Press, 1988), and Edward T. Chang, "Jewish and Korean Merchants in African American Neighborhoods: A Comparative Perspective," in *Los Angeles—Struggles Toward Multiethnic Community*, edited by Edward T. Chang and Russell C. Leong (Seattle: University of Washington Press, 1995), 5–22. For a study of political dynamics, see Leland T. Saito, "Asian Americans and Latinos in San Gabriel Valley, California: Interethnic Political Cooperation and Redistricting 1990–92," in Chang and Leong, 55–68. For studies of multiracial identity, see Karen I. Leonard, *Making Ethnic Choices: California's Punjabi Mexican Americans* (Philadelphia: Temple University Press, 1992), and Maria P. P. Root, ed. *Racially Mixed People in America* (Newbury Park, Calif.: Sage. 1992).

7. The statewide exit poll of the *Los Angeles Times*, November 10, 1994, indicated that 63 percent of Whites, 47 percent Blacks, 23 percent Latinos, and 47 percent Asians voted for Proposition 187, while *USA Today*, November 11, 1994, found that 64 percent of Whites, 56 percent Blacks, 31 percent Latinos, and 57 percent Asians supported it. At this writing, Proposition 187 is being reviewed by the courts and is yet to be implemented. "The Times Poll. Most Call Prop. 187 Good, Want It Implemented Now," *Los Angeles Times*, March 13, 1995. The *Los Angeles Times* affirmative action poll has been criticized for poorly worded questions that may have confused respondents. "The Times Poll. Most Back Anti-Bias Policy but Spurn Racial Preferences," *Los Angeles Times*, March 30, 1995.

8. The view that the differential outcomes of racial groups is based upon biology persists. Recent examples include *The Bell Curve* by Richard J. Herrnstein and Charles Murray (New York: Free Press, 1994). The authors argue that I.Q. scores are race-based and that African

Americans are intellectually inferior. Similarly, in the November 1994 remarks of President Francis Lawrence of Rutgers University, he stated that black students did not have the "genetic, hereditary background" to have a higher average on their SAT scores. See "Lawrence Must Go," *New York Times*, February 11, 1995. Both the book and Lawrence's remarks have been soundly challenged.

9. Michael Omi and Howard Winant, *Racial Formation in the United States* (New York: Routledge and Kegan Paul, 1986).

10. See, for example, *The State of Asian Pacific America: Policy Issues to the Year 2020* (Los Angeles: LEAP Asian Pacific American Public Policy Institute and UCLA Asian American Studies Center, 1993); Paul Ong, ed., *The State of Asian Pacific America: Economic Diversity, Issues and Policies* (Los Angeles: LEAP Asian Pacific American Public Policy Institute and UCLA Asian American Studies Center, 1994); and Robert D. Bullard, ed., *Confronting Environmental Racism* (Boston: South End Press, 1993).

11. Timothy P. Fong, *The First Suburban Chinatown* (Philadelphia: Temple University Press, 1994).

12. Paul Ong, ed., *Beyond Asian American Poverty* (Los Angeles: LEAP Asian Pacific American Public Policy Institute, 1993).

13. Evelyn Nakano Glenn, *Issei, Nisei, Warbride* (Philadelphia: Temple University Press, 1986), and Nazli Kibria, *Family Tightrope: The Changing Lives of Vietnamese Americans* (Princeton, N.J.: Princeton University Press, 1993).

14. Recent rural studies include Valerie J. Matsumoto, *Farming the Home Place* (Ithaca, N.Y.: Cornell University Press, 1993), and Gary Y. Okihiro, "Fallow Field: The Rural Dimension of Asian American Studies" in *Frontiers of Asian American Studies*, edited by Gail M. Nomura, Russell Endo, Stephen H. Sumida, and Russell C. Leong (Pullman: Washington State University Press, 1989). The emergence of "middle-class" Asian American communities in the suburbs is discussed, for example, in Timothy P. Fong, *The First Suburban Chinatown: The Remaking of Monterey Park, California* (Philadelphia: Temple University Press, 1994), and in Hsiang-shui Chen's *Chinatown No More: Taiwan Immigrants in Contemporary New York* (Ithaca, N.Y.: Cornell University Press, 1992).

15. Yen Le Espiritu, *Asian American Panethnicity* (Philadelphia: Temple University Press, 1992).

16. Shirley Hune, *Pacific Migration to the United States: Trends and Themes in Historical and Sociological Literature* (Washington, D.C.: Research Institute on Immigration and Ethnic Studies, Smithsonian Institution, 1977), 1–21. Also reprinted in *Asian American Studies: An Annotated Bibliography and Research Guide*, edited by Hyung-chan Kim (New York: Greenwood Press, 1989), 17–30.

17. See, for example, the articles in the special issue of *Amerasia Journal—Asians in the Americas* 5:2 (1989), including a discussion of diaspora in Russell C. Leong's "Asians in the Americas: Interpreting the Diaspora Experience," vii–xviii.

18. See, for example, Haiming Liu, "The Trans-Pacific Family: A Case Study of Sam Chang's Family History," *Amerasia Journal* 18:2 (1992), and Paul Ong, Edna Bonacich, and Lucie Cheng, ed., *The New Asian Immigration in Los Angeles and Global Restructuring* (Philadelphia: Temple University Press, 1994).

19. For a discussion of the different origins, missions, and frameworks of ethnic studies and area studies, see *Asian Americans: Comparative and Global Perspectives*, edited by Shirley Hune, Hyung-chan Kim, Stephen S. Fugita, and Amy Ling, "Part One, Comparing Old and New Area Studies" with articles by Shirley Hune, Evelyn Hu-DeHart, Gary Y. Okihiro, and Sucheta Mazumdar (Pullman: Washington State University, 1991), 1–44. See also Shirley Hune,

"Opening the American Mind and Body: The Role of Asian American Studies," *Change* (November/December 1989): 56–63.

20. See, for example, Omi and Winant, 1986, and Mari J. Matsuda, Charles R. Lawrence III, Richard Delgado, and Kimberle Williams Crenshaw, *Words That Wound: Critical Race Theory, Assaultive Speech and the First Amendment* (Boulder, Colo.: Westview Press, 1993).

21. In a controversial book in 1978, William J. Wilson noted the improving position of the black middle class in contrast to the deteriorating circumstances of the black underclass. *The Declining Significance of Race* (Chicago: The University of Chicago Press) launched a debate as to the relative importance of race and class in the African American community. By 1993, Cornell West (*Race Matters*, Boston: Beacon Press) was reminding the nation that race still matters for African Americans. See also Dana Y. Takagi, *The Retreat from Race* (New Brunswick, N.J.: Rutgers University Press, 1992), and Kenyon S. Chan and Shirley Hune, "Racialization and Panethnicity: From Asians in America to Asian Americans" in *Toward a Common Destiny: Improving Race and Ethnic Relations in America*, edited by W. Halley and A. W. Jackson (San Francisco: Jossey-Bass, 1995), 205–233, for a discussion of the significance of race for Asian Americans in education admissions.

22. Russell Endo and William Wei, "On the Development of Asian American Studies Programs" in *Reflections on Shattered Windows*, edited by G. Okihiro, S. Hune, A. Hansen, and J. Liu (Pullman: Washington State University Press, 1988), and Hune, *Change*, 1989.

Chapter Thirty-three

Heterogeneity, Hybridity, Multiplicity
Marking Asian American Differences

Lisa Lowe

In a recent poem by Janice Mirikitani, a Japanese-American nisei woman describes her sansei daughter's rebellion.[1] The daughter's denial of Japanese American culture and its particular notions of femininity reminds the nisei speaker that she, too, has denied her antecedents, rebelling against her own more traditional issei mother:

> I want to break tradition—unlock this room
>   where women dress in the dark.
>   Discover the lies my mother told me.
>   The lies that we are small and powerless
>   that our possibilities must be compressed
>   to the size of pearls, displayed only as
>   passive chokers, charms around our neck.
> Break Tradition.
>   I want to tell my daughter of this room
>   of myself
>   filled with tears of shakuhatchi,
>
>   . . . .
>
>   poems about madness,
>   sounds shaken from barbed wire and
>   goodbyes and miracles of survival.
>   This room of open window where daring ones escape.
> My daughter denies she is like me . . .
>   her pouting ruby lips, her skirts
>   swaying to salsa, teena marie and the stones,
>   her thighs displayed in carnivals of color.
>   I do not know the contents of her room.
> She mirrors my aging.
> She is breaking tradition. (9)

The nisei speaker repudiates the repressive confinements of her issei mother: the disciplining of the female body, the tedious practice of diminution, the silences of obedience. In turn, the crises that have shaped the nisei speaker—internment camps, sounds of threatening madness—are unknown to, and unheard by, her sansei teenage daughter. The three generations of Japanese immigrant women in this poem are separated by their different histories and by different conceptions of what it means to be female and Japanese. The poet who writes "I do not know the contents of her room" registers these separations as "breaking tradition."

In another poem, by Lydia Lowe, Chinese women workers are divided also by generation, but even more powerfully by class and language. The speaker is a young Chinese American who supervises an older Chinese woman in a textile factory.

> The long bell blared,
> and then the *lo-ban*
> made me search all your bags
> before you could leave.
>
> Inside he sighed
> about slow work, fast hands,
> missing spools of thread—
> and I said nothing.
>
> I remember that day
> you came in to show me
> I added your tickets six zippers short.
> It was just a mistake.
>
> You squinted down
> at the check in your hands
> like an old village woman peers
> at some magician's trick.
>
> That afternoon
> when you thrust me your bags
> I couldn't look or raise my face.
> *Doi m-jyu.*
>
> Eyes on the ground,
> I could only see
> one shoe kicking against the other. (29)

This poem, too, invokes the breaking of tradition, although it thematizes another sort of stratification among Asian women: the structure of the factory places the English-speaking younger woman above the Cantonese-speaking older one. Economic relations in capitalist society force the young supervisor to discipline her elders, and she is acutely ashamed that her required behavior does not demonstrate the respect traditionally owed to parents and elders. Thus, both poems foreground commonly thematized *topoi* of diasporan cultures: the disruption and distortion of traditional cultural practices—like the practice of parental sacrifice and filial duty, or the practice of respecting hierarchies of age—not only as a consequence of immigration to the United States but as a part of entering a society with different class stratifications and different constructions of gender roles. Some Asian American discussions cast the disruption of tradition as loss and represent the loss in terms of regret and shame, as in the latter poem. Alternatively, the traditional practices of family continuity and hierarchy may be figured as oppressively confining, as in Mirikitani's poem, in which the two generations of daughters contest the more restrictive female roles of the former generations. In either case, many Asian American discussions portray immigration and relocation to the United States in terms of a loss of the "original" culture in exchange for the new "American" culture.

In many Asian American novels, the question of the loss or transmission of the "original" culture is frequently represented in a family narrative, figured as generational conflict between the Chinese-born first generation and the American-born second generation.[2] Louis Chu's 1961 novel *Eat a Bowl of Tea*, for example, allegorizes in the conflicted relationship between father and son the differences between "native" Chinese values and the new "westernized" culture of Chinese Americans. Other novels have taken up this generational theme; one way to read Maxine Hong Kingston's *The Woman Warrior* (1975) or Amy Tan's recent *The Joy Luck Club* (1989) is to understand them as versions of this generational model of culture, refigured in feminine terms, between mothers and daughters. However, I will argue that interpreting Asian American culture exclusively in terms of the master narratives of generational conflict and filial relation essentializes Asian American culture, obscuring the particularities and incommensurabilities of class, gender, and national diversities among Asians; the reduction of ethnic cultural politics to struggles between first and second generations displaces (and privatizes) intercommunity differences into a familial opposition. To avoid this homogenizing of Asian Americans as exclusively hierarchical and familial, I would contextualize the "vertical" generational model of culture with the more "horizontal" relationship represented in Diana Chang's "The Oriental Contingent." In Chang's short story, two young women avoid the discussion of their Chinese backgrounds because each desperately fears that the other is "more Chinese," more "authentically" tied to the original culture. The narrator, Connie, is certain that her friend Lisa "never referred to her own background because it was more Chinese than Connie's, and therefore of a higher order. She was tact incarnate. All along, she had been going out of her way not to embarrass Connie. Yes, yes. Her assurance was definitely uppercrust (perhaps her father had been in the diplomatic service), and her offhand didacticness, her lack of self-doubt, was indeed characteristically Chinese-Chinese" (173). Connie feels ashamed because she assumes herself to be "a failed Chinese"; she fantasizes that Lisa was born in China, visits there frequently, and privately disdains Chinese Americans. Her assumptions about Lisa prove to be quite wrong, however; Lisa is even more critical of herself for "not being genuine." For Lisa, as Connie eventually discovers, was born in Buffalo and was adopted by non–Chinese American parents; lacking an immediate connection to Chinese culture, Lisa projects upon all Chinese the authority of being "more Chinese." Lisa confesses to Connie at the end of the story: "The only time I feel Chinese is when I'm embarrassed I'm not more Chinese—which is a totally Chinese reflex I'd give anything to be rid of!" (176). Chang's story portrays two women polarized by the degree to which they have each internalized a cultural definition of "Chineseness" as pure and fixed, in which any deviation is constructed as less, lower, and shameful. Rather than confirming the cultural model in which "ethnicity" is passed from generation to generation, Chang's story explores the "ethnic" relationship between women of the same generation. Lisa and Connie are ultimately able to reduce one another's guilt at not being "Chinese enough"; in one another they are able to find a common frame of reference. The story suggests that the making of Chinese American culture—how ethnicity is imagined, practiced, continued—is worked out as much between ourselves and our communities as it is transmitted from one generation to another.

In this sense, Asian American discussions of ethnicity are far from uniform or consistent; rather, these discussions contain a wide spectrum of articulations that includes, at one end, the desire for an identity represented by a fixed profile of ethnic traits and, at another, challenges to the very notions of identity and singularity which celebrate ethnicity as a fluctuating composition of differences, intersections, and incommensurabilities. These latter efforts attempt to define ethnicity in a manner that accounts not only for cultural inheritance but for active cultural construction, as well. In other words, they suggest that the making of Asian American culture may be a much "messier" process than unmediated vertical transmission from one generation to another, including practices that are partly inherited and partly modified, as well as partly invented.[3] As the narrator of *The Woman Warrior* suggests, perhaps one of the more important stories of Asian American experience is about the process of receiving, refiguring, and rewriting cultural traditions. She asks: "Chinese-Americans, when you try to understand what things in you are Chinese, how do you separate what is peculiar to childhood, to poverty, insanities, one family, your mother who marked your growing with stories, from what is Chinese? What is Chinese tradition and what is the movies?" (6). Or the dilemma of cultural syncretism might be posed in an interrogative version of the uncle's impromptu proverb in Wayne Wang's film *Dim Sum*: "You can take the girl out of Chinatown, but can you take the Chinatown out of the girl?" For rather than representing a fixed, discrete culture, "Chinatown" is itself the very emblem of fluctuating demographics, languages, and populations.[4]

I begin my chapter with these particular examples drawn from Asian American cultural texts in order to observe that what is referred to as "Asian America" is clearly a heterogeneous entity. From the perspective of the majority culture, Asian Americans may very well be constructed as different from, and other than, Euro-Americans. But from the perspectives of Asian Americans, we are perhaps even more different, more diverse, among ourselves: being men and women at different distances and generations from our "original" Asian cultures—cultures as different as Chinese, Japanese, Korean, Filipino, Indian, and Vietnamese—Asian Americans are born in the United States and born in Asia; of exclusively Asian parents and of mixed race; urban and rural; refugee and nonrefugee; communist-identified and anticommunist; fluent in English and non-English speaking; educated and working class. As with other diasporas in the United States, the Asian immigrant collectivity is unstable and changeable, with its cohesion complicated by intergenerationality, by various degrees of identification and relation to a "homeland," and by different extents of assimilation to and distinction from "majority culture" in the United States. Further,

the historical contexts of particular waves of immigration within single groups contrast with one another; the Japanese Americans who were interned during World
War II encountered quite different social and economic barriers than those from
Japan who arrive in southern California today. And the composition of different
waves of immigrants differs in gender, class, and region. For example, the first groups
of Chinese immigrants to the United States in 1850 were from four villages in Canton
province, male by a ratio of ten to one, and largely of peasant backgrounds; the more
recent Chinese immigrants are from Hong Kong, Taiwan, or the People's Republic
(themselves quite heterogeneous and of discontinuous "origins"), or from the Chinese diaspora in other parts of Asia, such as Macao, Malaysia, or Singapore, and they
are more often educated and middle-class men and women.[5] Further, once arriving
in the United States, very few Asian immigrant cultures remain discrete, inpenetrable
communities. The more recent groups mix, in varying degrees, with segments of the
existing groups; Asian Americans may intermarry with other ethnic groups, live in
neighborhoods adjacent to them, or work in the same businesses and on the same
factory assembly lines. The boundaries and definitions of Asian American culture are
continually shifting and being contested from pressures both "inside" and "outside"
the Asian origin community.

I stress heterogeneity, hybridity, and multiplicity in the characterization of Asian
American culture as part of a twofold argument about cultural politics, the ultimate
aim of that argument being to disrupt the current hegemonic relationship between
"dominant" and "minority" positions. On the one hand, my observation that Asian
Americans are heterogeneous is part of a strategy to destabilize the dominant discursive construction and determination of Asian Americans as a homogeneous group.
Throughout the late nineteenth and early twentieth centuries, Asian immigration to
the United States was managed by exclusion acts and quotas that relied upon racialist
constructions of Asians as homogeneous;[6] the "model minority" myth and the
informal quotas discriminating against Asians in university admissions policies are
contemporary versions of this homogenization of Asians.[7] On the other hand, I
underscore Asian American heterogeneities (particularly class, gender, and national
differences among Asians) to contribute to a dialogue within Asian American discourse, to negotiate with those modes of argumentation that continue to uphold a
politics based on ethnic "identity." In this sense, I argue for the Asian American
necessity—politically, intellectually, and personally—to organize, resist, and theorize
as Asian Americans, but at the same time I inscribe this necessity within a discussion
of the risks of a cultural politics that relies upon the construction of sameness and
the exclusion of differences.

The first reason to emphasize the dynamic fluctuation and heterogeneity of Asian
American culture is to release our understandings of either the "dominant" or the
emergent "minority" cultures as discrete, fixed, or homogeneous, and to arrive at a
different conception of the general political terrain of culture in California, a useful
focus for this examination since it has become commonplace to consider it an
"ethnic state," embodying a new phenomenon of cultural adjacency and admixture.[8]
For if minority immigrant cultures are perpetually changing—in their composition,

configuration, and signifying practices, as well as in their relations to one another—
it follows that the "majority" or dominant culture, with which minority cultures are
in continual relation, is also unstable and unclosed. The suggestion that the general
social terrain of culture is open, plural, and dynamic reorients our understanding of
what "cultural hegemony" is and how it works in contemporary California. It
permits us to theorize about the roles that ethnic immigrant groups play in the
making and unmaking of culture—and how these minority discourses challenge the
existing structure of power, the existing hegemony.[9] We should remember that
Antonio Gramsci writes about hegemony as not simply political or economic forms
of rule but as the entire process of dissent and compromise through which a
particular group is able to determine the political, cultural, and ideological character
of a state (*Selections*). Hegemony does not refer exclusively to the process by which a
dominant formation exercises its influence but refers equally to the process through
which minority groups organize and contest any specific hegemony.[10] The reality of
any specific hegemony is that, while it may be for the moment dominant, it is never
absolute or conclusive. Hegemony, in Gramsci's thought, is a concept that describes
both the social processes through which a particular dominance is maintained and
those through which that dominance is challenged and new forces are articulated.
When a hegemony representing the interests of a dominant group exists, it is always
within the context of resistances from emerging "subaltern" groups.[11] We might say
that hegemony is not only the political process by which a particular group constitutes itself as "the one" or "the majority" in relation to which "minorities" are
defined and know themselves to be "other," but it is equally the process by which
positions of otherness may ally and constitute a new majority, a "counterhege-
mony."[12]

The subaltern classes are, in Gramsci's definition, prehegemonic, not unified
groups, whose histories are fragmented, episodic and identifiable only from a point
of historical hindsight. They may go through different phases when they are subject
to the activity of ruling groups, may articulate their demands through existing parties,
and then may themselves produce new parties; in *The Prison Notebooks*, Gramsci
describes a final phase at which the "formations [of the subaltern classes] assert
integral autonomy" (52). The definition of the subaltern groups includes some
noteworthy observations for our understanding of the roles of racial and ethnic
immigrant groups in the United States. The assertion that the significant practices of
the subaltern groups may not be understood as hegemonic until they are viewed
with historical hindsight is interesting, for it suggests that some of the most powerful
practices may not always be the explicitly oppositional ones, may not be understood
by contemporaries, and may be less overt and recognizable than others. Provocative,
too, is the idea that the subaltern classes are by definition "not unified"; that is, the
subaltern is not a fixed, unified force of a single character. Rather, the assertion of
"integral autonomy" by not unified classes suggests a coordination of distinct, yet
allied, positions, practices, and movements—class-identified and not class-identified,
in parties and not, ethnic-based and gender-based—each in its own not necessarily
equivalent manner transforming and disrupting the apparatuses of a specific hegemony. The independent forms and locations of cultural challenge—ideological, as well

as economic and political—constitute what Gramsci calls a "new historical bloc," a new set of relationships that together embody a different hegemony and a different balance of power. In this sense, we have in the growing and shifting ethnic minority populations in California an active example of this new historical bloc described by Gramsci; and in the negotiations between these ethnic groups and the existing majority over what interests precisely constitute the "majority," we have an illustration of the concept of hegemony, not in the more commonly accepted sense of "hegemony-maintenance," but in the often ignored sense of "hegemony-creation."[13] The observation that the Asian American community and other ethnic immigrant communities are heterogeneous lays the foundation for several political operations: first, by shifting, multiplying, and reconceiving the construction of society as composed of two numerically overdetermined camps called the majority and the minority, cultural politics is recast so as to account for a multiplicity of various, nonequivalent groups, one of which is Asian Americans. Second, the conception of ethnicity as heterogeneous provides a position for Asian Americans that is both ethnically specific, yet simultaneously uneven and unclosed; Asian Americans can articulate distinct group demands based on our particular histories of exclusion, but the redefined lack of closure—which reveals rather than conceals differences—opens political lines of affiliation with other groups (labor unions, other racial and ethnic groups, and gay, lesbian, and feminist groups) in the challenge to specific forms of domination insofar as they share common features.

In regard to the practice of "identity politics" within Asian American discourse, the articulation of an "Asian American identity" as an organizing tool has provided a concept of political unity that enables diverse Asian groups to understand our unequal circumstances and histories as being related; likewise, the building of "Asian American culture" is crucial, for it articulates and empowers our multicultural, multilingual Asian origin community vis-à-vis the institutions and apparatuses that exclude and marginalize us. But I want to suggest that essentializing Asian American identity and suppressing our differences—of national origin, generation, gender, party, class—risks particular dangers: not only does it underestimate the differences and hybridities among Asians, but it also inadvertently supports the racist discourse that constructs Asians as a homogeneous group, that implies we are "all alike" and conform to "types"; in this respect, a politics based exclusively on ethnic identity willingly accepts the terms of the dominant logic that organizes the heterogeneous picture of racial and ethnic diversity into a binary schema of "the one" and "the other." The essentializing of Asian American identity also reproduces oppositions that subsume other nondominant terms in the same way that Asians and other groups are disenfranchised by the dominant culture: to the degree that the discourse generalizes Asian American identity as male, women are rendered invisible; or to the extent that Chinese are presumed to be exemplary of all Asians, the importance of other Asian groups is ignored. In this sense, a politics based on ethnic identity facilitates the displacement of intercommunity differences—between men and women, or between workers and managers—into a false opposition of "nationalism" and "assimilation." We have an example of this in recent debates where Asian

American feminists who challenge Asian American sexism are cast as "assimilation-ist," as betraying Asian American "nationalism."

To the extent that Asian American discourse articulates an identity in reaction to the dominant culture's stereotype, even to refute it, I believe the discourse may remain bound to, and overdetermined by, the logic of the dominant culture. In accepting the binary terms ("white" and "nonwhite," or "majority" and "minority") that structure institutional policies about ethnicity, we forget that these binary sche-mas are not neutral descriptions. Binary constructions of difference use a logic that prioritizes the first term and subordinates the second; whether the pair "difference" and "sameness" is figured as a binary synthesis that considers "difference" as always contained within the "same," or that conceives of the pair as an opposition in which "difference" structurally implies "sameness" as its complement, it is important to see each of these figurations as versions of the same binary logic. My argument for heterogeneity seeks to challenge the conception of difference as exclusively structured by a binary opposition between two terms by proposing instead another notion of difference that takes seriously the conditions of heterogeneity, multiplicity, and non-equivalence. I submit that the most exclusive construction of Asian American identity—which presumes masculinity, American birth, and speaking English—is at odds with the formation of important political alliances and affiliations with other groups across racial and ethnic, gender, sexuality, and class lines. An essentialized identity is an obstacle to Asian American women allying with other women of color, for example, and it can discourage laboring Asian Americans from joining unions with workers of other colors. It can short-circuit potential alliances against the dominant structures of power in the name of subordinating "divisive" issues to *the national question.*

Some of the limits of identity politics are discussed most pointedly by Frantz Fanon in his books about the Algerian resistance to French colonialism. Before ultimately turning to some Asian American cultural texts in order to trace the ways in which the dialogues about identity and difference are represented within the discourse, I would like to briefly consider one of Fanon's most important texts, *The Wretched of the Earth (Les damnés de la terre,* 1961). Although Fanon's treatise was cited in the 1960s as the manifesto for a nationalist politics of identity, rereading it now in the 1990s we find his text, ironically, to be the source of a serious critique of nationalism. Fanon argues that the challenge facing any movement dismantling colonialism (or a system in which one culture dominates another) is to provide for a new order that does not reproduce the social structure of the old system. This new order, he argues, must avoid the simple assimilation to the dominant culture's roles and positions by the emergent group, which would merely caricature the old colo-nialism, and it should be equally suspicious of an uncritical nativism, or racialism, appealing to essentialized notions of precolonial identity. Fanon suggests that another alternative is necessary, a new order, neither an assimilationist nor a nativist inver-sion, which breaks with the structures and practices of cultural domination and which continually and collectively criticizes the institutions of rule. One of the more remarkable turns in Fanon's argument occurs when he identifies both bourgeois assimilation and bourgeois nationalism as conforming to the same logic, as responses to colonialism that reproduce the same structure of cultural domination. It is in this sense that Fanon warns against the nationalism practiced by bourgeois neocolonial governments. Their nationalism, he argues, can be distorted easily into racism, territorialism, separatism, or ethnic dictatorships of one tribe or regional group over others; the national bourgeois replaces the colonizer, yet the social and economic structure remains the same.[14] Ironically, he points out, these separatisms, or "micro-nationalisms" (Mamadou Dia, qtd. in Fanon 158), are themselves legacies of colonialism. He writes: "By its very structure, colonialism is regionalist and separatist. Colonialism does not simply state the existence of tribes; it also reinforces and separates them" (94). That is, a politics of ethnic separatism is congruent with the divide-and-conquer logic of colonial domination. Fanon links the practices of the national bourgeoisie that has assimilated colonialist thought and practice with nativist practices that privilege one tribe or ethnicity over others; nativism and assimilationism are not opposites but similar logics both enunciating the old order.

Fanon's analysis implies that an essentialized bourgeois construction of "nation" is a classification that excludes other subaltern groups that could bring about substantive change in the social and economic relations, particularly those whose social marginalities are due to class: peasants, workers, transient populations. We can add to Fanon's criticism that the category of nation often erases a consideration of women and the fact of difference between men and women and the conditions under which they live and work in situations of cultural domination. This is why the concentration of women of color in domestic service or reproductive labor (child care, home care, nursing) in the contemporary United States is not adequately explained by a nation-based model of analysis (see Glenn). In light of feminist theory, which has gone the furthest in theorizing multiple inscription and the importance of positionalities, we can argue that it may be less meaningful to act exclusively in terms of a single valence or political interest—such as ethnicity or nation—than to acknowledge that social subjects are the sites of a variety of differences.[15] An Asian American subject is never purely and exclusively ethnic, for that subject is always of a particular class, gender, and sexual preference and may therefore feel responsible to movements that are organized around these other designations. This is not to argue against the strategic importance of Asian American identity, nor against the building of Asian American culture. Rather, I am suggesting that acknowledging class and gender differences among Asian Americans does not weaken us as a group; to the contrary, these differences represent greater political opportunity to affiliate with other groups whose cohesions may be based on other valences of oppression.

As I have already suggested, within Asian American discourse there is a varied spectrum of discussion about the concepts of ethnic identity and culture. At one end, there are discussions in which ethnic identity is essentialized as the cornerstone of a nationalist liberation politics. In these discussions, the cultural positions of nationalism (or ethnicism, or nativism) and of assimilation are represented in polar opposition: nationalism affirming the separate purity of its ethnic culture is opposed to assimilation of the standards of dominant society. Stories about the loss of the "native" Asian culture tend to express some form of this opposition. At the same time, there are criticisms of this essentializing position, most often articulated by feminists who charge that Asian American nationalism prioritizes masculinity and does not account for women. At the other end, there are interventions that refuse static or binary conceptions of ethnicity, replacing notions of identity with multiplicity and shifting the emphasis for ethnic "essence" to cultural hybridity. Settling for neither nativism nor assimilation, these cultural texts expose the apparent opposition between the two as a constructed figure (as Fanon does when he observes that bourgeois assimilation and bourgeois nationalism often conform to the same colonialist logic). In tracing these different discussions about identity and ethnicity through Asian American cultural debates, literature, and film, I choose particular texts because they are accessible and commonly held. But I do not intend to limit *discourse* to only these particular textual forms; by *discourse*, I intend a rather extended meaning—a network that includes not only texts and cultural documents but social practices, formal and informal laws, policies of inclusion and exclusion, and institutional forms of organization, for example, all of which constitute and regulate knowledge about the object of that discourse, Asian America.

The terms of the debate about nationalism and assimilation become clearer if we look first at the discussion of ethnic identity in certain debates about the representation of culture. Readers of Asian American literature are familiar with attacks by Frank Chin, Ben Tong, and others on Maxine Hong Kingston, attacks which have been cast as nationalist criticisms of Kingston's "assimilationist" works. Her novel/ autobiography *The Woman Warrior* is the primary target of such criticism, since it is virtually the only "canonized" piece of Asian American literature; its status can be measured by the fact that the Modern Language Association is currently publishing *A Guide to Teaching "The Woman Warrior"* in its series that includes guides to Cervantes's *Don Quixote* and Dante's *Inferno*. A critique of how and why this text has become fetishized as the exemplary representation of Asian American culture is necessary and important. However, Chin's critique reveals other kinds of tensions in Asian American culture that are worth noting. He does more than accuse Kingston of having exoticized Chinese American culture; he argues that she has "feminized" Asian American literature and undermined the power of Asian American men to combat the racist stereotypes of the dominant white culture. Kingston and other women novelists such as Amy Tan, he says, misrepresent Chinese history in order to exaggerate its patriarchal structure; as a result, Chinese society is portrayed as being even more misogynistic than European society. While Chin and others have cast this conflict in terms of nationalism and assimilationism, I think it may be more productive to see this debate, as Elaine Kim does in a recent essay (" 'Such Opposite' "), as a symptom of the tensions between nationalist and feminist concerns in Asian American discourse. I would add to Kim's analysis that the dialogue between nationalist and feminist concerns animates precisely a debate about identity and difference, or identity and heterogeneity, rather than a debate between nationalism and assimilationism; it is a debate in which Chin and others stand at one end insisting upon a fixed masculinist identity, while Kingston, Tan, or feminist literary critics like Shirley Lim and Amy Ling, with their representations of female differences and their critiques of sexism in Chinese culture, repeatedly cast this notion of identity into question. Just as Fanon points out that some forms of nationalism can obscure class, Asian American feminists point out that Asian American nationalism—or the construction of an essentialized, native Asian American subject—obscures gender. In other words, the struggle that is framed as a conflict between the apparent opposites of nativism and assimilation can mask what is more properly characterized as a struggle between the desire to essentialize ethnic identity and the fundamental condition of heterogeneous differences against which such a desire is spoken. The trope that opposes nativism and assimilationism can be itself a colonialist figure used to displace the challenges of heterogeneity, or subalternity, by casting them as assimilationist or anti-ethnic.

The trope that opposes nativism and assimilation not only organizes the cultural debates of Asian American discourse but figures *in* Asian American literature, as well. More often than not, however, this symbolic conflict between nativism and assimilation is figured in the *topos* with which I began, that of generational conflict. Although there are many versions of this *topos*, I will mention only a few in order to elucidate some of the most relevant cultural tensions. In one model, a conflict between generations is cast in strictly masculinist terms, between father and son; in this model, mothers are absent or unimportant, and female figures exist only as peripheral objects to the side of the central drama of male conflict. Louis Chu's *Eat a Bowl of Tea* (1961) exemplifies this masculinist generational symbolism, in which a conflict between nativism and assimilation is allegorized in the relationship between the father, Wah Gay, and the son, Ben Loy, in the period when the predominantly Cantonese New York Chinatown community changes from a "bachelor society" to a "family society."[16] Wah Gay wishes Ben Loy to follow Chinese tradition, and to submit to the father's authority, while the son balks at his father's "old ways" and wants to make his own choices. When Wah Gay arranges a marriage for Ben Loy, the son is forced to obey. Although the son had had no trouble leading an active sexual life before his marriage, once married, he finds himself to be impotent. In other words, Chu's novel figures the conflict of nativism and assimilation in terms of Ben Loy's sexuality: submitting to the father's authority, marrying the "nice Chinese girl" Mei Oi and having sons, is the so-called traditional Chinese male behavior. This path represents the nativist option, whereas Ben Loy's former behavior—carrying on with American prostitutes, gambling, etc.—represents the alleged path of assimilation. At the nativist Chinese extreme, Ben Loy is impotent and is denied access to erotic pleasure, and at the assimilationist American extreme, he has great access and sexual freedom. Allegorizing the choice between cultural options in the register of Ben Loy's sexuality, Chu's novel suggests that resolution lies at neither pole but in a third "Chinese American" alternative, in which Ben Loy is able to experience erotic pleasure with his Chinese wife. This occurs only when the couple moves away to another state, away from the father; Ben Loy's relocation to San Francisco's Chinatown and the priority of pleasure with Mei Oi over the begetting of a son (which, incidentally, they ultimately do have) both represent important breaks from his father's authority and from Chinese tradition. Following Fanon's observations about the affinities between nativism and assimilation, we can understand Chu's novel as an early masculinist rendering of culture as conflict between the apparent opposites of nativism and assimilation, with its oedipal resolution in a Chinese American male identity; perhaps only with hindsight can we propose that the opposition itself may be a construction that allegorizes the dialectic between an articulation of essentialized ethnic identity and the context of heterogeneous differences.

Amy Tan's much more recent *The Joy Luck Club* (1989) refigures this *topos* of generational conflict in a different social context, among first- and second-generation Mandarin Chinese in San Francisco and, more importantly, between women. Tan's *Joy Luck* displaces *Eat a Bowl* not only because it deviates from the figuration of Asian American identity in a masculine oedipal dilemma by refiguring it in terms of mothers and daughters but also because *Joy Luck* multiplies the sites of cultural conflict, positing a number of struggles—familial and extrafamilial—as well as resolutions, without privileging the singularity or centrality of one. In this way, *Joy Luck* ultimately thematizes and demystifies the central role of the mother-daughter relationship in Asian American culture.

Joy Luck represents the first-person narratives of four sets of Chinese-born mothers and their American-born daughters. The daughters attempt to come to terms with their mothers' demands, while the mothers simultaneously try to interpret their daughters' deeds, expressing a tension between the "Chinese" expectation of filial respect and the "American" inability to fulfill that expectation. By multiplying and subverting the model of generational discord with examples of generational concord, the novel calls attention to the heterogeneity of Chinese American family relations. On the one hand, mothers like Ying-ying St. Clair complain about their daughters' Americanization:

> For all these years I kept my mouth closed so selfish desires would not fall out. And because I remained quiet for so long now my daughter does not hear me. She sits by her fancy swimming pool and hears only her Sony Walkman, her cordless phone, her big, important husband asking her why they have charcoal and no lighter fluid.
>
> . . . because I moved so secretly now my daughter does not see me. She sees a list of things to buy, her checkbook out of balance, her ashtray sitting crooked on a straight table.
>
> And I want to tell her this: We are lost, she and I, unseen and not seeing, unheard and not hearing, unknown by others. (67)

The mother presents herself as having sacrificed everything for a daughter who has ignored these sacrifices. She sees her daughter as preoccupied with portable, mobile high-tech commodities which, characteristically, have no cords, no ties, emblematizing the mother's condemnation of a daughter who does not respect family bonds. The mother implies that the daughter recognizes that something is skewed and attempts to correct it—balancing her checkbook, straightening her house—but, in the mother's eyes, she has no access to the real problems; being in America has taken this understanding away. Her daughter, Lena, however, tends to view her mother as unreasonably superstitious and domineering. Lena considers her mother's concern about her failing marriage as meddlesome; the daughter's interpretation of their antagonism emphasizes a cultural gap between the mother who considers her daughter's troubles her own and the daughter who sees her mother's actions as intrusive, possessive, and, worst of all, denying the daughter's own separate individuality.

On the other hand, in contrast to this and other examples of disjunction between the Chinese mothers and the Chinese American daughters, *Joy Luck* also includes a relationship between mother and daughter in which there is an apparent coincidence of perspective; tellingly, in this example the mother has died, and it is left to the daughter to "eulogize" the mother by telling the mother's story. Jing-mei Woo makes a trip to China, to reunite with her recently deceased mother's two daughters by an earlier marriage, whom her mother had been forced to abandon almost forty years before when fleeing China during the Japanese invasion. Jing-mei wants to fulfill her mother's last wish to see the long-lost daughters; she wishes to inscribe herself in her mother's place. Her narration of the reunion conveys her utopian belief in the possibility of recovering the past, of rendering herself coincident with her mother, narrating her desire to become again "Chinese."

> My sisters and I stand, arms around each other, laughing and wiping the tears from each other's eyes. The flash of the Polaroid goes off and my father hands me the snapshot. My sisters and I watch quietly together, eager to see what develops.
>
> The gray-green surface changes to the bright colors of our three images, sharpening and deepening all at once. And although we don't speak, I know we all see it: Together we look like our mother. Her same eyes, her same mouth, open in surprise to see, at last, her long-cherished wish. (288)

Unlike Lena St. Clair, Jing-mei does not seek greater autonomy from her mother; she desires a lessening of the disparity between their positions that is accomplished through the narrative evocation of her mother after she has died. By contrasting different examples of mother-daughter discord and concord, *Joy Luck* allegorizes the heterogeneous culture in which the desire for identity and sameness (represented by Jing-mei's story) is inscribed within the context of Asian American differences and disjunctions (exemplified by the other three pairs of mothers and daughters). The novel formally illustrates that the articulation of one, the desire for identity, depends upon the existence of the others, or the fundamental horizon of differences.

Further, although *Joy Luck* has been heralded and marketed as a novel about mother-daughter relations in the Chinese American family (one cover review characterizes it as a "story that shows us China, Chinese-American women and their families, and the mystery of the mother-daughter bond in ways that we have not experienced before"), I would suggest that the novel also represents antagonisms that are not exclusively generational but are due to different conceptions of class and gender among Chinese Americans.

Toward the end of the novel, Lindo and Waverly Jong reach a climax of misunderstanding, in a scene that takes place in a central site of American femininity: the beauty parlor. After telling the stylist to give her mother a "soft wave," Waverly asks her mother, Lindo, if she is in agreement. The mother narrates:

> I smile. I use my American face. That's the face Americans think is Chinese, the one they cannot understand. But inside I am becoming ashamed. I am ashamed she is

ashamed. Because she is my daughter and I am proud of her, and I am her mother but she is not proud of me. (255)

The American-born daughter believes she is treating her mother, rather magnanimously, to a day of pampering at a chic salon; the Chinese-born mother receives this gesture as an insult, clear evidence of a daughter ashamed of her mother's looks. The scene not only marks the separation of mother and daughter by generation but, perhaps less obviously, their separation by class and cultural differences that lead to different interpretations of how female identity is signified. On the one hand, the Chinese-born Lindo and American-born Waverly have different class values and opportunities; the daughter's belief in the pleasure of a visit to an expensive San Francisco beauty parlor seems senselessly extravagant to the mother whose rural family had escaped poverty only by marrying her to the son of a less humble family in their village. On the other hand, the mother and daughter also conflict over definitions of proper female behavior. Lindo assumes female identity is constituted in the practice of a daughter's deference to her elders, while for Waverly, it is determined by a woman's financial independence from her parents and her financial equality with men and by her ability to speak her desires, and it is cultivated and signified in the styles and shapes that represent middle-class feminine beauty. In this sense, I ultimately read *Joy Luck* not as a novel which exclusively depicts generational conflict among Chinese American women but rather as a text that thematizes the trope of the mother-daughter relationship in Asian American culture; that is, the novel comments upon the idealized construction of mother-daughter relationships (both in the majority culture's discourse about Asian Americans and in the Asian American discourse about ourselves), as well as upon the kinds of differences—of class and culturally specific definitions of gender—that are rendered invisible by the privileging of this trope.[17]

Before concluding, I want to turn to a final cultural text which not only restates the Asian American narrative that opposes nativism and assimilation but articulates a critique of that narrative, calling the nativist/assimilationist dyad into question. If *Joy Luck* poses an alternative to the dichotomy of nativism and assimilation by multiplying the generational conflict and demystifying the centrality of the mother-daughter relationship, then Peter Wang's film *A Great Wall* (1985)—both in its emplotment and in its very medium of representation—offers yet another version of this alternative. Wang's film unsettles both poles in the antinomy of nativist essentialism and assimilation by performing a continual geographical juxtaposition and exchange between a variety of cultural spaces. *A Great Wall* portrays the visit of Leo Fang's Chinese American family to the People's Republic of China and their month-long stay with Leo's sister's family, the Chao family, in Beijing. The film concentrates on the primary contrast between the habits, customs, and assumptions of the Chinese in China and the Chinese Americans in California by going back and forth between shots of Beijing and Northern California, in a type of continual filmic "migration" between the two, as if to thematize in its very form the travel between cultural spaces. From the first scene, however, the film foregrounds the idea that in the opposition between native and assimilated spaces, neither begins as a pure,

uncontaminated site or origin; and as the camera eye shuttles back and forth between, both poles of the constructed opposition shift and change. (Indeed, the Great
Wall of China, from which the film takes its title, is a monument to the historical
condition that not even ancient China was "pure," but coexisted with "foreign
barbarians" against which the Middle Kingdom erected such barriers.) In this regard,
the film contains a number of emblematic images that call attention to the syncretic,
composite quality of all cultural spaces: when the young Chinese Liu finishes the
university entrance exam his scholar-father gives him a Coco Cola; children crowd
around the single village television to watch a Chinese opera singer imitate Pavarotti
singing Italian opera; the Chinese student learning English recites the Gettysburg
Address. Although the film concentrates on both illustrating and dissolving the
apparent opposition between Chinese Chinese and American Chinese, a number of
other contrasts are likewise explored: the differences between generations both within
the Chao and the Fang families (daughter Lili noisily drops her bike while her father
practices tai chi; Paul kisses his Caucasian girlfriend and later tells his father that he
believes all Chinese are racists when Leo suggests that he might date some nice
Chinese girls); differences between men and women (accentuated by two scenes, one
in which Grace Fang and Mrs. Chao talk about their husbands and children, the
other in which Chao and Leo get drunk together); and, finally, the differences
between capitalist and communist societies (highlighted in a scene in which the
Chaos and Fangs talk about their different attitudes toward "work"). The representations of these other contrasts complicate and diversify the ostensible focus on
cultural differences between Chinese and Chinese Americans, as if to testify to the
condition that there is never only one exclusive valence of difference, but rather
cultural difference is always simultaneously bound up with gender, economics, age,
and other distinctions. In other words, when Leo says to his wife that the Great Wall
makes the city "just as difficult to leave as to get in," the wall at once signifies the
construction of a variety of barriers—not only between Chinese and Americans but
between generations, men and women, capitalism and communism—as well as the
impossibility of ever remaining bounded and inpenetrable, of resisting change, re-
composition, and reinvention. We are reminded of this impossibility throughout the
film, but it is perhaps best illustrated in the scene in which the Fang and Chao
families play a rousing game of touch football on the ancient immovable Great Wall.

The film continues with a series of wonderful contrasts: the differences in the
bodily comportments of the Chinese American Paul and the Chinese Liu playing
ping pong, between Leo's jogging and Mr. Chao's tai chi, between Grace Fang's and
Mrs. Chao's ideas of what is fitting and fashionable for the female body. The two
families have different senses of space and of the relation between family members.
In one subplot, the Chinese American cousin Paul is outraged to learn that Mrs.
Chao reads her daughter Lili's mail; he asks Lili if she has ever heard of "privacy."
This later results in a fight between Mrs. Chao and Lili in which Lili says she has
learned from their American cousins that "it's not right to read other people's mail."
Mrs. Chao retorts: "You're not 'other people,' you're my daughter. What is this
thing, 'privacy'?" Lili explains to her that "privacy" can't be translated into Chinese.
"Oh, so you're trying to hide things from your mother and use western words to

trick her!" exclaims Mrs. Chao. Ultimately, just as the members of the Chao family are marked by the visit from their American relatives, the Fangs are altered by the time they return to California, each bringing back a memento or practice from their Chinese trip. In other words, rather than privileging either a nativist or assimilationist view, or even espousing a "Chinese American" resolution of differences, *A Great Wall* performs a filmic "migration" by shuttling between the various cultural spaces; we are left, by the end of the film, with a sense of culture as dynamic and open, the result of a continual process of visiting and revisiting a plurality of cultural sites.

In keeping with the example of *A Great Wall*, we might consider as a possible model for the ongoing construction of ethnic identity the migratory process suggested by Wang's filming technique and emplotment: we might conceive of the making and practice of Asian American culture as nomadic, unsettled, taking place in the travel between cultural sites and in the multivocality of heterogeneous and conflicting positions. Taking seriously the heterogeneities among Asian Americans in California, we must conclude that the grouping "Asian American" is not a natural or static category; it is a socially constructed unity, a situationally specific position that we assume for political reasons. It is "strategic" in Gayatri Spivak's sense of a "strategic use of a positive essentialism in a scrupulously visible political interest" (205). The concept of "strategic essentialism" suggests that it is possible to utilize specific signifiers of ethnic identity, such as Asian American, for the purpose of contesting and disrupting the discourses that exclude Asian Americans, while simultaneously revealing the internal contradictions and slippages of Asian American so as to insure that such essentialisms will not be reproduced and proliferated by the very apparatuses we seek to disempower. I am not suggesting that we can or should do away with the notion of Asian American identity, for to stress only our differences would jeopardize the hard-earned unity that has been achieved in the last two decades of Asian American politics, the unity that is necessary if Asian Americans are to play a role in the new historical bloc of ethnic Californians. In fact, I would submit that the very freedom, in the 1990s, to explore the hybridities concealed beneath the desire of identity is permitted by the context of a strongly articulated essentialist politics. Just as the articulation of the desire for identity depends upon the existence of a fundamental horizon of differences, the articulation of differences dialectically depends upon a socially constructed and practiced notion of identity. I want simply to remark that in the 1990s, we can afford to rethink the notion of ethnic identity in terms of cultural, class, and gender differences, rather than presuming similarities and making the erasure of particularity the basis of unity. In the 1990s, we can diversify our political practices to include a more heterogeneous group and to enable crucial alliances with other groups—ethnicity based, class based, gender based, and sexuality based—in the ongoing work of transforming hegemony.

NOTES

Many thanks to Elaine Kim for her thought-provoking questions and for asking me to deliver portions of this essay as papers at the 1990 meetings of the Association of Asian

American Studies and of the American Literature Association; to James Clifford, who also gave me the opportunity to deliver a version of this essay at a conference sponsored by the Center for Cultural Studies at UC Santa Cruz; to the audience participants at all three conferences who asked stimulating questions which have helped me to rethink my original notions; and to Page duBois, Barbara Harlow, Susan Kirkpatrick, George Mariscal, Ellen Rooney, and Kathryn Shevelow, who read drafts and offered important comments and criticism.

1. Nisei refers to a second-generation Japanese American, born to immigrant parents in the U.S.; Sansei, a third-generation Japanese American. *Issei* refers to a first-generation immigrant.

2. See Kim, *Asian,* for the most important book-length study of the literary representations of multi generational Asian America.

3. Recent anthropological discussions of ethnic cultures as fluid and syncretic systems echo these concerns of Asian American writers. See, for example, Fischer; Clifford. For an anthropological study of Japanese American culture that troubles the paradigmatic construction of kinship and filial relations as the central figure in culture, see Yanagisako.

4. We might think, for example, of the shifting of the Los Angeles "Chinatown" from its downtown location to the suburban community of Monterey Park. Since the 1970s, the former "Chinatown" has been superceded demographically and economically by Monterey Park, the home of many Chinese Americans as well as newly arrived Chinese from Hong Kong and Taiwan. The Monterey Park community of 63,000 residents is currently over 50 percent Asian. On the social and political consequences of these changing demographics, see Fong.

5. Chan's history of the Chinese immigrant populations in California, *Bittersweet,* and her history of Asian Americans are extremely important in this regard. Numerous lectures by Ling-chi Wang at UC San Diego in 1987 and at UC Berkeley in 1988 have been very important to my understanding of the heterogeneity of waves of immigration across different Asian-origin groups.

6. The Chinese Exclusion Act of 1882 barred Chinese from entering the U.S., the National Origins Act prohibited the entry of Japanese in 1924, and the Tydings-McDuffie Act of 1934 limited Filipino immigrants to fifty people per year. Finally, the most tragic consequence of anti-Asian racism occurred during World War II when 120,000 Japanese-Americans (two-thirds of whom were American citizens by birth) were interned in camps. For a study of the anti-Japanese movement culminating in the immigration act of 1924, see Daniels. Takaki offers a general history of Asian origin immigrant groups in the United States.

7. The model minority myth constructs Asians as aggressively driven overachievers; it is a homogenizing fiction which relies upon two strategies common in the subordinating construction of racial or ethnic otherness—the racial other as knowable, familiar ("like us"), and as incomprehensible, threatening ("unlike us"); the model minority myth suggests both that Asians are overachievers and "unlike us" and that they assimilate well and are thus "like us." Asian Americans are continually pointing out that the model minority myth distorts the real gains, as well as the impediments, of Asian immigrants; by leveling and homogenizing all Asian groups, it erases the different rates of assimilation and the variety of class identities among various Asian immigrant groups. Claiming that Asians are "overrepresented" on college campuses, the model minority myth is one of the justifications for the establishment of informal quotas in university admissions policies, similar to the university admission policies which discriminated against Jewish students from the 1930s to the 1950s.

8. In the last two decades, greatly diverse new groups have settled in California; demographers project that by the end of the century, the "majority" of the state will be comprised of

ethnic "minority" groups. Due to recent immigrants, this influx of minorities is characterized also by greater diversity within individual groups: the group we call Asian Americans no longer denotes only Japanese, Chinese, Koreans, and Filipinos but now includes Indian, Thai, Vietnamese, Cambodian and Laotian groups; Latino communities in California are made up not only of Chicanos but include Guatemalans, Salvadorans, and Colombians. It is not difficult to find Pakistani, Armenian, Lebanese, and Iranian enclaves in San Francisco, Los Angeles, or even San Diego. While California's "multiculturalism" is often employed to support a notion of the "melting pot," to further an ideological assertion of equal opportunity for California's different immigrant groups, I am, in contrast, pursuing the ignored implications of this characterization of California as an ethnic state: that is, despite the increasing numbers of ethnic immigrants apparently racing to enjoy California's opportunities, for racial and ethnic immigrants there is no equality but uneven development, nonequivalence, and cultural heterogeneities, not only between but within groups.

9. For an important elaboration of the concept of "minority discourse," see JanMohamed and Lloyd.

10. This notion of "the dominant"—defined by Williams in a chapter discussing the "Dominant, Residual, and Emergent" as "a cultural process . . . seized as a cultural system, with determinate dominant features: feudal culture or bourgeois culture or a transition from one to the other"—is often conflated in recent cultural theory with Gramsci's concept of hegemony. Indeed, Williams writes:"We have certainly still to speak of the 'dominant' and the 'effective,' and in these senses of the hegemonic" (121), as if the dominant and the hegemonic are synonymous.

11. See Gramsci, "History." Gramsci describes "subaltern" groups as by definition not unified, emergent, and always in relation to the dominant groups:

The history of subaltern social groups is necessarily fragmented and episodic. There undoubtedly does exist a tendency to (at least provisional stages of) unification in the historical activity of these groups, but this tendency is continually interrupted by the activity of the ruling groups; it therefore can only be demonstrated when an historical cycle is completed and this cycle culminates in a success. Subaltern groups are always subject to the activity of ruling groups, even when they rebel and rise up: only "permanent" victory breaks their subordination, and that not immediately. In reality, even when they appear triumphant, the subaltern groups are merely anxious to defend themselves (a truth which can be demonstrated by the history of the French Revolution at least up to 1830). Every trace of independent initiative on the part of subaltern groups should therefore be of incalculable value for the integral historian. (54–55)

12. "Hegemony" remains a suggestive construct in Gramsci, however, rather than an explicitly interpreted set of relations. Contemporary readers are left with the more specific task of distinguishing which particular forms of challenge to an existing hegemony are significantly transformative and which forms may be neutralized or appropriated by the hegemony. Some cultural critics contend that counterhegemonic forms and practices are tied by definition to the dominant culture and that the dominant culture simultaneously produces and limits its own forms of counterculture. I am thinking here of some of the "new historicist" studies that use a particular notion of Foucault's discourse to confer authority to the "dominant," interpreting all forms of "subversion" as being ultimately "contained" by dominant ideology and institutions. Other cultural historians, such as Williams, suggest that because there is both identifiable variation in the social order over time, as well as variations in the forms of the counter-culture in different historical periods, we must conclude that some aspects of the oppositional forms are not reducible to the terms of the original hegemony.

Still other theorists, such as Ernesto Laclau and Chantal Mouffe, have expanded Gramsci's notion of hegemony to argue that in advanced capitalist society, the social field is not a totality consisting exclusively of the dominant and the counterdominant but rather that "the social" is an open and uneven terrain of contesting articulations and signifying practices. Some of these articulations and practices are neutralized, while others can be linked to build important pressures against an existing hegemony. See Laclau and Mouffe, especially pp. 134–45. They argue persuasively that no hegemonic logic can account for the totality of "the social" and that the open and incomplete character of the social field is the precondition of every hegemonic practice. For if the field of hegemony were conceived according to a "zero-sum" vision of possible positions and practices, then the very concept of hegemony, as plural and mutable formations and relations, would be rendered impossible. Elsewhere, in "Hegemony and New Political Subjects," Mouffe goes even further to elaborate the practical dimensions of the hegemonic principle in terms of contemporary social movements.

13. Adamson reads *The Prison Notebooks* as the postulation of Gramsci's activist and educationalist politics; in chapter 6, he discusses Gramsci's two concepts of hegemony: hegemony as the consensual basis of an existing political system in civil society, as opposed to violent oppression or domination, and hegemony as a historical phase of bourgeois development in which class is understood not only economically but also in terms of a common intellectual and moral awareness, an overcoming of the "economic-corporative" phase. Adamson associates the former (hegemony in its contrast to domination) with "hegemony-maintenance," and the latter (hegemony as a stage in the political moment) as "hegemony-creation." Sassoon provides an excellent discussion of Gramsci's key concepts; she both historicizes the concept of hegemony and discusses the implications of some of the ways in which hegemony has been interpreted. Sassoon emphasizes the degree to which hegemony is opposed to domination to evoke the way in which one social group influences other groups, making certain compromises with them in order to gain their consent for its leadership in society as a whole.

14. Amilcar Cabral, the Cape Verdean African nationalist leader and theorist, echoes some fundamental observations made by Fanon: that the national bourgeoisie will collaborate with the colonizers and that tribal fundamentalism must be overcome or it will defeat any efforts at unity. In 1969, Cabral wrote ironically in "Party Principles and Political Practice" of the dangers of tribalism and nativism: "No one should think that he is more African than another, even than some white man who defends the interests of Africa, merely because he is today more adept at eating with his hand, rolling rice into a ball and putting it into his mouth" (57).

15. I am thinking here especially of de Lauretis; Spivak; and Minh-ha. The last explains the multiple inscription of women of color:

[M]any women of color feel obliged [to choose] between ethnicity and womanhood: how can they? You never have/are one without the other. The idea of two illusorily separated identities, one ethnic, the other woman (or more precisely female), partakes in the Euro-American system of dualistic reasoning and its age-old divide-and-conquer tactics. . . . The pitting of anti-racist and anti-sexist struggles against one another allows some vocal fighters to dismiss blatantly the existence of either racism or sexism within their lines of action, as if oppression only comes in separate, monolithic forms. (105)

16. For a more extensive analysis of generational conflict in Chu's novel, see Gong. Gong asserts that "The father/son relationship represents the most critical juncture in the erosion of a traditional Chinese value system and the emergence of a Chinese American character. Change from Chinese to Chinese American begins here" (74–75).

17. There are many scenes that resonate with my suggestion that generational conflicts cannot be isolated from either class or the historicity of gender. In the third section of the novel, it is class difference in addition to generational strife that founds the antagonism between mother and daughter: Ying-ying St. Clair cannot understand why Lena and her husband, Harold, have spent an enormous amount of money to live in a barn in the posh neighborhood of Woodside. Lena says: "My mother knows, underneath all the fancy details that cost so much, this house is still a barn" (151). In the early relationship between Suyuan Woo and her daughter, Jing-mei, the mother pushes her daughter to become a success, to perform on the piano; we can see that such desires are the reflection of the mother's former poverty, her lack of opportunity as both a poor refugee and a woman, but the daughter, trapped within a familial framework of explanation, sees her mother as punishing and invasive. Finally, the mother-and-daughter pair An-mei and Rose Hsu dramatize a conflict between the mother's belief that it is more honorable to keep personal problems within the Chinese family and the daughter's faith in western psychotherapy: the mother cannot understand why her daughter would pay a psychiatrist, a stranger, to talk about her divorce, instead of talking to her mother: the mother who was raised believing one must not show suffering to others because they, like magpies, would feed on your tears says of the daughter's psychiatrist, "really, he is just another bird drinking from your misery" (241).

REFERENCES

Adamson, Walter. *Hegemony and Revolution: A Study of Antonio Gramsci's Political and Cultural Theory.* Berkeley: University of California Press, 1980.

Cabral, Amilcar. *Unity and Struggle: Speeches and Writings of Amilcar Cabral.* Trans. Michael Wolfers. New York: Monthly Review, 1979.

Chan, Sucheng. *Asian Americans: An Interpretive History.* Boston: Twayne, 1991.

———. *This Bittersweet Soil: The Chinese in California Agriculture, 1860–1910.* Berkeley: University of California Press, 1986.

Chang, Diana. "The Oriental Contingent." In *The Forbidden Stitch,* edited by Shirley Geok-Lin Lim, Mayumi Tsutakawa, and Margarita Donnelly. Corvallis: Calyx, 1989. 171–177.

Chu, Louis. *Eat a Bowl of Tea.* Seattle: University of Washington Press, 1961.

Clifford, James. *The Predicament of Culture: Twentieth Century Ethnography, Literature, and Art.* Cambridge: Harvard University Press, 1988.

Daniels, Roger. *The Politics of Prejudice.* Berkeley: University of California Press, 1962.

Fanon, Frantz. *The Wretched of the Earth.* Trans. Constance Farrington. New York: Grove, 1961.

Fischer, Michael M. J. "Ethnicity and the Post-modern Arts of Memory." In *Writing Culture,* edited by James Clifford and George Marcus. Berkeley: University of California Press, 1986.

Fong, Timothy. "A Community Study of Monterey Park, California." Dissertation, University of California, Berkeley.

Glenn, Evelyn Nakano. "Occupational Ghettoization: Japanese-American Women and Domestic Service, 1905–1970." *Ethnicity* 8 (1981): 352–386.

Gong, Ted, "Approaching Cultural Change Through Literature: From Chinese to Chinese-American." *Amerasia* 7 (1980): 73–86.

Gramsci, Antonio. "History of the Subaltern Classes: Methodological Criteria." *Selections* 52–60.

———. *Selections from the Prison Notebooks.* Edited and translated by Quinton Hoare and Geoffrey Nowell Smith. New York: International, 1971.

Great, Wall, A.. Dir. Peter Wang. New Yorker Films, 1985.

JanMohamed, Abdul, and David Lloyd (eds.). *The Nature and Context of Minority Discourse.* New York: Oxford University Press, 1990.

Kim, Elaine. "'Such Opposite Creatures': Men and Women in Asian American Literature." *Michigan Quarterly Review* (1990): 68–93.

———. *Asian American Literature: An Introduction to the Writings and Their Social Context.* Philadelphia: Temple University Press, 1982.

Kingston, Maxine Hong. *The Woman Warrior.* New York: Random House, 1975.

Laclau, Ernesto, and Chantal Mouffe. *Hegemony and Socialist Strategy.* London: Verso, 1985.

Lauretis, Teresa de. *Technologies of Gender.* Bloomington: Indiana University Press, 1987.

Lowe, Lydia. "Quitting Time." *Ikon 9, Without Ceremony: A Special Issue by Asian Women United.* Special issue of *Ikon* 9 (1988): 29.

Minh-ha, Trinh T. *Woman, Native, Other: Writing Postcoloniality and Feminism.* Bloomington: Indiana University Press, 1989.

Mirikitani, Janice. "Breaking Tradition." *Without Ceremony.* 9.

Mouffe, Chantal. "Hegemony and New Political Subjects: Toward a New Concept of Democracy." In *Marxism and the Interpretation of Culture*, edited by Cary Nelson and Lawrence Grossberg. Urbana: University of Illinois, 1988. 89–104.

Sassoon, Anne Showstack. "Hegemony, War of Position and Political Intervention." *Approaches to Gramsci*, edited by Anne Showstack Sassoon. London: Writers and Readers, 1982.

Spivak, Gayatri. *In Other Worlds.* London: Routledge, 1987.

Takaki, Ronald. *Strangers from a Different Shore: A History of Asian Americans.* Boston: Little, Brown 1989.

Tan, Amy. *The Joy Luck Club.* New York: Putnam's, 1989.

Williams, Raymond. *Marxism and Literature.* Oxford: Oxford University Press, 1977.

Yanagisako, Sylvia. *Transforming the Past: Kinship and Tradition Among Japanese Americans.* Stanford: Stanford University Press, 1985.

1. What are the limitations of the Black-White paradigm outlined by Hune? What are the limitations of existing historical narratives that frame the experiences of Asian Americans from the standpoint of "victims"? What does Hune mean when she argues for emergent paradigms that treat power within the community as fluctuating and differential? How do these emergent paradigms attempt to rearticulate Asian American experiences, and how may they alter our perception of Asian American community dynamics? What theoretical concerns does Hune suggest are important to consider in theorizing about the Asian American experience? What are the limitations of these emergent paradigms?

2. What is Lisa Lowe's core argument in this article? What kinds of essentializing themes in Asian American culture does she try to subvert? How are the emergent themes in her discourse, which are framed in a post-1965 context, relevant to the historical experiences of pre–World War II immigrants to the United States from Asia?

3. What is Lowe's purpose is invoking the debate that emerged around Maxine Hong Kingston's *Woman Warrior*? To what extent is this argument cast about issues pertaining to "nationalisms" and "assimilation"? What, according to the author, is a more appropriate reading of this text? What are the implications of these lessons for the development of an Asian American identity?

SUGGESTED READINGS

Chang, Gordon. 1995. History and Postmodernism. *Amerasia Journal* 21(1–2): 89–93.

Chang, Jeff. 1994. Race, Class, Conflict and Empowerment: On Ice Cube's 'Black Korea.' Pp. 87–107 in Edward T. Change and Russell C. Leong (eds.), *Los Angeles: Struggles Toward Multiethnic Community*. Seattle: University of Washington Press.

Hirabayashi, Lane. 1995. Back to the Future: Reframing Community-Based Research. *Amerasia Journal* 21(1–2): 103–118.

Horton, John. 1995. *The Politics of Diversity: Immigration, Resistance, and Change in Monterey Park, California*. Philadelphia: Temple University Press.

Kim, Elaine H. 1995. Beyond Railroads and Internment: Comments on the Past, Present, and Future of Asian American Studies. Pp. 11–21 in Gary Y. Okihiro, Marilyn Alquizola, Dorothy Fujita-Rony, and K. Scott Wong (eds.), *Privileging Positions: The Sites of Asian American Studies*. Pullman: Washington State University Press.

Kondo, Dorinne. 1995. Poststructuralist Theory as Political Necessity. *Amerasia Journal* 21(1–2): 95–100.

Lowe, Lisa. 1996. *Immigrant Acts: On Asian Cultural Practices*. Durham: Duke University Press.

Omi, Michael, and Howard Winant. 1994. *Racial Formation in the United States: From the 1960s to the 1990s*. Second Edition. New York: Routledge.

Osajima, Keith. 1995. Postmodernism and Asian American Studies: A Critical Appropriation. Pp. 21–36 in Gary Okihiro et al. (eds.), *Privileging Positions: The Sites of Asian American Studies*. Pullman: Washington State University Press.

Palumbo-Liu, David. 1995. *The Ethnic Canon: Histories, Institutions and Interventions*. Minneapolis: University of Minnesota Press.

San Juan, E. 1998. *From Exile to Diaspora: Veterans of the Filipino Experience in the United States.* Boulder: Westview Press.

Spickard, Paul R., and Rowena Fong. 1995. Pacific Islander Americans and Multiethnicity: A Vision of America's Future. *Social Forces* 73(4): 1365–1383.

Wang, L. Ling-Chi. 1995. The Structure of Dual Domination: Toward a Paradigm for the Study of the Chinese Diaspora in the United States. *Amerasia Journal* 21(1–2): 149–169.

FILM

Tajima-Peña, Renee. 1998. *My America . . . or Honk If You Love Buddha* (87-minute documentary).

Contributors

Carl L. Bankston III is Assistant Professor of Sociology at Tulane University.

Lucie Cheng is Professor of Sociology at University of California, Los Angeles.

Colleen Fong is Associate Professor of Ethnic Studies at California State University, Hayward.

James V. Gatewood is a graduate student in Asian American Studies at University of California, Los Angeles.

Alice Y. Hom is a doctoral student in U.S. history at the Claremont Graduate School.

Shirley Hune is Professor of Urban Planning and Associate Dean for Graduate Programs in the Graduate Division at the University of California, Los Angeles.

Nazli Kibria is Assistant Professor of Sociology at Boston University.

Dorinne Kondo is Professor of Anthropology and American Studies and Ethnicity at the University of Southern California.

Jennifer Lee is a President's Postdoctoral Fellow at the University of California, Los Angeles.

John M. Liu is Associate Professor of Sociology and Asian American Studies at the University of California, Irvine.

Lisa Lowe is Professor of Comparative Literature at the University of California, San Diego.

Martin F. Manalansan IV teaches Asian American Studies at New York University.

Pyong Gap Min is Professor of Sociology at Queen College of the City University of New York.

Deborah N. Misir was a law student at University of Minnesota at the time she wrote this article.

Don T. Nakanishi is Professor of Education and Director of the Asian American Studies Center at the University of California, Los Angeles.

Regina Nordquist is a graduate student at the Wagner School of Public Service at New York University.

Gary Y. Okihiro is Professor of International and Public Affairs at Columbia University.

Glenn Omatsu is Associate Editor of *Amerasia Journal* at the University of California, Los Angeles.

Paul Ong is Professor of Urban Planning and Director of the Lewis Center for Regional Policy Studies at the University of California, Los Angeles.

Keith Osajima is Professor of Race and Ethnic Studies at the University of Redlands.

Lisa Park (pseudonym) is a mixed-heritage Asian American writer.

Rhacel Salazar Parreñas is Assistant Professor of Women's Studies and Asian American Studies at the University of Wisconsin, Madison.

Rubén G. Rumbaut is Professor of Sociology at Michigan State University.

Paul R. Spickard is Professor of History and Chair of Asian American Studies at the University of California, Santa Barbara.

Dana Y. Takagi is Associate Professor of Sociology at the University of California, Santa Cruz.

Ronald Takaki is Professor of Ethnic Studies at the University of California, Berkeley.

Yasuko I. Takezawa teaches at the Institute of Modern Language and Cultures, University of Tsukuba, Japan.

James A. Tyner is an Assistant Professor of Geography at Kent State University.

Karen Umemoto is Assistant Professor Urban and Regional Planning at the University of Hawai'i at Manoa.

L. Ling-chi Wang is Professor of Ethnic Studies at the University of California, Berkeley.

Raymond Brady Williams is LaFollette Distinguished Professor in the Humanities and Professor of Religion at Wabash College.

Philip Q. Yang is Associate Professor of Sociology and Social Work at Texas Woman's University.

Judy Yung is Associate Professor of American Studies at the University of California, Santa Cruz.

Min Zhou is Associate Professor of Sociology and Asian American Studies at the University of California, Los Angeles.

Permissions

Index

Abbott, M. R., 604
Abella, M., 207, 224
Abelmann, N., 292
Abrahamic religions: of Christianity, 392, 393, 398–399; of Islam, 392, 398, 404; of Judaism, 392, 393
Absentee owners, 279
Activism, 1, 95
Activist strategies, 636
Actors' Equity, 637, 638
Adamson, W., 695, 696
Adaptation, 472, 473, 474, 477
Admissions quotas, 483, 484, 486, 487, 489, 490, 491, 492, 493, 494, 495
Advocacy Group, 580
Aesthetics, 632
Affirmative action, 95, 97, 486, 659
African American: communities, South Central Los Angeles, 242; community, 107; ghetto, 236; movements, 50, 54, 62; neoconservatives, 96, 97; slavery, 303, 312
African Americans, 2, 37, 49, 83, 90, 91, 95, 100, 134, 142, 233, 236, 303, 312, 394, 400, 404, 615, 668; comparison to Asian Americans, 450
After-school programs, 383
Agarwal, V., 165, 174
Agbayani-Siewart, P., 295, 336, 350
Agnew, S., 89
Agostinelli, G., 224
Agresta, A., 182, 202
Agricultural Workers Organizing Committee (AFL-CIO), 105, 106
Aguayo, S., 177, 193, 206
Aguilar, D., 207, 215, 218, 224
Ahlstrom, G., 161, 170
AIDS, 556, 572, 578, 579, 580, 582, 630
Akimoto, B., 303
Alarcon, R., 44
Alba, R., 28, 43
Aldrich, H., 279, 294, 250n, 253
Alegado, D., 225
Alexander, Meena, 229, 627–629
Alexander the Great, 135–136
Almirol, E. B., 336, 350, 352
Almquist, E., 258, 275
Alquizola, M., 698
Amarles, B., 210, 220, 223, 224, 225

Amazon expansion, 137
Amerasian culture, 613
Amerasian Homecoming Act, 176, 180, 181
Amerasian League, 612
Amerasians, 609
American: autonomy, 647; birth, 684; creed, 132; dream, 244, 278, 577, 578, 579; exceptionalism, 671, 672; gay culture, 573; individualism, 383
American Catholicism, 374
American Federation of Labor (AFL), 157
American Federation of Teachers (AFT), 71
American Hospital Association (AHA), 166
American Indians, 83, 95
American Presbyterian missionaries, 378
American West, 145
Americanization, 394, 688
Americans for Immigration Control, 339
Amott, T., 209, 225
Anaheim-Santa Ana, Calif., 17
Ancheta, A. N., 543
Andall, J., 218, 222, 225
Anderson, B., 516n, 543, 572, 583
Anderson, K., 413, 428
Angel Island, Calif., 132
Angels in America, 659
Anglo-American culture, 562
Anglo-Saxon peoples, 144
Anti-Asian: legislation, 95, 150, 229; sentiment, 454; violence, 501–505, 630, 507–509, 511–515
Anti-Chinese movement, 157
Anti-immigrant sentiment, 339
Anti-imperialism, 54
Anti-miscegenation law, 589–590, 603
Anti-Oriental riot in Vancouver (1907), 393
Antislick ideal, 634
Antonovsky, A., 358, 370
Aoki, G., 653, 661
Arax, M., 481n
Archimbault, C., 361, 369
Archive research, 301, 312
Arcinas, F., 225
Areza, P. D., 342
Argiros, R., 191, 202
Aristotle, 135, 136
Armenians, 125
Arnold, F., 207, 225, 376, 377, 391

Arranged marriages, 402
Arrian, 135, 136
Art system, 632
Artistic: freedom, 638; intervention, 637
Asia Pacific entrepreneurship, 240, 242, 243, 244
Asian America, 551, 552, 553, 554, 680
Asian American: 549, 550, 551, 552, 554, 555, 556, 557, 558, 606, 684; activism, 80; admissions debate, 37, 483; aesthetics, 41, 627, 629, 631; art, 632; artists, 41, 630; cinema, 41, 633; communities, 93, 94, 100, 547, 548, 556, 562, 629, 683; consciousness, 80, 87; conservatism, 92; culture, 552, 634, 679, 680–681, 683, 685, 686, 688, 690, 692; discourse, 557, 687, 683, 684, 685, 686; empowerment, 87, 91, 94; enrollment, 37, 118; experience, 558, 554, 680; gay men, 576; gay politics, 577; gays and lesbians, 38–39, 556, 561; gays and lesbians, writings of, 556–558; history, 424, 547–548, 549, 551, 556; identity, 1, 42, 459, 556, 557, 681, 683, 684, 685, 688, 692; labor market, 471; literature, 6, 41; masculinity, 686; men, 552, 686; narrative, 690; nationalism, 686; neo-conservatives, 94, 95, 96, 100, 107; parents, 561, 566, 567, 568, 569; political activists, 576; population, 99; population, bifurcation in, 480; representation, 41; responses to multicultural Asians, 613; roles, 639; second generation, 33–34; stereotype, 106; student enrollment, 3, 4; subculture, 547; subject, 685, 687; success, 449, 455, 464, 467; theater, 41; values, 98; voting bloc, 37; women, 35, 472, 550, 552, 553; women's history, 413–414; work ethic, 453; young professionals, 94
Asian American Movement, 1, 2, 5, 23, 24, 30–31, 42, 80, 81, 93, 105, 108, 402
Asian American Political Alliance (AAPA), 60–62, 65, 67, 70, 71
Asian American Studies, 1, 3, 4, 6, 8, 35, 41, 42, 80, 547, 548, 553, 554, 606, 667, 671–672, 673, 674; at UCLA, 80
Asian Americans, 49, 302, 303, 307, 310, 312, 315; diversity of, 452; national origins of, 15; public perception of, 450; proportion of foreign-born, 13; voting behavior of, 488
Asian culture, 106
Asian cultures, original, 680
Asian exclusion acts, 9, 31. *See also* Chinese Exclusion Act of 1882
Asian immigrant entrepreneurs, 476
Asian Immigrant Women Advocates (AIWA), 101–103
Asian immigration, 8–20, 31, 32, 88, 473, 629, 680, 155, 159
Asian Indian Americans, 462, 465, 467, 469, 474
Asian Indians, 119, 120, 128, 501–515
Asian newly industrialized countries (NICs), 169
Asian origin community, 683
Asian Pacific Alliance for Creative Equality (APACE), 656, 657
Asian Pacific American Coalition U.S.A., 481
Asian Pacific Americans, 233, 234

Asian Pacific Student Alliance, 627
Asian Pacifica Sisters in San Francisco, 561
Asian Studies, 671, 672
Asian Women United of California, 426, 428
Asian-origin population, diversity of, 175
Asia-Pacific Triangle, the, 9, 126, 135, 158, 159
Asiatic Barred Zone, 393
Assimilation, 6, 21, 24, 29, 40, 301, 318, 325, 332, 374, 439, 451, 506, 536, 552, 562, 680, 683, 684–685, 686, 687, 688, 690, 692; the problem of, 27–29
Association of Lesbians and Gay Asian (ALBA), 548
Australia, 158
Authenticity, 554, 556, 557, 558
Autonomy, 418, 421
Aven, R., 76
Avila, E., 349, 350
Awasthi, S., 170
Azarcon-dela Cruz, P., 225
Azores, T., 230, 337, 351

Bach, R. L., 189, 191, 202, 249n, 252, 256, 276
Bachelor's societies, 317, 416
Baci ceremony, 362, 367, 368
Baker, L., 170
Baker, R. P., 183, 202
Bakersfield, Calif., 106
Bakla tradition, 573, 574, 575, 582
Ballescas, M. P., 221, 223, 225
Bangladesh, 210, 394; immigrants from, 394, 398, 402, 405
Bankston, C. L. III, 34, 46, 261, 277, 296, 352, 357–358, 362, 364, 369–371, 420, 430, 701
Barlow, W., 76
Barnett, L. D., 603
Barnhardt, J. L., 583
Barrett, J. M., 415, 428
Barringer, H., 13, 43, 467, 468, 469, 481
Bar-Yosef, R. W., 363, 370
Basch, L., 337–340, 350
Baskir, L. M., 177, 202
Bates, T., 292
Batholdi, F. A., 133
Battistella, G., 207, 223, 224, 225
Batung, M., 347–348
Bautista, P., 585
Bean, F., 169, 170
Becker, E., 202
Becker, G., 255, 275
Beeghley, L., 259, 277
Bell, D. A., 331, 334, 456n, 457n
Bellah, R. N., 358, 370
Bender, E. I., 283, 293
Bengali, 402
Bennett, M. T., 158, 159, 161, 170
Bensinger, T., 583
Benson, J., 192, 202, 422, 428
Beresford, M., 434, 442
Berger, P. L., 358, 368, 370

Berges, P. M., 664
Bernard, J., 256, 275
Berthoff, R., 123, 130
Bertolucci, B., 553
Berzon, B., 583
Betancur, J., 250
Bhaba, H., 645
Bhagwati, J., 171
Bicultural: adjustment, 328; biculturalism, 630; con-
  flicts, 328–329
Binder, F., 148n
Biologically based abilities, 209
Biracialism, 611
Bisaya, 576
Black(s), 301, 303; nationalists, 279; neighborhoods,
  N.Y. City, 279, 284; neighborhoods, Philadelphia,
  279
Black Panther Party, 60, 62, 68, 87
Black Power, 60, 450
Black Student Union (BSU), 55, 62, 64, 65, 66–67, 70,
  72, 73, 77
Black Studies, 64, 74
Black-Asian conflict, 99
Black-Jewish relationships, 288–291
Black-Korean tension, 33, 279, 286, 290
Black-White dichotomy, 42
Blakely, E., 235, 250
Blauner, R., 130
Bluestone, B., 164, 171, 235, 251
Boat people, 11, 32, 176
Bodhisattva, 361
Bodin, A., 165, 171
Bogardus, E., 590, 604
Bombay, India, 399
Bonacich, E., 101, 124, 243, 244, 249n, 250, 255, 256,
  258, 275, 278, 280, 281, 285, 292, 295, 476, 482, 675
Borjas, G., 259, 275
Borsellino, R., 517n
Bottomley, G., 583
Bourgeois: assimilation, 684, 686; construction of na-
  tion, 685; nationalism, 684, 685, 686
Bouvier, L. F., 155, 171, 182, 202
Bowlby, S., 225
Bowles, S., 456n
Bozorgmehr, M., 481n
Brain drain, 166, 474
Breines, W., 82, 83
Brettel, C. B., 208, 228
Briggs, V., 171
Bronx High School of Science, N.Y., 332
Brooklyn, N.Y., 317, 320, 324, 333
Brown, L., 618
Brown, R., 204
Brown University, 483, 490, 494
Brown, W., 560
Brown, T., 96
Buchanan, P., 96, 606, 617
Buckley, W., 96

Buddhism, 362, 392, 408; "folk," 361, 368; Mahayana,
  361
Buddhist: monks, 361; temples, 408
Buenaventura, S. S., 409, 559
Buffon, G., 142
Bui doi, 176
Bulatao, R., 225
Bulosan, C., 5, 128, 229, 296, 628
Burma, 425; Buddhism in, 361
Burma, J., 603, 604
Burstein, P., 158, 171
Bush, G., 299
Busto, R., 602
Butler, J., 559
Butterfield, F., 457n
Buzz Off, Butterfly, 645–646

Cabezas, A., 457n
Cabral, A., 54, 87, 695, 696
Calavita, K., 156, 171
California, 99, 102, 574, 575, 681, 682, 683, 691–692;
  gold rush, 120; junior college systems, 53
California Civil Rights Initiative (Proposition 209),
  668
California Master Plan, 53, 63
California State University, 53
Cambodia, 11, 17, 32; Buddhism in, 361
Cambodian Americans, 14, 16, 18, 29, 422, 463, 478
Cambodian community, Long Beach, Calif., 184, 238
Campaign finance scandal, 38, 518–527
Campbell, M. B., 135, 136, 147n, 259, 276
Canada, 8, 393, 397, 406
Canda, E. R., 409
Cape Horn, South America, 143
Capitalism, 256, 460, 477, 691
Caplan, N., 192, 200, 202
Caplovitz, D., 290, 292
Caribbean, the, 338
Carmichael, S., 69, 456n
Carradine, D., 638
Carroll-Seguin, R., 189, 202
Castells, H., 251
Castells, M., 256, 275
Catholic: churches, 379, 380; fraternity organizations,
  375; immigrant groups, 374
Catholicism, 369; Syro-Malabar, 395. *See also* Mis-
  sionaries, Roman Catholic
Catholics, 374, 377
Caucasian, 126
Cauce, A. M., 619
CCBA. *See* Chinese Consolidated Benevolent Associ-
  ation
Center on Budget and Policy, 90
Cerritos, City of (Calif.), 246, 247
Cha, P., 409
Chafetz, J., 441, 442
Chai, A., 418, 420, 424, 428
Chai, L., 603, 604

Chan, C. S., 562, 570, 583
Chan, D., 592
Chan, K. S., 676
Chan, S., 11, 12, 21, 43, 150, 151, 419, 428, 559, 693, 696
Chan, Y., 532n
Chanda, N., 202
Chang, D., 679, 696
Chang, E. T., 674
Chang, G., 150, 698
Chang, J., 698
Chang, K. S., 296
Change, E. T., 698
Chant, S., 208, 221, 225
Chao, C., 352
Chao Pa guerrilla resistance (Laos), 179
Chatterjee, G., 627
Chau, F., 641
Chavez, C., 106
Chavez, L., 191, 205, 337, 339, 350
Chen, H., 675
Cheng, C. K., 603, 604
Cheng, L., 11, 23, 36, 37, 44, 45, 460, 474, 481, 482, 497, 675, 701
Cheung, K. K., 584
Chicago, 17, 375, 398; Southside, 236
Chicano, 49, 143
Chicanos/Latinos, 90, 95
Chien, W., 352
Chiengkul, W., 225
Child-care, 257, 268
Child-rearing, 419, 436–438
Children of inmates, 299, 302
Chin, F., 552, 584, 634, 686
Chin, V., 28, 454, 488
China, 9, 10, 92, 415, 526, 553, 687–688, 689, 690, 691; Buddhism in, 361; immigrants from, 175, 315, 317
China's "Open Door," 144, 145
Chinatown, 17, 36, 55, 56, 57, 58, 59, 86, 87, 92, 315, 316, 680; after-school programs, 320, 322; crisis-oriented programs, 322; economic structure of, 318; ethnic economy of, 318; Equal Opportunity Council, 58; Free University for Chinatown Kids, 57; garment industry, 318; kinship network, 316; laundry business, 318; religious institutions, 321; satellite, 317, 319; social capital, 315, 316; transformation of, 319; voluntary associations, 319; women, 33; youth gangs, 319
Chinatown Chinese American Planning Council (CPC), 320, 331
Chinatown History Museum, 321, 331, 334
Chinatown, Los Angeles, 237, 238, 239, 477
Chinatown, N.Y. City, 118, 234, 254, 259, 261, 262, 269, 270, 271, 272, 315–333, 687; high school dropouts, 331; language school, 320; satellite, 317
Chinatown, San Francisco, 117, 234, 237, 238, 239, 240, 241, 425, 687; Hwa Ching youth, 57; Six Companies, 55, 56, 57, 58
Chinatown Today Publishing, 319, 320, 334

Chinese, 119, 120, 121, 122, 125, 128; from Cambodia, 82, 183; cultural values, 143, 266, 325–327, 679; gangs, 118; language classes, 320; laundries, 242; from Vietnam, 179, 182, 183; women workers, 678
Chinese American families, 32–333; adjustment problems, 327; cultural identities, 325; distinctive characteristics, 325–327; parent-child relationship, 326, 327, 329, 332, 334
Chinese American Planning Council, 320–322, 327, 331, 334; branch offices, 320; youth-targeted programs, 320
Chinese American Studies, 56
Chinese American women, 424
Chinese Americans, 10, 13, 14, 18, 25, 40, 94, 99, 301, 304, 307, 315, 419, 425, 426, 449, 451, 459, 460, 462–465, 467, 468, 471, 474–476, 479, 614, 678, 679, 680, 687; educational achievement, 315; fastest-growing minority groups, 315; in New York City, 315; San Francisco, 237, 238; socioeconomic background, 317, 324; younger-generation, 315, 327–333
Chinese children, 330–333; English language deficiency, 330, 331, 334; gang subculture, 330; search for identity, 330, 334; views, 330
Chinese Christian Herald Crusade (N.Y.), 321, 331, 333
Chinese Consolidated Benevolent Association (CCBA), 319–321, 331
Chinese Exclusion Act of 1882, 9, 14, 22, 125, 132, 146n, 156, 317, 417, 681
Chinese immigrants, 315, 317; garment workers, 84; women, 318, 324
Chinese Progressive Association (CPA), 101–105
"Chineseness," 679
Chinese-owned garment factories, 261, 262
Ching, M., 102
Cho, M., 352
Chouy, L. S., 662
Chow, E., 444
Chow, H., 445
Chow, R., 553, 559
Choy, B. Y., 372, 390
Choy, C., 445, 543, 585
Choy, K., 641, 645, 646, 660
Choy, M. H., 192, 200, 202
Christian imperialism, 139
Christianity, 369, 392, 395, 398; Orthodox, 395
Chu, L., 5, 679, 695, 696
Chung, C., 570
Chung, P., 662
Chuong, C. H., 619, 620
Church functions: fellowship, 373–374, 381–382; maintenance of tradition, 374, 382–384; social services, 374–375, 384–387; social status, 375, 387–389
Cimmarusti, R. A., 352
Civil rights, 51, 53, 83, 96, 107, 392, 460
Civil Rights Act of 1964, 158
Civil Rights Movement, 2, 9, 155, 450

Civil War, 156
Claremont Colleges, 41, 655, 660
Clark, M., 610
Class, 417, 460, 501–502, 506, 511–512, 522–523, 572, 574, 575, 576, 591, 668, 669–670, 671–673, 678, 679, 680, 681, 683, 684, 685, 687, 689, 690; differences, between merchants and customers, 287; resources, 281
Class war, one-sided, 89, 90
Cleveland, G., 133
Client Referral Assistance (CRA), 222
Clifford, J., 693, 696
Clines, F. X., 530n
Clinton administration, 525
Clinton, W., 177, 518–519, 521
Coachella vineyards (Calif.), 106
Coalition of the International Majority/National Minority, 655, 656
Coalition-building, 640, 657
Cohen, A., 300, 313
Cohen, E., 559
Cohen, S., 377, 390
Cold War, 53, 177, 180, 522, 526; paradigm, 671, 673
Coleman, J., 282, 292, 316, 334
Collective action, 572, 576, 581, 582
College admission, 50, 53
College of San Mateo, 69
Collier, J., 431, 442
Collins, S., 82, 83
Colonialism, 684, 685, 687
Colonization, 140, 141, 142, 150
Columbia University, 378
Columbus, 138, 139
Coming out, 551, 552, 553, 554, 561, 562, 563, 566, 567, 568, 569, 573, 576
Commission on Wartime Relocation and Internment of Civilians, 305
Communist subversion, 523
Communities, Asian Pacific American, 668–670, 673–674
Community: -based organization, 315, 318–319, 322–323, 333, 352; building, 87; imagined, 572
Community Involvement Program, 52
Compadrazgo kin system, 341
Comparison of immigrants vs. U.S.-born workers, 260, 263–265
Comprehensive Training and Employment Act (CETA), 364
Concentration effects, 236
Concerned Chinese for Action and Change, 56
Conflict mediation, 244
Confucianism, 380; Confucius values, 325
Congress for Industrial Organization (CIO), 157
Connery, S., 652, 663
Conquergood, D., 192, 202
Conze, E., 361
Coolidge, M., 157, 171
Cooney, R., 258, 275

Cooper, A. J., 134
Cooper, E., 67
Cooper, N., 620
Cooperstein, R. A., 184, 203, 432, 442
Cordes, C., 607, 608
Cordova, F., 150, 419, 424, 425, 428
Cordova, T., 236, 250
Core cultural group, 28
Corporate offensive, 89, 91, 93
Council of Korean Churches in Greater New York, 375, 390
Counterculture, 51
Counterhegemonic, 50; strategies, 636
Countries of first asylum, 179
Crafting Selves (Kondo), 654
Crenshaw, K. W., 676
Crichton, M., 646, 648, 652, 654, 660, 663
Cross-dressing, 573, 574, 580, 582
Cruz, P. V., 105–109
Cruz, V., 207, 225
CSUH Affirmative Action Faculty Development Program, 602
Cuban women in Miami, 257
Cultural: analysis, 358; anthropology, 300; broker, 290; essentialism, 651; heritage, 25; organizations, 395; orientations in ethnic communities, 316; politics, 658, 681; production, 642, 659; revolution, 85, 86, 87; space, 690, 691; symbols, 359; tradition, 358; unity, 631; workers, 86
Culture, 451, 592–593, 679, 680
Curry, J., 337, 350
Curthoys, A., 209, 225

Daniels, R., 5, 131, 150, 229, 559, 693, 696
Danis, K., 517n
David, R., 214, 226
Davis, C., 129
Davis, D., 148n
Day of Rememberance (1978), 304, 305, 310
de Crevecoeur, J. H., 21, 43, 133
de Dios, A., 207, 214, 216, 220, 221, 223, 224, 226
de Guzman, A., 207, 223, 226
de Lauretis, T., 558, 695, 697
De Vos, G., 300, 311, 313
Dearman, M., 372, 376, 390
Decolonization, 157, 628
Defoe, D., 141
Deinard, A. S., 192, 203
Delgado, R., 676
Democratic fever, 90
Democratic National Committee, 518, 520, 522
Democratic Party, 94, 488
Denationalization, 7
Denton, N., 19, 45, 251, 516n
Desai, V., 627
Desbarats, J., 202
Despres, L., 300, 313
Devasahayam, T., 210, 220, 223, 228

di Leonardo, M., 431, 442
Dia, M., 685
Diaspora, 582, 678; diasporic experiences, 6, 7
Diaz, G., 342
Diaz, V., 344–347
Dillon, R. H.319
Dim Sum (film), 680
Ding, L., 151, 445, 498, 663
Dirlik, A., 230
Discrimination, 303, 307, 309, 455, 459, 472, 473, 518–525, 538, 638. *See also* Racism
Displaced Persons Act of 1948, 161
Diversity, 473, 558; population, 15–19
Divorce, 416, 421, 423, 436
Doeringer, P., 249n, 250
Dohrenwend, B. P., 196, 204
Dole, B., 519, 521
Domestic: economy, 436–440; obligations, 422; violence, 416, 423, 426, 435, 439; work, 419
Dominican Republic, the, 210
Dong, A., 151
Dong, B., 533n
Donnelly, N. D., 422, 428, 444
Dotbusters, 501–506
Dou, T., 258, 275
Double consciousness, 607
Double disadvantage, 258
Douglass, F., 87
Dower, J., 661
Downing, B. T., 192, 203
Downward mobility, 258, 474; and Korean immigrants, 387, 389
Drinnon, R., 144, 148n, 149n
Du, P. L., 543
Du, S. J., 245
Duarte, I., 226
DuBois, W. E. B., 87, 606, 607, 617; *The Philadelphia Negro*, 373–374, 390n
Duffy, B., 530n
Duffy, L. K., 619
Dumke, G. S., 64, 68, 70, 77
Dunning, B. B., 202
Durand, J., 44
Durkheim, E., 316, 334, 358, 370; theory of social integration, 316, 358, 361–363
Durkheimian. *See* Durkheim, E., theory of social integration
Dworkin, A., 441, 442
Dylan, B., 599

East African, 406
Easterly, D. P., 607, 617
Eat a Bowl of Tea (Chu), 679, 687, 688
Eaton, E. M., 611
Eck, D., 395
Economic: niche, 93; refugees, 221; restructuring, 164, 235, 256, 262; stability, 259; transformation, 235
Edmonston, B., 14, 45

Education, 450, 452, 465, 474, 483, 484; educational achievement, 36
Educational Council for Foreign Medical Graduates, 166
Edwards, H., 76
Edwards, R., 249n, 251
Eelens, F., 211, 226
Effeminacy, 573
Ehrenreich, B., 256, 275, 441, 442
El Centro, Calif., 117
Eldridge, K. T., 618
Elkhanialy, H., 515n
Ellis Island, N.Y., 132, 146n
Ellison, C. G., 358, 370
Ellison, E. K., 283, 292
Ellsworth, E., 549, 558
Elmhurst, N.Y., 380
Emergent paradigms, 667, 669, 670
Emigrant train, 143
Empirical sociology, 358
Employer-sponsored: immigrants, 323; migrants, 10, 11, 12
Empowerment, 81, 87, 105, 106, 108, 415, 419, 523, 573
Enclave economy, 240, 254, 261
Endo, M. J., 95
Endo, R., 6, 43, 603, 675, 676
Eng, D., 584
Engel, M. H., 374, 391
England, P., 255, 258, 275
Enlightenment deism, 393
Entitlement Program, 299, 312
Entrepreneurship, 460
Epstein, J. E., 558
Equal Employment Opportunity Programs (EEO), 476
Espiritu, Y. L., 26, 27, 44, 337, 350, 352, 414, 415, 419, 420, 428, 444, 460, 482, 497, 583, 616, 675
Essentialism, 690
Ethnic: antagonism, 124; caucuses, 520–521; consciousness movement, 1, 5; culture, 685; economy, 241, 254, 261, 460; enclave, 25, 26; identity, construction of, 460; niches, in occupation, 475; resources, 281; separatism, 685; solidarity, 241, 244
Ethnic churches, 372–390; fellowship, 373–374; maintaining cultural tradition, 373, 374; providing social status/positions, 373, 375; social services, 373, 374–375; structure of, 372
Ethnic communities, 307, 308, 316, 414, 423, 424, 425, 427, 567, 568, 670, 680
Ethnic Studies, 667
Ethnicity, 406, 628, 680, 683, 684, 686; emergent, 21, 24; instrumental, 26; Pan-, 26–27; symbolic, 26
Eugenics, 608
Eurasians, 639
Euro-American aesthetics, 631
Euro-American neighborhoods, 20
Eurocentrism, 631; Eurocentric model, 105, 120
Europe, 89

European: immigrants, 120, 124, 125, 127; invention, 135; migration, 123

Europe's Other, 136, 140

Evans, L., 45, 482

Evers, M., 51

Eviota, E., 211, 215, 226

Executive Order 8802, 157

Executive Order 9066, 22, 126, 299, 305, 310, 314

Exhibition Planning Student Committee, 321

Exoticization, 686

Experimental college, 52, 54, 64

Exploitation of women, 207

Extended family, 342, 343

Extraterritoriality, 525–527

Faderman, L., 296

Fadiman, A., 409

Families: behavioral standards, 323, 325–328; roles of women, 324–325

Family, 315, 320, 323, 414, 416, 419, 420, 423, 427, 437–438, 452, 567, 569, 579; businesses, 420; chain migration, 323; cohesion, 95, 106; reunification, 323; strategy, 259; ties, 402; values, 106, 323, 325–328

Family-sponsored migrants, 10, 12

Fanon, F., 54, 60, 87, 628, 684, 685, 687, 696

Far, S. S., 611, 618

Farkas, G., 258, 275

Father-son relationship, 687

Fawcett, J., 208, 226, 376, 377, 391

Feagin, J., 339, 350

Federal Licensure Examination, 166

Female migration, 221–223

Femininity, 677, 679, 688

Feminism, 416, 548, 557, 595, 683, 684

Feminist: discourse, 655; theory, 685; feminists, 558, 686

Feminization, 552

Fenton, J. Y., 374, 390, 409

Ferguson, J., 8, 44

Fernandez-Kelly, M. P., 256, 257, 258, 276, 316, 334

Ferree, M. M., 257, 258, 276

Fertility, 176

Fictive kinship, 336, 337

Fiedler, L., 148n

Filial piety, 418, 453

Filipina: domestic workers, 336, 339, 341; entertainers, 213, 218, 219, 220, 222, 223; maids, 218, 219, 220; overseas contract workers to Europe, 214; provincial girls, 218, 219; women, 336

Filipina Americans, 424

Filipino: cultural tradition, 39; family values, 336, 341; gay community, 572, 573, 580, 581, 582; gay identity, 572, 580, 581; gay men/community, 572, 582, 583; household, viewed as egalitarian, 215; immigrants, 10, 32, 33, 336–349; male overseas contract workers, 215; migrants, 337, 348; swardspeak, 574, 575, 576, 578; women, 32

Filipino Americans, 13, 14, 18, 25, 29, 40, 301, 419, 451,

459, 460, 462, 463, 465, 467, 469, 471, 472, 474, 475, 613

Filipino transitional family, 336–349; background, 337–338; broken homes, 341; cultural factors, 336, 340–343; formation, 336–337, 340–341; reproduction, 336, 340–341; responsibilities, 337; segregation, 340; structural factors, 336, 338–340

Filipinos, 119, 120, 122, 125, 128, 145

Fillmore Tutorial, 52, 54

Fink, P., 165, 171

Finn, M., 163, 171

Finnan, C. R., 184, 203, 432, 442

Fire Island, N.Y., 572

First World, 392

First-generation, 511–512

Fischer, M. J., 693, 696

Fitzgerald, F. S., 124, 128

Flatbush, N.Y., 279

Floro, M. S., 211, 215, 226

Flushing, N.Y., 118, 237, 317, 320, 333, 380

Fong, C., 40, 589, 622, 701

Fong, L., 593

Fong, T. P., 43, 230, 675, 693, 696

Fong, Wayne, 600, 604

Fong, Winston, 597

Fong-Torres, B., 600, 604

Forbes, D., 434, 443

Forbes, S. S., 183, 184, 191, 203

Foreign medical graduates (FMGs), 164, 166

Foreigners, 20, 22, 23, 28, 38

Form, W. H., 276

Foucault, M., 502, 559

Four prisons, 80

Fowler, D., 603

Fowler, G., 618

Frame of reference, 259

Franklin, B., 126

Fraser, R., 82, 83

Frazier, E. F., 375, 390

Free University for Chinatown Kids, Unincorporated, San Francisco, 57

Freedom Rides of 1962, 51

Freeman, J. M., 192, 203

Freer, R., 250n, 250

Freire, P., 87

Fresno, Calif., 18

Friday, C., 150

Friendship networks, 381–382

Frobisher, M., 138

Frost, R., 628

Fu Manchu, 644

Fuentes, A., 256, 275

Fugita, S. S., 675

Fujimoto, M., 594

Fujino, D. C., 622

Fujita, D. C., 622

Fukiai, J., 304

Fulbeck, K., 622

Fung, R., 584, 663
Furutani, W., 92
Fuss, D., 552, 559, 584

Gabaccia, D., 414, 417, 426, 428
Ganatra, N., 585
Gangs, Chinese, 118
Gans, H., 26, 28, 43, 288, 291, 292n, 293
Garcia, A. M., 256, 257, 258, 276
Gardner, R. W., 26, 43, 155, 171, 376, 391, 457n, 481
Garment industry, 88, 102, 103, 255, 256, 261, 264, 267, 272; Chinese-owned factories, 261, 262
Garment Workers' Justice Campaign, 103
Gatewood, J. V., 701
Gay: bashing, 563, 564; community, mainstream, 574; culture, hypermasculine, 573; gays and lesbians, 426, 645; icons, 582; identity, 550, 551, 552, 556, 557, 563; movements, 557; sexuality, 554
Gay America, 551
Gay and Lesbian Studies, 6
Gay Asian organizations, 547
Gay Asian Pacific Alliance Community HIV Project (San Francisco), 561
Gay Asian Pacific Islander Men of New York (GAPIMNY), 577
Gay, D. A., 358, 370
Gay Pride Day, 572
Gee, D., 664
Gee, E., 418, 428
Geertz, C., 300, 313, 358, 370
Gehrig, L., 166, 171
Gelder, V., 559
Gender, 415, 425, 552, 563, 564, 579, 670, 672, 673, 679, 681, 683, 684, 685, 687, 689, 690, 691; constructions of, 413, 425; division of labor, 209, 215, 216; oppression, 550; relations, 423, 425, 431–434, 589; roles, 215, 413, 414, 420, 436–437, 630; subordination, 209
Gender Studies, 6
Gendered migration, 207, 229; from the Philippines, 207–223
Gender-neutral terms in Tagalog, 215
Gender-role reversal, 564
Generational: conflict, 630, 687, 688–690; differences, 24–26, 678, 679, 680, 683, 691; status, Asian immigrants, 630
Gentleman's Agreement of 1907, 156
German immigrants, 261
Geschwender, J., 276
Ghosh, B. N., 171
Gibney, M., 177, 203
Gibson, M. A., 296
Giddings, P., 146n
Gillette, R., 171
Gin, W., 593, 598
Gintis, H., 456n
Gitlin, T., 82, 458n
Gittlesohn, J., 171
Givens, H., 250

Glass ceiling, 97, 461, 475
Glass, T. A., 358, 370
Glazer, N., 28, 44
Glenn, E. N., 216, 217, 224, 226, 296, 338, 350, 352, 417, 421, 422, 428, 675, 696
Global: capitalism, 338–341, 343, 671, 672; cities, 339; economy, 92; forces, 155; labor market, 340; political economy, 460
Globalization, 10, 234, 235, 256. *See also* Global, capitalism
Gluck, J., 600
Gock, T., 583
"Gold Mountain," 120, 134
Gold, S. J., 192, 203, 432, 442
Goldberg, D., 515n
Goldsmith, W., 235, 250
Gong, S., 663
Gong, T., 695, 696
Gonzalez, H., 44
Goodman, L. W., 173
Gordon, A., 585
Gordon, D., 249n, 251
Gordon, L. W., 189, 203
Gordon, M., 28, 44, 590, 604
Gosei generation, 352
Gosha, J. D., 230
Gospel churches, 379
Government reception centers, 183
Gramsci, A., 641, 682, 683, 694, 695, 696
Grassroots organizing, 93, 99, 100, 101, 103, 105
Great Depression, 393
Great Khan, 138
Great Wall, A (film), 690
Greeley, A., 374, 390
Green, J., 215, 226
Greenberg, D., 559
Greenwood, L., 129
Griffin, C. W., 562, 570
Guangdong, China, 122
Guest, P., 226
Guest workers, 338
Guevara, C., 54, 87
Gujarat, India, 399; Gujarati, 399, 402
Gulick, S. L., 609, 618
Gupta, A., 8, 44
Guthrie, P., 602

Haddad, Y. Y., 358, 370
Haines, D. W., 192, 203, 432, 442
Haiti, 337
Hajj pilgrimage, 398
Hall, C. C. I., 615, 619, 620, 621
Hall, J., 144
Hall, S., 549
Halley, W., 676
Halpern, J. M., 361, 370
Hamamoto, D., 664
Hamilton, C. V., 456n, 616

Handlin, O., 120
Haney-Lopez, I., 44
Hansen, A. A., 559, 676
Hapa identity, 607
Haraway, D., 548, 558, 560
Harding, V., 91
Haring, M. J., 358, 371
Harkess, S., 255, 276
Harlem, N.Y., 236, 284
Harlins, Latasha, the fatal shooting of, 245, 279, 286
Harper, E., 171
Harrison, B., 164, 171, 235, 251
Hart, D., 583
Hart, H., 138, 583
Hart-Cellar Act of 1965, 9, 10, 12, 32, 119, 155, 159, 162, 165, 415, 451. *See also* Immigration and Nationality Act of 1965
Harvard University, 484, 485, 490, 491, 493, 495
Hashimoto, K., 302, 308
Hatanaka, H., 603, 604
Haub, C., 129
Hawaii, 40, 99, 562–563, 565, 566, 567, 614; Oahu, 117
Hay, J., 144, 145
Hayakawa, S. I., 61, 70, 71, 72
Hayama, D., 307, 308
Hayashi, B., 409
Hayashi, D., 302, 306, 430
Hayden, T., 82
Health care, 426
Health Professional Educational Assistance Act of 1976, 165
Hebrew, 374
Hee, S., 245, 252, 279, 293, 464, 471, 482
Hegemony, 413, 456, 636, 658, 682
Hein, J., 177, 203
Hemphill, E. A., 620
Hendricks, G. L., 192, 203
Hendry, J. B., 433, 442
Hernton, C., 618
Herrnstein, R. J., 674
Hess, G., 150, 177, 203
Heston, C., 638
Heterogeneity, 557, 670, 671, 677, 680, 681, 683, 684, 687, 688, 689, 692
Heterosexuality, discourse of, 555
Hickey, G. C., 433, 442
Higa, K., 664
High-skill occupations, 468, 469
High Technology Recruitment Index, 164
Higham, J., 124, 130, 146n
Hill, K., 159, 172
Hiller, D., 259, 276
Hinduism, 392, 395–396, 400–406, 408; Hindu temples, 395–396
Hing, A., 76
Hing, B. O., 230, 497
Hippocrates, 134, 136, 139
Hirabayashi, L. R., 6, 7, 44, 698

Hirokawa, D., 603
Hirschman, C., 464, 467, 482, 497
Hispanic population, 119
Historical memory, 535
Hmong(s), 11, 14, 16, 18, 29, 32, 178; American, 422; community in Fresno, 184
Hoare, Q., 696
Hoff, J., 517n
Holley, D., 249n, 251
Holocaust, the, 312
Hom, A., 39, 556, 584, 701
Hom, M. K., 129
Homeland, the, 680
Homelessness, 107
Homoerotic, 549
Homophobia, 553, 564, 566, 569, 574, 576
Homosexual: identities, 549, 552; tradition, 573, 574
Homosexuality, 554, 561, 564, 572, 576
Hondagneu-Sotelo, P., 337, 349, 350, 417, 428
Hong Kong, 11, 210, 211; Chinese immigrants from, 315, 317
Hong, P., 44
Honolulu, 17, 462
Hook, J. N., 124
Hooper, B., 413, 429
Hoover, D. W., 141, 148n
Hope, T. L., 352
Horton, J., 698
Hosokawa, B., 551
Hossfield, K., 216, 226
Hotel Employees and Restaurant Employees (HERE), 104
Hourglass economy, 20
House Un-American Activities Committee (HUAC), 51
Household: responsibilities, 257; as safe space for women, 423
Houston, 17
Houston, V. H., 638, 664
Houstoun, M. F., 415, 428
Howard, K., 192, 203
Huang, J., 38, 518, 521, 523–524, 527–529
Huber, J., 255, 276
Hu-Dehart, E., 675
Huguet, J. W., 226
Human capital, 259
Human rights, 101
Humphrey, M., 218, 26
Hune, S., 7, 35, 41, 413, 428, 444, 559, 674, 675, 676, 701
Hunger of Memory (Rodriguez), 606
Hunter College High School, N.Y., 332
Hunter College, N.Y., 41
Huntington, S., 90
Hurh, W. M., 293, 358, 370, 372, 377, 381, 382, 387, 388, 389, 390, 409, 444, 457n, 497
Hurley, R., 559
Hutchinson, E. P., 161, 171
Huynh, C., 421, 428

Hwa Ching youth. *See* Chinatown, San Francisco
Hwang, D. H., 129, 642, 662
Hwang, J., 622
Hybridity, 677, 681, 683, 686, 692
Hyperagamy, 40, 590–591, 601

Iberia Parish, La., 364, 367
Ichioka, Y., 150, 418, 428
Idealism, 51, 113
Identities: conflicting, 23; ethnic, 33, 40
Identity, 1, 5, 6, 21, 23, 332, 510–515, 537, 538, 606, 636, 681, 684, 686, 689; biracial, 40, 616; crises, 24; double, 607; emergent, 21; ethnic, 299, 300, 301, 311, 366, 576, 685, 687, 688, 692; ethnic/racial, 572; female, 690; homosexual, 39; lesbian, 553, 554, 555, 556, 557; multiethnic, 40, 606, 608; Pan-Asian, 36, 37; politics, 550, 557, 558, 683, 684; private and public, 606
Iizuka, S., 306
Ilongo, 576
Ima, K., 200, 201, 205, 497
Immigrant: disadvantages, 255, 260, 265, 274; entrepreneurs, Korean, 278, 280, 281, 284, 291, 292; entrepreneurship, 101, 102; religion, plausibility structures, 401–402; religions, 392–407; survival needs, 257, 259; women, 431–438
Immigration, 416, 461, 575, 576, 577, 578, 579, 670, 671, 672, 679, 681; from Asia, 8–20; from China, 155, 158, 168; from Hong Kong, 155, 168; of highly skilled workers, 162–164, 166–168; from India, 155, 158, 169; from Korea, 169; legislation, 9, 31–32, 92; national-origin quotas, 159; from Philippines, 155, 158, 169; from Taiwan, 155, 158; of women, 418, 427
Immigration Act of 1924, 156, 158, 160, 161, 393
Immigration Act of 1990, 156, 477
Immigration and Nationality Act of 1965, 394. *See also* Hart-Cellar Act of 1965
Immigration and Naturalization Act of 1952 (McCarren-Walter Act), 158, 159, 161, 162
Immigration Nursing Relief Act of 1989, 156
Immigration Reform and Control Act of 1986 (IRCA), 160, 461
Impelido, Cecilia, 342
Independent migration of women, 210
India, 9, 10, 13, 17, 392–393, 394, 395, 401–406; British colonial rule, 399; cultural centers, 395; immigrants from, 175, 393, 394, 398, 401, 402, 405; indigenous religion, 392; Punjab religion, 397
Indian: Christianity, 398, 399; hating, 144; Parsis, 399–400; Zoroastrians, 399–400
Indian Americans. *See* Asian Indians
Indispensable enemy, 21, 260
Individualism, 106
Indochina, 88
Indochina War, 175, 176, 177
Indochinese Refugee Act (1978), 479
Indochinese refugees, 177–201; population size, 181
Indonesia, 11, 415

Inferiority complex, 611
Informal economy, 420, 422
In-group virtues, 288
Inner-city neighborhoods, 32, 233
Institute of Electrical and Electronic Engineers, 166
Institutional racism, 514, 656
Instrumentalists, 300
Intercollegiate Chinese for Social Action (ICSA), 55, 57, 63
Interdependency, 341, 343
Interethnic conflict, 278, 286
Intergenerational conflicts, 384
Intermarriage, 40, 374, 608, 611. *See also* Interracial marriage
Internal colonialism, 6, 54, 669
International Hotel, 524
International Hotel, San Francisco, 86, 117
International Society of Krishna Consciousness, 400–401, 404
Internment, 299, 300, 301, 302, 303, 307, 311, 312; camps, 299, 301, 677
Interpretative memories, 25
Interpretive sociology, 357
Interracial marriage, 589; factors contributing to, 592–601; female perspectives on, 592–597; male perspectives on, 597–601
Interracial relations, 668
Interracial tensions, 233, 245
Intra-Asian American diversity, 468
Intra-Asian ethnic relations, 613
Iran, 399
Irish immigrants, 261
Ishizuka, K., 151
Islam: Shi'a, 395; Suni, 395
Islamic Society of North America, 398
Issacs, A. R., 203
Issacs, H., 300, 313
Issei, 22, 425, 677; Japanese American, 299, 305, 312; psychological effects on, 299
Italian: Catholic parishes, 374; immigrants, 261
Iyori, N., 223, 226

Jackson, A. W., 676
Jackson Heights, Queens, N.Y., 246, 247
Jackson, J., 83, 92
Jackson, P., 207, 209, 210, 227
Jacobs, J. A., 603, 604, 622
Jacobson, C. K., 352
Jaffe, E. M., 283, 292
Jain Association in North America, 397
Jain Study Circle, 397
Jainism, 392, 395, 396–397, 400–406, 408
James, C. L. R., 99, 100
JanMohamed, A., 694, 697
Japan, 9, 10, 13, 17, 89, 415, 563; Buddhism in, 361
Japan-bashing, 652
Japanese American: identity, 311; incarceration, 22, 25, 33; internment, 93

Japanese American Children's Village, 608
Japanese American Citizens League, 62, 123, 304
Japanese American National Museum in Los Angeles, 25
Japanese American Redress Movement, 487
Japanese Americans, 13, 14, 18, 25, 40, 92, 99, 299–305, 310, 377, 419, 422, 424, 425, 449, 451, 459, 460, 463–465, 468, 471, 474, 479, 614, 677, 678; assimilation, 299; communities, 299, 304; success story, 299, 312, 314; third-generation (*see also* Sansei), 299; wartime incarceration, 609
Japanese culture, 648
Japanese immigrants, 13, 117, 119, 120, 123, 128
Japanese internment, evacuation order, 302, 312
Japantown, 36, 60
Jaret, C., 292n
Jasso, G., 172
Javate de Dios, A., 227
Javillonar, G. V., 215, 227
Jaynes, G. D., 44
Jefferson, T., 127, 142
Jen, G., 352
Jenkins, S., 375, 390
Jensen, J., 230
Jensen, L., 249n, 252
Jersey City, N.J., 501
Jewish: diaspora, 374; immigrants, 278; synagogue, 374, 377
Jewish Americans, 485
Jews, 123, 312, 402
Jian, S., 517n
Jo, M. H., 293
Job "mismatch," 235–236
Johnson, J. Jr., 102
Johnson, K. A., 433, 442
Johnson, R. C., 619
Johnson, S., 141
Jones, L., 295
Jones, V., 286, 293
Jones, W. H. S., 147n
Jones, W. Jr., 205
Jordan, W. D., 148n, 618
Joy Luck Club, The (Tan), 679, 688, 689, 690
Judeo-Christian: ethos, 408; tradition, 393
Jung, C., 593, 598–599, 600
Juvenile delinquency, 385

Kagiwada, G., 543
Kain, J., 236, 251
Kambal sa Lusog, 572, 573, 583
Kamen, A., 517n
Kamo, Y., 29, 46, 498
Kandiyoti, D., 431, 433, 442
Kaneko, V., 597
Kang, C. K., 352
Kang, L., 6, 44
Kang, M., 285, 293
Karnow, S., 203

Kasarda, J., 236, 251
Kashima, T., 300, 409
Kasindorf, M., 331, 334
Kato, M., 594–595
Katsiaficas, G., 82
Katz, A. H., 283, 293
Katz, J., 559
Katzenelson, I., 456n
Kawakami, C., 618
Kawakami, K. K., 610, 618
Keely, C., 160, 169, 170
Kelly, G. P., 203
Kelly, K., 662
Kelly, N., 151
Kennedy, J. F., 51, 394
Kennedy, R., 67
Kesselman, M., 456n
Keyes, C. F., 301, 311, 313, 433, 442
Keywords, 87
Khare, B. B., 444
Khmer Guided Placement Project, 184
Khmer Rouge, 179
Khomeini, A., 399
Khoo, S. E., 208, 226
Kiang, P., 6, 44
Kibria, N., 192, 201, 203, 352, 422, 423, 424, 429, 432, 442, 444, 675, 701
Kich, G. K., 616, 619, 621
Kikumura, A., 415, 429, 603
Kilbourne, B., 258, 275
Kim, A., 570
Kim, B. L., 377, 390
Kim, D., 584
Kim, E., 296, 602, 686, 692, 697, 698
Kim, H., 675
Kim, I., 87, 249n, 251, 293, 372, 373, 377, 381, 387, 390, 534n
Kim, J. H., 409
Kim, K. C., 280, 293, 358, 370, 372, 377, 381, 382, 387, 388, 389, 390, 444, 457n, 497
Kim, S., 22, 44
Kim, Y. Y., 192, 203
Kimmel, M. S., 605
King, M. L. Jr., 50, 67, 81, 96, 108, 109
Kingston, M. H., 634, 120, 129, 131, 266, 444, 679, 686, 697, 698
Kinship, 317, 319, 340, 364, 381–382; networks, 12, 25; ties, 424
Kirschenman, J., 236, 251
Kitano, H., 5, 22, 44, 469, 482, 603, 604
Kitano, S., 622
Kitsuse, J., 5
Kivisto, P., 358, 370
Klatch, R. E., 441, 442
Kobayashi, M., 618
Kogawa, J., 129, 352
Kolko, G., 177, 204
Kondo, D., 41, 701

Kondo, S., 302, 307
Konvitz, M., 156, 172
Korea, 9, 10, 13, 361, 415; Christians of, 372, 376, 377;
  immigrants from, 175
Korean: Buddhists, 376; community, 567; Confucians,
  377; conversion, 377; cultural traditions, 382–384;
  family problems, 384; identity, 384; marital con-
  flicts, 385; merchants, 279, 281–284, 287, 288
Korean Americans, 13, 14, 18, 92, 94, 97, 419, 424, 426,
  451, 459, 463, 465, 467, 471, 474, 476, 479, 614
Korean Catholic church, 386
Korean Central Intelligence Agency, 98
Korean Christian Institute for the Study of Justice
  and Development, 378, 379, 380
Korean church: in Chicago, 372, 388; in Connecticut,
  374; functions, 372–390; in New Jersey, 376; in New
  York, 372, 375–390; services, 379; structure, 372–390.
  See also Korean immigrant churches
Korean Churches Directory of New York, 375, 380
Korean immigrant churches, 34, 372–390; fellowship,
  381–382; maintaining cultural tradition, 382–384;
  providing social status/positions, 387–389; social
  services, 384–387
Korean Immigrant Worker Advocates (KIWA), 101–
  105
Korean immigrants, 22,33, 119, 120, 121, 372–390;
  church affiliations, 376–377
Korean Independence Day, 384
Korean March First Independence Movement Day,
  384
Korean Methodist denomination, 378
Korean National Bureau of Statistics, 376, 390
Korean War, 11, 377, 463
Koreana Wilshire Hotel, 104
Koreatown, Los Angeles, 118, 234, 237, 238, 239
Korn, P., 204
Kotkin, J., 201, 204
Kozak, T., 516n
Kramer, R., 415, 428
Krieger, L. L., 664
Kudaka, G., 584
Kuhn, T., 667, 672, 674
Kuo, C. L., 317, 319–320, 330–331, 334
Kurahashi, Y., 664
Kwang, H. K., 409
Kwong, D., 646, 661
Kwong, P., 249n, 251, 318, 334, 533n
Kyes, 281–283

Labor, 420, 426, 427, 460, 468;-exporting countries,
  219, 221;-importing countries, 214, 219, 221
Labor force: participation of women, 208, 259, 264,
  269; participation rates, 240
Labor migration, from the Philipines, 207, 212–215
Labov, T., 603, 604, 622
Laclau, E., 695, 697
Laguerre, M., 337, 350
Lai, H. M., 146n

Lam, A., 204
Lamanna, M., 204
Lamphere, L., 431, 433, 442
Lance, J., 601
Landale, N. S., 29, 45
Lane, A., 602
Lane, W., 602
Lang Xang ("Million Elephants") Village, 365, 366,
  367
Language school. *See* Chinatown, N.Y. City
Laos, 11, 17, 32, 357, 360
Lao-style Buddhist temple, 365
Laotian Americans, 463, 478
Laotian Buddhism, 357, 359–366, 369; animism, 360;
  canonical, 360, 363; belief system, 361. *See also* Lao-
  tian-American Buddhism
Laotian community, moral order of, 357, 360, 364–
  369
Laotian pre-Buddhist rituals, 361
Laotian refugees, 408
Laotian resettlement in the U.S., 363–364
Laotian-American Buddhism, 364–369; construction
  of community, 364–365; moral order and identity,
  365–367
Laotians, 14, 16, 18, 29; community, 408; religious
  practices, 34
Last Emperor, The (film), 553
Latent functions, 388
Latin American Students Organization (LASO), 65,
  77
Latino, 49, 83; immigration, 160
Latino Americans, 2, 37
Latinos, 576
Lau, W., 274n
Lavelle, J. P., 192, 204
Lawrence, C. R. III, 676
Lawrence, F., 674
Law-Yone, W., 543
Layador, M. A. G., 207, 227
Lazarus, E., 132, 133
LeBar, F. M., 360, 370
Lee, A., 585
Lee, B., 601
Lee, C. F., 603, 605
Lee, C. R., 230
Lee, G. L., 296
Lee, H. C., 293
Lee, J., 33, 278, 279, 285, 290, 293, 664, 701
Lee, J. F., 517n
Lee, J. S., 601
Lee, K. W., 107, 620
Lee, L. C., 622
Lee, M. P., 150, 352
Lee, P. R., 164, 172
Lee, Q., 585
Lee, R. H., 5, 248n, 664
Lee, S. M., 497, 634, 603, 622
Lee, Wen Ho, 28

LeMay, M., 172
Lemp, G. F., 583
Lemshewsky, A. K., 570
Lenin, V., 87
Leon, J. J., 603
Leonard, K. I., 150, 296, 444, 674
Leonetti, D. L., 603
Leong, R. C., 3, 45, 558, 584, 674, 675, 698
Lesbian and gay communities, 562
Lesbianism, 548, 563, 565, 567, 568, 573
Lessinger, J., 352
Levin, M. J., 43, 481
Levine, D., 159, 172
Liberal Asian American establishment, 95
Liberation movement, 91, 106, 108
Lie, J., 292
Liebow, E., 283, 293
Lien, P., 543
Light, I., 249n, 251, 280, 281, 285, 293, 476, 482
Lim, G., 146n
Lim, S., 686
Lim-Hing, S., 584
Lin, K, 204
Lindquist, B., 227
Ling, A., 618, 686, 675
Ling, H., 423, 424, 429
Link, B., 196, 204
Linkh, R. M., 374, 375, 390
Lipsitz, G., 85
Little Manila, 17
Little Saigon, Calif., 17, 118, 184
Little Tokyo, Los Angeles, 17, 87, 118, 236
Liu, H., 417, 429, 675
Liu, J. M., 11, 31, 43, 155, 166, 172, 230, 460, 482, 559, 701
Liu, W. T., 204
Live-in domestic workers, 224
Lloyd, D., 694, 697
Local interventions, 658, 659
Loewen, J. W., 620, 674
Logan, J. R., 249n, 253, 257, 277, 318, 335
Loo, C., 6, 44
Loo, M. L., 248n, 251
Looney, J., 204
Lopata, H. Z., 375, 390
Lopez, D., 27, 44
Lorden, D. M., 617
Los Angeles, 36, 462, 471, 473, 476; riots, 33, 279, 286, 291; South Central, 286; uprising, 673
Los Angeles-Long Beach, 17
Los Angeles Times, 478, 639
Louie, E., 618
Louisiana, 357, 360, 364–369
Lovejoy, A., 148n
Lowe, F., 151
Lowe, L., 7, 8, 42, 103, 557, 558, 560, 677, 678, 698, 701
Low-skill occupations, 478
Lui, J., 676

Lummis, A. T., 358, 370
Luu, V., 423, 429
Luzon, 563
Lyman, S., 5
Lyu, K., 372, 391

Ma, S. M., 230
Ma, T., 660
Machida, M., 627, 629–631
Mackintosh, C., 637, 638
Madame Butterfly, 639, 641, 642, 643, 644, 645, 646, 660
Mahu Sisters and Brothers Alliance at UCLA, 561
Majority/dominant culture, 681, 682, 683, 684
Makeda, S., 570
Making Waves (Asian Women United), 553
Malayalam, 402
Malaysia, 11, 415
Malcolm X, 54, 67, 81, 87, 108, 109, 400, 606, 617
Male sexuality, 687
Manalansan, M. F., 39, 583, 584, 701
Mandeville, J., 138, 139
Mangiafico, L., 377, 389, 391
Manhattan, N.Y., 316
Manila, the Philippines, 343, 563
Manilatown, 59, 86, 87
Mann, A., 172
Manongs, 117; *manong* generation, the, 105
Mao, Z., 54, 60, 87, 100; Red Book of, 60
Mar, D., 6, 44, 249n, 251
Marable, M., 97, 109
March on Washington (1963), 51
Marchetti, G., 664
Marginalization, 548, 555, 557
Marisol (Rivera), 659
Markusen, A., 251
Marr, D. G., 433, 435, 442
Marriage, 416, 418; partners, 592
Marriott, M., 516n
Martin, B., 559
Martin, E. P., 435, 443
Martin, G., 204
Martin, J. M., 435, 443
Martin, P., 340, 351
Martinez, J., 58, 62
Marx, K., 87
Marxism, 6, 87, 95
Masaoka, J. G., 618
Masculine subjectivity, 648
Masculinity, 413, 574, 651, 684
Mason, L., 204
Mass, A. I., 300, 313, 611, 616, 618, 620, 621
Mass marketing, 285
Mass media, 577, 594, 600, 628, 630
Mass student organization, 49
Massey, D., 8, 12, 19, 44, 45, 251, 337, 351, 516n
Masuda, M., 204
Materialism, 107

Mathy, R., 583

Matsuda, M. J., 676

Matsumoto, V. J., 45, 352, 419, 429, 675

Matsuoka, F., 409

Matthaei, J., 209, 225

Maykovich, M. K., 301, 313

Mazumdar, S., 150, 675

McBee, S., 456n, 457n

McCarren-Walter Act, 9, 229. *See also* Immigration
   and Naturalization Act of 1952

McClain, C. J., 543

McClelland, K., 337, 351

McClintock, J., 103

McCunn, R. L., 415, 429

McDowell, L., 209, 227

McGurn, W., 98

Media Action Network for Asian Americans
   (MANAA), 653, 661

Media representation, 426

Medina, B. T., 215, 216, 227, 341, 351

Megwili, D., 638

Meinhardt, K., 192, 204

Melting pot, 133, 134

Melville, H., 127, 144, 148n

Memmi, A., 139, 140, 148n

Mengel, L., 618

Mental illness, 450, 535, 536

Mercato, G., 138

Merced, Calif., 18

Merchant-customer relationships, 286

Merchant's associations, 317, 319

Meritocracy, 460

Merton, R. K., 288, 293, 388, 391

Messner, M. A., 605

Mexican: *braceros*, 338; immigrants, 106

Mexican American Student Confederation (MASC),
   65, 77

Mexico, 337

Mick, S., 167, 173

Middle East, 392

Middle-class people of color, 94

Middleman minority, 242, 243, 244, 245

Mieszkowski, P., 234, 251

Migration: invasion, 222; network, 12

Mikado, The, 41, 637, 654, 655, 656, 657, 658

Miller, J., 82, 310

Miller, P., 131, 170

Miller, S. C., 140, 142, 148n

Mills, E., 234, 251

Min, K. B., 376, 391

Min, P. G., 34, 279, 280, 292n, 293, 296, 372, 377, 387,
   389, 391, 408, 421, 429, 476, 482, 701

Mincer, J., 258, 276

Mincy, R., 234, 236, 251

Mineta, N., 119

Minh-Ha, T. T., 549, 556, 558, 559, 664, 695, 697

Minidoka, 304

Mink, G. R., 172

Minneapolis, 17

Minnesota, 99

Minority: culture, 681, 682; discourse, 655; faculty, 50

Mirak, R., 131

Mirikitani, J., 677, 679, 697

Mishan, Ahrin, 296

Misir, D. N., 37, 701

Miss Saigon, 39, 41, 572, 576, 577, 578, 580, 582, 640,
   656, 657, 659, 660, 661; controversy, 613, 637, 639,
   640, 641

Missionaries, Roman Catholic, 398

Mitchel, C., 517n

Miyagawa, J., 303, 308

Miyamoto, F., 5

Miyatake, H., 304

Model minority, 92, 278, 301, 331, 452, 463, 535–537,
   551, 552, 643, 655, 681

Model minority thesis, 449, 451, 453, 455, 464, 468,
   473; deconstruction of, 36, 38; discrimination, 454;
   political implications of, 453

Modell, J., 5, 295

Modern Language Association (MLA), 686

Mohanty, C. T., 558, 559

Mollenkopf, J., 251

Mollica, R. F., 192, 204

Monaghan, P., 4, 45

Monasticism, 366

Mongol invasion, 137

Monsivais, C., 634

Monterey Park, Calif., 22, 477

Montero, D., 204

Moore, H. A., 256, 276

Moore, J., 236, 251

Moore, M., 130

Morales, R., 236, 251

Morawska, E., 283, 293

Morgan, D., 147

Morishima, J., 300, 620

Morokvasic, M., 227, 255, 276, 442, 443

Morris, M., 155, 172

Morris, Y., 618

Moser, R. J., 191, 205

Moss, P., 252

Mosses, G., 148n

Mother-daughter relationship, 679, 688, 689, 690

Mouffe, C., 695, 697

Moy, J. S., 664

Much Ado About Nothing, 642

Mueller, C., 259, 276

Muller, A., 570

Multiculturalism, 81, 100, 557, 634, 683

Multiethnic neighborhoods, 307

Multiplicity, 627, 669, 677, 681, 684; of voices, 629

Multiracial Asian Americans, 612, 638

Muni, C., 396

Muni, S. K., 396

Mura, D., 585, 641, 646, 664

Murata, A., 204

Murphy-Shigematsu, S., 611, 616, 618, 619, 621
Murray, C., 674
Murray, G., 68
Museum of the Chinese in the Americas in New York, 25
Muslim, 392, 398, 400
Muslim Student Association, 398
Mutiracial, 668, 669, 673
Muto, S., 662
Mutual aid, 424
Myrdal, G., 132

Nagata, D. K., 300, 314
Nagoshi, C. T., 619
Nair, M., 230
Nakanishi, D. T., 3, 37, 45, 95, 701
Nakasako, S., 230, 296, 498
Nakashima, C., 608, 616, 617, 618, 619, 620
Namiki, C., 301, 312
Narasaki, D., 311, 313, 314
Nash, J. W., 358, 370, 409
Nash, P., 45
Nash, R. N., 358, 370
Nation of nations, 127
National Asian Pacific American Legal Consortium, 543
National Board of Medical Examiners, examination of, 165
National Coalition for Redress and Reparation (NCRR), 548
National Defense Education Act (NDEA), 53
National Farm Workers Association, 52
National Origins Act of 1924, 13, 125, 133
National Origins Quota System, 317
National Rainbow Coalition, 82
National Research Council, 172
National Science Foundation, 172
Nationalism, 513–514, 520, 630, 683, 684, 685, 686; in Third World nations, 157
Native Americans, 2, 49
Native Asian culture, 685
Nativism, 125, 461, 520, 684, 685, 686, 687, 688, 690, 692
Neckerman, K., 236, 251, 292n
Nee, B., 130
Nee, V., 130, 249n, 252
Nelson, H. L., 416, 429
Neoconservatism, 94
Neo-Marxist approach, the, 255, 256–257, 259
Neu, C., 157, 172
New England, 143
New Frontier, 51
New historical bloc, 683
New Orleans, La., 17
New Phnom Penh, Long Beach, Calif., 234, 238, 239
New political animals, 94
New World, 126, 142
New World consciousness, 50, 58, 84

New yellow peril, 520
New York, 17, 99, 462, 471, 572, 578
New York Harbor, 141
New Zealand, 158
Newell-Morris, L., 603
Newfield, C., 585
Newman, K., 292n
Ng, R., 207, 216, 227
Ngaosyvathn, M., 362, 370
Nguyen, V., 433, 443
Nicassio, P. M., 192, 203
Nicholas, R., 515n
Nichols, B., 375, 391
Nikkei, 306, 352
Niland, J., 172
Nirvana, 361, 363
Nisei, 306, 425, 551, 610, 612, 677; childhood and adolescence, 301; impact of internment, 300, 302; intergenerational ties, 308; Japanese American, 300, 301, 308, 309, 310, 311, 312; psychological effects on, 299; reaction toward redress payment plan, 304
Nishi, N., 5, 45
Nishida, Mo, 84
Nixon, R., 71, 72, 89
Njeri, I., 279, 286, 293
Noda, B., 556
Noel, P., 286, 293
Noguchi, I., 618
Nomura, G. M., 422, 429, 675
Non-European immigration, 8
Non-Hispanic white women, 258
Nordquist, R., 33, 254, 701
Norris, Bahar, 255, 275
North, D. S., 183, 202
North, O., 119
Nostalgia, 366
Nunokawa, J., 556, 559
Ny, Sokly, 296
Nyland, C., 434, 443

Oakland, Calif., 17, 462, 471
Occupational mobility, 450, 468
Ochiai, S., 305, 307, 308, 309
Odo, F., 45, 604
Office of Refugee Resettlement, 180, 181, 188, 189, 190
Oh, E. T. *See* Yellow discrimination
Ohama, C., 151
Okada, J., 5
Okamoto, P. M., 248n, 252
Okamura, J. Y., 423, 429
Okazaki, S., 497, 543
Okihiro, G. Y., 31, 132, 150, 444, 559, 618, 619, 668, 674, 675, 676, 698, 702
Okun, M. A., 358, 371
Old World, 142
Ollenburger, J.C., 256, 276
Omatsu, G., 1, 2, 30, 31, 80, 113, 702

Omi, M., 6, 45, 313, 429, 453, 457n, 516n, 669, 675, 676, 698
Ong, M., 592, 594, 596
Ong, P., 11, 31, 32, 45, 155, 166, 172, 230, 233, 236, 240, 241, 243, 245, 249n, 250n, 251, 252, 279, 293, 337, 351, 460, 461, 464, 469, 471, 474, 482, 675, 702
Oppression, 220–221, 550
Orange County, Calif., 478
Orderly Departure Program (ODP), 179, 181
Ordway Theatre, 641
"Oriental Contingent, The," 679
Oriental problem, 8, 31
Orientalism, 136, 140, 578, 630, 637, 647, 648, 651, 656, 657, 661
Oropesa, R. S., 29, 45
Orozco, W., 208, 221, 227
Orru, M., 363, 370
Ortiz, V., 258, 275
Osajima, K., 36, 559, 698, 702
Osofsky, G., 248n, 2
Osuga, K., 592
Osumi, M. D., 603
Out-group vices, 288
Outweek, 576
Overseas contract workers (OCW), 207, 208
Owan, T. C., 192, 204
Oxnam, R., 457n

Pacific Century, the, 93
Paganoni, A., 207, 221, 223, 225
Pakikisama, 340, 341
Pakistan, 392–407, 408; immigrants from, 393, 394, 398, 401, 402, 405
Pali, 362
Palma-Beltran, M., 207, 208, 221, 227
Palmer, A. H., 145
Palolo Valley, 117
Palumbo-Liu, D., 698
Pan Asian Voices for Equality (PAVE), 640
Pan-Asianism, 426, 459–461, 480, 502, 507, 606
Pang, G. Y., 601, 602, 603, 604, 605
Papademetriou, D., 155, 172
Paradigm shift, 667
Parental pressure, 332, 334
Parent-child: relations, 402, 403; tensions, 385
Parents and Friends of Lesbians and Gays in Los Angeles (PFLAG), 561, 562
Parisi, A., 516n
Park, A. S., 409
Park, H., 372, 388, 391
Park, I. S., 376, 377, 391
Park, K., 241, 243, 249n, 250n, 252, 293, 416, 423, 429
Park, L., 23, 38, 702
Park, R. E., 124, 130
Parreñas, R. S., 34, 292n, 336, 338, 350, 352
Parsis, 399–400
Participatory democracy, 50, 87
Partison politics, 488

Pascoe, P., 602, 603
Paterson, W., 372, 391
Pathet Lao, 178
Patriarchal bargain, 431–432, 438
Patriarchy, 209, 210, 416, 419, 423, 425, 427, 431, 589, 594, 602, 632
Patriotism, 90, 133
Patterson, W. K., 150
Payne, S. F., 583
Paz-Cruz, V., 337, 351
Pearl Harbor, 29, 303, 304, 310, 311
Pedraza-Bailey, S., 177, 204
Pegues, J., 641
Pekarik, A., 627, 632–633
Pennsylvania, 99
Penrose, J., 207, 209, 210, 227
Pentony, D. V., 76
Perea, J., 339, 351
Perez, L., 257, 258, 276
Performance art, 645, 646
Perot, R., 519, 521
Perry, I., 85
Perry, M. C., 144
Personal interviews, 301, 312
Peru, 210
Pessar, P. R., 423, 429, 431, 443
Petersen, W., 449, 450, 456n, 481n, 497
Peterson, J. T., 341, 343, 351
Pfeiffer, P., 627, 631–632
Phabtong, T., 409
Phi, 362, 368
Philadelphia Negro, The. See Dubois, W.E.B.
Philippine Independence Day, 572
Philippine labor migration industry, 217
Philippine Overseas contract workers (OCW), 213, 217, 218 222, 223
Philippine Overseas Employment Administration (POEA), 217, 219, 220, 222, 223, 224n
Philippine-American Collegiate Endeavor (PACE)58–59, 62, 63, 68, 77, 84
Philippines, the, 8, 10, 13, 32, 92, 336–349, 415, 574, 575, 576, 577, 578, 581; immigrants from, 175; labor migration from, 207, 212, 215; Marcos dictatorship, 106
Philliber, W., 259, 276
Phizacklea, A., 208, 227
Phnom Penh, 11
Physiognomy, 615
Pickwell, S. M., 191, 205
Picture brides, 416, 417
Pido, A. J. A., 377, 391
Pilipino, 576; farm workers, 58, 84; immigrants, 106
Pilipino-American experience, 59
Piore, M., 249, 250
Pittin, R., 210, 227
Plastic surgery, 535
Plato, 135
Pleck, E. H., 443

Pluralism, 120
Pluralism Project, of Diane Eck, 395
Pol Pot labor camps (Cambodia), 179
Polacheck, S., 258, 276
Polatnick, R., 602
Political: fundraising, 521–523; mobilization, 641; organizing, 487; participation, 502; strategy, 88
Politics of pleasure, 651
Pollner, M., 358, 370
Polo, V. M., 137, 138, 139
Polynesian, 144
Population dynamics, 12
Population growth, distorted, 14
Portes, A., 19, 45, 163, 172, 177, 197, 199, 204, 249n, 252, 256, 261, 276, 283, 294, 316, 334, 340, 351
Posadas, B., 619
Post–1965 Asian immigration, 460, 462, 463
Postcolonialism, 6
Postmodernism, 6
Potvin, R. H., 603
Poverty, 99, 233
Power relations, 639
Powesland, P., 148n
Prabhudhanitisarn, N., 211, 228
Pratt, M. B., 559
Prentice, D., 593
Primordial ties, 374
Primordialists, 300
Princeton University, 490, 493
Prison Notebooks, The (Gramsci), 682
Professionalization, 6
Proposition 187, Calif., 340, 652, 668
Proposition 209, Calif. *See* California Civil Rights Initiative
Prospero, 141
Pryce, J., 637, 638, 639
Pryer, J., 227
Pseudo-extended family, 381
Public: media, 485; policy, 233, 235, 243, 245; television, 635
Puerto Ricans, 117
Punjabi, 397
Punjabi American, 422
Push-pull, 120

Quayle, D., 177
Queens, N.Y., 246, 317, 320, 324, 333
Queer, 553; androgyny, 574

Race, 578, 632, 642, 643, 644, 669; and popular culture, 636
Race relations, 502–503; model/theory, 667, 669, 672
Racial: antagonisms, 244; association, 426; discrimination (*see also* Racism), 303, 307, 309, 310, 313, 578; division of labor, 210; domination, 636; harmony, 50; identity, 549, 550, 552; paradigms, 668; restriction in U.S. immigration policies, 156; stereotypes, 217, 578

Racialism, 684
Racialization, 224, 501–502; of Asian Americans, 519
Racially coding economic arguments, 288–290
Racism, 37, 90, 94, 97, 155, 419, 451, 461, 464, 578, 636, 648, 649, 650; state-sponsored, 237
Radcliffe, S., 208, 209, 210, 221, 227
Rahe, R. H., 204
Rainbow Coalition, 92
Rajadhon, A., 362, 370
Raleigh, W., 138
Ramirez, A., 457n
Reagan, R., 54, 70, 72, 75, 88, 90, 92, 454, 634
Reaganomics, 97
Reclaim history, 558
Redress movement, 299, 300, 303, 304–311
Reeducation camps, 178
Reference-group approach, 255, 258, 259, 272
Refugee Act of 1980, 169n
Refugee settlement, 183
Refugees, 478, 451; from Cambodia, 175–201, 229; from Cuba, 176, 177, 229; from the former Soviet Union, 176, 229; from Laos, 175–201, 229; from Vietnam, 175–201, 229
Reginald, D. G., 622
Regional realignment, 234
Reich, M., 249n, 251
Reimers, D., 159, 162, 172
Reiss, A., 279, 294
Reitz, J., 389, 391
Religion, 34, 576; Asian Indian, 392–407, 408; neoclassical theories, 358
Religious: ceremonies, 366; imagery, 582; institutions, 321; organizations, 395; pluralism, 395
Religious faith: cultural affairs, 392; experiences of recent immigrants, 401–403; self-identification, 392
Representation, 639
Republican Party, 94
Republicans, 98
Residential: enclaves, 460; segregation, 96–97
Retail niches, 285
Return migration, 123
Reuter, E. B., 609, 617, 618
Revilla, L., 336, 350
Reyes, N., 576, 583
Reynold, W. B., 543
Rieder, J., 287, 294
Riggs, F., 157, 173
Rising Sun (film), 41, 646–654, 661
Roberts, A. E., 86, 192, 204
Robey, B., 457n
Rodney King case, 279, 286
Rodriguez, R., 606, 617
Roosevelt, T., 144
Root, M. P. P., 617, 618, 622, 674
Rosenbaum, D. E., 530n
Rosenberg, N., 173
Rosenberg, S., 374, 375, 391
Rosenfeld, S., 531n

Rosenstein, C., 166, 172, 230
Rosenzweig, M., 172
Rotating credit associations, 93, 281–284, 424
Rothenberg, N., 296
Rouse, R., 423, 429
Route 128, Mass., 118
Roy, S., 585
Rumbaut, R. G., 32, 45, 175, 177, 178, 181, 183, 191, 192, 196, 197, 199, 200, 201, 204, 316, 334, 340, 351, 364, 370, 432, 443, 702
Russell, J., 662
Russian Jews, 261
Russo, A., 558
Rutherford, D., 432, 442
Rutherford, G. W., 583
Rutledge, P., 358, 370, 374, 390, 409
Ryan, W., 456n

Sacramento, 18
Safire, W., 529n
Said, E. W., 135, 147n, 650
Saigon, 11; fall of, 177, 178
Saiki, P., 489
Saito, L. T., 296, 674
Sakoda, J., 5
Salazar, R., 702
Saliba, J., 227
Salyer, L. E., 150
San Diego, Calif., 17
San Francisco, Calif., 17, 304, 462, 471, 688
San Francisco State College, 1, 2, 3, 30, 42, 60, 61, 63; President Smith, 69; School of Ethnic Studies, 49, 64, 84; strike, 49, 50, 51, 83, 84, 113
San Francisco State University, 595
San Gabriel Valley, Calif., 477
San Jose, Calif., 17, 69
San Juan, E., 699
Sanchez, A., 293
Sancho, N., 207, 208, 227
Sanders, J., 249n, 252
Sangha, 361
Sansei, 300, 301, 303, 307, 548, 677; adolescence, 301–302; childhood, 301; ethnic awareness, 303; intergenerational ties, 308, 313; Japanese American, 299, 312; model minority, 301; psychological effects on, 299; ties to community, 309
Santacruzan, 573, 680, 581, 582
Santos, R., 352
Sassen, S., 10, 45, 285, 294, 339, 351
Sassen-Koob, S., 235, 252
Sassoon, A. S., 695, 697
Sato, M., 415
Sawada, M., 151
Sawers, L., 252
Saxton, A., 5, 156, 173, 227, 260, 276, 543,
Scapegoating, 519
Scardino, A., 129
Scharlin, C., 105

Scully, M., 166, 173
Seattle, Wash., 17
Second generation, 502, 511–512, 514–515. *See also* Nisei
Second-generation immigrants, 323
Secondary migration, 364
Secondary wage-earners, 255
Sectarianism, 82
Secular/profane, 582
See, L., 429
Segawa, A., 307
Self-determination, 49, 50, 54, 55, 59, 63, 66, 68
Self-employment, 274, 278, 280, 291, 420
Self-empowerment, 636
Seller, M. S., 374, 391
Selznick, G. J., 294
Sensenbrenner, J., 316, 334
Seoul, South Korea, 564
Sephardic Jews, 374
Service programs. *See* Chinese Consolidated Benevolent Association (CCBA)
Sethi, R. C., 543
Sexism, 101, 413, 686
Sexist: ideologies, 209; stereotypes, 210, 211, 216, 217, 220
Sexual division of labor, 211
Sexual identities, parent's view, 39
Sexual identity, 549, 550, 553, 573
Sexual orientation, 565, 569
Sexuality, 547, 548, 549, 552, 561, 565, 579, 630, 684, 685
Shah, N., 207, 225
Shah, S., 425, 426, 427, 429, 444
Shakespeare, W., 141
Shankar, L. D., 585
Shapiro, P., 76
Shariati, A., 80
Shawcross, W., 205
Shelley, M., 627
Shen, C. *See* "Smell of the Wet Grass, The,"
Shibutani, T., 5
Shifting paradigms, 667
Shin, E. H., 372, 388, 391, 296
Shinagawa, L., 601, 602, 603, 604, 605
Shinto, B., 409
Shoplifting, 287
Shulman, S., 166, 173
Siddhachalam, Pa., 396
Siegel, T., 543
Sigmund, S., 662
Sikh temple, 117
Sikhism, 392, 395, 397, 400–406, 408
Silent Minority, the, 98, 551, 552, 554, 555
Silverberg, M., 652
Simmel, G., 124
Simon, R. J., 228
Sin, P. C. P., 242
Sing, W. A., 634
Singapore, 11, 210, 211, 217

Singhanetra-Renard, A., 211, 228
Single parenthood, 287
Sino-Vietnamese, 179, 182
Situational ethnicity, 611
Siu, C. P., 252
Siu, P., 5
Skeldon, R., 213, 228
Skrentny, J., 292n
"Smell of the Wet Grass, The," 328, 334
Smith, A., 141
Smith, G. N., 696
Smith, J. P., 14, 45, 173
Smith, P. C., 226, 457n
Smith, R. J., 76, 292n, 652
Smith, W. C., 618
Smith-Hefner, N., 230
SNCC, 69
Snipes, W., 652
Social: capital, 281–284, 316, 423; change, 358; clubs, 425; justice, 426; mobility, 483; networks, 432–438; structure, 324
Social construction of gender, 209, 211
Social construction theory, 207, 208, 210
Social Darwinism, 608
Social Distance Scale, 590
Socialization, 215–216, 222
Socio-cultural approach, the, 255, 257–258, 259, 272
Soe, V., 543, 622, 664
Soja, E., 413, 429
Sojourners, 122
Solomon, N., 534n
Soloutos, T., 123
Sone, M., 5
Soukhouan, 362, 367
South Asian Americans, 502
South Asians, 37, 393; in California, 393; in Oregon, 393; in the U.S., 392–407; in Washington, 393
South Korean dictatorship, 92
South Vietnam, 176, 178
Southeast Asia, 92
Southeast Asian Americans, 419, 426, 451, 480
Southeast Asian refugees, 11, 12, 14, 25, 32, 35, 229; first-wave, 176, 192
Space race, 53
Spain, D., 413, 429
Spear, A., 252
Spicer, E., 300, 314
Spickard, P. R., 40, 590, 601, 604, 606, 617, 618, 619, 620, 622, 699, 702
Spitze, G., 255, 257, 258, 276
Spivak, G., 549, 692, 695, 697
Split households, 338, 417
Sputnik, 53
Sri Lanka, 210, 211, 394; Buddhism in, 361
Srikanth, R., 585
Srole, L., 374, 391
St. Martinville, 364
Stack, C. B., 283, 294

Stack, S., 358, 370
Stacks, C., 435, 443
Stahl, C., 228
Stalin, J., 87
Stanford University, 490, 494
Stanley, S., 584
Starr, P. D., 192, 204
Statue of Liberty, 128, 132, 146, 393, 394
Status symbol, 218
Status-attainment, 257, 259
Steele, S., 96
Stein, A., 596
Steinberg, S., 292n, 294
Steltenkamp, M. F., 369, 370
Stephen, C. W., 619, 622
Stephen, W. G., 619, 622
Stereotype, the model minority, 28
Stereotypes, 20, 329, 331, 334, 455, 552, 563, 639, 640, 644, 648, 651, 653, 684, 686; the Chinese, 143
Stereotyping, 452, 464, 609, 610, 630
Stevens, R., 166, 173
Stevens, W., 628
Stevenson, R. L., 143, 148n
Stewart, B., 69
Stier, H., 276
Stock, W. A., 358, 371
Stockton, Calif., 18, 51
Stonequist, E. V., 617
Stop the Out-of-Control Problems of Immigration Today, 339
Strand, P. J., 205
Strategic essentialism, 692
Strauss, A., 603
Strauss, W. A., 177, 202
Street gangs, 98
Street of the Sun, The (Rivera), 659
Stromberg, A., 255, 276
Strong, N. D., 619, 620
Student Nonviolent Coordinating Committee (SNCC), 51
Student strike, 2
Student-initiated programs, 52
Students for a Democratic Society (SDS), 64, 65, 82
Stuyvesant High School, N.Y., 332
Subaltern groups, 682
Subalternity, 687
Subcultures, 547
Subjectivity, 558, 572
Suburban settlement, 92
Suburbanization, 234, 235
Suddard, A., 360, 370
Sue, S., 497
Suhrke, A., 177, 193, 206
Suicide, 535–541
Sullivan, J., 145
Sullivan's Island, 146n
Sumida, S. H., 151, 675
Summerskill, J., 64

Sung, B. L., 24, 45, 259, 262, 268, 276, 317, 319, 323–324, 326, 328, 330, 334, 352, 591, 601, 603, 604, 619, 622
Sunoo, S., 418, 429
Sunset District, San Francisco, 246
Sunset Park, N.Y., 320, 333
Support systems in ethnic communities, 318
Sur, M., 415
Susman, W., 87
Suzuki, L. E., 409
Swidler, A., 358–359, 367
Swift, J., 141
Symbolic: compensation, 261; interpretation, 300
Synagogue, 374

Ta, V. T., 435, 443
Tabb, W., 252
Tachiki, A., 4, 45, 604
Tadiar, N. X., 341, 351
Tagalog, 576
Taiwan, 9, 10, 17; Kuomintang party, 97; Taiwanese immigrants, 10
Tajima-Pena, R., 543, 585, 627, 633–635, 699
Takagi, D. Y., 6, 38–39, 45, 497, 543, 676, 702
Takahashi, J., 423, 429, 622
Takaki, R., 31, 45, 117, 148, 150, 151, 351, 415, 429, 464, 469, 471, 482, 693, 697, 702
Takei, P., 305
Takeshita, L., 618
Takeuchi, D. T., 481
Takezawa, Y. I., 21, 22, 26, 33, 299, 300, 314, 352, 702
Tam, A., 627
Tamagawa, K., 610
Tambiah, S. J., 360, 361, 371
Tamil, 402
Tamura, E., 352
Tan, A., 352, 679, 686, 688, 697
Tan, T., 210, 220, 223, 228
Tanaka, G., 302, 303, 306
Tanaka, R., 599–600, 604
Taplin, R. C., 517n
Tartars, 137
Tateishi, J., 304, 314
Tatsuno, S., 248n, 252
"Tawneys," 126
Tazuma, L., 204
Teach-ins, 656
Temple Corporation, 365
Terris, D., 201, 205
Texas, 99
Thadani, V., 208, 228
Thai refugee camps, 178
Thai workers to the Middle East, 211
Thailand, 11, 12, 360, 364
Thaker, S., 421, 429
Theravada Buddhism, 34; identity, 364–369; moral order, 357, 360–363, 365–366

Third World, 339, 549; consciousness, 4, 30, 87; movements, 49, 54; strike, 595, 606
Third World Communications Collective, 61
Third World Liberation Front (TWLF), 1, 49, 55, 56, 57, 62–64, 65, 66, 67, 70, 71, 72, 74
Third World Women's Coalition, 61
Third-generation, 312. *See also* Sansei
Thomas, C., 96
Thomas, P., 432, 442
Thompson Committee, 520, 527
Thornton, M. C., 615, 619, 620
Thrift, N., 434, 443
Tiana, S., 256, 276
Tiananmen Square, 132, 146
Tibrewal, C. S., 296
Tien, C. L., 522
Tilly, C., 236, 252
Tinker, J. N., 603, 604
Tobin, M., 234, 252
Todaro, M., 208, 228
Toji, D., 102
Tom, S., 192, 204
Tom, T., 594
Tomasi, S. M., 374, 391
Tong, B., 457n, 686
Tong, J., 241, 243, 249n, 250n, 252
Tong War, 319
Tongs, 317, 319
Tono, H., 218, 228
Torres, L., 558
Torres, M., 236, 250
Trade wars, 647
Tradition, 677–679
Traditional American values, 90, 97
Tran, T. V., 352
Tranh, D., 646, 648
Transcontinental Central Pacific, 119
Transnational: capitalism, 651; communities, 6, 33
Transnational households, 344, 350; adult-children-abroad, 344, 347–348; one-parent-abroad, 344–347
Transnationalism, 352, 405–4–6, 417, 426, 459, 460, 480, 518–519, 521–526, 671
Transpacific families, 417
Transvestites, 574
Trautmann, M., 192, 206
Trie, C. Y., 38, 518, 523–524, 529n
Tripmaster Monkey (Kingston), 634
Trounson, R., 249n, 252
Trueba, H. T., 497
Truman, H., 158, 159
Tse, P., 192, 204
Tsuchida, N., 603
Tsui, K., 556, 570
Tsui, N., 594, 595, 601
Tsutakawa, M., 664
Tuan, M., 26, 45, 498
Tung, T. M., 204
Twentieth Century Fox, 653

Twilight: Los Angeles 1992, 640, 654, 659
Tydings-McDuffie Act of 1934, 125, 156, 338, 350
Tyner, J. A., 32, 207, 223, 228, 229, 702
Tyrell, W. B., 147
Tzu, S., 76

Ube, C., 309
Ui, S., 422, 430
Umemoto, K., 2, 30, 32, 49, 113, 233, 250n, 252, 532n,
    604, 702
Underclass, 91; urban, 236
Underemployment, 29
Unemployment, 107
United Farm Workers (UFW), 105, 106
United Kingdom, 406
United States: effects on religion and society, 403–
    406; growth of South Asian community, 394–395;
    immigrant religions, 395; immigration from India
    and Pakistan, 393; religious pluralism, 395
University of California, 53
University of California, Berkeley, 60, 483, 485, 490,
    494
University of California, Los Angeles (UCLA), 2, 3, 4,
    85, 483, 484, 490, 491, 494
University of California, Los Angeles, Asian Ameri-
    can Studies Center, 2
University of California, Santa Barbara, 69
University of Chicago, 124
Uno, E., 304, 313
Uno, M., 352
Unpaid family labor, 261
Upward mobility, 258, 271–272, 273, 280
Urban: poverty, 290, 292; renewal, 237; revitalization,
    234, 242, 244; riots, Los Angeles, 243, 244; under-
    class, 236
U.S.: citizenship, 125; colonization, 176; foreign poli-
    cies, 175; imperialism, 550; involvement in Indo-
    china, 81, 177–178; labor shortage, 161; military in-
    tervention, 81; ruling elite, 90; as world leader, 155;
U.S. Bureau of the Census, 357, 361–362, 369
U.S. Commission on Civil Rights, 45, 518, 543
U.S. Congress, Joint Committee on Atomic Energy161
U.S. Department of Health, Education, and Welfare
    (HEW), 165
U.S. Department of Labor's Schedule A, 162, 166
U.S. Immigration Act of 1965, 315, 323. *See also* Hart-
    Cellar Act of 1965
U.S. Immigration Act of 1990, 167, 168
U.S. Immigration and Naturalization Act, 323
U.S. Immigration and Naturalization Service (INS),
    180, 315, 318, 334, 393, 394; (USINS), 9, 45
U.S. immigration law, 315; quota systems, 315, 317
U.S. immigration policies, 155, 175; family unification
    provisions, 160; occupational preferences, 160, 163;
    political-economic objectives, 155; preference cate-
    gories, 167
U.S. Marshall Plan, 162
U.S. Naturalization Act of 1790, 125, 134

U.S. Peace Corps, 357, 364, 371
U.S. v. Bhagat Singh Thind, 127
Uyeki, E., 5

Vaid, J., 426, 430
Valverde, K. C., 619, 620
Van Velsor, E., 259, 277
Vasquez, N., 207, 228
Vega, W. A., 197, 206
Verdieck, M. J., 603
Vernez, G., 160, 169, 170
Versluis, A., 409
Vicente, R. Jr., 517n
Vientiane, 11; fall of, 178
Vietnam, 9, 35, 160, 360, 415; Buddhism in, 361
Vietnam syndrome, 177
Vietnam War, 9, 11, 64, 177, 463
Vietnamese, 14, 16, 18, 119, 120; community, 97, 567;
    invasion of Cambodia, 179; in Philadelphia, 35; ref-
    ugees, 14, 16; society, 433–434; in Texas, 184;
    women, 35
Vietnamese Americans, 14, 16, 422, 423, 424, 431–443,
    451, 459, 462, 465, 469, 475, 478, 479, 614
Vigil, J. D., 330, 335
Violence, 37
Visa Qualifying Exam, 165
Visual culture, 41
Voluntarism, 550
Vose, C., 236, 52
Voting Rights Act of 1965, 158
Vu, T. M., 543

Wage system, 420, 421
Wakabayashi, R., 123
Waldinger, R., 249n, 250, 253, 256, 262, 277, 284, 292n,
    294, 481n
Walker, A., 547, 558
Walker, R., 227
Walker-Moffat, W., 498
Walsh, J., 603
Walt, V., 517n
Walters, R., 620
Walton, J., 163, 172
Wang, A., 361
Wang, L. L., 7, 45, 534n, 699, 702
Wang, P., 690, 697
Wang, W., 230, 680
War brides, 463
War Brides Act of 1945, 14, 317, 590
War of position, 641
War of the Flea, 69–70
War Relocation Authority (WRA), 609–610
Ward, D., 253
Ward, H. W., 204
Ward, K., 256, 277
Ward, R., 253
Warner, R. S., 363, 370
Warner, W. L., 28, 45, 374, 391

Warren, R., 159, 172
Washburn, W., 148n
Washington, D.C., 17
Washington, G., 140, 142
Wasson, E. H., 54
Wat, E. C., 6, 45, 585
Watanabe, C., 457n
Watanabe, M. E., 543
Watanabe, T., 166, 170, 174
Water Festival, 366–367
Waters, M. C., 26, 46, 310, 314, 622
Weber, M., 373, 391
Wechsler, J., 664
Week, J., 559
Weeks, J. R., 181, 183, 197, 206
Weglyn, M., 151
Wehman, J., 151
Wehrle-Einhirn, J., 258, 275
Wei, W., 6, 43, 604, 616, 676
Weinberg, S., 417, 423, 430
Weinberger, C., 165, 174
Welaratna, U., 296
Welch, F., 173
Welfare dependency, 233, 287
Westermeyer, J., 192, 206
Westinghouse Science and Talent Search, 315
Whitam, W., 583
White: American, 307, 308; conservatives, 96; masculinity, 652; whiteness, 637
White-Parks, A., 618
Whitman, W., 127, 131
Whitmore, J. K., 183, 192, 193, 200, 202
Whiz kids, 106
Wickham, D., 617
Wiener, S., 234, 236, 251
Wilkinson, C., 210, 228
Willette, J., 129
William, F., 137
Williams, J. K., 192, 206
Williams, M., 422, 430
Williams, R., 87, 697, 702
Williams, R. B., 35, 374, 391, 392, 408, 409
Williams, T. K., 615, 619, 620
Williamson, J., 516n
Wilson, K., 252
Wilson, W. J., 236, 248n, 249n, 253, 287, 294, 676
Winant, H., 413, 429, 453, 457n, 516n, 669, 675, 676, 698
Wing, M. G., 430
Winkler, J., 147
Wirth, A. G., 562, 570
Wirth, M. J., 562, 570
Wishik, S. M., 191, 205
Witter, R. A., 366–367
Wittig, M., 555, 559
Wittner, J. G., 358, 371
Wolf, D. L., 498
Wolf, M., 431, 433, 443

Wollenberg, C. M., 498
Wollstonecraft, M., 627
Woman Warrior, The (Kingston), 679, 686
Women: dual workload, 421; formal association, 425; and immigration, 414; independent migration of, 210; as overseas contract workers, 207; sexuality of, 414; as unpaid labor, 420; and work, 414
Women's: multiple roles, 255, 267–268, 274; resources, 43; triple role, 267–268
Women's liberation, 83, 87
Wong, B., 45, 46, 249n, 253, 604
Wong, B. D., 642
Wong, B. P., 317, 335
Wong, C., 444
Wong, D., 422, 430
Wong, E., 45, 604
Wong, J. S., 5
Wong, K. S., 151, 698
Wong, M. G., 45, 622, 464, 467, 482, 497
Wong, R., 601
Wong, S. L., 7, 46, 604
Wong, W., 129
Woo, B., 592
Woo, D., 422, 430, 602
Woo, J. M., 583
Woo, M., 92, 556
Woo, W., 409
Wood, P. H., 146n
Woodside, N.Y., 380
Woodward, B., 530n
Wordsworth, D., 627
Work ethic, 469
Working: career, 257; poor, 102; women, 255, 258, 264
World capitalist system, 107
World system, 155
World War II, 155, 156, 169, 229, 317, 299, 300, 309, 310, 338, 393, 404, 405, 408, 609, 614, 621
Wretched of the Earth, The (Fanon), 684
Wu, J. Y. S., 618
Wu, P., 638, 660
Wu, W., 498
Wuthnow, R., 357, 371, 374, 391

Xavier, L., 342
Xenophobia, 648
Xenos, P., 481
Xiong, G., 296

Yaffe, D., 517n
Yale University, 490
Yamada, M., 444
Yamamoto, E., 46, 151
Yamamoto, K., 151
Yamamura, D. S., 603, 604, 605
Yamanaka, K., 337, 351, 603, 622
Yamanaka, L. A., 543
Yambe, J. A., 310, 313

Yanagisako, S. J., 7, 46, 352, 414, 423, 424, 430, 693, 697
Yancey, W., 24, 25, 46
Yang, F., 409
Yang, P. Q., 23, 36, 37, 474, 481, 702
Yankee traders, 134, 142, 143
Yap, S., 426, 430
Yasui, L., 352
Ybarra, L., 442, 443
Ybarra-Frausto, T., 634
Yellow discrimination, 327, 334
Yellow peril, 21, 28; new, 520
Yep, J., 409
Yeung, W., 603, 604
Yim, S., 617
Ying, Y. W., 352
Yinger, M., 389, 391
Yochum, G., 165, 174
Yonemoto, B., 230
Yonsei generation, 312
Yoo, D., 409
Yoon, I. J., 280, 294
Yoshikawa, Y., 664
Young, D., 296
Young Koreans United, 92

Young Lords, 87
Young, M. B., 177, 206
Young, W., 551, 559
Youth Center of the Chinese Christian Herald Crusade (YCCCHC), 321, 331; crisis-orientated programs, 321
Youth gangs, 330–331
Yu, C. Y., 192, 204
Yu, E. Y., 296, 387, 391
Yu, H., 8, 46
Yu, R., 149n
Yuan, D., 603, 604
Yun, S., 330, 335
Yung, J., 40, 146n, 417, 419, 425, 426, 430, 445, 589, 622, 702

Zane, Nolan W. S., 622
Zangwill, I., 21, 46
Zhou, M., 14, 17, 19, 20, 29, 33, 45, 46, 315, 317, 318, 335, 352, 358, 371, 419, 430, 498, 702
Zia, H., 517n
Zigman, L., 292n, 294
Zolberg, A. R., 177, 193, 206
Zucker, N. F., 177, 206
Zucker, N. L., 177, 206